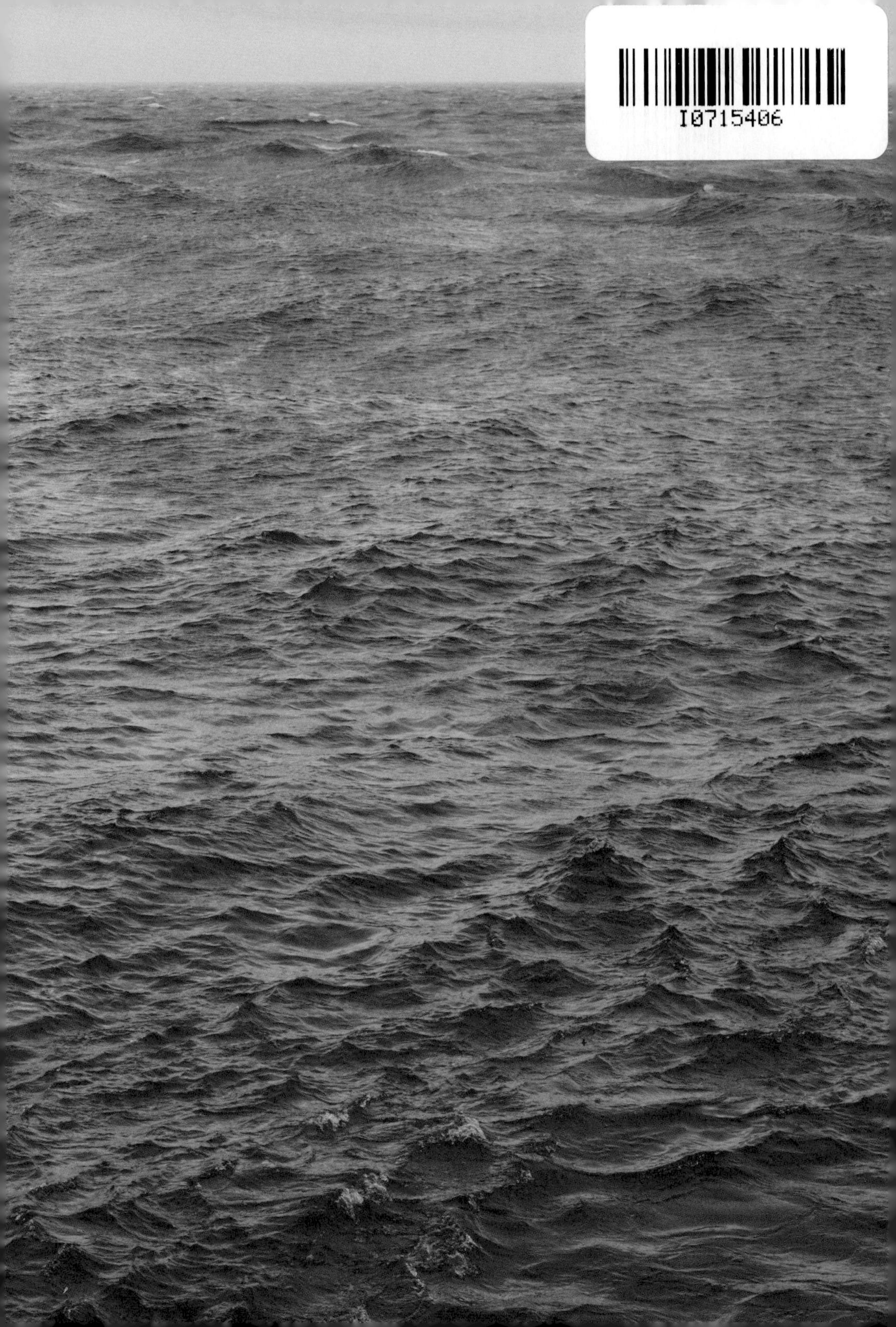
I0715406

Wolfgang Tillmans

four books

Wolfgang Tillmans 1995

Burg 1998

truth study center 2005

Neue Welt 2012

abridged, additions 2020

TASCHEN

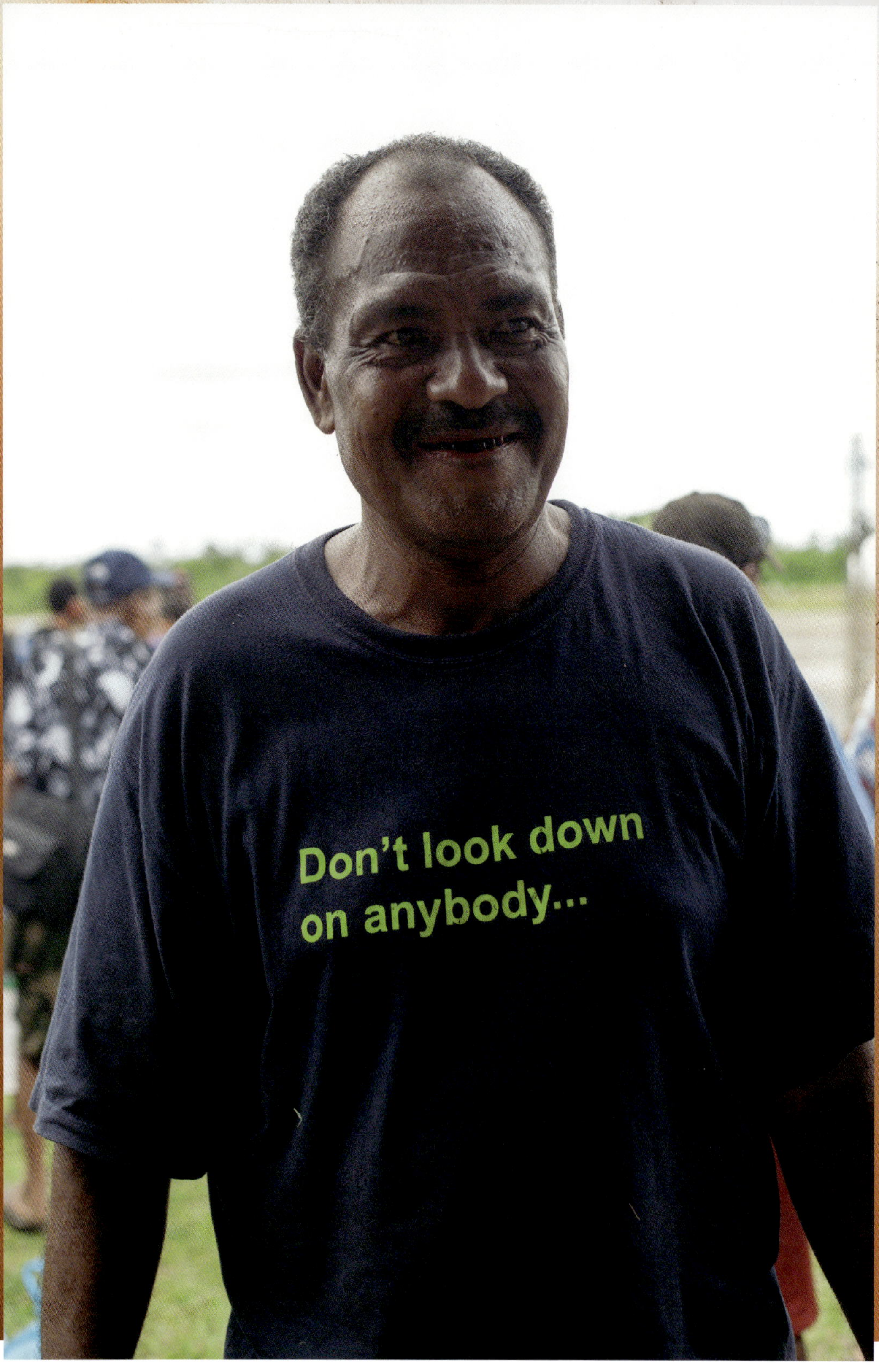

Don't look down
on anybody...

8 years ago was the year 2012.

8 years from now is the year 2028.

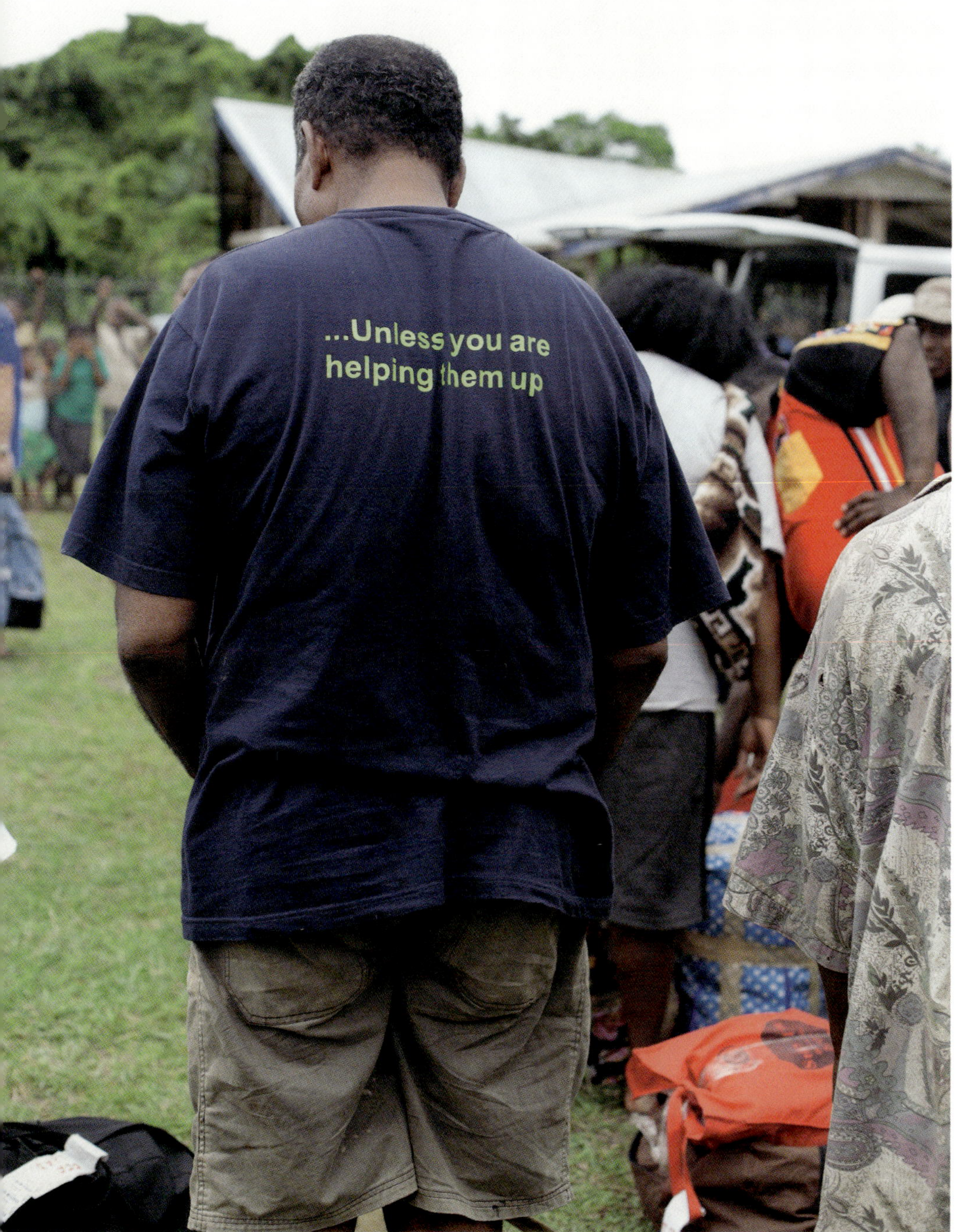

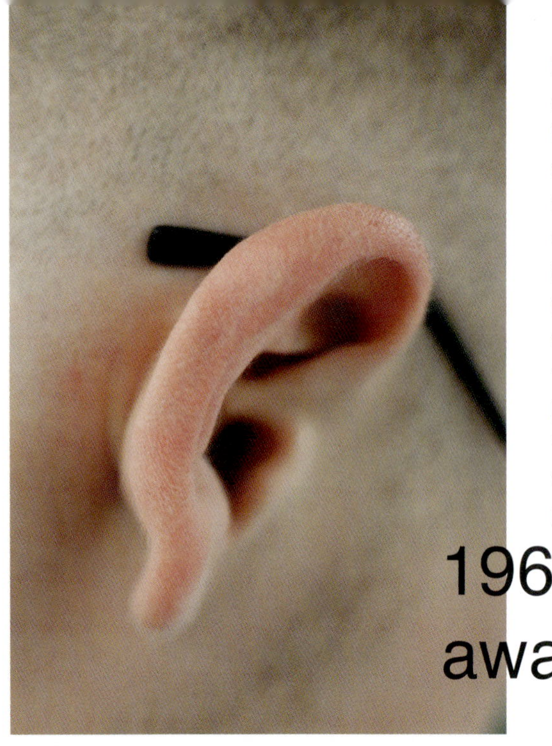

Fast Lane   1986
Approaches   1988
Like brother, like sister   1992
social fabric   1994
for when I'm weak I'm strong   1996
On the Verge of Visibility   1996
if one thing matters, everything matters   2003
truth study center   2005
What's wrong with redistribution?   2005
To know when to stop   2006
Life is astronomical   2012
Your Body is Yours   2015
What is lost is lost forever   2016
Rebuilding the future   2017

1968 was 23 years away from 1945.

23 years back from now is 1997.

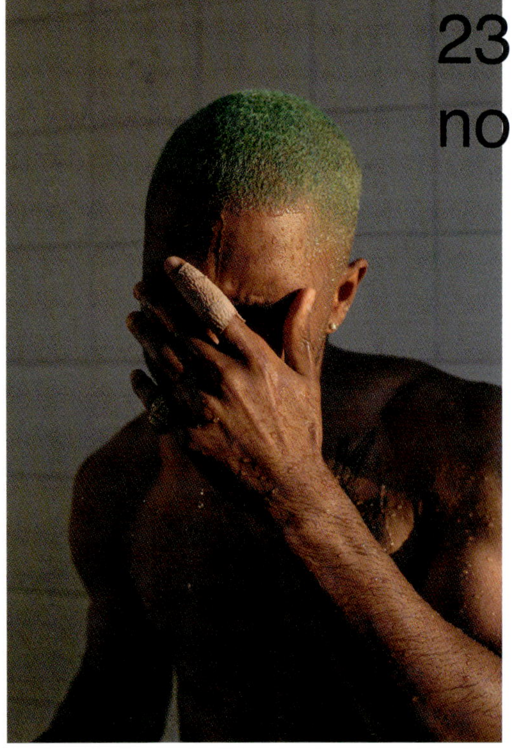

What does it feel like to flex a muscle?
What is the movement of a bowel?
Where is awareness located in my brain?
Can a heart feel itself?
What if?

Greifbar 74, 2018   Papua New Guinea, T-shirt, 2011
Outer Ear, 2012   Frank in the shower, 2015

I'm aware how my brain fails me.
I think I said something, but I hadn't.
I thought I saw something, but I didn't.
I believe you said this, but in fact you said that.
The eyes are optical 'instruments'; by default they are impartial.
They project light that falls through their lenses onto the retina.
I need to know what the brain does to what my eyes see.
To observe what do I want to see.
What do I really see.
What do I see, and what do I want to see.
What is in the picture?
What is in the room, on the walls? And what does the visitor see,
what does she want to see?
What do I need her for to complete the picture?
This sounds like a flaw, an exception.
But different people see different things in the same picture.
I act surprised, but I should really view it as normal.
And then discuss this.
We need to discuss the fact that humans seem to function like this.
Not discuss the opposing views and records,
but let's discuss the very fact that the same and similar humans
come to such different conclusions.
For that we need humility.
Progress can only begin when I start to accept
that all humans are born equal.
When I start observing how I observe.
I need to observe. Not just talk and shout.
Careful observation, with the openness
to change my mind, when results differ from my preconceived ideas.
Allow evidence.

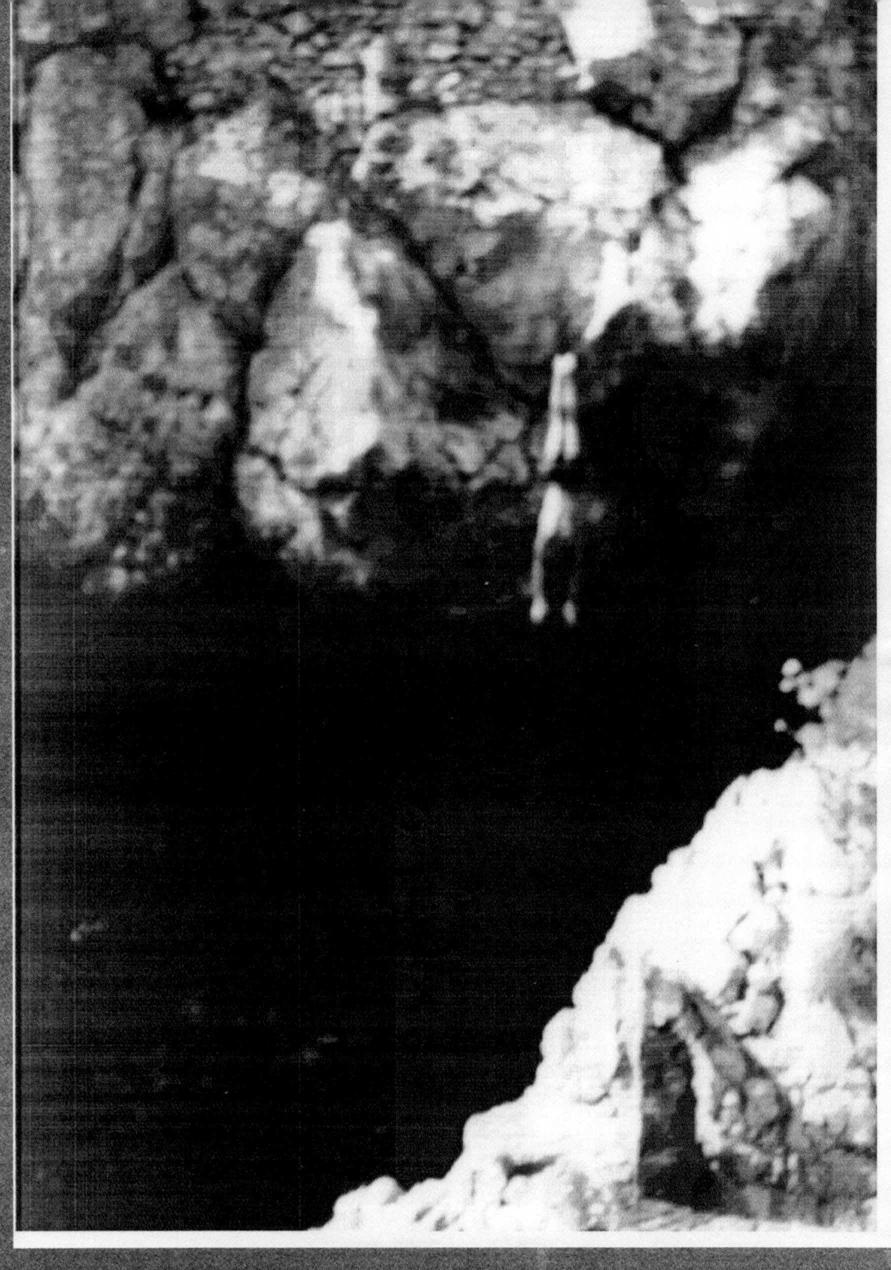

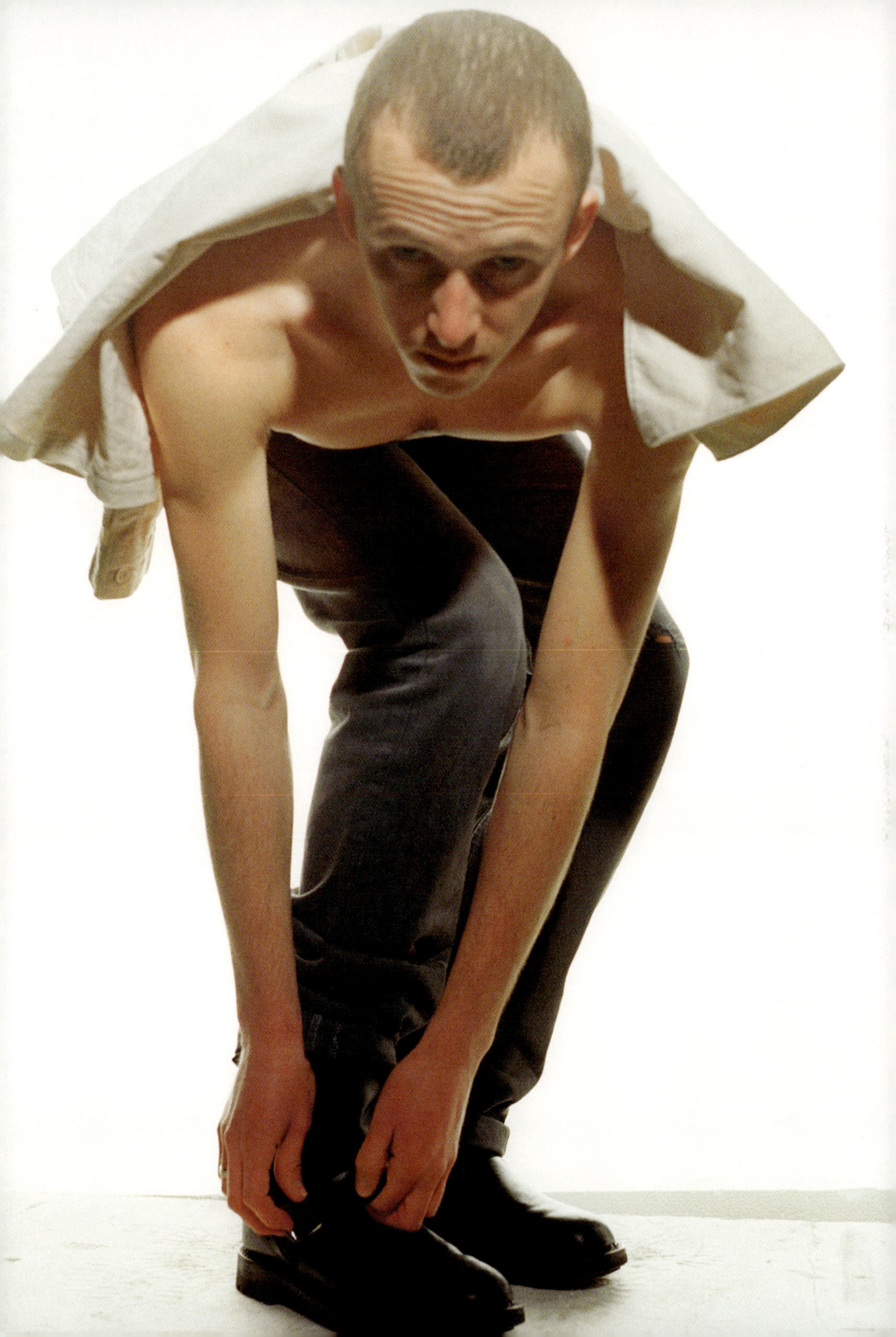

Sun, 1987
Christos, Athens, 1992
Oscar Niemeyer, 2010

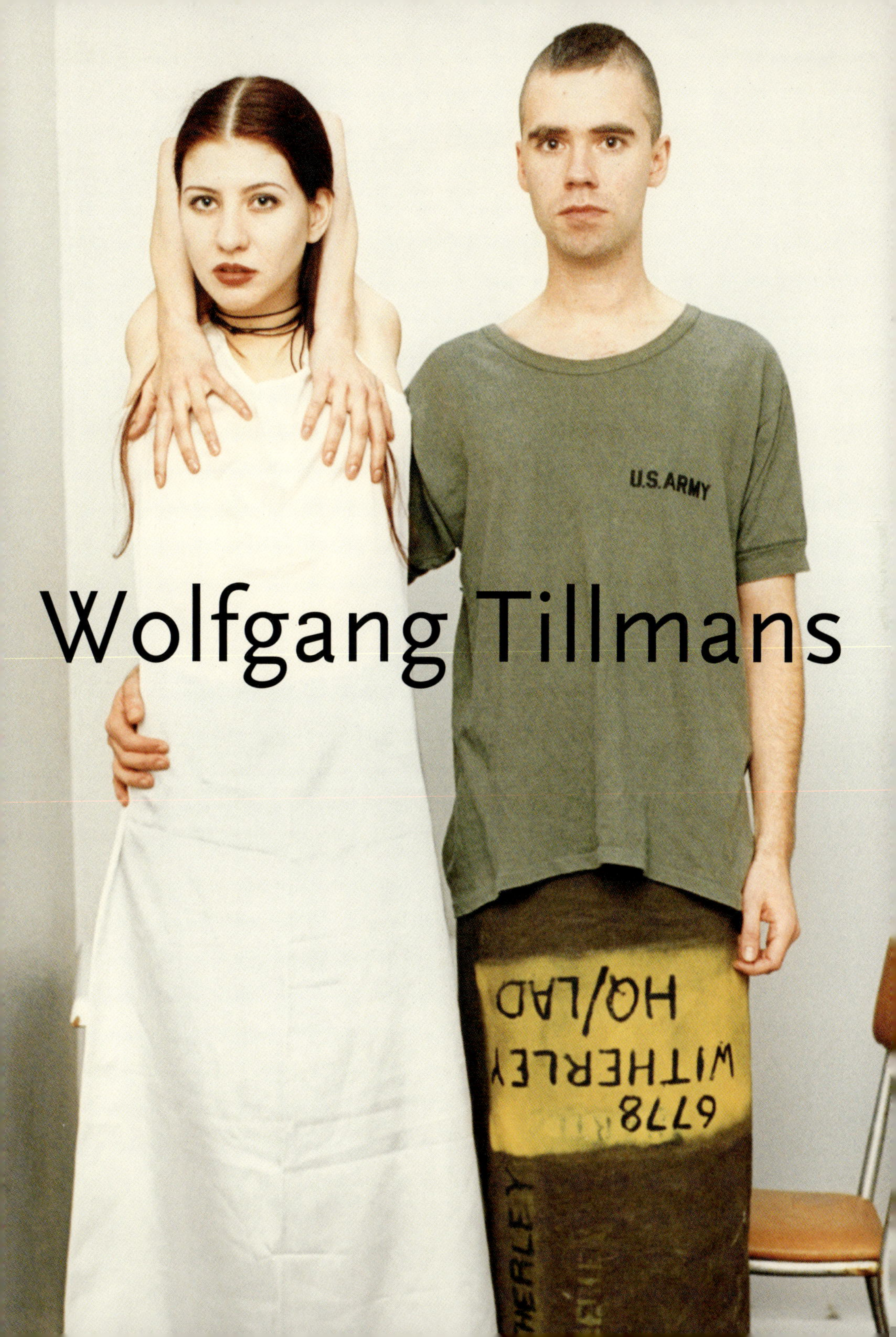

Wolfgang Tillmans
U.S. ARMY
6778
WITHERLEY
HQ/LAD

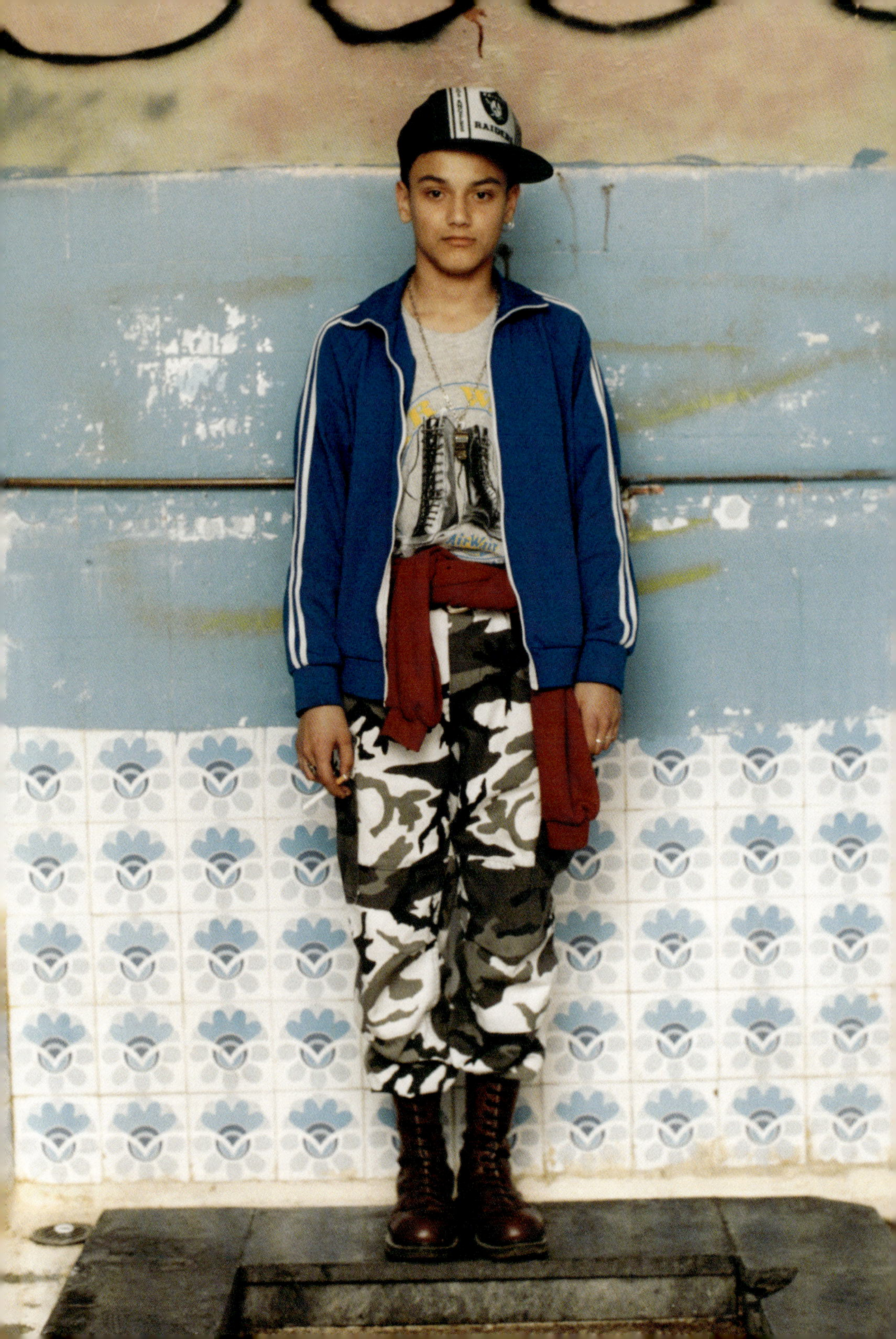

Oscar Niemeyer died in 2012,
aged 104.

104 years prior to his birth
was the year 1803.

TASCHEN

Professional fashion photography is frequently caught between two conflicting imperatives. First, to describe clothes and accessories in relation to their materials, cut, stitching... Second, to provide cultural associations of sexiness, taste, class, contemporaneity, and so on. The first tends to encourage the photographer towards detail, while the second involves skills of generalization. Successful fashion photographers have often imitated the stylistic characteristics of other branches of photography in order to attract attention to clothes in new and often surprising ways, following in the footsteps of Cecil Beaton's slinky models, stepping out over the ruins of London after the Blitz.

Such images lent post-war fashion the associations of contemporary reportage documentary photography, and seemingly admitted fashion into the domain of serious photojournalism. Thus we have seen commercial fashion photography imitate the style of almost every branch of professional photography, and better known styles of painting. As an artist, Wolfgang Tillmans might initially be seen to be enjoying a form of aesthetic revenge on this predatory appropriative process. He uses the opportunity to publish his photographs in the context of fashion stories, the only full-page photo-spreads available in mainstream culture, as an armature on which he can carefully hang his extremely personal view of the world he lives in. His insistence on styling every aspect of the shoot makes clothes and fashion a catalyst and vehicle for content.

Born in Remscheid, Germany, in 1968, he moved to Hamburg in 1987. At school, he had specialized in natural sciences, and with no immediate encouragement he began to experiment in his mid-teens with photocopies, learning about layout and the ways in which the meanings of individual images are affected – often dramatically – by their immediate relations with other images. In a sense, he was teaching himself the basic principles of how sequences of photographs can be made to narrate ideas and values according to the way in which they are arranged and edited. For the young Tillmans there was a great deal of pleasure in this process of rearrangement and reorganization – constantly moving images around in front of him in different combinations. It was a natural, and at the time exciting development to actually get hold of a camera – an SLR – and start making his own photographs, rather than relying on found images as he had done previously.

From the beginning, Tillmans' own colour photographs revealed an intense interest in the day-to-day elements of domestic life, and this has continued to inform much of his subsequent work. While much of his later work is also very intimate, it also quietly insists that intimacy is not necessarily a property of private spaces. Most of his early work took the form of the diptych, hinging different images together in pairs, or longer sequences, many of which explored his own immediate domestic world. For example, objects in his mother's kitchen, a hotel room window which contains a trapped bat, his bedroom, and so on. Rejecting more conventional professional or academic alternatives, he was soon supporting himself (to his own surprise) from his photography, especially his early pictures of club life in Hamburg in the late eighties.

Tillmans first visited England as a language student in 1983, and he was deeply influenced by this early acquaintance with London and its highly diversified youth culture – the music of Boy George, and style magazines such as *The Face*, and especially *i-D*, which he bought regularly after he returned to Germany. Meanwhile, his skills as both a photographer and picture editor quickly led to commercial success in Hamburg, where he worked with local fashion and lifestyle magazines. Yet this was not ultimately satisfying for him, since he had never set out to become a professional photographer as such. In 1988, he met some of the staff of *i-D*, and since then has regularly produced work for the magazine. As he remarked: "I became a photographer before I even noticed".

Tillmans, however, remained unseduced by the tackier aspects of lifestyle magazine production, and at the same time he began to put together exhibitions in galleries where he would show his work in a very different manner to the forms of display used in conventional photographic exhibitions. By mixing photographs with large-size inkjet prints and actual magazine pages in his installations, he made clear his intention to allow both worlds, publishing and art, to influence each other in his work. His photographs of the European club scene since 1989 are never in the least voyeuristic. On the contrary, he was simply exploring his own culture, and that of his German and British contemporaries. As well as sharing a social life revolving around House music, he is also actively involved with other social and political issues, ranging from housing and environmentalism to anti-racism and gay rights. In this respect, it is important to recognise that his work is never simply didactic. Tillmans sees his own work as being political in its totality, rather than equally in all its individual component parts. He is interested in the relation between the different parts of people's lives – the ways in which he and his friends live lives that are at once political, sexual, spiritual.

In conversation, he uses the term "parallelism" to express this sense of the inner diversity of the individual, as opposed to the idea that any one personal characteristic necessarily dominates or determines all the others. His work makes no grand, inflated claims to be revealing essential truths about particular groups of people, nor is he seeking to present individuals as representatives of larger social groups or constituencies. His well-known club pictures should not, therefore, be regarded as some kind of "document" of urban youth dance culture in the late eighties and nineties. Rather, these pictures simply show us something of the intensity and heightened intimacy of club culture – its integrity and its breadth. For Tillmans, such pleasures are one aspect of life, lived in parallel with an equally strong interest in science, religion, politics and art making. The close relationship between Tillmans and his models also takes him far from the familiar conventions of "hidden camera" documentary photography. For we are usually aware that his models are themselves well aware of being photographed. There is thus also a form of submerged narrative running through much of his work, as it traces his own movement and that of his friends between London, Berlin, Cologne, Amsterdam and other major cities.

At first, Tillmans used photography in a semi-magical mode, seeking to directly hard-copy his own, newly adopted world and the freedoms to which it gave access. Hence his attraction to the self-creating, self-sustaining cultural tribes which flourish and proliferate in urban Britain. Indeed, he is the principal photographic poet of Europe's resurgent nightlife, as well as of the daylight lives of those who flourish under the strobes. In all of this, technique has never been an end in itself for Tillmans. Rather, it is the means by which he can realize his images, which may subsequently be used in many different ways, from magazine layouts and photo-spreads to installations in white-wall galleries. Or, as now, in book form. In this respect, he also differs greatly from those who seek a fixed, easily identifiable style in which to make gimmicky, "interesting" pictures. The effect of contemporaneity has never been his principle goal, though much of his work is closely continuous with contemporary life, which he steadfastly refuses to over-simplify. This is an especially significant aspect of his work, since the subject of youth culture is so frequently trivialized and/or sensationalized. This is to acknowledge the great challenge of working in the domain of contemporary life and lifestyles, which in the work of others can easily become merely vogueish and ephemeral.

Thus Tillmans does not strive for the obvious, glossy colours of much fashion photography. His sense of colour is intense but low-key, sumptuous and associative, rather than narrowly descriptive – the sensibility of someone for whom colour-xeroxing has always been readily available. This in itself parallels something of the ways in which many of his sitters, consciously or unconsciously, model their appearance on the visual rhetoric of pop and fashion photography, constantly creating and recreating themselves from the stylistic elements of other places and other times, "re-mixed" in ever changing assemblages, questioning the possibility of personal invention or newness.

It is therefore not surprising that in 1990 he began to produce his first staged images, though he feels there is no important distinction to be made in his own work between "found" and "made" images. Both types of photography are continuous, parallel and related aspects of his personal project as an artist. He does not, however, work in a photographic studio, preferring whenever possible to use available light. Setting up his images also allows him to employ the range of colour he prefers, and to select environments that he finds appropriate to different models. His pictures of friends taken in the British seaside town of Bournemouth, where he was a student from 1990 until 1992, differ, therefore, from photographs which respond to London or Berlin. The reticent, unpretentious quality of Tillmans' best work leaves the degree of his involvement in questions of mise-en-scène unanswered, as he intends. For example, the Chinese woman TV reporter whom he photographed in a Hong Kong meat market was in fact found there by chance. The image, however, is strictly continuous with his staged work. This unwillingness to take a restrictively narrow, doctrinaire approach towards photography is a fundamental characteristic of his art.

For several years, Tillmans has exhibited pictures and picture sequences in Cologne, New York and Paris, among other places. In these installations he has been able to fully express his continuing exploration of the roles and potentials of enlargement and printing, exercising great control over the choice, combination and eventual siting of images in a given space and context. Such work clearly develops ideas originating from the beginning of his career, when he instinctively found that certain images worked well together, and belonged (for the time being) in a particular grouping. Questions of relative size and scale therefore become increasingly important for him, as will also be apparent from the meticulous layout of the images in this published collection. When working on a gallery installation, he will typically select a substantial number of images in boxes, and then take anything up to a week in the actual gallery space, selecting and positioning and repositioning images in what he has described as "an intense, full-time experience". Sometimes an entire exhibition will migrate from one wall to another in this demanding process of installation. The varied opportunities to recontextualize the images is in some way as important as printing or taking new pictures.

In a wider sense, Tillmans might also be seen to be hinging together seemingly distinct yet in fact overlapping domains of social experience. We can directly compare and interweave how he, for instance, uses photography as an opportunity to explore his relationship to lovers, the longing for idyllic love, the specificity of personal attraction, with, shall we say, his parallel involvement in the art world: dealers, fellow artists, their art works, a sense of the wider impact of art in everyday life. He is continually finding new subject areas which also involve new possibilities for displaying photographs. In his photographs made for a Swiss work-clothing company, he seems as interested in the scientific aspects of the clothes' manufacture as in the dignity of the factory workers who both make and wear them. The world of political activism and the gay community also provide him with opportunities to make his own images which are also always portraits. Yet he has no desire to present "types", and his highly personal approach to his subjects could hardly be more different from the taxonomic gaze of his fellow countryman, August Sander.

Moreover, as his experience has broadened and deepened, so his work has become more playful and, at times, more serious. He has a remarkable eye for the overall look of the image, and is often unaware of details that may stand out for others, such as car number-plates or graffiti. For example, he had not been aware of the sign that reads "Live and let spy" in the well-known picture of *Lars in the Tube* (1993). Following his own intuition, he presents something of the dignity and complexity of the lives of those who have grown up under the shadow of the economic recession of the nineties, who remain unimpressed by the ethos of rampant commercialism and double standards which survives from the eighties. His subjects are rarely "worldly". Life for most of his sitters is evidently not conventionally comfortable or easy, but it is not overly solemn either. They are neither complacent nor nihilistic.

It is Wolfgang Tillmans' particular gift to be able to present something of the richness and diversity of his generation with a deceptively laconic intensity. Distrusting rhetoric and excessive verbal contextualization or "explanation", Tillmans provides us with a dense tapestry of sumptuous images which go some way to restore our sense of the dignity and integrity of a generation which is so frequently represented only in banal clichés and stereotypes. His work positively bursts with a sense of the contradictory times in which we live – a sense conveyed specifically through photography by an artist whose personal modesty is as remarkable and unusual as his creative gifts. Just look at these pictures.

Simon Watney, London, July 1994

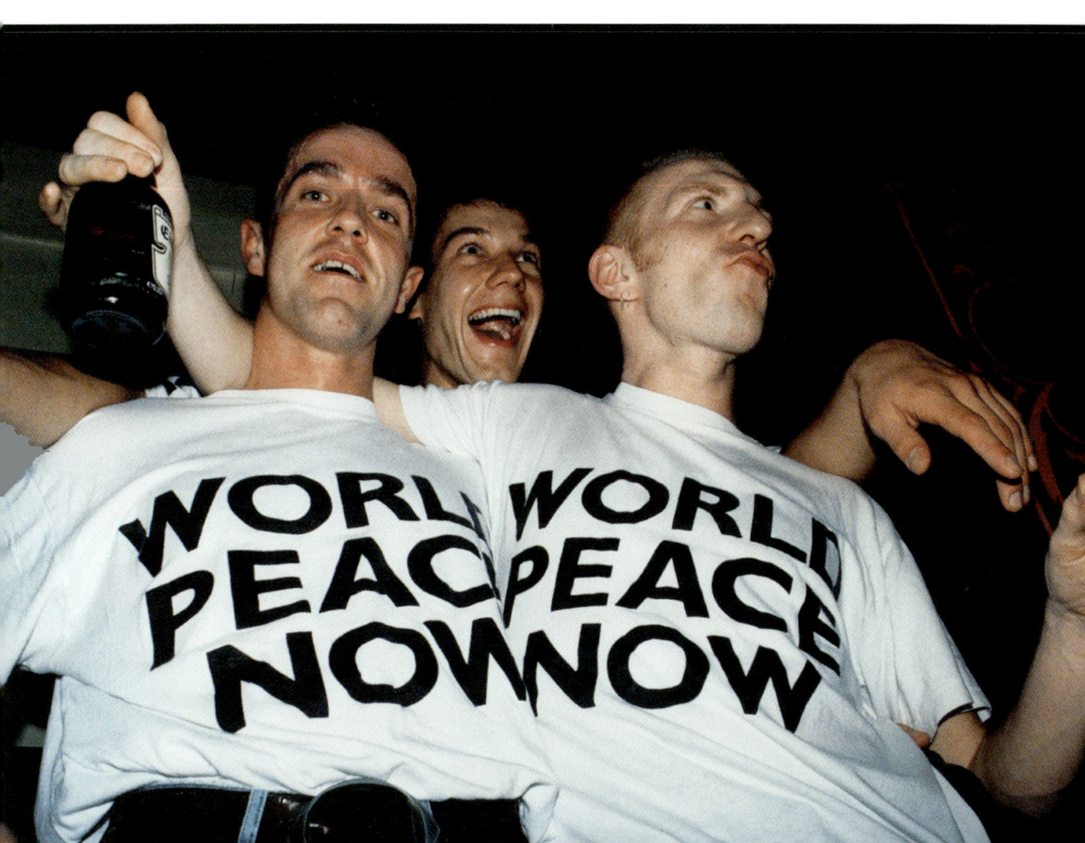

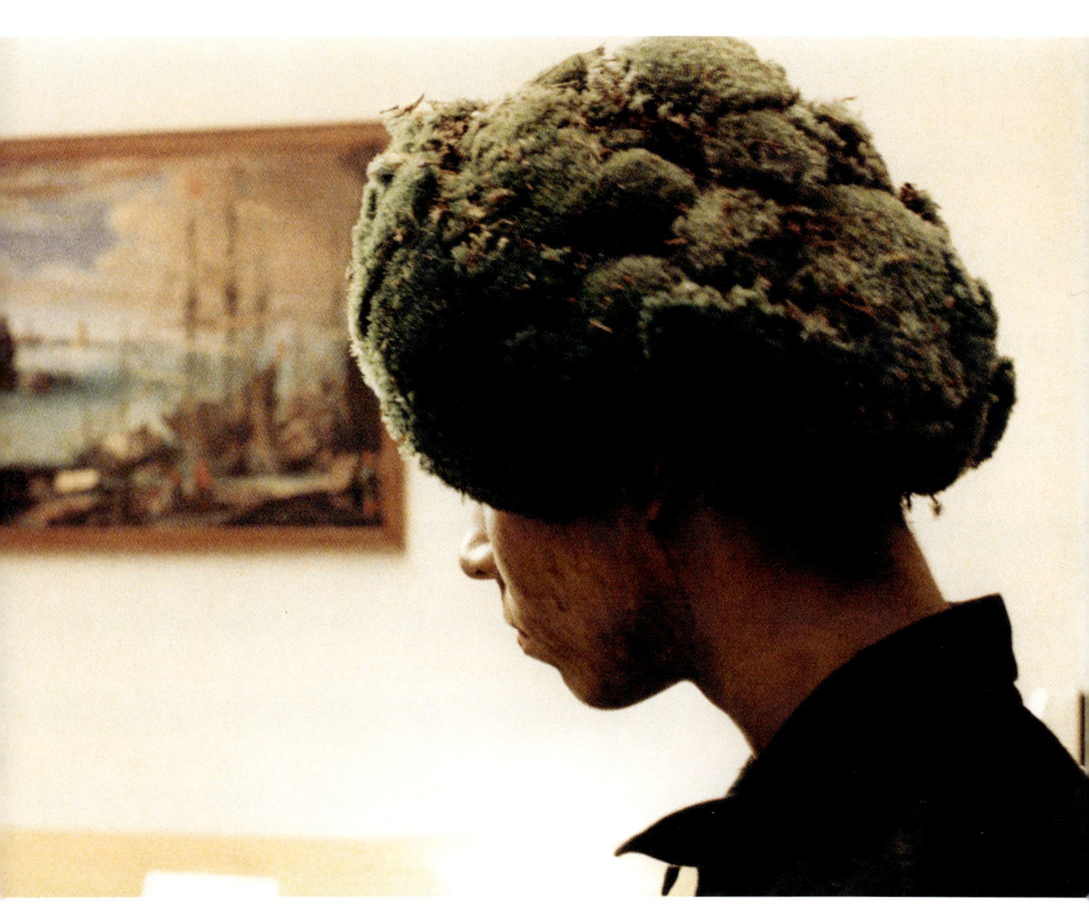

Opera House (Ingo), 1989
Mosshat, 1988

dancer, Opera House, 1989

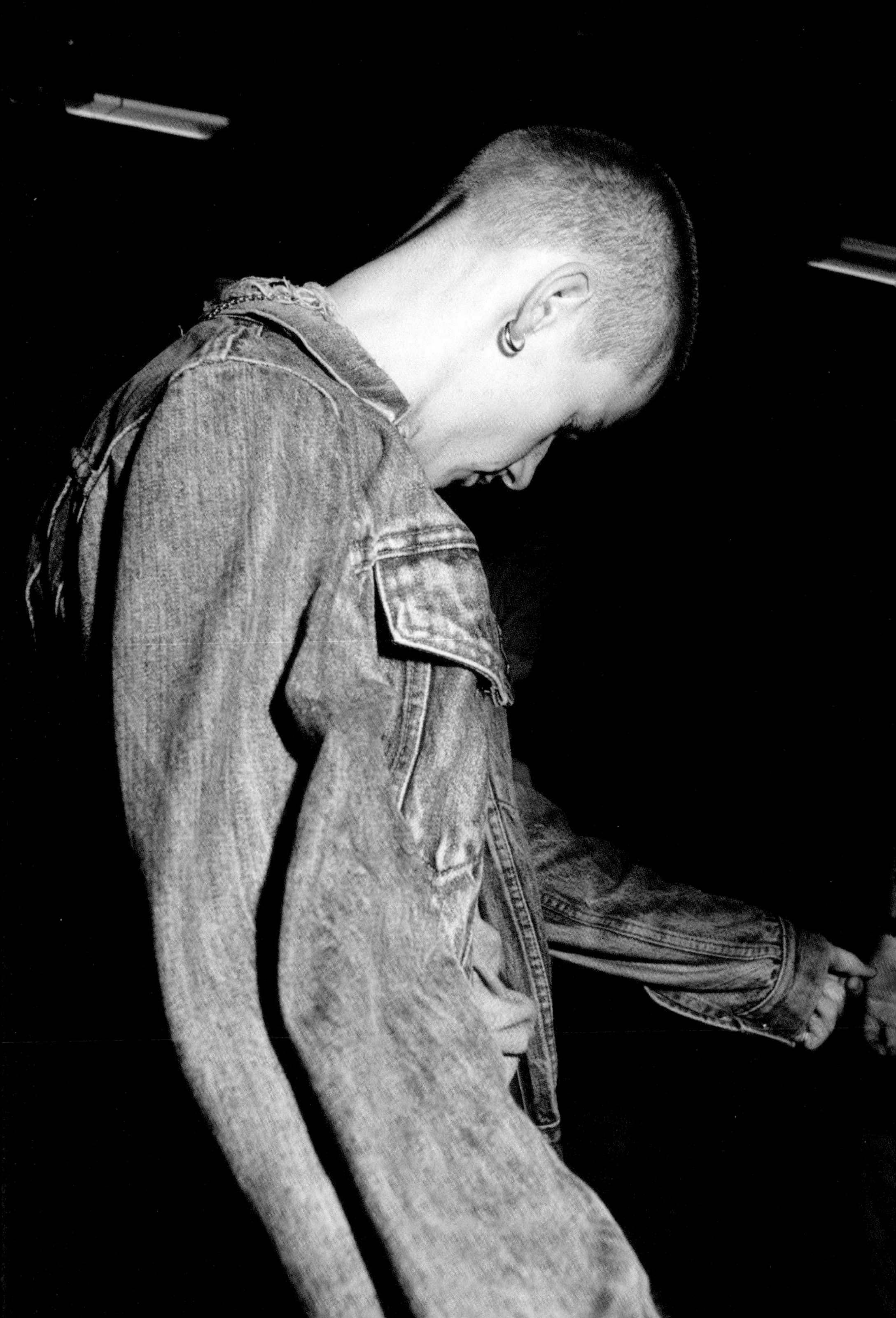

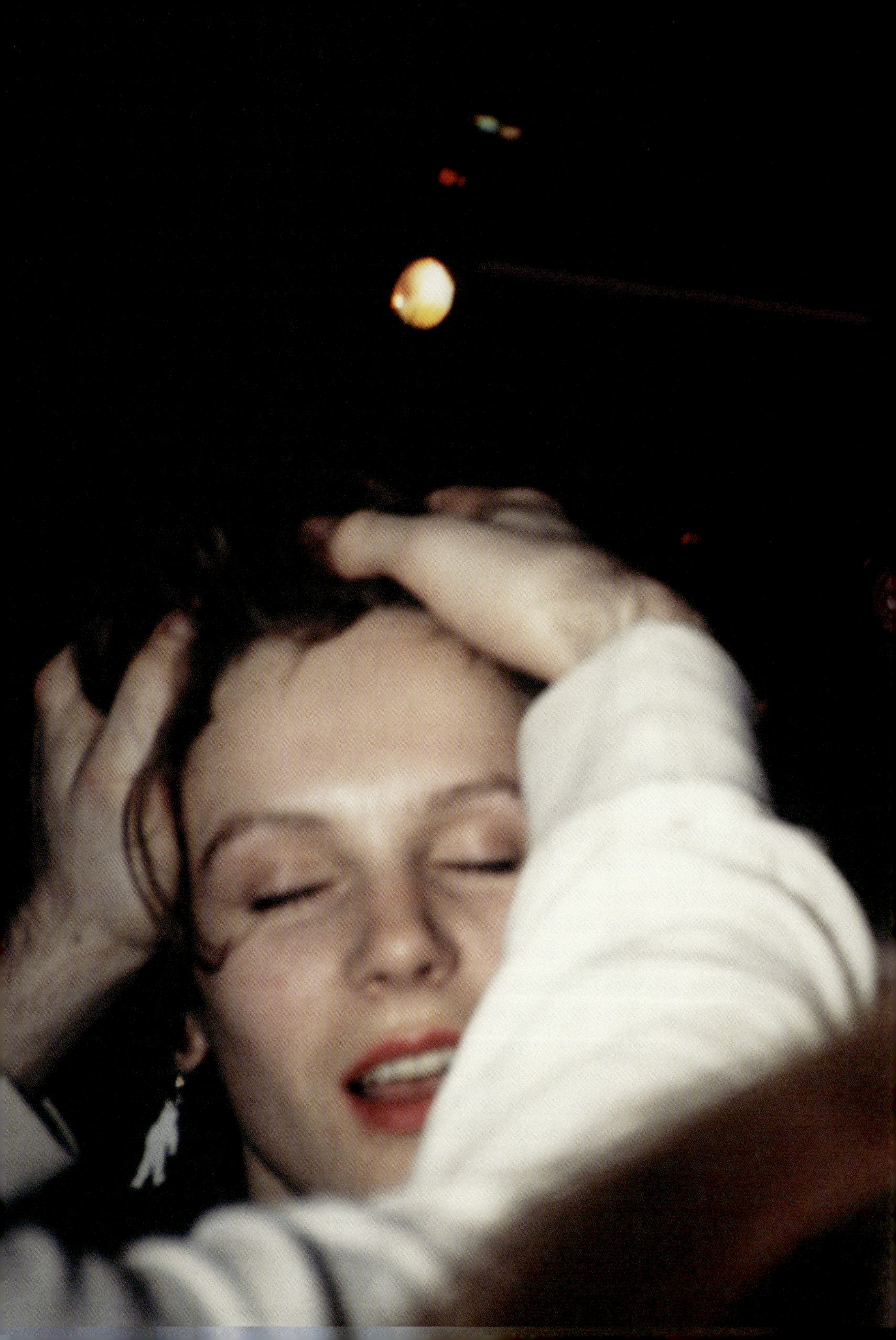

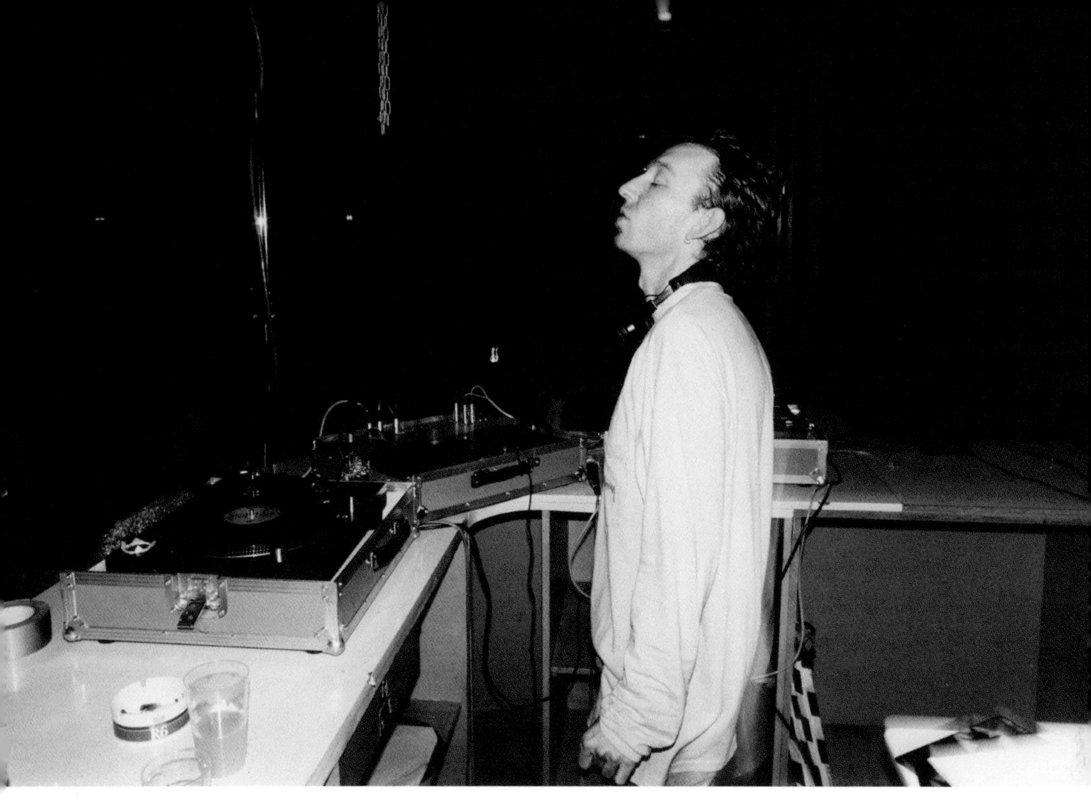

Love (hands in hair), London, 1989
Mike Pickering, Hamburg, 1989

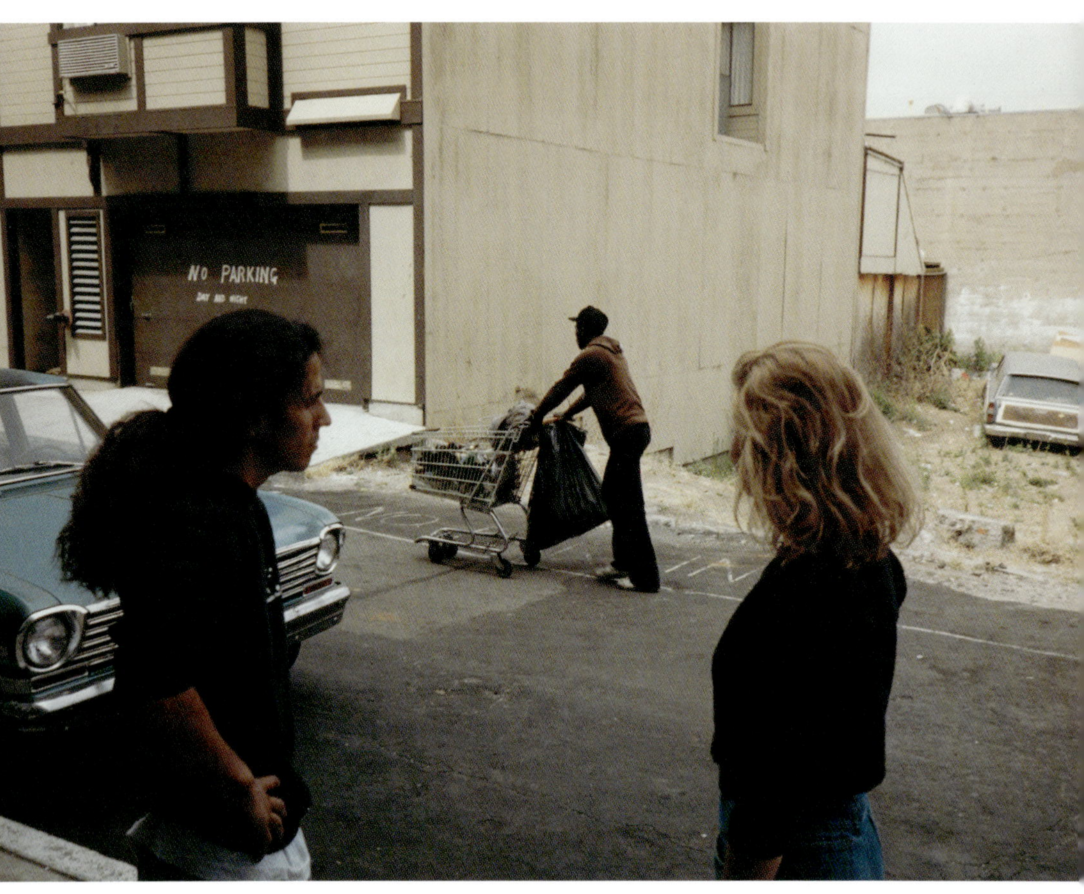

outside Globe, SF, 1990
Rob Greig, Talbot Road, 1991
Joy Ray, 1990
Princess Julia & Vaughan Toulouse, 1989

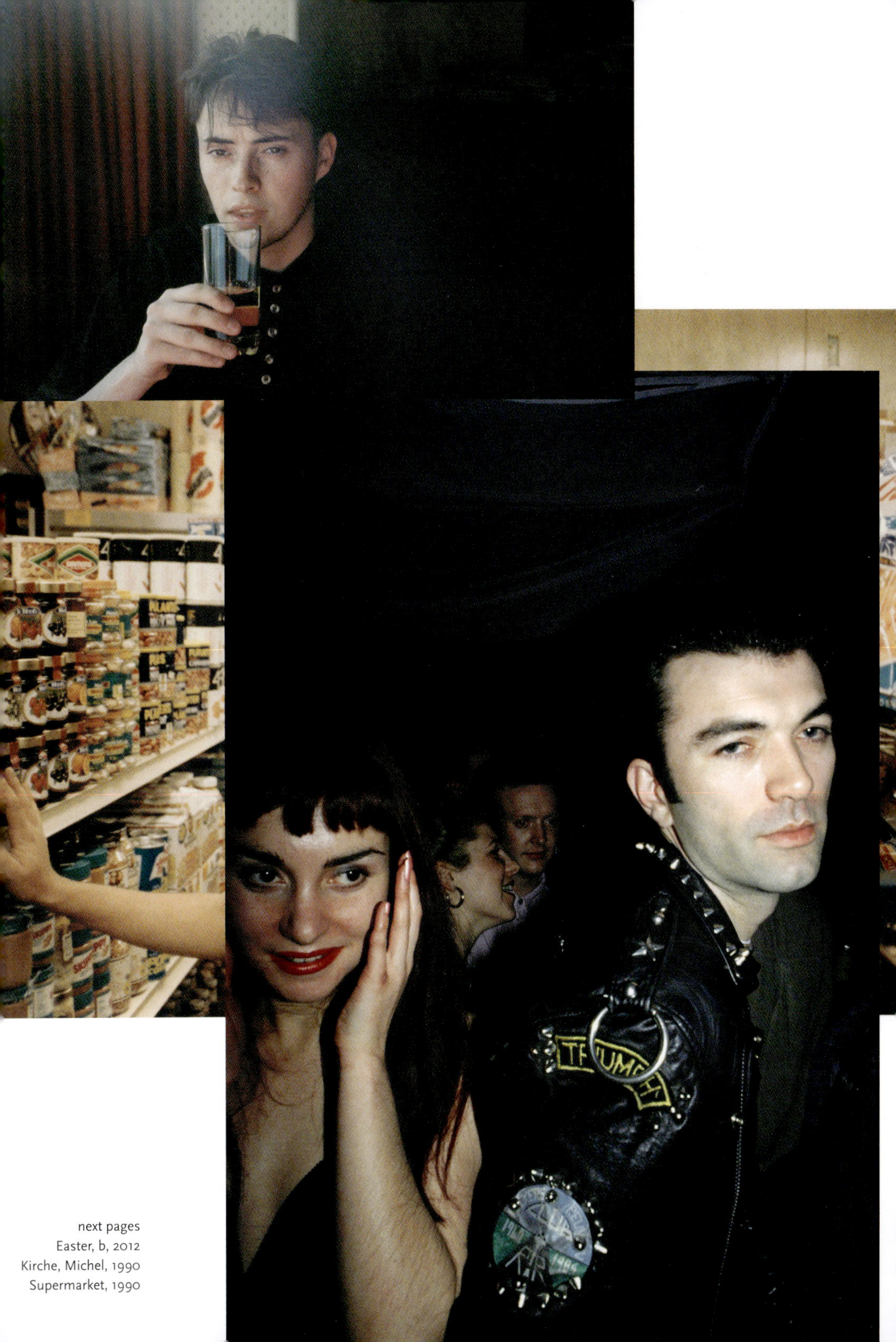

next pages
Easter, b, 2012
Kirche, Michel, 1990
Supermarket, 1990

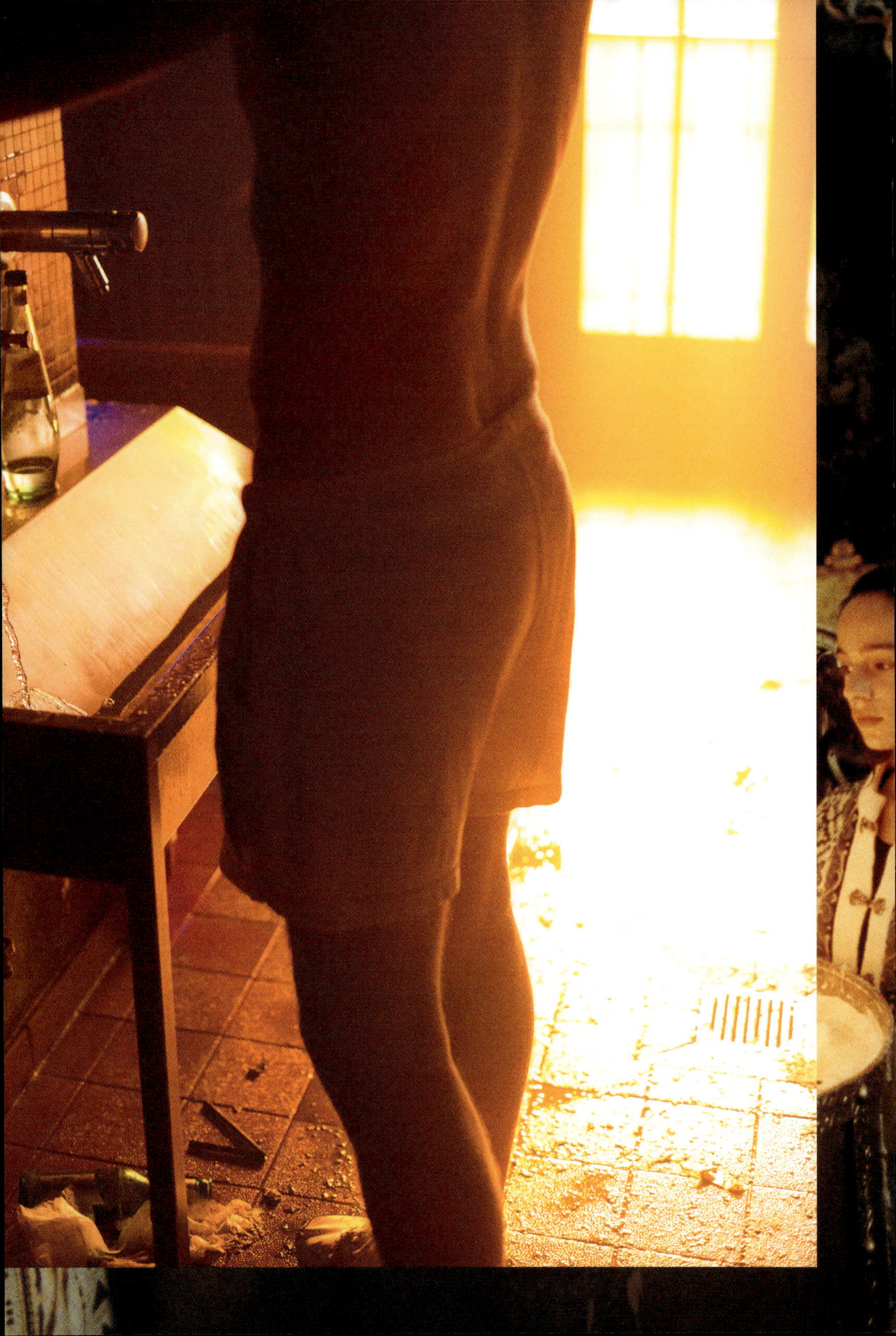

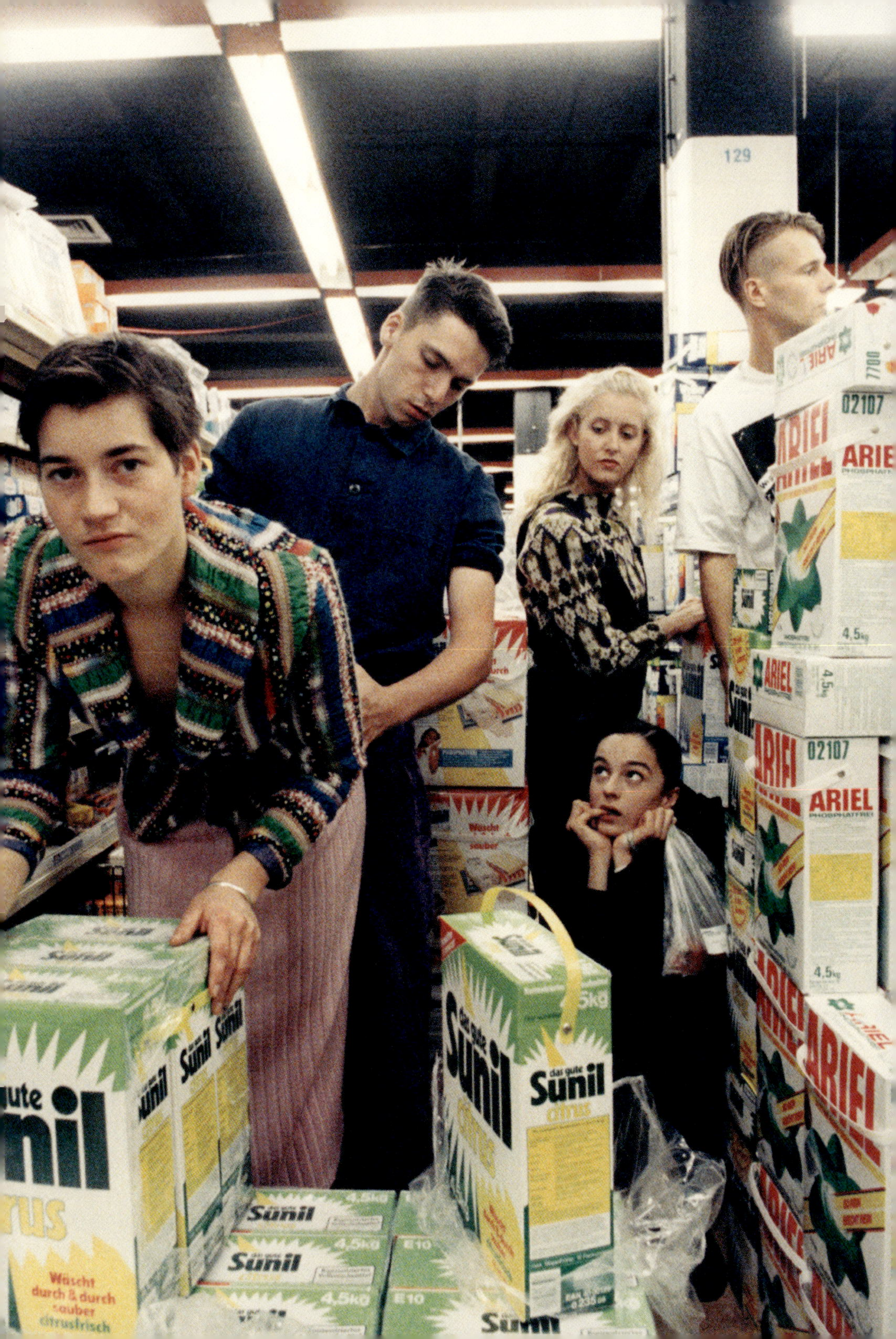

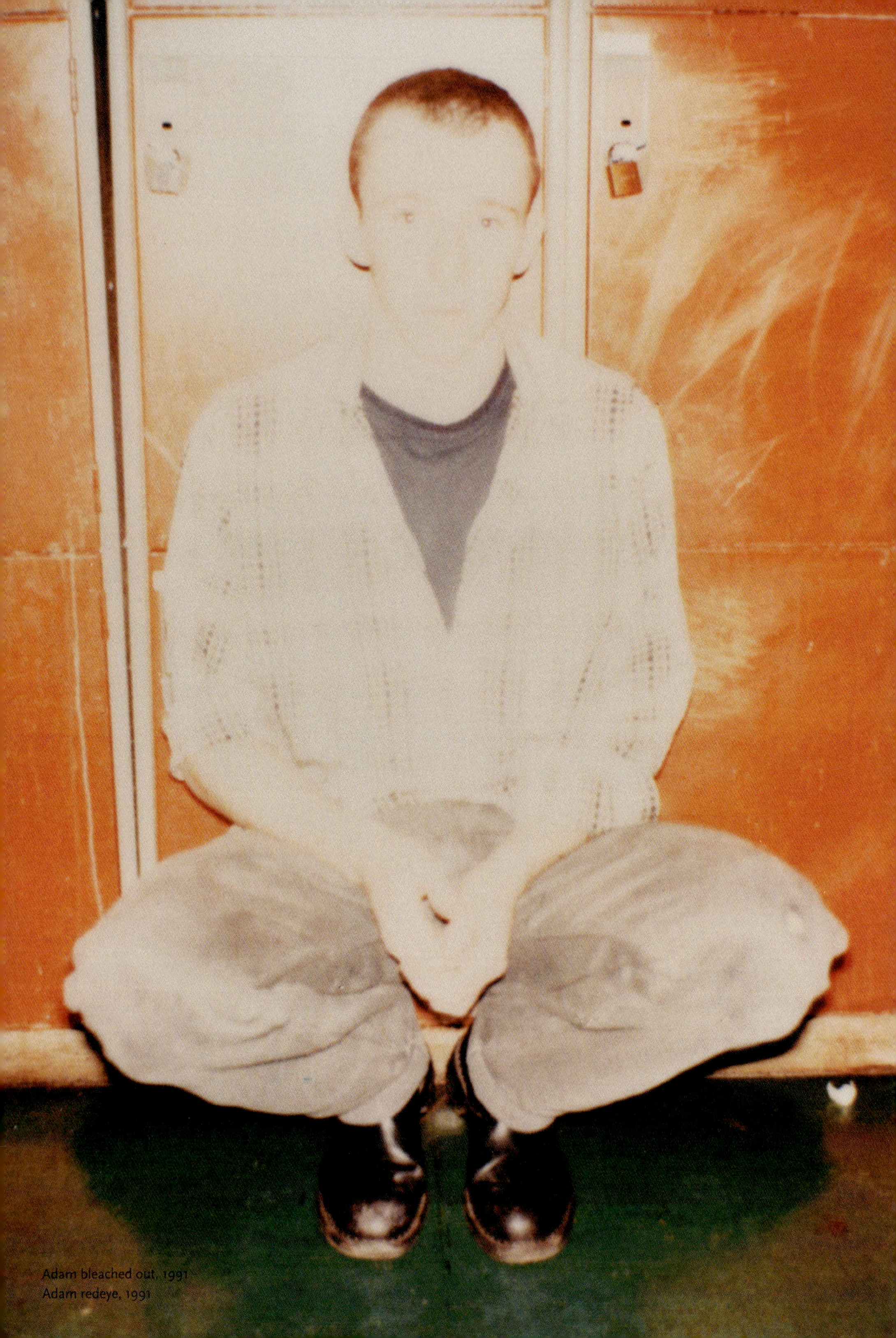

Adam bleached out, 1991
Adam redeye, 1991

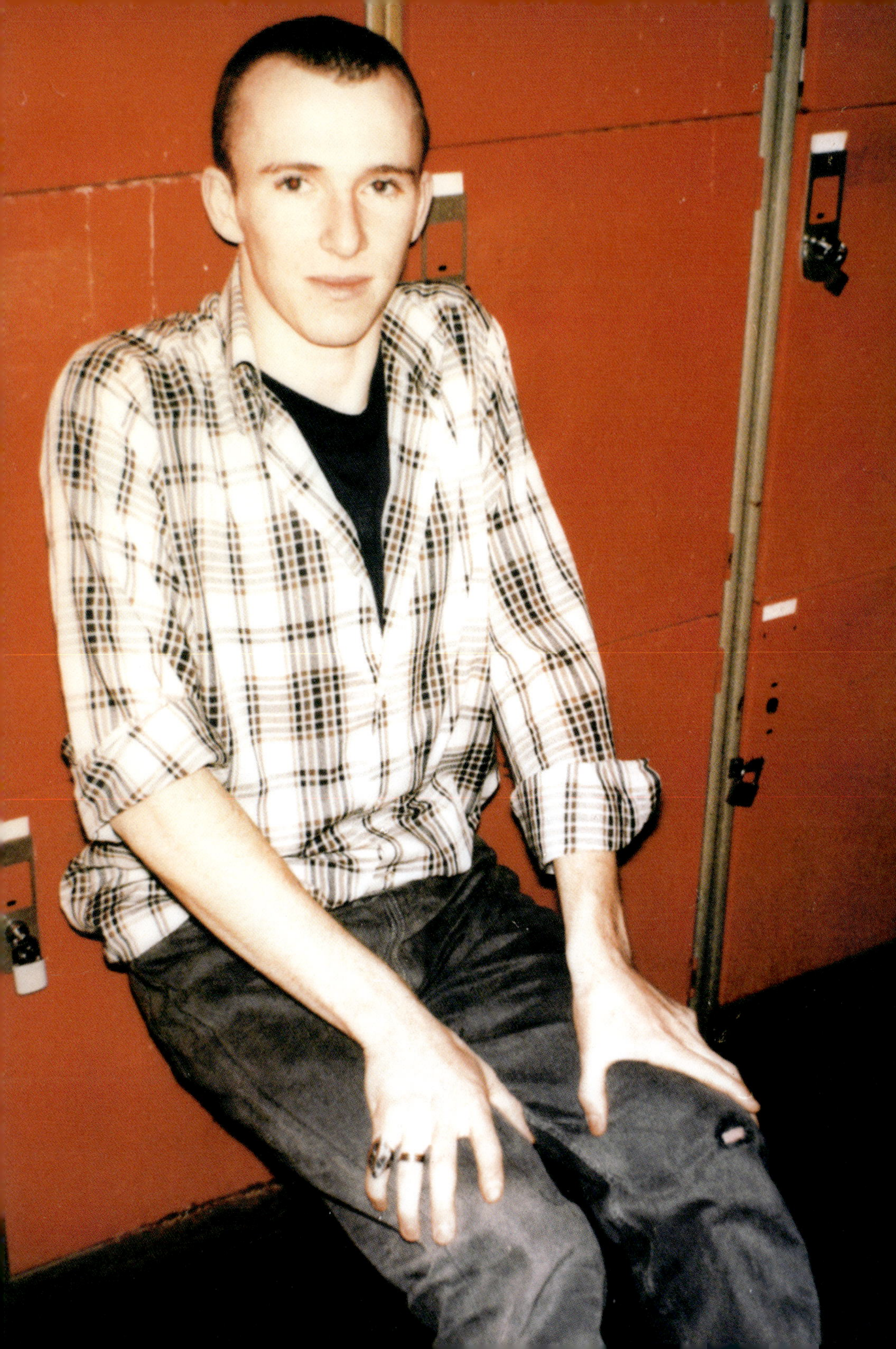

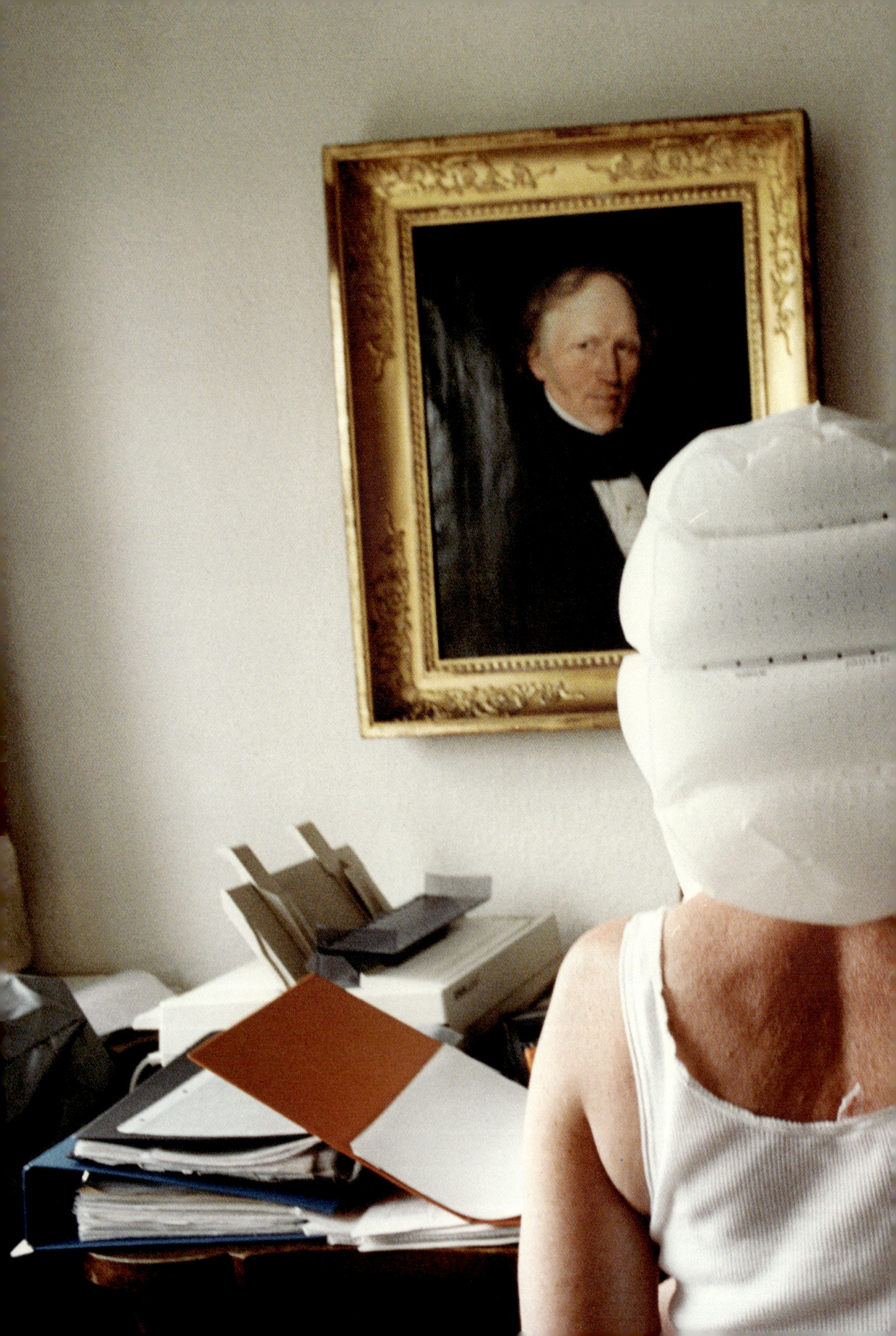

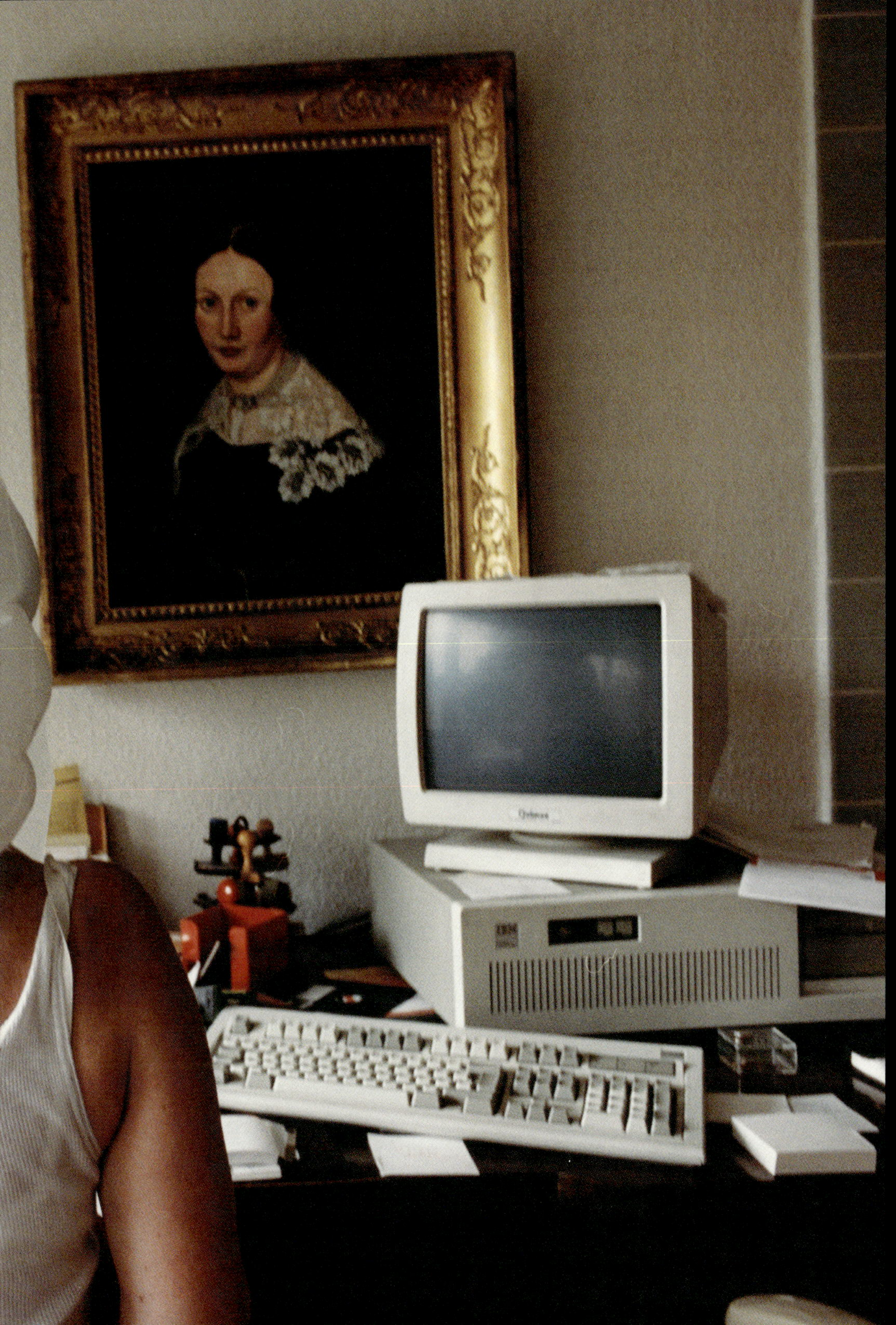

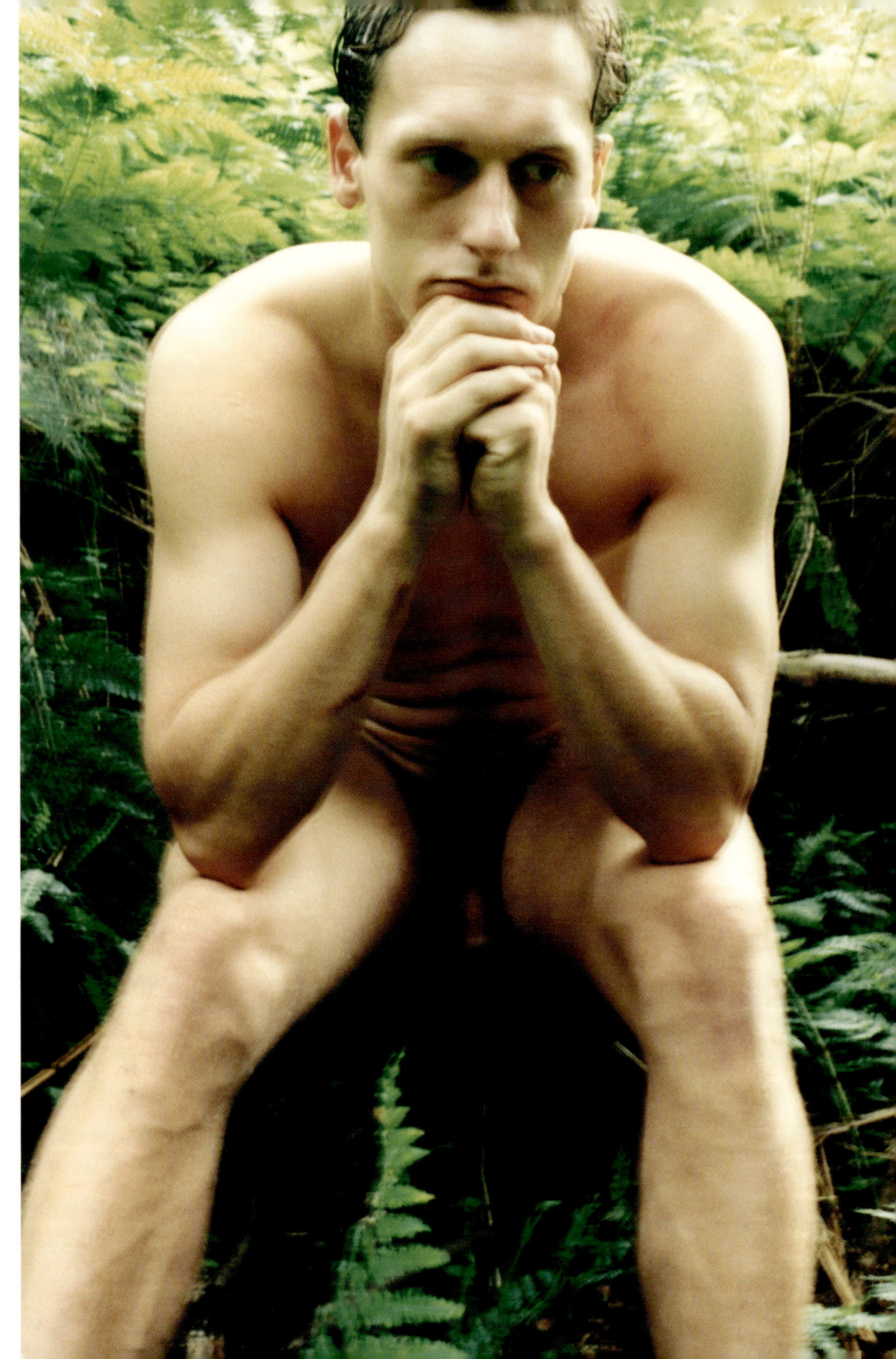

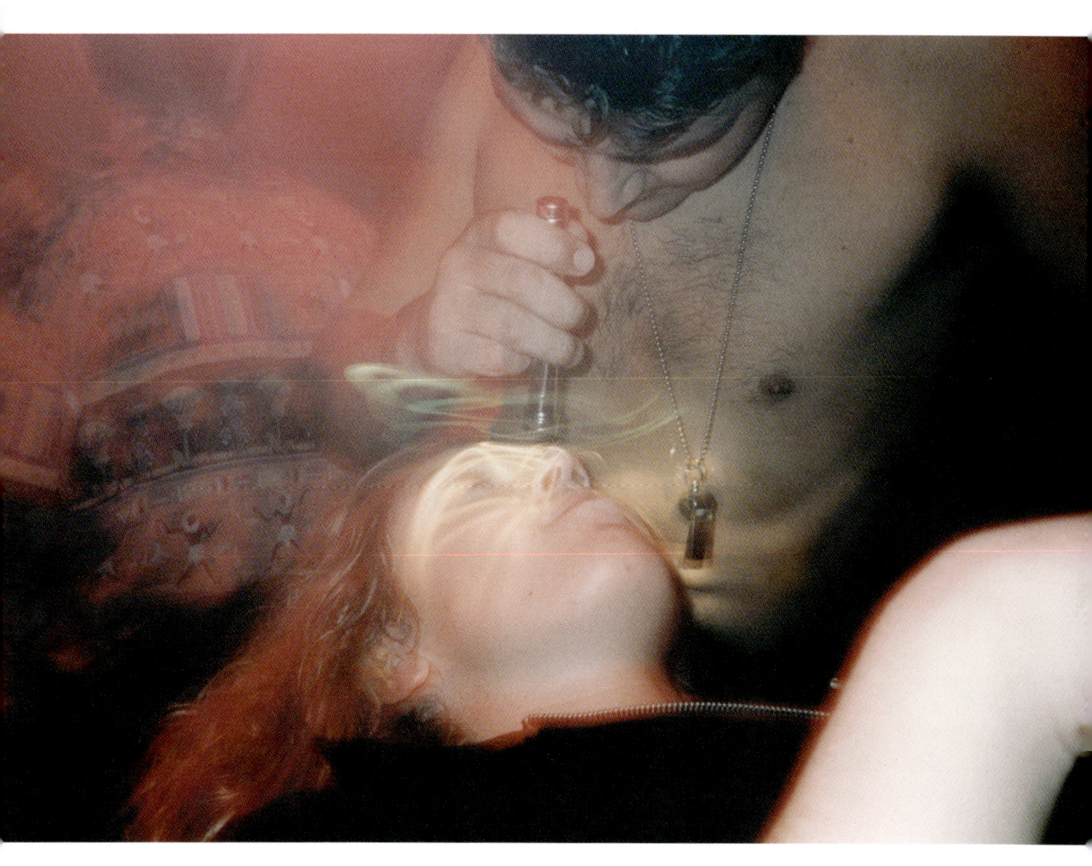

domestic scene, Remscheid, 1991
Arnd, nude sitting, 1991
Dorian Gray, Frankfurt, 1991

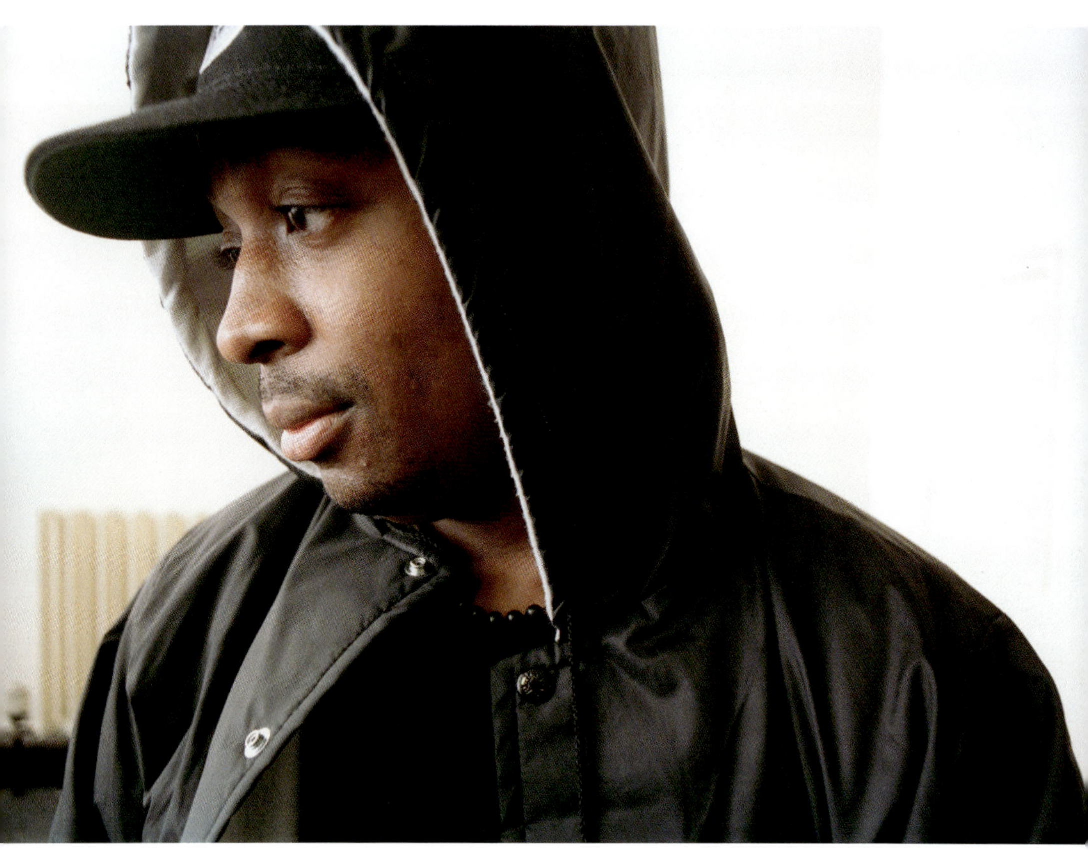

Chuck D, 1992

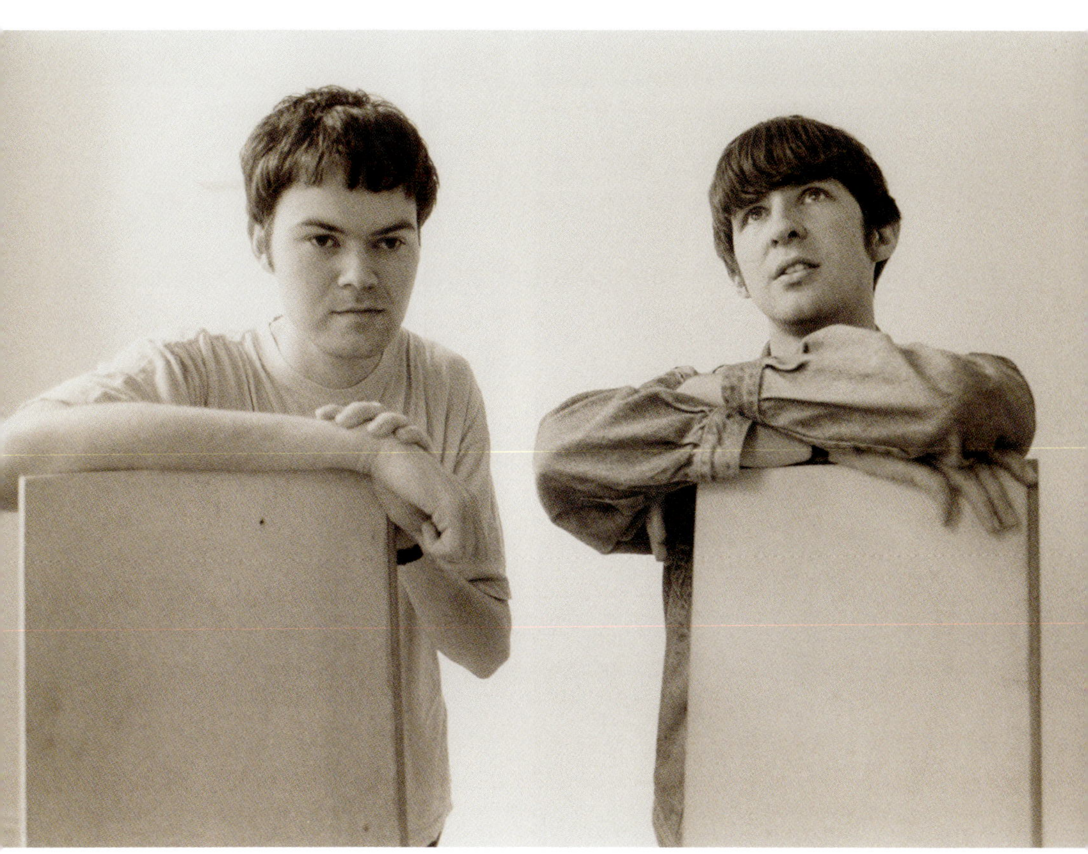

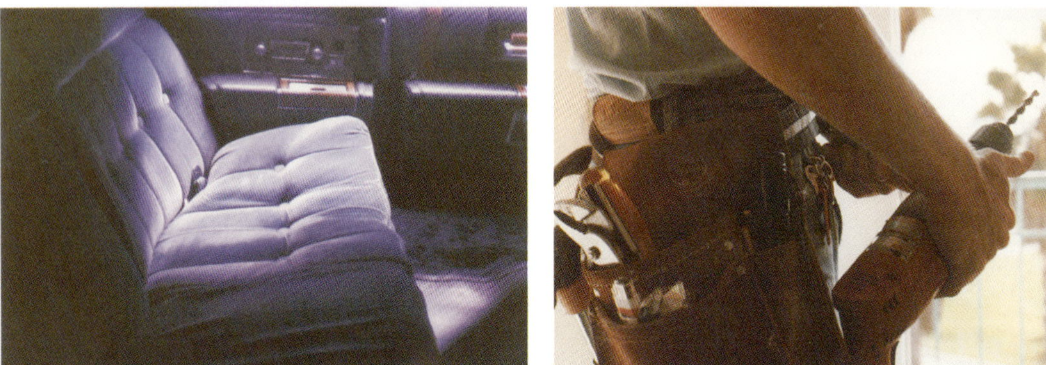

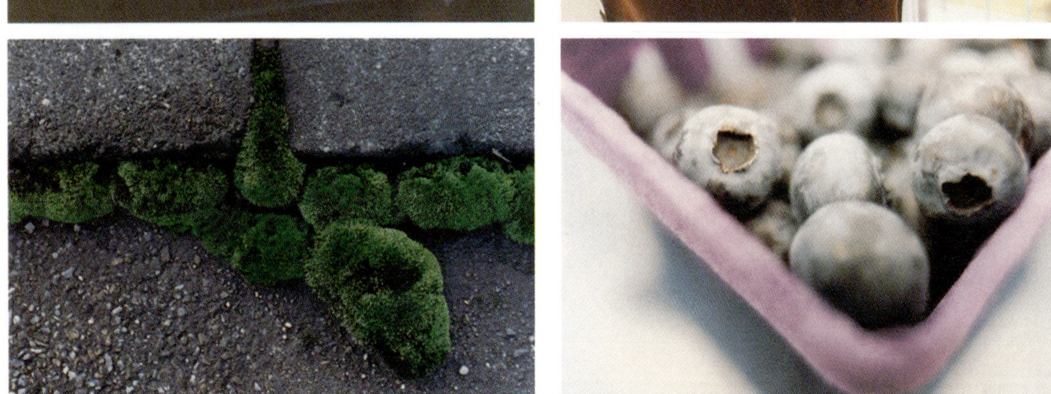

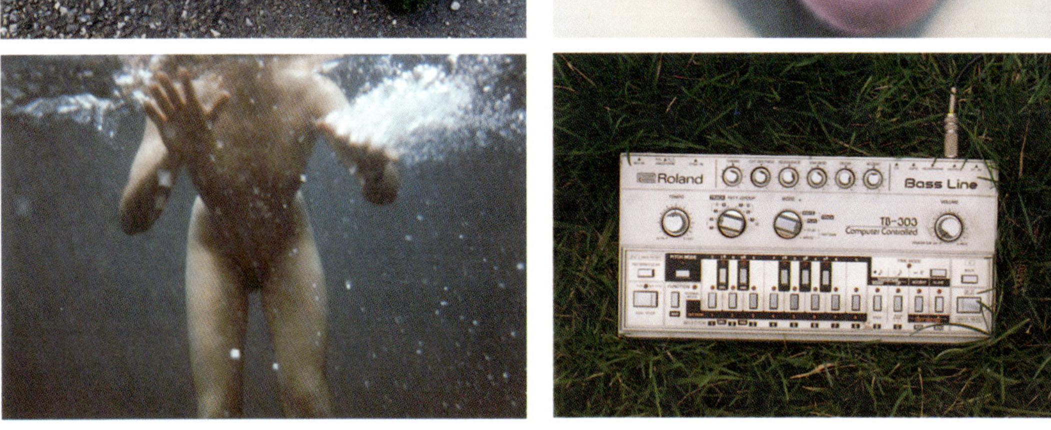
Roland
Bass Line
TB-303
Computer Controlled

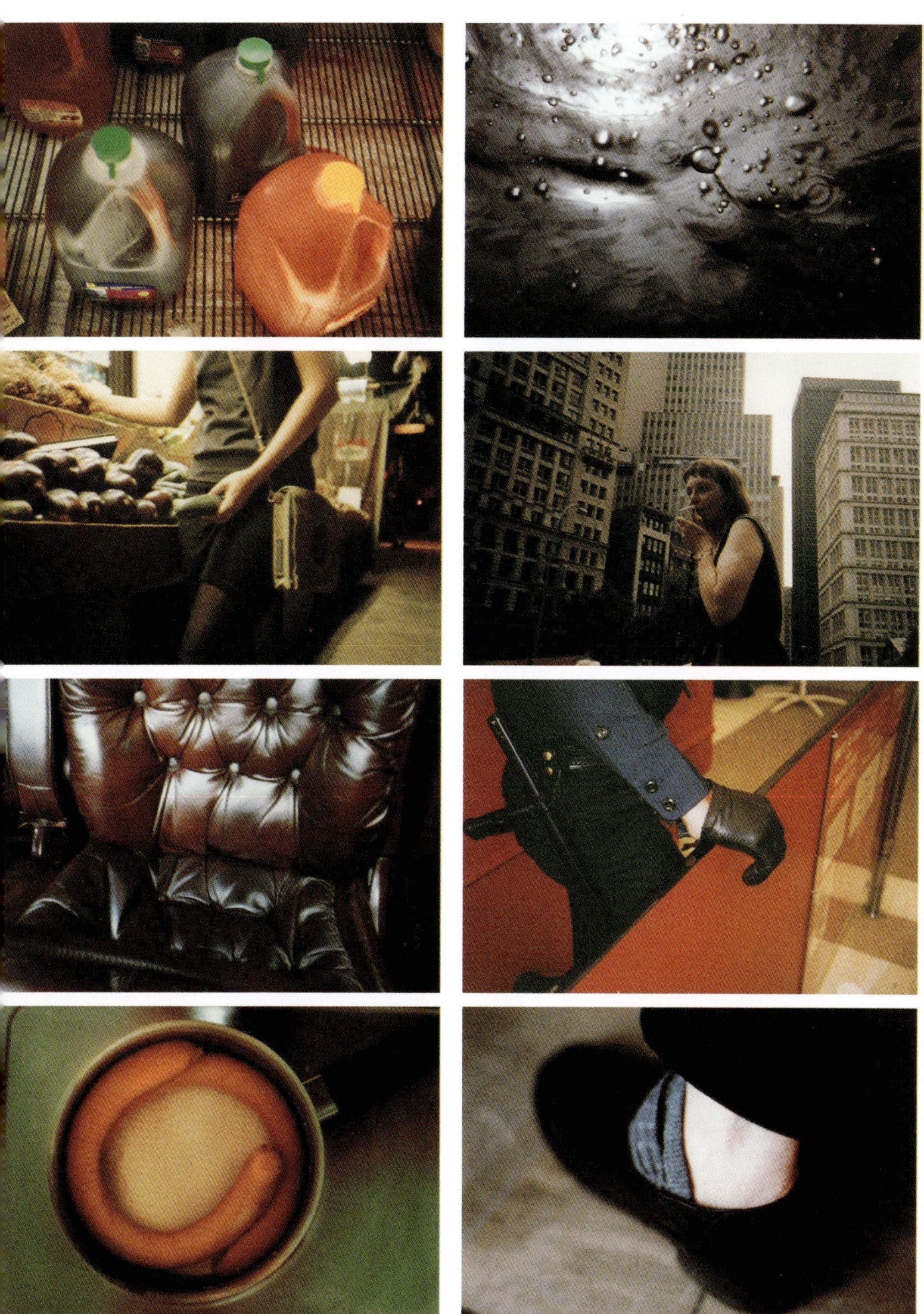

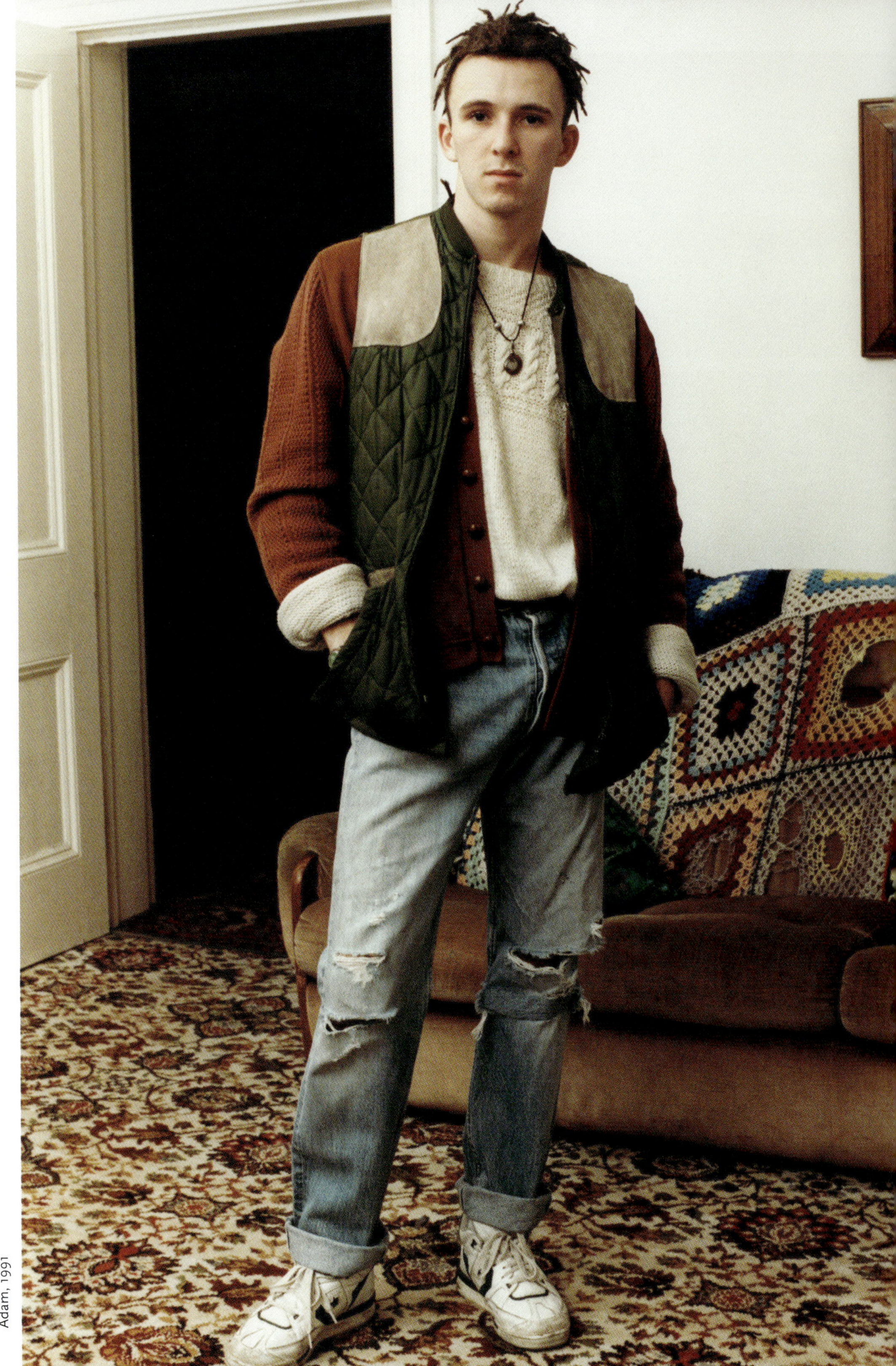

Adam, 1991

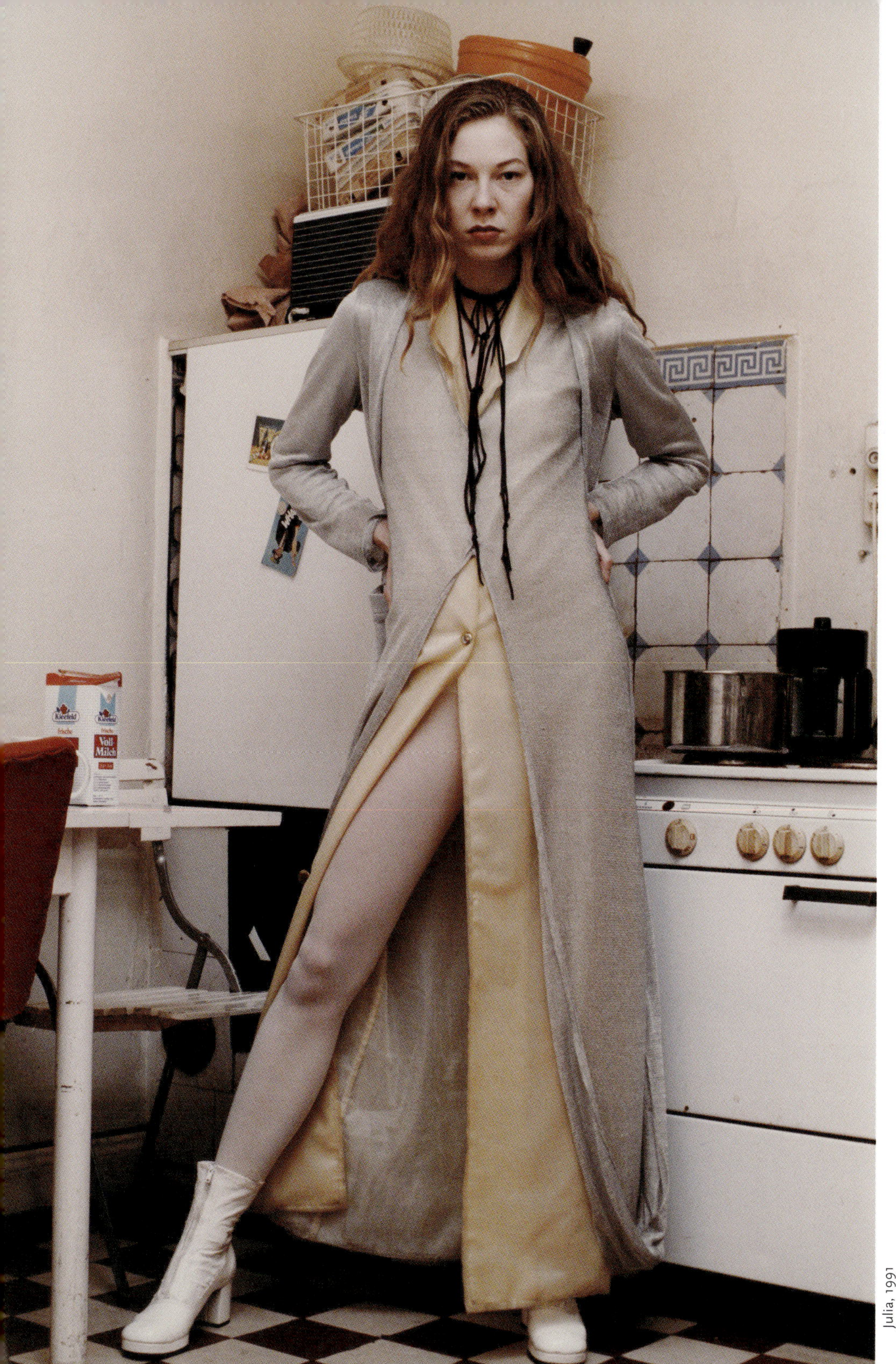

Julia, 1991

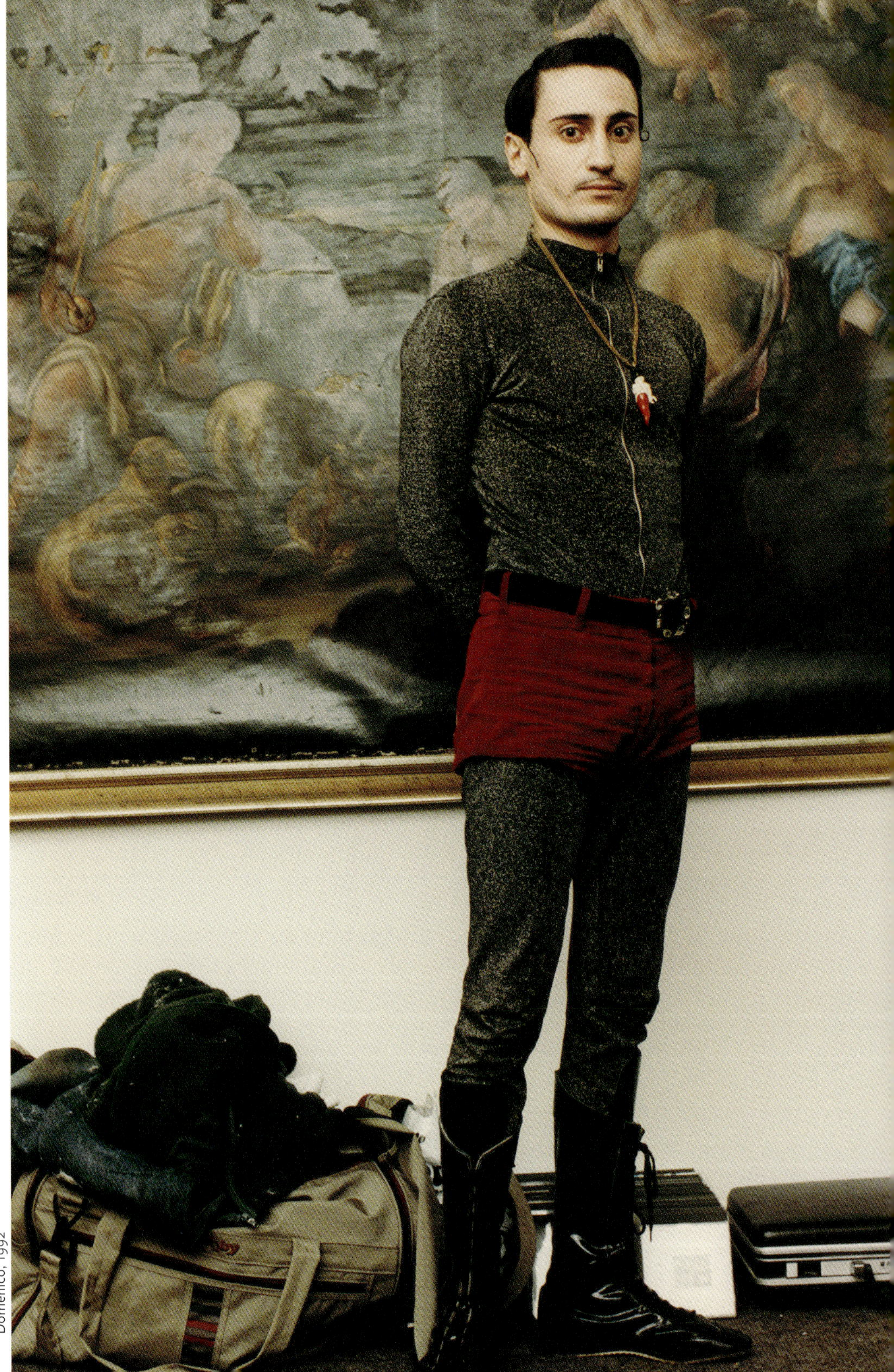

Domenico, 1992

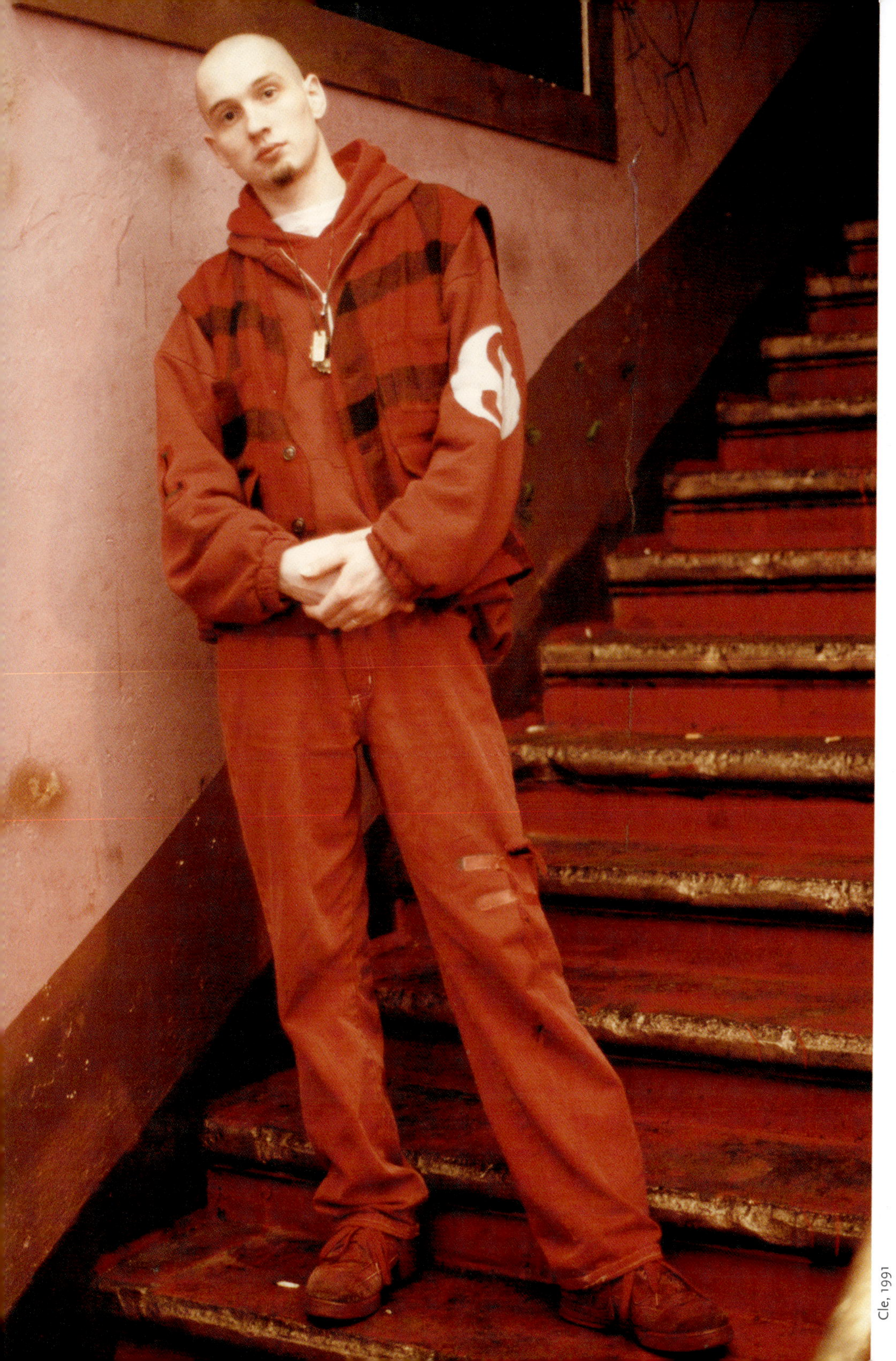

Cle, 1991

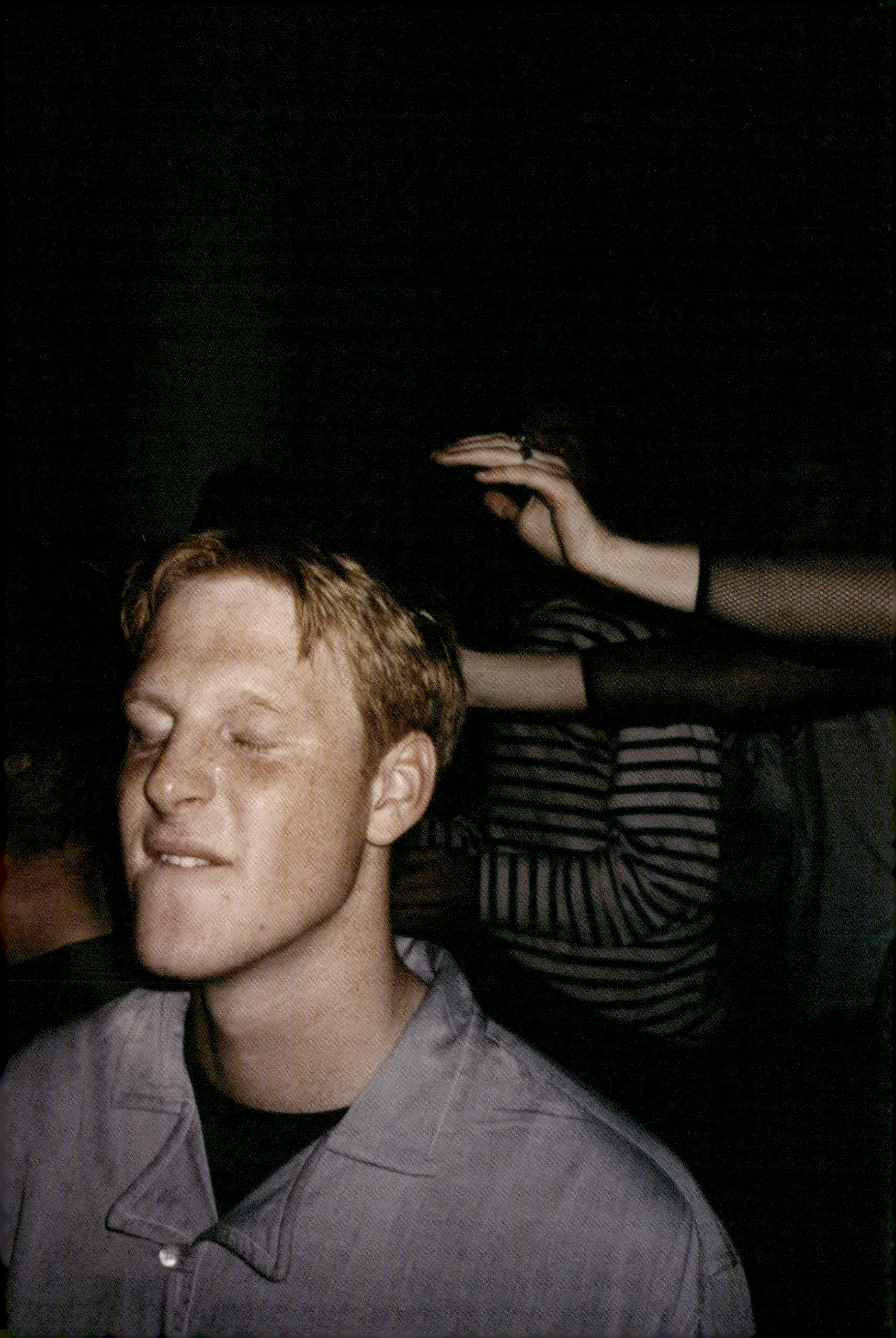

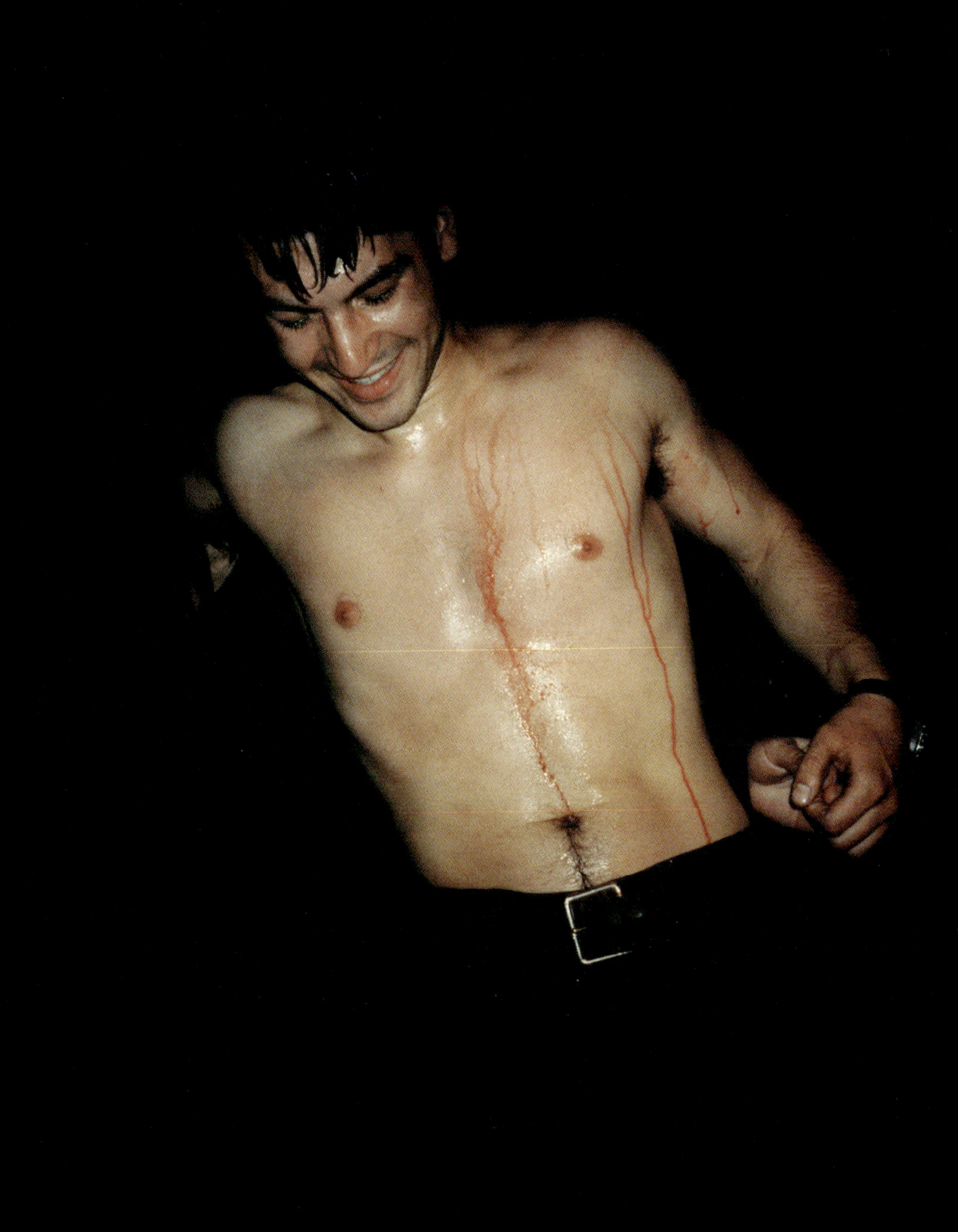

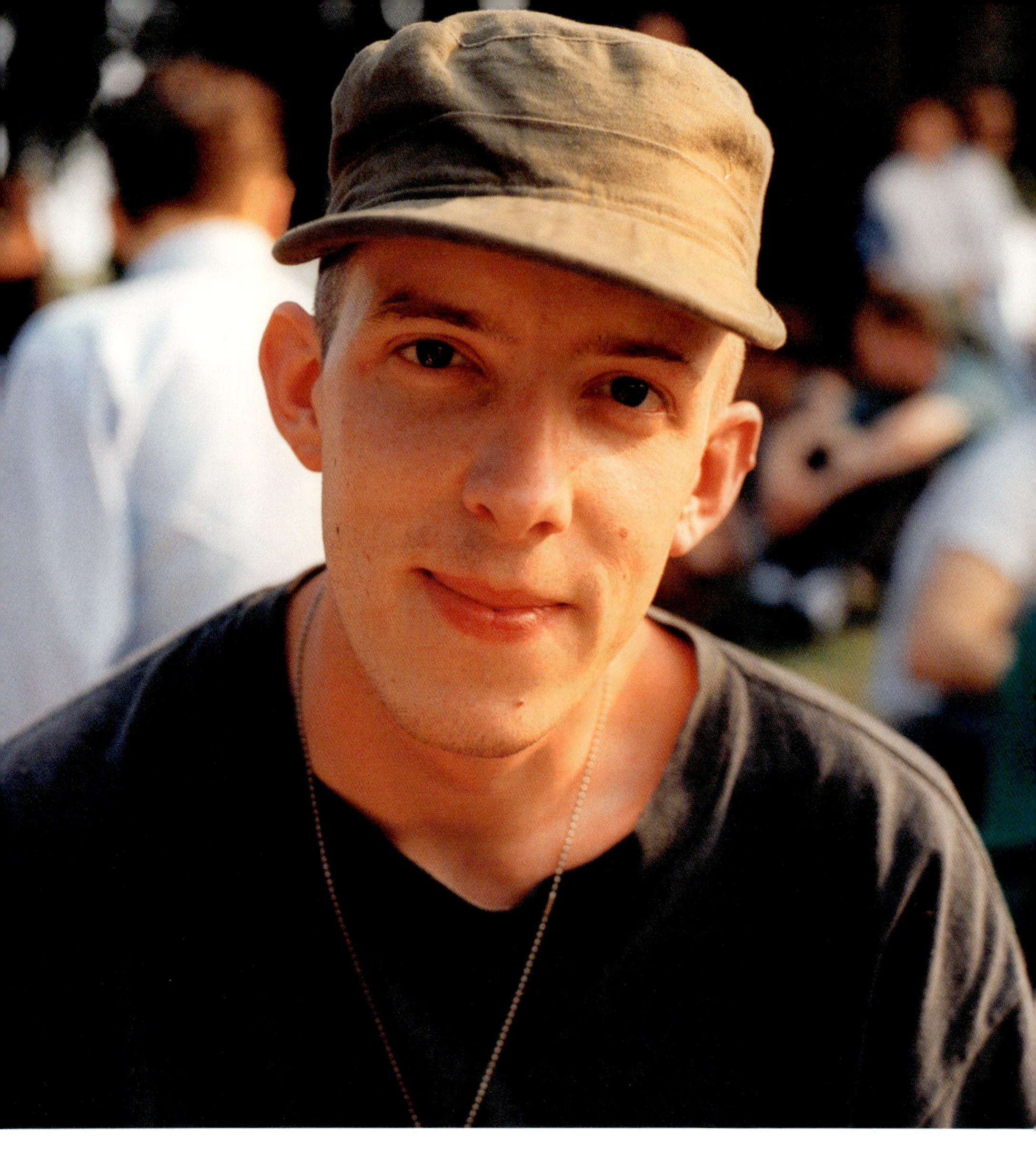

Brighton Raver, 1992
blood dancer, 1992
Craig, Pride, 1992
European Gay Pride, London, 1992
London Olympics, 2012

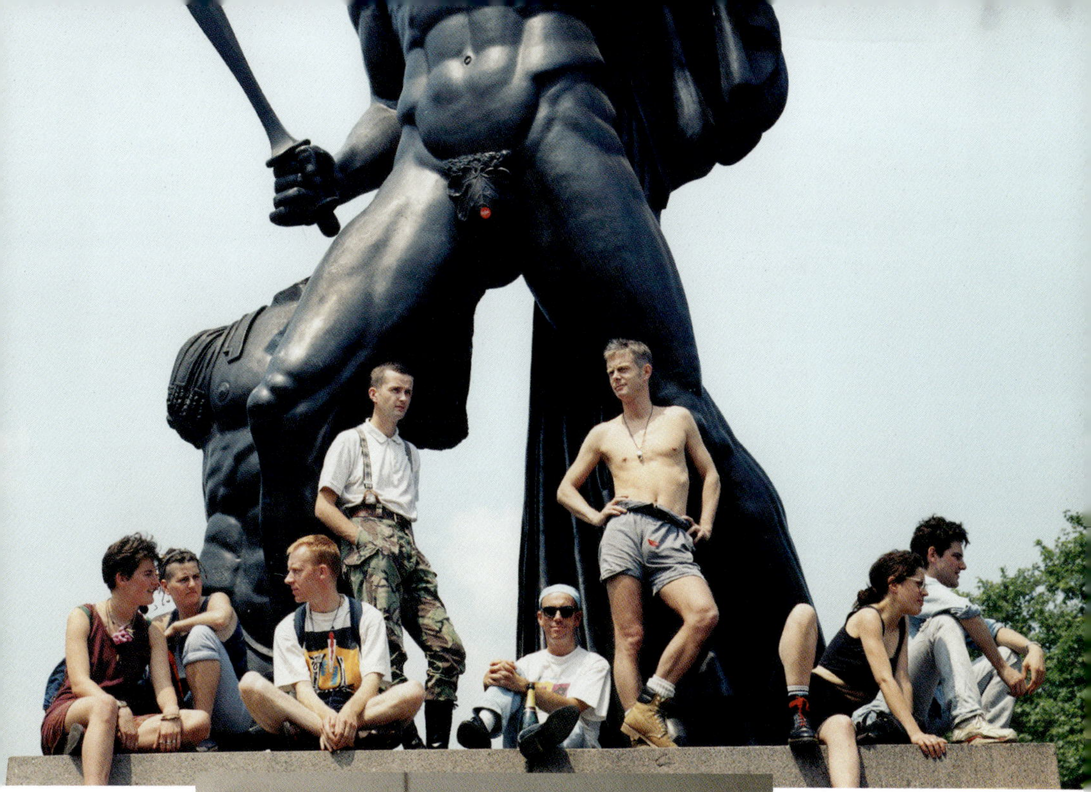

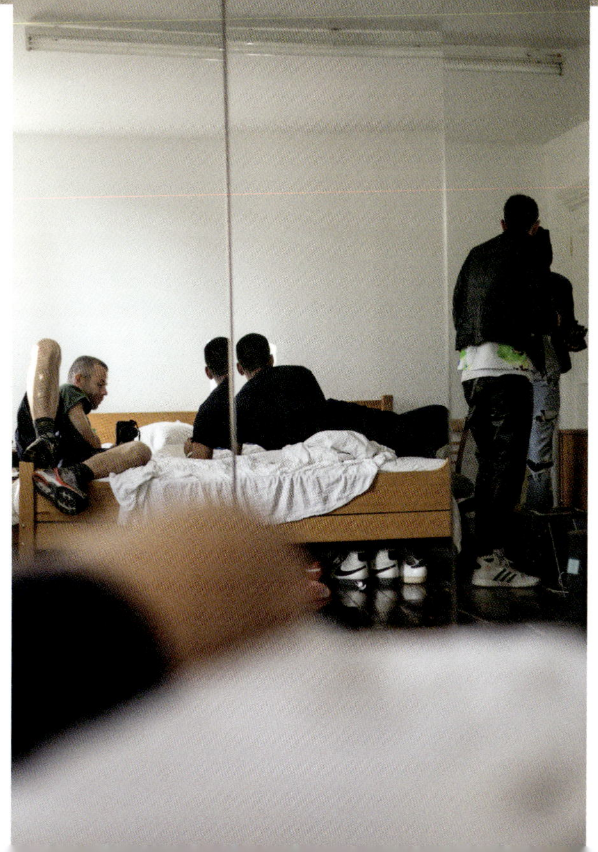

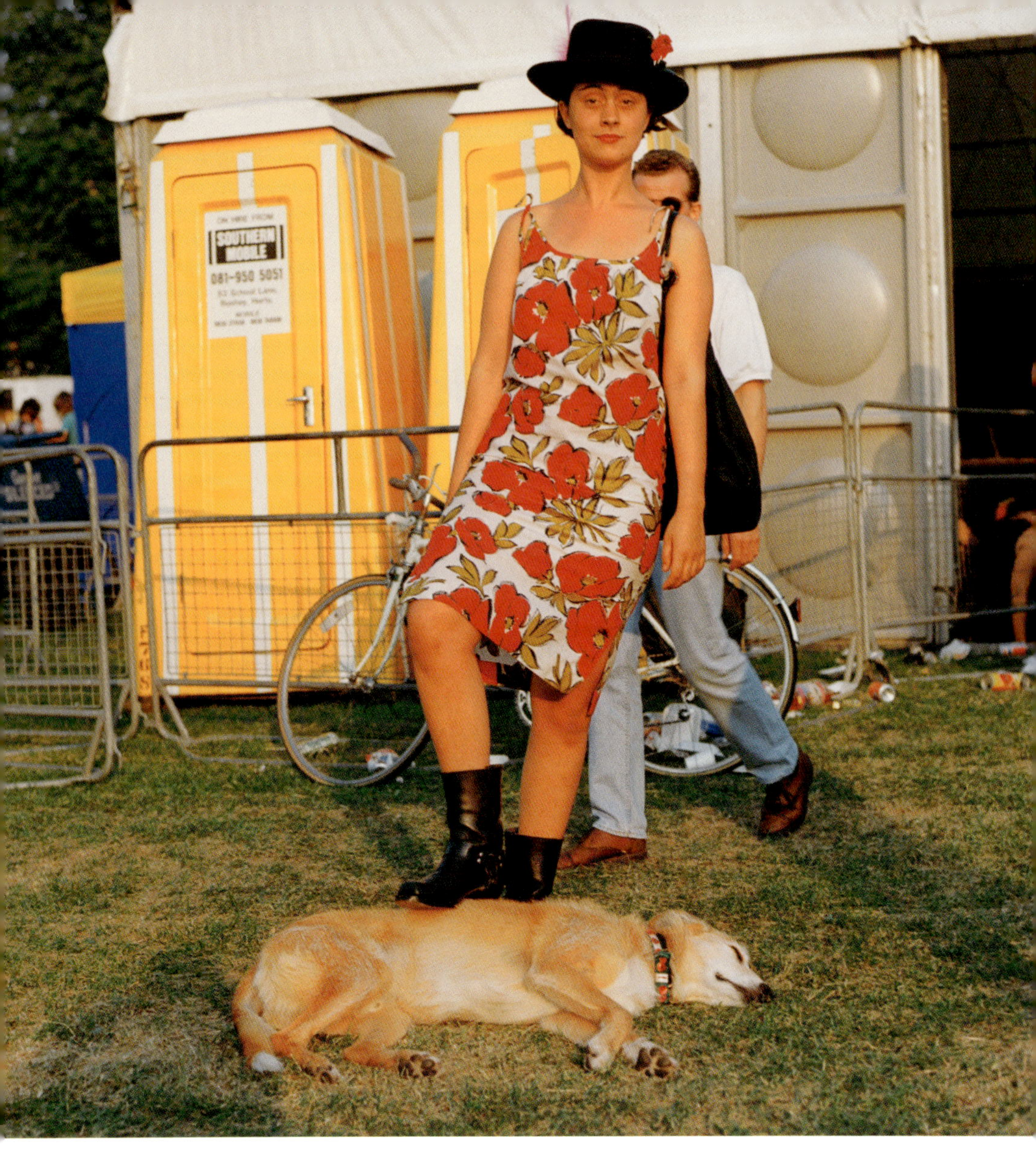

Misri (Europride), 1992

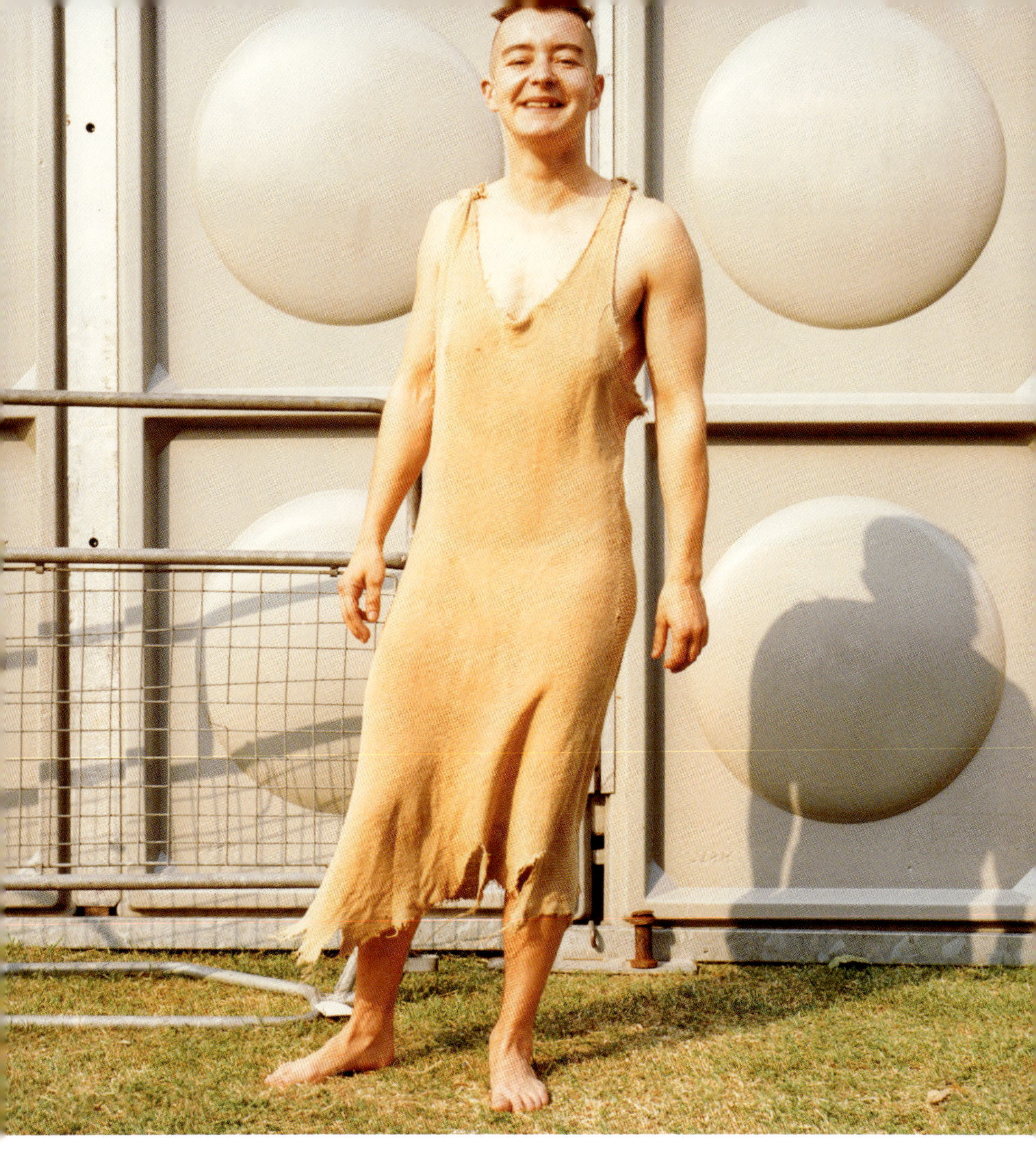

Eddie (Europride), 1992

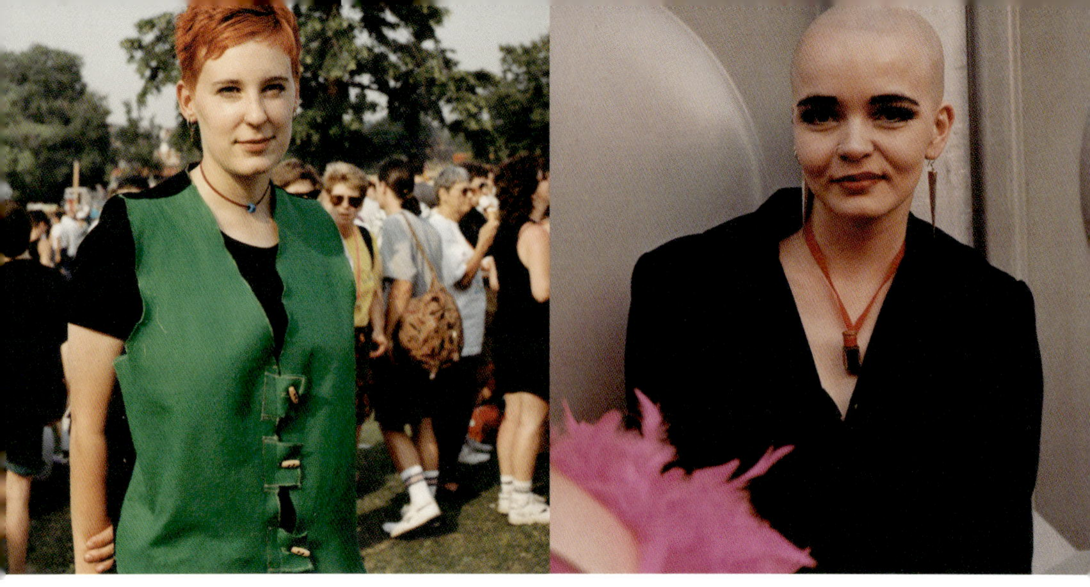

Rachel (Europride), 1992
Kaisu (Europride), 1992
Christoph & Alex (Europride), 1992

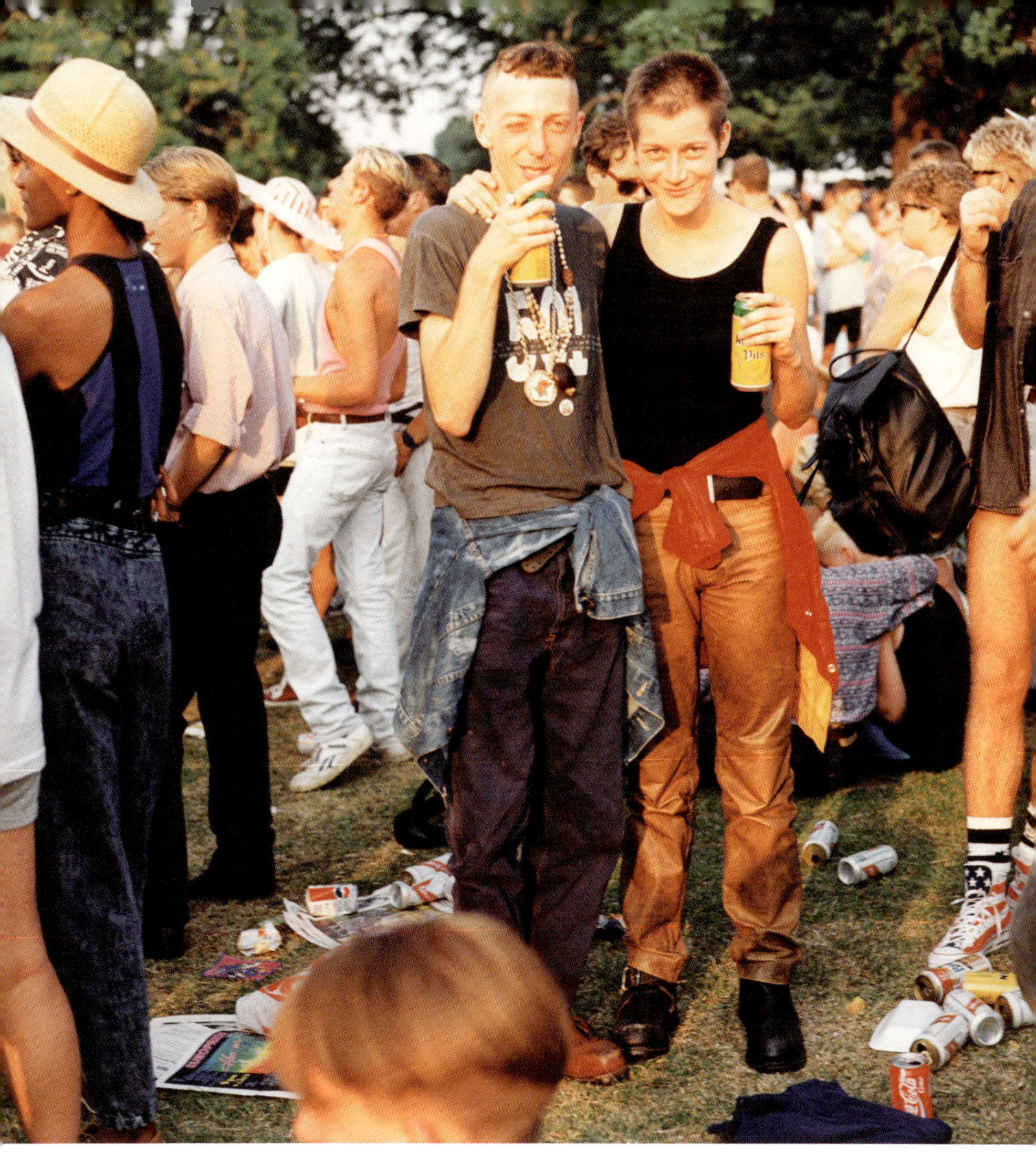

Love Parade, woman dancing in rain, 1992
Love Parade, guy dancing in rain, 1992

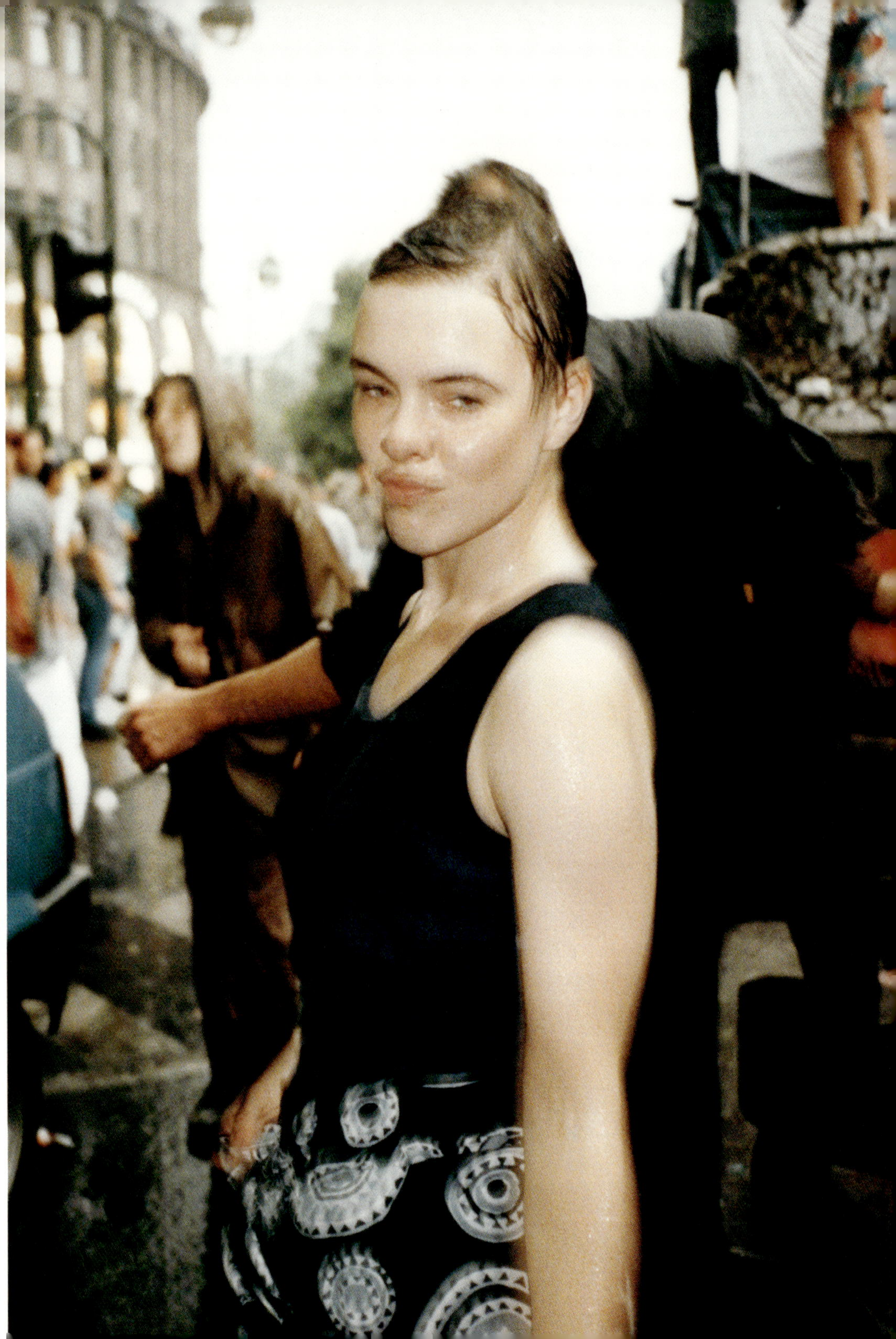

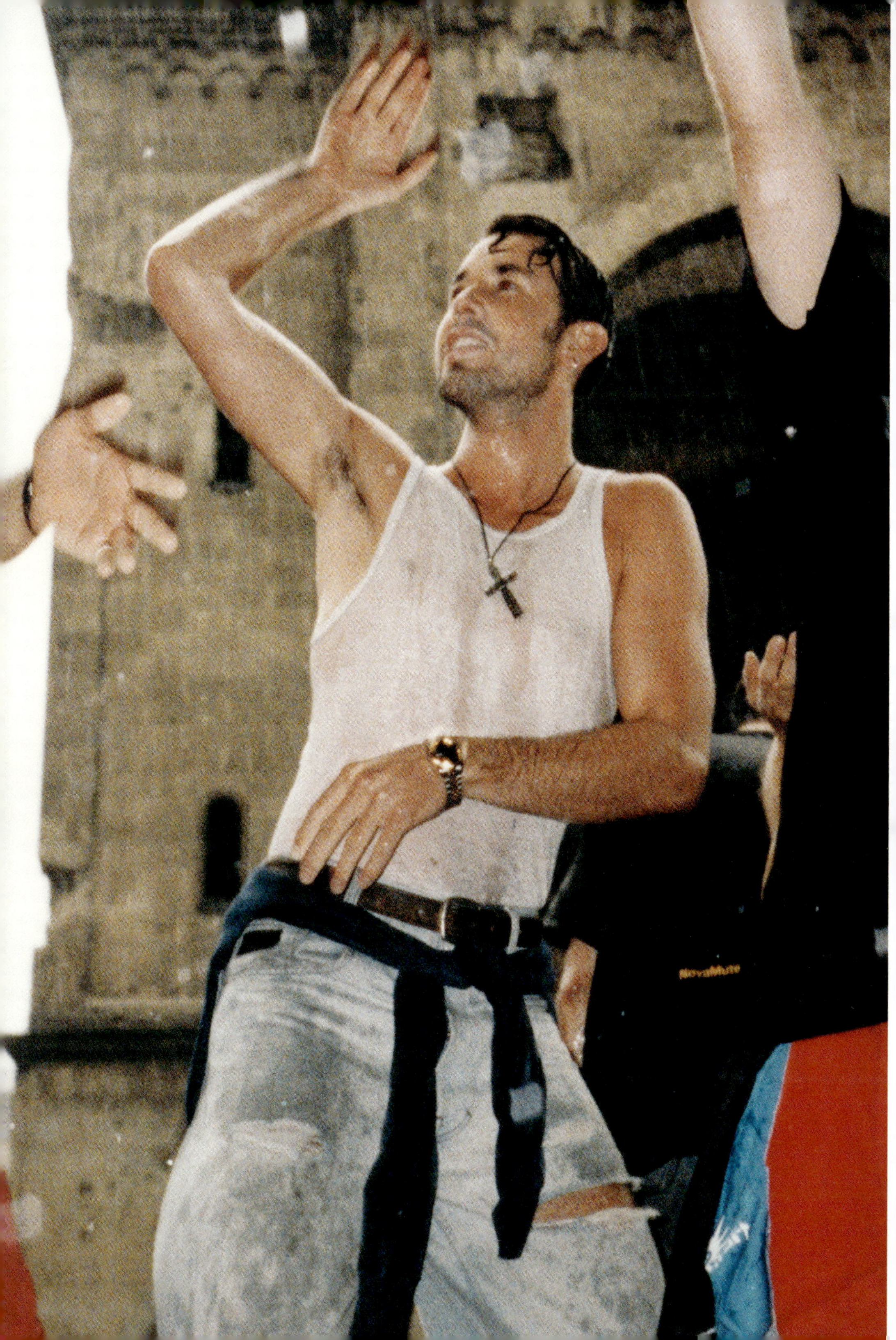

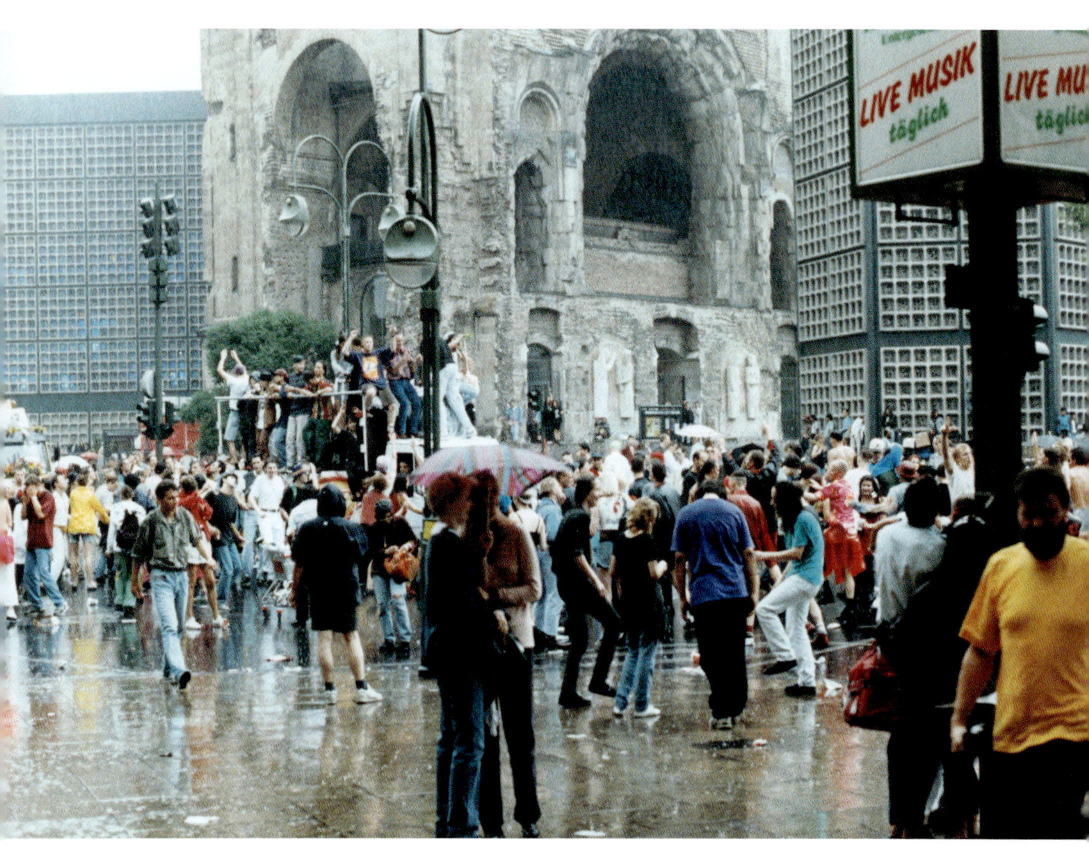

Love Parade, rain, 1992

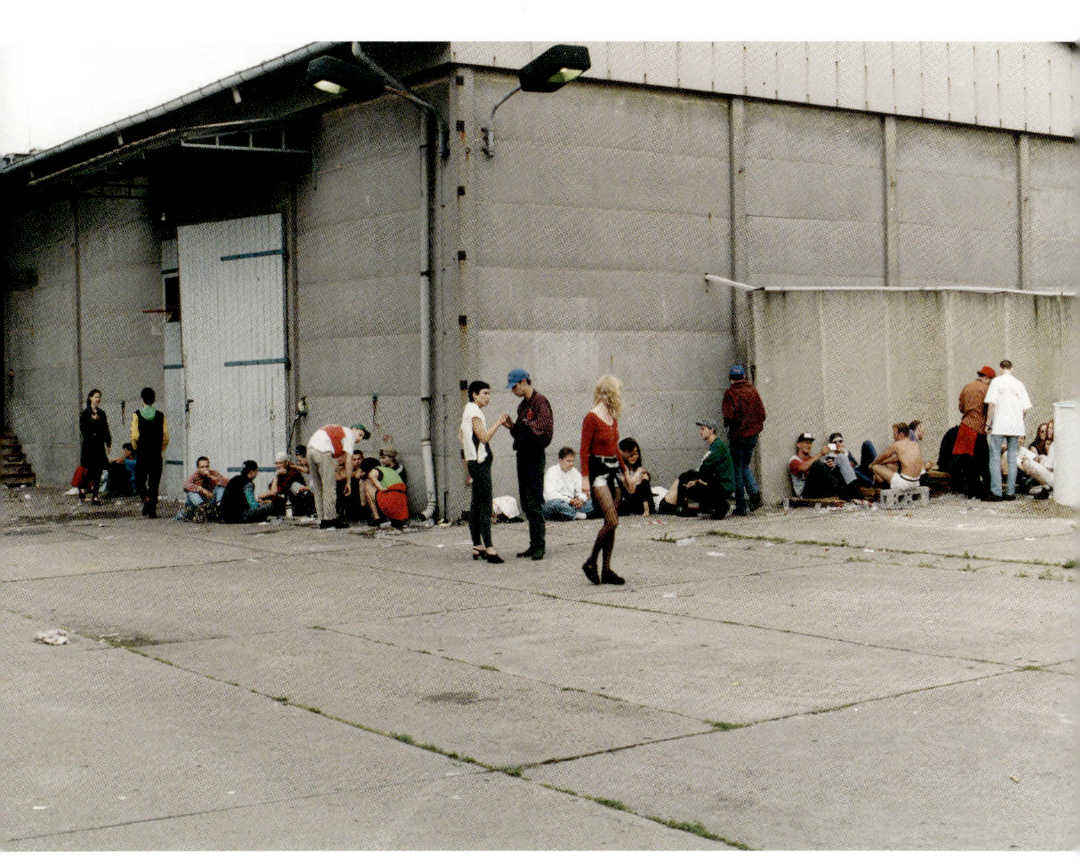

outside Planet, view, 1992

Friends outside Planet, 1992

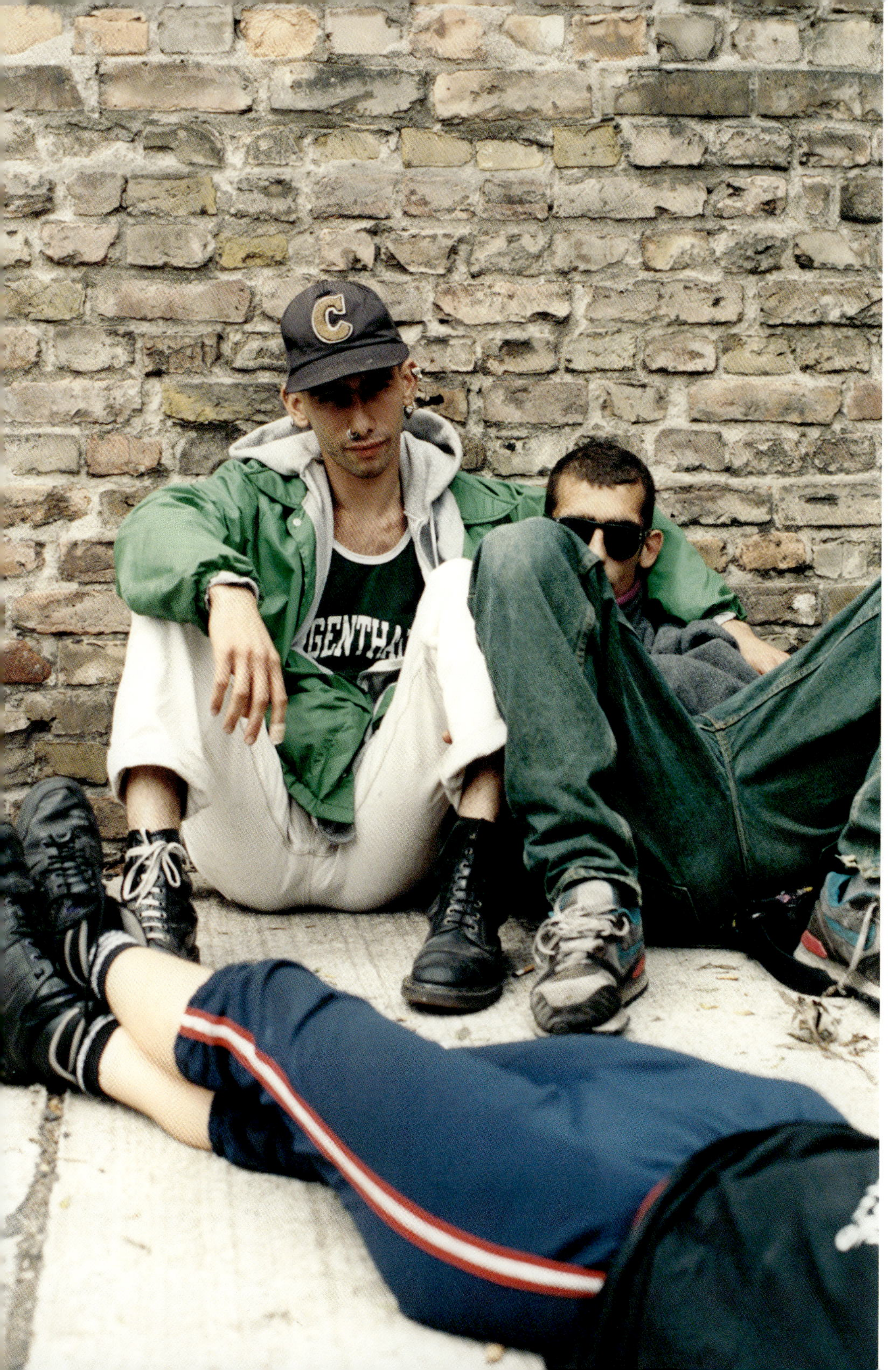

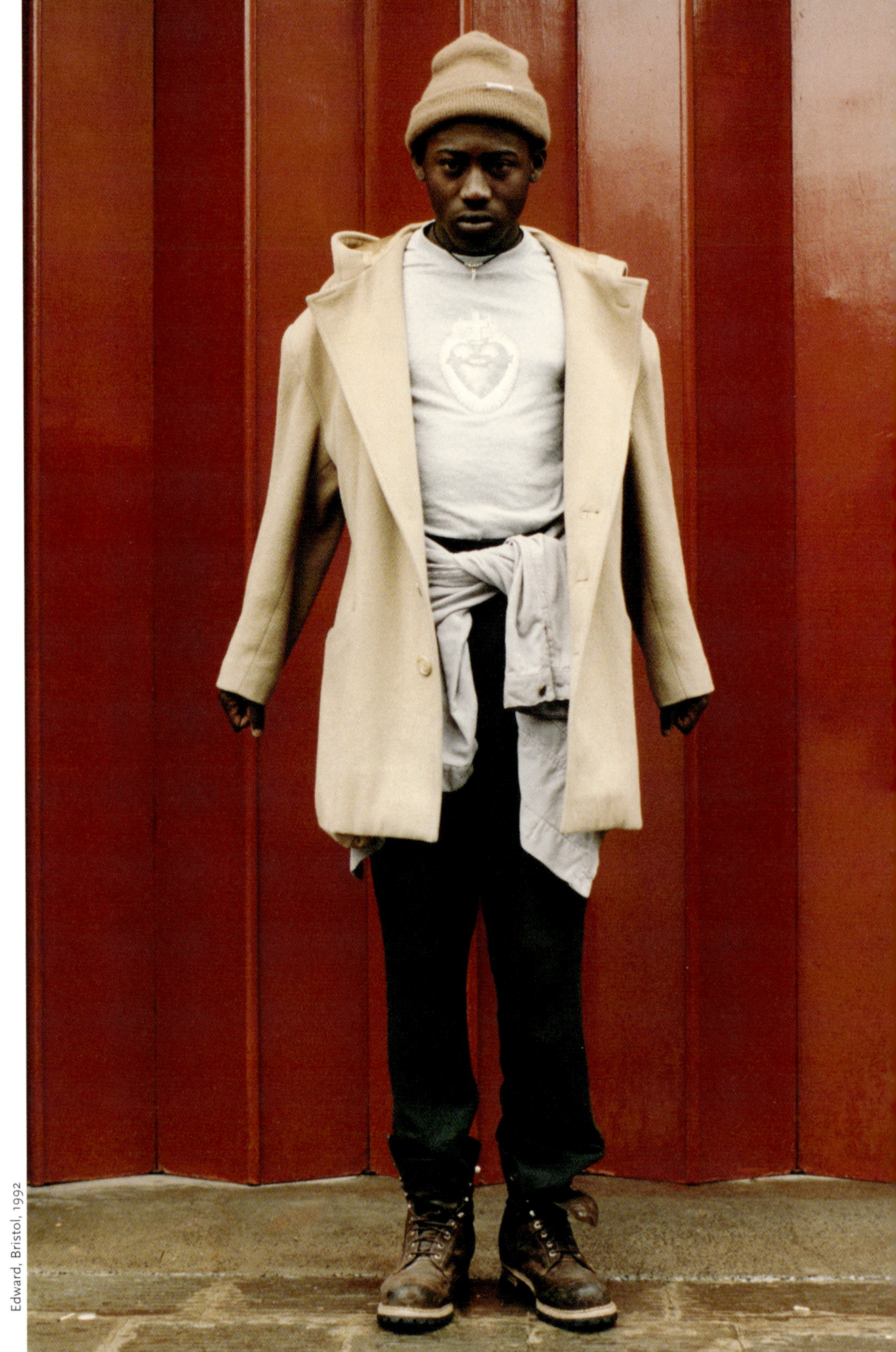

Edward, Bristol, 1992

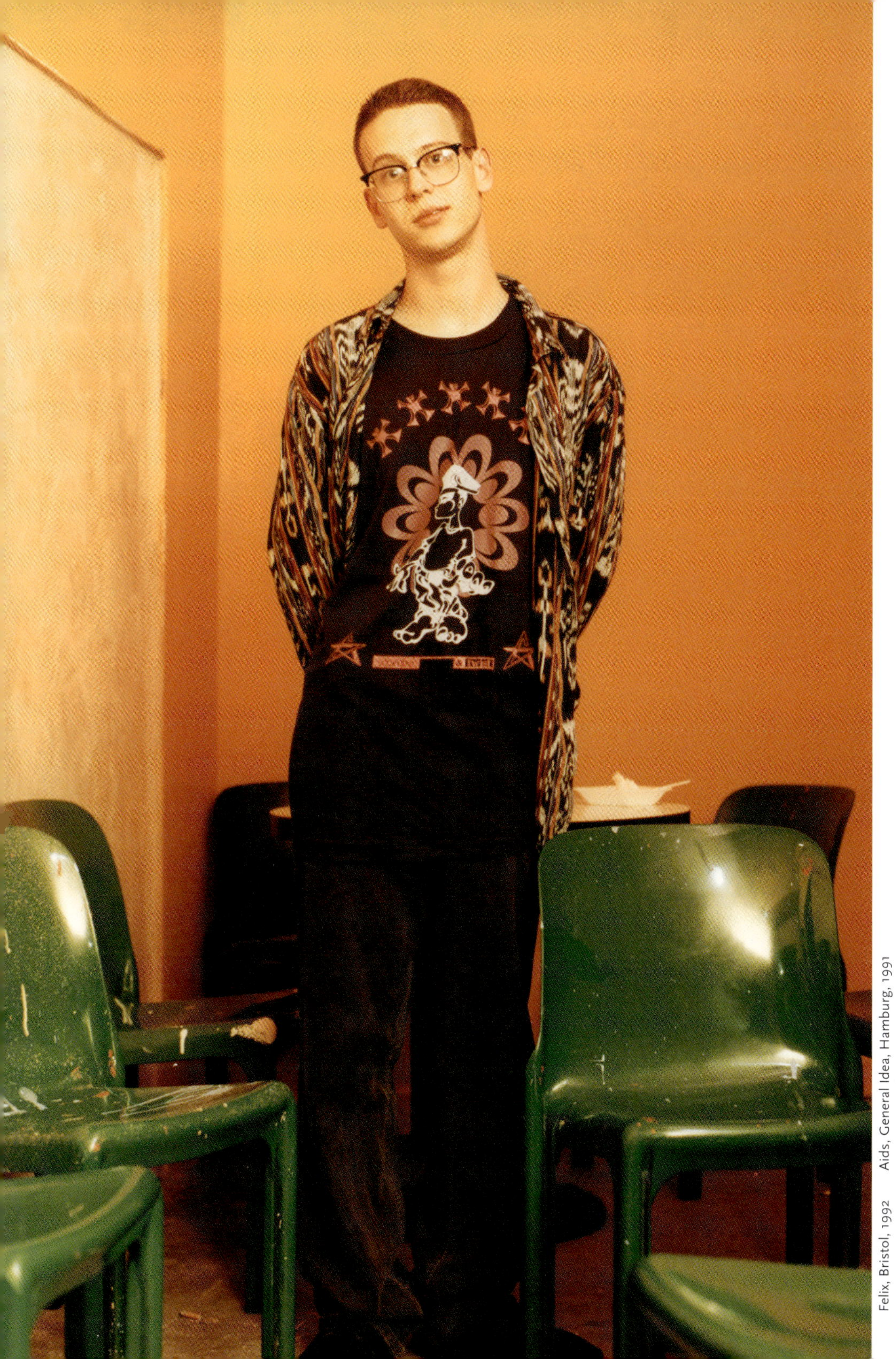

Felix, Bristol, 1992   Aids, General Idea, Hamburg, 1991

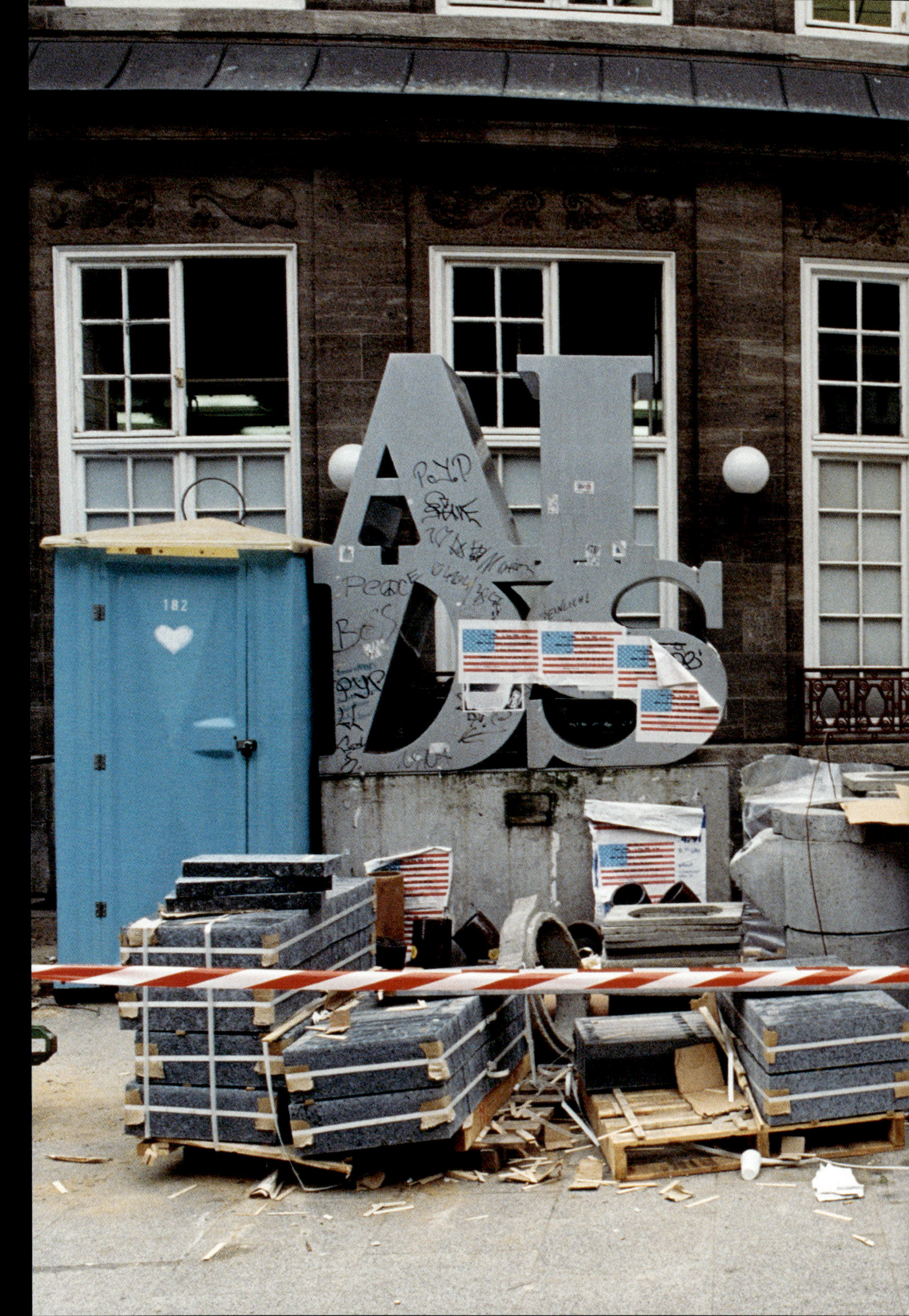

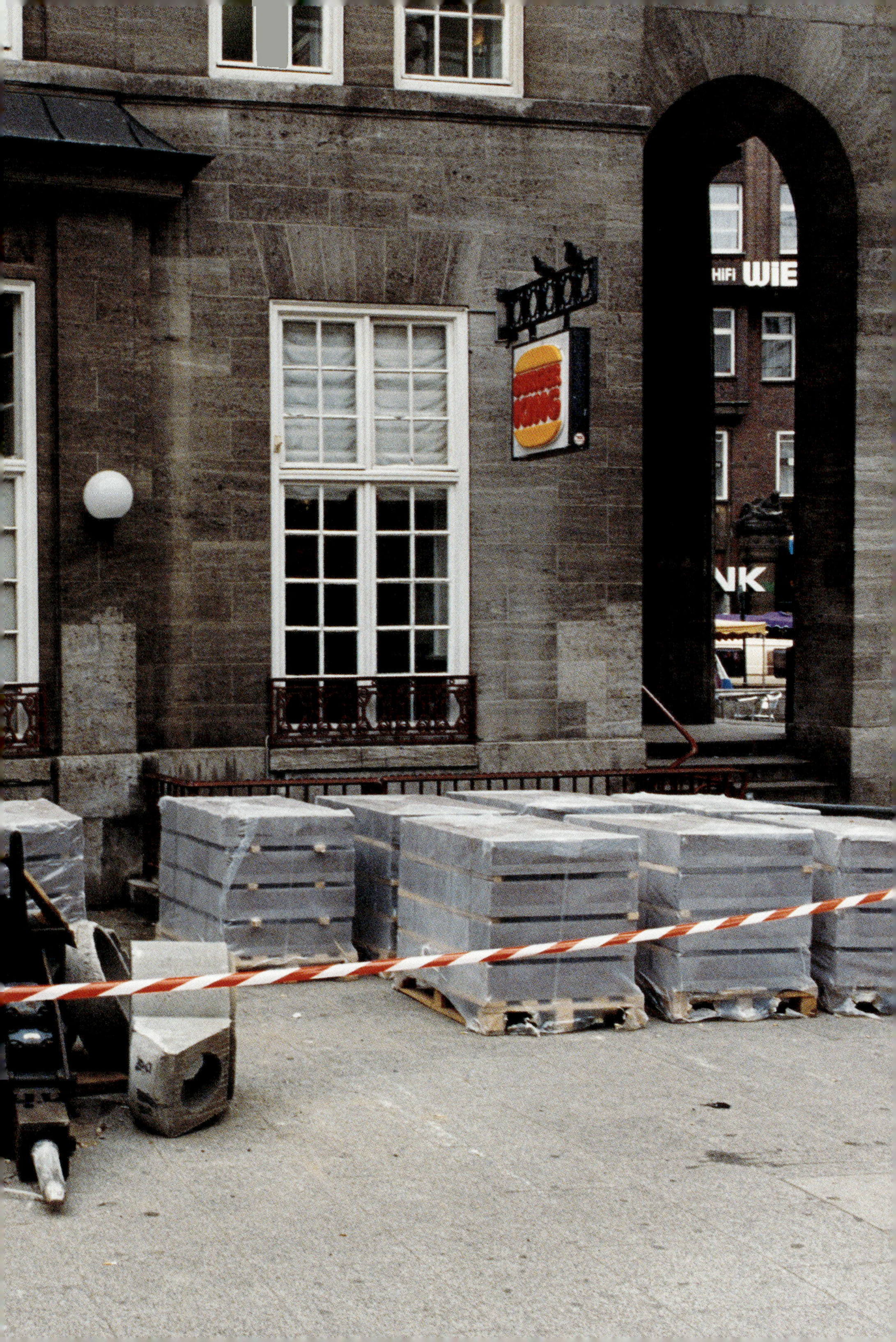

HIFI WIE
NK

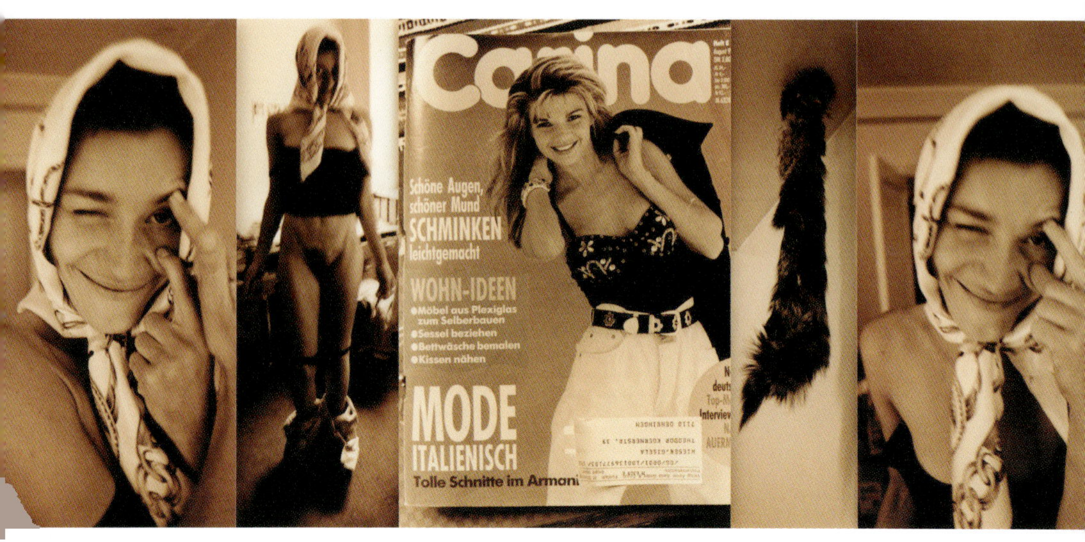

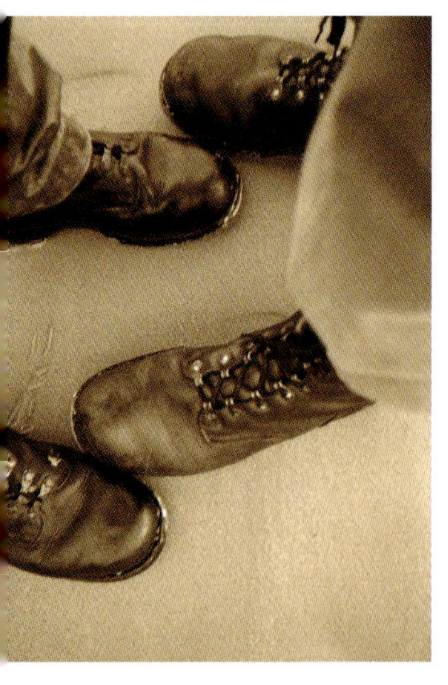

Carina, 1992
four boots, 1992

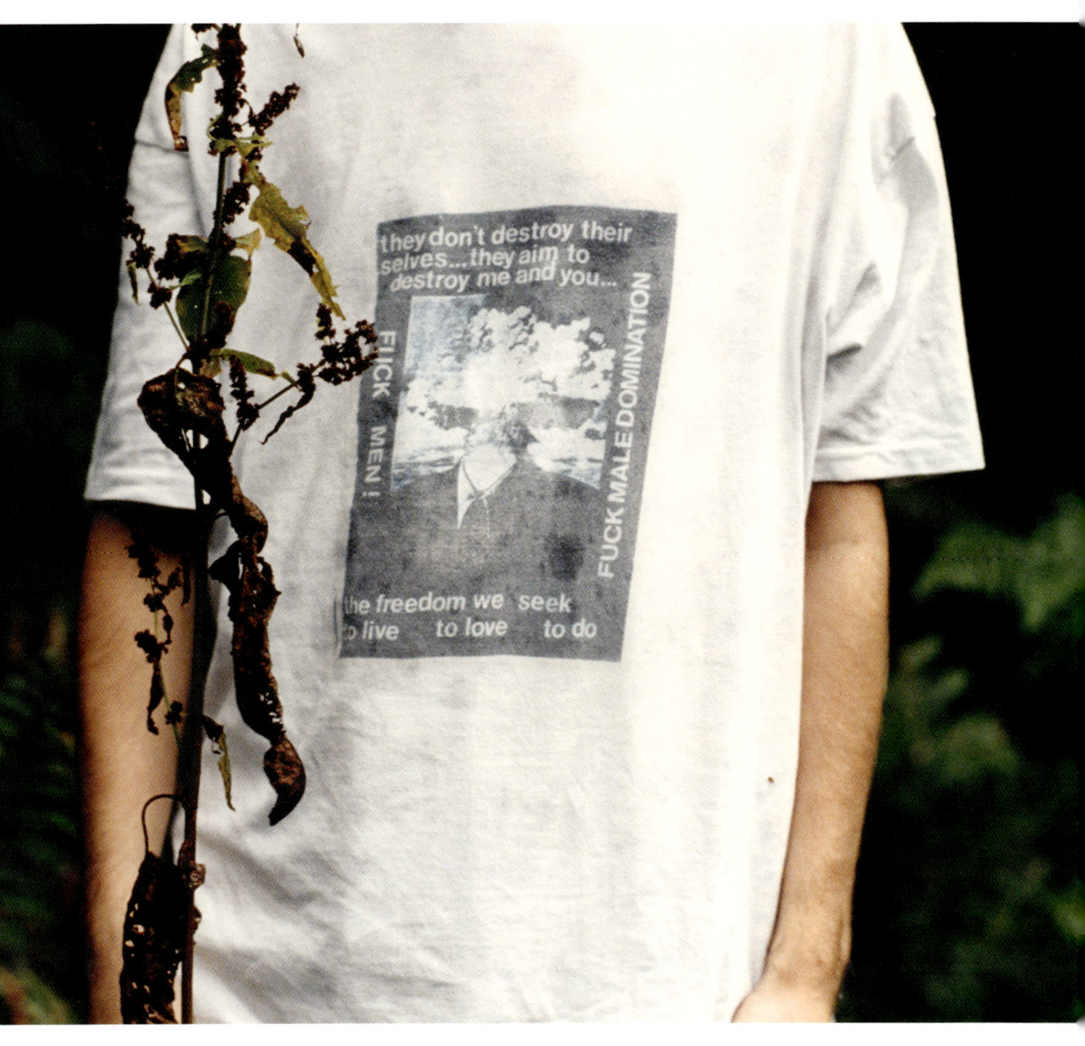

Fuck Men, 1992
Alex with cock plant, 1992
Lutz & Alex holding cock, 1992
Lutz wanking, 1991
Alex & Lutz holding each other, 1992

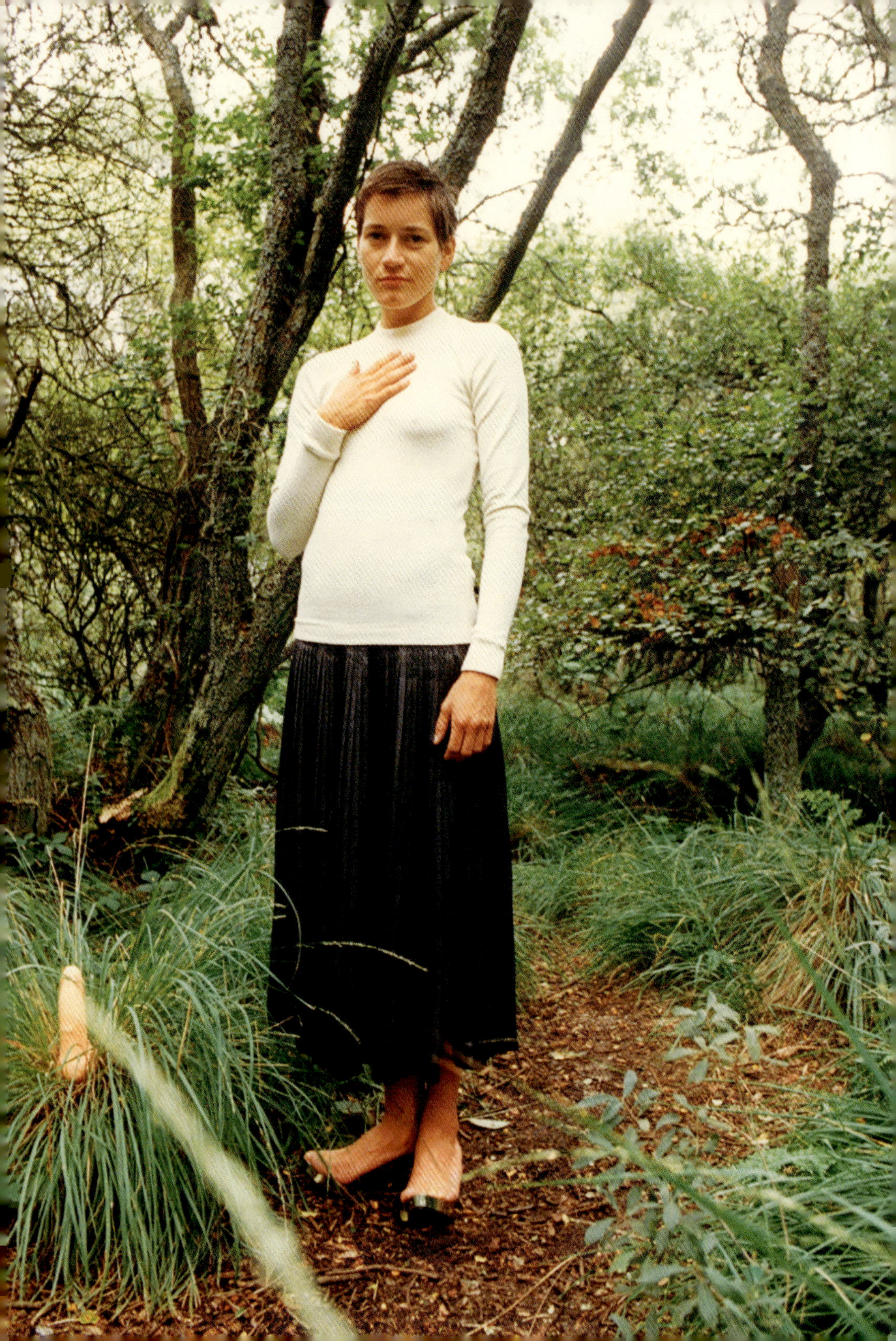

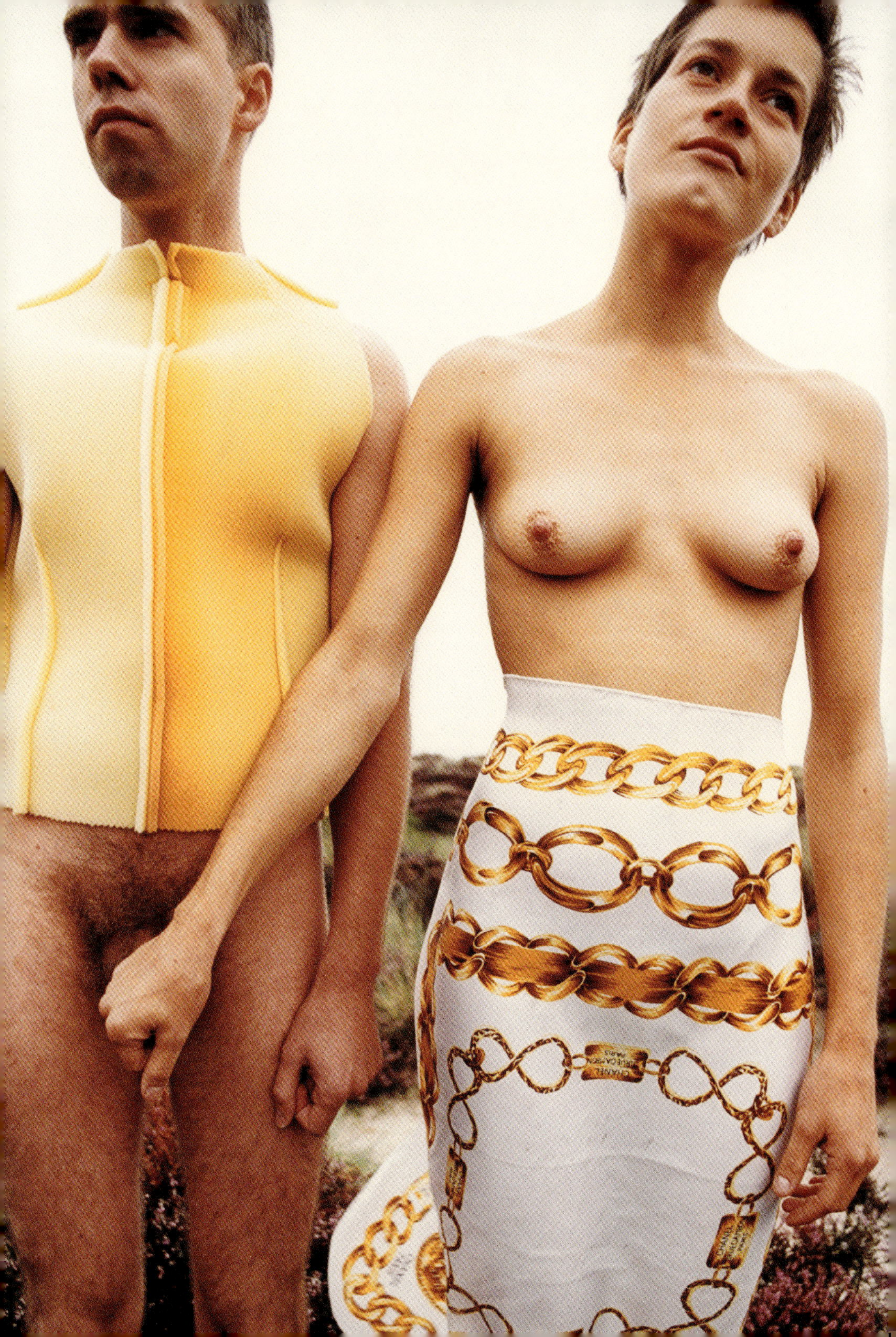

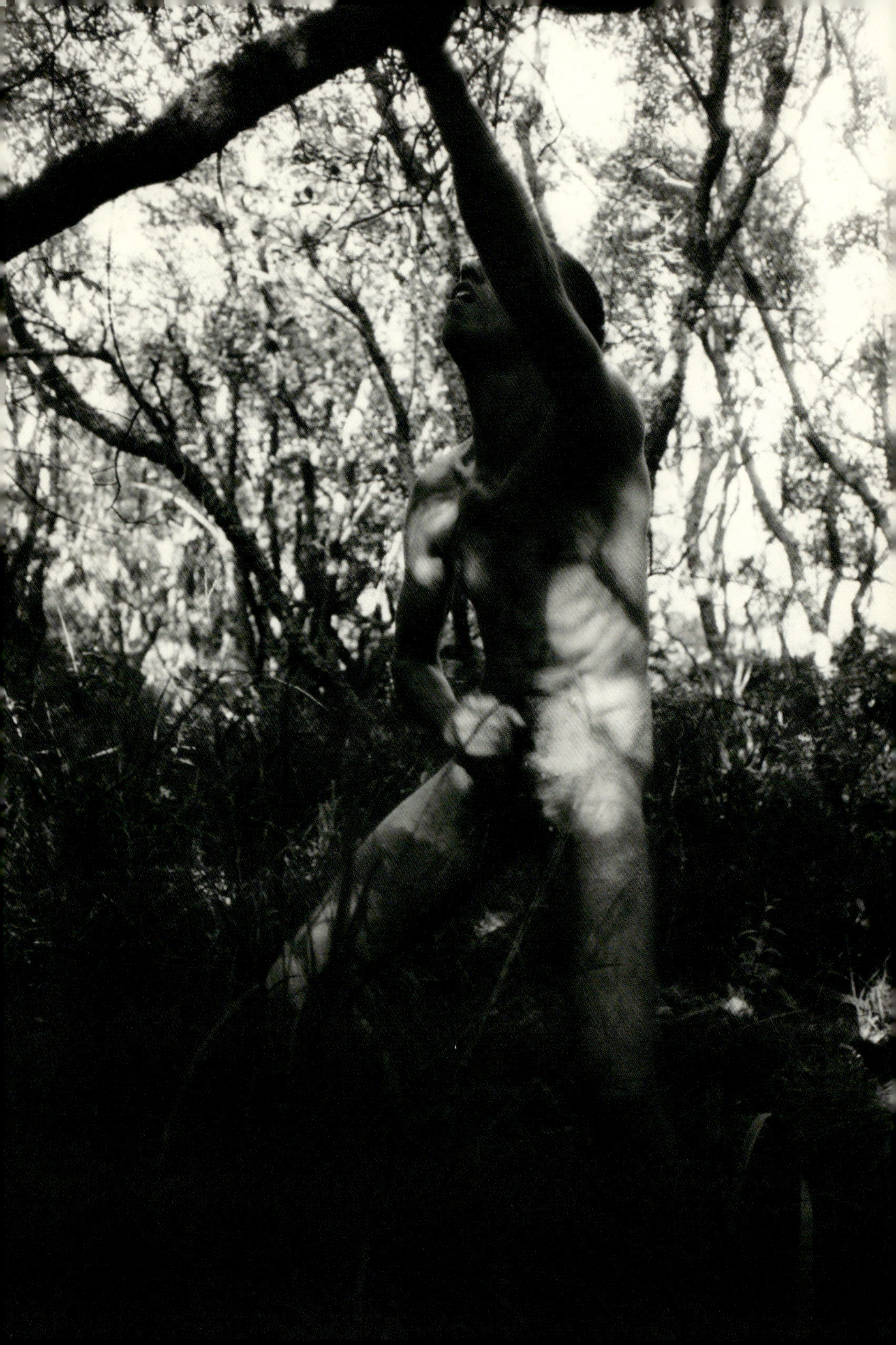

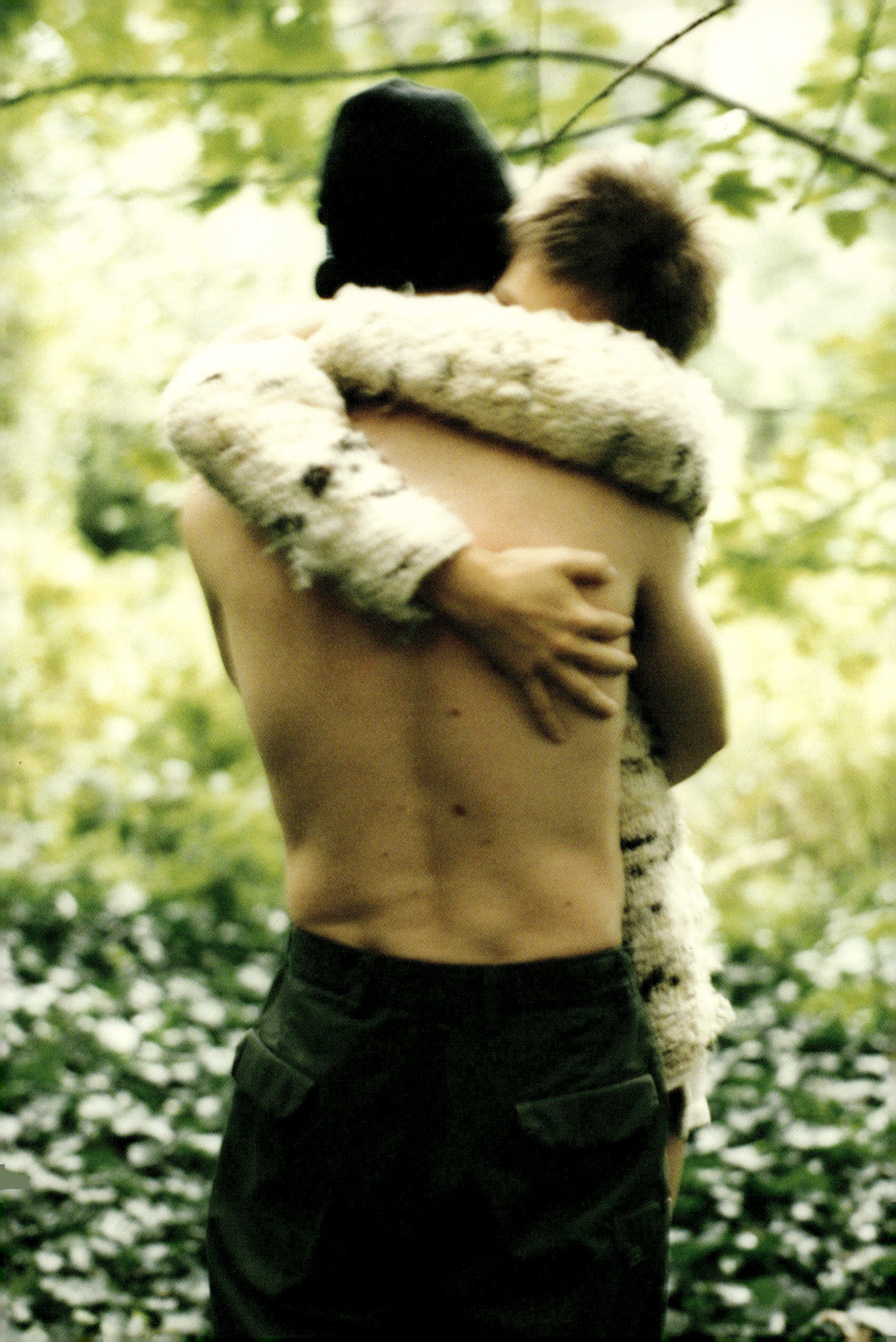

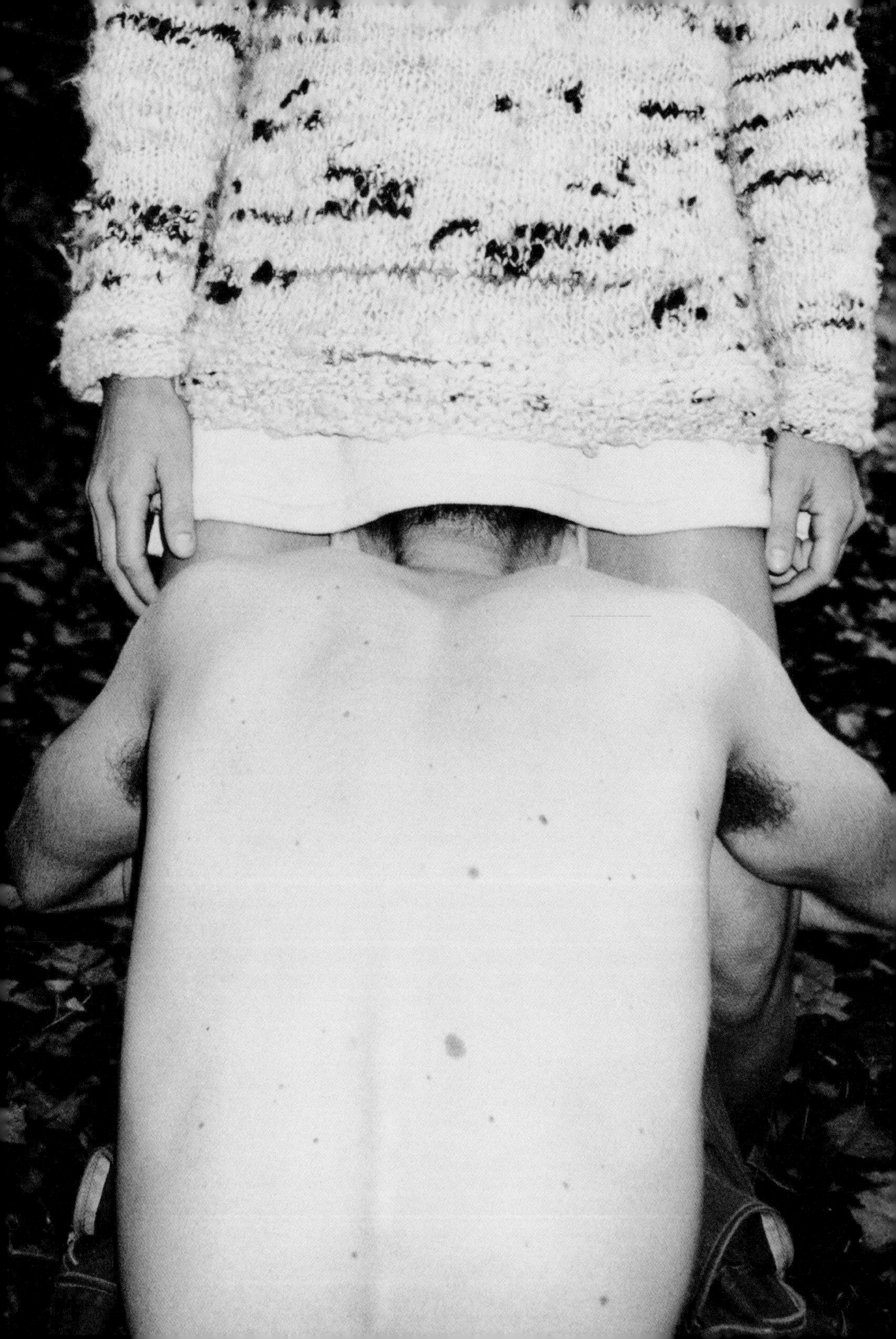

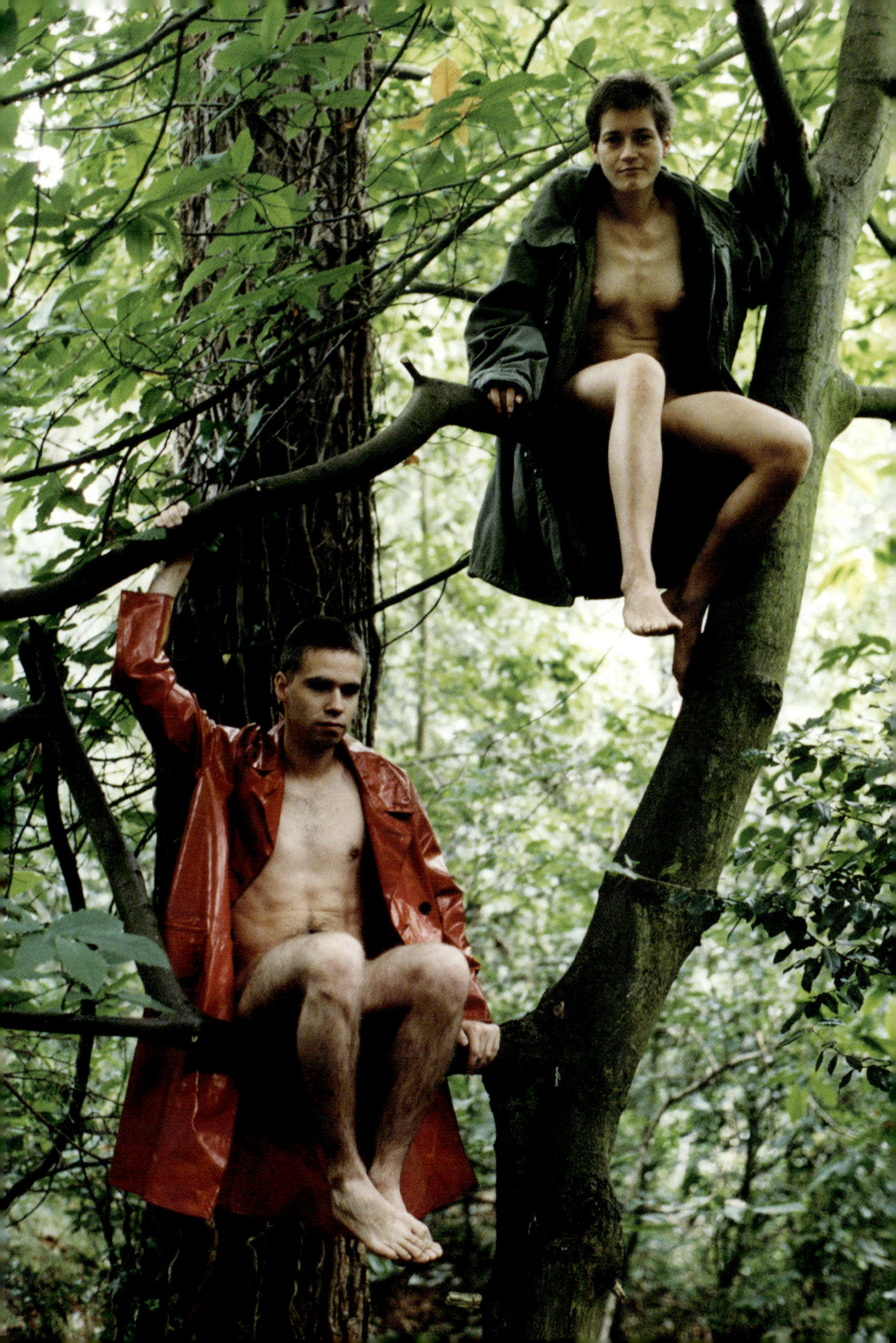

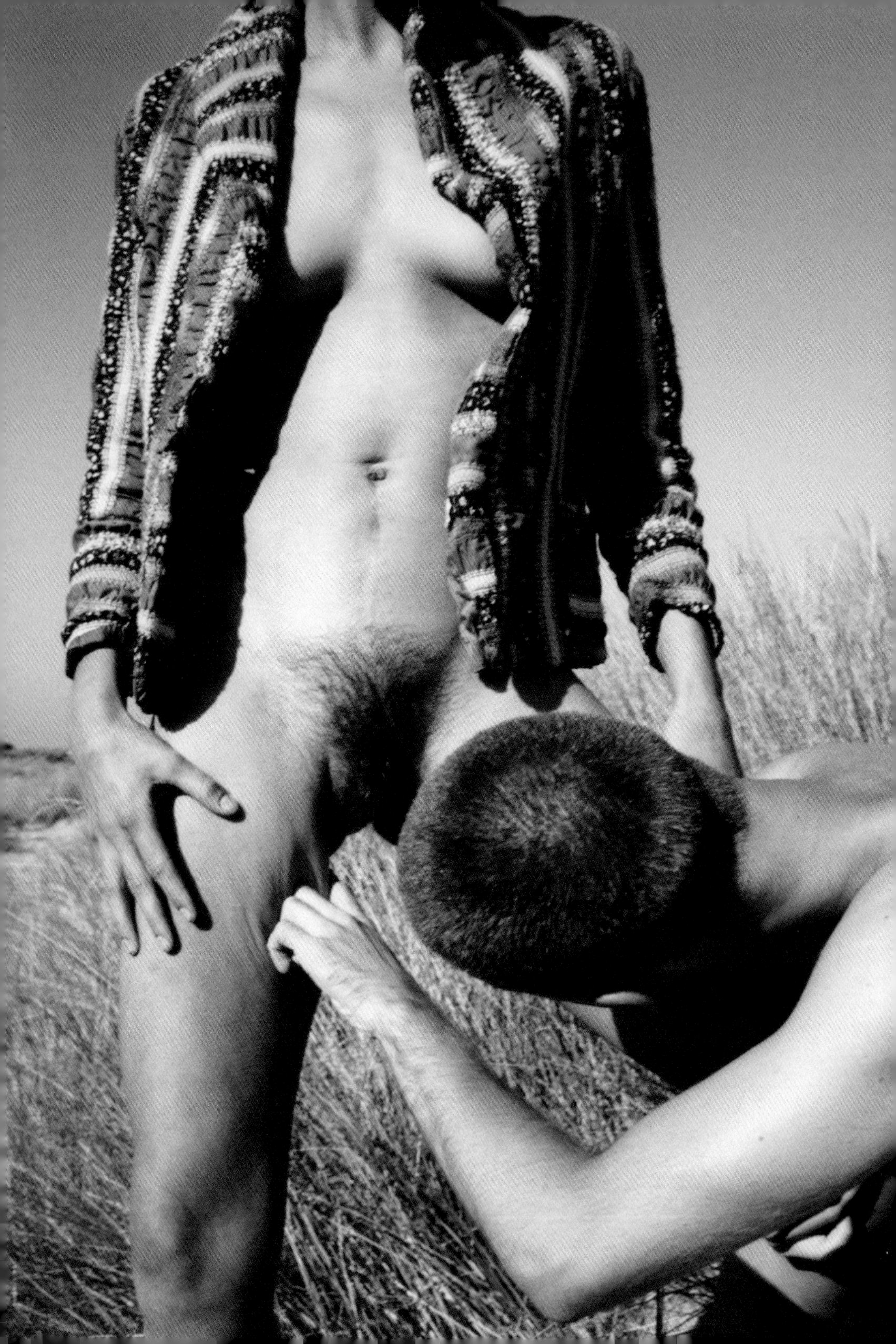

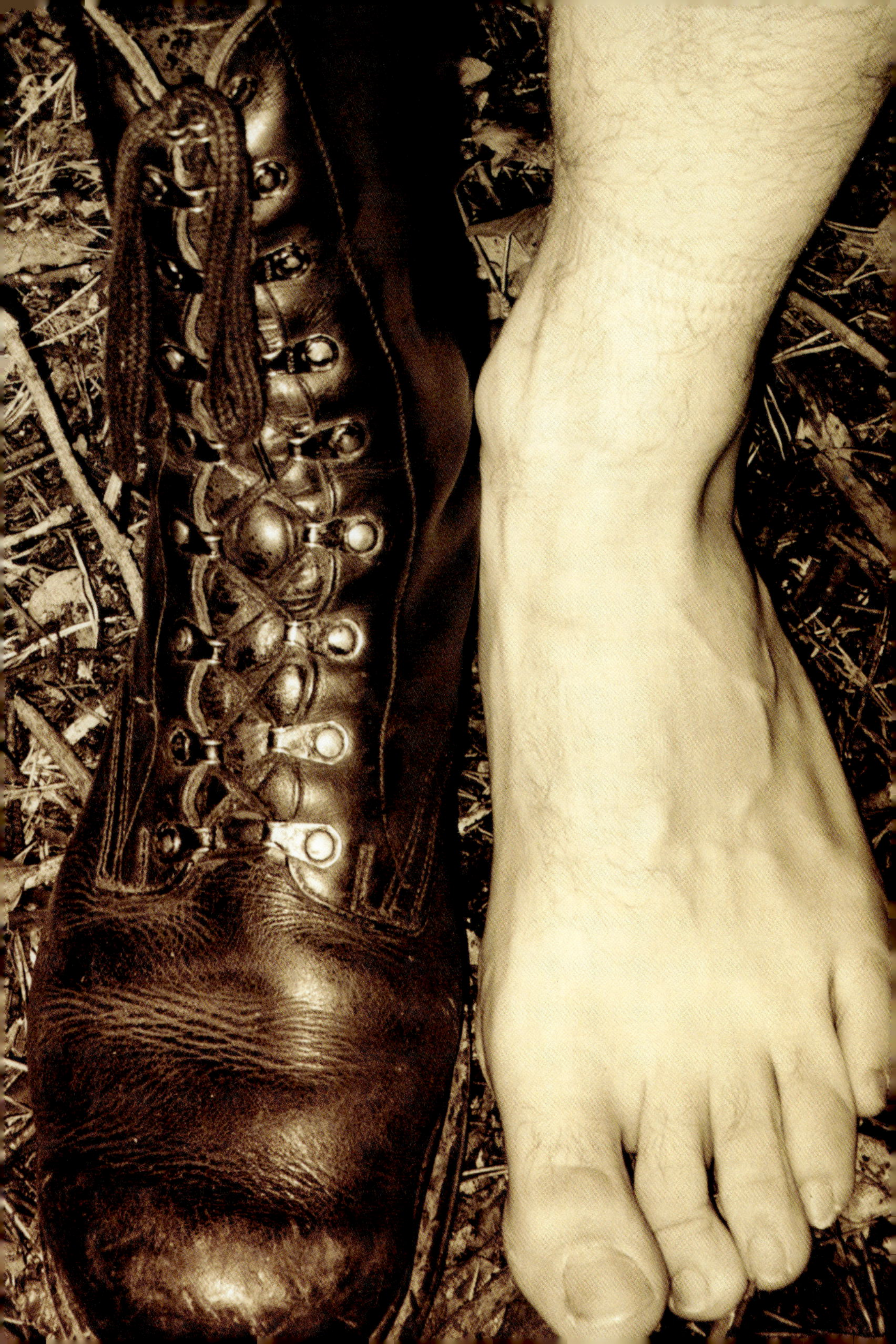

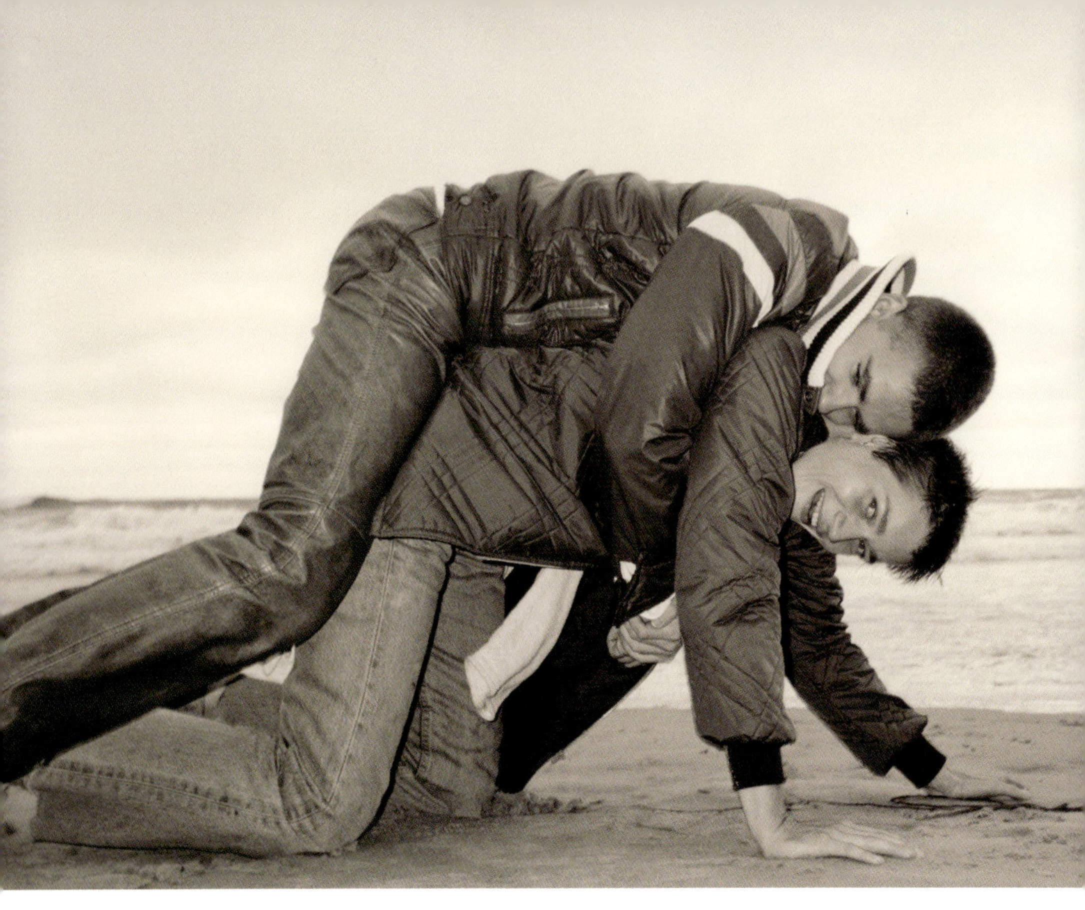

Alex & Lutz, back, 1992
Lutz & Alex sitting in the trees, 1992
Lutz & Alex looking at crotch, 1991
boot/foot, 1992
Lutz & Alex on beach, 1992

guys on beach, 1992
Chemistry (view), 1992
Chemistry squares, 1992
young woman, Chemistry, 1992
young man, Chemistry, 1992

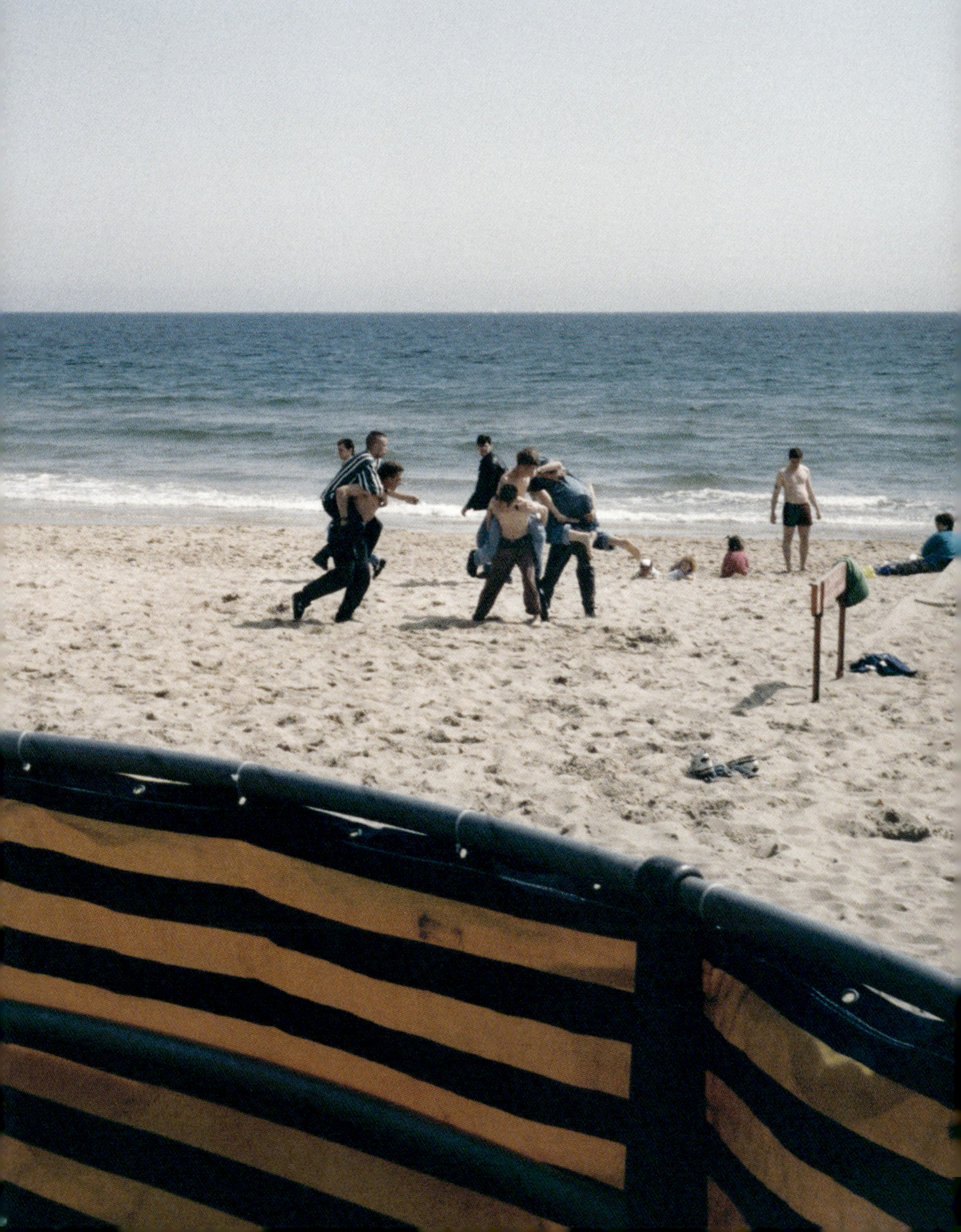

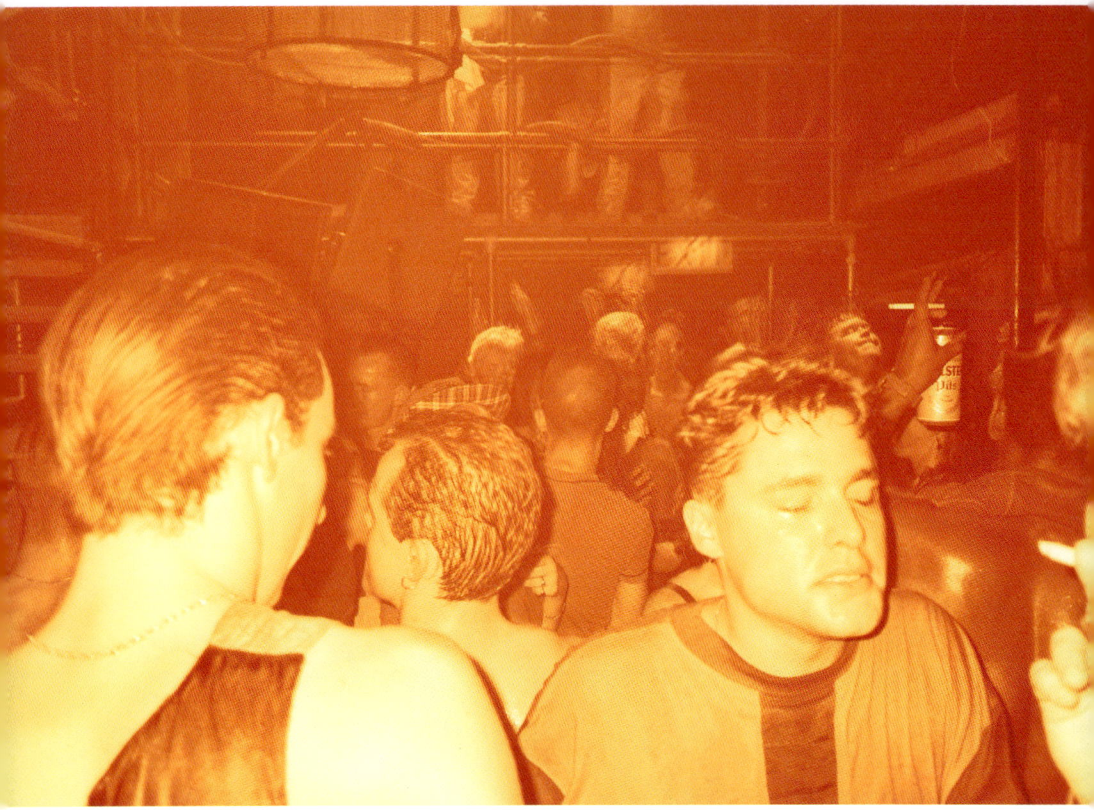

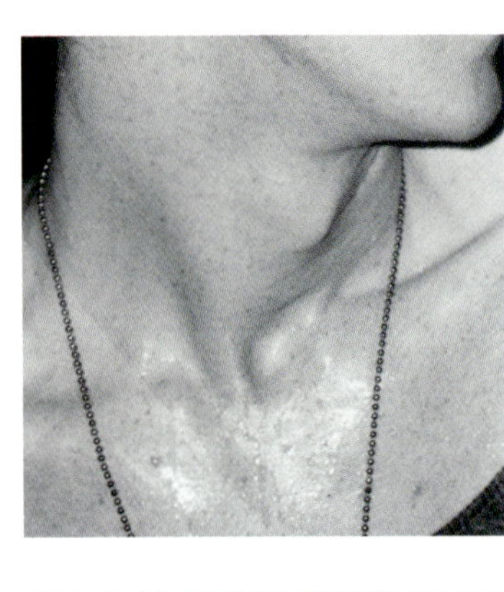
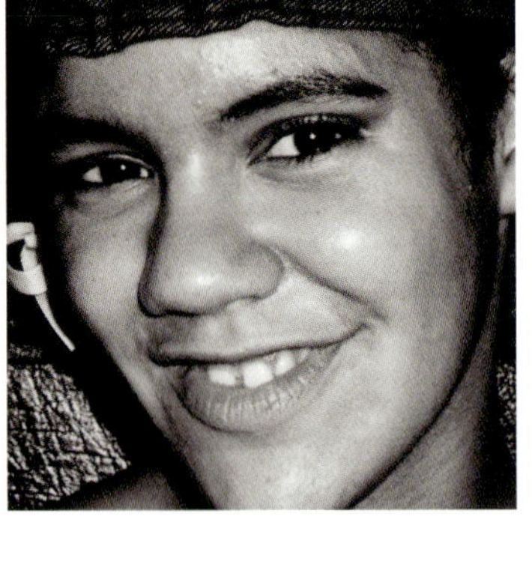
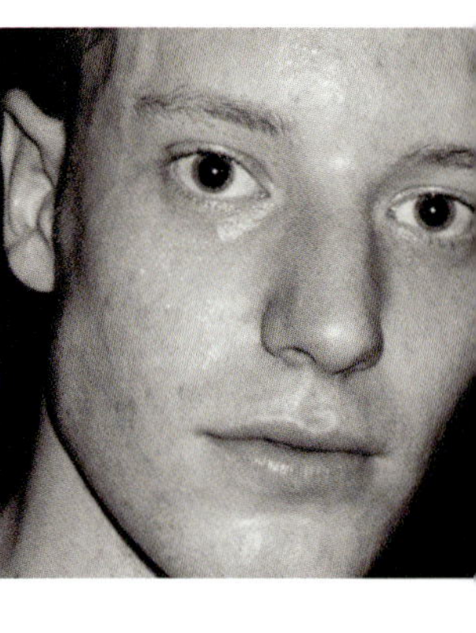
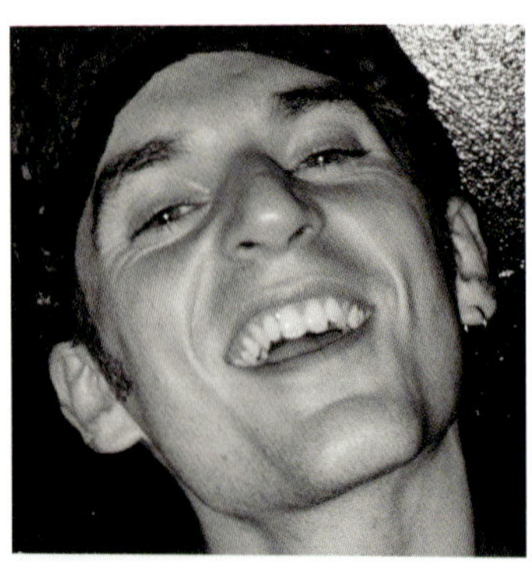
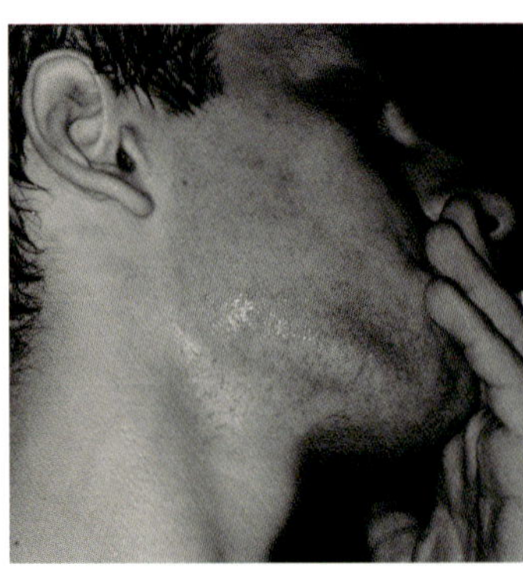
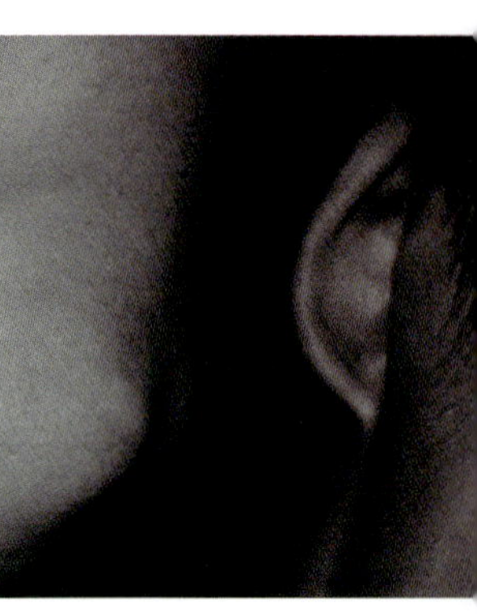

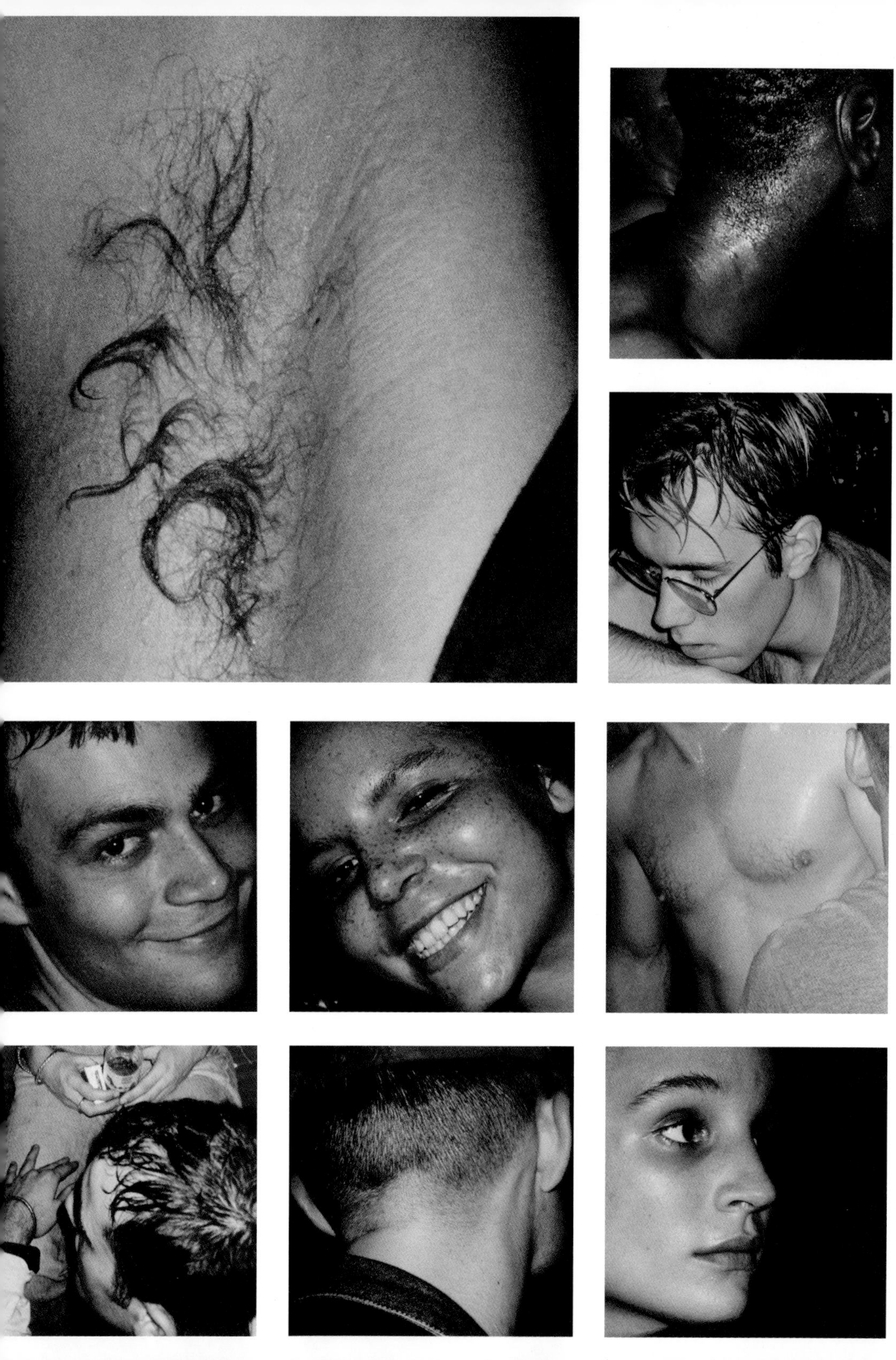

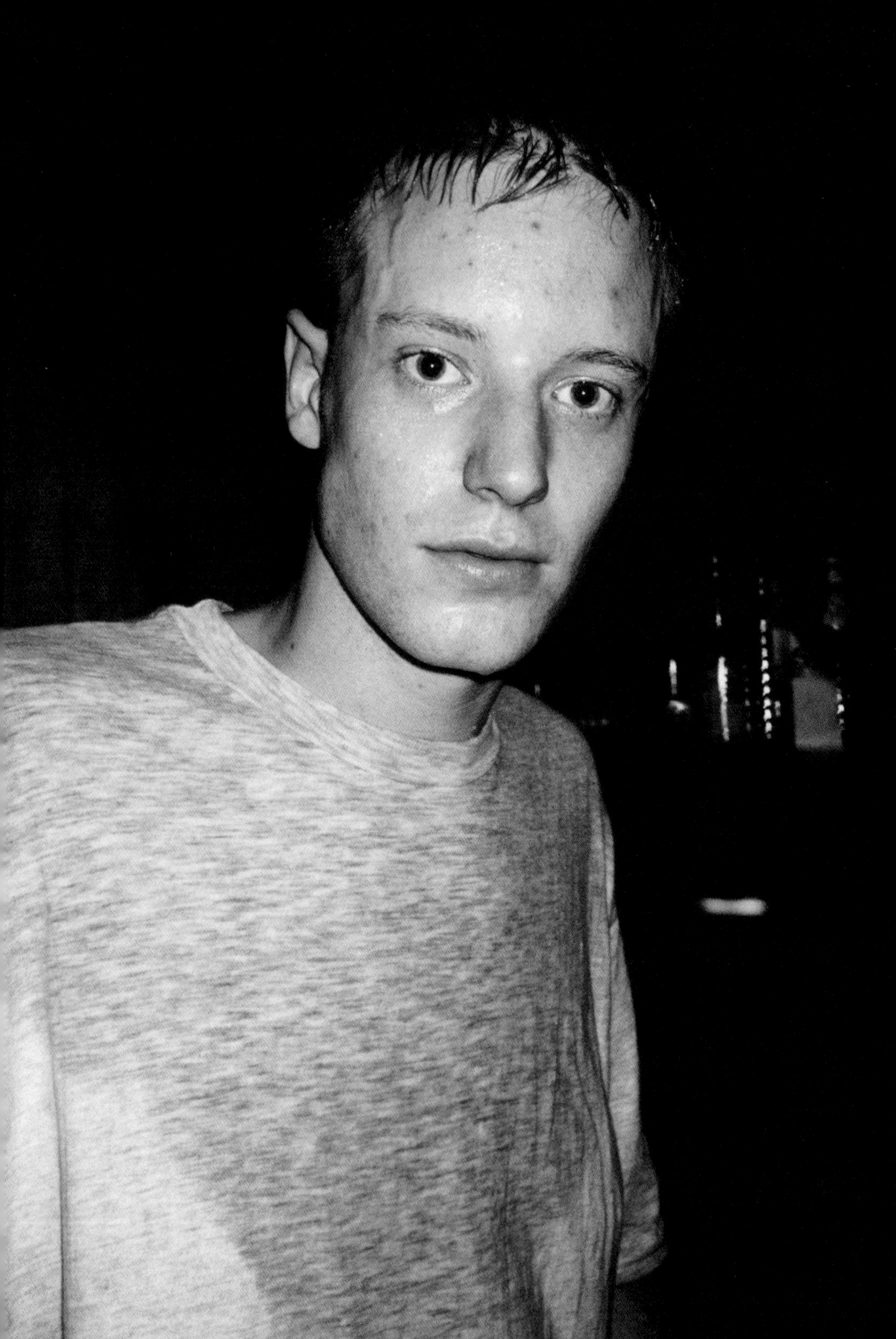

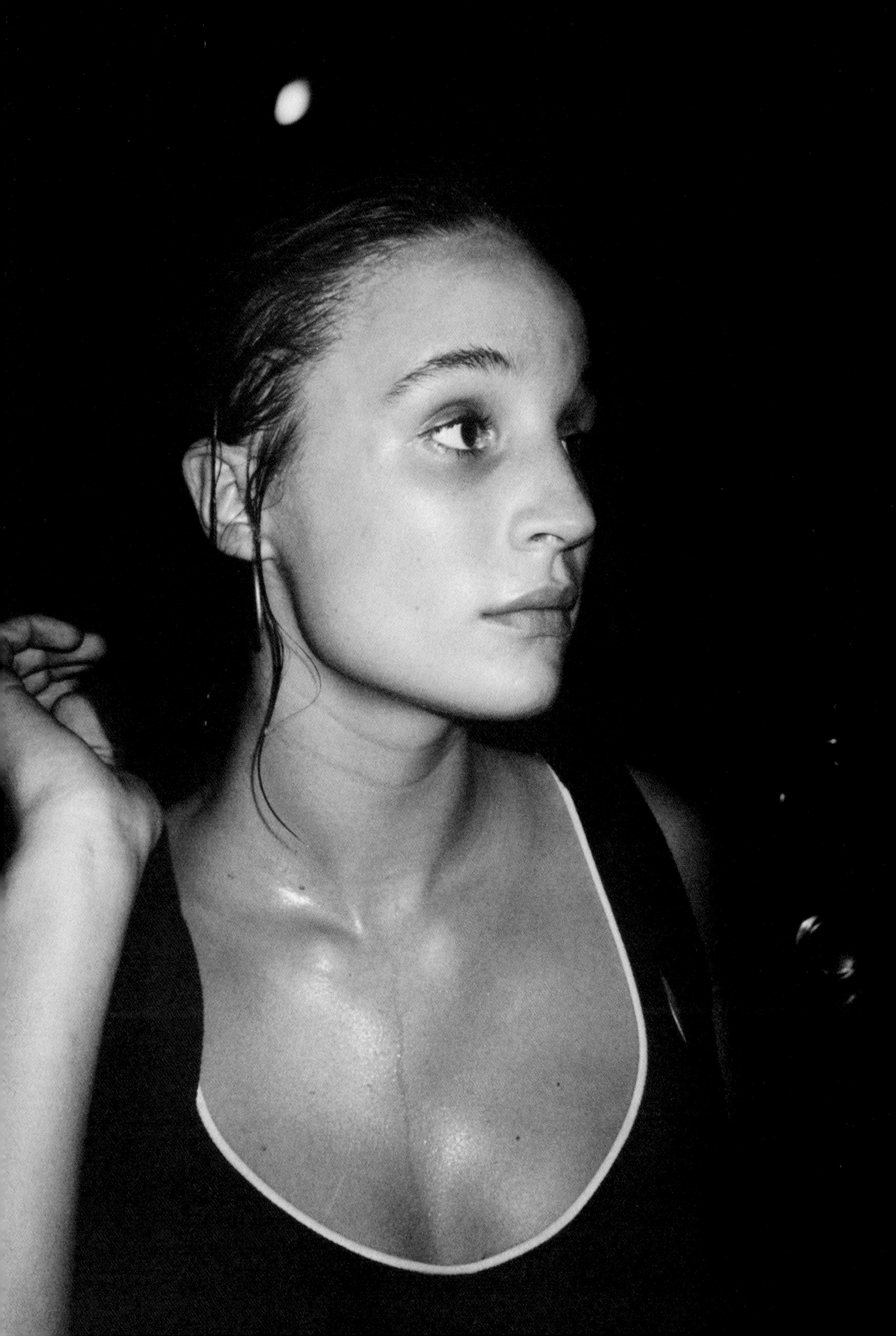

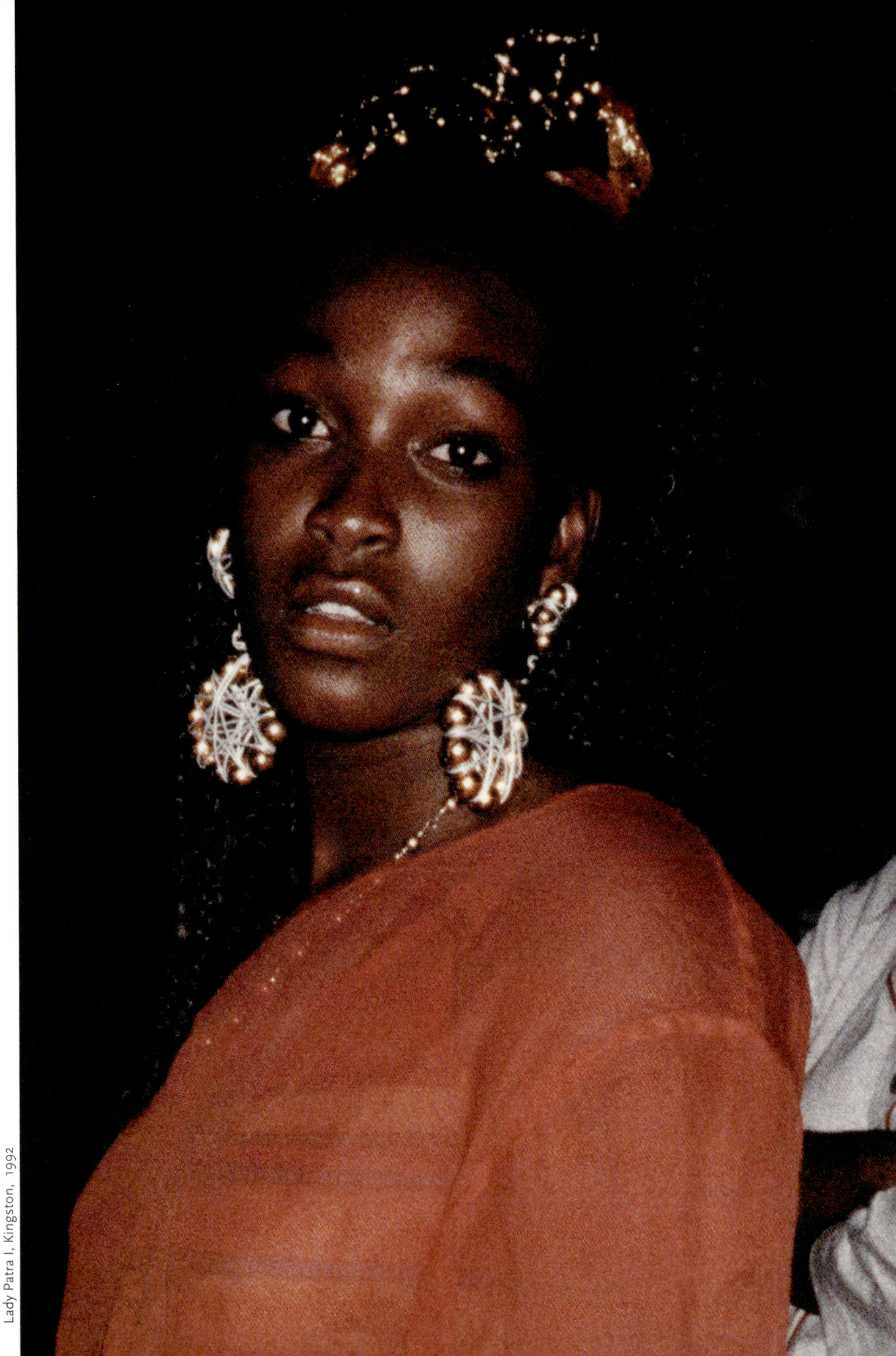

Lady Patra I, Kingston, 1992

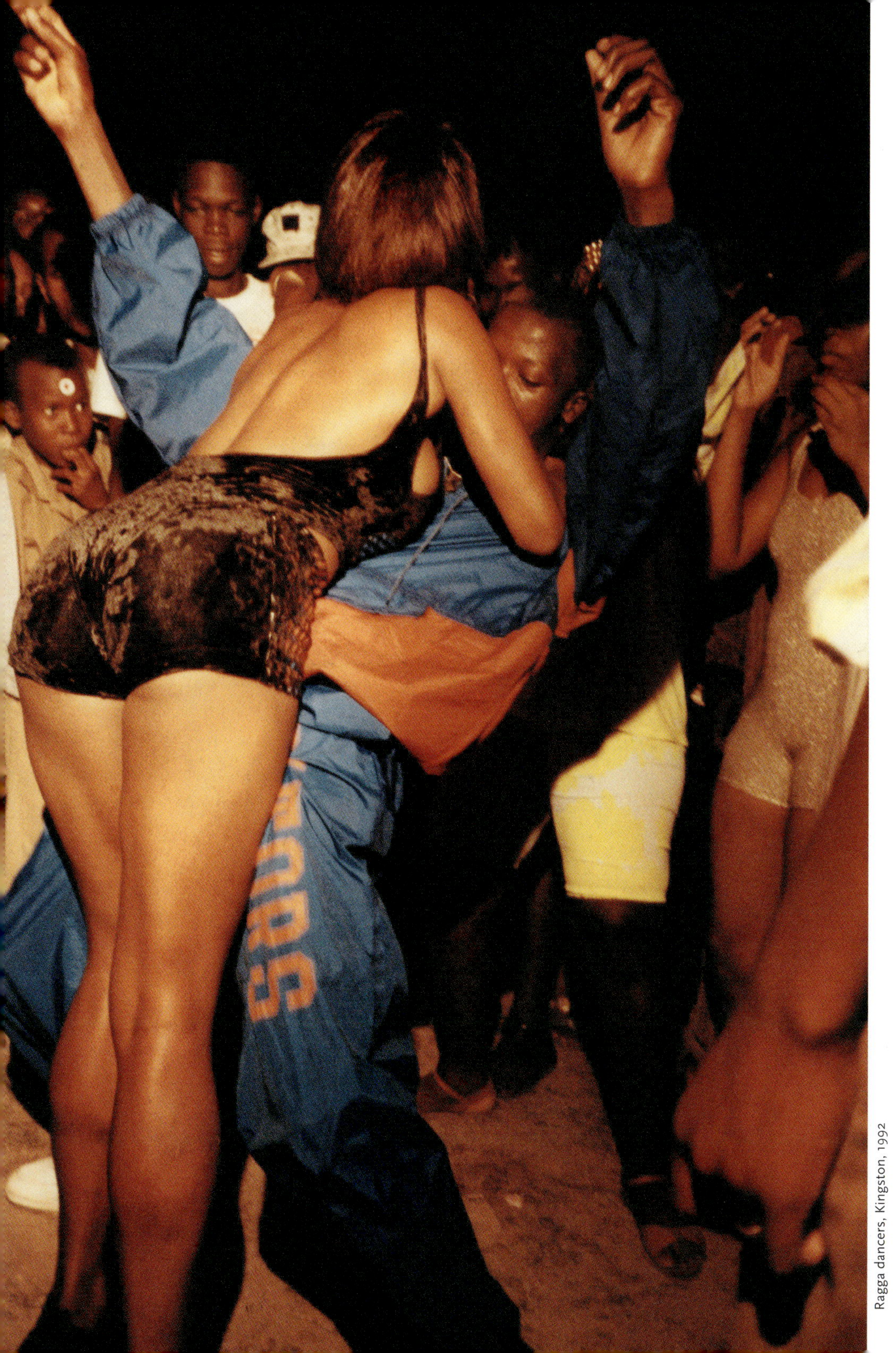

Ragga dancers, Kingston, 1992

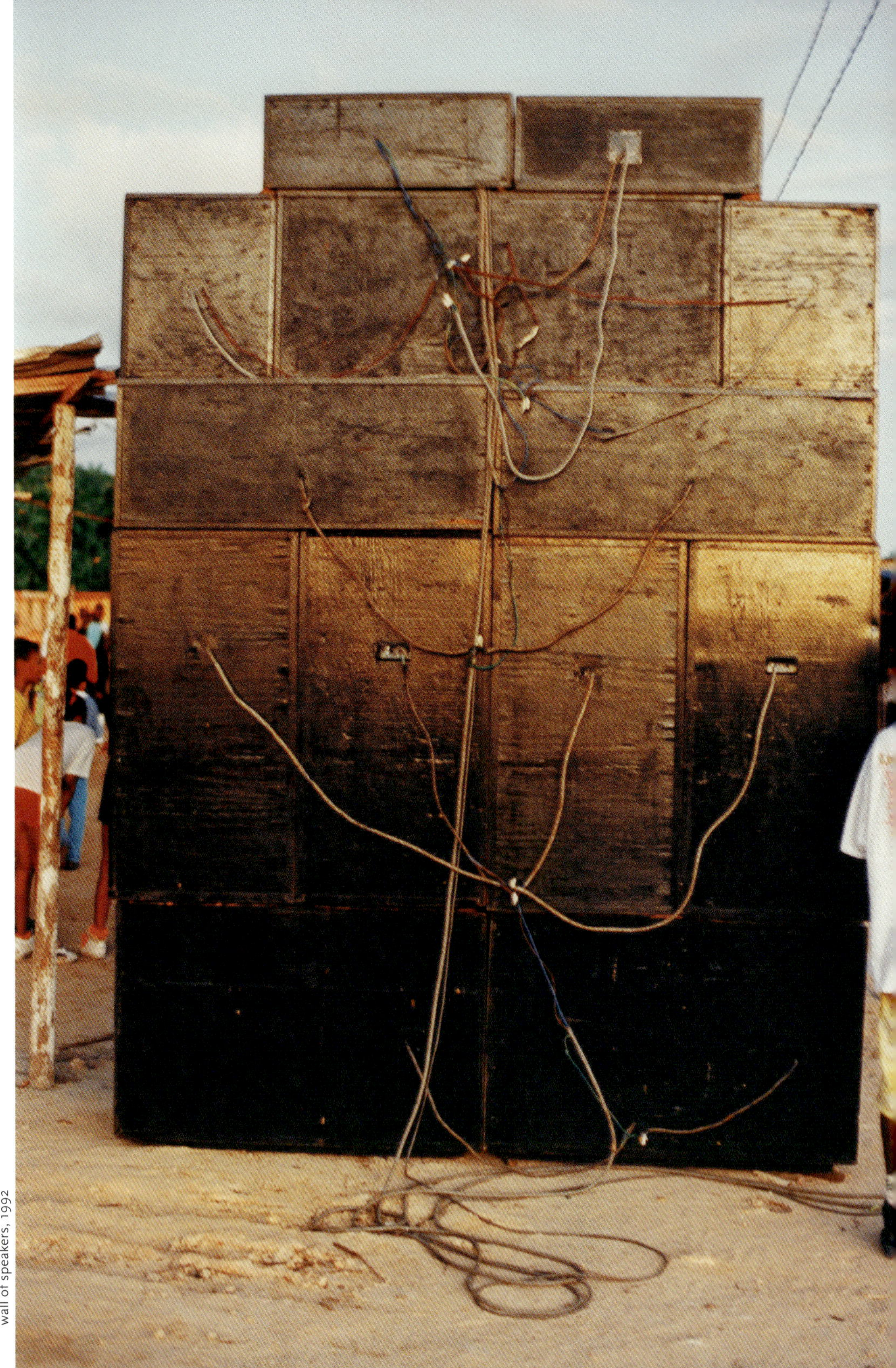

wall of speakers, 1992

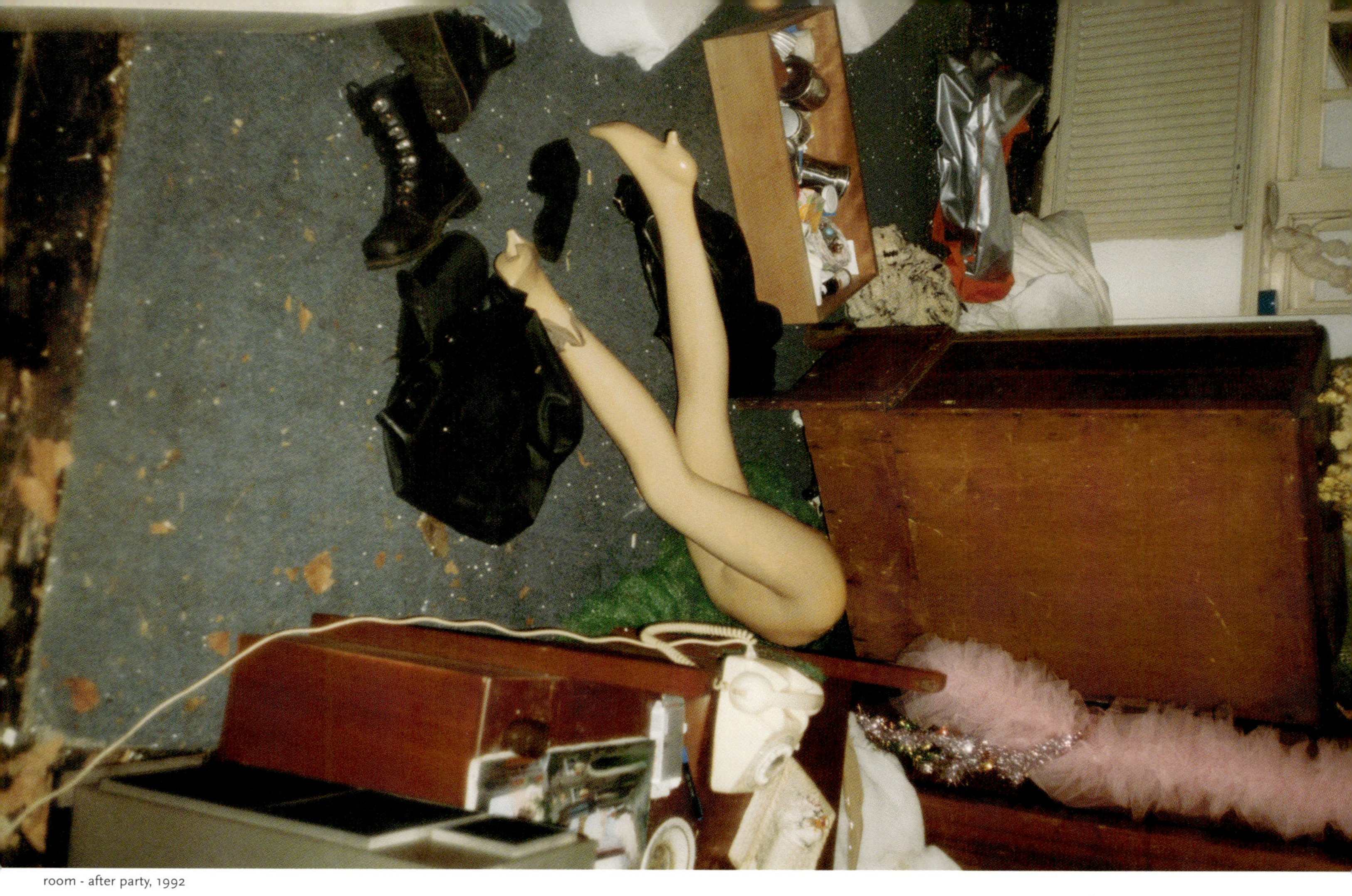

room - after party, 1992

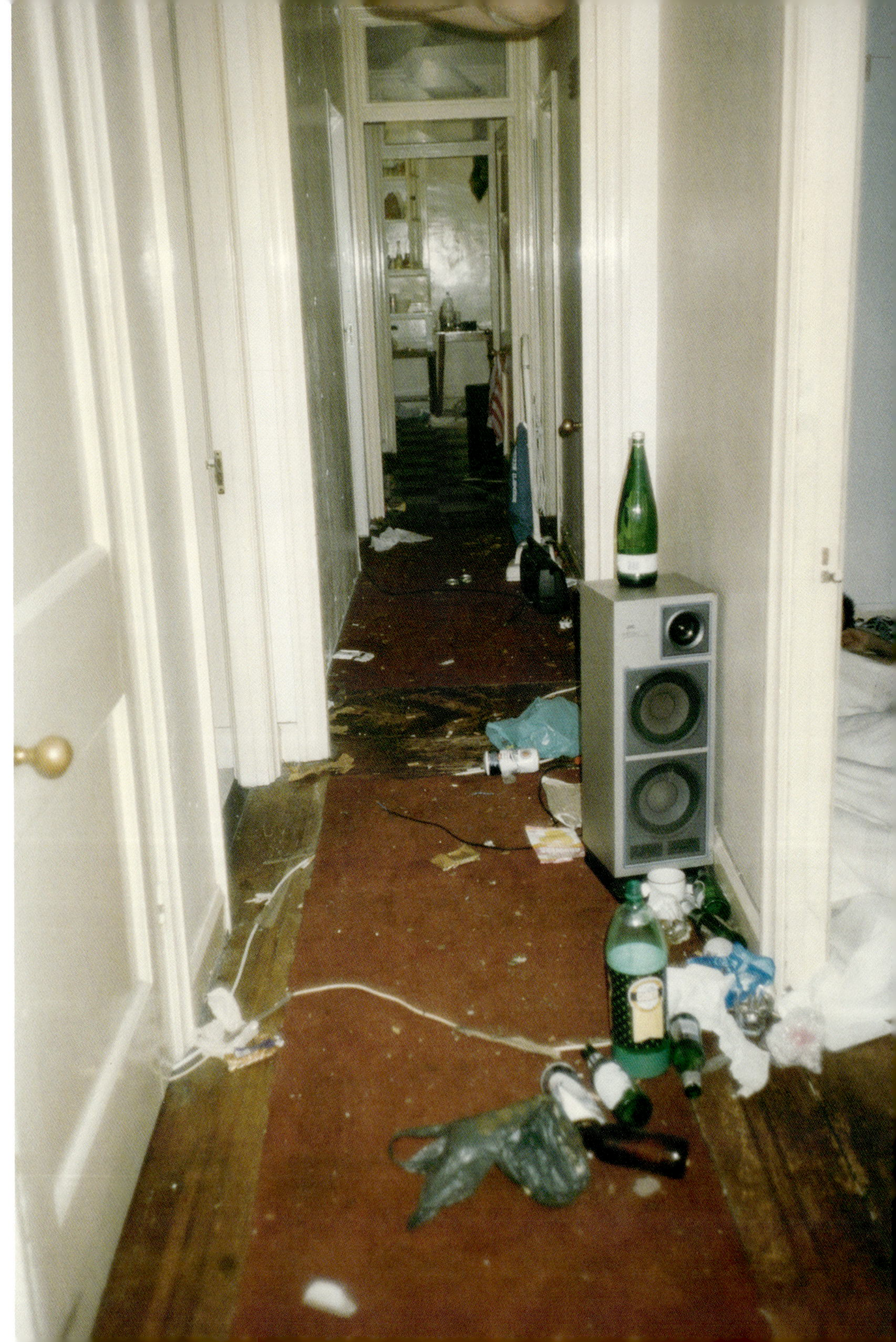

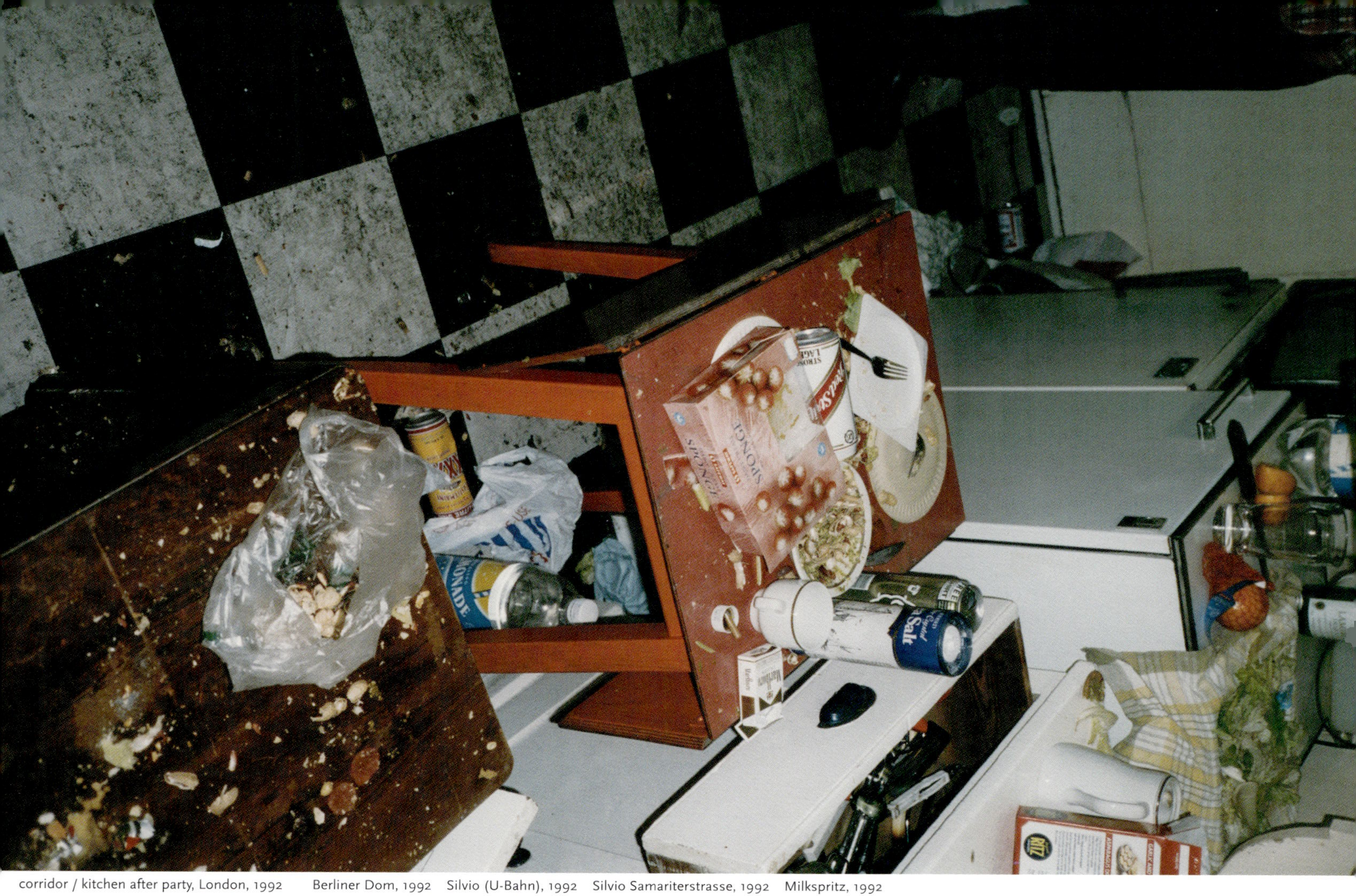

corridor / kitchen after party, London, 1992   Berliner Dom, 1992   Silvio (U-Bahn), 1992   Silvio Samariterstrasse, 1992   Milkspritz, 1992

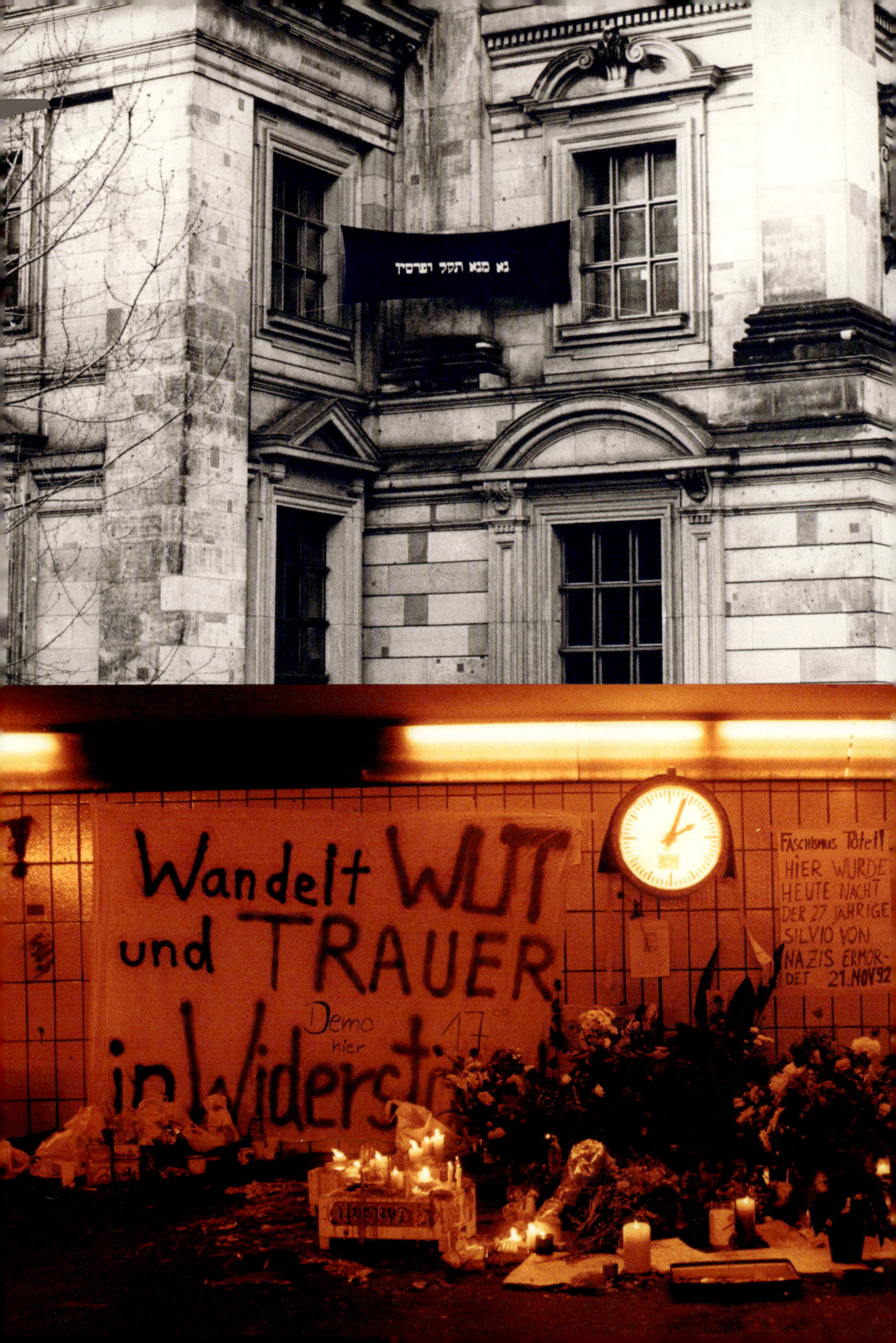

Wandelt WUT und TRAUER in Widerst
Demo hier 17⁰⁰
FASCHISMUS TÖTET!
HIER WURDE HEUTE NACHT DER 27 JÄHRIGE SILVIO VON NAZIS ERMORDET 21.NOV 92

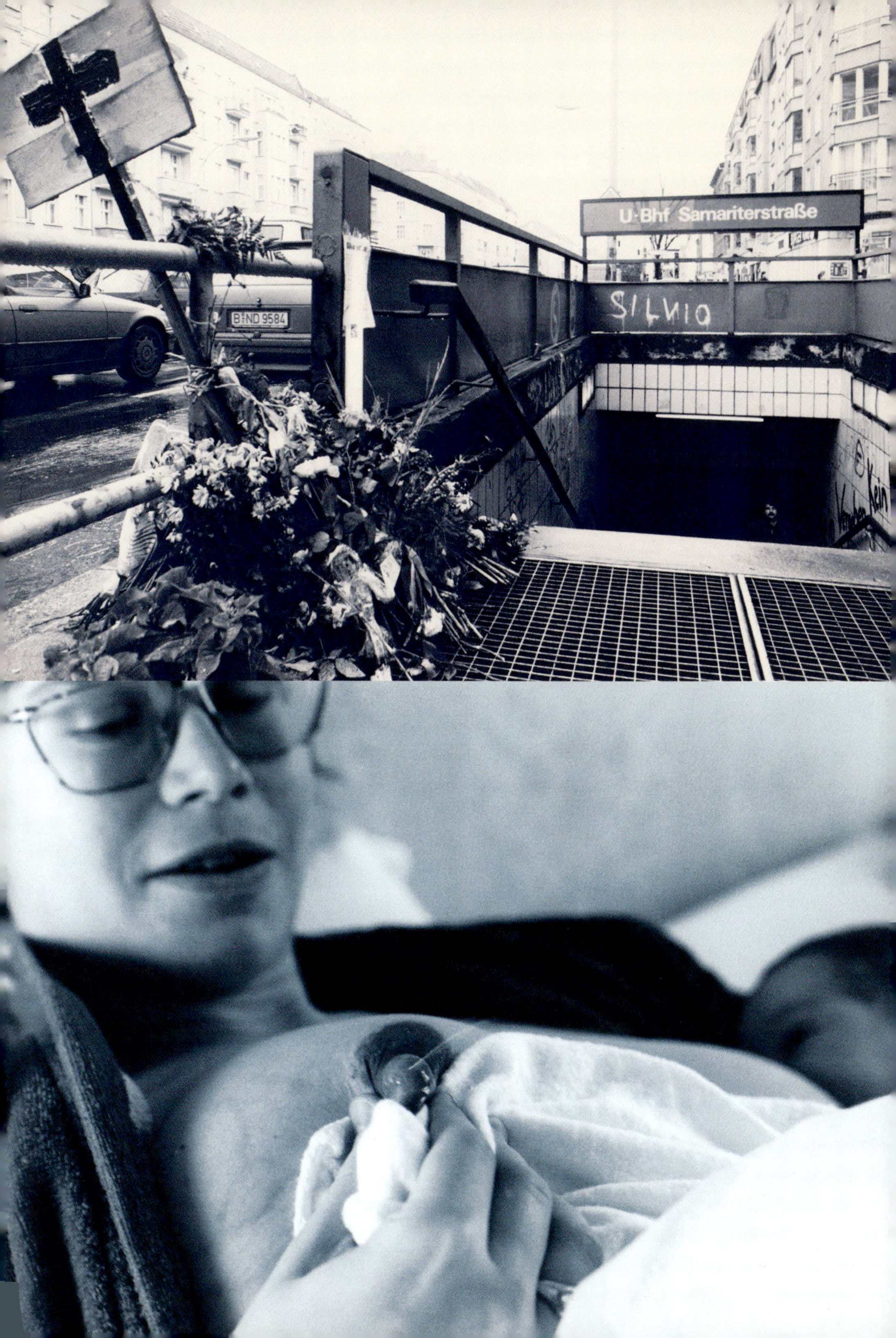
U-Bhf Samariterstraße
SILVIO
B·ND 9584

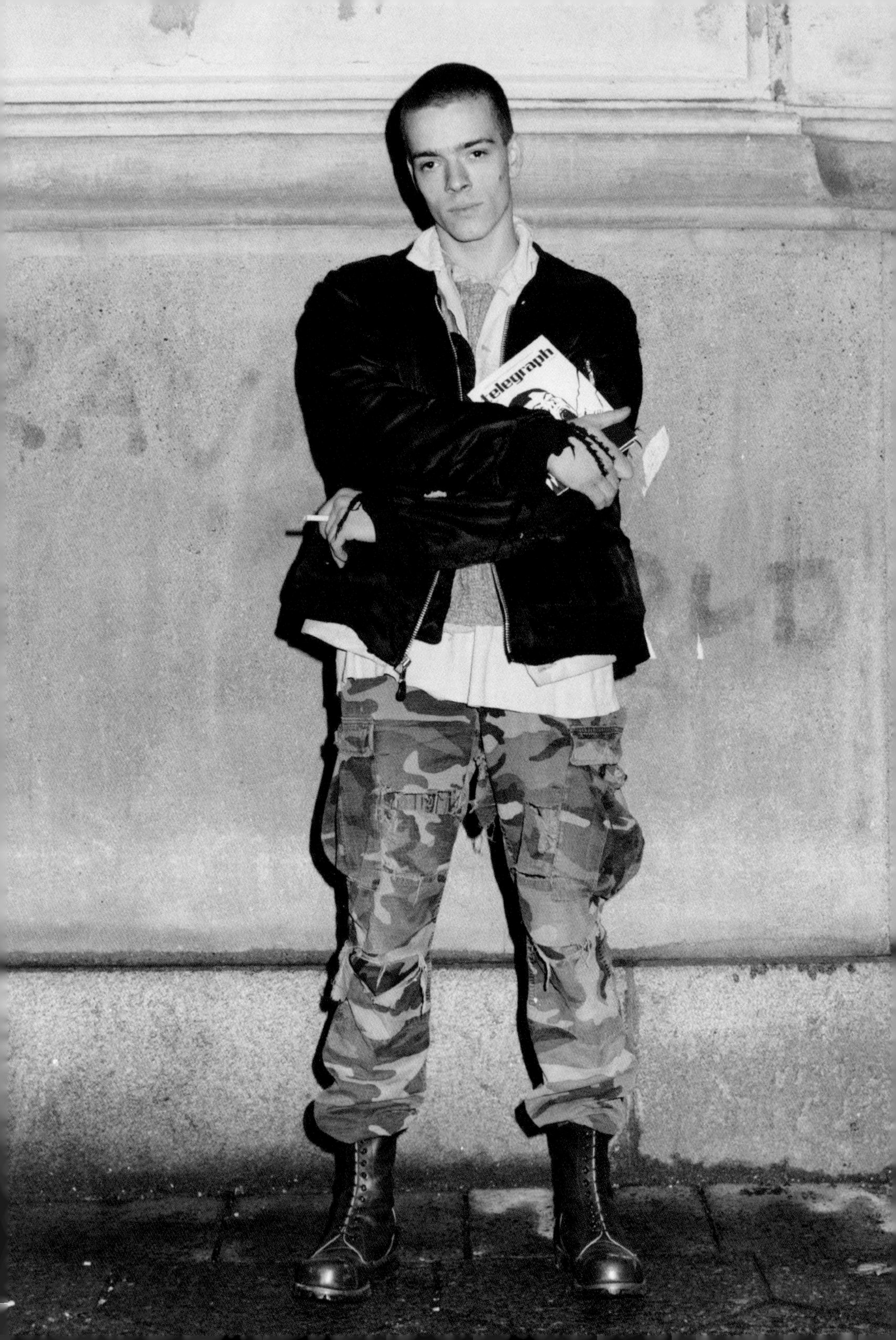
telegraph

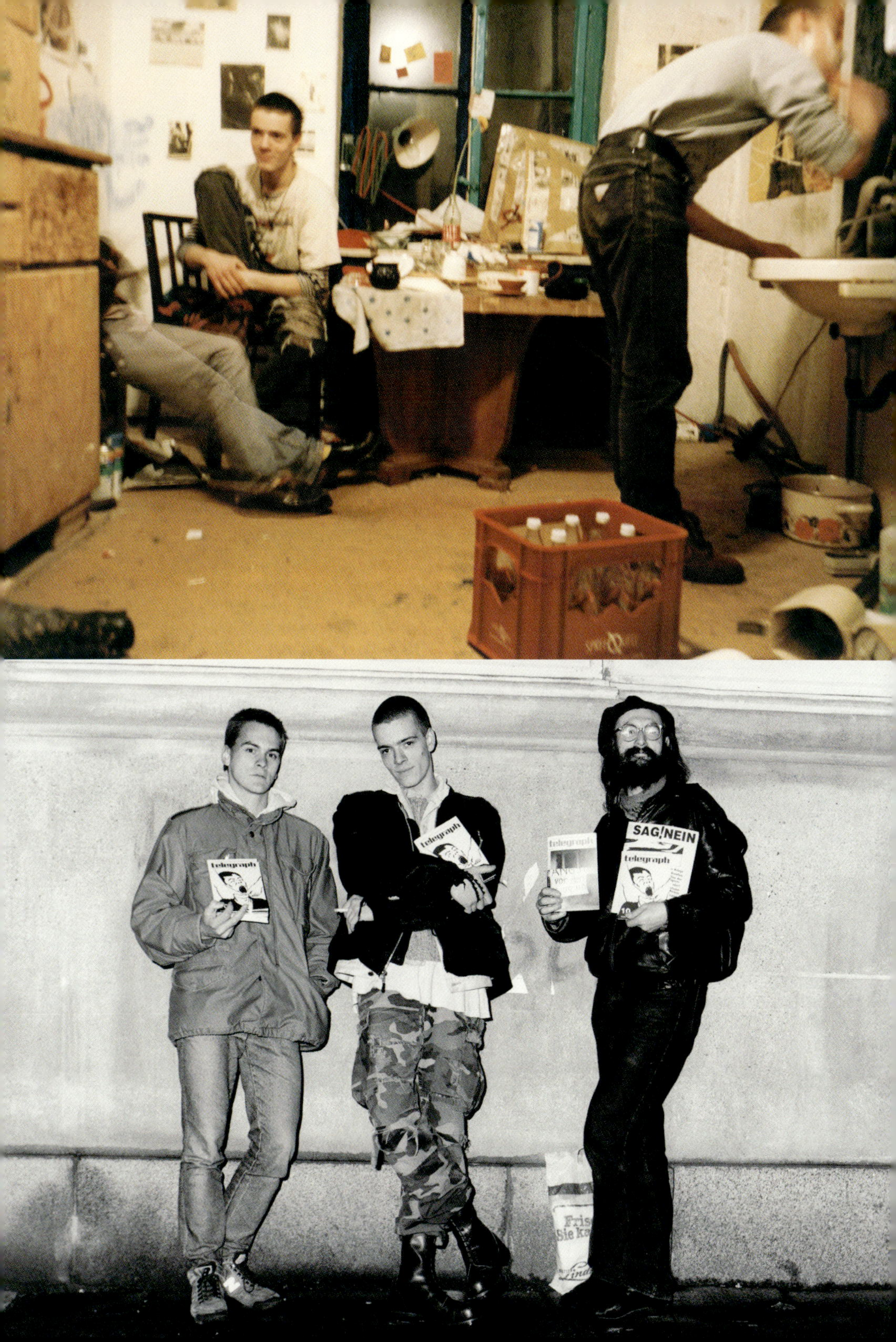

SAG!NEIN
telegraph
telegraph
telegraph

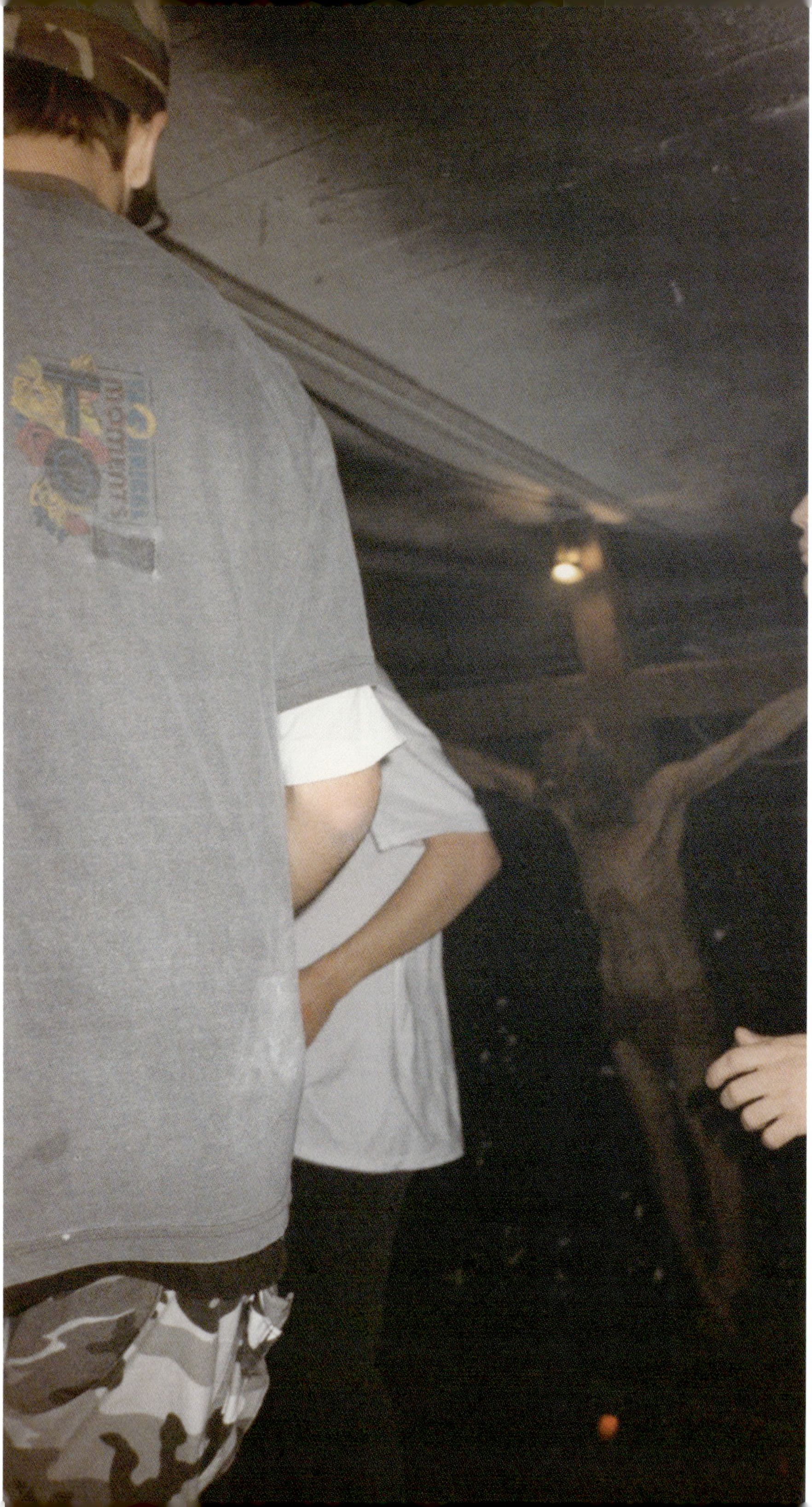

Bono, antifacist punk, Berlin, 1992   Bono Wohnung, 1992   telegraph, 1992
Bunker, Crucifix, 1992

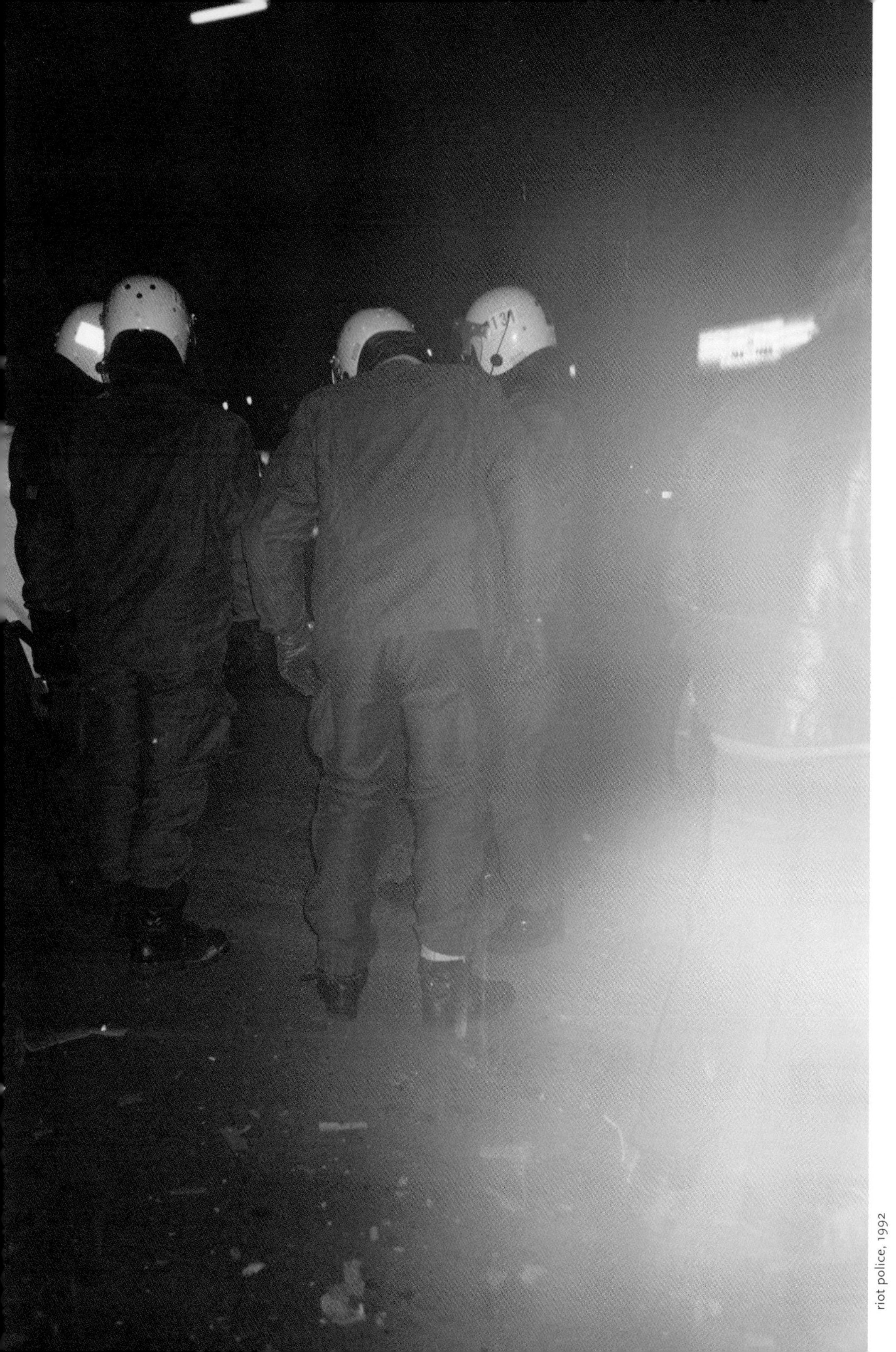

riot police, 1992

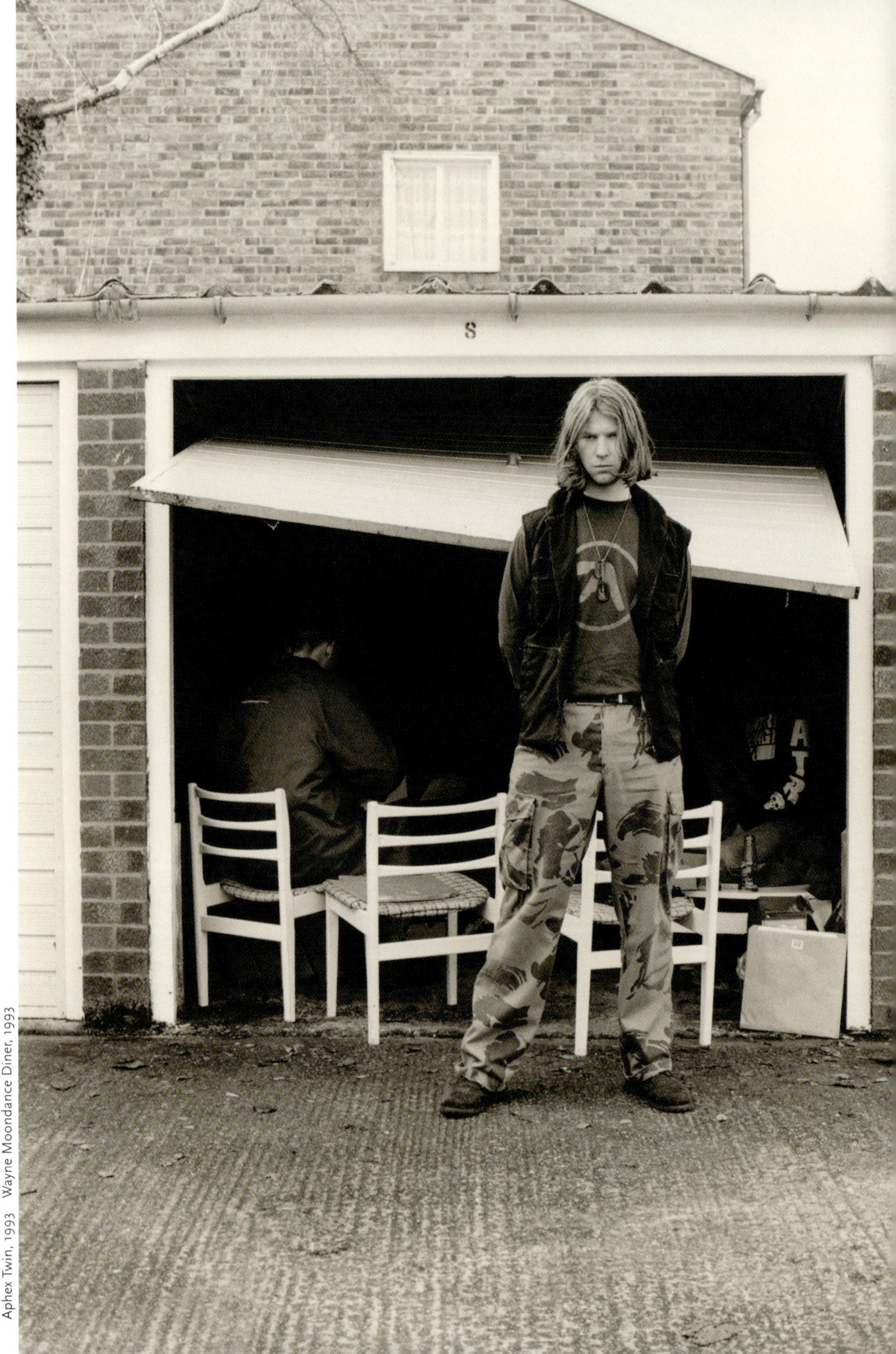

Aphex Twin, 1993   Wayne Moondance Diner, 1993

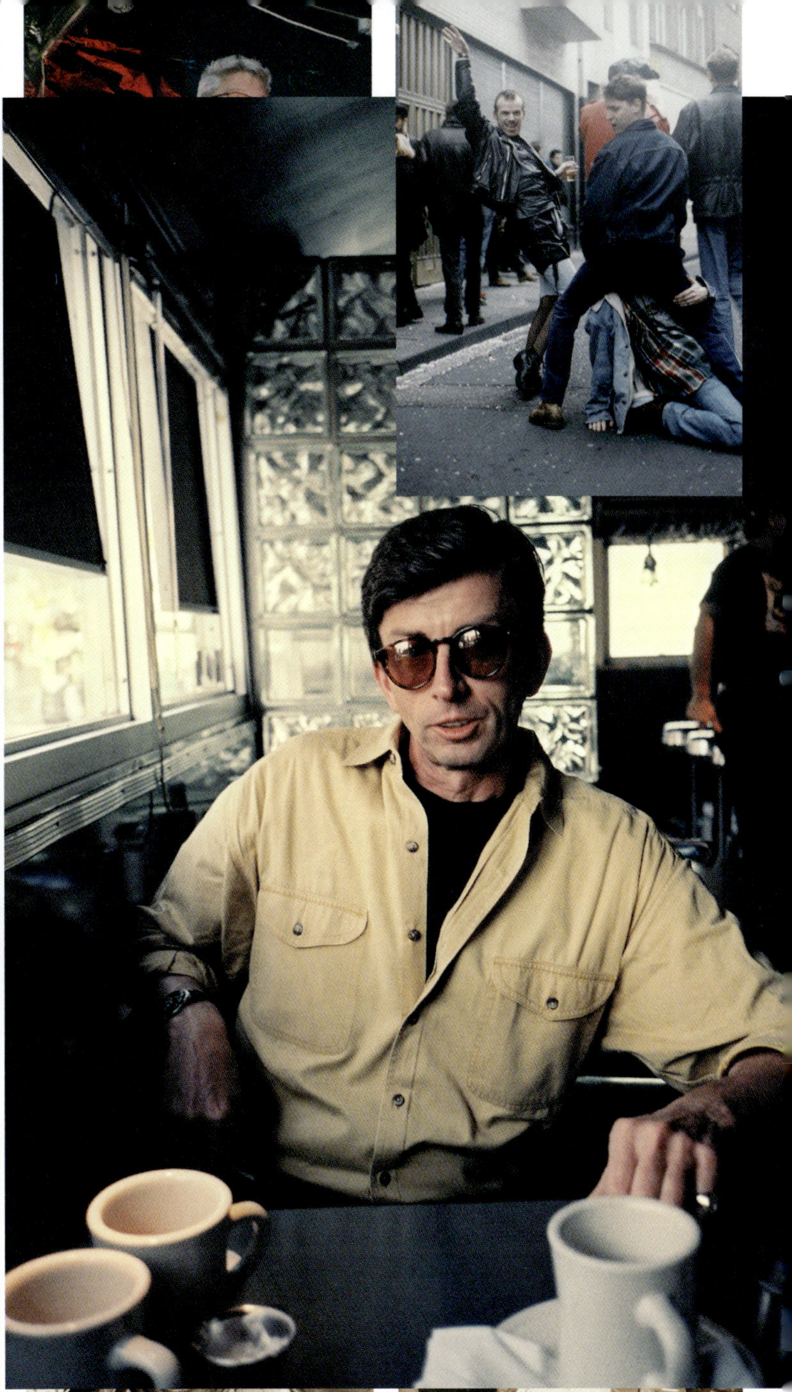

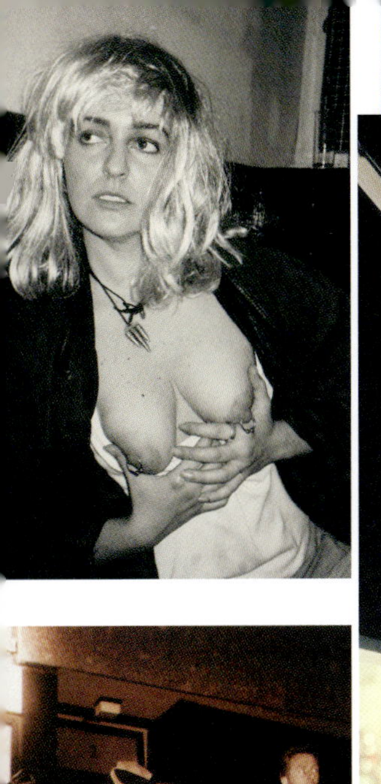
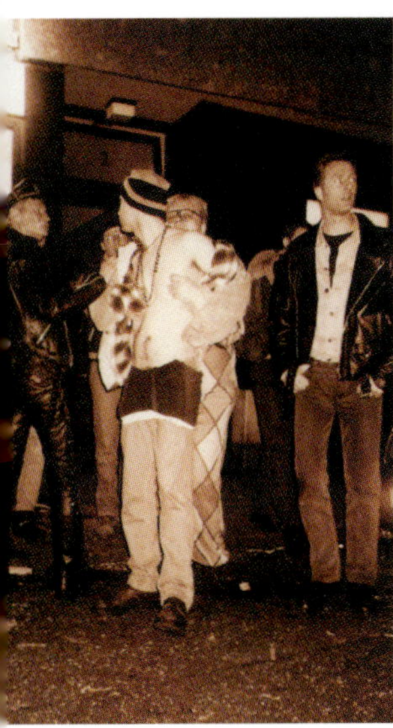
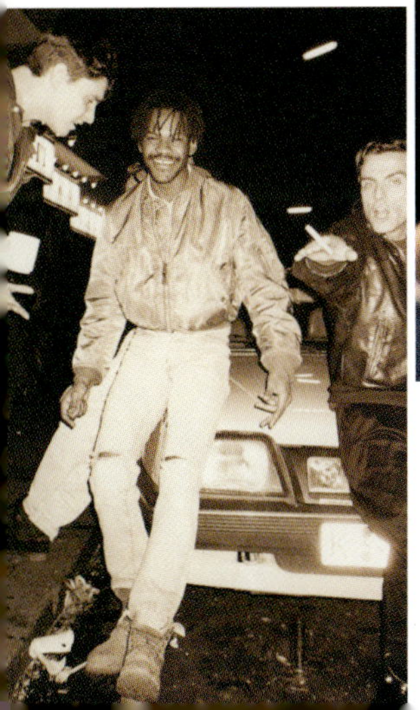

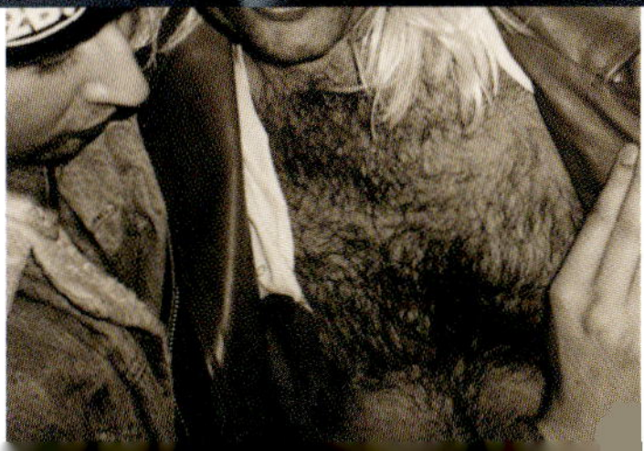

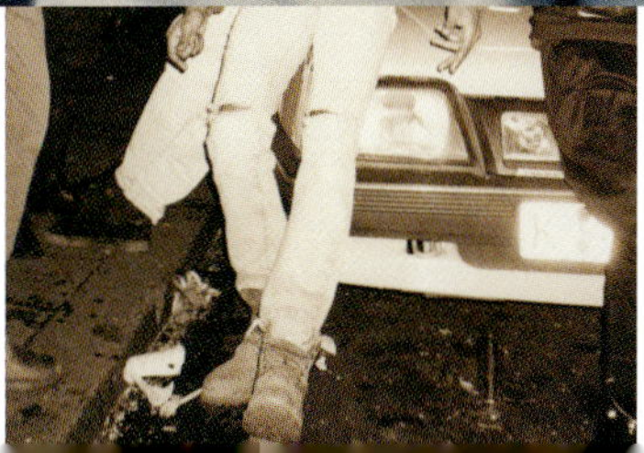

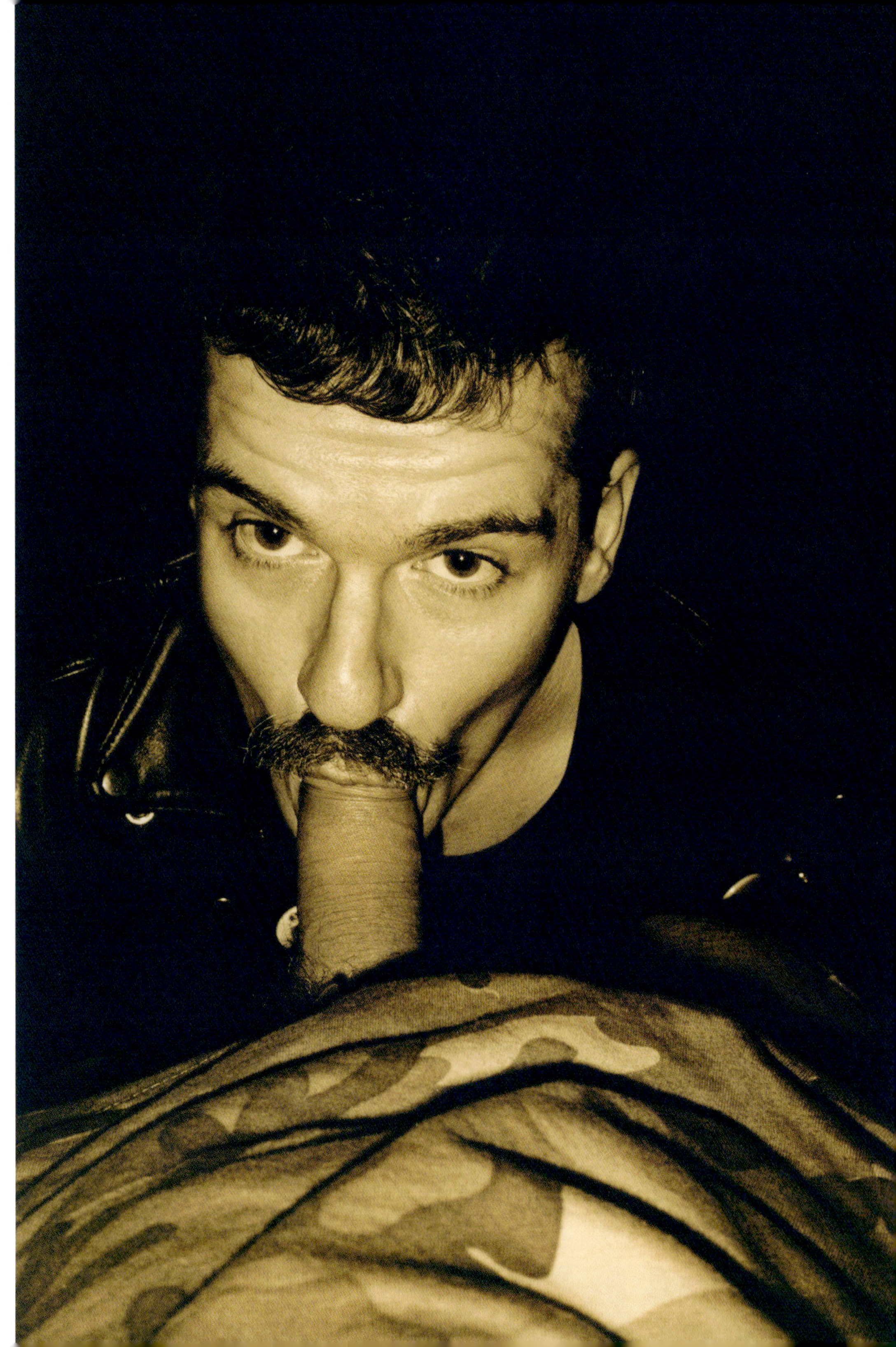

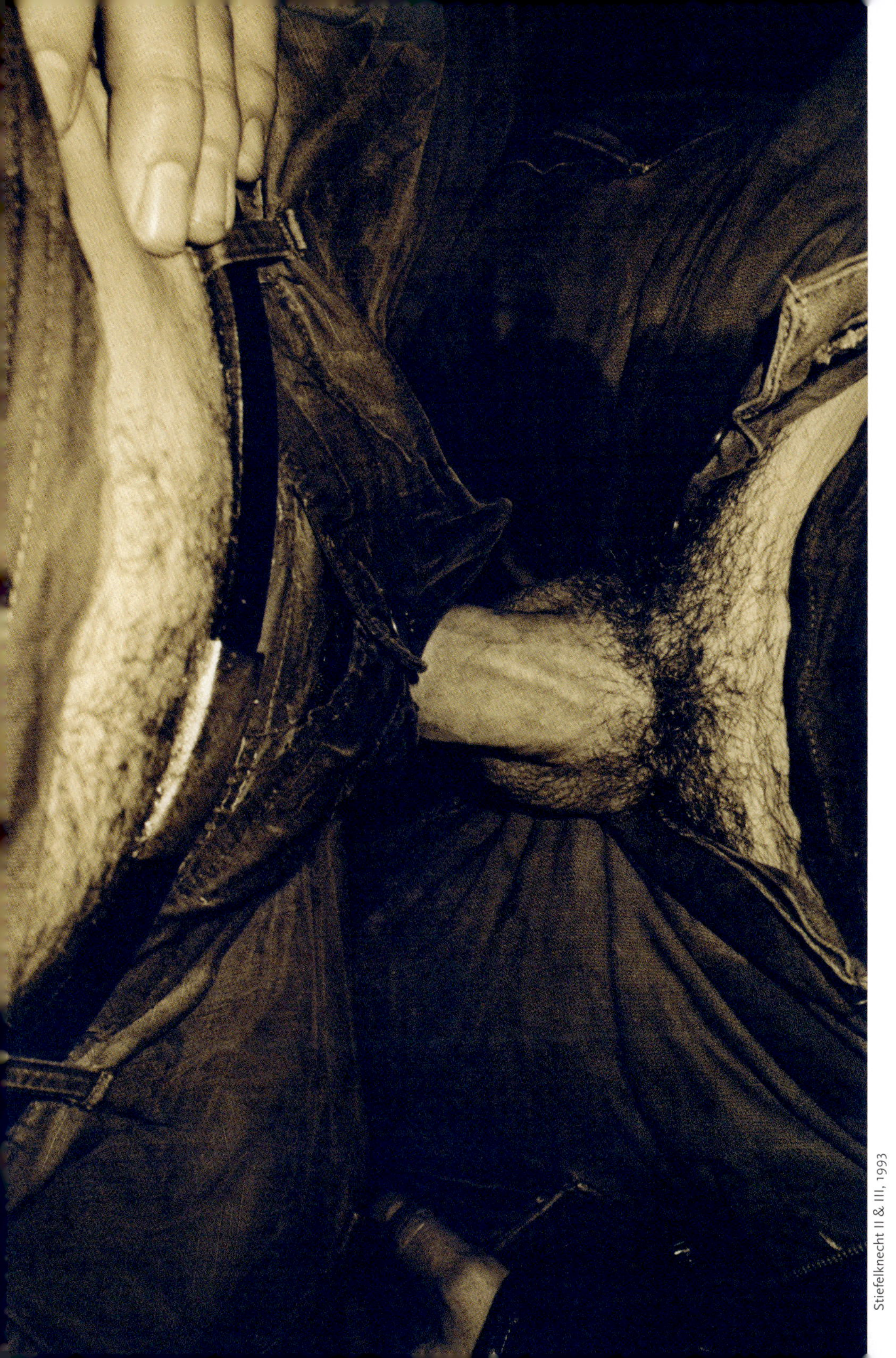

Stiefelknecht II & III, 1993

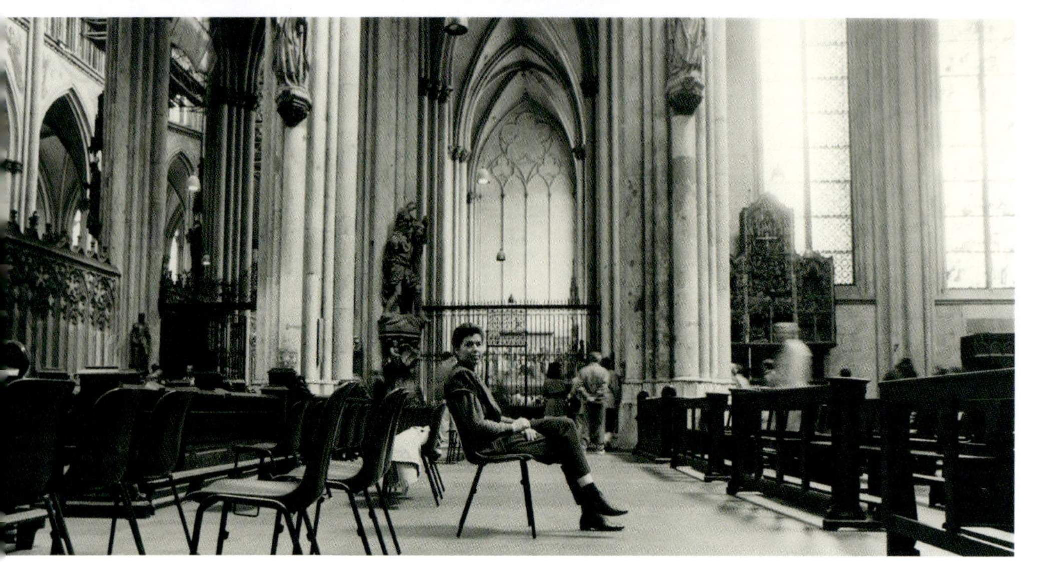

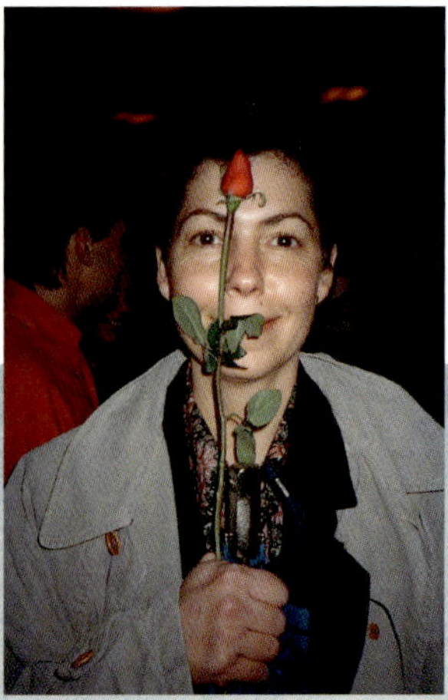

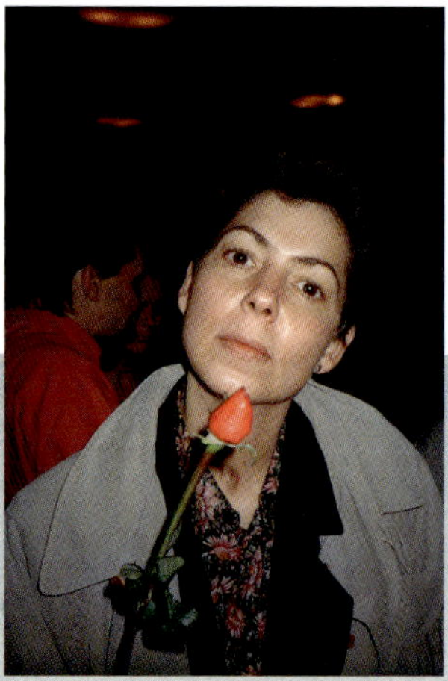

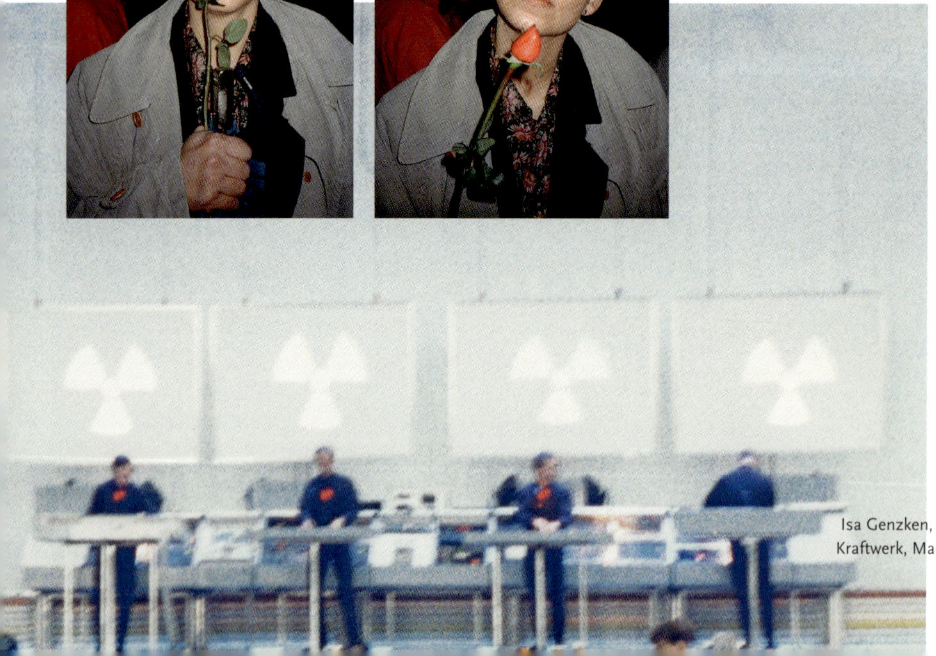

Isa Genzken, Cologne, 1993
Kraftwerk, Manchester, 1992

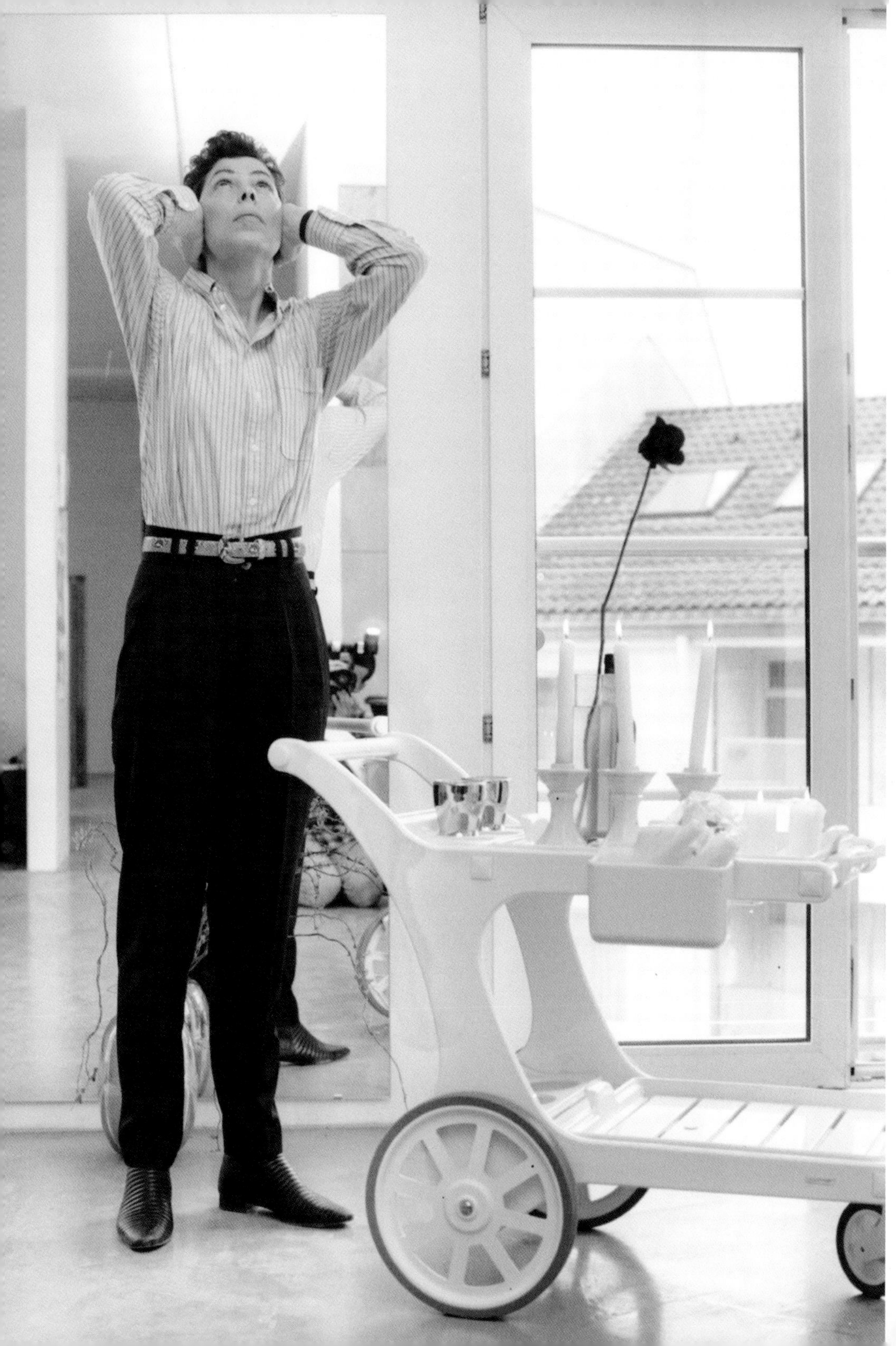

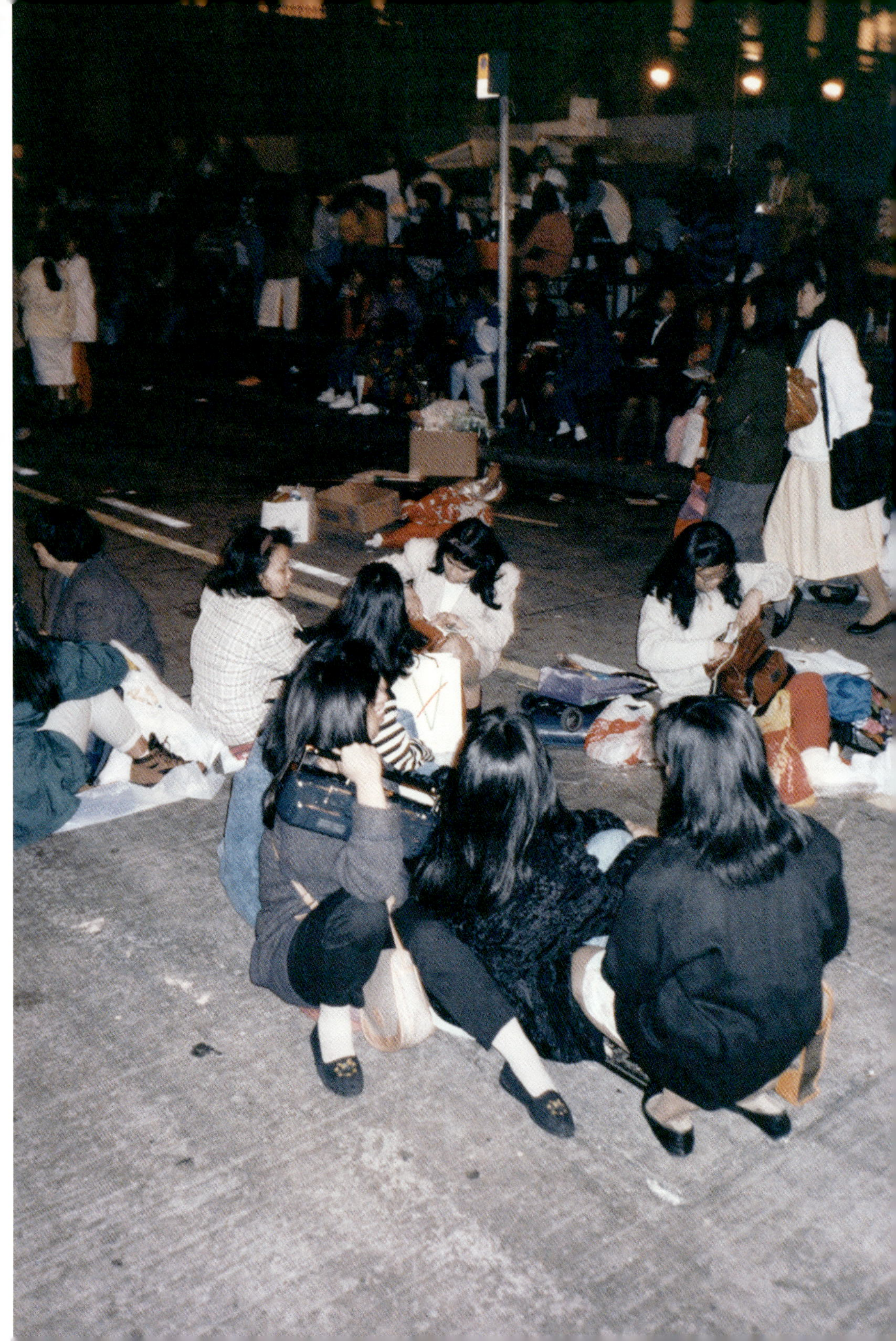

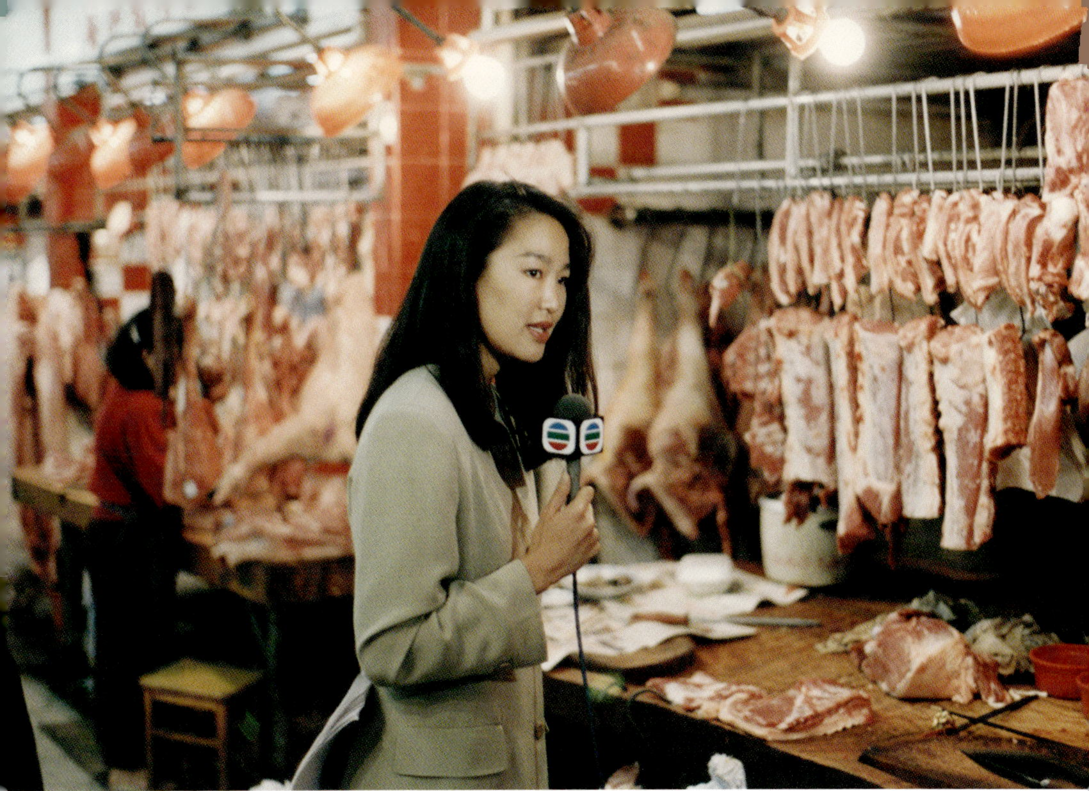

Hong Kong, Phillipinas on street, 1993
Hong Kong TV reporter, 1993

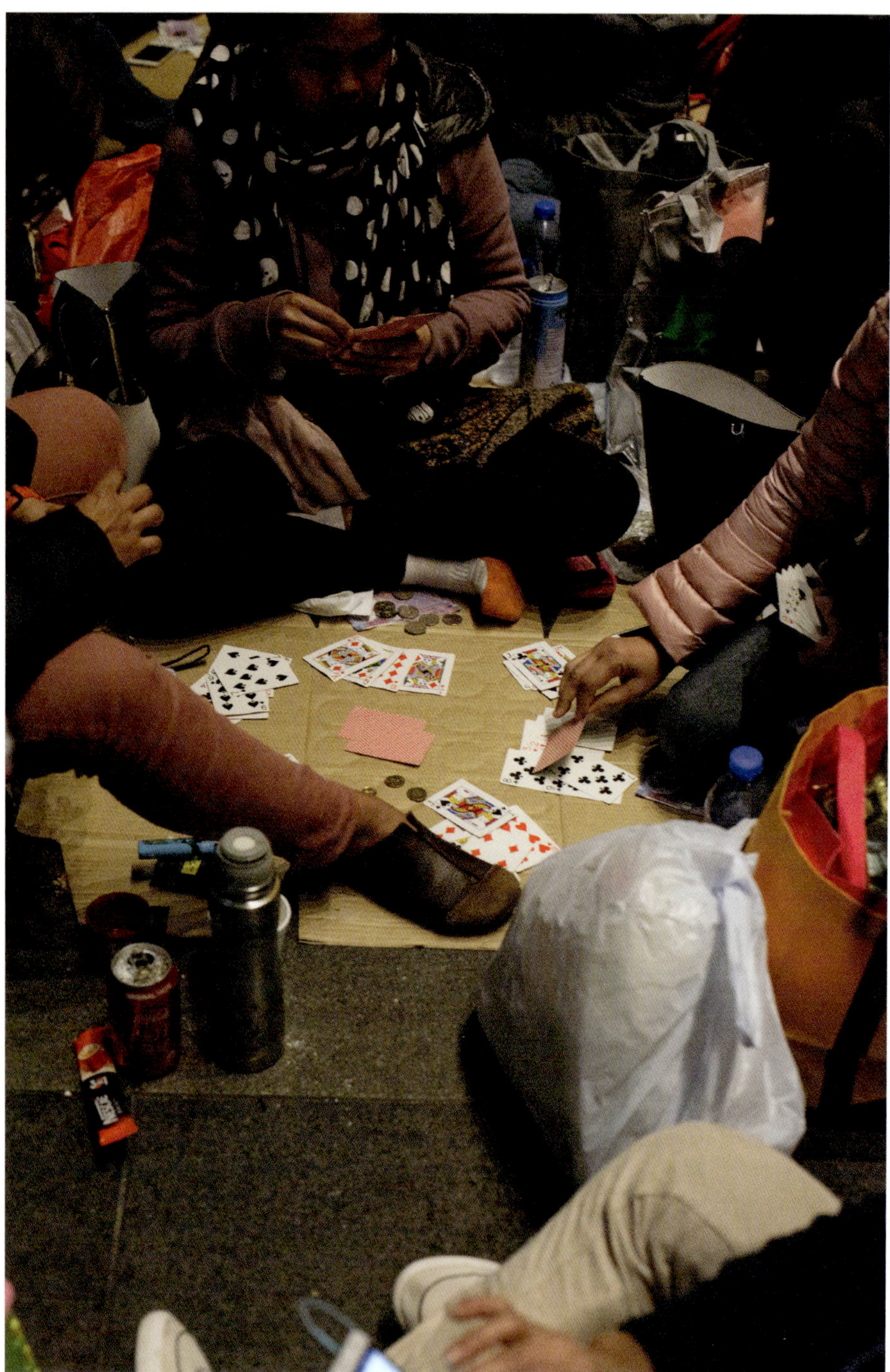

Playing cards, Hong Kong, 2018

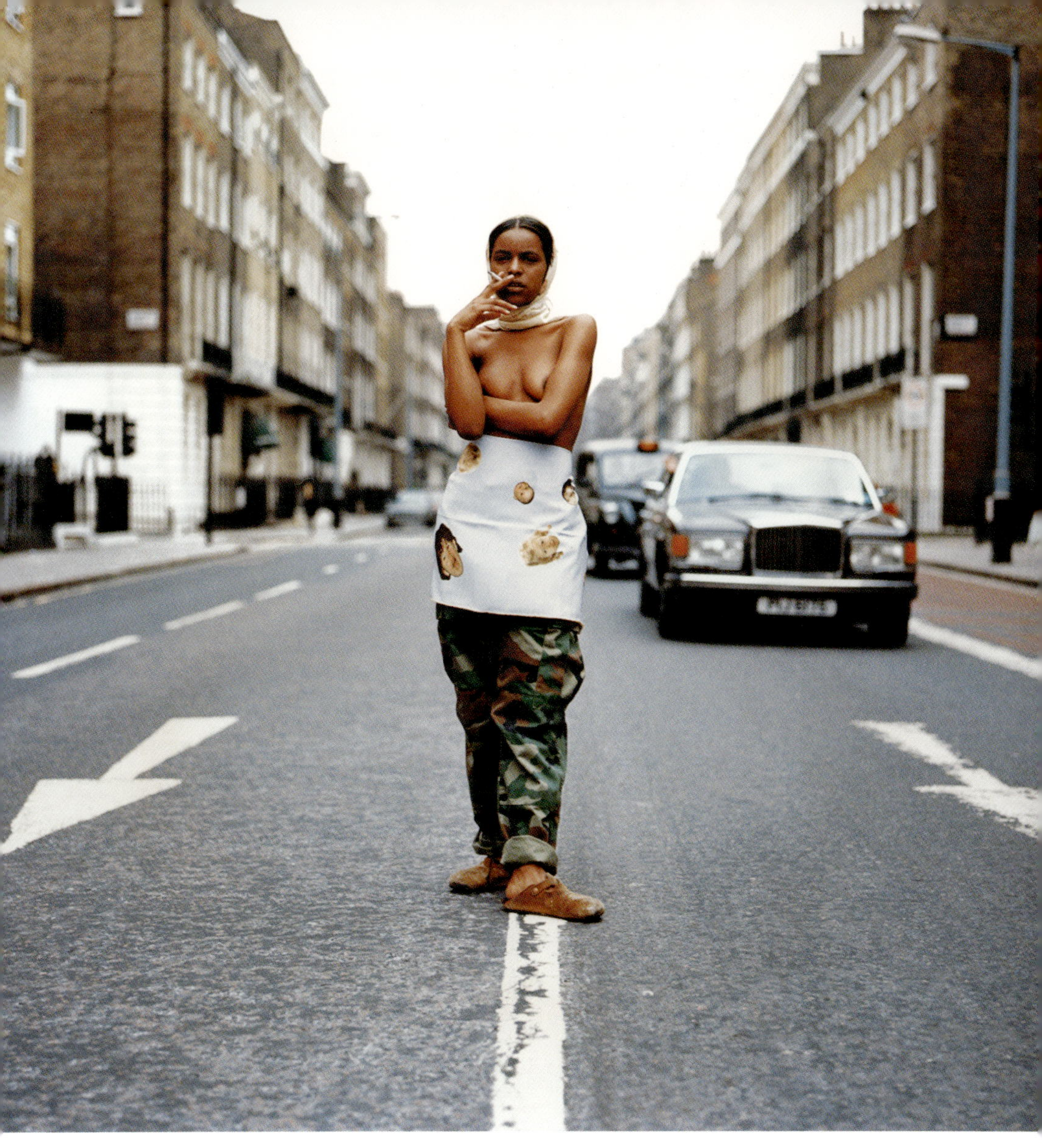

Corinne on Gloucester Place, 1993

Suzanne & Lutz, white dress, army skirt, 1993
Lutz, Alex, Suzanne & Christoph on beach (b/w), 1993

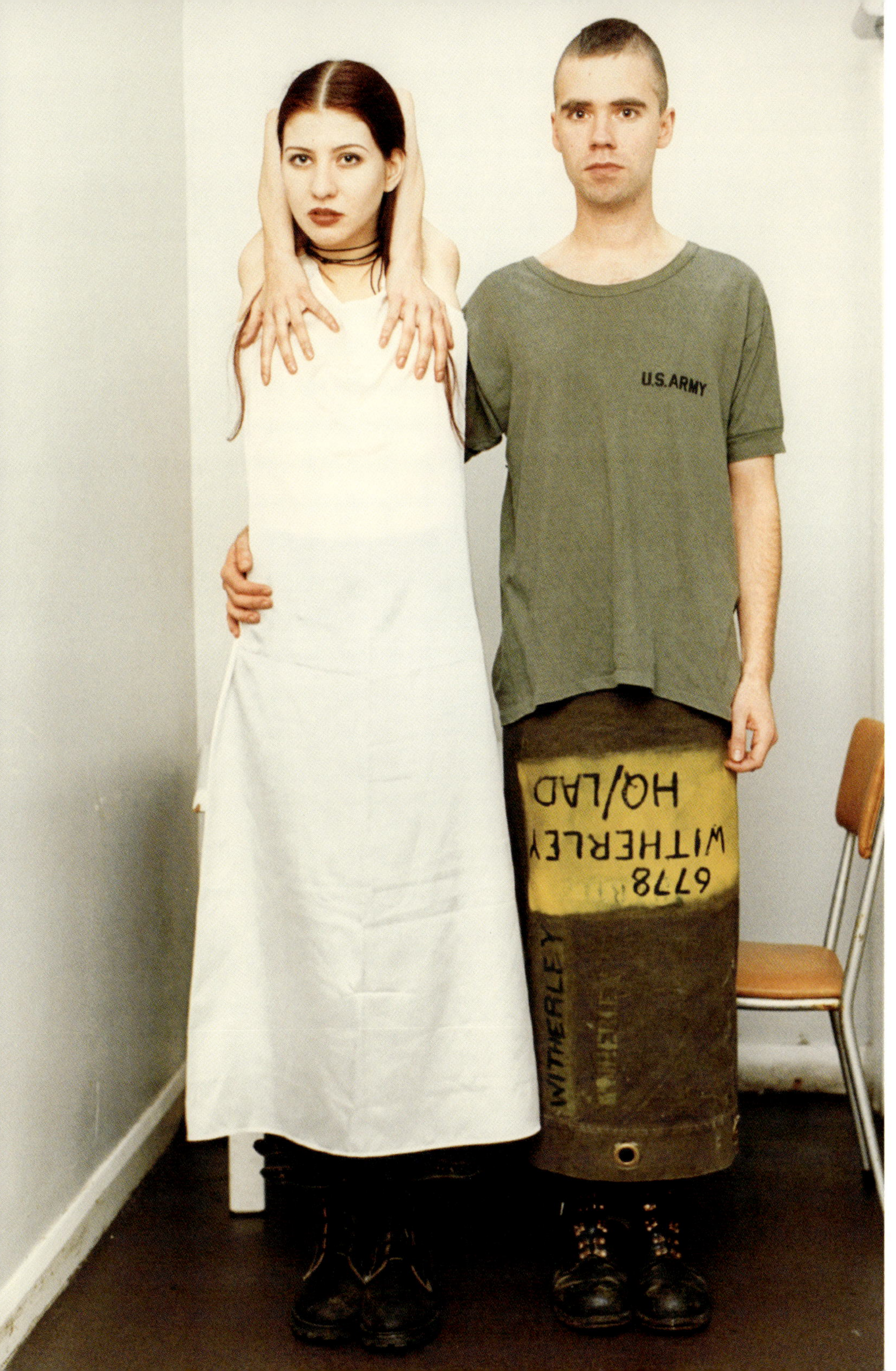

U.S.ARMY
HQ/LAD
WITHERLEY
6778
WITHERLEY

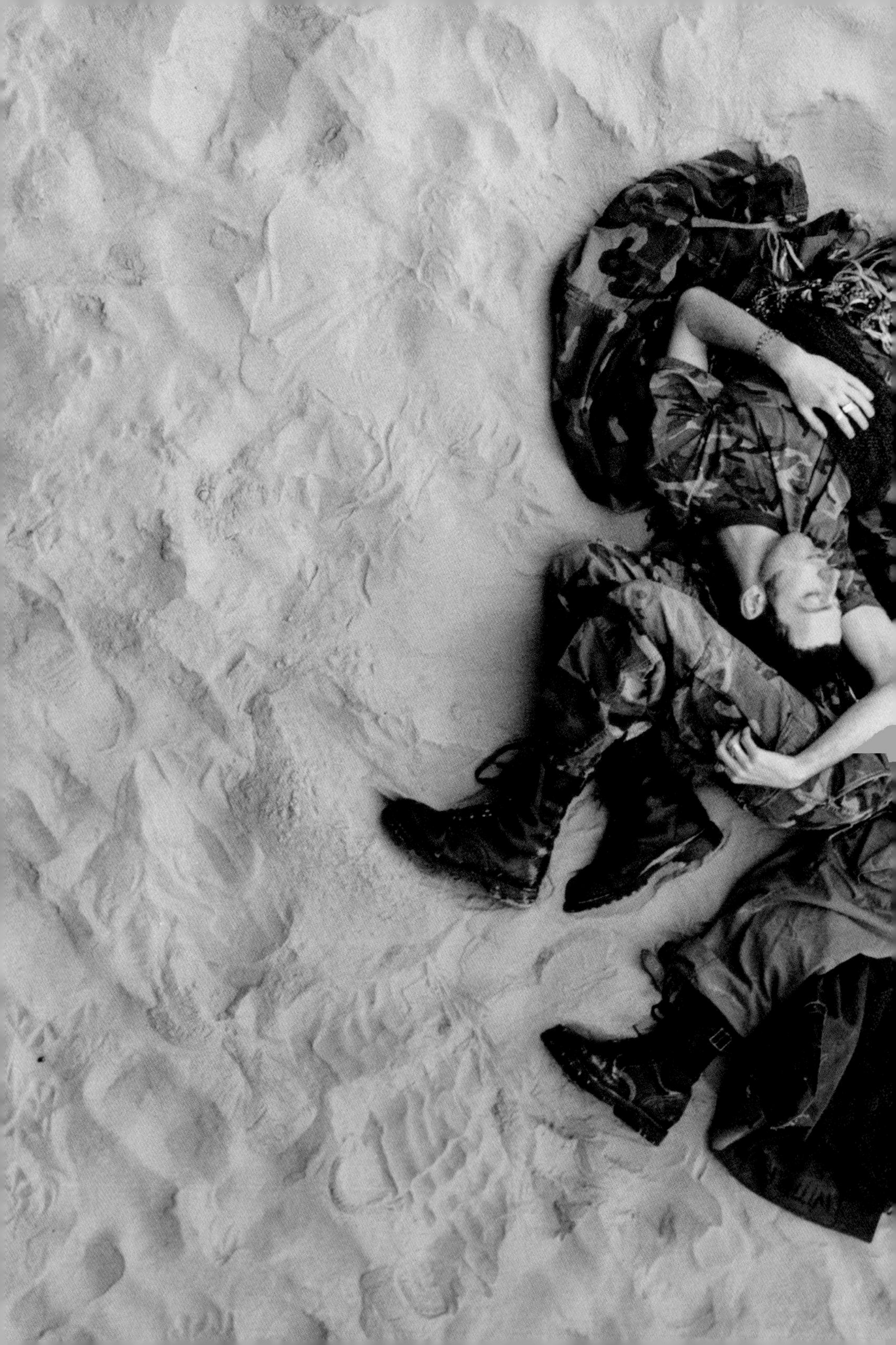

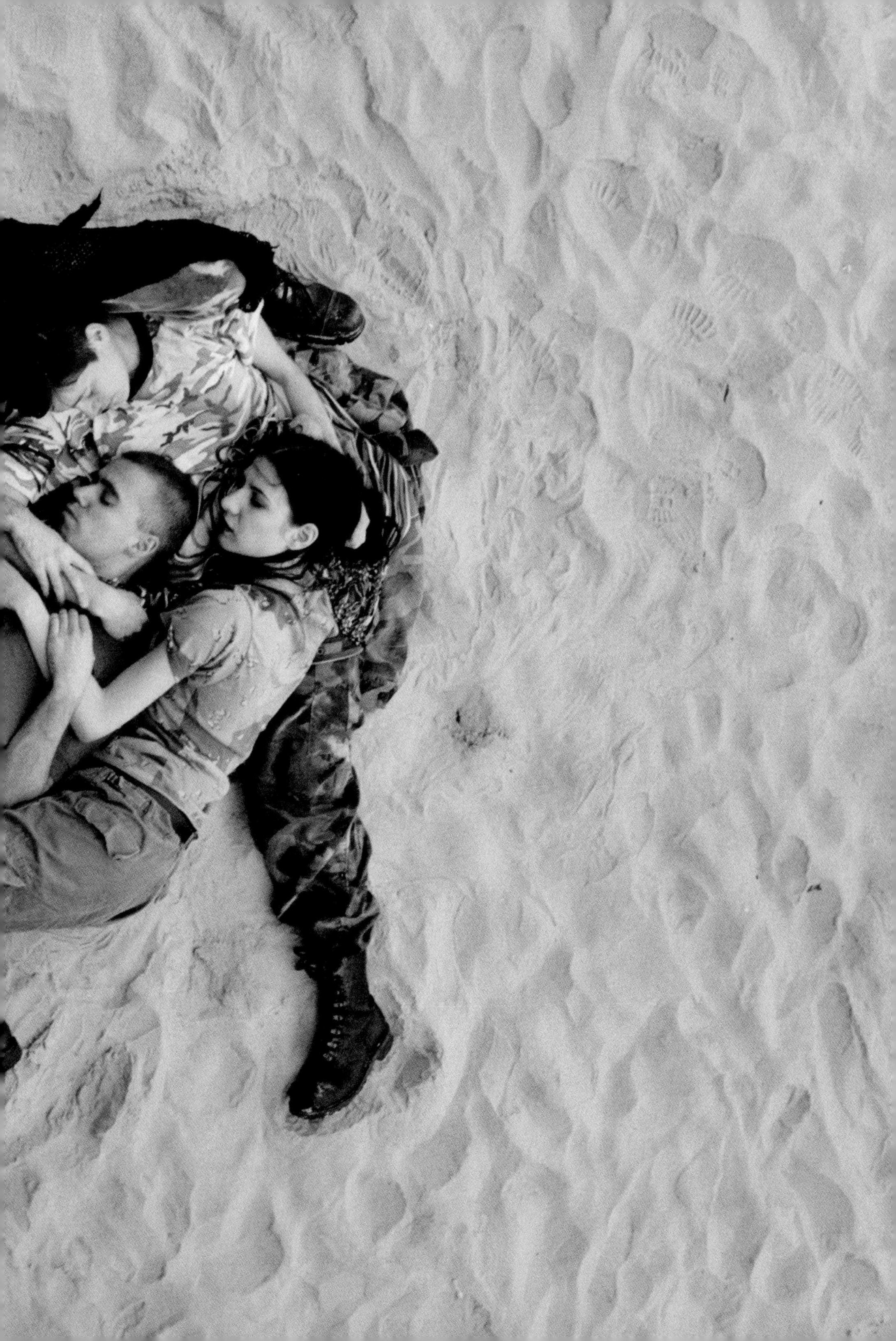

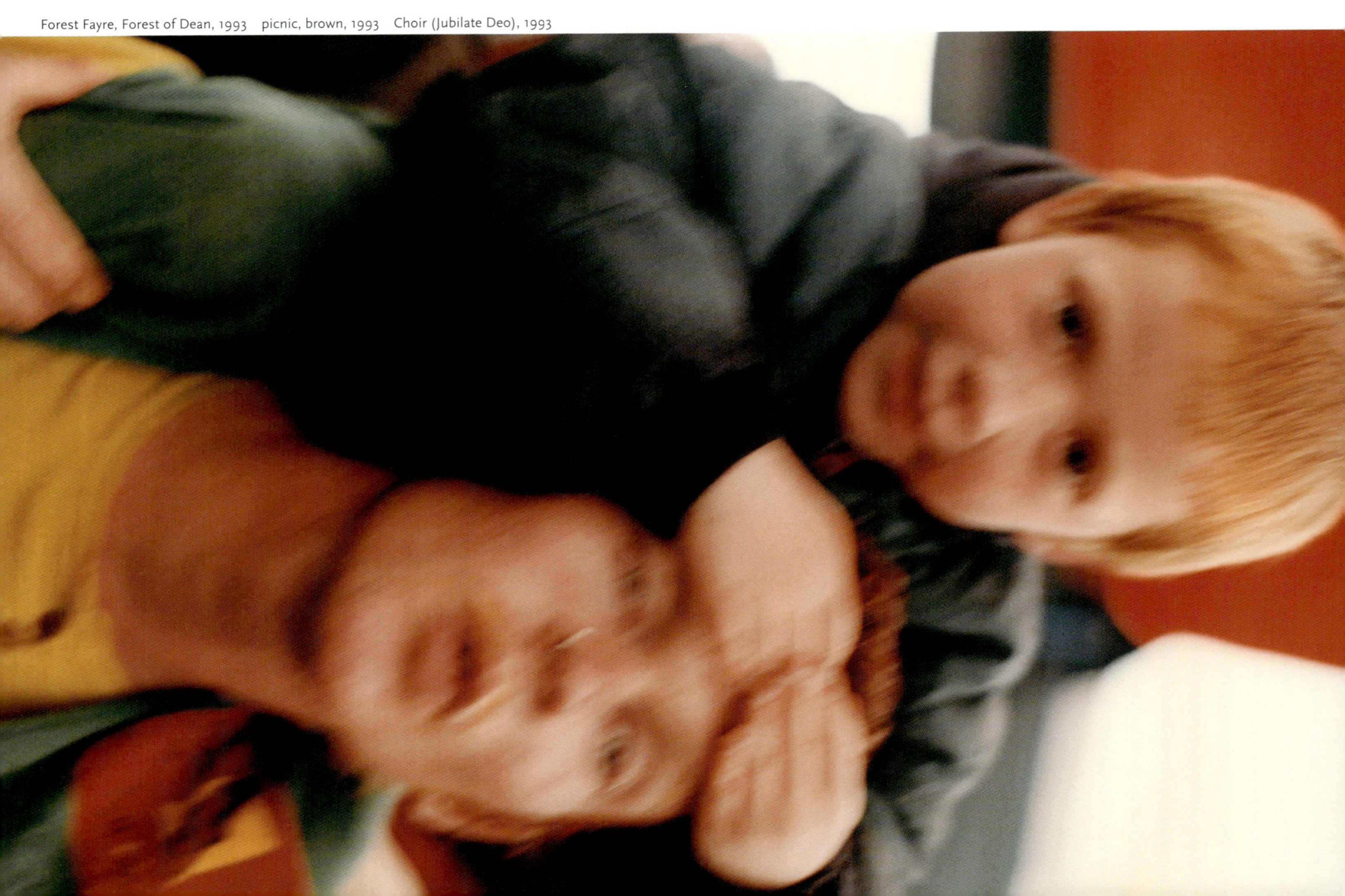

Forest Fayre, Forest of Dean, 1993   picnic, brown, 1993   Choir (Jubilate Deo), 1993

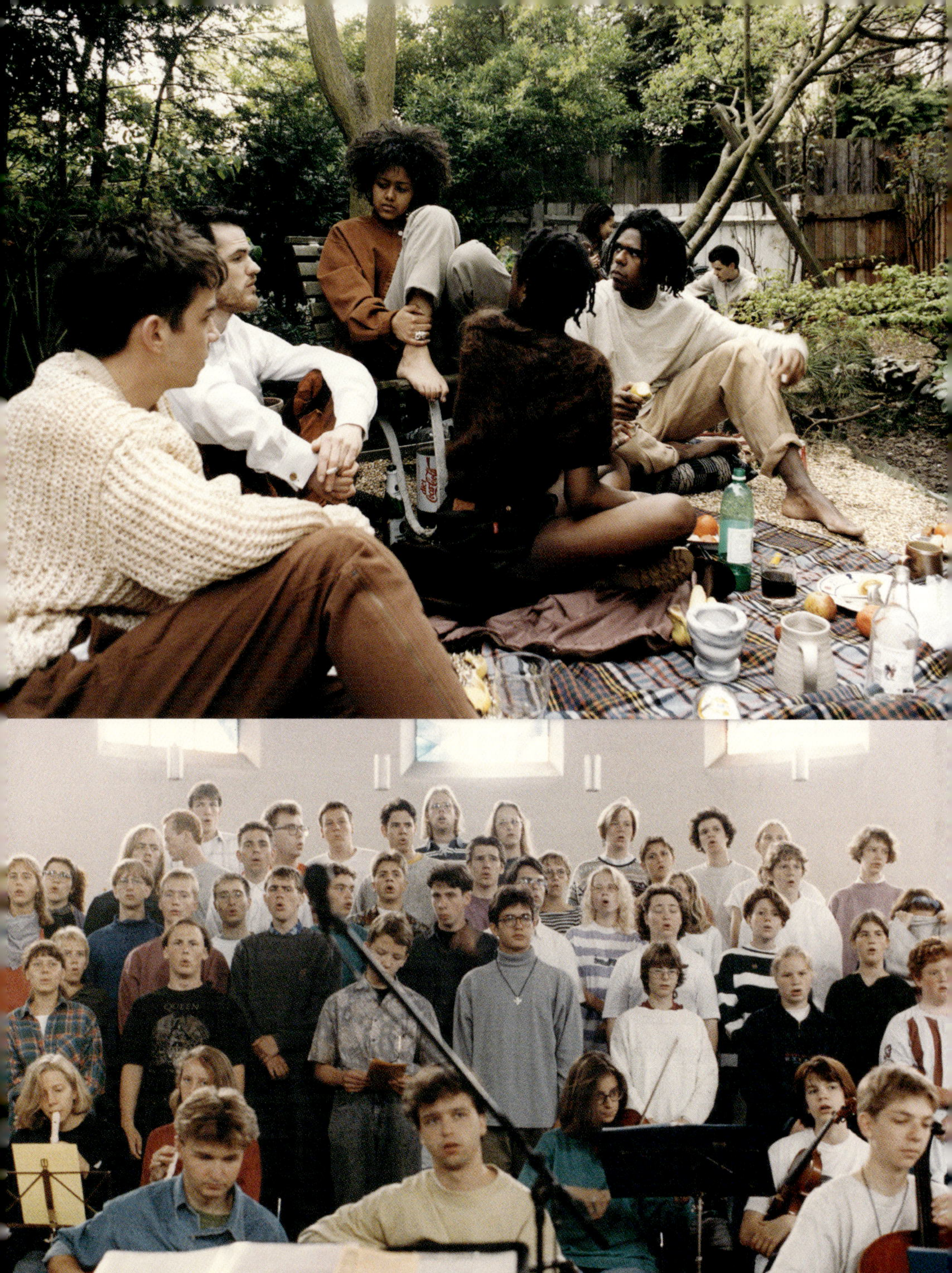

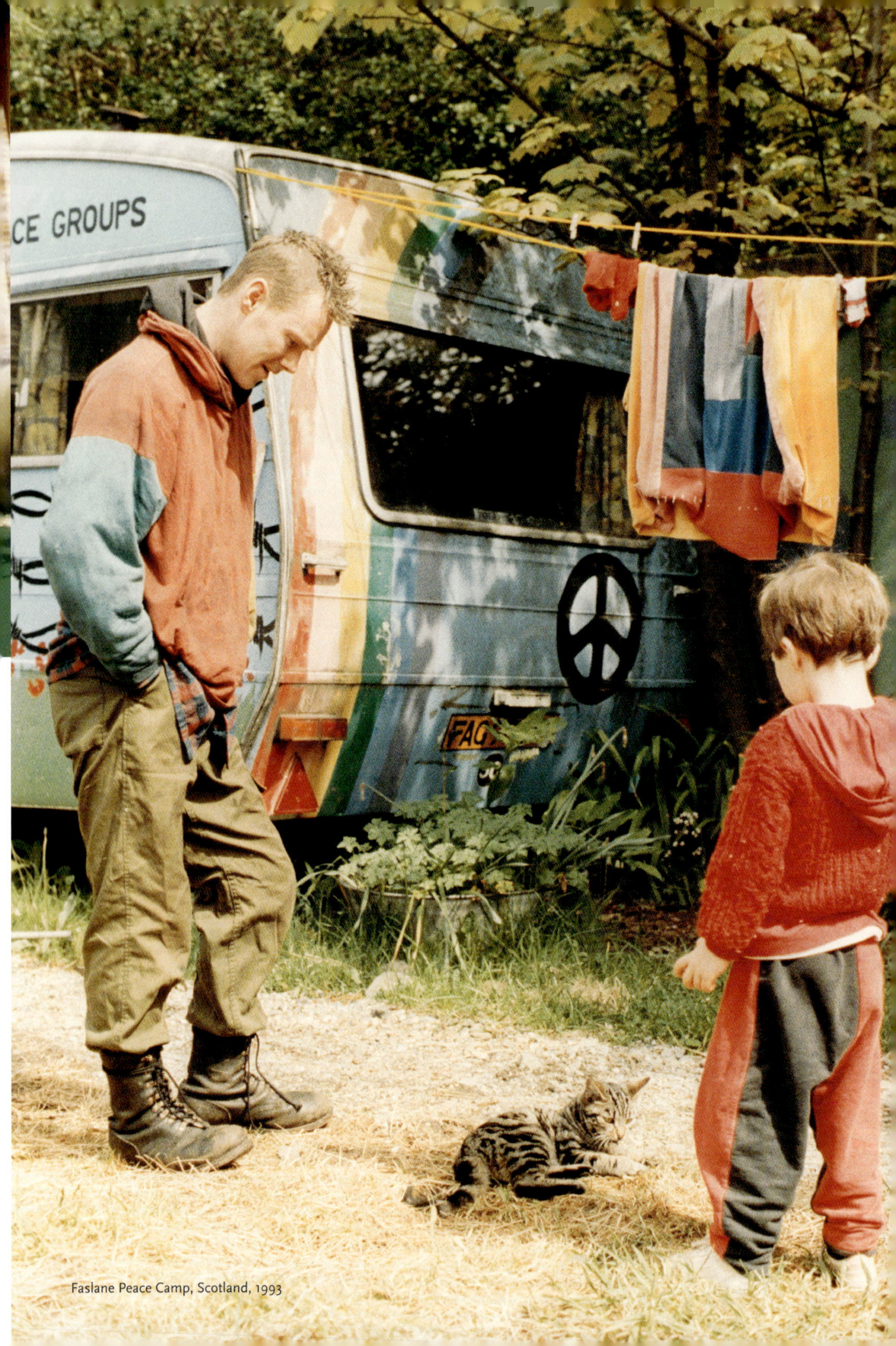

Faslane Peace Camp, Scotland, 1993

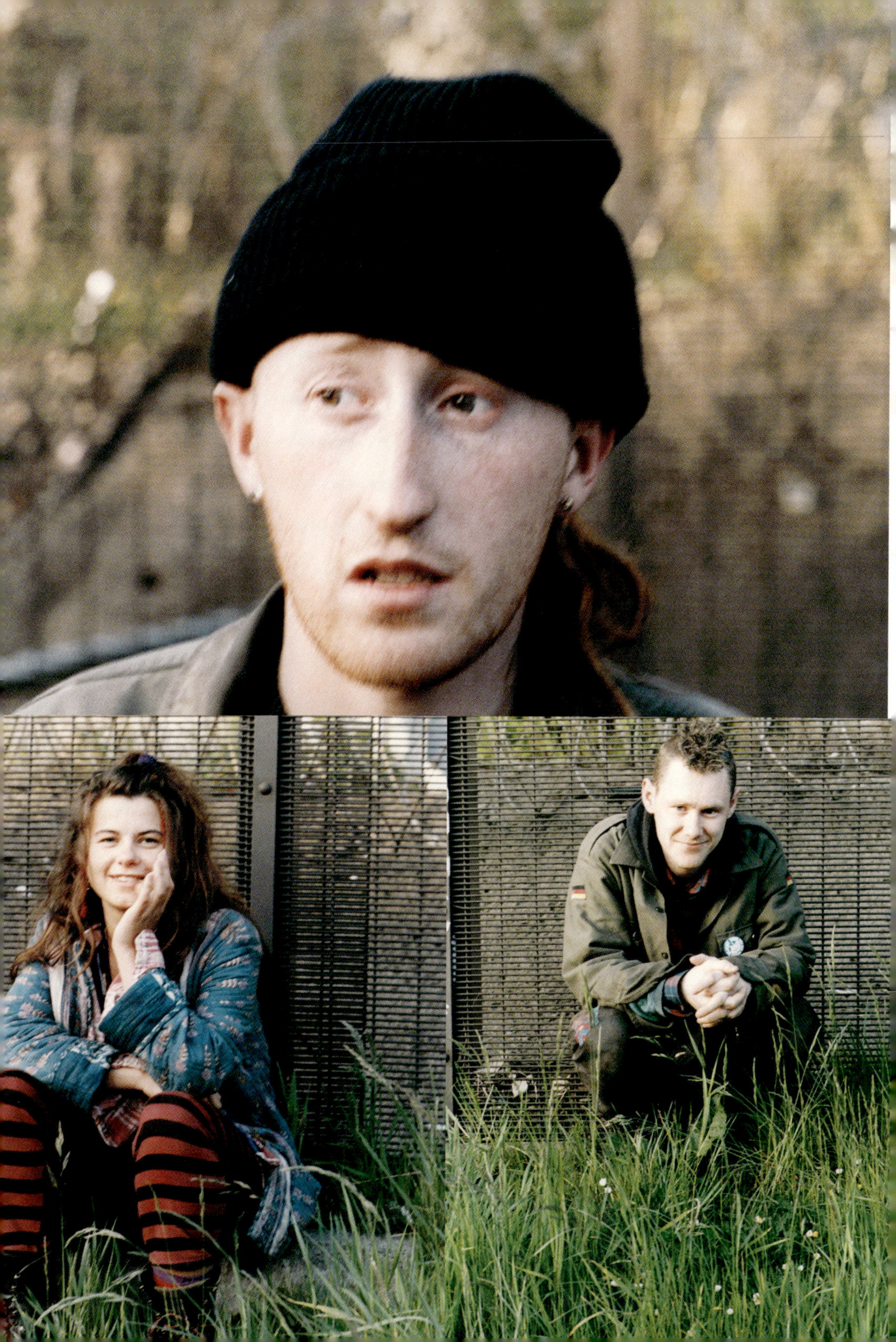

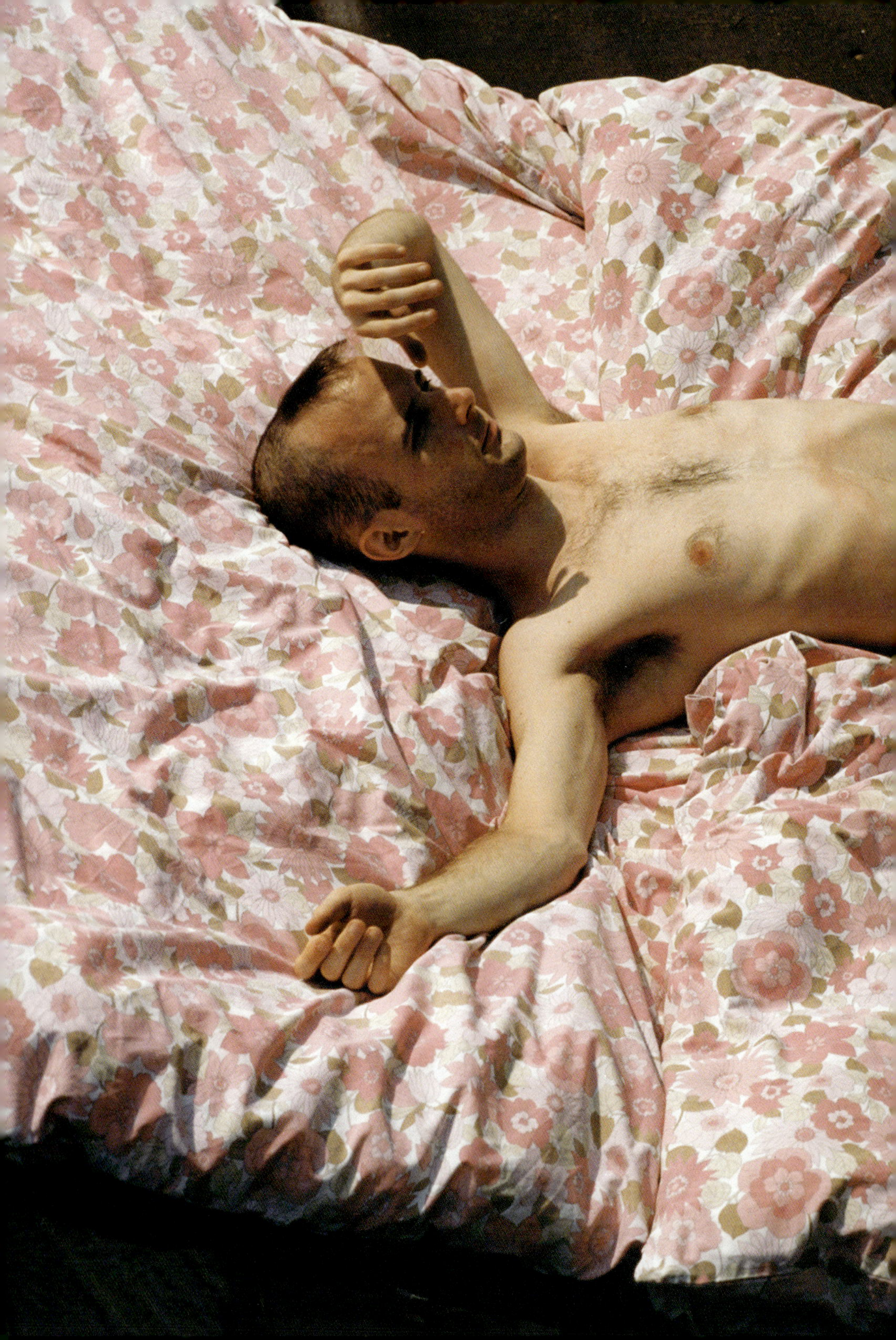

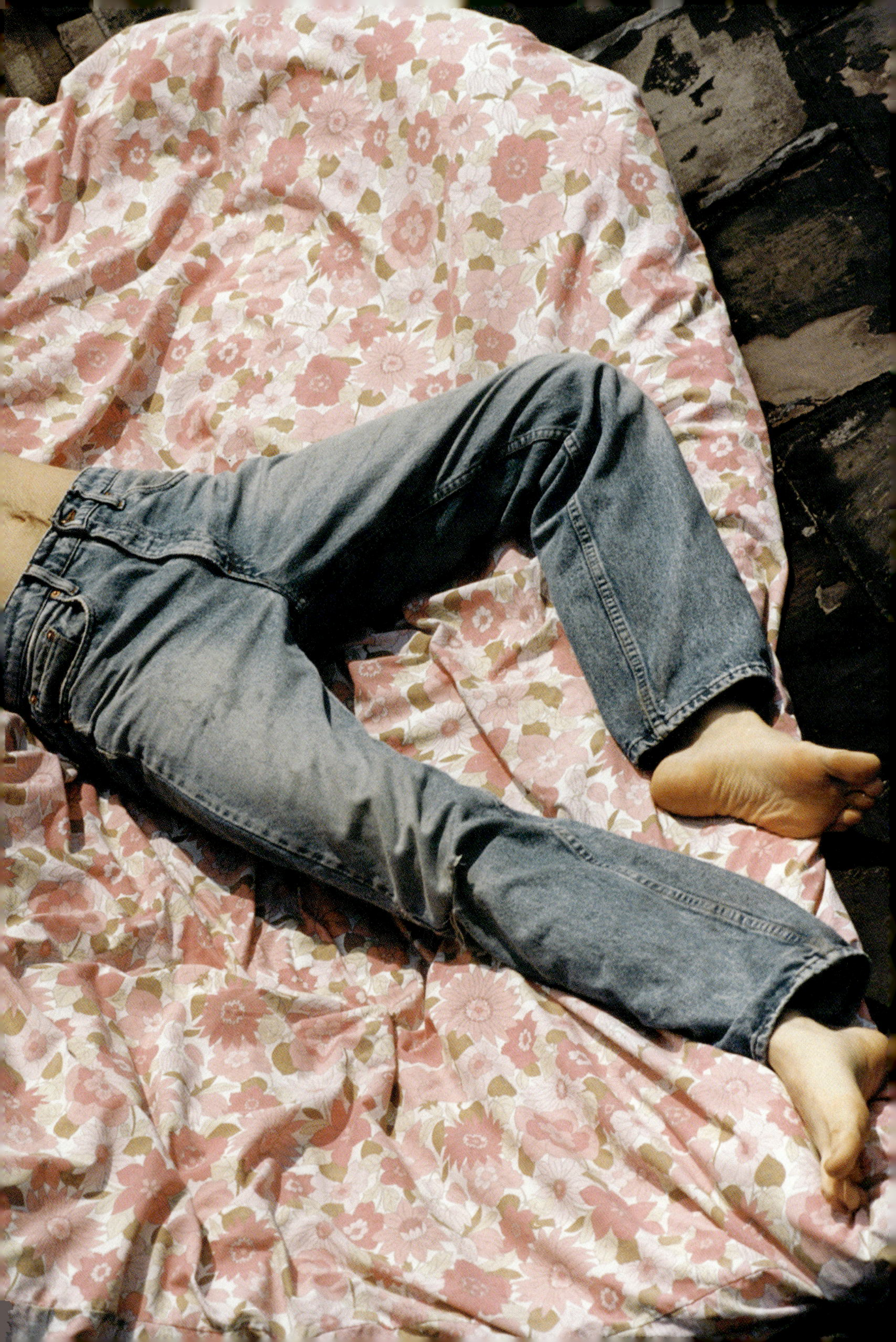

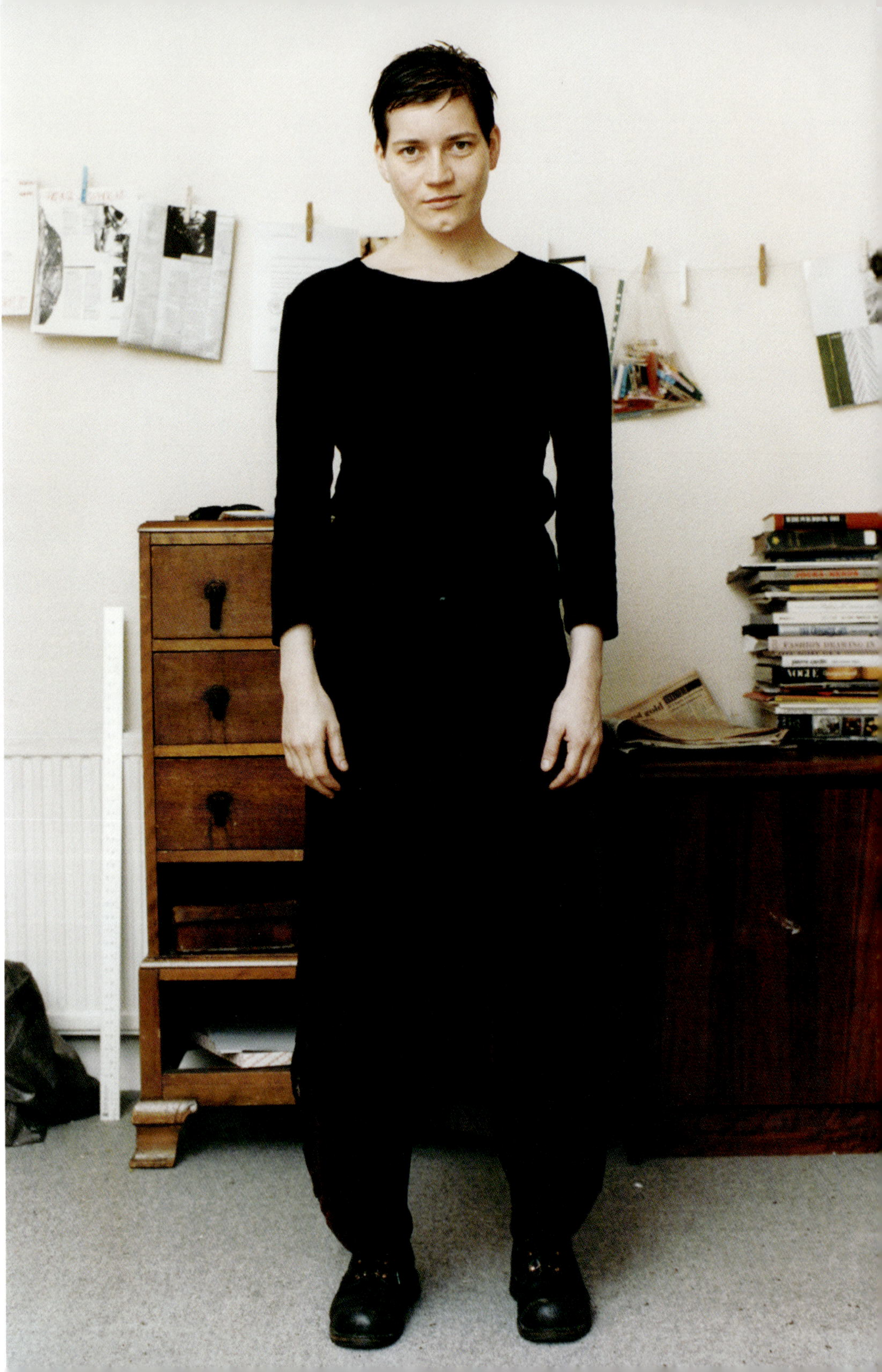

Moby (lying), 1993   Alex in her room, 1993

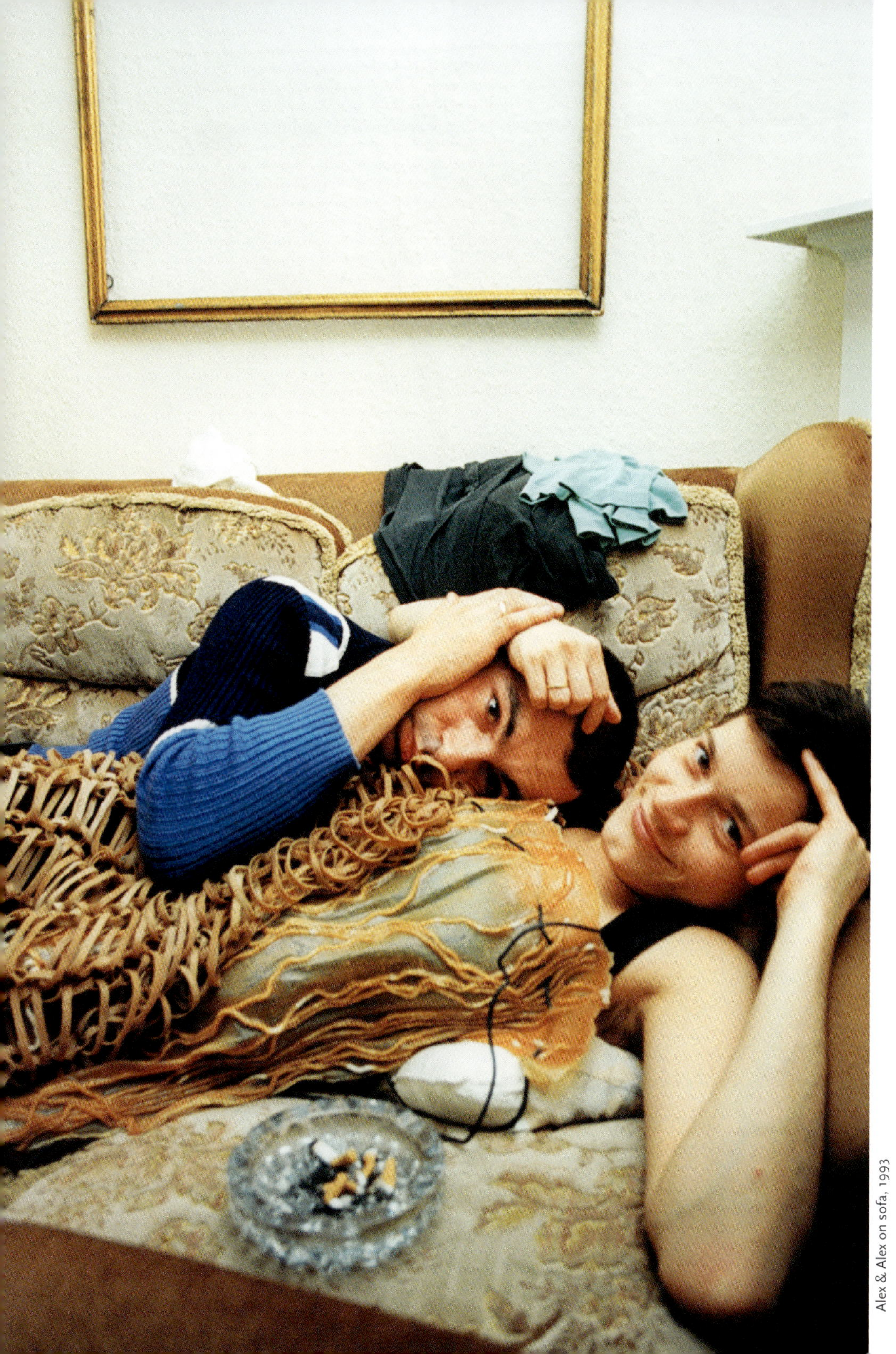

Alex & Alex on sofa, 1993

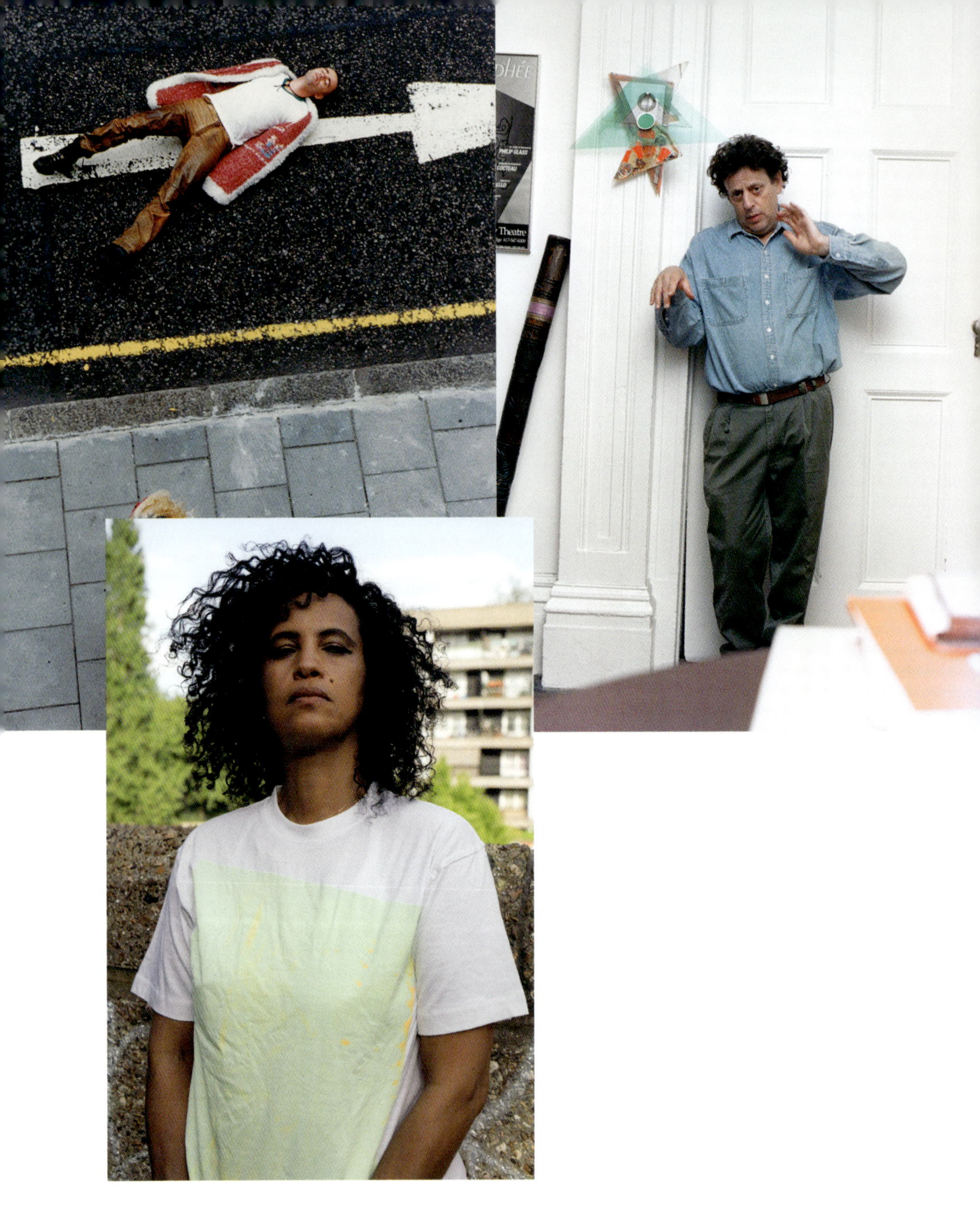

Lutz, sidewalk, 1993
Philip Glass, 1994
Neneh Cherry, 2018
Lars in tube, 1993

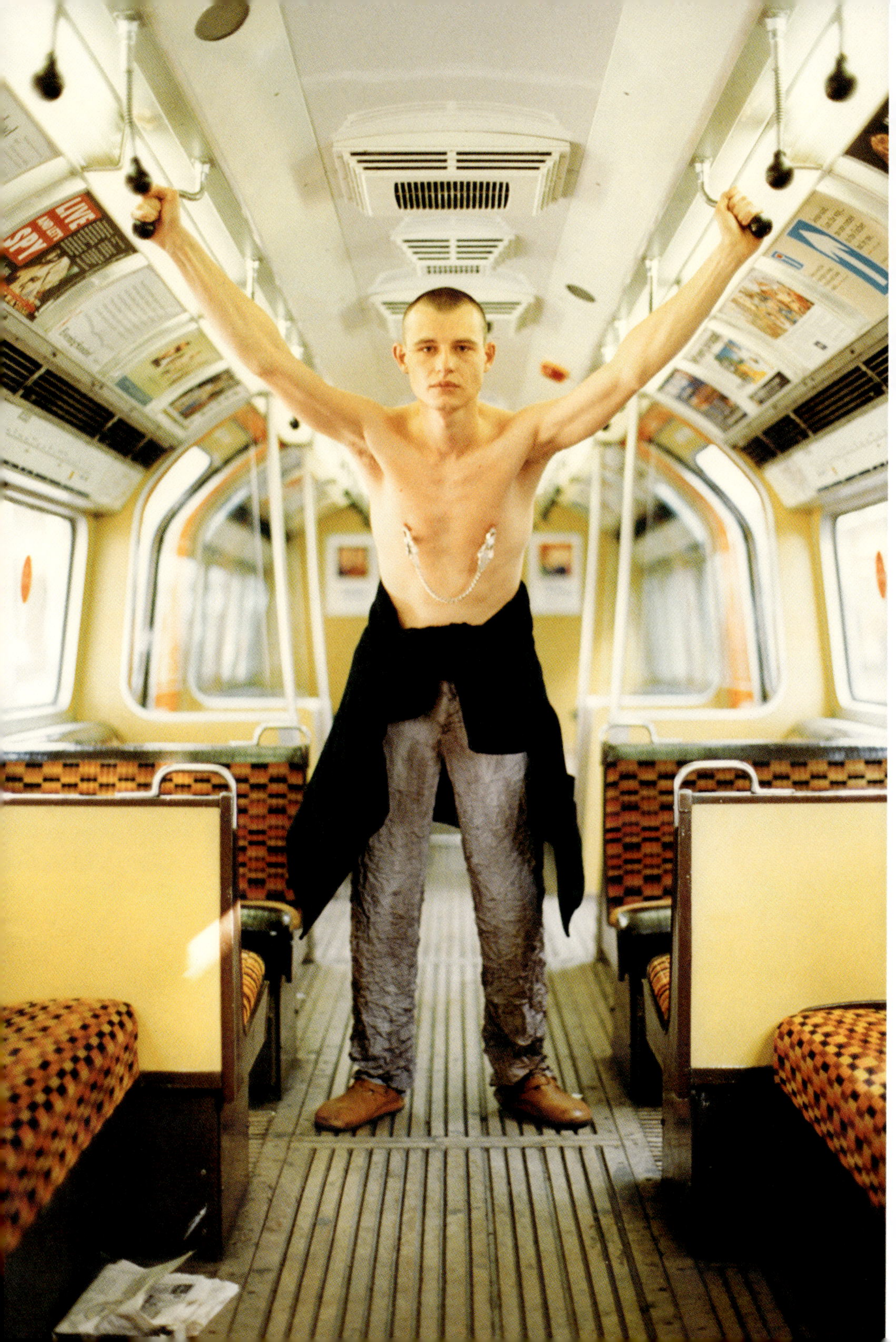

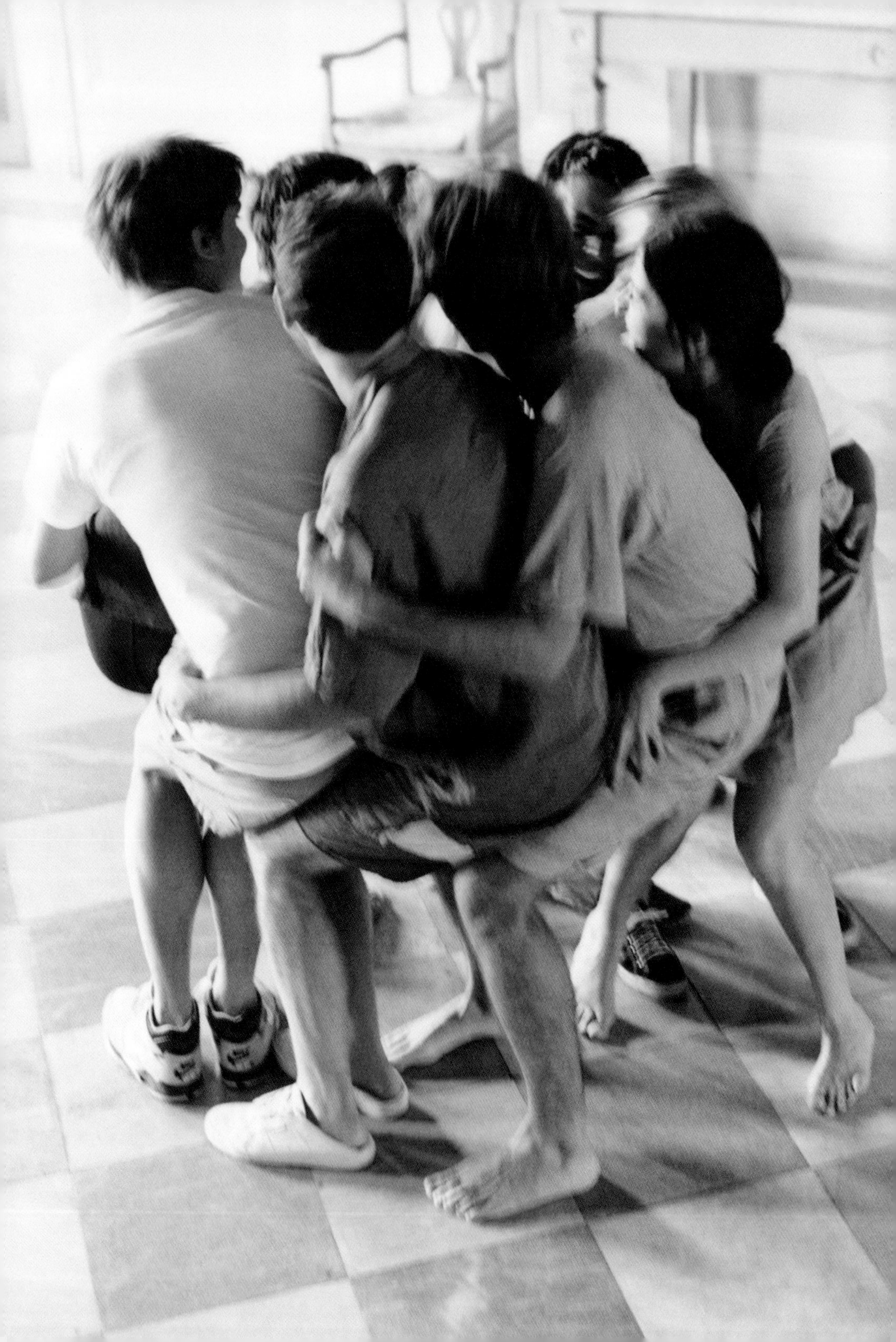

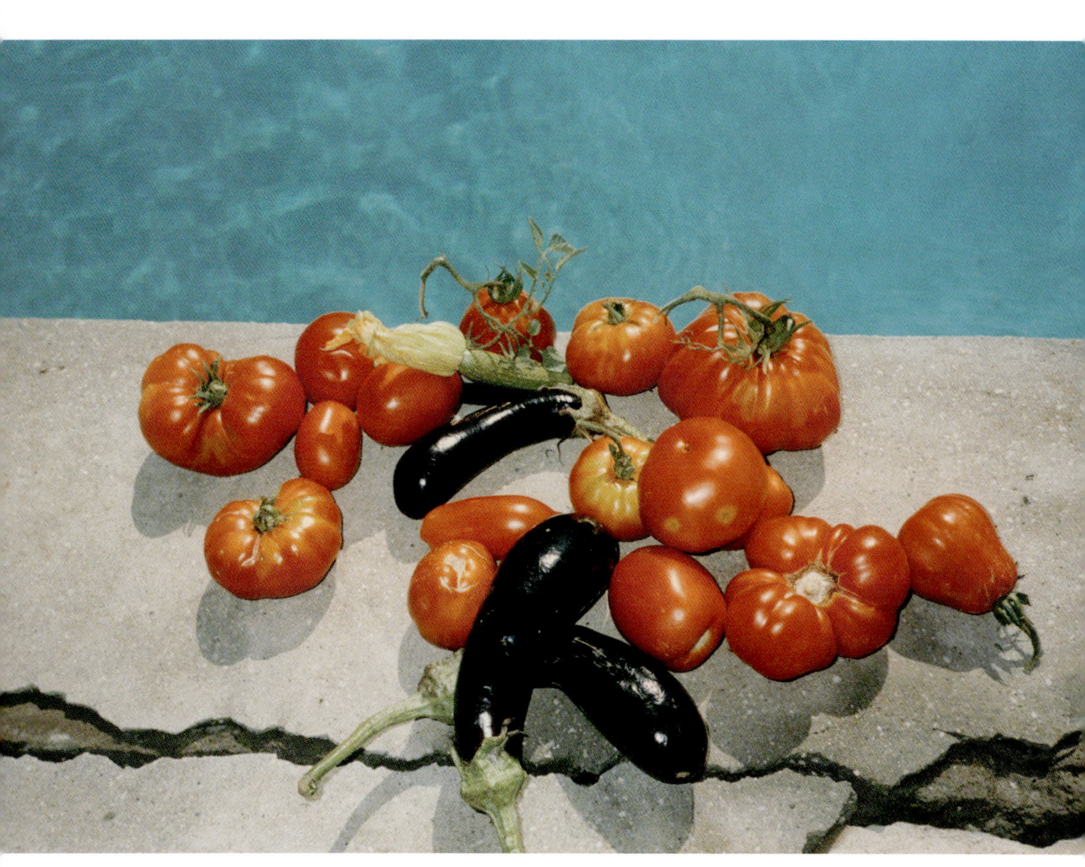

Sitzkreis, 1993   Pomodoro, 1993

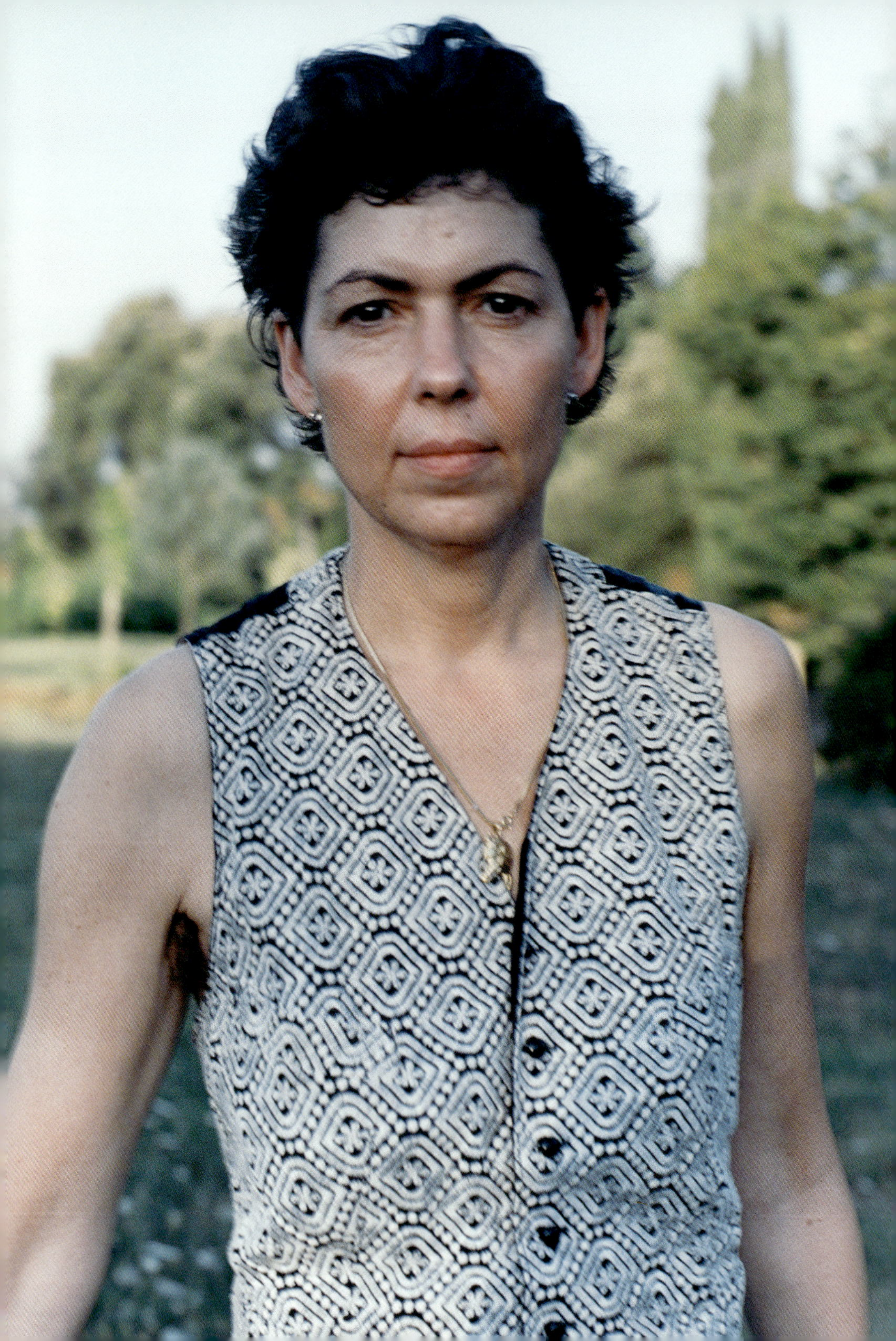

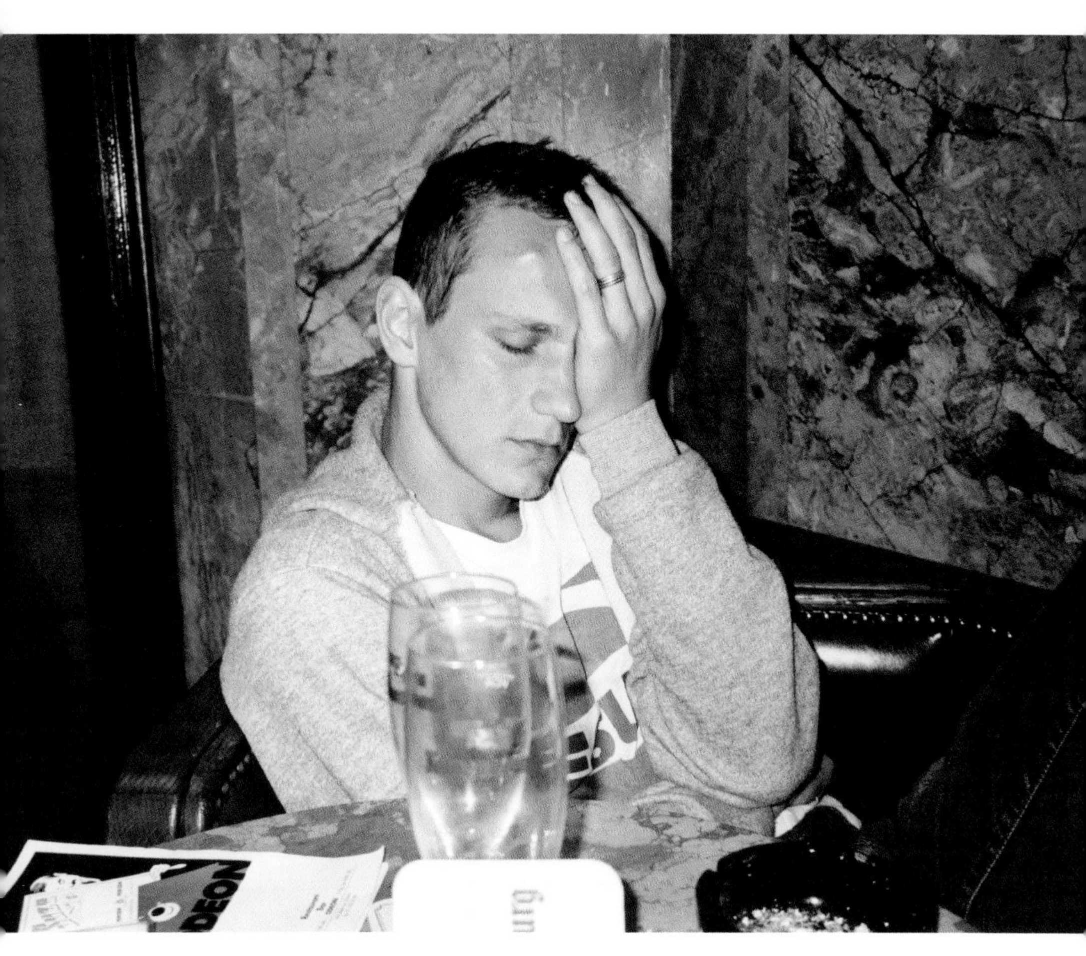

Isa Genzken, Atelier, part 11, 1993
Cornel, Zurich, 1993

petition, Camden Market, 1993
Andy on Baker Street, 1993

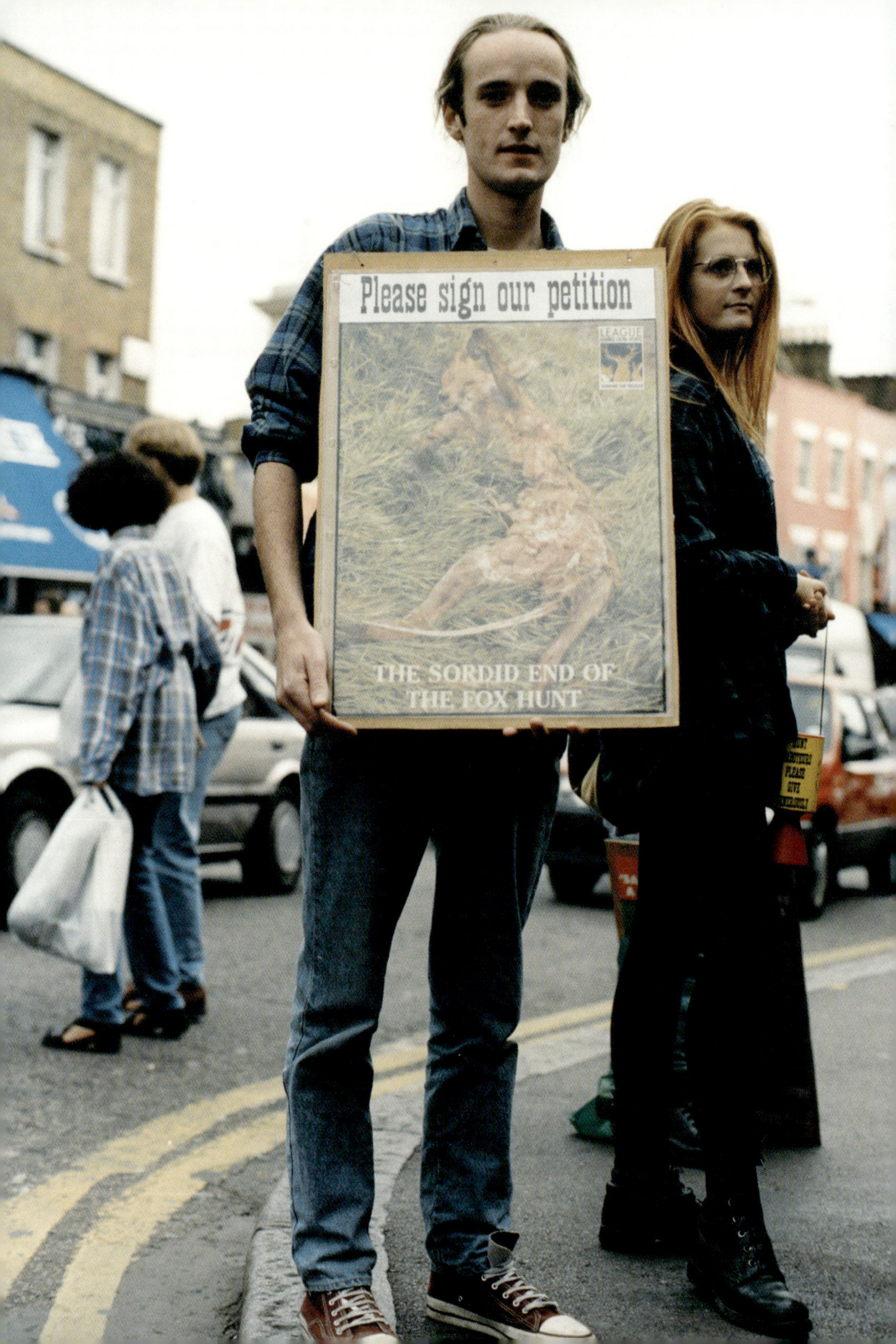
Please sign our petition
LEAGUE
THE SORDID END OF
THE FOX HUNT

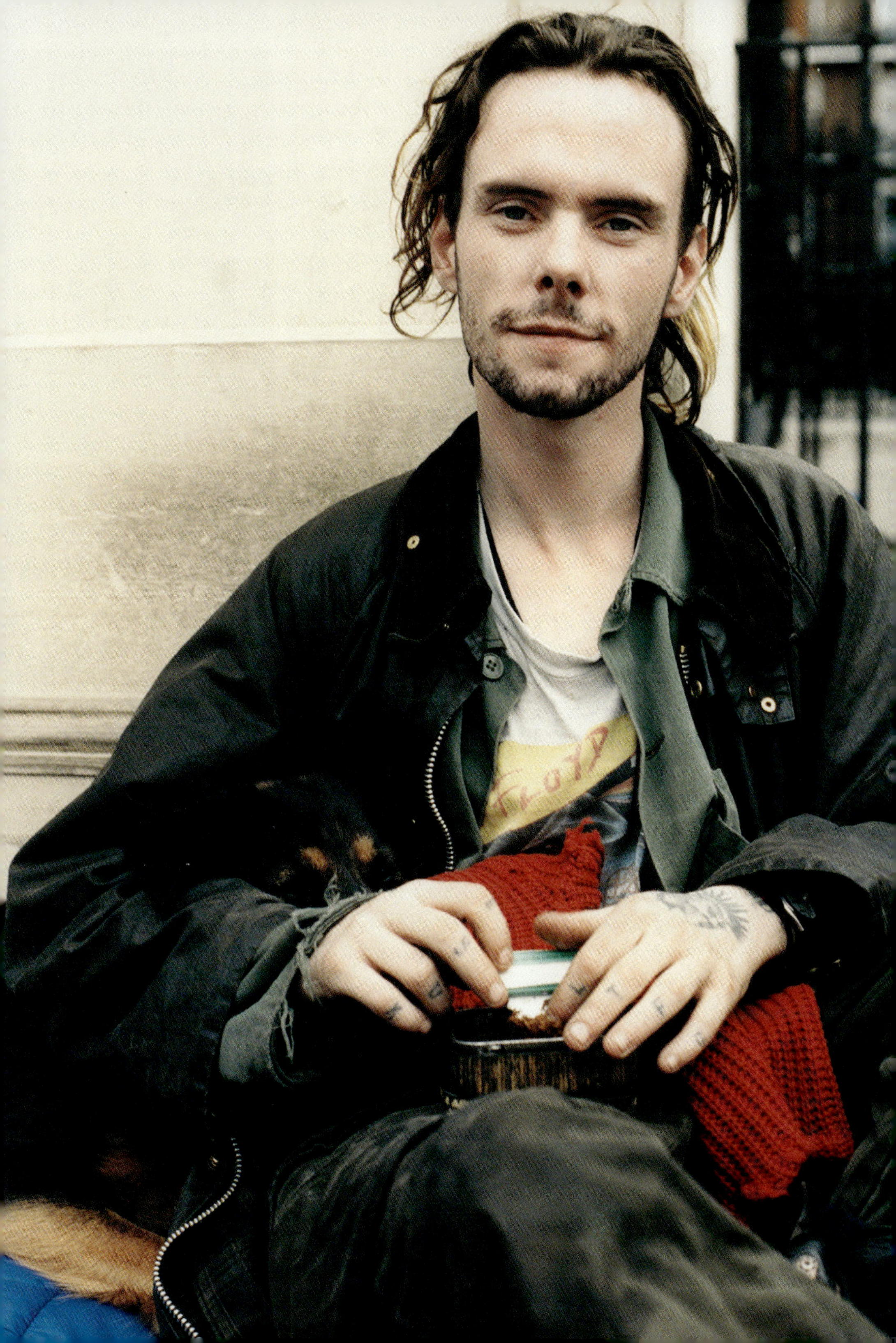

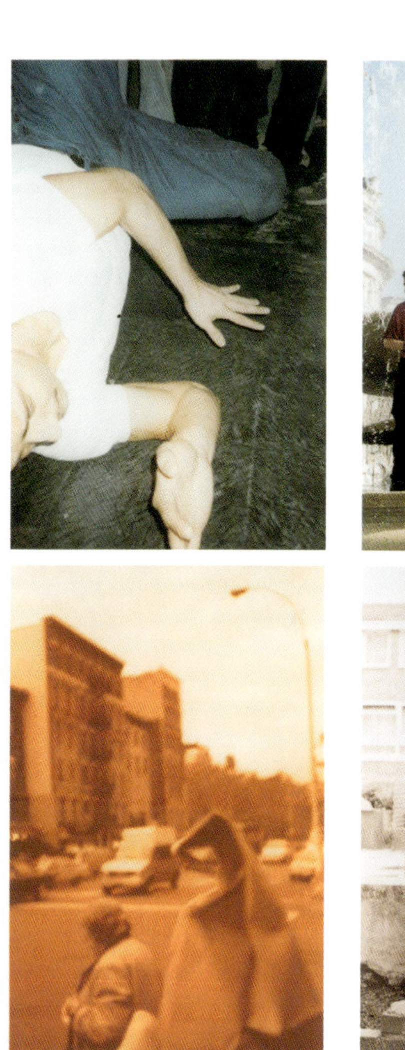
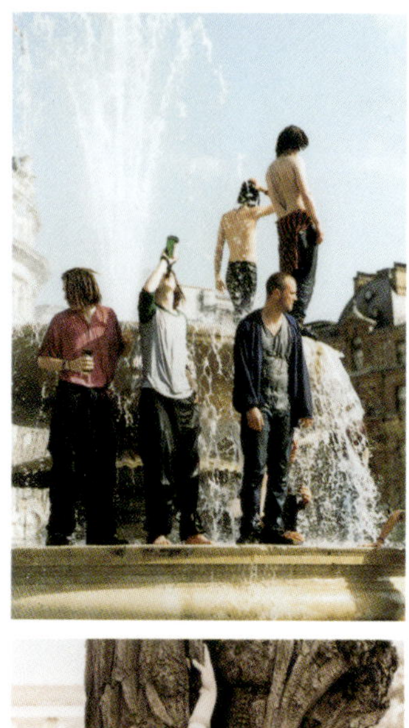
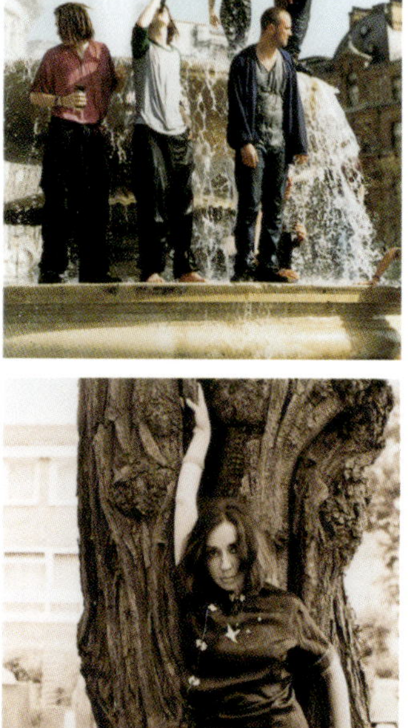
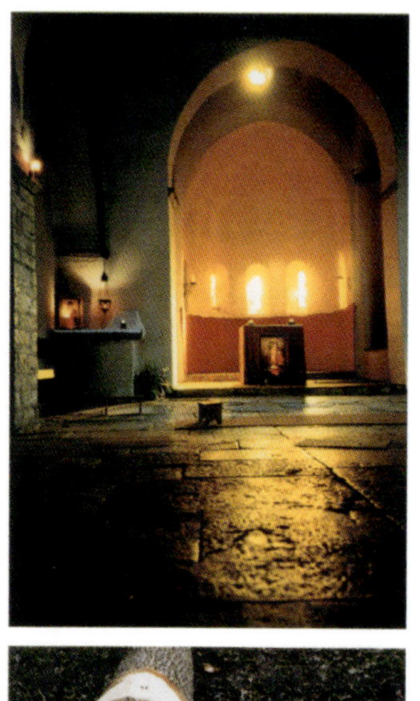
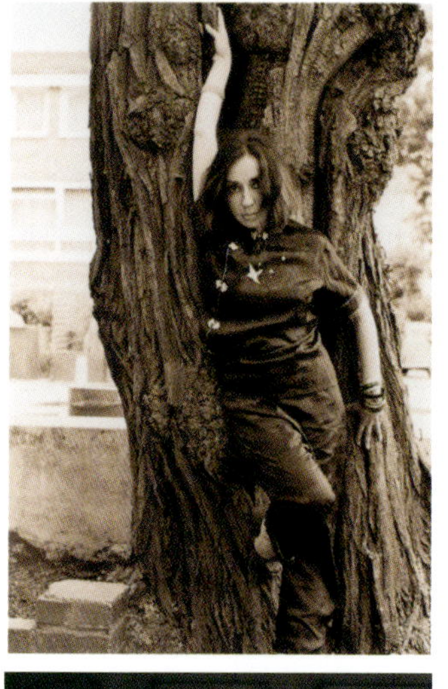
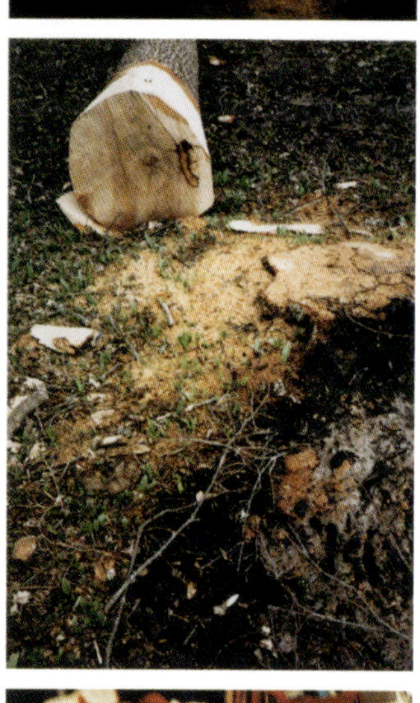
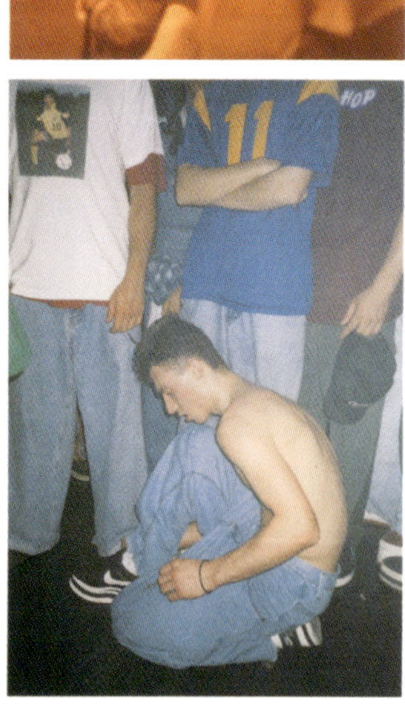
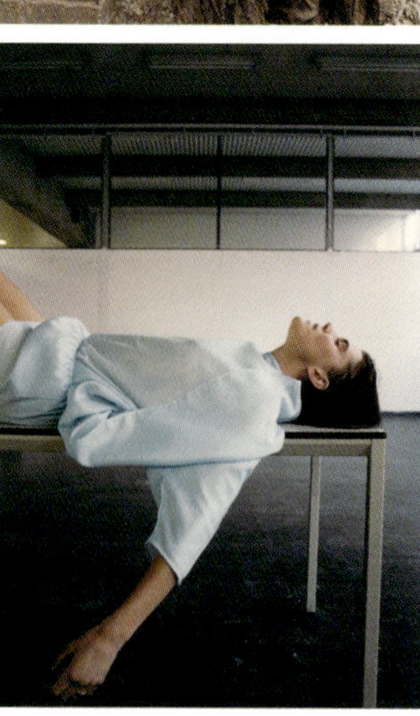
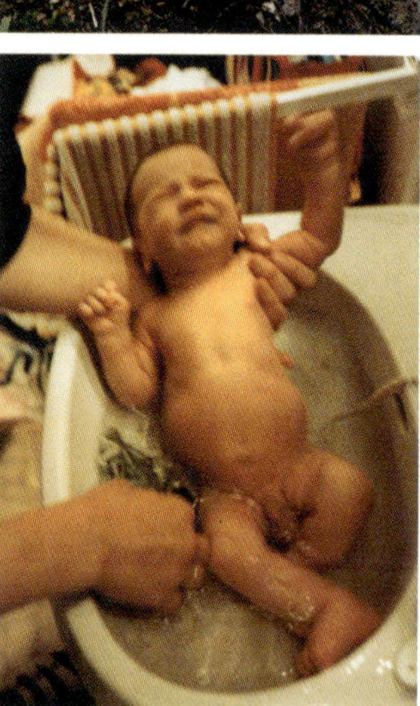

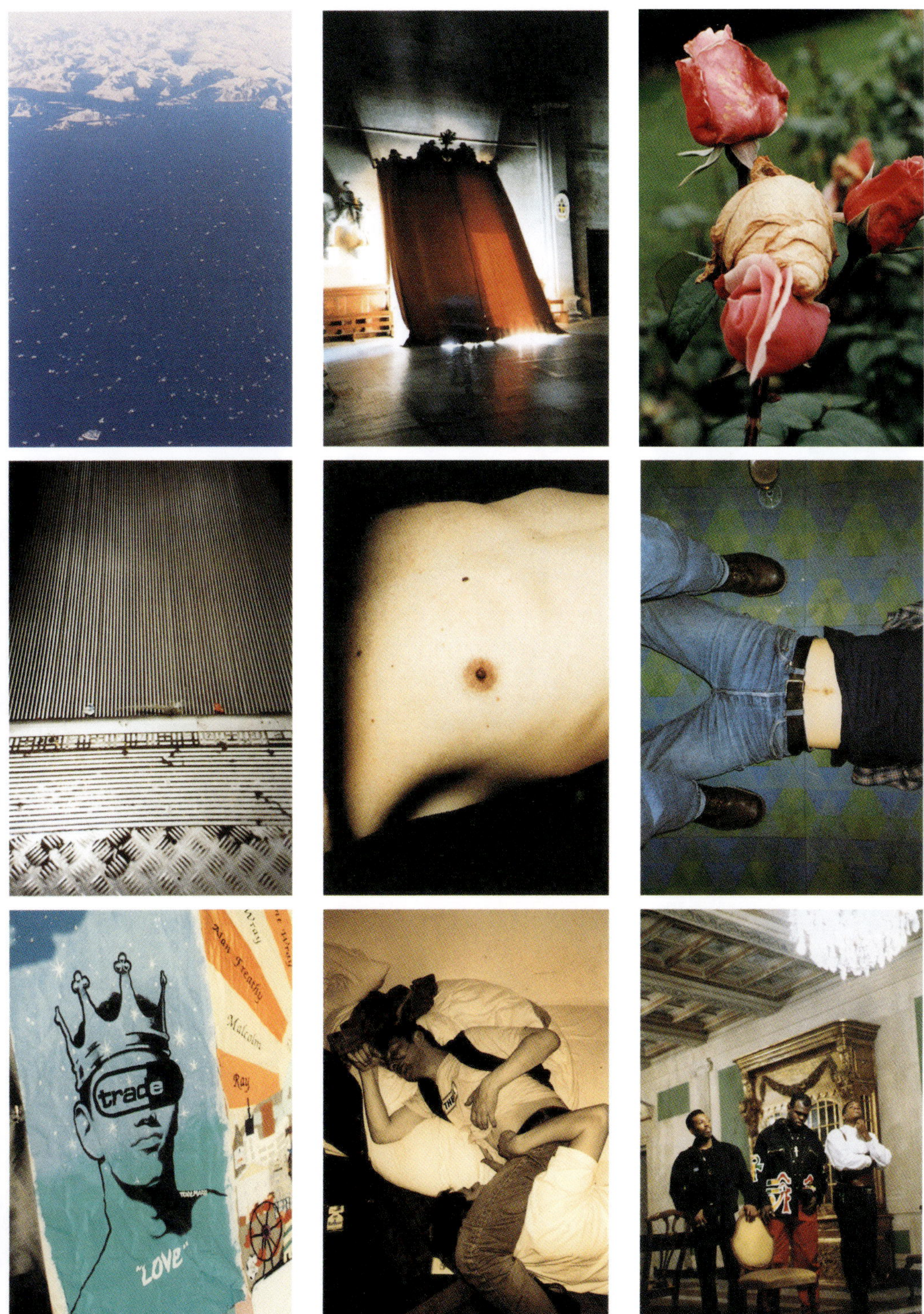
Alan Freathy
Malcolm
Ray
trade
"LOVE"

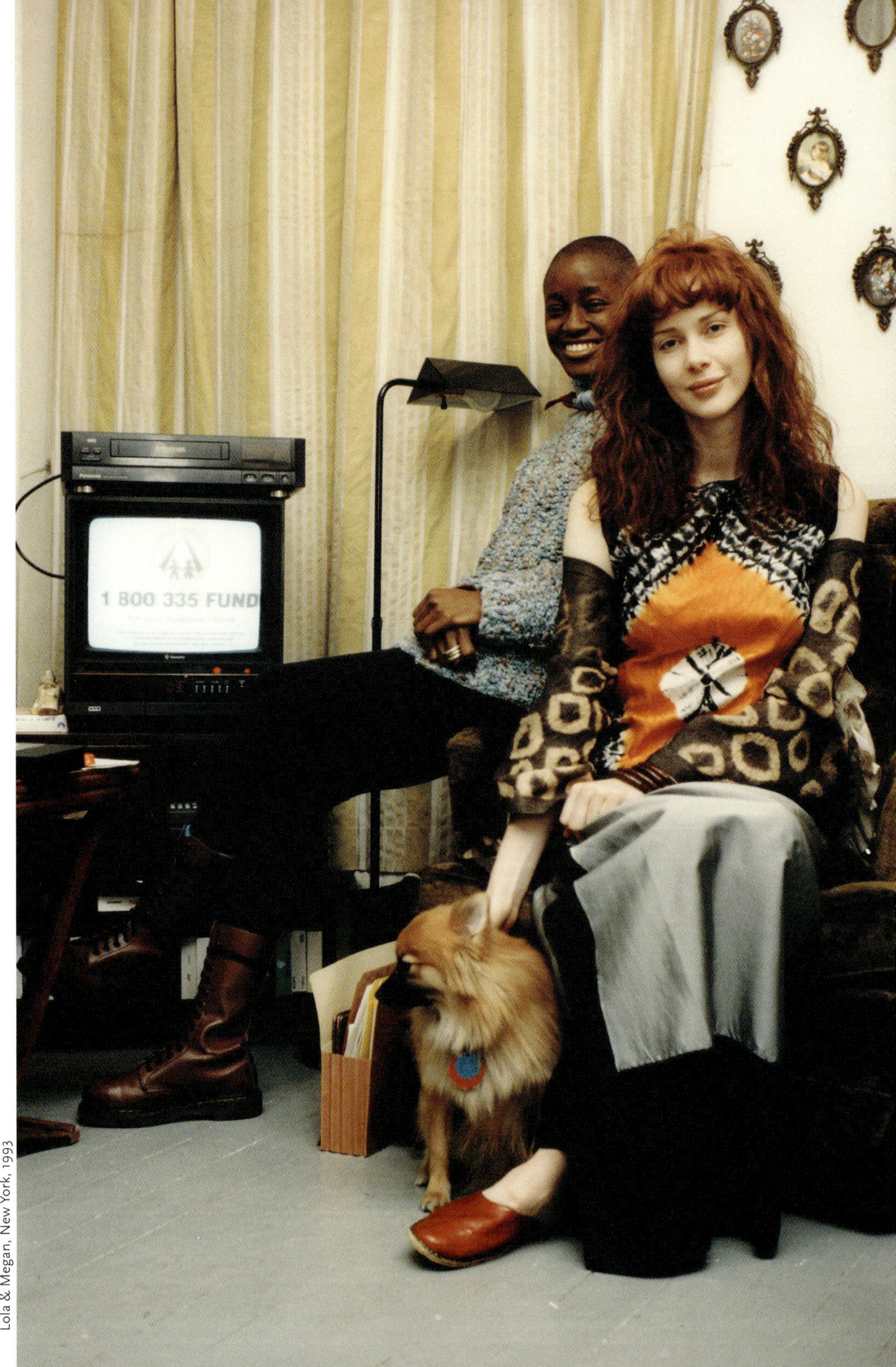

Lola & Megan, New York, 1993

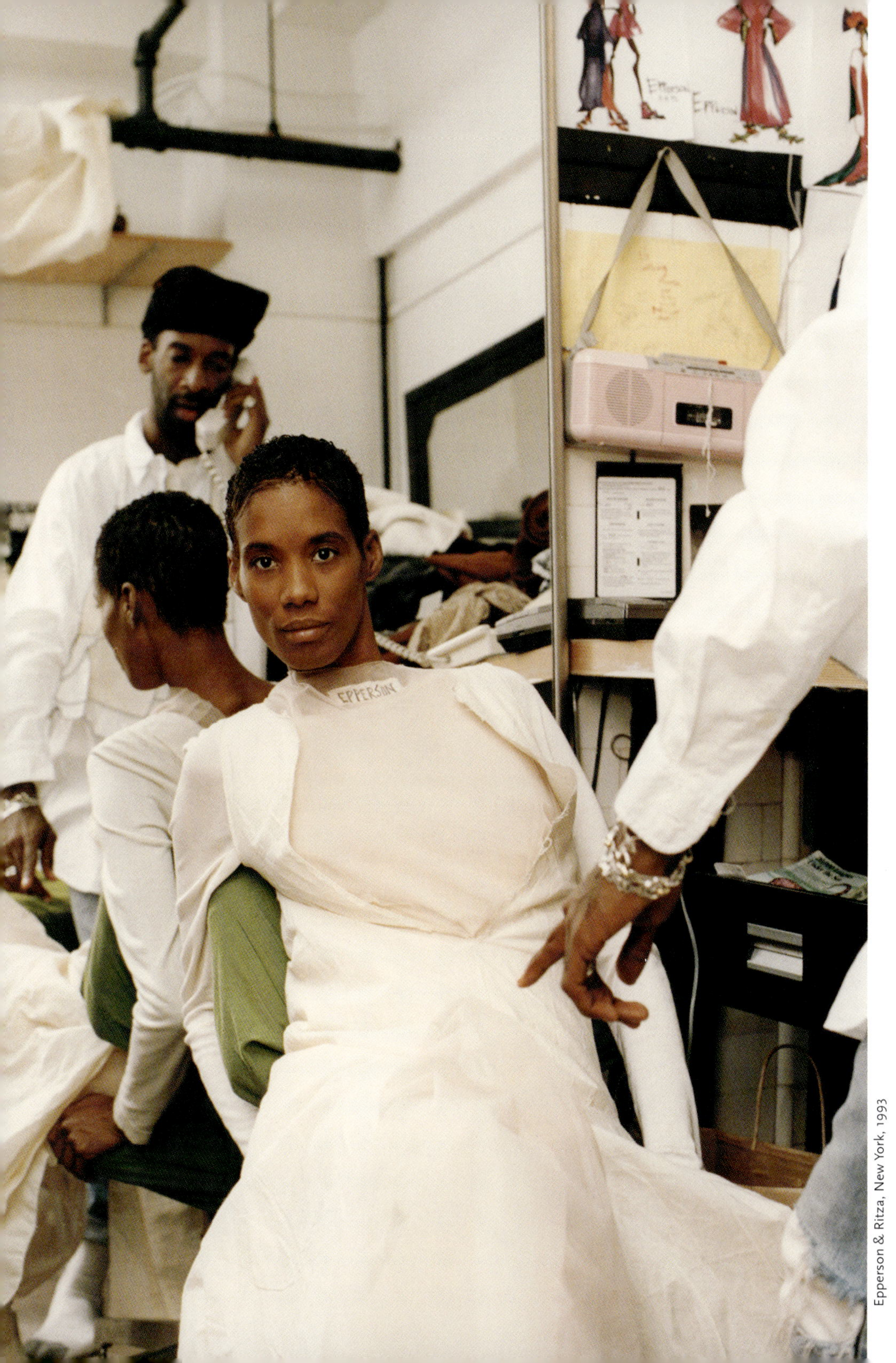

Epperson & Ritza, New York, 1993

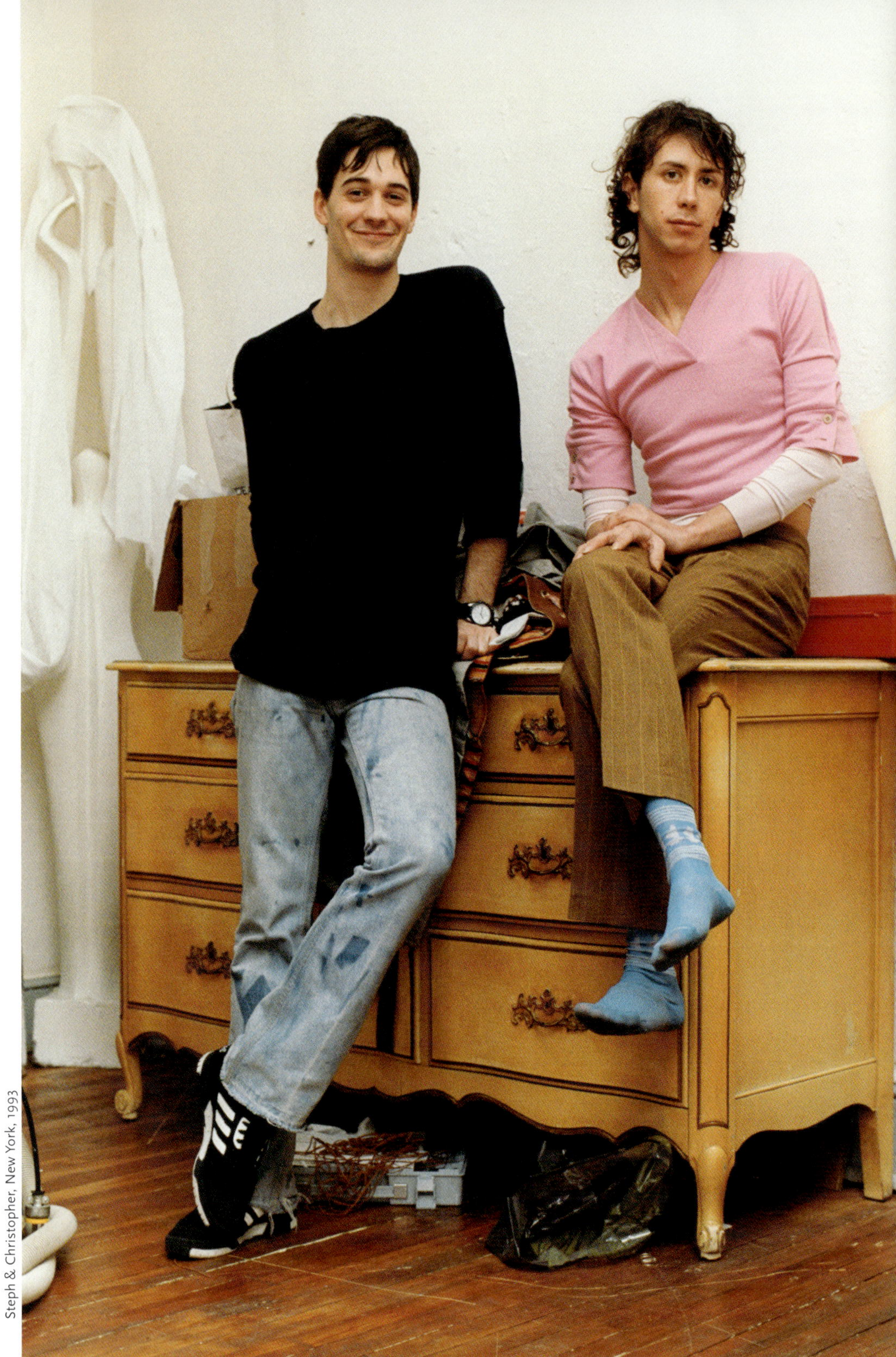

Steph & Christopher, New York, 1993

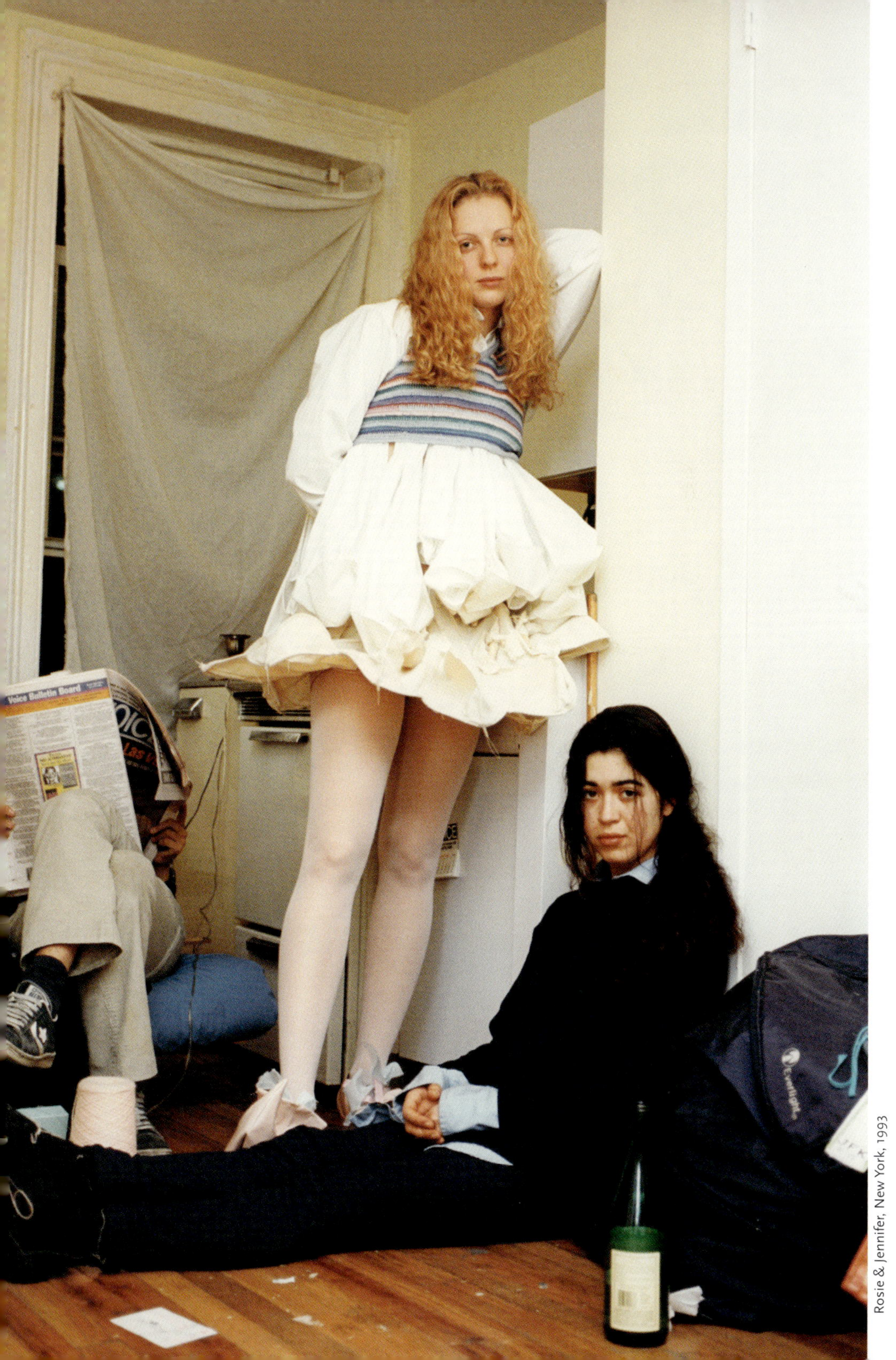

Rosie & Jennifer, New York, 1993

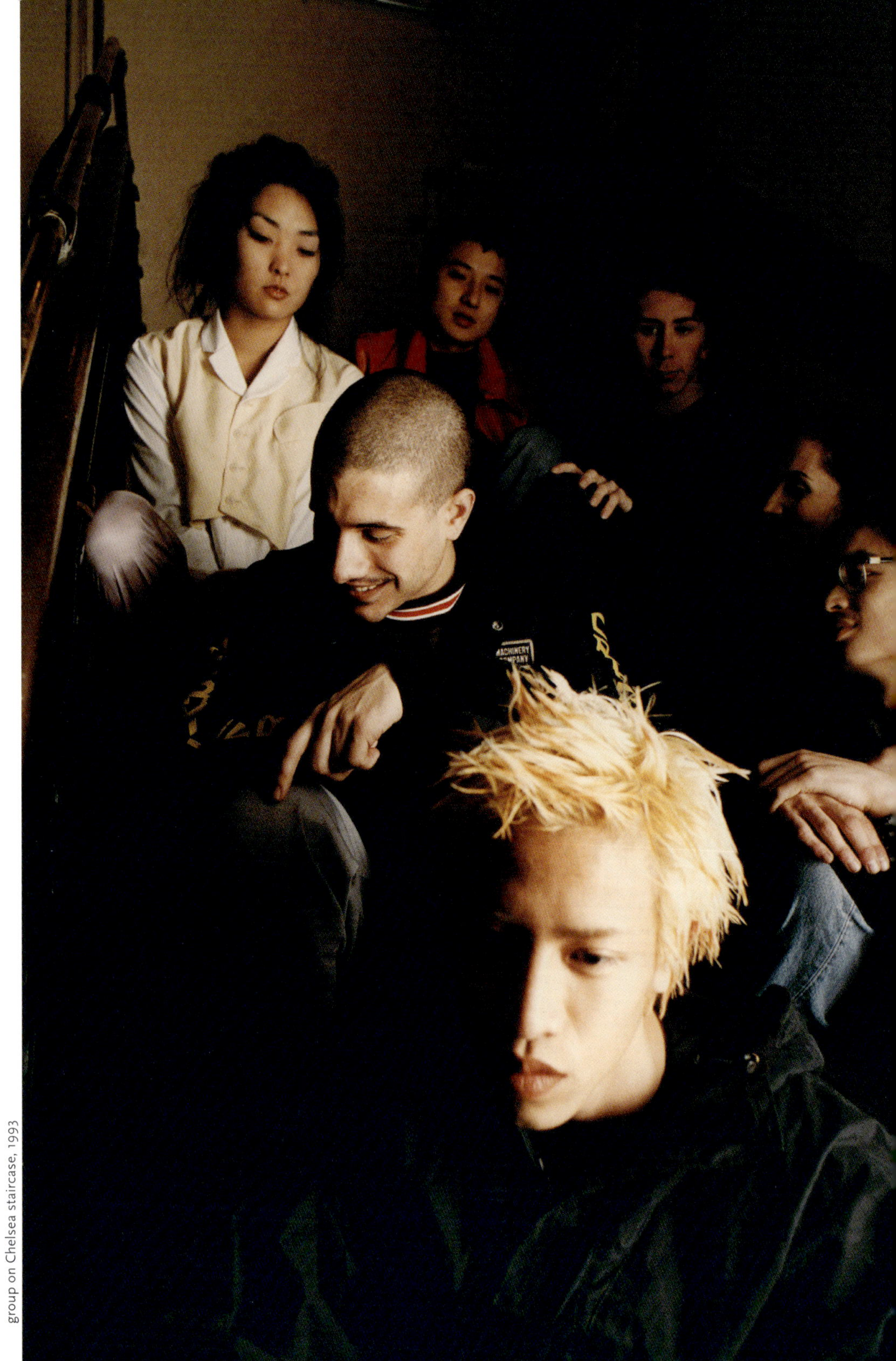

group on Chelsea staircase, 1993

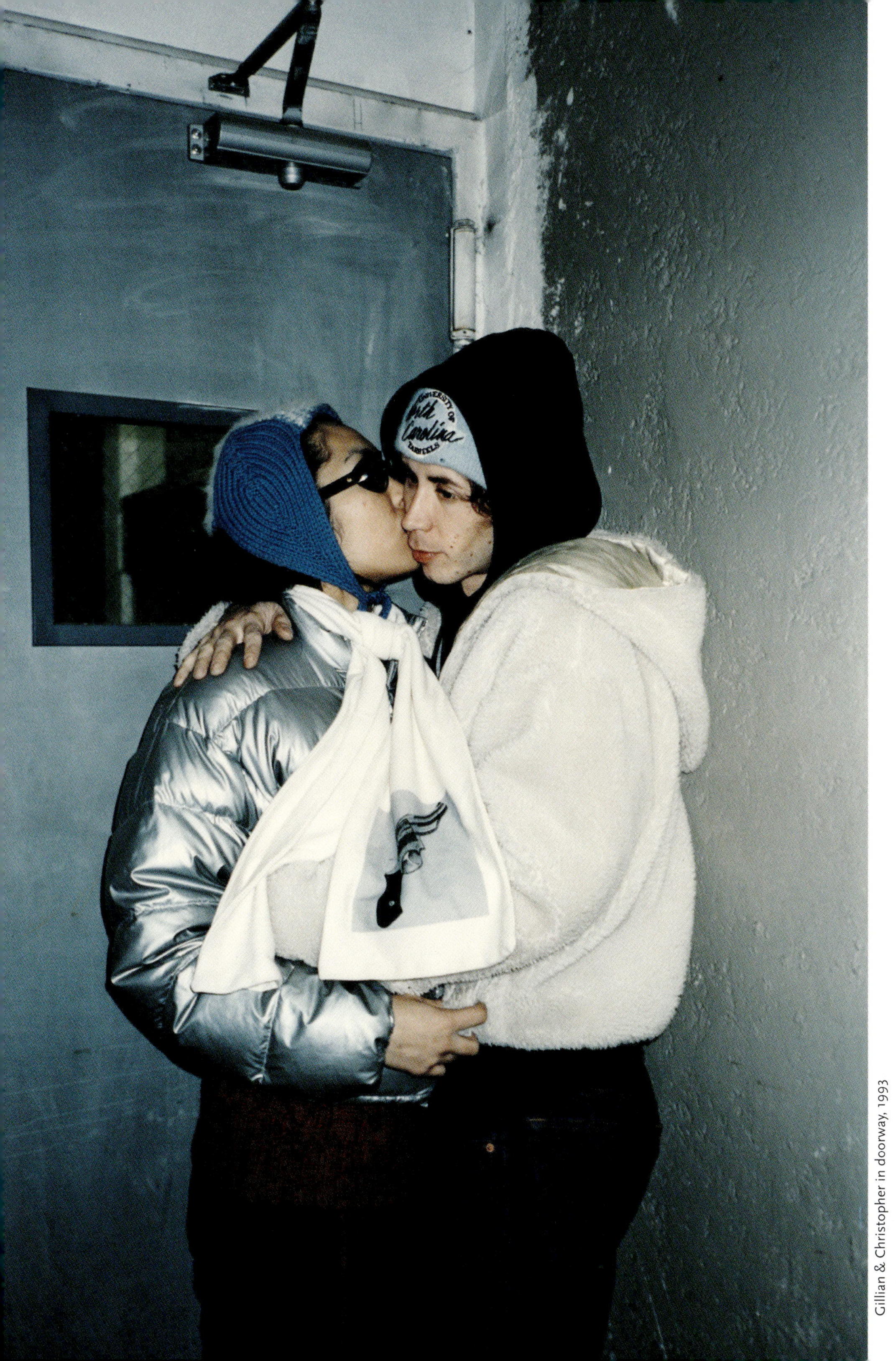

Gillian & Christopher in doorway, 1993

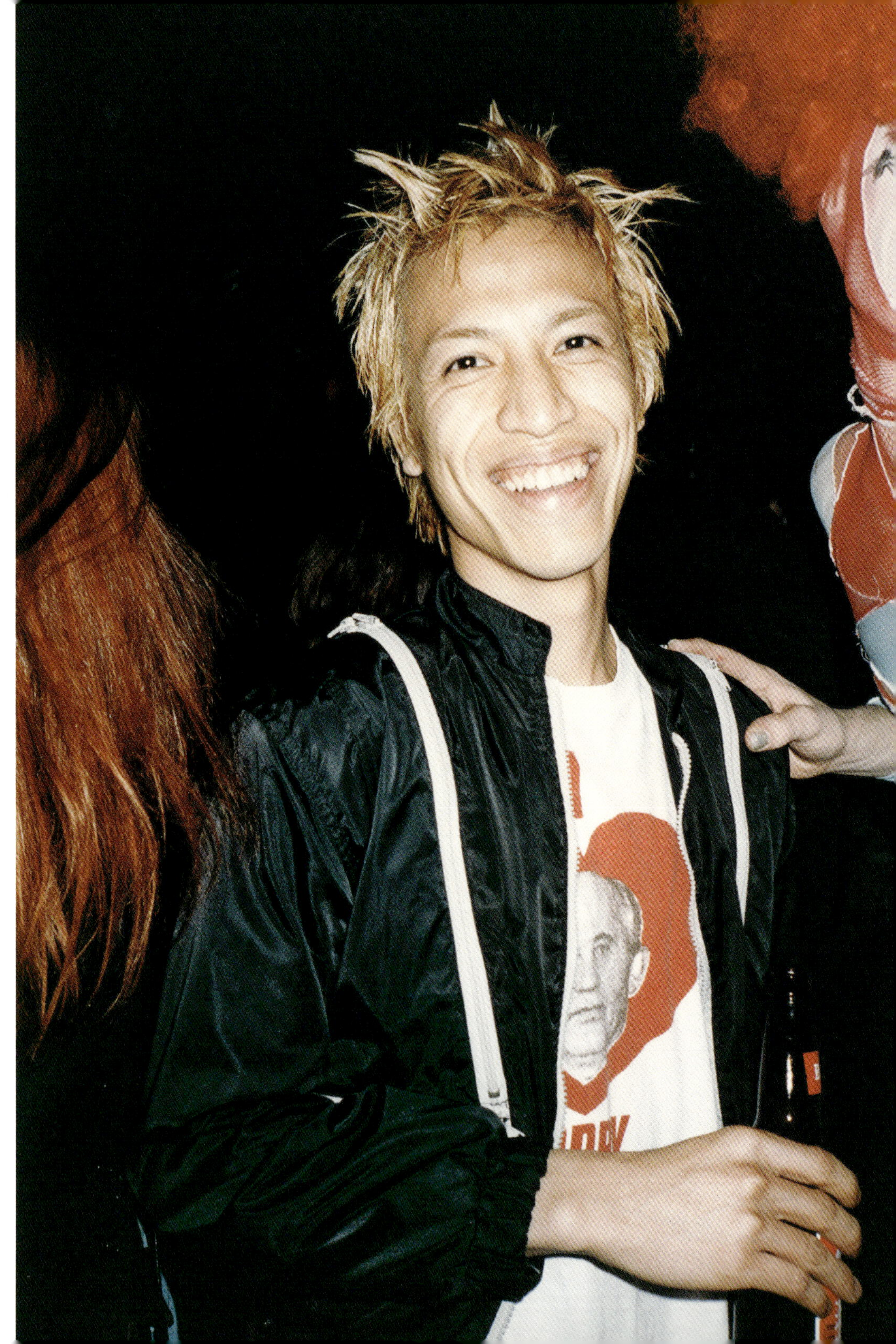

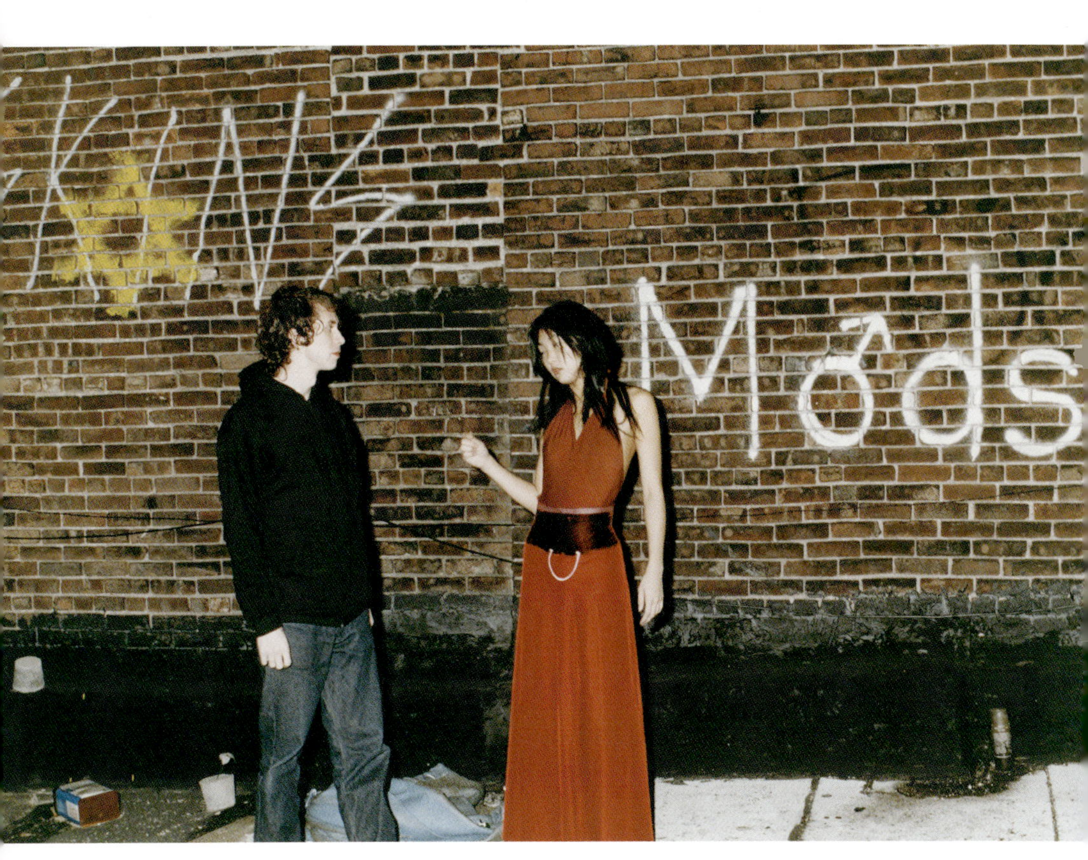

Thuy in Make-up Room, 1993
Skins/Mods, 1993

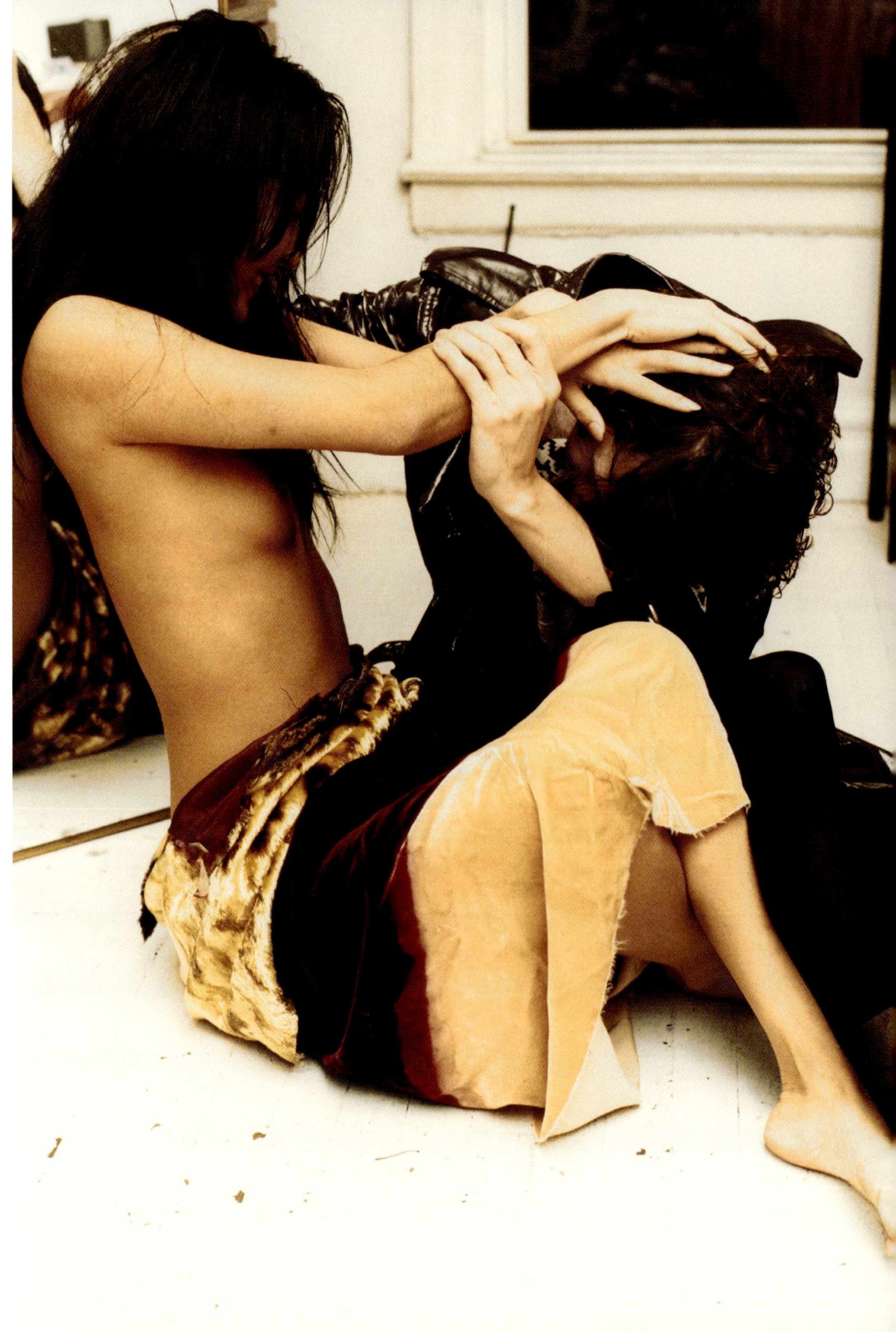

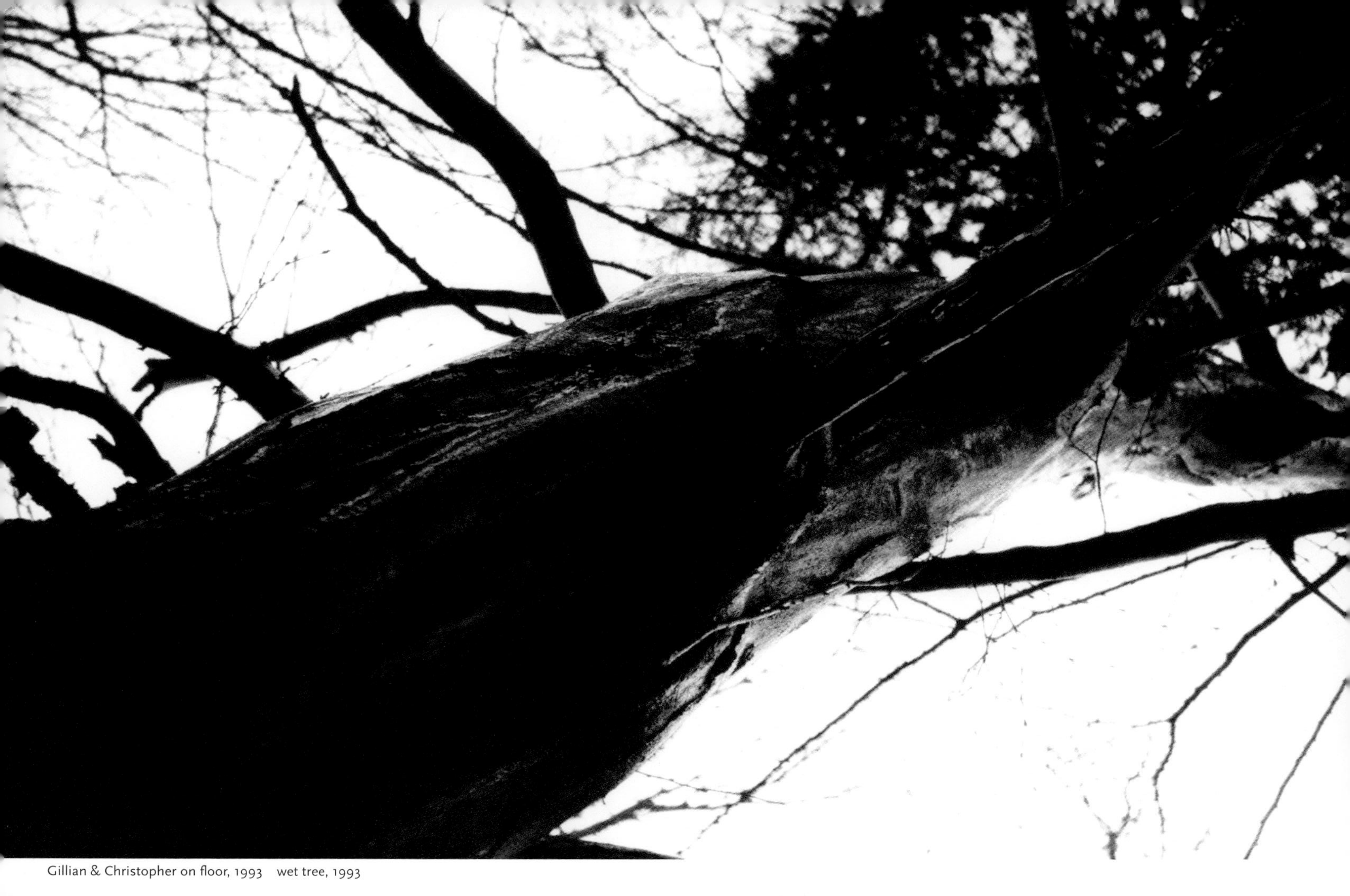

Gillian & Christopher on floor, 1993   wet tree, 1993

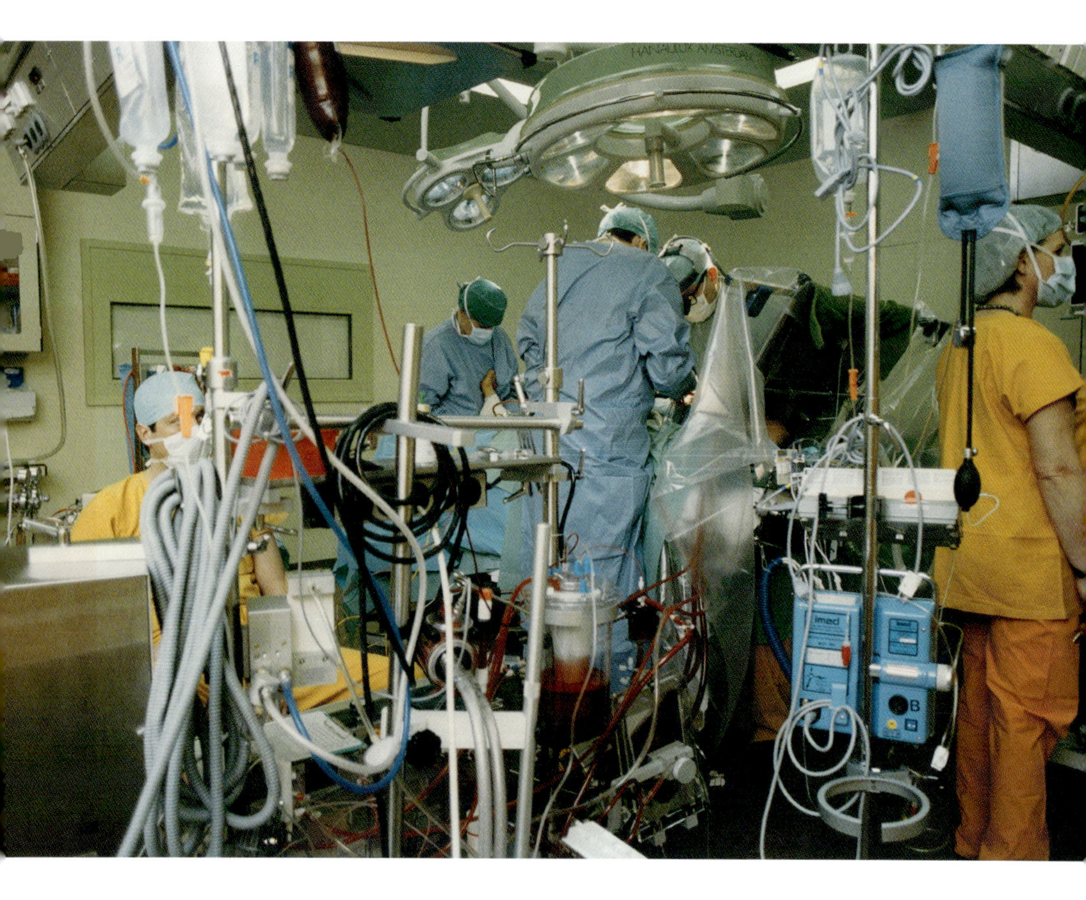

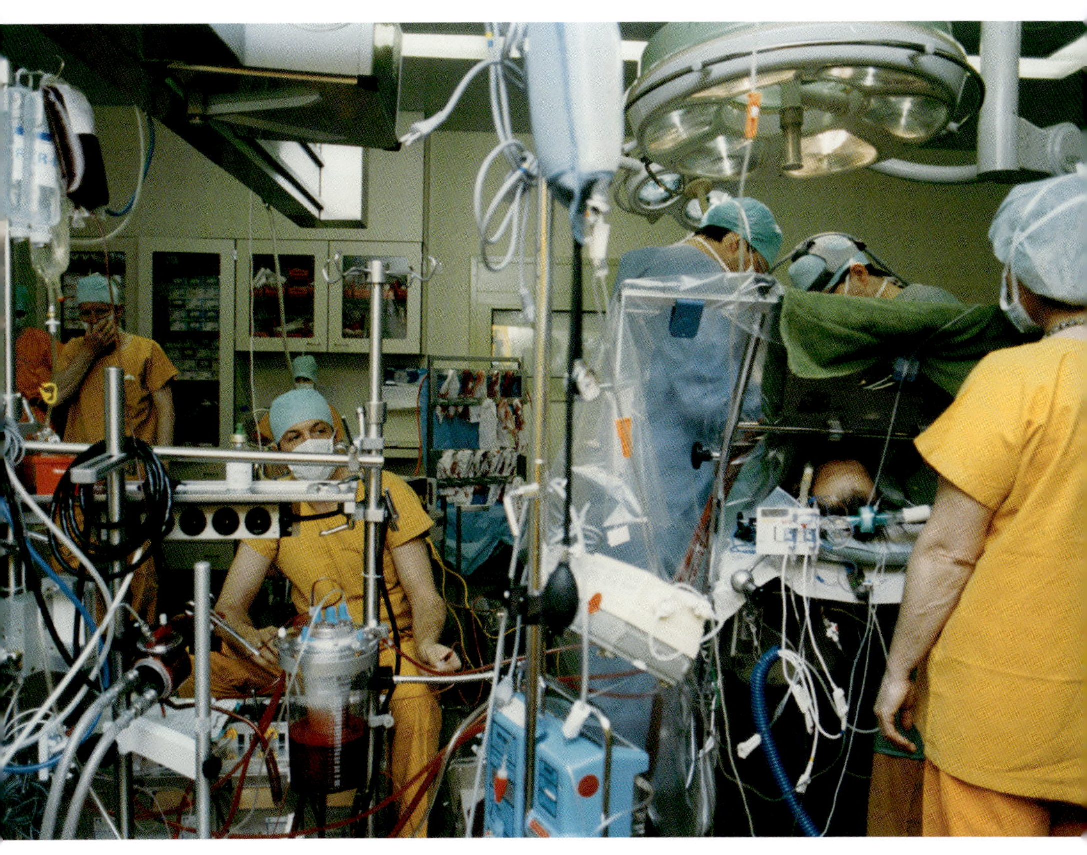

Operation theatre II & I, 1994   Knotenmutter, 1994

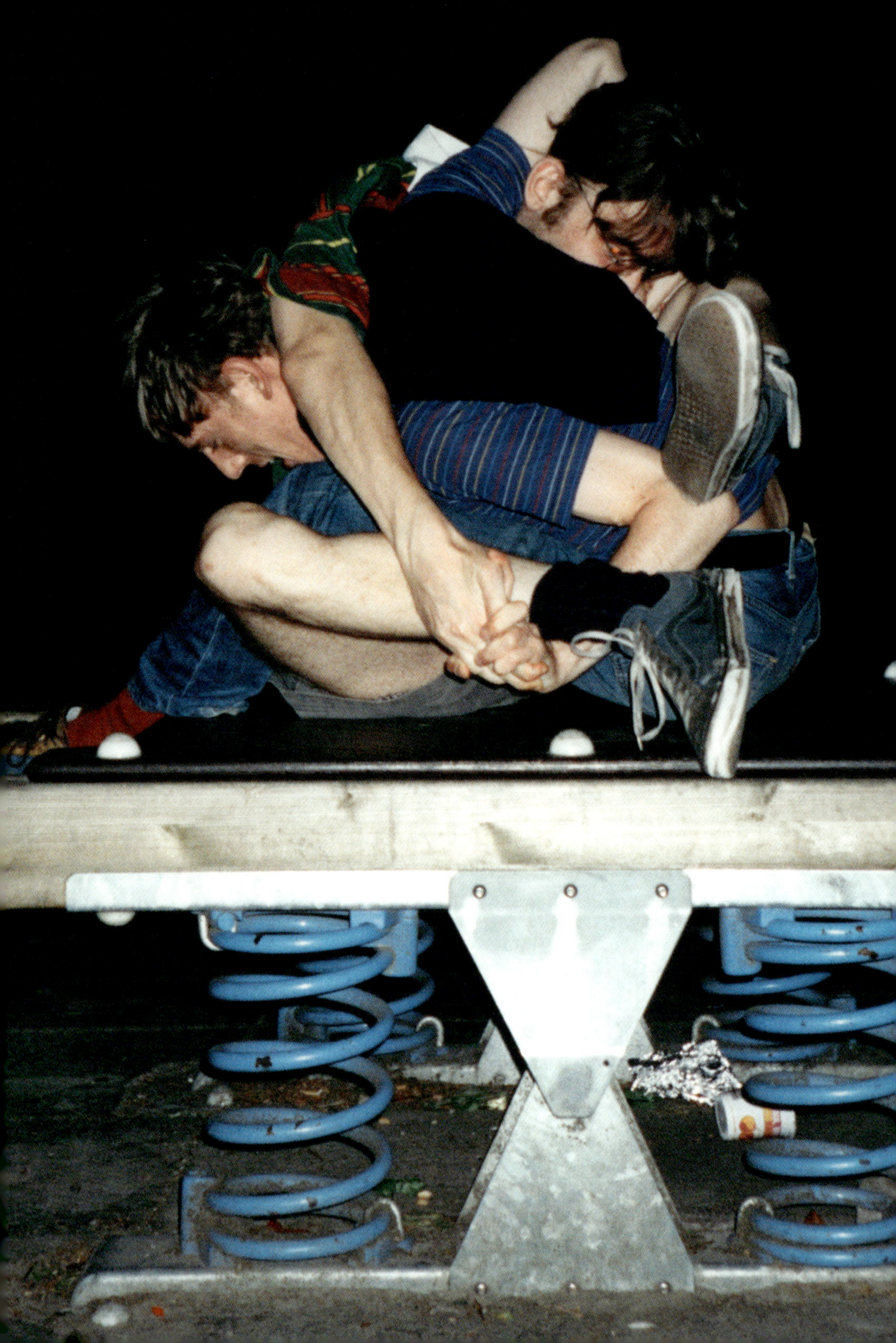

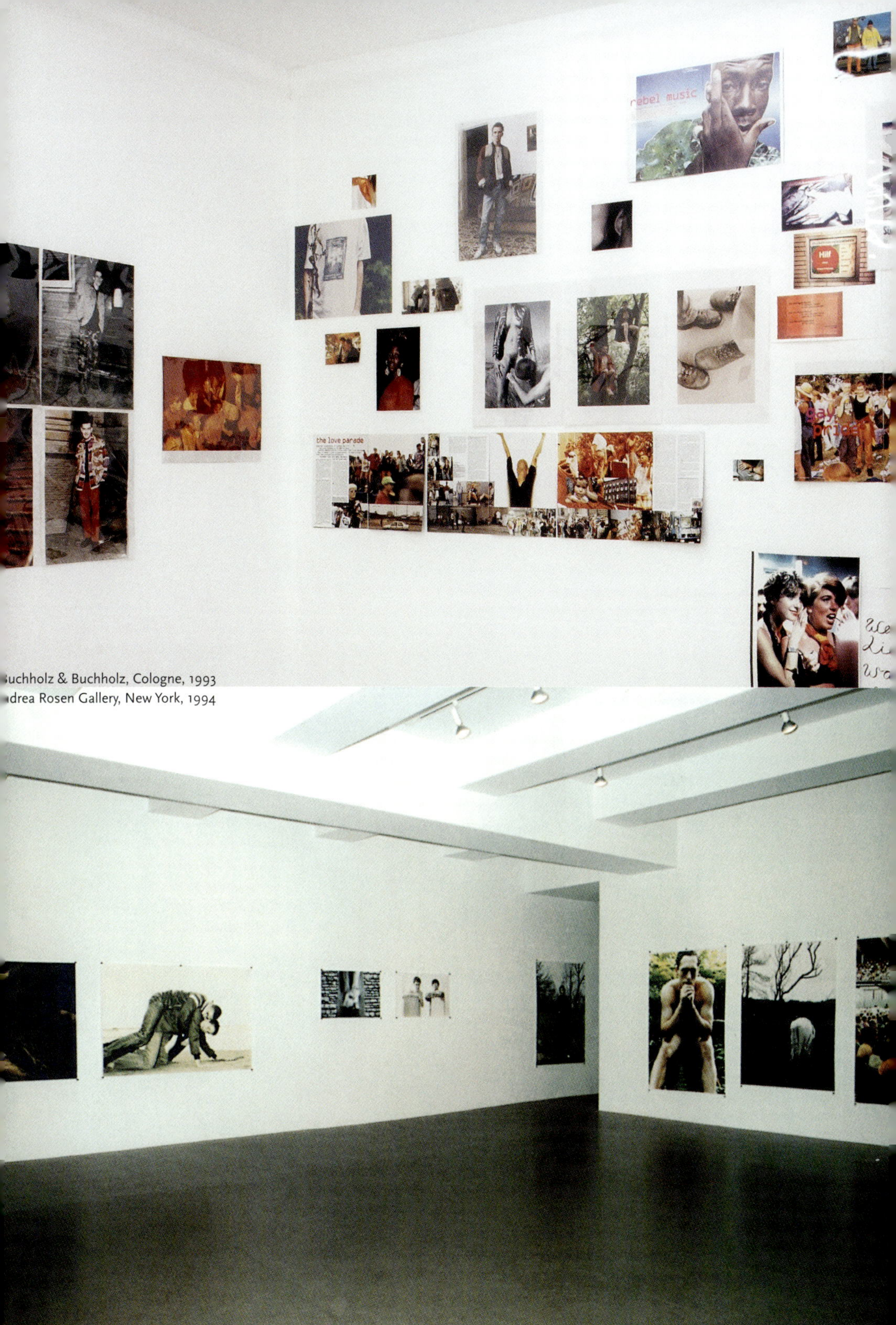

Buchholz & Buchholz, Cologne, 1993
Andrea Rosen Gallery, New York, 1994

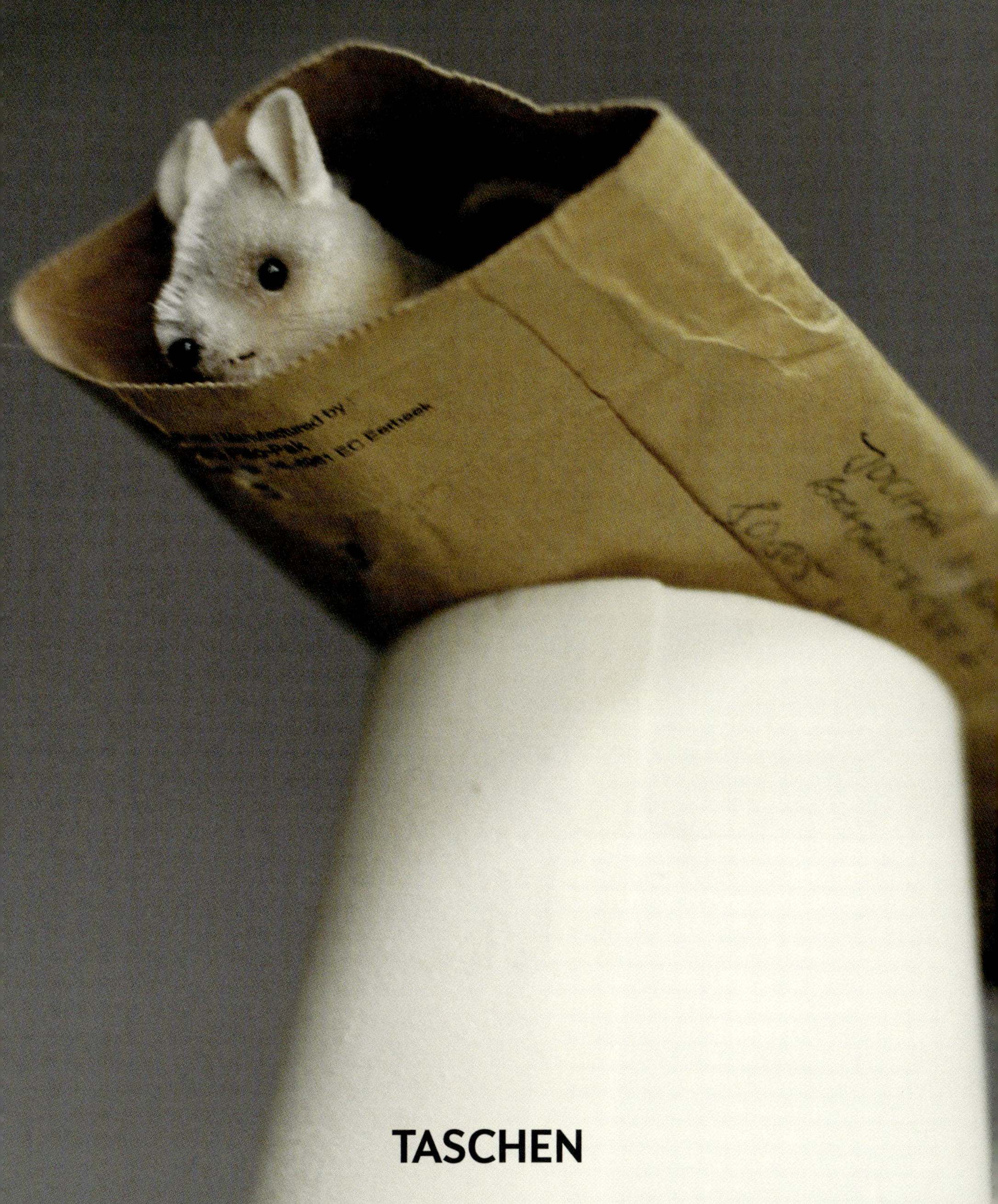

WOLFGANG TILLMANS BURG
TASCHEN

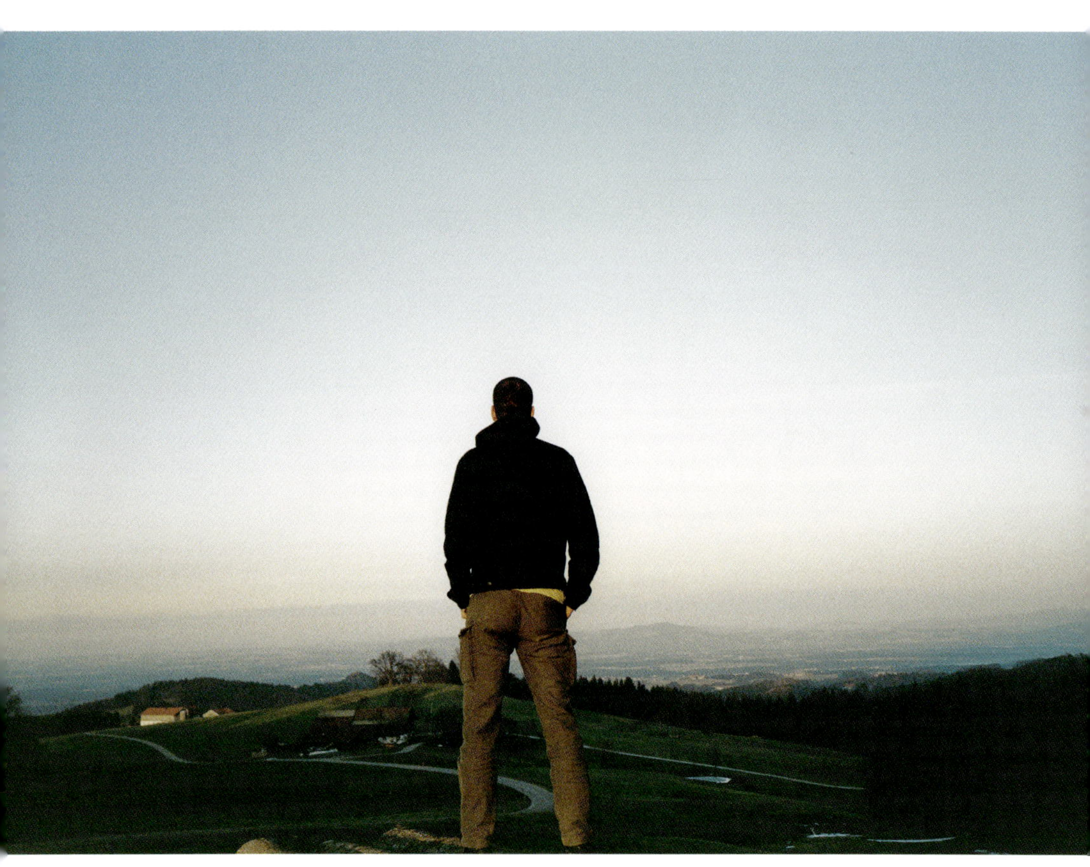

← Maus, 1997
Valentine, 1998

WOLFGANG TILLMANS
BURG

edited and designed by Wolfgang Tillmans   with an essay by David Deitcher

TASCHEN

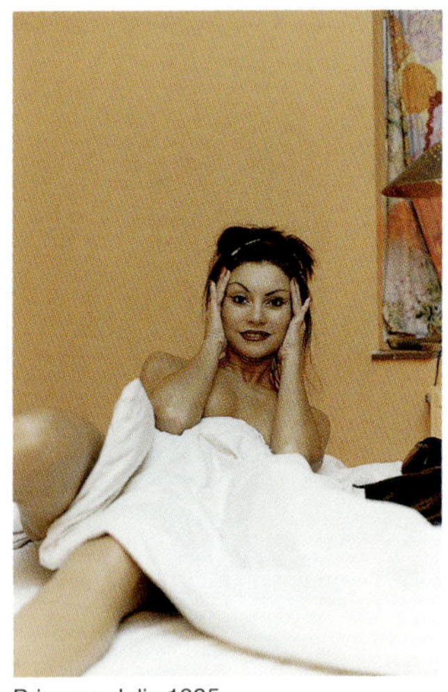

Princess Julia 1995

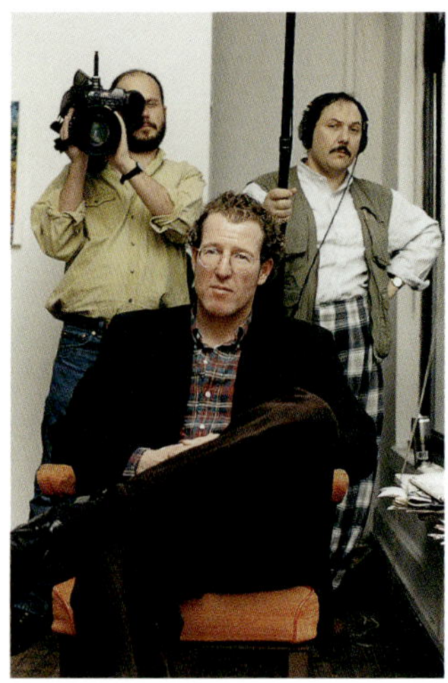

Kultur Report 1995

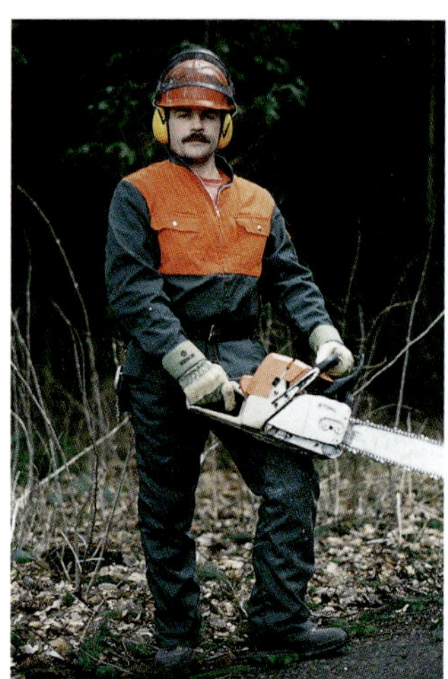

Förster 1994

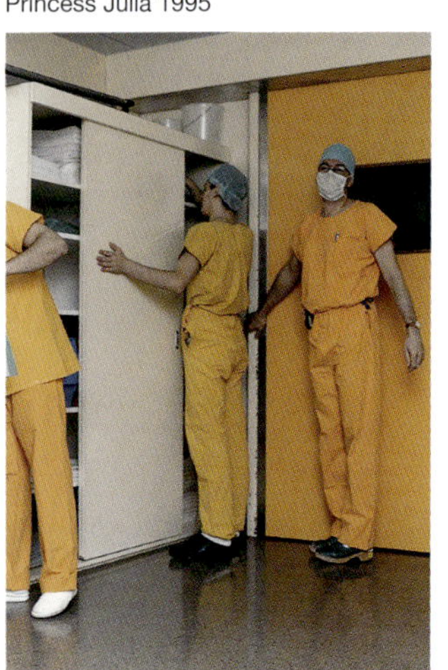

OP Schleuse 1994

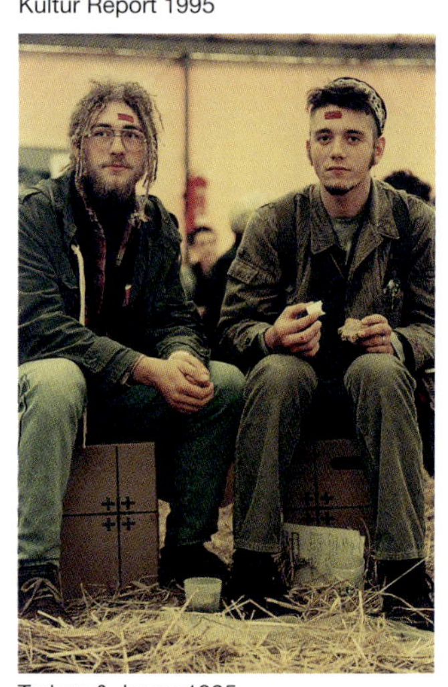

Torben & Jonas 1995

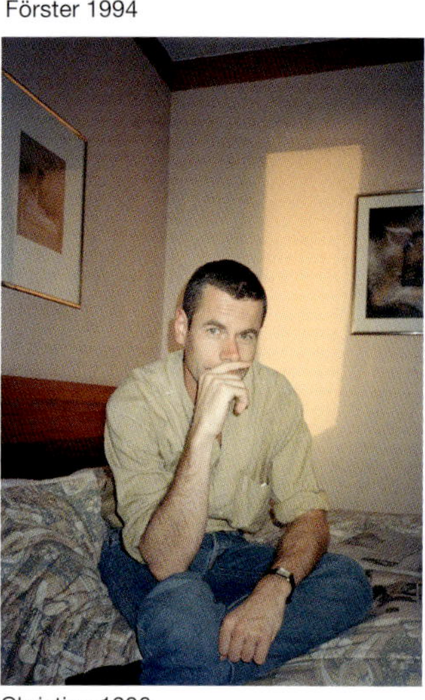

Christian 1996

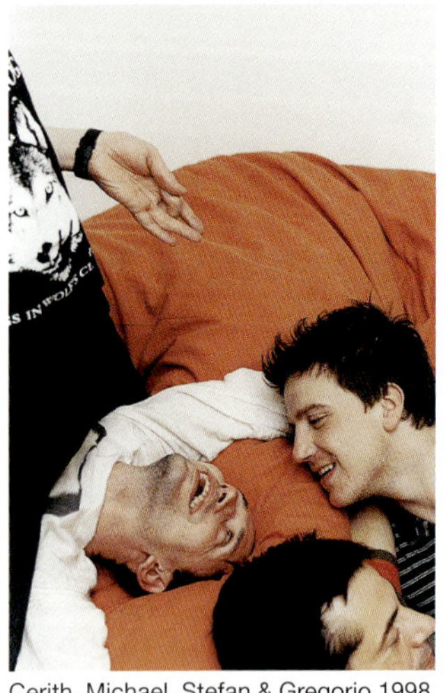

Cerith, Michael, Stefan & Gregorio 1998

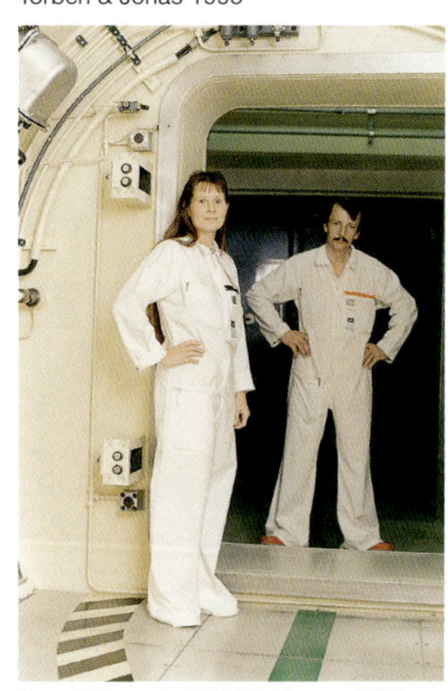

Frau & Mann in KKW Schleuse 1994

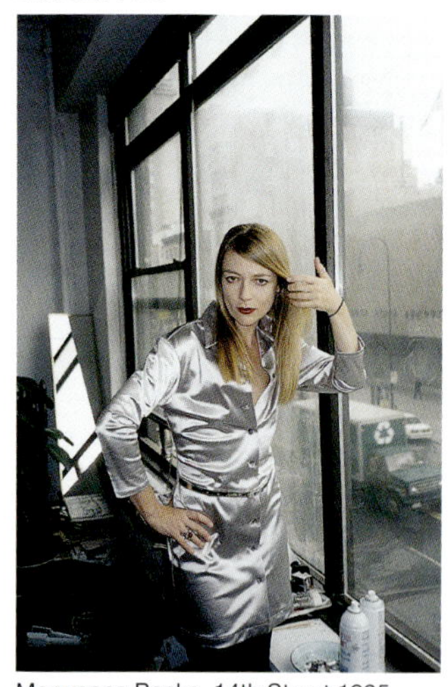

Morwenna Banks, 14th Street 1995

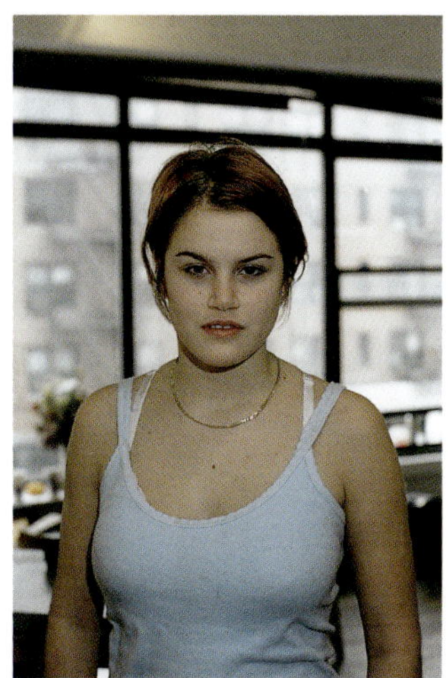

Alison Folland Index Cover 1995

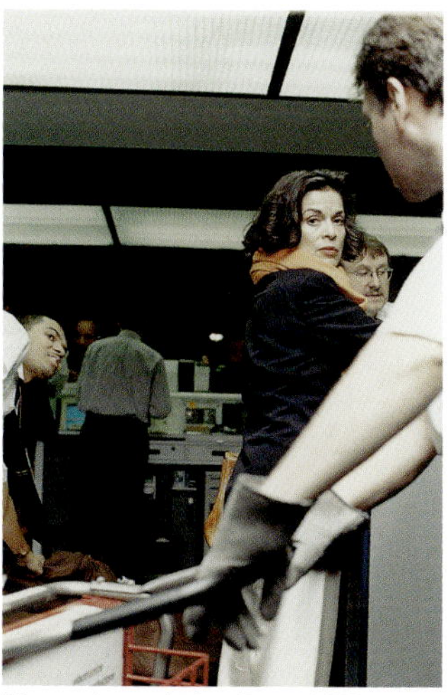

Bianca Jagger Index Cover 1998

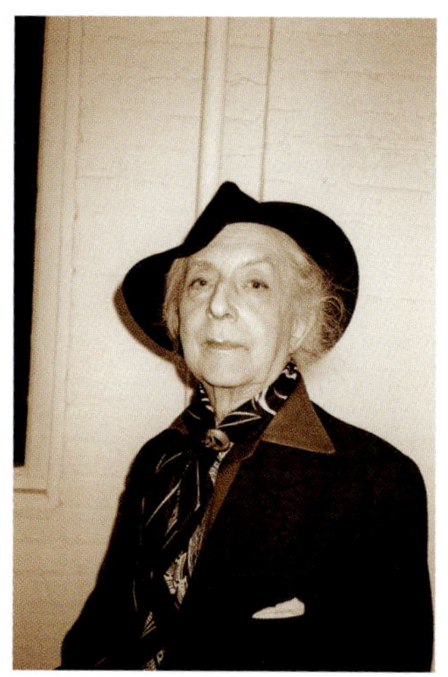

Quentin Crsip, 1996

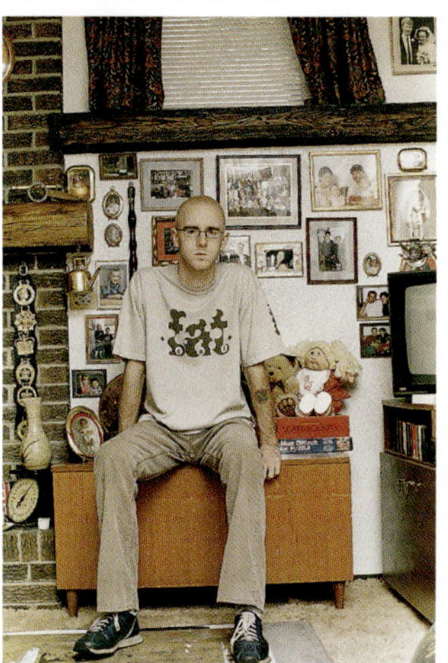

Richie Hawtin, home, sitting 1994

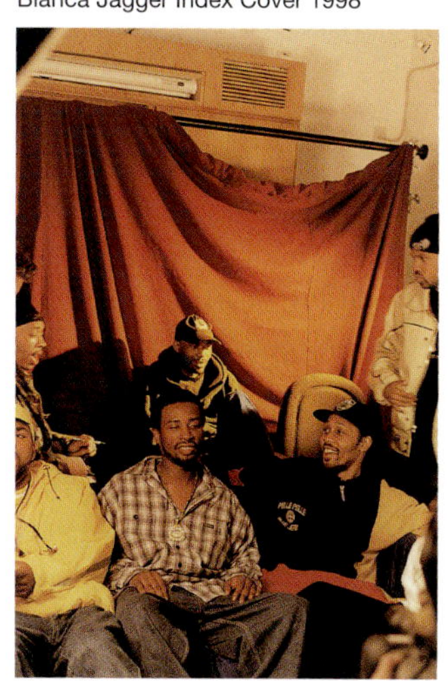

Wu Tang Clan 1997

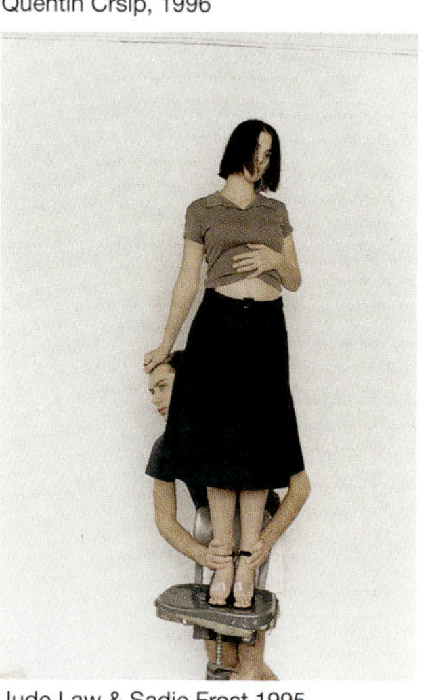

Jude Law & Sadie Frost 1995

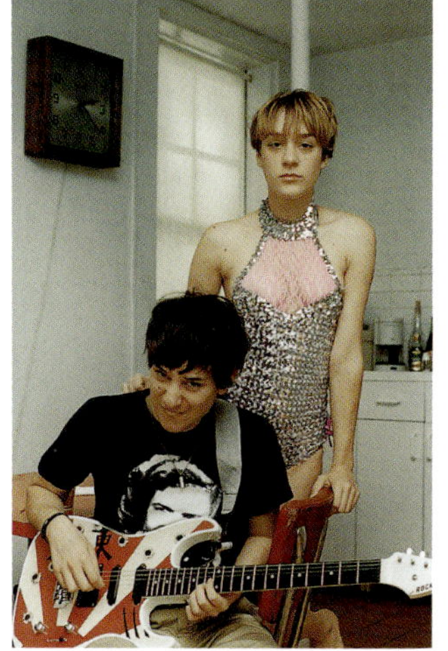

Harmony & Chloe 1995

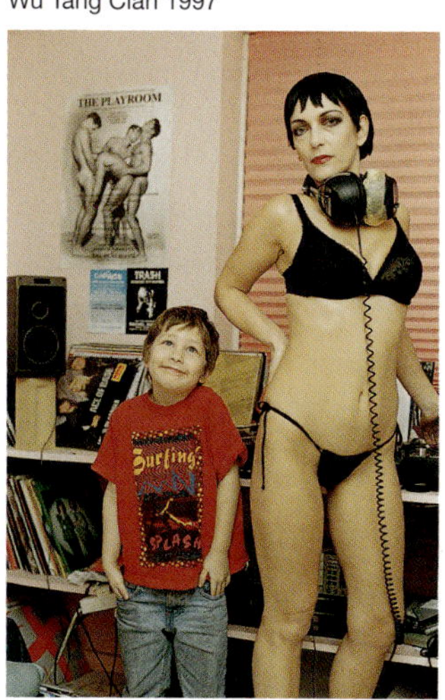

Rachel Auburn & son 1995

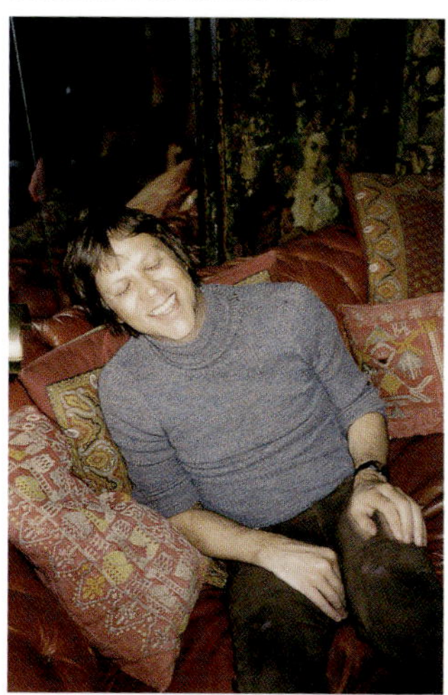

Todd Haynes 1998

LOST AND FOUND

BY DAVID DEITCHER

N ot too long ago I was speaking with a friend about the photographs of Wolfgang Tillmans. Late in our conversation, my friend – himself a photographer – summarized his feelings by declaring with more than a trace of annoyance, "I don't get it. Why does Tillmans show the same pictures over and over again?" I too had noticed Tillmans' propensity for showing old pictures in combination with new ones, especially in the extensive installations he creates for his gallery and museum shows. Nor had it escaped my attention that Tillmans has documented these installations in photographs that he publishes not just in the relevant exhibition catalogue but in other catalogues and in books like this one together with other photographs of other installations. Unlike my friend, however, I am not annoyed by these aspects of Tillmans' practice, that strike me as more significant than bothersome. In fact, the meanings I associate with this method inform much of what I value most about Tillmans' work.

Confronted by a wall of his photographs, or by the sequences of images he has published in magazines and books, I want to find the common denominator, to make sense of the whole. In short, I am possessed by a powerful desire to know things. In a situation like this, I become like an amateur detective, combing through the evidence in an effort to uncover meaning. I look for patterns in the formal correlations between pictures that otherwise appear to have nothing in common. I consider hierarchies of scale and other ways of granting priority to some pictures over others. Given a profusion of images, I look for the links between them: are there, I wonder, individuals who appear in more than one picture? And if so under what circumstances? What geographical locales do the pictures represent? And what social milieus? Even while attending to the beauty and plainness of the everyday objects that Tillmans has singled out for posterity, I look for the significant detail, as if it might provide me with access to domestic spaces and private rituals. Finally, I wonder, does the whole somehow add up to something greater than the sum of its parts?

Such a desire to know is analogous to the structure of narrative. Writing about the works of Henry James, literary theorist Tzvetan Todorov once observed that narrative is based on the quest for an "absent cause"; the absence of that cause is what sets the machinery of the story in motion and keeps it grinding along. Once the cause is identified or otherwise made present, narrative ceases. The desire for narrative ceases. The desire for narrative induced by Tillmans' photographic practice results in part from a structural idiosyncrasy of photographs: that they are, as Susan Sontag once observed, powerless to explain anything.[1] But the ensuing flood of speculation about the meaning of the photographs is sustained and itensified by Tillmans' various ways of rearranging his work, which keep meaning in a state of flux. "As an artist," he has said, "I am interested not in singular readings, but in constructing networks of images and meanings capable of reflecting the complexity of the subject."[2]

If Tillmans' photographs suggest any kind of narrative it would be the chronicle. But for a number of reasons, the kind of chronicle his practice suggests is perhaps the memoir more than a journal, and certainly more than photojournalism and documentary. Eager to classify the work of this younger photographer, early observers quickly noticed the prevalence of young people in his seemingly spontaneous photographs and labeled Tillmans a documentarian of his generation. The truth was more complex, and not just because of the extent to which Tillmans was actually collaborating with his friends to ensure that they properly "impersonated" the idea of the conception of themselves that they and Tillmans were interested in seeing.[3] In fact, Tillmans was adjusting the sober code of documentary in order to register in his photographs a measure of emotional engagement with his youthful subjects who often displayed self-conscious, awkward and exhibitionistic modes of self-presentation with which he identified. Tillmans specifically resents the wholesale dismissal of this aspect of youth as only a "phase". In this regard it is interesting that he has noted the use of the same form of patronizing devaluation in relation to his experience of growing up gay.

The process of youthful self-constitution through manipulation of one's public image provided Tillmans with his own self-defining motif from the beginning of the '90s. This process, and its ritualization in subcultural formations, are not just theatrically riveting but can be politically resistant as well as they occur in the context of a predatory commodity culture that is perpetually pursuing the next trend, fad and fashion, and the next label through which these fads and fashions can be neutralized and marketed to the lucrative mass market of youth. As Neville Wakefield has perceptively observed, Tillmans was investigating the tension between "desire as it has been commercialized within the image and the sanctity of the self as something apart from its myriad representations."[4]

What Tillmans found, and photographed, in that space of tension was beauty and grace. His photographs of young lives being shaped through resistant engagement with the prescriptive codes of mainstream representation reflected his effort to expand on what he has referred to as the "climate of possibility". And while it was above all Tillmans' individual pictures of young people that made visible the extent to which the self is always a work in progress, his thoughtful (re-)arrangements of those pictures in magazine spreads, books and installations were providing him with a means of coming to grips with his own mutable state of selfhood, as he has said, at any given moment in time.

Since the mid-1990s, Tillmans' has moved on somewhat from his former tendency to focus on the formation of the youthful self in the city square, the dance club, and the crash pad. Intimacy and reflectiveness which were always implicit in his work have become explicit as he has shifted his focus to describe what might in every sense be termed "interiority." To be sure, Tillmans has by no means constructed a vision of a literally sedate or securely settled existence. There has always been visual evidence of travel in his photographs, and these traces have lately become even more apparent. But only now have they clearly coalesced to form a visual trope, a metaphor in which the photographer's restlessness takes on the significance of a search – whether for intimate contact and meaning, or for rare experiences of transport, by which I refer to transcendence.

Transport of both kinds is the subject of *Haselmaus* (1995), a photograph of the pale young man who warranted this affectionate, and slightly antiquated, sobriquet (roughly: honeymouse). Wearing only blue bathing trunks and a beatific expression, he stands on a rock before a tropical waterfall, arms raised and head tilted back in delight. Inasmuch as the work's title declares Tillmans' love for this man, the word "transport" applies on both sides of the camera.

Travel also promises a sense of unfettered possibility – of ungroundedness – that crystallizes in the idea of flight. Transport of this kind is the subject of *JAL* 1997, an improbably beautiful view from the window of a jet at cruising altitude, showing the gleaming, streamlined engines and wing sandwiched comfortably between a bed of clouds and an azure sky. But on the ground as well, Tillmans' nomadism has afforded him occasions to contemplate and record beautiful vistas that recall and happily seculurize the romantic tradition of the sublime (*Louisiana* (1996), *Moonrise, Puerto Rico* (1995), *Porte La Galère* (1996)).

Tillmans manages to maintain a certain reflectiveness in the midst of a life that now more than ever could be consumed by distraction. Among his many portraits, the appearance of unmistakably familiar faces from the worlds of fashion, art, and popular music attests to the photographer's success. Tillmans' portrait style does little to diminish the high voltage of celebrity, but it does manage to instill some doubt in the viewer's mind about whose "aura" is a product of fame and whose is not. This effect is partly the result of his collaboration with sitters who seem innately to know how to deliver what the camera and the man behind it want. But it is also due to the fact that his photographs of the famous people are inevitably seen in the company of other images. In his installations and photo spreads Tillmans creates such a mix of ordinary people and living legends that in this realm of the symbolic he manages a partial leveling of the social field.

Tillmans' unconventional sense of beauty, combining with his work's increased focus on the practice of everyday life, has produced an extensive body of still lifes. "I want to reflect the way I look at the world," Tillmans has said. "That I am aware of the fact that I'm now looking at the sky, but now I'm looking at my feet.... I'm interested in various aspects of life, and I want to give them space and representation."[5] At first glance, the still lifes have a primarily abstract visual appeal partly because they are so frequently photographed from overhead. *Naoya Tulips* (1997), for example, is an aerial shot of radiant flowers encircled by the debris of a busy life. But the flowers are also bracketed by bare feet – the photographer's own – and part of his right leg, and this makes explicit a quality that is present in most of his still lifes and that sets them apart: they convey a strong sense of the photographer's physical and emotional relationship with the inanimate objects he pictures.

Although Tillmans' views from above emphasize the abstract qualities of his "motifs," the same vantage also promotes an awareness of these objects' integration within the patterns of everyday life. The wealth of vernacular debris (price stickers, plastic containers, skimpy paper napkins, plastic spoons, elastic bands, disposable lighters...) that accompanies his fruits, flowers and vegetables anchors these arrangements securely in the everyday. Combining with the sense of seeing the objects in *Last Still Life* (1995) through Tillmans' eyes, the presence of the small dish containing four spent cigarettes deepens this otherwise merely elegant composition by ensuring that it is grasped on an emotional level as the residue of an experience that has passed and with which the viewer can identify through the agency of his or her own private associations.

Tillmans' still lifes are also enlivened by his playful, sometimes eccentric way of interacting with the objects that inhabit the world around him. This is evident in his placement of a used makeup pad, that hides in plain sight among the otherwise banal flesh tones and bone-dry textures of *Shells* (1995); or in the two-dimensional raspberries that adorn the top of a yogurt container and that now – seen from overhead – blend right in among the (originally) three-dimensional cherries, roses and half-eaten grapefruit of *Stilleben Marktstrasse* (1997). Tillmans also played with the expectations and challenged the perceptions of the viewer in the photographs he shot for American *Vogue* in 1996: only an attentive viewer will find the cluster of homely new potatoes nestling among the strawberries that provide a properly colorful counterpoint to a beaming Kate Moss. Only a formalist and a prankster would think to situate the supermodel behind a "still life" of shrinkwrapped artichokes and a head of broccoli. This *Arte povera* direction provides the required spot of texture and color while also functioning as a rudimentary eye test to see if any fashion enthusiast either notices this impropriety or cares.

The life that Tillmans describes in his photographs reveals other, more serious signs of being at odds with middle-class convention. Which, thankfully, is not to say that he has in any way turned this into a pretext for solemnity. Consider, for example, two photographs of a youth who sports a trim Mohawk. The interior is recognizable from other photographs of Kate Moss and Michael Stipe: both sat for Tillmans in a "modern" armchair with a cantilevered green upholstered seat and back and that chair figures significantly in one of the pictures of this self-styled punk. Was it, I wonder, before or after Tillmans photographed those luminaries that this multiply pierced, shirtless young man dropped his trousers and aimed to make sure that not a drop of his piss would miss that seat? A second photograph shows the same rebellious young man masturbating on his knees in front of a storage unit. To intensify his pleasure, he has fastened a chain and tit clamps to his pierced nipples. To intensify ours, Tillmans has photographed him so as to show the blue jeans bunched between his alabaster thighs, and red suspenders that echo in reverse the angle and color of his cock.

A potentially hazardous incident of queer attraction provides the occasion for *Soldaten I* and *II* (1997): while riding on a train somewhere in German, Tillmans seems to have positioned his camera only inches from the beefy, camouflage-clad thighs of a soldier. Both photographs emit an incendiary sexual charge, which is not entirely due to the fetishized appeal of this big man in uniform; it also derives from the pleasure Tillmans evidently took in stealing a sideways glance at this man who, though put together to elicit admiration, might not have welcomed it from a "fag".

Soldaten I and *II* are extremely rare images for Tillmans in one respect: they convey an enthrallment to a kind of hypermasculinity that for once is completely consistent with the construction of the contemporary gay male ideal in gay market culture and pornography. Tillmans' photographs more often describe a queer sexuality that within the context of this discussion can be seen as being doubly transgressive, for not only does it violate the coercive code of compulsory heterosexuality, it also resists the blandishments of a gay sexual culture that Tillmans, along with many other young and insightful same-sexers, rightly find oppressive.

As I survey Tillmans' photographs of young men, none of them – not even the punk who pissed on Tillmans' chair and jerked off beside his closet – adheres to the gay sexual ideal as embodied in the pages of your average glossy gay skin magazine. One has only to look at the studies of the young man identified as "Paul" to conclude that Tillmans' photographs of the male nude are not erotic, or certainly not in any conventional sense. When Tillmans wants to project sexual longing, he focuses on the fetish instead of the man. In *Jeremy* (1993), for example, he directs the viewer's gaze to the thick black leather belt with an eagle-emblazoned buckle that encircles the man's waist; to the tattoos that coil up an arm; and only then to the smoothly muscled torso of this faceless young man.

The erotic charge of the fetish also informs the many photographs that Tillmans has taken of clothing. (He has said that sexuality for him is located "on the surface of the clothes".[6]) In *Gray Jeans over Stair Post* (1991) the post supports the jeans like a blunt armature, and in so doing suggests the legendary phallus whose absence, according to Freud, brings the fetish to life. But the photographs of fallen garments are not always so illustratively fetishistic: as often as they may elicit sexual longings in the viewer, they can also inspire more tender longings and associations about the circumstances that led to their being cast off in the first place. Whether hung over a radiator to dry or tossed casually to the floor, the button-fly jeans, shorts and T-shirts Tillmans photographs give him a concise and evocative way of demonstrating the permeation of everyday life by the erotic. *Sportflecken* (1996), a monumentalizing closeup of a plain white T-shirt, focuses on the soft folds of the collar, the fabric below that (puckers in places), and the ivory spots that hint at the presence of sex. In its evocation of purity and comfort, *Sportflecken* is emblematic of the increasingly visible importance of romantic love in Tillmans' work, as is plainly evident in photographs in which the body of the loved one is immersed within the fullness and complexity of a shared life. Thus, *Sleep* (1995), *Haselmaus, Jochen Taking a Bath* (1997), and *New Inn Broadway* (1997).

To look at *Sportflecken* is to imagine the body of the person who once filled that T-shirt. In this sense, the work recalls another well-known picture, the photograph that the artist Felix Gonzalez-Torres took of an unmade bed in 1991. There, two dented pillows conjure the heads of now absent occupants. Enlarged to billboard scale and exhibited that way in streets throughout New York, this work has been interpreted primarily, though not exclusively, in relation to disappearances brought on by AIDS.

Throughout the decade of Tillmans' photographic activity, AIDS has been a prominent fact of life, though not one that he has made a point of chronicling directly. Nevertheless, the photographs of discarded clothing are so redolent with desire and loss that I cannot help but relate them to AIDS. This association is only intensified by the fact that the articles of clothing that Tillmans photographs and transforms into fetishes are for some observers especially encoded as queer. In this context it is helpful to recall Freud's analysis of the fetish once again: he observed of these inanimate objects that they stand in for absences that are felt by the subject to be intolerable. Looking at Tillmans' photographs of cast-off clothing, one can be reminded of the fact that now it is death, rather than the threat of castration, that the fetish simultaneously acknowledges and disavows.

Tillmans has been extremely careful to facilitate identification with his work even among viewers who do not share in the particularities of his life. This is even true of the single photograph that is almost literally cast in shadow by the presence of AIDS, an image of a robust hand reaching across a bed to make contact with the hand of another. The thumb of this second hand is connected to an electronic device that emits a red glow against the institutional blue of the bedding, signaling that this transitory connection between two human beings is occuring within the antiseptic chill of a hospital room. Personally, I would find it impossible not to identify this photograph with the prevalence of AIDS in my life. That said, I would find it presumptuous and wrong to use that historical context to foreclose on the capacity of this photograph to generate other meanings. For one thing, such a foreclosure would contradict Tillmans' statement about being interested "not in singular readings, but in constructing networks of images and meanings capable of reflecting the complexity of the subject".

Tillmans' installations, with their elaborate recombination of old and new photographs, demonstrate his belief in the capacity of such networks of images and meanings to suggest the multivalent complexity of a life. But another effect of these installations is to deflect the viewer's attention away from the individual photograph and onto the ensemble of which it is a part. Combined with the fact that their photographs are unframed, and merely fastened by adhesive to the wall, the installations undermine the authority of the individual work, underscoring the extent to which its meaning is dependent on both context and the experiences of the viewer. In these situations Tillmans has found, not just a new and challenging way to work with photographs in the spaces of galleries and museums, but to underscore the depth of his engagement with contingency. By "contingency" I mean the way in which meaning, but also subjectivity, sexuality, gender and identity, are all the unstable and temporary results of dynamic processes at the heart of which is difference.

Tillmans' apparent willingness to embrace contingency rubs against the grain of such quintessentially Western values as permanence, stability, commitment, and rooted-ness, just as it also contradicts such articles of faith within the dominant ideology of capitalist democracies as the belief in self-sufficiency, autonomy, and freedom – this last considered to have been already accomplished. To embrace contingency can be exhilarating, as is evident in the photographs that describe flirtation and sexual adventure, travel and sublime transport; in a word, liberation. To judge from the photographs it can be beautiful and sad to surrender to the cadences of everyday life. But to embrace contingency is also frightening, inasmuch as it implies transitoriness and death. The great modern invention of photography can be identified with just such an attempt, if not to stop time, then at least to preserve that which was. Yet even as the camera records the object, the resulting photograph can only be the mark of its passage. "To take a photograph," Sontag has written, "is to participate in another person's (or thing's) mortality, vulnerability, mutability. Precisely by slicing out this moment and freezing it, all photographs testify to time's relentless melt."[7]

Tillmans has evolved a practice that requires constant returns to the past and equally constant reconsiderations of how the events of the past, and one's thoughts and feelings about them, relate to those of the present. What results is therefore something more than a photocollage of a life; something other than a cumulative portrait of the artist as a complexly constituted young man. Tillmans' recombinatory practice extends the dialectic of desire and loss that informs the practice of photography. As such, it constitutes not just a way of maintaining in consciousness cherished aspects of the past but a way of managing the trauma of their perpetual loss. It is ultimately essential to the serious beauty of Tillmans' project that even as the individual photographs record sensual pleasure and intimate connection they simultaneously represent the fear of their imminent loss, a fear that should be familiar to all people who have been fortunate enough to have found what they are looking for in life.

1   "Photographs, which cannot themselves explain anything, are inexhaustible invitations
     to deduction, speculation and fantasy." See: Susan Sontag, *On Photography*
     (New York, Farrar Straus and Giroux, 1977), p. 23
2   "Neville Wakefield in conversation with Wolfgang Tillmans," in: Brigitte Kölle (ed.),
     Wolfgang Tillams (Frankfurt/M., Porticus, 1995), n. p.
3   "I don't photograph them as friends. They are impersonators of their own and my ideas." Ibid.
4   Ibid.
5   "Wolfgang Tillmans with Peter Halley and Bob Nickas," *Index,* March 1997, p. 42
6   Wakefield and Tillmans, op. cit.
7   Sontag, op. cit., p. 15

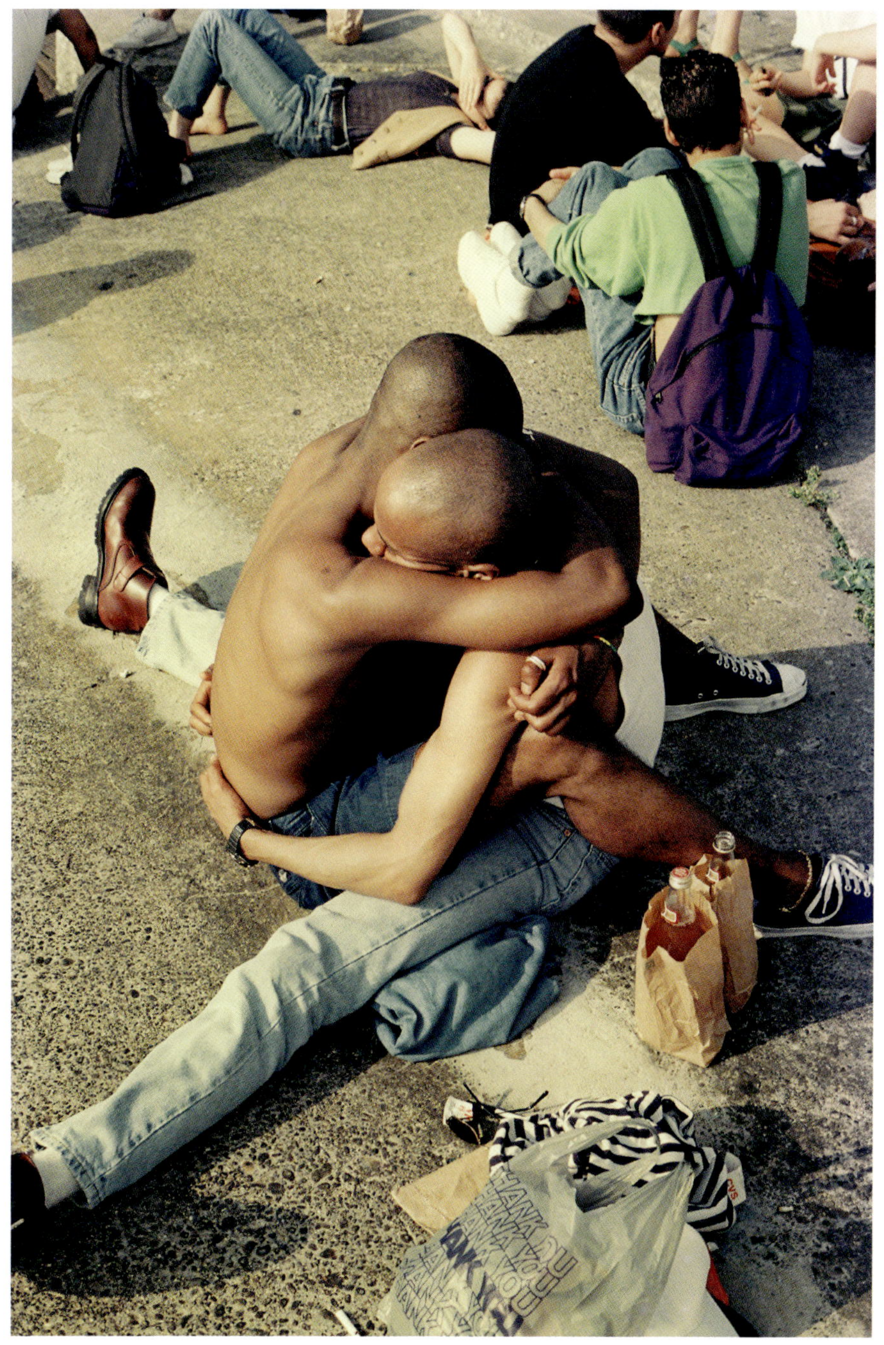

Christopher Street Pier, 1995

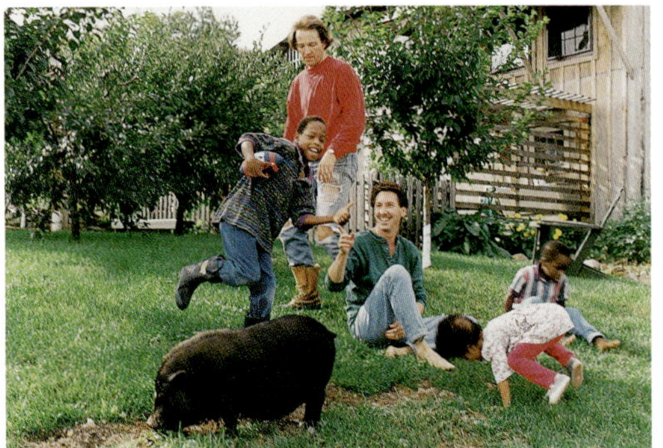

The Day Family 1995

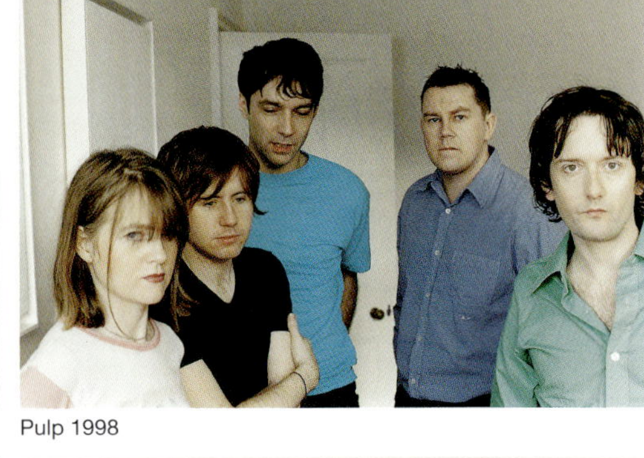

Pulp 1998

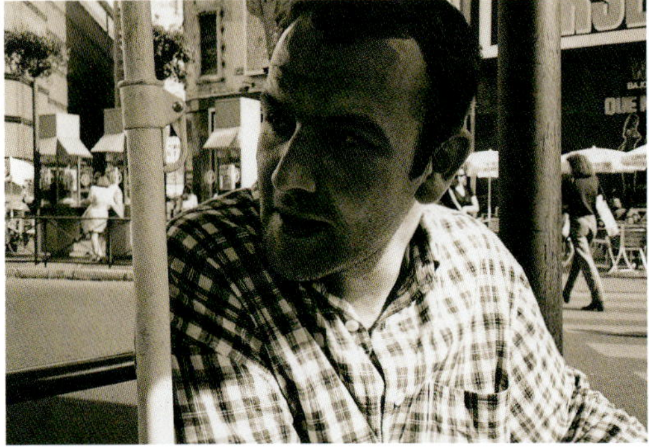

Scott in Madrid 1994

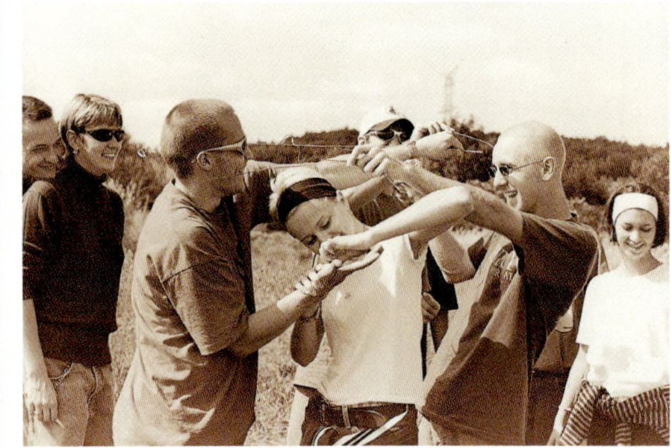

Plus 8 friends + family 1994

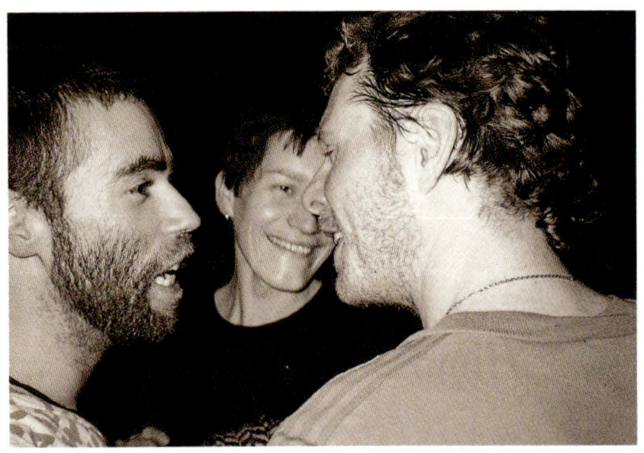

Lutz, Alex & David 1997

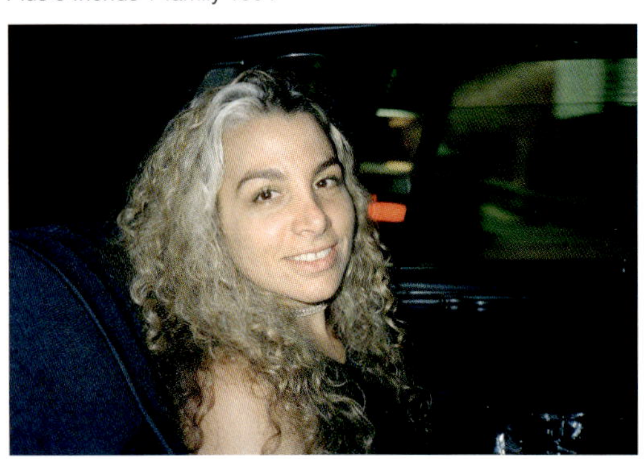

Andrea, 1996

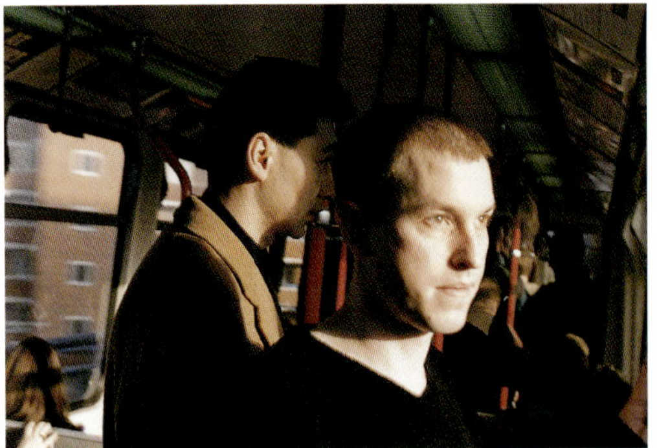

John & Matthew in DLR train 1997

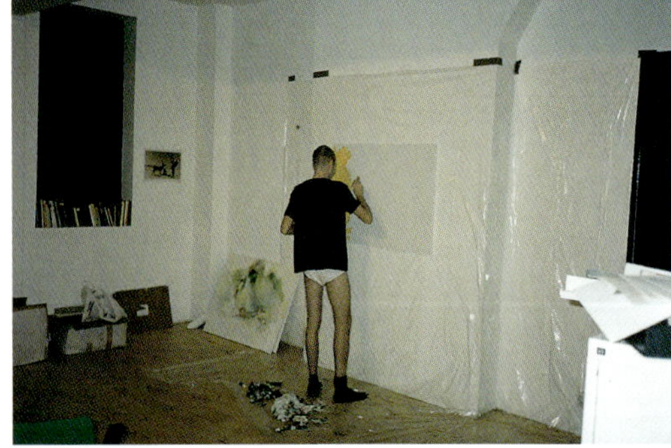

New Inn Yard 1996

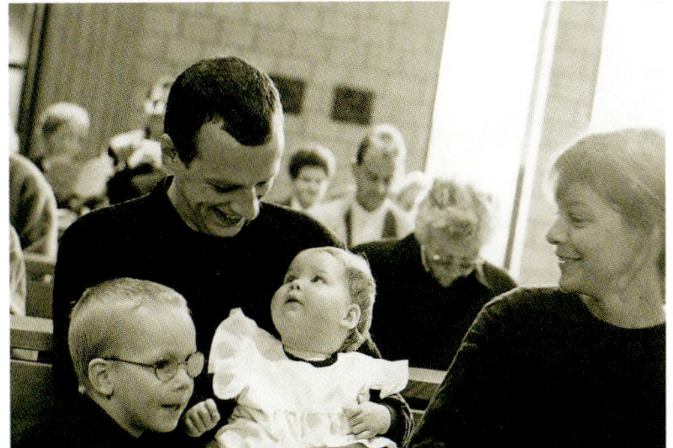

Karl, Georg, Rosa & Ute, Rosas Taufe 1996

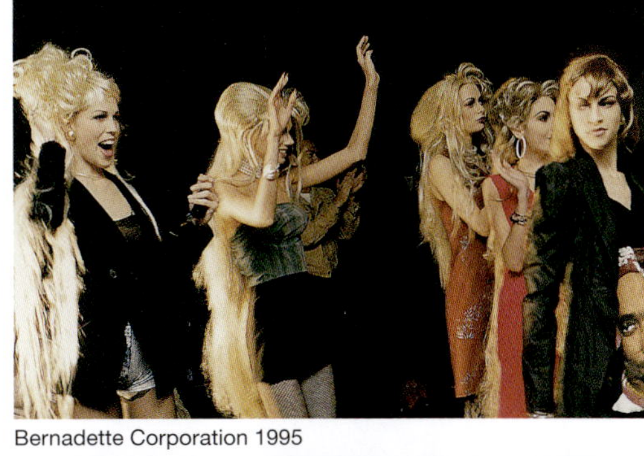

Bernadette Corporation 1995

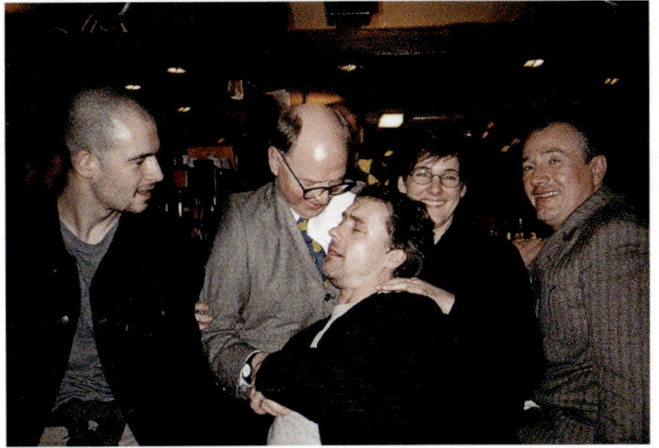

Jake, George, Damien, Sadie & Gilbert at Päff 1993

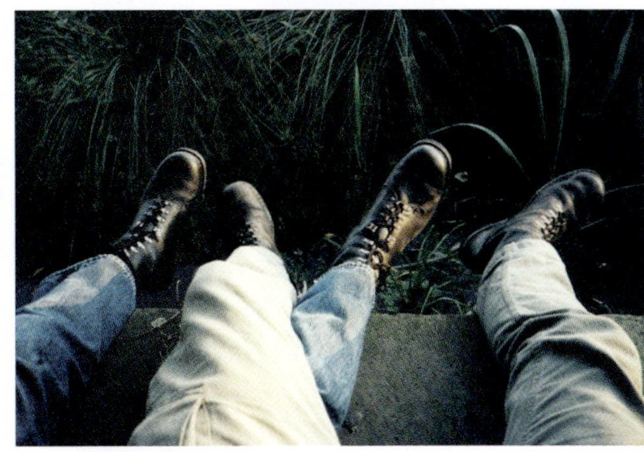

An der Alster, 1994

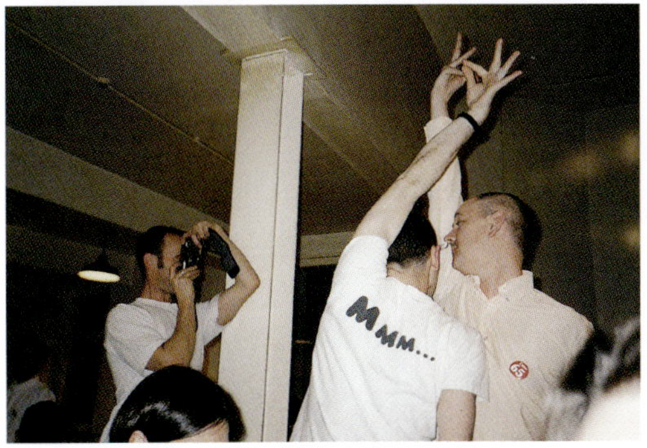

Johnnie, Michael & Cerith at St. Johns 1998

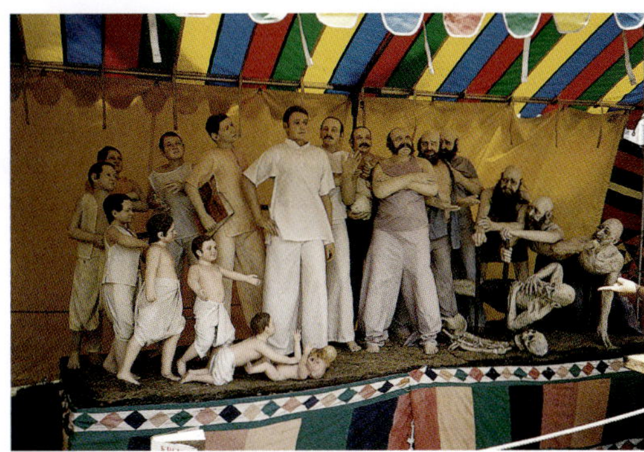

Krsna Display, Venice Beach 1990

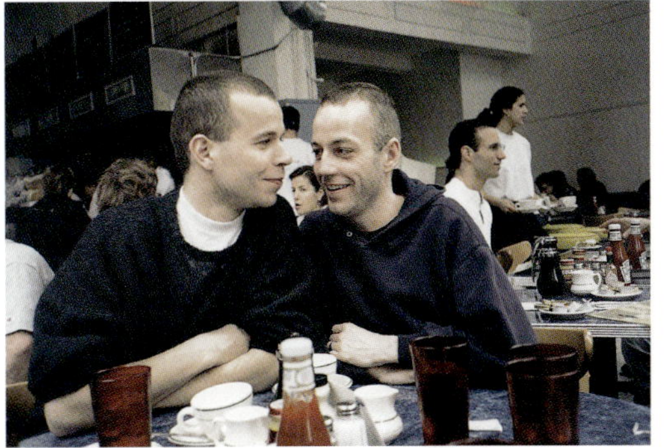

Mayrose 1996

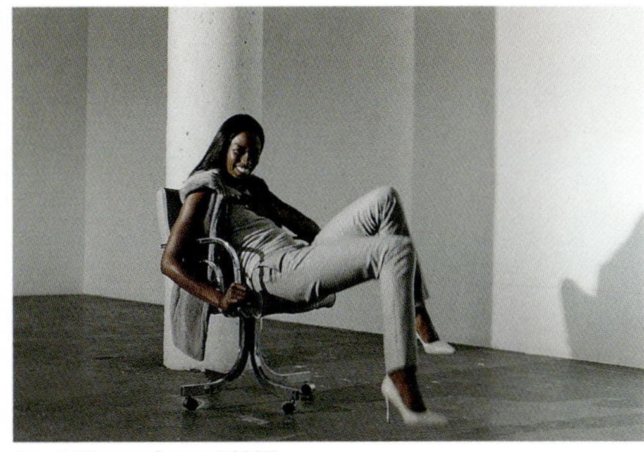

Naomi Vogue Spread 1997

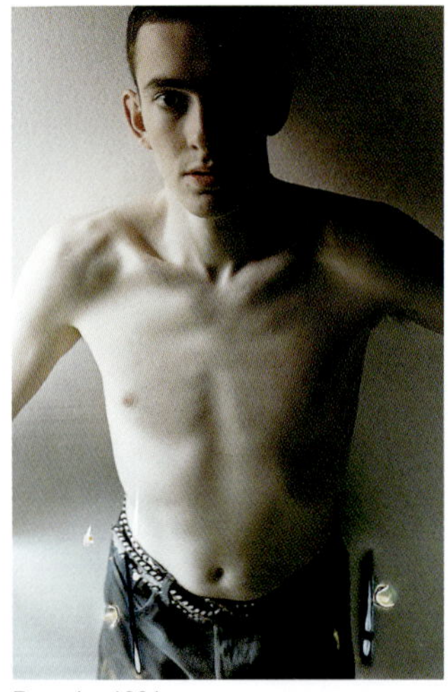

Barnaby 1991

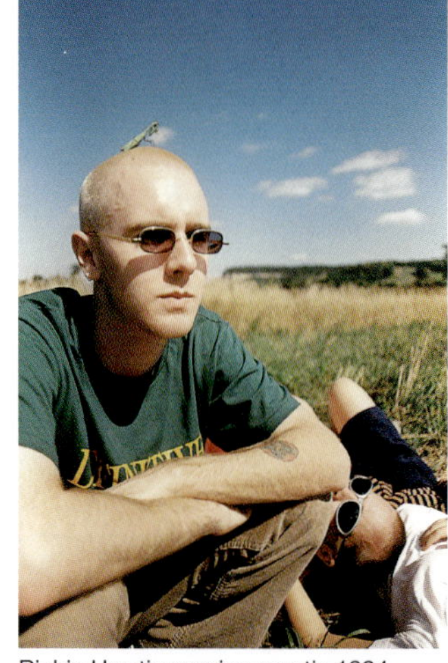

Richie Hawtin praying mantis 1994

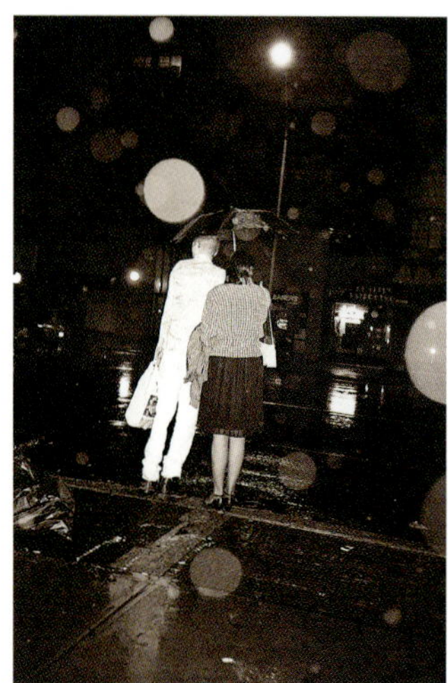

Leaving Ciel Rouge 1996

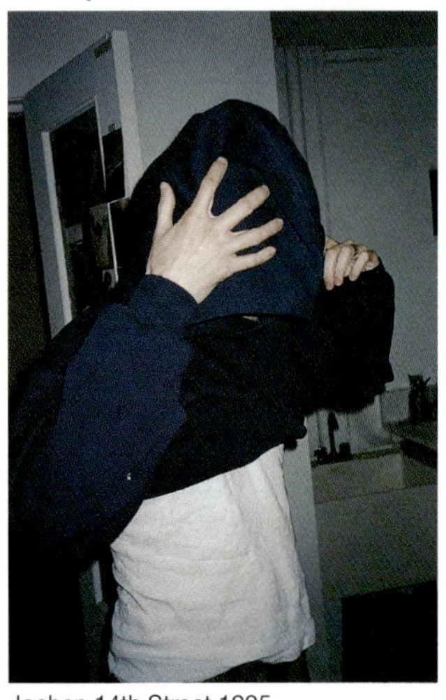

Jochen 14th Street 1995

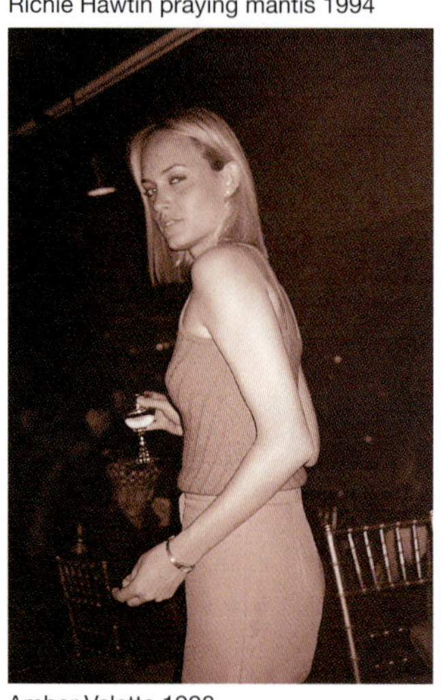

Amber Valetta 1998

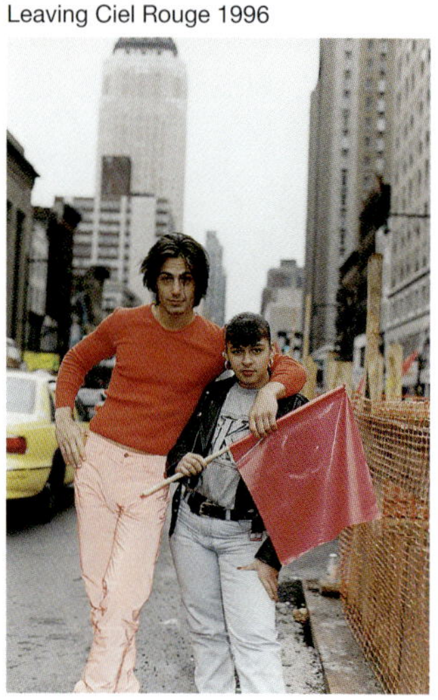

Michael Bergin & Fan 1995

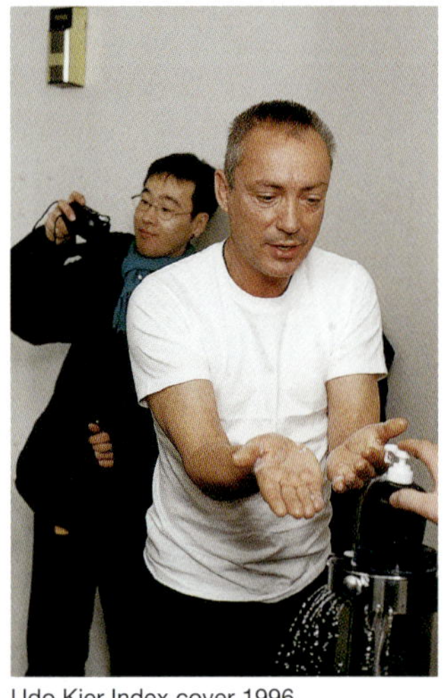

Udo Kier Index cover 1996

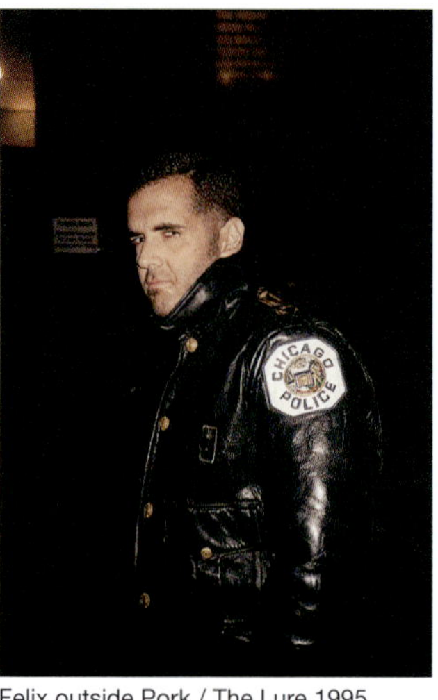

Felix outside Pork / The Lure 1995

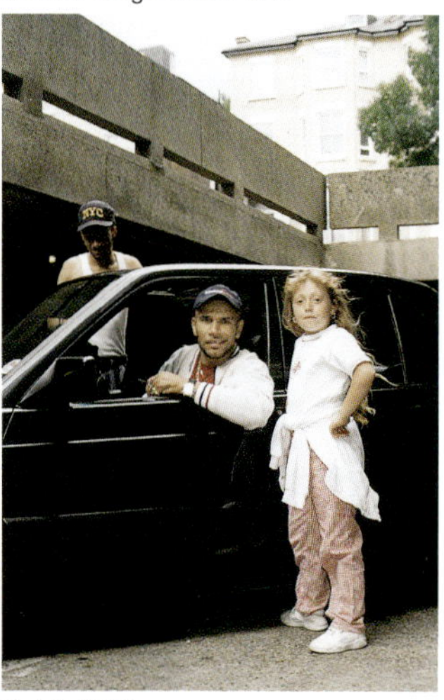

Goldie 1996

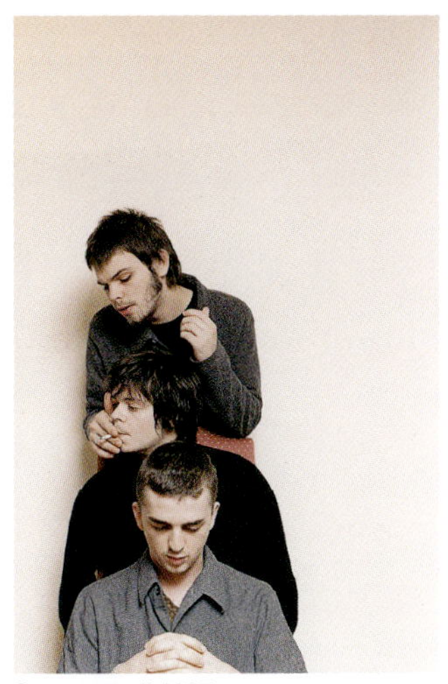

Supergrass II 1997

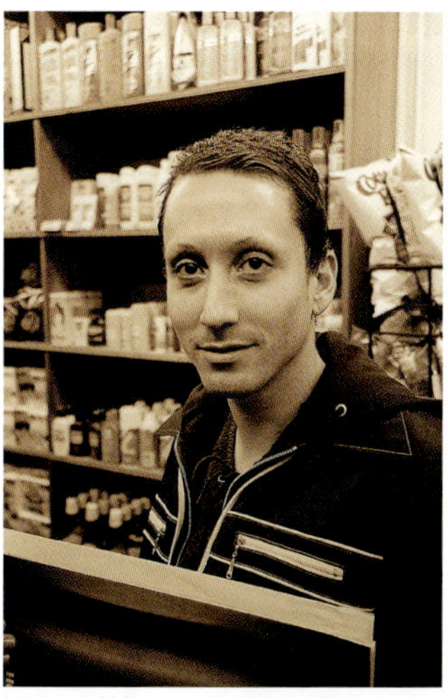

Michael / Mistress Formica 1995

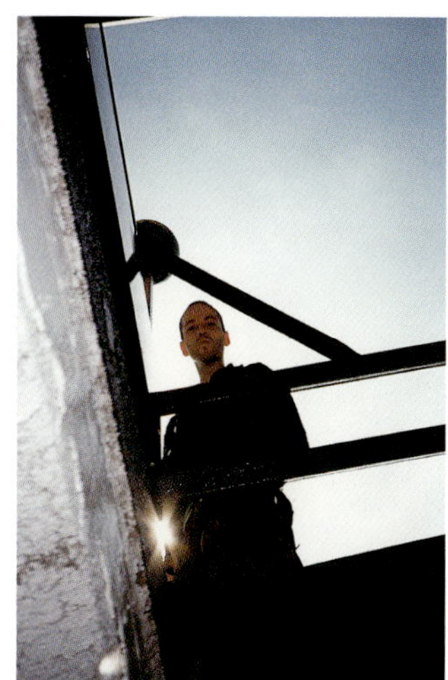

Seventh Ave/Ninth St 1996

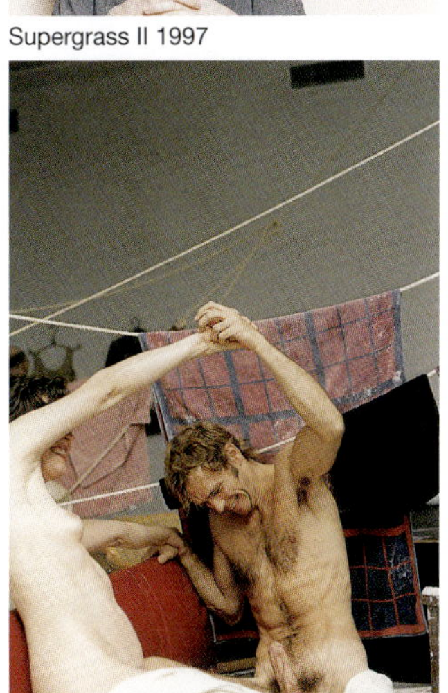

Paula & John, hardon 1994

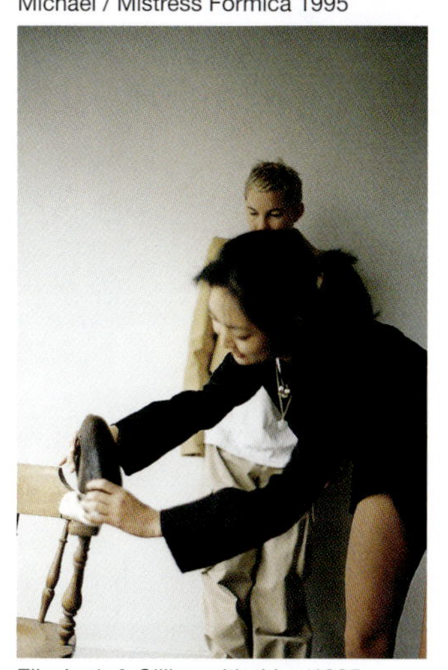

Elisabeth & Gillian with thing 1995

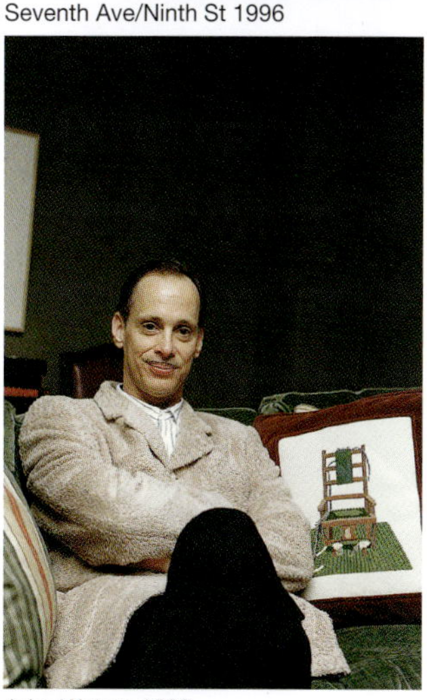

John Waters 1996

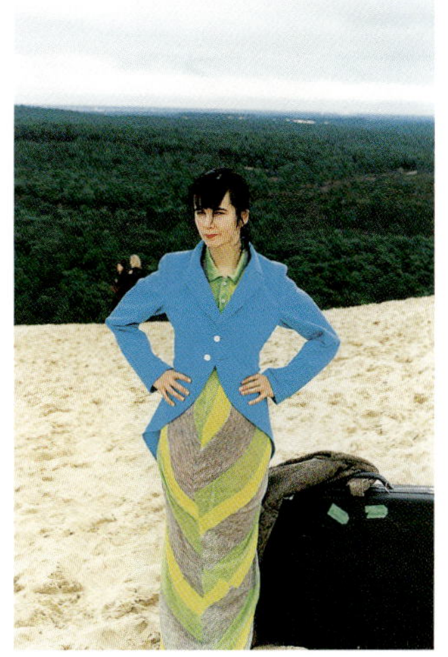

Gillian on dune, 1996

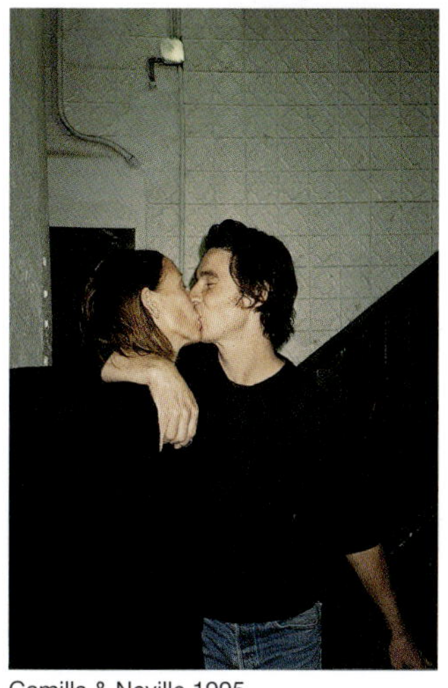

Camilla & Neville 1995

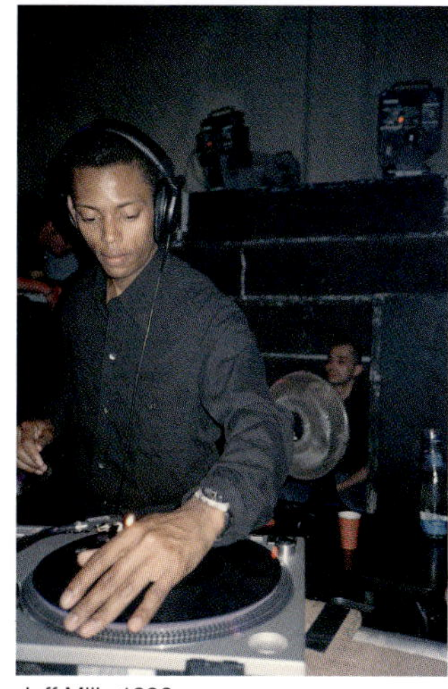

Jeff Mills 1996

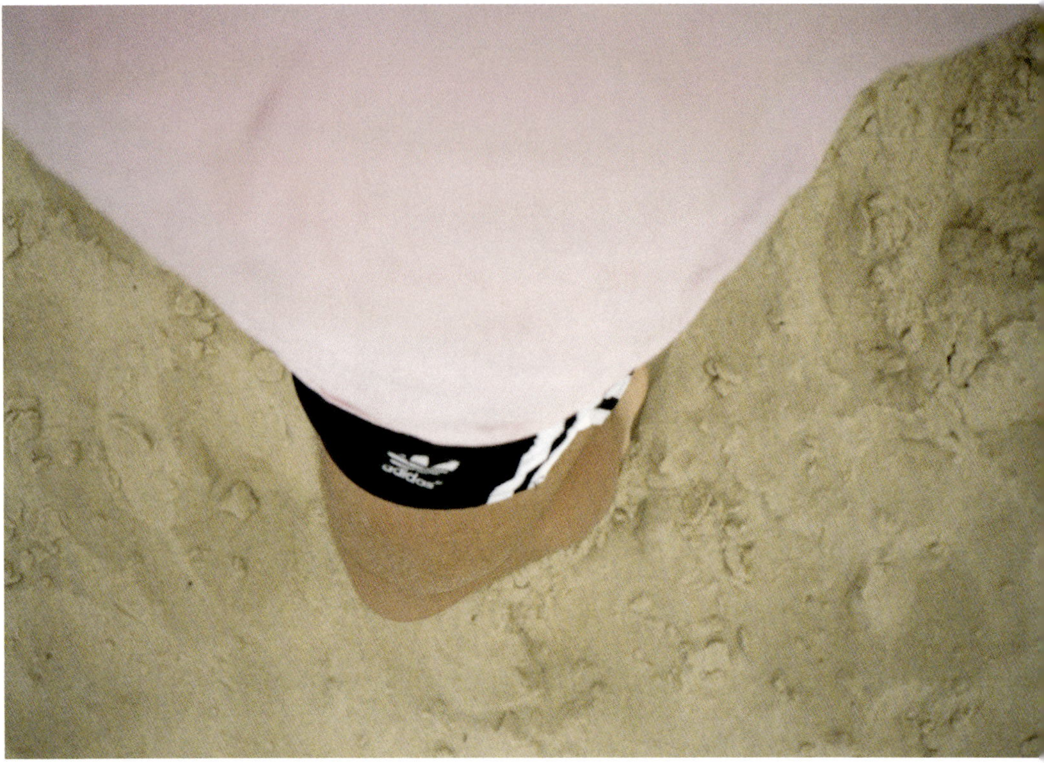

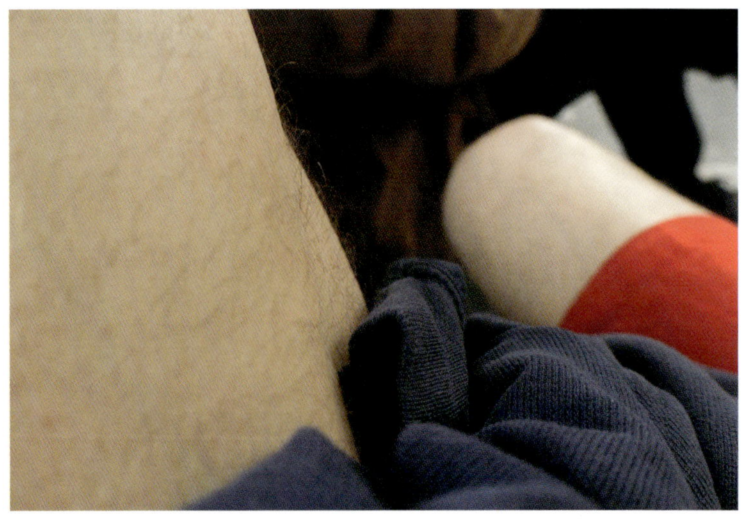

Lacanau (self), 1986   Basilea, 2017

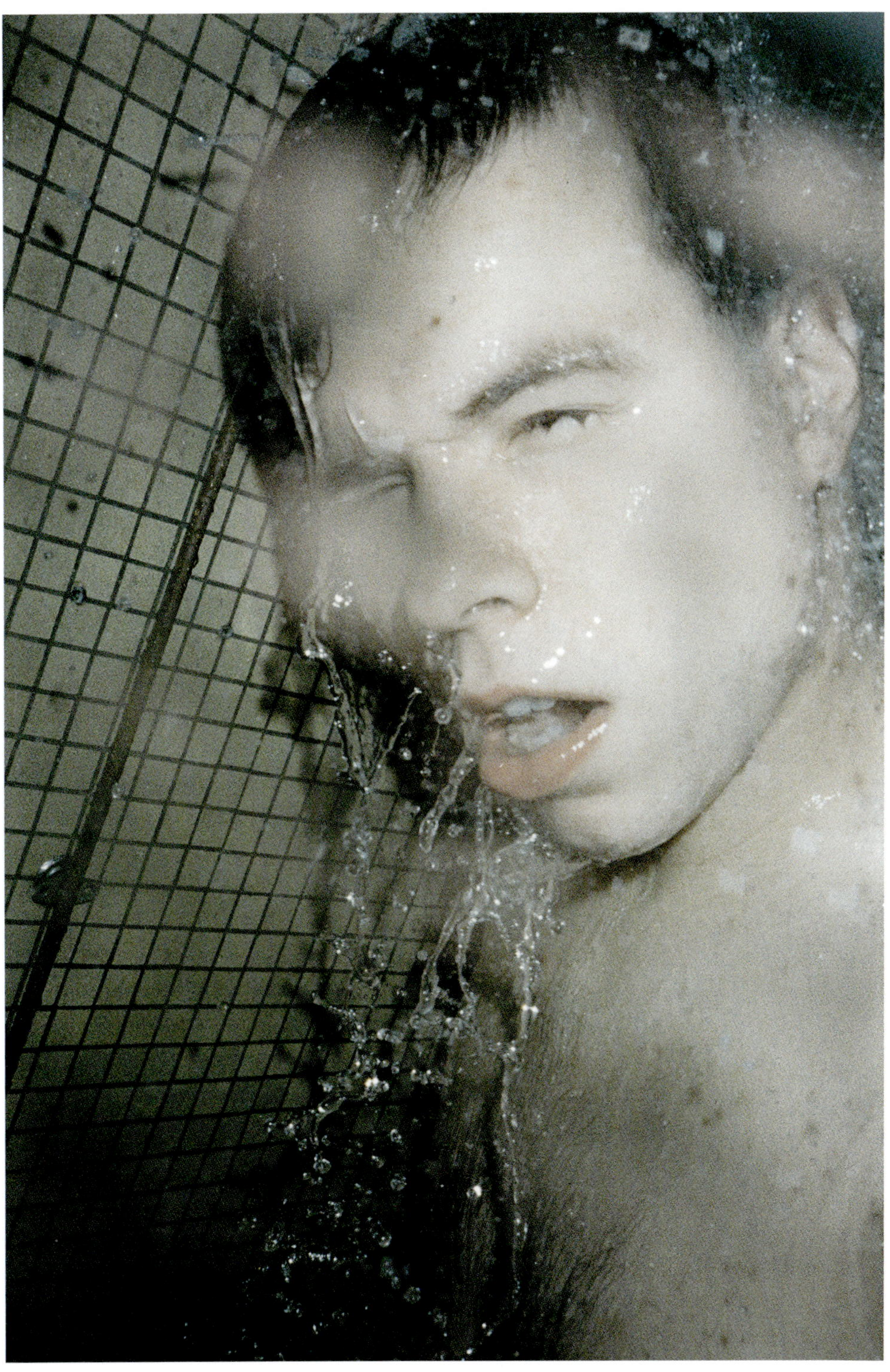

me in the shower, 1990

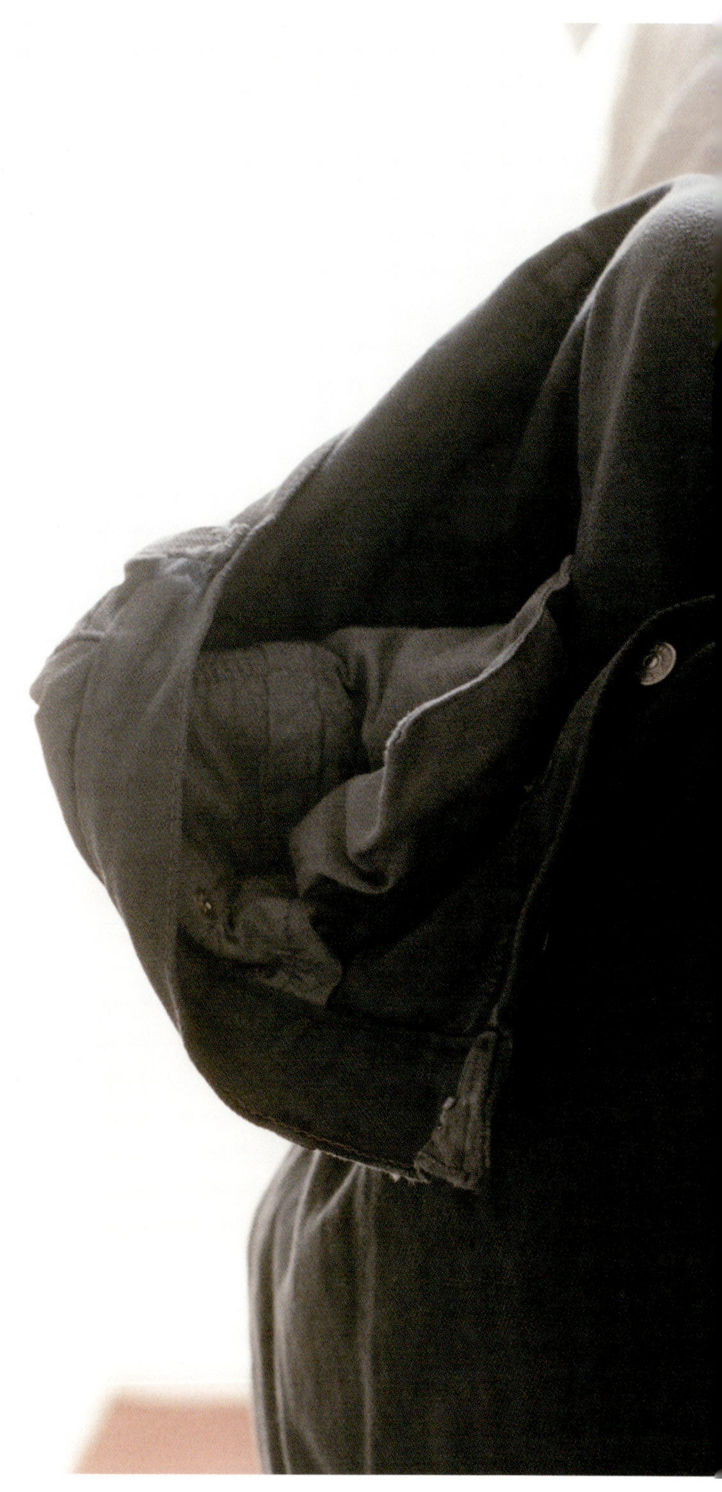

grey jeans over stairpost, 1991

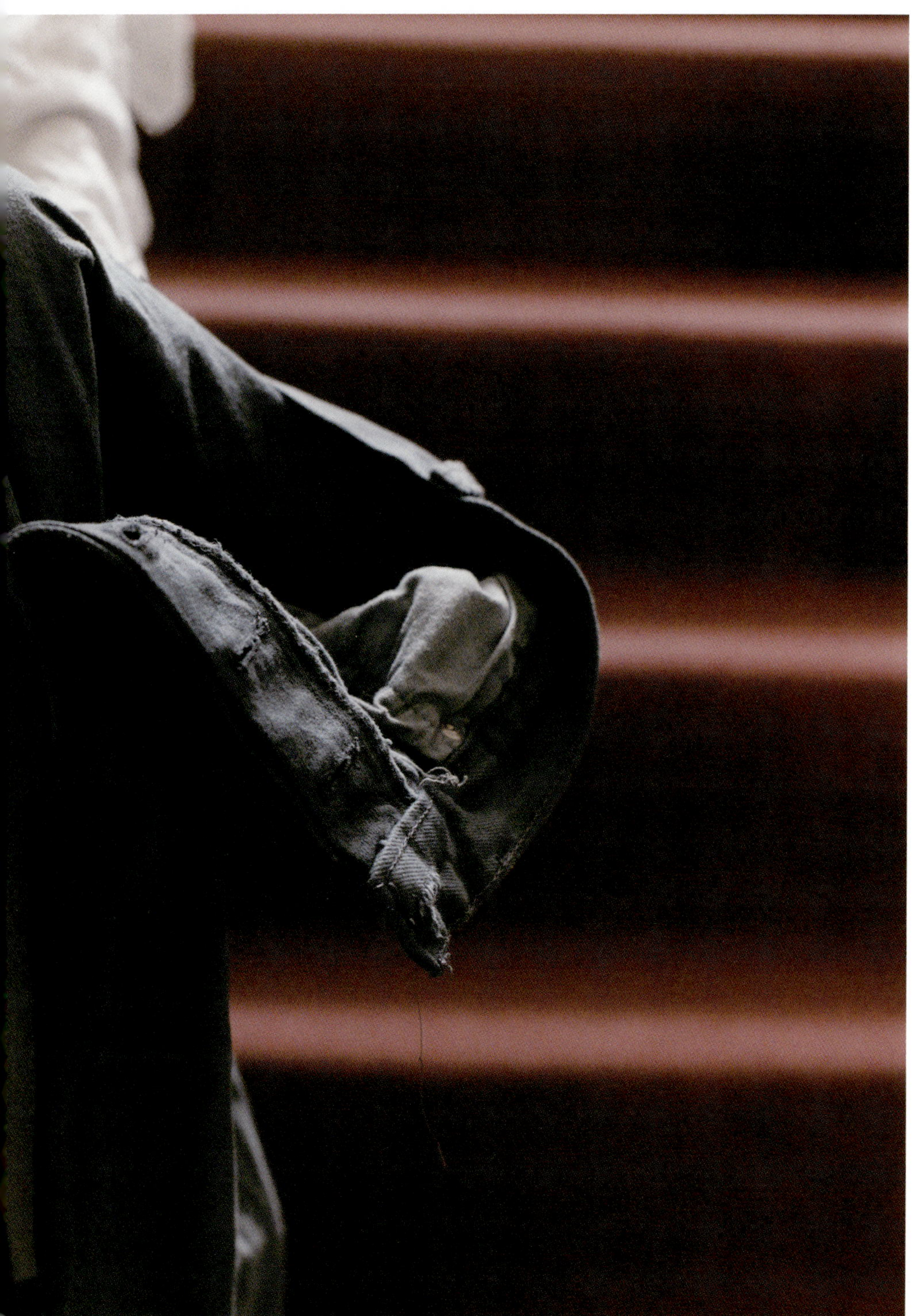

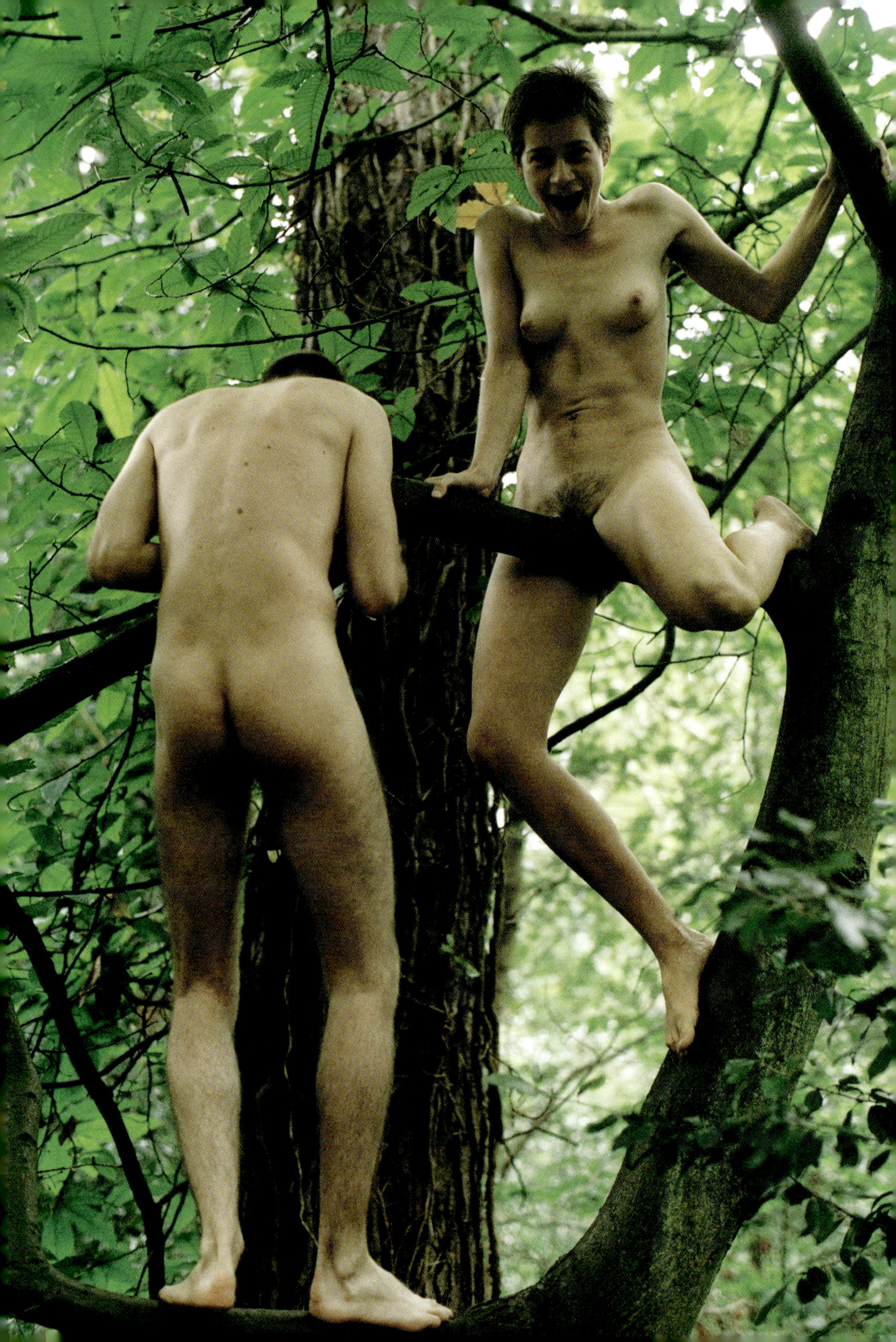

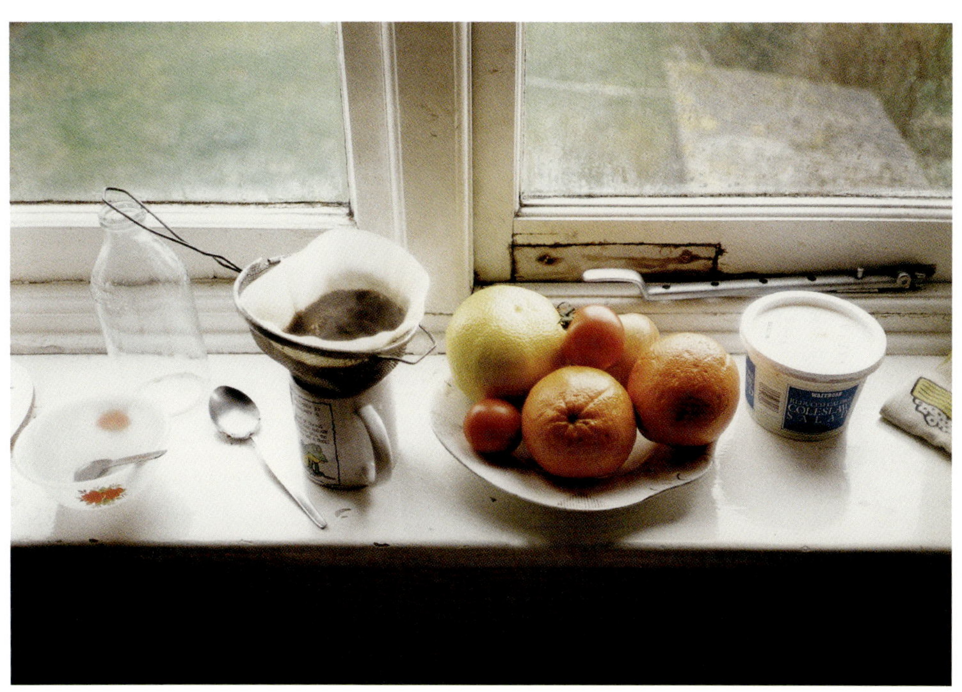

Lutz & Alex climbing tree, 1992
still life Talbot Road, 1991

Turnhose (Sandalen), 1992

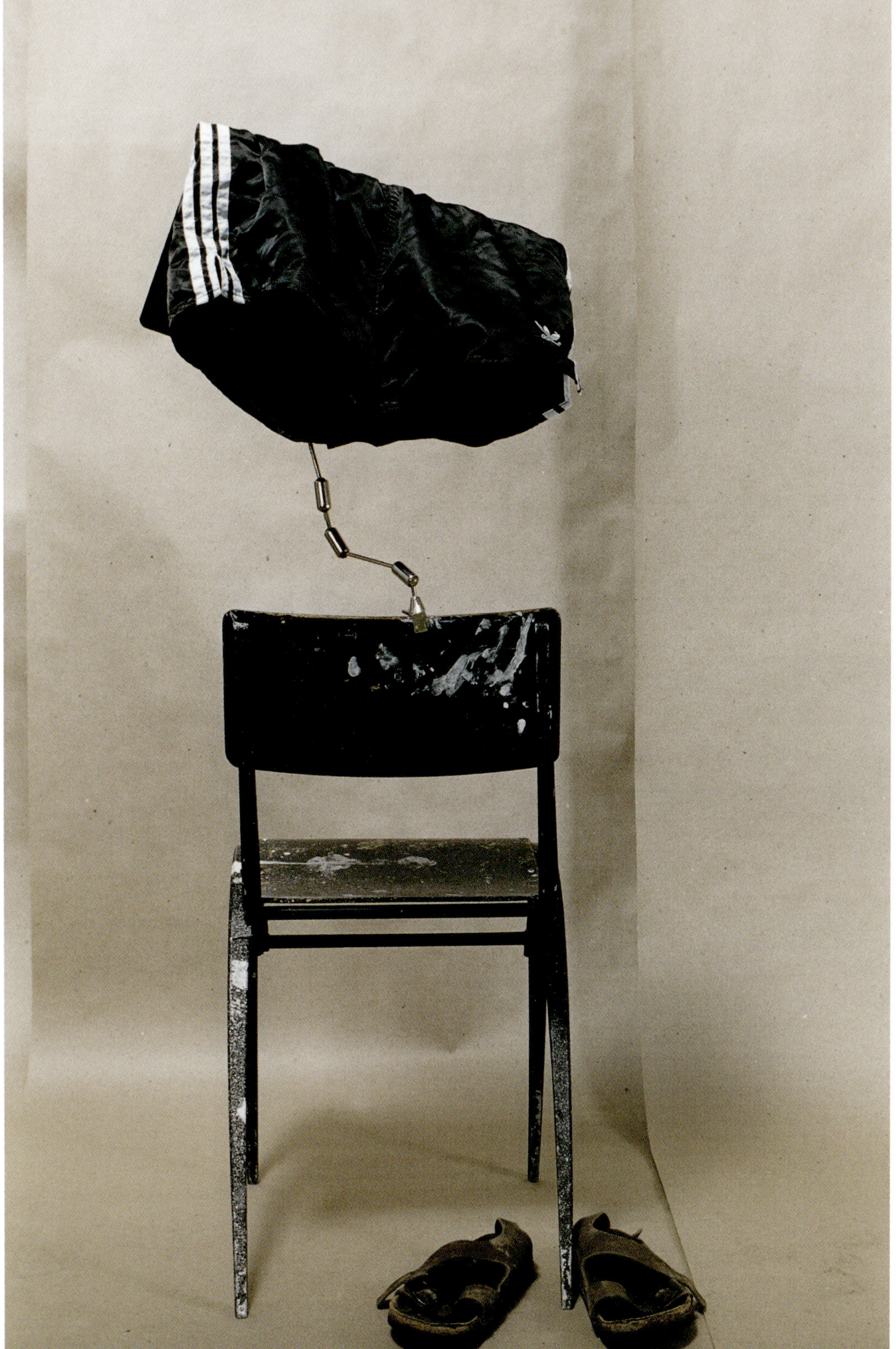

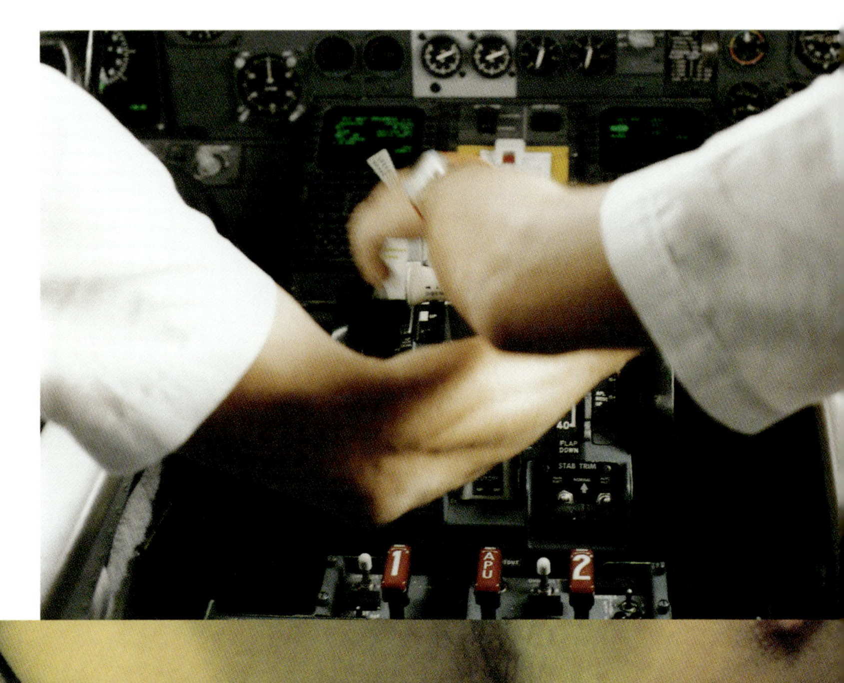

Piloten, 1993
Jeremy, 1993
Jason in skatepipe, 1993

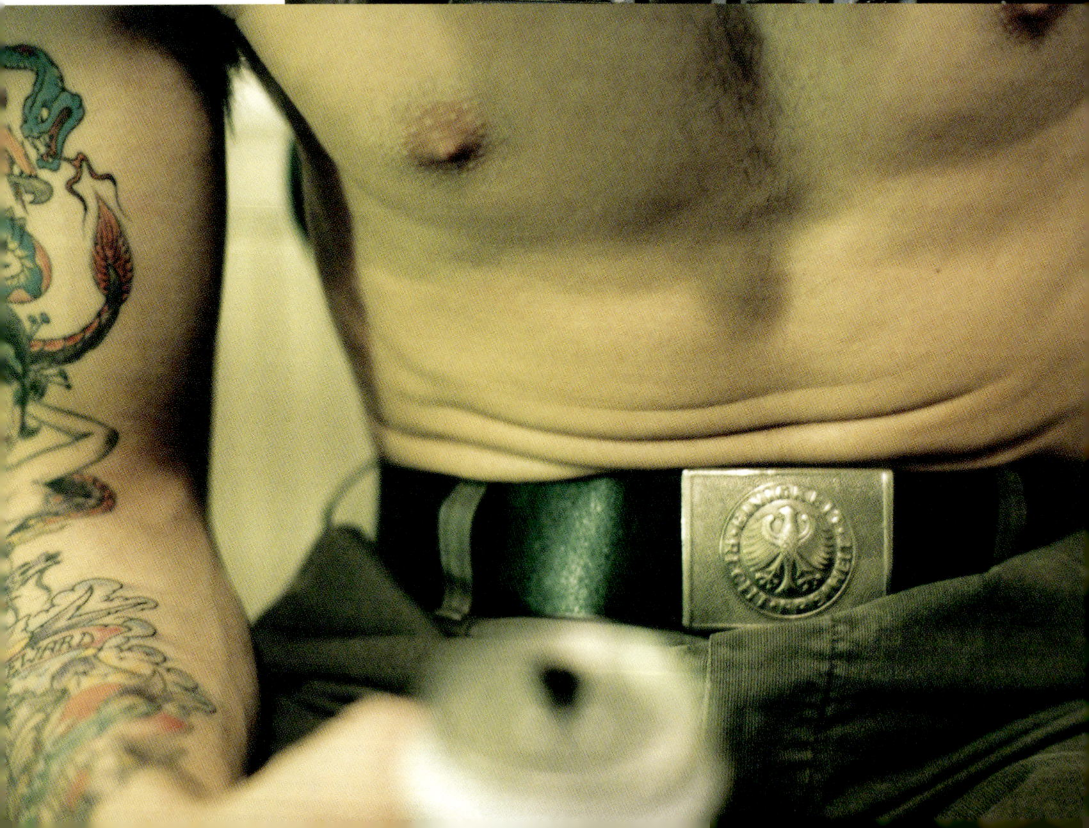

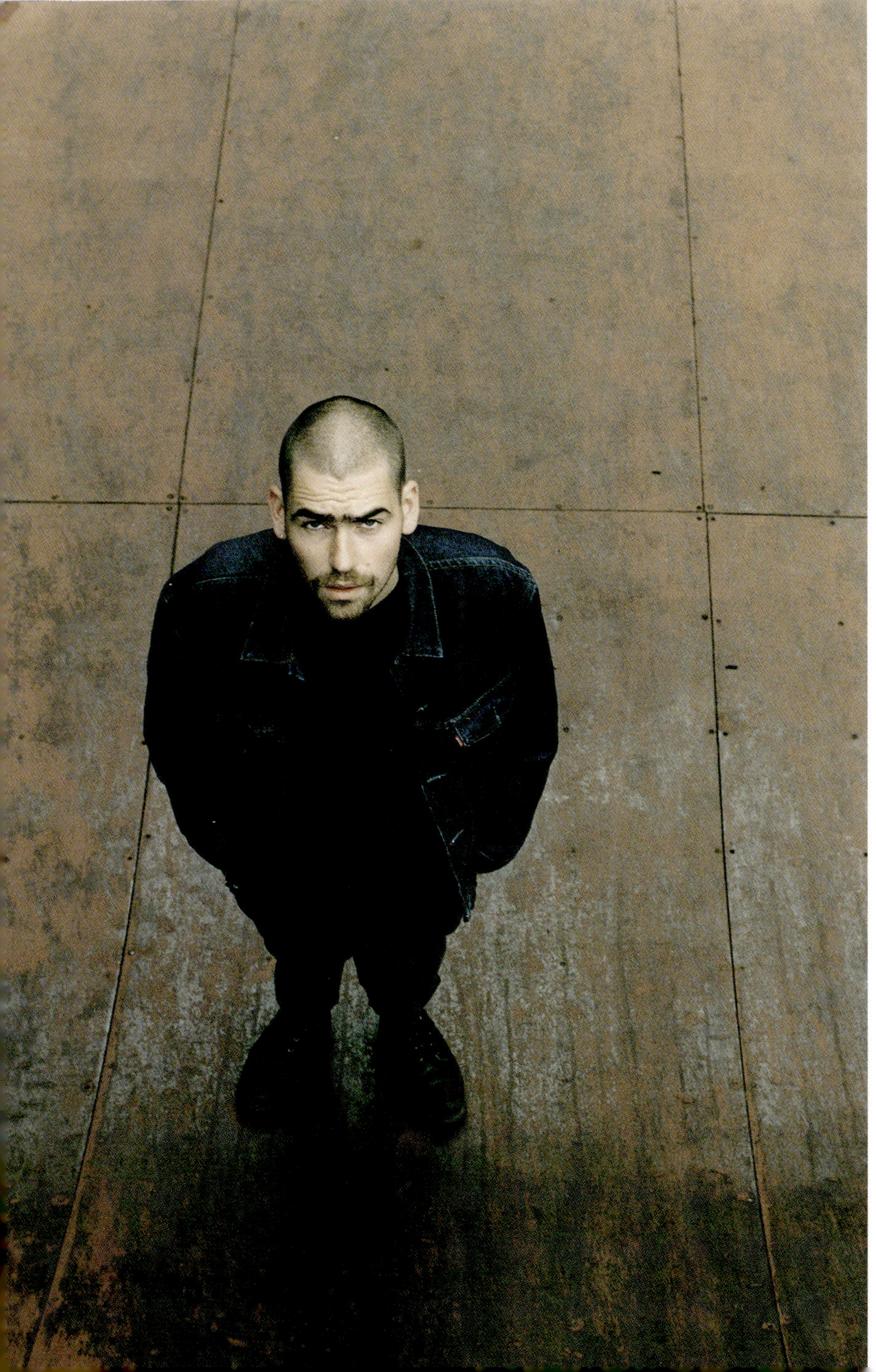

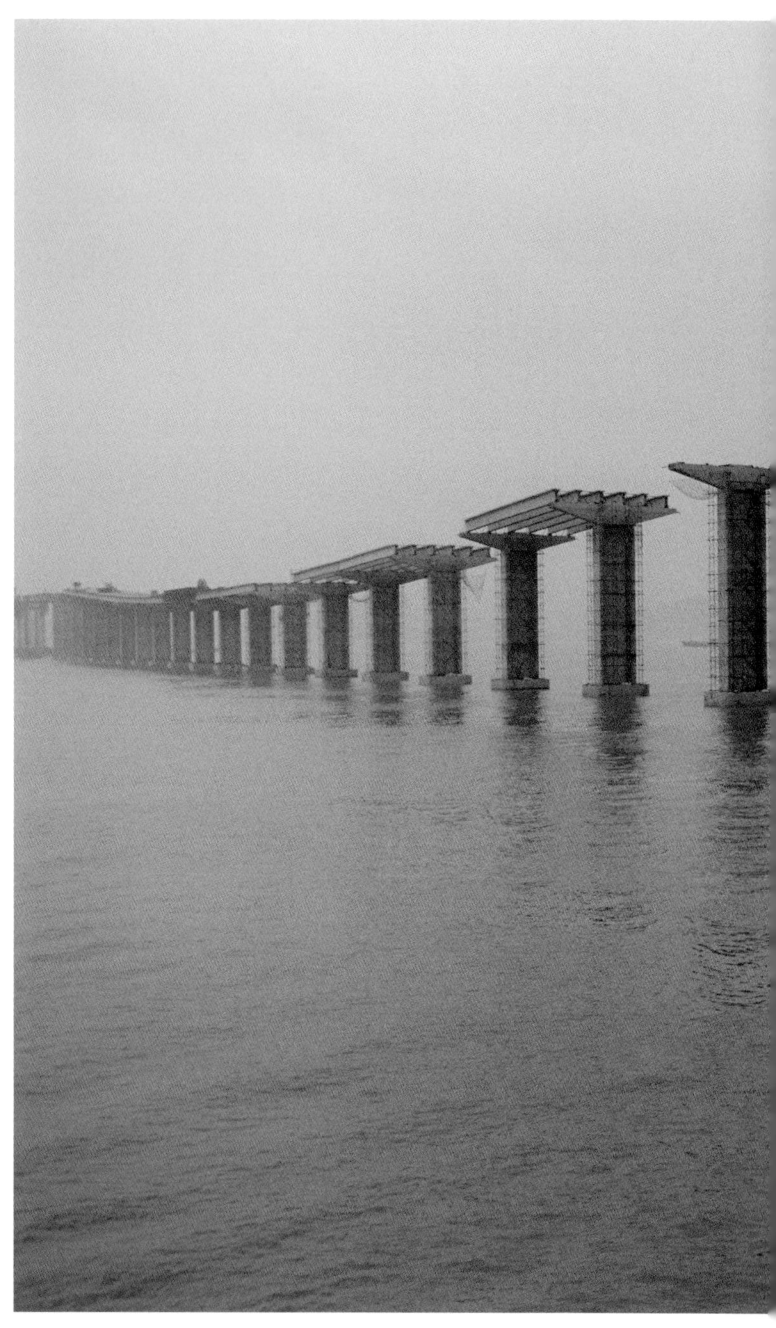

Macau Bridge, 1993

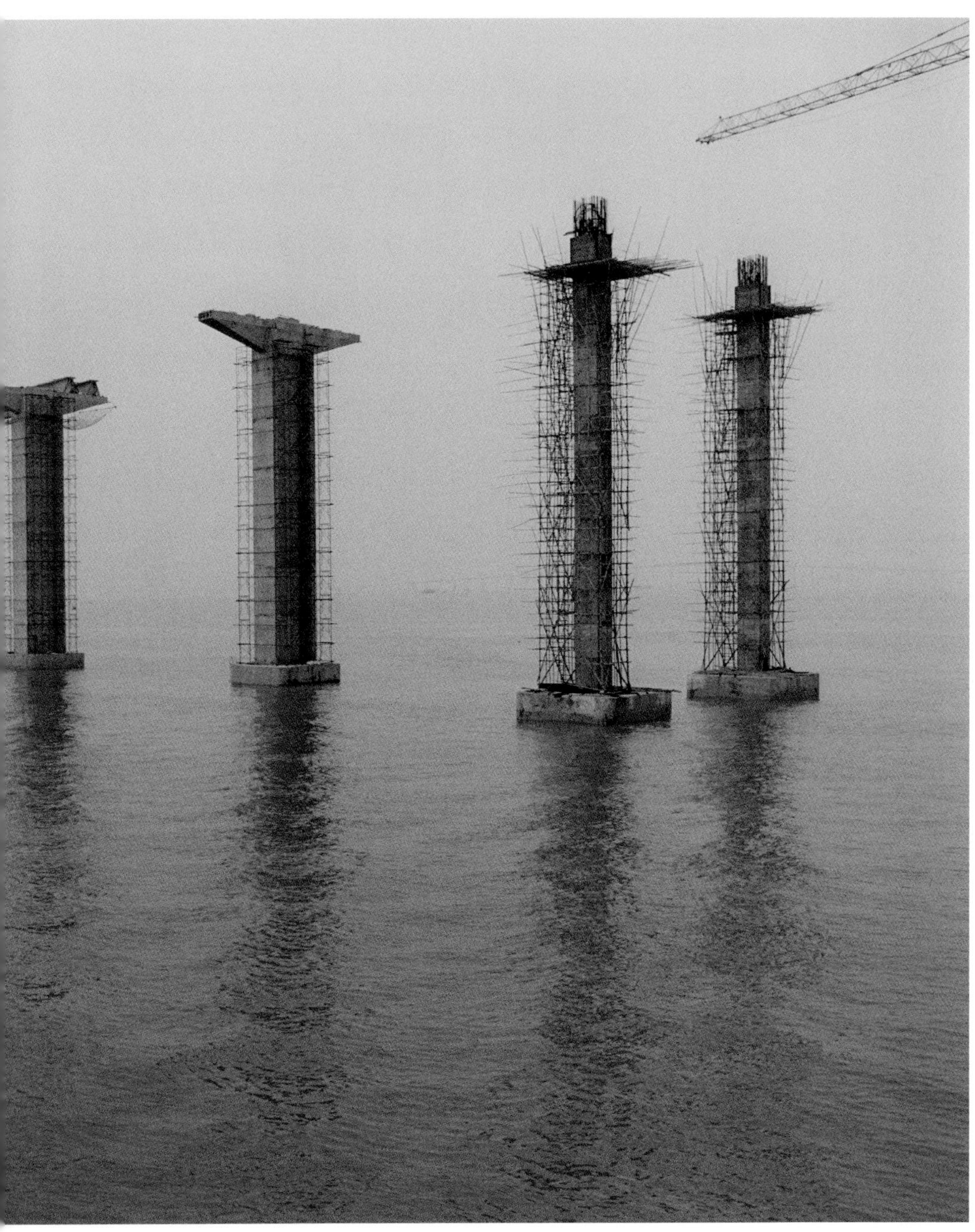

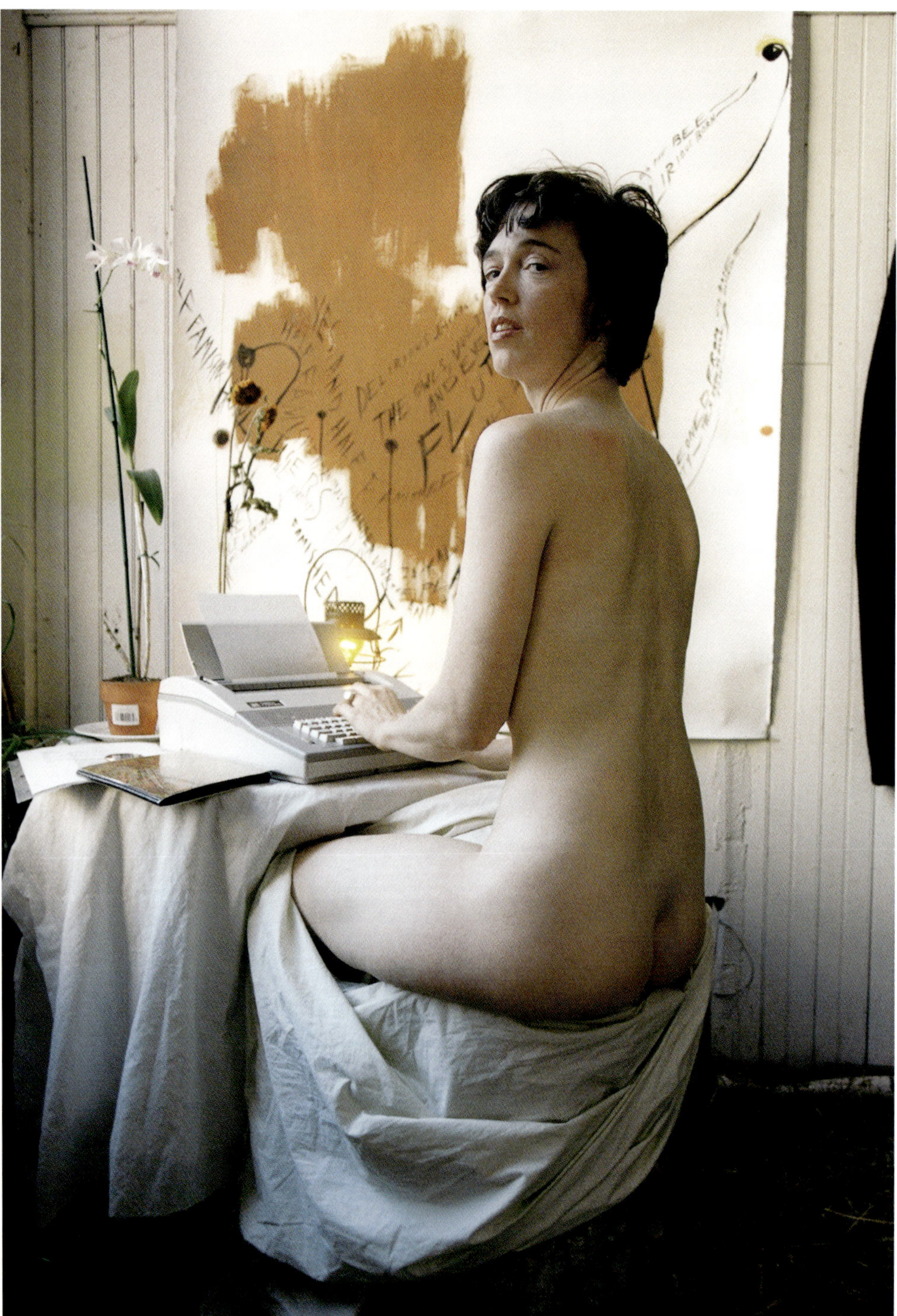

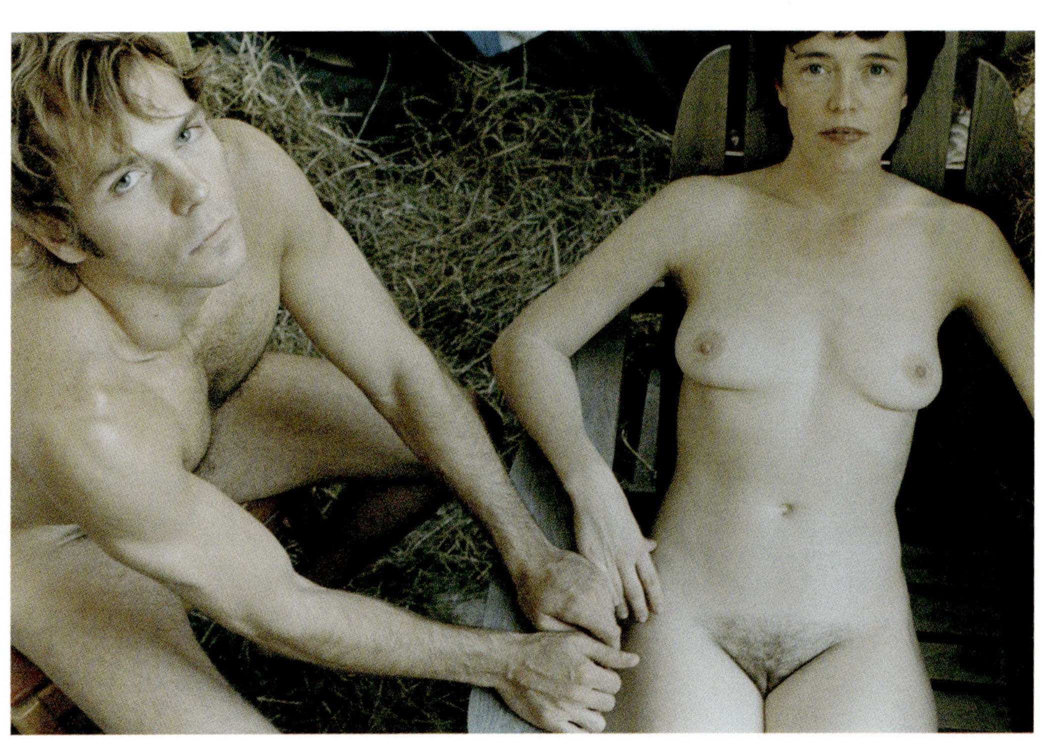

Paula with typewriter, 1994
John & Paula, hay, CX 1000, 1994

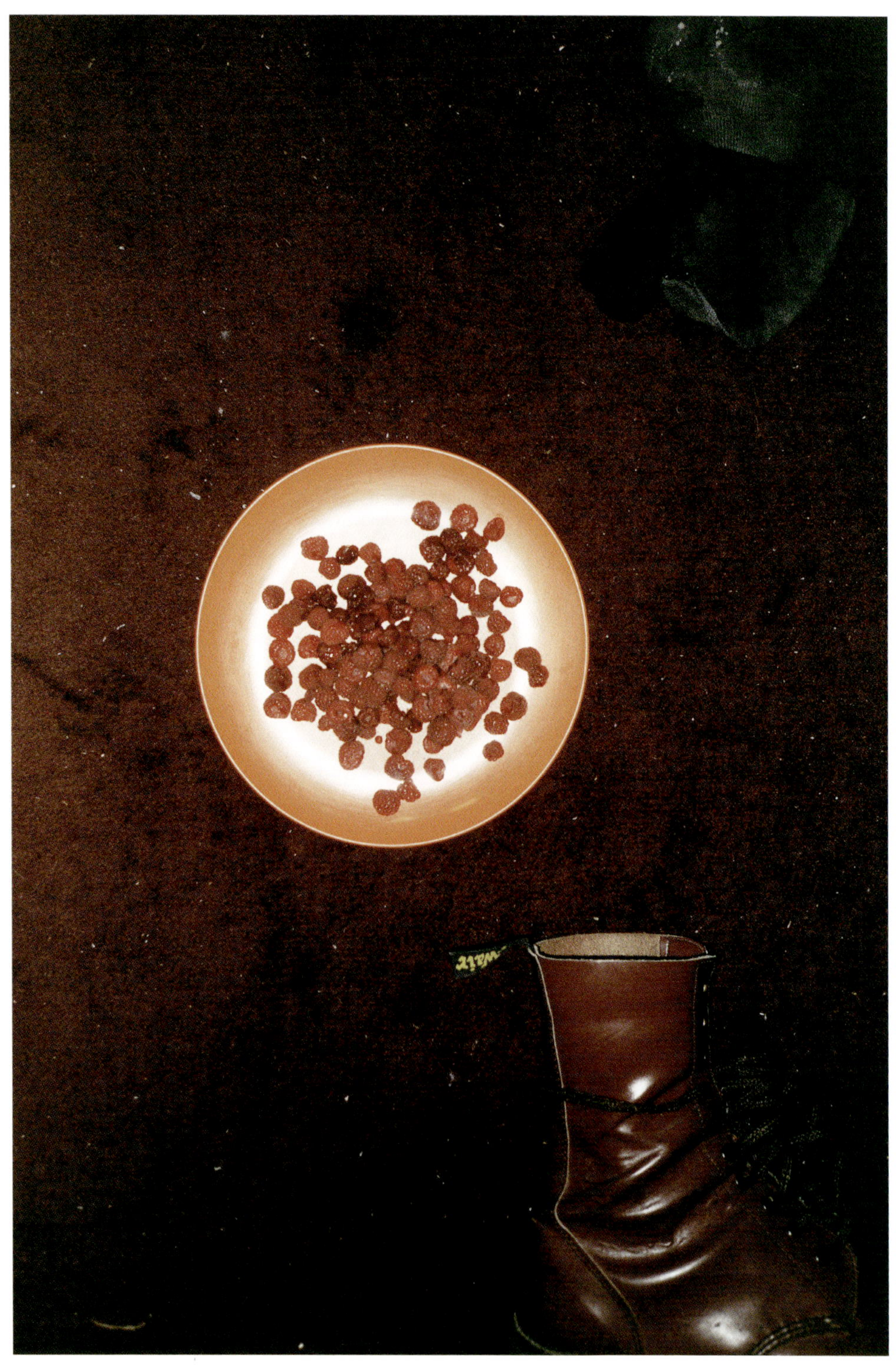

raspberries & boot, 1994

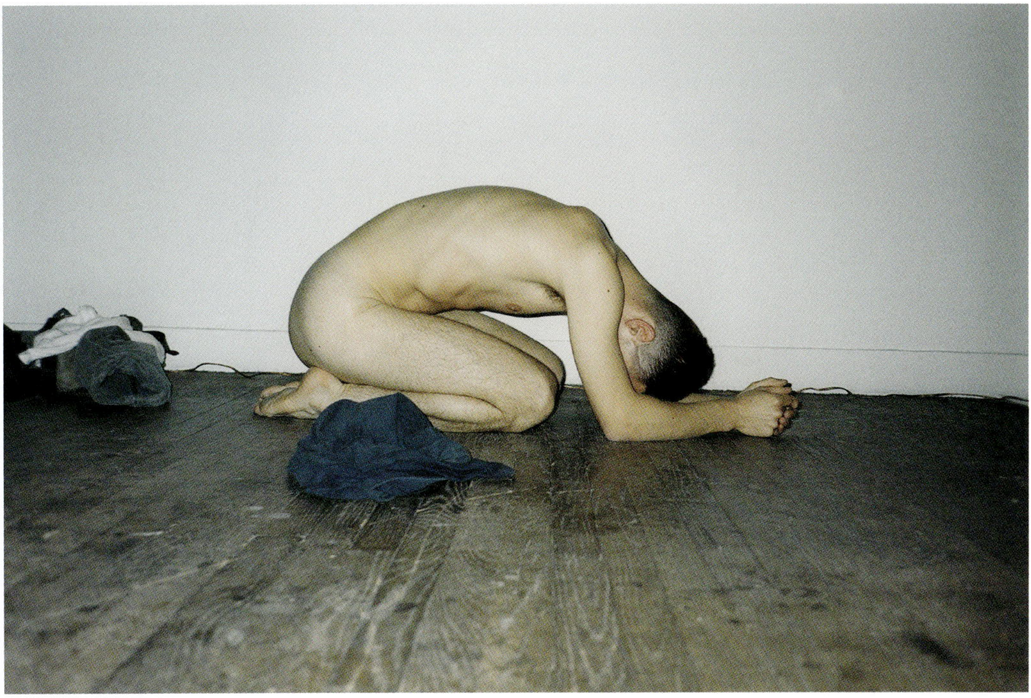

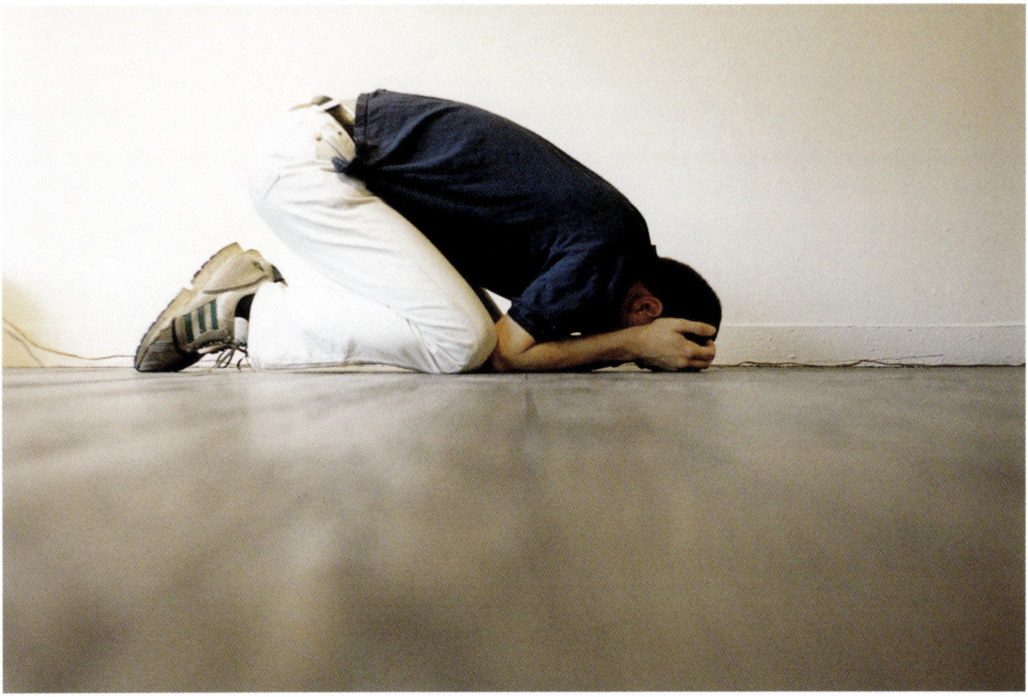

like praying I & II, 1994

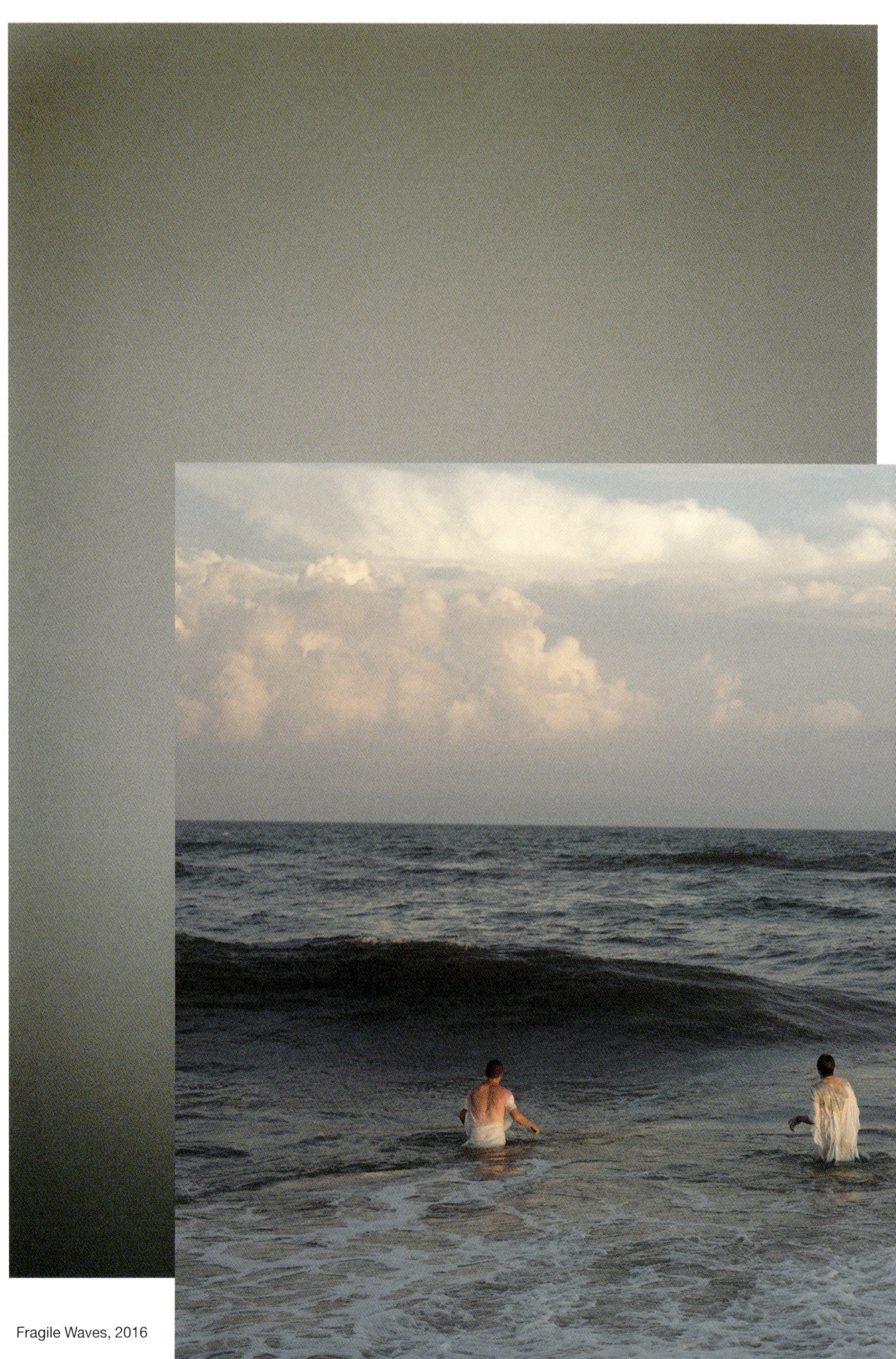

Fragile Waves, 2016

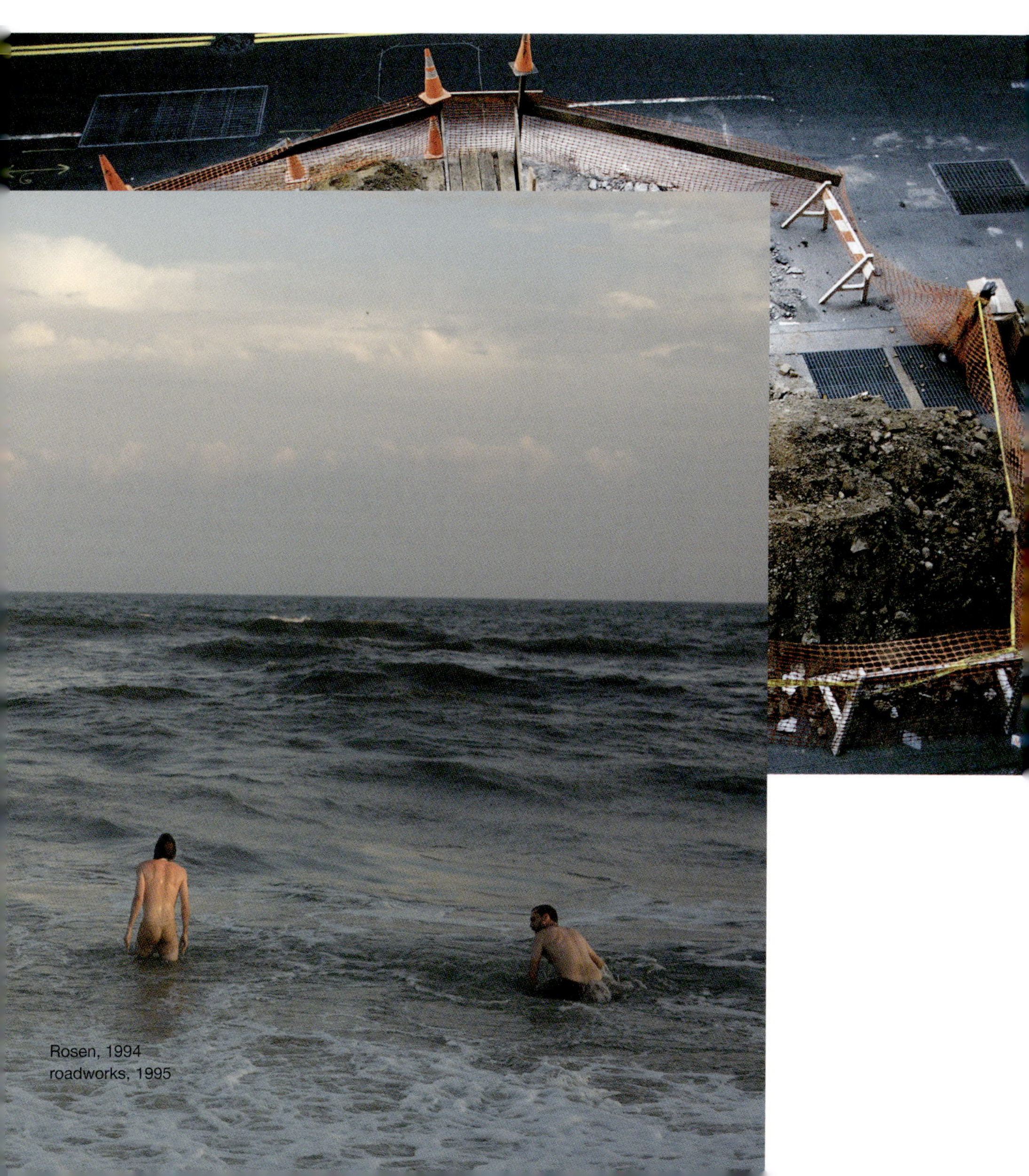

Rosen, 1994
roadworks, 1995

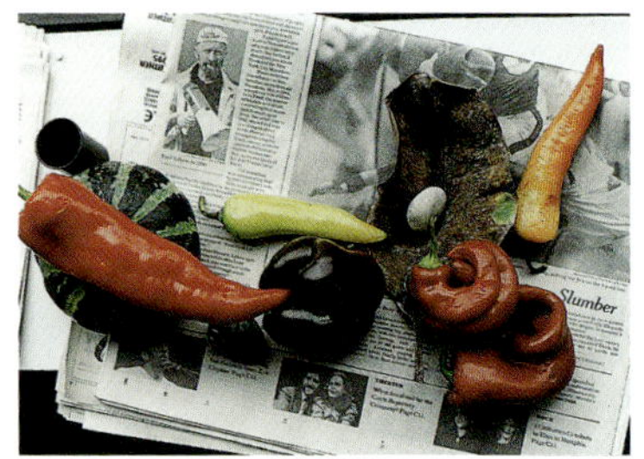

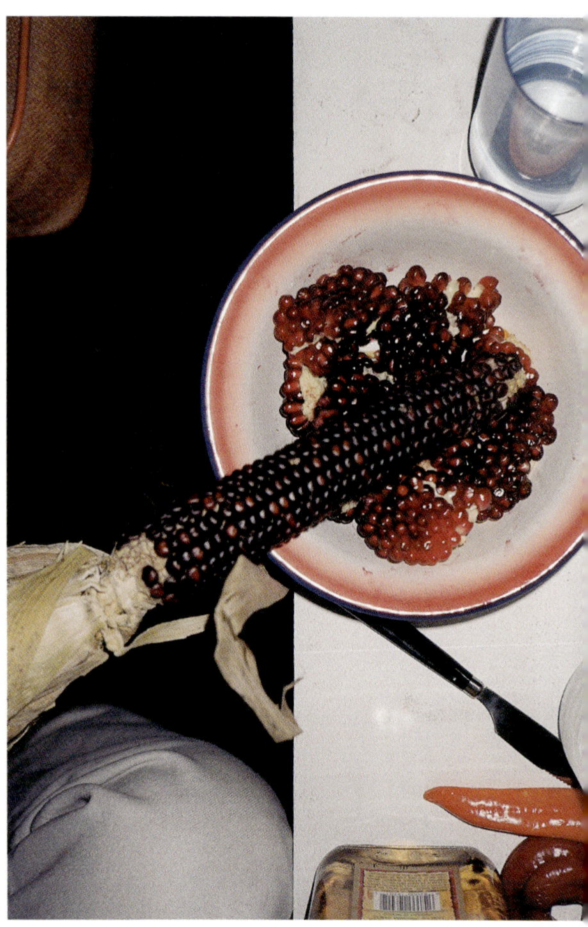

Peppers, 1994
indian corn & pomme granate, 1994

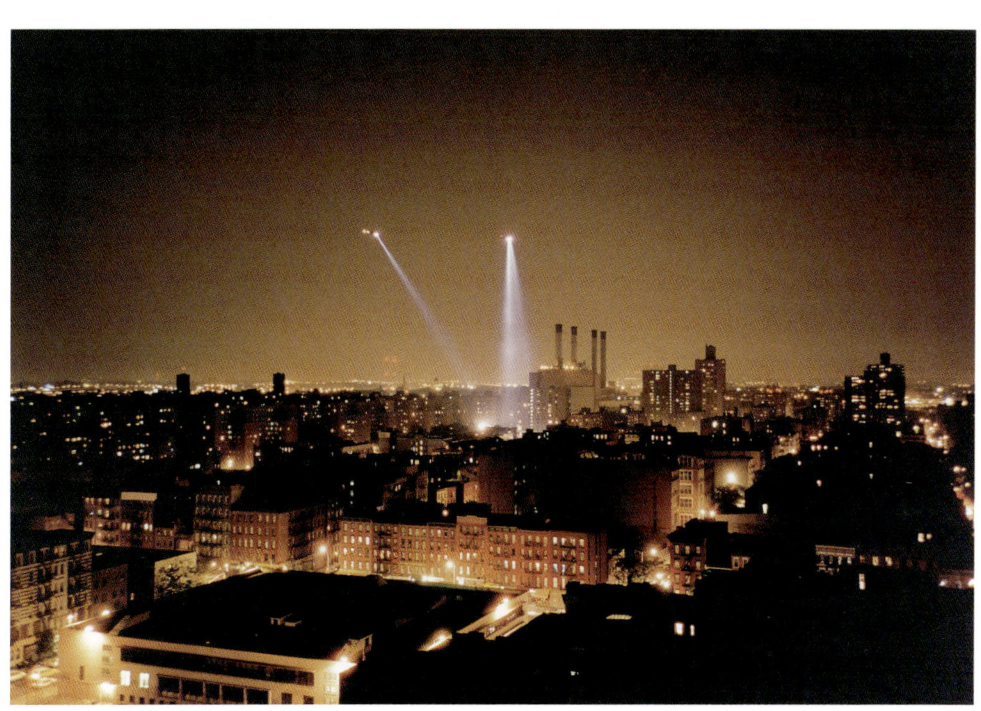

police helicopter, 1995

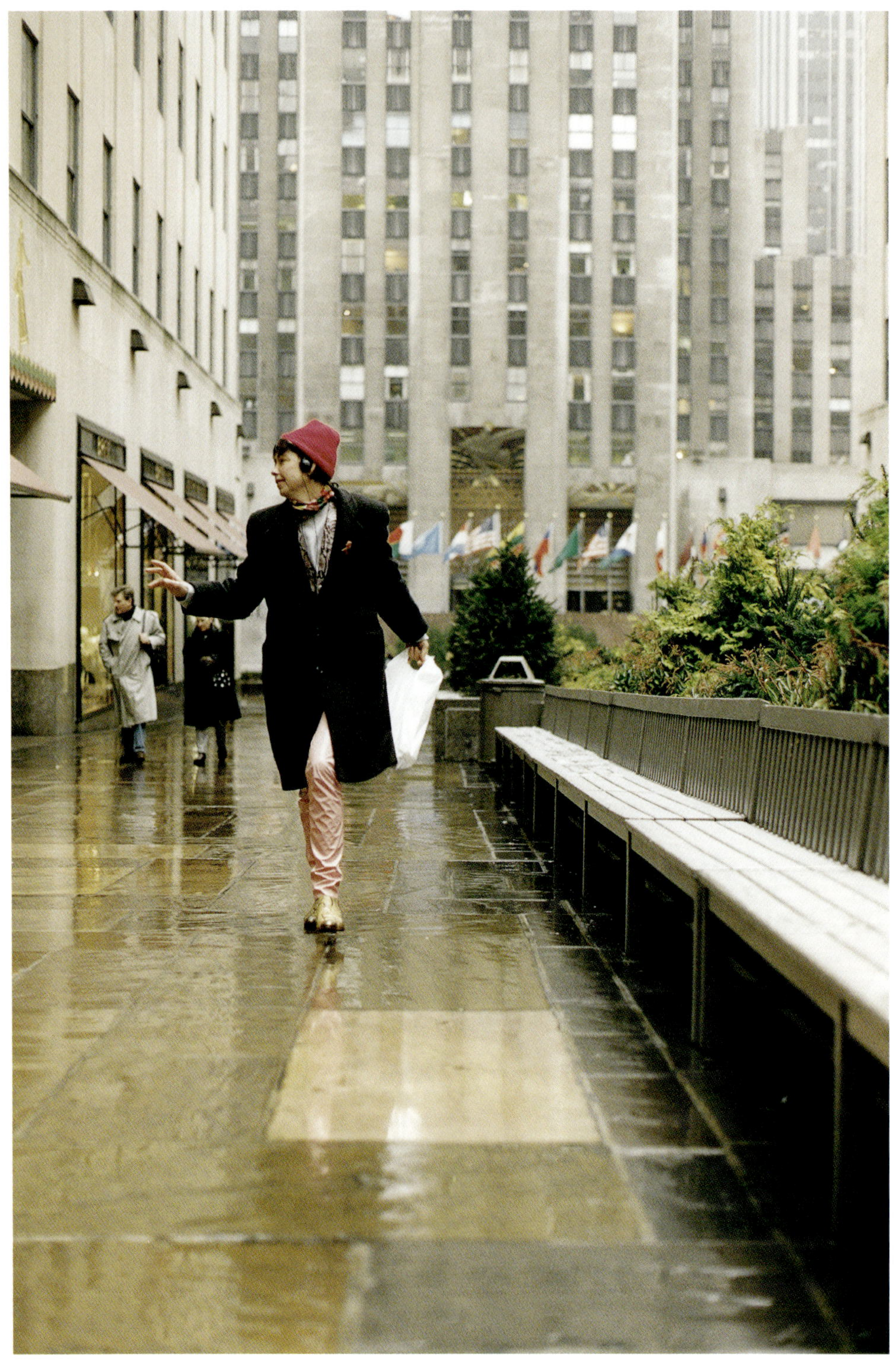

Isa dancing, 1995

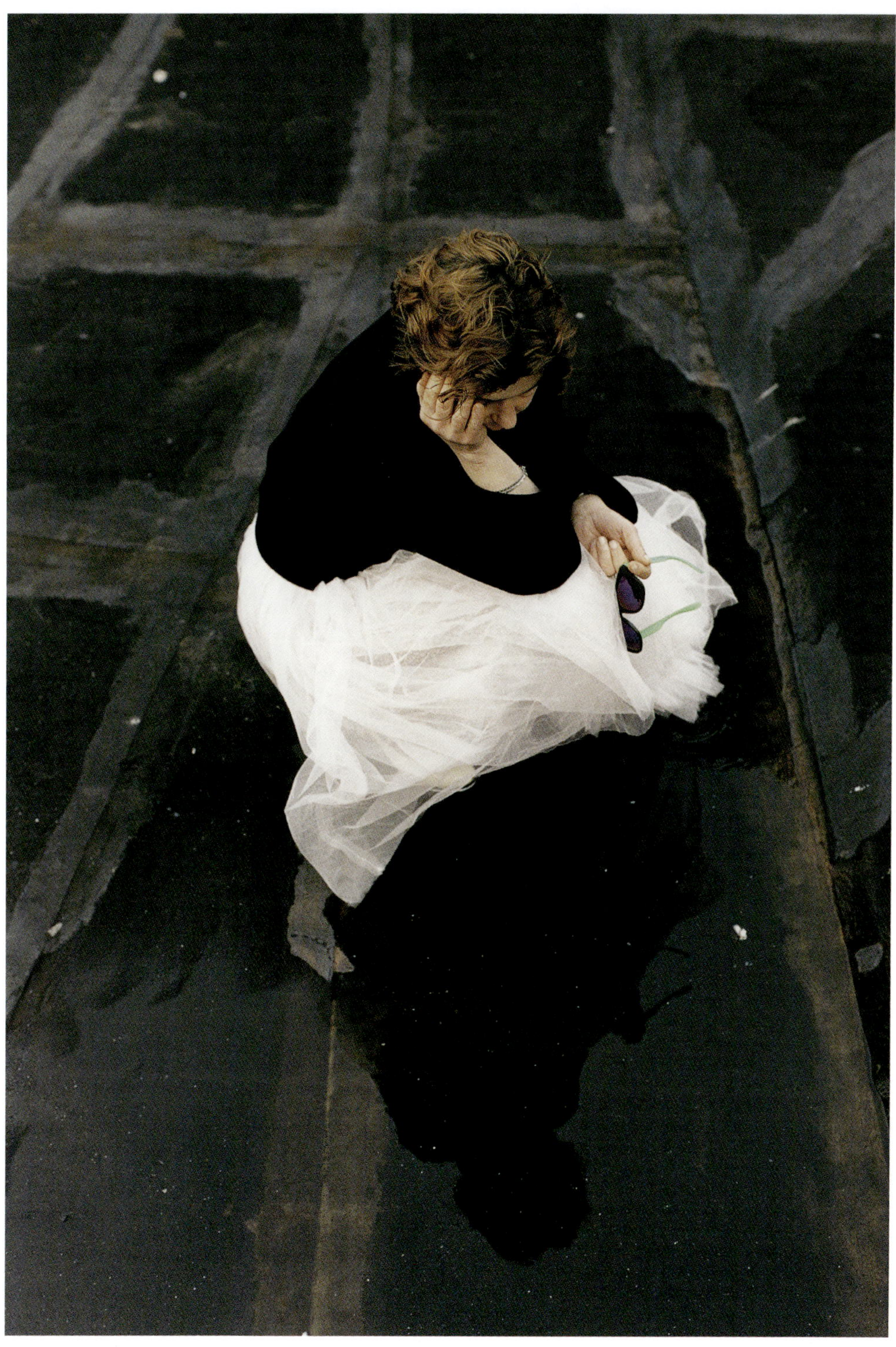

Isa with pool of water, 1995

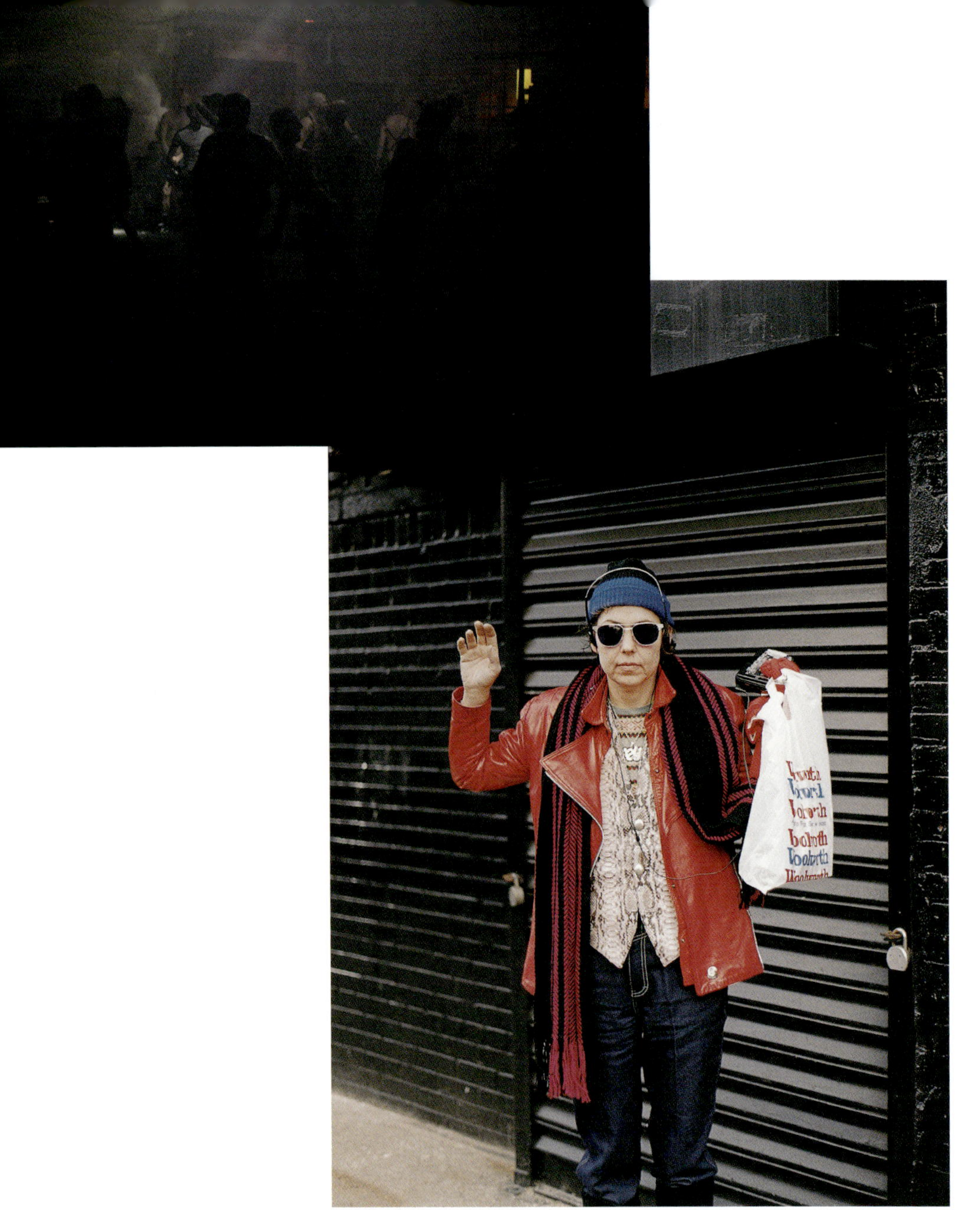

Easter, a, 2012
Isa vor Sound Factory, 1995
Haselmaus, 1995

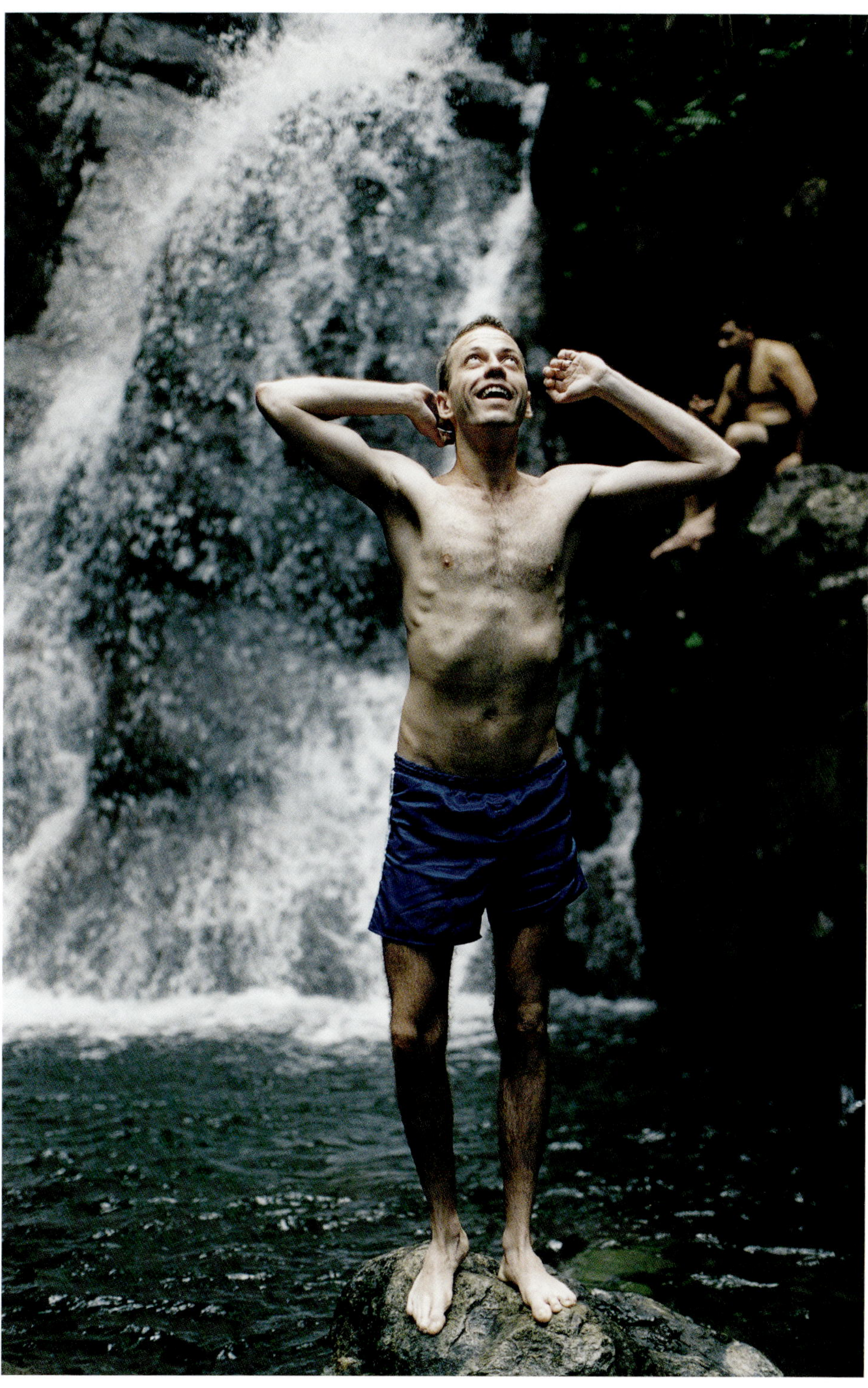

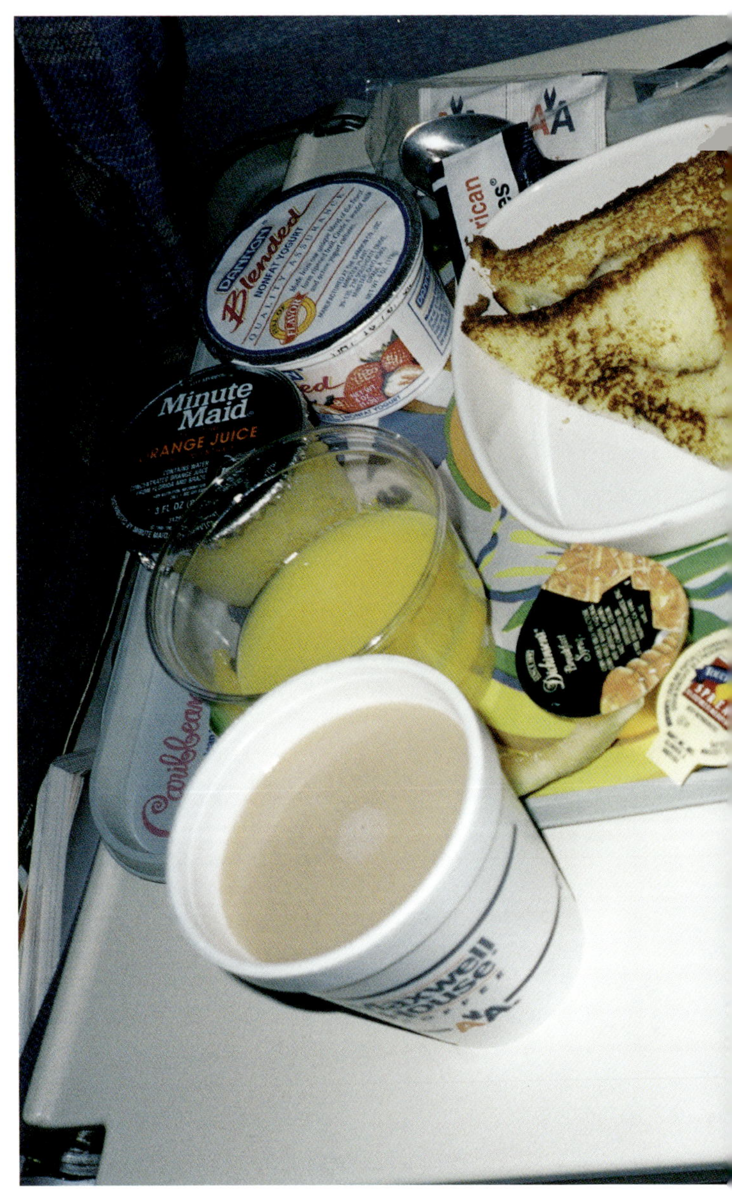

AA Breakfast, 1995

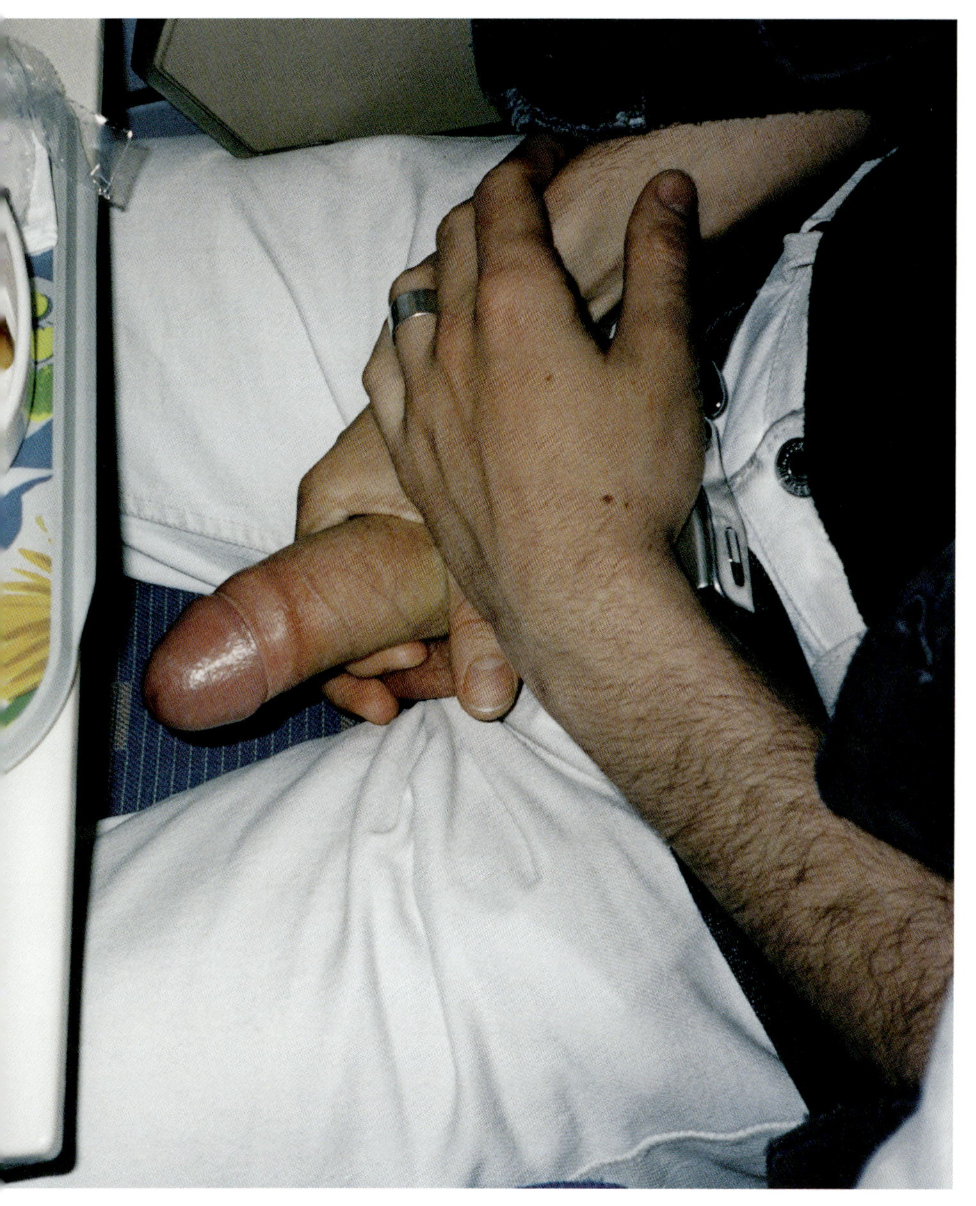

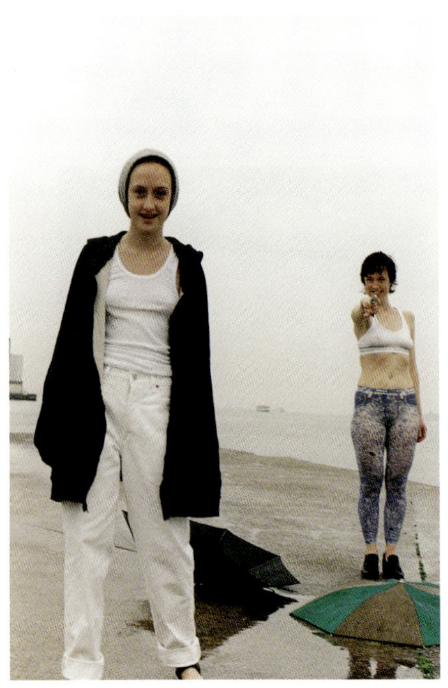

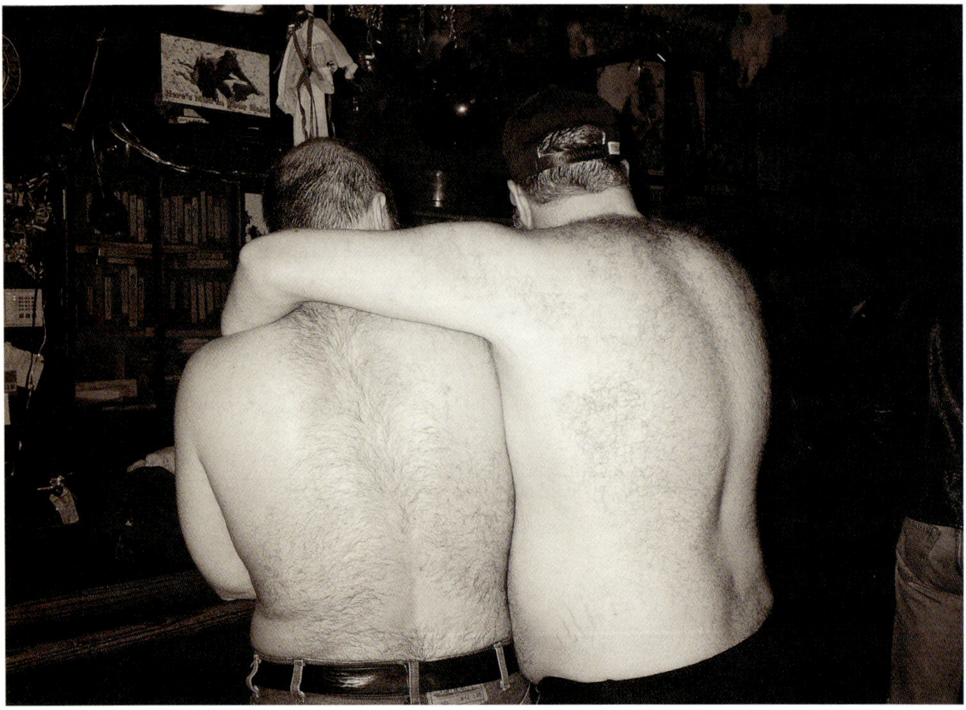

Rylan & Paula shooting, 1995
Hole In The Wall, 1995

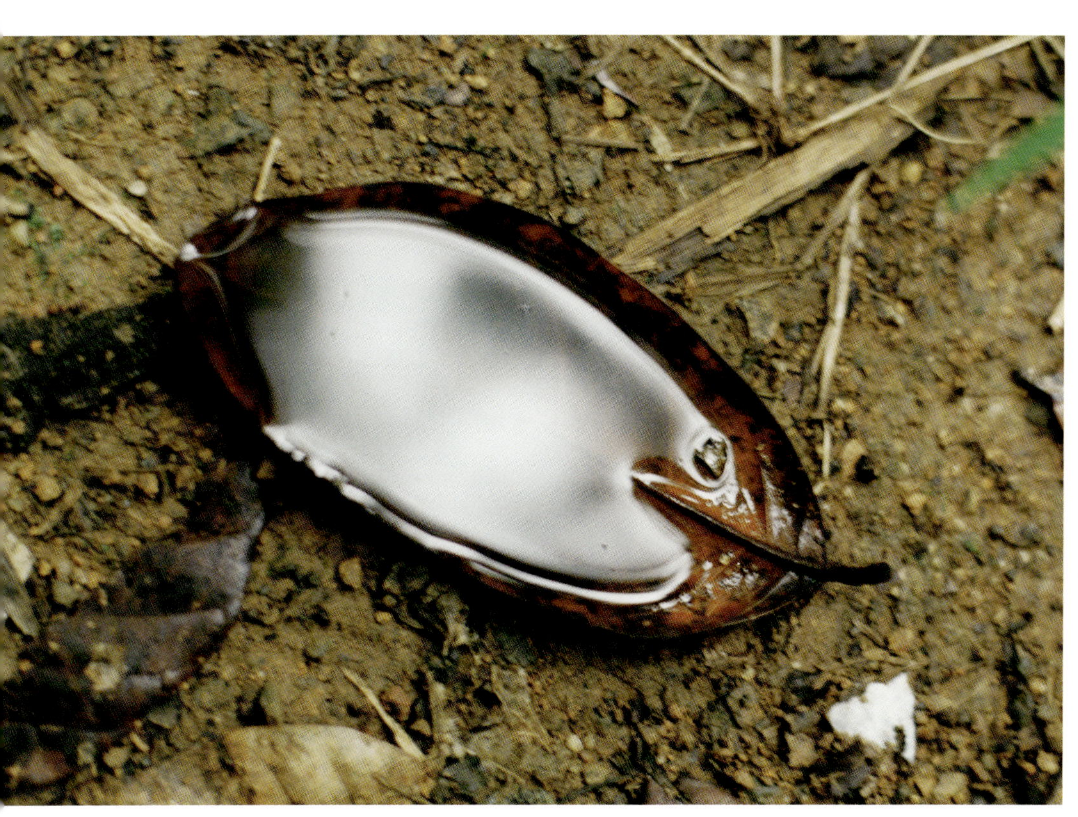

Leaf, 1995
moonrise, Puerto Rico, 1995 →

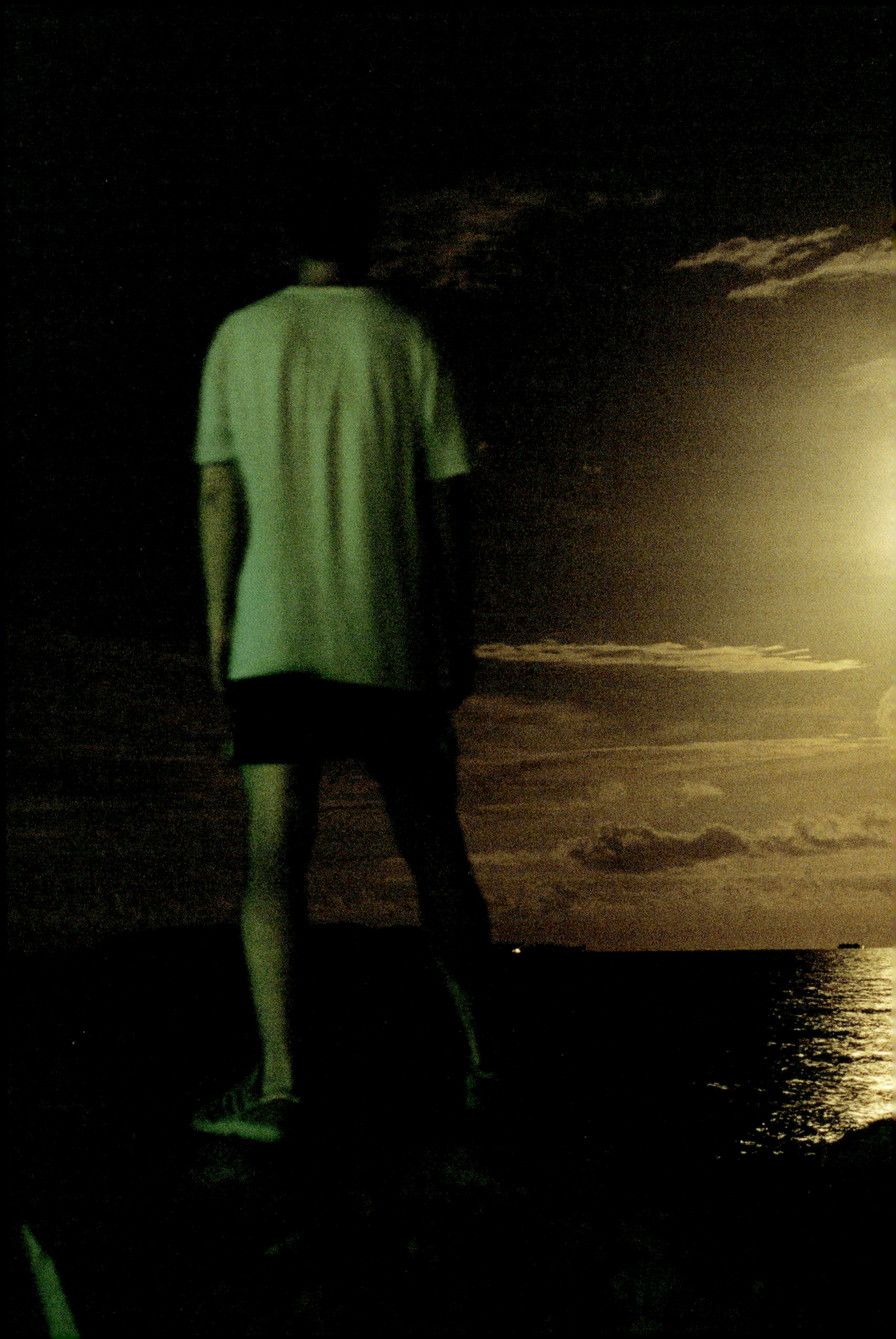

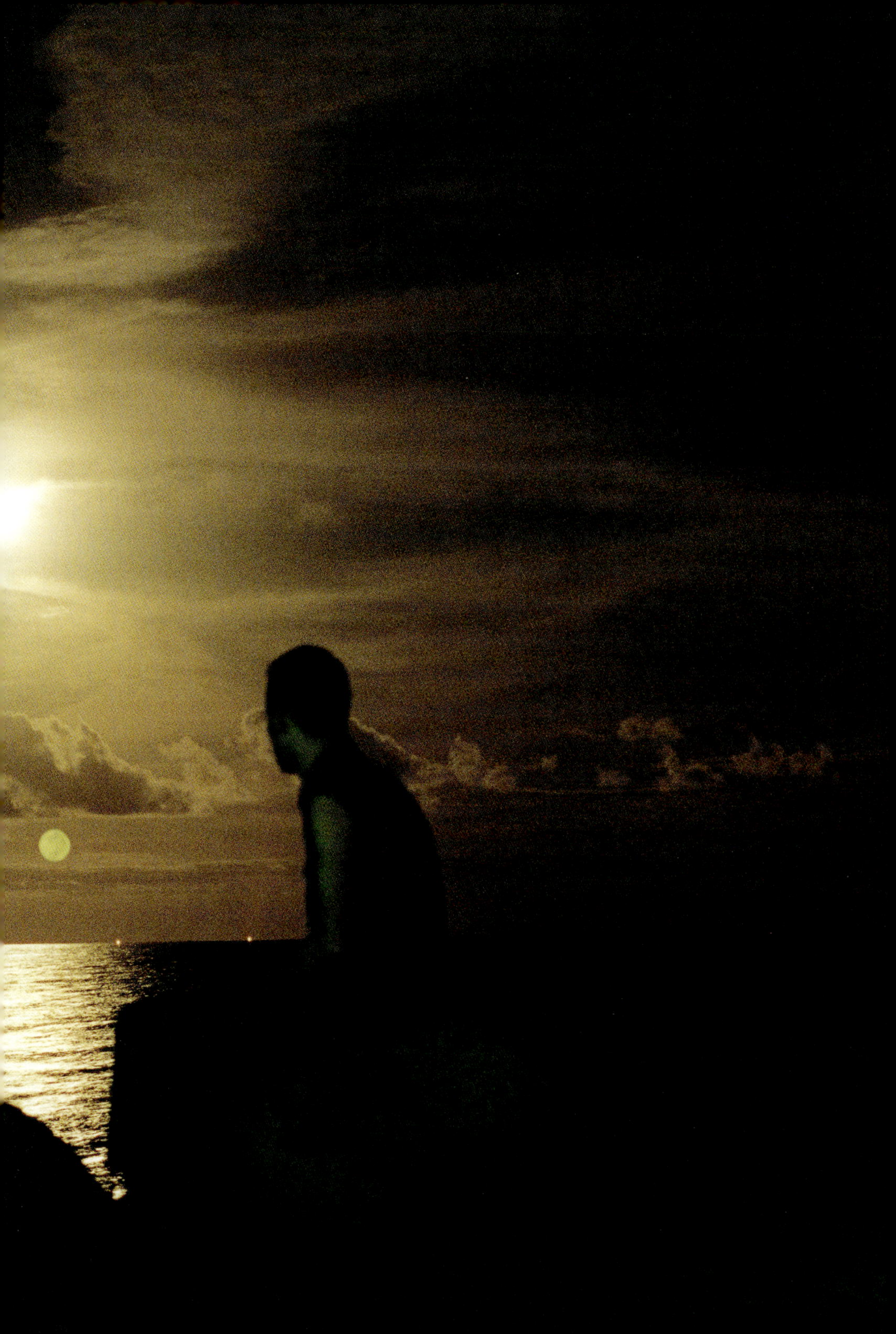

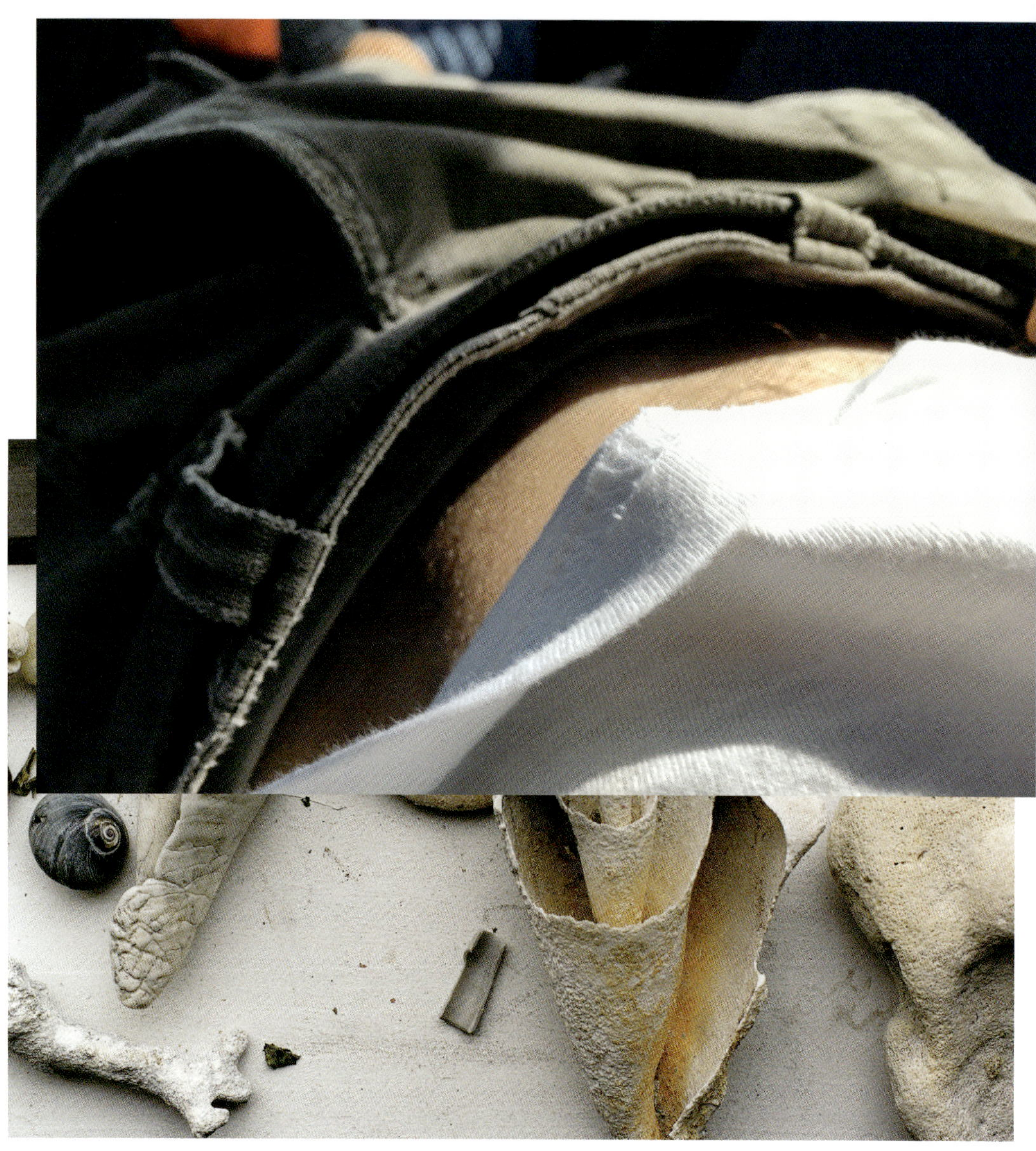

Shells, 1995   The Air Between, 2016

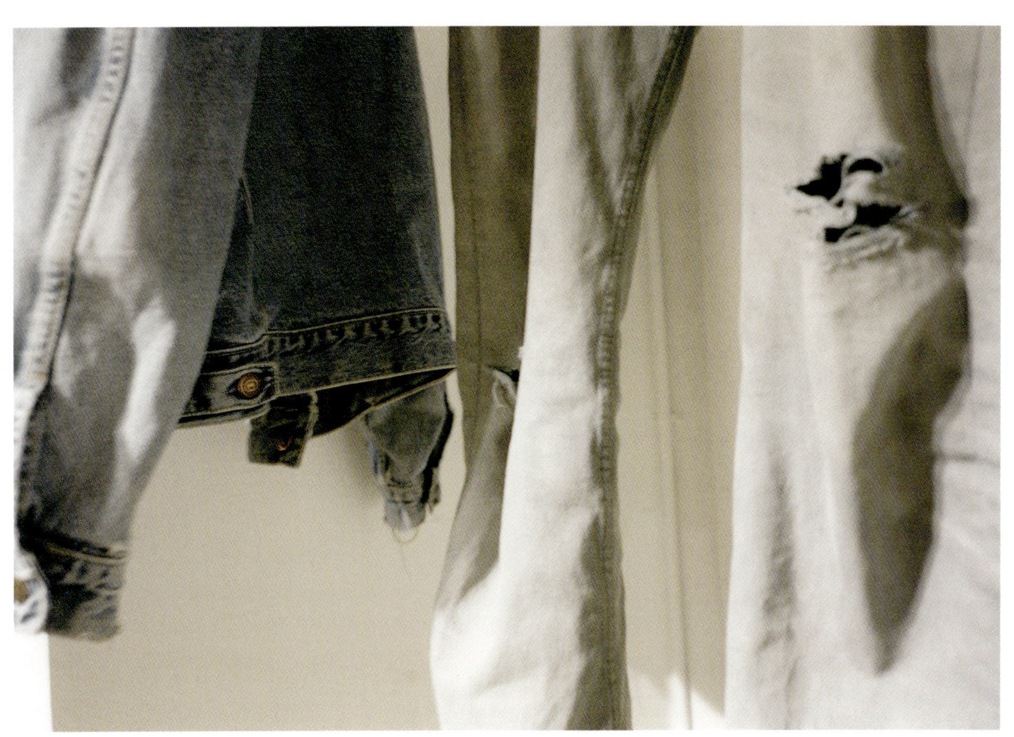

blue jacket, grey jeans, 1995

Liv Tyler, 1995

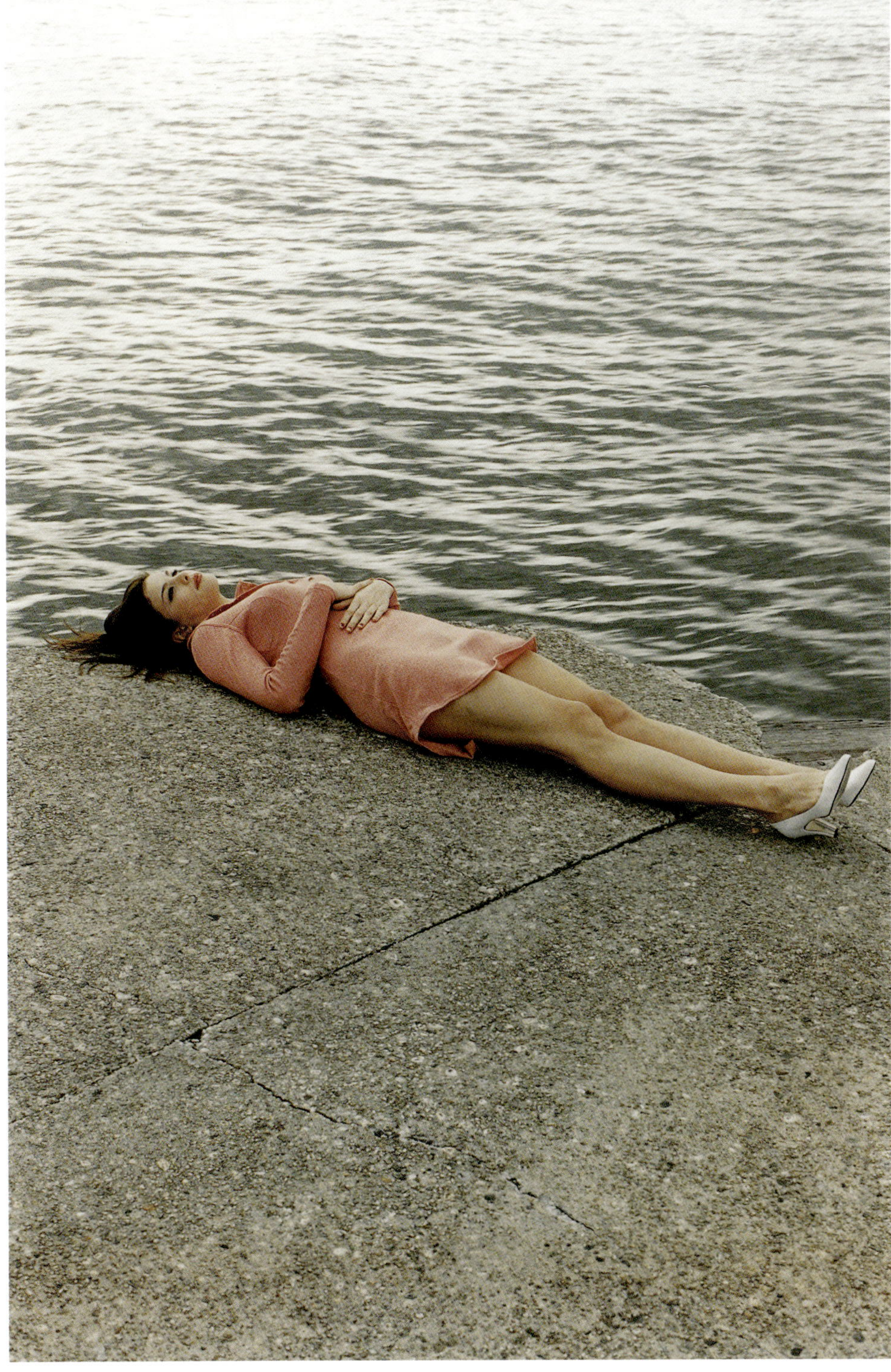

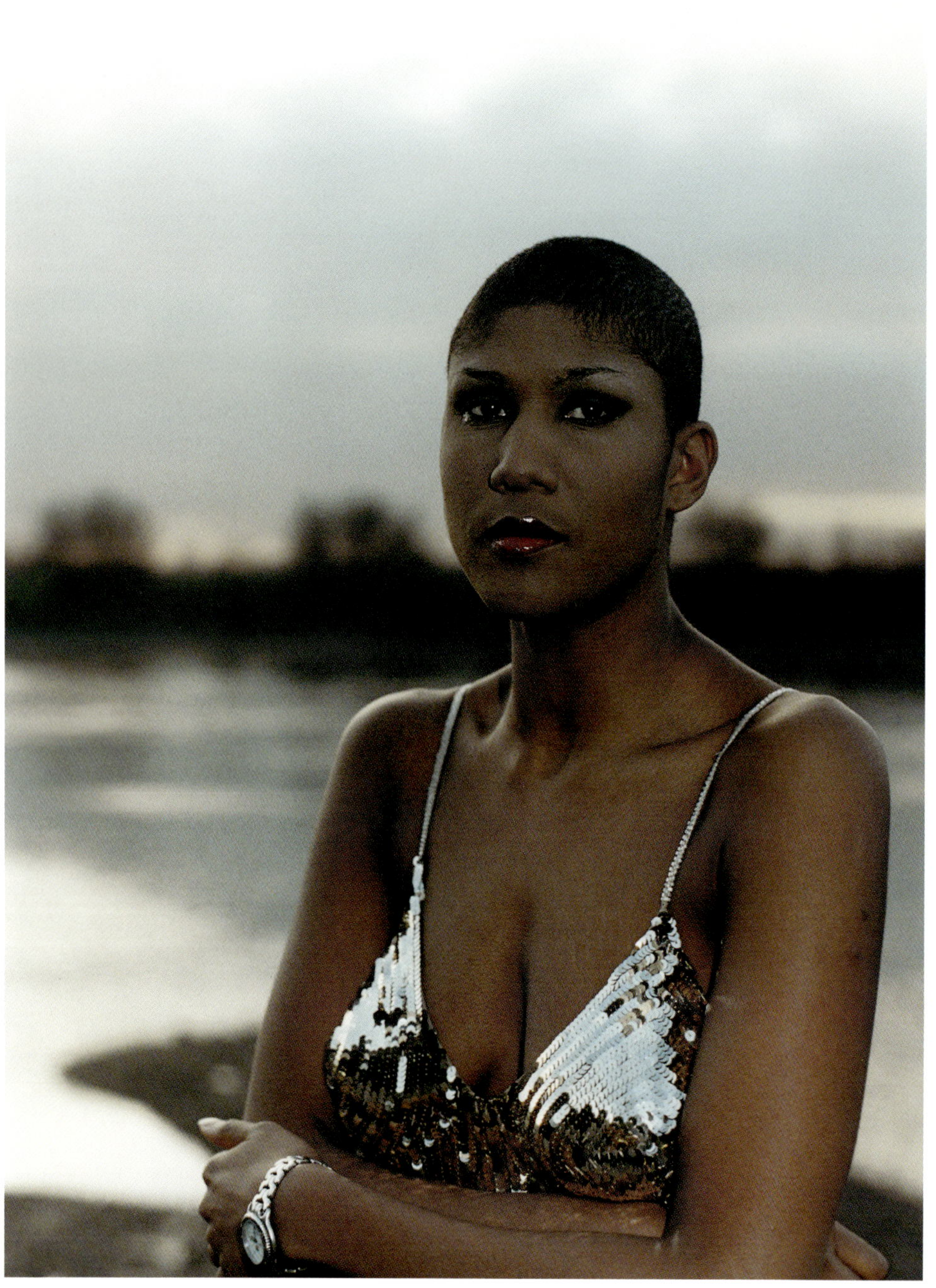

Smokin' Jo, 1995

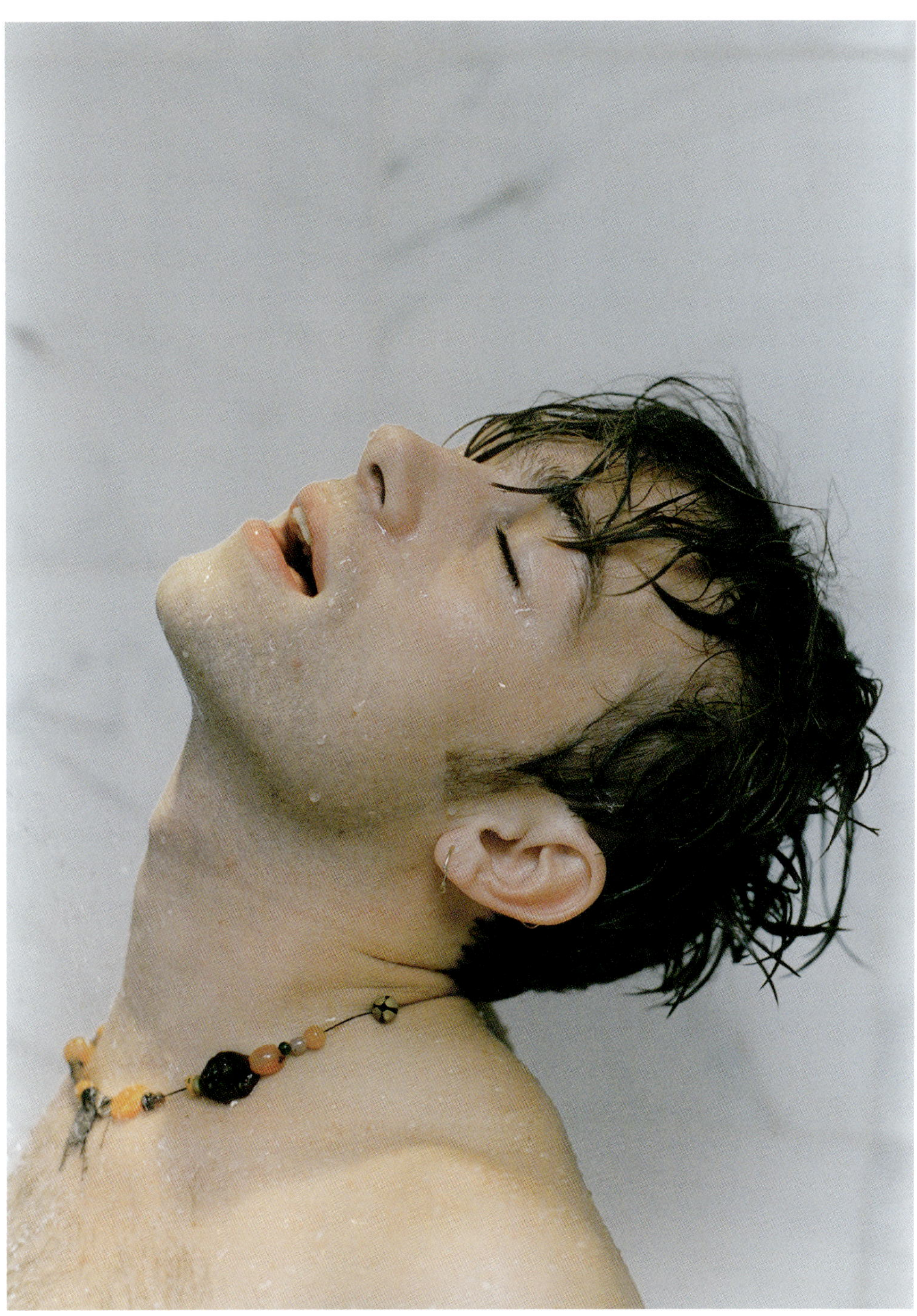

Damon, shower, head up, 1995

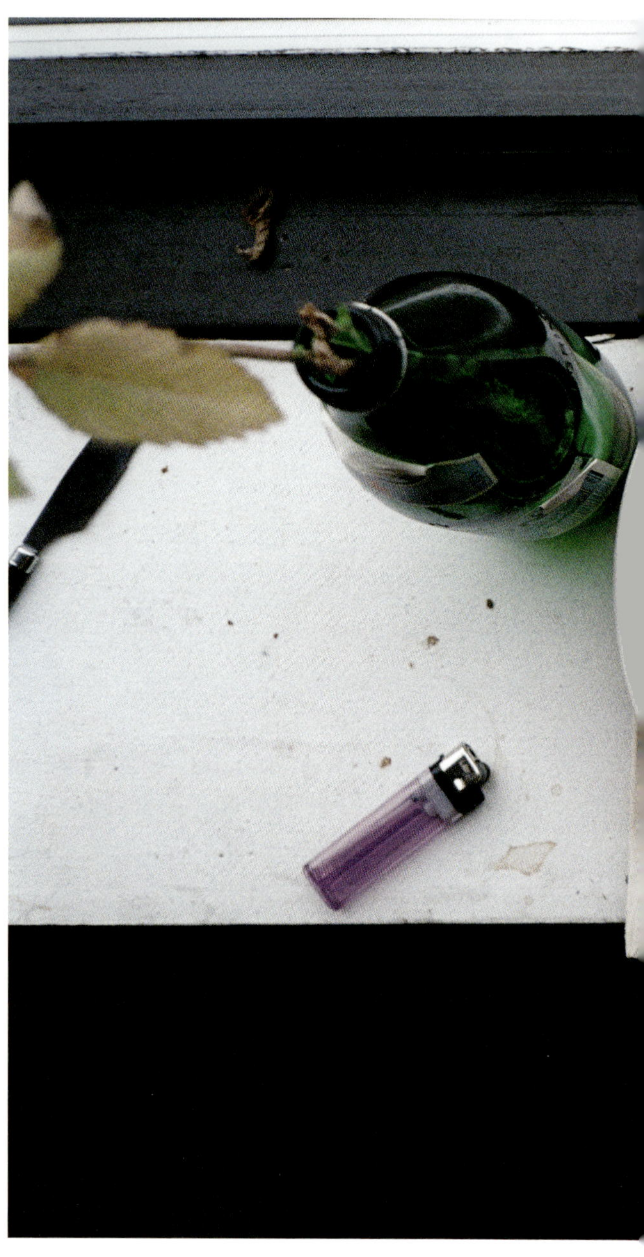

summer still life, 1995
Deer Hirsch, 1995 →

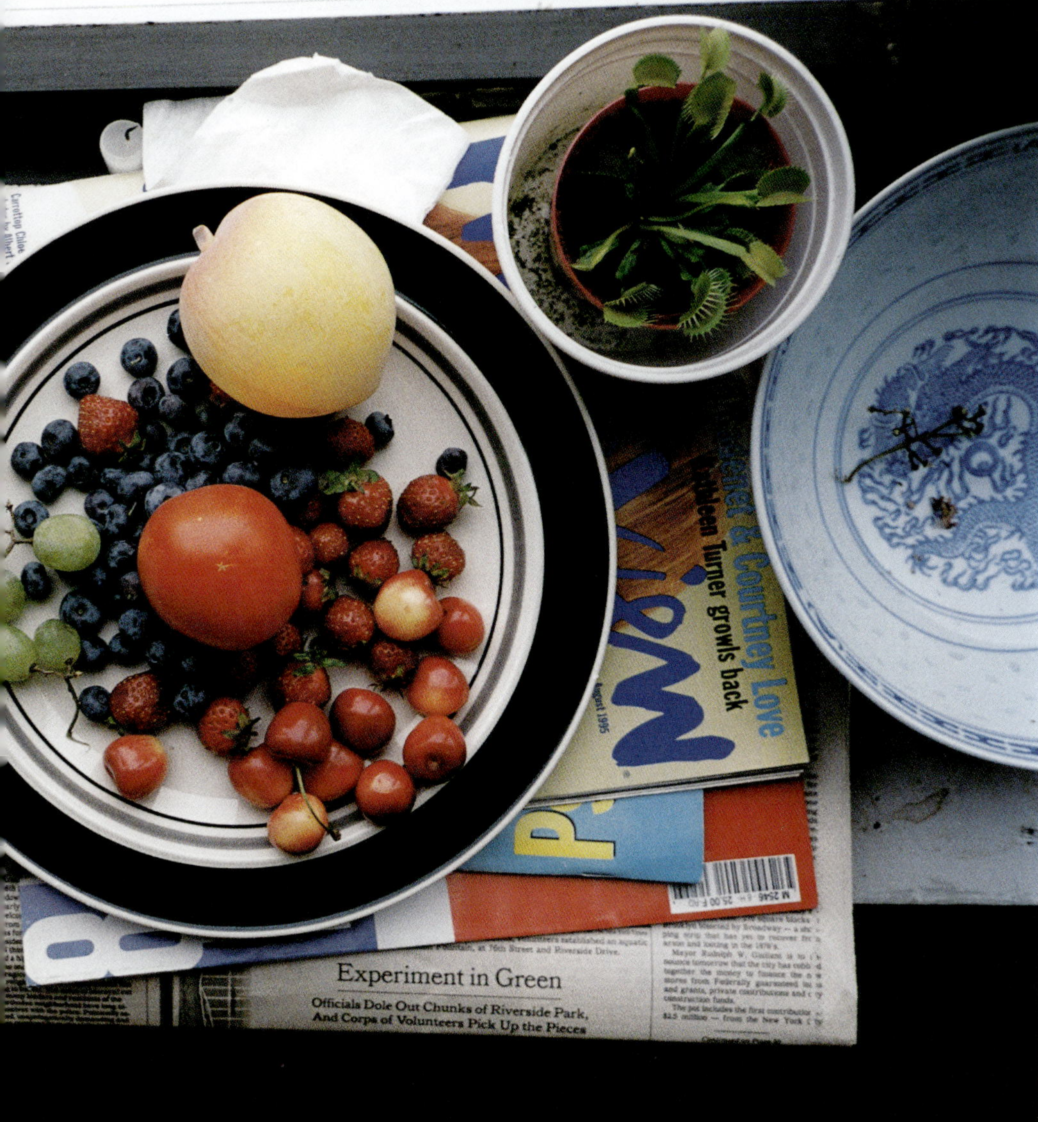
Courtney Love
Kathleen Turner growls back
August 1995
PaperView
P
Experiment in Green
Officials Dole Out Chunks of Riverside Park,
And Corps of Volunteers Pick Up the Pieces

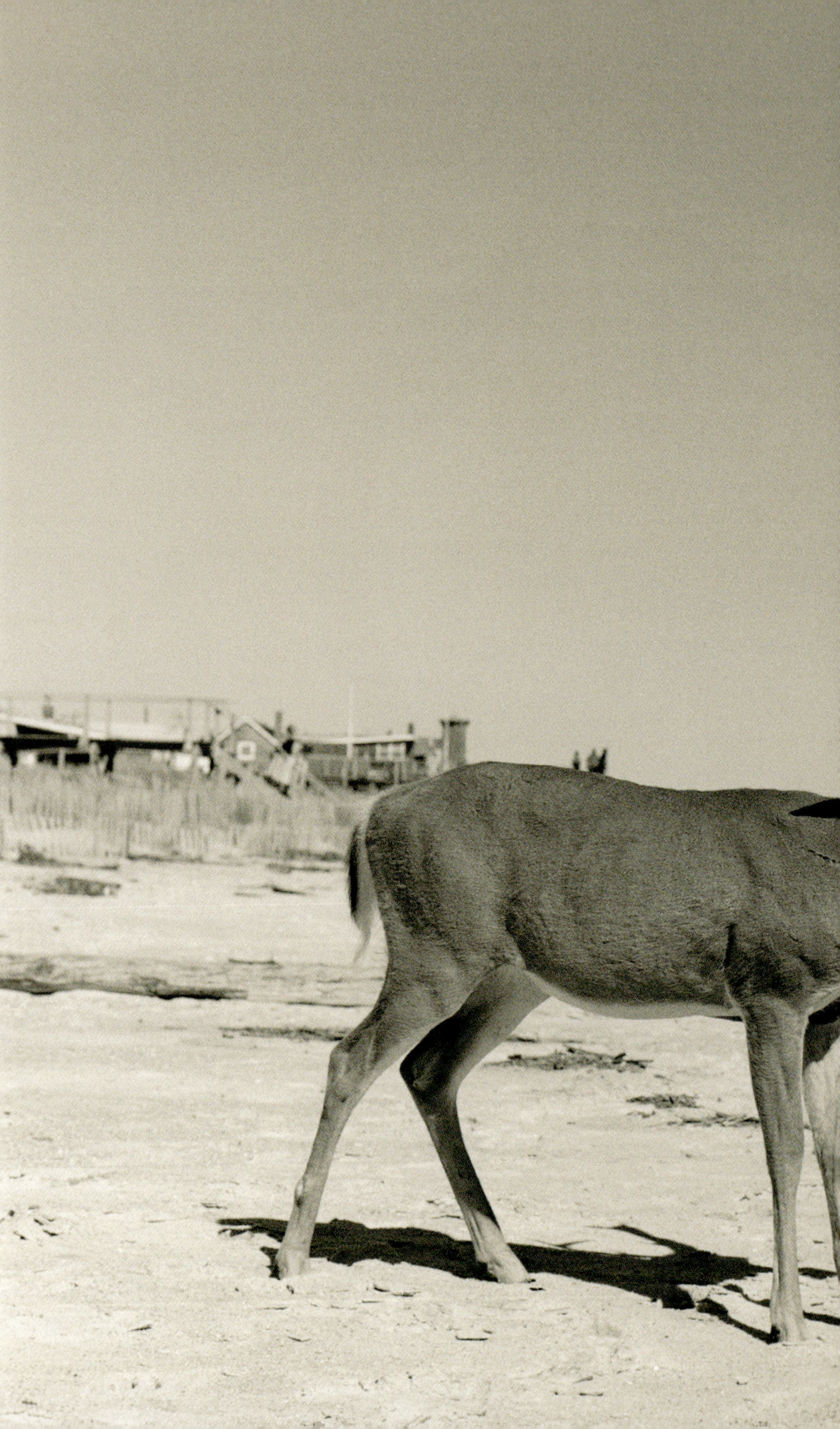

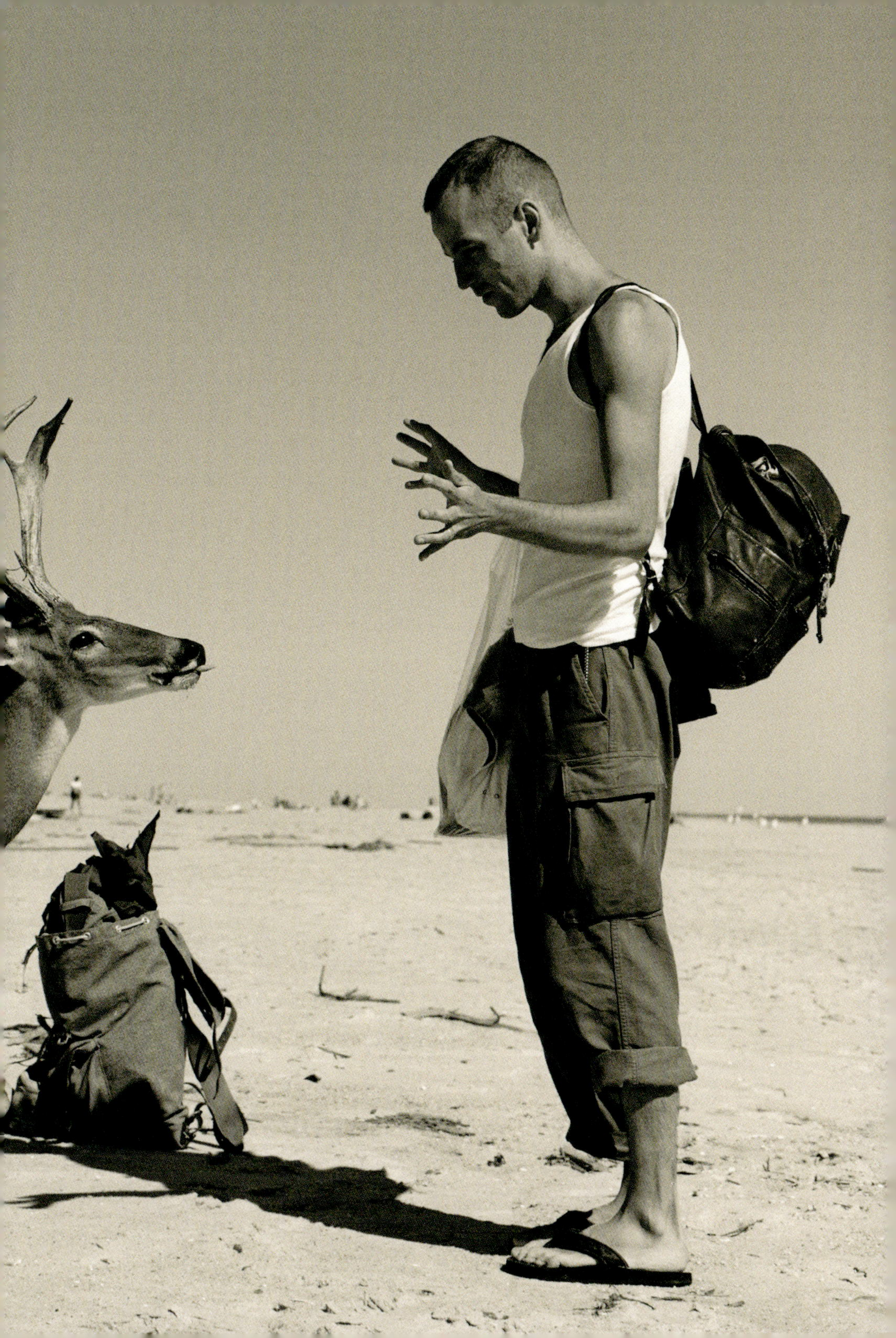

Hallenbad Detail, 1995

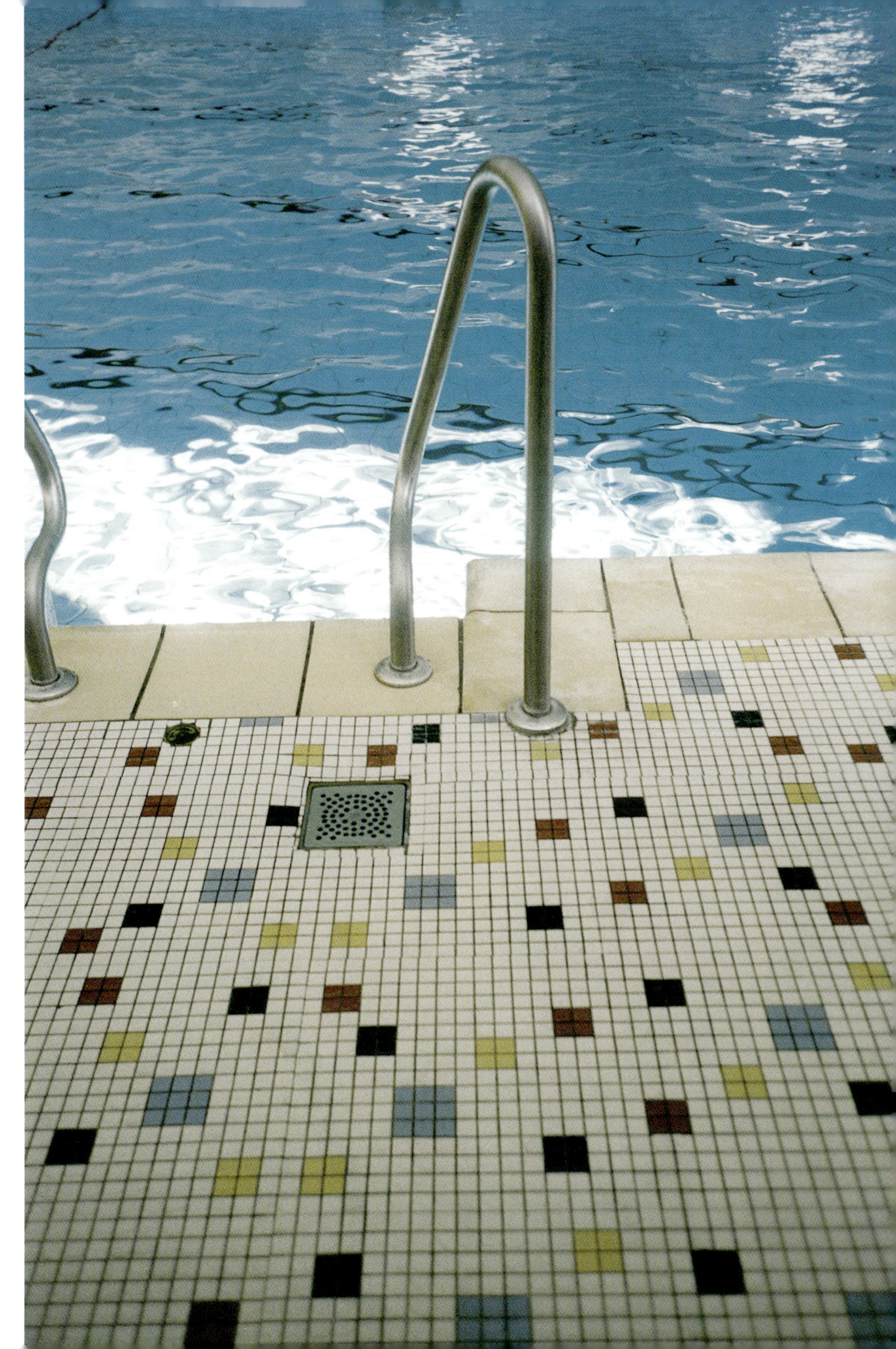

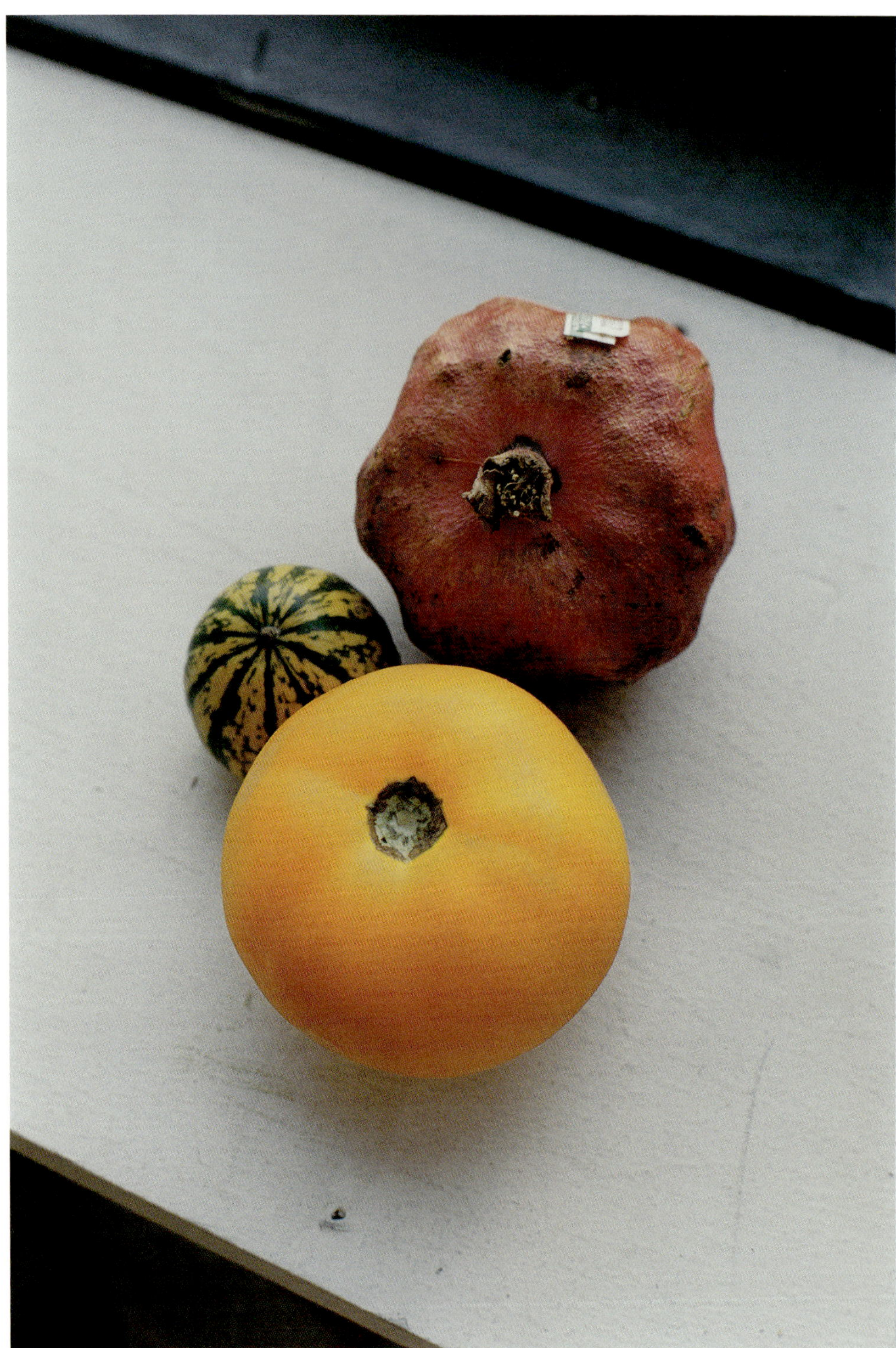

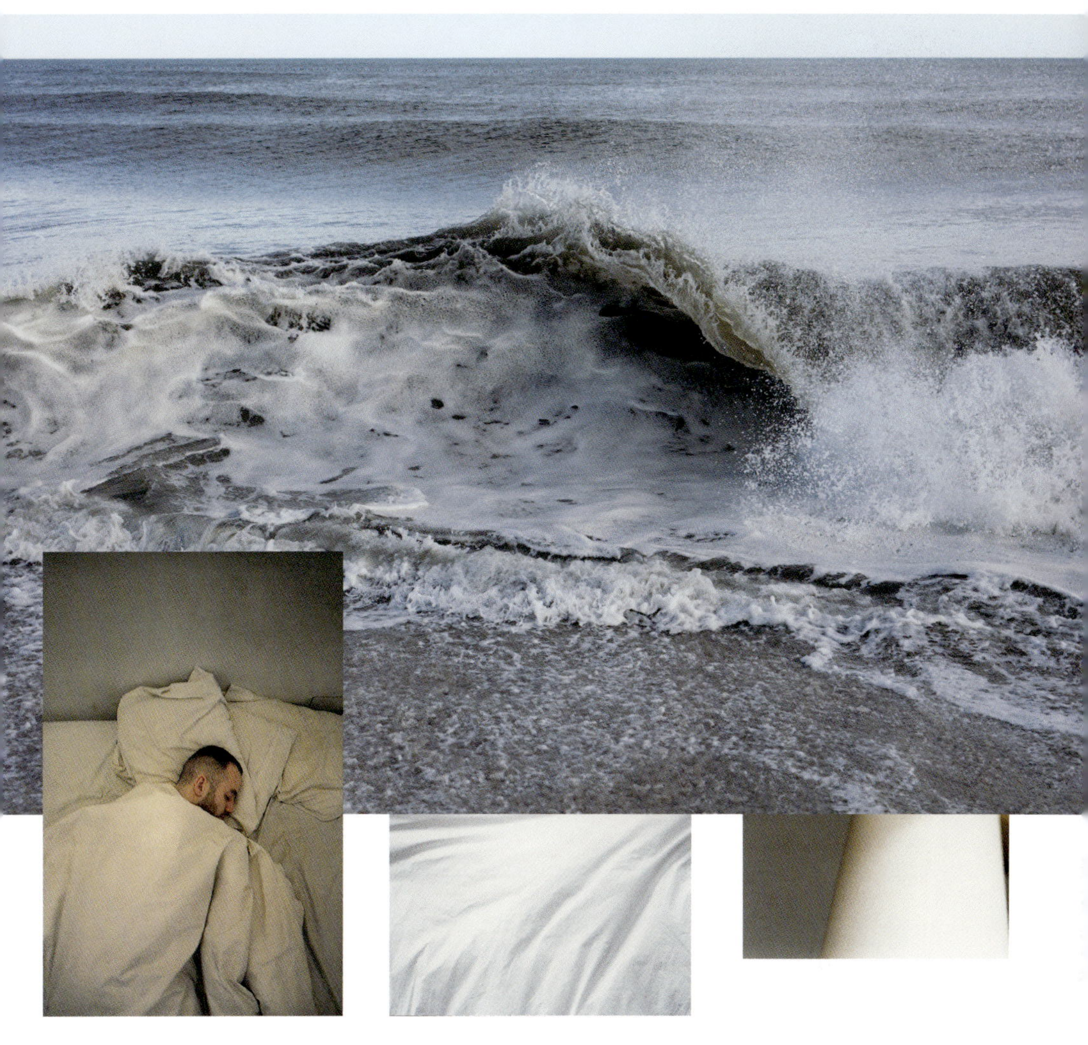

Pumpkin, tomato & pomme granate, 1995
sleep, 1995
Atlantique, b, 2016

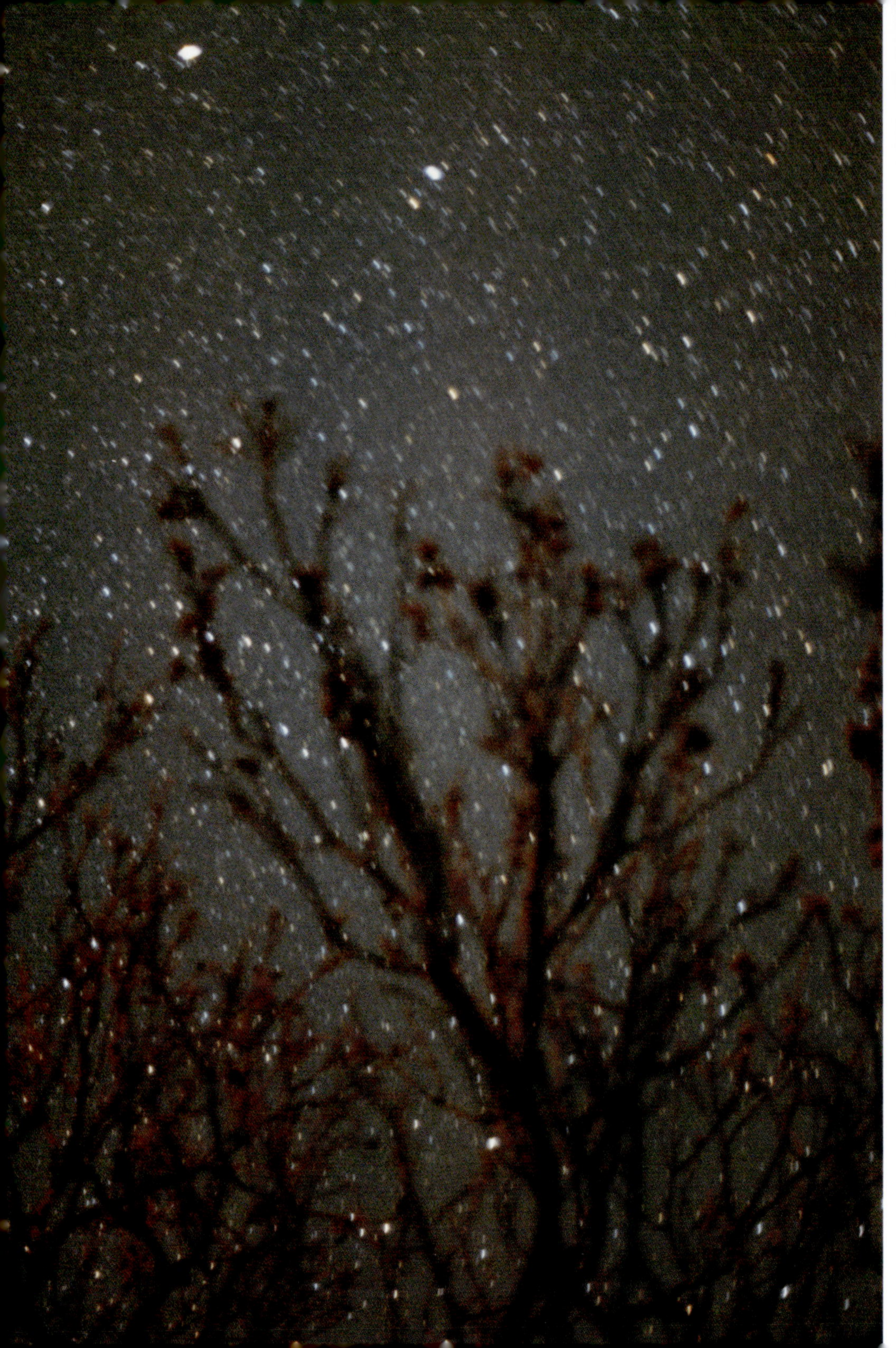

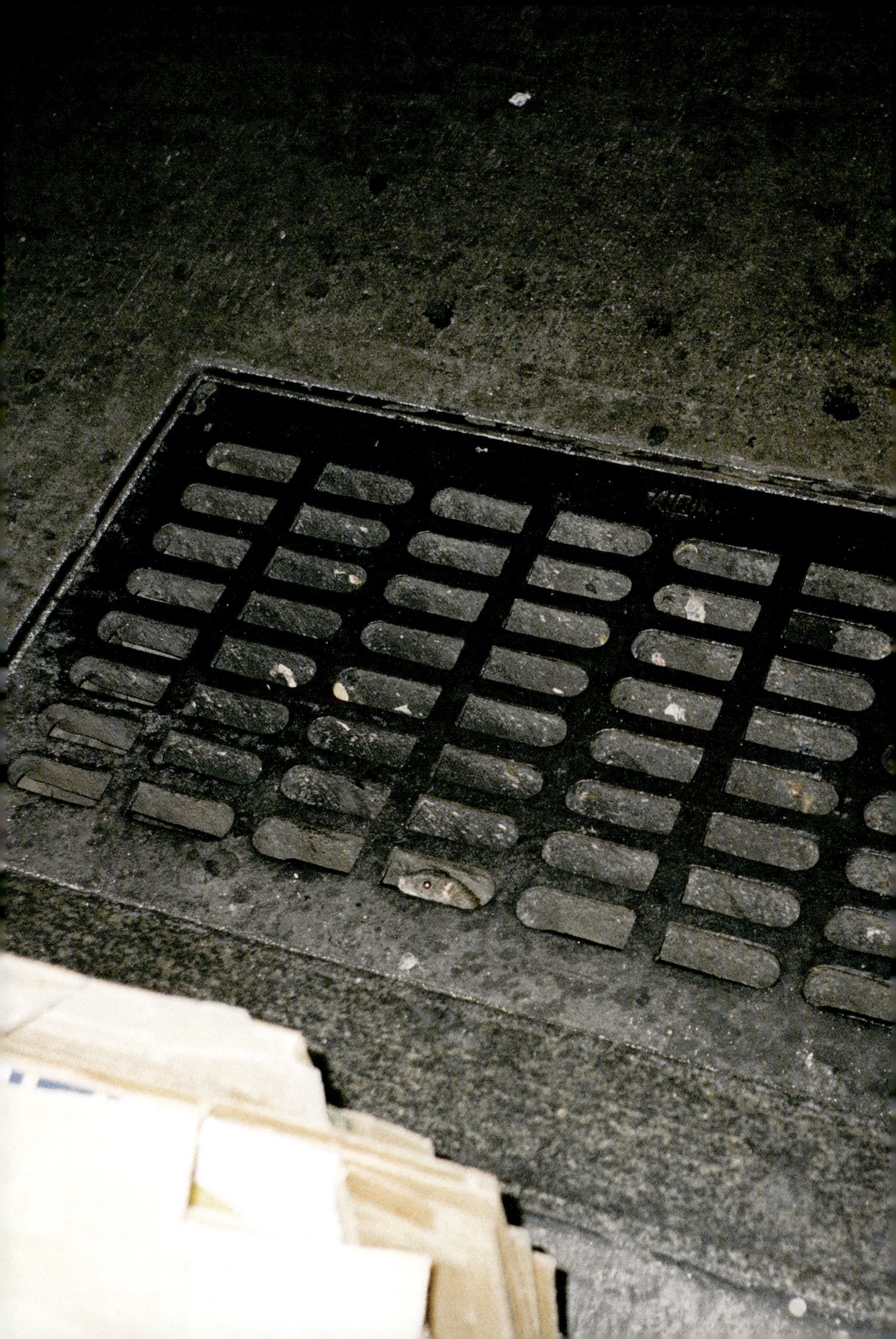

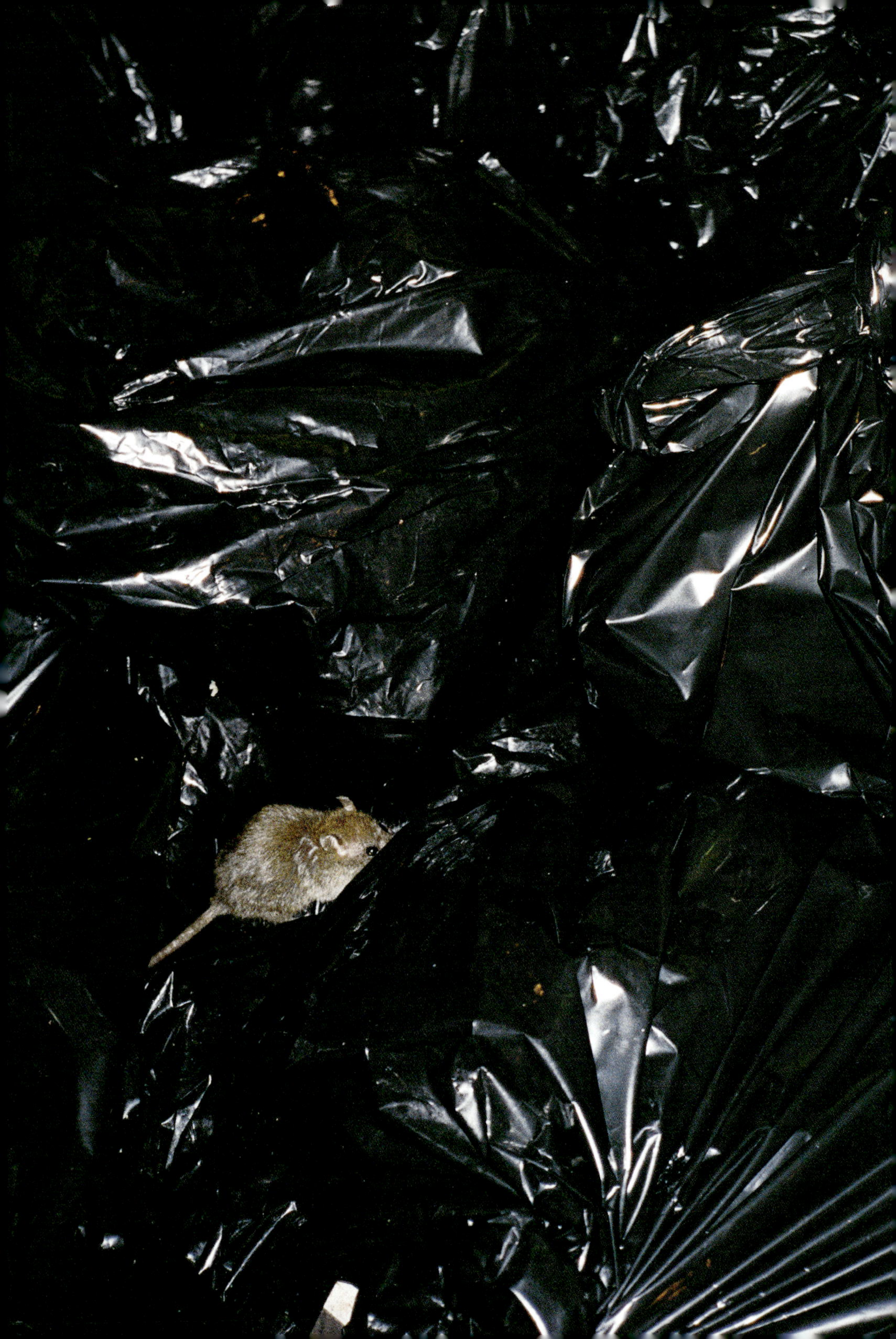

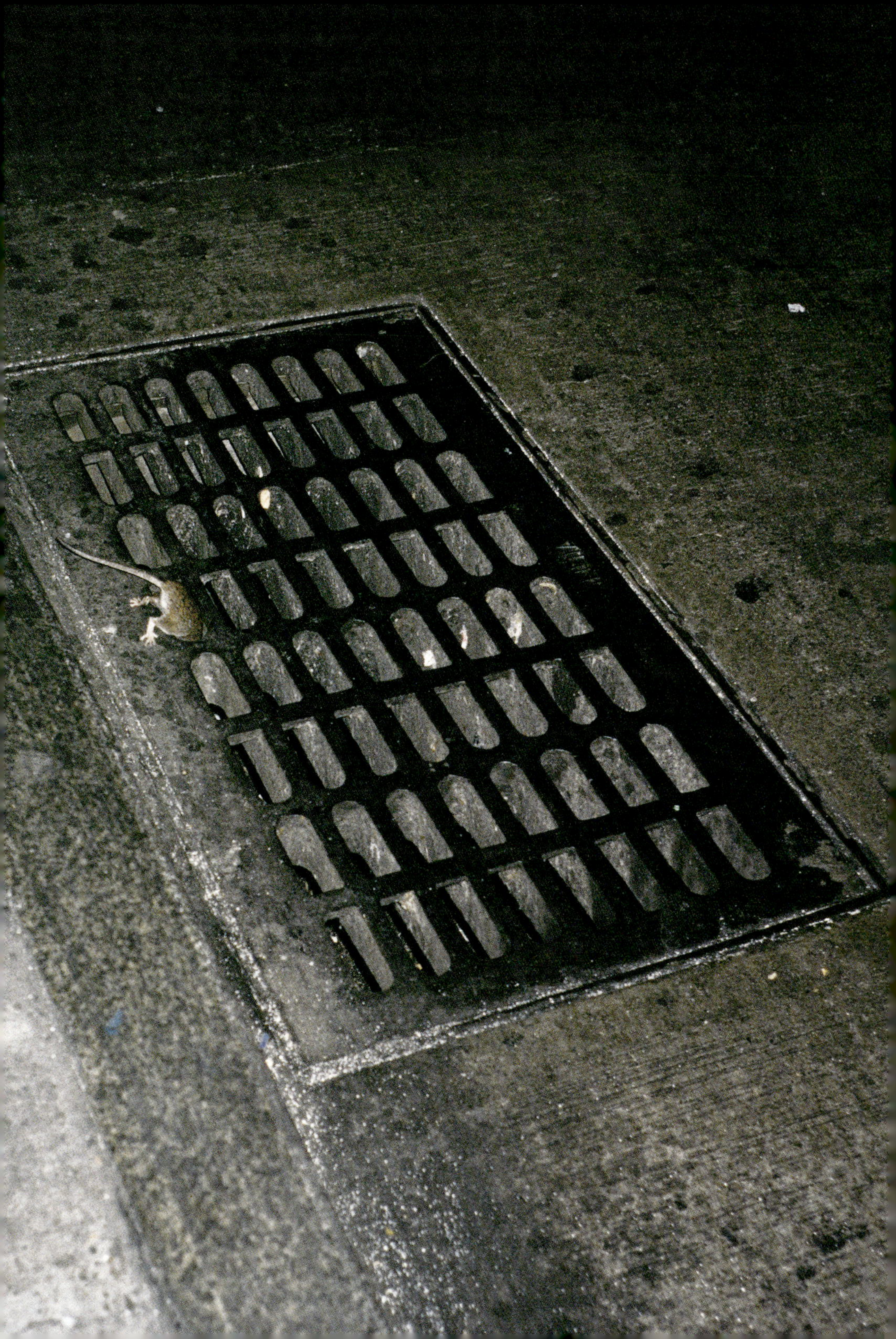

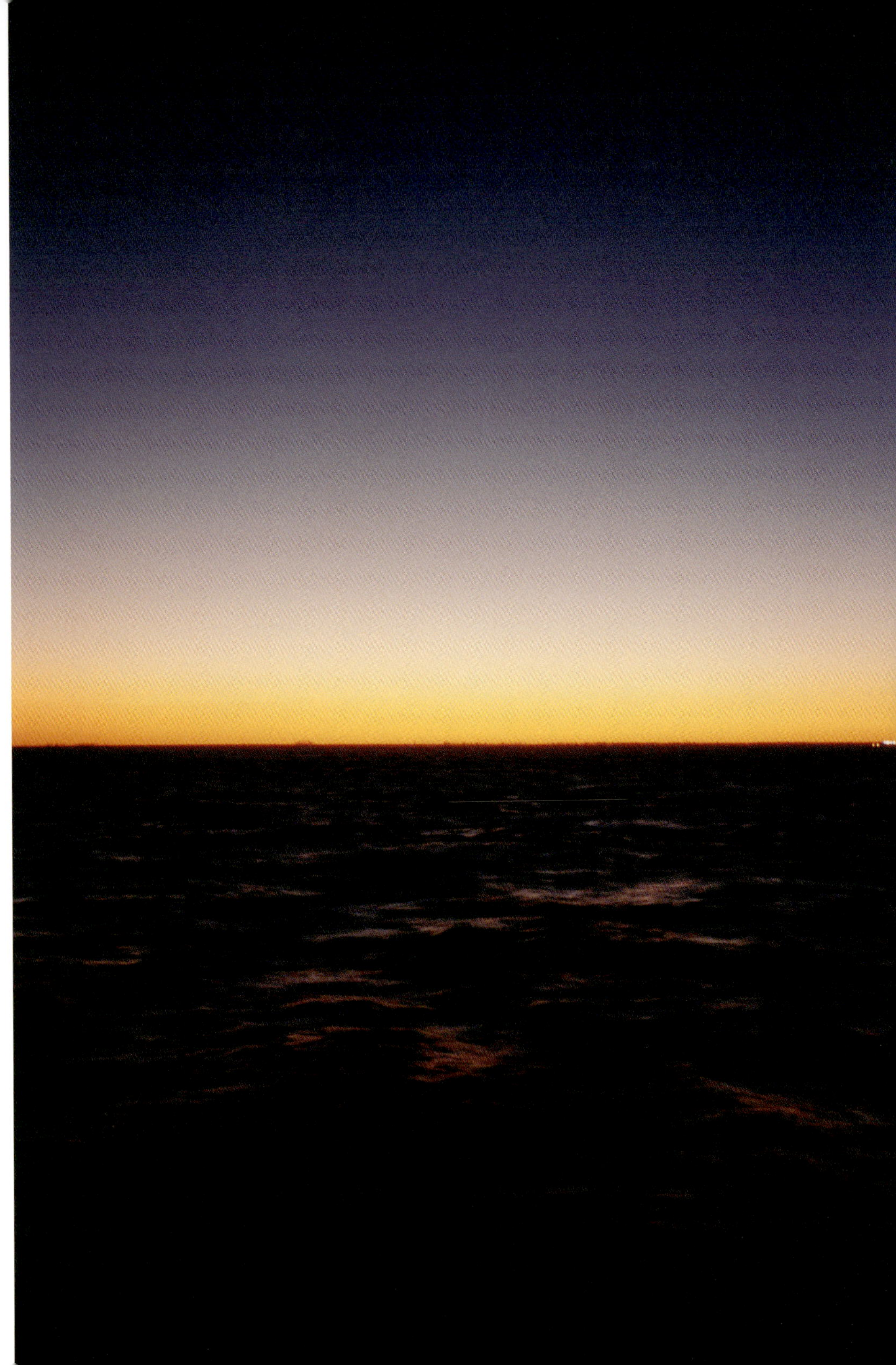

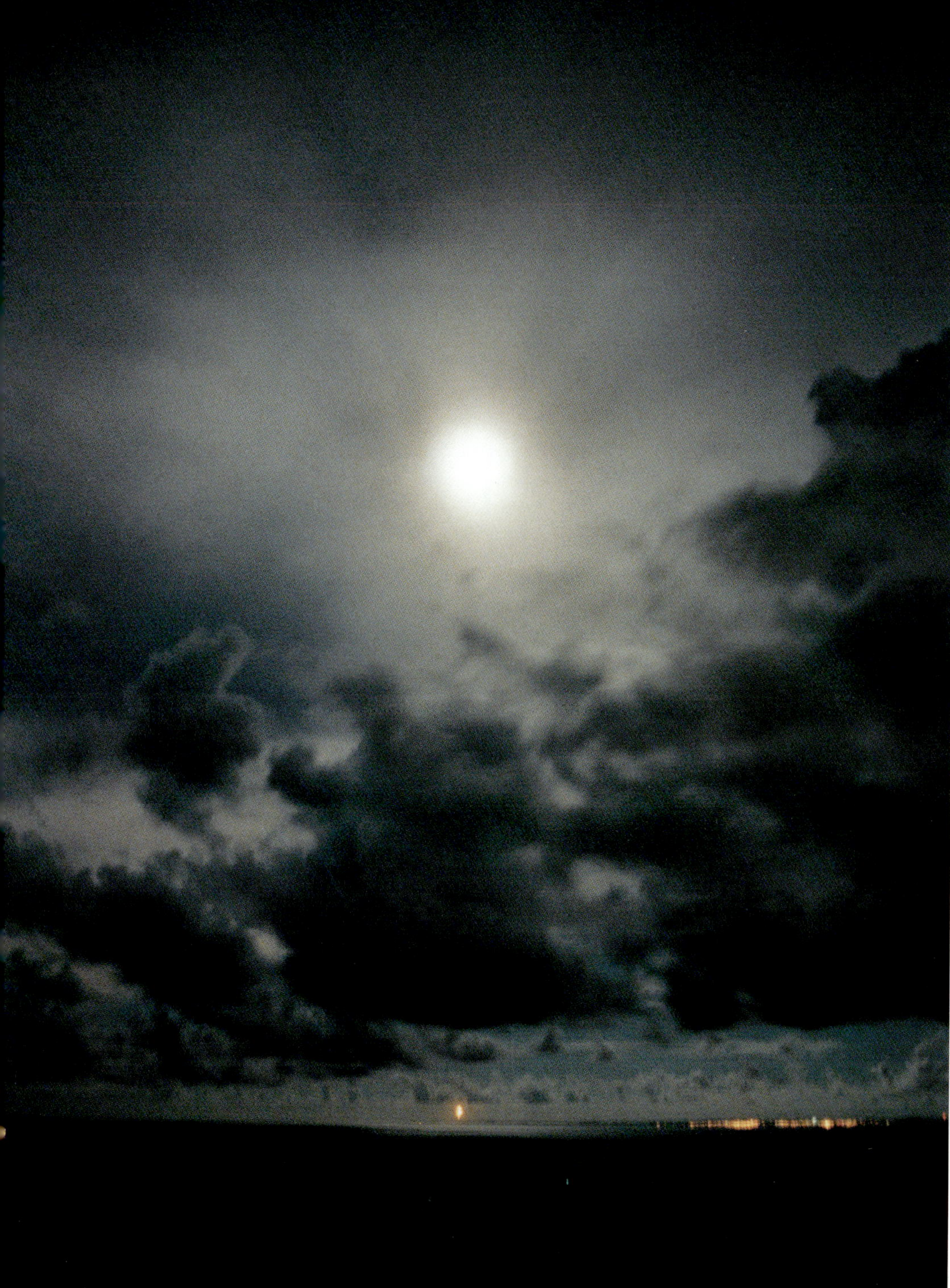

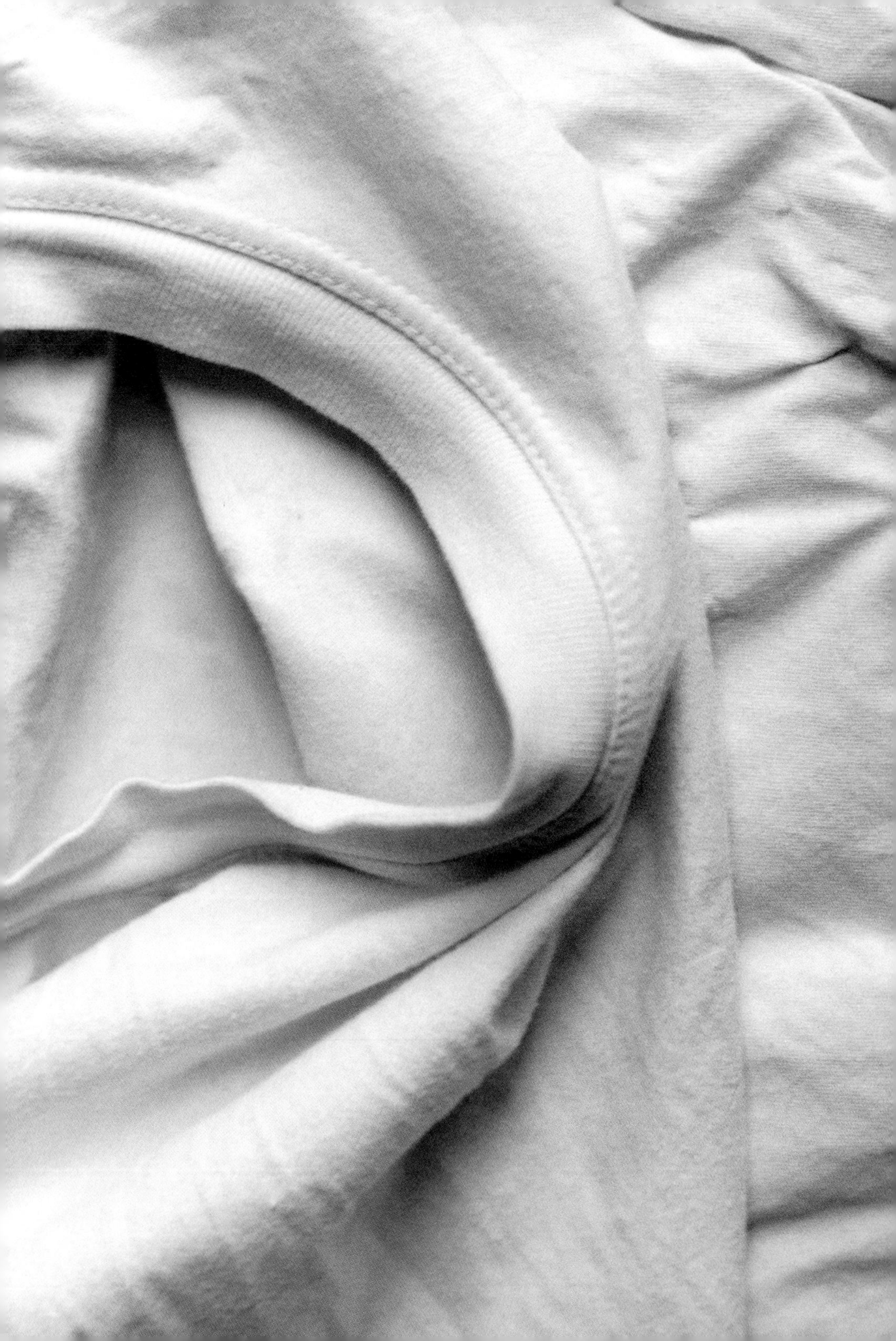

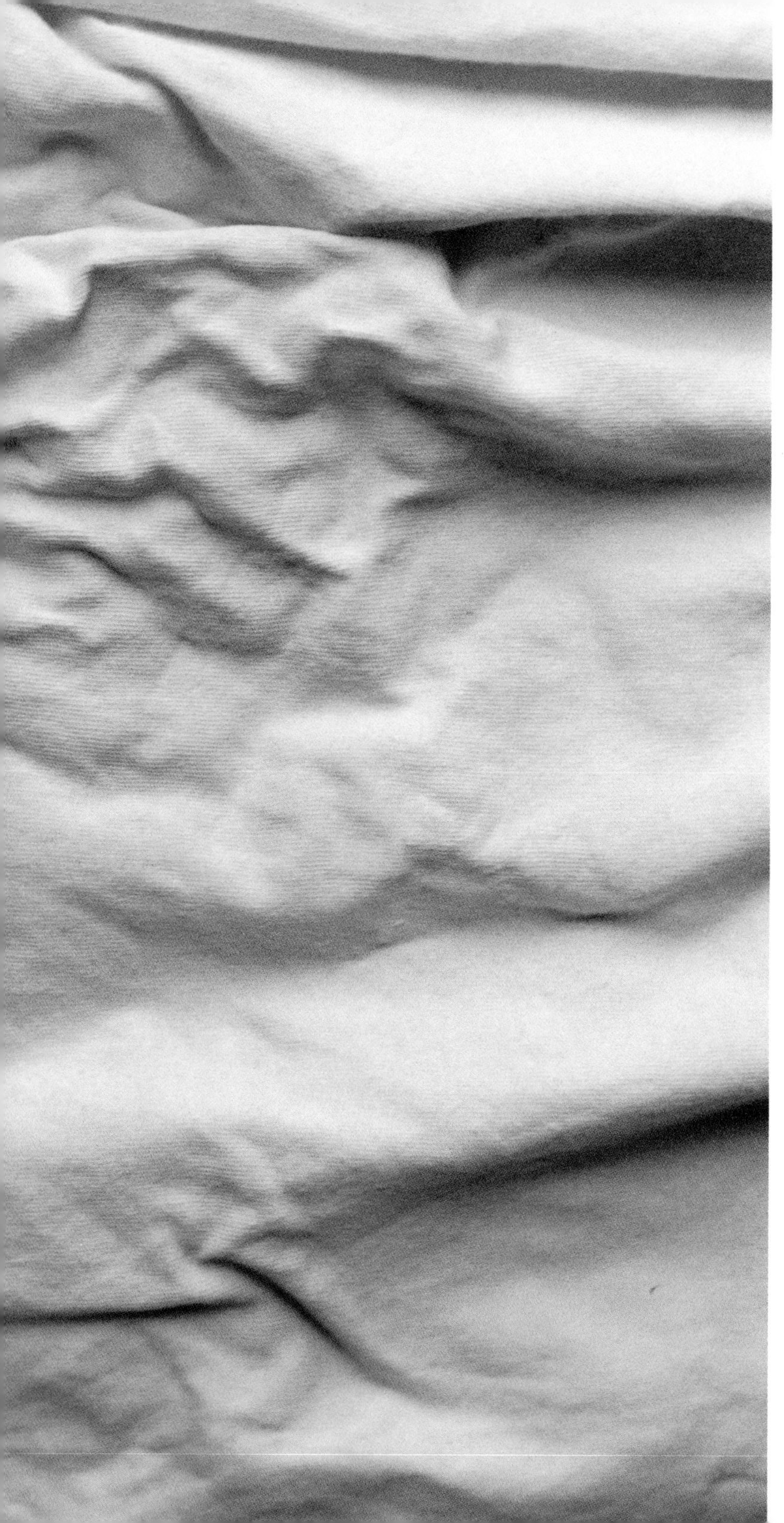

Sportflecken, 1996

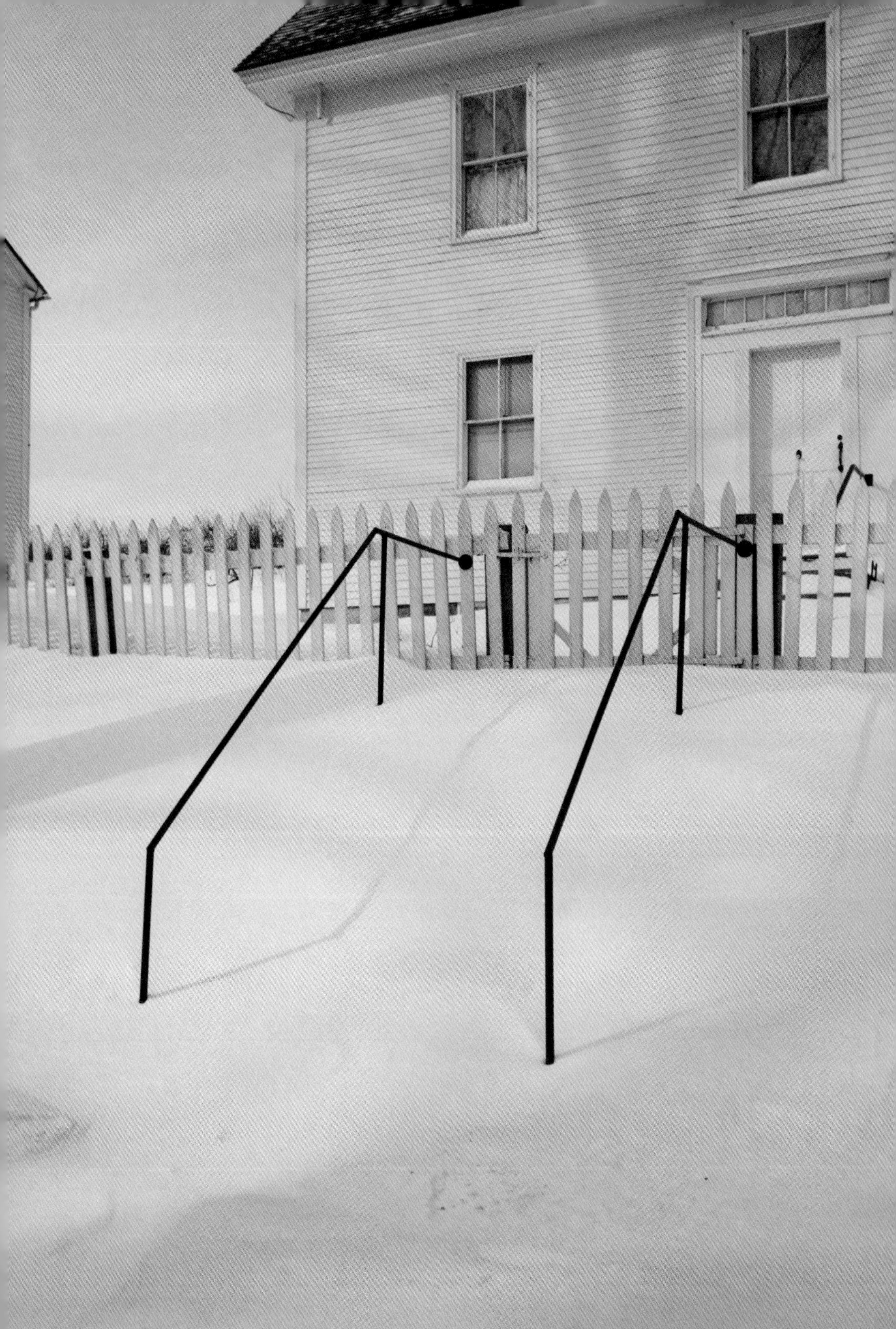

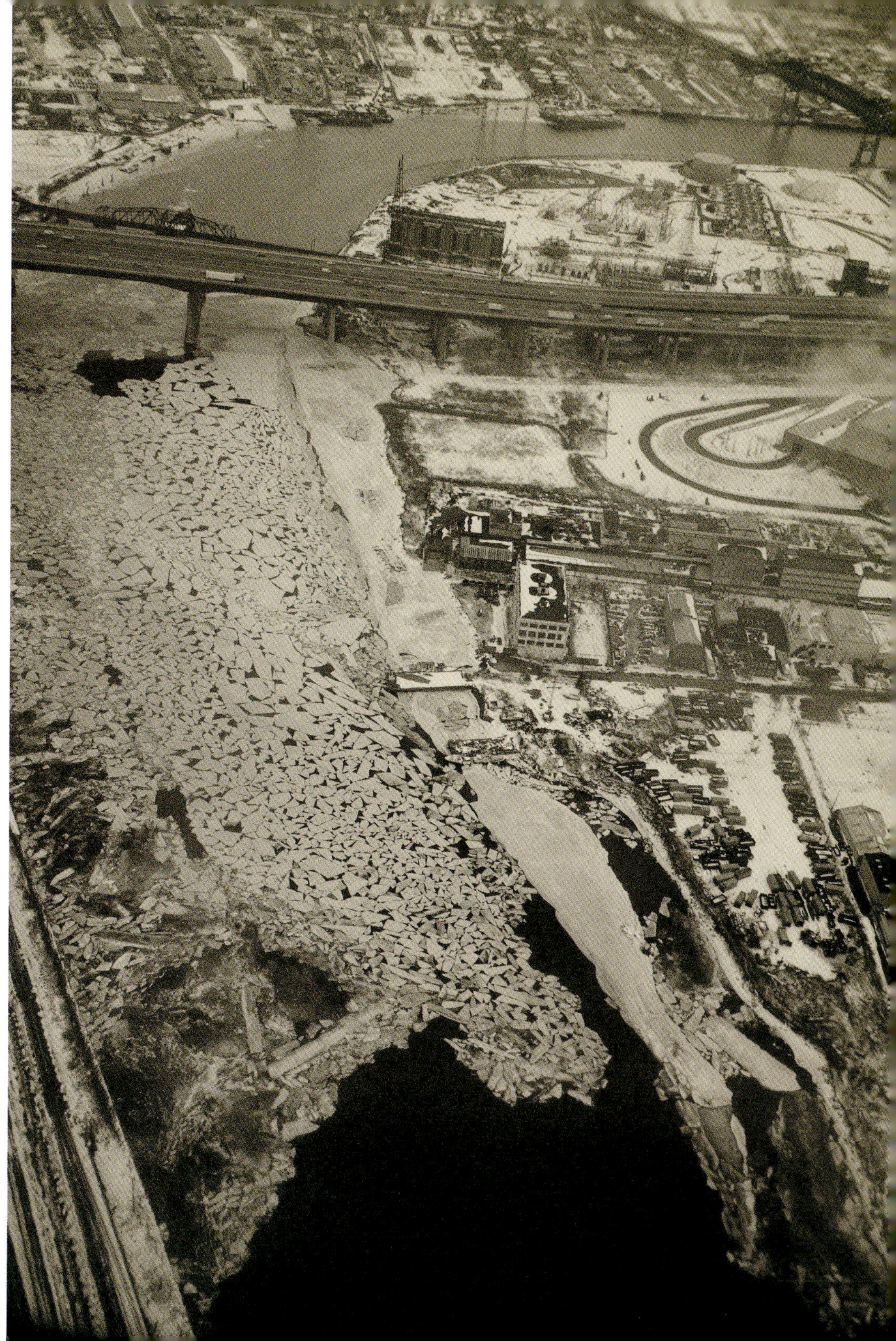

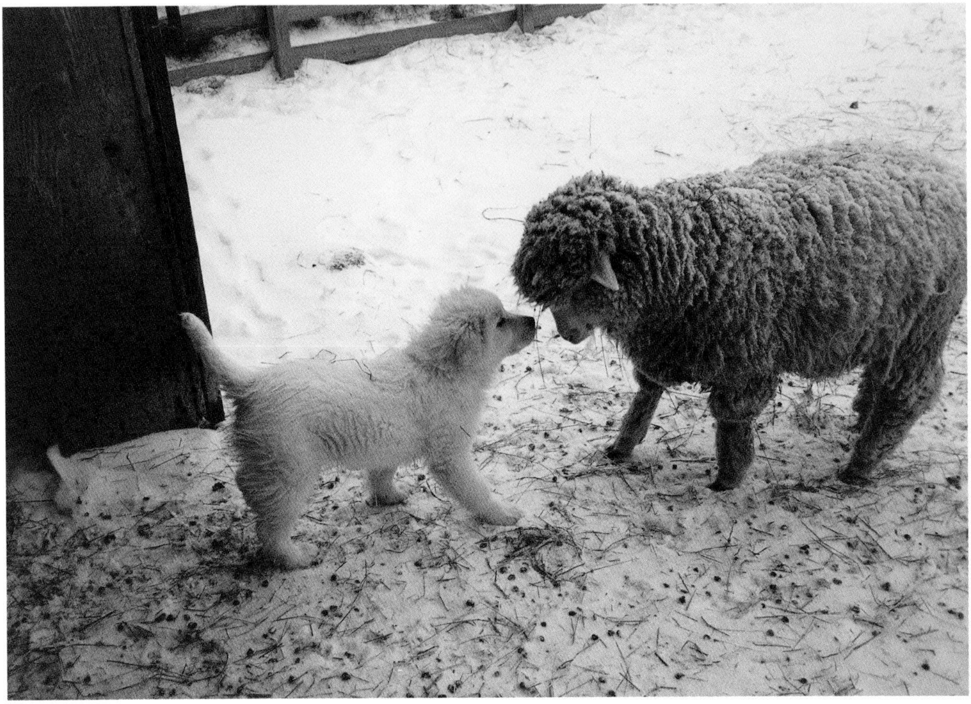

Habakkuk & Cherubim, 1996
Space Between Two Buildings, 1996

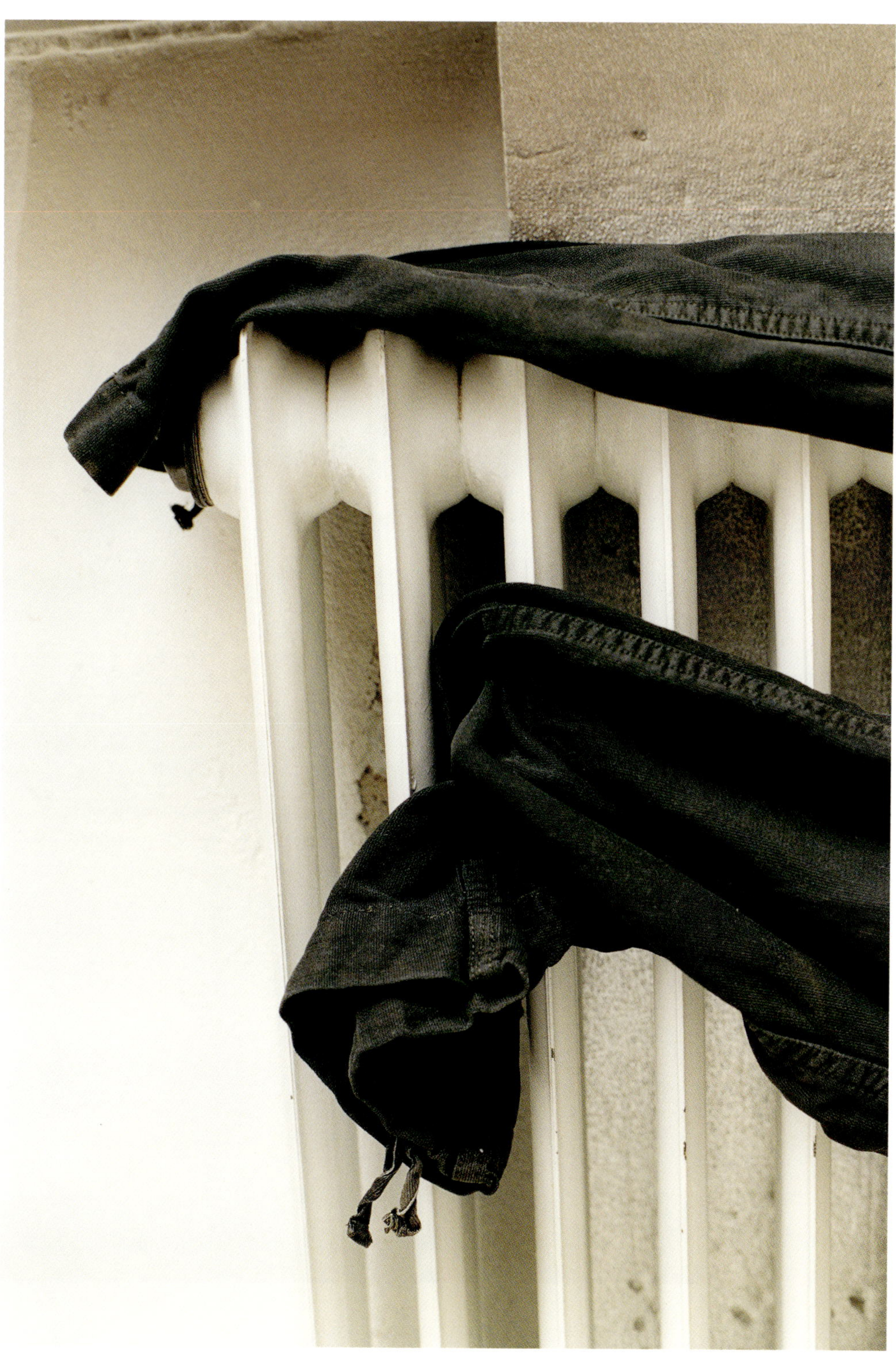

Faltenwurf (oliv), 1996

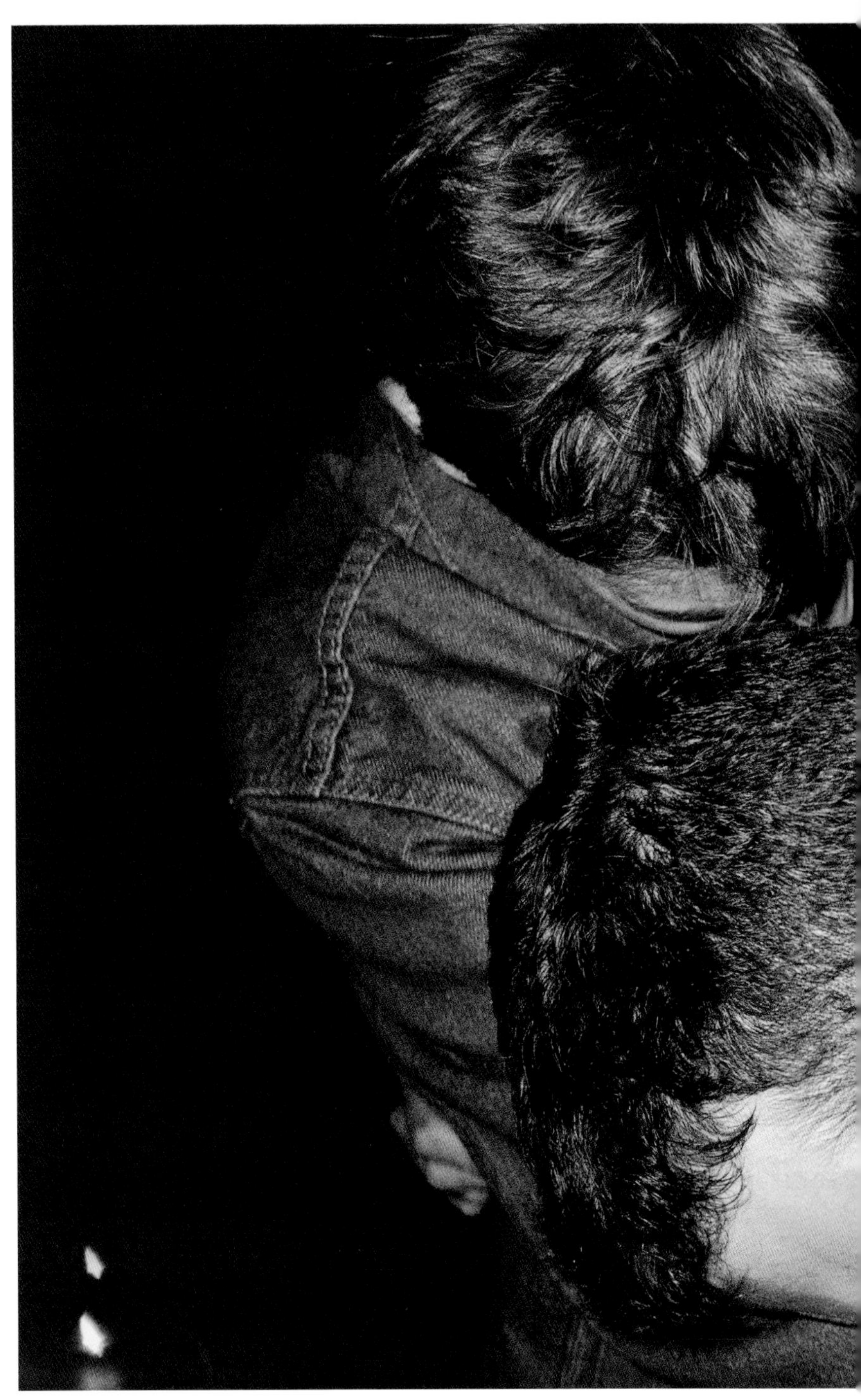

Arkadia I, 1996
The Point II, 1996   Faltenwurf (off Soho), 1996 →

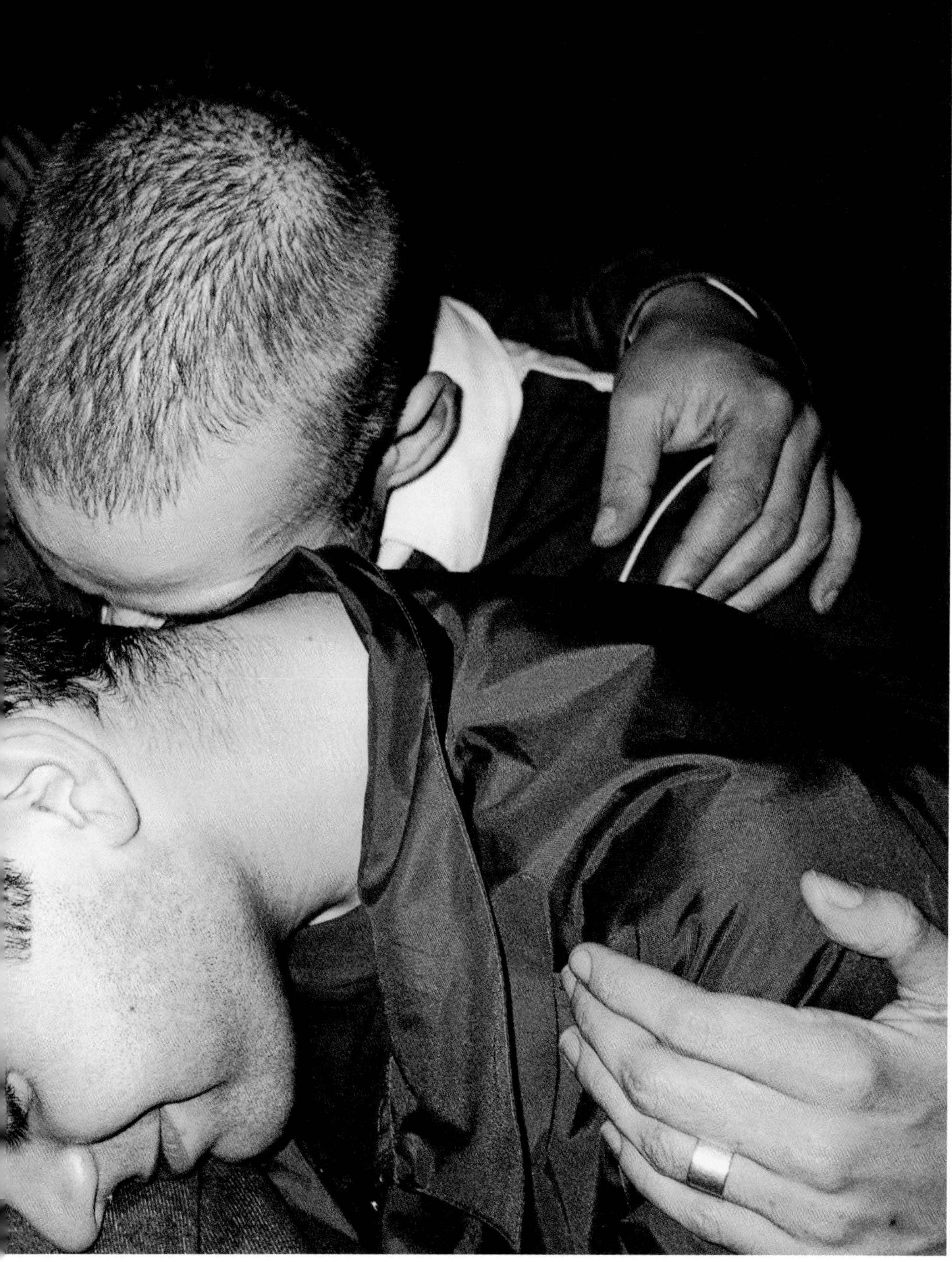

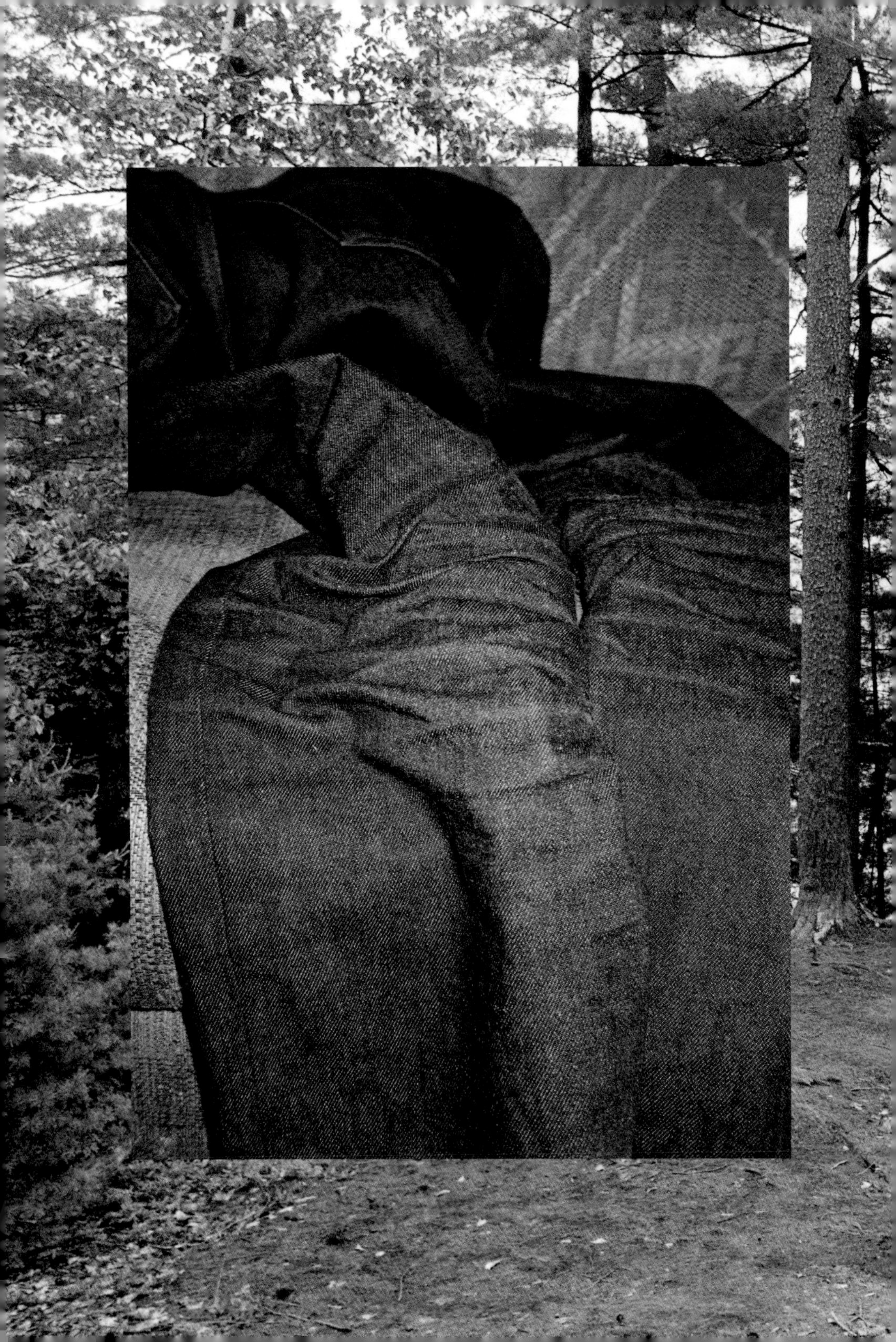

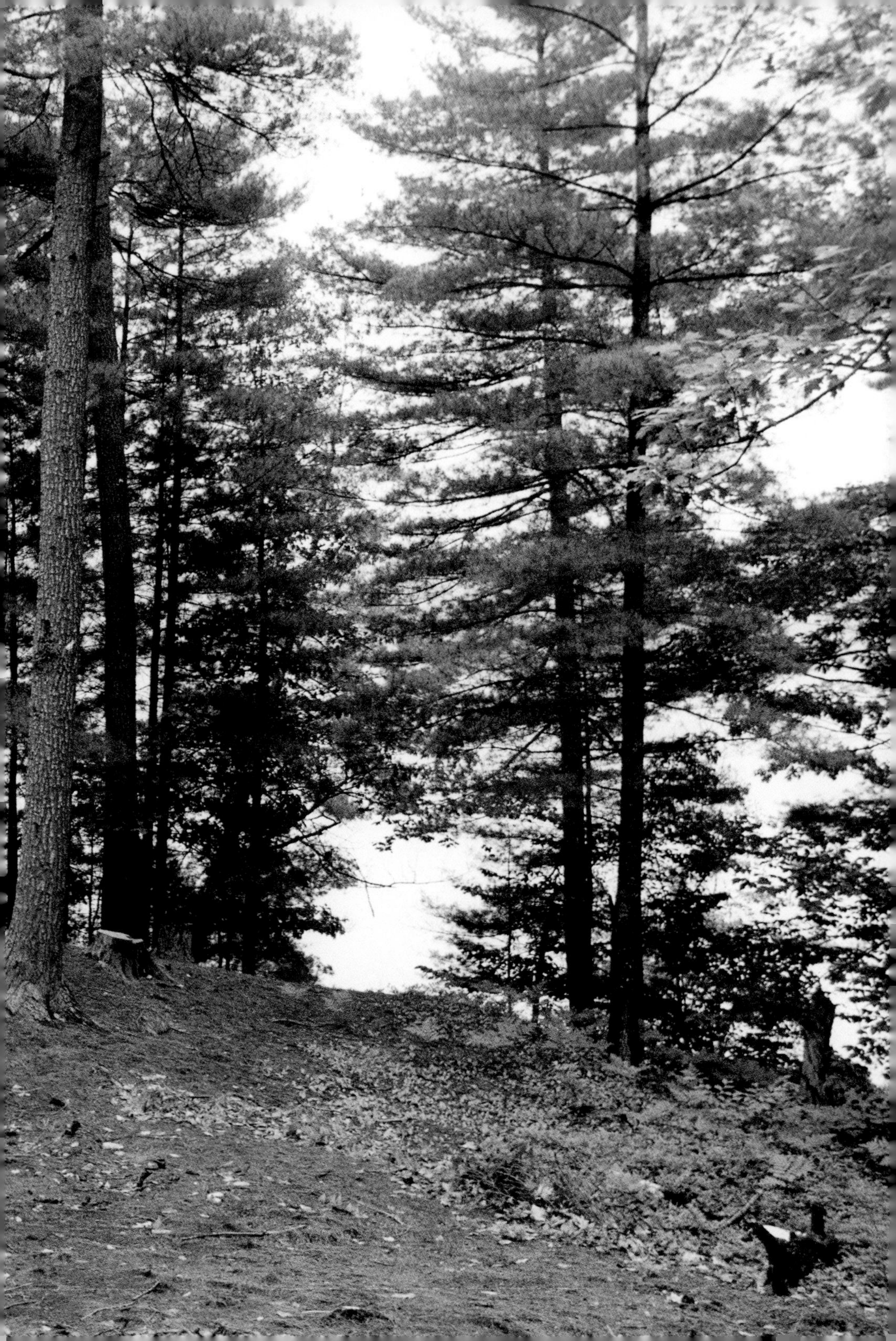

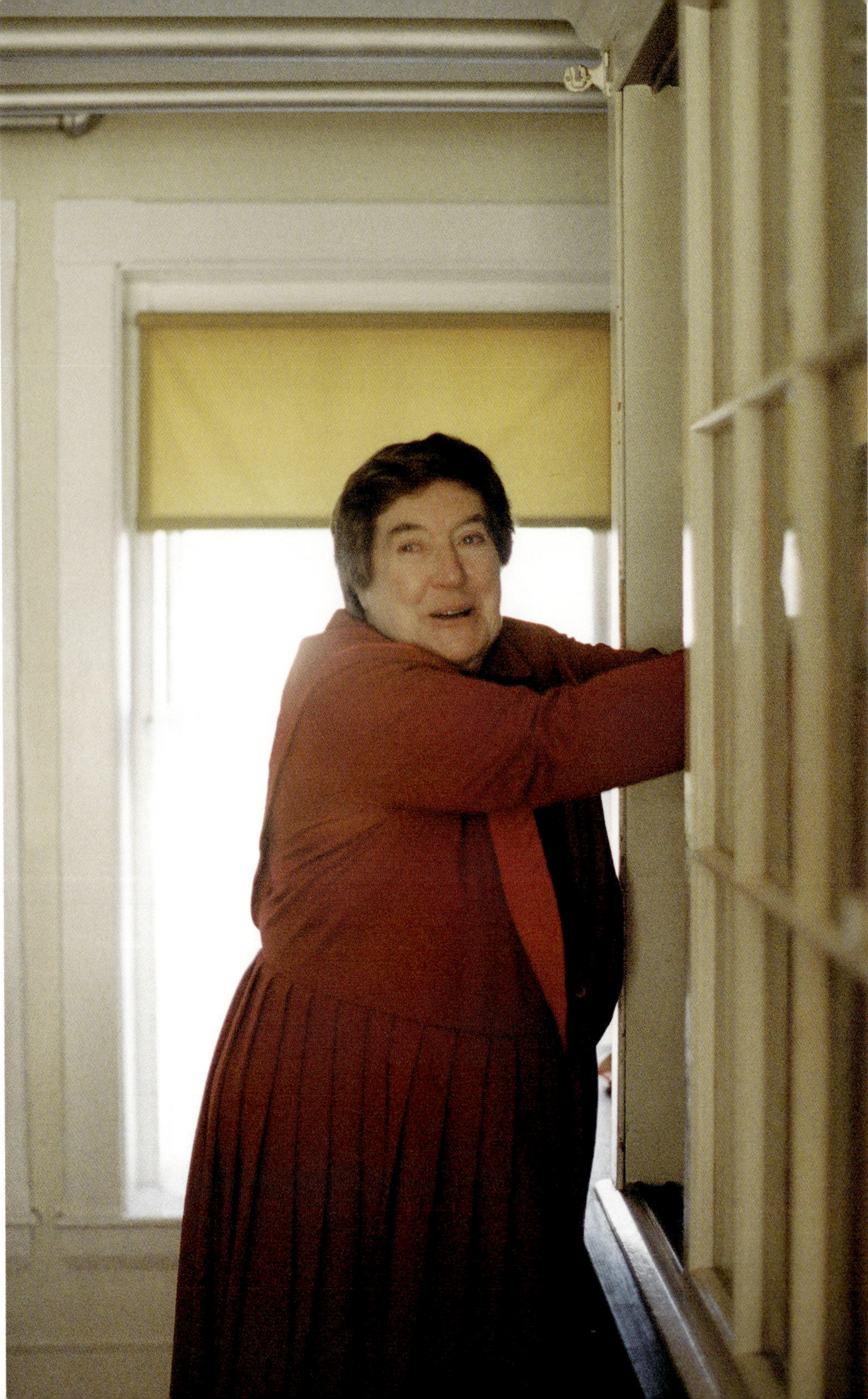

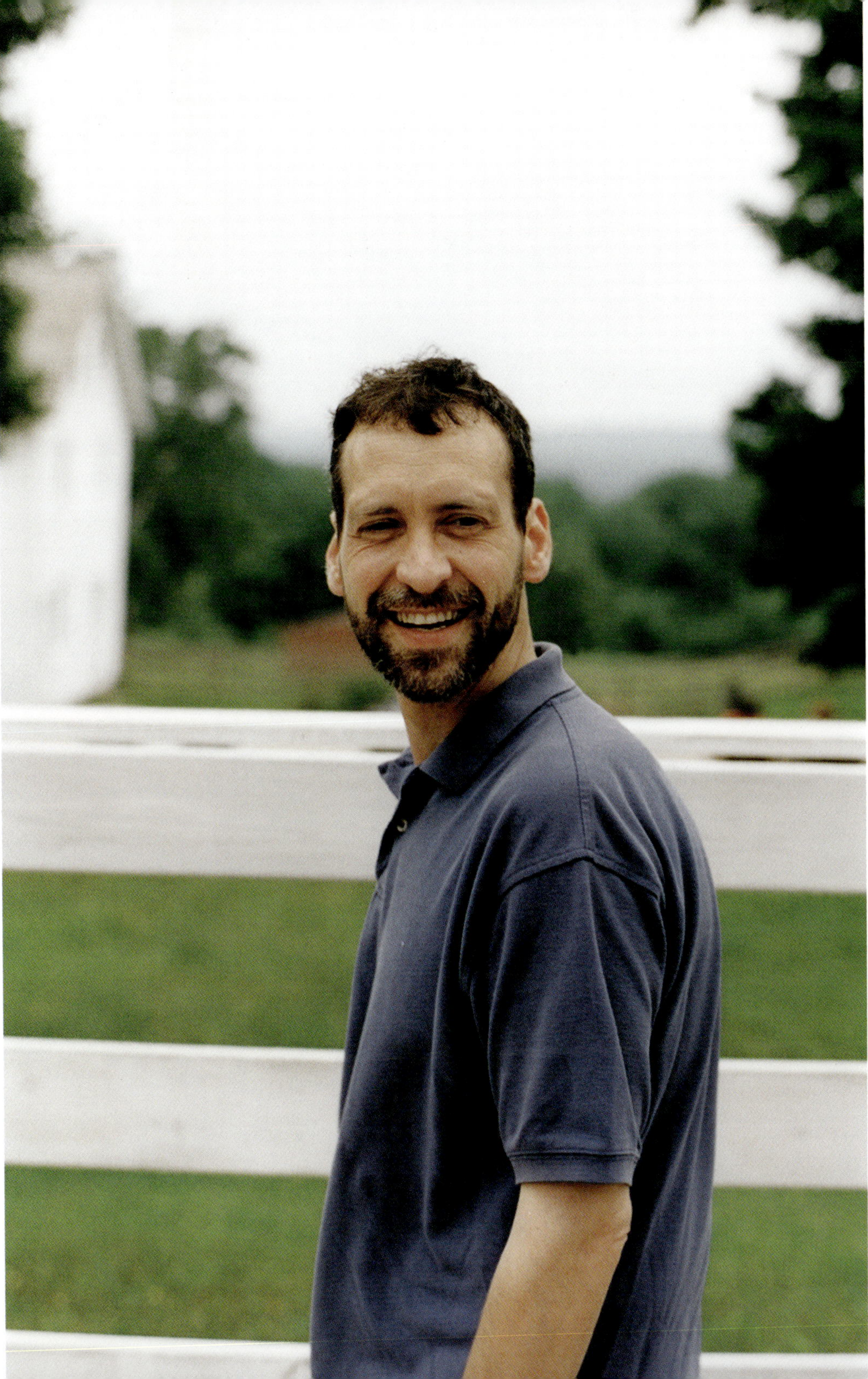

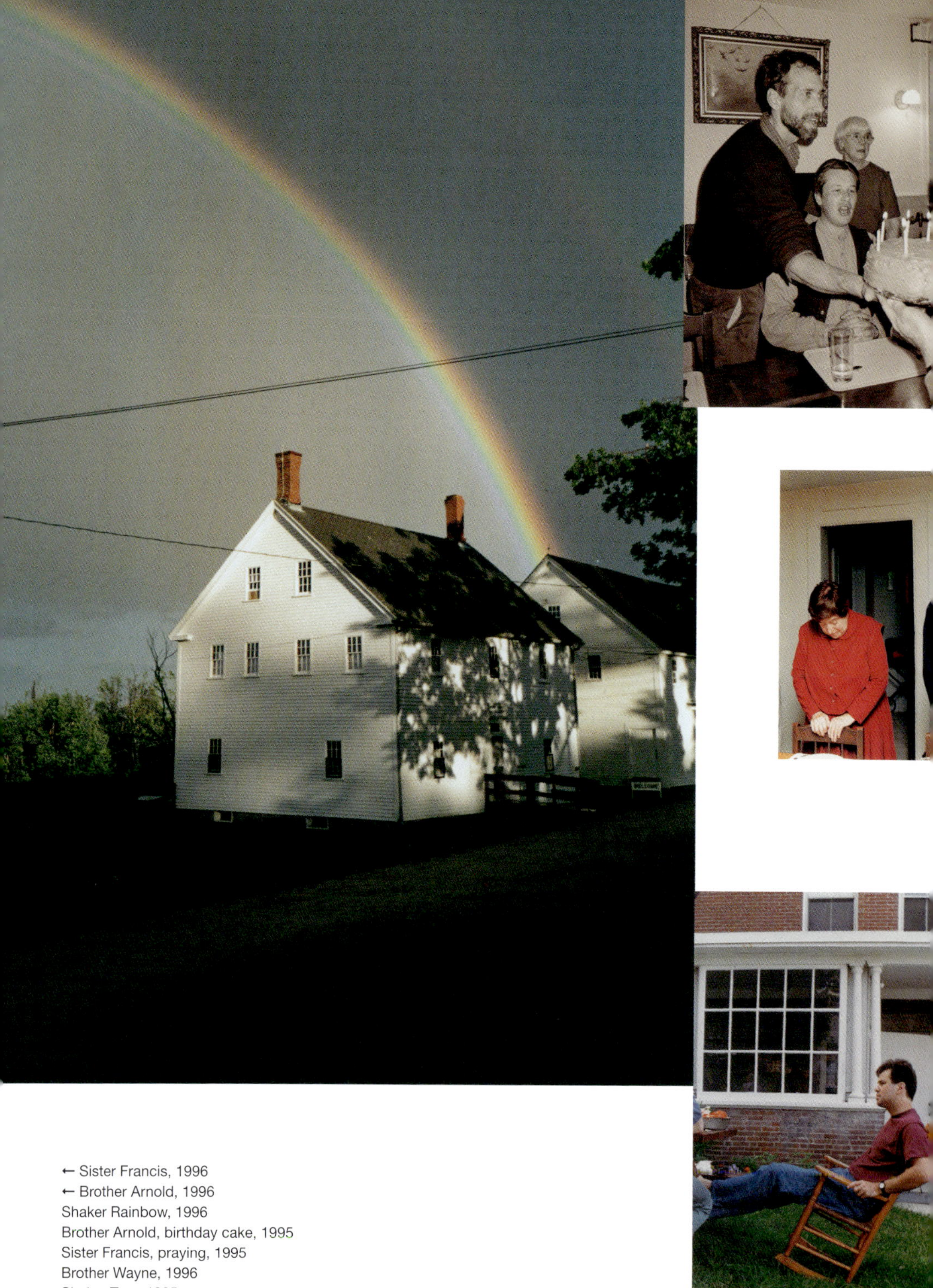

← Sister Francis, 1996
← Brother Arnold, 1996
Shaker Rainbow, 1996
Brother Arnold, birthday cake, 1995
Sister Francis, praying, 1995
Brother Wayne, 1996
Shaker Tree, 1995

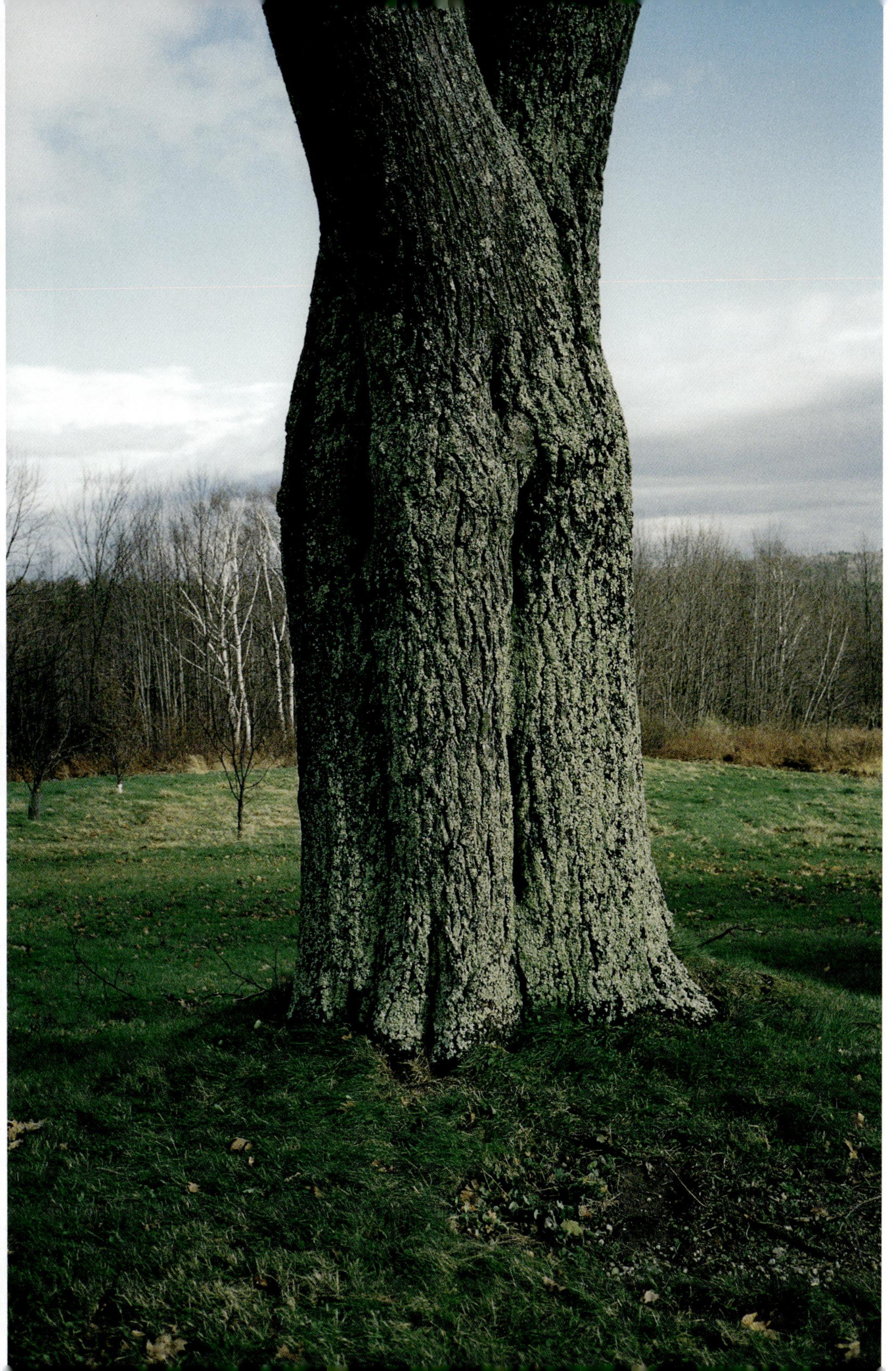

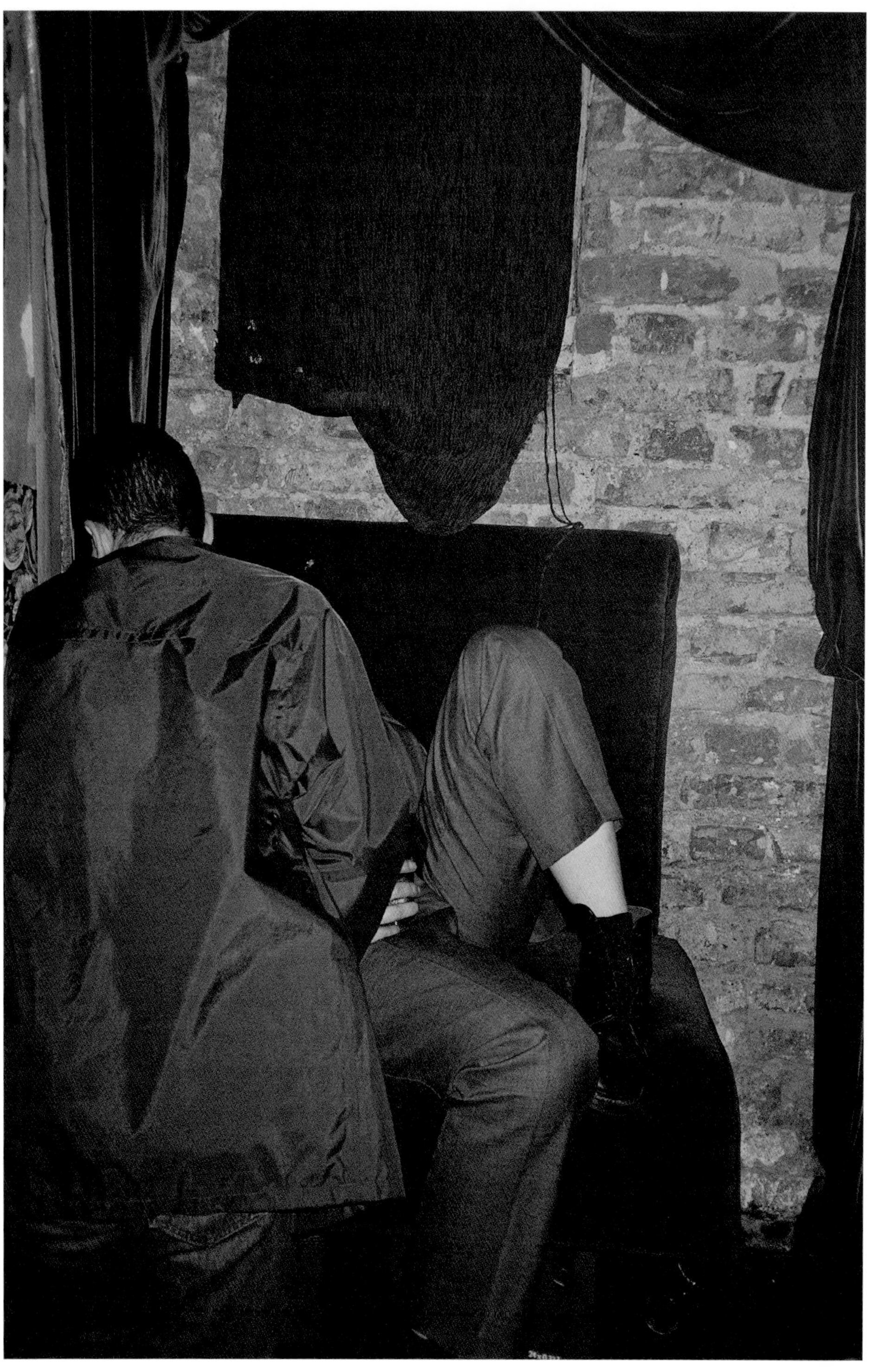

Arkadia III, 1996

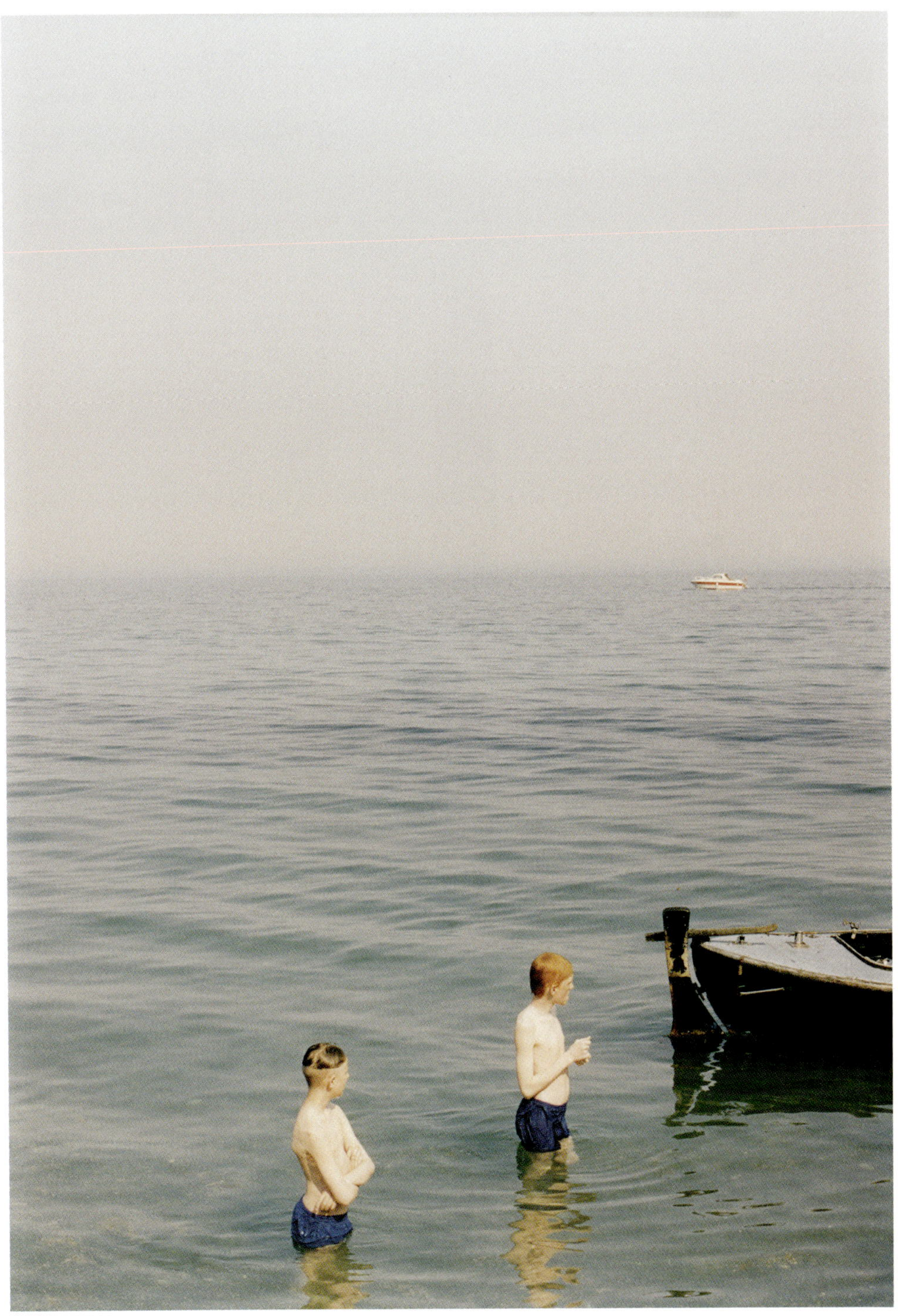

Louisiana, 1996

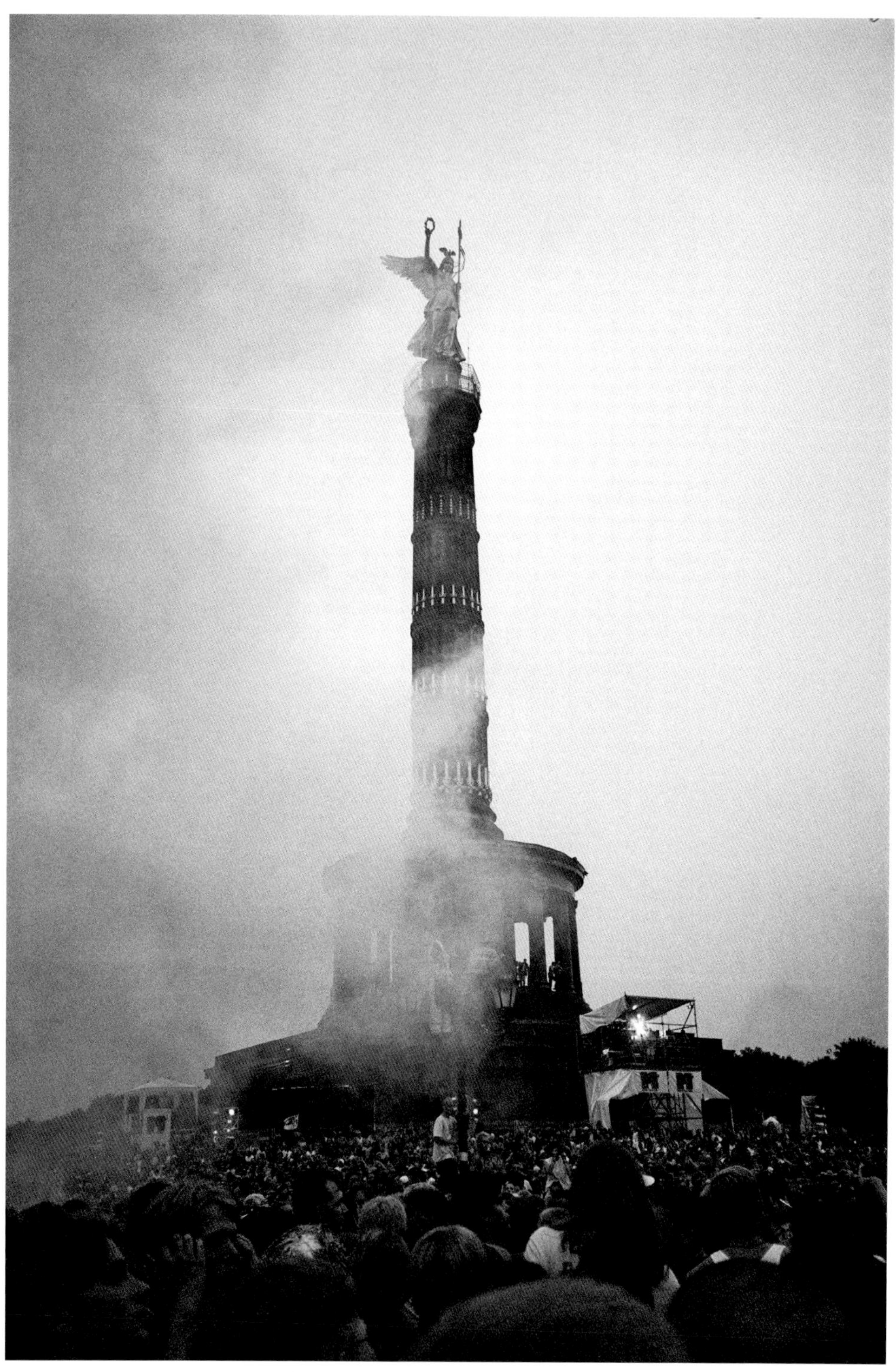

Love Parade, Siegessäule, 1996
Concorde, 1996

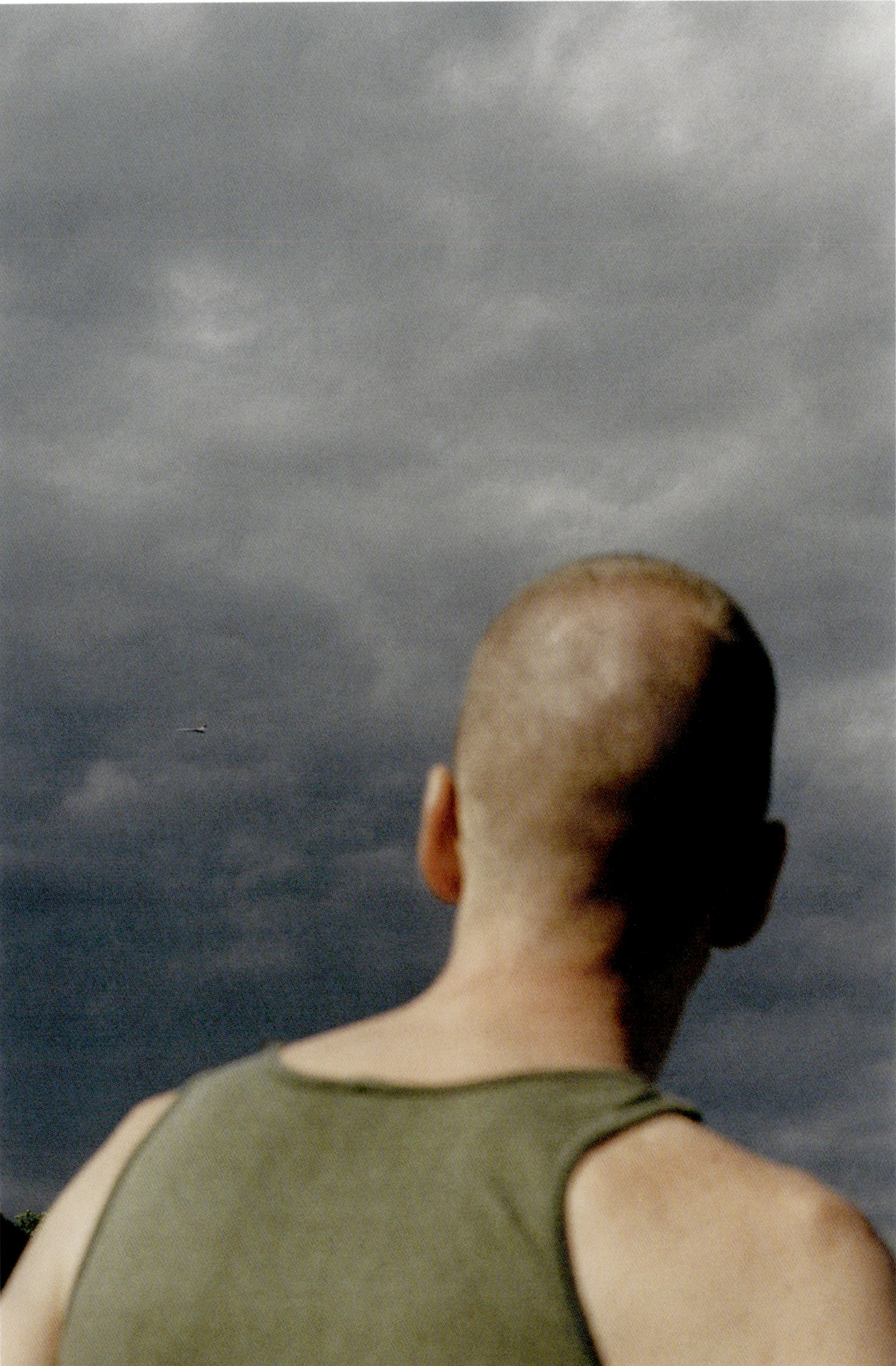

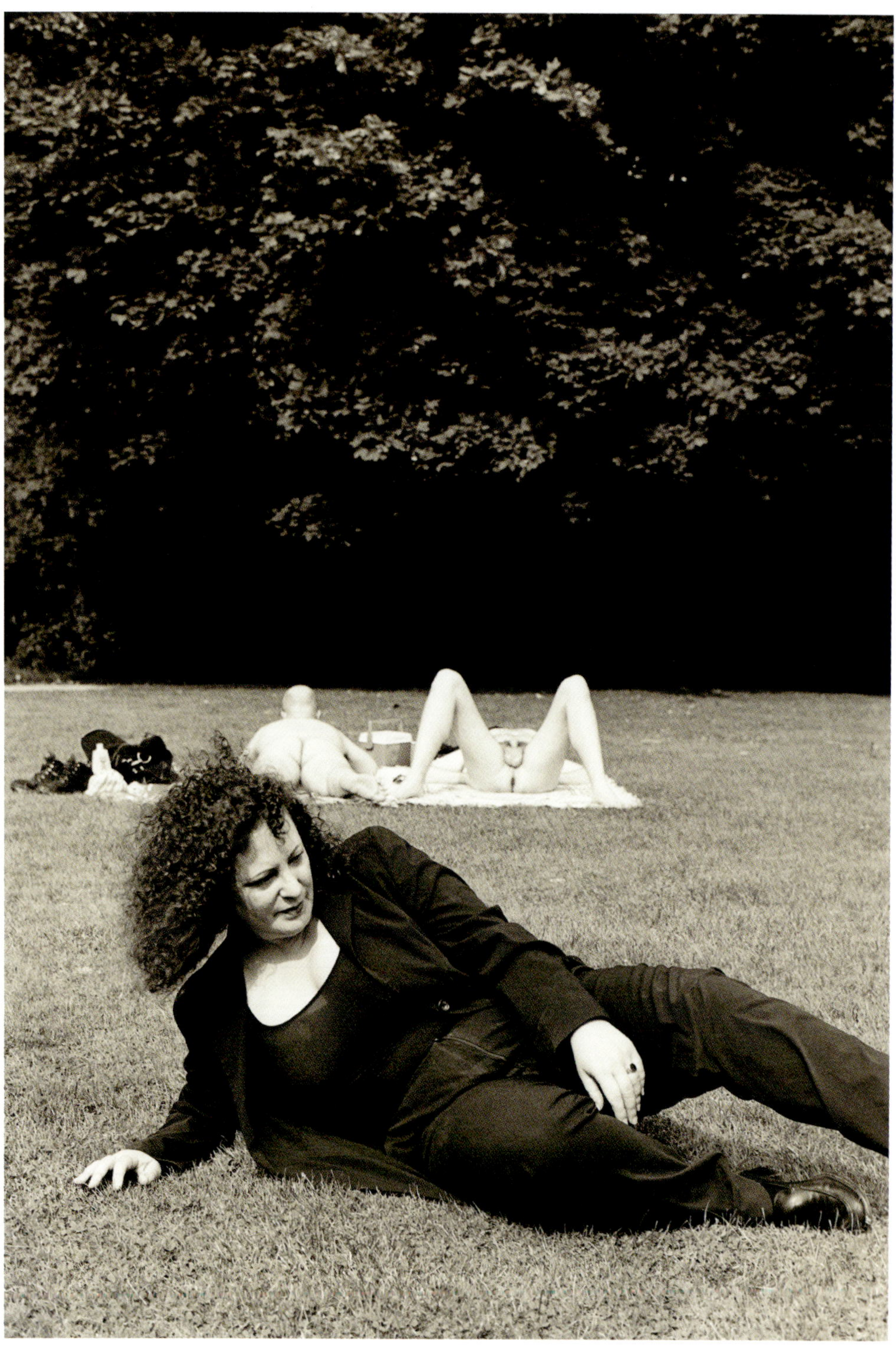

Nan reclining, 1996

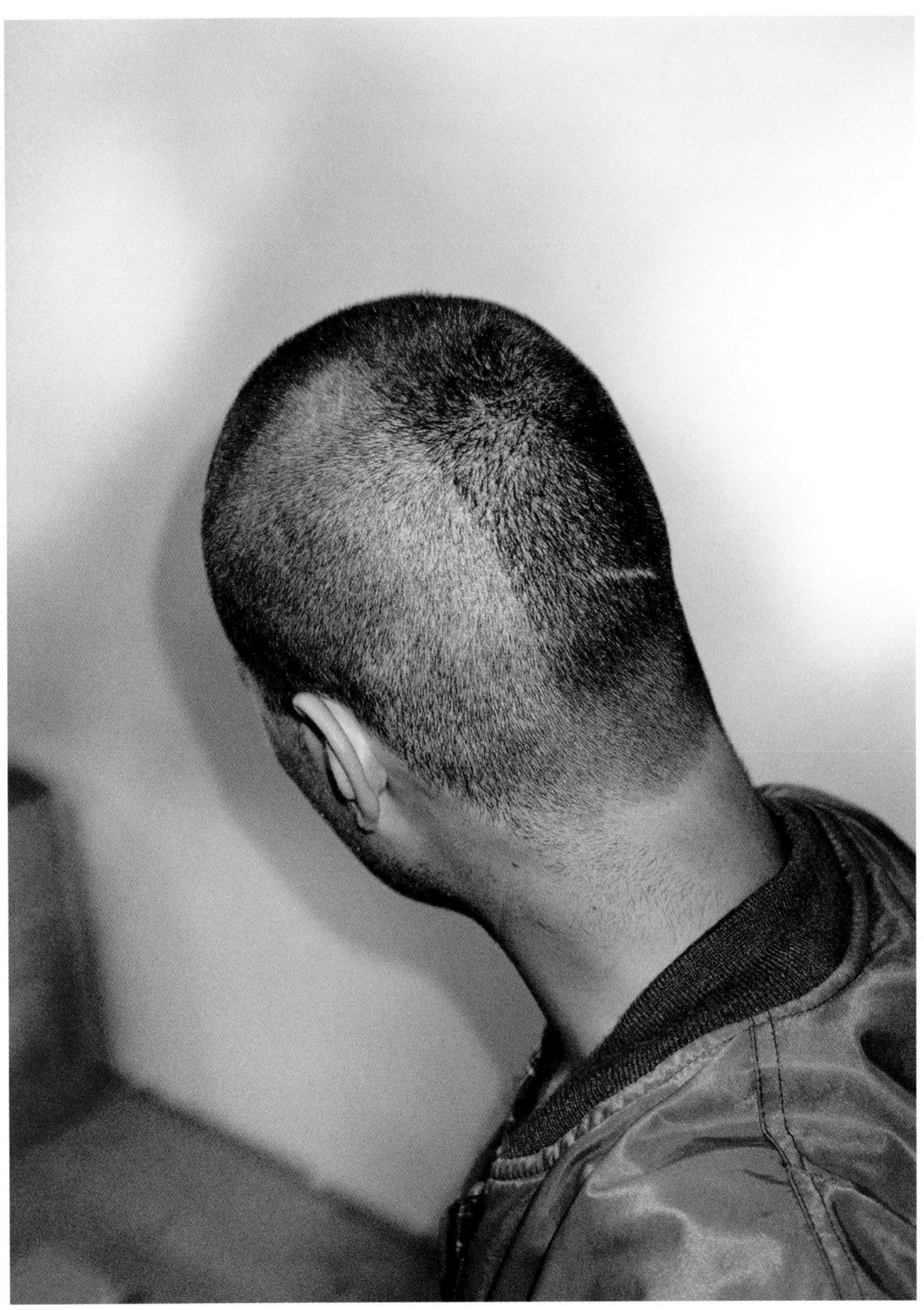

After Warriors, 1996

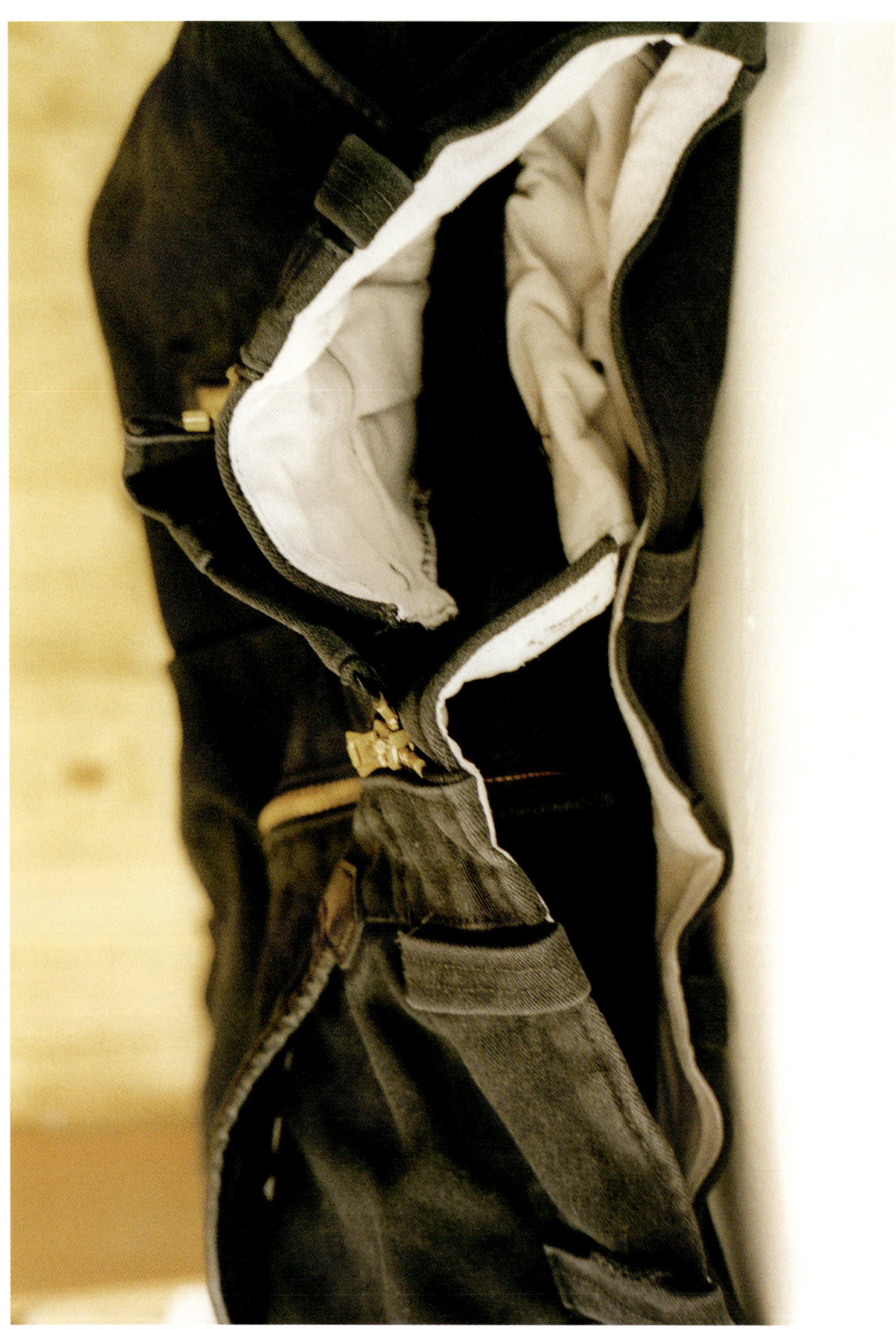

Zimmerer, 1996

Still Home, 1996

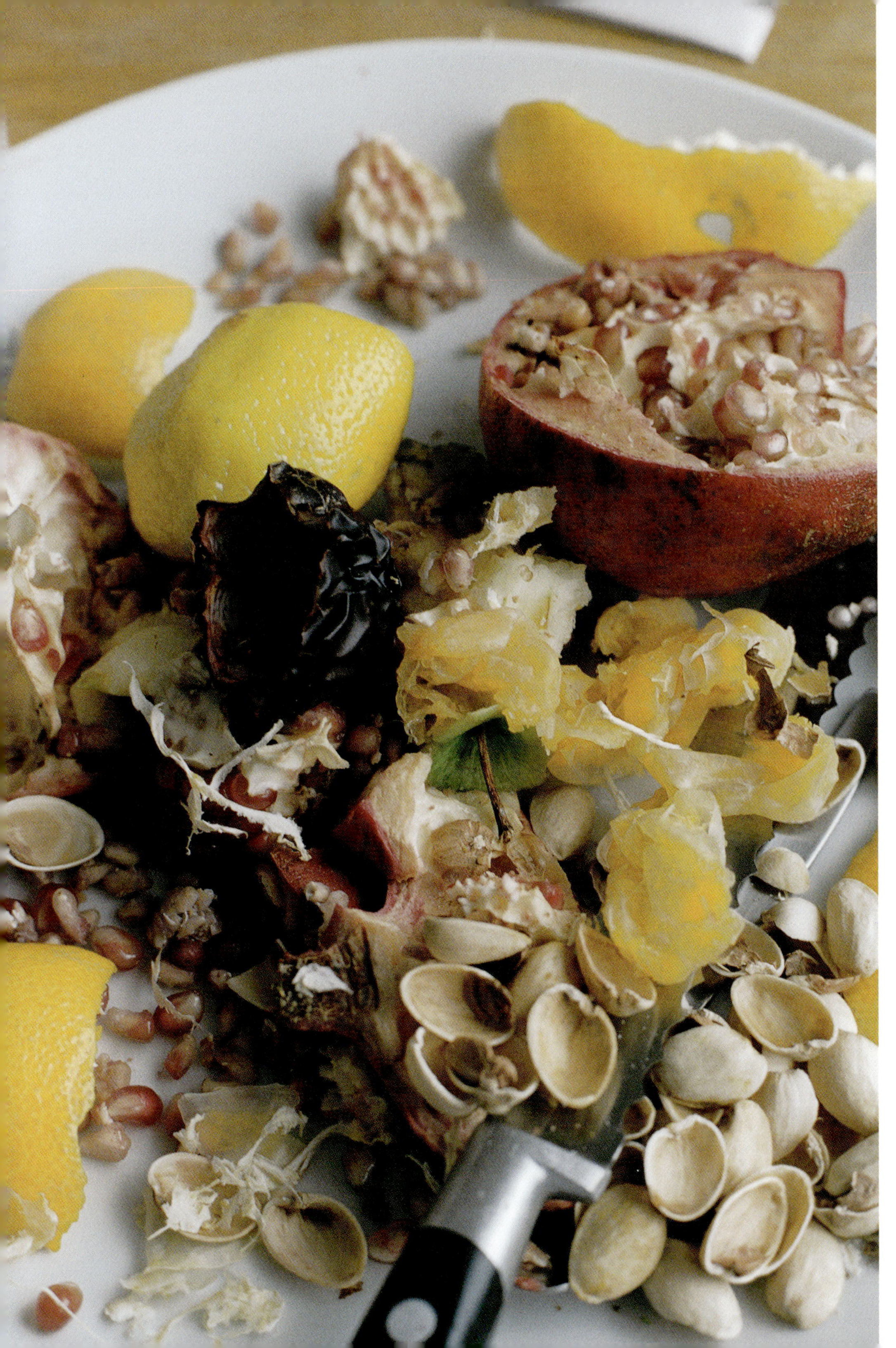

Kate McQueen, 1996

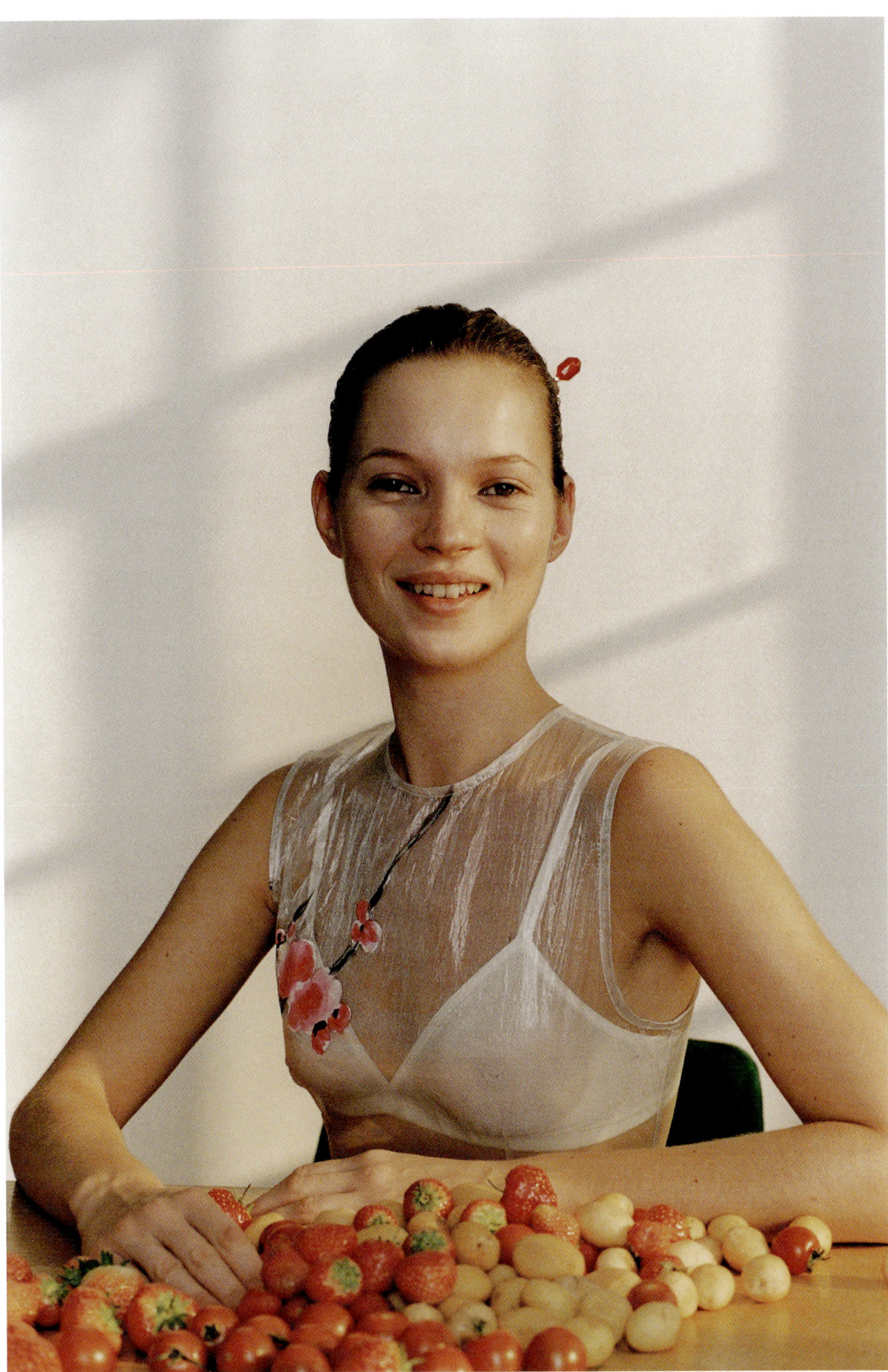

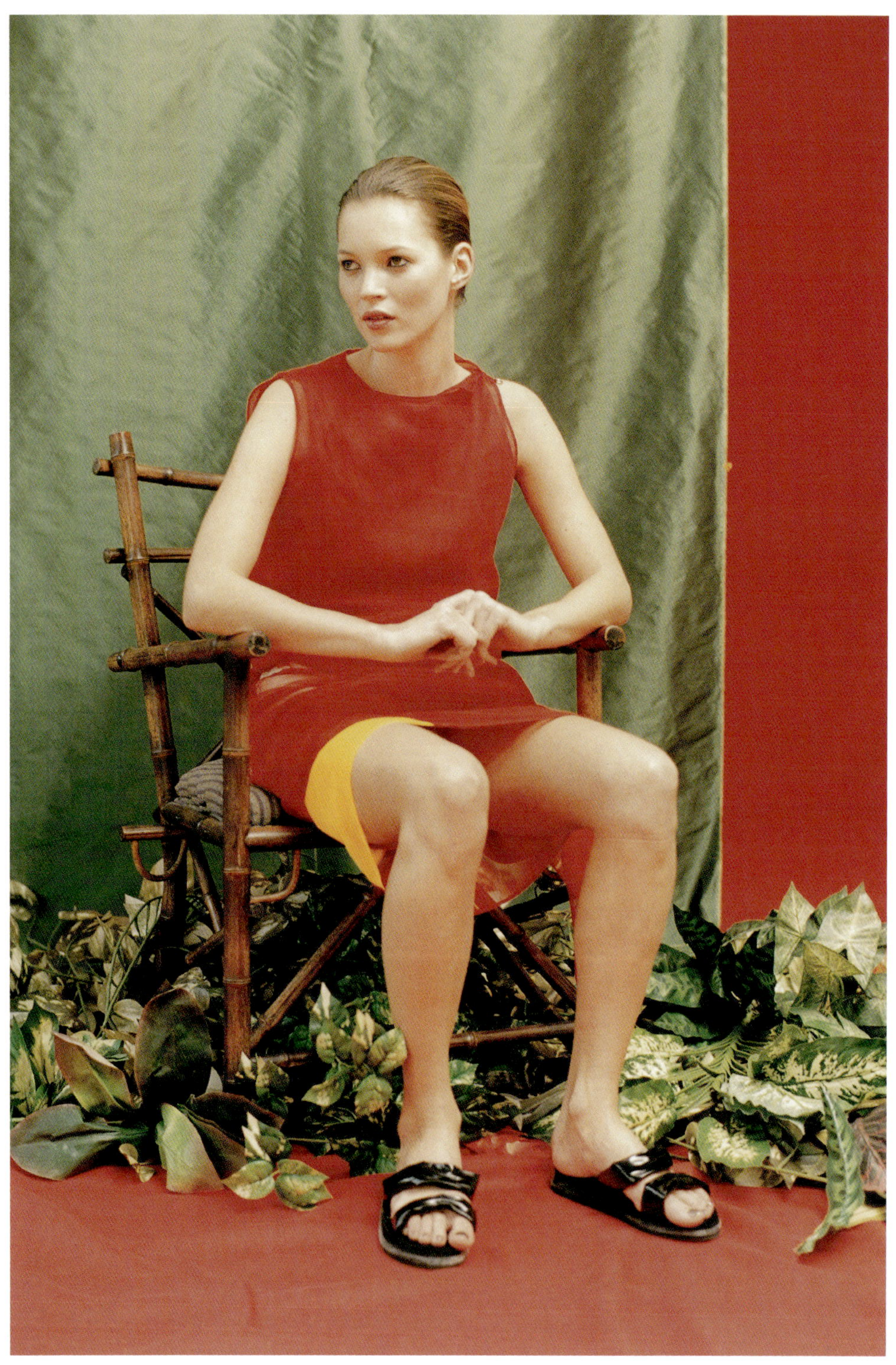

Kate sitting, 1996

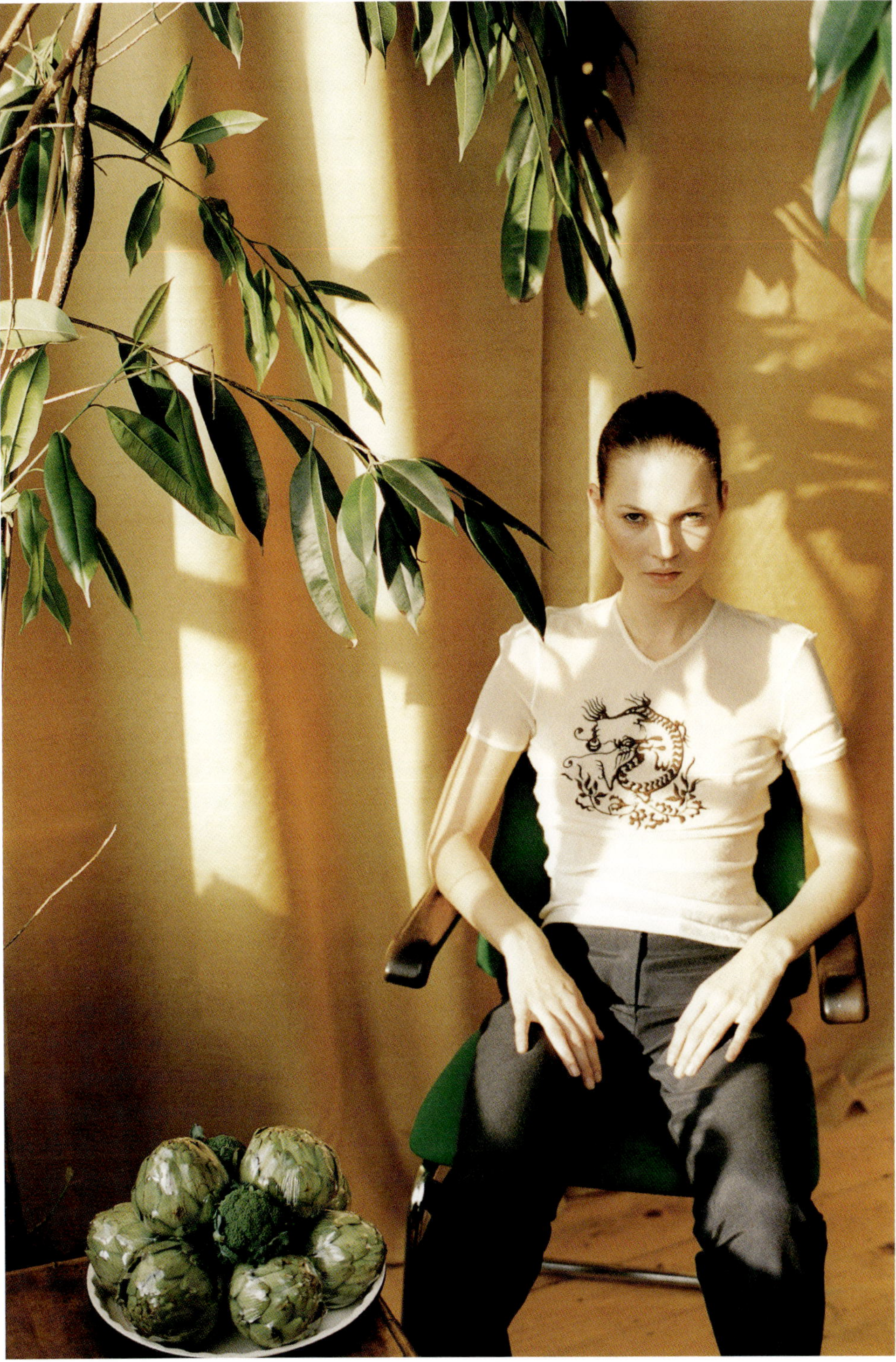

Kate with tree, 1996

Kate with broccoli, 1996   The London Apprentice, 1996 →

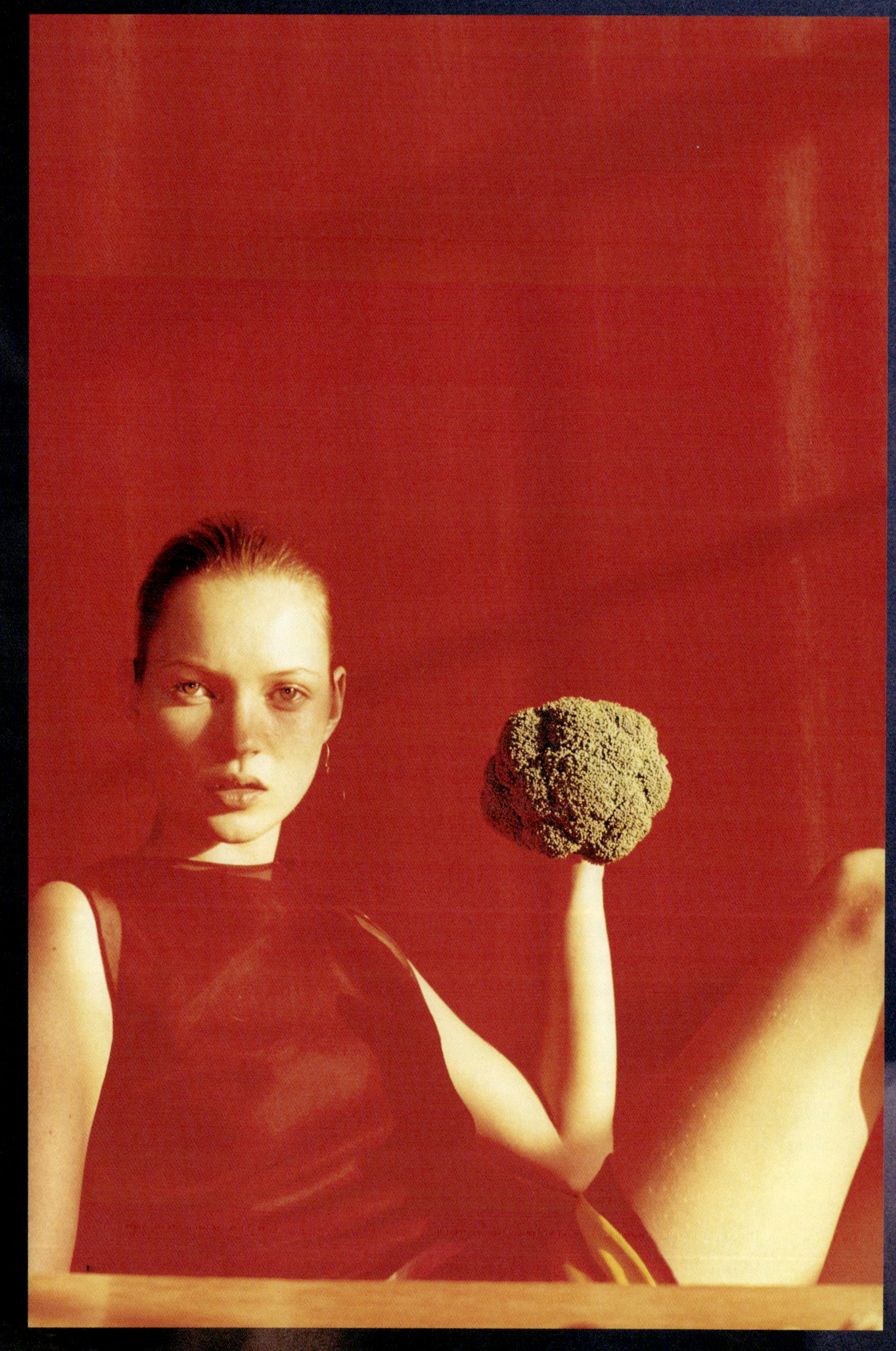

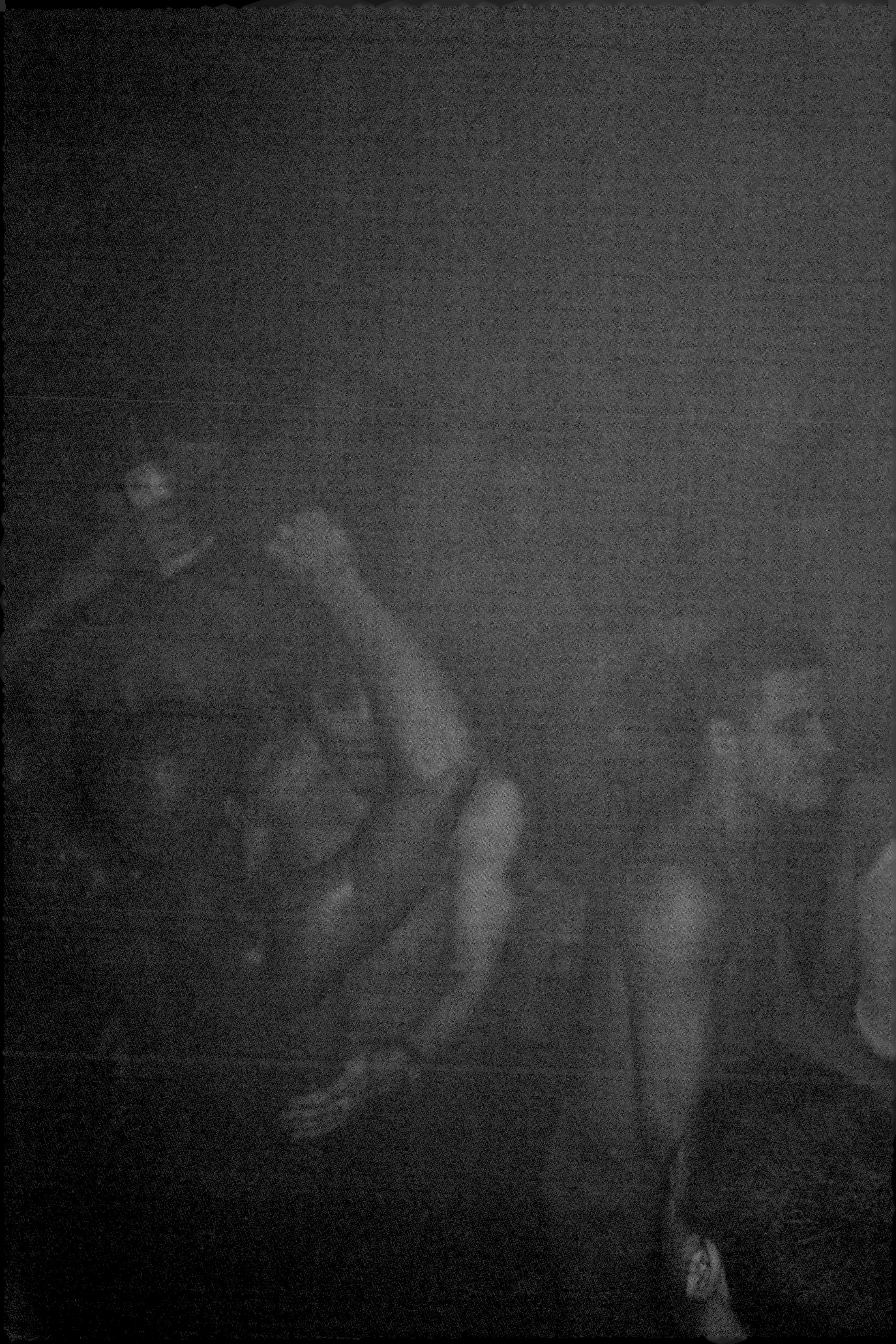

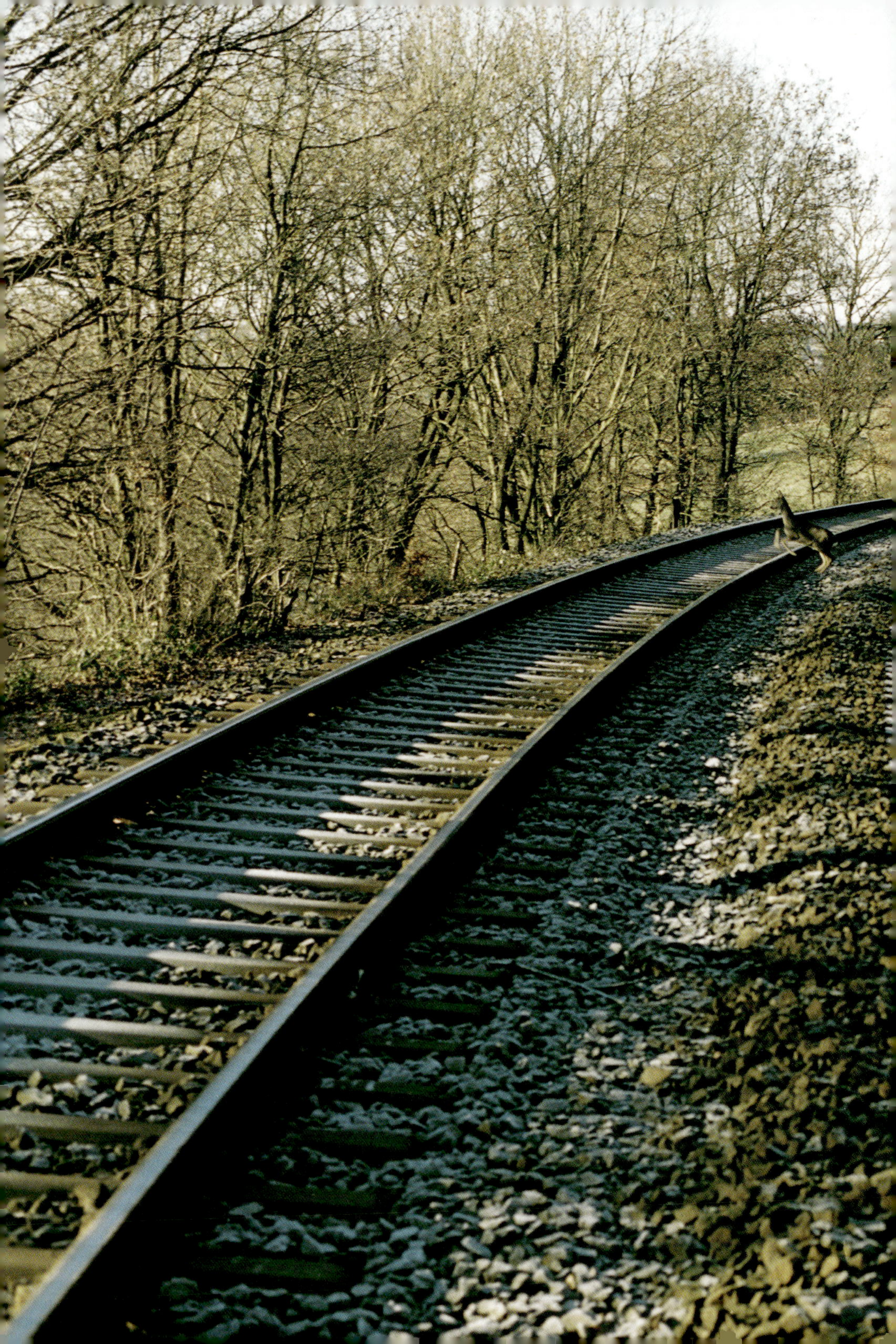

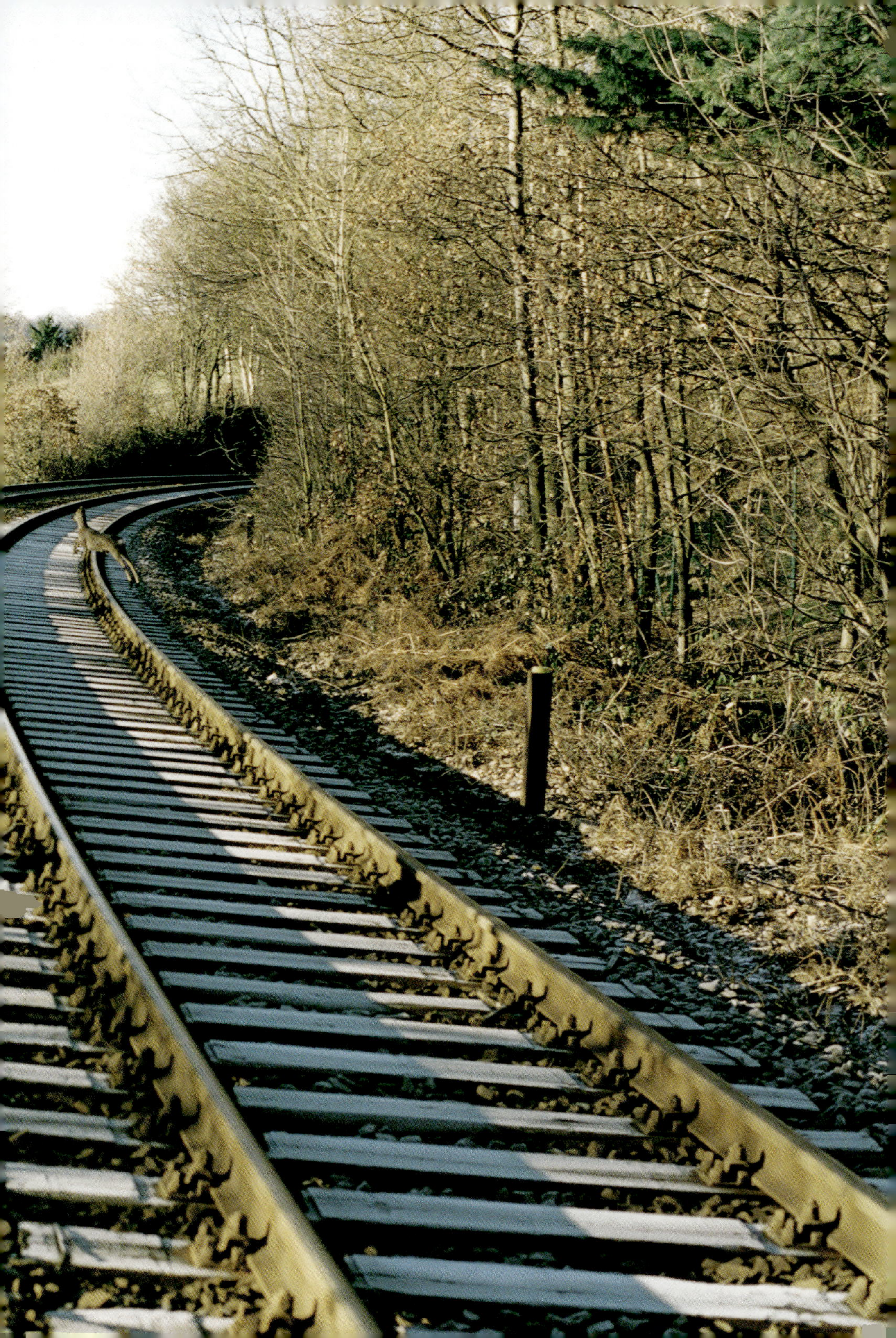

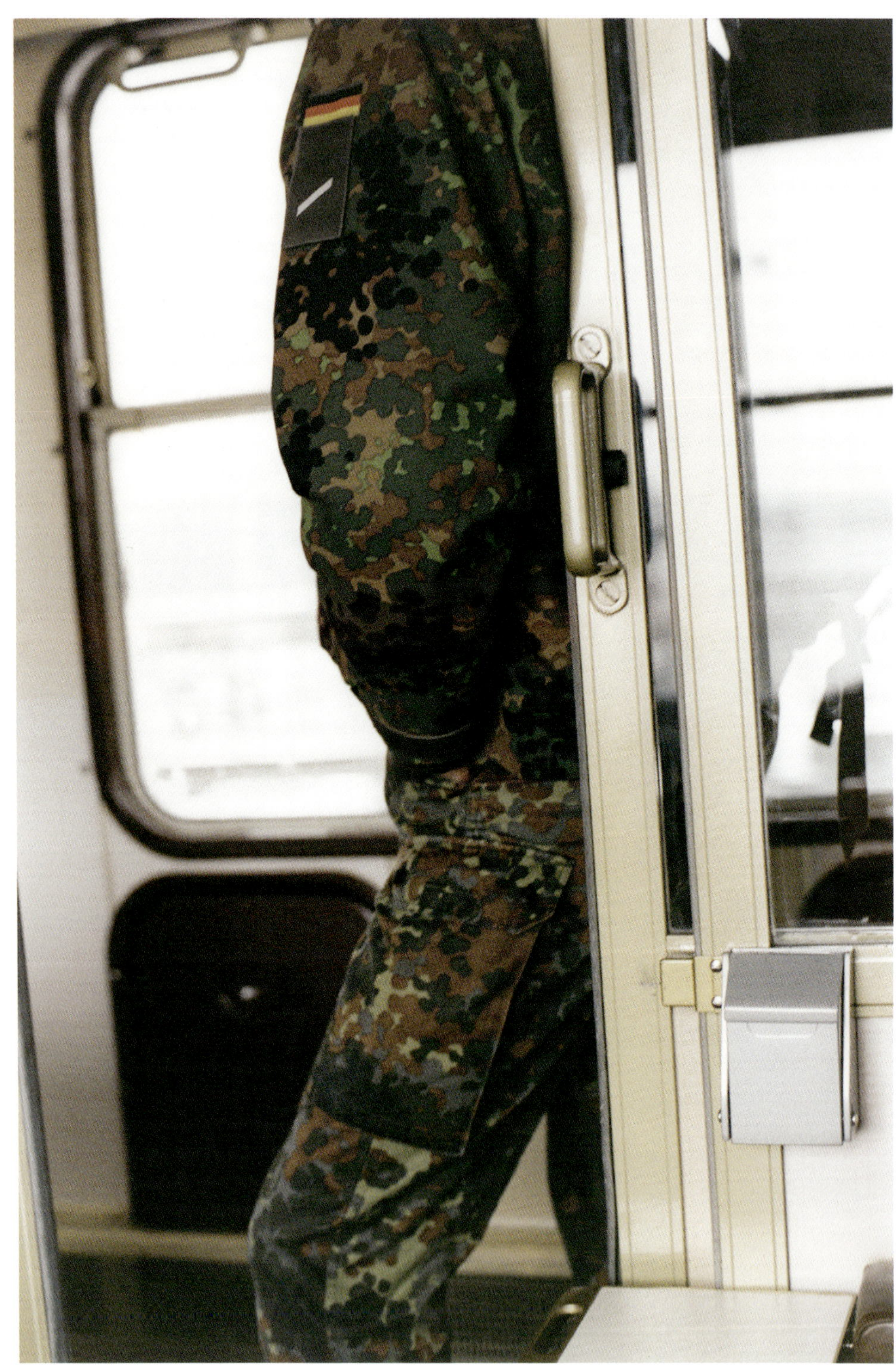

← Bahndamm, 1996

Soldat I, 1996

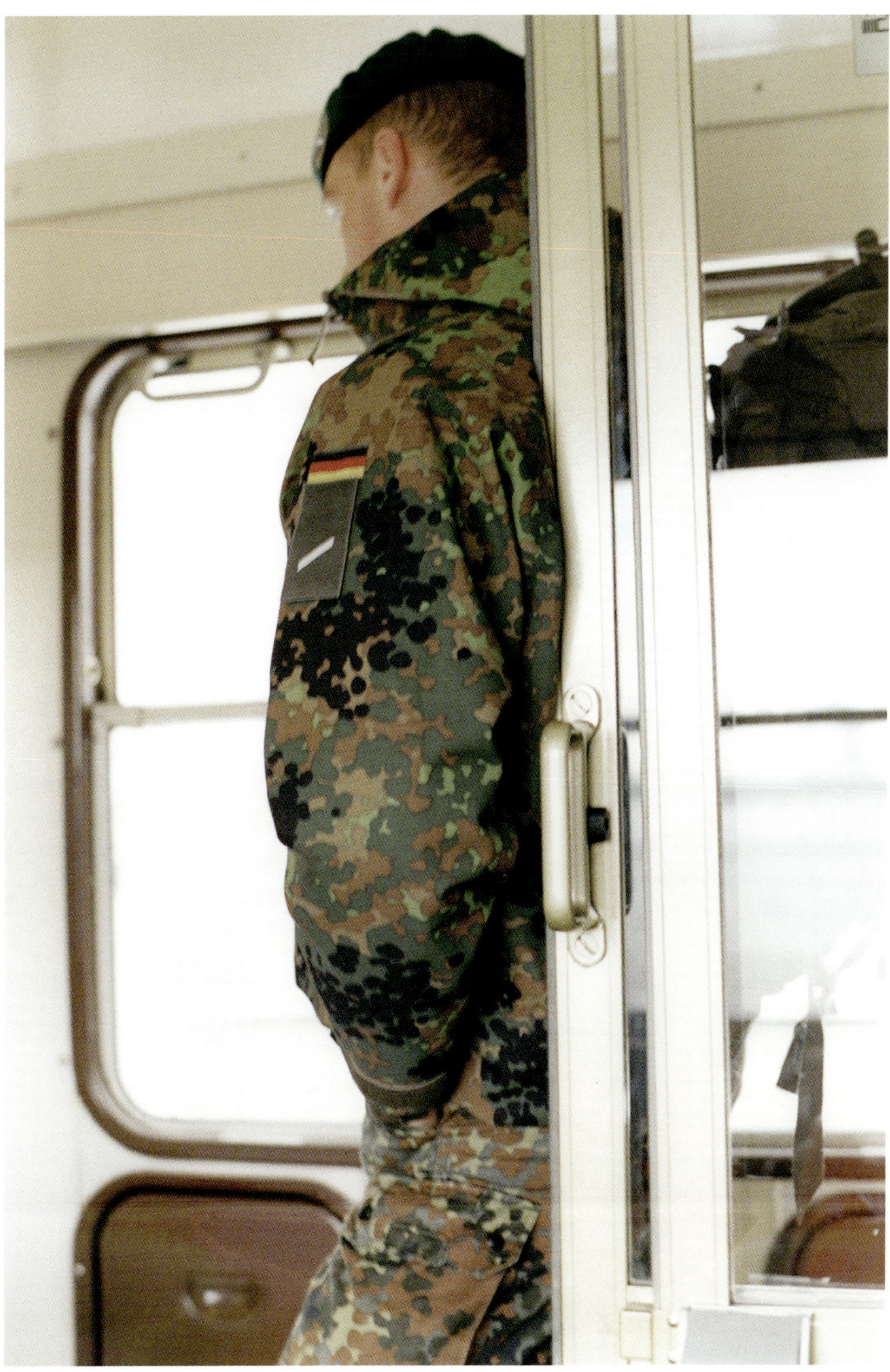

Soldat II, 1996

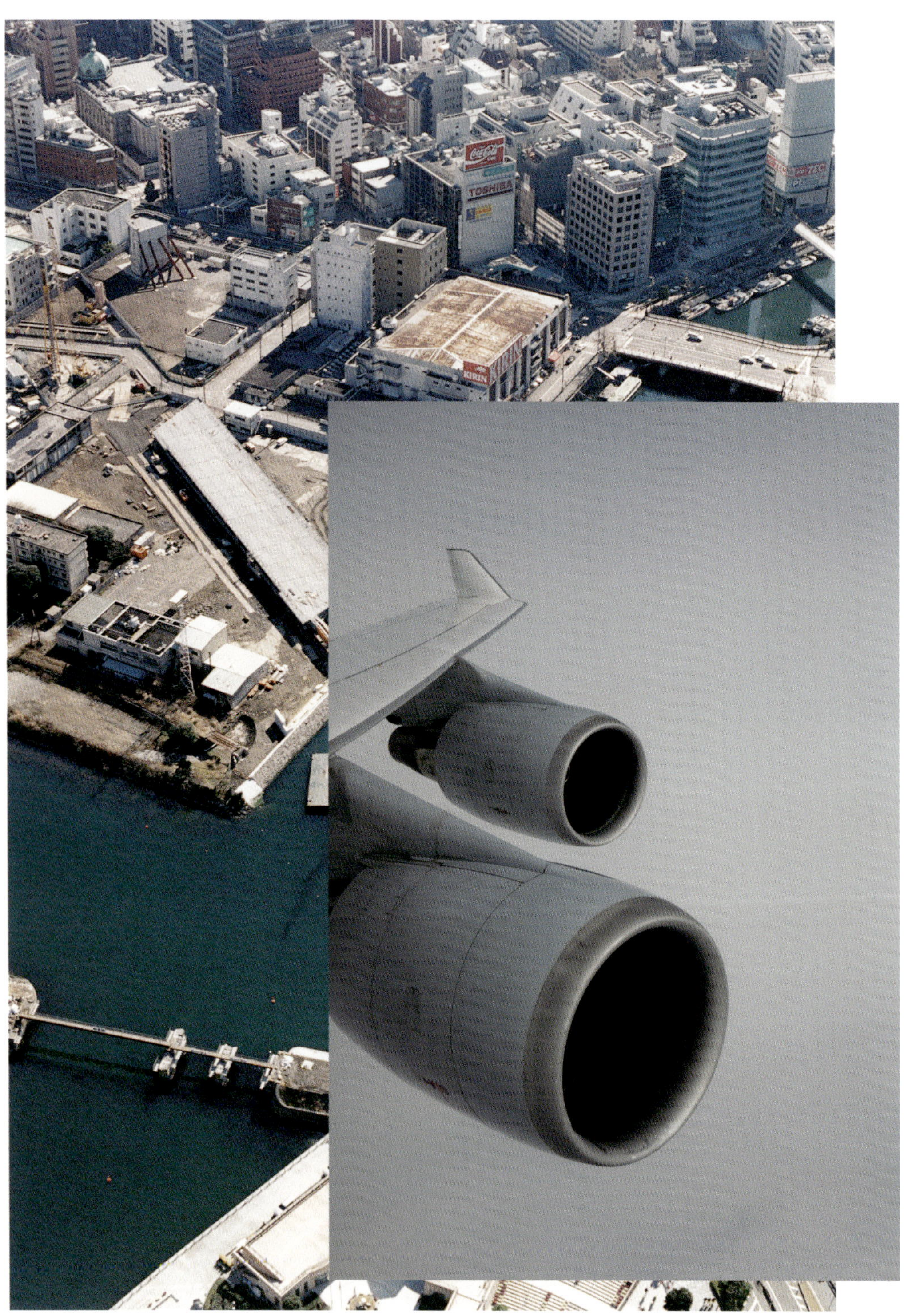

Minato Mirai 21, 1997   JAL II, 2016   JAL, 1997

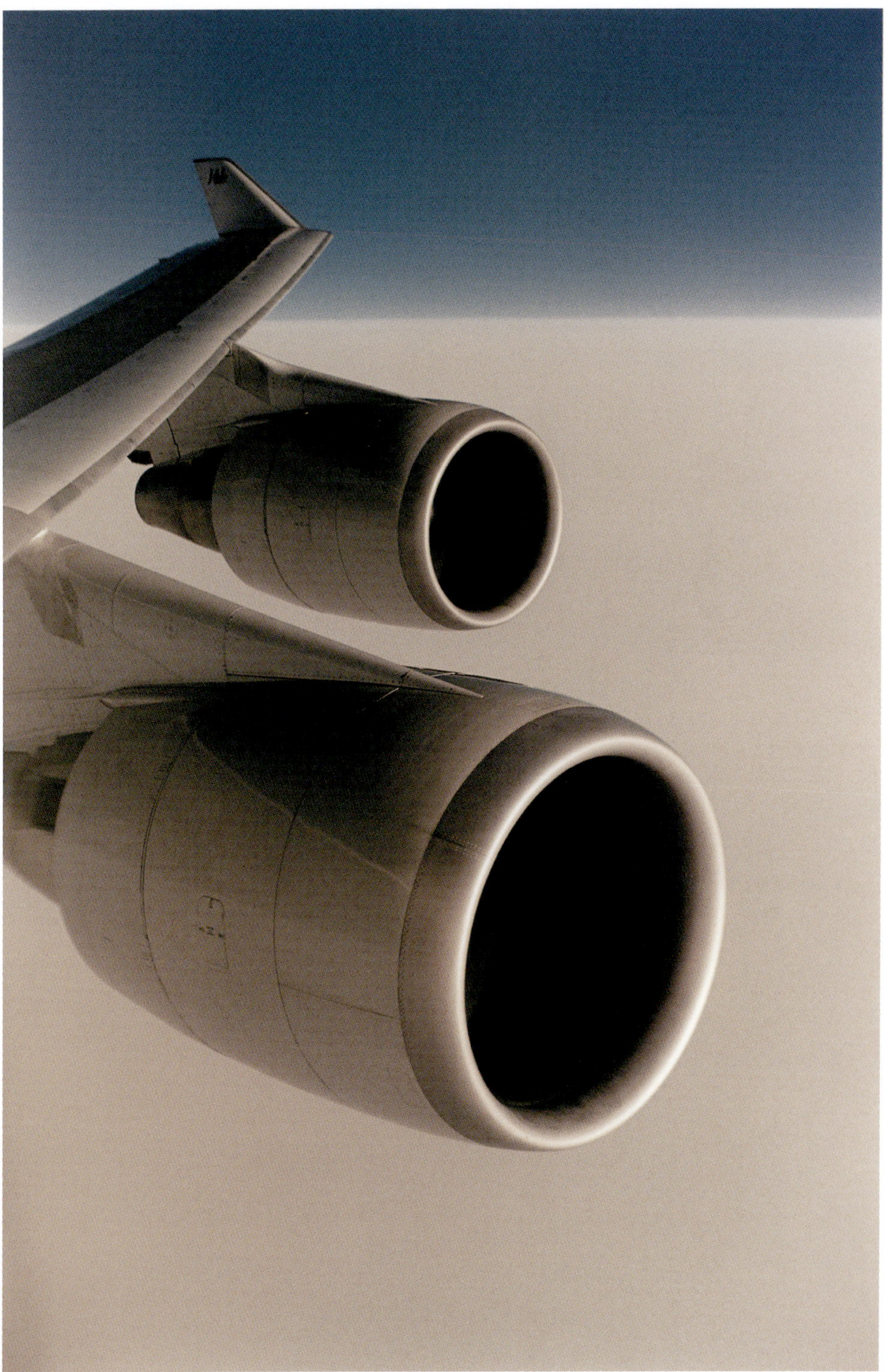

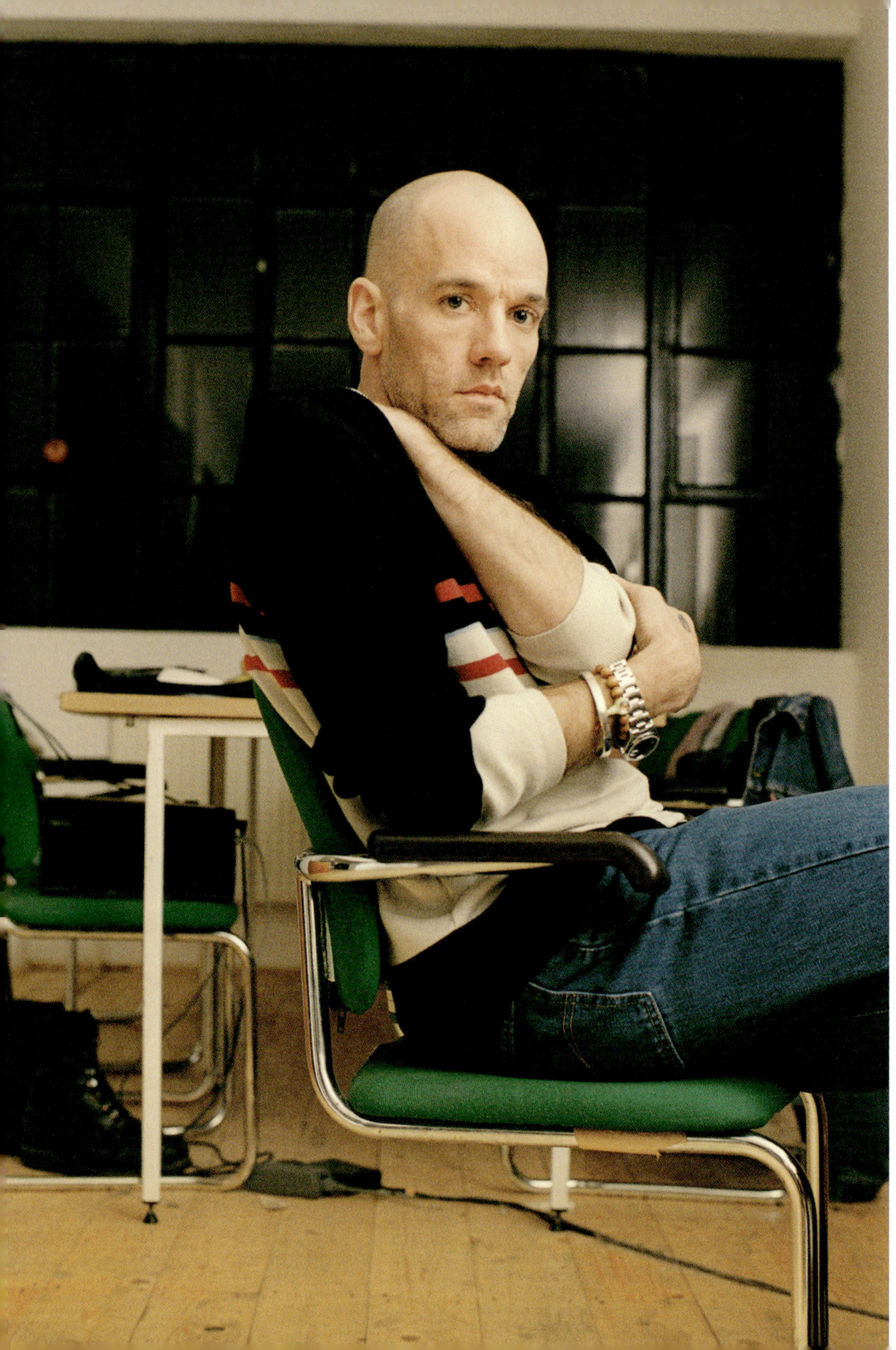

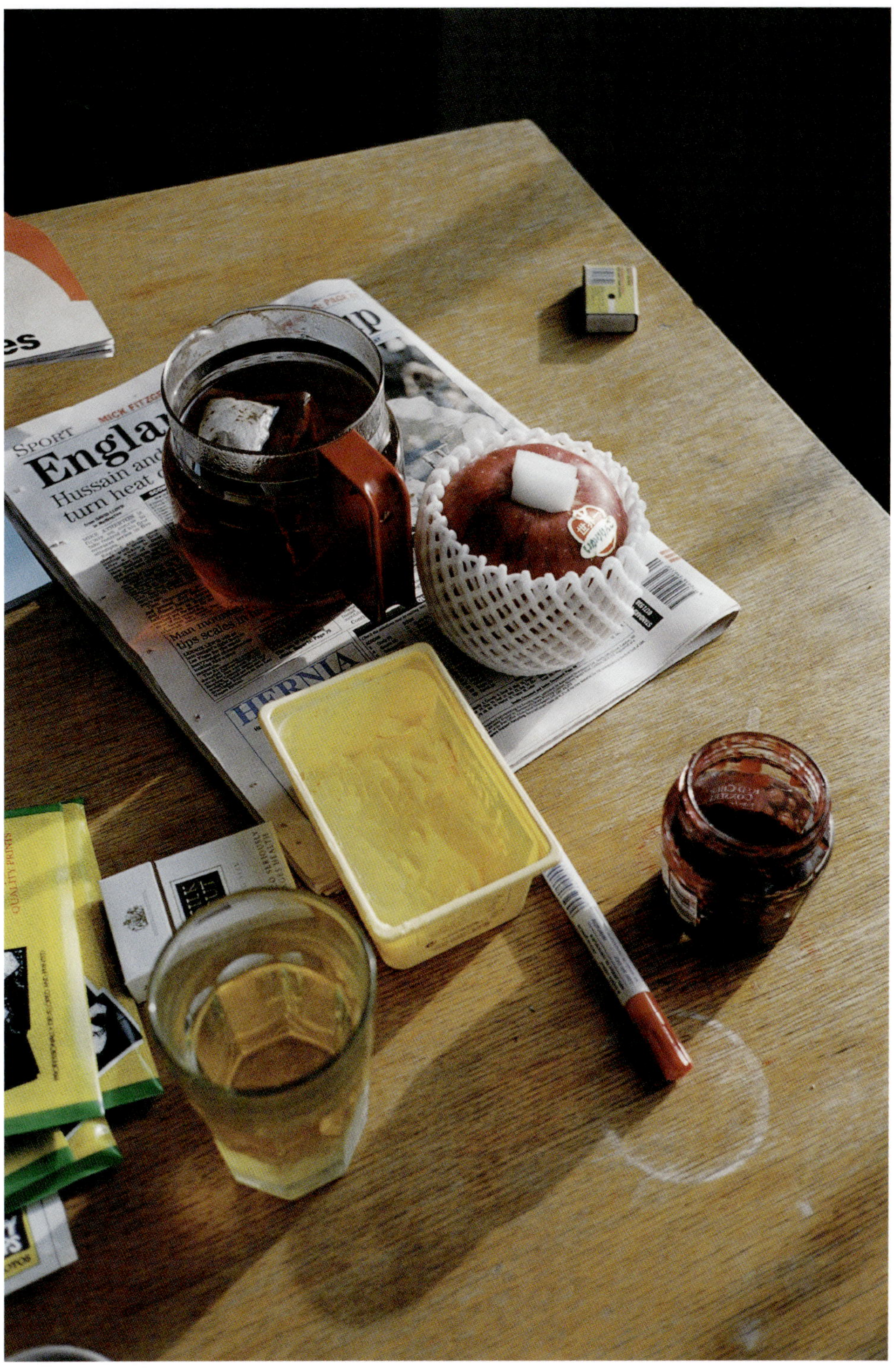

Michael, New Inn Yard, 1997   on the verge of visibility, 1997

window Caravaggio, 1997

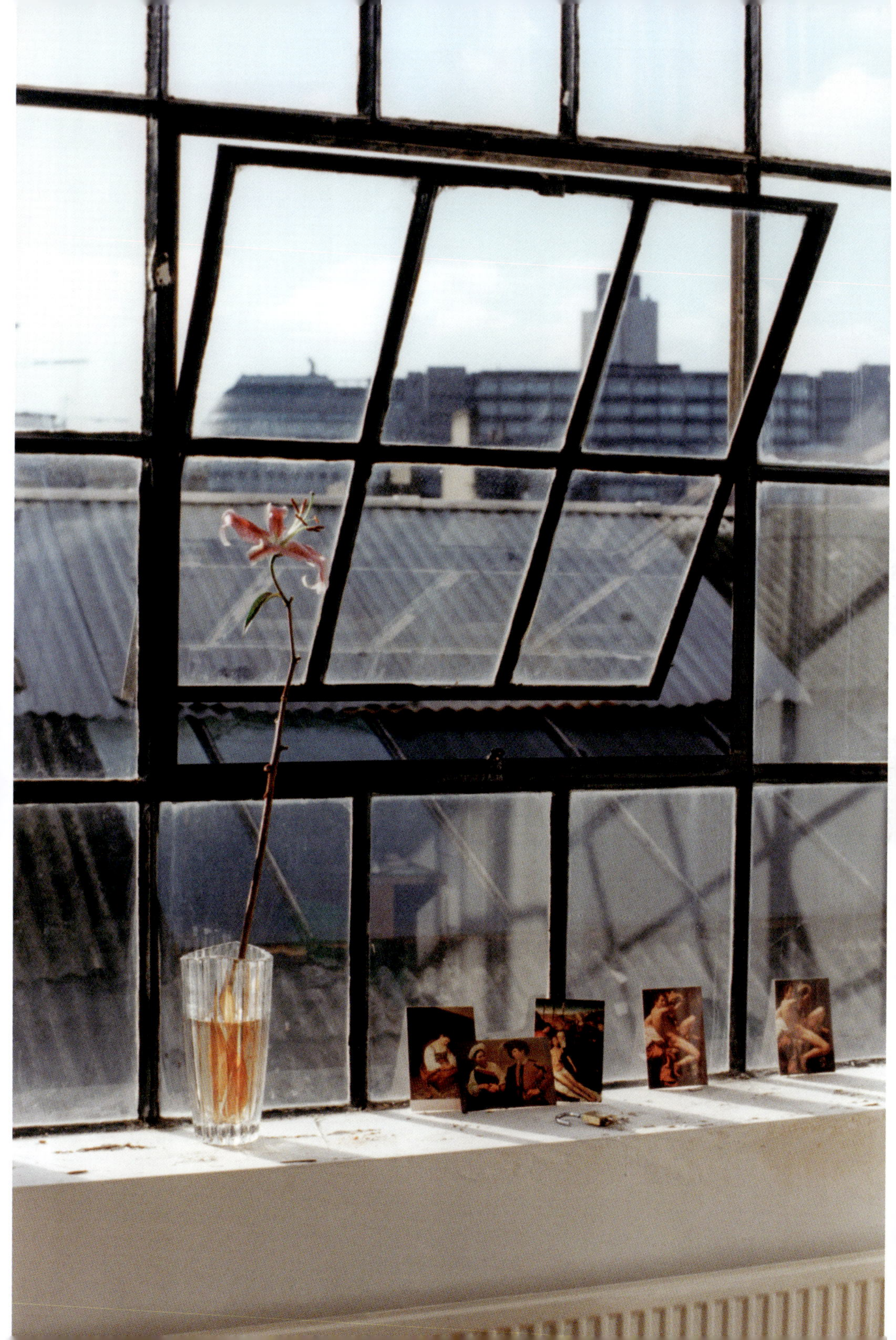

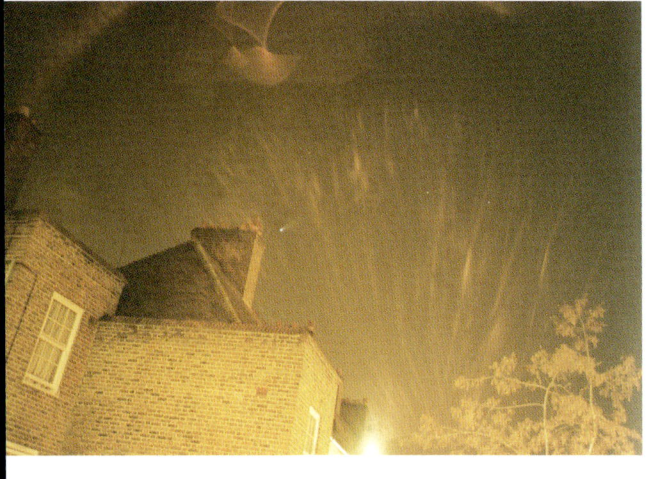

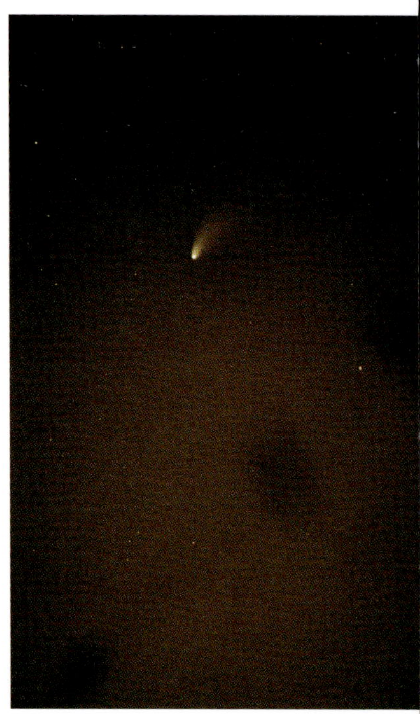

Hale-Bopp, 1997

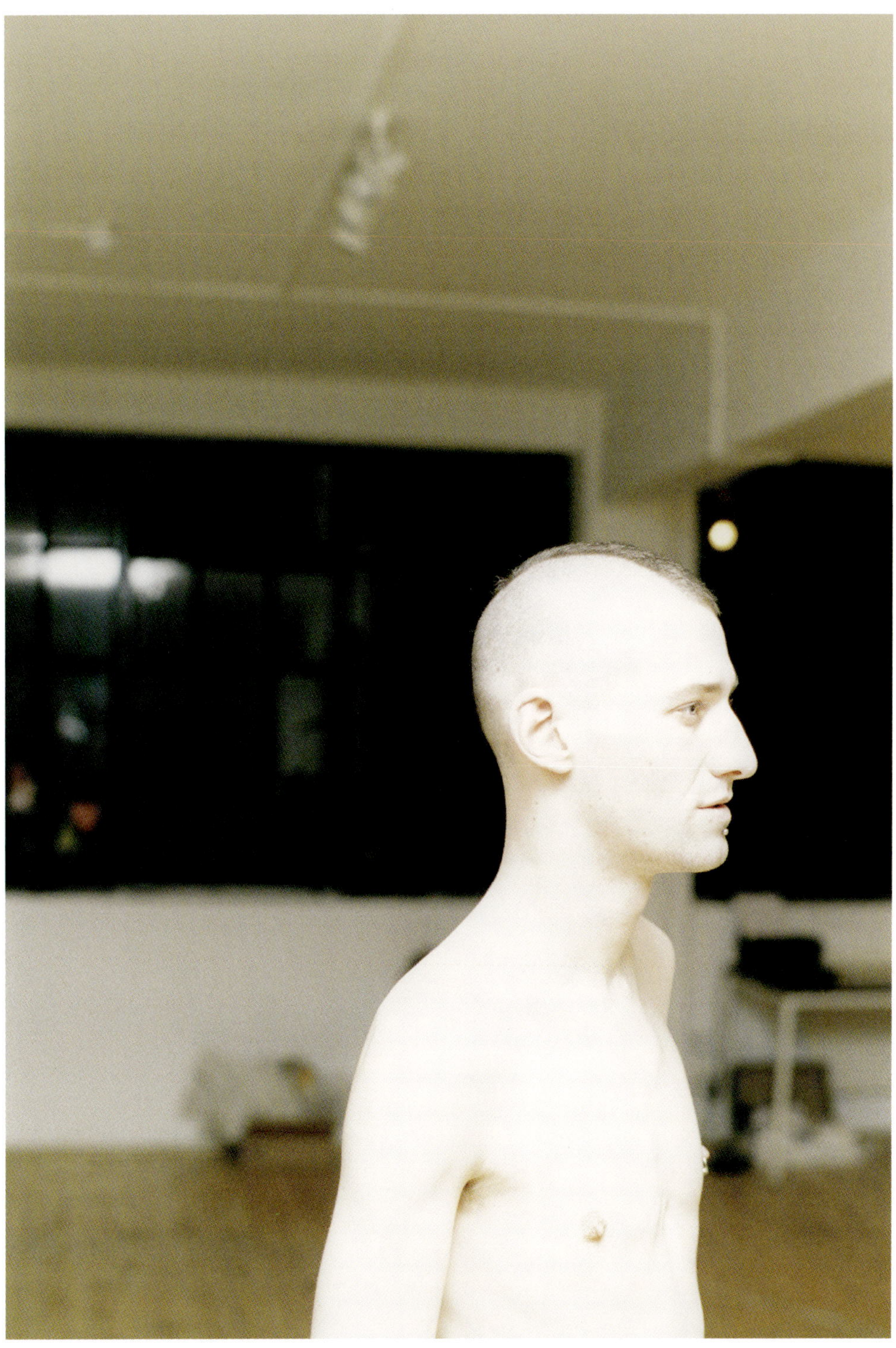
Philip Light, 1997

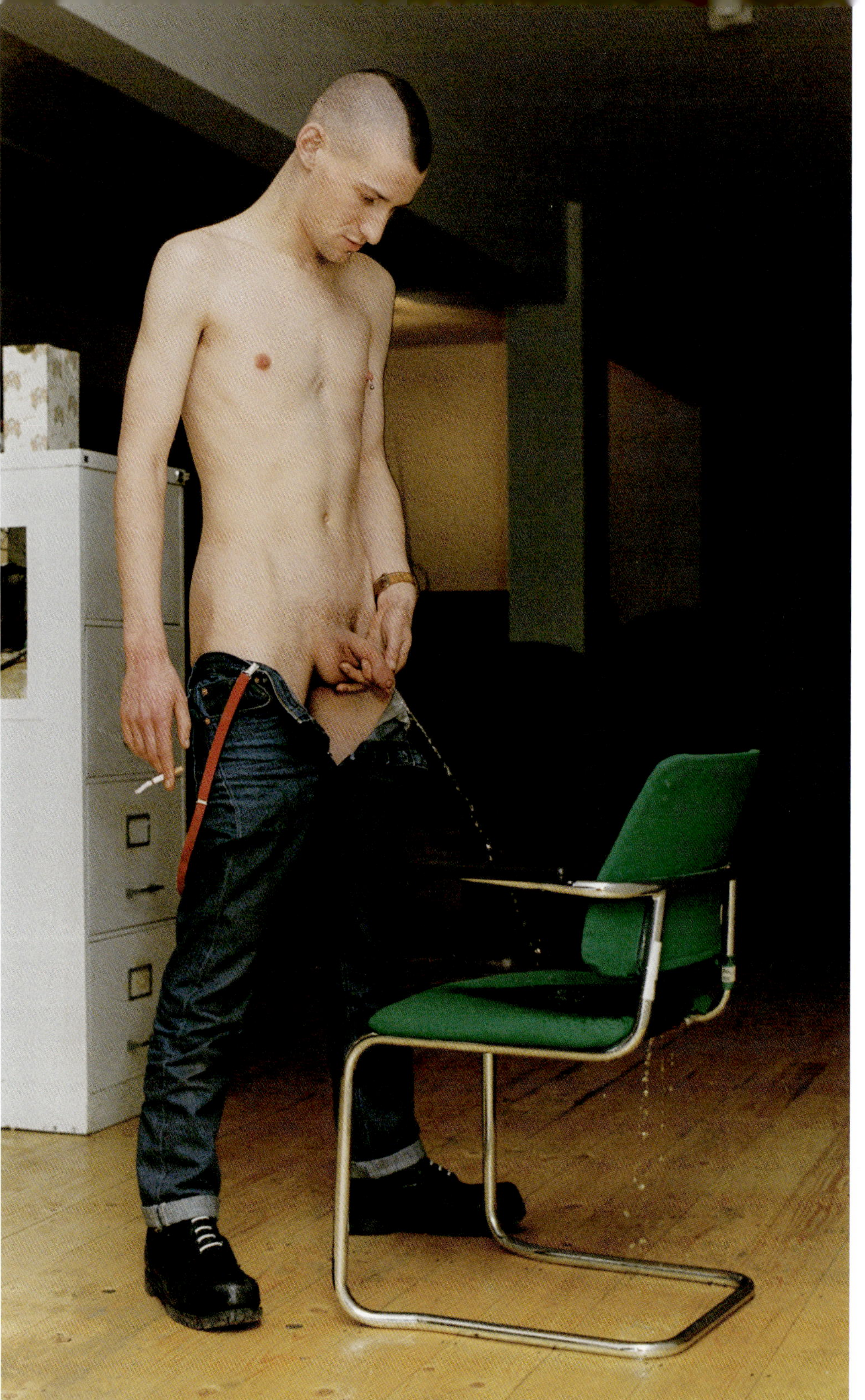

man pissing on chair, 1997

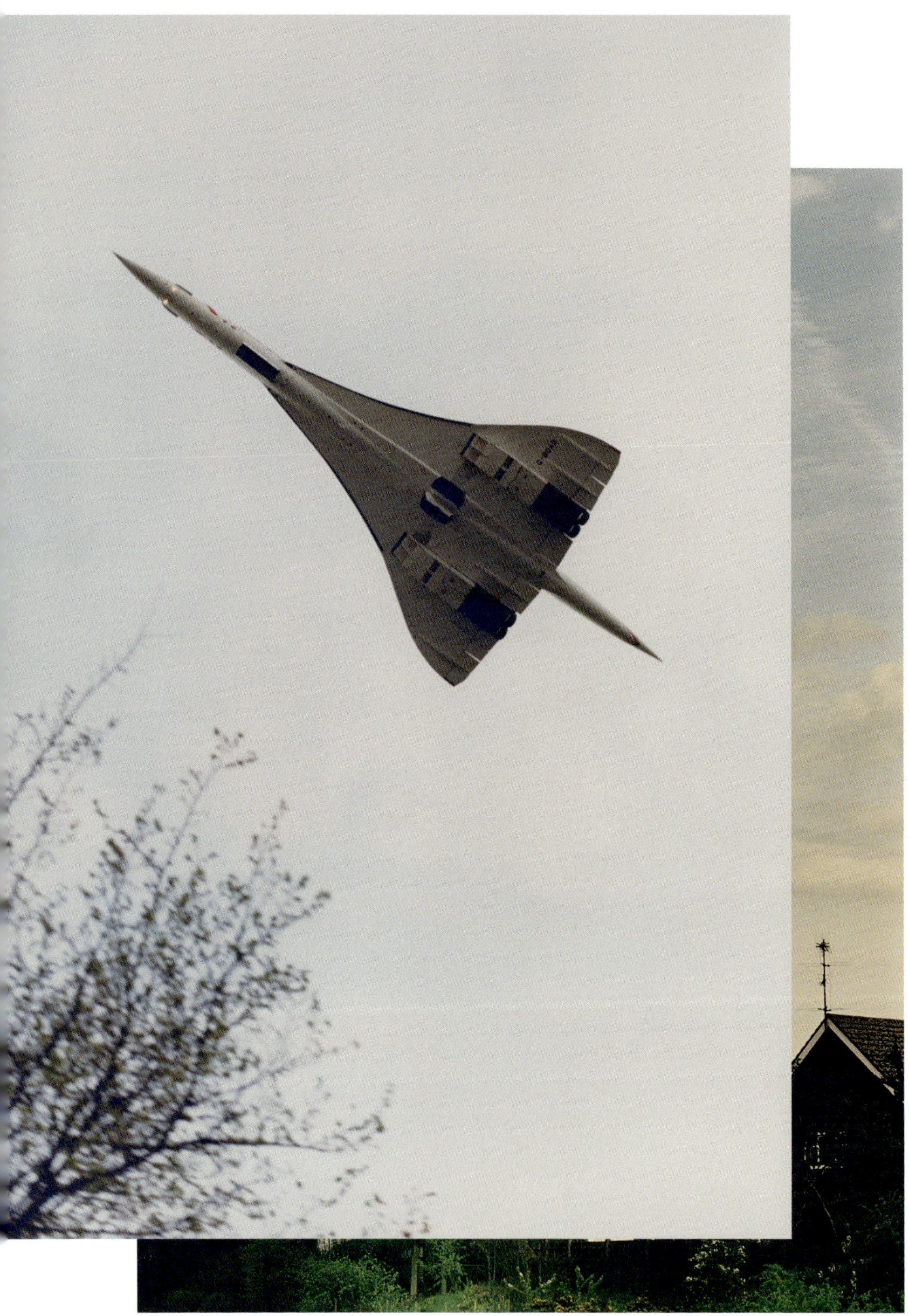

Concorde L 449-15A, 1997

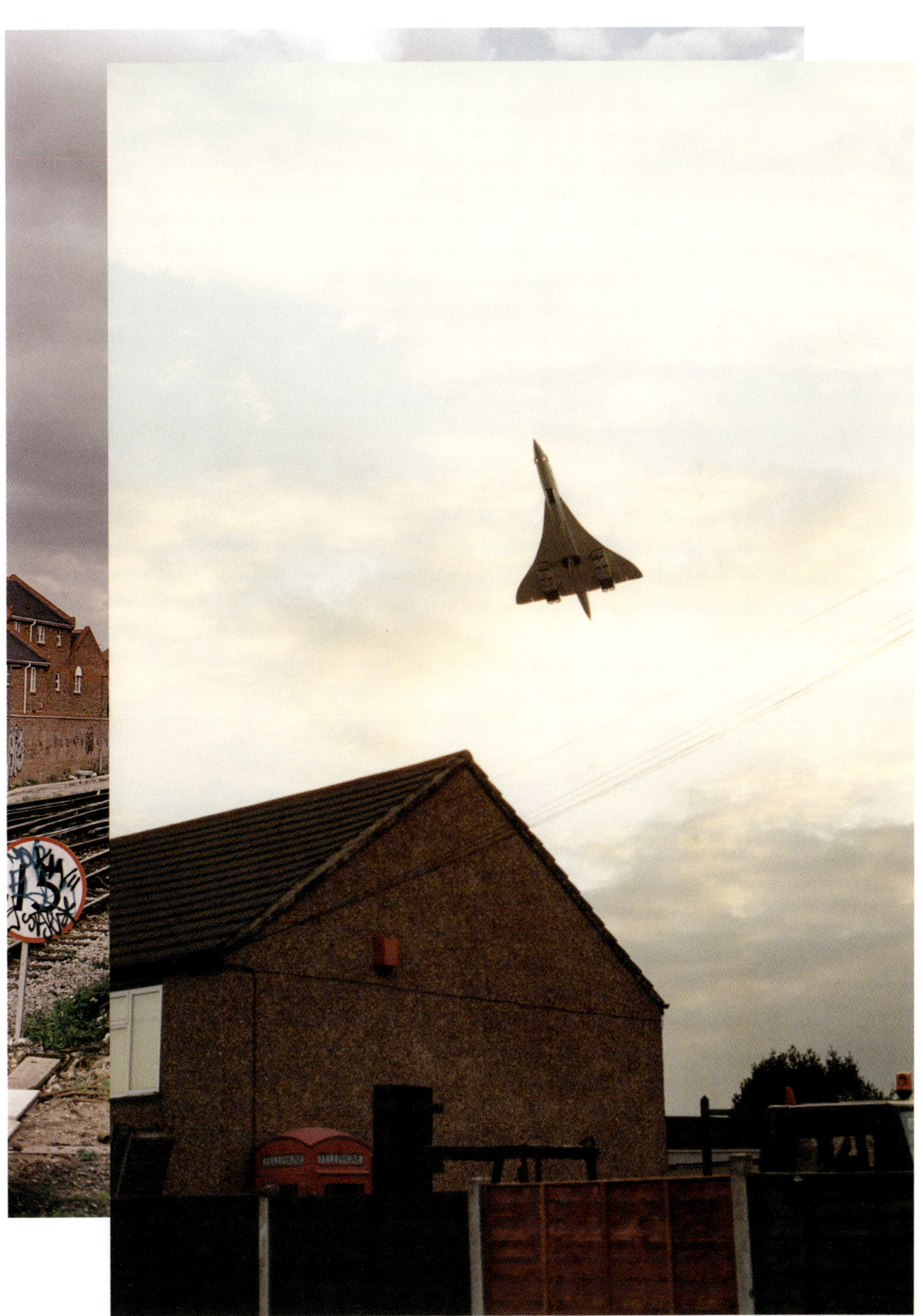

Concorde L 449-12, 1997

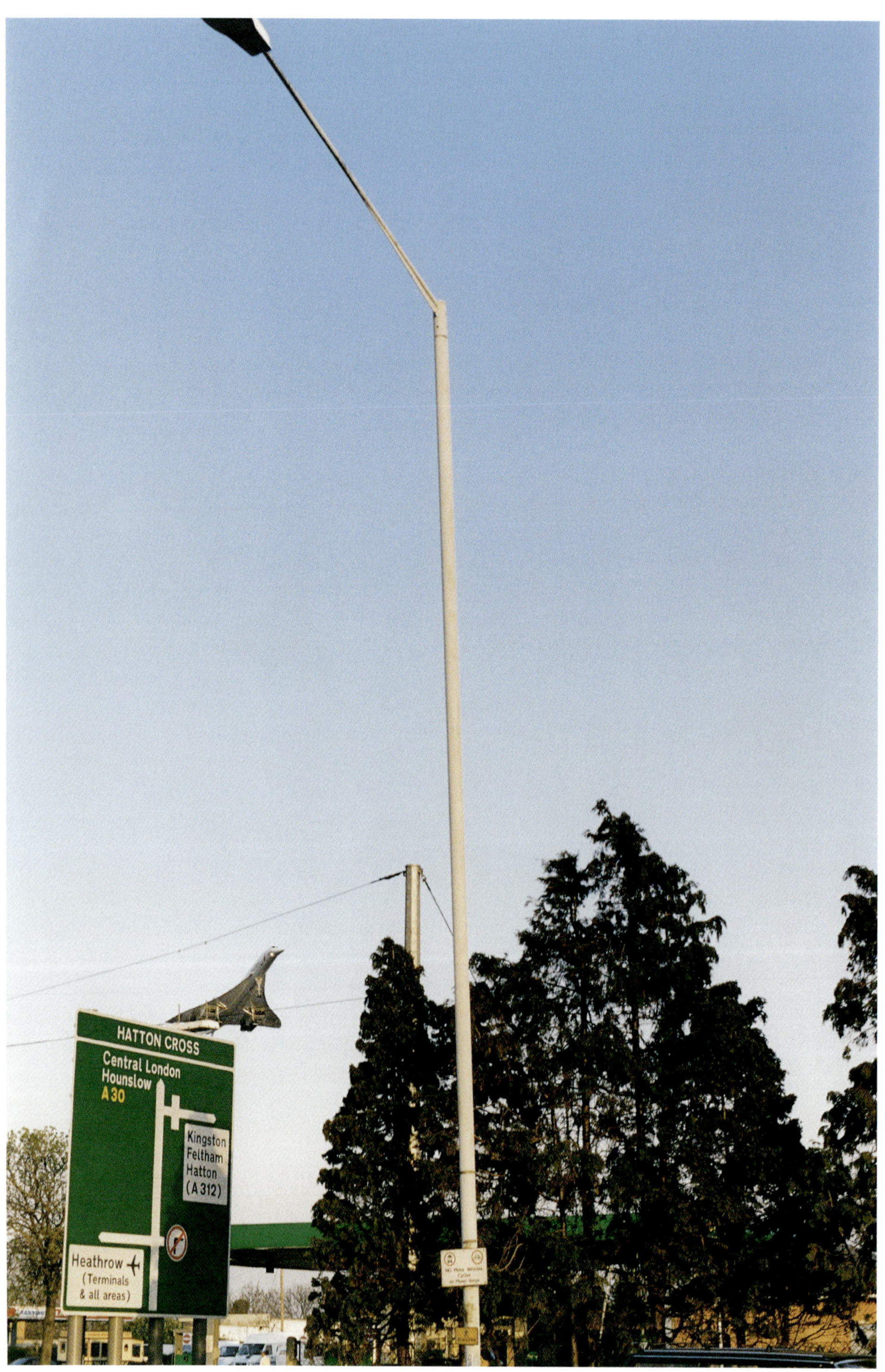

Concorde L 432 - 6, 1997

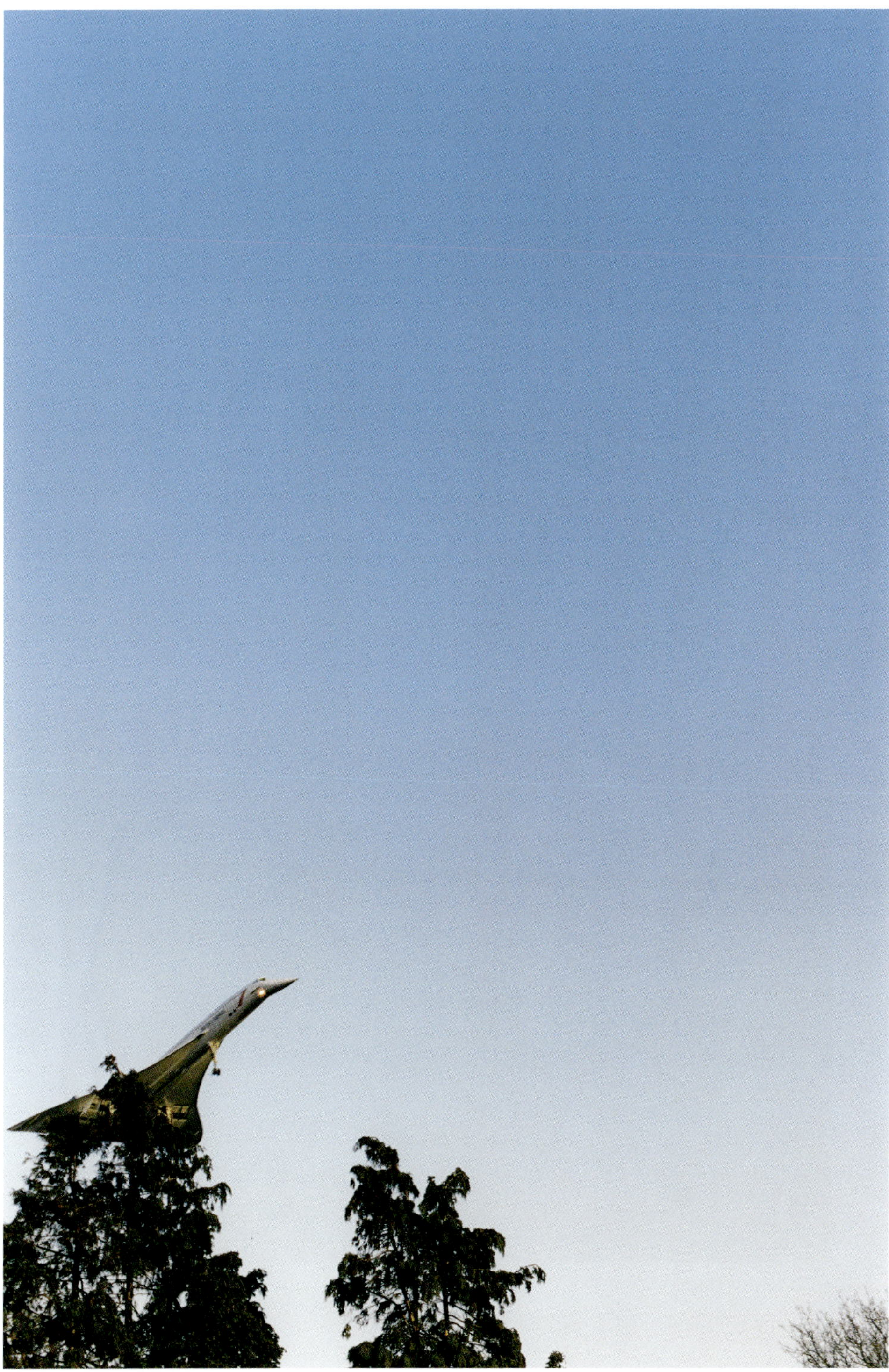

Concorde L 432 - 7, 1997

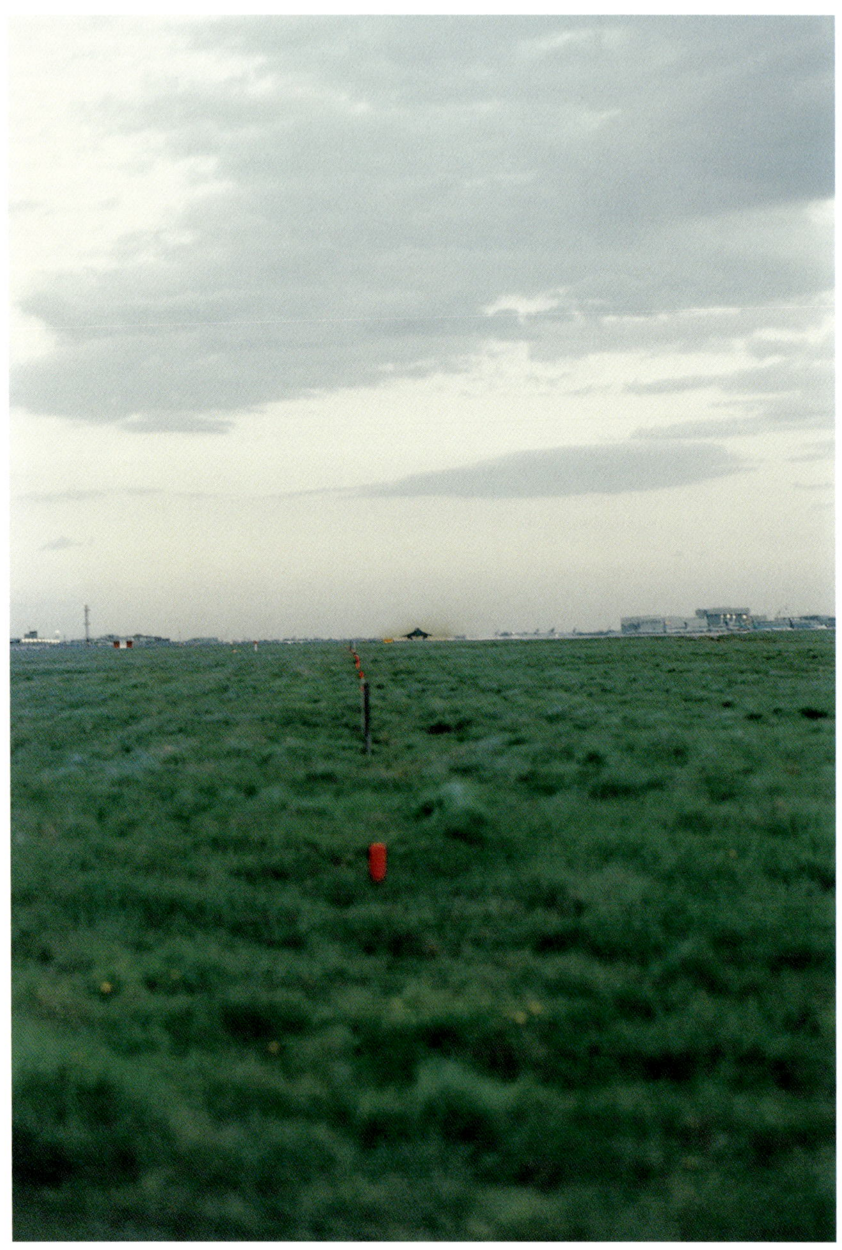

Concorde L 441 - 1 A, 1997

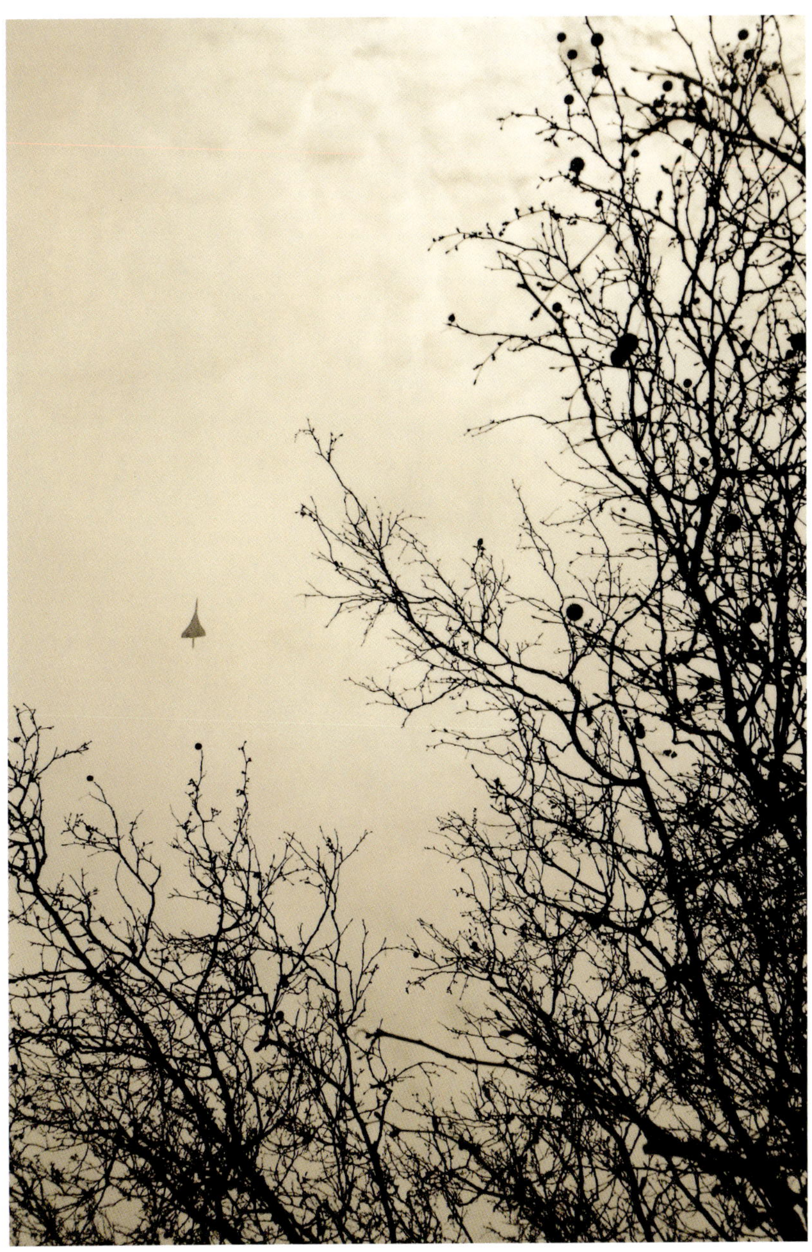

Concorde L 444 - 9, 1997

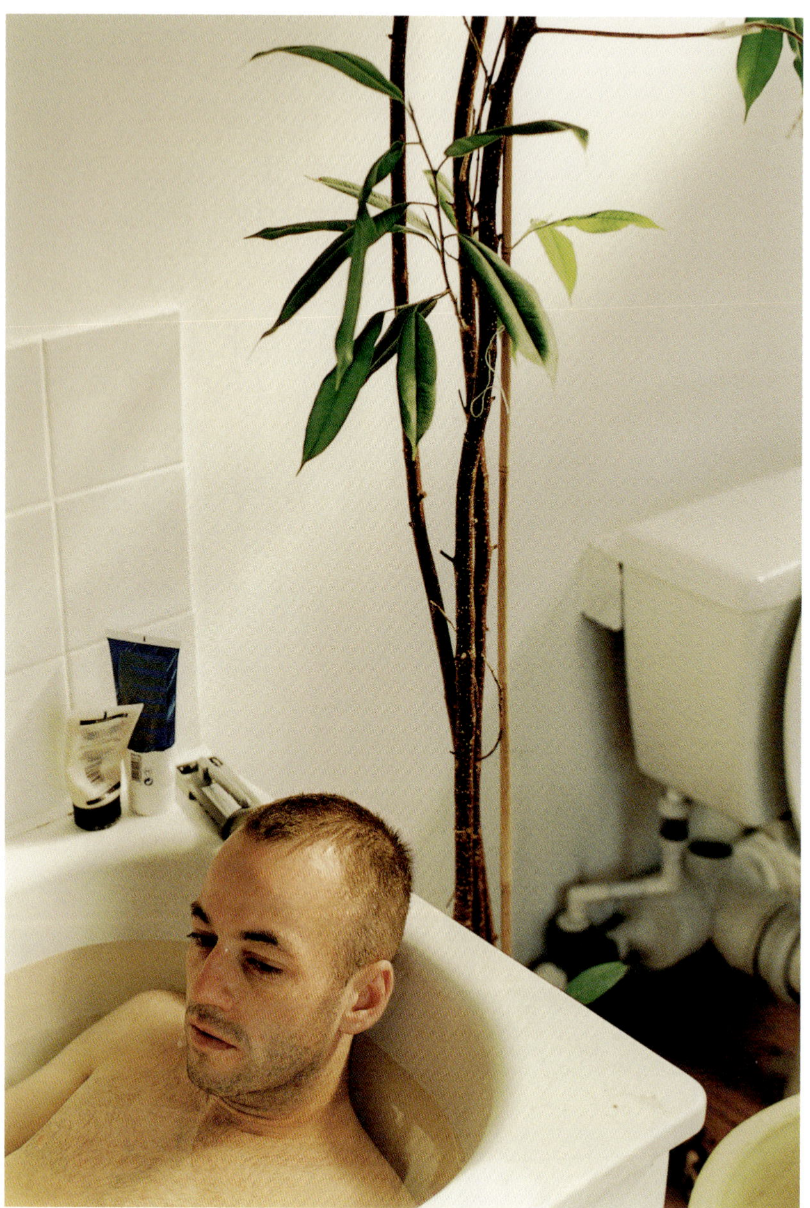

Jochen taking a bath, 1997

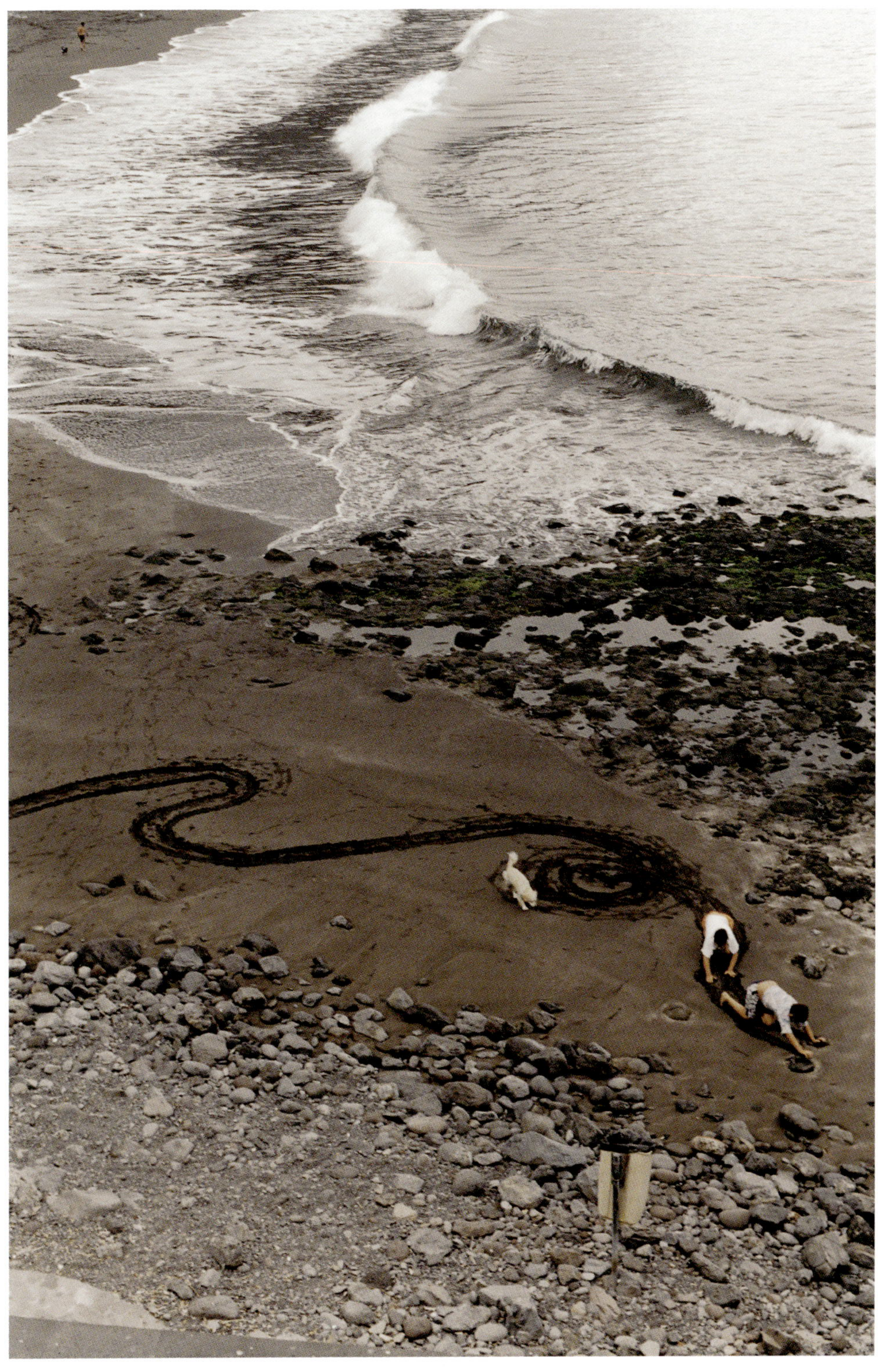

untitled (La Gomera), 1997

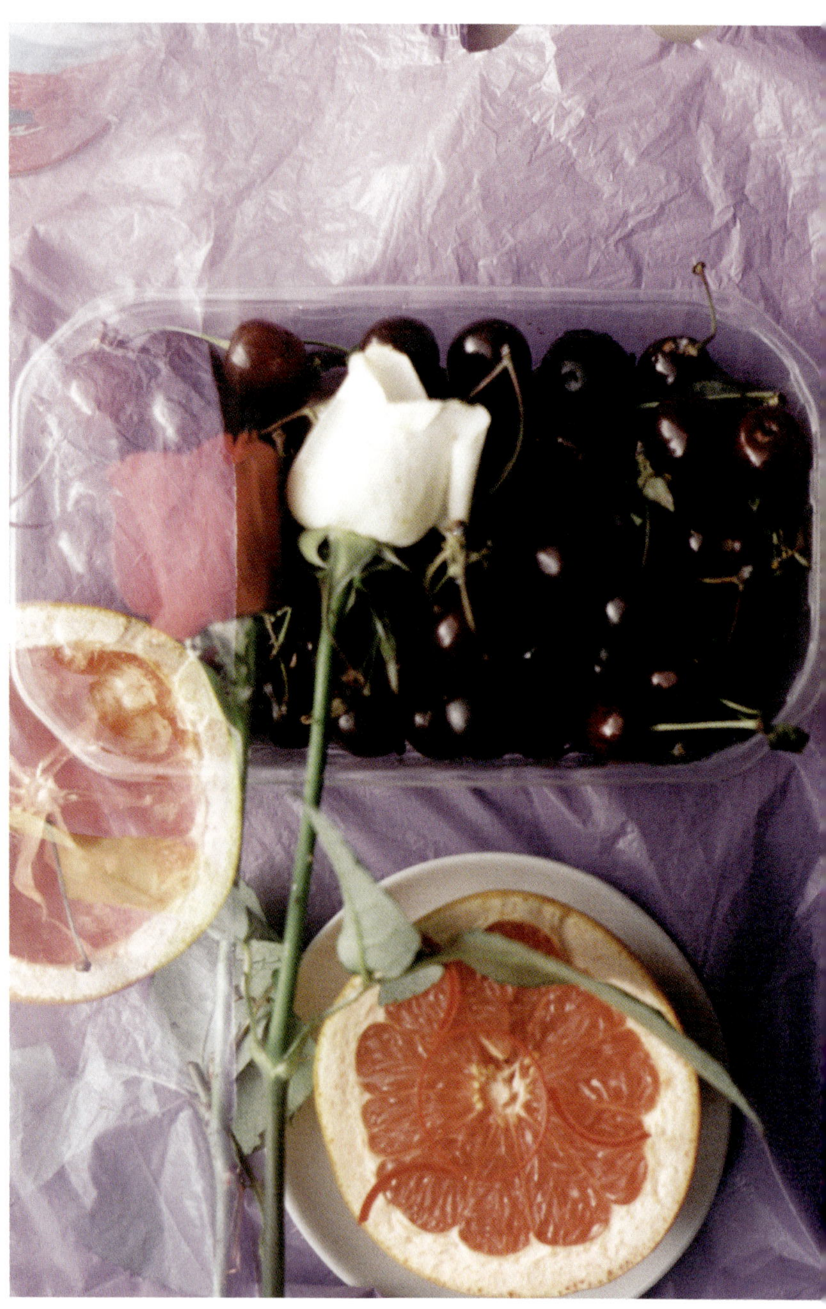

Stilleben Marktstrasse, 1997
Für Immer Burgen, 1997 →

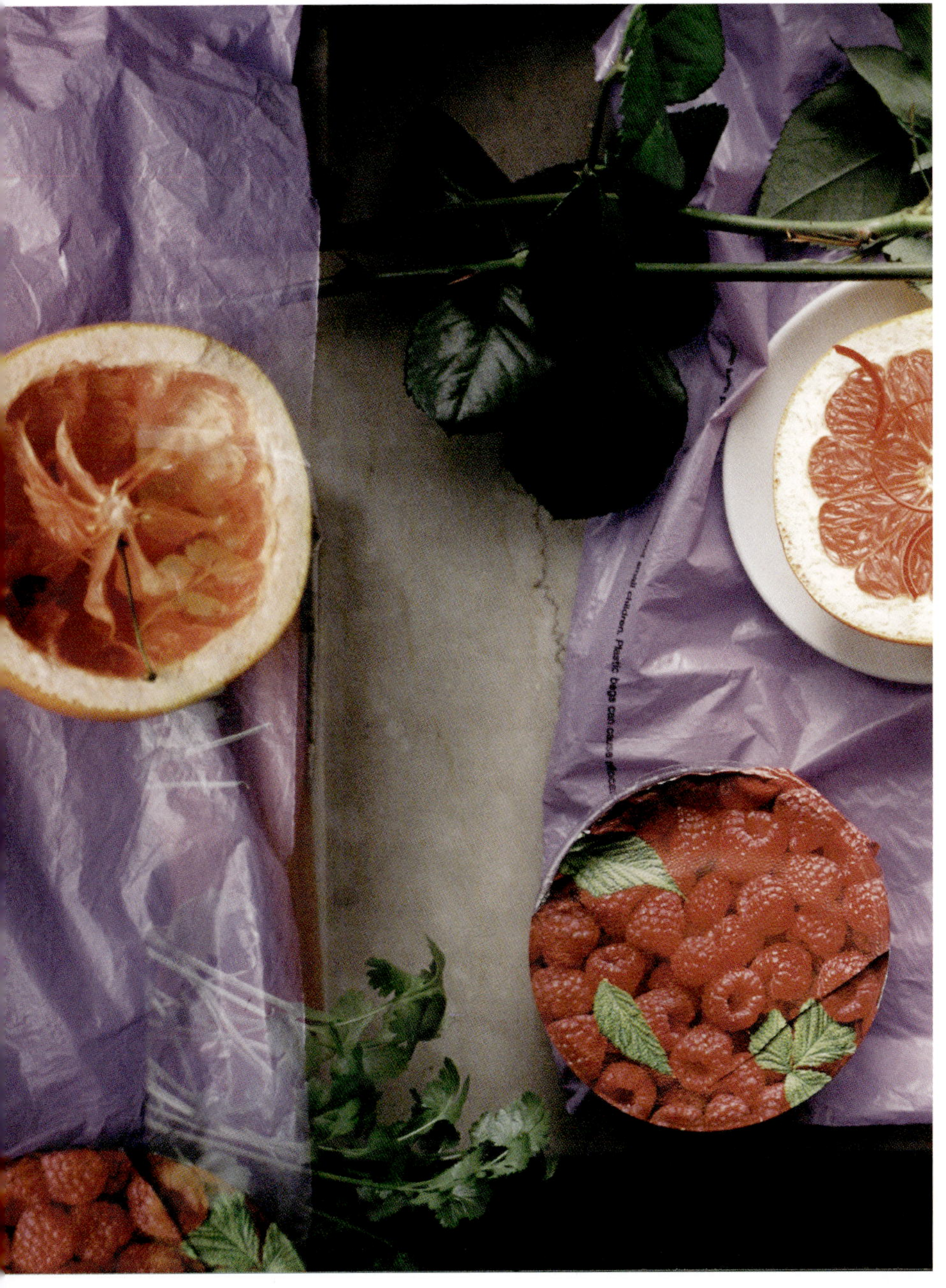

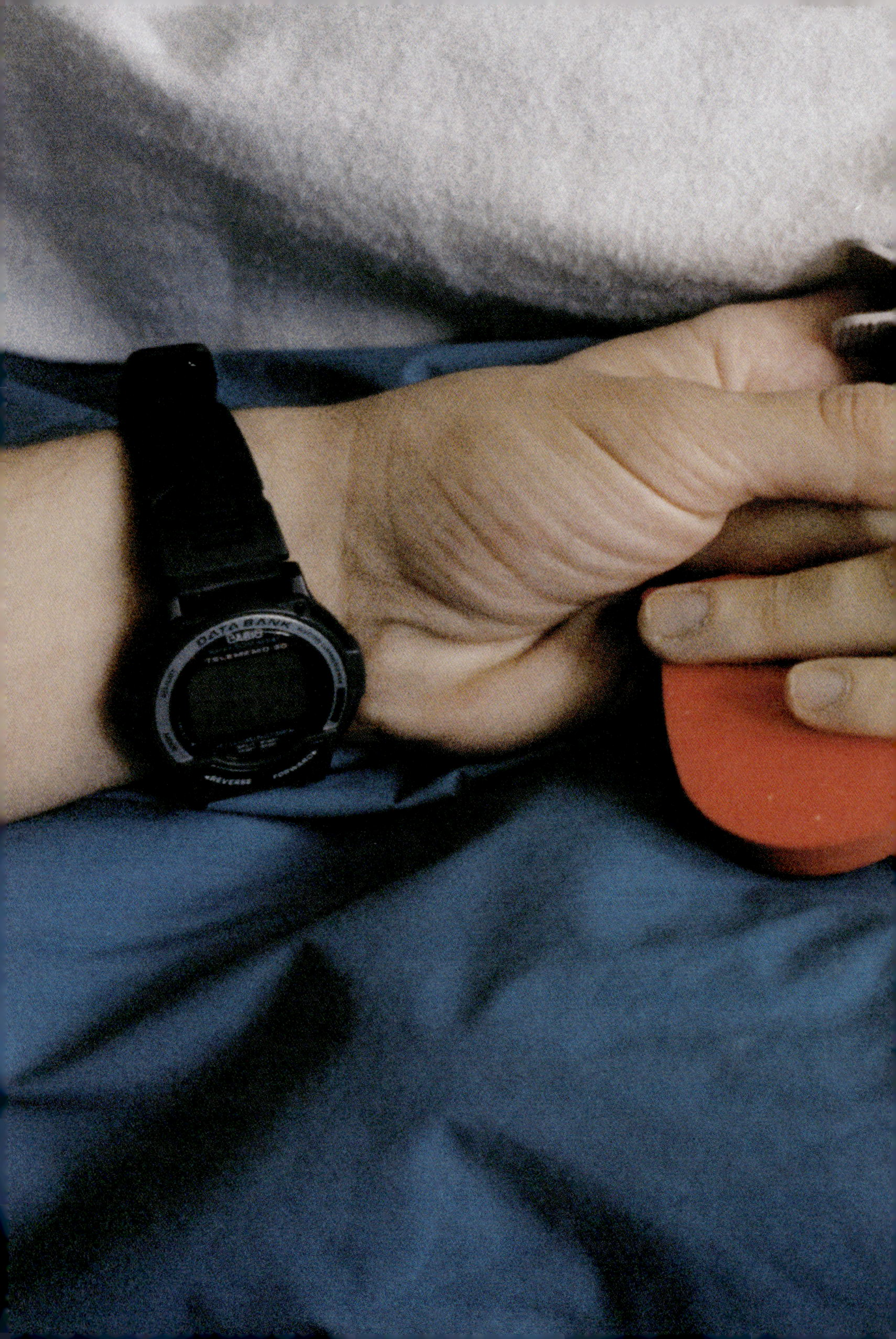

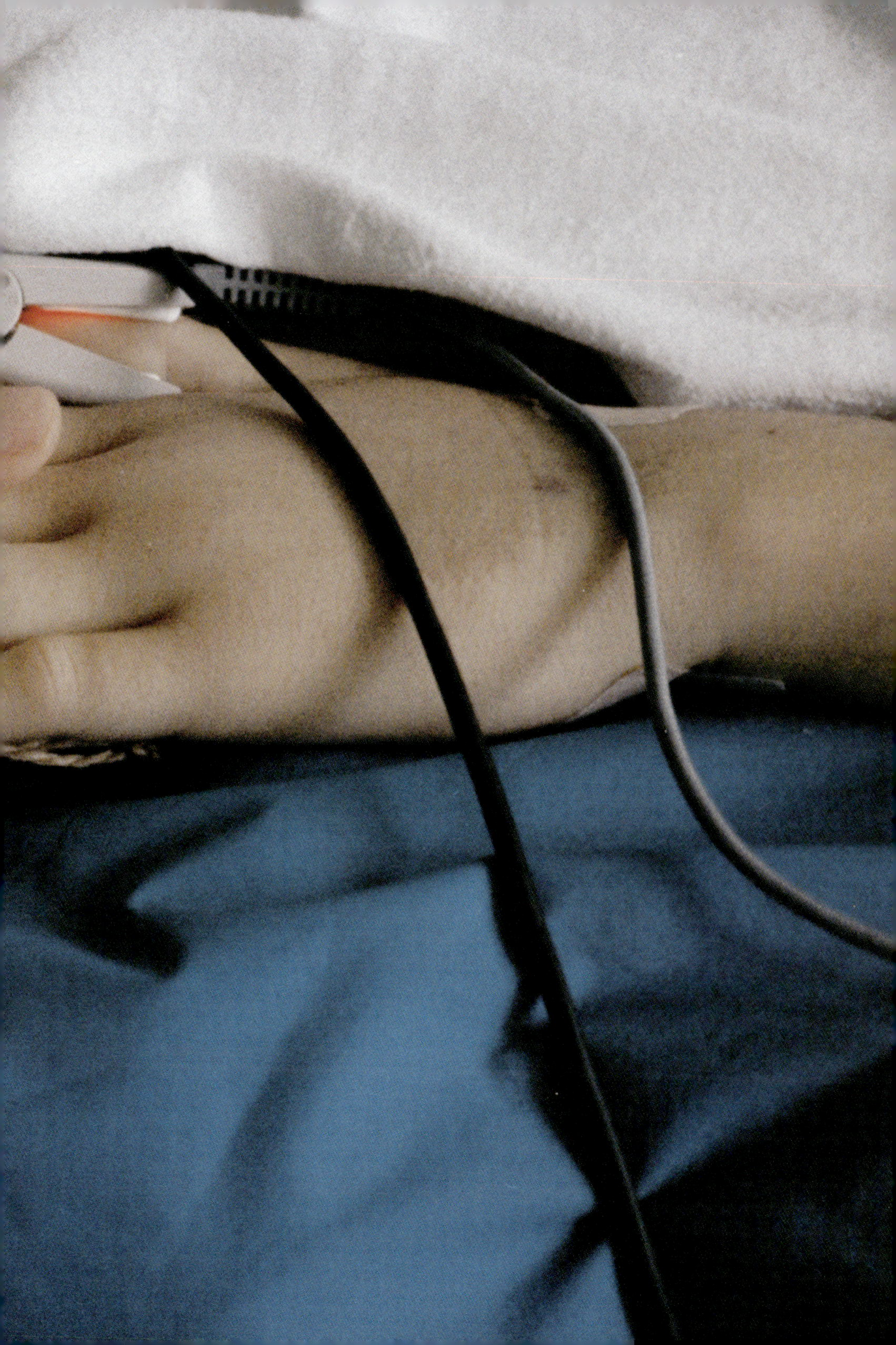

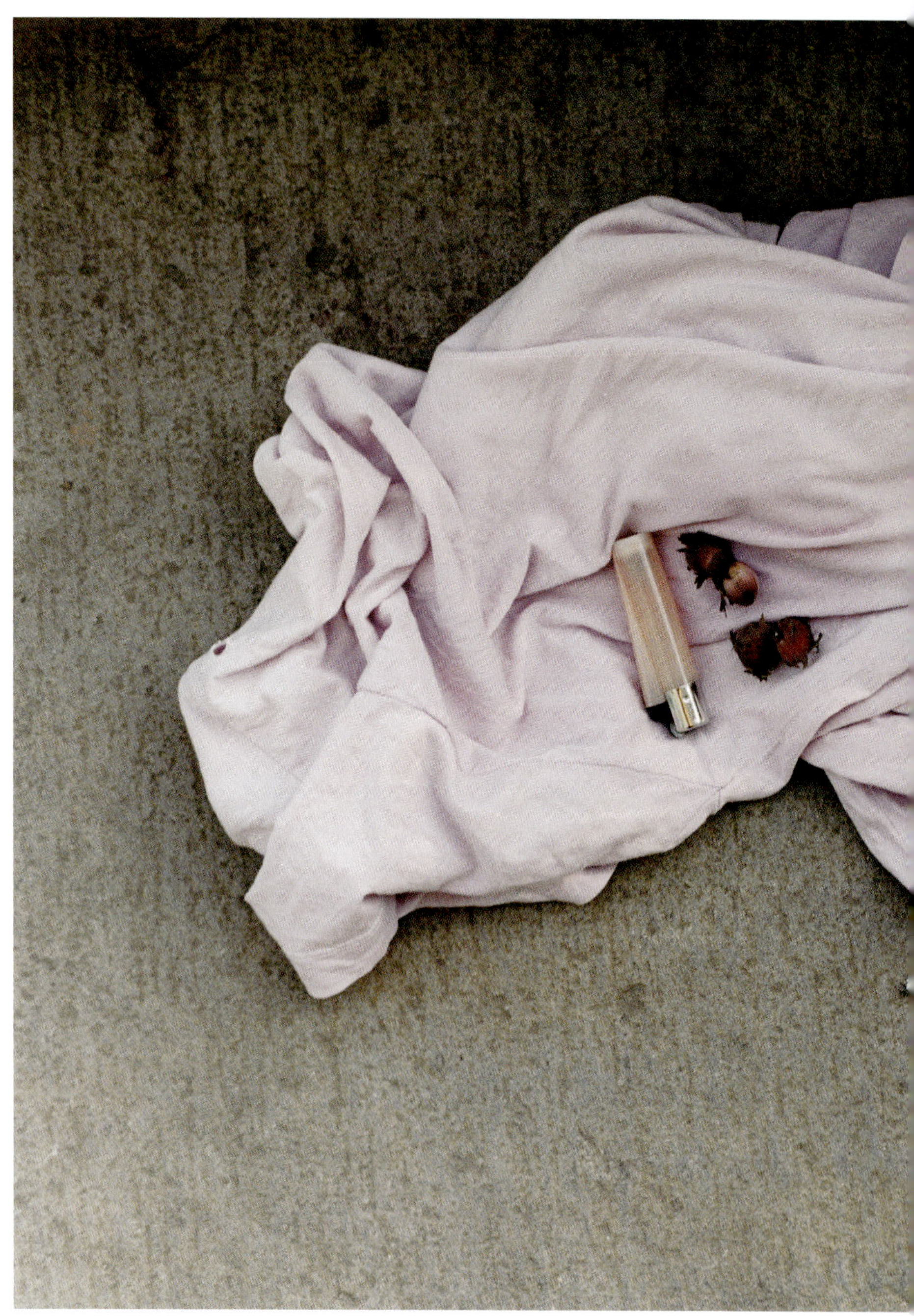

Stilleben Nüsschen II, 1997   Flatsedge, 2019

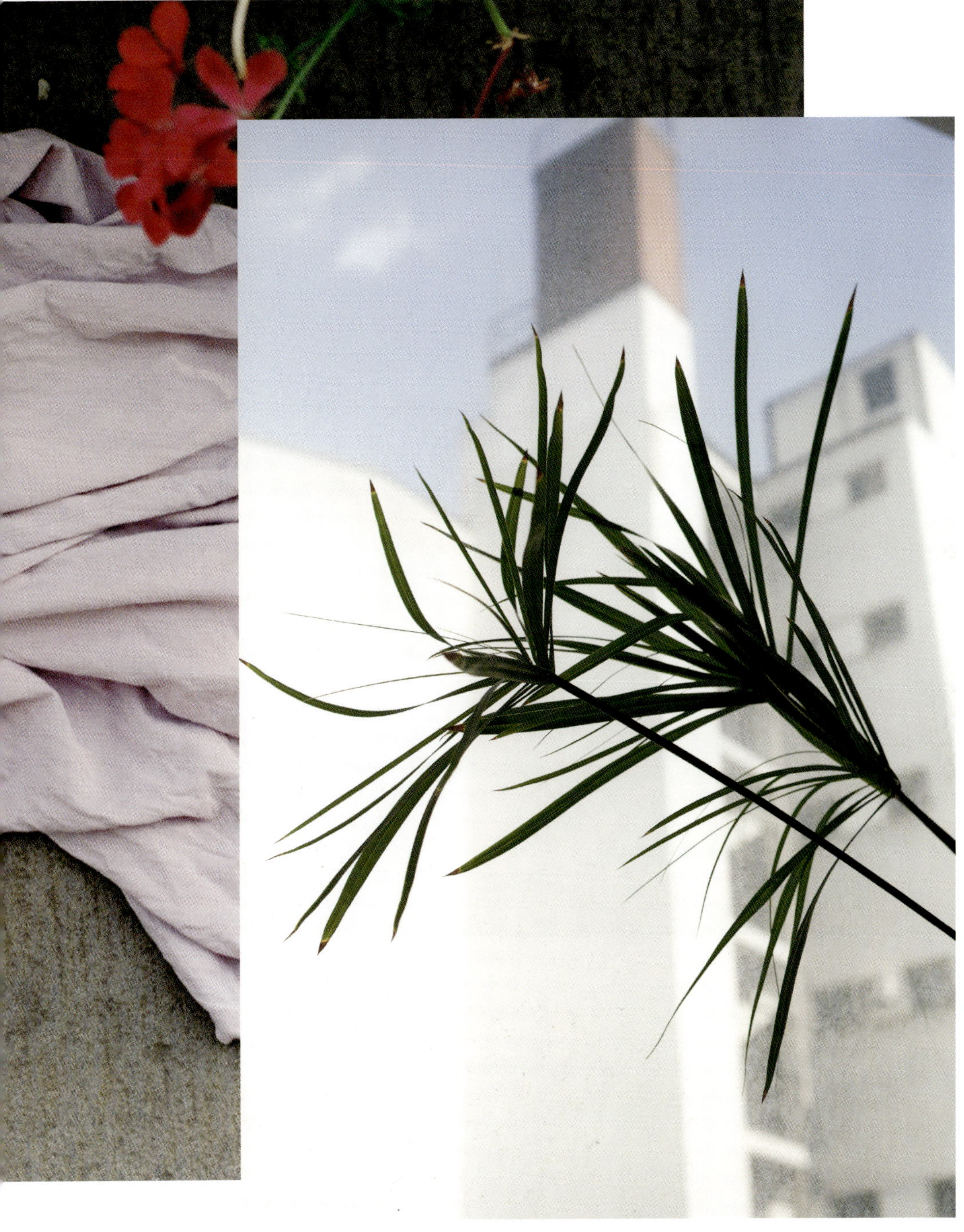

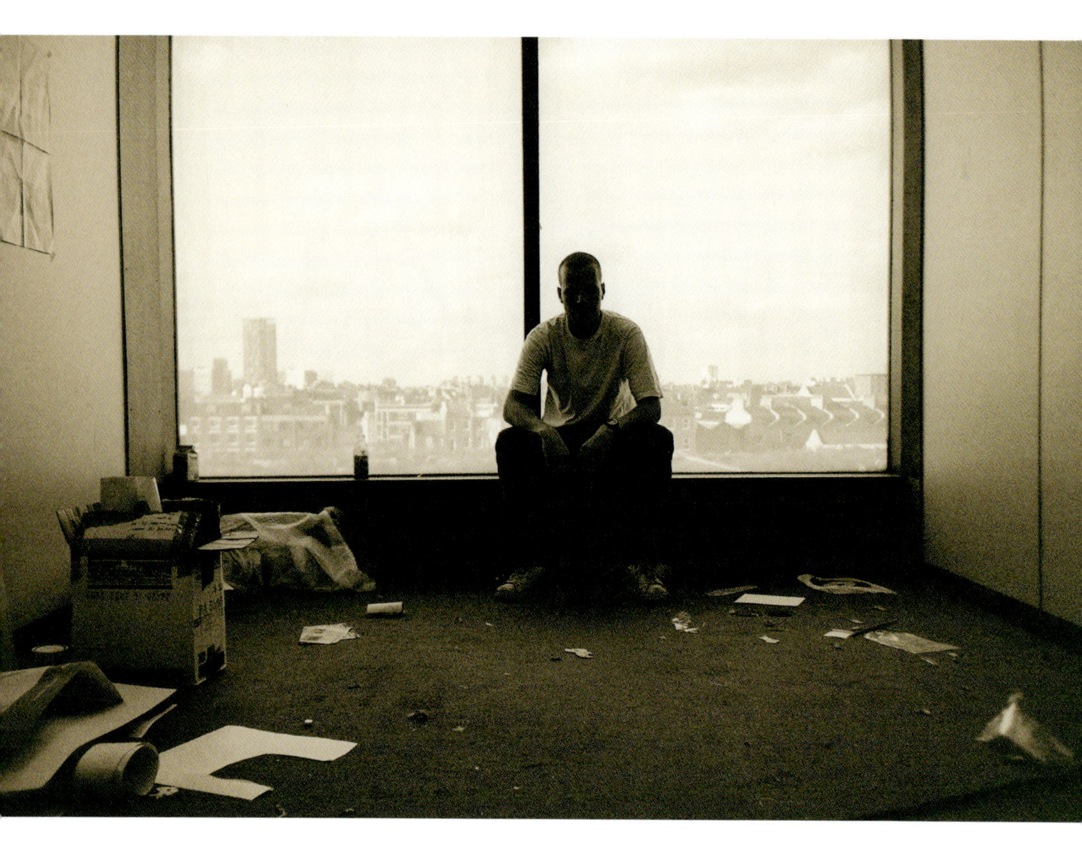

o.M., 1997

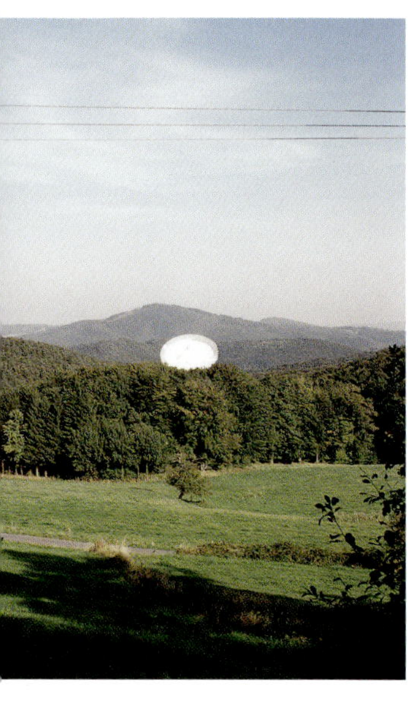

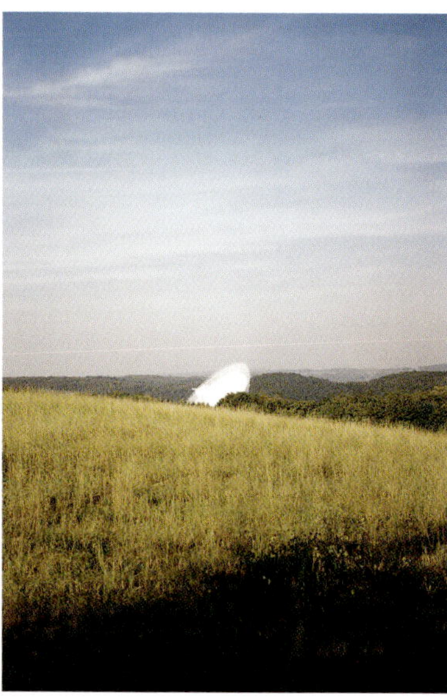

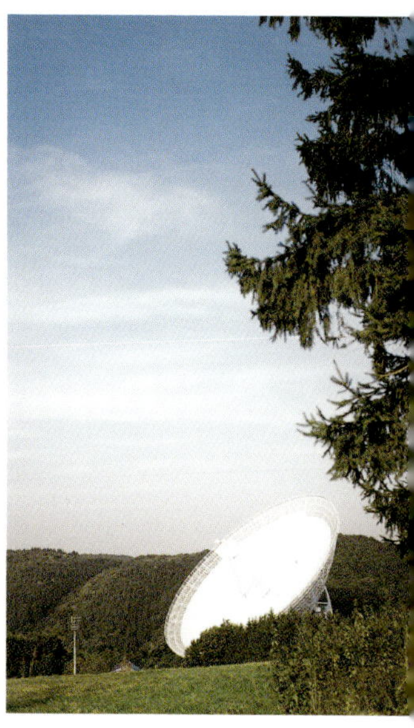

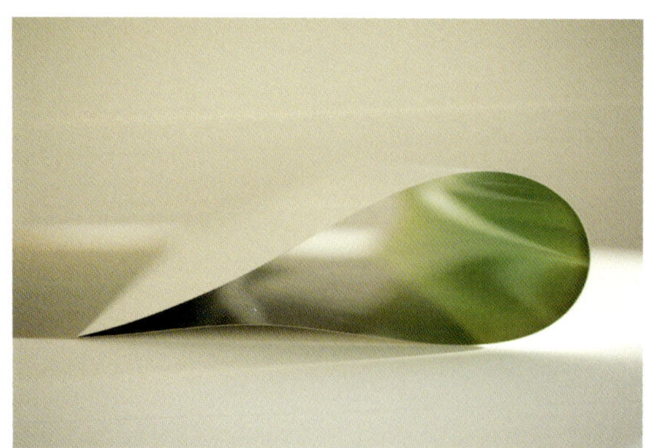

Radioteleskop Effelsberg I - VI, 1997   paper drop (passage) I, 2019   Pear Cut, 2019

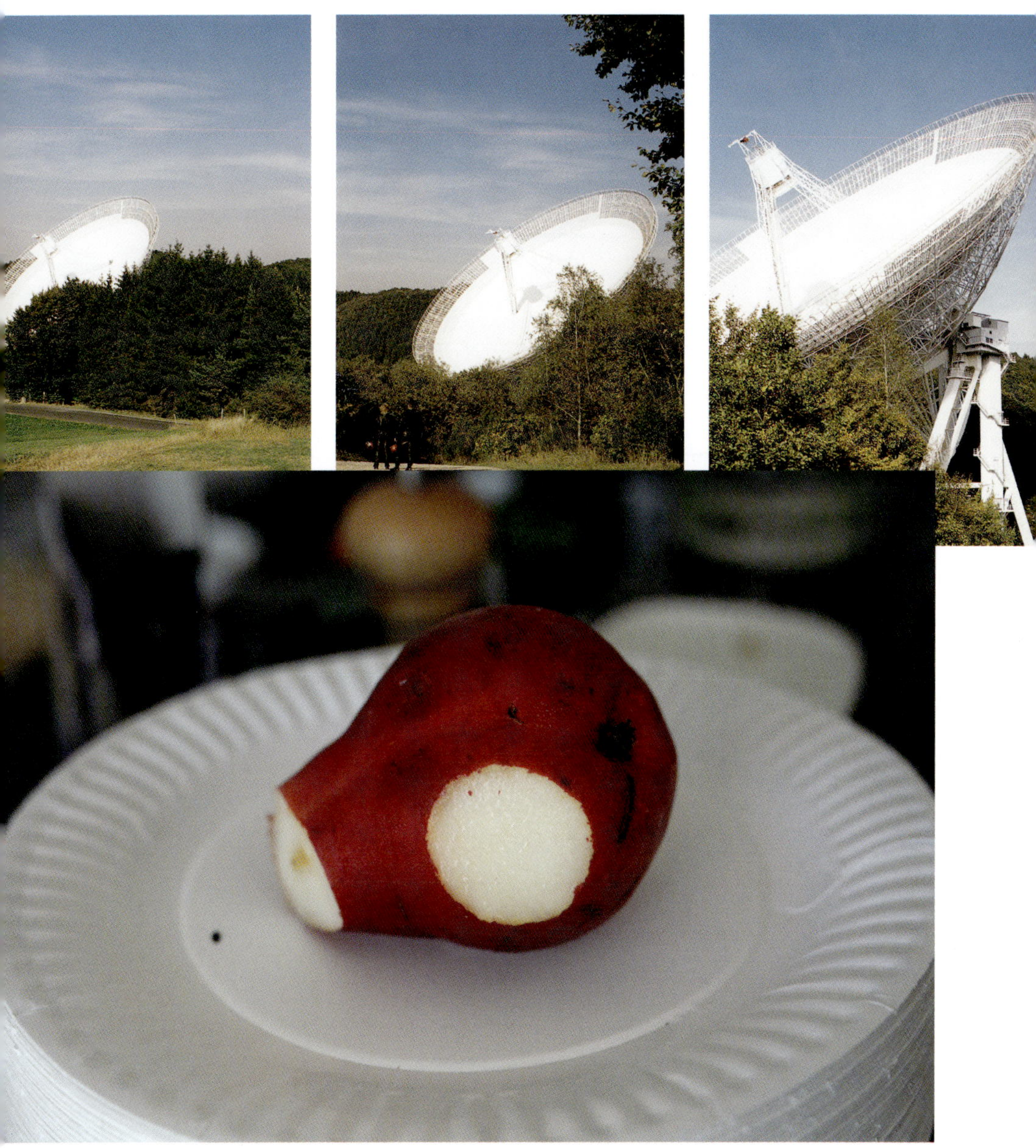

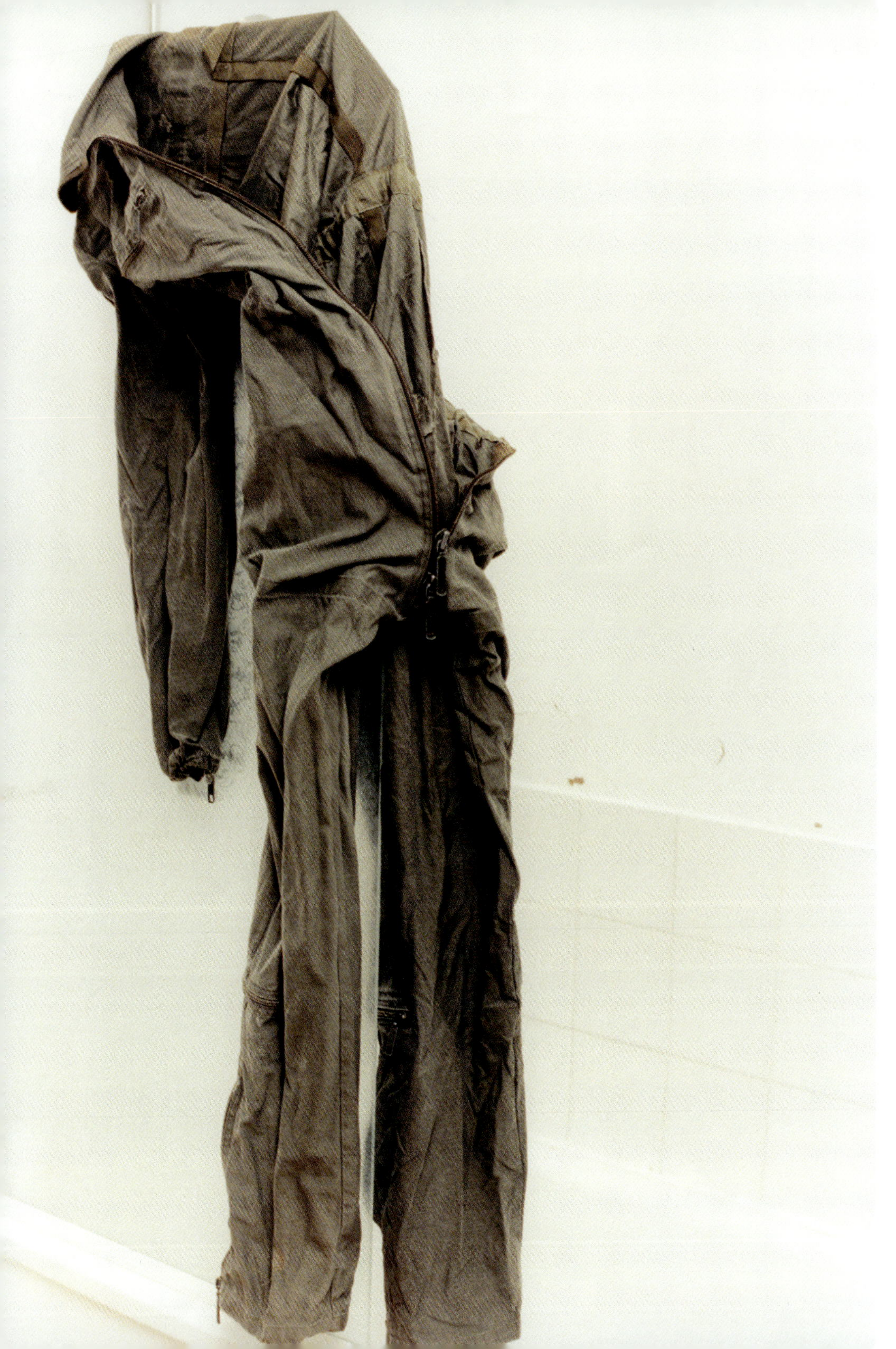

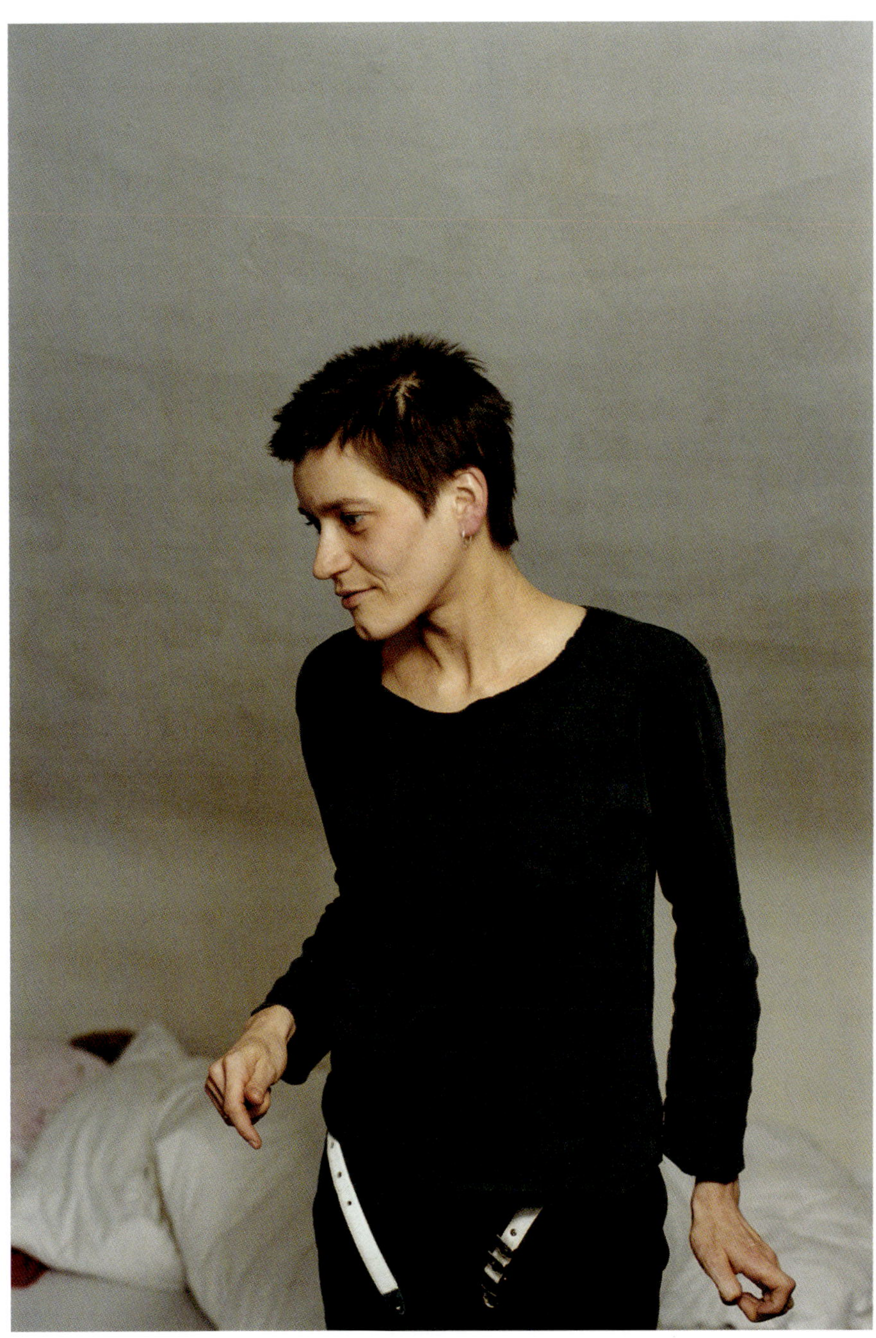

suit, 1997   Alex, 1997

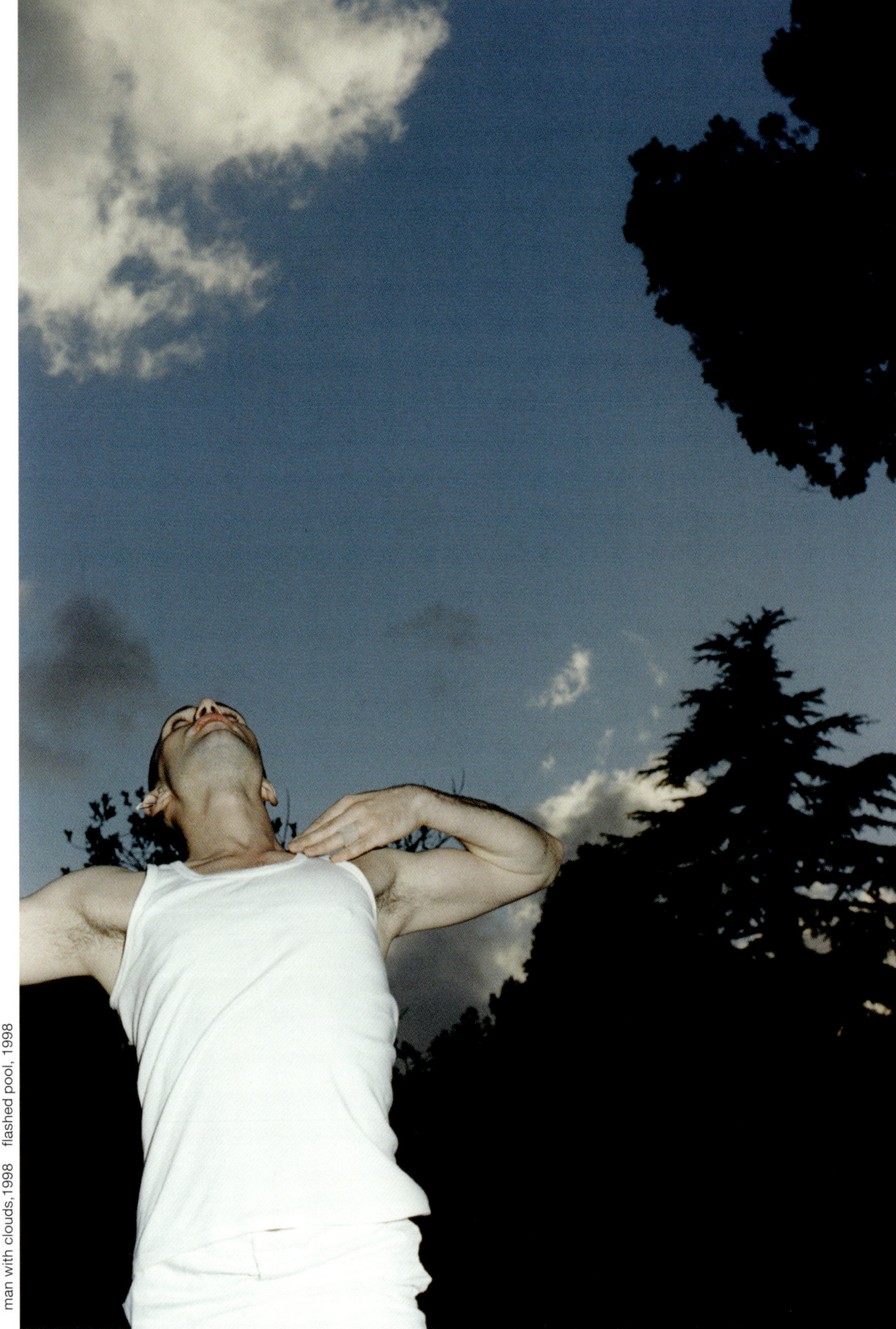

man with clouds,1998   flashed pool, 1998

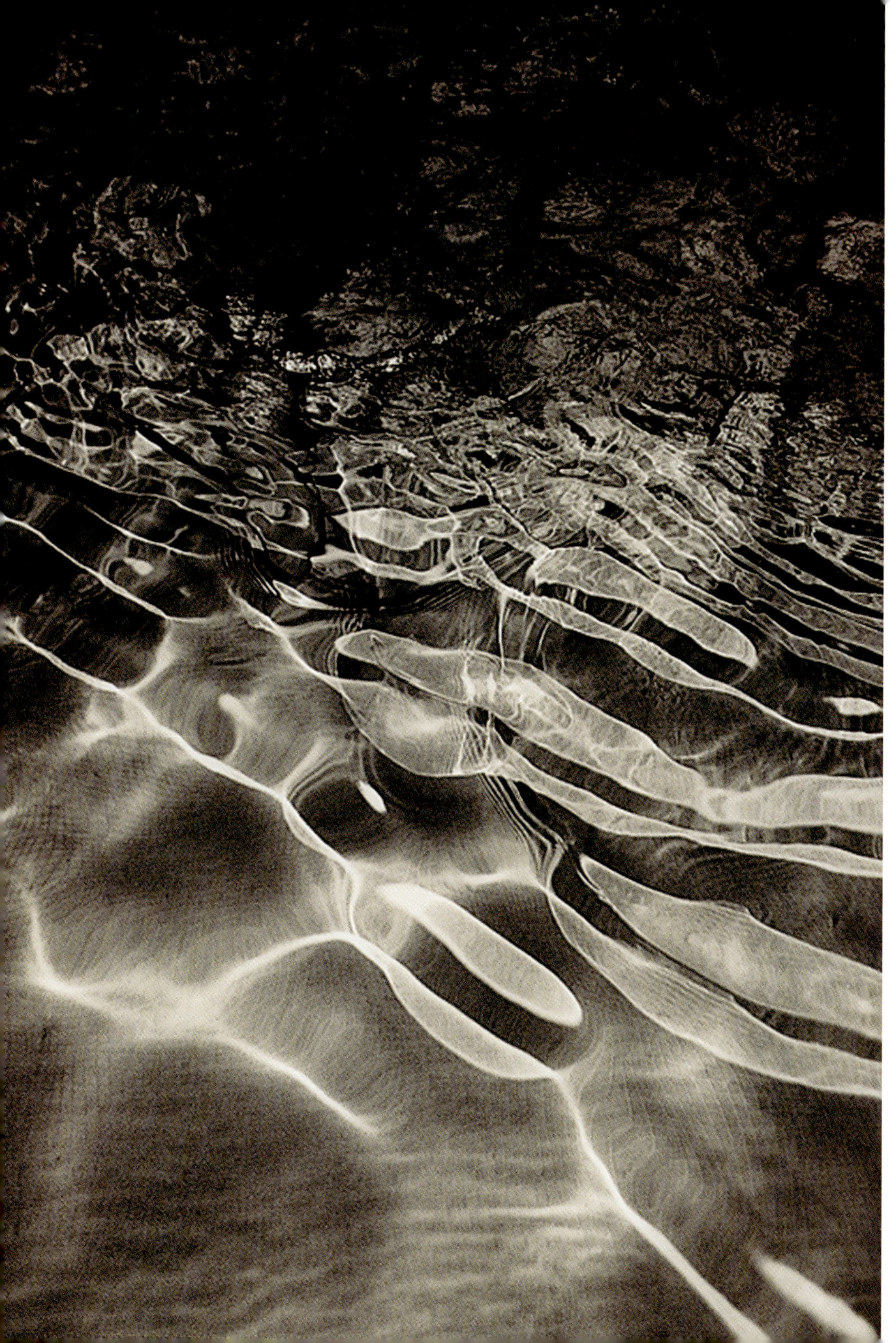

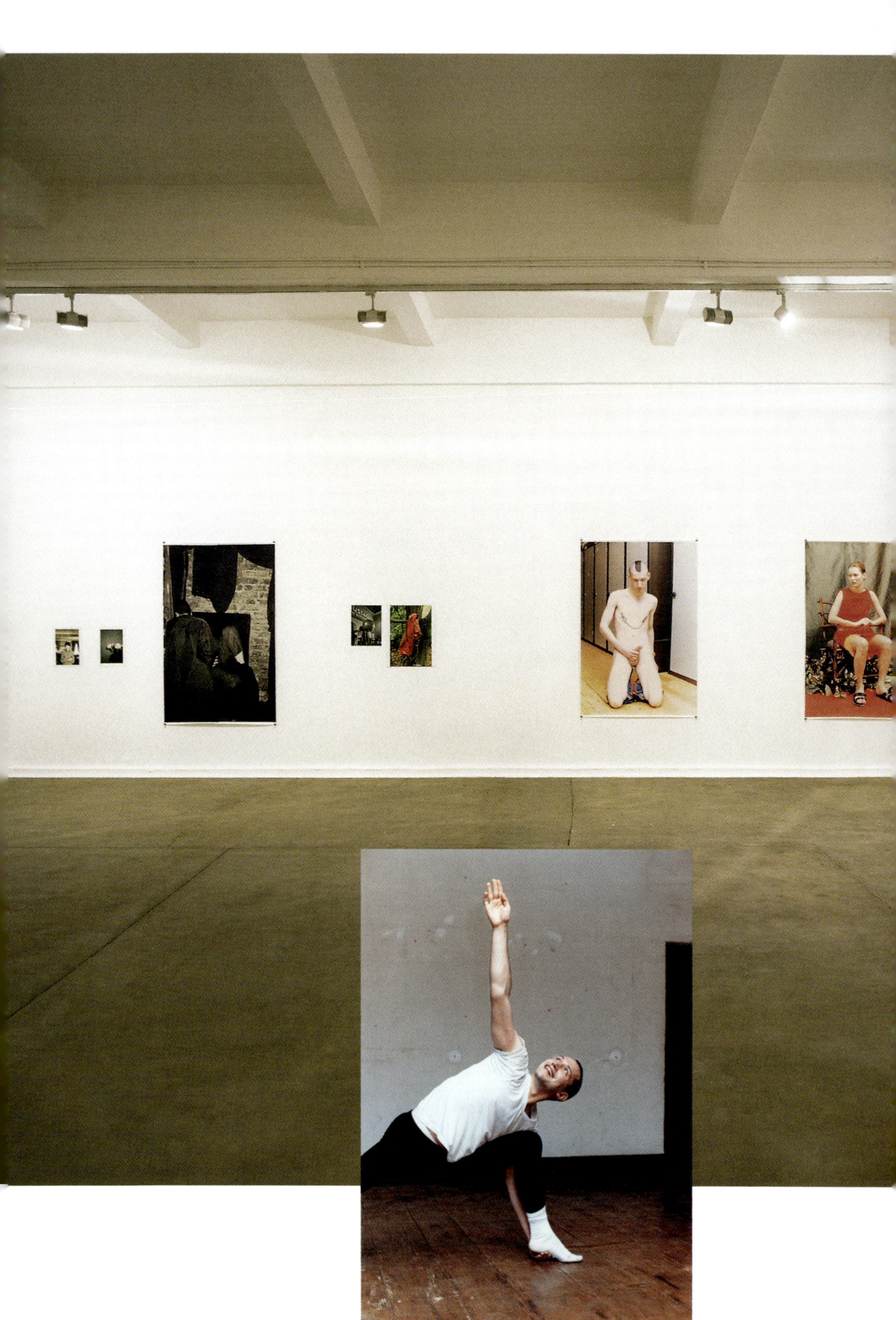

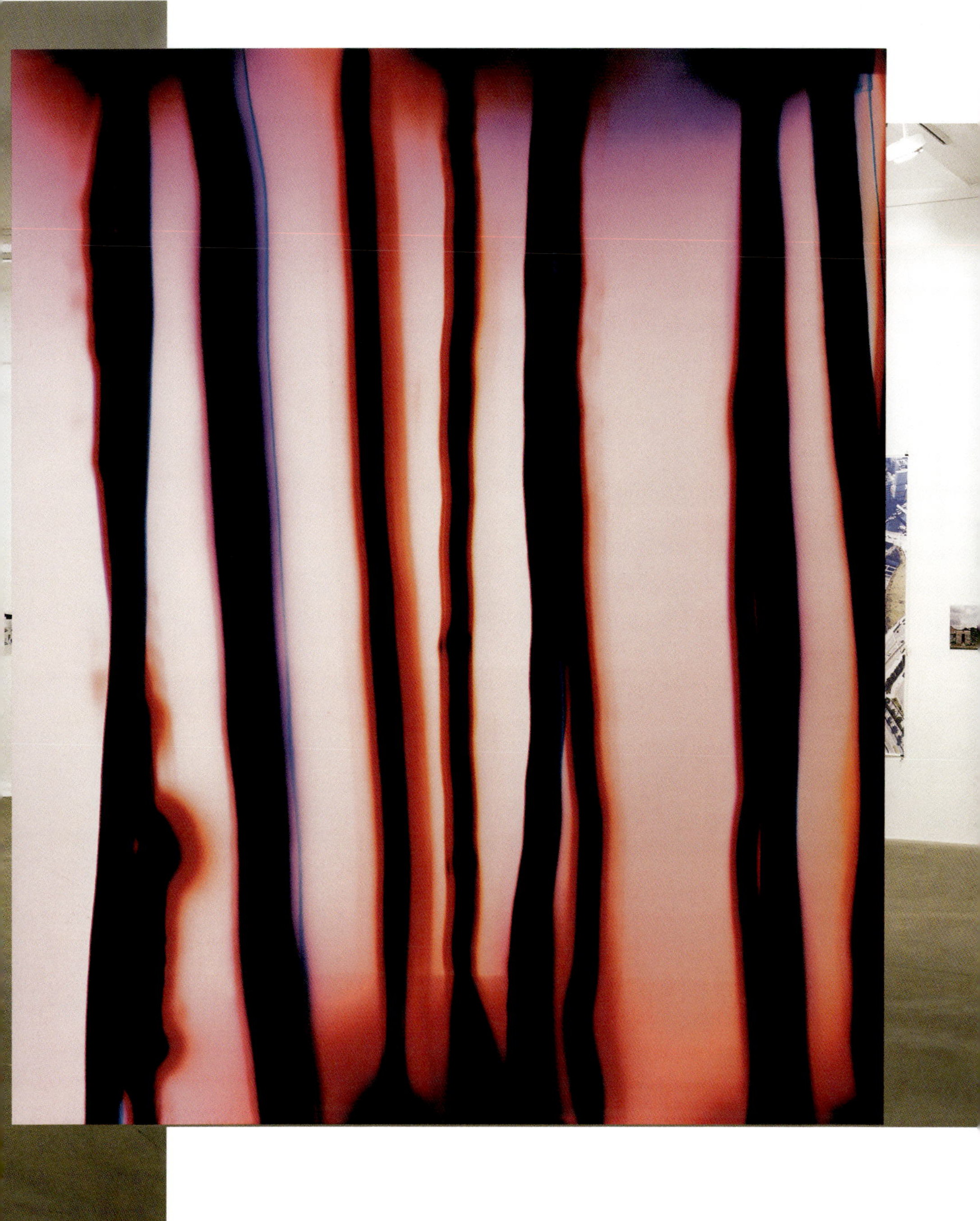

"I Didn't Inhale", Chisenhale Gallery, 7.6.-3.8.1997
Michael Clark, 1998
Strings of Life, 1999

Wolfgang Tillmans
truth study center

TASCHEN

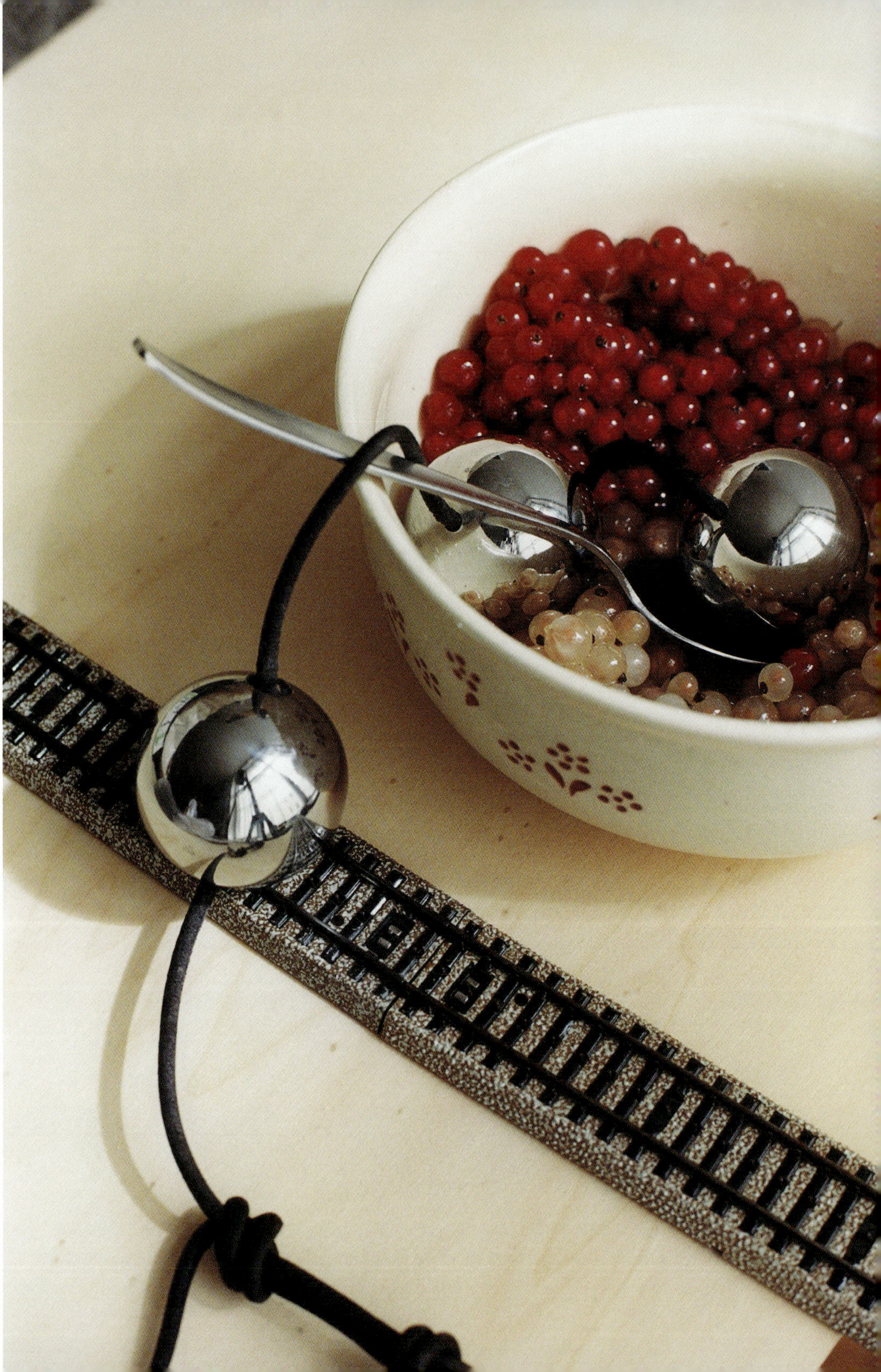

Venus transit, 2004 ⌃ Sommer, 2004

Wolfgang Tillmans
truth study center

edited and designed by Wolfgang Tillmans
with an essay by Minoru Shimizu

TASCHEN

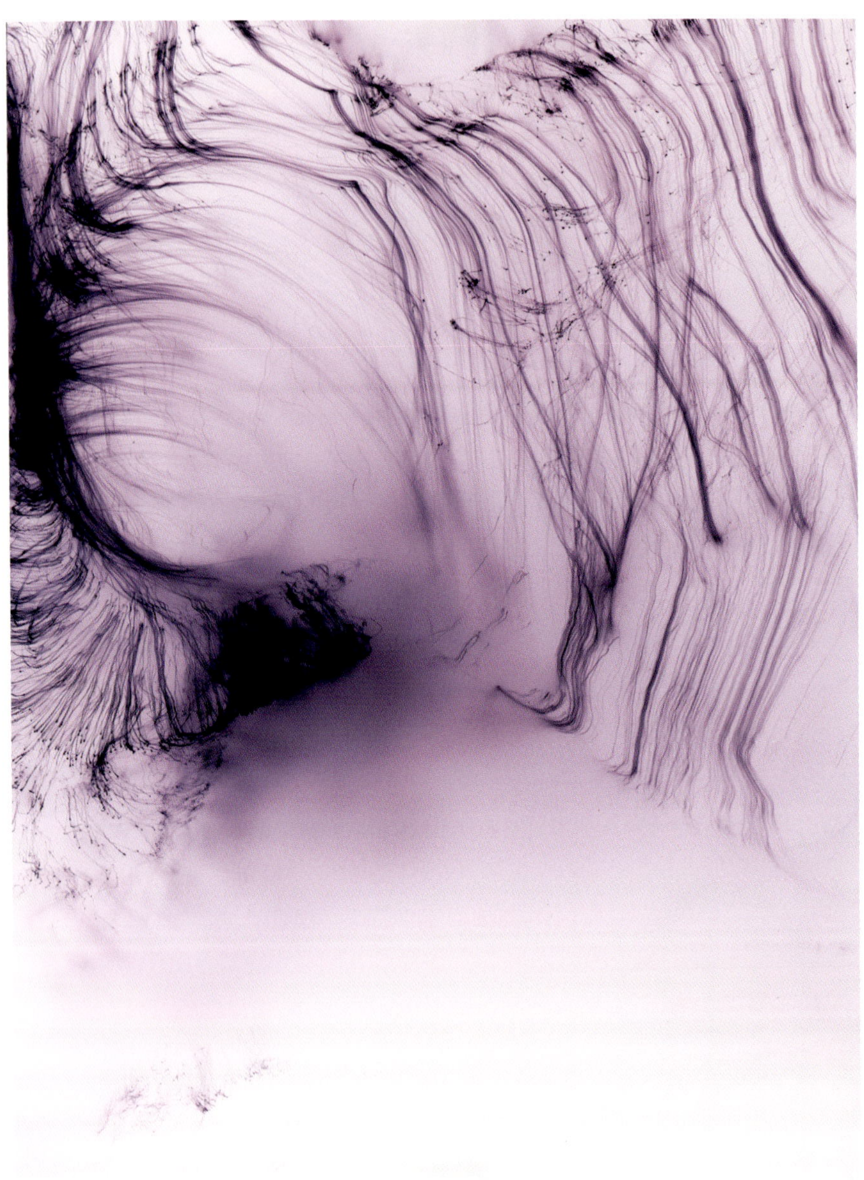

It's only love, give it away, 2005

A transit of Venus happens when the Sun, Venus and Earth are in perfect alignment. Observed from Earth it manifests itself as the small black disk of the planet Venus slowly wandering over the bright disk of the Sun in the course of several hours. This is an extremely rare phenomenon because the planes of the orbits of Earth and Venus are slightly tilted to each other and a transit can only occur when both planets are exactly at the point where the planes of their orbits meet. This happens in a regular cycle of 122 years, then eight years later, after which it takes another 105 years, then again eight years and then again 122 years and so on. The last transit took place on 8 June 2004. This was also the first that any human being alive at that time on Earth could have seen. In effect, evidence of transits of Venus actually occurring has only been given through historical written reports or drawings, beginning from the time of the invention of the telescope and later through photographic images of the two transits which occurred after the invention of photography. Only six transits have been observed in human history, which were those of 1639, 1761, 1769, 1874, 1882 and 2004.

In the 18th and 19th centuries the observation of this geometrical phenomenon had a huge scientific importance. Researchers understood that they could calculate the distance between the Earth and the Sun through the exact observation and comparison of the passage times of Venus over the disk of the sun as recorded from distant points on Earth. At that time it was considered to be the only way to more or less exactly establish our own absolute position in relation to the Sun and hence to the universe around us. Only the relative distances in our solar system were known, measured in multiples of the distance between the Earth and the Sun, not the absolute distances. It was like having a map without scale.

Various ambitious expeditions, for example Captain Cook's first one in 1769, were undertaken for the sole purpose of observing the transit of Venus from a point as far away from Europe as possible. The idea was to measure the parallax, which, in simple terms, can be described as observing the displacement of a nearer object in front of a more distant object viewed from two different points; like for example observing the changing position of a thumb held up in front of a house on the horizon alternately viewed with one or the other eye shut.

The exactness of clocking the event was impaired by the black drop effect, which caused Venus' disk to be seemingly connected to the sky around the Sun for a while longer than should be expected from its predicted position. Even though it was supposed to be already clearly 'inside' the Sun's disk, Venus' disk was deformed into a drop-like shape. Only through photographic observation of the two transits of the 19th century was it established that the drop effect was actually an illusion caused by the human brain.

Observing the transit of 2004 through the telescope, which I still have from my astronomy-obsessed teenage days, had of course no scientific value, but it was a moving experience to see the actual mechanics of the sky work in front of my eyes. To see a planet actually move in front of another defined object that is part of the solar system gave me as an earthbound human a visual sense of my location in space. Despite the flatness of the telescopic image one could experience space as three-dimensional space. The next transit of Venus will occur on 6 June 2012. WT

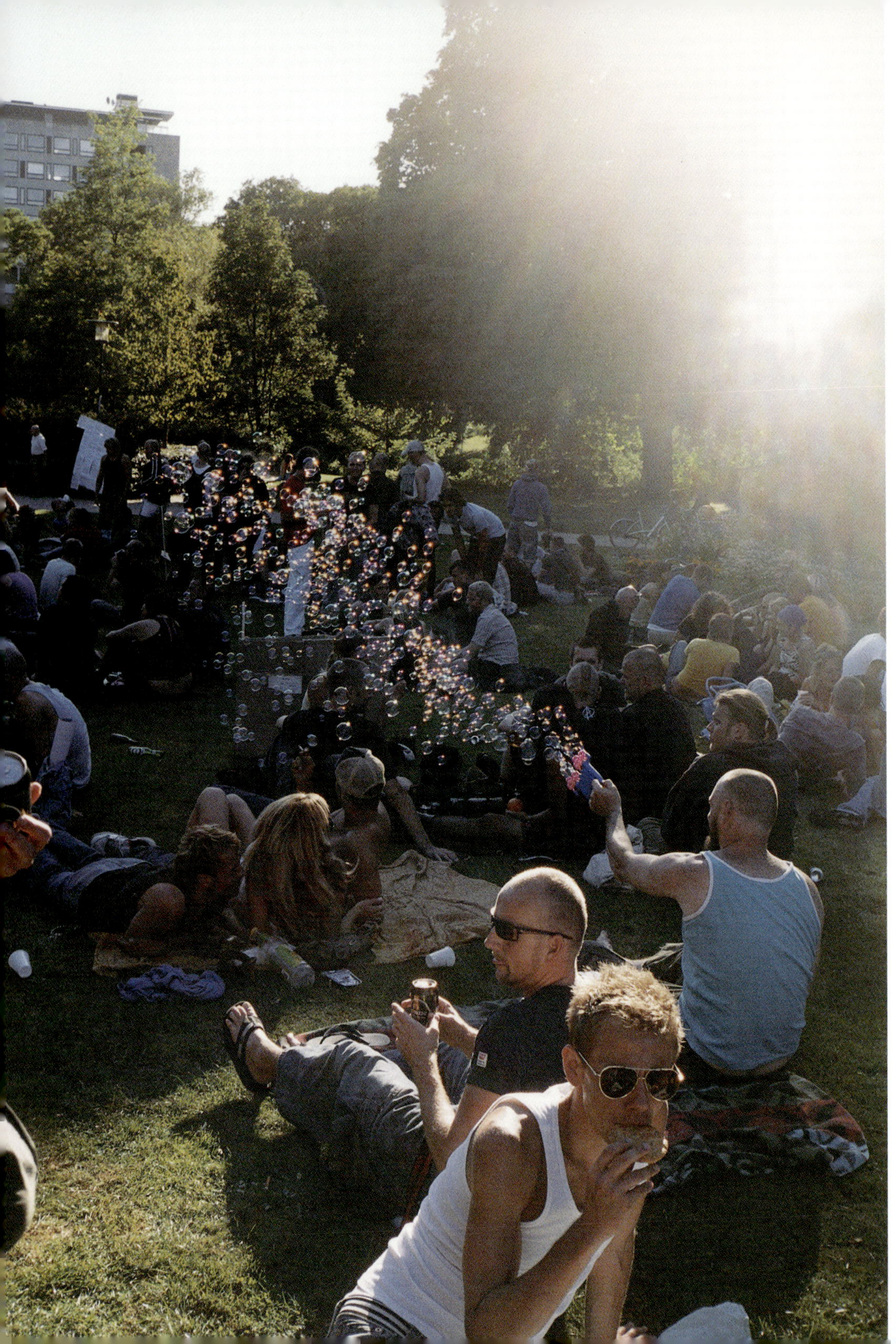

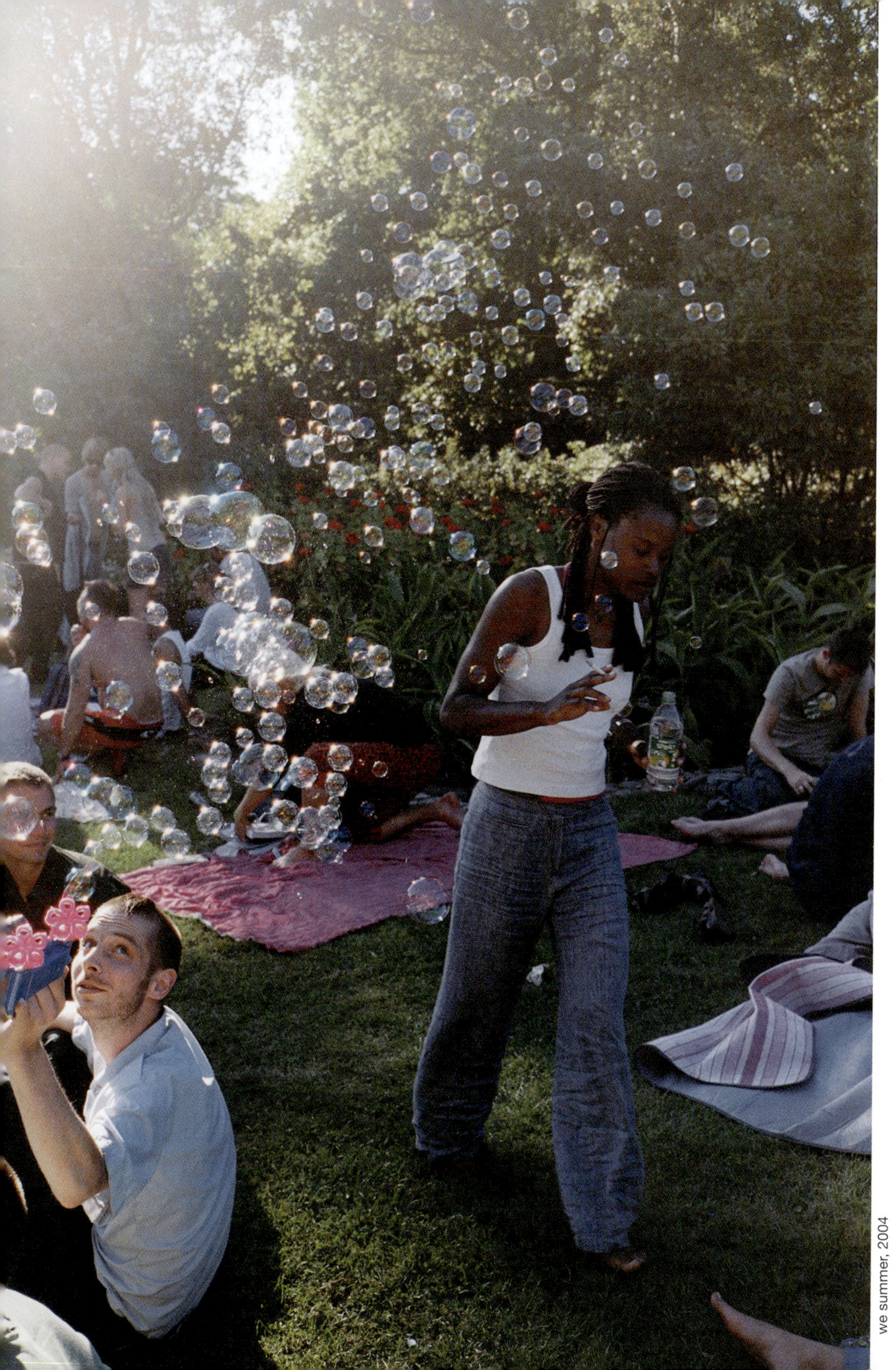

we summer, 2004

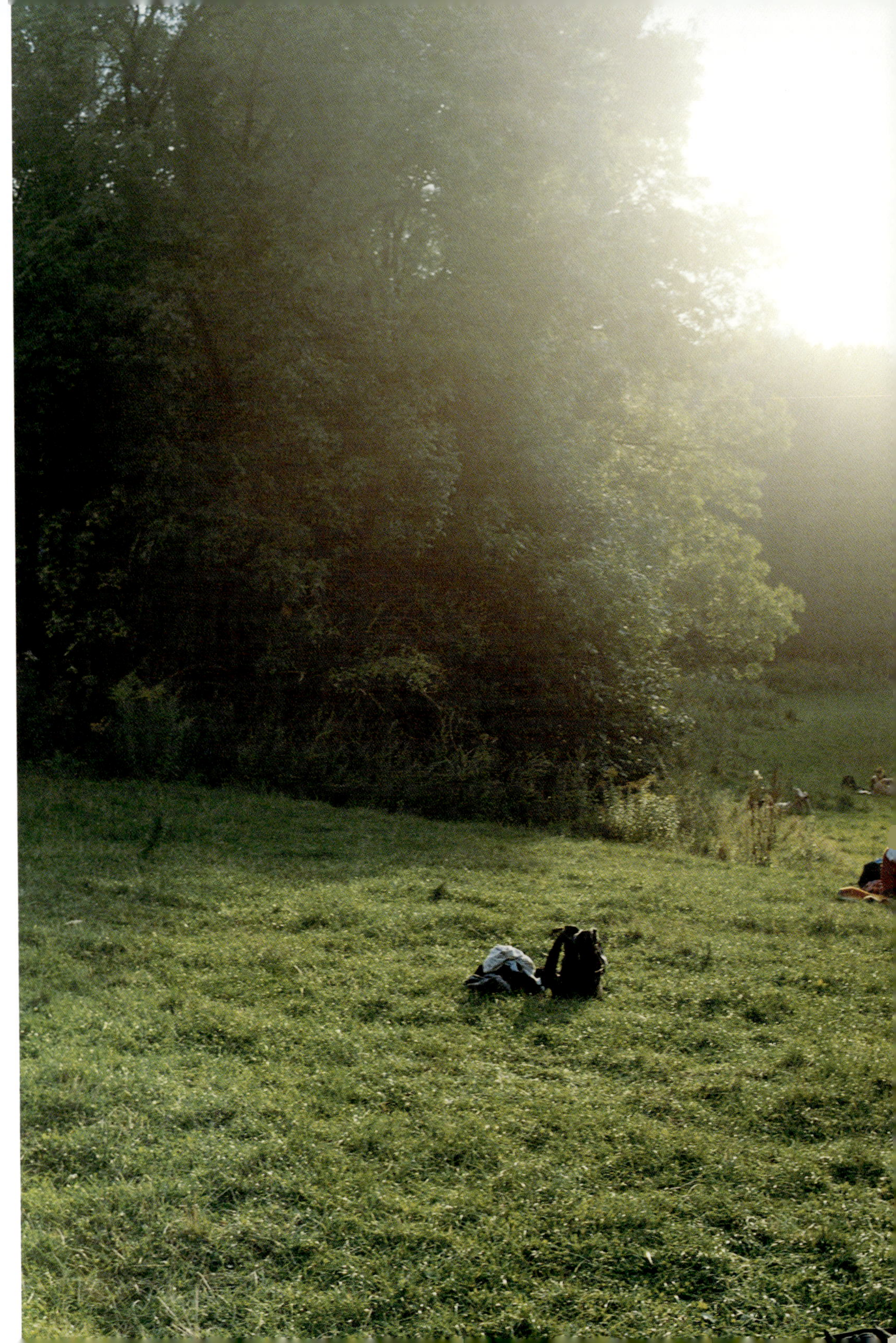

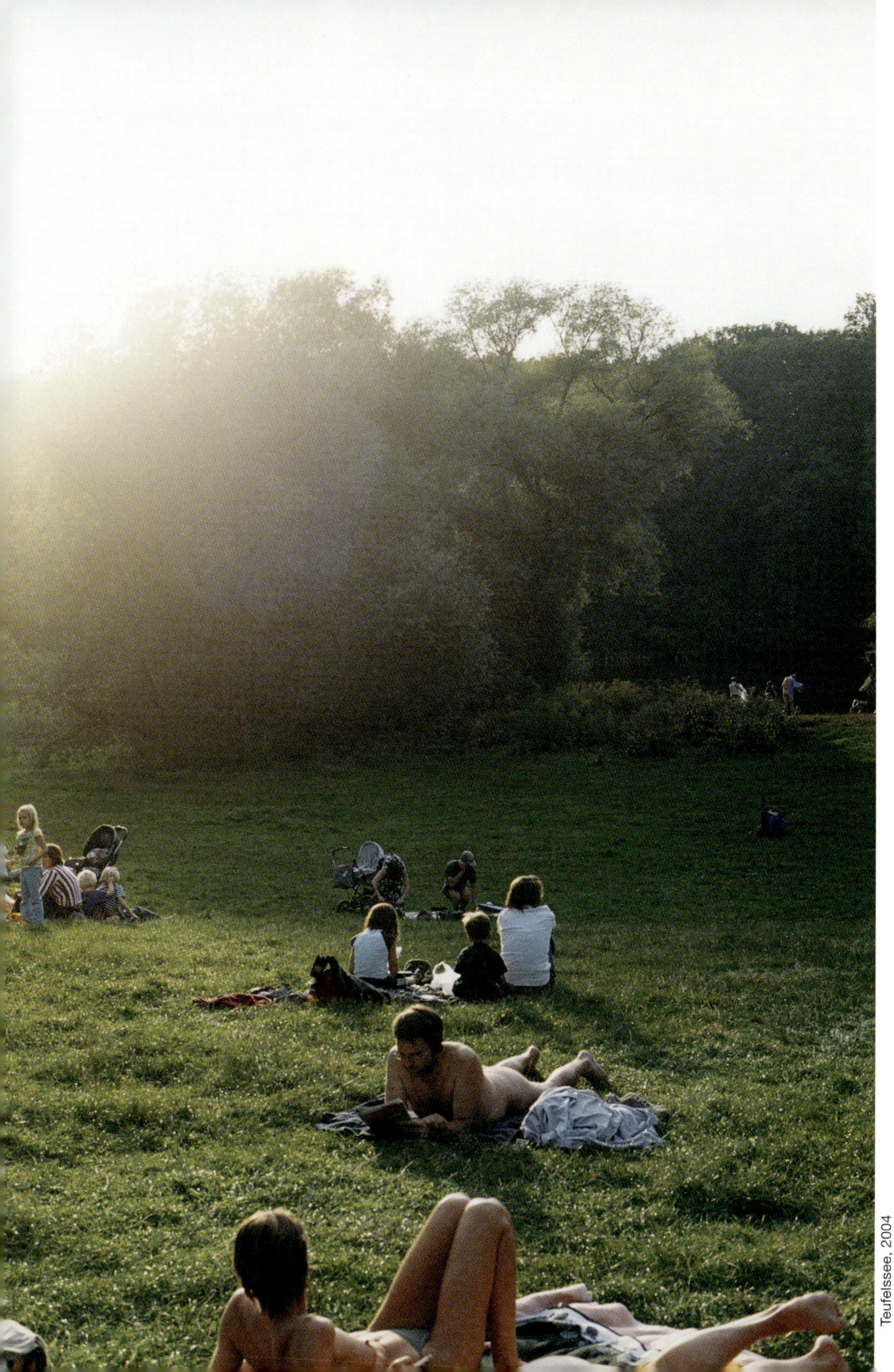

Teufelssee, 2004

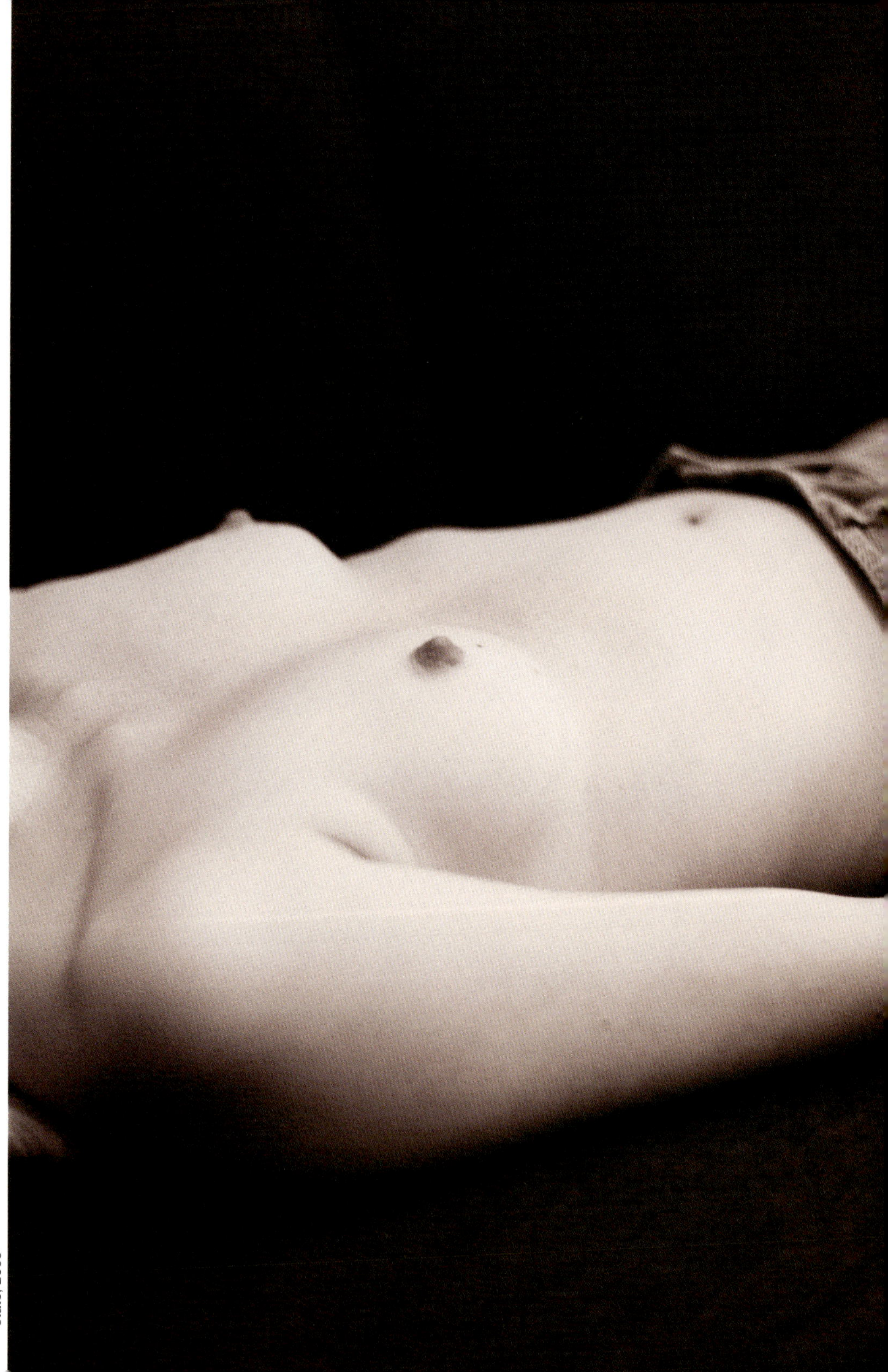
state, 2005

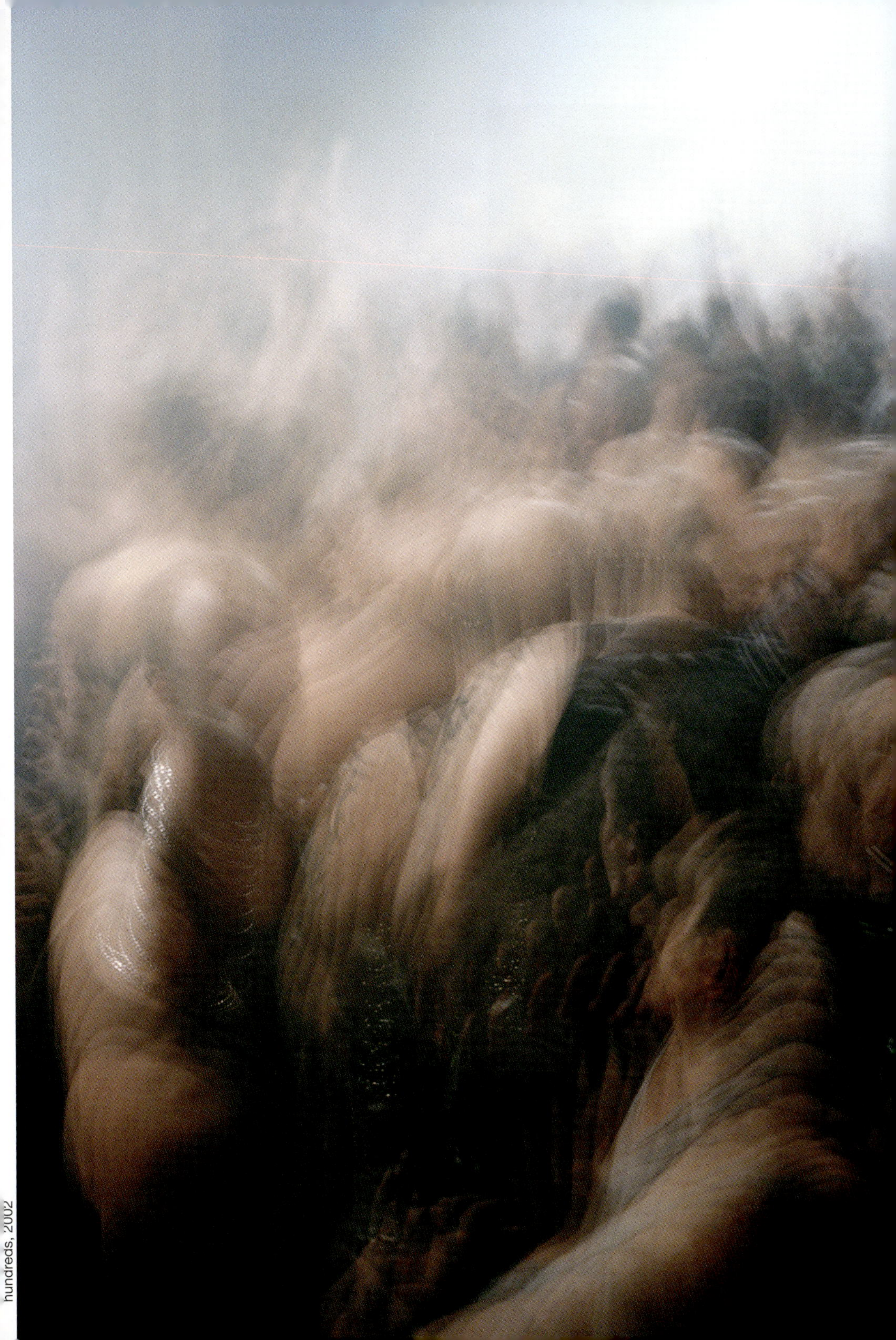

hundreds, 2002

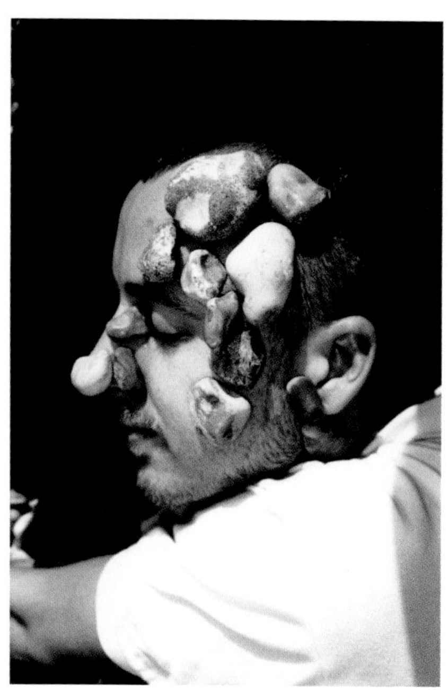

Anders (Brighton Arcimboldo), 2005   Elephant Man, 2002

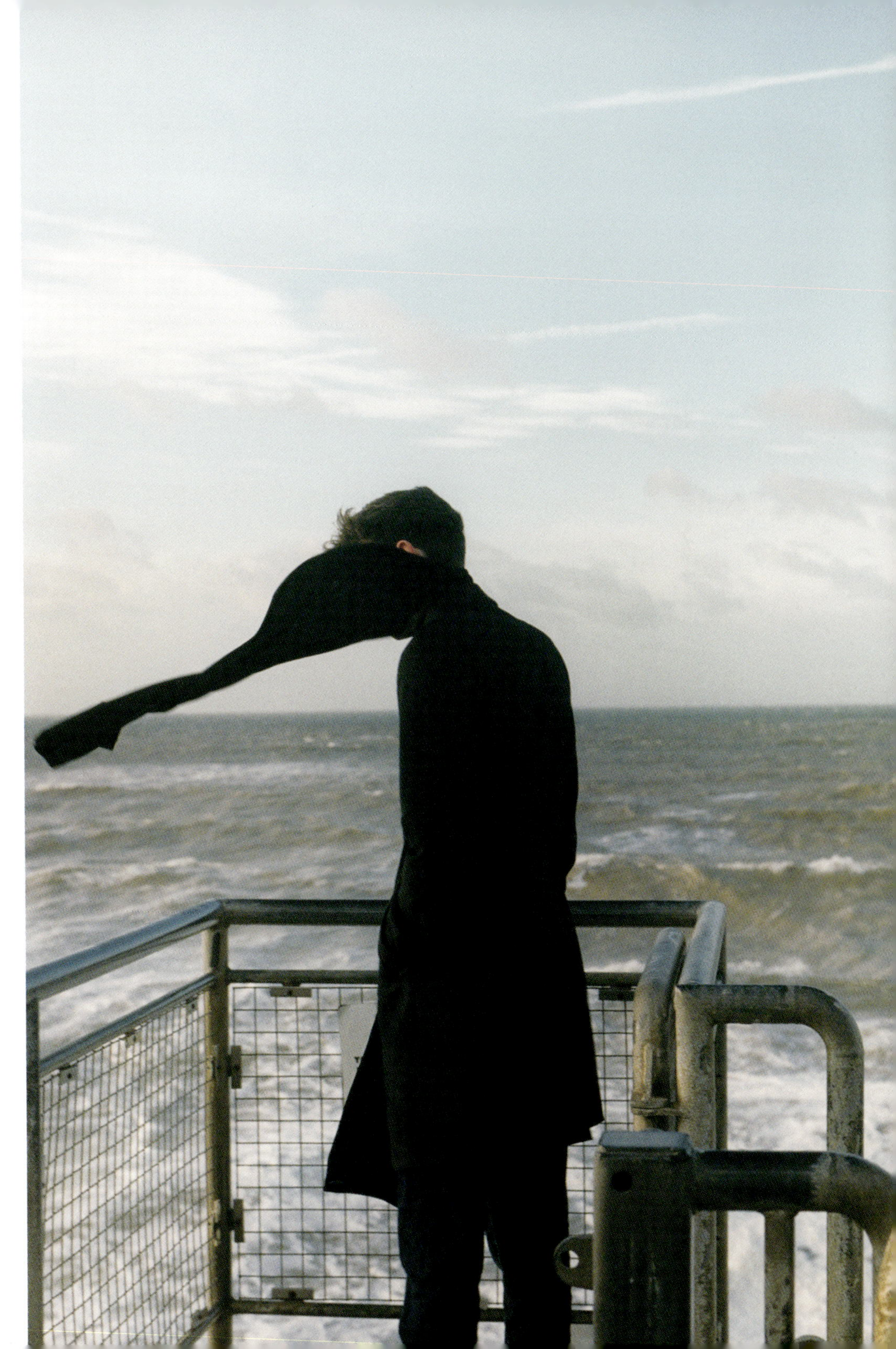

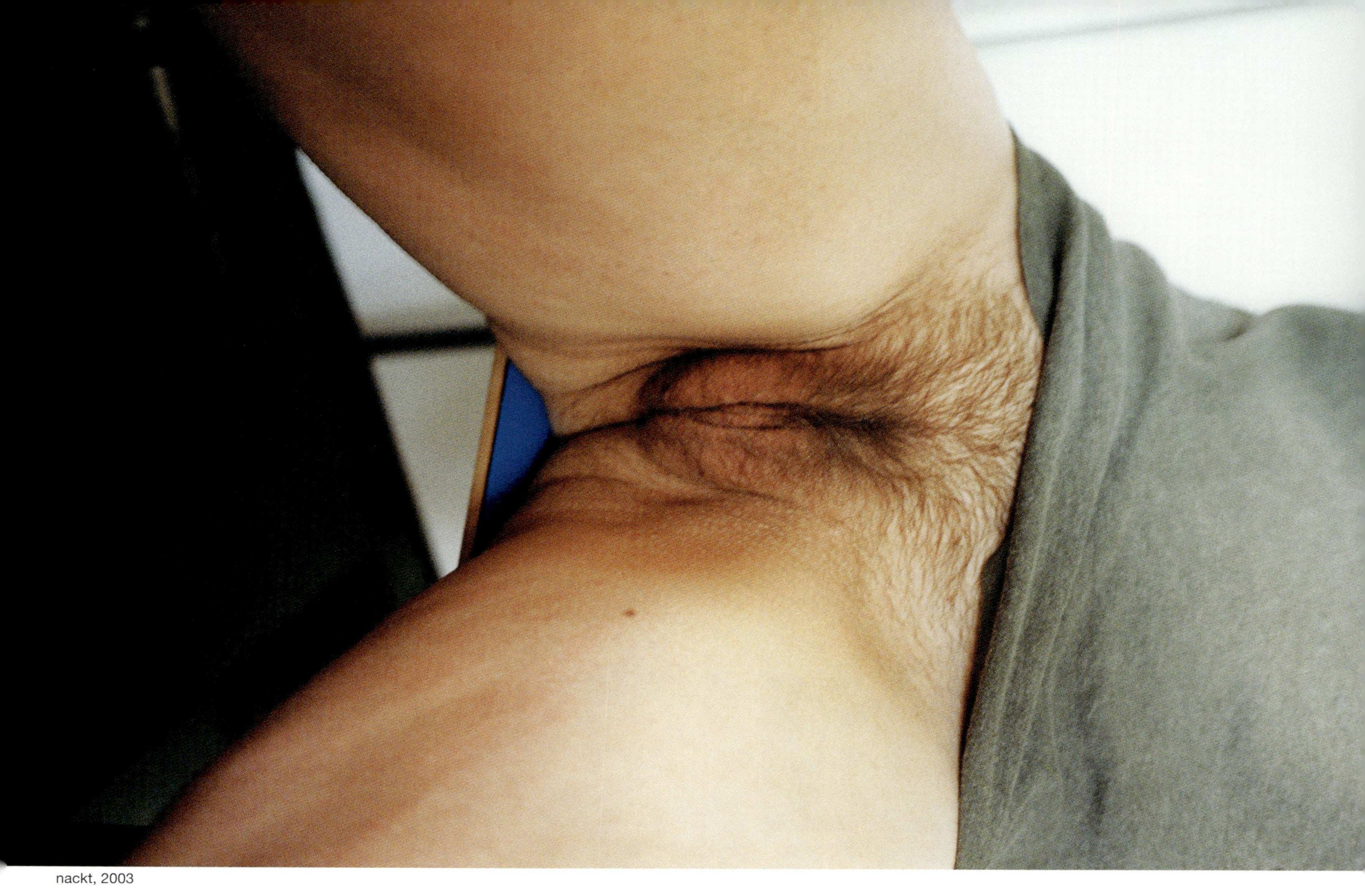

nackt, 2003

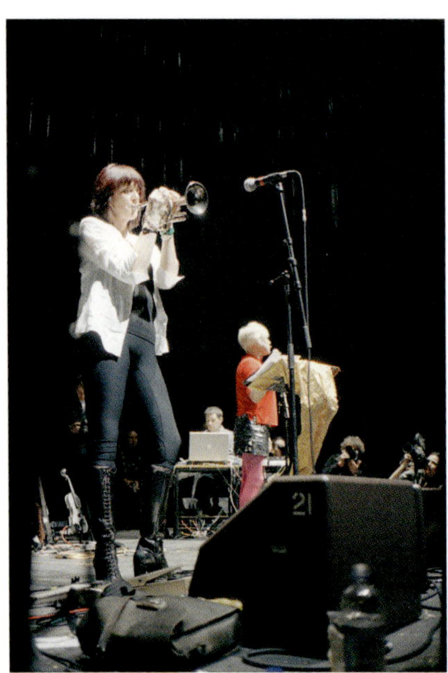

Throbbing Gristle, 2005   Anders pulling splinter from his foot (b/w), 2004

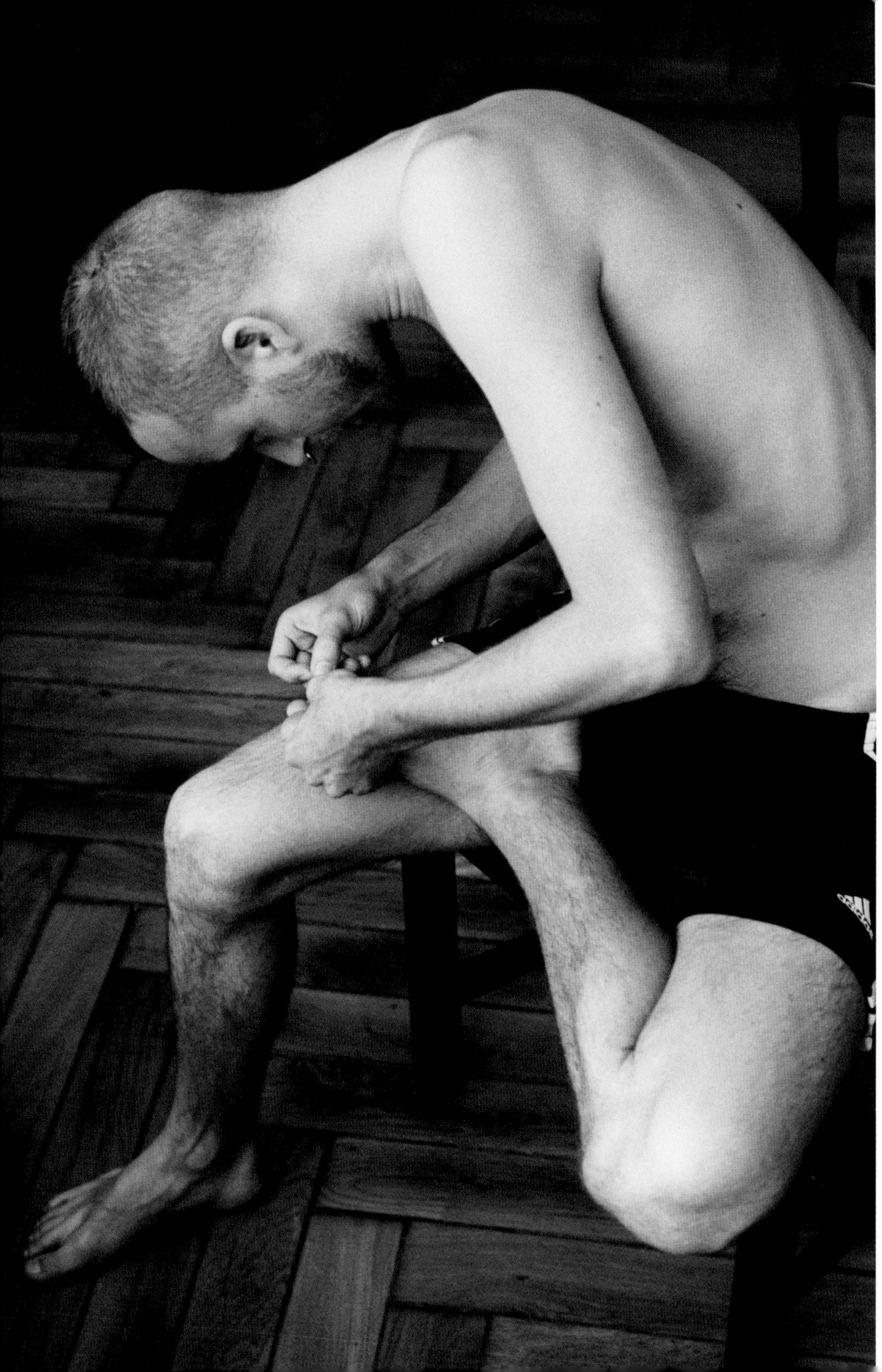

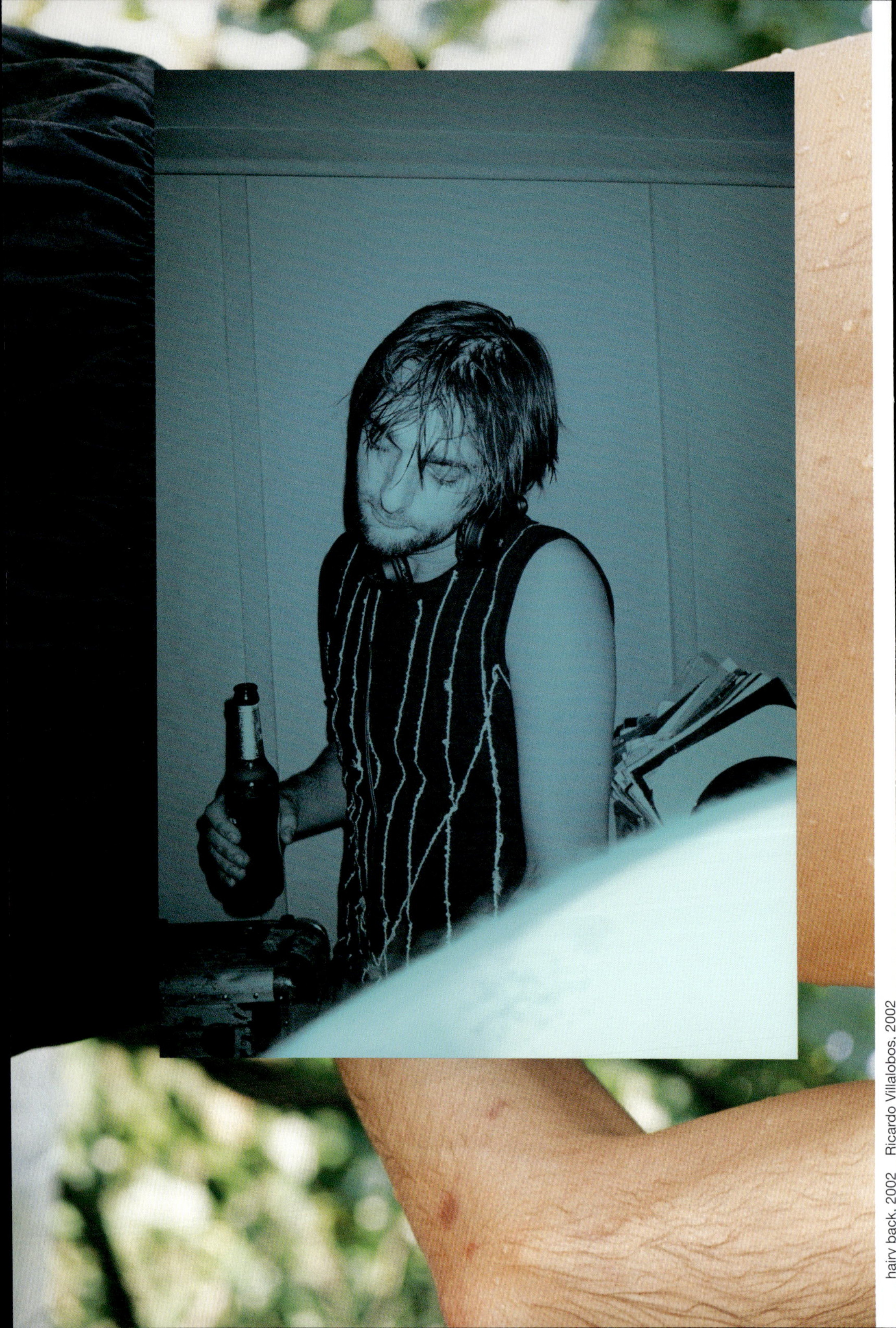

hairy back, 2002   Ricardo Villalobos, 2002

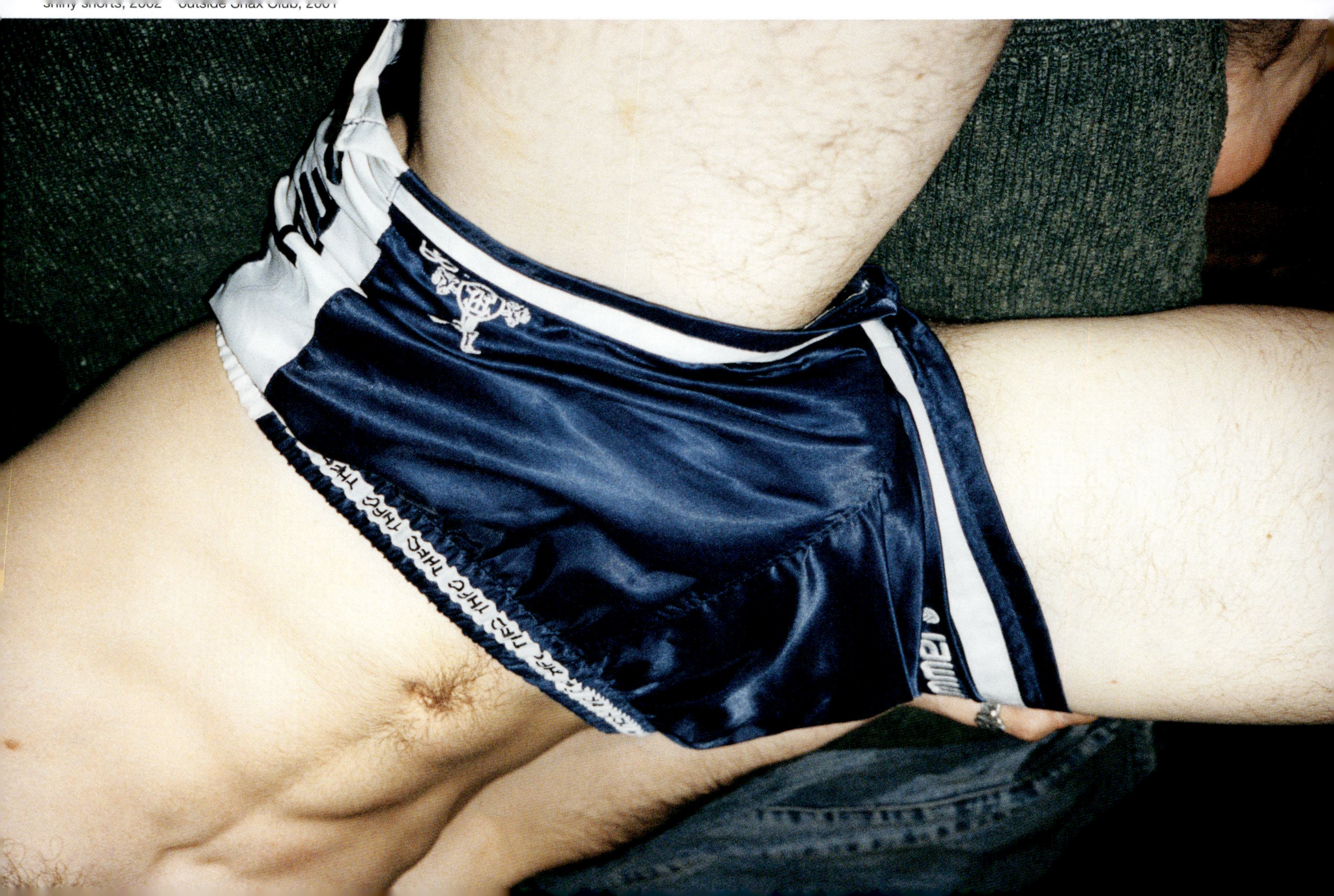

Shiny Shorts, 2002   Outside Shax Club, 2001

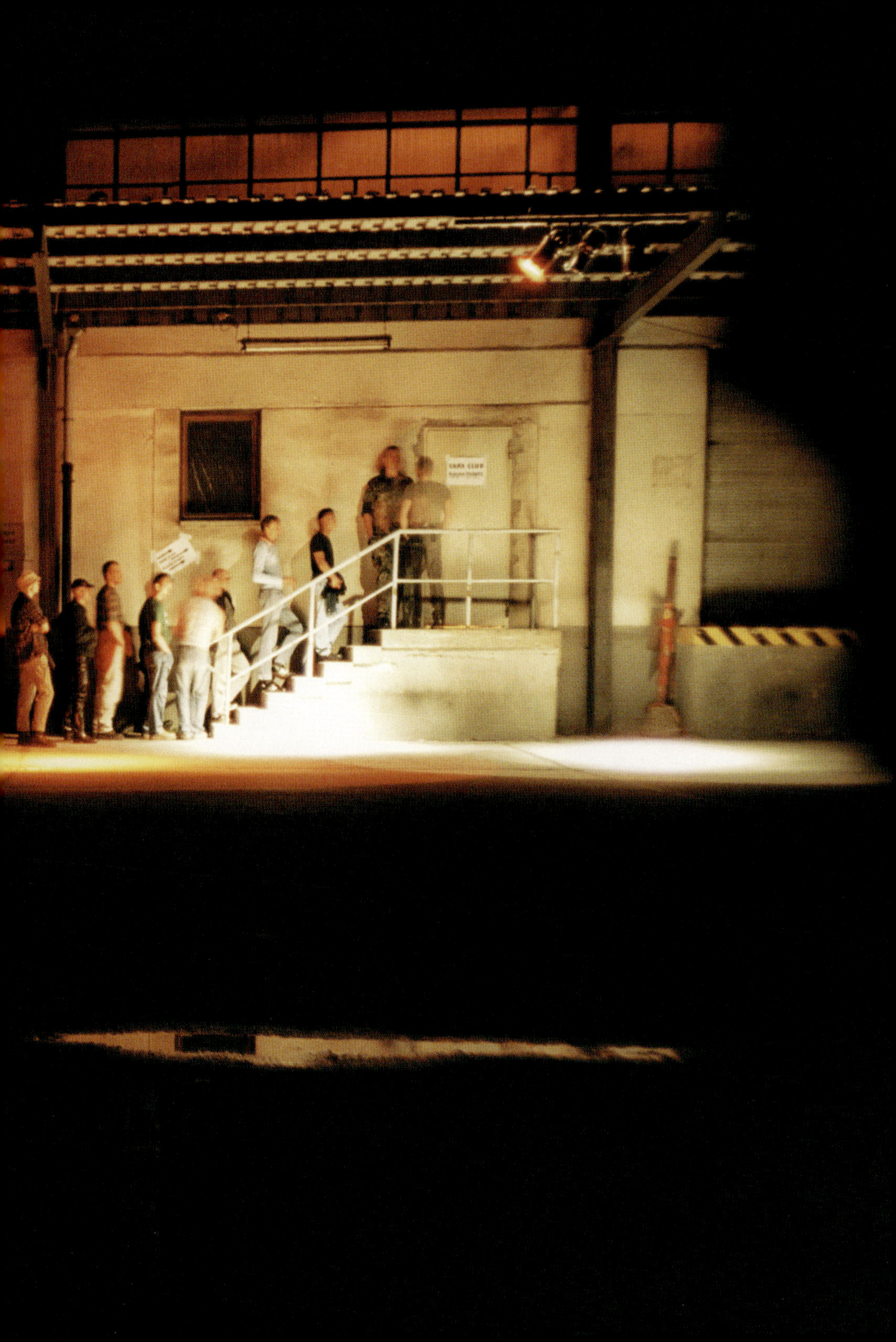

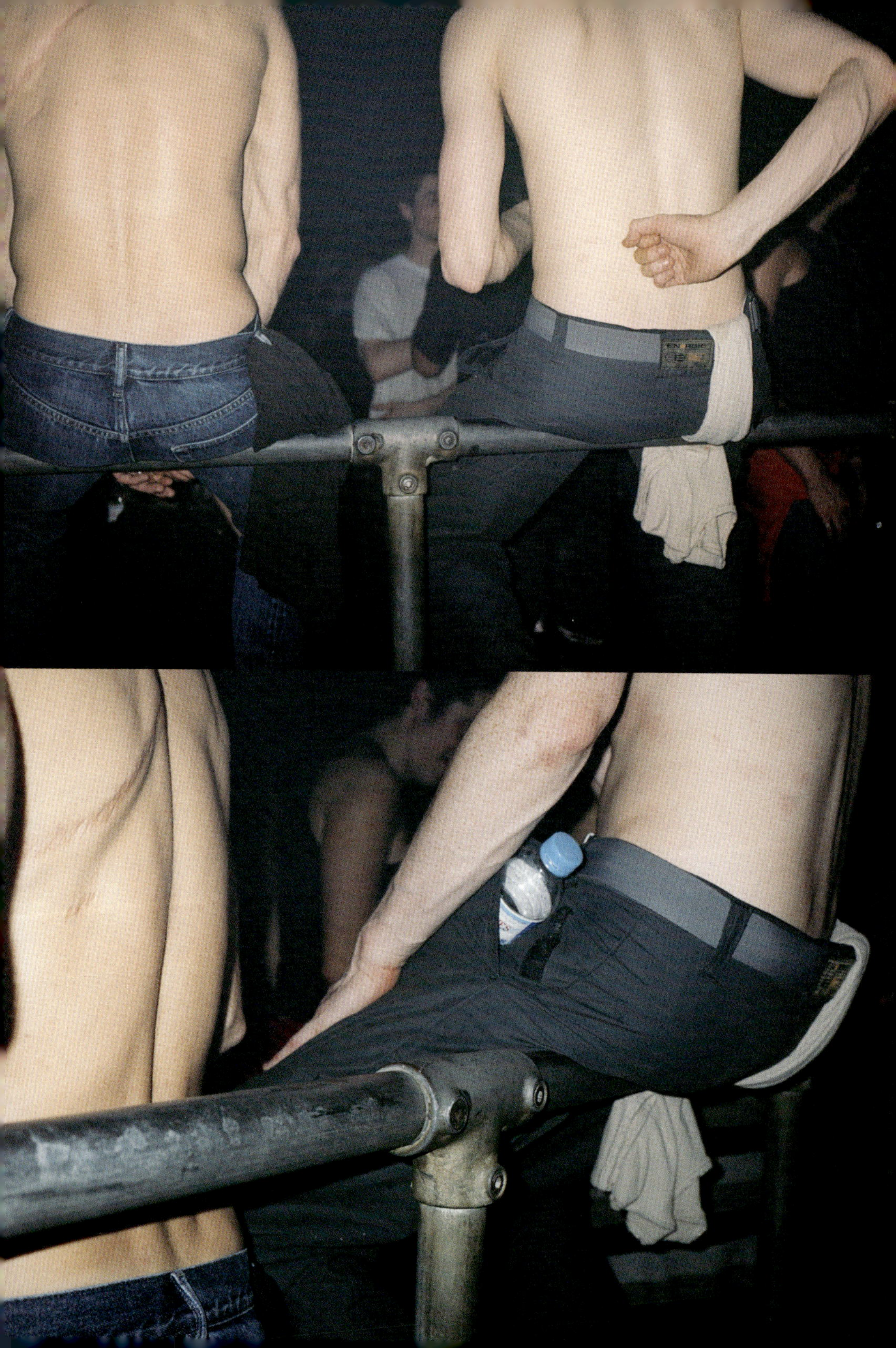

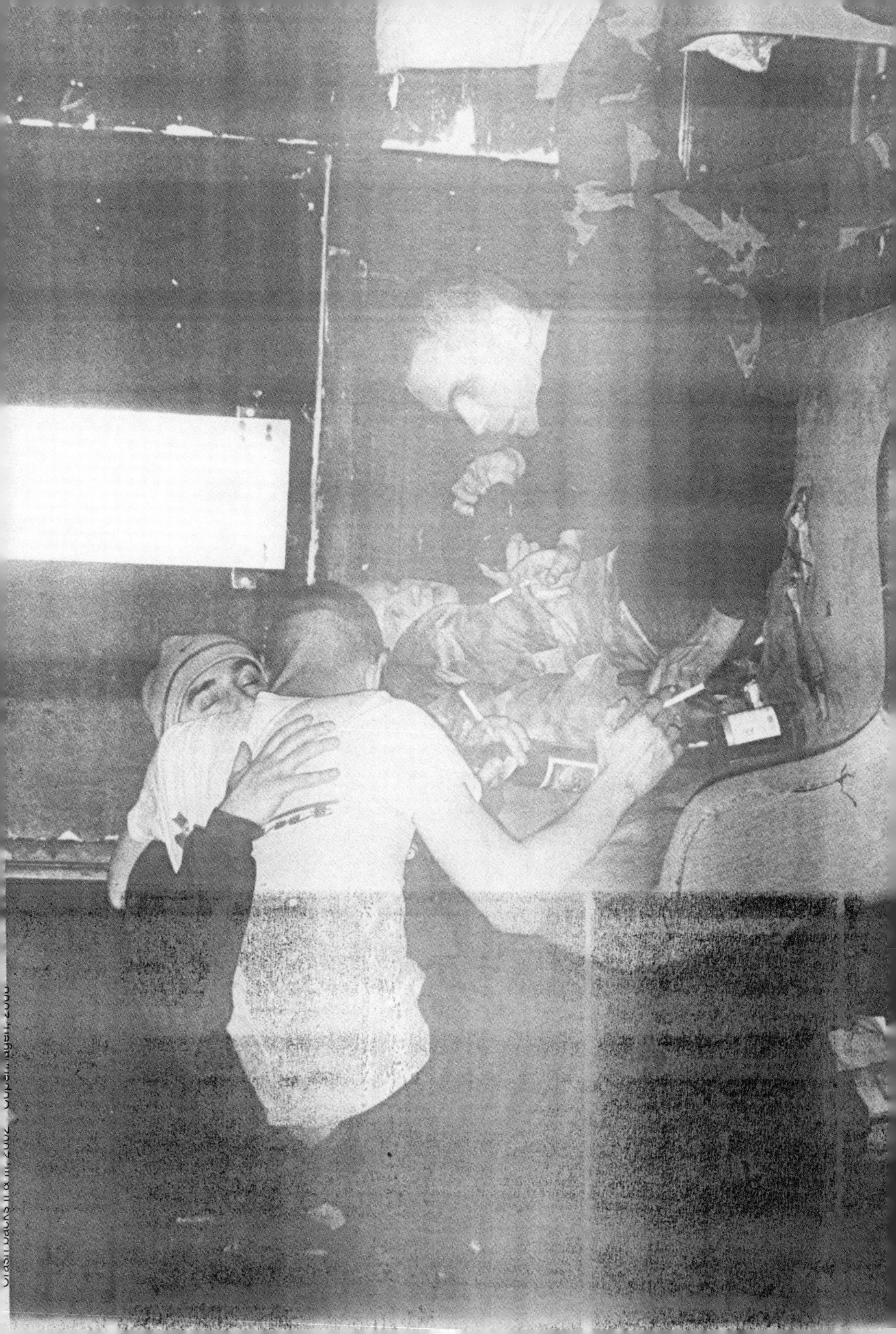

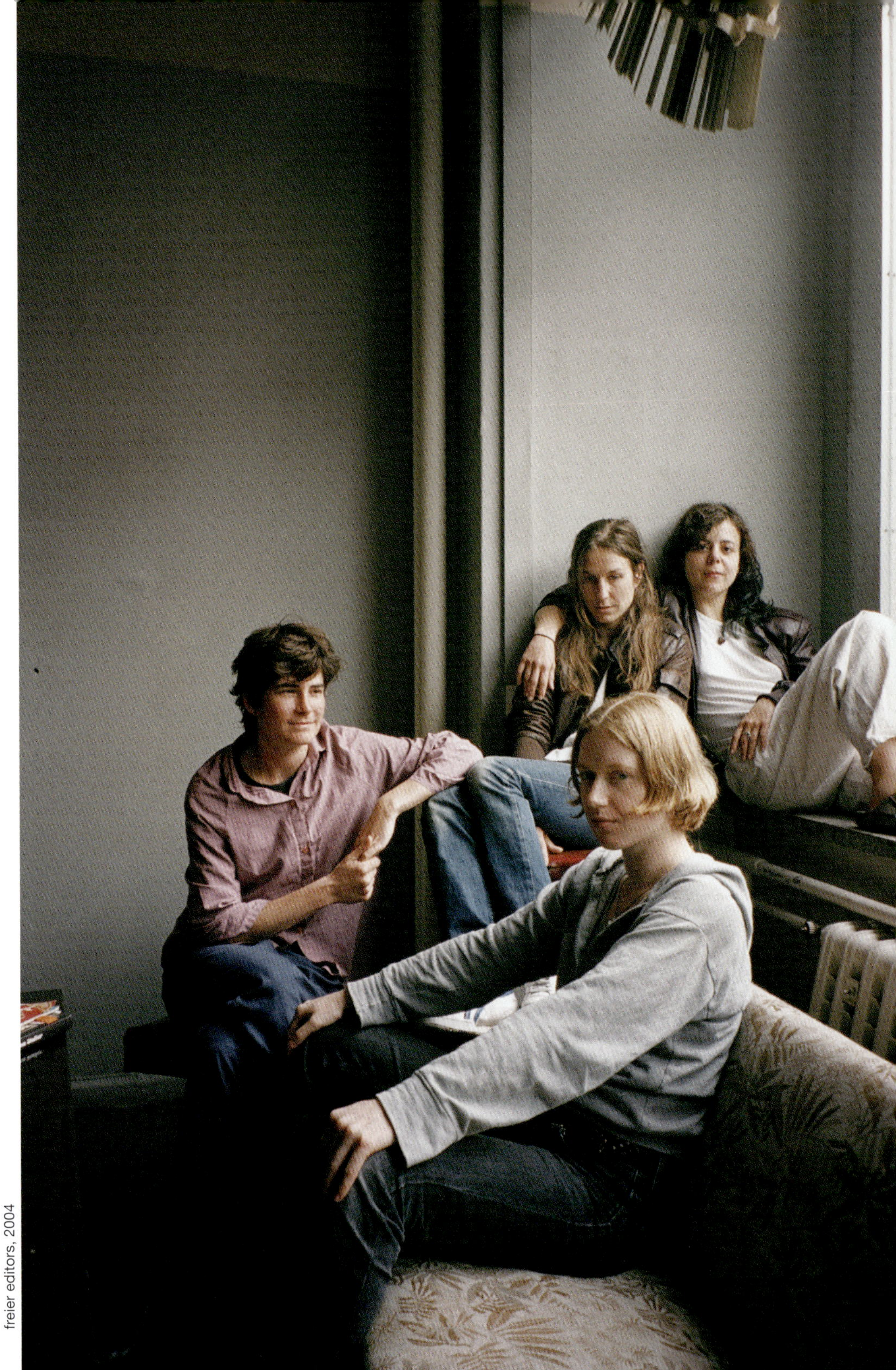

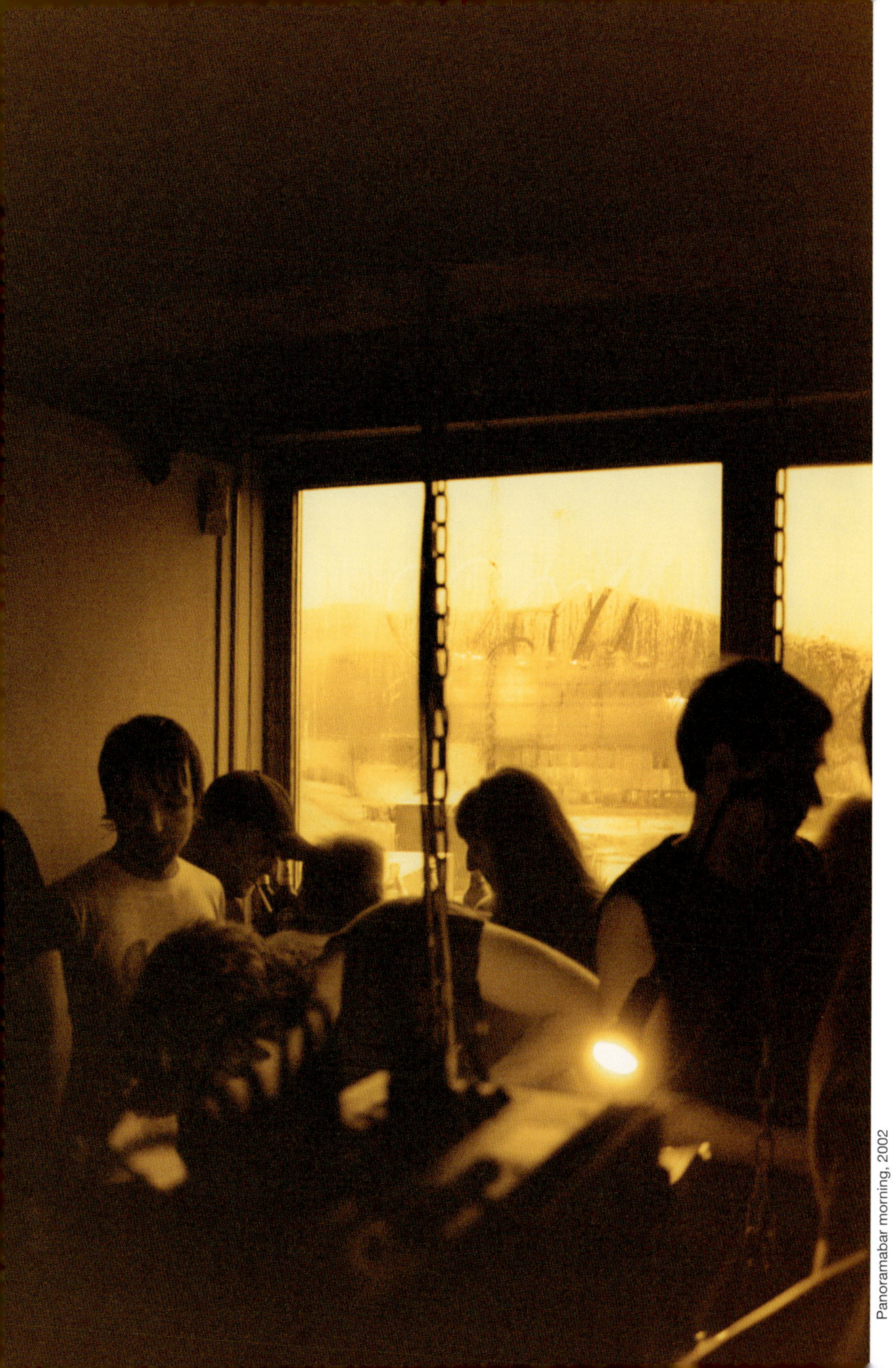

Panoramabar morning, 2002

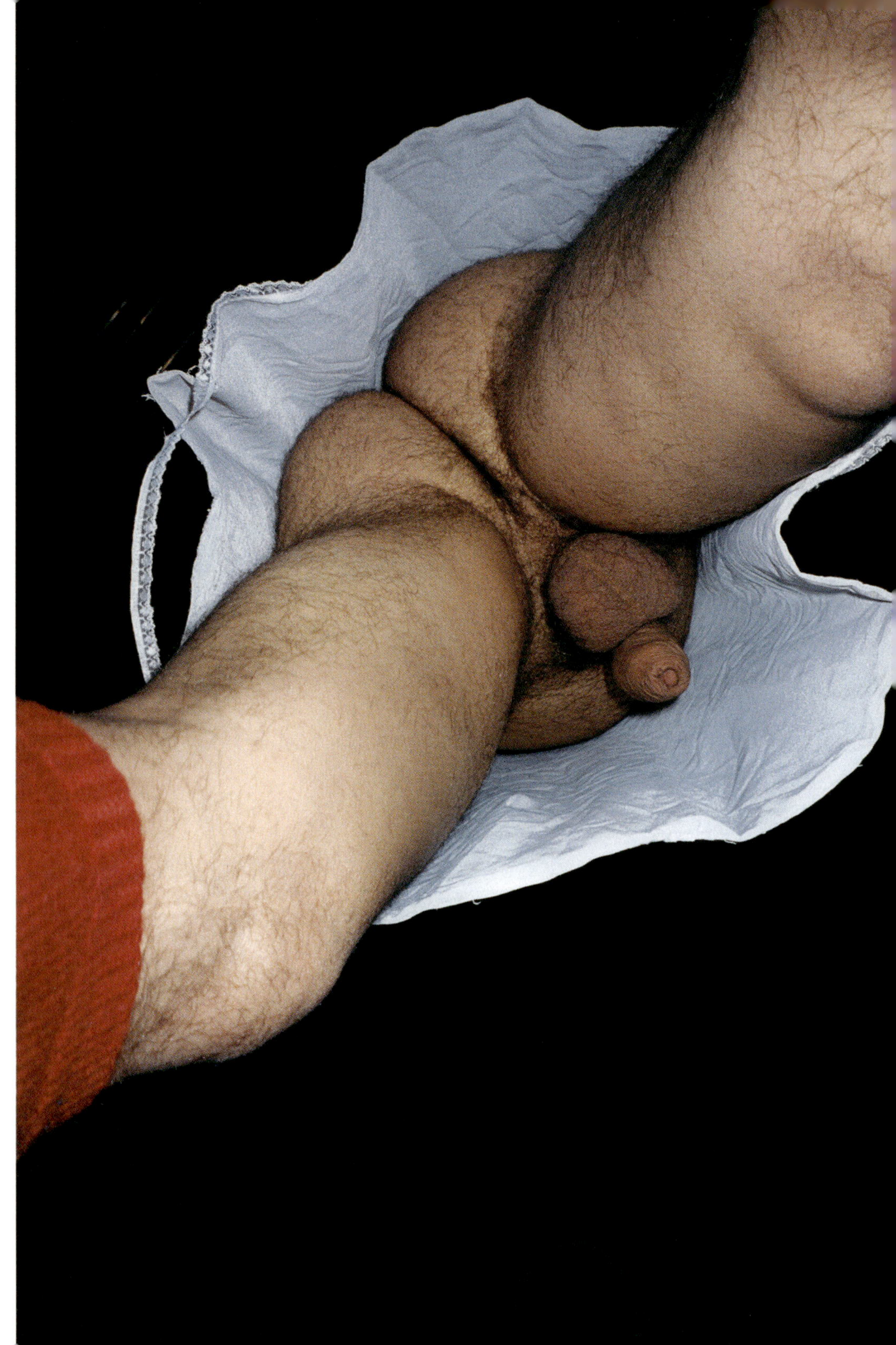

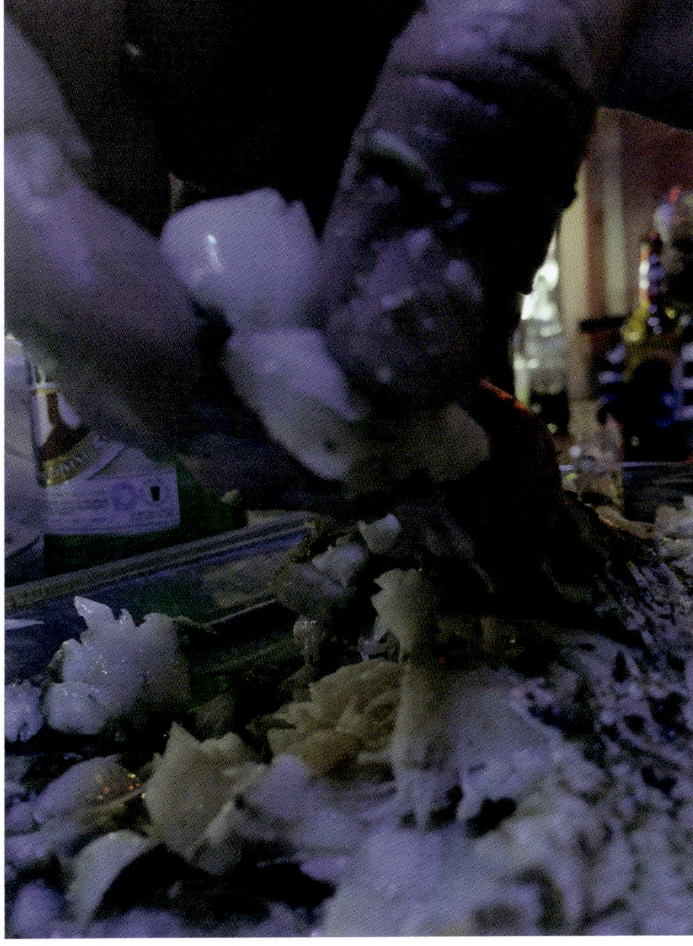

Dunst I, 2004   Yaounde dinner, 2019

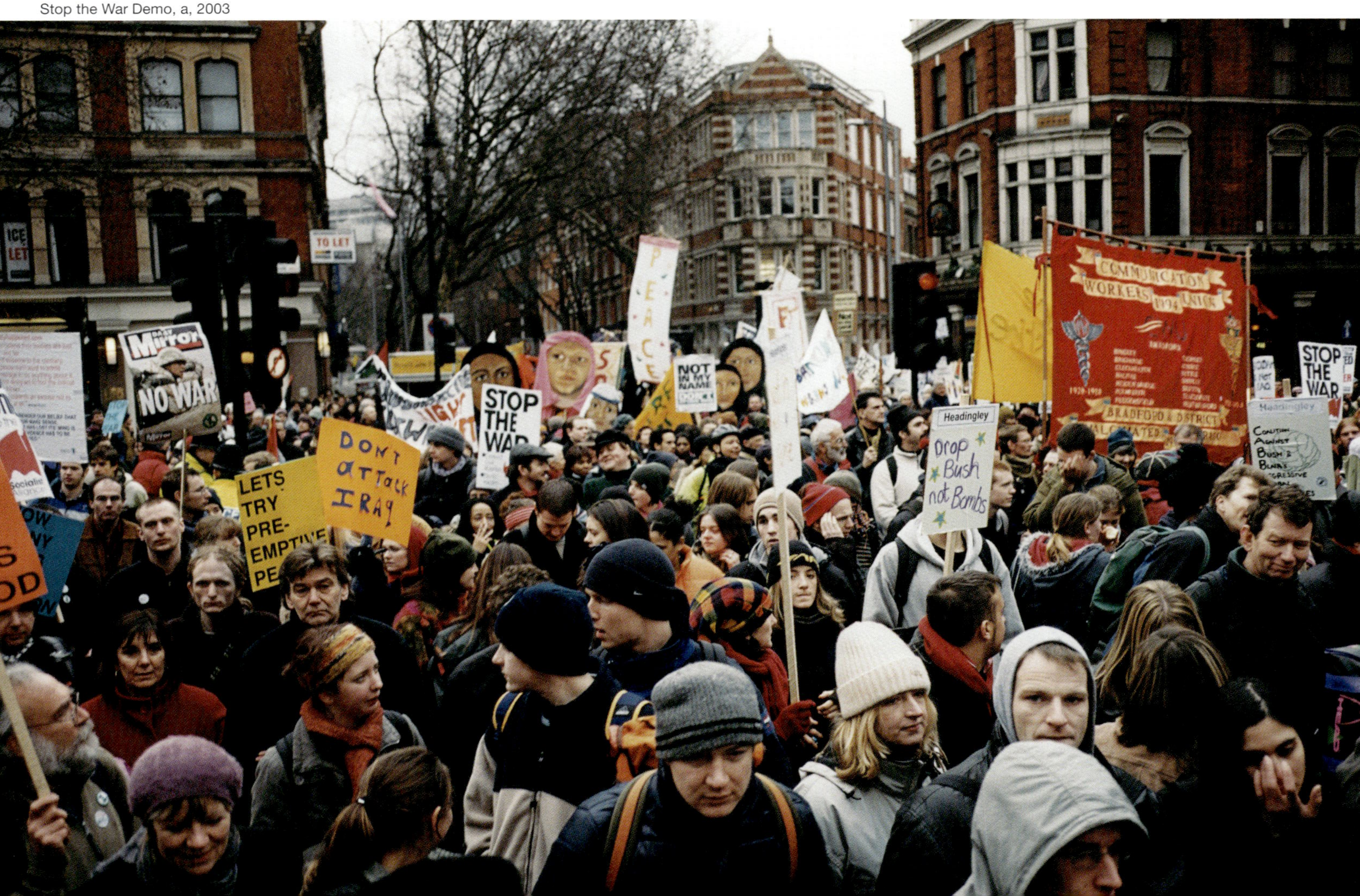

Stop the War Demo, a, 2003

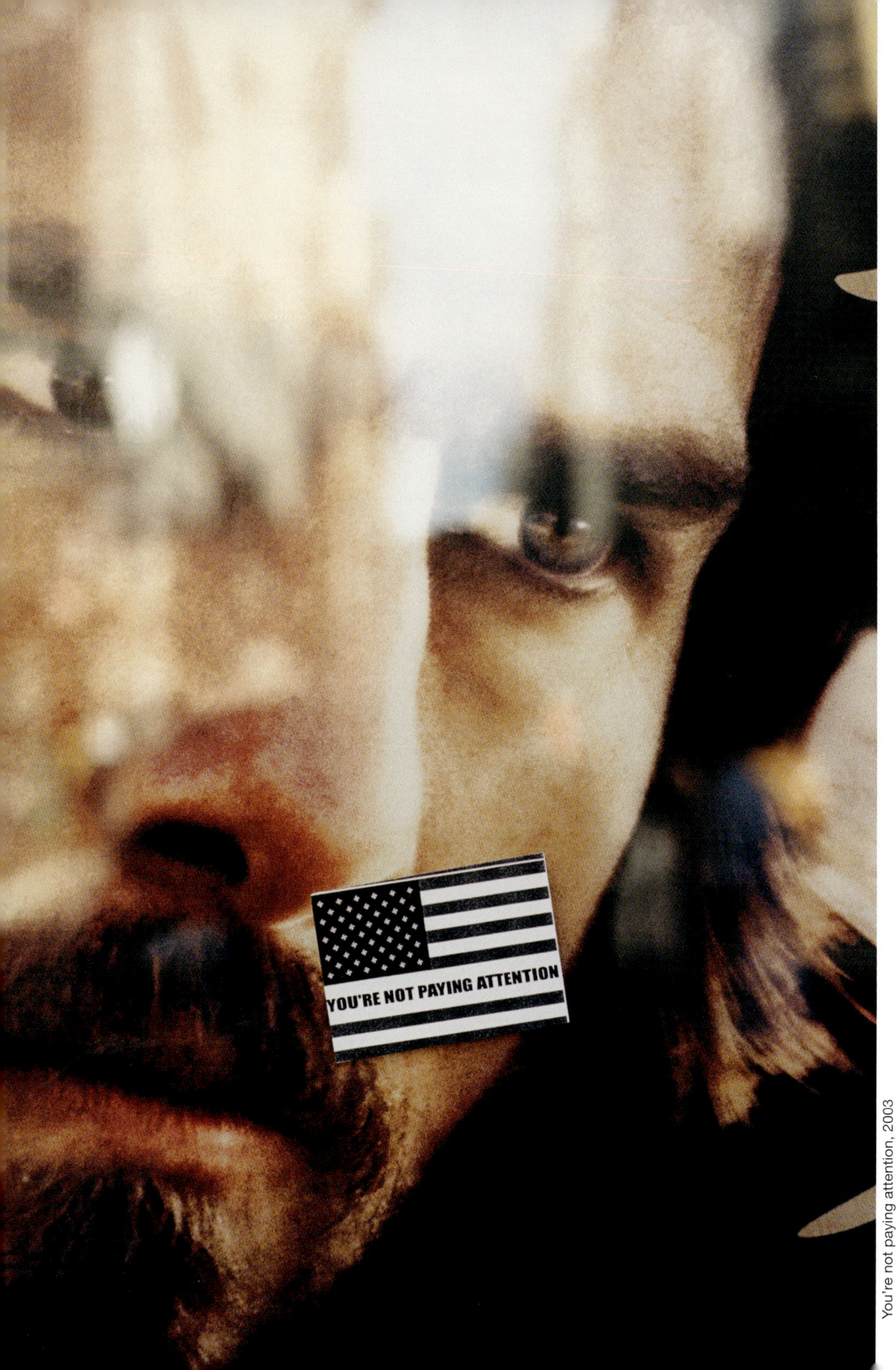

YOU'RE NOT PAYING ATTENTION

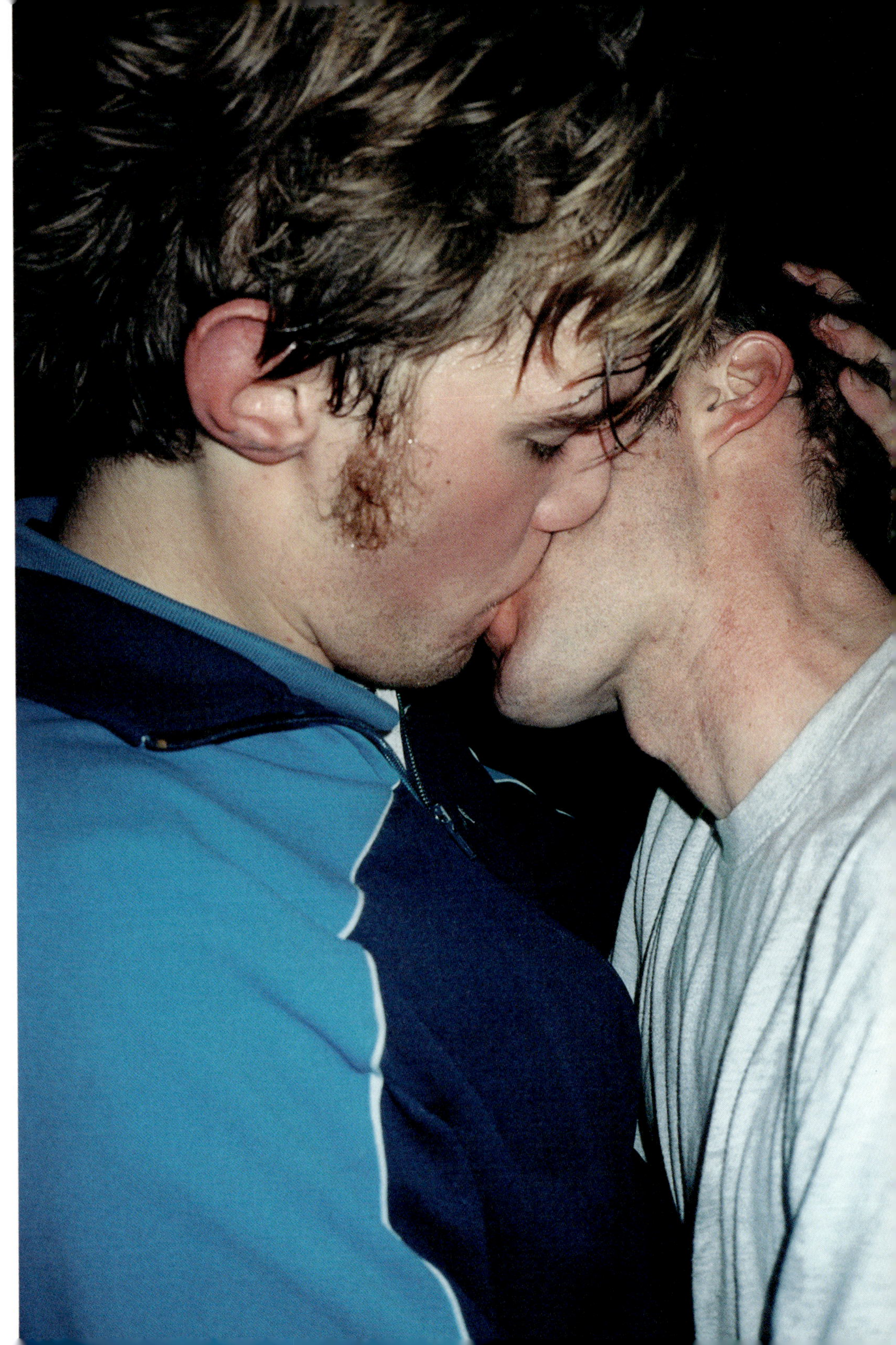

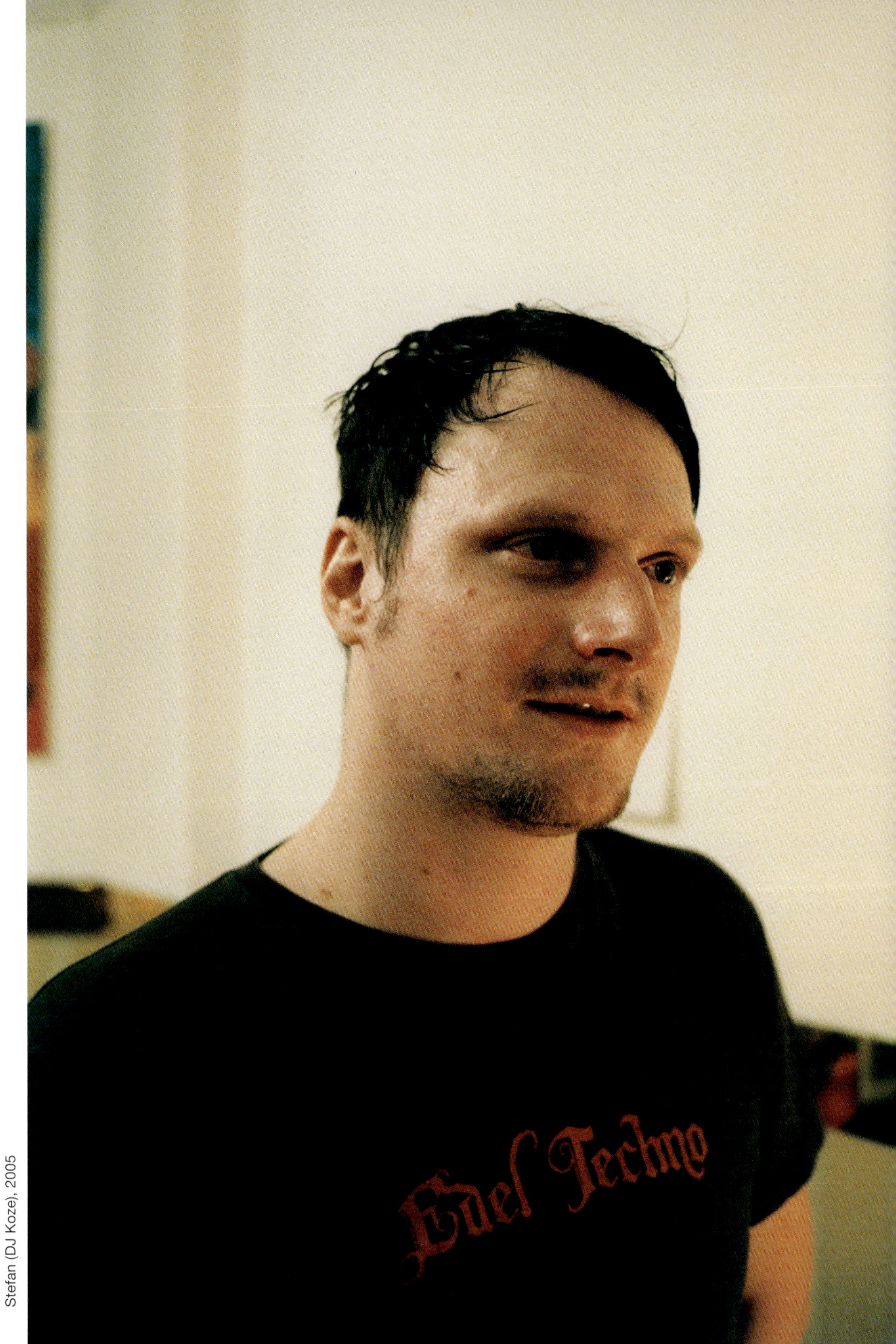

Stefan (DJ Koze), 2005

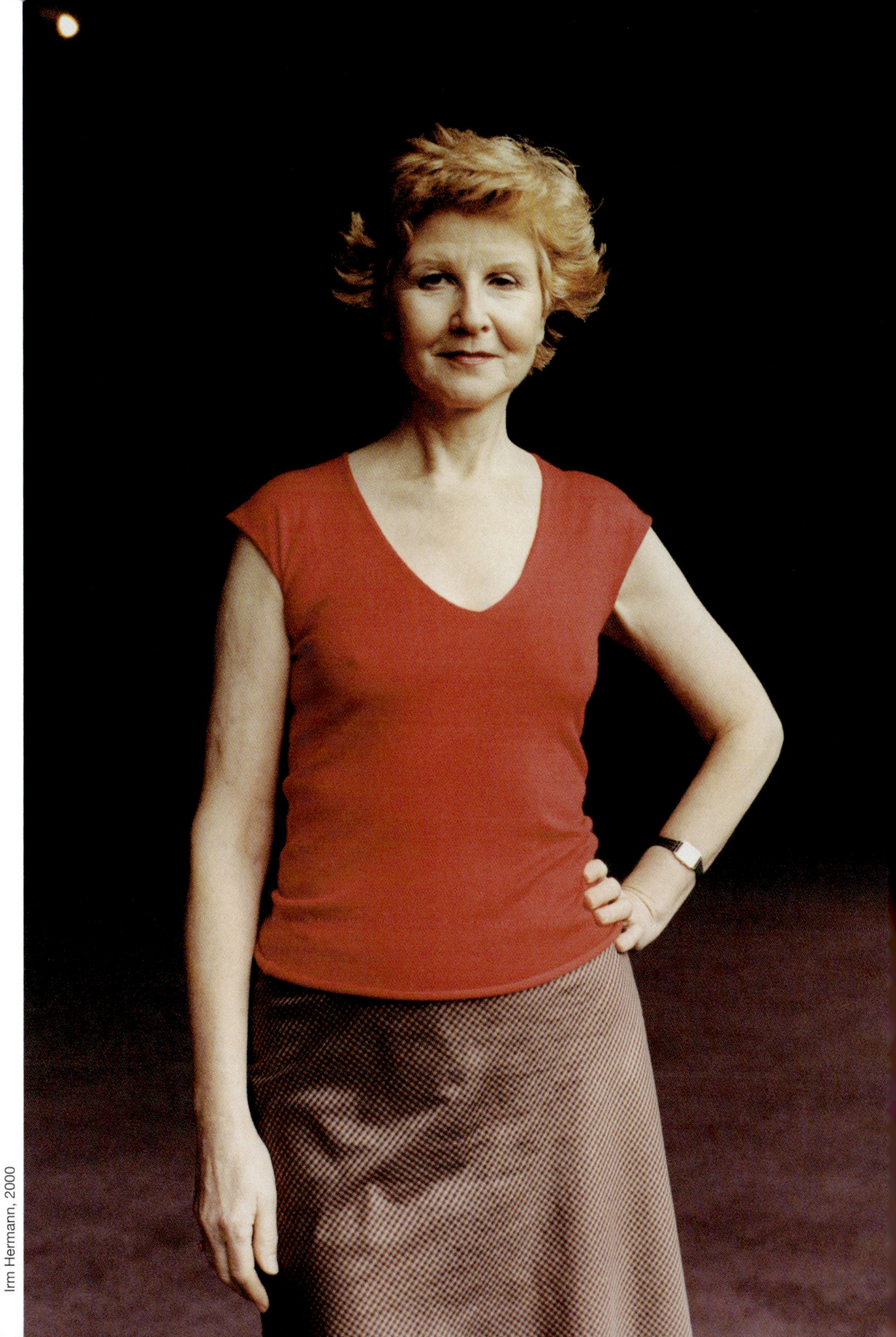

Irm Hermann, 2000

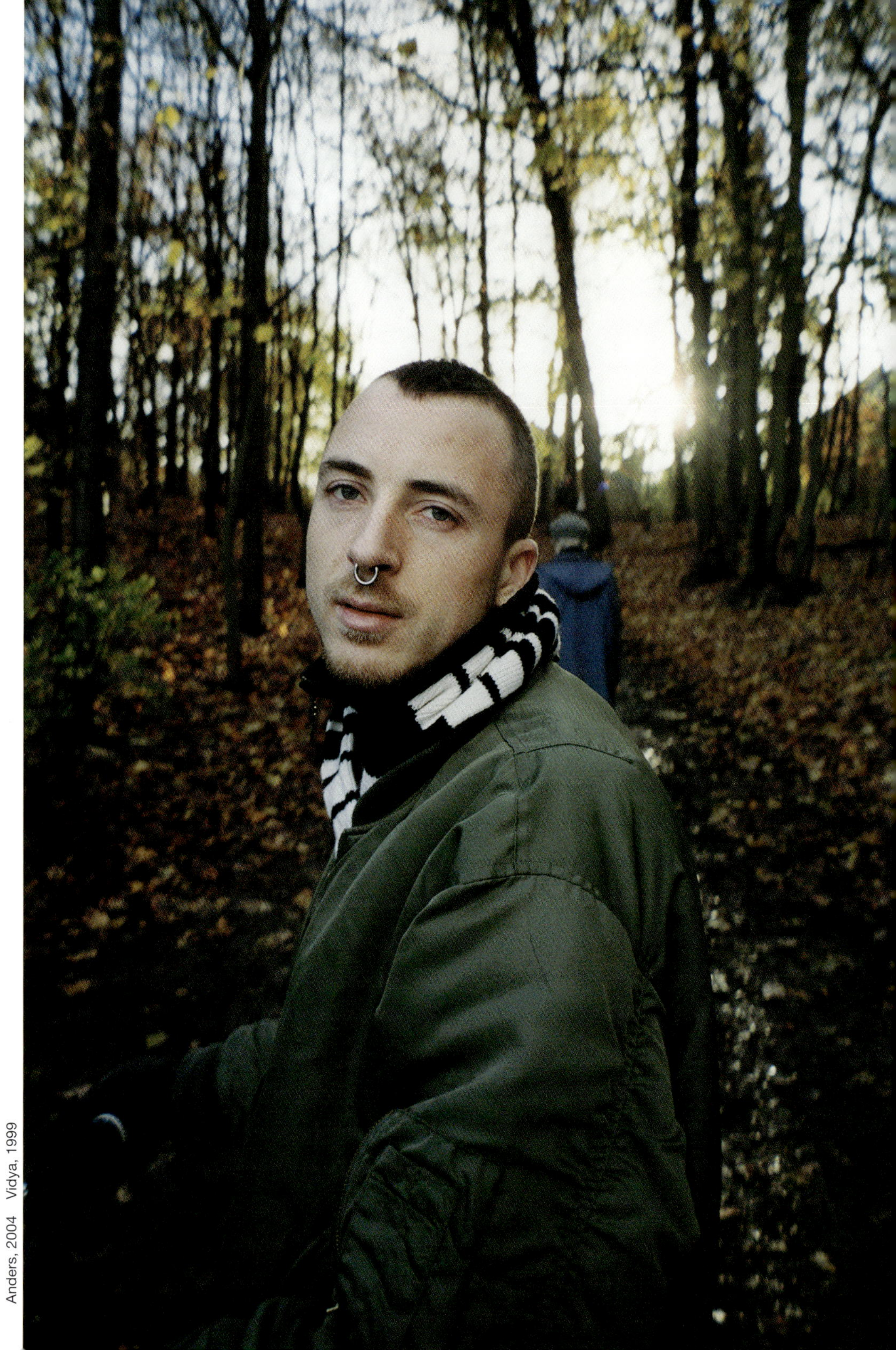

Anders, 2004   Vidya, 1999

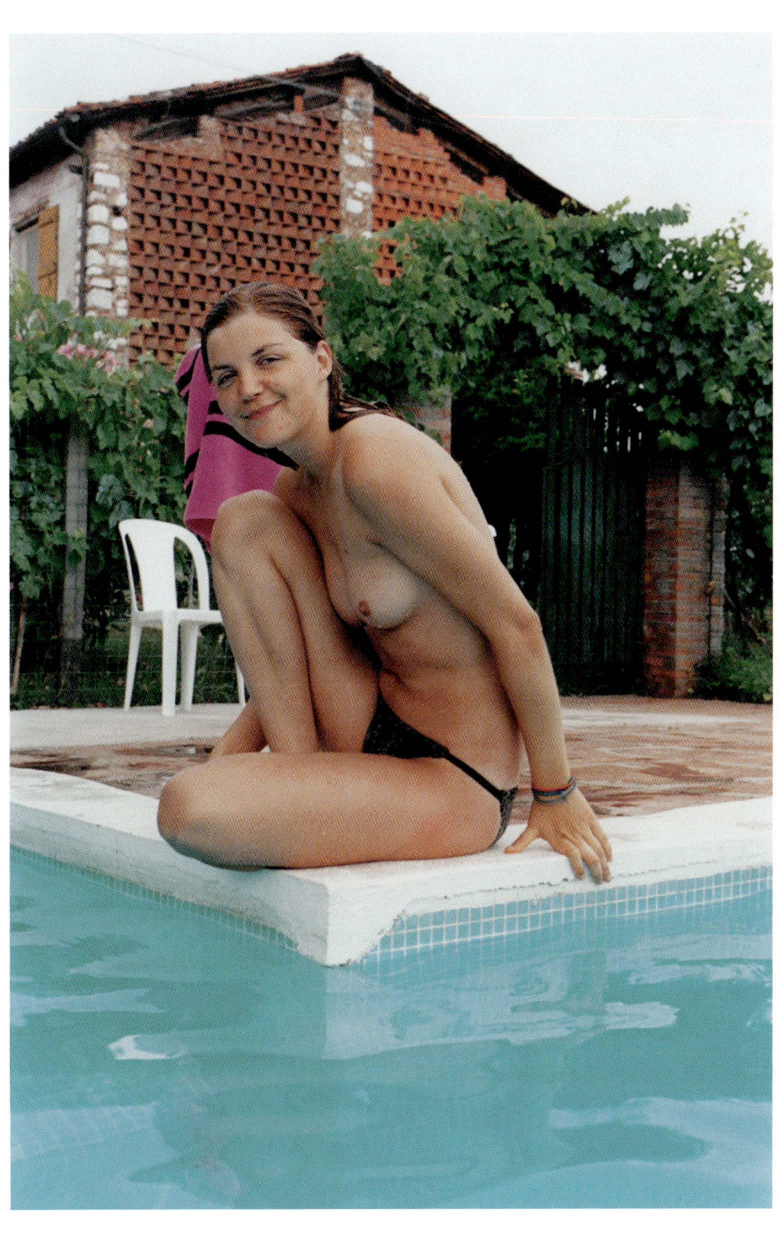

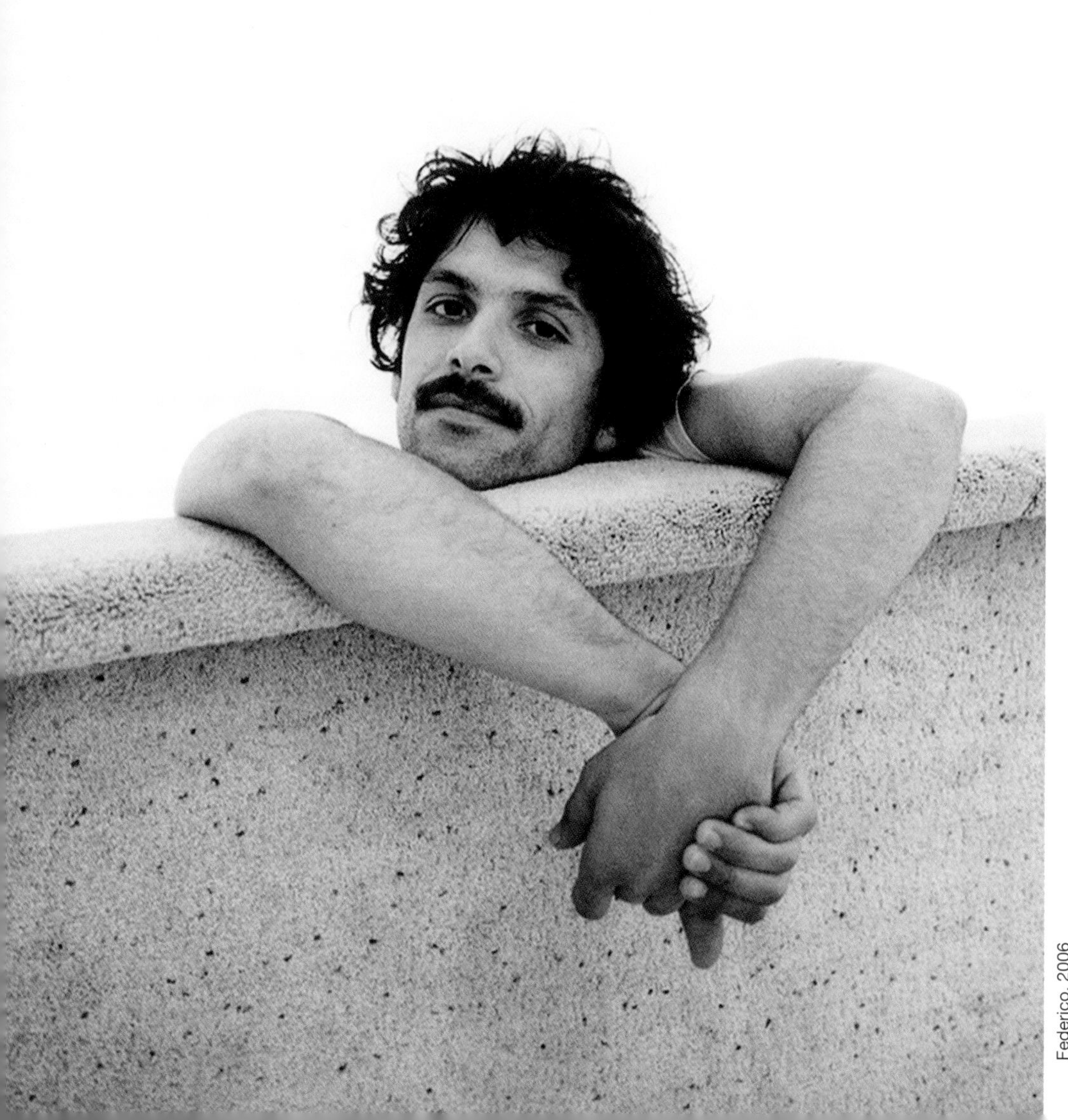

Federico, 2006

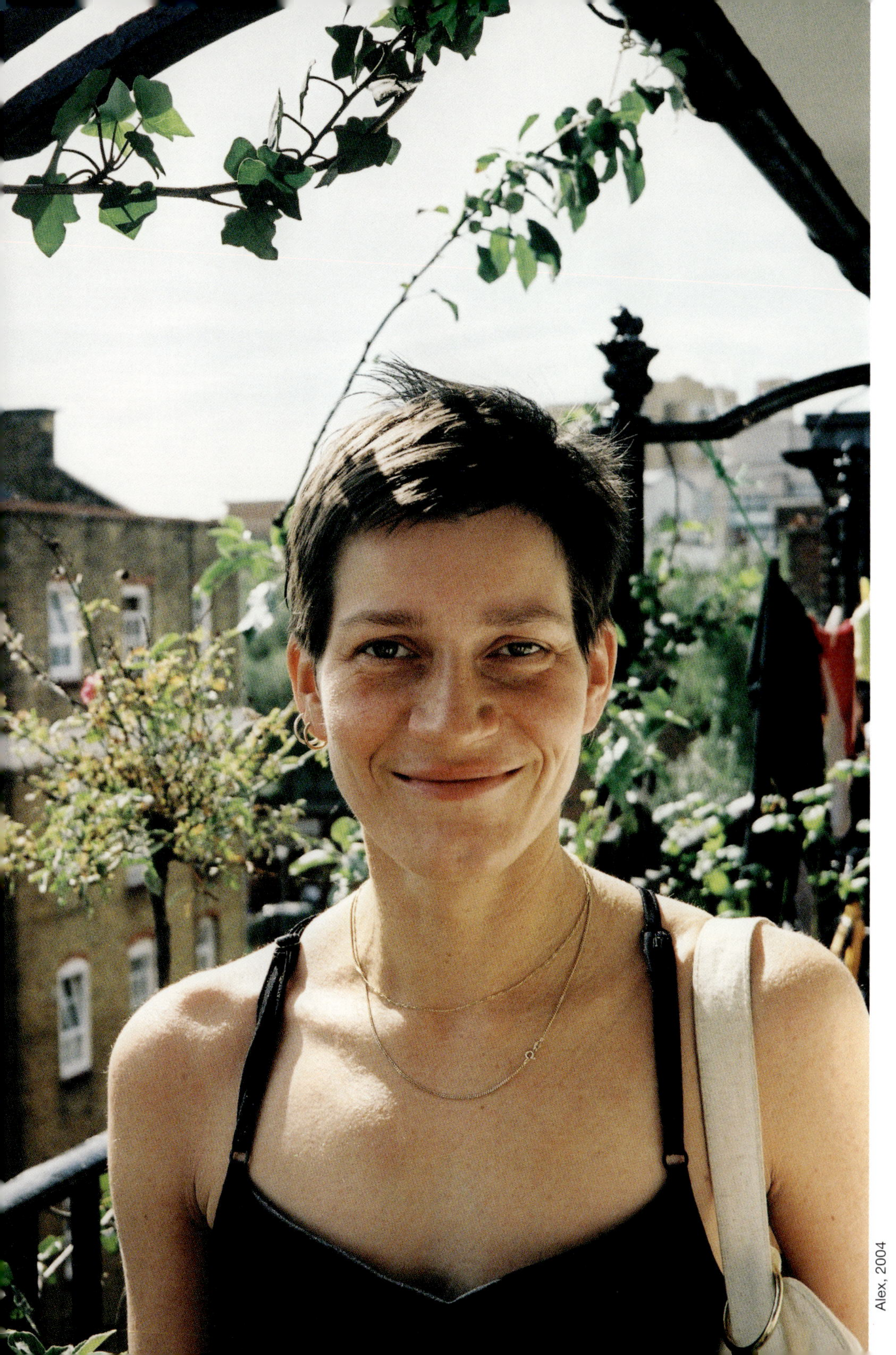

Alex, 2004

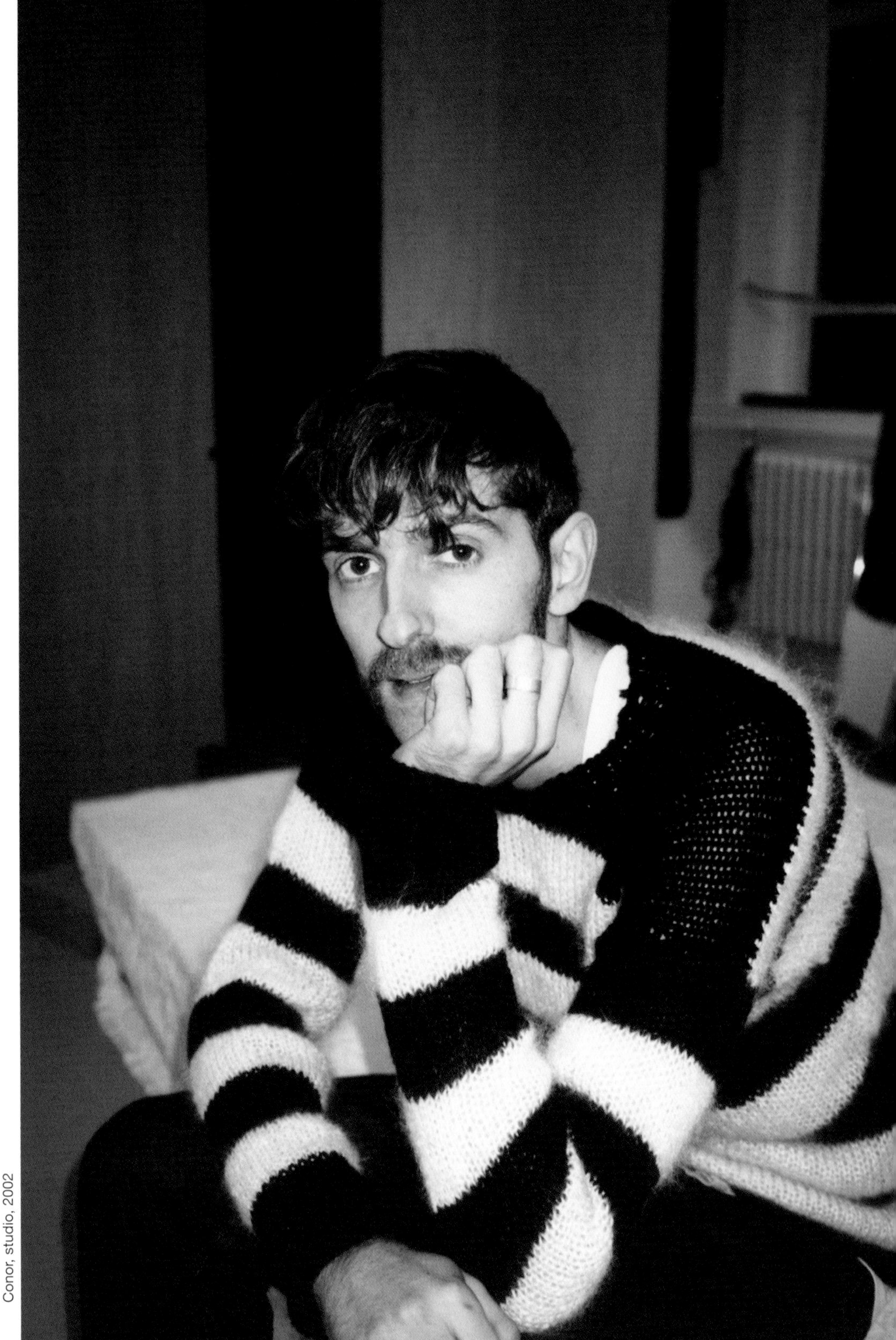

Conor, studio, 2002

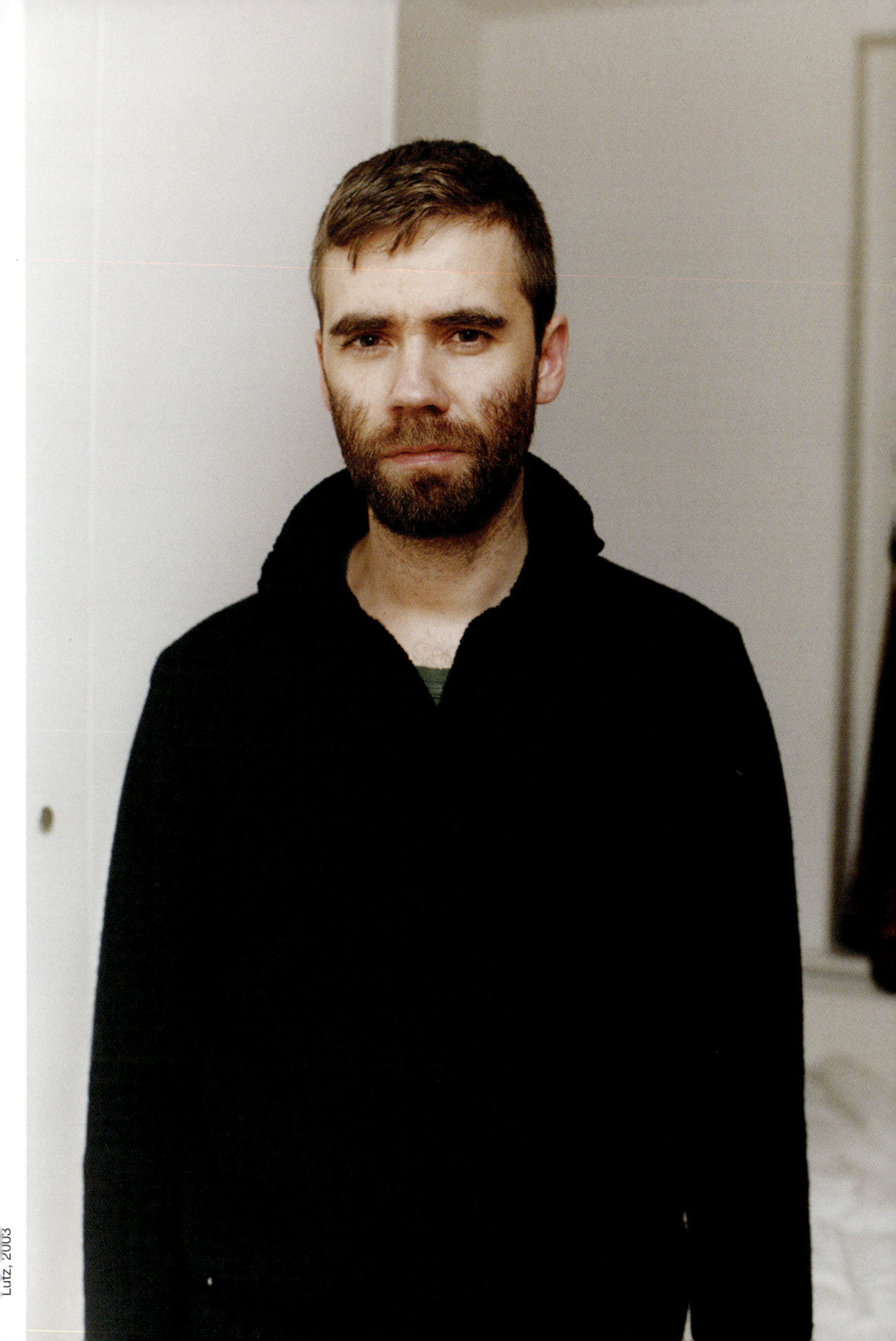

Lutz, 2003

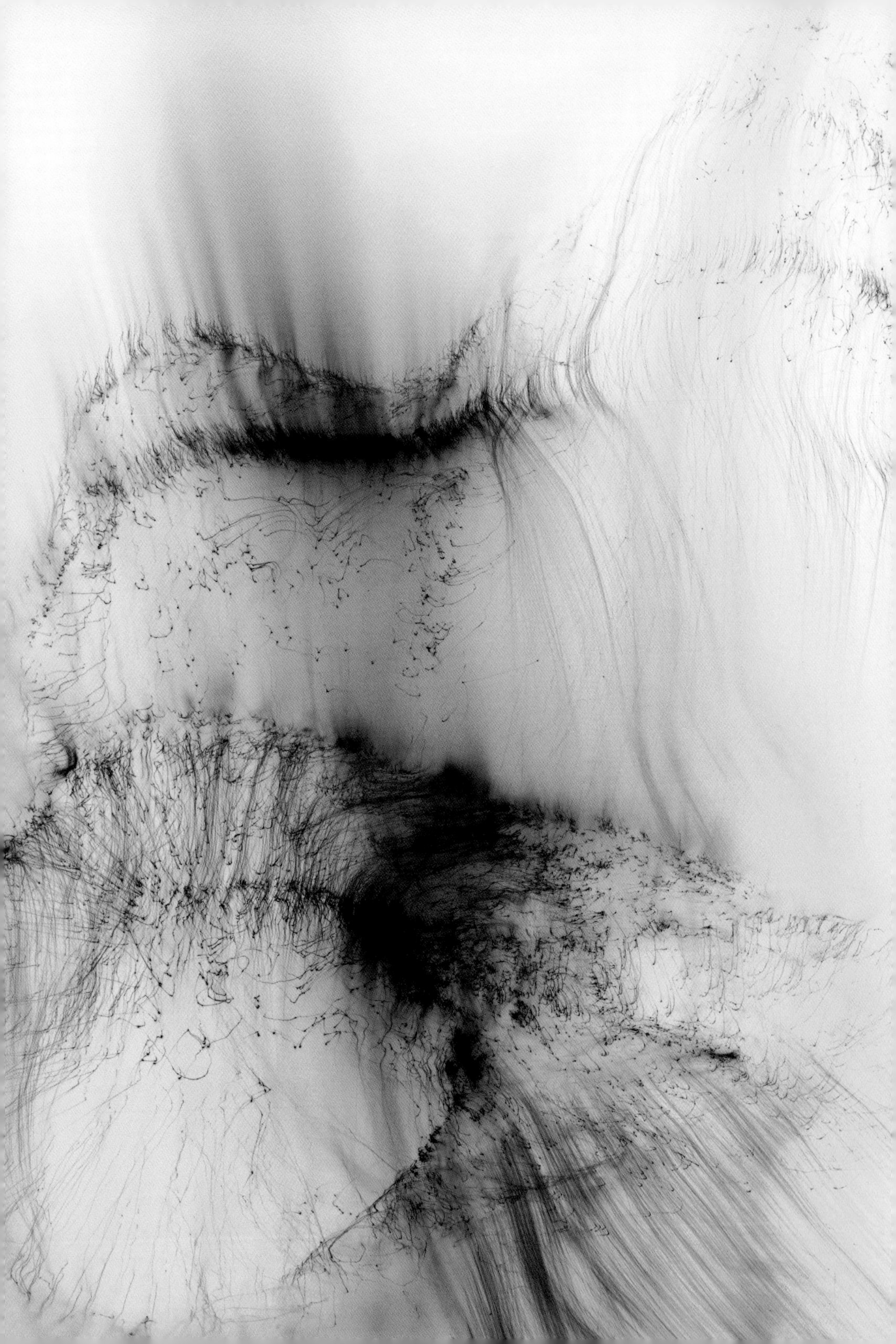

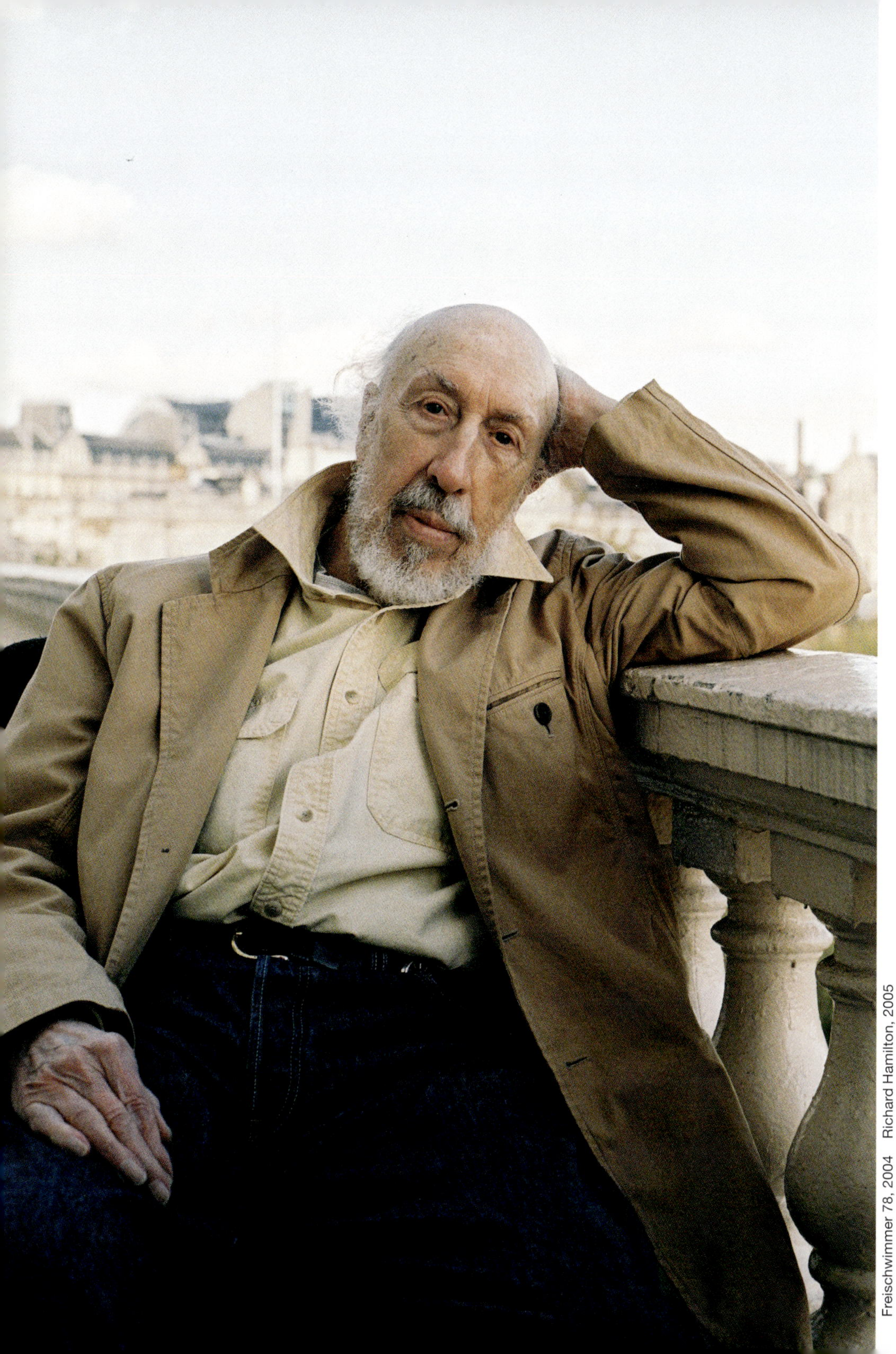

Freischwimmer 78, 2004   Richard Hamilton, 2005

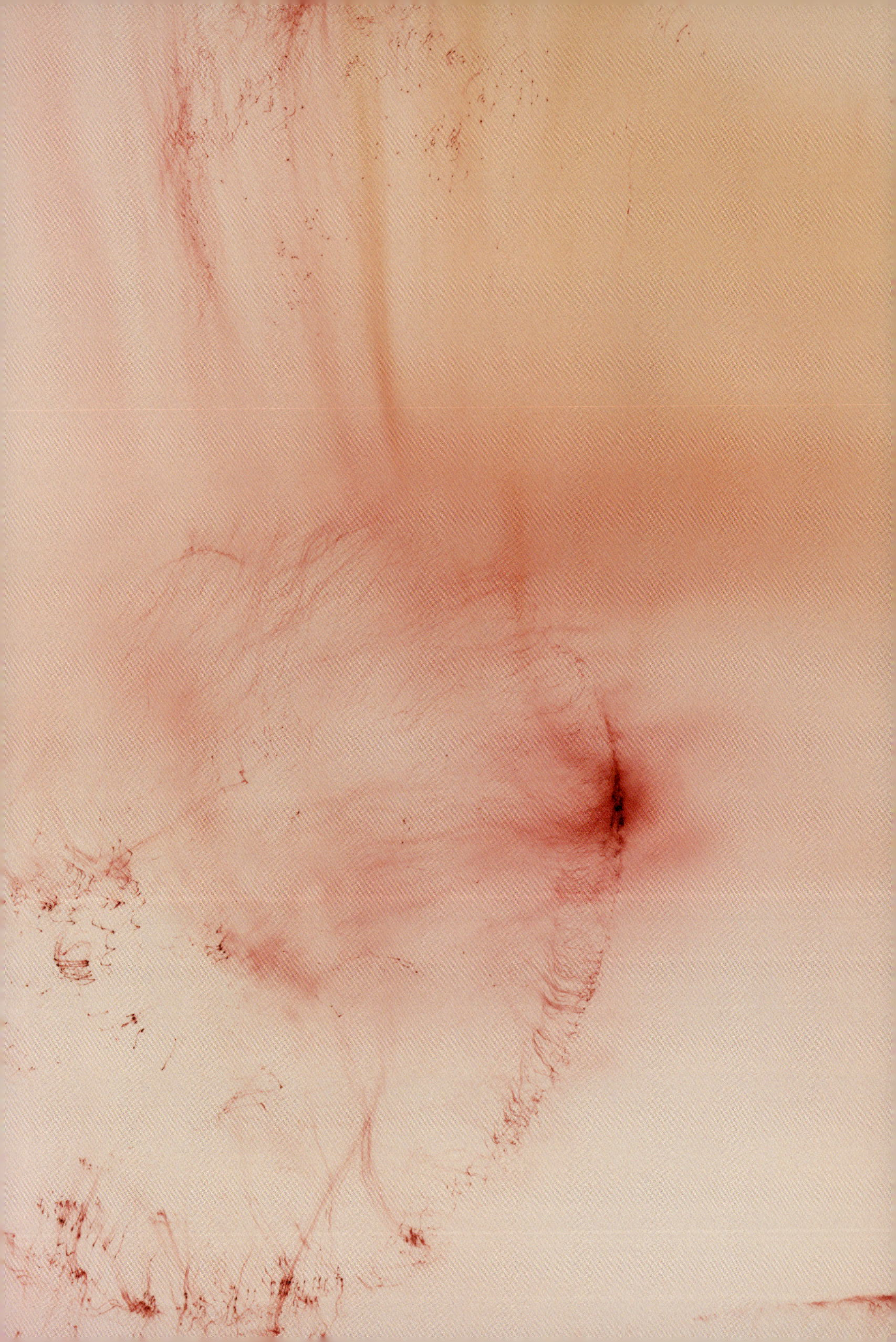

Urgency I, 2006   Freischwimmer 16, 2003

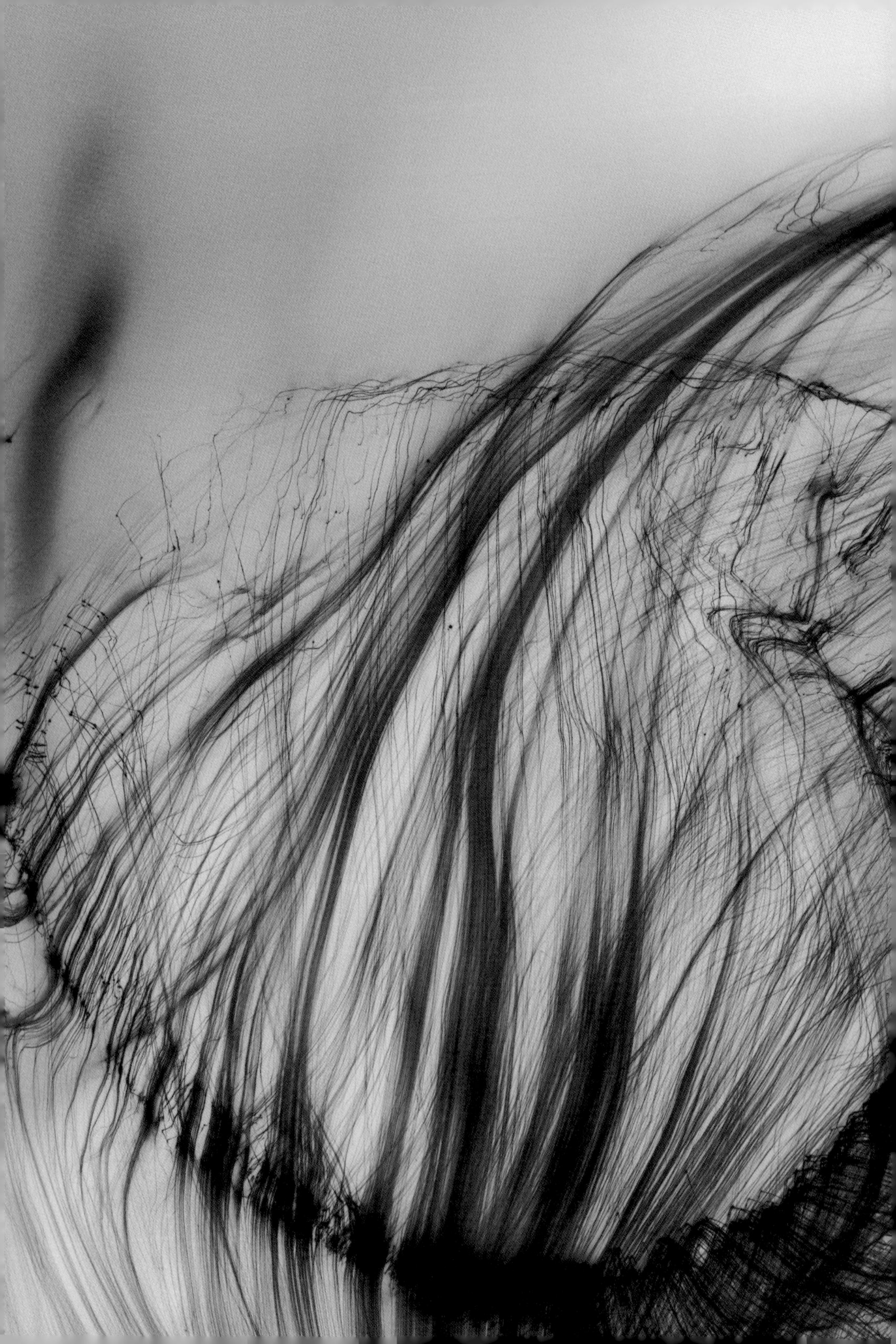

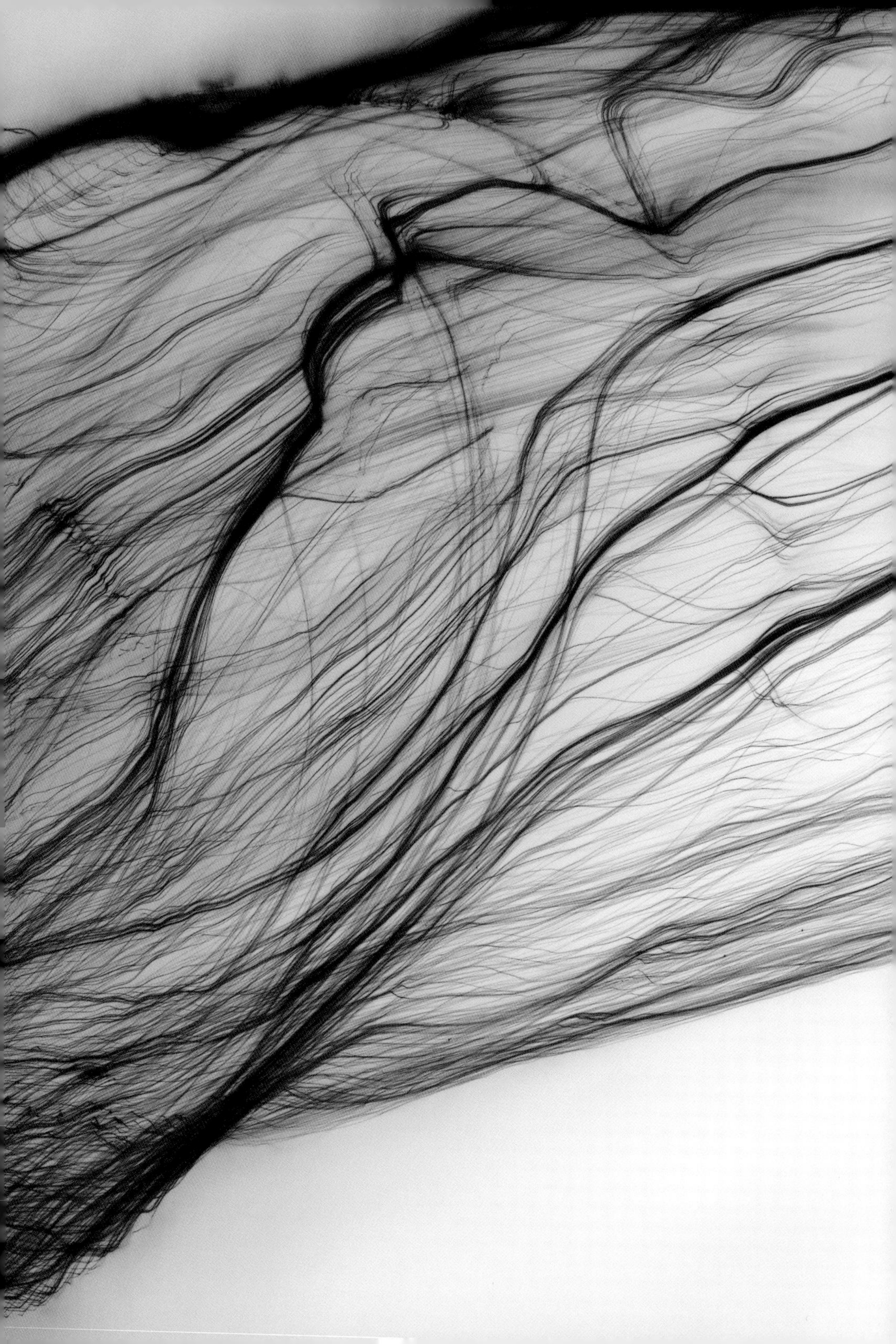

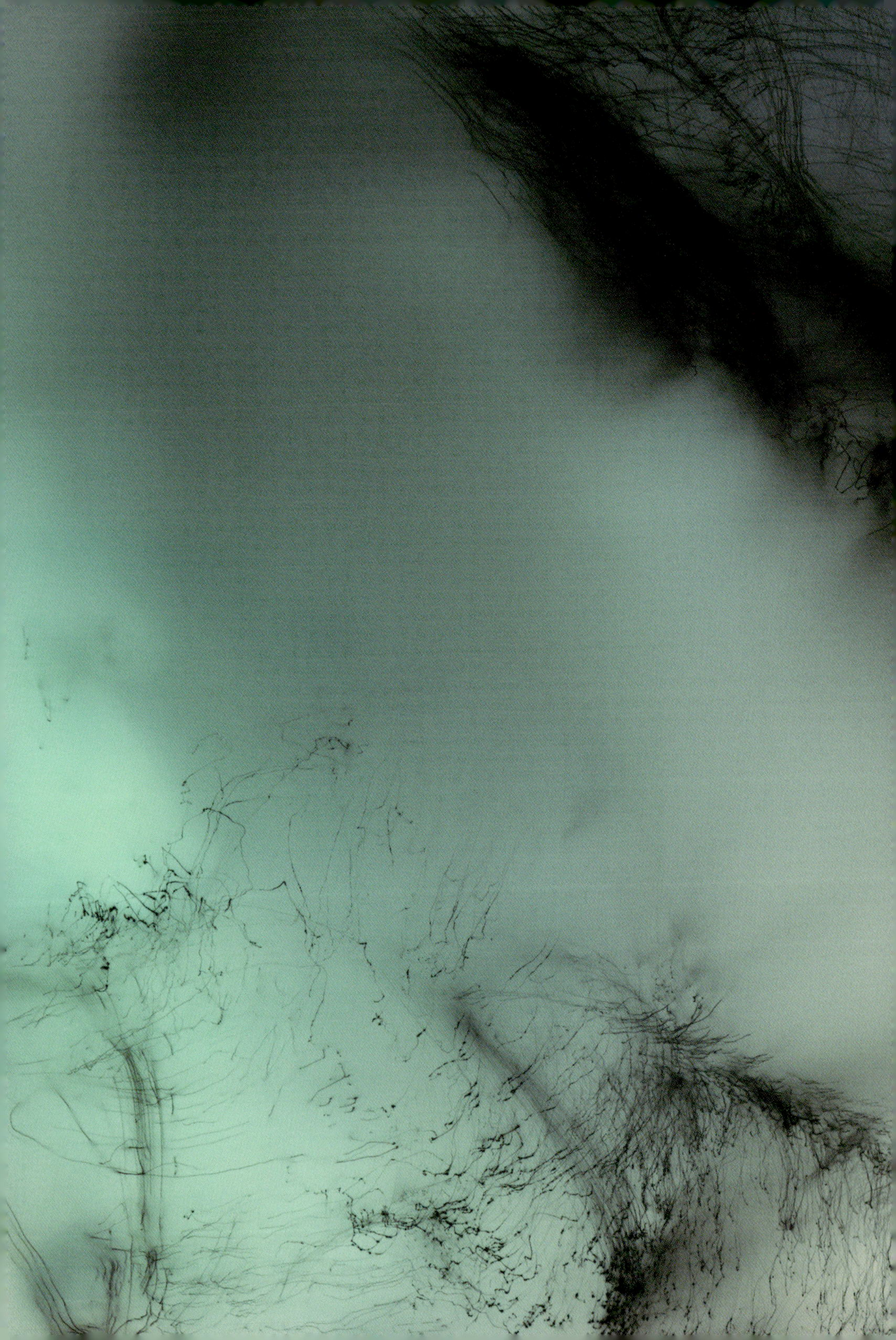

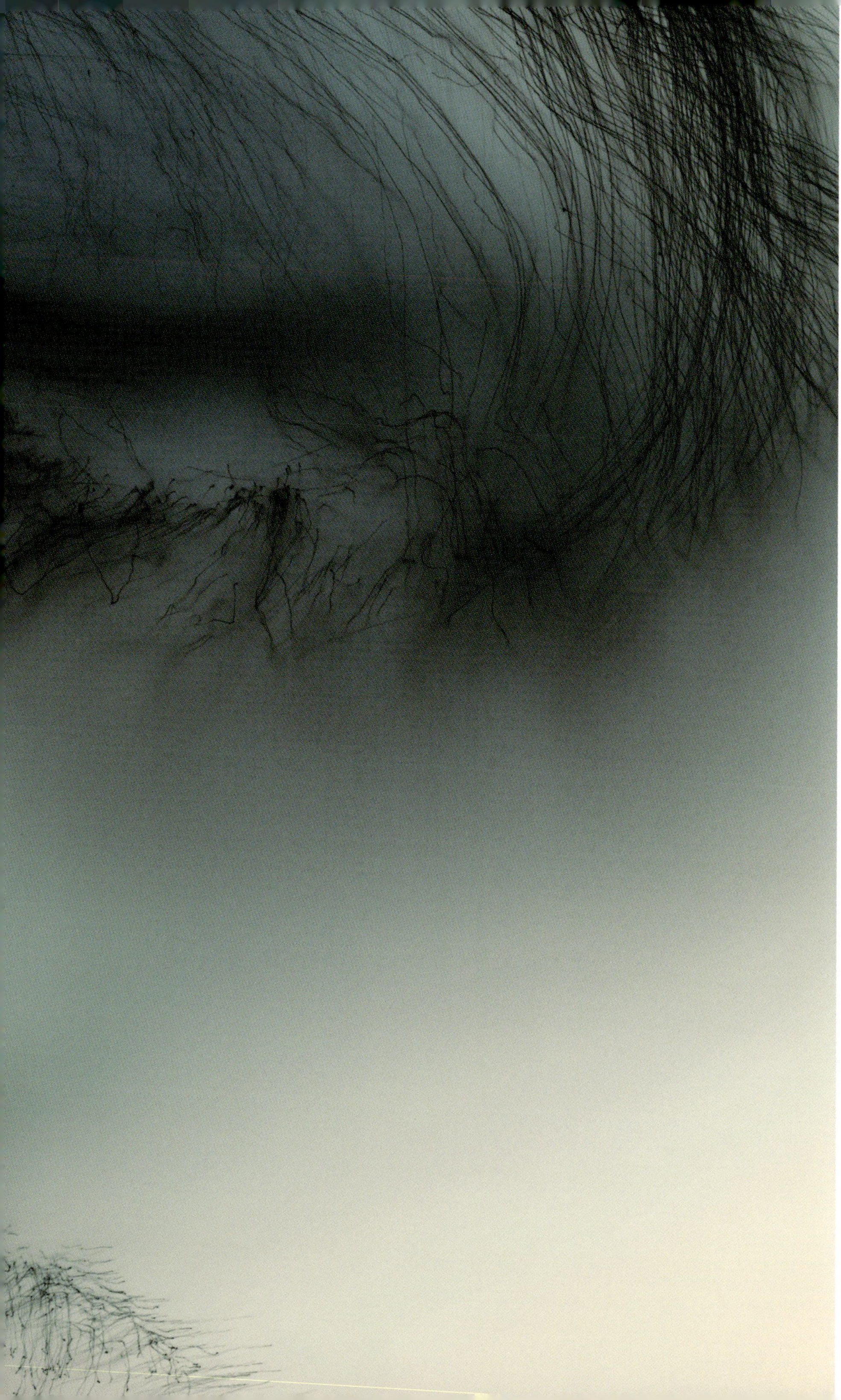

Freischwimmer 151, 2010

Peaches V, 2001
Blushes # 66, 2000
Freischwimmer 54, 2003
Greifbar 104, 2020

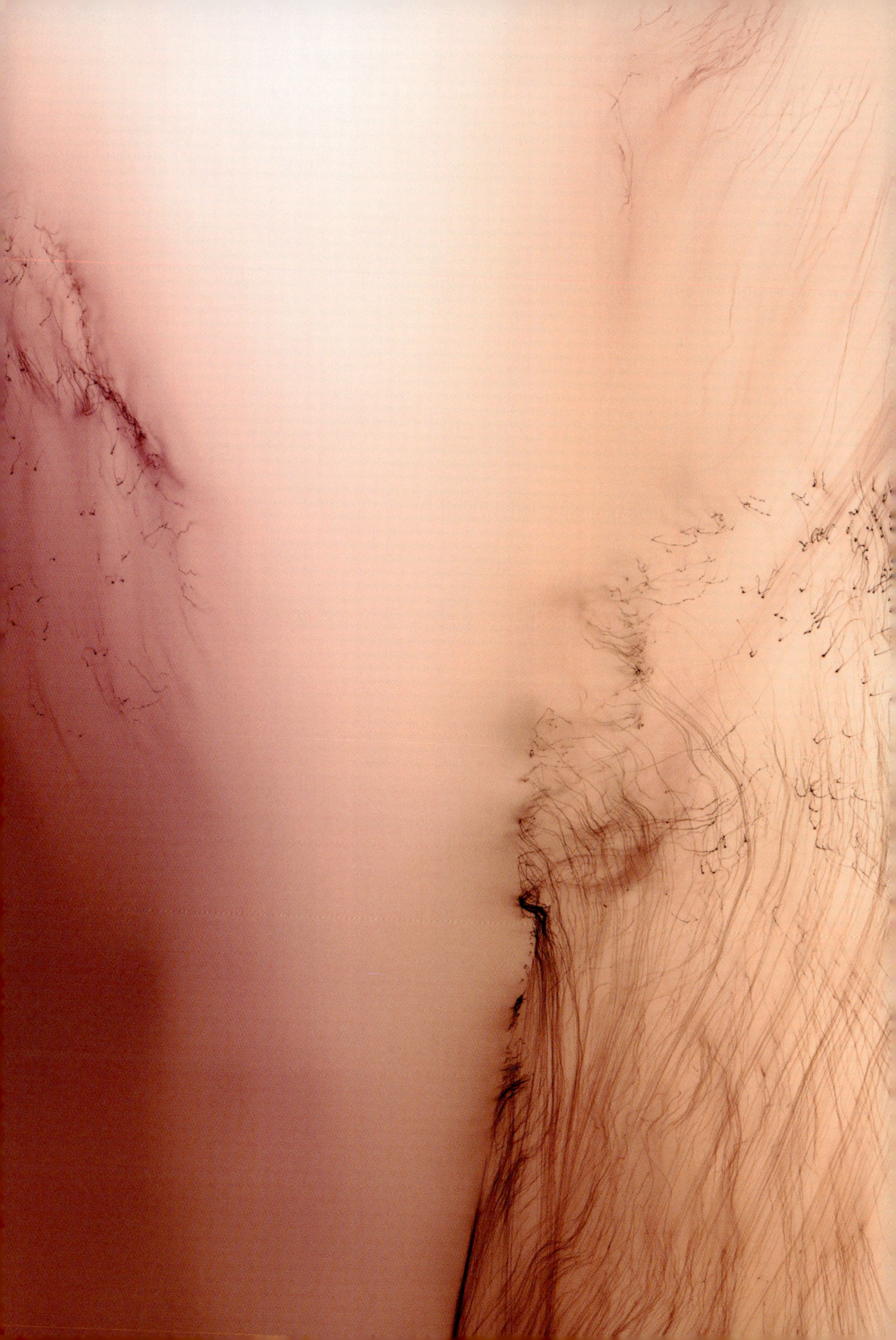

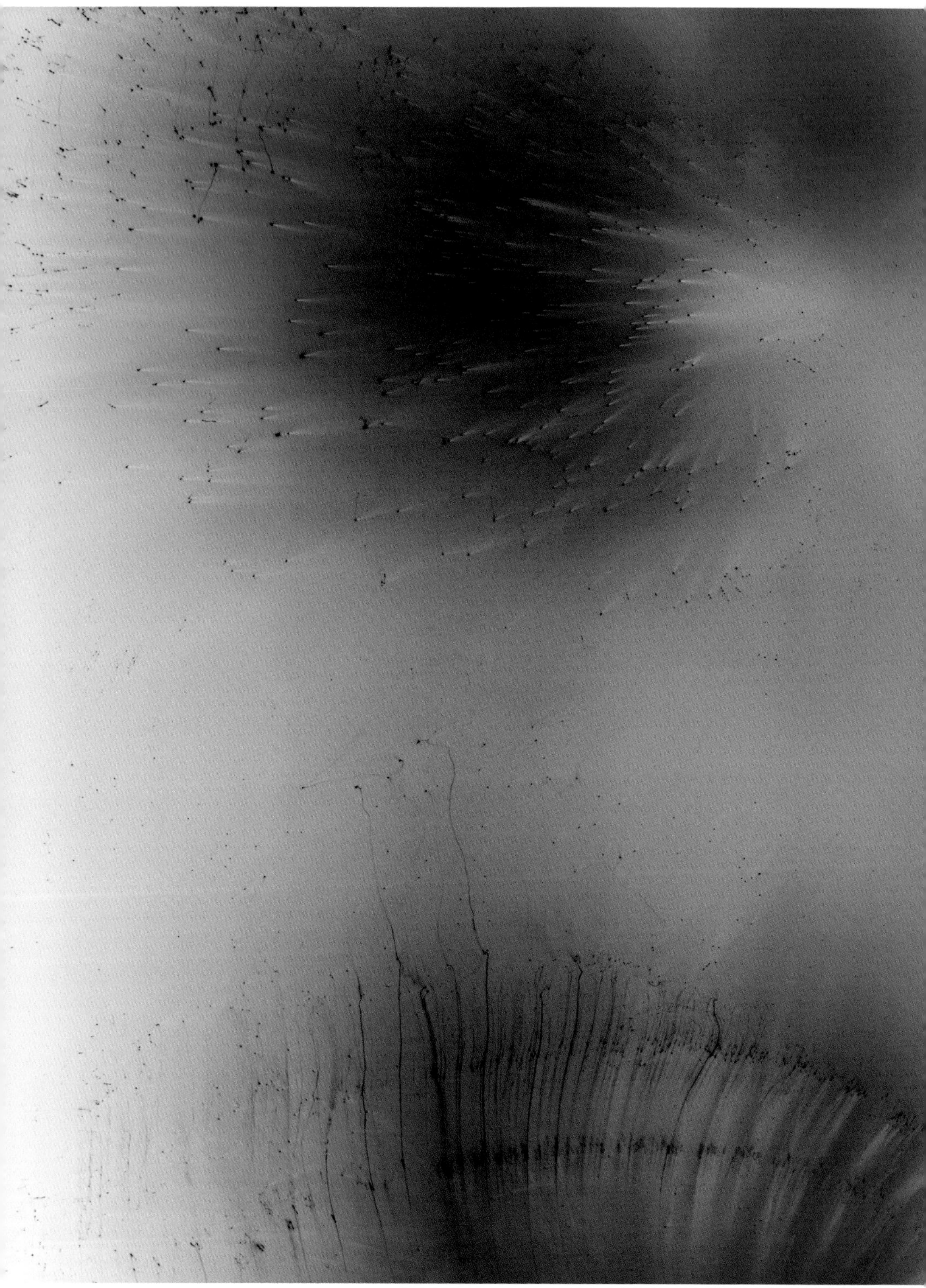

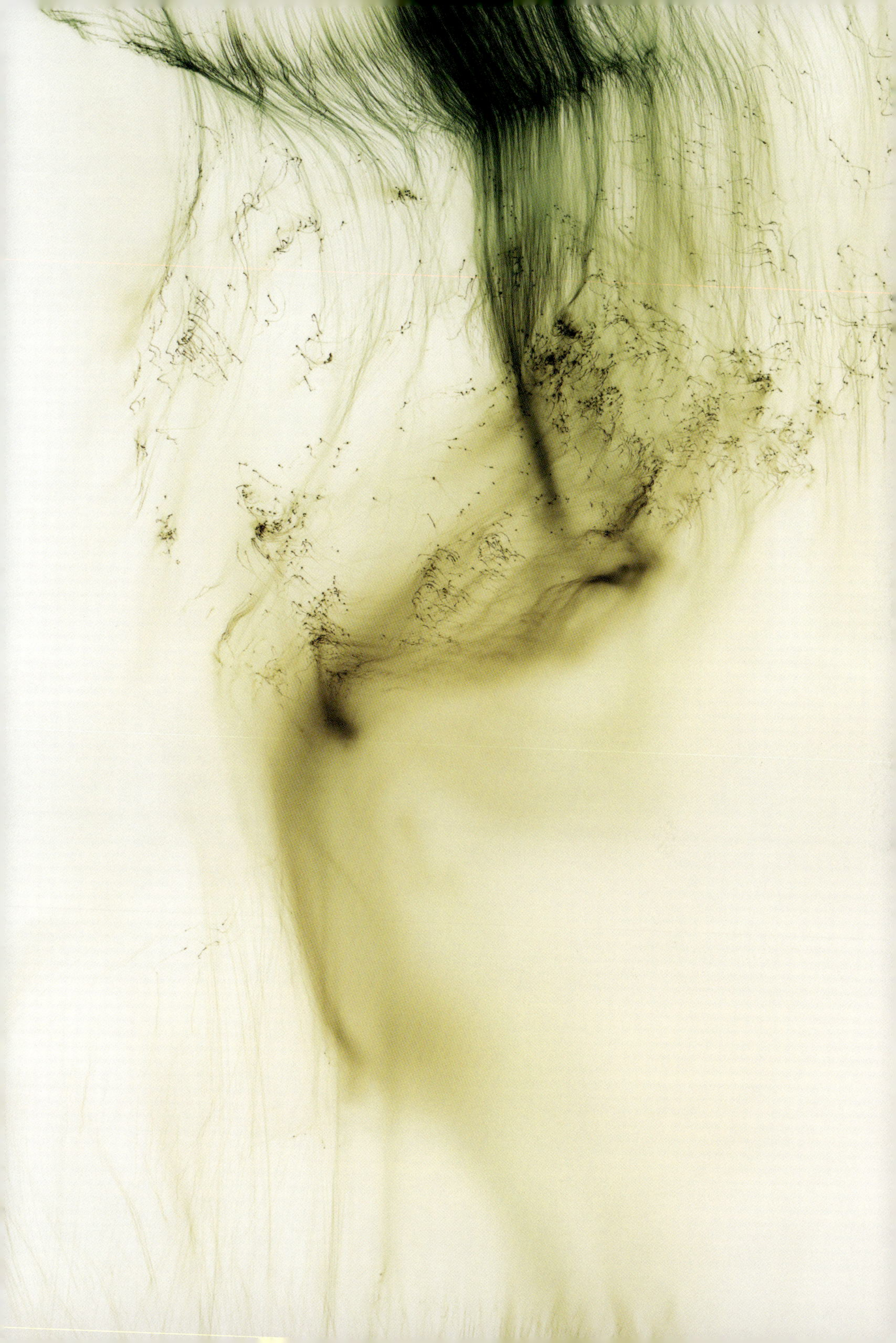

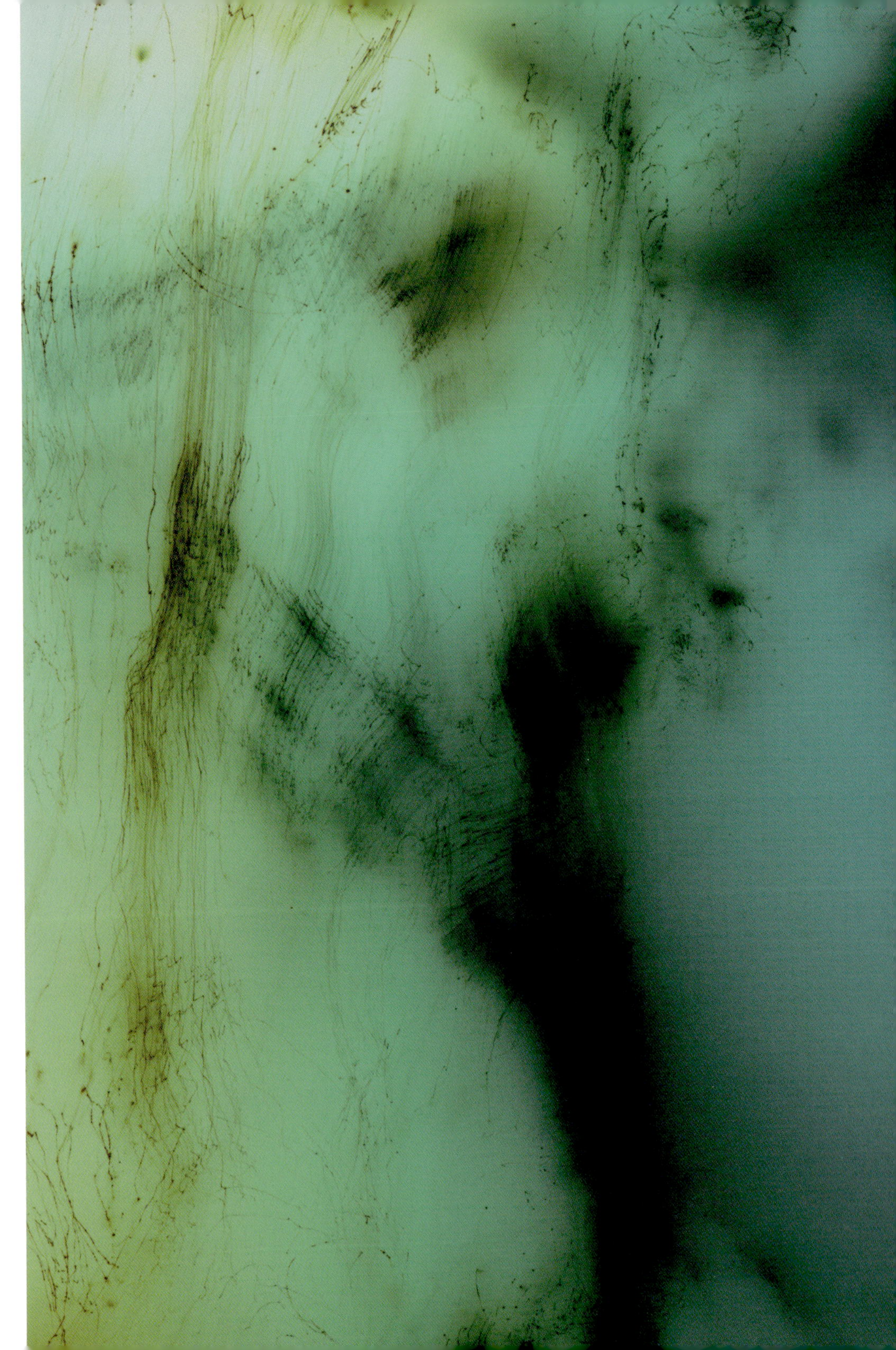

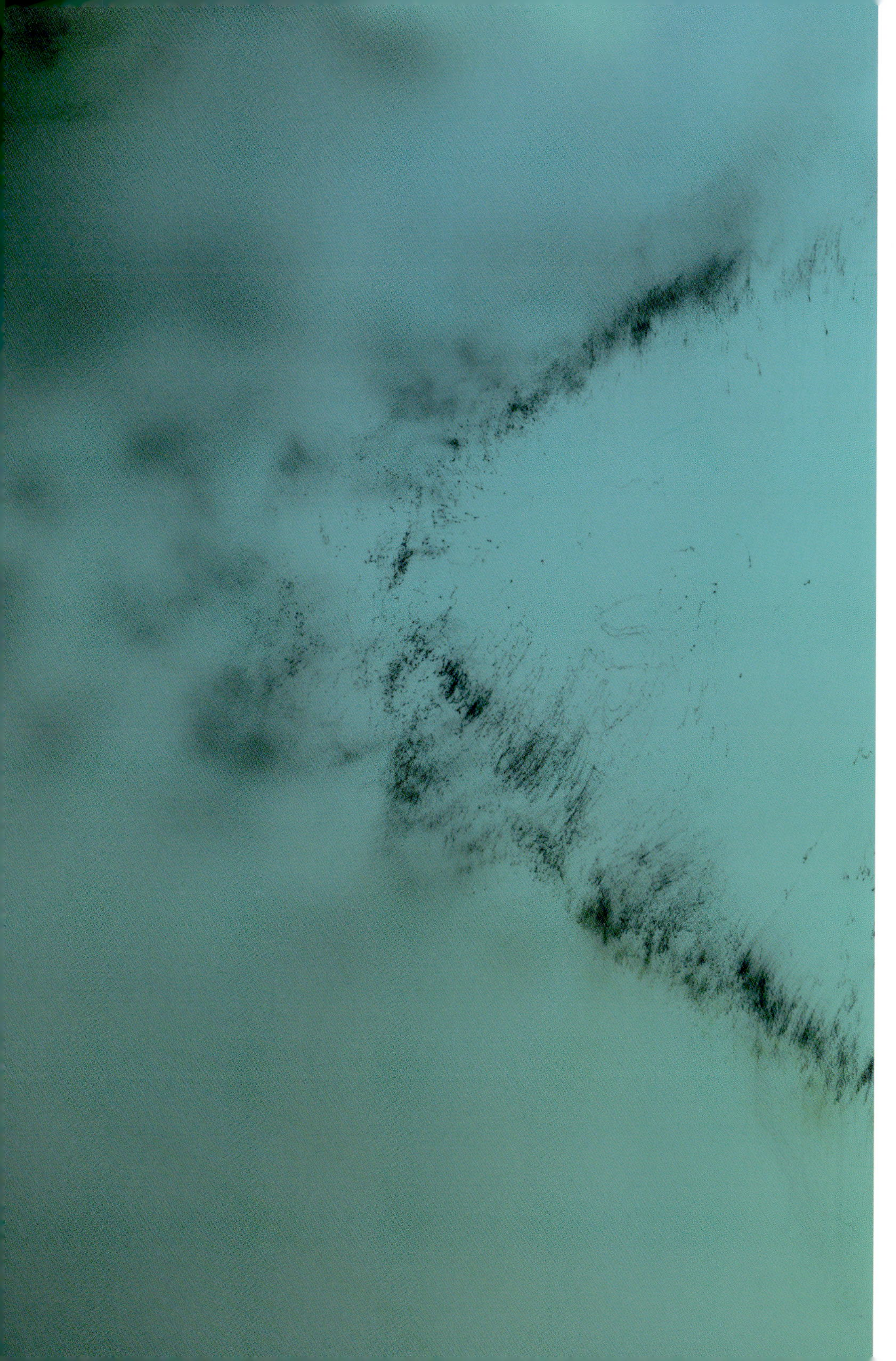

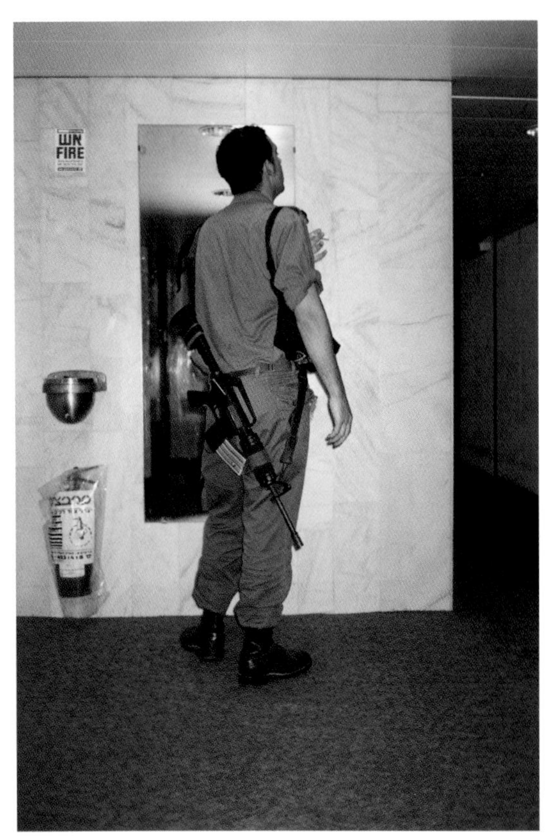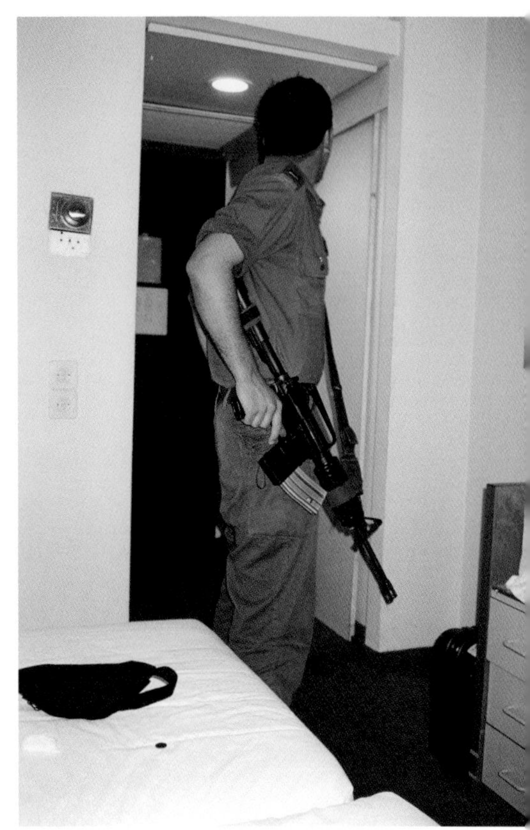

Shay I - IV, 2002

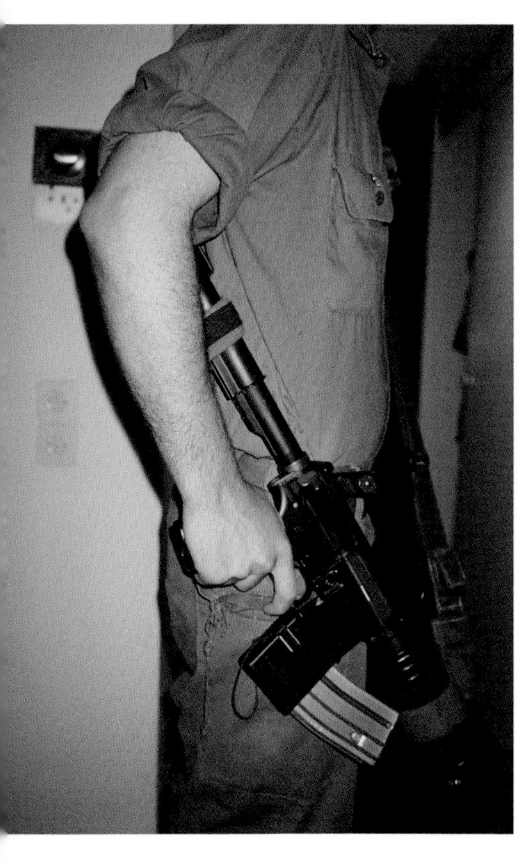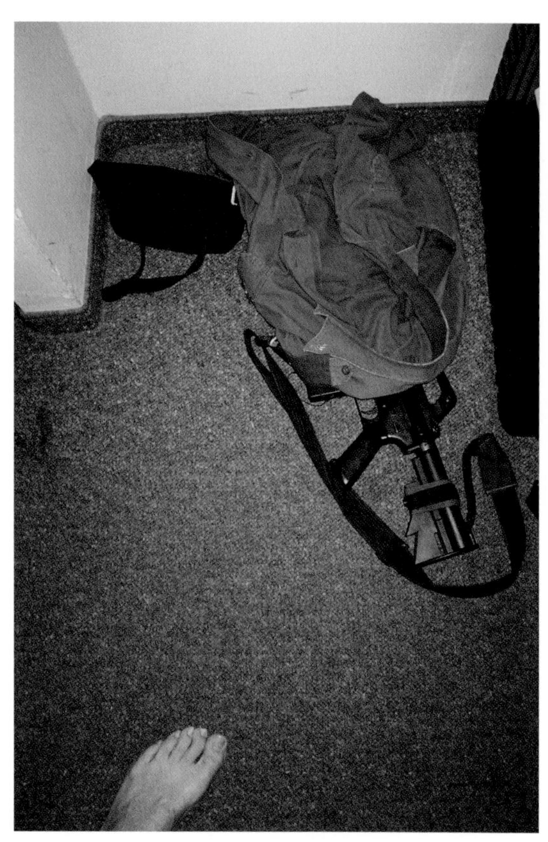

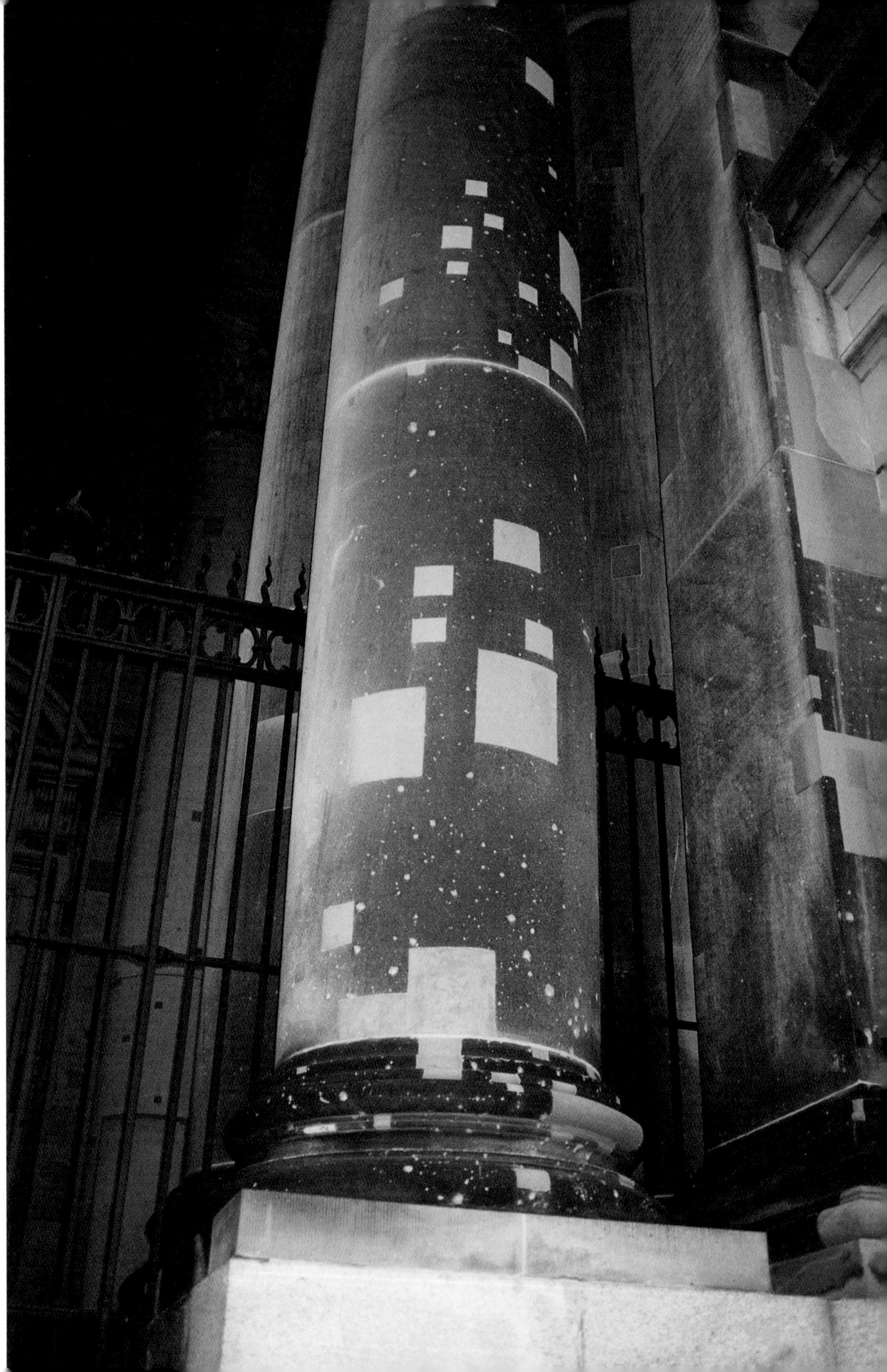

pixel bullet holes I (b/w), 2002   pyramids, 2005

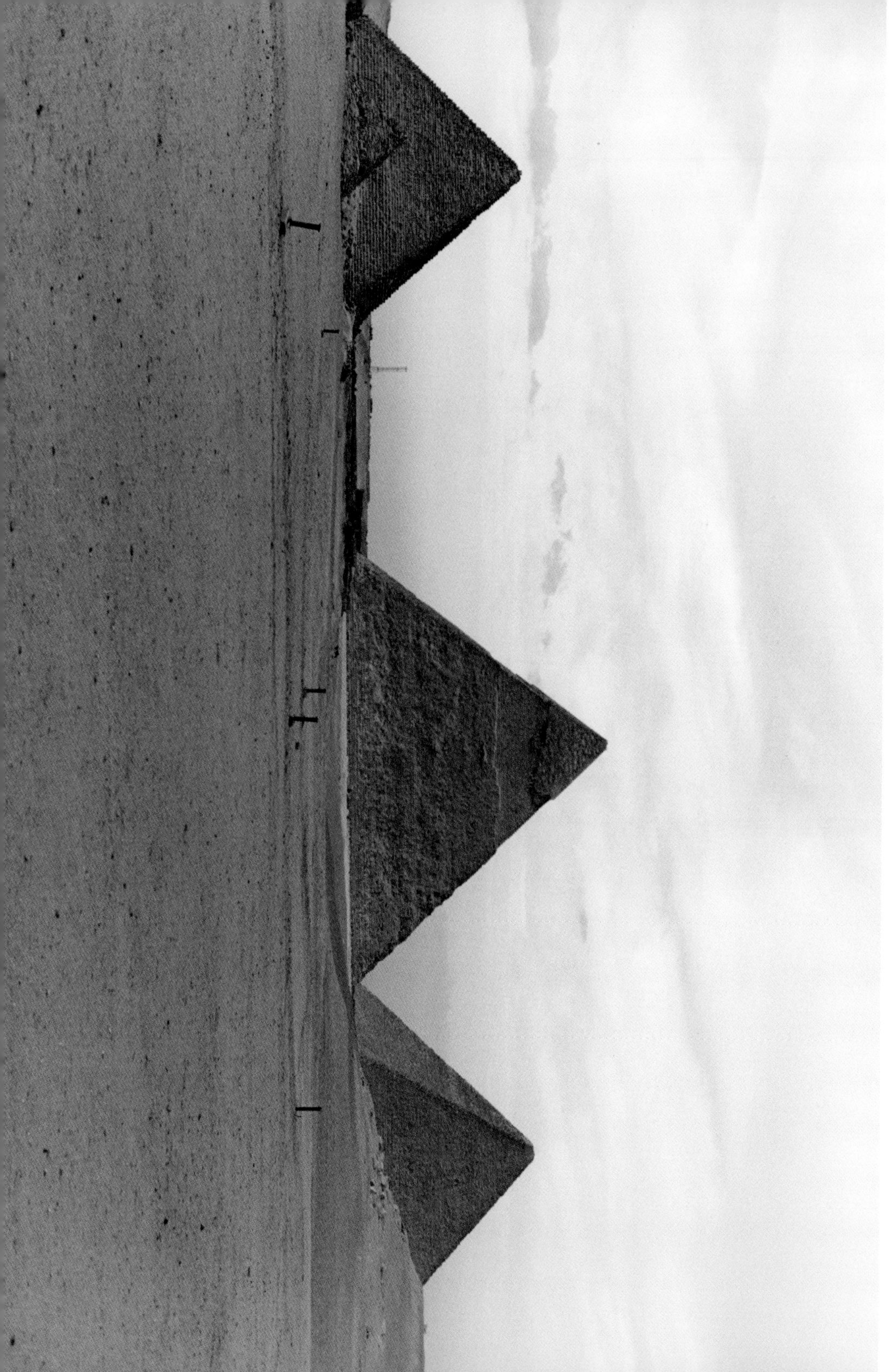

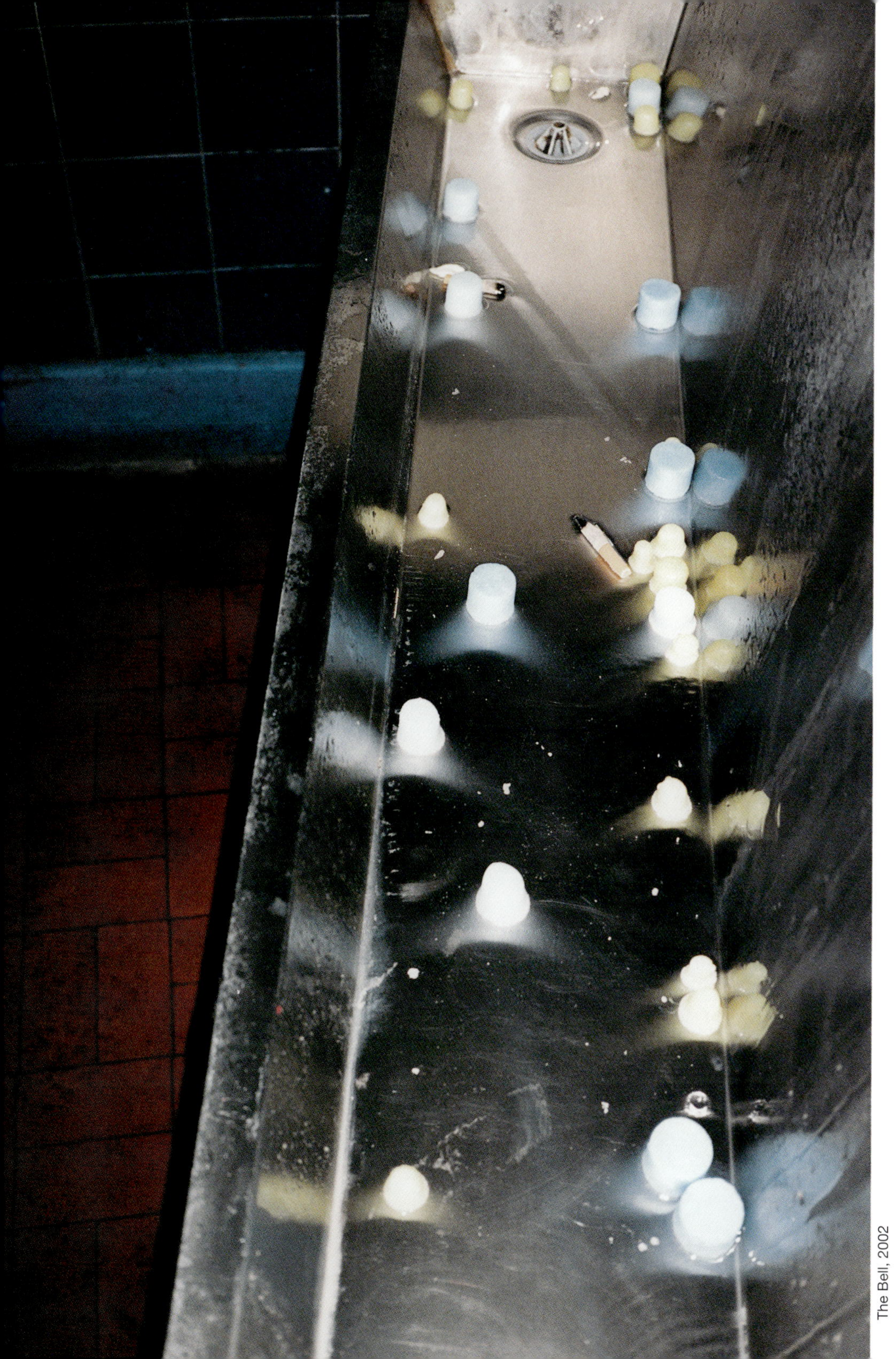

The Bell, 2002

anti-homless device, 2000   device control, 2005

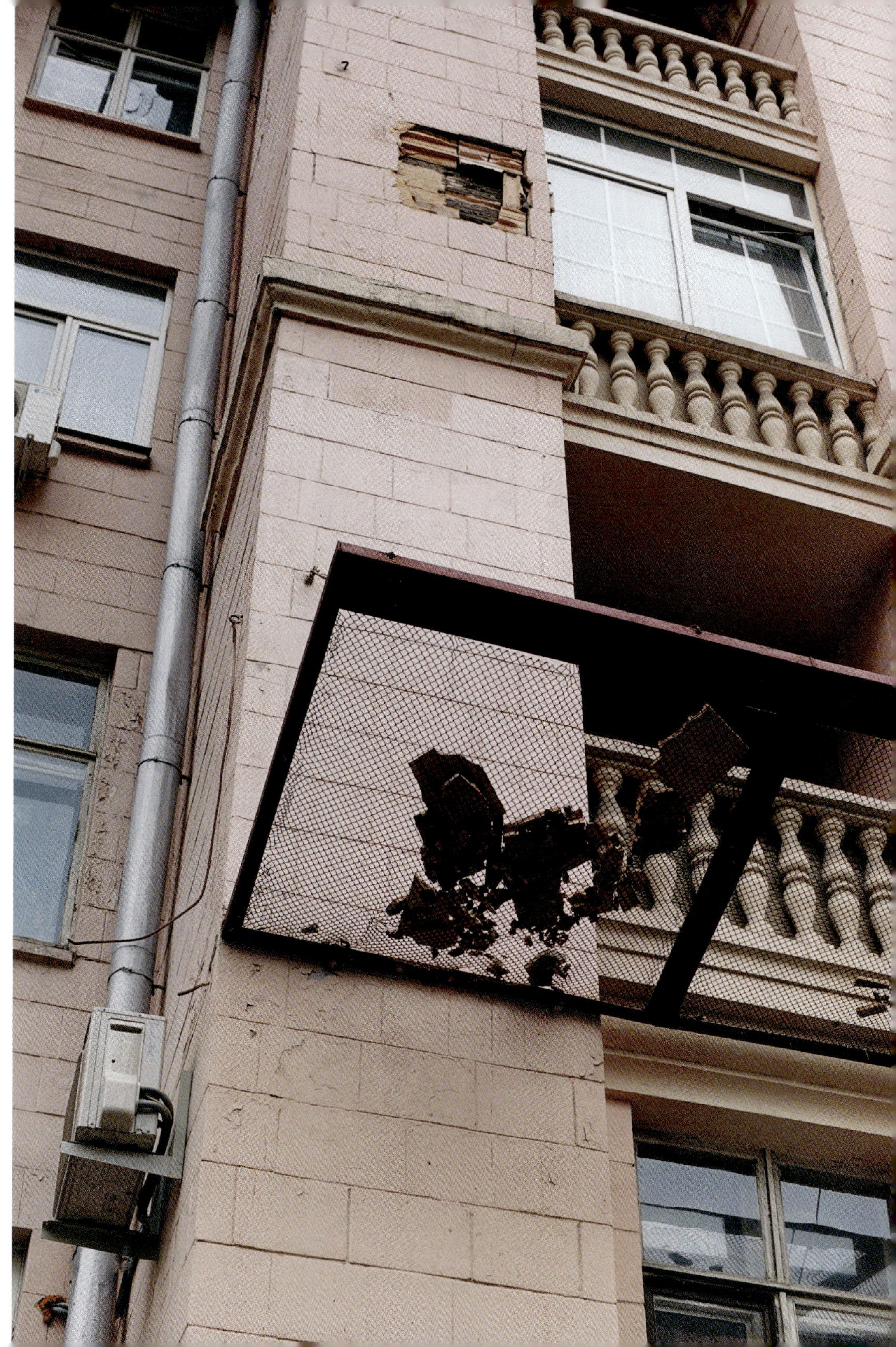

tree filling window, 2002   Sahara, horizontal center line thirty kilometers, a, 2018

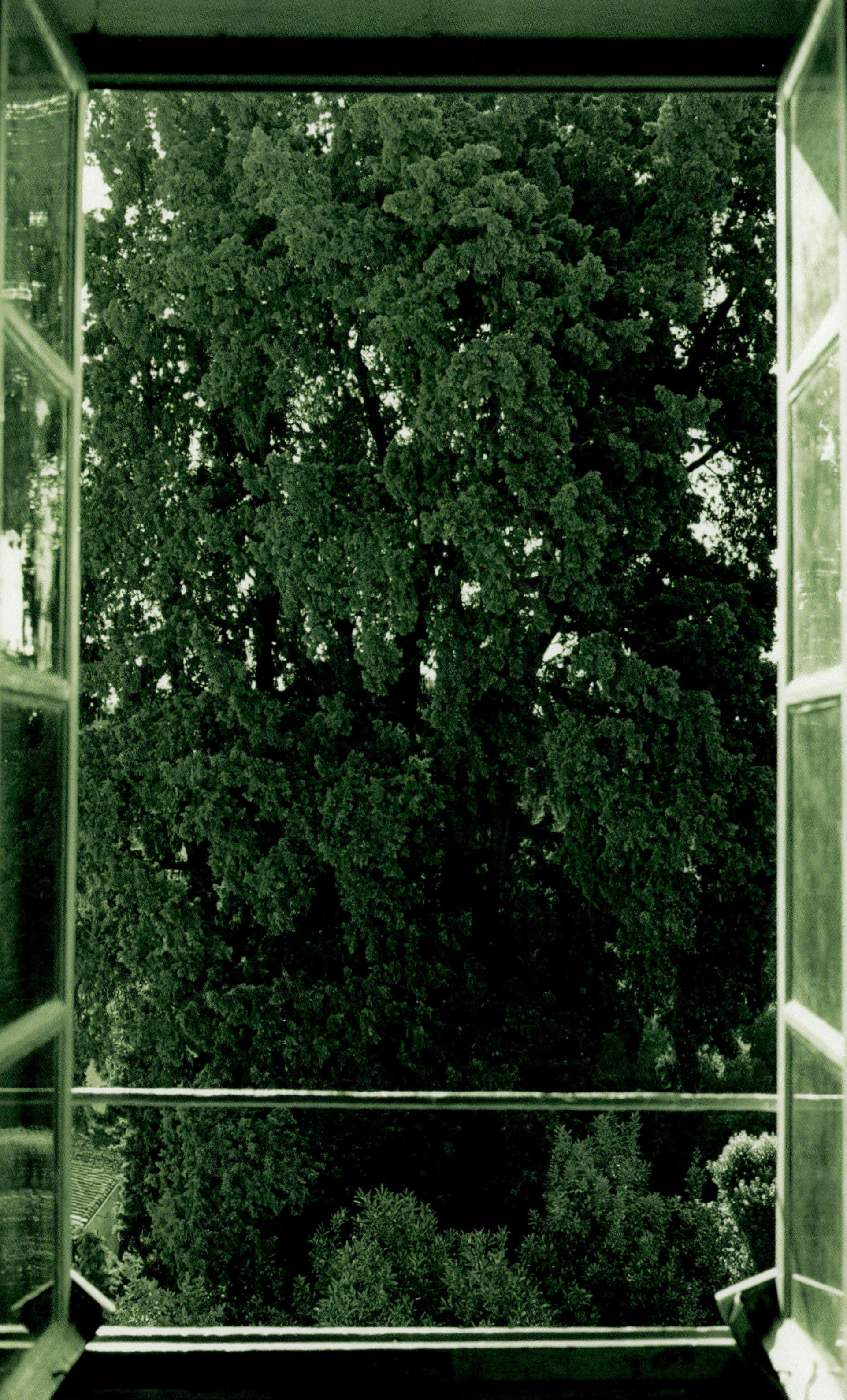

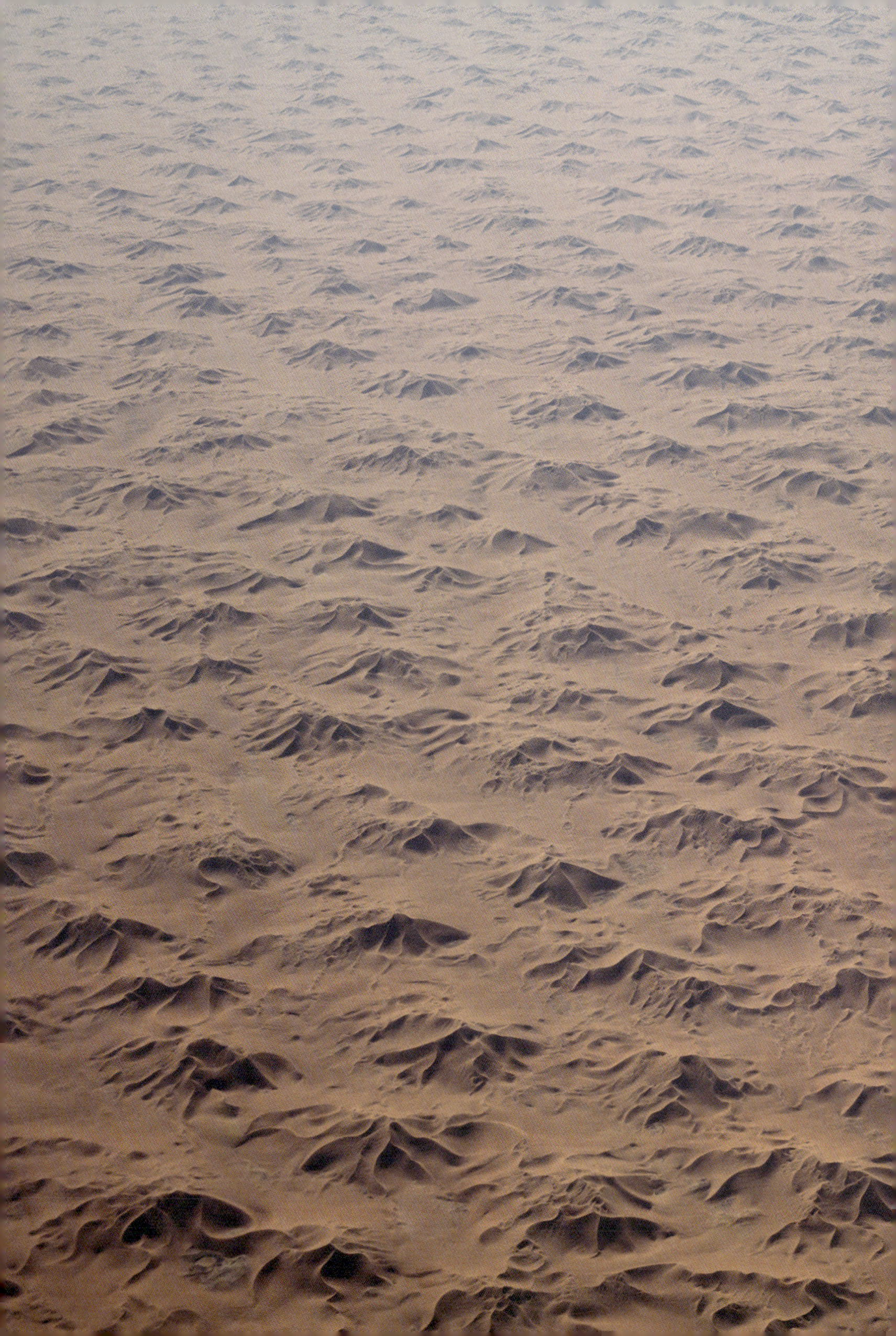

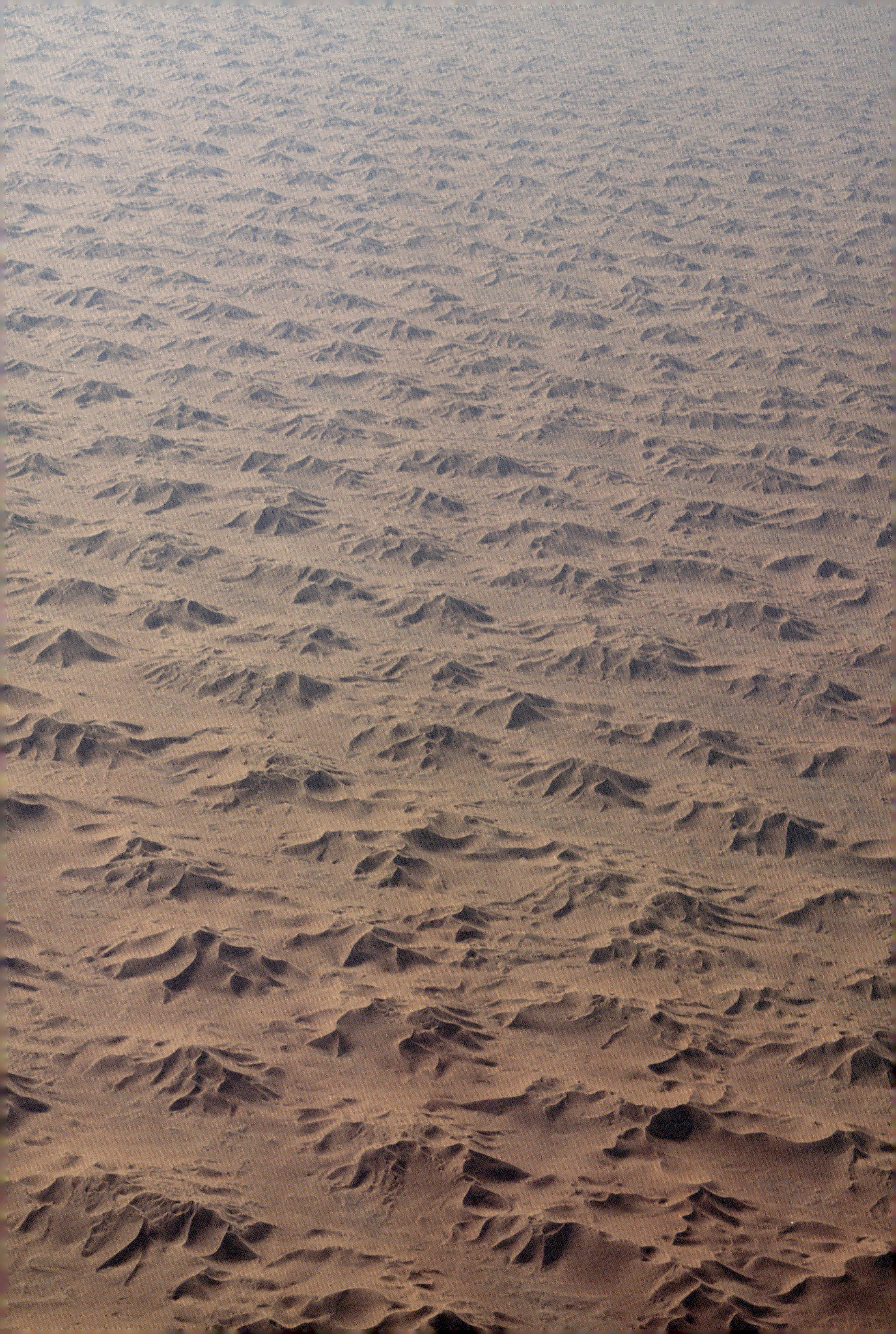

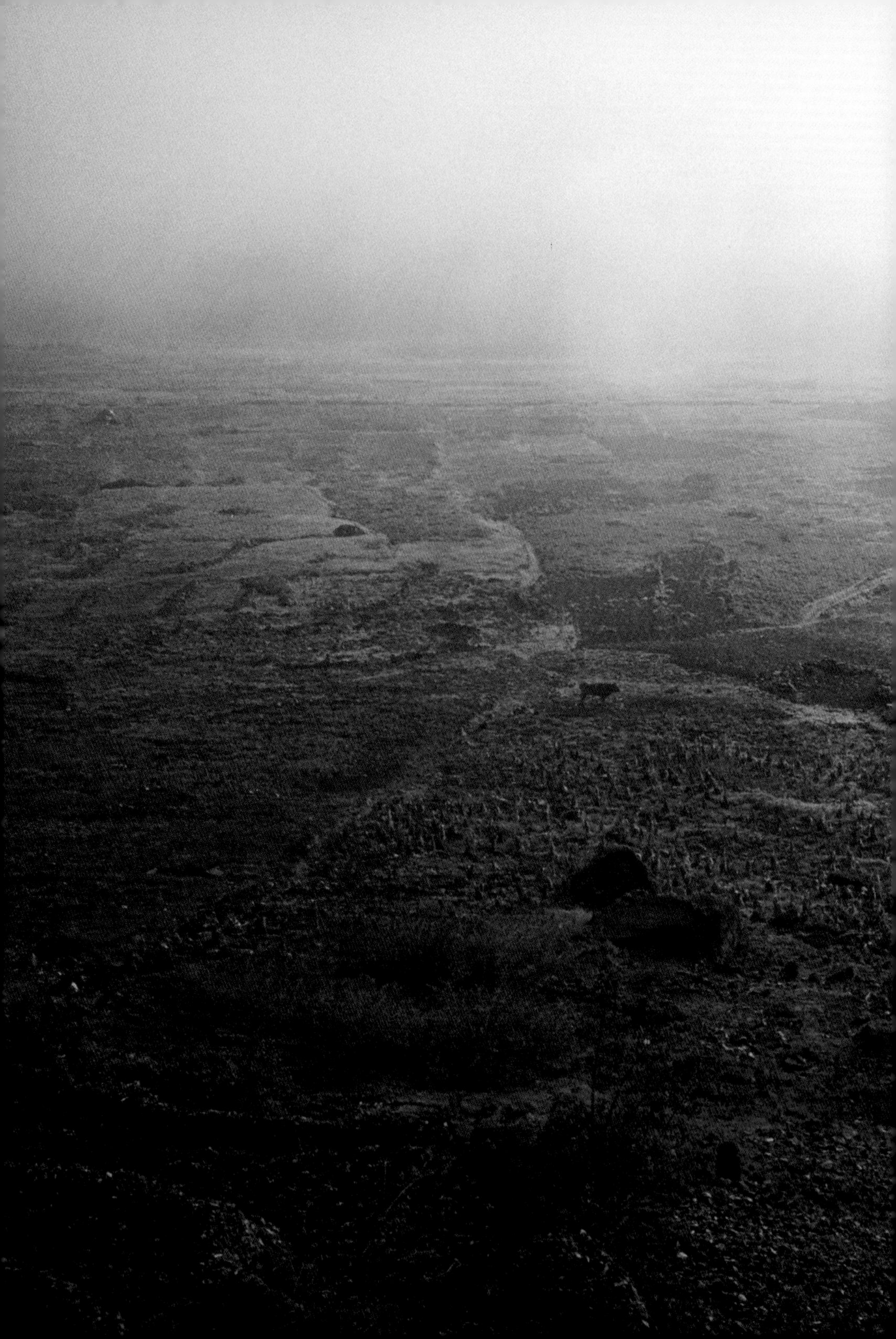

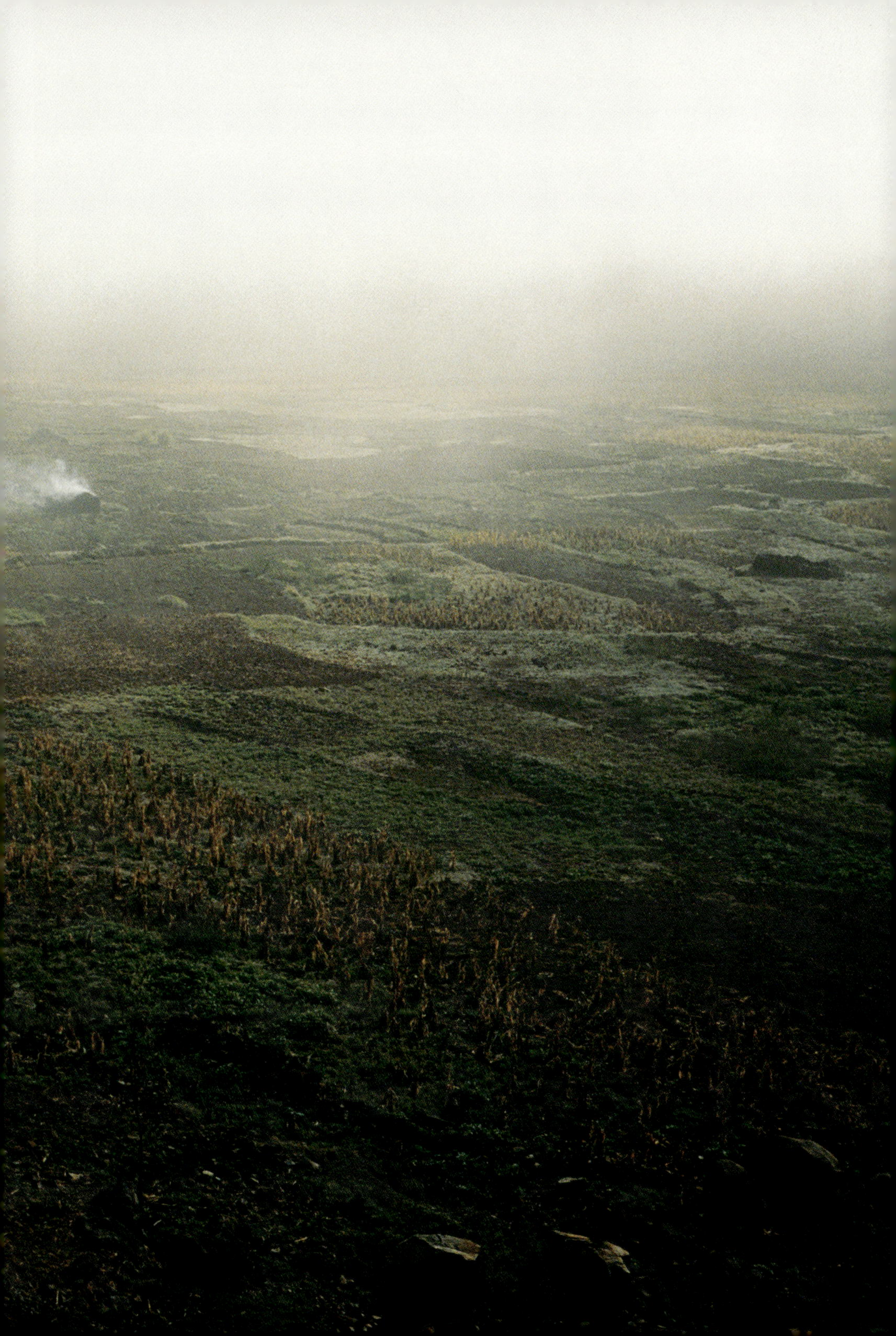

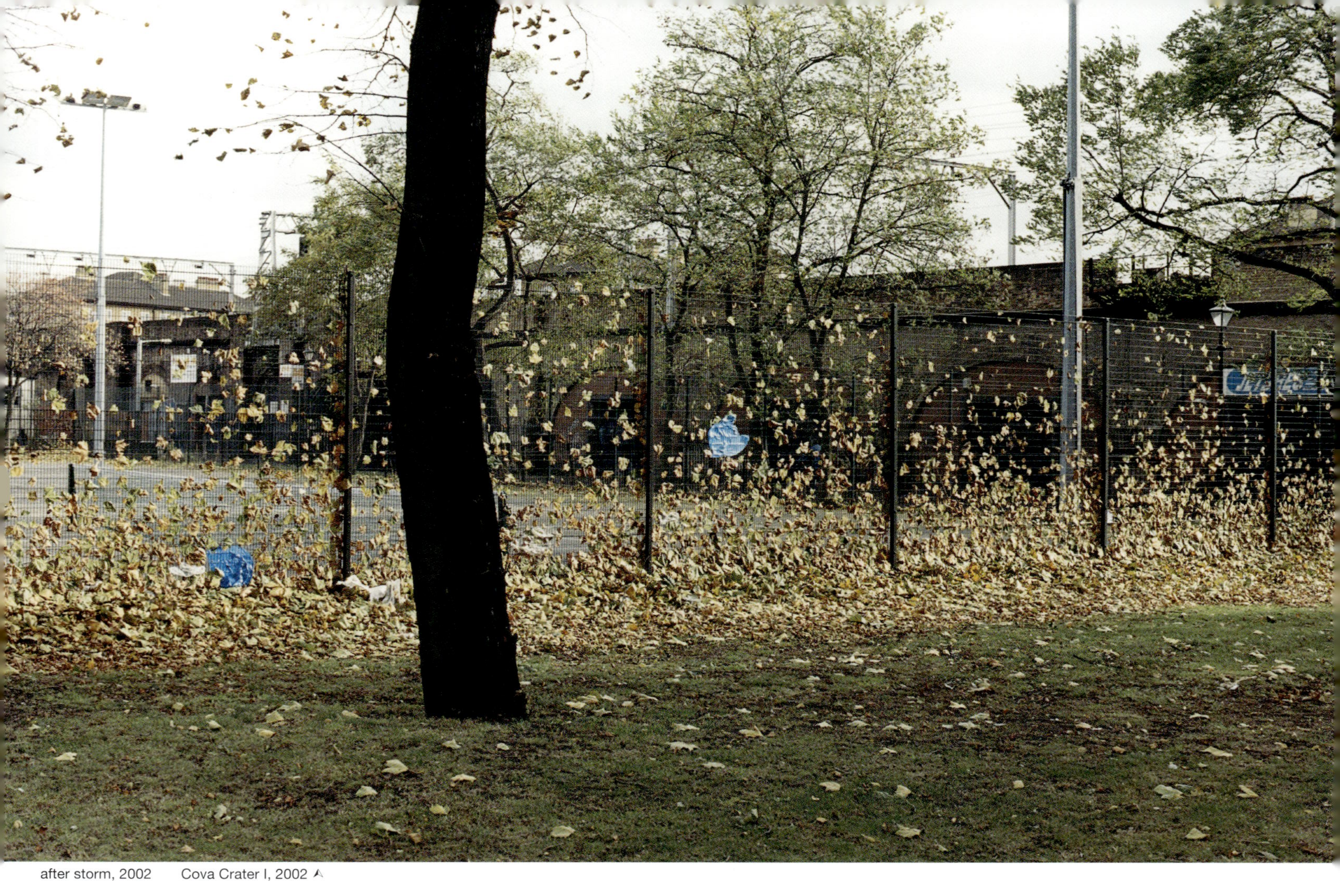

after storm, 2002   Cova Crater I, 2002 ⌐

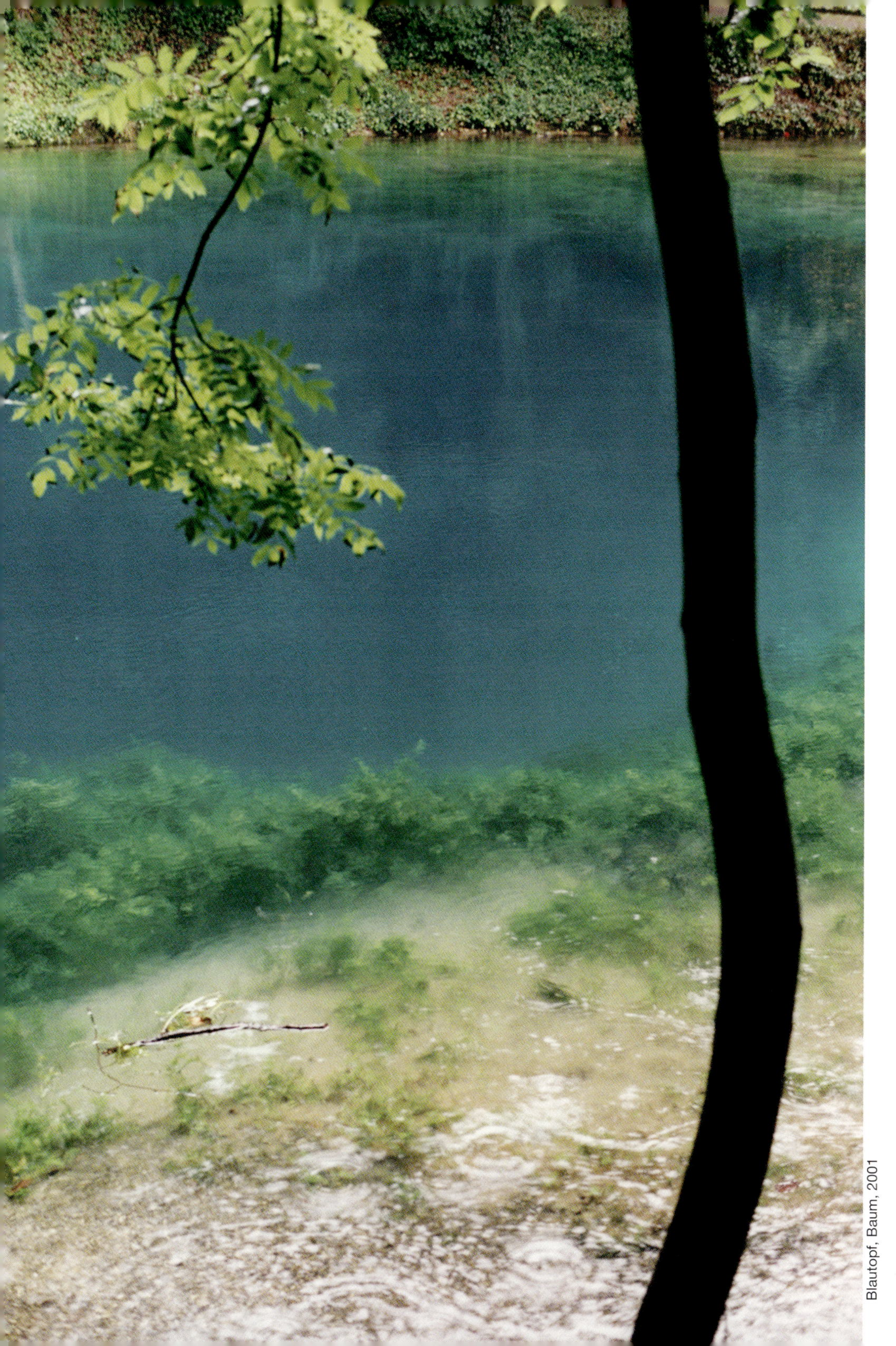

Blautopf, Baum, 2001

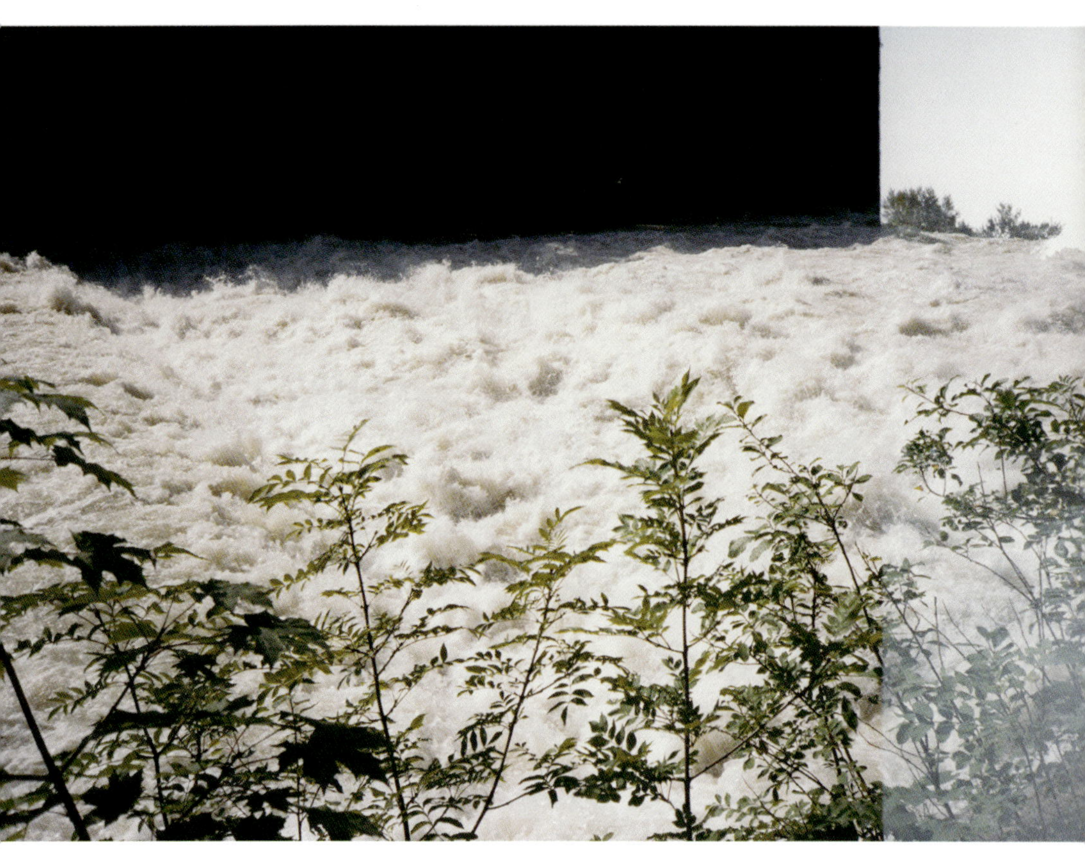

Fluten, 1997

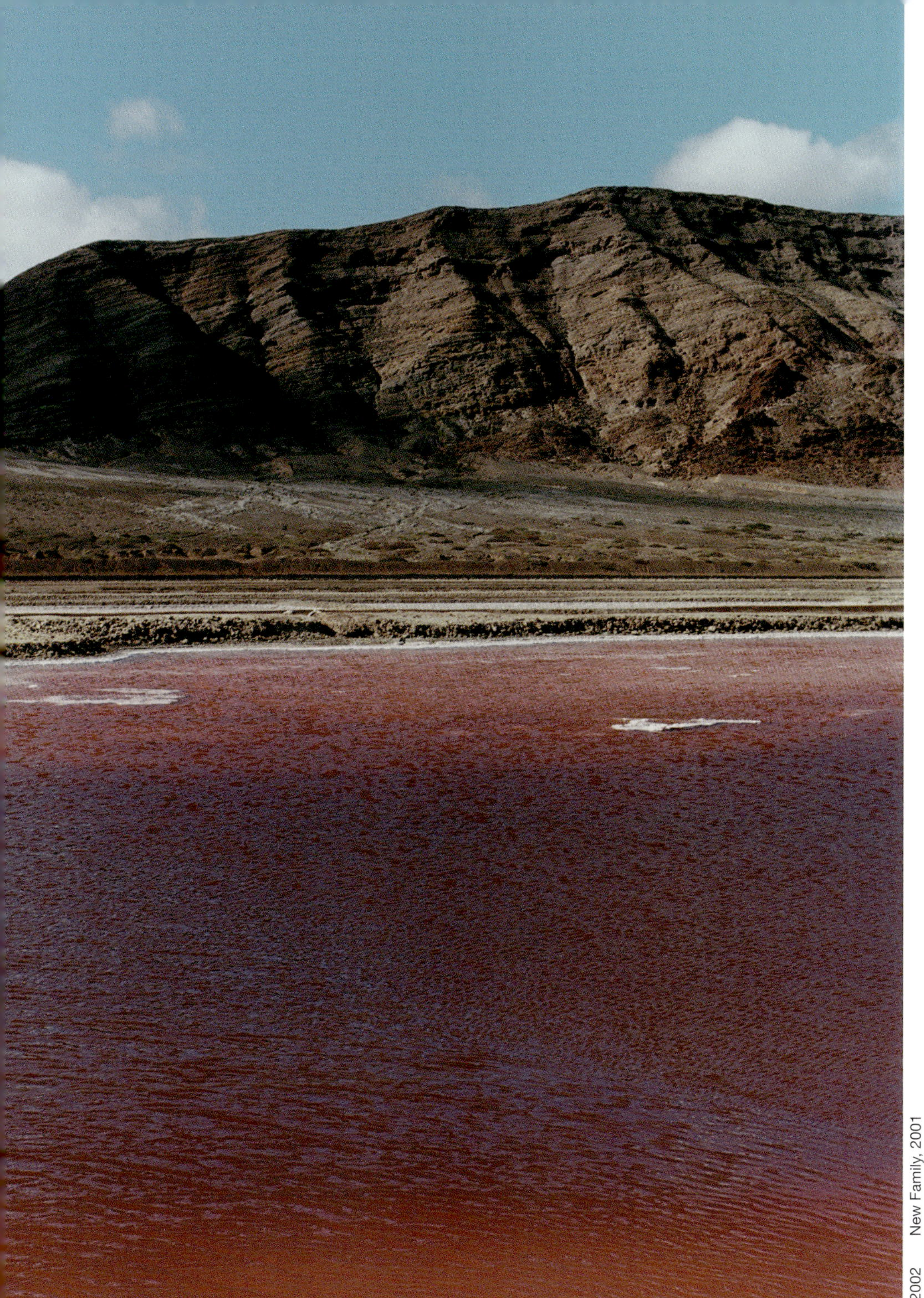

red lake, 2002   New Family, 2001

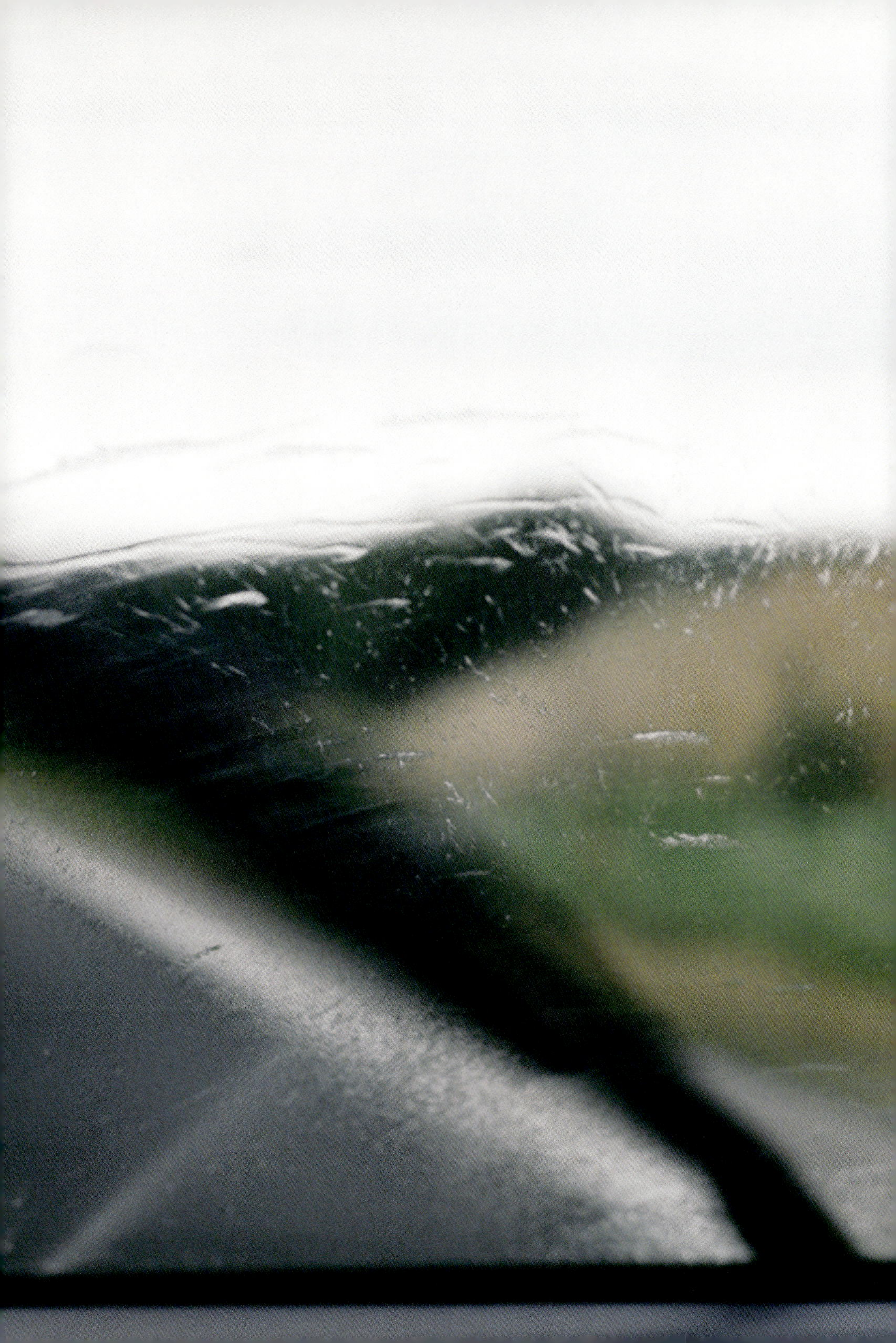

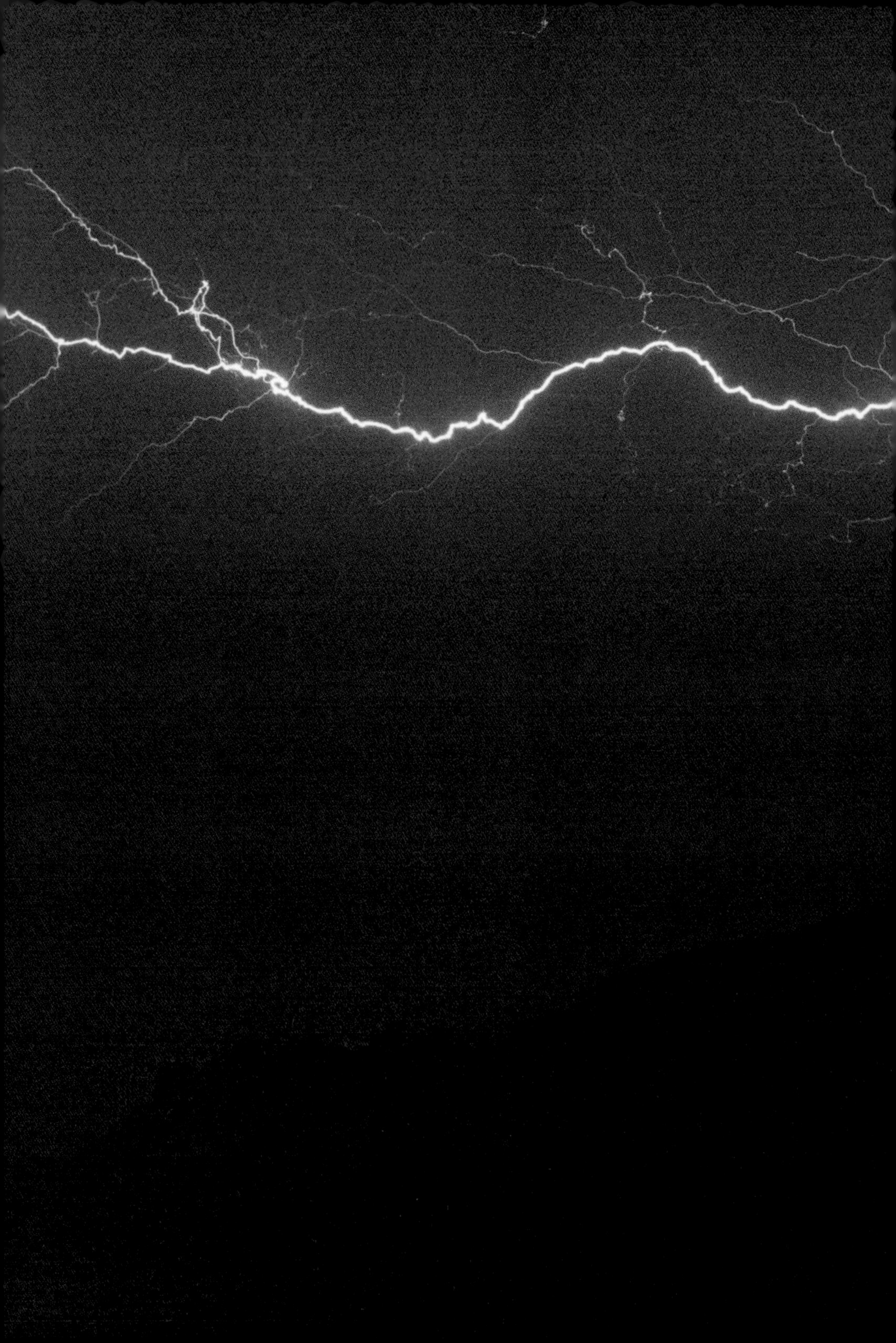

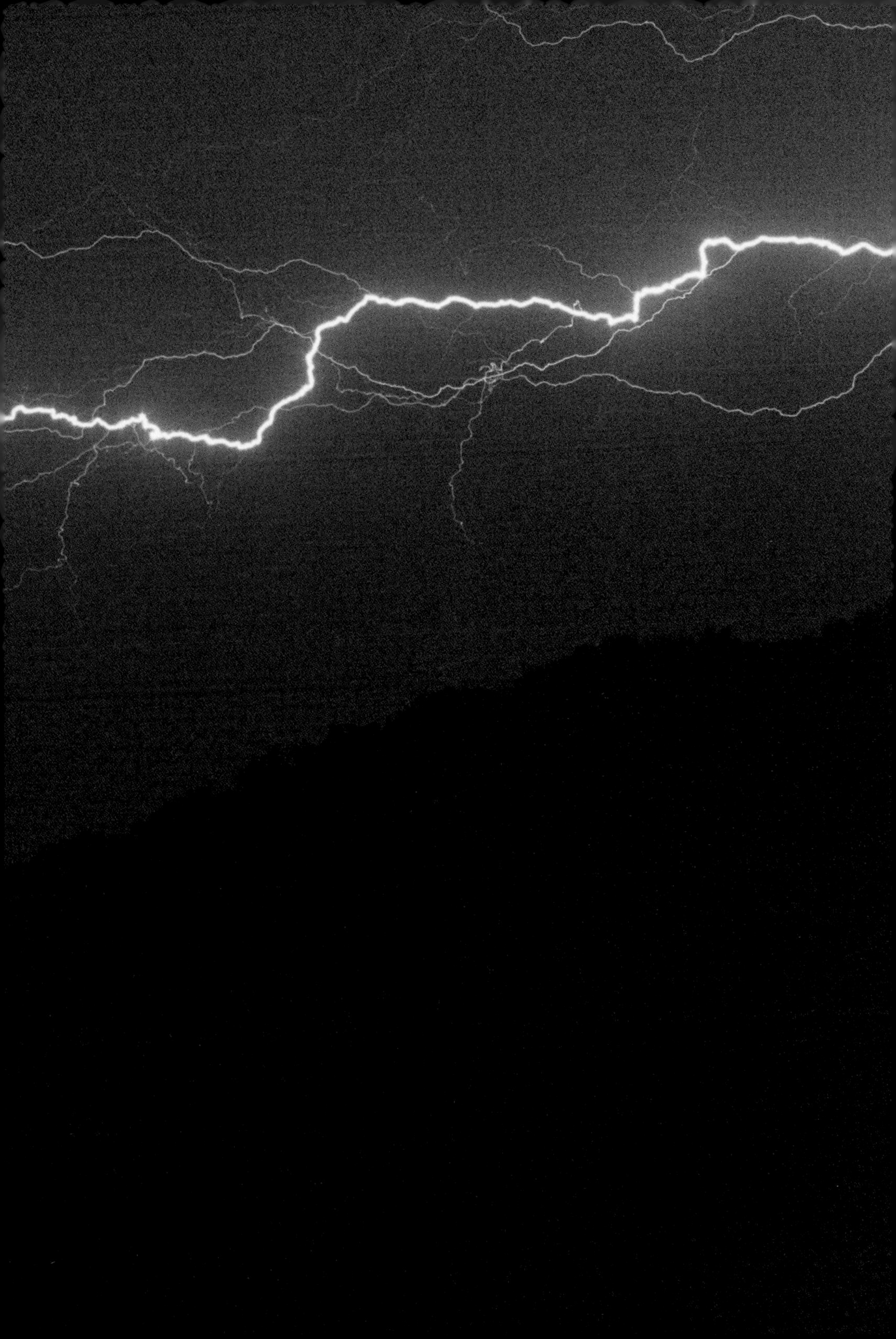

Lightning I, 2002
Venus transit, edge, 2004

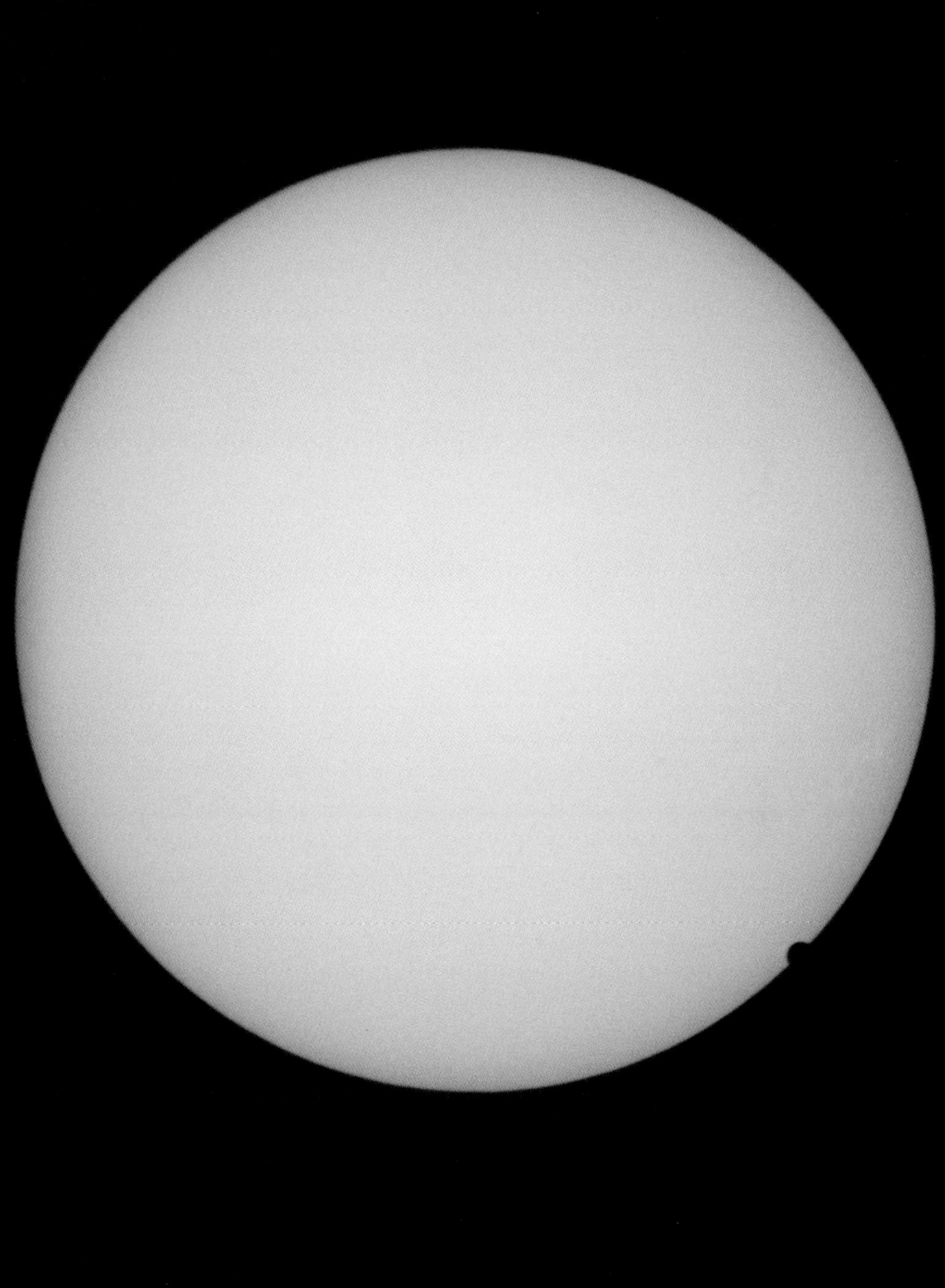

Venus transit, 2004
Venus transit, clouds, 2004
Venus, drop, 2004

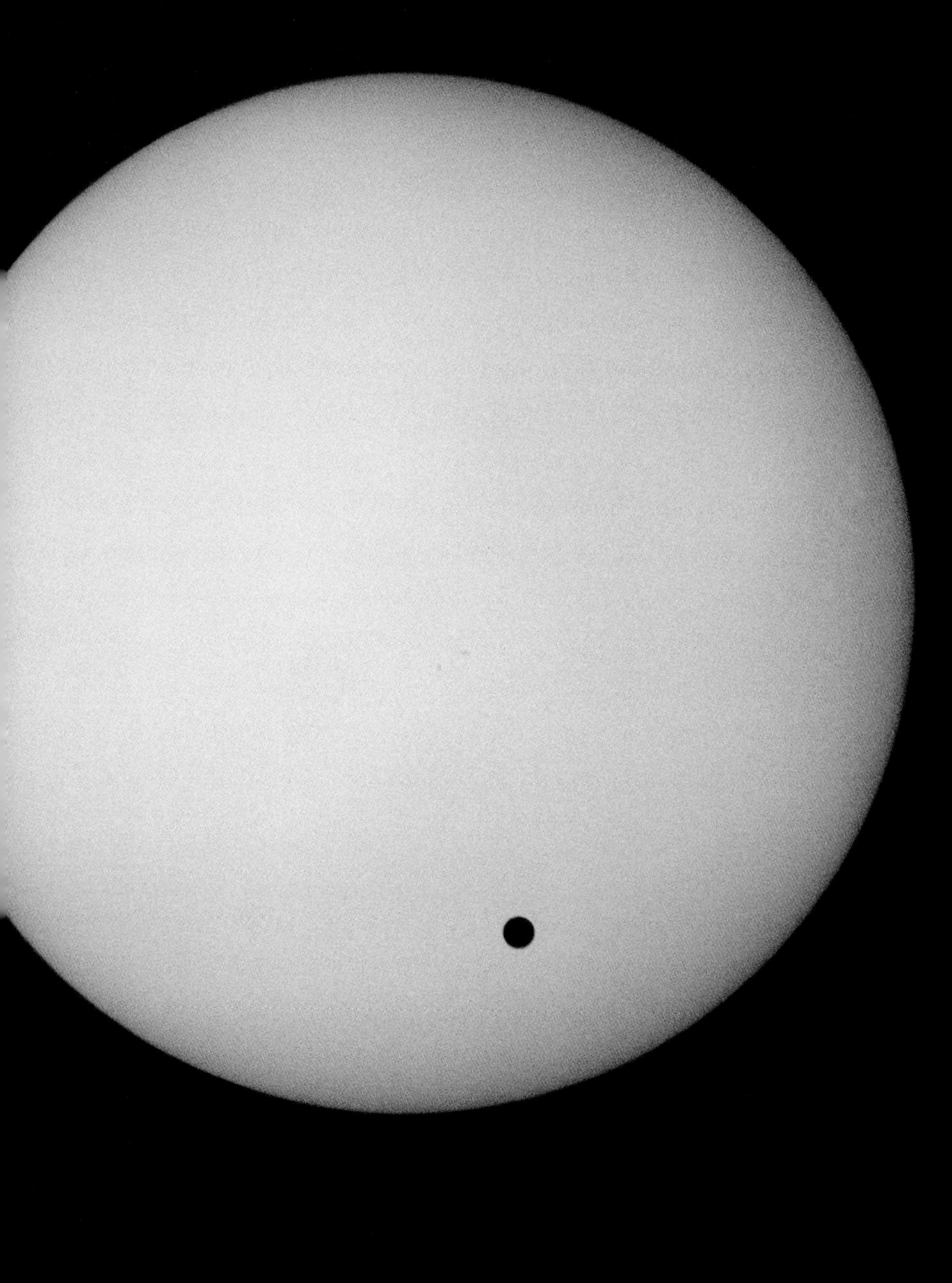

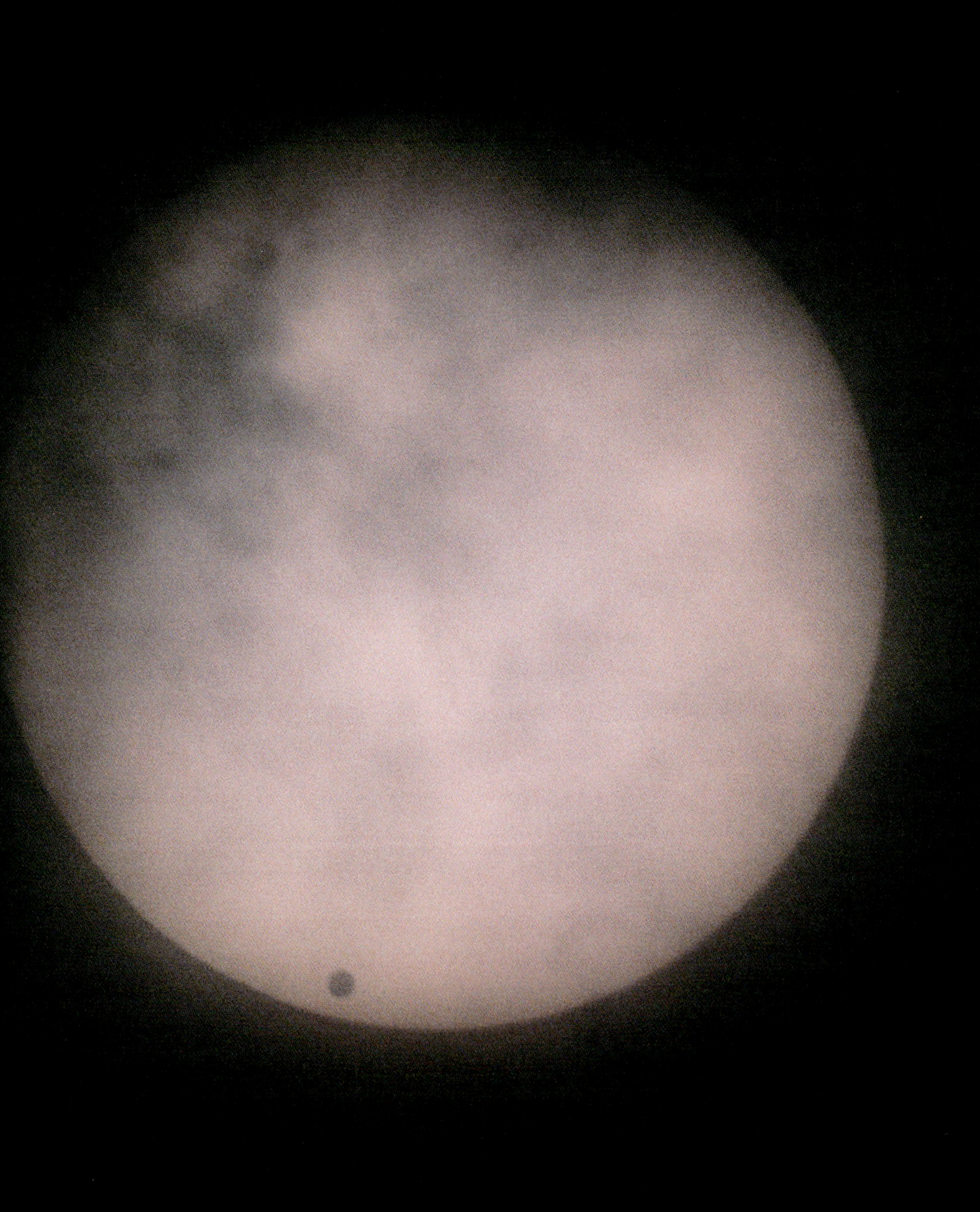

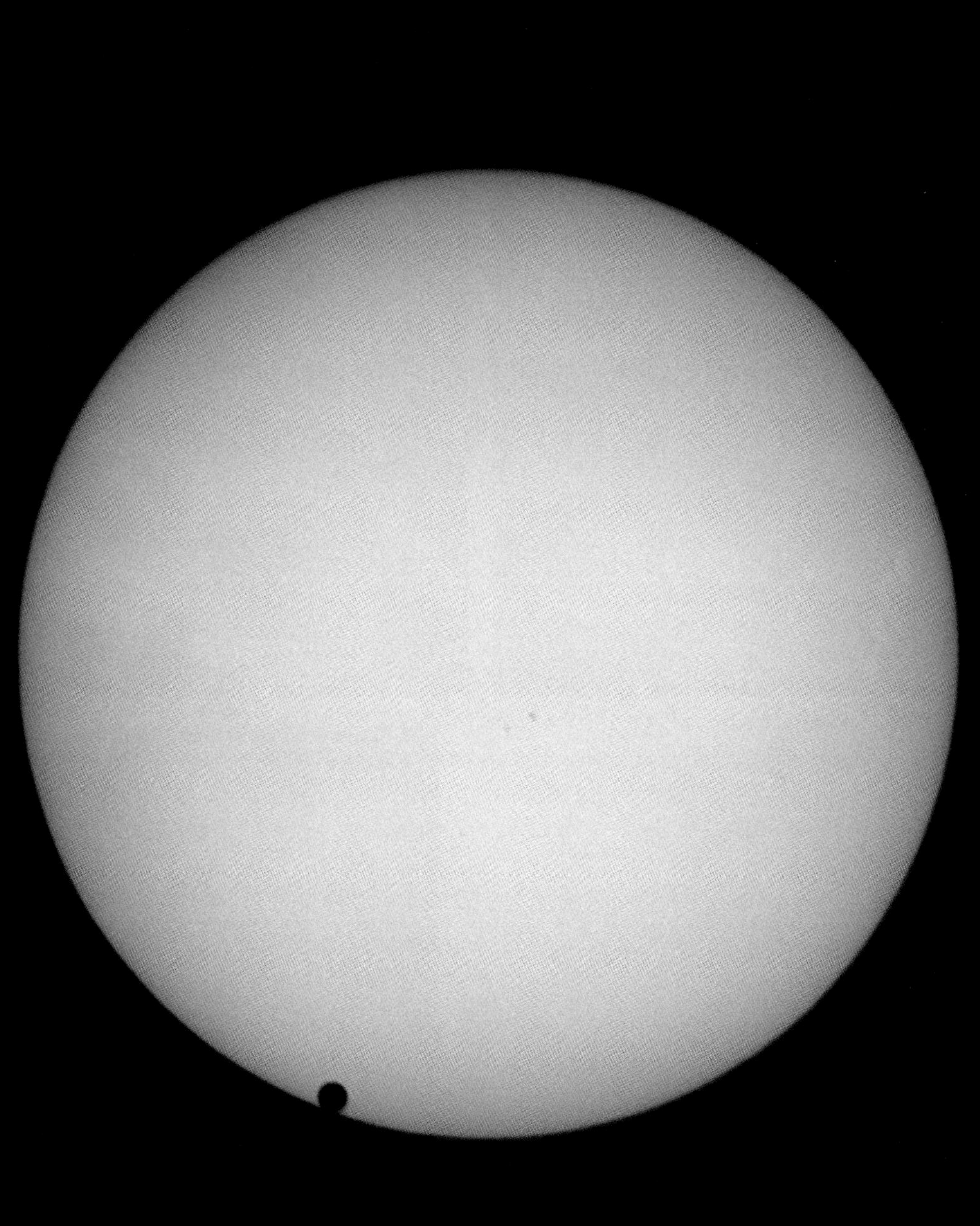

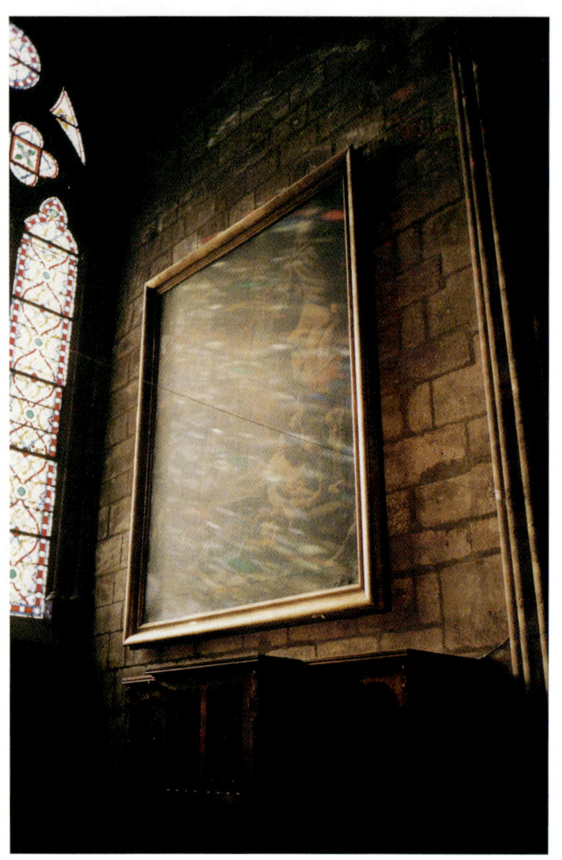
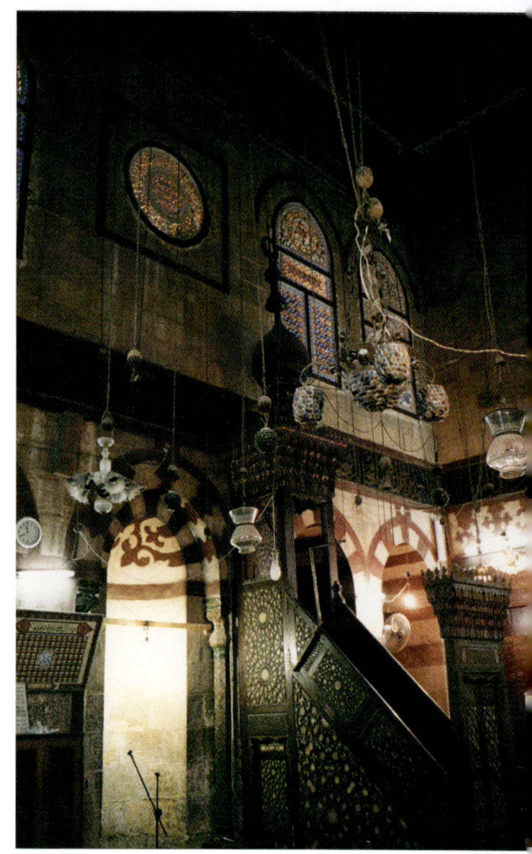
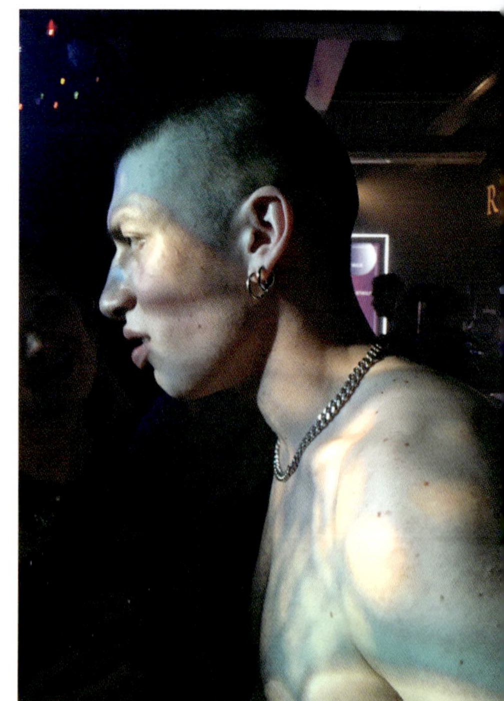

Dans nos obscurités, 2004   Egypt lights II, 2005
Olly at Adonis, 2019

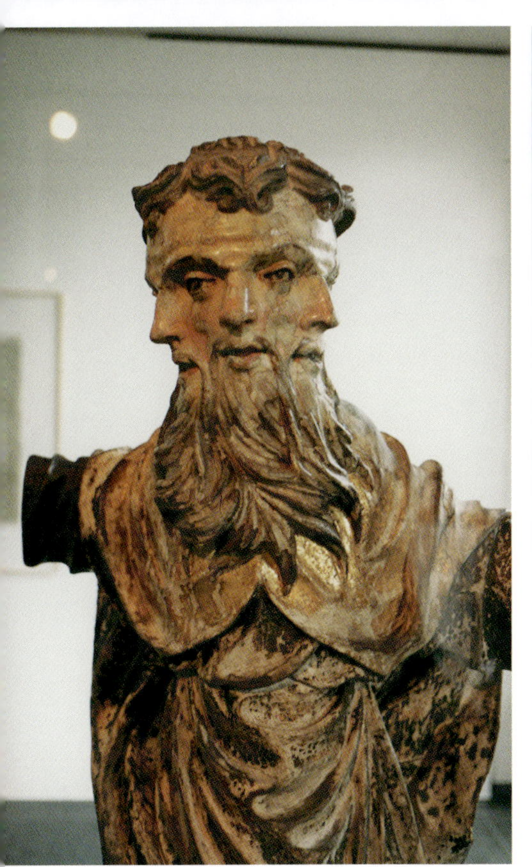

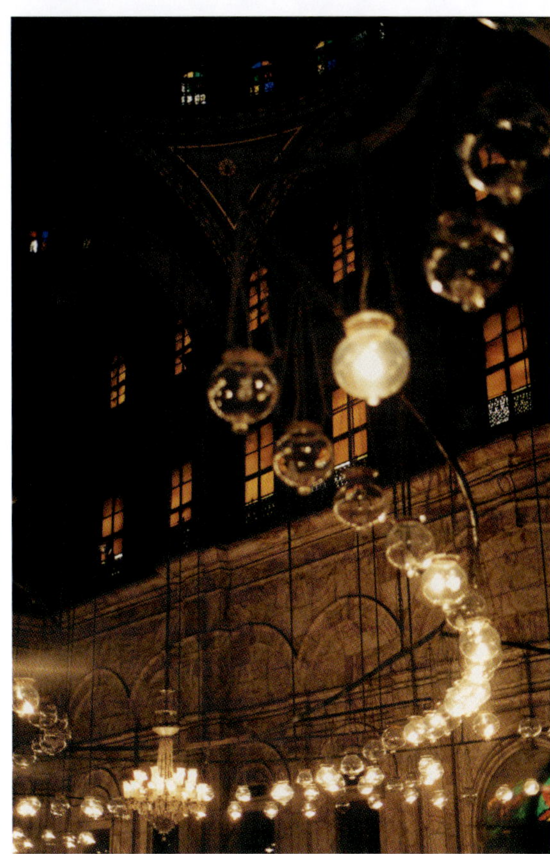

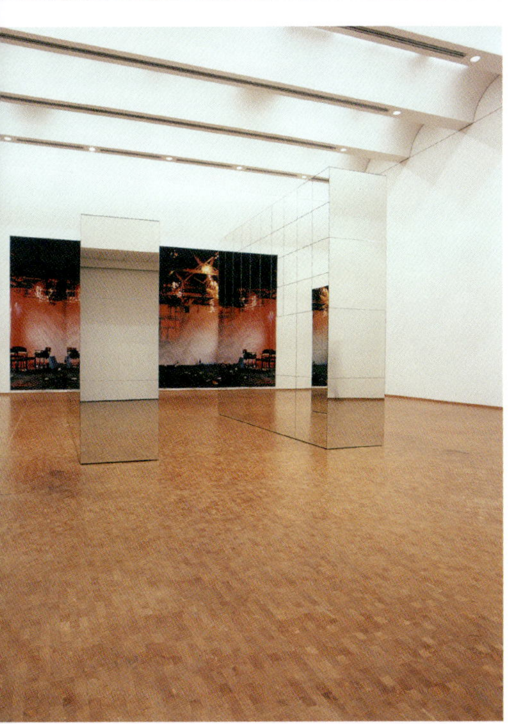

Trinitatis, 2002   Egypt lights I, 2005
Science Fiction / Hier und jetzt zufrieden sein, Museum Ludwig (Cologne), 2001
wake, 2001 ⌄

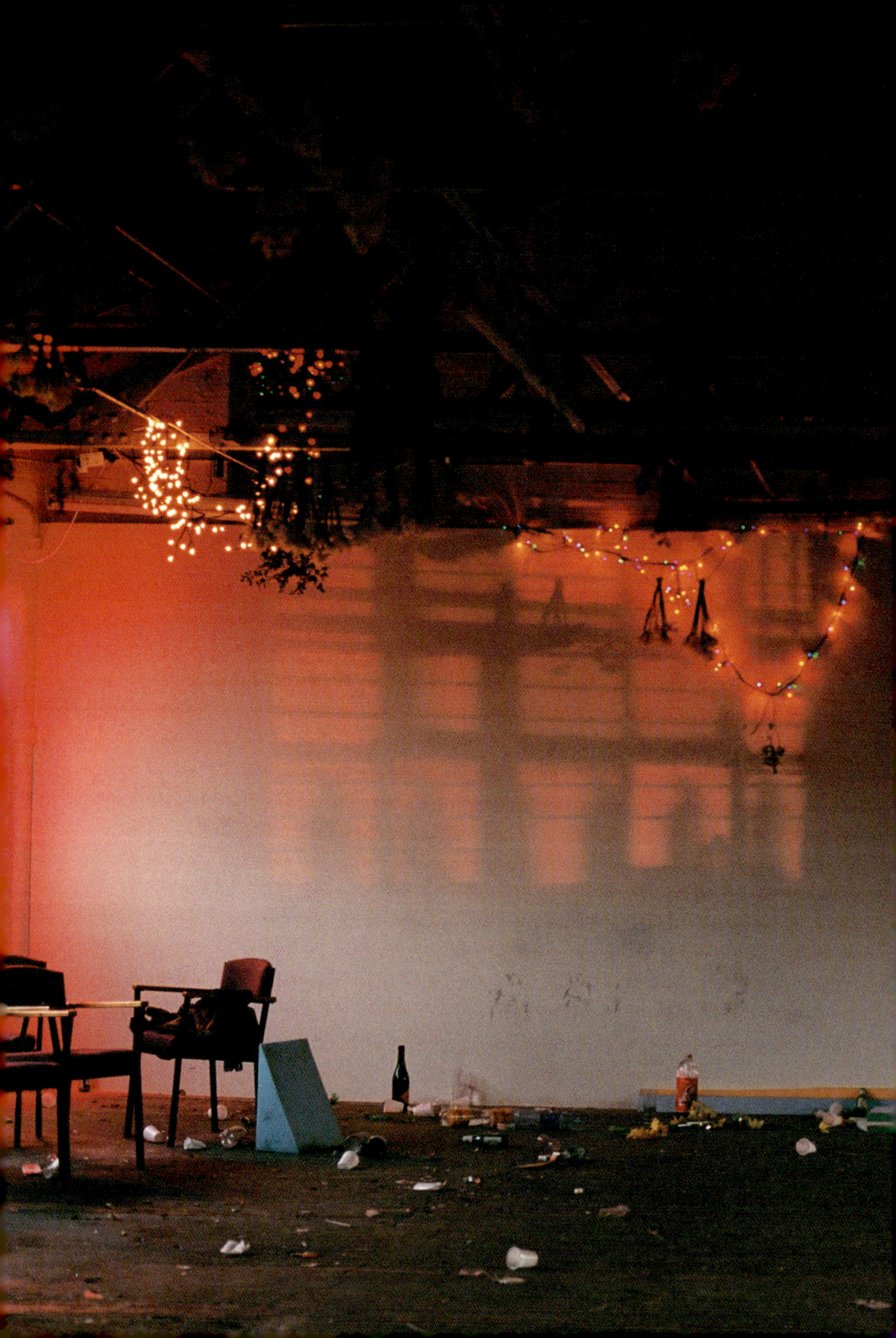

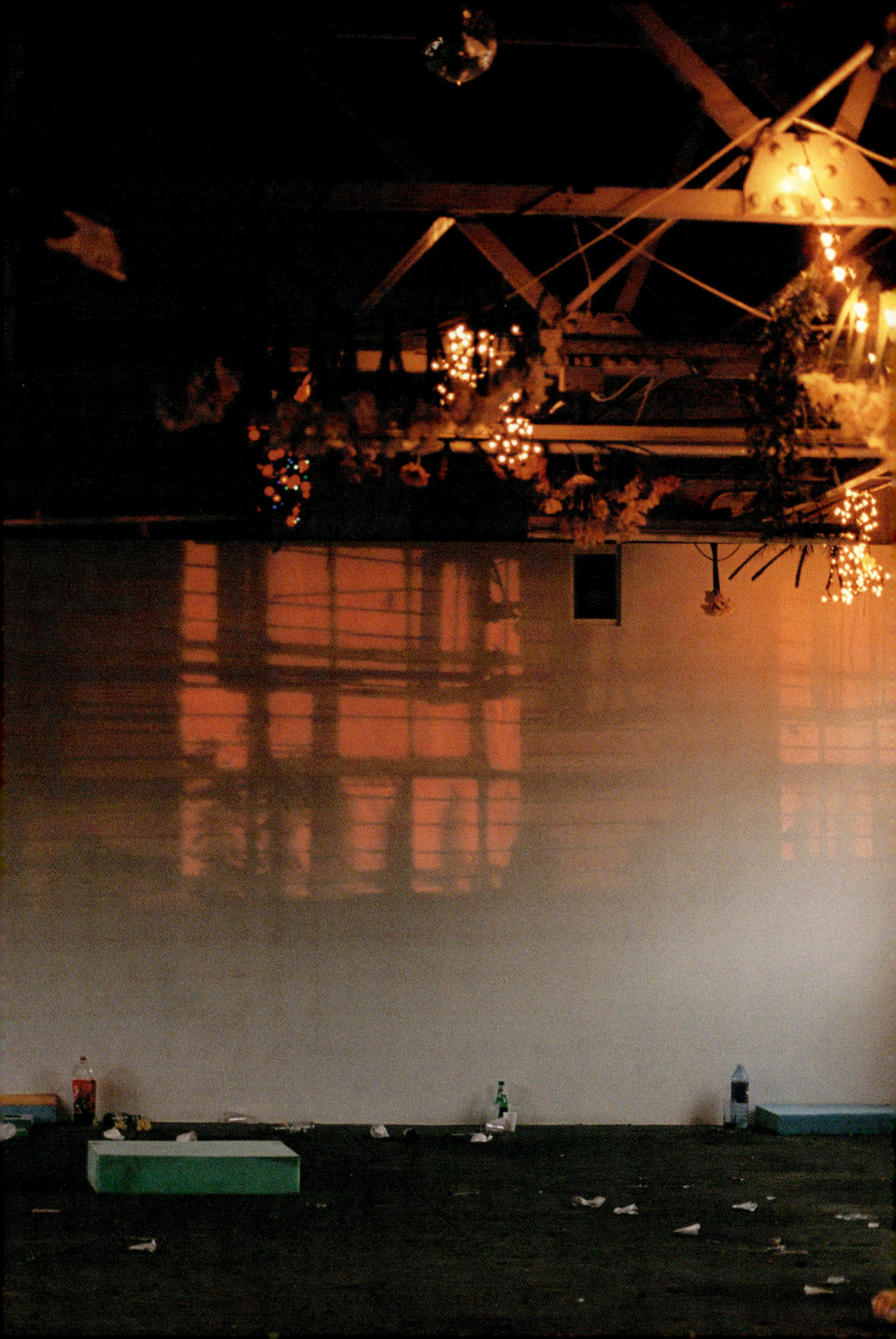

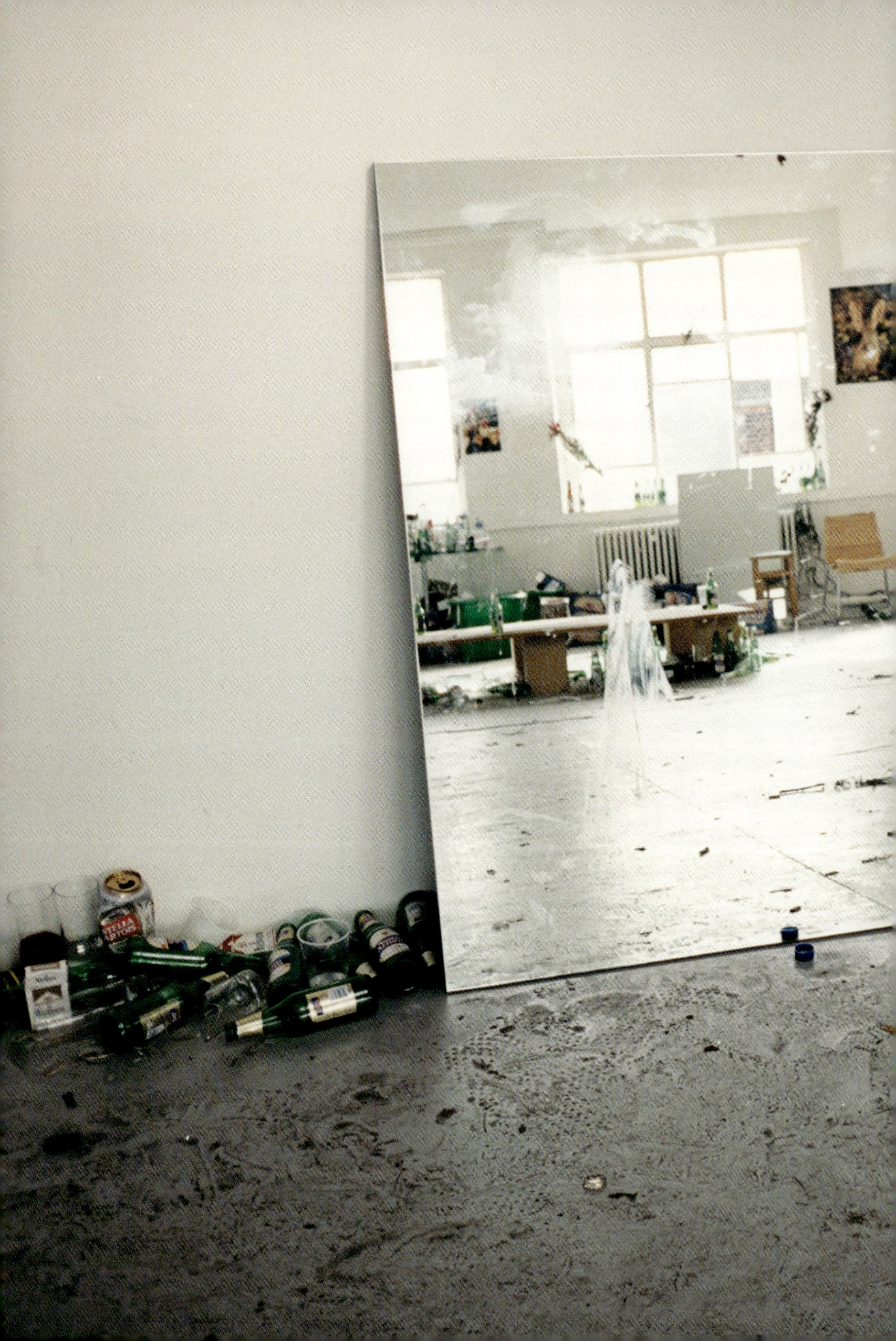

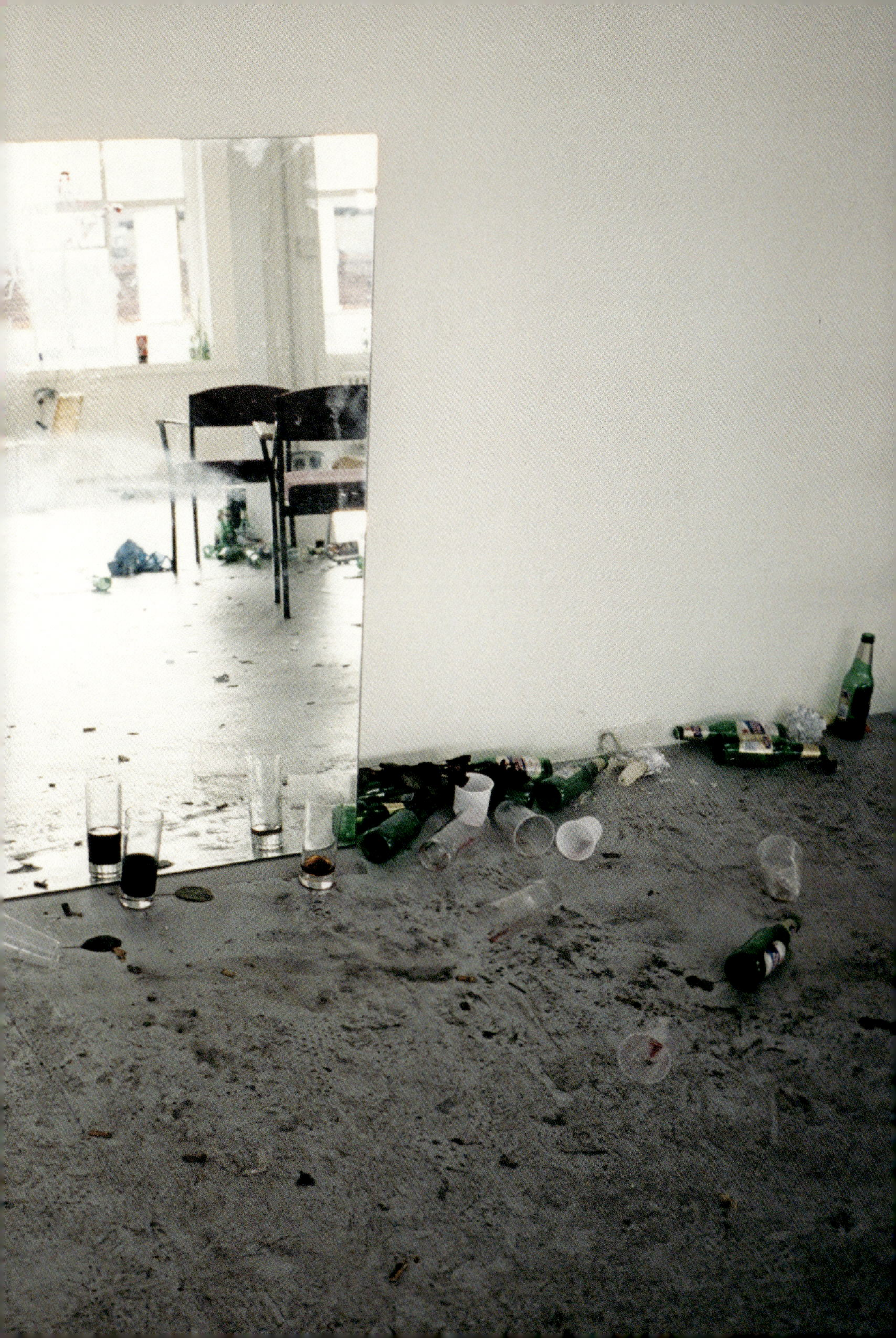

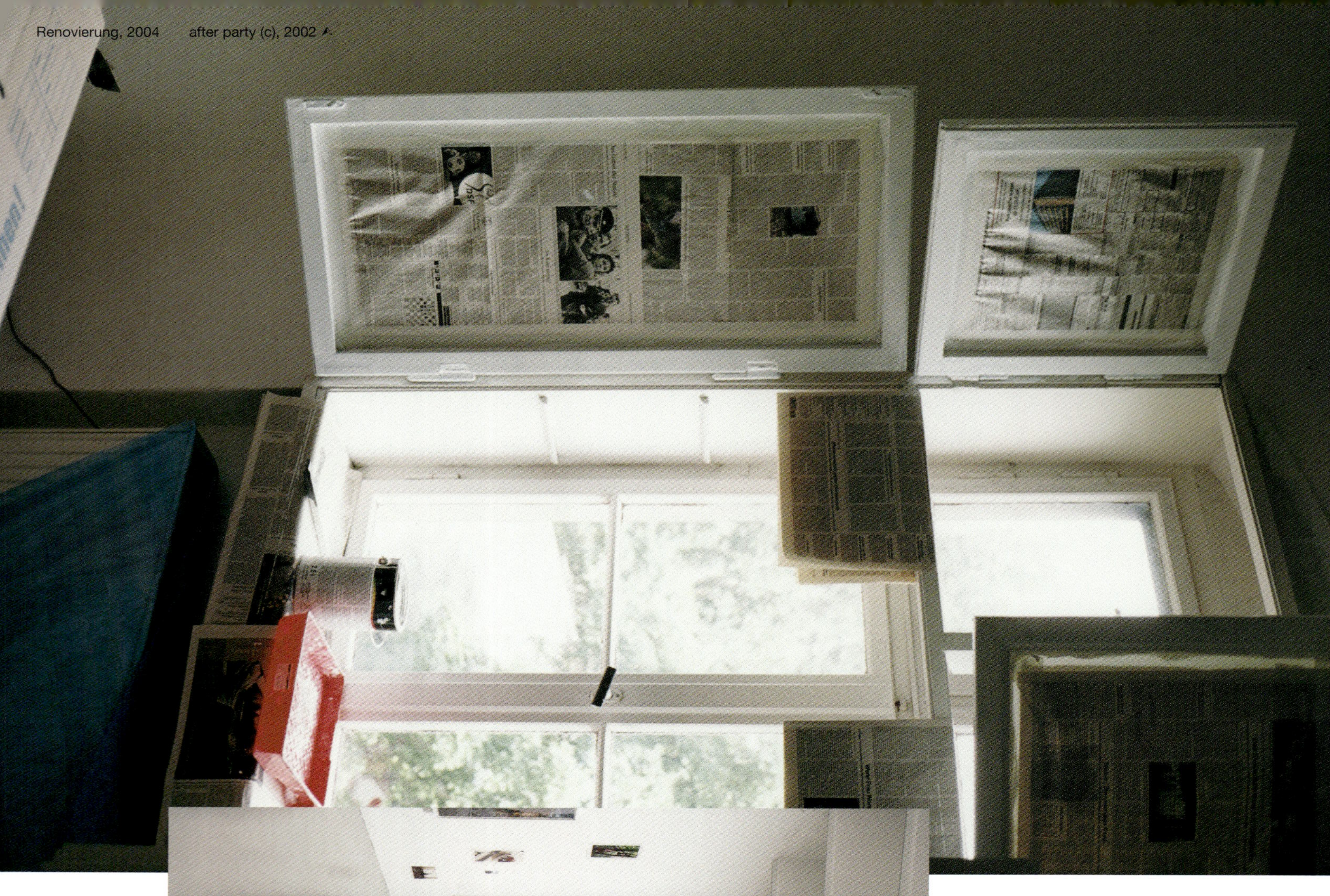

Renovierung, 2004   after party (c), 2002

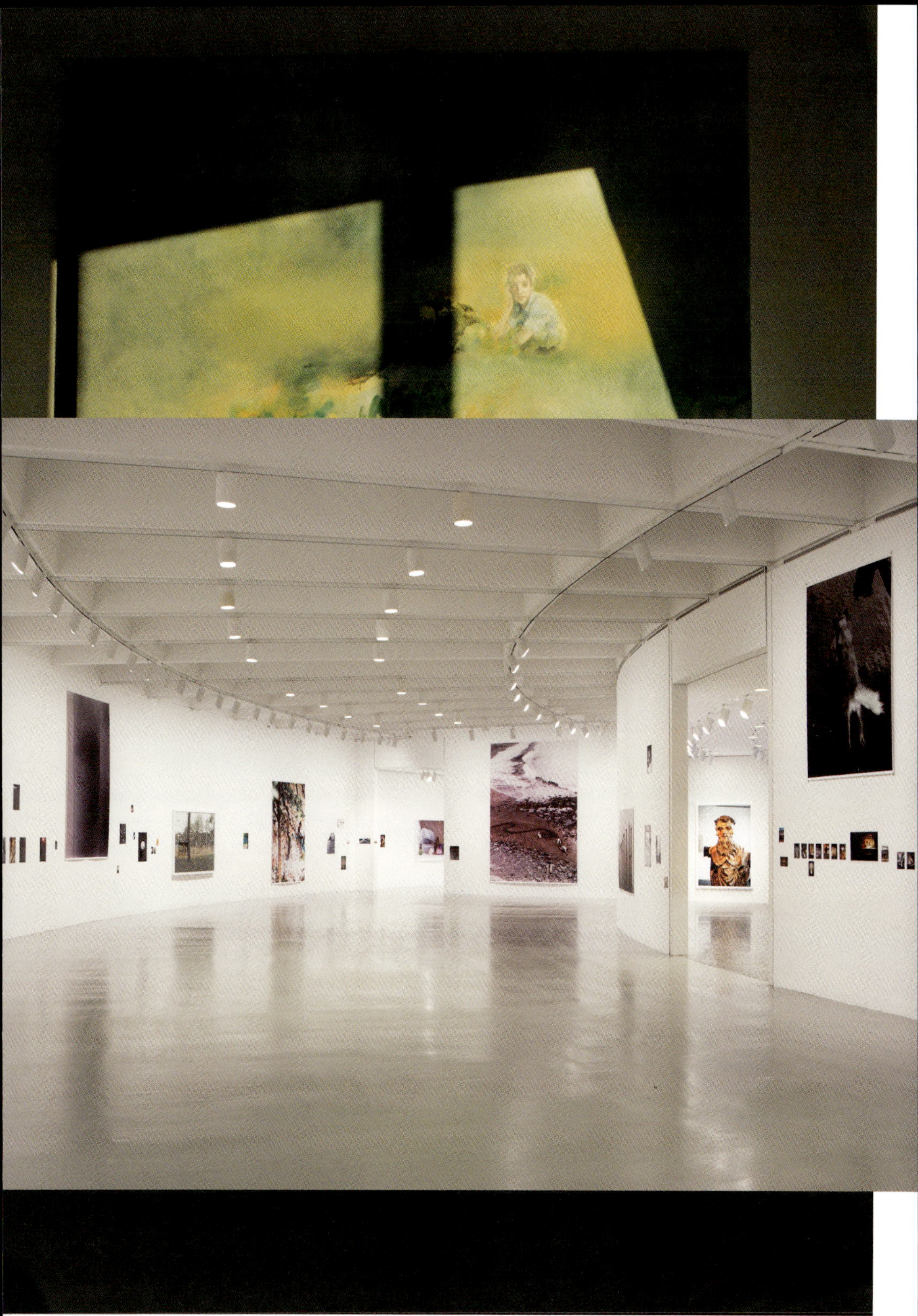

painting in sunlight, 2000   Installation view Hirshhorn Museum (Washington D.C.), 2007   windowbox, 2000

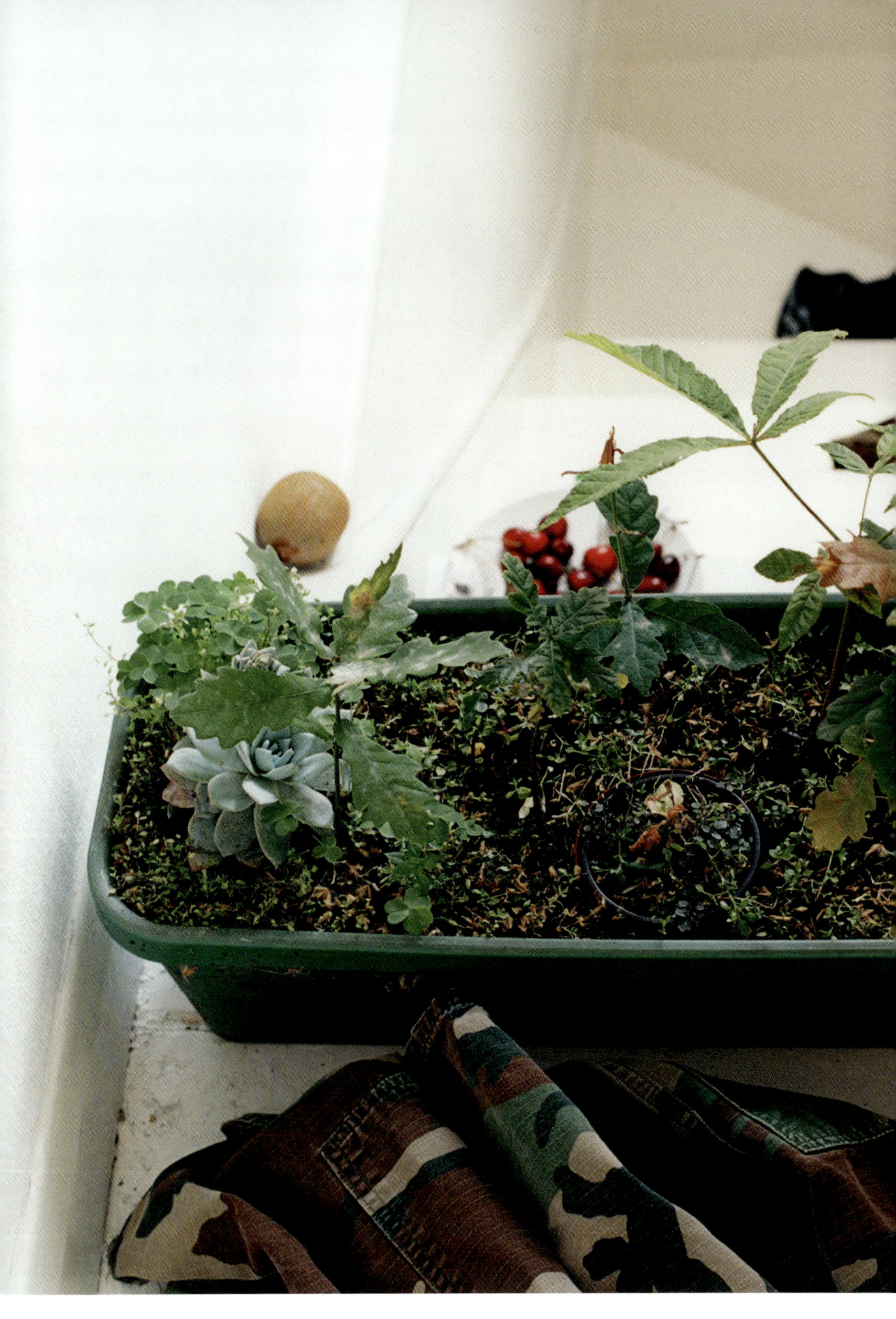

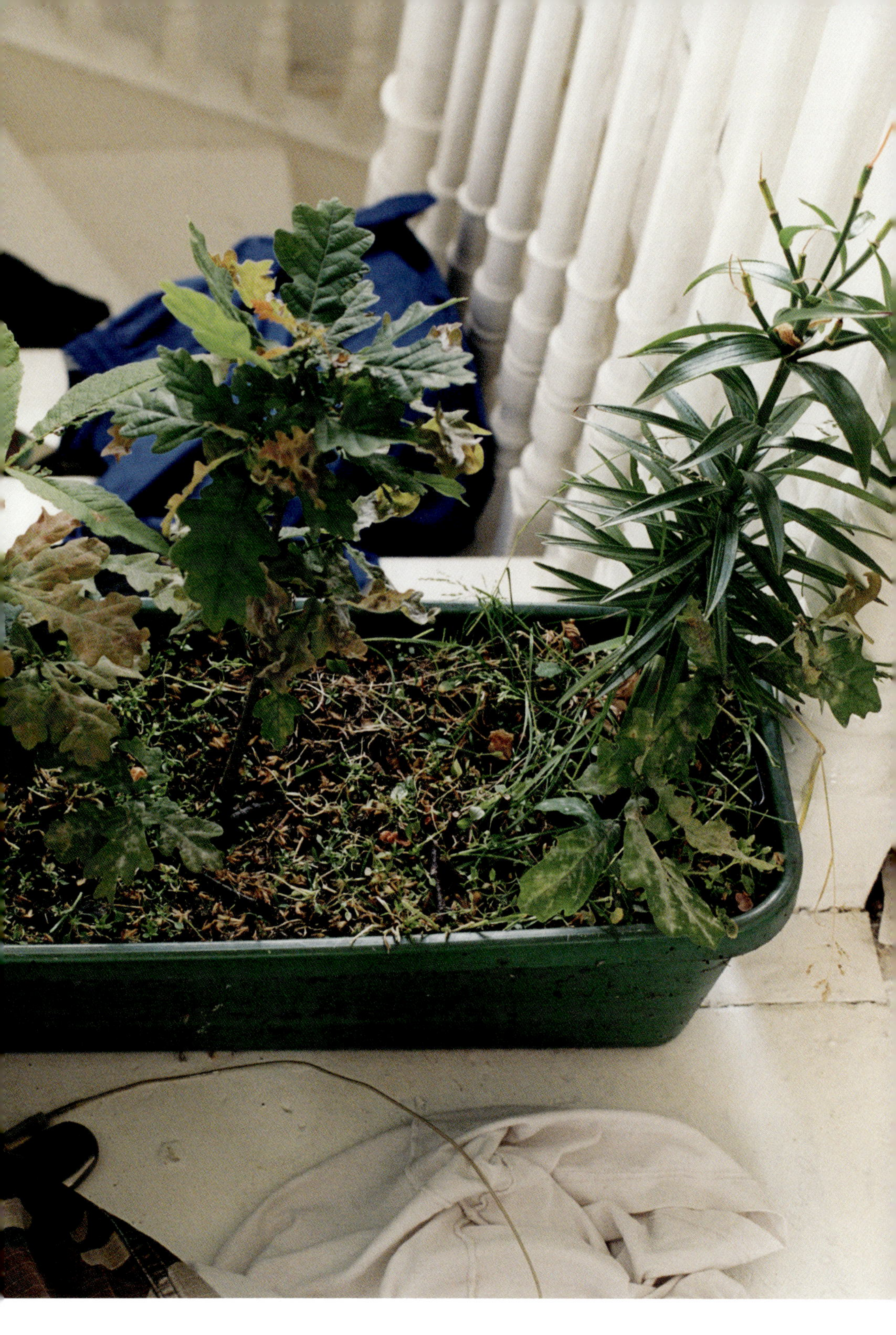

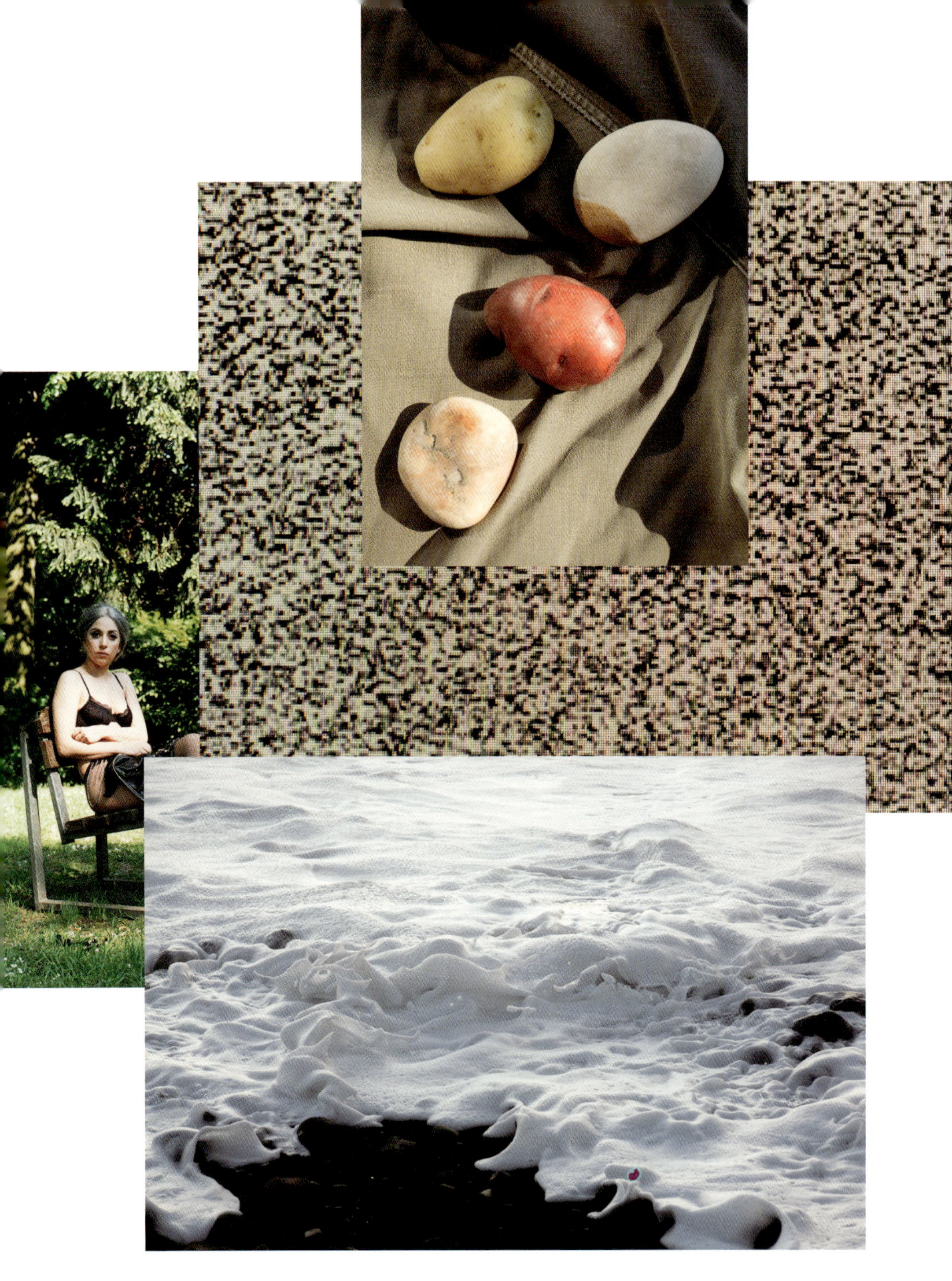

Gaga sitting in park, 2010   La Palma, 2014
Far away inside (Echo Beach), 2017   Sendeschluss / End of Broadcast II, 2014
Schneckenstilleben, 2004   Argonaut, 2017

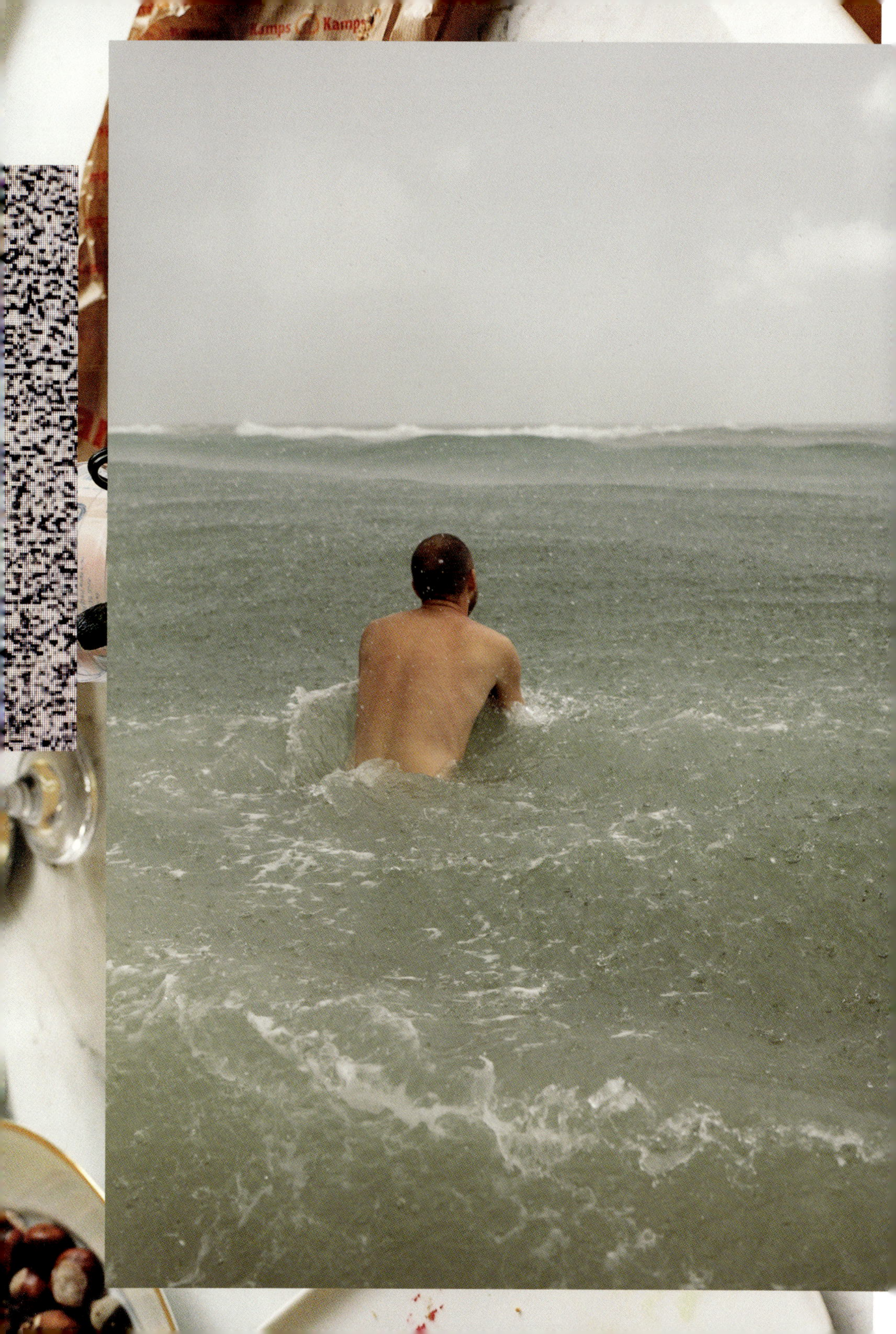

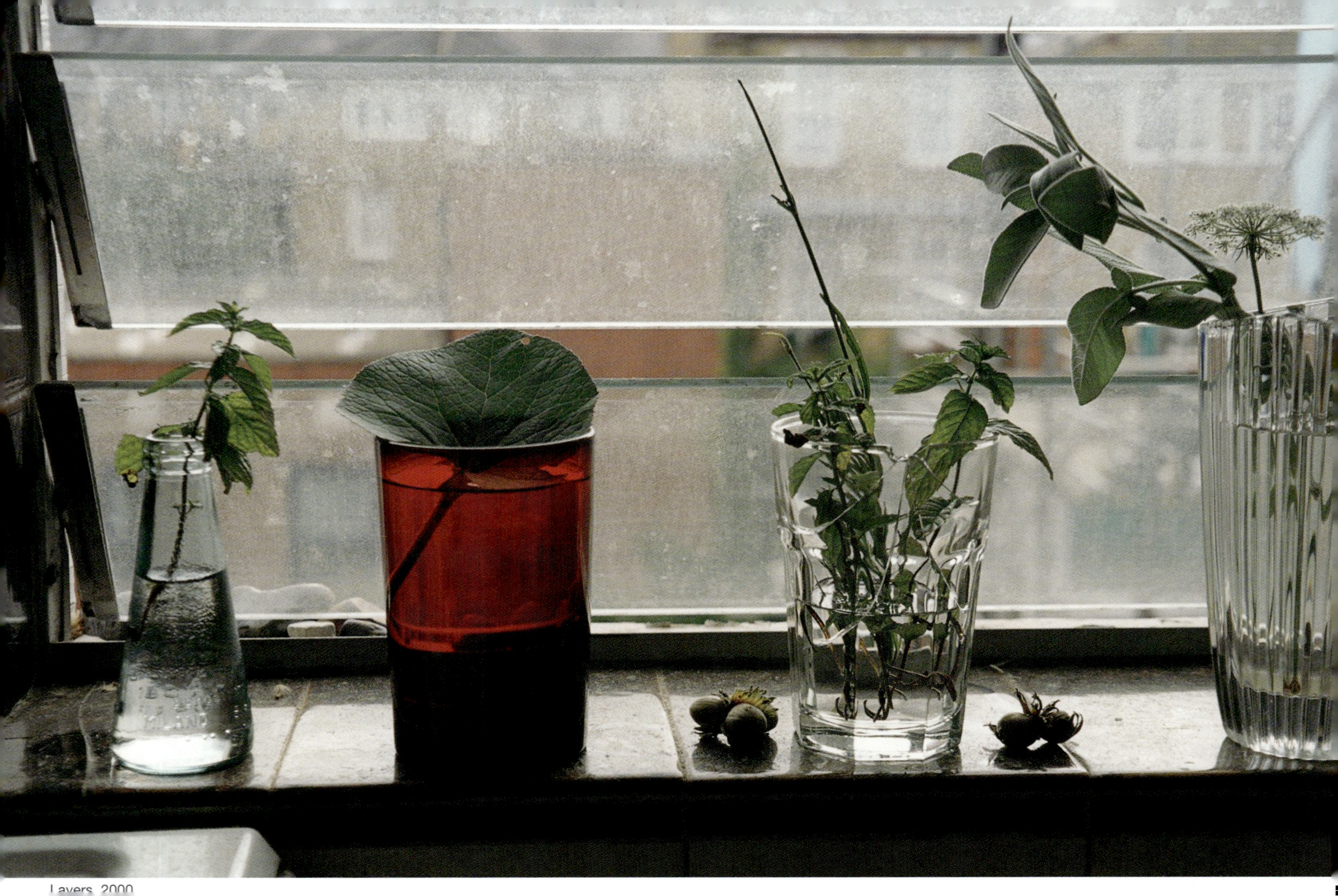

Lavers 2000

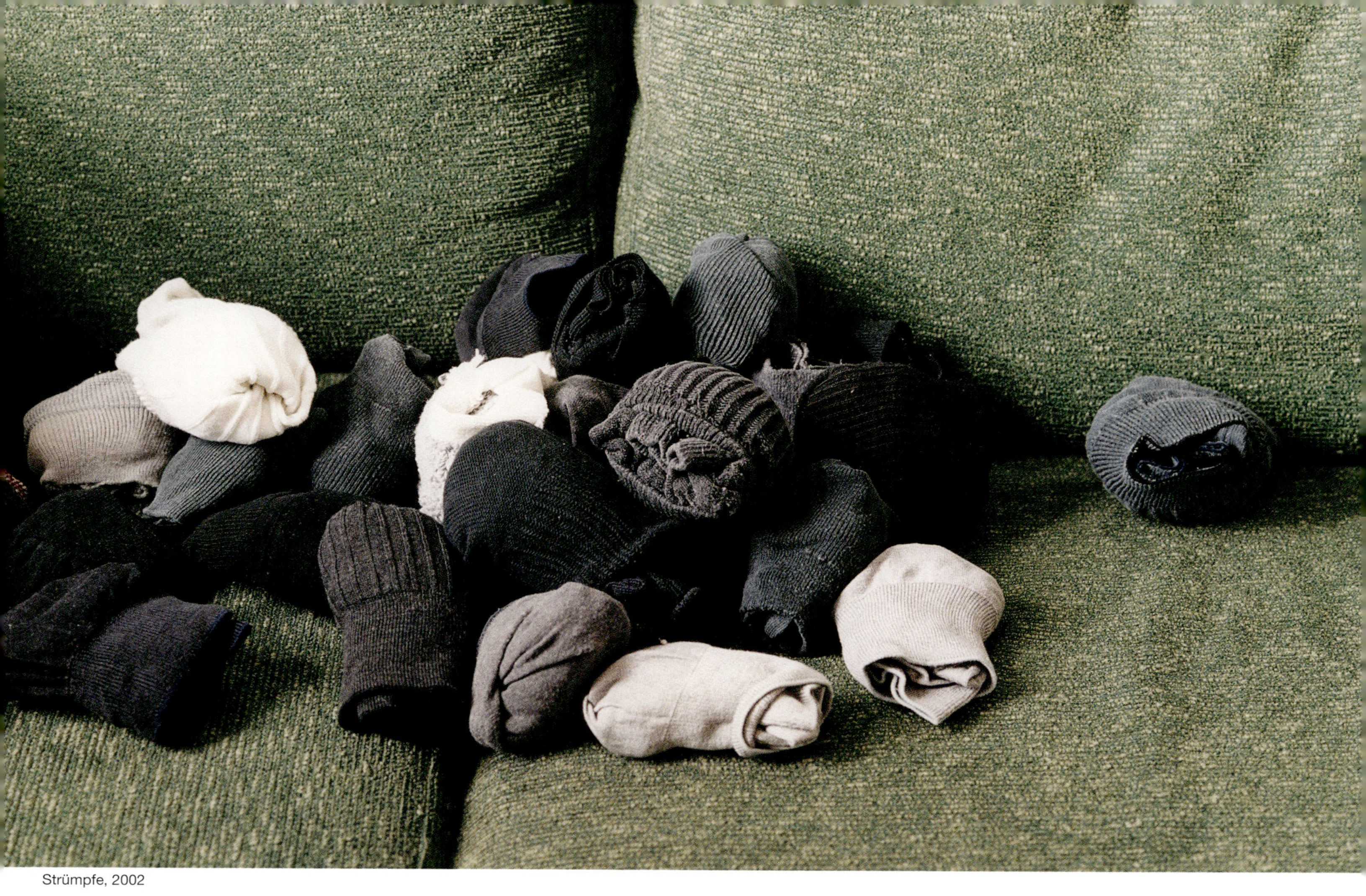

Strümpfe, 2002

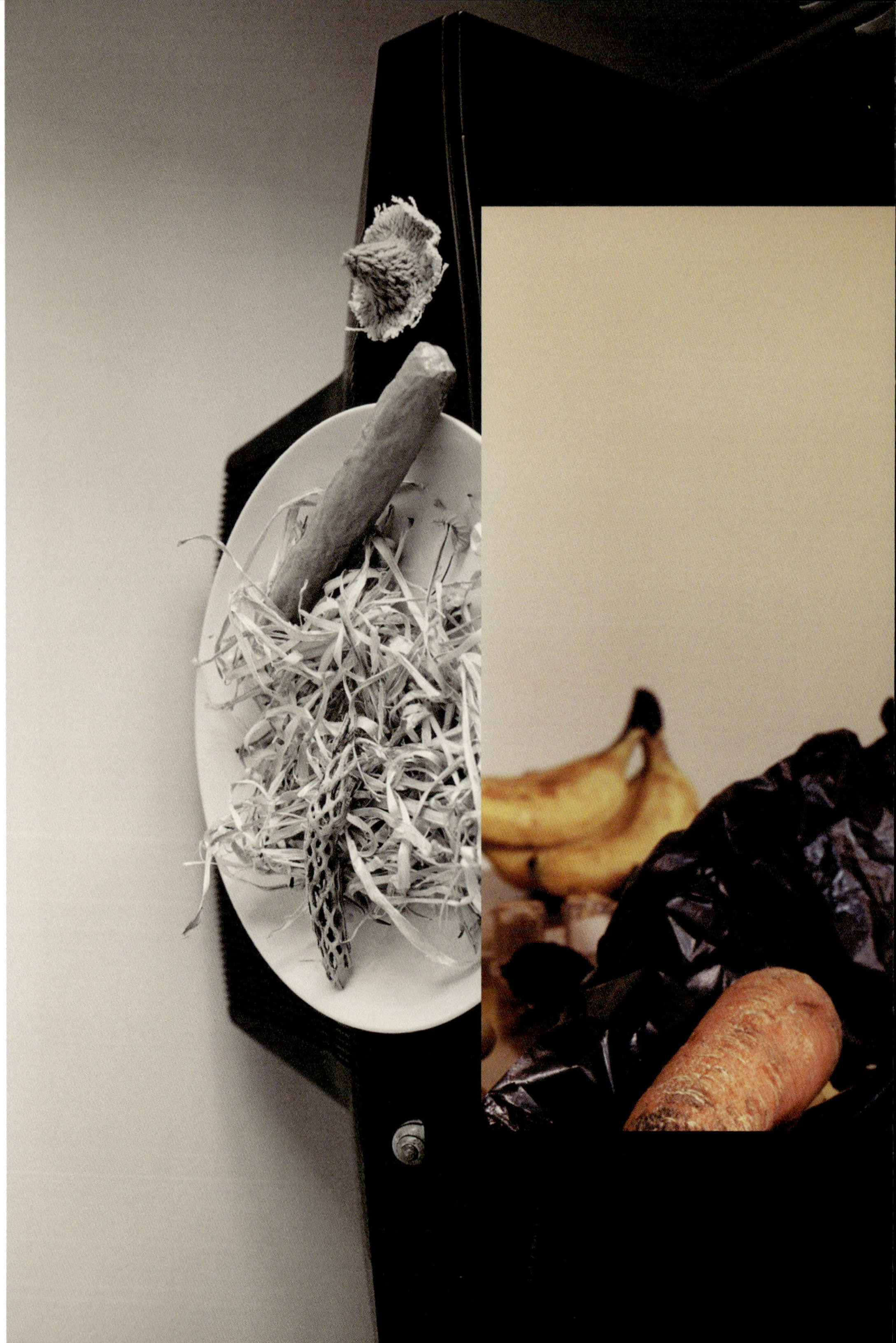

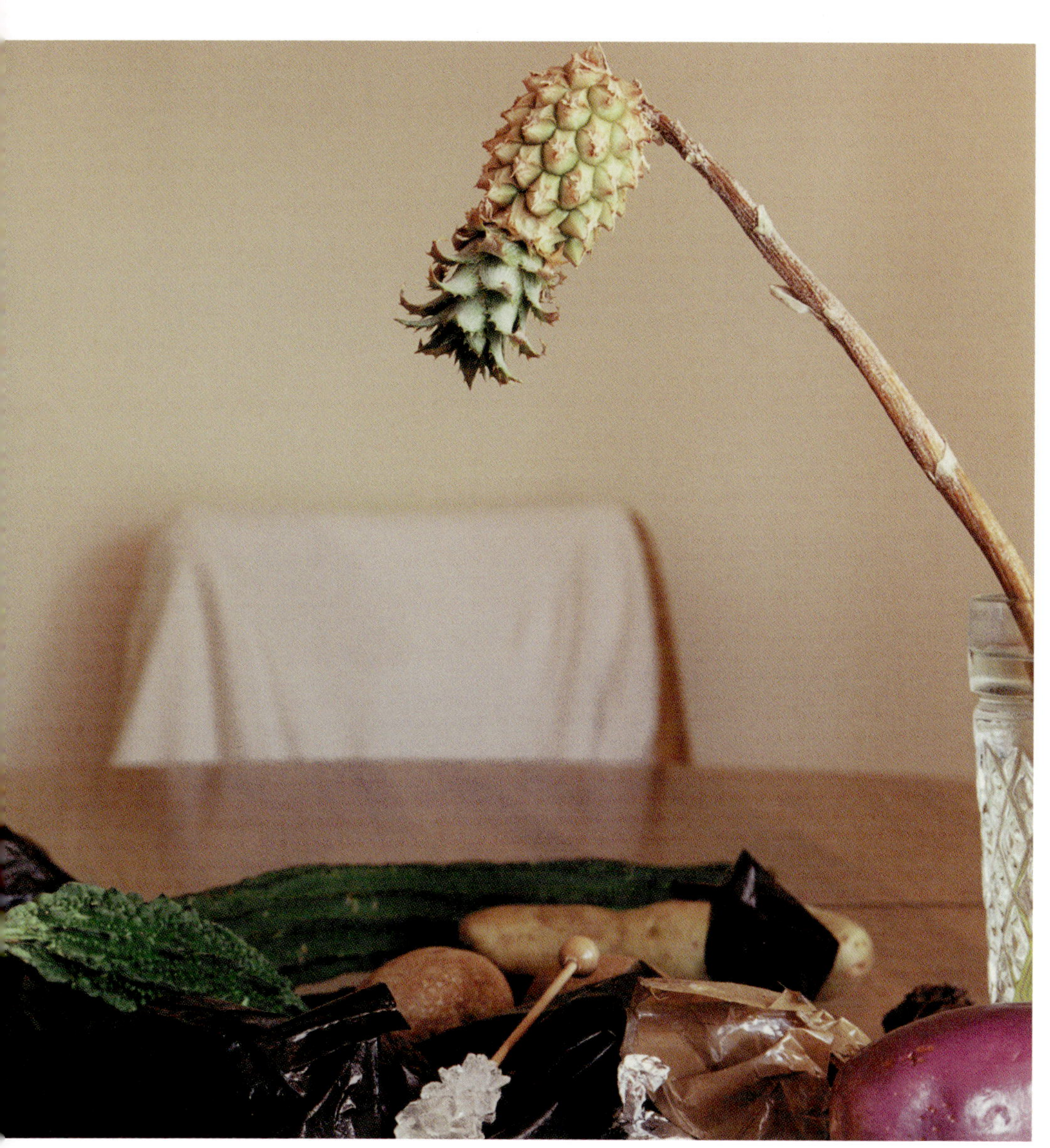

asparagus still life, 2005   new LA still life, 2001

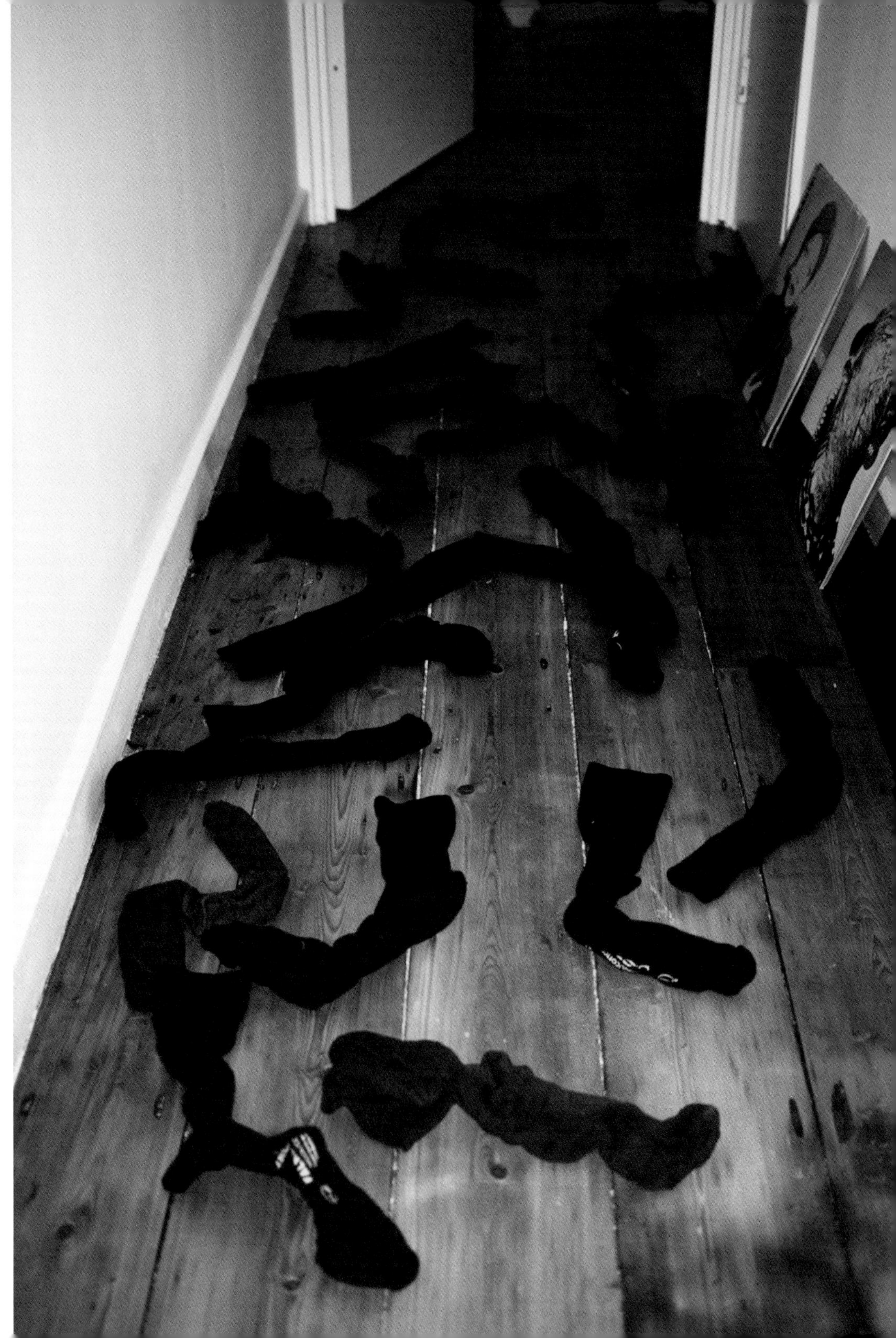

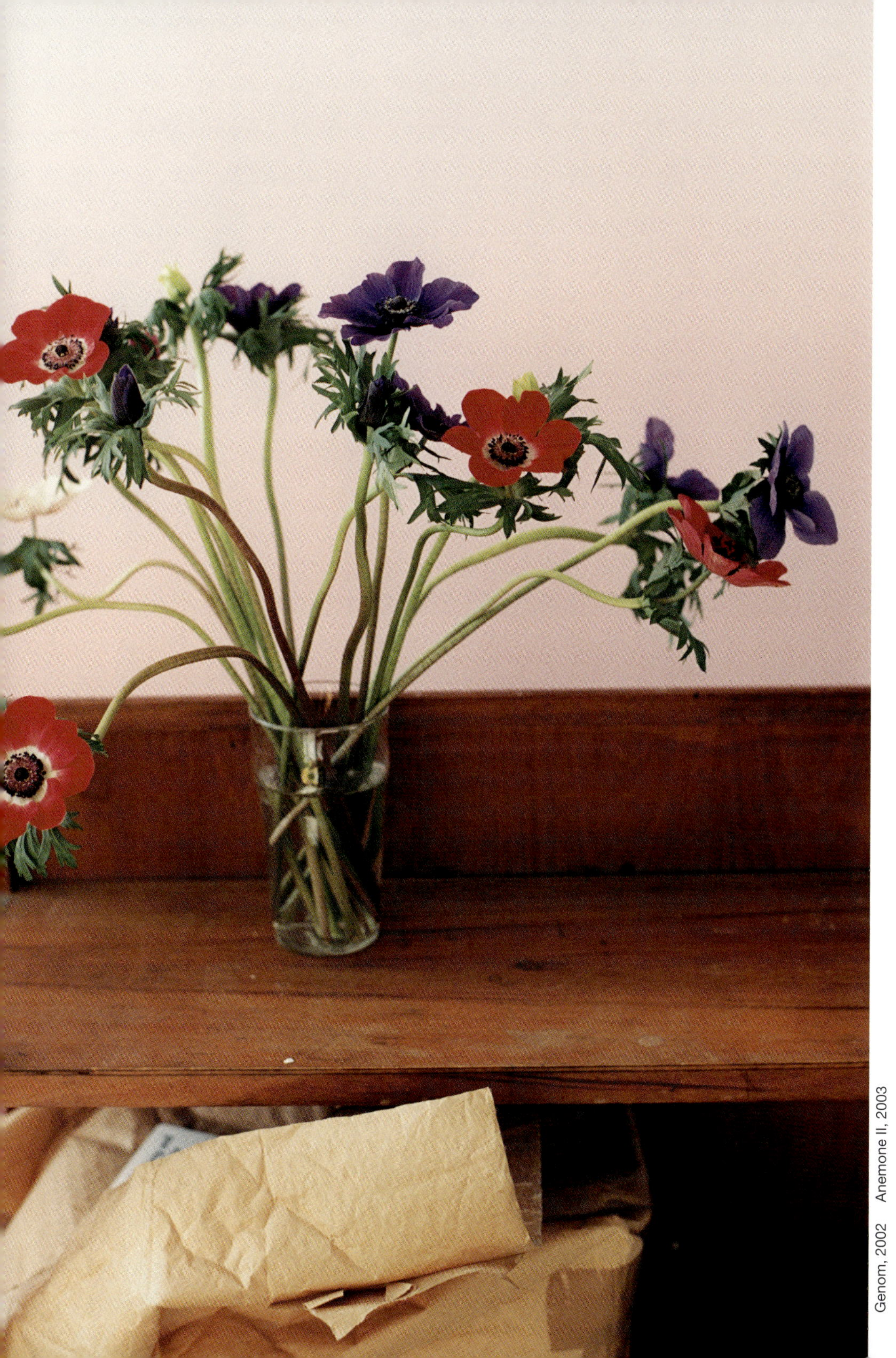

Genom, 2002   Anemone II, 2003

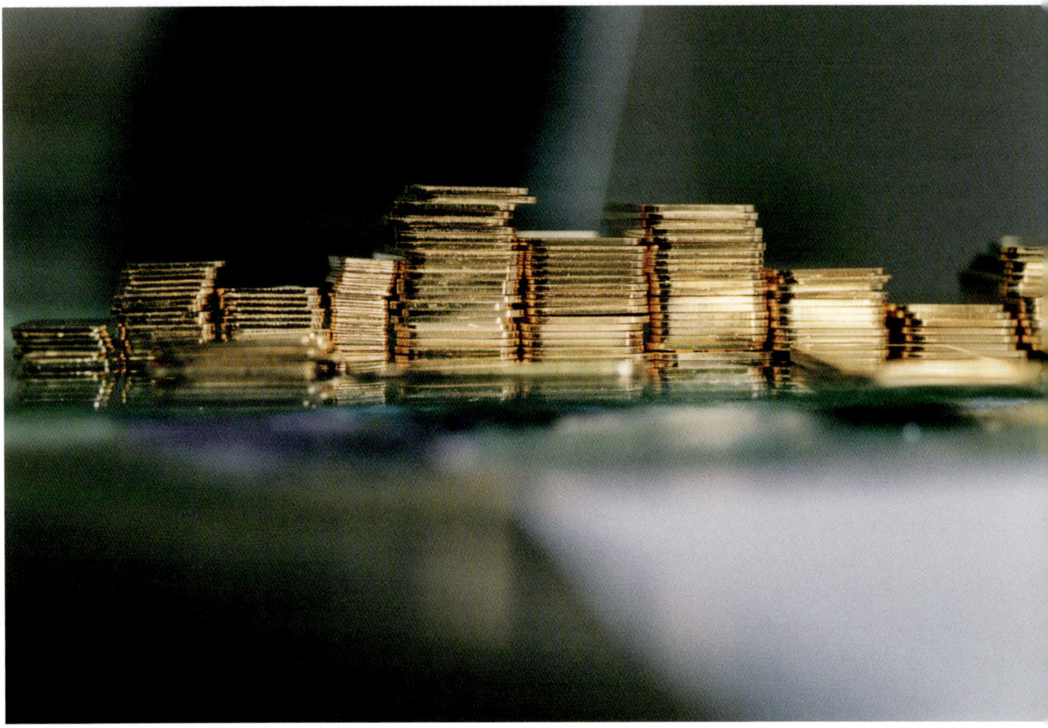

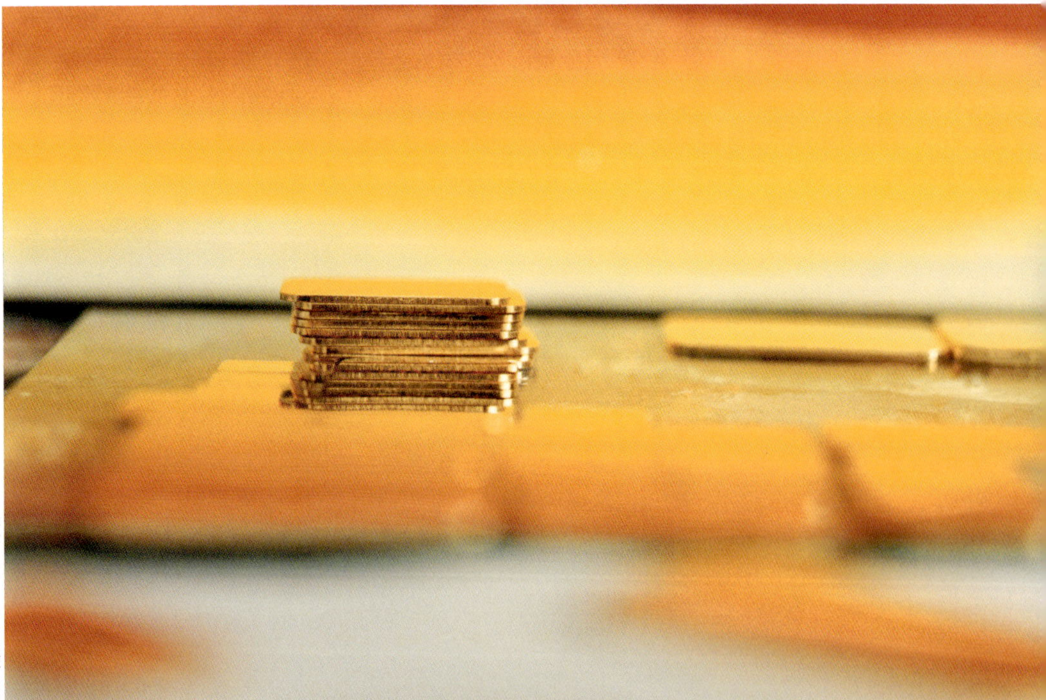

Gold (a), 2002   Gold (c), 2002

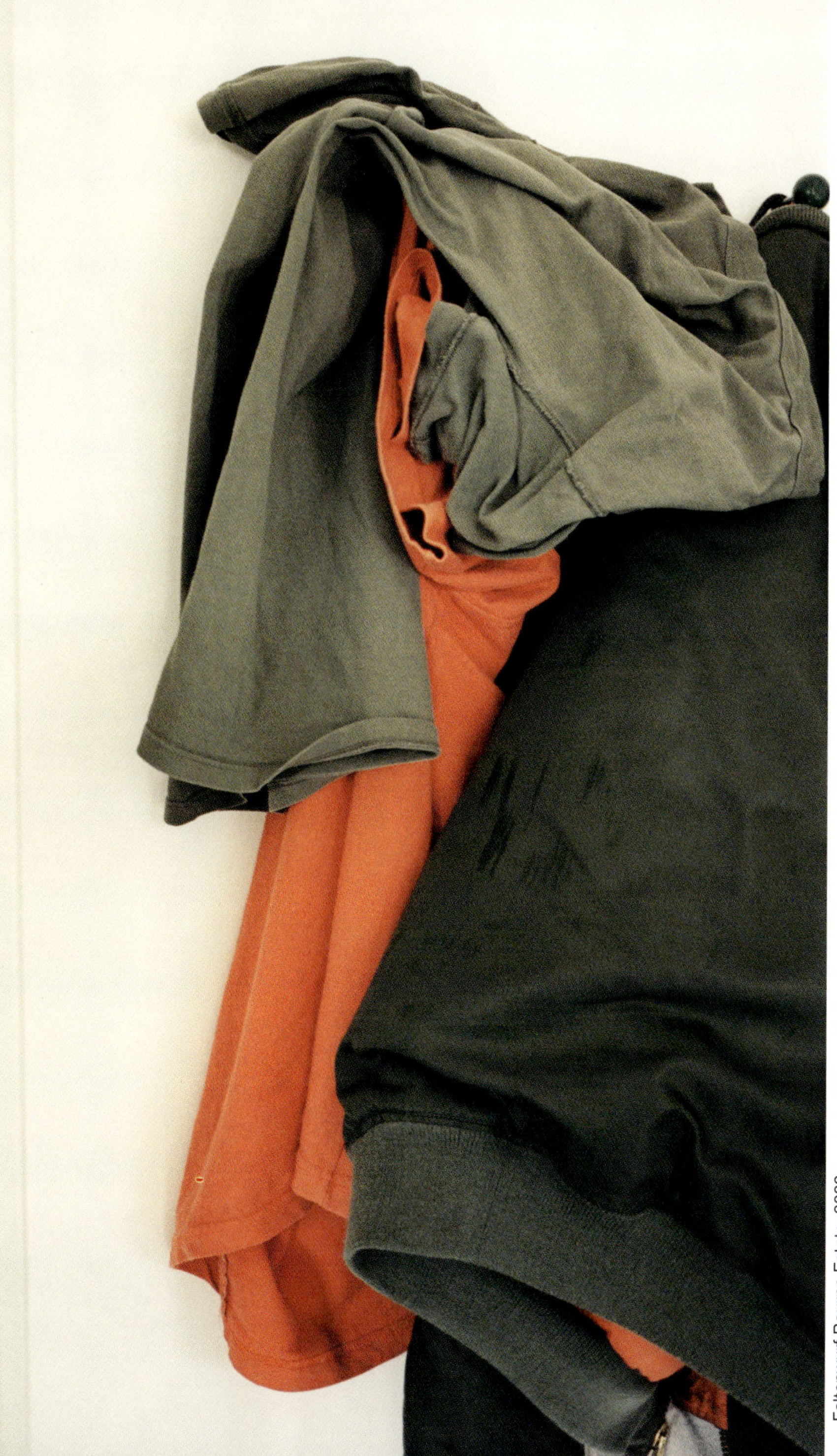

Faltenwurf Bourne Estate, 2002

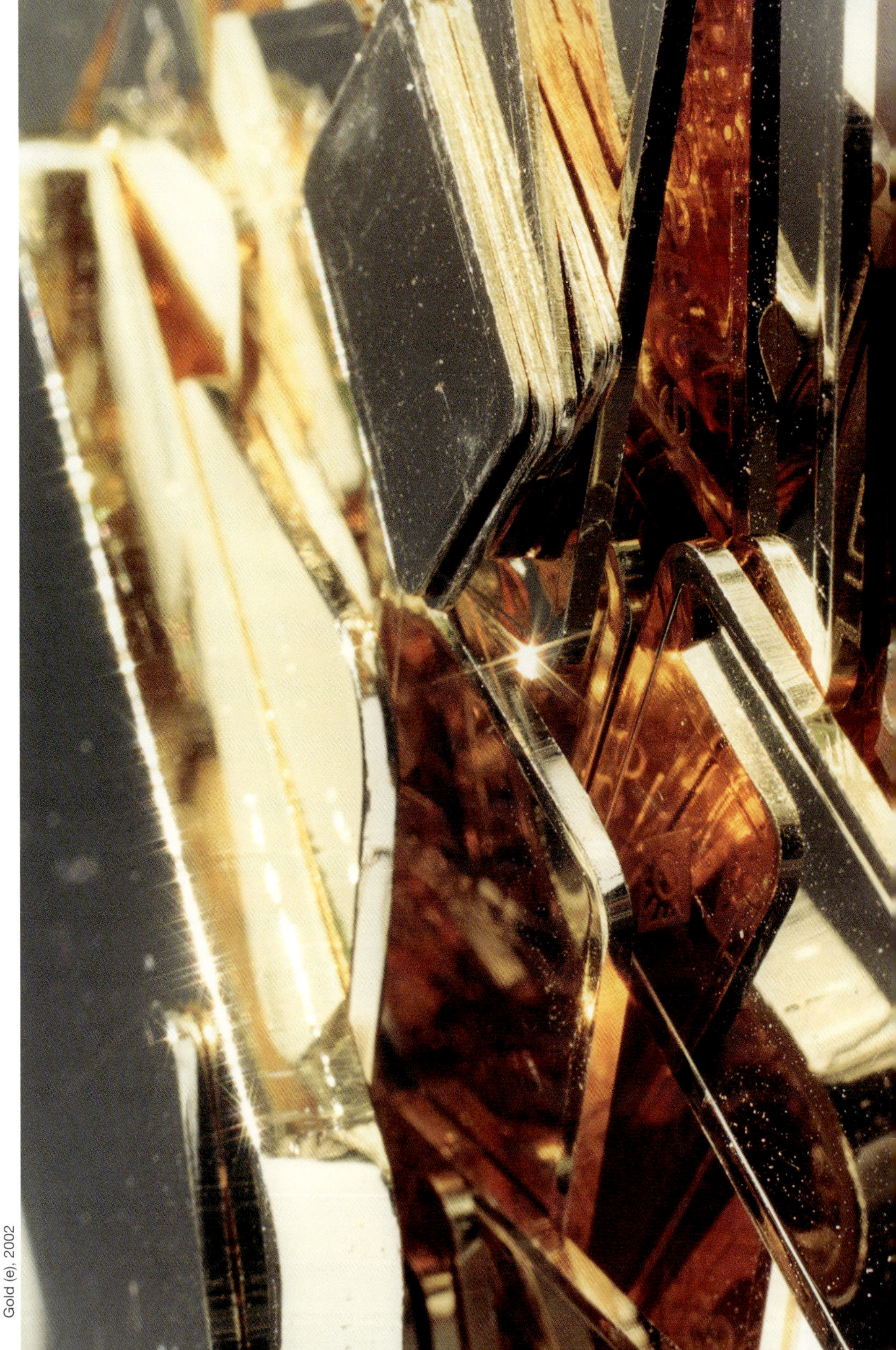

Gold (e), 2002

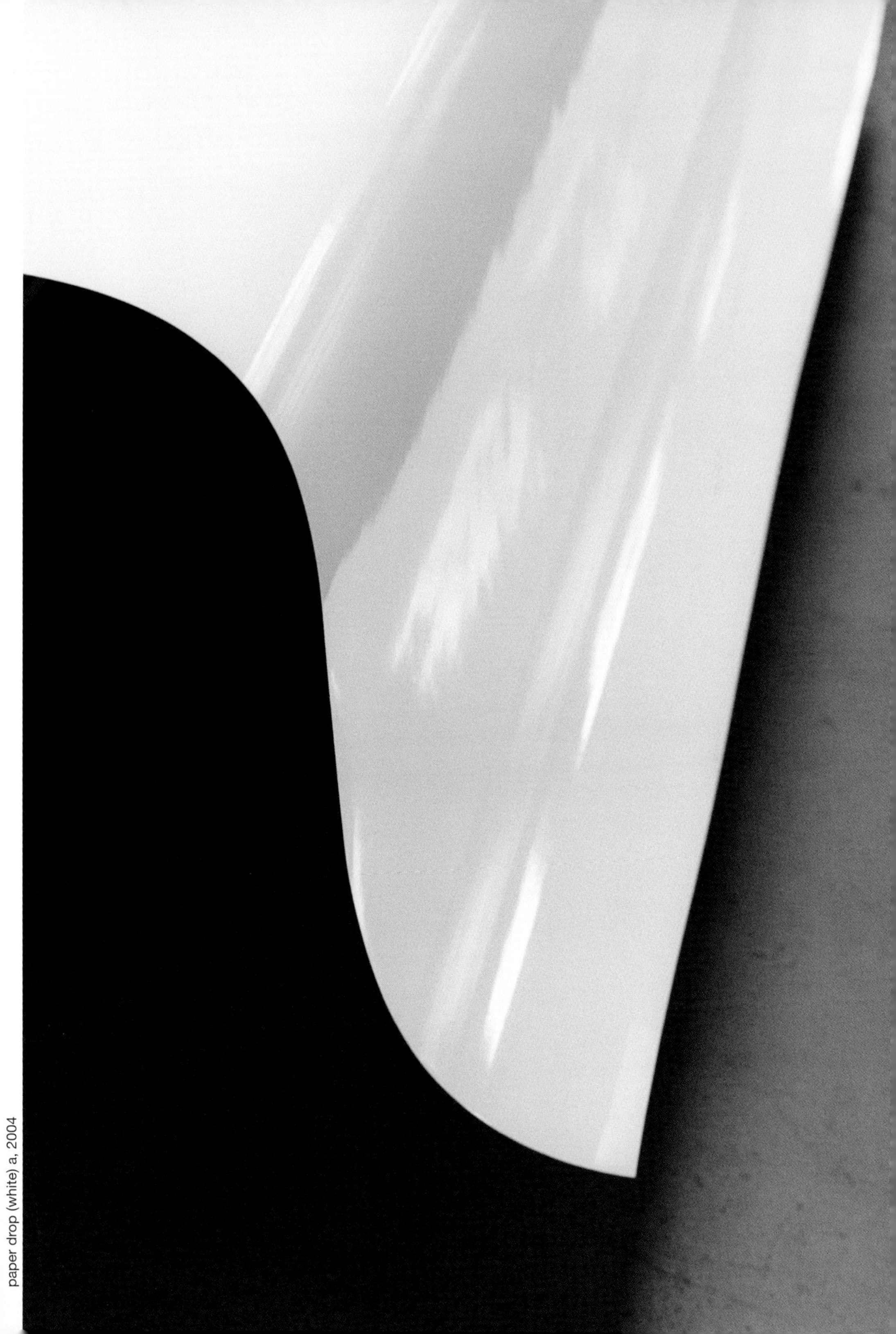

paper drop (white) a, 2004

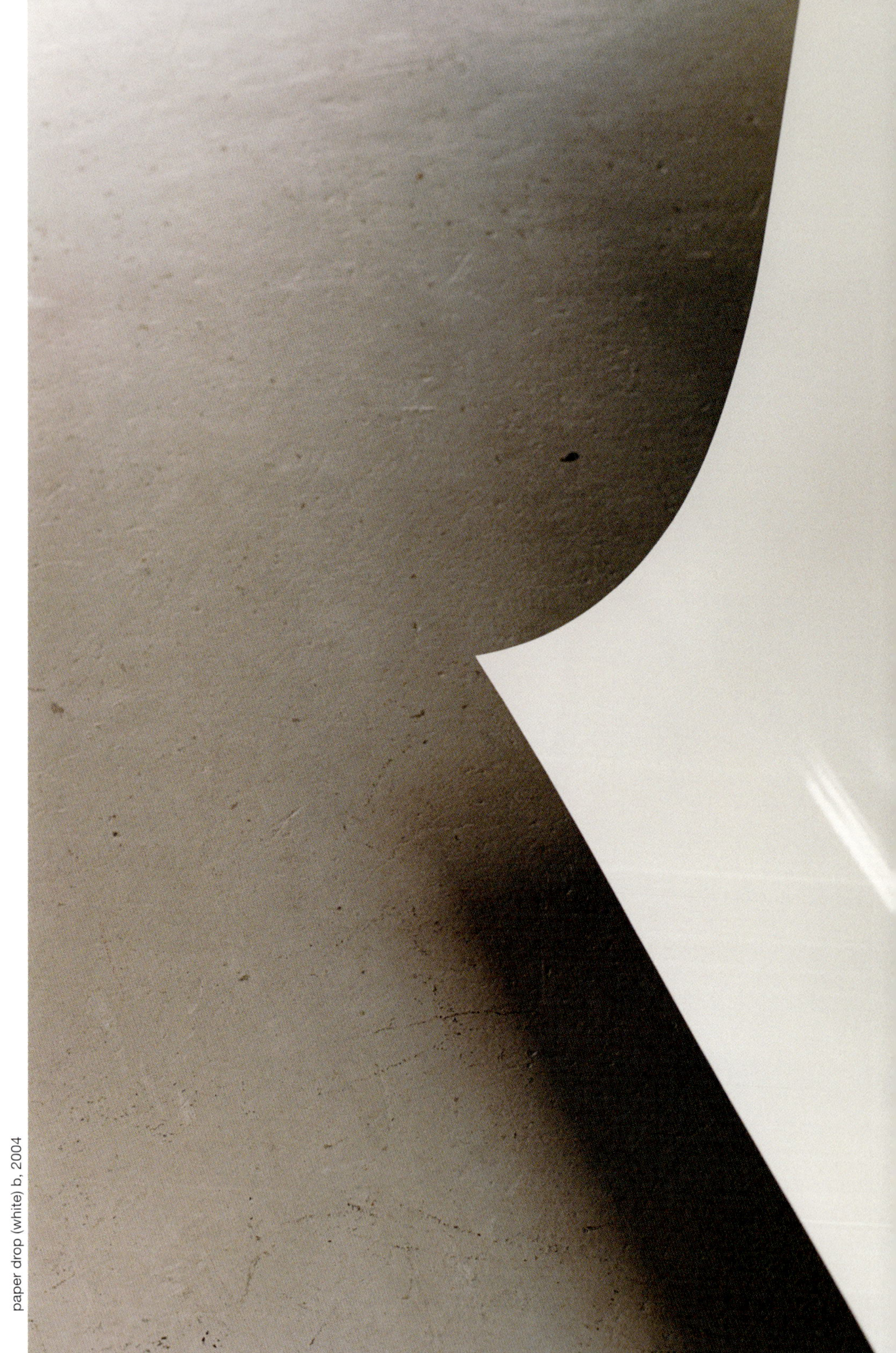

paper drop (white) b, 2004

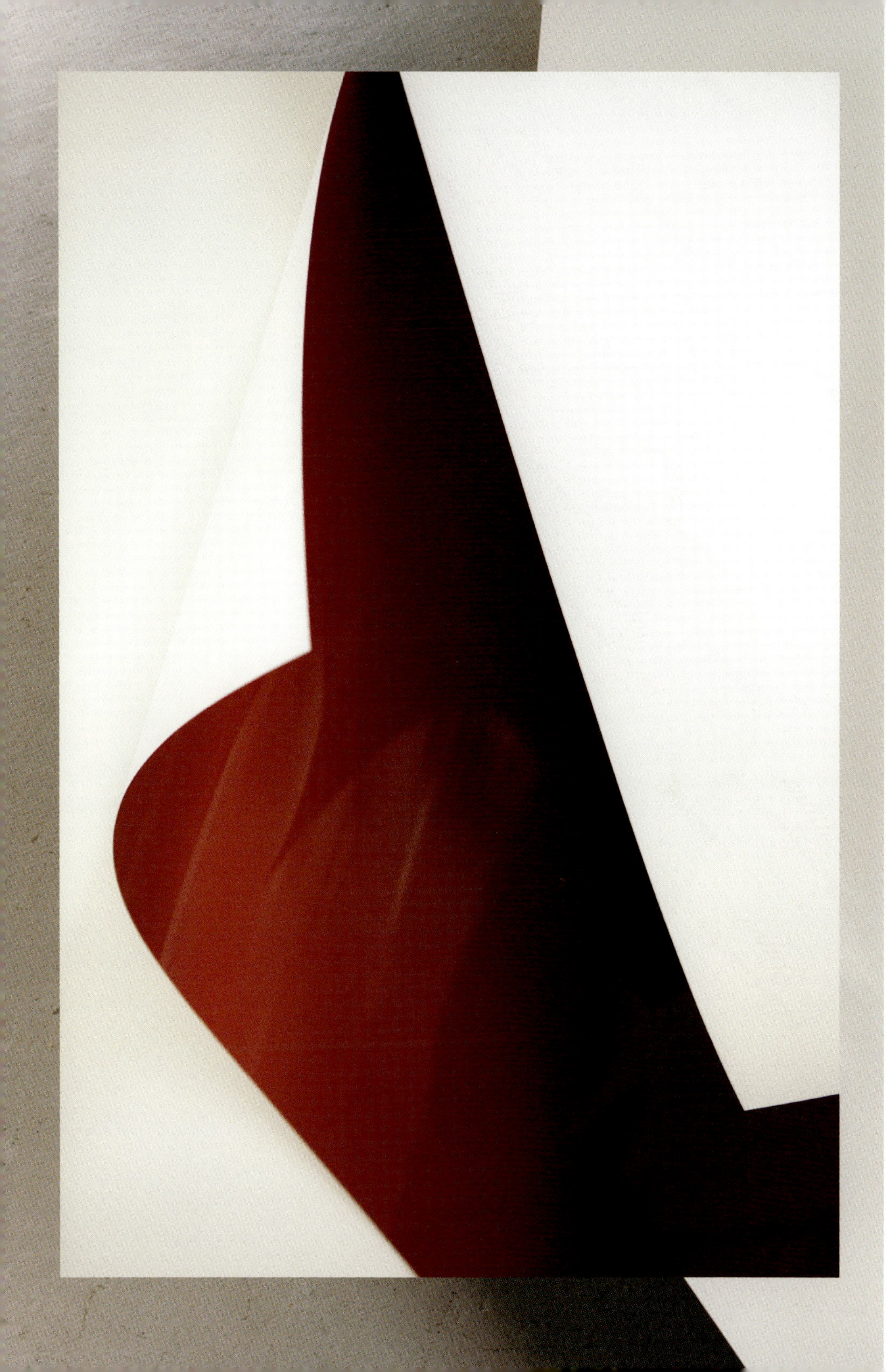

paper drop (white) c, 2004   paper drop (London) II, 2011

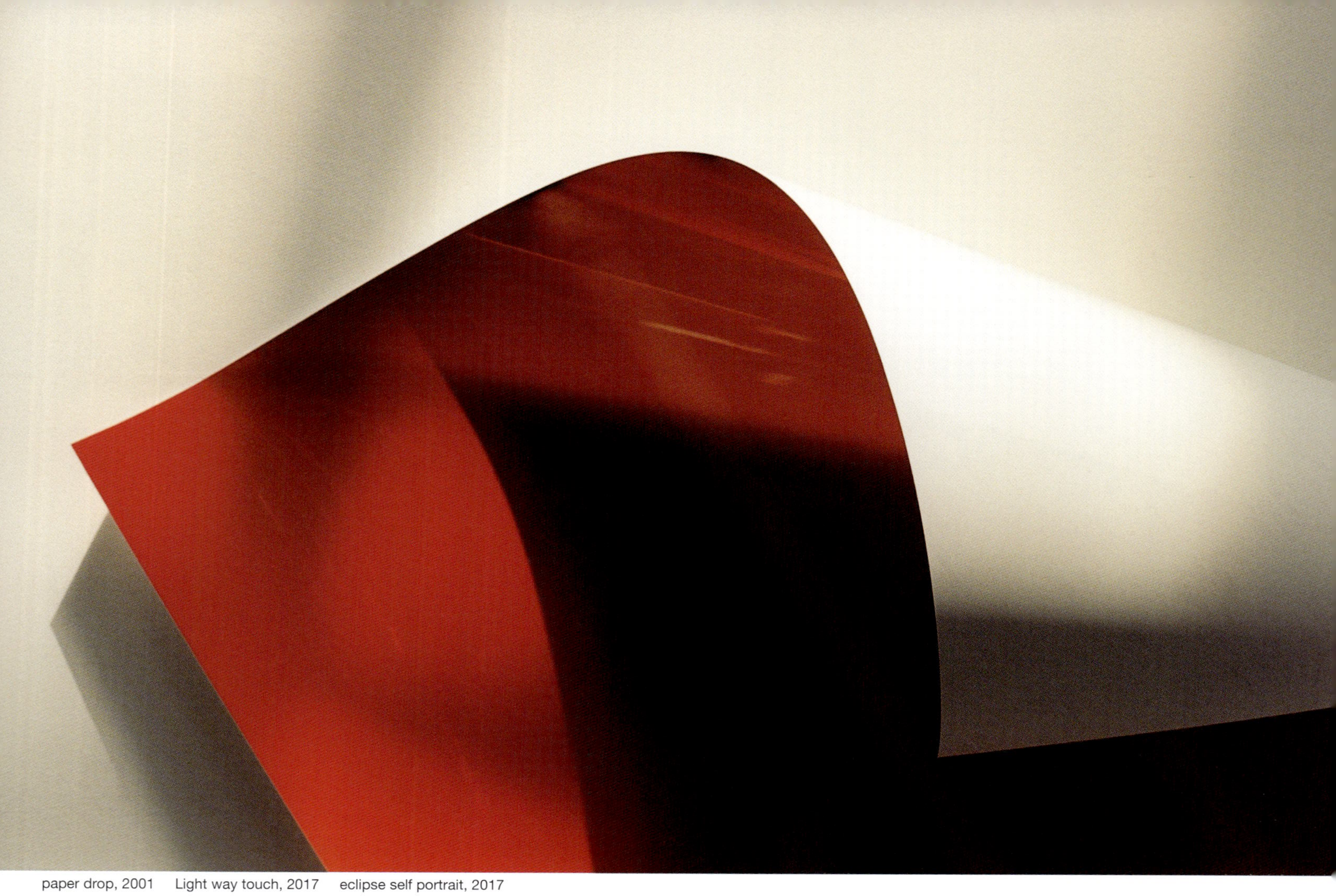

paper drop, 2001   Light way touch, 2017   eclipse self portrait, 2017

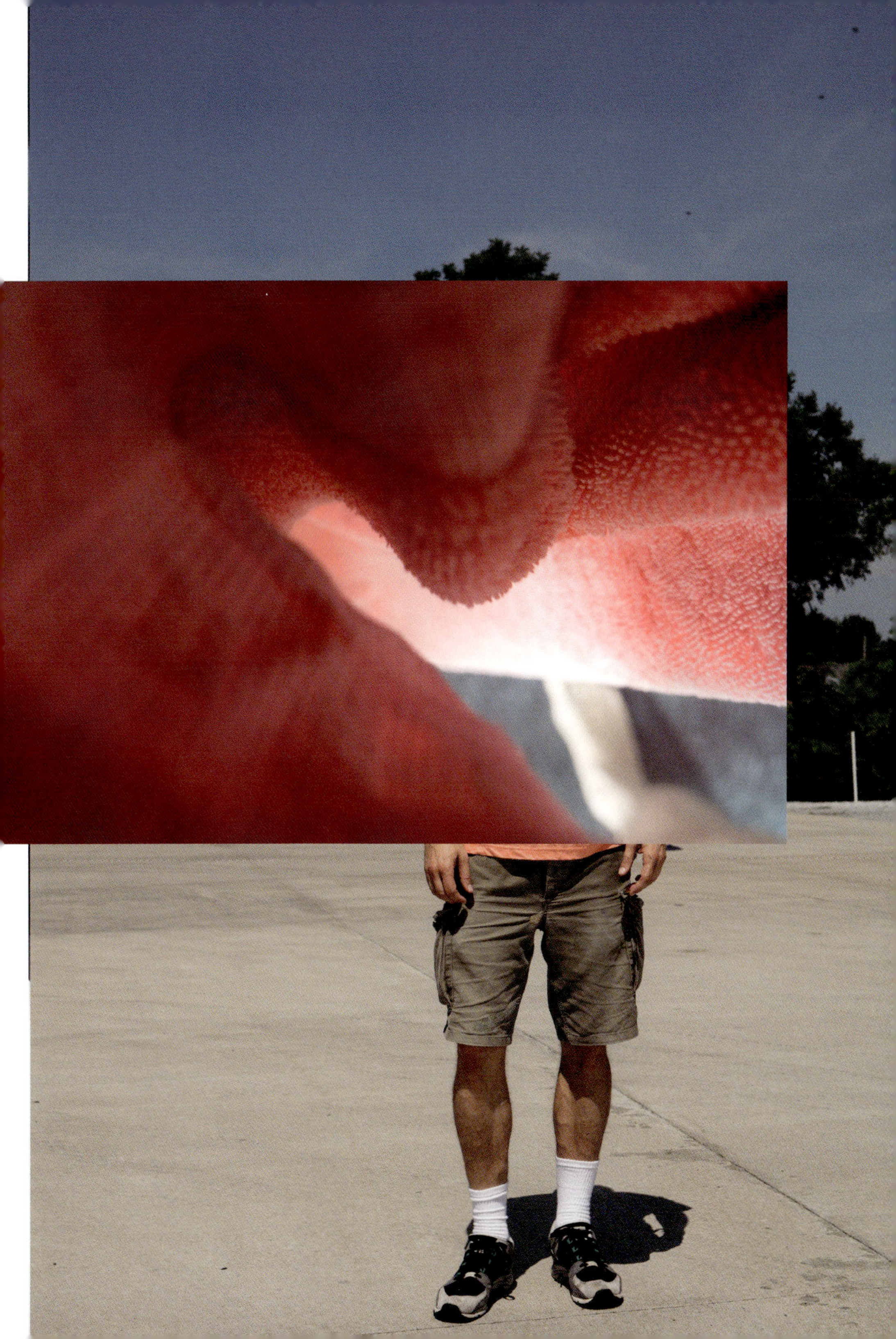

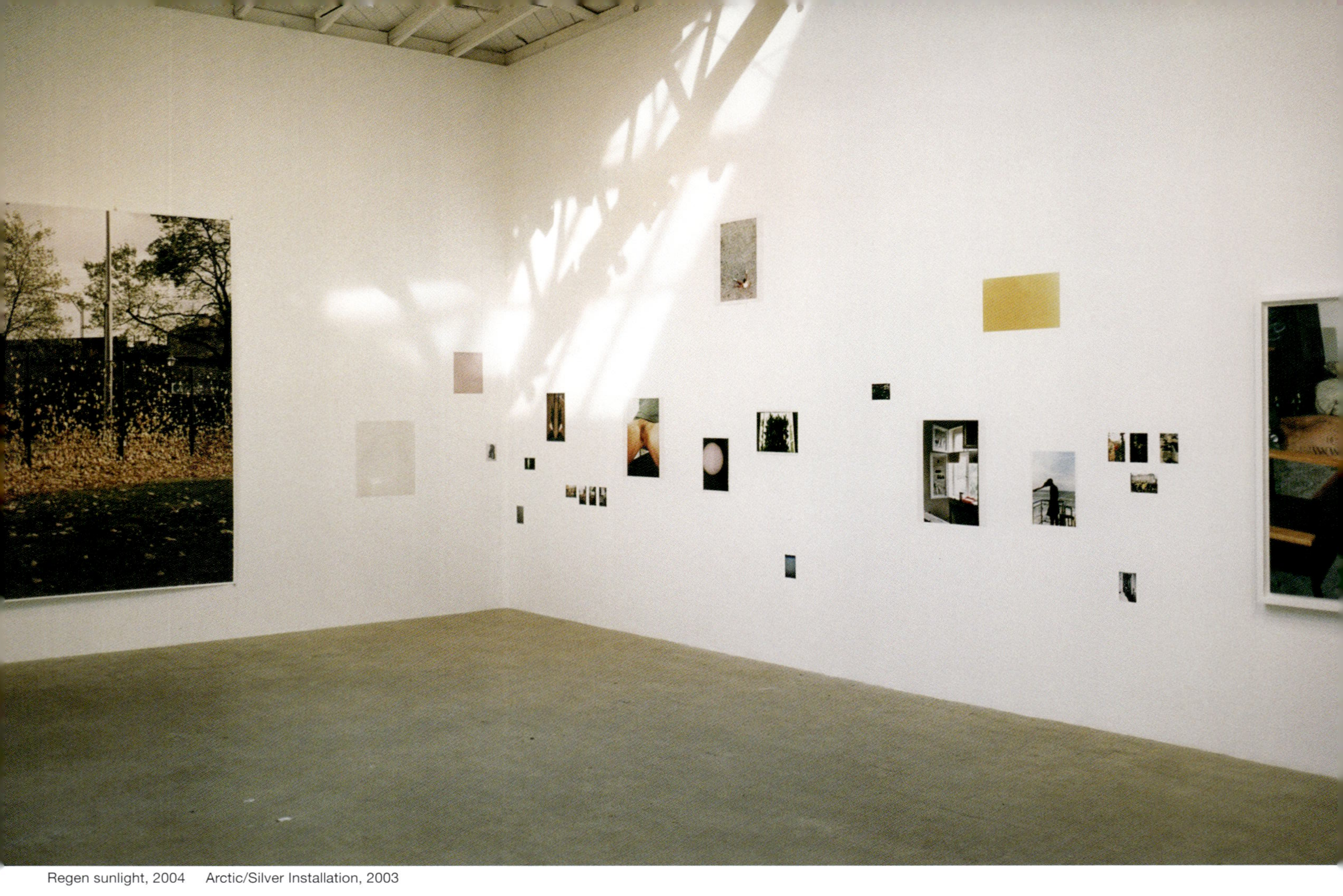

Regen sunlight, 2004   Arctic/Silver Installation, 2003

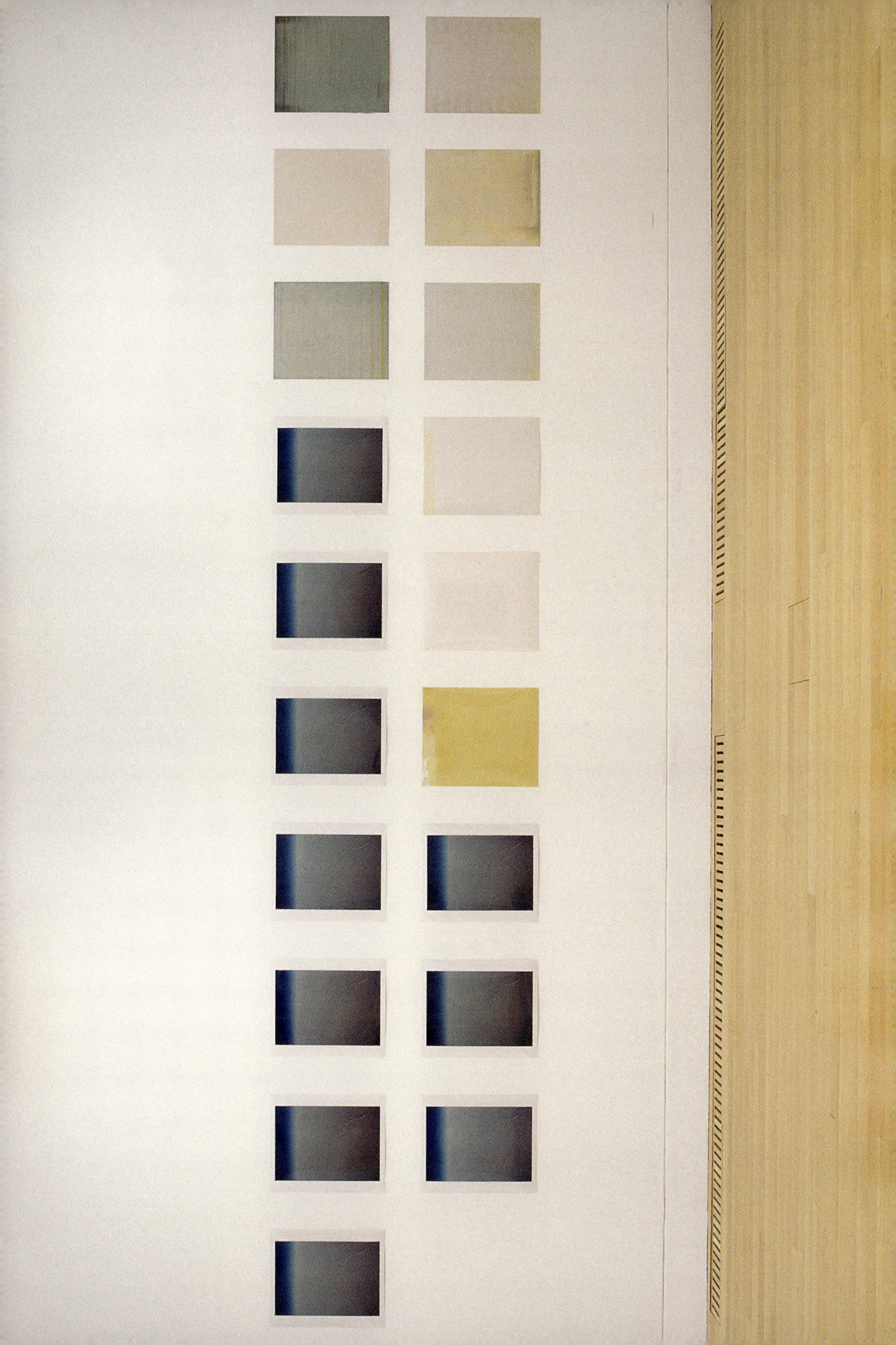

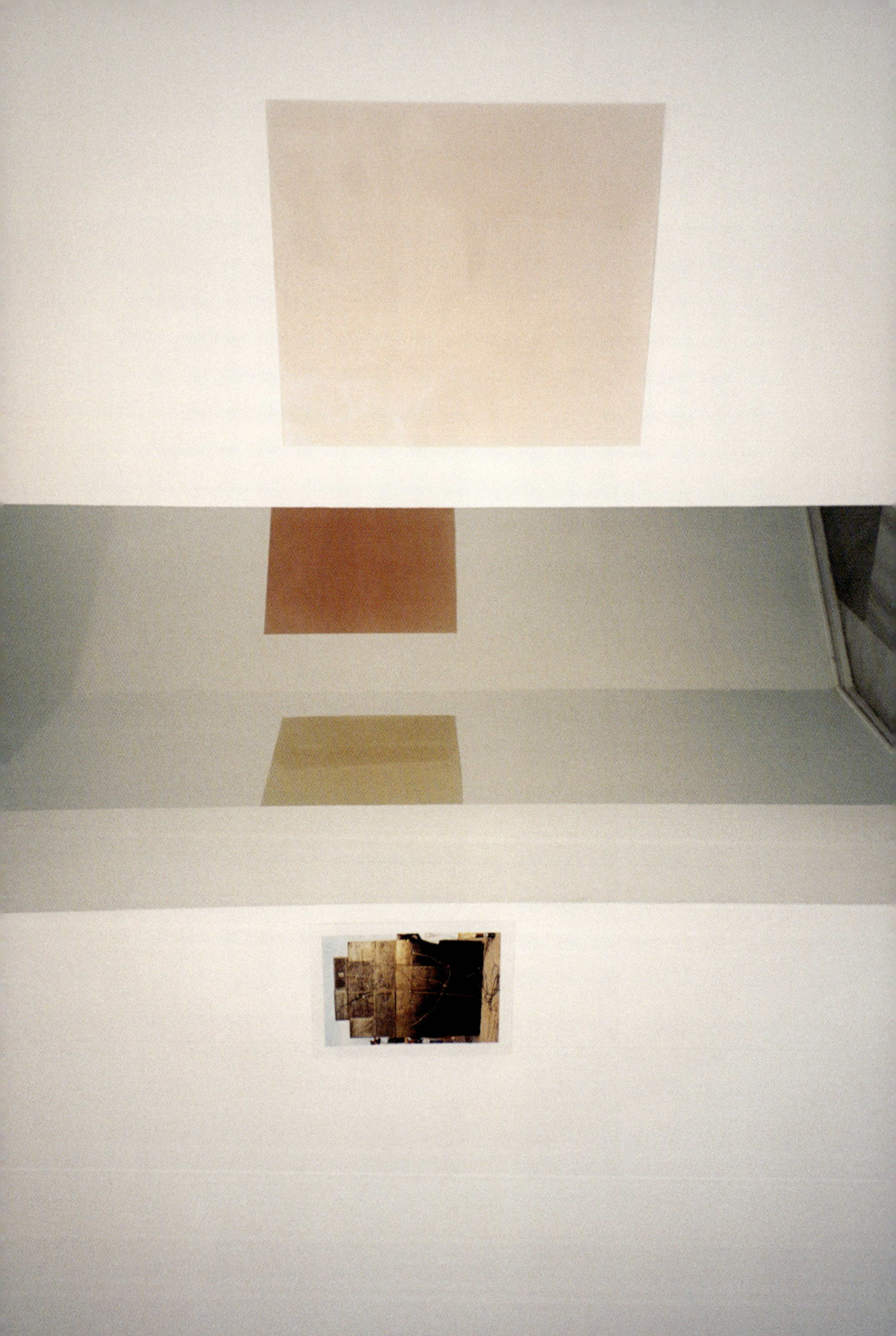

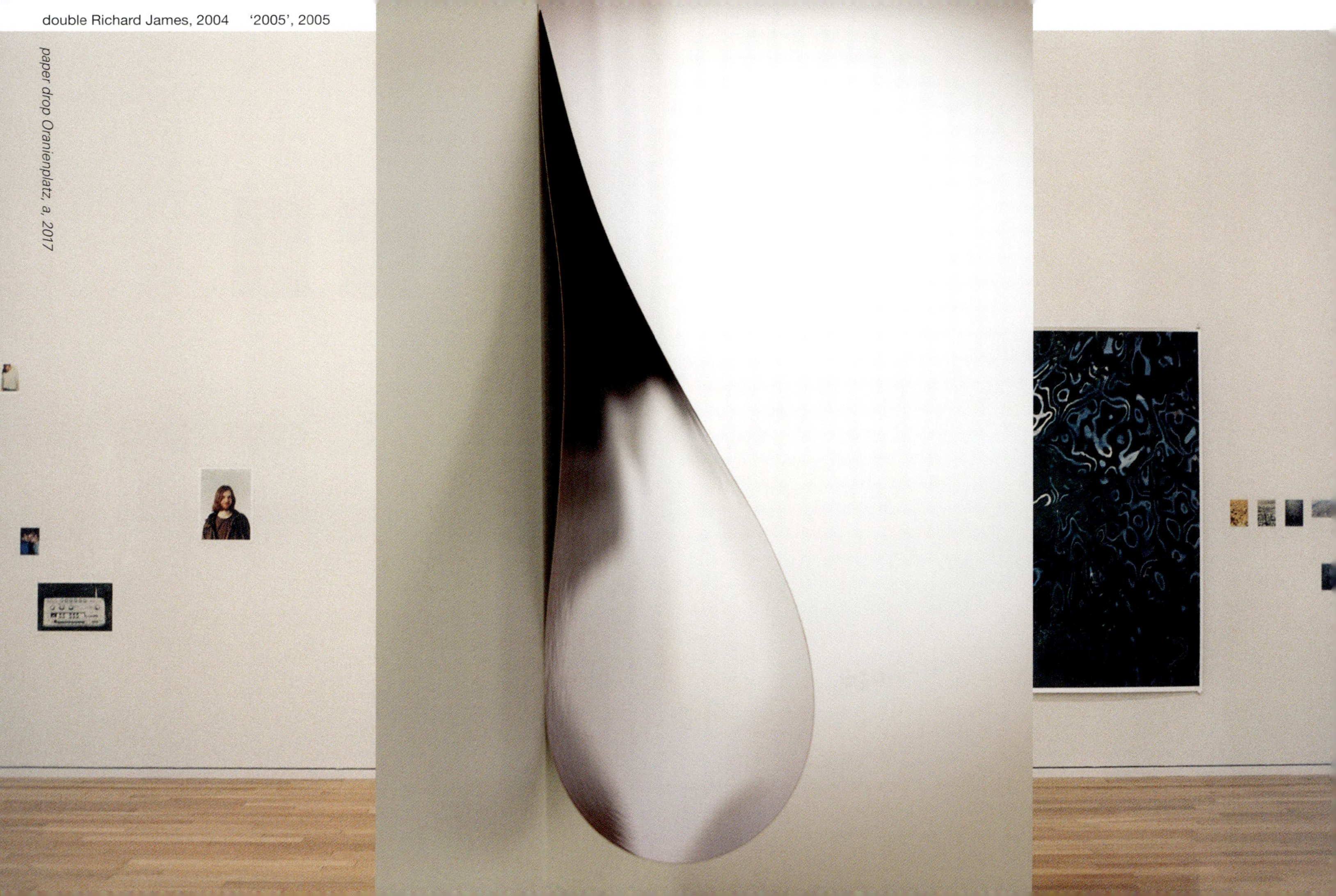

double Richard James, 2004   '2005', 2005

paper drop Oranienplatz, a, 2017

Silver Installation X, 2010   Installacion dos, 2005   impossible colour (green) a, 1997   Silver 36, 2004
Kinshasa still life, 2018   corrugated structure, 2019   Silver 37, 2004   impossible colour II, 2001

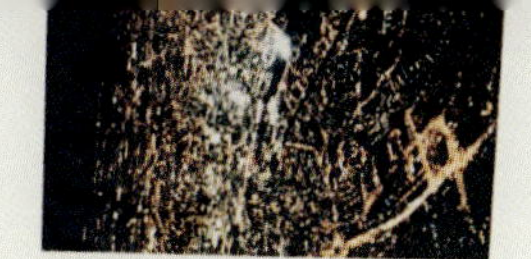
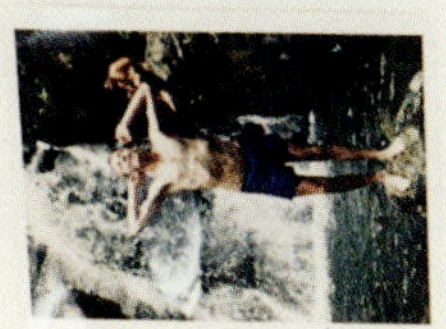
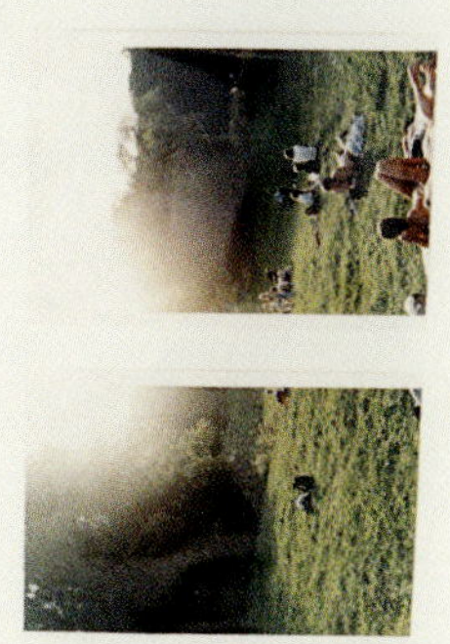
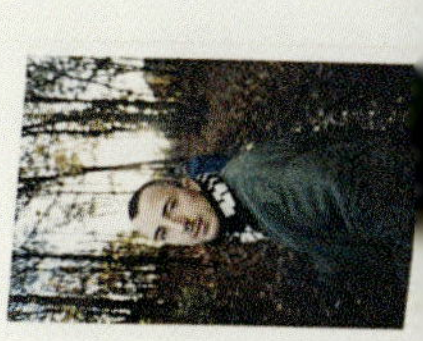

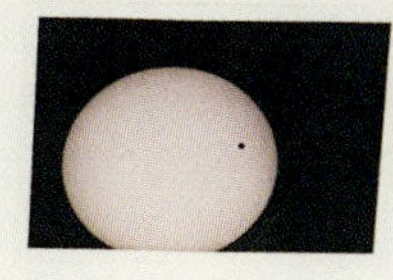
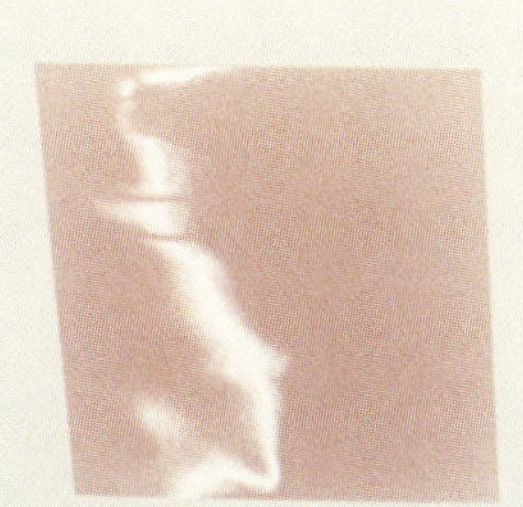
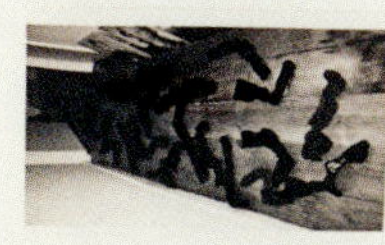
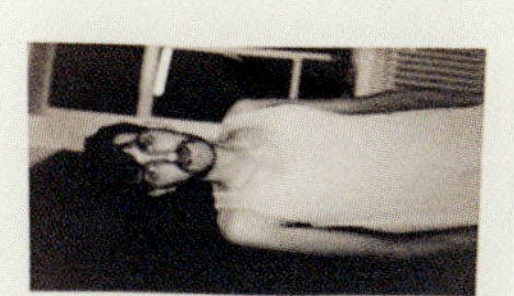
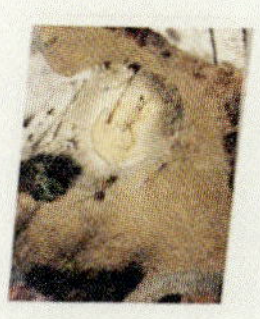
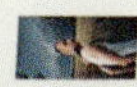

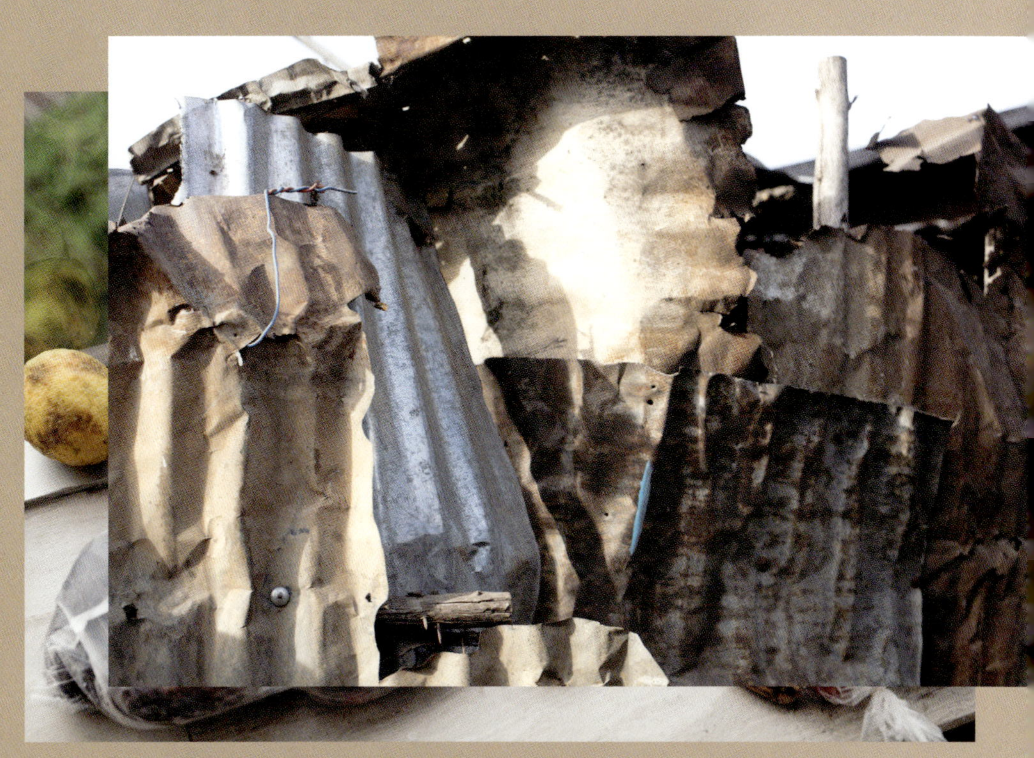

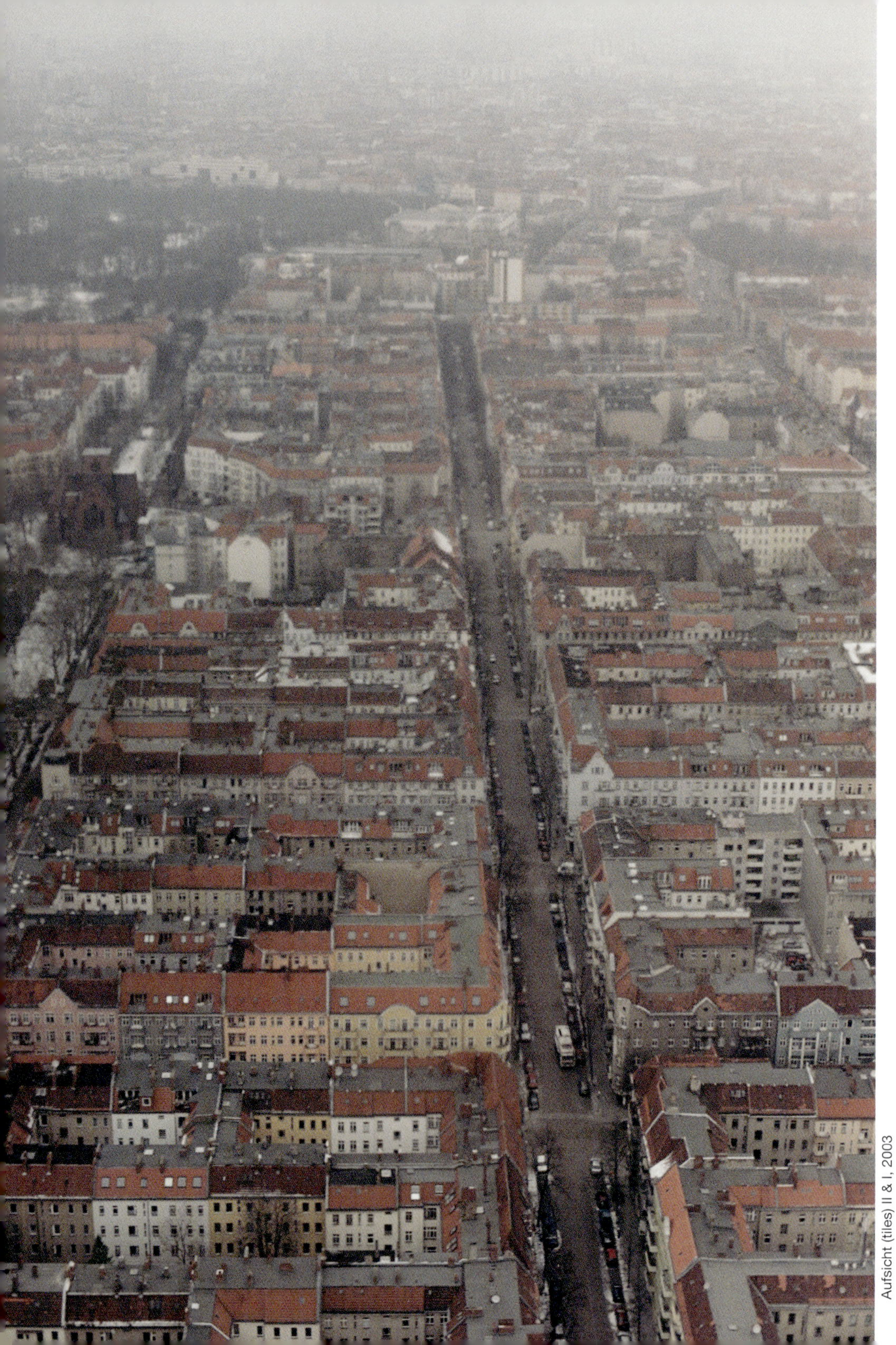

Aufsicht (tiles) II & I, 2003

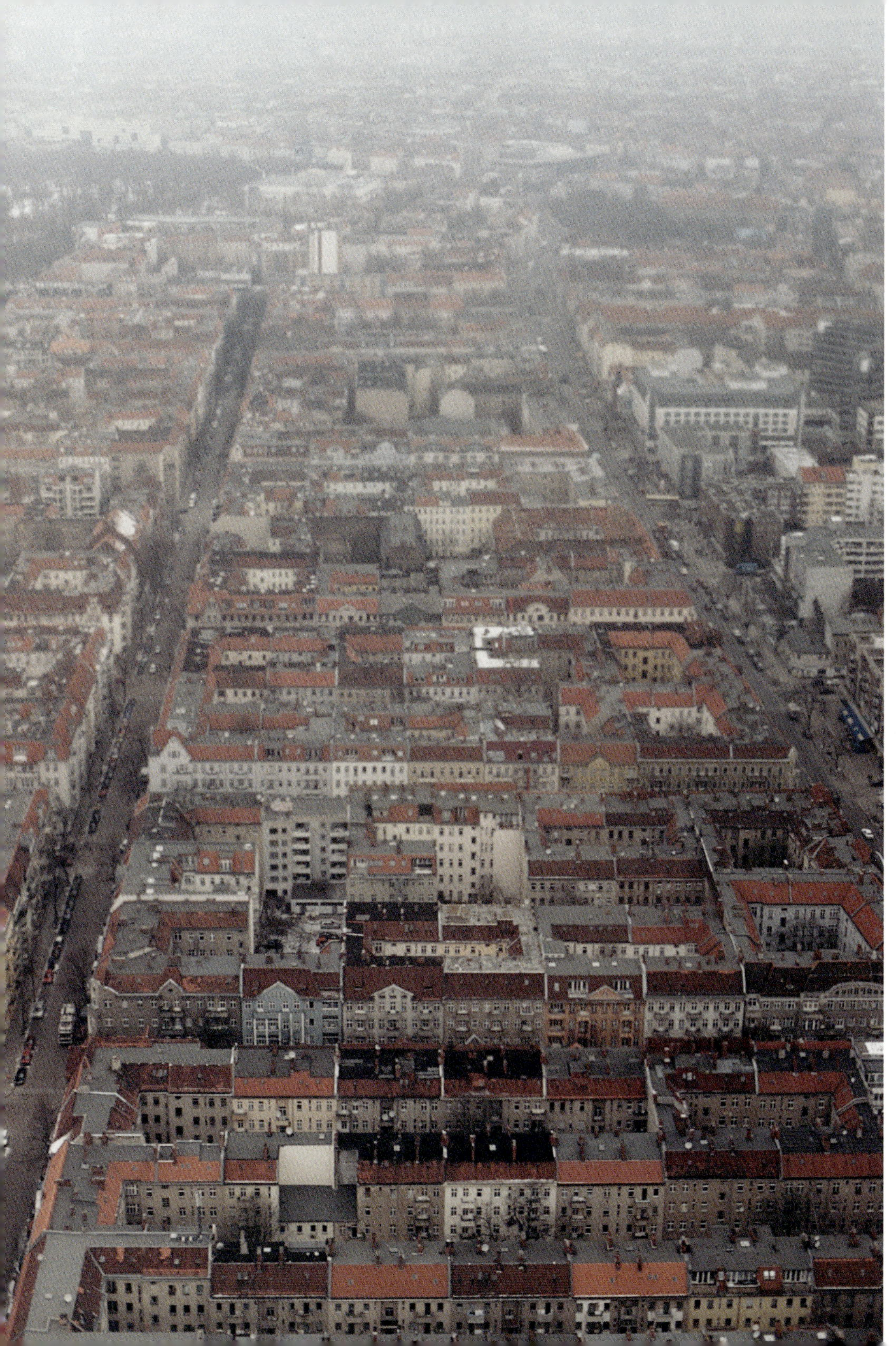

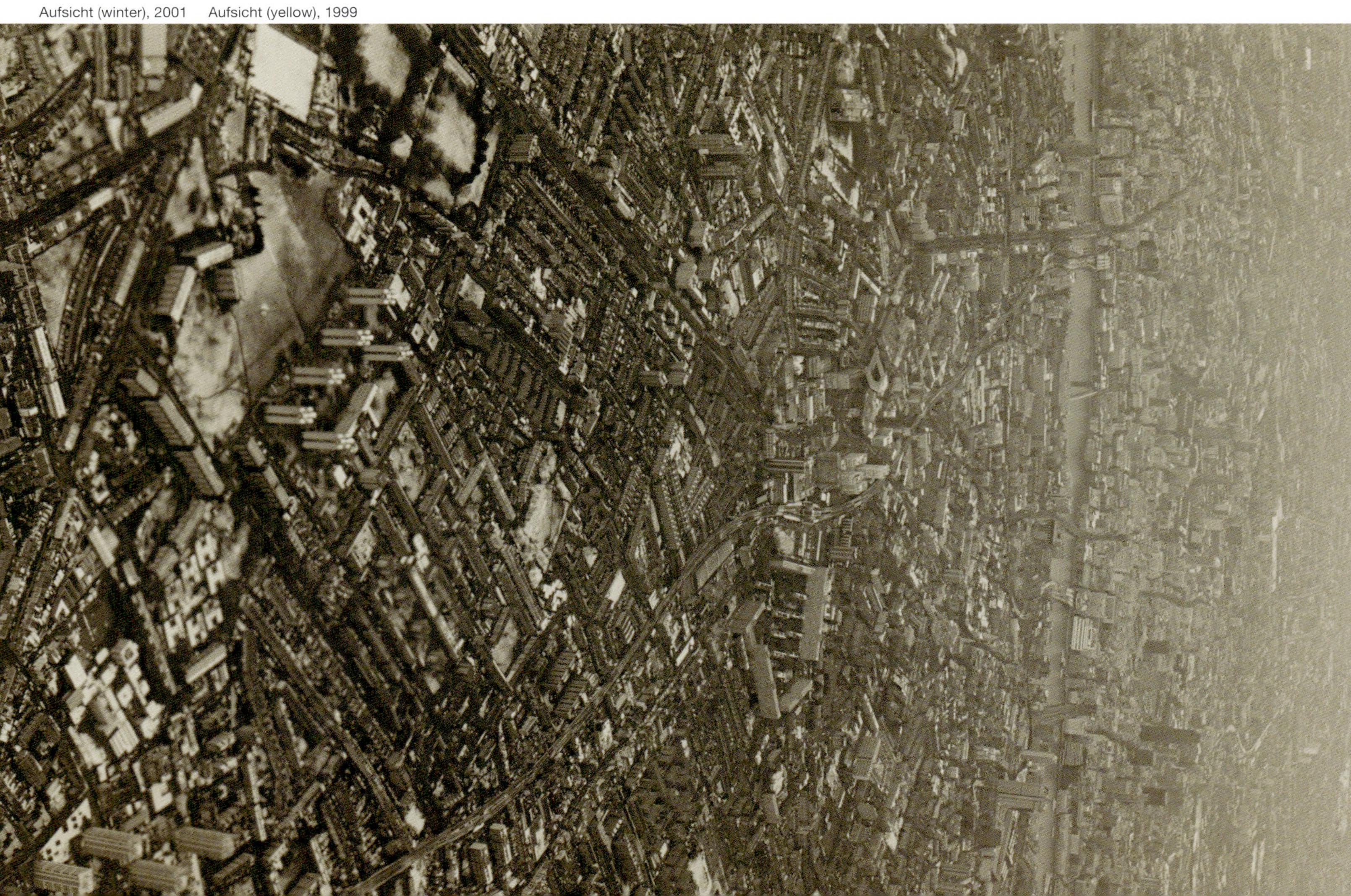

Aufsicht (winter), 2001　Aufsicht (yellow), 1999

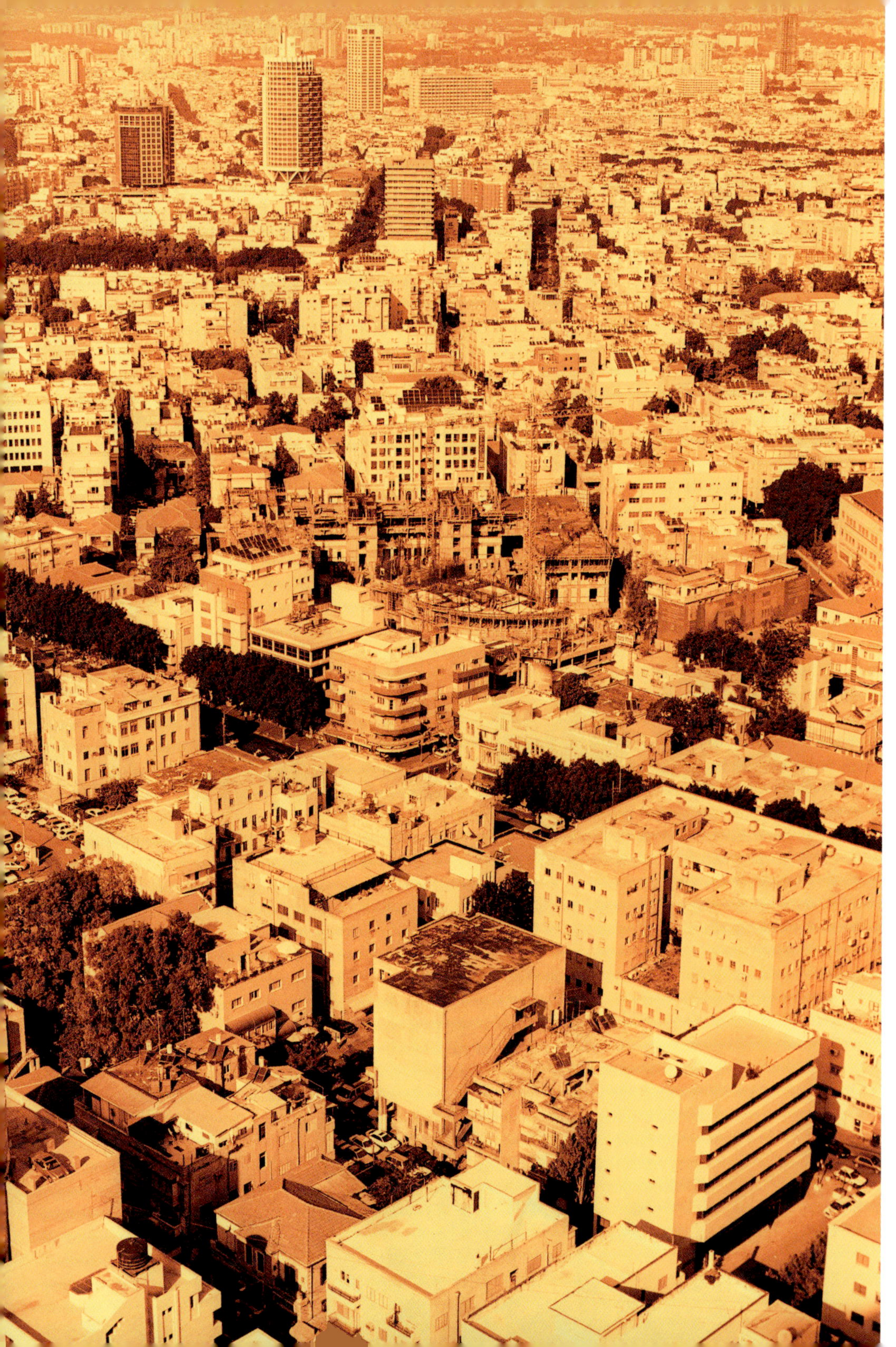

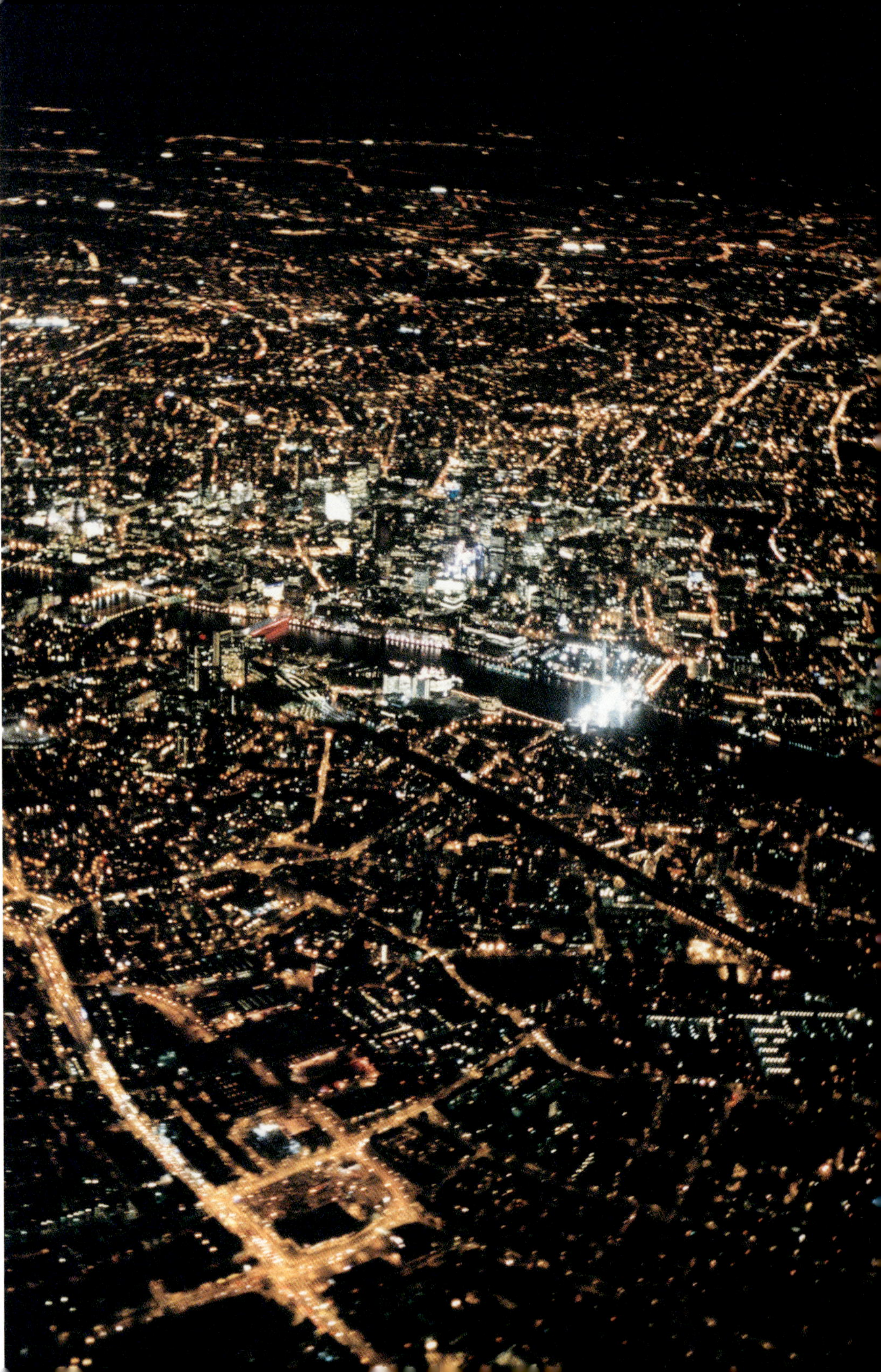

Germany Valley, West Virginia, 2017

The Colour of Money, 2004   suburban/urban, 1999

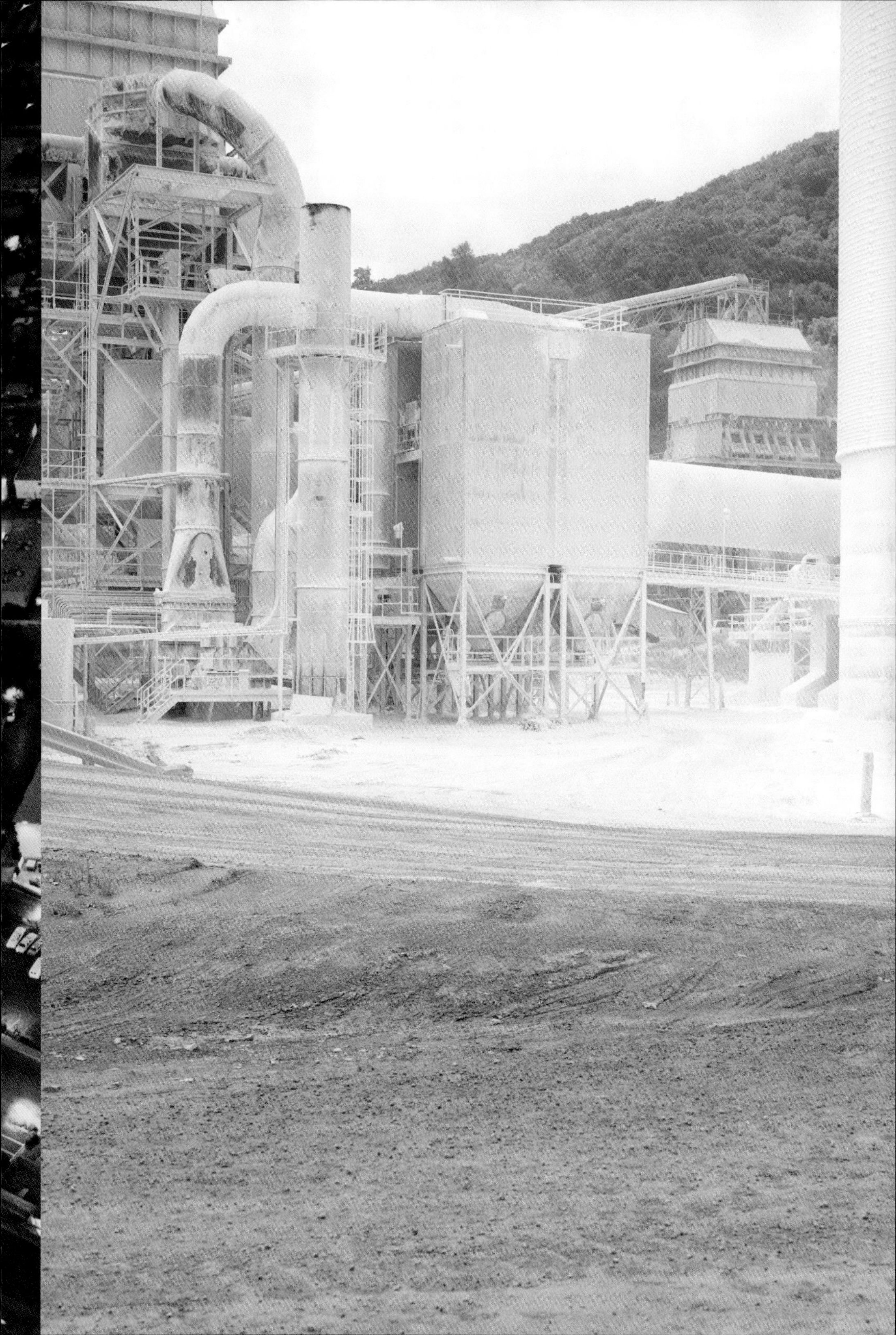

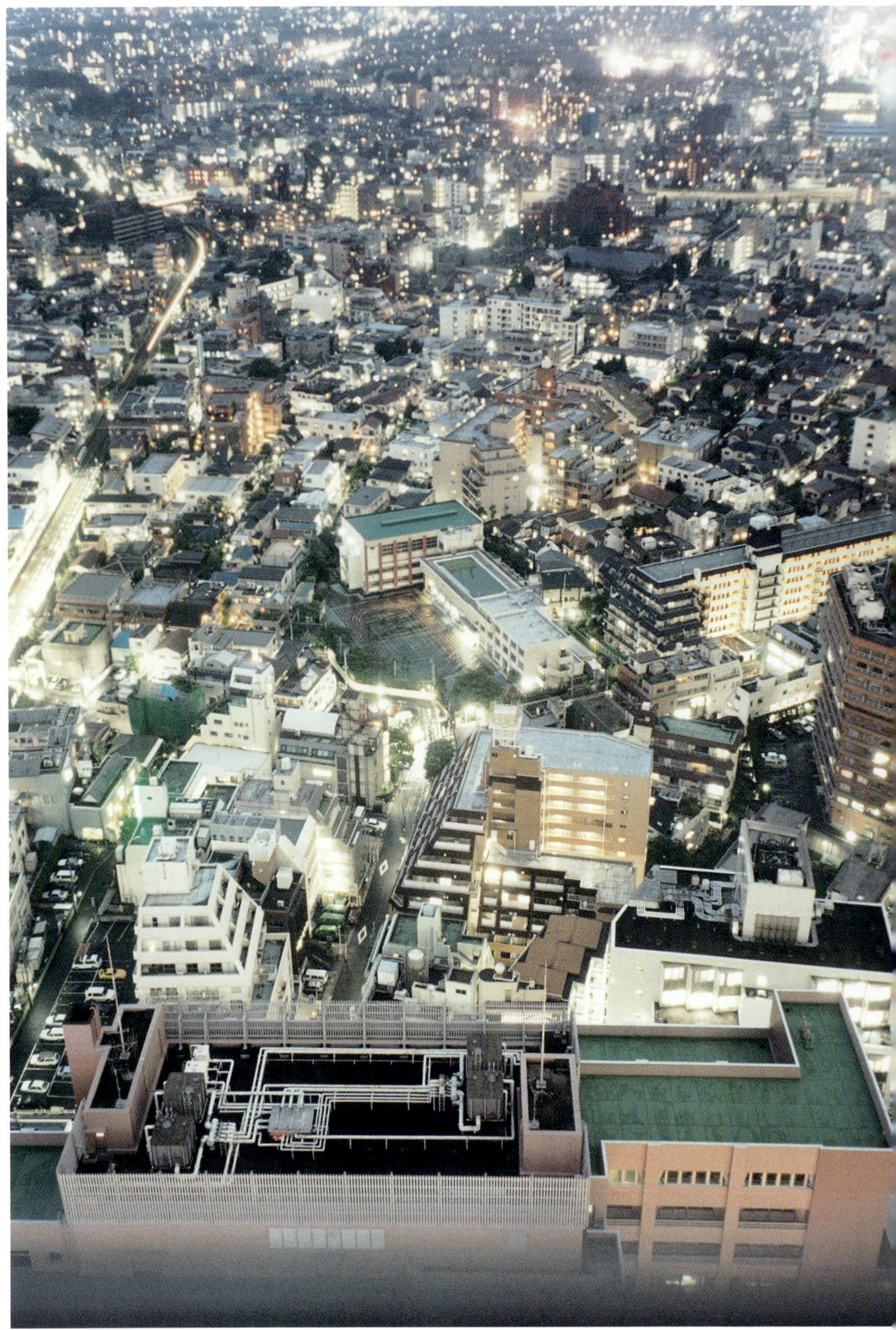

Aufsicht, green, 1999

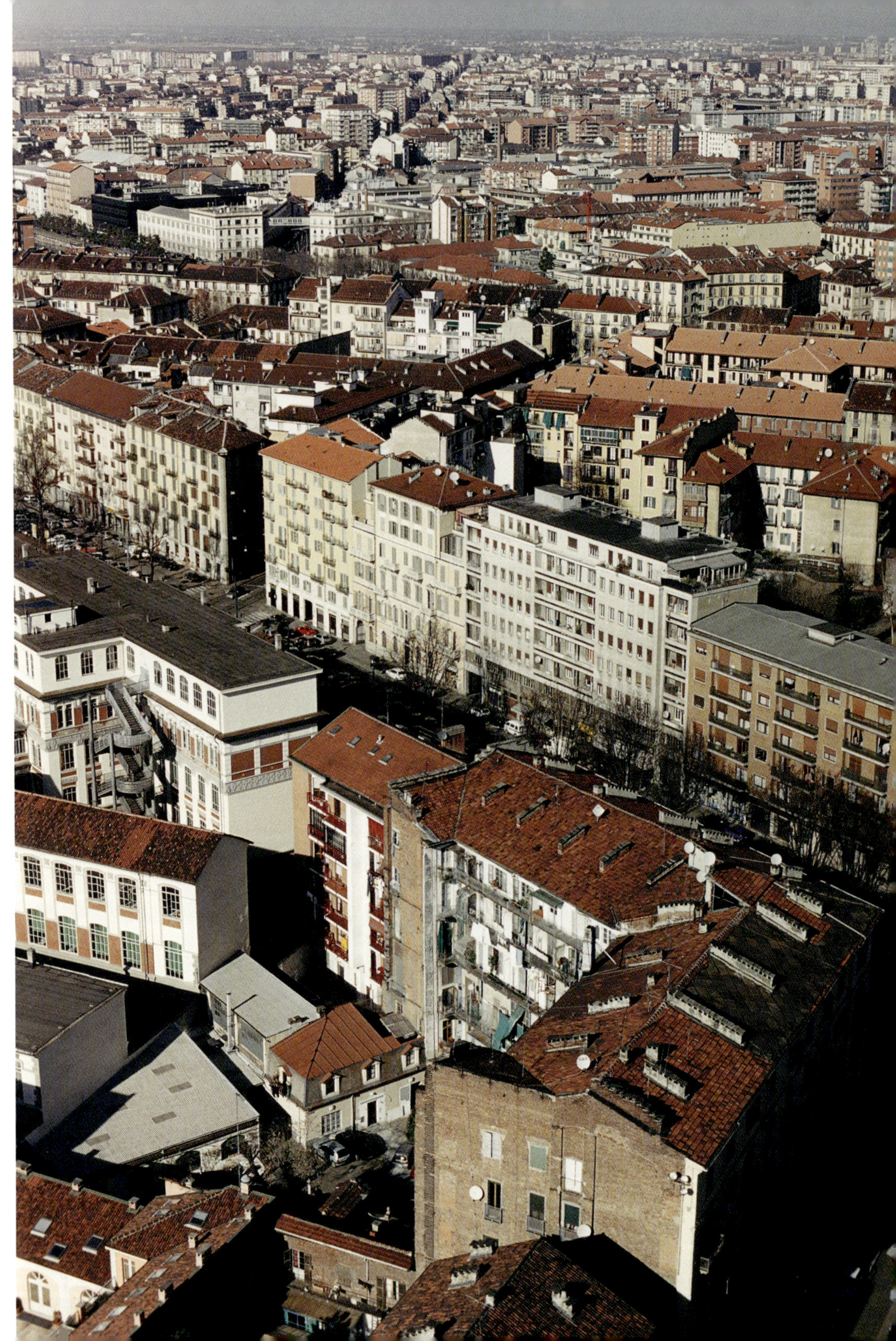

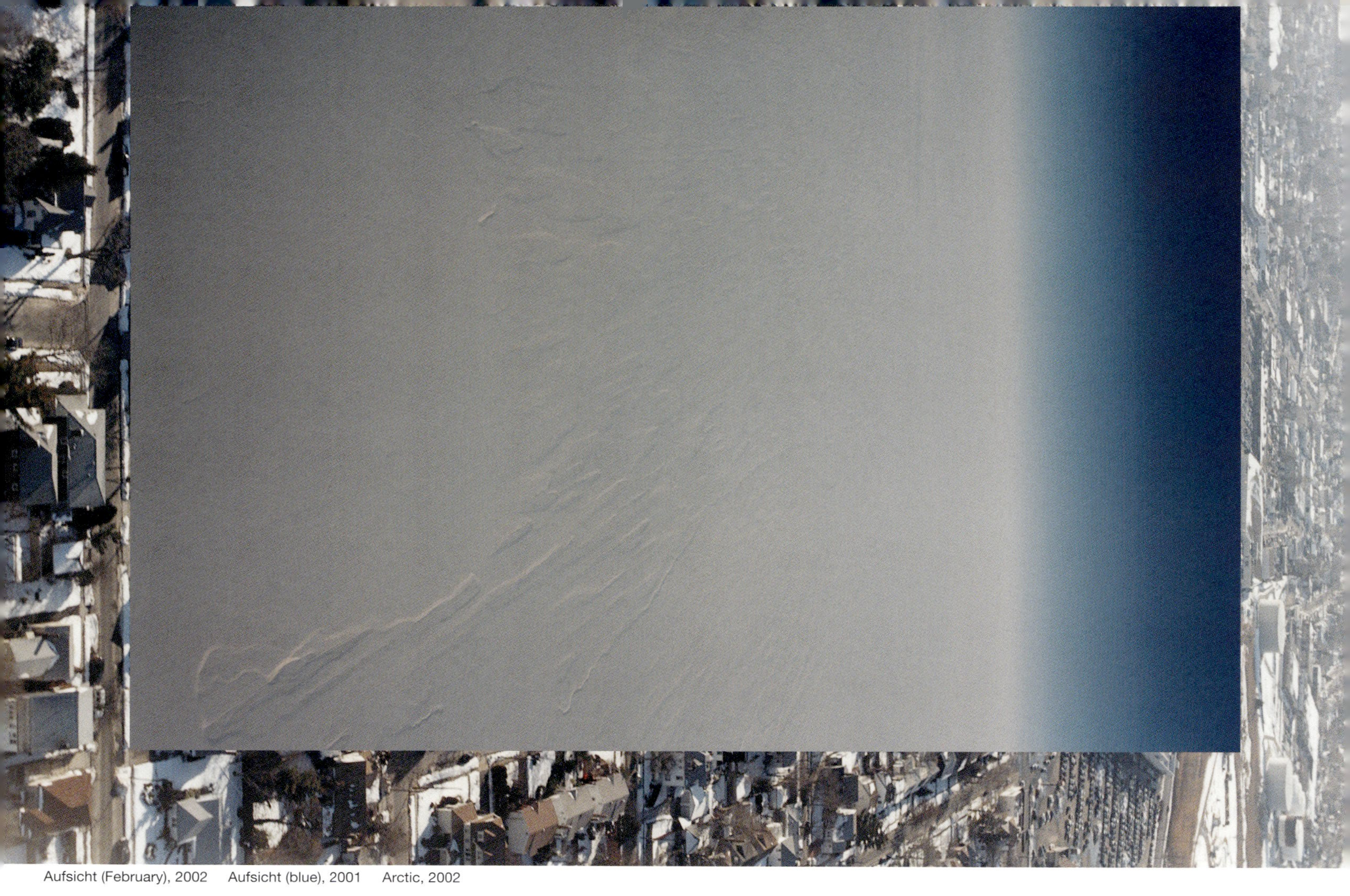

Aufsicht (February), 2002   Aufsicht (blue), 2001   Arctic, 2002

I don't want to get over you, 2000

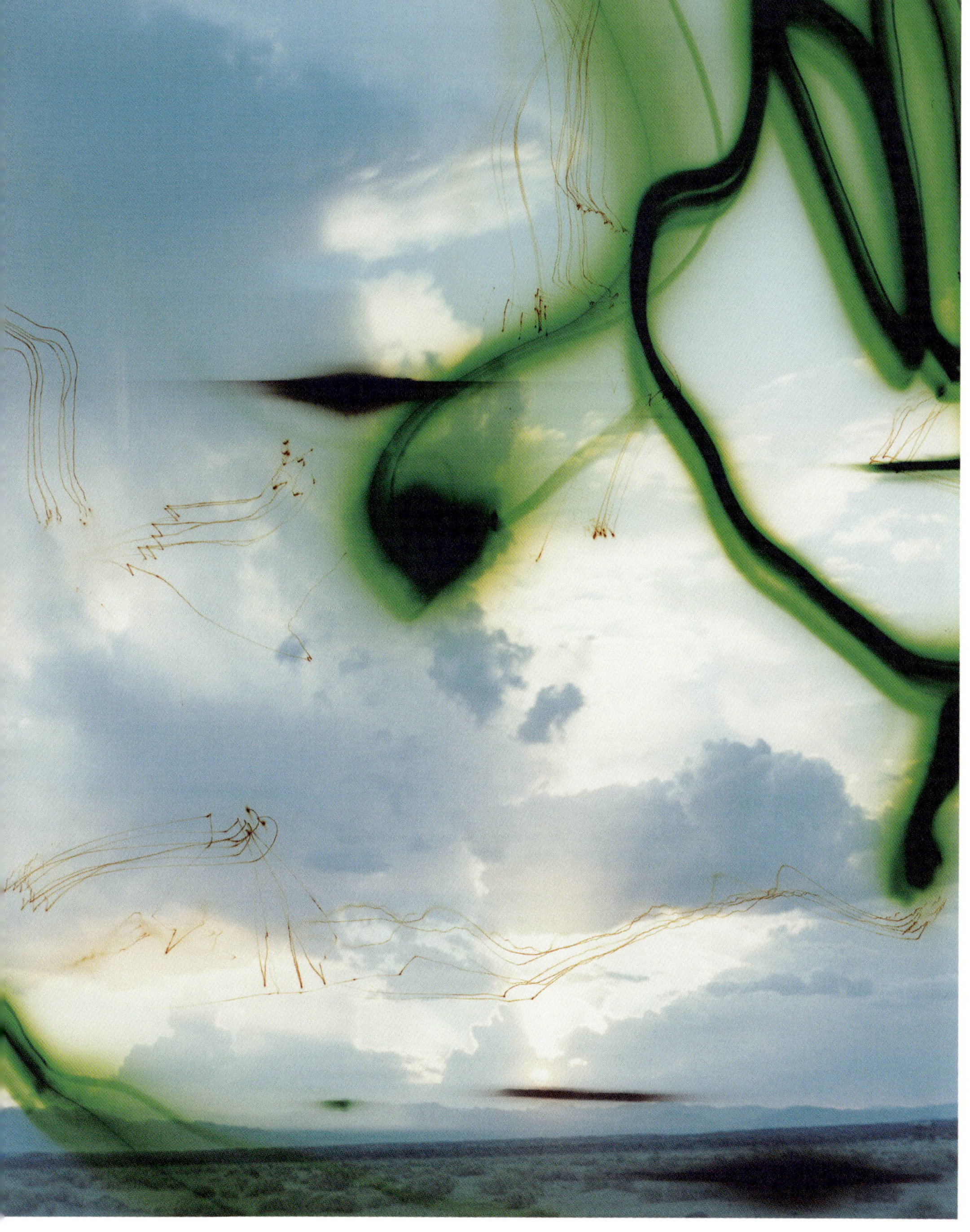

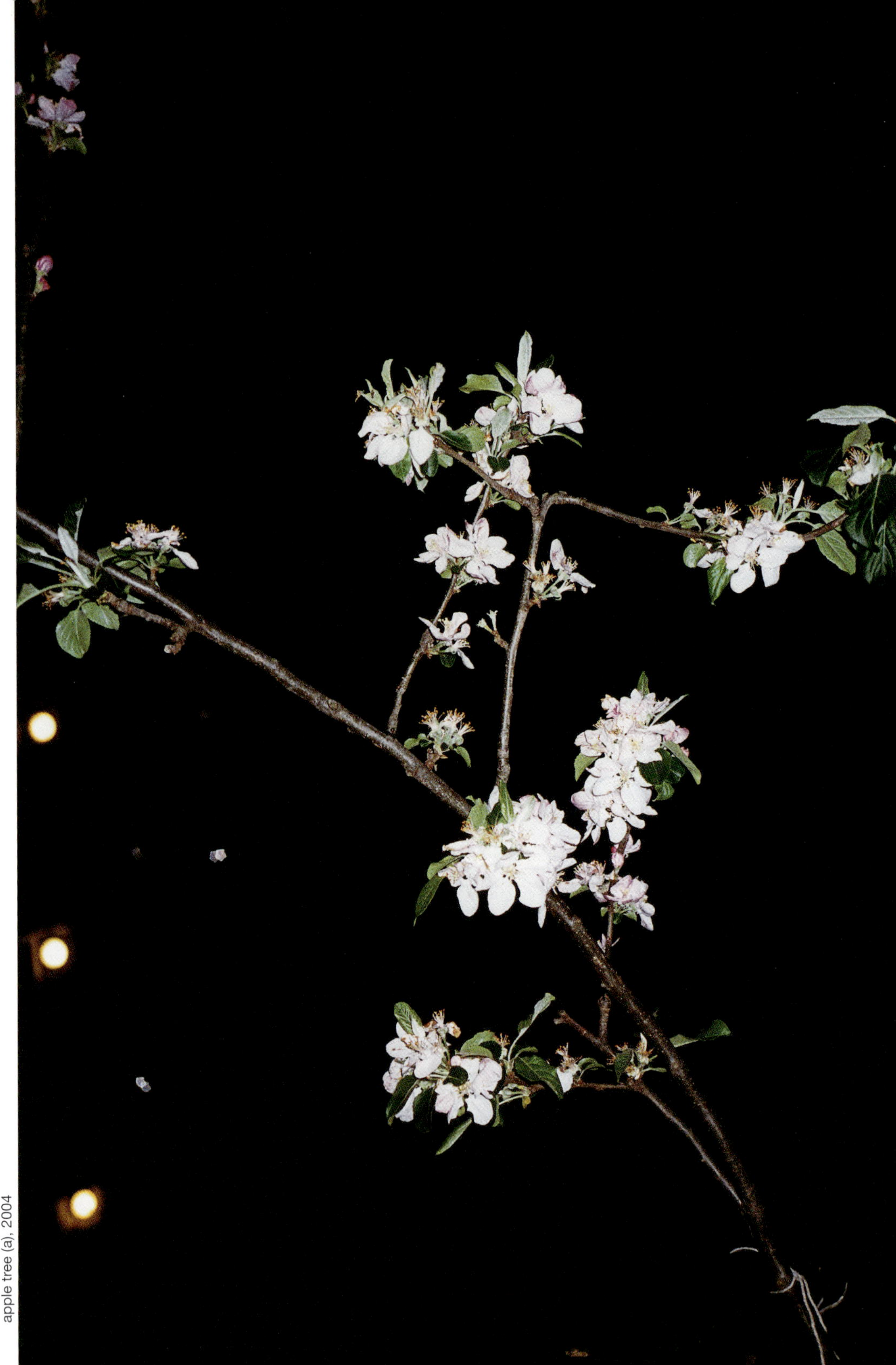

apple tree (a), 2004

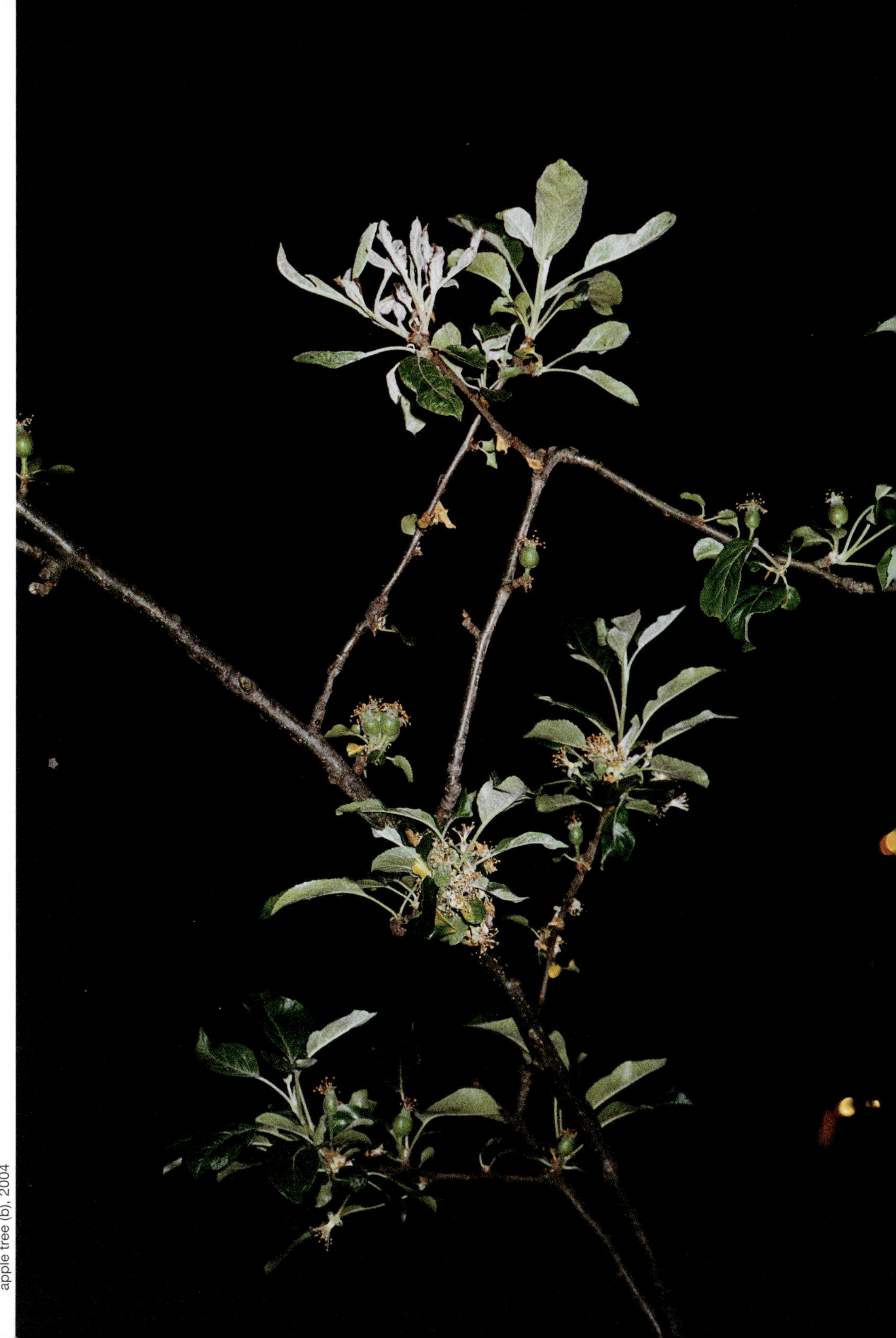

apple tree (b), 2004

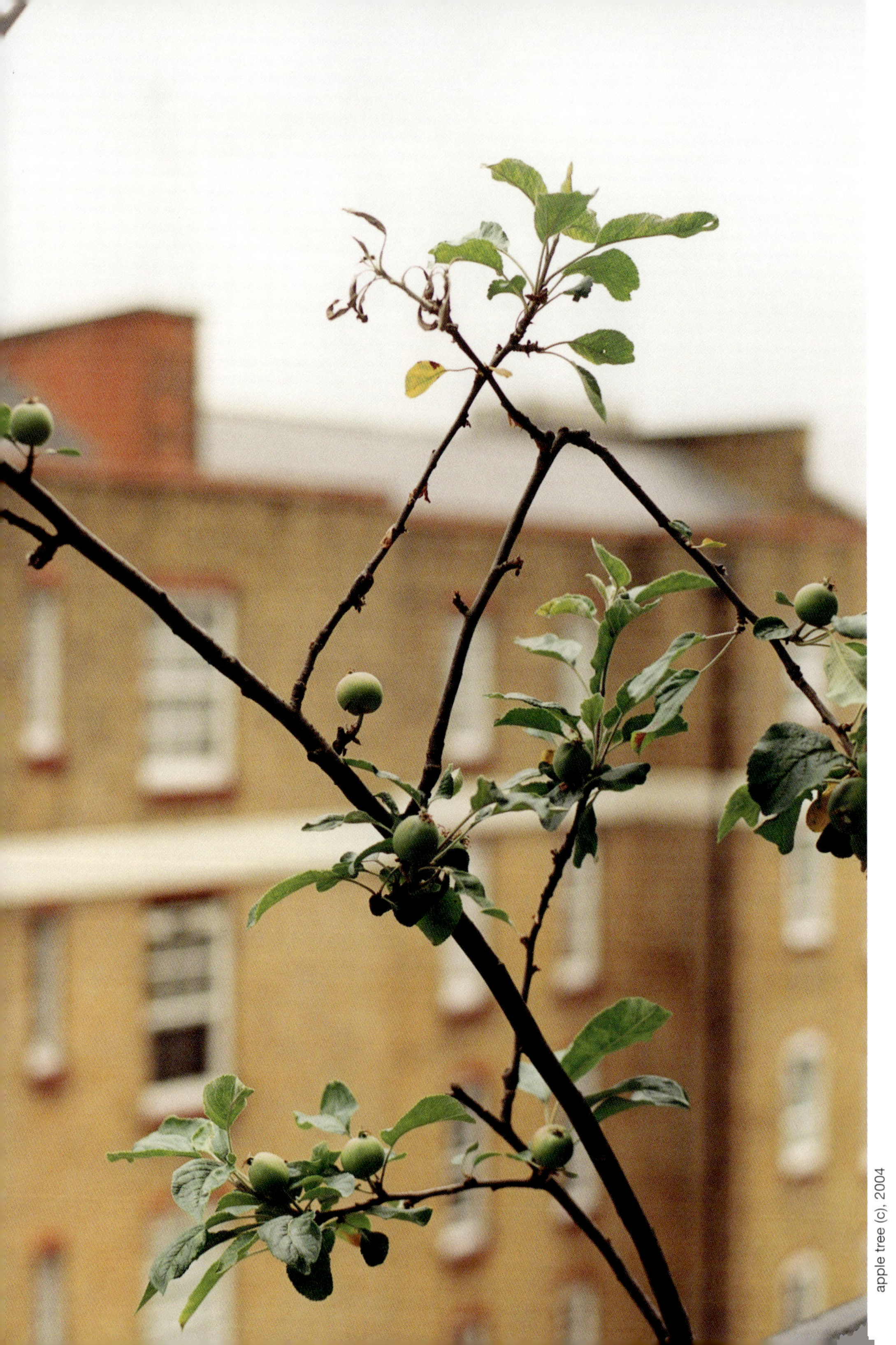

apple tree (c), 2004

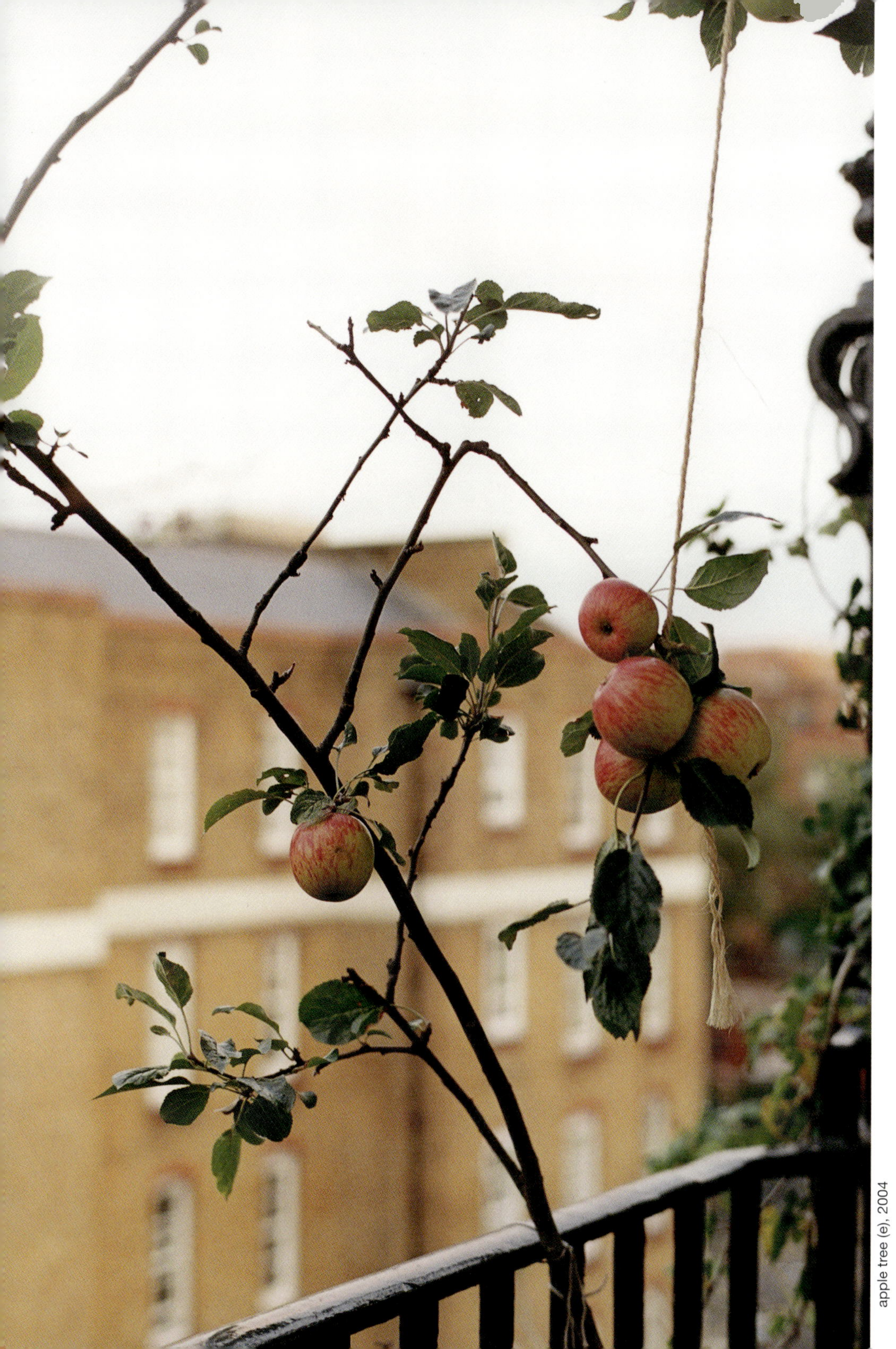

apple tree (e), 2004

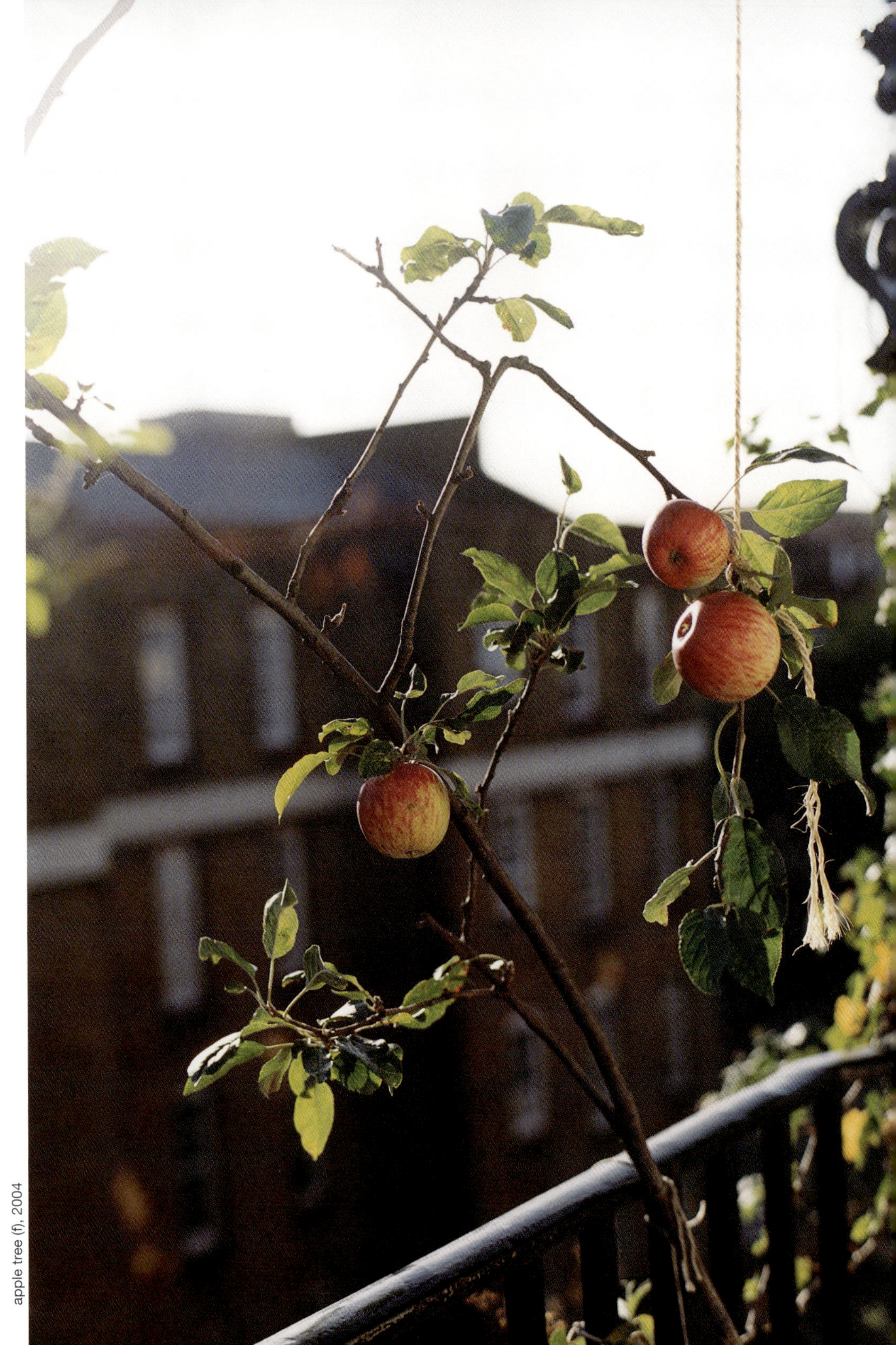

apple tree (f), 2004

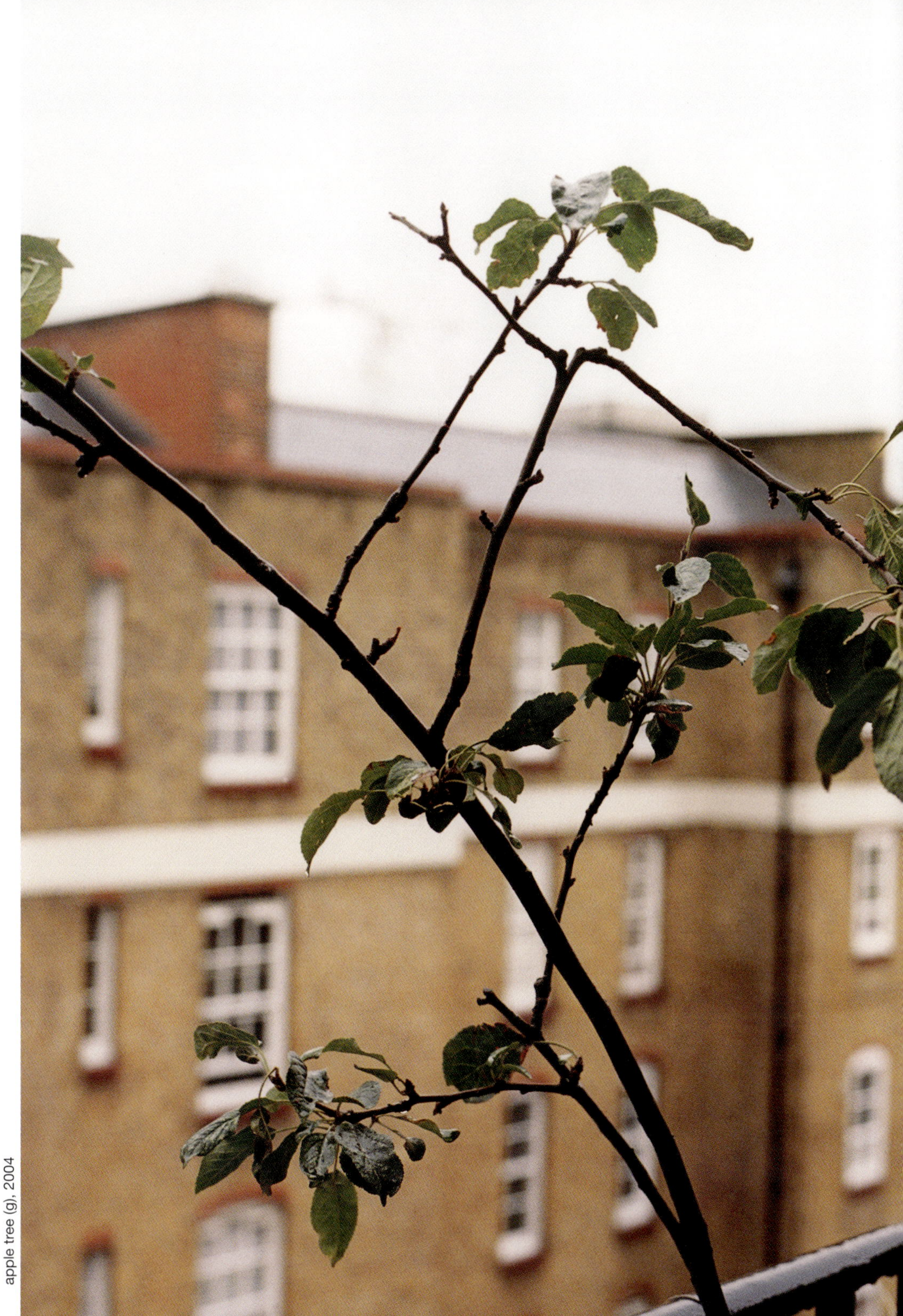

apple tree (g), 2004

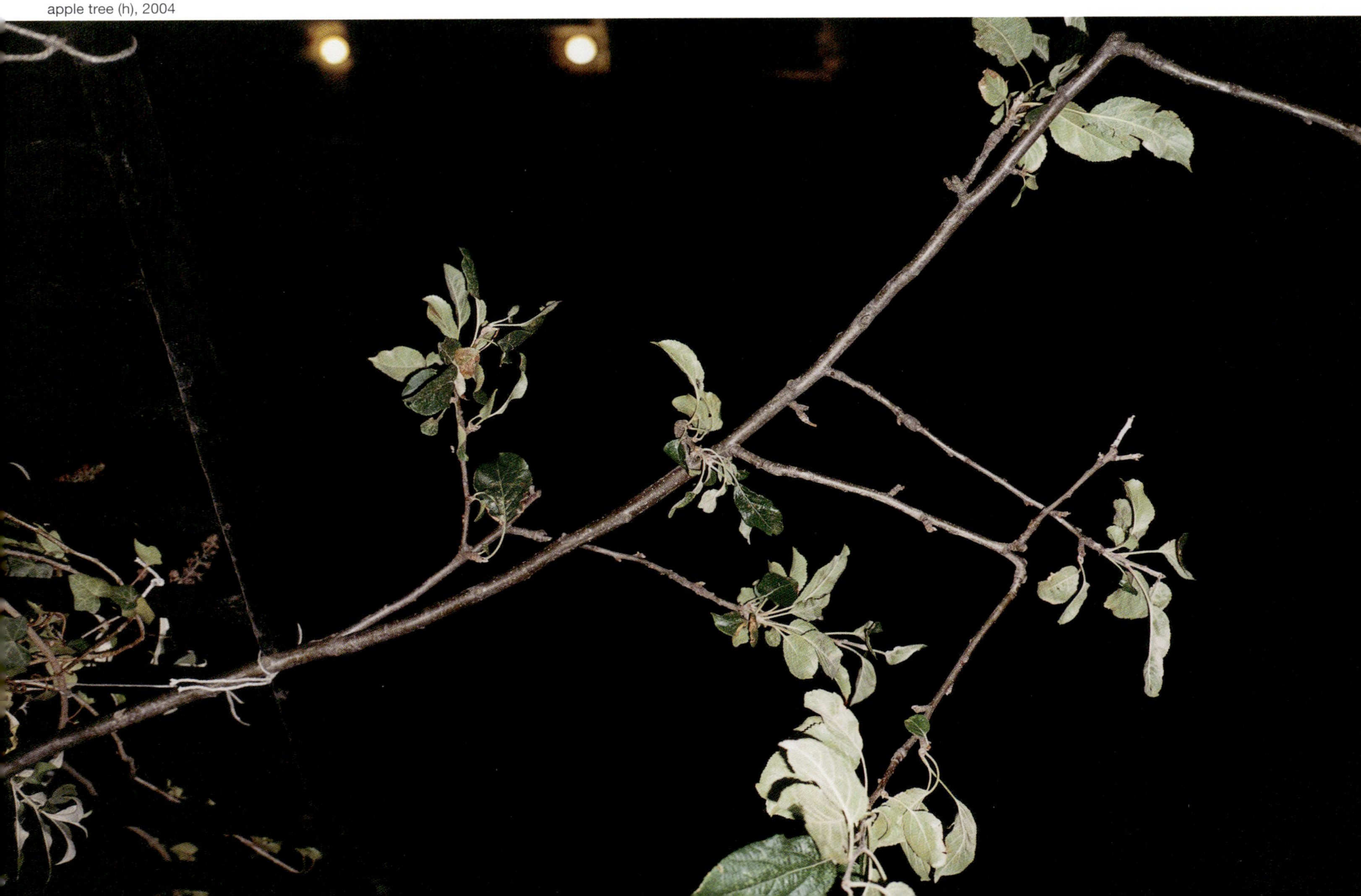

apple tree (h), 2004

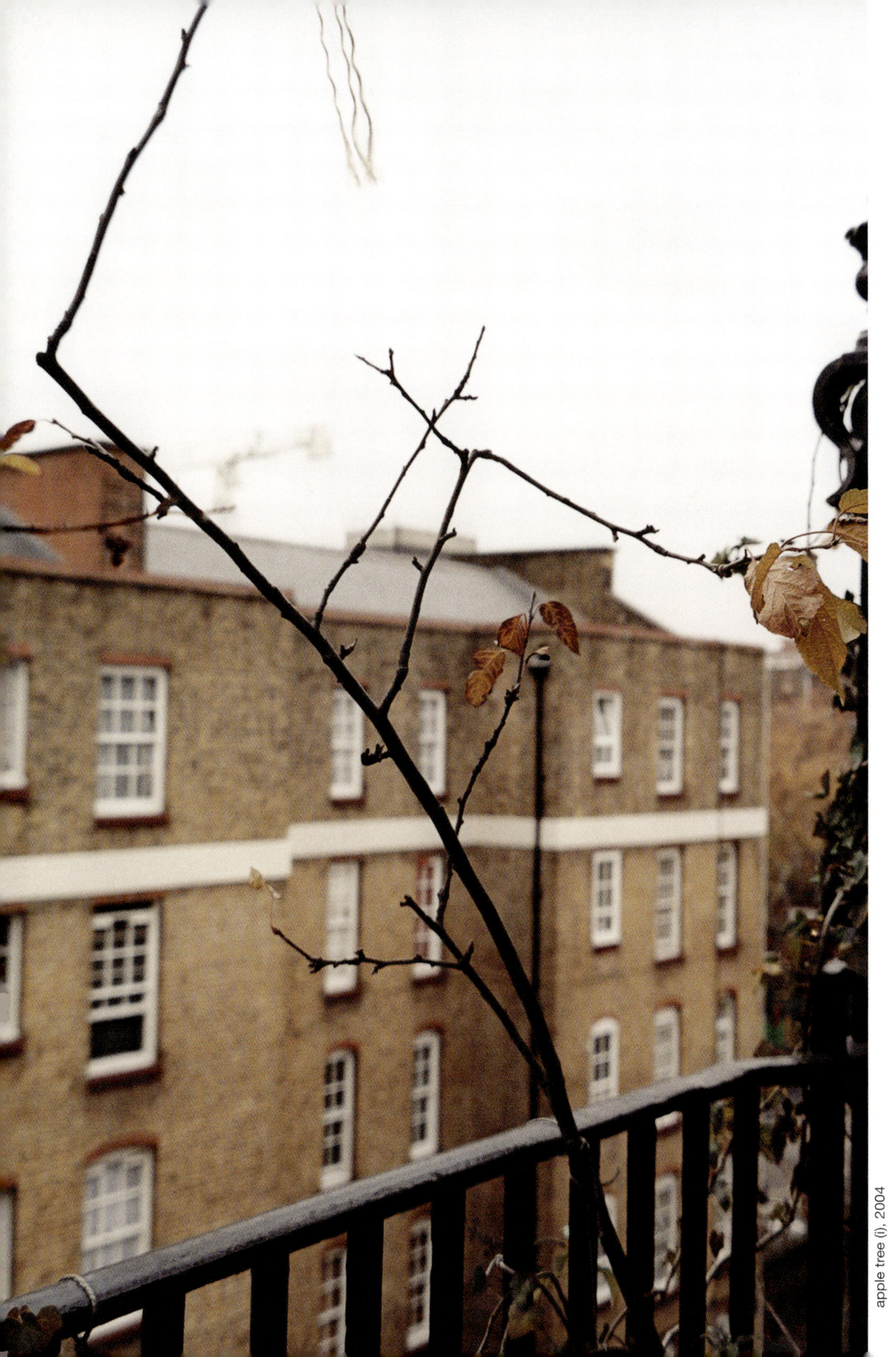

apple tree (i), 2004

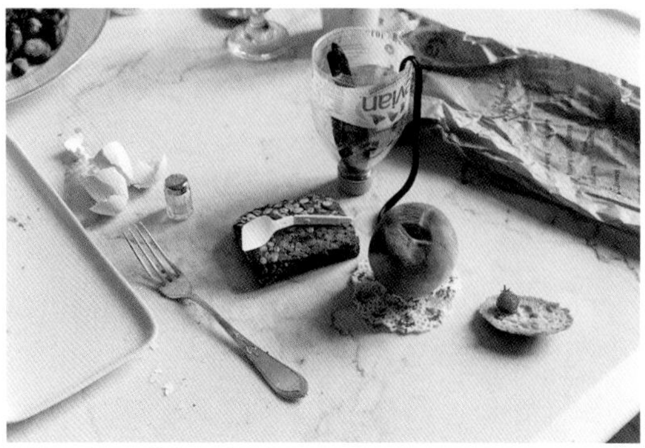

1 Schneckenstilleben, 2004

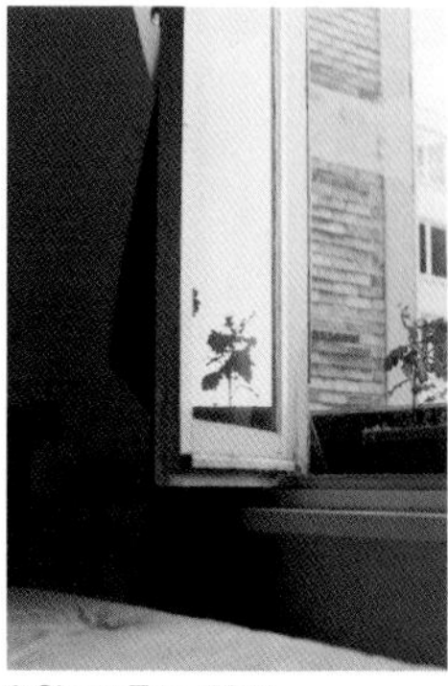

2 Sheet Two, 2001

Wolfgang Tillmans: The Art of Equivalence

Minoru Shimizu

The Politics of Everyday Life

Wolfgang Tillmans creates his photographs by carefully selecting, arranging, and manipulating the motif in order to express a consistent concept. This concept is the violation and transformation of the border between public and private.

Even when antiwar or anti-Nazi demonstrations appear as subject matter, Tillmans' concern is not the obvious, symbolic political events but the politics that are an unobtrusive part of everyday life. This sort of politics has an inherent tendency to self-concealment. A situation that people regard as natural without thinking deeply about it is actually produced by politics. If a person is gay, what does it mean to "come out" (or be made to "come out")? Isn't it just a kind of confession? Whether you like men or women is a private matter. Why make it public? Such a response may be considered natural, but it is a form of discrimination. Discrimination is always hidden in what seems natural. Coming out is not just a confession. It challenges a boundary, the line that is generally drawn between the public and the private, the things that one calls private and must be changed if one is to live as a gay person. Privacy is fundamentally a political concept. Etymologically, it is derived from the Latin word "privare," meaning "to deprive." There is no privacy that is not taken forcibly from the public realm. When we use the word "private," it is always based on the premise of public power. To problematize my privacy is to question the power relationships that have been hypothesized as natural in the past. This politics of private life is relevant to the condition of an alternative self or individuality in an age when egotism and individuality are best-selling products, the period from the 1990s to the present, in which capitalist societies have achieved dominance through the spread of information technology.

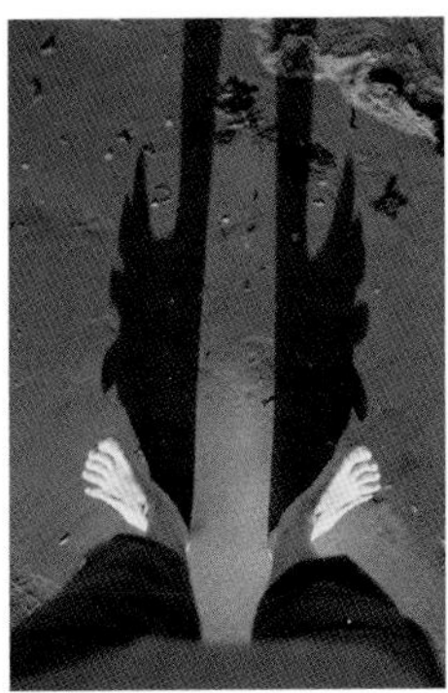

3 sunset feet, 2004

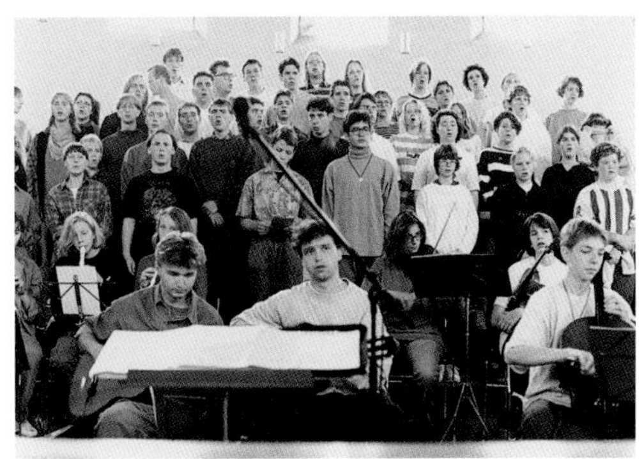

4 choir (Jubilate Deo), 1993

> The endless industry thirst for labels, trends, and fashions turns every individual style into another benign marketing plot. In a way I try to channel attention to the multi-layeredness of personality and identity …[1]

In contrast to the humorous, peaceful surface of Tillmans' work, its transformation and violation of the political structures and boundaries of everyday life has the ability to shock profoundly. This is because Tillmans is not concerned with creating a new independent ego as an alternative to the "self as consumer." By "multi-layeredness," he does not mean that a person has many different faces. His concept of multilayeredness is not oriented toward the establishment of differences and divisions, that is, the establishment of separate identities, but arises from the transformation and violation of these divisions and boundaries. His aim is to break up the outlines of people's identities, making them coexist and fuse with the outlines of others, thus creating multiple layers. Tillmans' political principle is not the principle of difference or identity but the principle of "sameness."[2] He does not see every person as different but views (not identifies) each arbitrary entity as being equivalent to and the same as every other arbitrary entity. "Sameness" is a concept that opposes "identity." This sameness is scandalous because it subverts the idea of individual character.

Tillmans' work can be divided into five main categories, which are best understood in terms of this concept.

1. Photographs that "perform" the conditions of an alternative, utopian lifestyle: *Faltenwurf* (the creases and folds of clothing that has been taken off),[3] still lifes (fig. 1), window planters, nudes, friends, models, etc.

> It (the European club culture of the eighties) definitely seemed to be for a better society, a better understanding, it was a utopian ideal of togetherness. That's how living together could be: being peaceful and enjoying the senses. It seemed a very tangible and inherently political thing to me.[4]

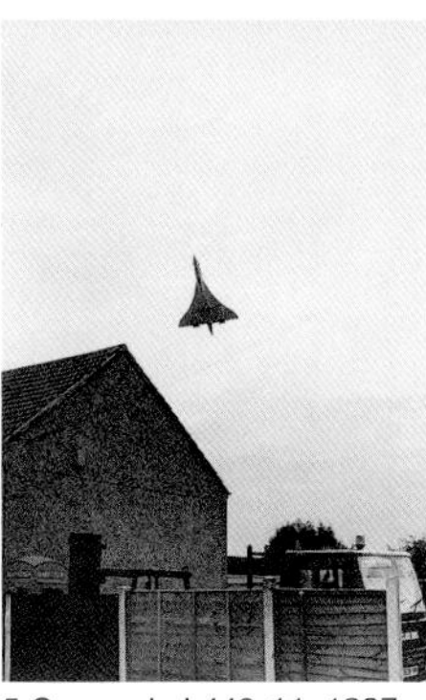

5 Concorde L449-11, 1997

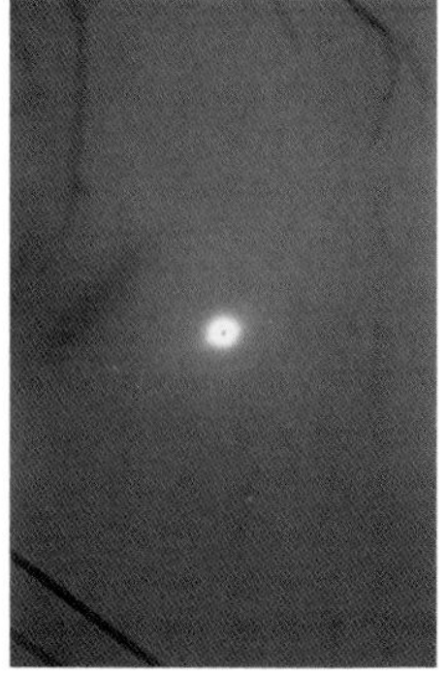

6 Total Solar Eclipse Aruba, 1998

2. Performative strategies. Adding or inserting something (for example, a penis) to a given situation as an element that oversteps boundaries: the *Concorde* series (fig. 5), photographs in which part of his own body (a self-portrait) appears, the stuffed mouse doll picture. Intervention in the developing process, changing colors in the printing process.

3. Becoming one: "This idea of melting into one … That idea of being together, of fusion."[5] Direct physical expression of a sense of fusion (fig. 4). Games such as Knotenmutter, in which bodies are pressed together. Embracing lovers, political demonstrations, soldiers.

4. Sameness: photographs in which the same situation is shared by many people. For example, images of uniforms (military uniforms, work clothes), astronomical phenomena (comets, eclipses (fig. 6), sunsets), "views from above," in which it is possible to see and be seen in a comprehensive way, crowded underground cars (figs. 8, 9, 18), world events (such as 9/11).

> But maybe part of my idea of nothingness is that ultimately everything is pretty much the same in terms of physical presence. In other words, even the most uninteresting stuff … is actually physically as present as a diamond, or as a person …

> I think one of the unifying things is that they are a representation of an unprivileged gaze or view. "The unprivileged view" may be applied to all my works.

> I have always associated the Underground with incredible intimacy among people, without them wanting to be intimate with each other. It's a weird phenomenon, whereby men and women standing incredibly close to each other and looking into each other's shirts and ears and hair is acceptable, and we've all decided not to think it odd as a sensual experience because a taboo is at work.[6]

5. Portraits: Tillmans' working concept is to break down the outlines of identity and personality, leading to a multilayered condition, violating and transforming boundaries between self and others,

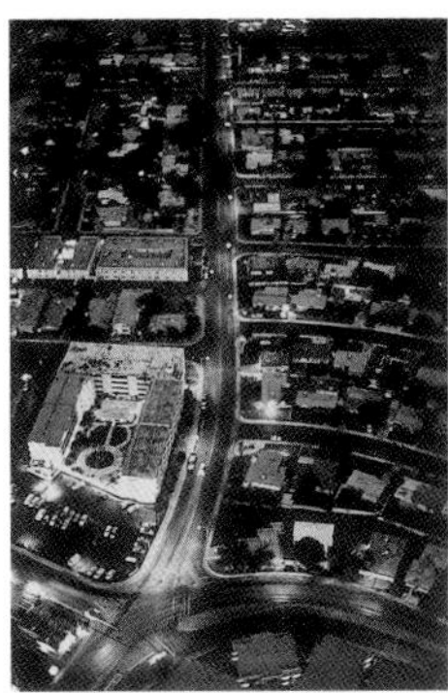

7 suburban/urban, 1999

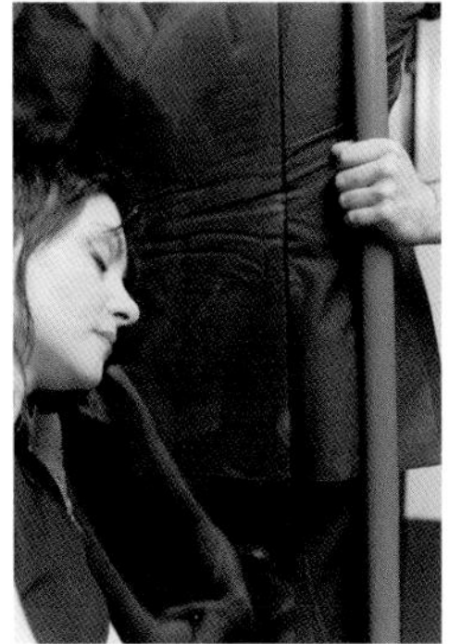

8 Victoria Line, glass partition, 2000

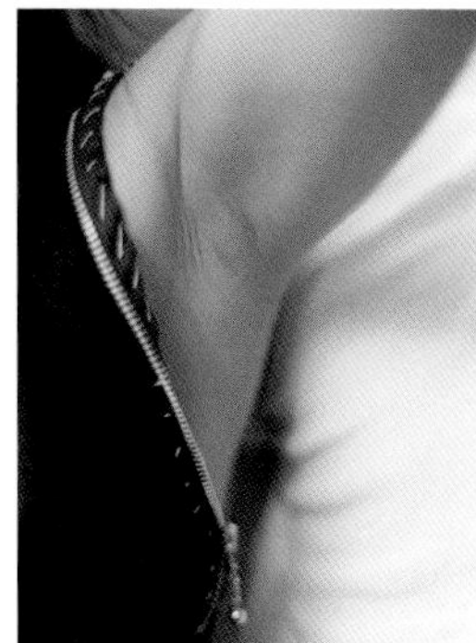

9 Circle Line, 2000

and making everything "one" and "the same." In this context, the essence of portraiture can be expressed by the word "vulnerability": that is, the fragility and vulnerability of the outlines of a human being, and the vulnerability and insecurity of accepting multilayeredness. He has spoken of this as follows:

> I think, corny as this sounds, I need to love, respect, or in some way to embrace all the people that I photograph. That really is a very, very strong criterion, so when asked about who do you photograph it really boils down to that sort of essential sympathy ... For a person to communicate this basic fragility and insecurity—to me, as I do to him or her—is the foundation of most of my pictures. I can really say that nothing bores me more in people than the assumption of security and certainty.[7]

In his portraits, the outlines of identity are distorted. The subject of the photograph is opened up and broken down, turning into a variety of equivalent things.

> Nearer still to nature—and the multiplicity of these analogies is itself all the more natural in that the same man, if we examine him for a few minutes, appears in turn a man, a man-bird, a man-fish, a man-insect ...[8]

> What I always look for are the complexities within people.[9]

Photographs about Photographs

Born in 1968, Tillmans belongs to a generation that has grown up surrounded by proliferating media images. His photographs have their origin in the act of looking at photographs rather than capturing the real world with them. This essential quality means that Tillmans' photographs are far removed from snapshots that document reality.

> No one now can be unselfconscious of photographs taken before. There is an encyclopedia of representation that is in our heads almost from the day we were born.[10]

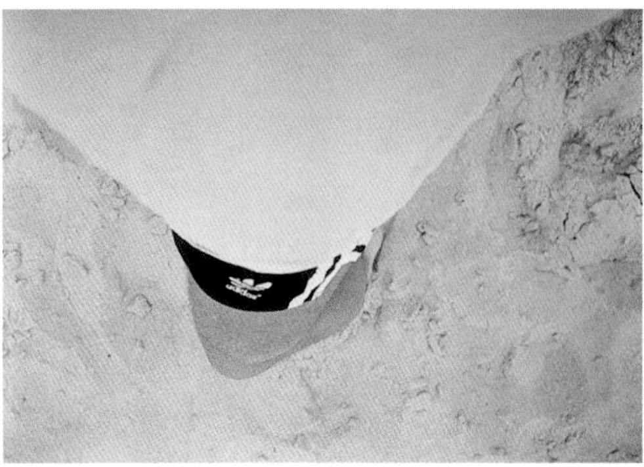

10 Lacanau (self), 1986

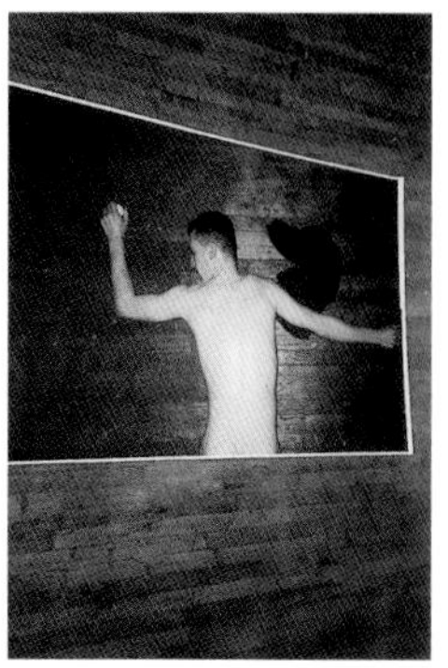

11 Paul, arm right angle,
on floor, 1995

In Tillmans' case, this statement refers to a synchronicity in taking and looking at photographs rather than visual intertextuality. There is no opposition between the photographer and the subject. They are one. The position that Tillmans takes as a photographer is to be half photographer and half subject. His work is based on the idea that the viewer is the photographer or, to put it another way, part of the photographer is always in the photograph.

In this context, a photograph does not capture and preserve something in the real world; it is the photograph that the artist wanted to see. "Seeing" a photograph is a complex experience. It cannot be summed up in such simple terms as "framing," "freezing," or "mapping" reality. That is, even if Tillmans adopts the utopian sensibility of youth culture, as represented by raves, his work is not fundamentally intended to reflect the worldview, life awareness, zeitgeist, or esthetic sensibility of a particular generation. Nor does it aim to pick out fresh bits of everyday life.

> That it happens now, here, this second, doesn't make it any better or more authentic. I think that is what I wanted to say …[11]

> I am not gathering memories. The point is not to possess or experience something by seizing it with the camera.[12]

In "taken" photographs, the subject and the photographer are joined in a straight-line, one-to-one relationship. The gaze in "seen" photographs travels in a curved line that wanders freely (*frei schwimmen*) and becomes entwined with the subject. To Tillmans, photographs that are worth "seeing" are located somewhere between pure snapshots, photographs found in magazines, set-up photographs, or photographs manipulated in the darkroom. Ultimately, the work appears when the image floats up in the developing solution. Developing and printing are also extremely important to him.

> I guess I could have an easier life if I didn't care so much about all the different manifestations of an image, if I didn't care about making the prints myself or in my studio, but somehow I see that as being part of my work, and the time spent dealing with a print is also time spent with the work. I understand my work better through this process.[13]

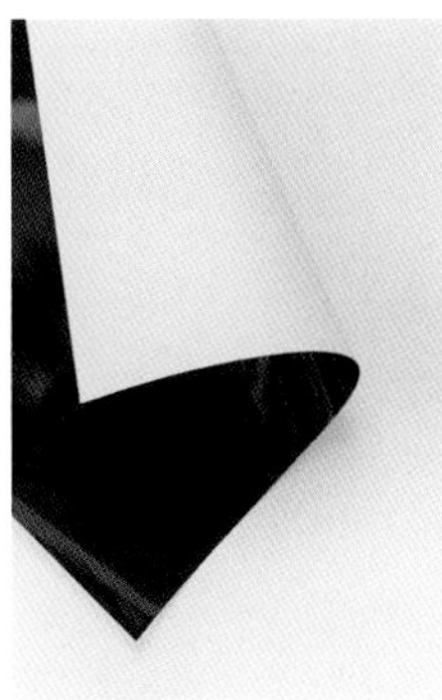

12 paper drop (black), 2001

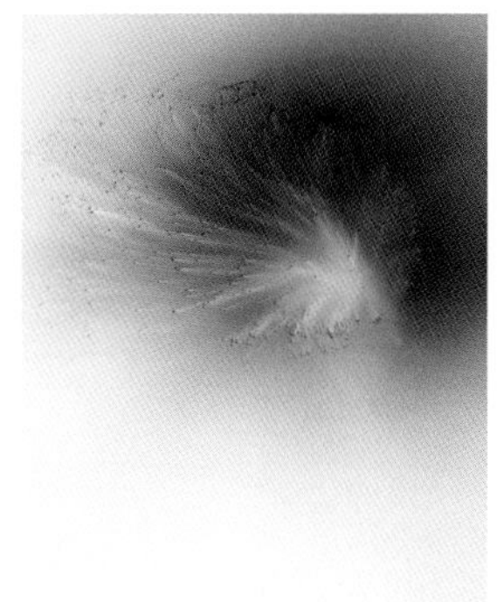

13 Blushes # 59, 2000

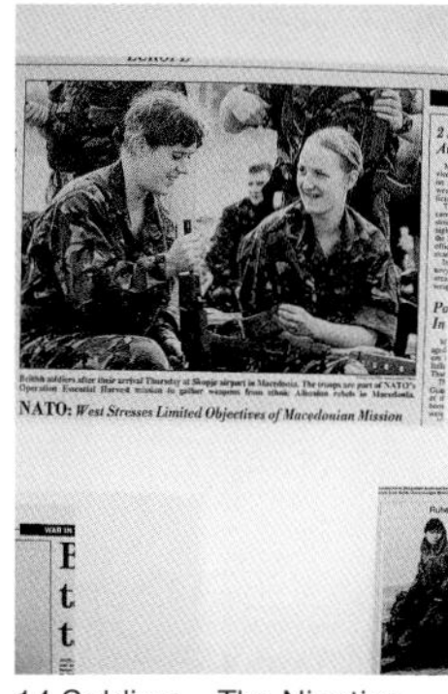

14 Soldiers – The Nineties,
1999 (detail)

There are four ways that Tillmans creates photographs that express the meaning of photography, photographs about photographs.

1. Photographs including images of the photographer: Tillmans sometimes includes part of his own body in his photographs. This basic motif recurs consistently in Tillmans' work (figs. 3, 10). The viewer of such an image naturally shares the photographer's point of view, but the point of Tillmans' photographs of himself is that the body that is photographed can be only that of the photographer. The viewer shares the body of the photographer. That is, photographs that include the photographer have the effect of fusing the viewer and the photographer.

2. Framed images: Newspaper photo clippings (*Soldiers: The Nineties* (fig. 14)), window frames (fig. 2), photographs of photographs (fig. 11) or posters, photographs of television screens, self-constructed photographs (fig.12), boxed images.

3. Views from above: Photographs taken from an elevated angle are metaphors for seeing the image appearing in the developing solution (fig. 7).

4. Photographs that demonstrate the basic principle of photography, the effect of light on photo-sensitive materials: Intervention and manipulation in the developing process, many purely abstract photographs made with light (fig. 13).

Equivalence
Equivalence is the central principle of Tillmans' photography, which has moved from one motif to another, from representation to abstraction. In a manner of speaking, it is the equal sign that joins his political and esthetic subjects. His photographs are transformed through the principle of equivalence and "swim freely" from one photograph to another. What is this equivalence, this principle of the *Freischwimmer*?

Transformation and development of expression through equivalence was also a major feature of the prose of Jean Genet. Here are some examples:

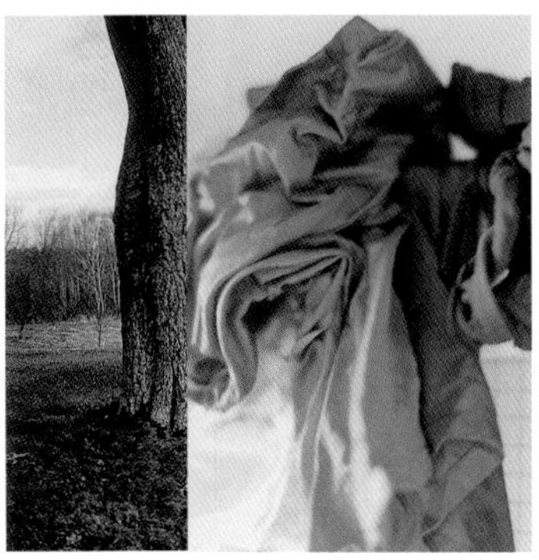

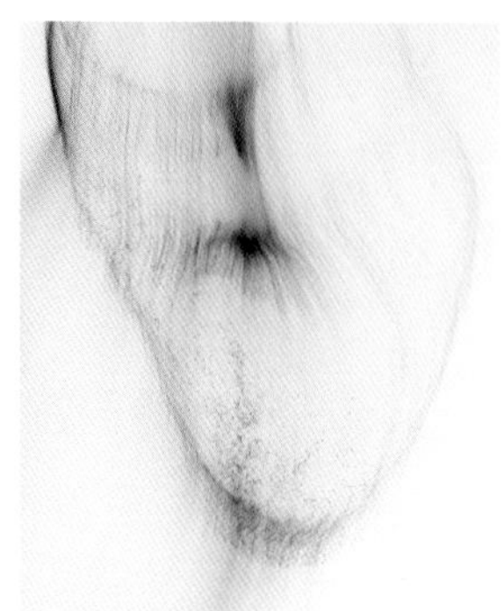

15 Shaker Tree, 1995
16 Faltenwurf, shiny, 2001

17 elbow, 2001

Staves (*verges*) and orchards (*vergers*) grow from my mouth.[14]

In the triangle of the V-necked shirt, in the middle of a tuft of hair that implied a fleece all over him, I saw, snug and warm, a little gold medallion cuddling in that wool, which was fragrant with the odor of armpits, like a plaster Jesus in the straw and hay dazed by the smell of the droppings of ox and the ass.[15]

Mario's voice was broad and thick, like his hands—except that it carried no sparkle. It struck Querelle slap in the face. It was a brutal, callous voice, one capable of stirring up and scattering the scum of the earth.[16]

Vernacular Arabic sounds as if it ought to look like vermicelli when it's written down, and it is all twists and turns. The Lebanese refer to Hebrew script as "spare parts." Arriving in Beirut from Damascus and seeing those signposts at the crossroads was as painful as seeing Gothic lettering in Paris during the German occupation.[17]

The mere crease, though curiously precise in the left leg, of his blue denim trousers.[18]

Equivalence is fundamentally sexual, meaning, broadly, "the permeation of everyday life by the erotic."[19] This is a pansexuality in which sexuality permeates everything and is not focused only on the genitals. The final quote from Genet immediately recalls the *Faltenwurf* that frequently appears in Tillmans' photographs. The sexuality in these images is "located on the surface of the clothes."[20] Eros is not located only in the penis but in the swelling curves and volumes of the cloth covering it, not only in the physical body but in the creases and folds of clothing that the body fills. To state this position with some exaggeration, every place is an erogenous zone, not just nude bodies and genitalia. That is, the sexual qualities seen as being equivalent are ultimately superficial sensory qualities. The artist deals with all the senses in terms of these sexual qualities. Sight, touch, smell, pain, and memory are joined by the equivalence of eros. The qualities of a voice, of vowels and consonants, slide into tactile sensations, and the visual phenomenon of written letters

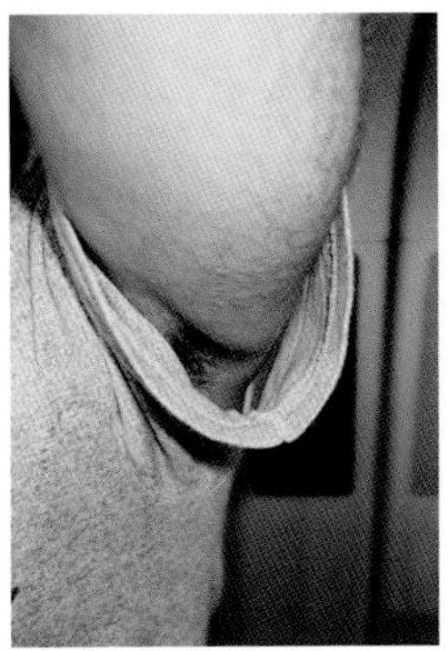
18 Bakerloo Line, 2000

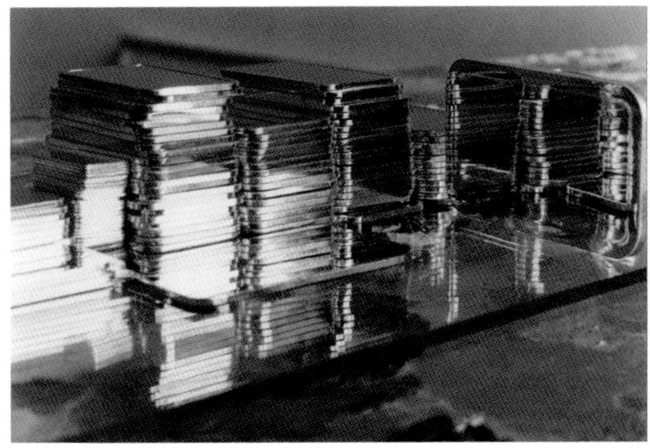
19 Gold (b), 2002

resurrects a sense of pain. The issue is not what or who is depicted in the photograph, its meaning or content. The work continues to change, to swim freely, through the equivalence of purely superficial sexual sensations.

Equivalence should not be confused with a chain of associations or modifications based on resemblance. Tillmans does not make use of similar images or descriptive elements to deal with and suggest the erotic qualities he perceives. The same, single eros, which is a common denominator between slightly disparate images, does not arise as identity among differences. The transformation through equivalence is like the equivalent transformation of a mathematical formula. Different images are not similar only in certain parts; they are entirely equivalent. For example, *verge* and *verger* (penis and orchard), vernacular and vermicelli (thin Italian pasta) do not resemble each other, but they are equivalent in the sensation produced in the mouth when they are pronounced. The image entitled *elbow* (fig. 17) in the *Blushes* series hardly resembles the underarm hair of the subway passenger (fig. 18), nor does his beard resemble *Zero Gravity*, but they are equivalent in their tactile erotic quality. As seen in the section on the politics of everyday life, the issue for Tillmans is not "identity" but the discovery of a "sameness" that shatters identity.

At present, I believe it is possible to find four kinds of equivalent qualities in the work of Tillmans.

1. Phallus: Images of horizontal and vertical protrusion (fig. 15). It may be thought that the queer imagination operates in a phallic way, but these photographs are not simply intended to suggest associations with the penis. They are photographs of equivalent qualities of hardness, thickness, and protrusion, the qualities that also make the penis erotic.

2. Tactility, subtle textures sensed by the fingertips: short hair, shaved whiskers, body hair, the *Blushes* (figs. 13, 18, 21).

3. Luster, wetness, sheen: Shiny surfaces, including cloth, metal, water surfaces, a sweaty back, luscious nature (figs. 16, 19, 20, 21).

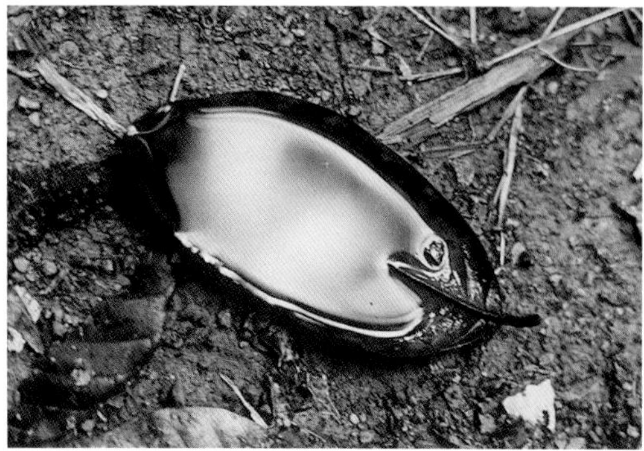

20 Leaf, 1995

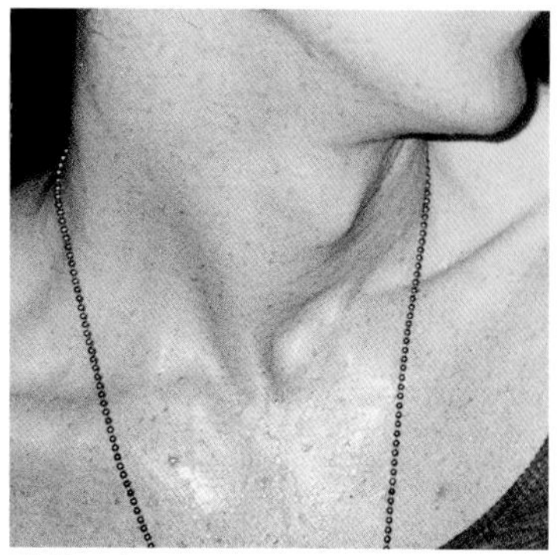

21 Chemistry square,
neck & chest, 1992

4. Strong curves, swelling, stretching, roundness: *Faltenwurf*, T-shirts, taut muscles (rivers, spheres, fruit) (figs. 7, 12, 21, 22, 23, 24).

The Art of Equivalence

We have looked at three elements of the art of Wolfgang Tillmans: the political nature of his concept; self-reflexivity in photographs about photographs and the phenomenon of photography; and equivalence, the principle he uses to work with a wide variety of motifs as he develops his art. A person looking at a collection of Tillmans' photographs will notice that five categories of motifs are expressed in four self-reflexive styles. There is no taxonomy for Tillmans' works, because his motifs are continuously connected with one another and are not divided into self-content categories (remember the polyvalence of the series *Concorde, View from above*, and self-portraits). Tillmans is making his current work according to the central concept of becoming the same, becoming one, and he continues to change and move on to different motifs or abstract images through the principle of equivalence. Politics and esthetics become one in his work through the principle of equivalence.

As a single sound is made of plenty of overtones, so a single photograph implies many qualities. Therefore, if a single work is virtually equivalent to a number of works, a number of works can be regarded as a single work, that is, an artist book and an installation (that is why sometimes installation views appear as photographic works). This part = whole relationship is characteristic of Tillmans. A sheet of photographic paper can act as a white wall and page, the relationship between the image and the margin can correspond to the balance of installation and layout, and equivalent qualities within a single work are projected as a constellation of several photographs onto pages and walls. Tillmans' installations and the layout of his books evoke something musical, but this music is the electronic music. They are not to be considered as compositions of separate units but as temporal and spacial developments of a single photograph. As dynamism and harmony of overtones produce a color of a sound, the continuous development of equivalences in a Tillmans installation or book allows us to experience an act of creation live.

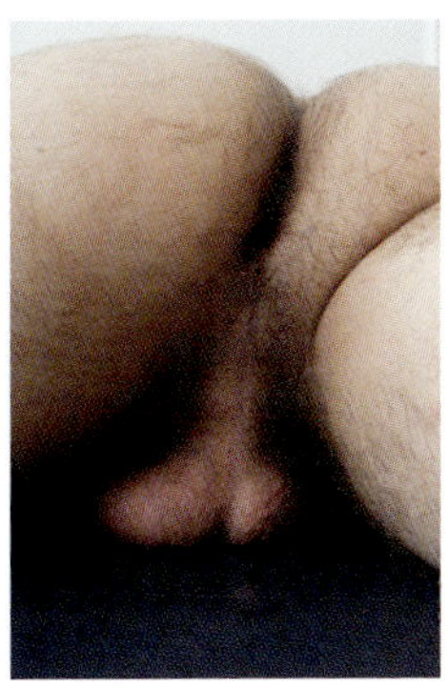
22 nackt, b, 2014

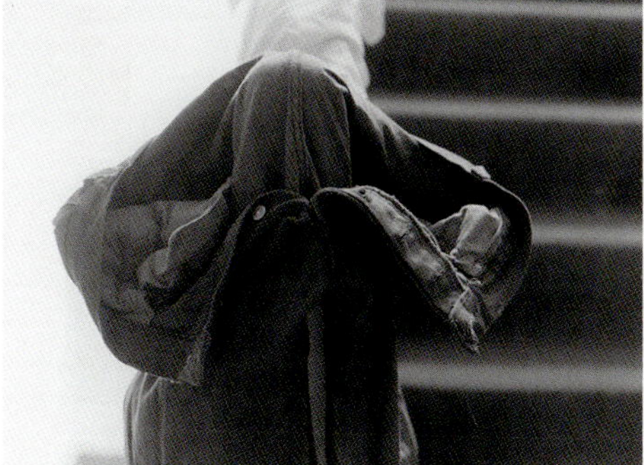
23 grey jeans over stair post, 1991

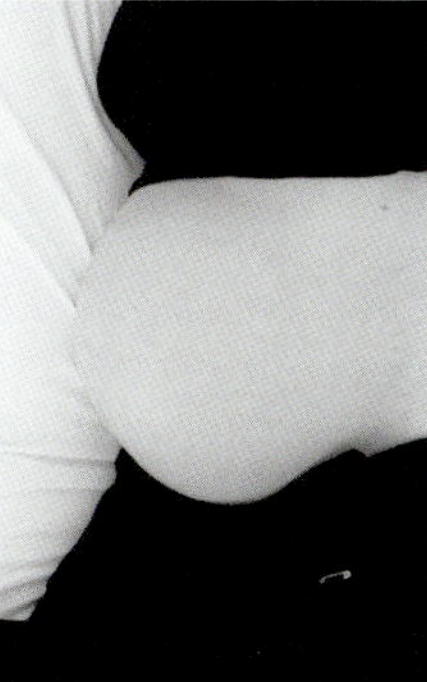
24 Womb, 1999

Notes

1 Wolfgang Tillmans, an interview with Neville Wakefield, in *Wolfgang Tillmans—Portikus Frankfurt*, Portikus Frankfurt, 1995.
2 Or, in the words of Leo Bersani, "homo-ness." Leo Bersani, *Homos*, Harvard University Press, 1995. In particular, see the chapter "The Gay Outlaw." Barsani's discussion of the disturbing qualities of "homo-ness" was extremely helpful to me in writing this essay.
3 *Faltenwurf* is also an art-historical term used to refer to the folds in garments on sculpture.
4 Wolfgang Tillmans, an interview with Peter Halley, in *Wolfgang Tillmans*, Phaidon Press, London, 2002, p. 13.
5 Ibid.
6 Wolfgang Tillmans, an interview with Nathan Kernan, in *Wolfgang Tillmans: View from above*, Hatje Cantz, Ostfildern-Ruit, 2001, p. 8.
7 Tillmans in conversation with Wakefield (see note 1).
8 Marcel Proust, *Remembrance of Things Past, Cities of the Plain*, vol. II, translated by C. K. Scott Moncrieff and Terence Kilmartin, Vintage Books, 1982, p. 628.
9 Tillmans in conversation with Wakefield (see note 1).
10 Ibid., p. 122.
11 Tillmans in conversation with Kernan (see note 6), p. 9.
12 Wolfgang Tillmans, an interview with Mary Horlock, in *Wolfgang Tillmans: if one thing matters, everything matters*, Hatje Cantz, Ostfildern-Ruit, 2003, p. 305.
13 Tillmans in conversation with Kernan (see note 6), p. 9.
14 Jean Genet, *Funeral Rites*, translated by Bernard Frechtman, Grove Press, 1969, p. 18.
15 Ibid., p. 38.
16 Jean Genet, *Querelle of Brest*, translated by Gregory Streatham, Faber and Faber, 2000, p. 30.
17 Jean Genet, *Prisoner of Love*, translated by Barbara Bray, *New York Review Books*, 2003, pp. 309–10.
18 Jean Genet, *The Thief's Journal*, translated by Bernard Frechtman, Grove Press, 1987, p. 23.
19 David Deitcher in: *Burg*, Taschen, Cologne, 1998.
20 Tillmans in conversation with Wakefield (see note 1).

How likely is it that only I am right in this matter?

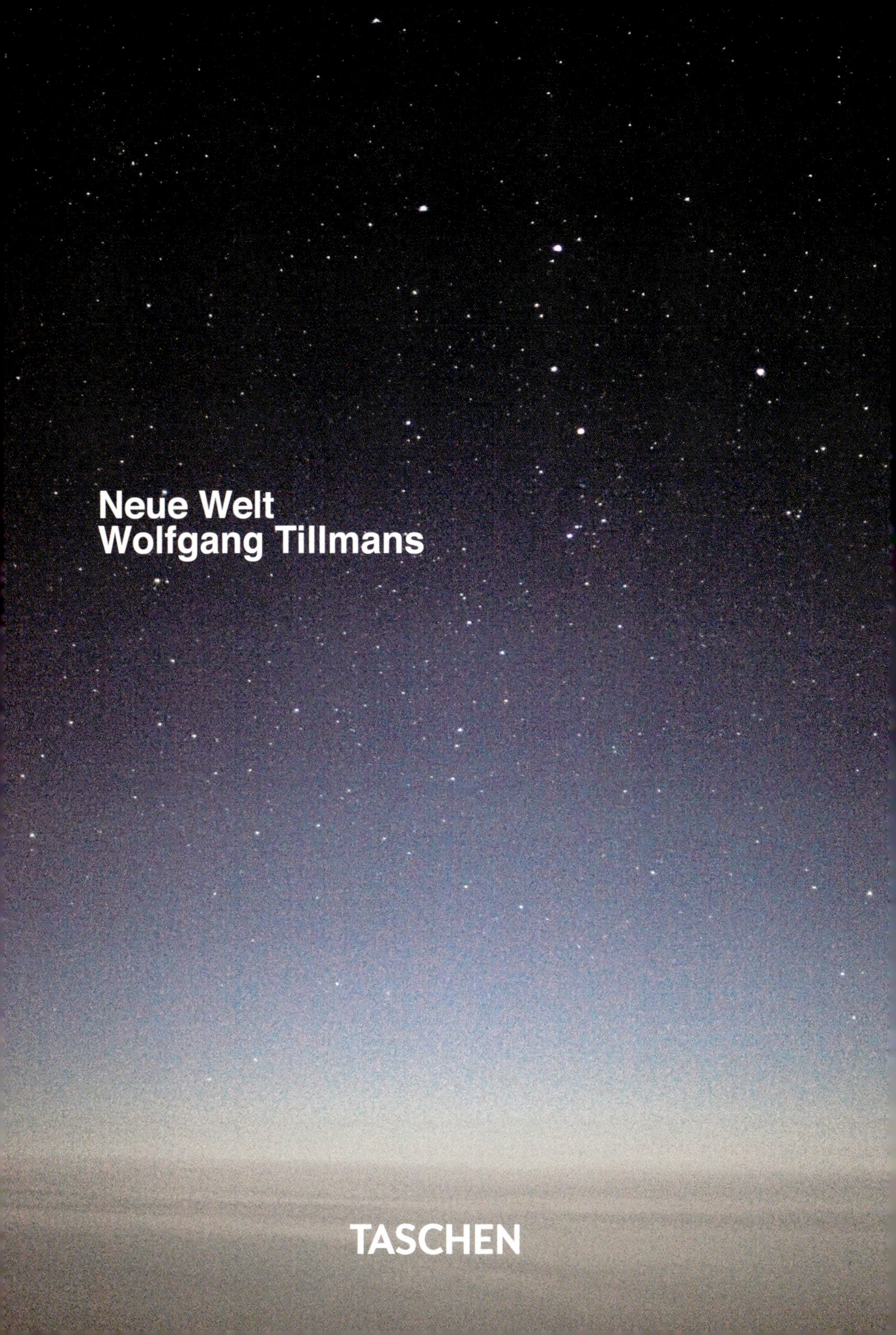

Neue Welt
Wolfgang Tillmans

TASCHEN

Wolfgang Tillmans

Neue Welt

Edited and designed by Wolfgang Tillmans

With an interview by Beatrix Ruf

Kunsthalle Zürich

TASCHEN

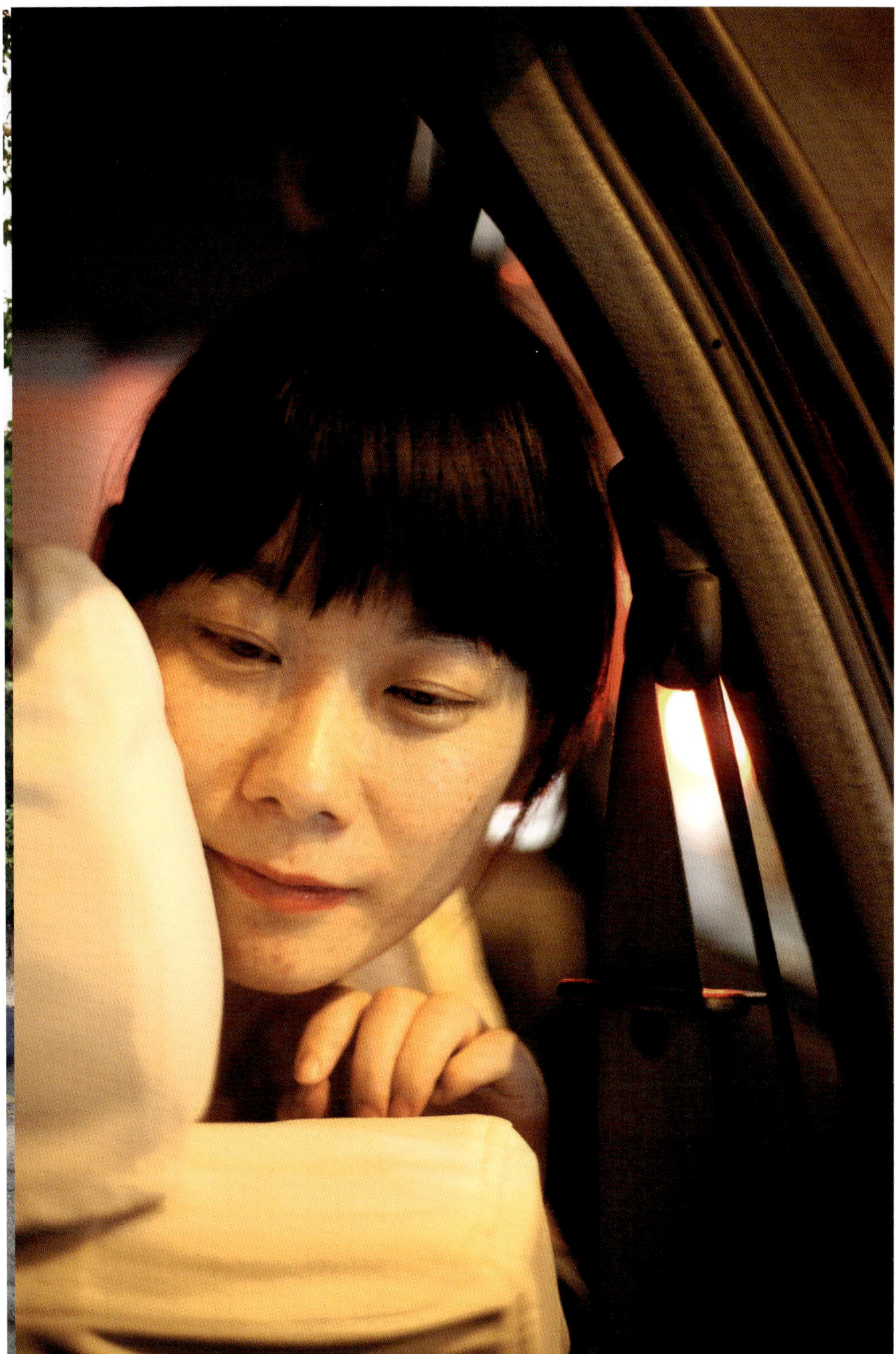

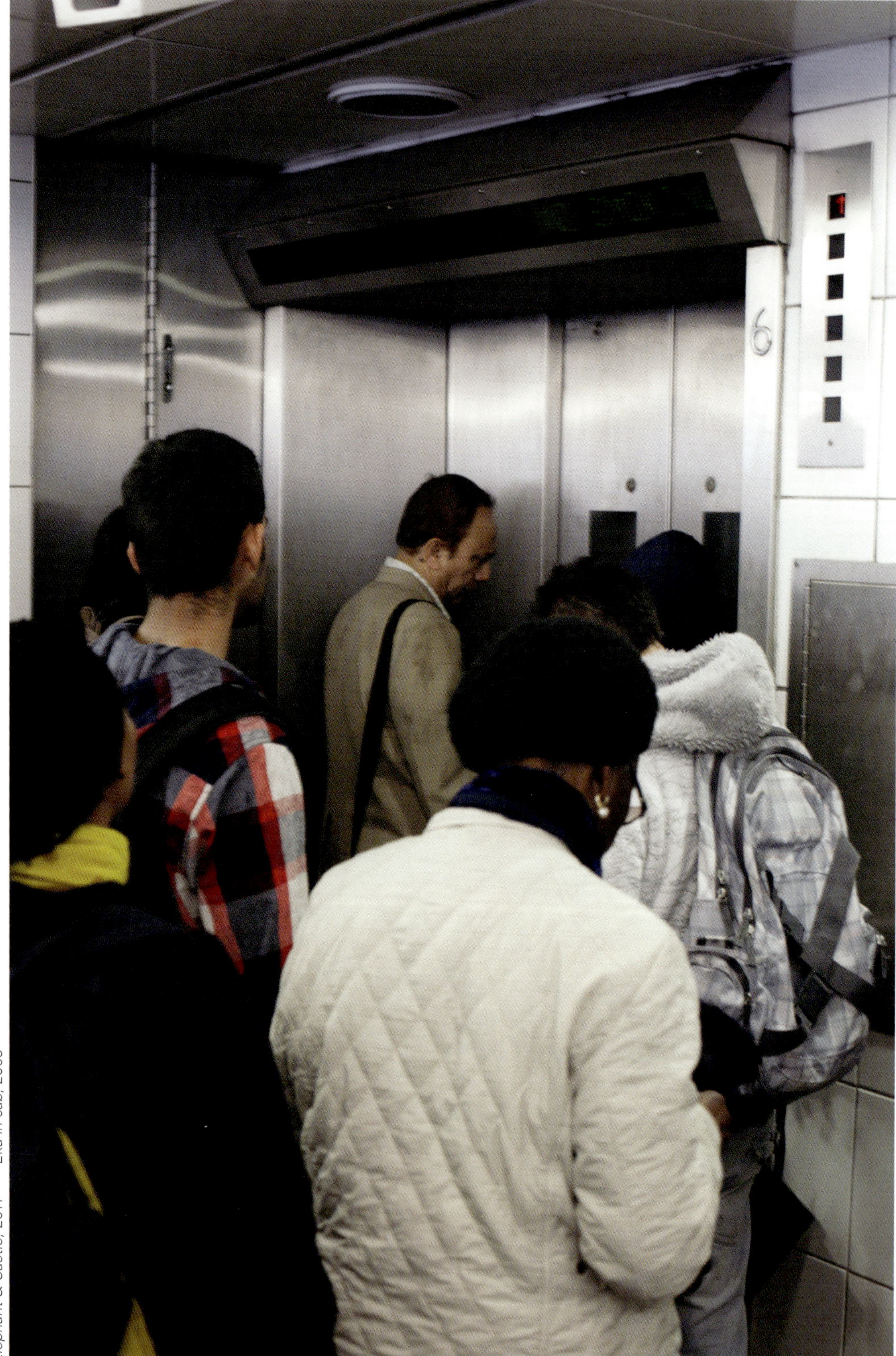

Elephant & Castle, 2011   Eka in cab, 2009

New World / Life is astronomical

Wolfgang Tillmans in conversation
with Beatrix Ruf

BR You call this book and the new series
Neue Welt [New World]. The title brings to
mind the 1928 photography book *Die Welt ist
schön* [The World is Beautiful] by Albert Renger-
Patzsch, in which he used 100 photographs
to depict the state of the world in motifs like
those of plants, people, landscapes, architecture, machinery, and industrial products.
It also reminds me of the 2002 publication
Sichtbare Welt [Visible World] by Peter Fischli
& David Weiss, in which they revisited every
sight seen hundreds of times already, every
longed-for mythologized location, and made
touristy, postcard images from them again.
What was your project? How can one grasp
the world today?

WT Recently, a friend referred to my studio
as a laboratory for the contemporary. What
is the current situation? From the start, I was
concerned with trying to answer this question
as a whole. In the process, I was constantly
aware of only being able to do this based on
selected motifs and significant fragments taken
from the world. For example, carefully studying
a single edition of a daily newspaper tells you
an amazing amount about the world. It poses
the question of how information is actually
processed. Information density nowadays is
incredibly high. For that reason, only fragments
can actually be processed. We might possess
more absolute knowledge than ever before,
but everything is fragmented—the same way
hard drives save "fragmented" files. There is no
longer a view of the totality, of the whole.
Until now, I had always found this whole in
facets of the private and the public, and I usually
remained close to my own living environment
at the same time. Foreign and exotic exceptions
to the rule have always existed. Of course, my

work was primarily an involvement with people
and things in some way close to me, or with
art-immanent questions concerning the picture,
the material, and the installation. Basically, to
study a wrinkle in a piece of cloth or a dent in an
unbroken surface is already enough to locate a
picture of the whole. It's all a matter of the gaze,
of an open, anxiety-free gaze.

BR So you have dealt extensively with
questions of medium, abstraction, and
representation.

WT For the last ten years I've been dealing
rather introspectively with abstract, medium-
reflexive images like those in *Blushes*, *paper
drop*, and *Lighter*. During that time, I also continued to photograph with the camera. But only
now, after years of studio practice, has a really
new, artistic interest in the outside world devel-
oped. The abstract works, too, were a reaction
to things in the world, but they confronted
paper and abstract compositions for the most
part. This is why, at the end of the last decade,
I arrived at the question of how the world actually appears when seen at a distance from my
usual beaten path. In this sense, I was gripped
by a restlessness and curiosity. I asked myself
why I shouldn't travel to places where I was
nothing but a traveler. I wanted to know: How
does the world appear twenty years after I've
begun to form a picture of it? Can there be a
"new" view of it? And "new" also in the sense
of greatly expanded technical possibilities. The
tremendous political and economic shifts of
recent years, and technical advancements, have
considerably altered the world's appearance.

BR You could have also said: The world is so
greatly altered that this even shows itself in
my immediate vicinity. We definitely see "old
friends," too, among the portraits in *Neue Welt*.

WT That's why I photographed simultaneously in London, New York, and Berlin, also

"old friends" whose world has likewise moved on, but also found as uncomplicated and, actually, as utterly wondrous as things like cell phones and flat-screen monitors.

BR   You repeatedly talk about the micro- and macrocosm connection that you reinvent in particular in the digital resolution of a high-resolution pictorial world. After these abstract worlds in the introspective space of the studio, did the new digital technology first inspire you to travel to take photographs?

WT   There was no direct connection. The wish to expand the field of vision was there first. I bought this digital camera before taking the first trip. That was in 2009, on the occasion of the total solar eclipse in Shanghai. I had always deprived myself of the China trend. But the total solar eclipse was different. That was my China moment. On my way back, I traveled through different Asian countries. During this trip, I took both analog and digital photographs. By the way, the photographs in this book are also, in part, analog prints.
Digital photography is not better than analog photography. It's just different. What mattered to me was looking at the "new world" through a contemporary medium that corresponds with the simplicity of a good reflex camera. The camera I chose for this cost 2,000 and not 15,000 euros. It's important to me that my medium delivers high-quality results without it settling into a world of "special effects." I always find technologies interesting when they arrive at the point of general use, because this is also when they have the potential to reach people with a generally accepted vocabulary.

BR   The attention to detail in digital pictures no longer corresponds to our everyday seeing experience, unless one consciously changes to extreme focusing. In your new photographs, one continually encounters this extreme perceptual density, for example, in the picture of the waterfall (*Iguazu*, 2010), where even the smallest spray of water surprises with its staggering resolution, or when microstructures become large-format images.

WT   This question deeply preoccupies me, now more than ever since I switched to the digital camera. It enables pictures to be taken with an almost endless information density, which only reveals all its details when enlarged to two meters. Even then, one doesn't see pixels! I had to learn from scratch how to take pictures. Thirty-five millimeter film is actually enough for me, since it corresponds to what my eye actually sees. Large-format images are, of course, impressive, but they don't usually move me because of their inhuman sharpness. Now I find myself in the situation of using a camera capable of achieving large-format sharpness. But now, too, the increased sharpness strikes me as being consistent, because everything in the world is "high definition" in the meantime. The increased sharpness corresponds to what feels like a new perception, and since I otherwise use the new camera like I did the other—without a tripod, et cetera—the former view remains the same.
I find it extremely challenging to generate photographs in an already overdepicted world using precisely these new technologies. Just the same, I often had my doubts and thought: What sort of randomness and complete worthlessness is this?

BR   The digitalized world archive is still physically and mentally impossible to grasp, as well as a disturbing model of an archive. Has digital photography changed your approach to taking pictures?

WT   I needed a year to ignore all feedback on the small display on the back of the camera, detailing what's being photographed at the moment. For me, photography is a dialogue between the photographed and the one

photographing—a projection, a hope, and a presumption, regardless of what emerges from it. With analog photography, this first becomes visible a few days later. In the viewfinder, you can see what you photograph, but the translation process constituting the magic and psychology of photography is not just optomechanical. Photographs are also spiritually charged objects. In the past, this idea had a space of its own. Today, however, you already see the image in the display a half second after taking the shot. For me, a customary approach encountered a great disturbance in this way. I had to learn to ignore this. Taping over the display is not the solution, because it also gives me access to important controls. Evaluating the deeper quality of the picture is done later on the computer.
That's one of the reasons why, on principle, I never retouch or alter anything afterwards. I believe in the magic of the picture's creation process at the moment the photograph is taken. One should be able to trust my pictures. Despite the vast photo-editing possibilities, as a matter of principle, I never remove, enhance, or smooth out any details. On those rare occasions when I did change something, the intervention was clearly recognizable, and it was usually meant tongue-in-cheek.

BR   Then you would say: You still make your decisions for the picture in the same manner?

WT   Exactly. It happens afterwards, weeks or months later. I don't take advantage of the possibilities of immediate processing. I always feel images somehow need time to mature. Of course, that's not true, since they don't really do that. But the more distance you have from the moment the image is photographed, the more you can separate yourself from your wishes and hopes.

BR   Like in your earlier work, similar to Renger-Patzsch, large thematic groups move through *Neue Welt* as well: people, social constellations, natural formations, plants, points of transit like airports, shopping malls, animals, means of transportation, technology, and science. How do you view these thematic groups, and what do you see happening when pictures are juxtaposed?

WT   I'm not concerned with completeness or a conceptual principle. Popular locations and landmarks can be followed the next day by a totally unfamiliar or banal place, perhaps some small town I hung around in because a friend of my parents lived there and I could stay a couple days. There is less of a system to my traveling. It has more to do with searching for possible flight routes: What lies over there? What could be connected to that? That's how I landed in unheard-of spots like Darwin in North Australia. And I'm not scared off by unusually popular locations like Iguazu Falls either, since I trust that many places are unusually popular simply because they are, in fact, special. For example, the Sydney Opera House is such a famous landmark that it shouldn't be necessary to see it in life. But it looked totally different from the well-known photographs of it, and felt totally different from the way I had imagined it.

BR   While searching out these well-known places again, you have neither a guiding concept nor any ethnological or investigative intentions. Also, you say that you don't stay very long in each of these locations.

WT   That's right. A short period of full immersion is enough for me. More isn't possible than simply being physically present, moving around as much as possible, gathering impressions, making contacts, and opening a few doors. It comes down to physically taking a good look at various things on location and confronting them as best you can. This was no touristy round-trip that forces the so-called foreign into familiar interpretive patterns, but rather the attempt to have a genuinely new experience.

The short stay can attain a special lucidity in the process. We're all like this: The first day of a trip feels like three days, the second day like two days, and the third like one. After that, the time passes like it does every day.

In the case of such a short stay, the surface of a place stands out most. The surfaces and even superficiality itself have always interested me, because we basically have to read the truth of things from the world's surface. There is a well-known quote by Bertolt Brecht about the exterior of a factory never depicting the work conditions inside it. Of course the photograph of a factory reflects only to a limited extent what happens inside, but its exterior is a reality, too, the way it stands there. And the double-page spread with both photographs of the foreign workers' dismal quarters in Dubai is to be understood this way (*workers' accommodation*, 2009).

BR   What also suggests itself here is the critical discourse on the exotic and the reception of the exotic. How do you deal with this difficult question? What does it mean today to travel and to grasp the world?

WT   The more interesting question is: "What is normal?" Who decides what is aestheticizing, what is research, what is familiar, what is exotic? Pictures are always the transcription of an experiencing of the world. Ideally, they pose the question of there possibly being another way to experience the world. It's not the world contained in the picture; the picture is a translation. A representational picture does no more and no less than form reality before our eyes. Even if this is fundamentally a platitude, it should always be kept in mind. Of course, I'm aware of the problem addressed here. It was even a key point for me, as a privileged individual travelling to places less connected to the West and suffering economically. Just the same, these places exist and people live here without seeing their existence purely as hardship.

What mattered to me was not losing sight of the respective social presence—without being, of course, able to penetrate it too deeply in such a short amount of time, but while, most of all, devoting myself to the question of what constitutes life on earth today, how one assesses and captures it, and perhaps, too, how a sense of the whole could be revealed. In connection with this, three or four years ago I came across the sentence "Life is astronomical." I see the earth and, most importantly, all living things as merely the formation of a particular astronomical condition, which specifically exists on this planet. The human assumption that we all heed, that life on earth is in and of itself separate: "We live on the earth," "We populate the earth," and "Save the planet!" just isn't so, because *we* are the planet; all of us are the formation of these conditions and, for that reason, only the expression of an astrogeological concoction. The same is inherent in the juxtaposition of people, plants, constructions, and technologies: Everything is matter continually renewing itself and transforming from one aggregate state into another. I even find that somewhat comforting. Naturally, we should make each other's life as pleasant as possible, and that's why I believe philosophy, politics, and the rest make sense. All this isn't just entropy and chaos—that we desire a sense of order and, for example, seek love, right?

BR   That sounds like a higher wisdom that ignores social conditions and relationships.

WT   The thought that "Life is astronomical" is not meant deterministically, implying that everything follows its "higher" path and no one can change the course of things and so forth. It's rather the question of: What can one know at all; what can and cannot be changed? In what position does one find oneself as an observer? In my experience, occurrence advances in its simultaneity and always remains ungraspable in its wholeness. Nevertheless, I was driven by the question of whether it might be possible to achieve the awareness and experience relevant to wholeness via a short-term visibility of things. In order to engage in such an "experiencing of the world," one has to physically move oneself to the most diverse places on earth.

My relationship to reality is always, above all, more ethical than technical, or purely aesthetic. I see and photograph the world in the same way that I otherwise react towards it. Essentially, this is about humanitarianism. I'm aware that one can easily succumb to ethnological temptations and glorify the exotic as such. But these photographs are also reactions to my own experiences, which are not always pleasant and familiar. In that respect, "Life is astronomical" deserves emphasis in larger brackets.

BR   What does photographing strangers mean for you at all? That's not exactly a problem-free activity. And you don't always ask for their permission beforehand.

WT   In my opinion, observing people and sometimes photographing them without their knowledge is acceptable when done with the kind of empathetic gaze just mentioned. Of course, each person has to decide this for himself. It could also be considered question-able, how people use posed profile pictures on Facebook in order to be appealing. I think the unobserved photographing of people in their everyday life can also contribute, in general, to a more empathetic understanding of the world. This should never be about capturing photographic "spoils." I realize I'm walking a thin line here, but I always try to remain aware of this. The moment I sense a lack of consent or catch people at a bad moment, I imme-diately delete the picture. That's good about the camera display. But this photography in a state of flux, which dives into life with the camera, risks embarrassment, and has no safety zone

whatsoever, continually brings forth something truthful, something genuine. I'm sure of that. It's also the joy of experiencing the unpredicta-bility and derangedness of life, the preposterous situations that arise, how bodies act among themselves, and how they dress, establish near-ness, or keep their distance. All this is infinitely fascinating. I find such contact with everyday life around the world endlessly inspiring.

BR   In the series and here, too, in the book, pictures of stellar constellations and night skies frequently appear. You have as strong an interest in astronomy, the universe, scientific research focused on perceiving the universe, and viewing the world we live in as scientifi-cally ascertained and ecologically endangered, as you do in basic questions concerning human existence in light of knowledge and non-knowledge.

WT   The question of knowledge and non-knowledge, of everything non-scientific ap-plied to the scientific and the reverse, naturally leads to an ironic way of dealing with knowl-edge and/or non-knowledge. This is the topic of my work *truth study center*. It opposes those people who accept nothing outside of their own truths and religions; it opposes an ideological understanding of knowledge and truth. Astronomy is my childhood obsession. I even believe it was my visual initiation into seeing: hours spent trying to distinguish between the finest of details, moving along the boundaries of the visible. Did I just see something or was that only a flicker in my eye? Since then, the question of perceptibility, of the ability to dis-tinguish between nothing and something, has been a central interest of mine. When do devel-opments become visible? What were they prior to being recognizable? This is as interesting politically as it is scientifically. In the series of night sky shots, I could specifically capture this borderline topic in pictures with the new cam-era. For these pictures, I adjusted the camera's sensor to such a high speed that it could record hundreds of stars in only one or two seconds. But at the same time, this extreme adjustment makes it hard to tell if what one sees is a star or nothing at all. When sensors see nothing, they create noise, and in these pictures the noise's pixels seamlessly merge with the real stars. At the European Southern Observatory, one could see that astronomers push their research to precisely this limit. What they see by night are not sparkling stars, but rather weak and pale-hued monitor images in which the noise is barely distinguishable from the stars. Not until several exposures are layered together does it stand out what is artifact and what is truly reality.

That today, twenty-five years later, I redis-covered a deep interest in astronomy also has to do with astronomy currently being at a point where it's paradigmatically changing the world again – as it last did in the times of Copernicus and Galileo. In this respect, I'm fascinated by exoplanet research. That now one can say, with relative certainty, that millions of earth-like planets exist in the universe, has actually changed the fundamental parameters for assessing human life. Until recently, only the guesswork of astronomers told us there were probably other planets with earth-like atmospheres, but this couldn't be proven. Today, one has proof—with almost absolute certainty—that among the countless planets in the uni-verse, the specific conditions for an earth-like surface character are repeated elsewhere.

This year, when I was able to visit the European Southern Observatory in Chile, an astronomer confirmed this for me. He said that, twenty-five years ago, when as a young physicist, he chose to become an astronomer, it was still a seemingly inert field of research, and it was unforeseeable that one would handle such fundamental questions today.

Naturally, this challenges religions and their leaders, who see human beings as the center of divine concerns. Something is fundamentally changing today. Without delving any further into this topic, let me briefly mention that I deliberately left religion out of *Neue Welt*. There are more relevant things.

BR   This seems to be just the beginning. In CERN, in Geneva, discussions in the area of the microcosm are opening up similar fundamental boundaries of our knowledge of the world.

WT   Yes, on a neighbouring mountain beside the one that is home to the largest ESO tele-scope to date, consisting of four mirrors, each one eight meters across, the E-ELT is going to be built and completed by 2022, with the telling name "Extremely Large Telescope." It will have the incredible reflector diameter of 40 meters. For a period of 40 years, the five-meter reflect-ing telescope at Mount Palomar was consid-ered astonishingly big. During the last fifteen years came the eight-meter reflectors, and today, thanks to further advancements, even 40 meters are possible. My guide at ESO spoke of being on the brink of a Galilean moment.

BR   This thought is directly realized in your new pictures: The conditions for creating the earth's surface and its extremes basically corre-spond with the conditions for creating images. The presence and absence of composition is definitely similar.

The world is incessantly recorded microscop-ically as well as macroscopically, for example, on the pages of *Google Earth*. Technology is everywhere nowadays. What exactly does it mean to produce pictures in this overdepicted and over-represented world, and to make physical and mental journeys? Couldn't you also make these pictures and journeys on the Internet?

WT   Not really. I still believe it's possible to show something new and say or find something inexpressible in pictures. There I have faith in the picture. In fact, I think a value is created when I "put myself in situations" and subject myself to unpredictable reactions. Taking a step on the Internet always means following the respective "command." Maybe you never know what follows on the next page, but you basically see only whatever you have asked about. Everything is predefined on the Internet. On the other hand, in the real world the possibility of a surprise is always immanent.

BR   The Swedish poet and artist Karl Holmqvist said that, provided the collectivization of a given world is advanced, the individual will become collectively meaningful again. Precisely because the overlapping, the collective authorship, like on the Internet, is so omnipotent regarding the simultaneity of all the "voices," the individual voice becomes relevant again in order to establish a connection to the collective as a dialogue factor. Today, the Internet is no longer the technical "other" or counterpart we imagined it to be ten years ago. Now it's a fully integrated aspect of reality—and for that reason has a completely different connection to the individual…

WT   …and perhaps even demands this. In any case, at the end of the 1990s, I sensed less of a need to photograph my contemporaries. I felt the parameters had changed. In the early 1990s, that was still the exception and it wanted to be visualized. Ten years later, however, to photograph a young European-American person meant something else, and we were only then on the road to the over-photographed state, which was nowhere near as far along as it is today. As a kind of counter-reaction, I slowed down my picture production and directed my attention more towards nonrepresentational, abstract photography. Now it strikes me as necessary to become active in such excessive background noise. And so I asked myself: Would it be possible not to filter out individual pictures, but rather to place them inside it, as individual pictures that "ring out" from the general noise?

BR   During your travels, you had to "resist" using your new digital camera's photo-editing possibilities. So which pictures surprised you most?

WT   Actually, everything continued to function the way it always does: When something interests me, or when I've thought about it long enough, I always find the right moment to photograph it, without having to force it in order to make the pictures.
In the process, I find especially interesting the observations that set me in motion without having to search for them. For example, over the last ten years, I have followed how car headlights have increasingly become highly technical and transformed to complex light sculptures, and have a more aggressive look about them now. They've been "overbred" far beyond the necessary technical requirements. I found the "right moment" in an underground garage in Hobart in Tasmania. The ambient lighting and absence of security guards let me give my full attention to the headlights. In this small detail, I saw a picture for a fundamental state of mind, for the technological fantasies of the entire world. It's interesting how, on this restless search for individuality and distinction, one falls for such cyber-light objects.
I see an immediate connection between this aggressive design and the increasingly tougher competition rhetoric in the world. While twenty years ago, most car headlights were round or rectangular, with a friendly look, today, nearly all of them are shark-eye headlights. There really is something detectable on the surface here. Cars have always interested me, these strange capsules always present in the street scene. Mankind's fundamental wish for individual and independent mobility is understandable, but the consequences of this are also so monstrous…

BR   You could have also photographed these headlights in an underground garage in Berlin.

WT   Yes, but somehow it needed …

BR   …Tasmania.

WT   There are many pictures in the series I could have made in London, a city I know better than any other, but nevertheless an endless, unfathomably deep, and intricate place that functions like a mirror reflecting the whole world, of course reinforced by the Commonwealth that practically was the whole world once.
In reality, it's not at all clear which place produced which pictures. Oddly enough, I rarely hear: "Where was that taken?" I often heard this with my earlier pictures, when the W-questions: Who? Where? Why? What? functioned as reflexive actions meant to give viewers access to the images.

BR   Let's go back to the photographs of the car headlights and the association with shark eyes it triggers in the viewer. The relationship of technology and nature, or the association made to this relationship, frequently appears in your work, for example, in the photographs of new technologies for food processing and packaging, but also with the copy and printing machines and high-tech settings. You often show transportation vehicles and technical facilities …

WT   It's amazing how high technology visually overpowers and spreads around the world. In the past, a smaller number of people participated in the use of high technology. Technical advancements were best recognized in connection with icons of sought-after achievements like space travel, the moon landing, and the Concorde. Today, billions of people communicate with the same cell phones. Even in poor countries, like Ethiopia, no one uses a cell phone from ten years ago.

I observed something similar in connection with sportswear, although sportswear doesn't immediately depict a sense of technology, but rather tries awakening the suggestion of technological advancement directly on the body. Wherever I went, people wore the same styles and materials—like a global uniform. This gave the impression that certain things are virally present. Of course, this corresponds with the intentions of corporations. But there's more to this simultaneous spreading of particular styles and technologies.
It's fascinating to observe how the world's surface is changing: For example, the color of light is drifting away from light-bulb yellow and towards the pallid, cold glow of the energy-saving lamp. At first, I wondered how someone could accept this lighting of a much lesser quality. Now it has become apparent that energy-saving lamps are just an intermediate phase, and that in the future all light will come from LED sources, which offer a broader spectrum of colors. In China, entire houses are decked with LEDs already. The cities there look totally unlike anything I've ever seen before. And the flatness fetish related to monitor screens is a similar global phenomenon. In Ushuaia, the world's southernmost city, I photographed a shanty town, where the heat insulation was made entirely of Styrofoam packaging from technical appliances (*Ushuaia Favela*, 2010).

BR   Surfaces, disguises, and architectural cladding constantly turn up in these pictures as well: designs evolving from folds, but also architectural facings like the Arabic architectural elements used as decorations in one of your photographs (*cladding*, 2009), taken in a new structure built of concrete; the radiant surfaces of the new hotel and merchandise temple, but also the forms and encasements of the world's surface in urban structures, shown from a bird's-eye view; or the Masai's hair sculpted into an artistic shape with mud (*Young Masai*, 2012).

WT   Cladding is not just a construction type, enormously popular and almost considered normal. It also grants expression to a specific attitude. Other similarly questionable attitudes are, in the Anglo-Saxon realm, exposed brickwork and the factory-building aesthetic in Berlin, both interesting at first, but later became the cliché of stifled forms. I always travel around the world with half an eye open only to architecture. What interests me is when something is pure facade and when something is "genuine," meaning when something is either false or honest. In my opinion, architecture often handles the expectations of its users very carelessly. In this respect, I consider deception, when it presents itself as such, much less problematic. But when everything is just curtain-walled slabs, my first reaction is that I don't feel taken seriously as a user. In the Anglo-Saxon realm, everything is completed with cladding or curtain walling. The Centre Pompidou-like approach is more to my taste, everything left open, or else everything permanently plastered. Of course, the "cladders" could say that they are being honest in their illusion, that it never lasts longer than five years anyway, and being fake is used in the same way to neatly plaster or cover with bricks.
This tension between constructions promising eternity and endurance and the pragmatism and practical constraints of money, the vagabonding use of it, is something I find mind-boggling. A strong motivation for traveling and taking trips to cities evolves from observing this in all its forms around the world. Built space always confronts viewers with the results of a multitude of creative decisions made by the most disparate people and their different approaches. A kind of visual polyphony reigns. Most people don't notice this at all, because it qualifies as the norm. But I constantly see and read the world in this way.
Other interesting "constructions" are blossoms. On the one hand, they envelop and adorn the real issue: the fertility pistil. On the other, blossoms are wondrously decorative deception devices for bees. But they never poison bees. This is less clear in many malls in the world of consumers. I am not, per se, against consumerism. I'm concerned with intensifying that point where the harmless enjoyment of packaging, advertising, and types of decoration shifts to exploitation and simulating false data. It always revolves around the same question: What is genuine?

BR   Alongside cosmological, technological, and organizational constellations you frequently express an interest in social constellations, groups of people entangled in everyday situations. Here, I'm thinking about the marketplace scene in Ethiopia (*Market I,* 2012). What I find especially interesting about this picture is that it makes an immense picture archive available as the basis of our perception: We encounter such a huge number of images. Unlike nineteenth-century ethnologists, we no longer bring home with us from our travels pictures that appear foreign in nature. A great deal of this comes across in the marketplace picture. On the one hand, this is your own "authentic" picture. But it also shows everything we know about composed imagery. One witnesses the interplay of everything possible: expressions of so-called "authentic" life or the not composed, art history, and a visual range spanning from our collective projections to the collapse of this acquired way of seeing. Like you mentioned earlier, the same scene, with people wearing different clothes and with other goods, could have taken place in a park in London, right? What role does the migration and globalization of pictures and merchandise play for you in this context?

WT   Markets and merchandise define people and cultures. People come together where trading takes place. Markets are economically vital for their participants, but also places of communication and places to ward off boredom with. People are never alone at markets, and they can hope to personally benefit from some part of the general activity.

BR   How and why do the photographs become specific?

WT   That's another important aspect. This has nothing to do with making a stereotypical image of the world, but rather with making something in the general realm of things visible. I don't think of this as a "balancing act." It's actually inherent in all things. For example, a hotel room is, first of all, nothing out of the ordinary and simply a standard. At the same time, however, it's this specific hotel room that prompted a reaction in me (*Jurys Inn*, 2010). So it's not just the idea "Ah yes, there are millions of hotel rooms like this one," but also the specific combination of red carpeting, offensive lamp stand, and this particular abstract painting on the wall.

BR   The Internet, perhaps the last twenty years of images and image transfer, has played a major role in establishing access to a different dimension of the subjective and the individual in order to enable other assertions again. In media theories, this is discussed in terms of new maneuvering space for the subjective. I can imagine that there must be more advanced theories of the subjective, theories we haven't actually read yet and therefore can't discuss.

WT   It is probably becoming increasingly difficult as an individual to make an individually valid depiction of the "world" because people are overrun, like never before, by an incredible number of preconceived opinions and pictures of an unknown magnitude, and these are constantly colliding and ending up beside and on top of one another within a sustained noise. What interested me was not only to passively submit to all this, but to consciously let things bump against each other and stand side by

side, even when—or precisely because—their references are so obvious.

In this book, for example, there is a double-page spread showing what appears to be one sheep, until its shadow reveals it to be two sheep. Beside this image is the picture of a beach cottage in Papua New Guinea, which is the epitome of the island paradise cliché, but, in reality, shows a family residence. Then there is also the photograph of a DeBeers jewelry store with a limousine driving by, taken on Fifth Avenue in New York City. Here, the contrasts are really too obvious. What excites me, however, is enduring this because it's somehow the full range: How far does it go? What can one endure? I can resist the judging-and-condemning impulse these contrasts provoke in me. Now I can leave everything the way it is.

BR   This is really about an altered reality and, therefore, having different experiences with this simultaneity.

WT   The simultaneity and availability of all things constitute our reality today. That hint of the didactic is gone: There are the poor and there are the rich, and so forth…

BR   …and the genuine and the perhaps no longer genuine. What does it mean when you refer to all three of these pictures without immediately activating the clichés of your existing or, to some extent, learned and educated criteria? The first time I saw these works, I had the impression they were about an emptying process—not of pictures, but rather an emptying of the clichés and stereotypes we are familiar with and readily approach.

WT   Essentially, artworks are only endowed with a soul and uniqueness when a specific set of criteria exists in the artist. I found it to be an enormous challenge, verging on frightening, to unlearn how to photograph, to ignore the criteria I felt secure with, and to expand my focus to the extreme: to the whole world, to the entire pixel and/or information density, and to the complete range of subject matter, while pulling out the rug of my own social environment from under my feet in the process. Added to that comes the hugely increased number of pictures, around three times as many as I normally used when I photographed with film…

BR   That means you must have had many more pictures to choose from…

WT   Exactly. Where image consumption is concerned, I believe there's a limit. Books with thousands of pages don't interest me. "A lot" has never really interested me. Even though I've always been very productive, I only fully utilize thirty to forty camera pictures a year as art works. As a viewer, you can't really process more than that.

BR   With your abstract works, the studio works, from the *Freischwimmer* series to the *Silver* works, there is a development linked to a material-induced composition. You didn't want the *Freischwimmer* series brought in connection with the "travel" pictures, but with the latest *Silver* works you did…

WT   …because the *Freischwimmer* series connects intention and wish to the uncontrollable with far more intensity. Ultimately, it deals with traces and compositions I actively bring into the picture manually. With the *Silver* works, my hands are involved only insofar as I expose some of the sheets to colored, homogeneous light. The imaging process is subjected to the inherent logic of the material purely mechanically. The undeveloped photo paper—sometimes exposed, sometimes unexposed—passes through a photo-developing machine, which I intuitively, or depending on my intention, leave dirty or clean to varying degrees. Because of the remnants of chemicals in the empty machine, filled with only water,

the photo paper continues to develop, but only partially. On the other hand, dirt and silver particles from the traces of chemicals settle on the paper's surface, and this often produces interesting scratches. The result is basically no less a piece of reality than the photograph of a tree, but one for which I also didn't create the depicted object.

BR   A self-depiction of the process?

WT   This is fundamentally something mineral, a piece of nature, genuine matter, a changing environment. Residues of every kind—dirt, remains, and scratches—are unavoidable, basic and intermediate states in nature. Even in the photo emulsion, I view color in exactly the same way—as a natural phenomenon. Placed in connection with the subject, this "natural autonomy" development of the *Silver* pictures' material perhaps transforms thinking and perceiving in the sense of a new subjectivity. Actually, here in the book, one always confronts a representational picture as though the main concern is likewise a kind of reflecting on reality. At the same time, one could view the *Silver* works as a farewell to the organic-chemical nature of photography.

BR   In books, you have recently begun to layer photographs onto the pages.

WT   The first time I did that was last year, in the catalog of the exhibition in the Zachęta National Gallery of Art in Warsaw. One naturally lessens the "preciousness" of the individual picture and uses it as pure image material. But we should also have confidence in the picture as simply an excerpt in a new relationship to other pictures, as able to be something entirely new. On the one hand, this might create an image from the simultaneity of pictures I sense. But, most of all, I believe this addresses an interest in new developments, in the question: "How does one arrive at new pictures?"

In some cases, I see these compositions and pages created from layering as new, individual works.

BR   For example, you have three technolog-ical pictures, headlights, and technical spaces overlap on the back cover. It looks as if cutting took place, but the pictures are no longer the classical, cut-out fragments of a collage technique, but rather layered images and visual simultaneities.
Then double-pages like these appear in the book: the photograph of an extremely intricate concrete mixer truck beside the page showing the interior of the driver's cabin of a bus, where images in the reinforced rearview mirror, tel-evision images above it, and the view outside layer the composition; or the image of the young man on the telephone, with the layered photograph of a copying machine behind it, and which you juxtapose with a hotel window's view of a city—but superimposed on the view is the reflection on the window's inside surface…
Can you say more about these layered images and overlaps? They not only seem to demon-strate your special perception, but also a transi-tion of this simultaneity to a picture.

WT   These layered images, the impure, the contaminated, and that which isn't compati-ble but which functions just the same, were present in my work from the start. This not only happens in the pictures, but has always been a central aspect of my installations. Books, too, if you turn the pages rapidly, have this simulta-neity. As a result, a new formation of some-thing that was there all along is currently in my work. Now my perception of the world has found this form.

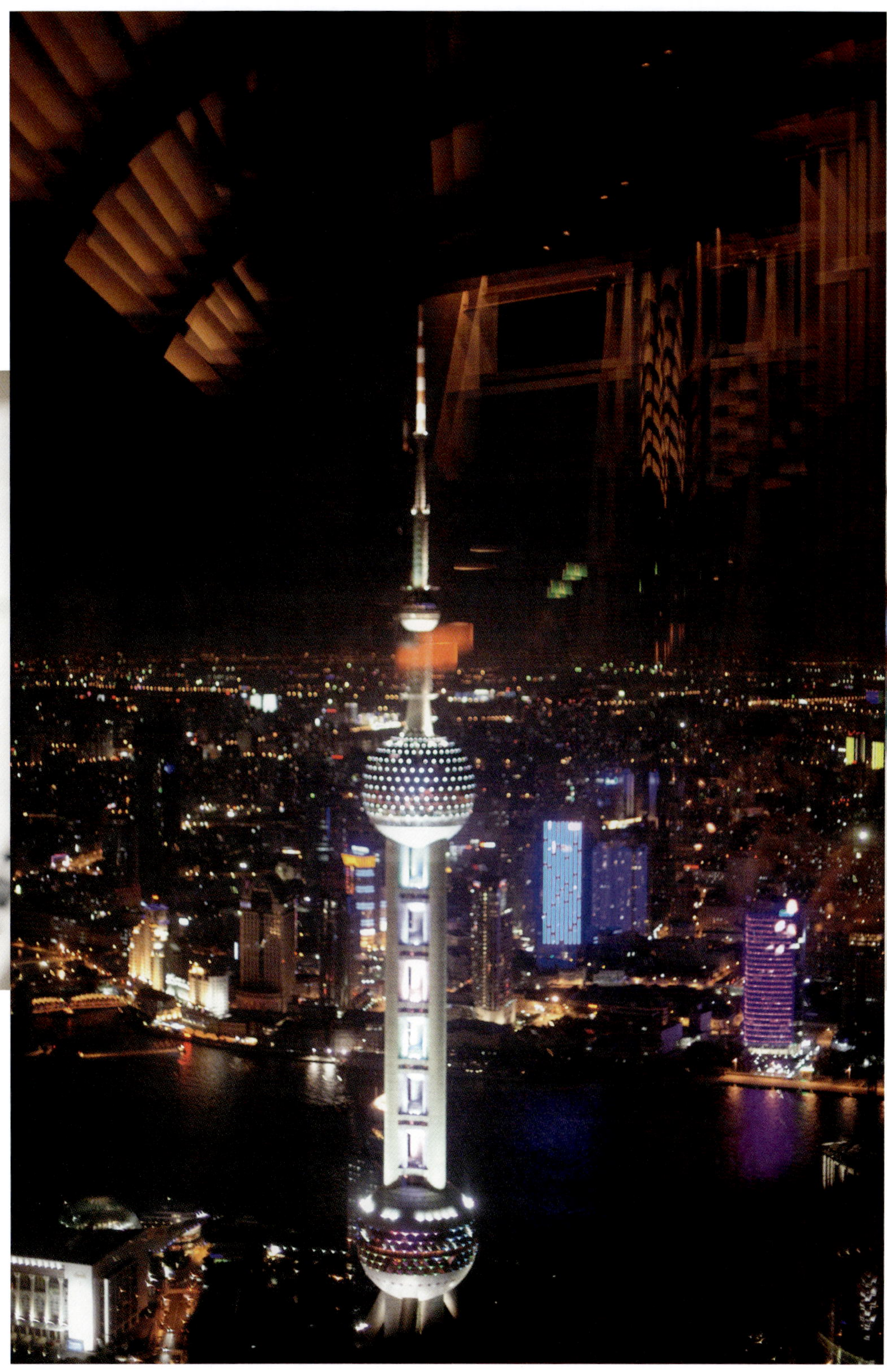

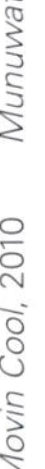

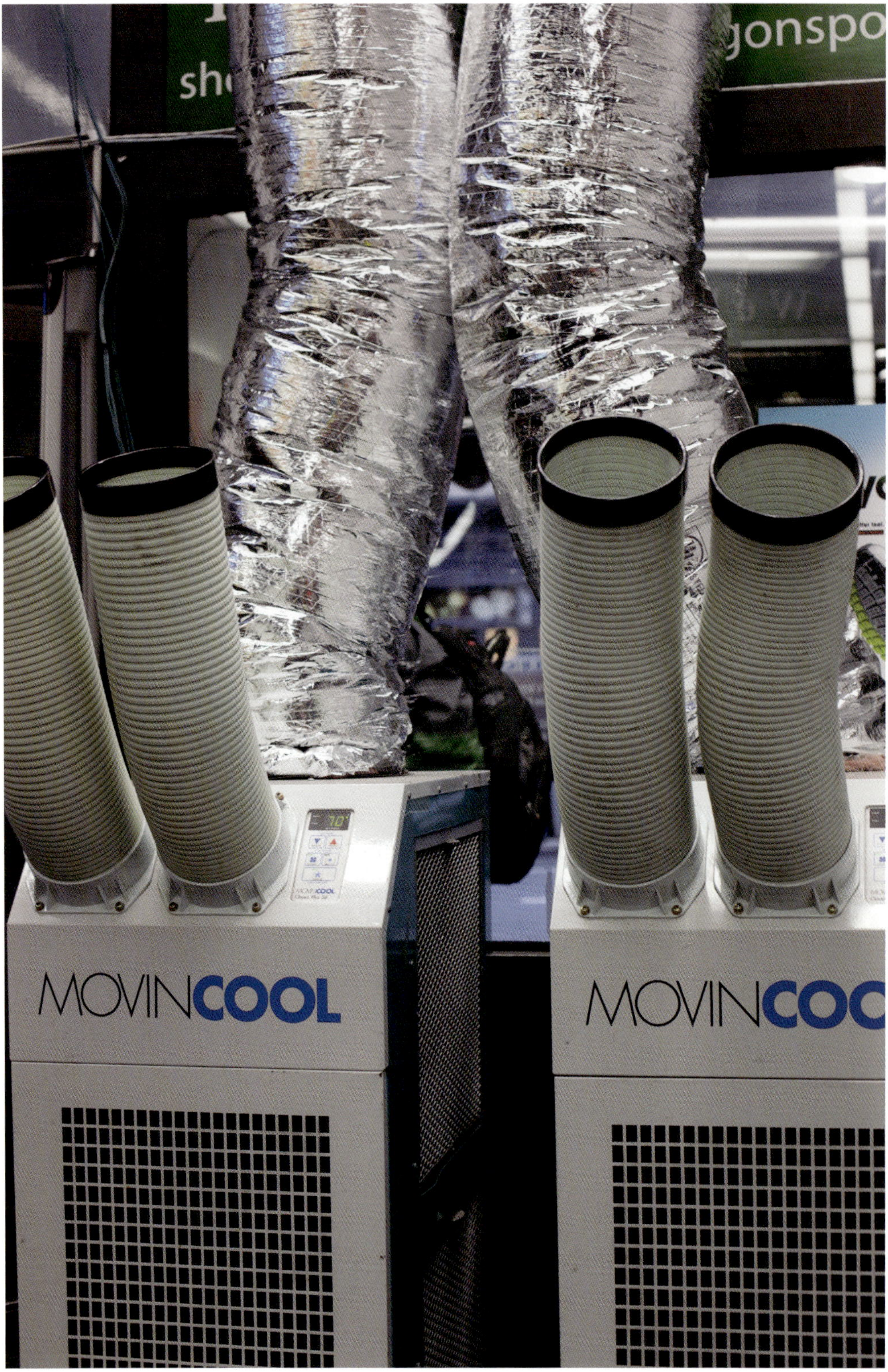

Movin Cool, 2010   Munuwata sky, 2011   Silver 84, 2011

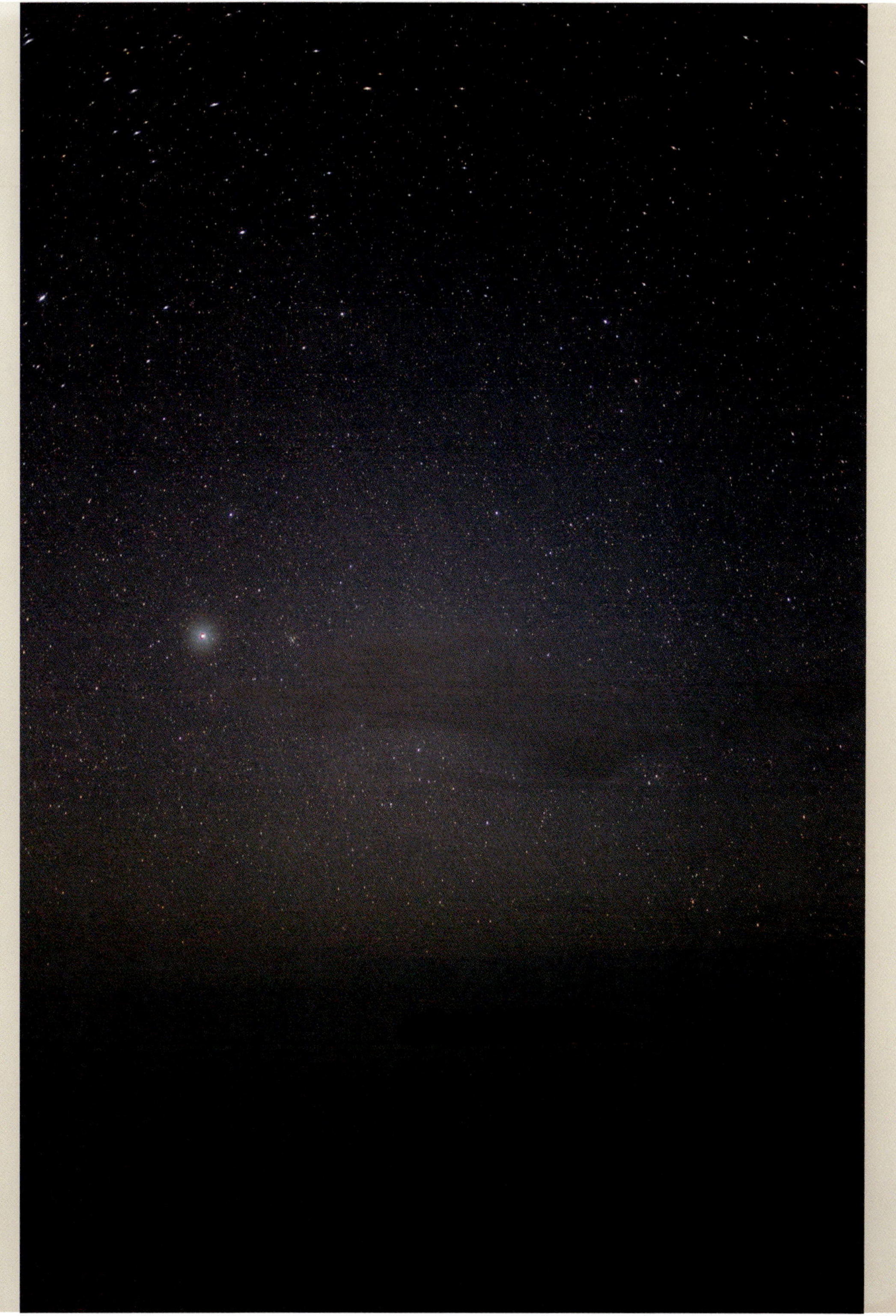

Headlight (d), 2012

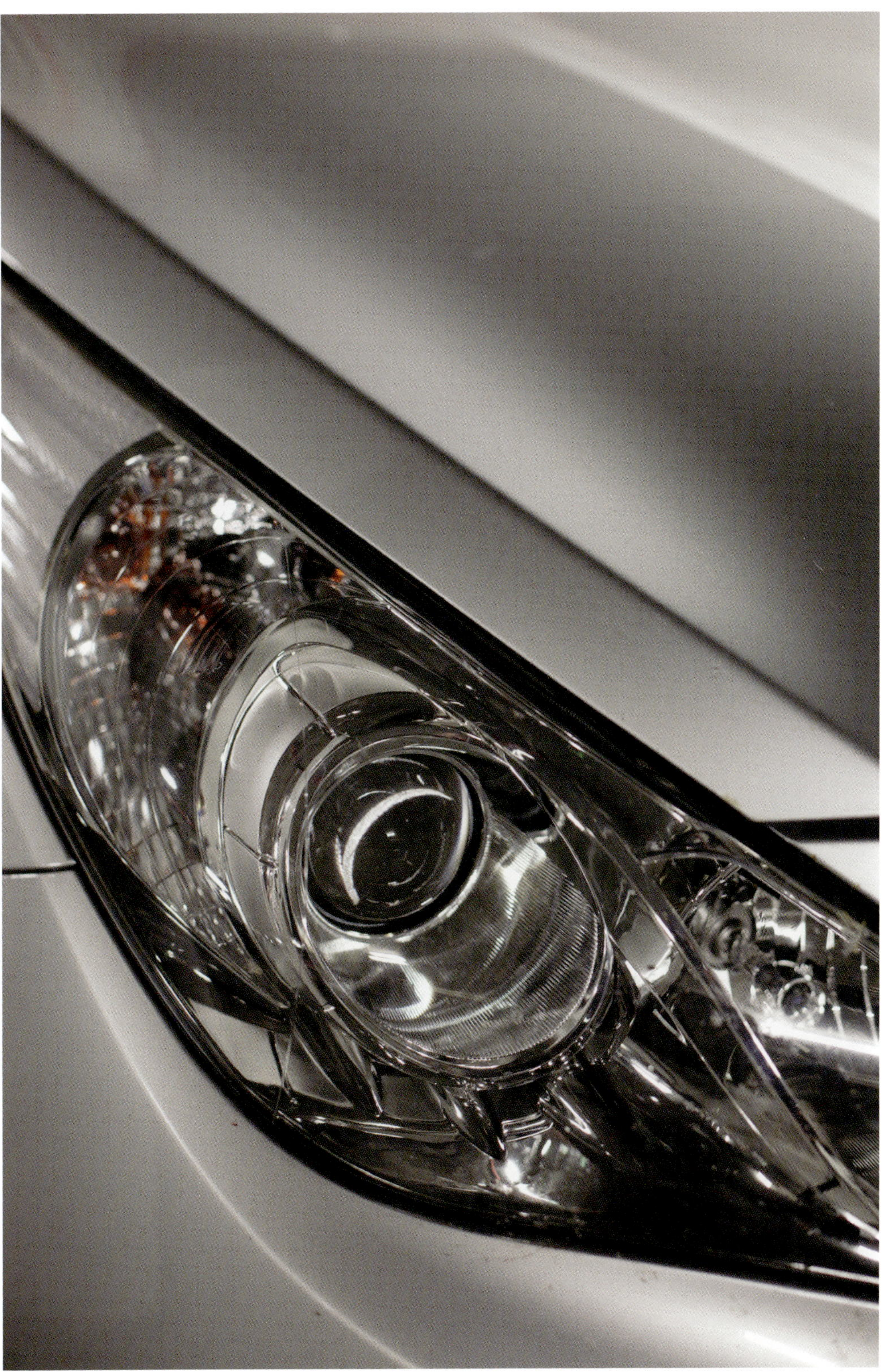

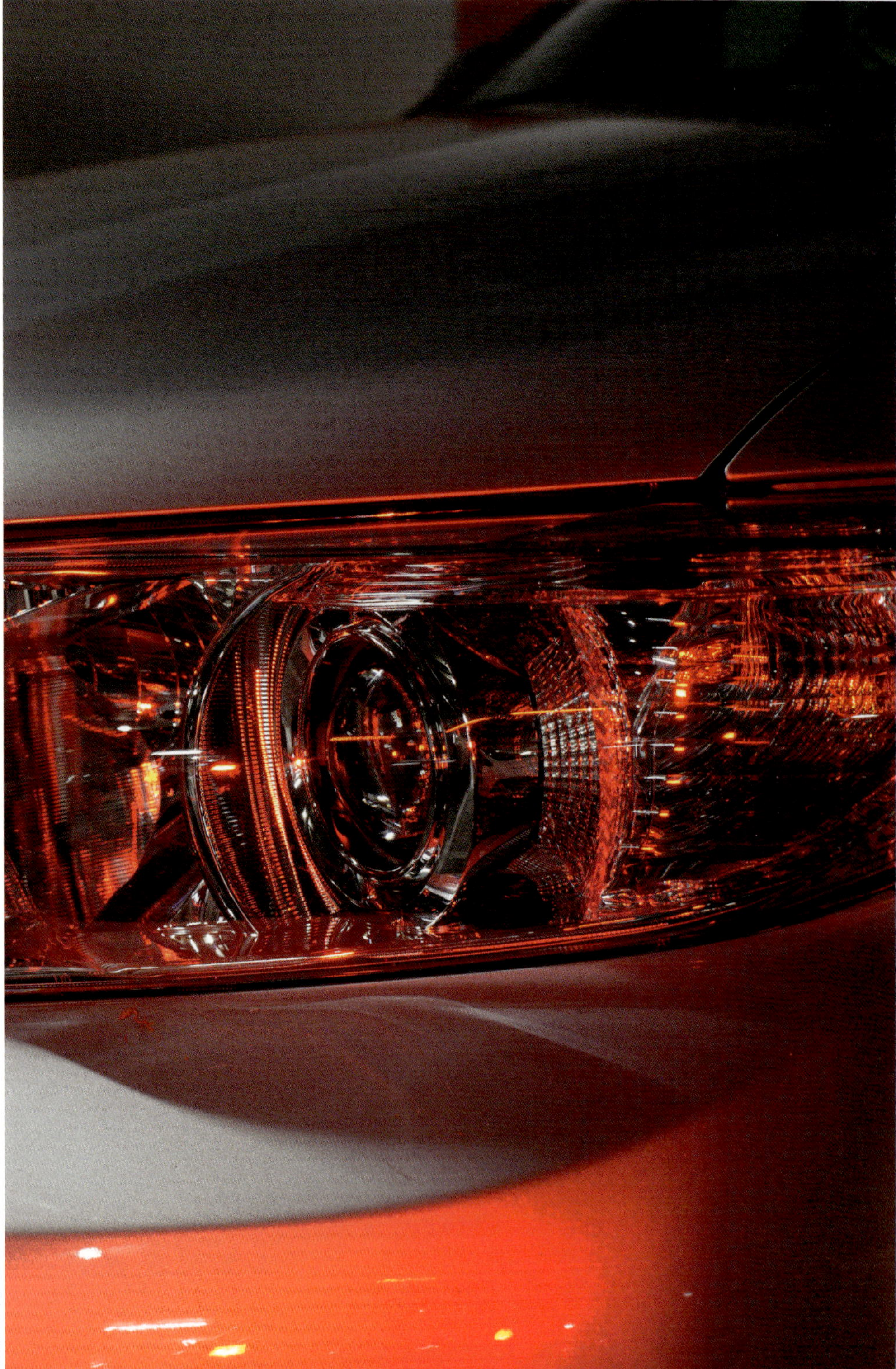

Headlight (a), 2012   Silver 83, 2011

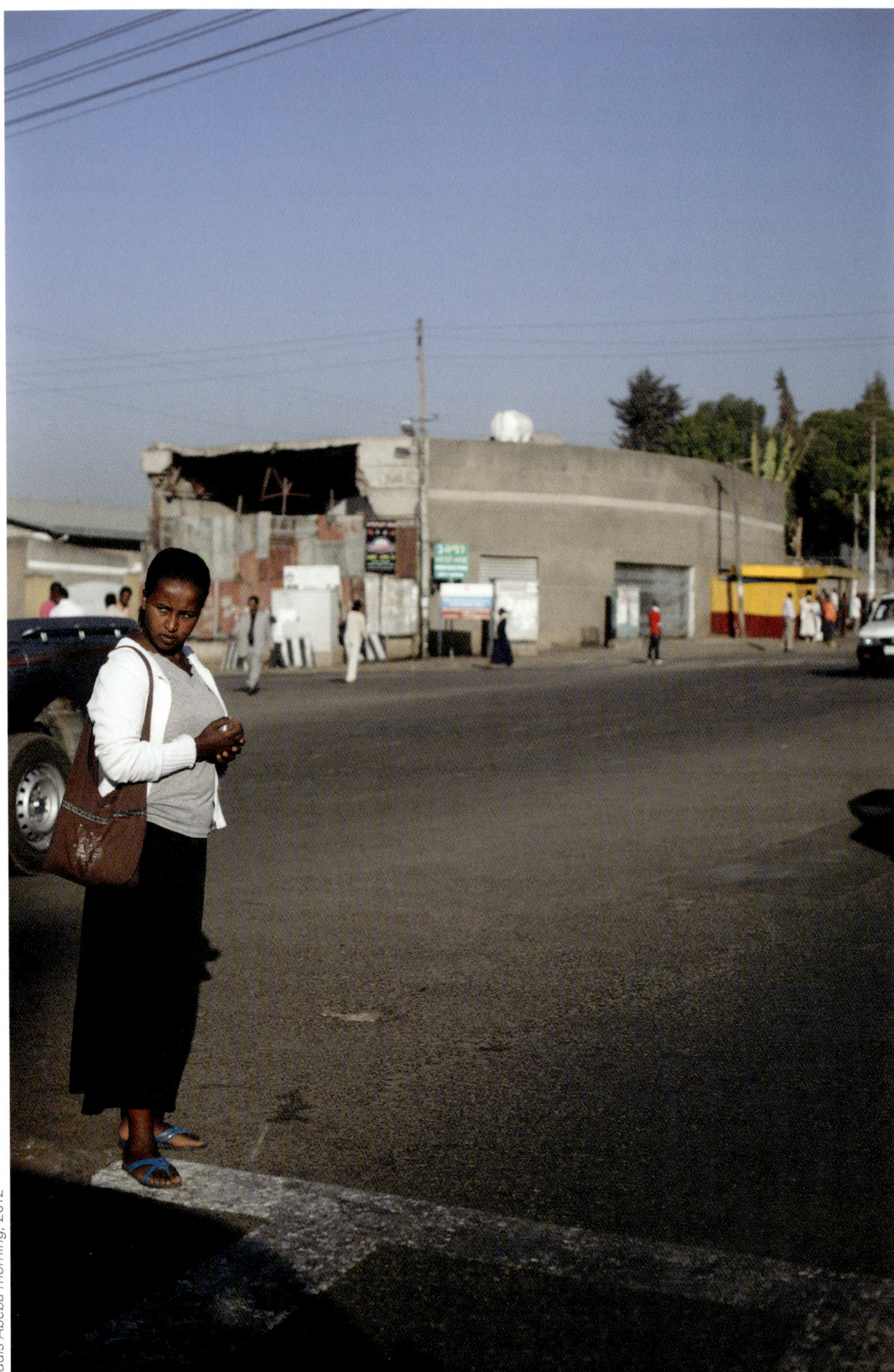

Addis Abeba morning, 2012

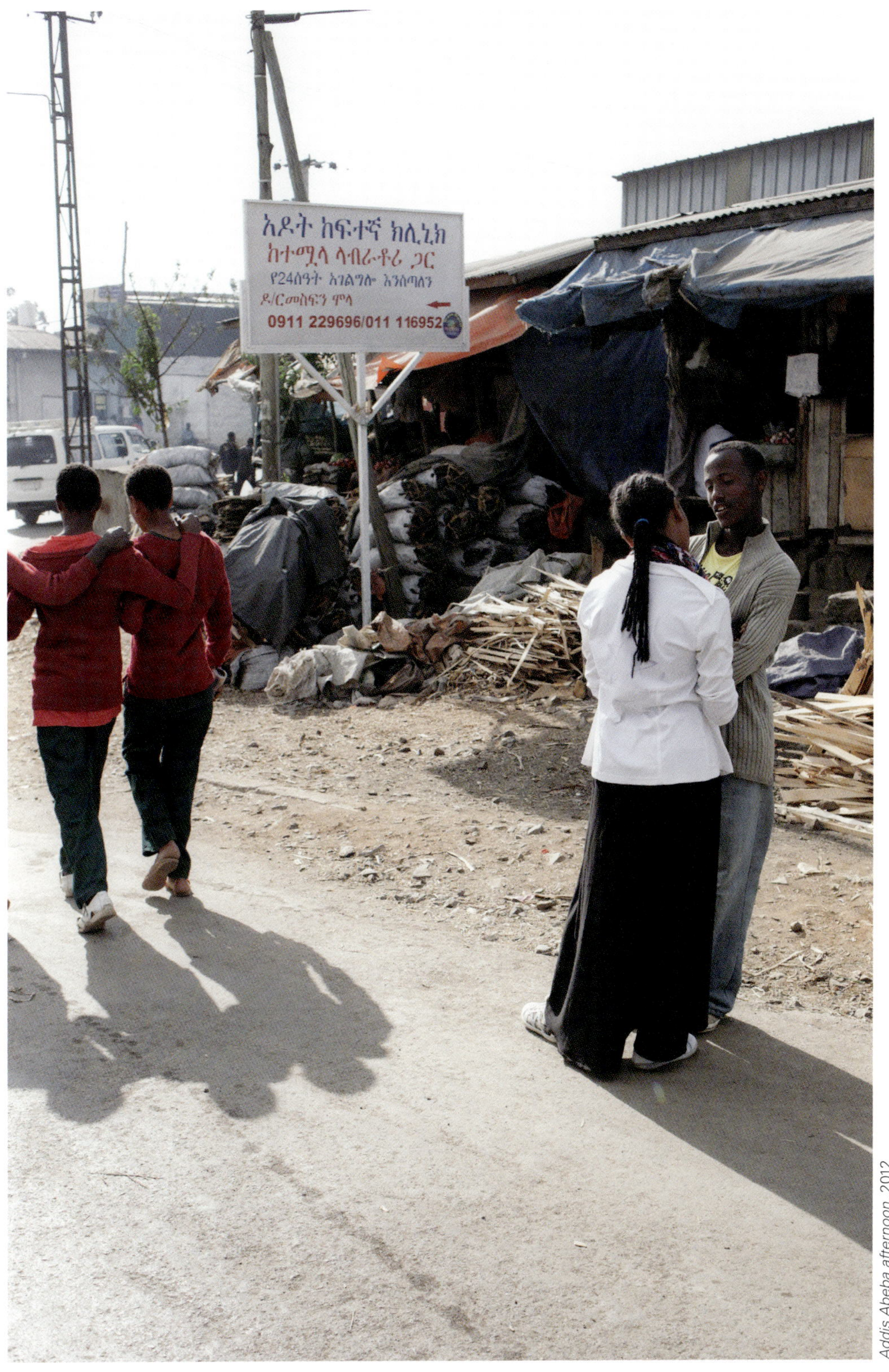

Addis Abeba afternoon, 2012

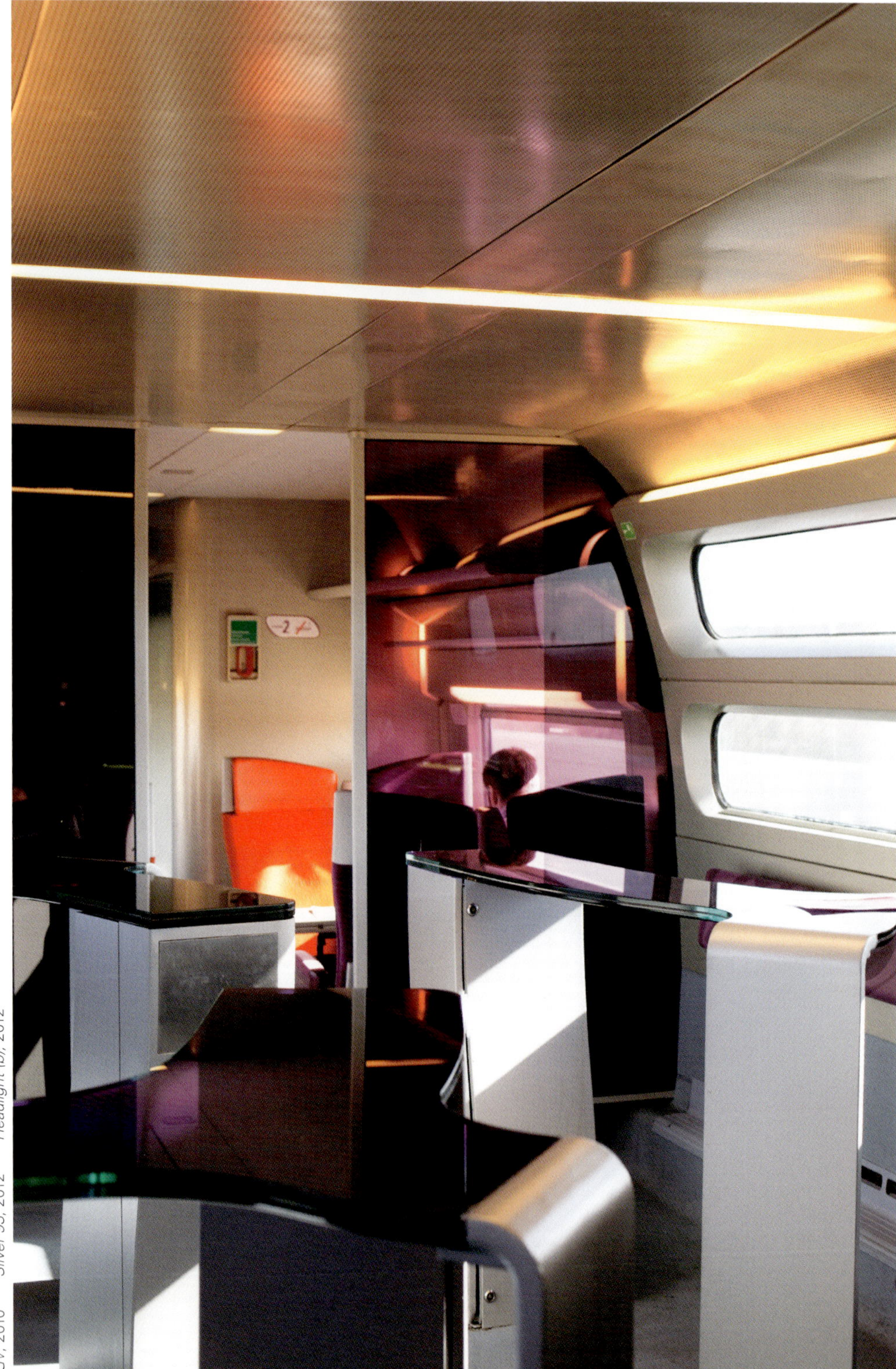

TGV, 2010   Silver 93, 2012   Headlight (b), 2012

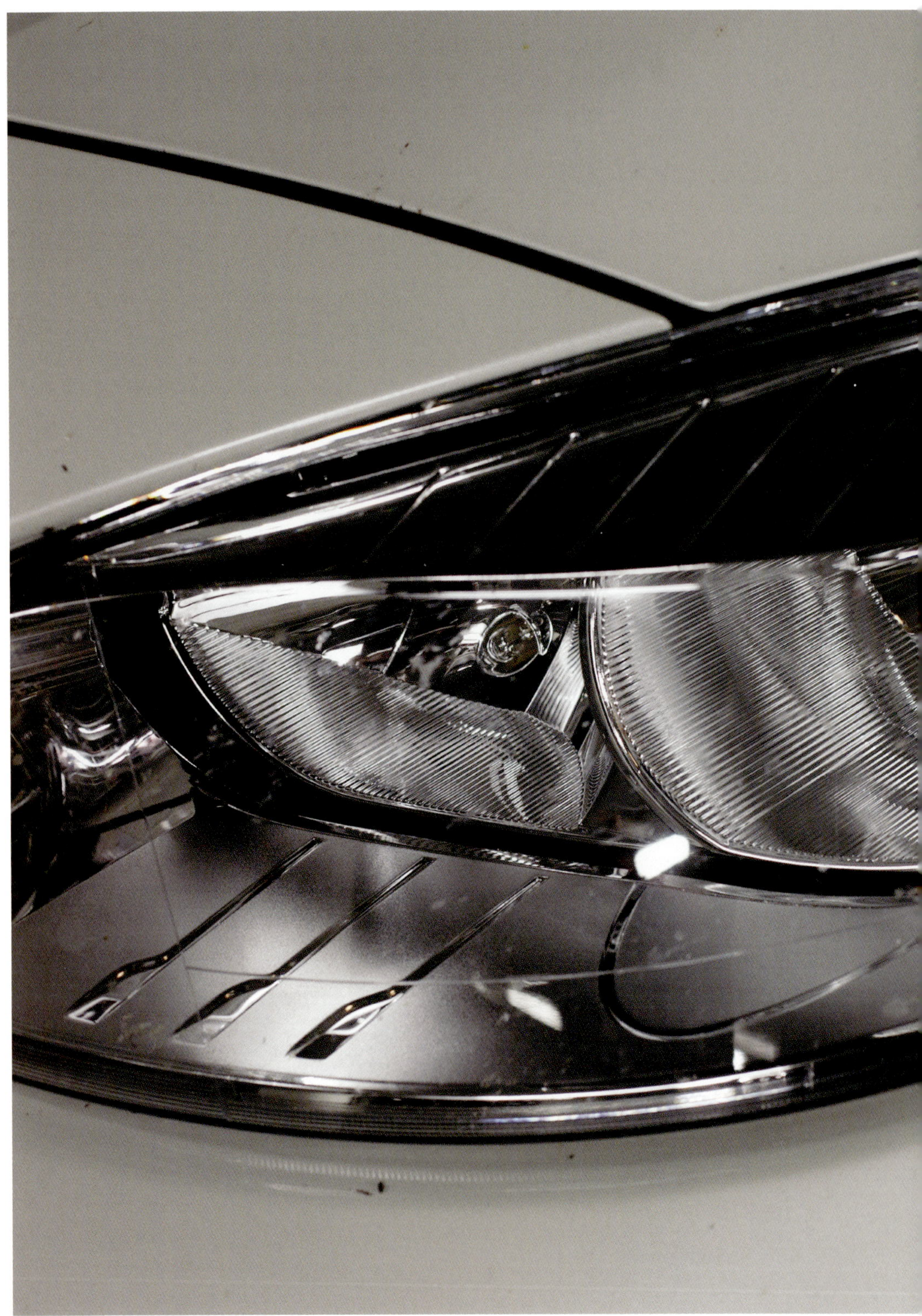

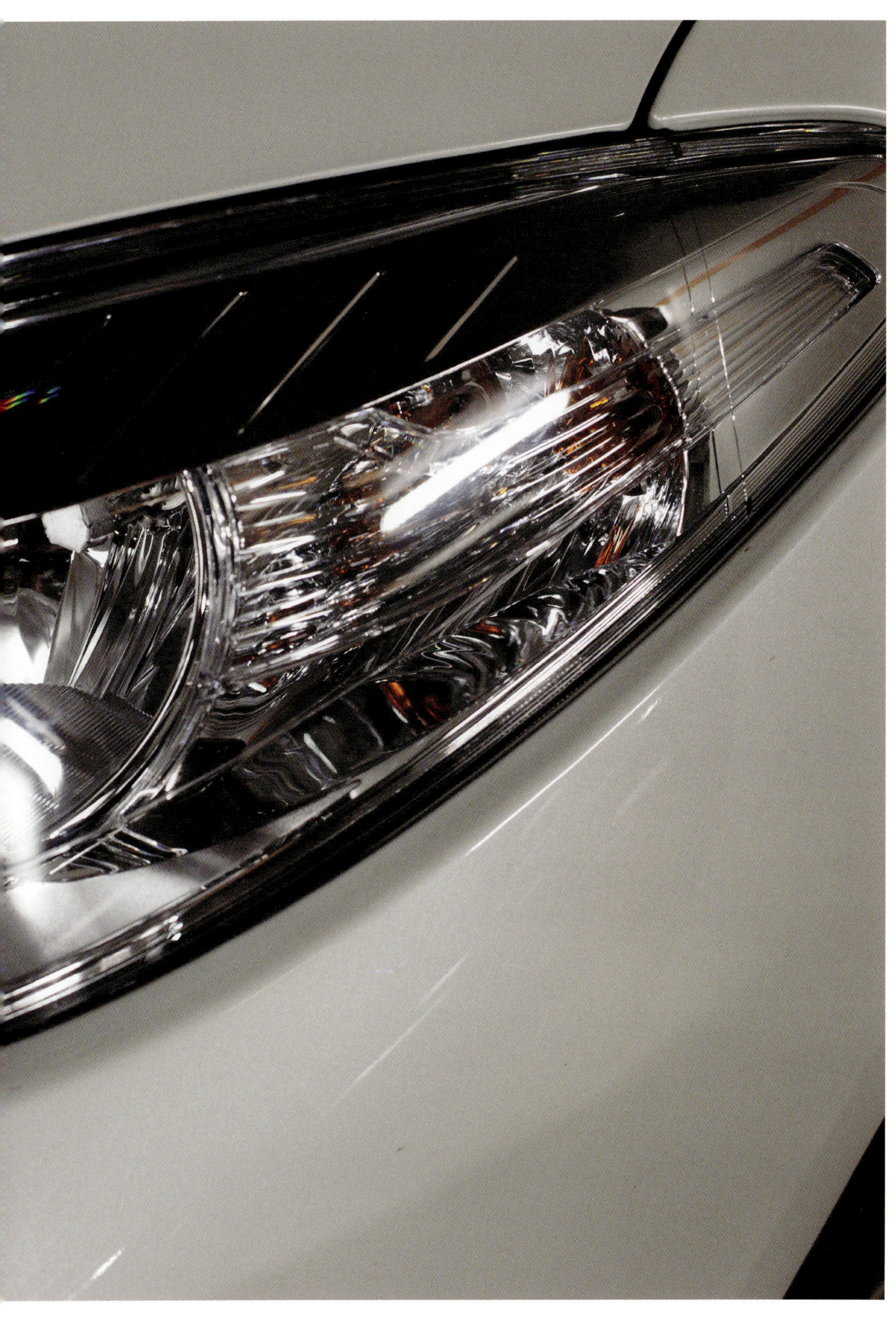

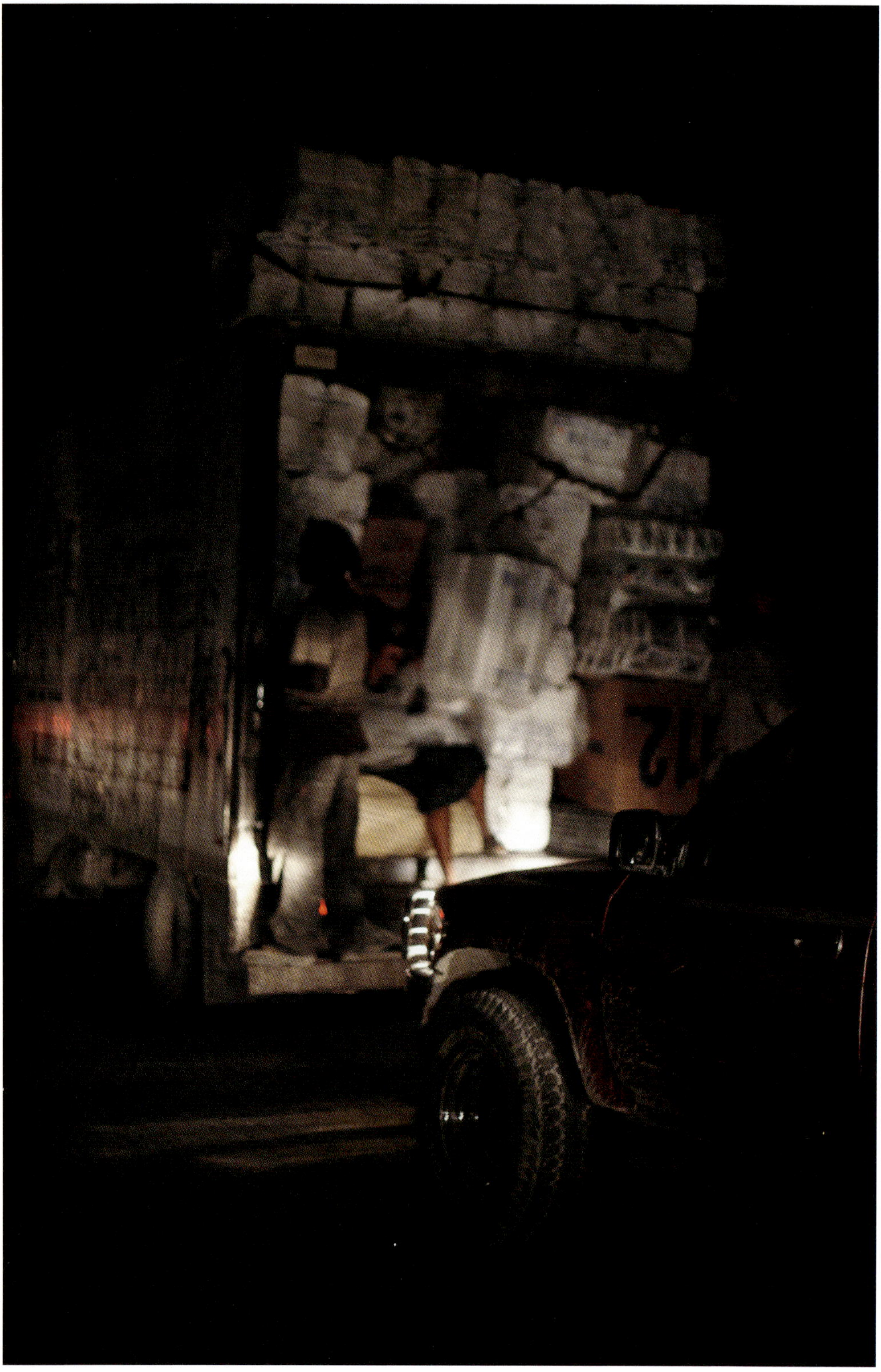

Nightfall (b), 2010   Freezer still life, 2017   Silver 82, 2011

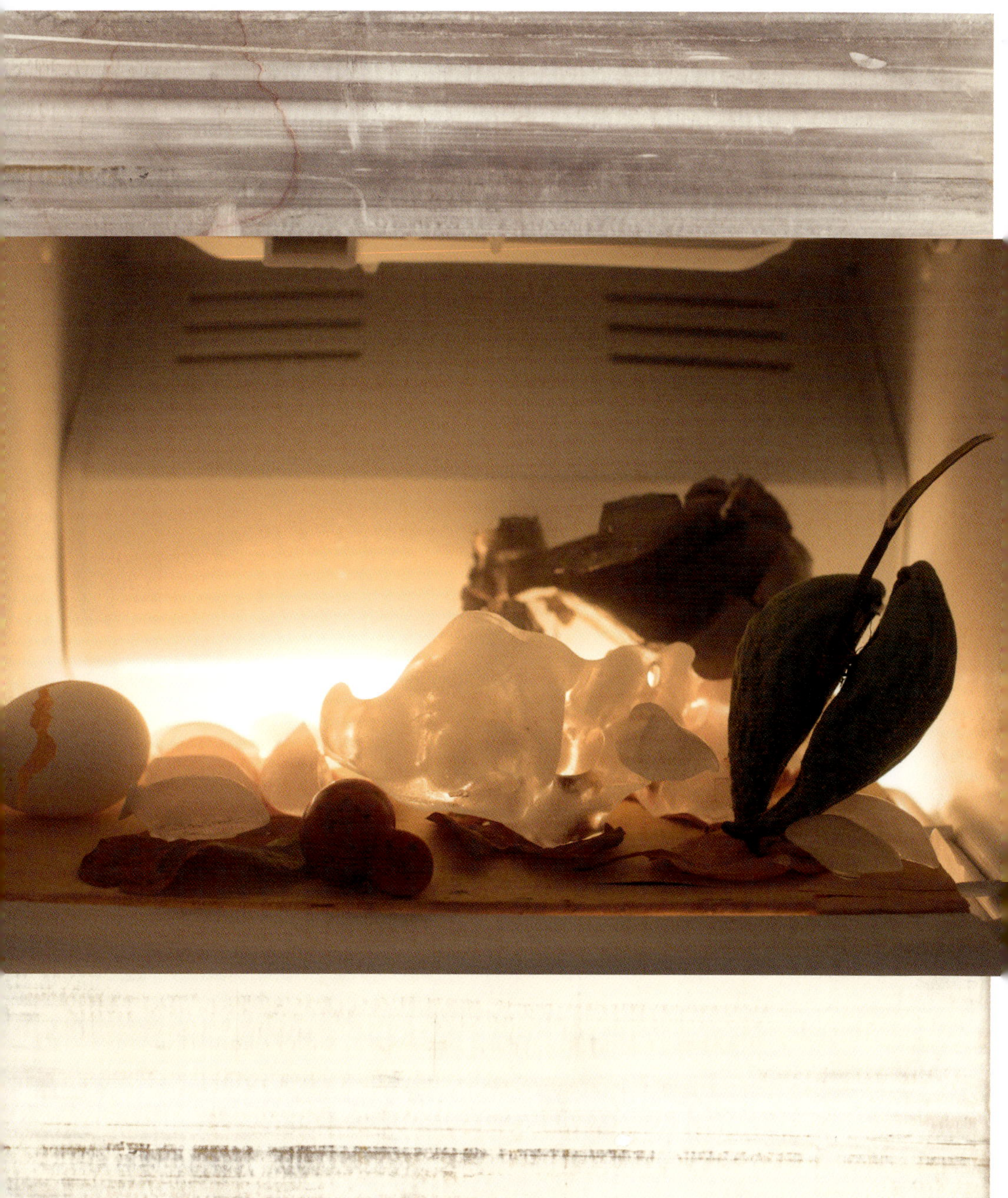

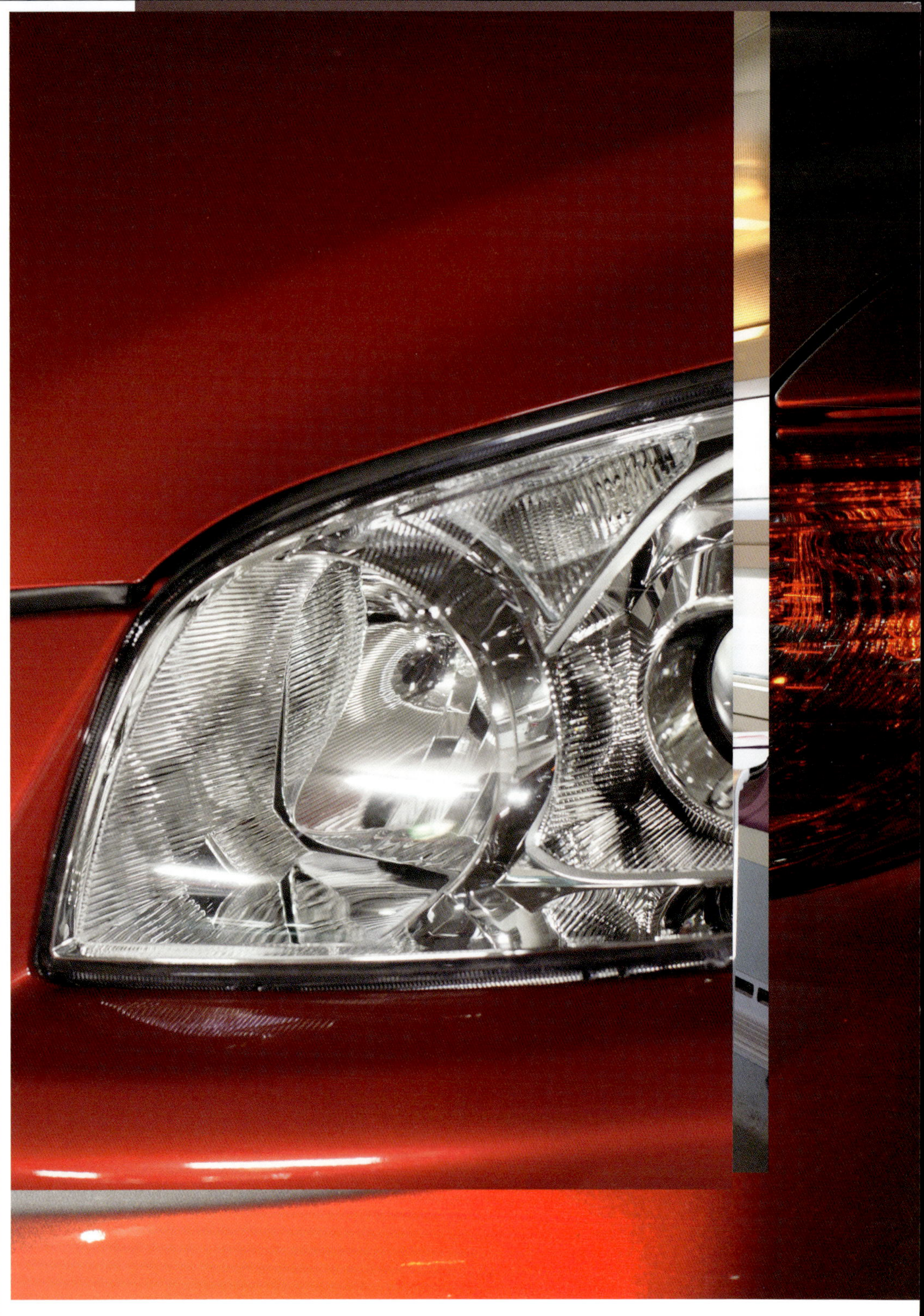

Headlight (f), 2012   _Gym (Santiago)_, 2012   _collage_, 2012

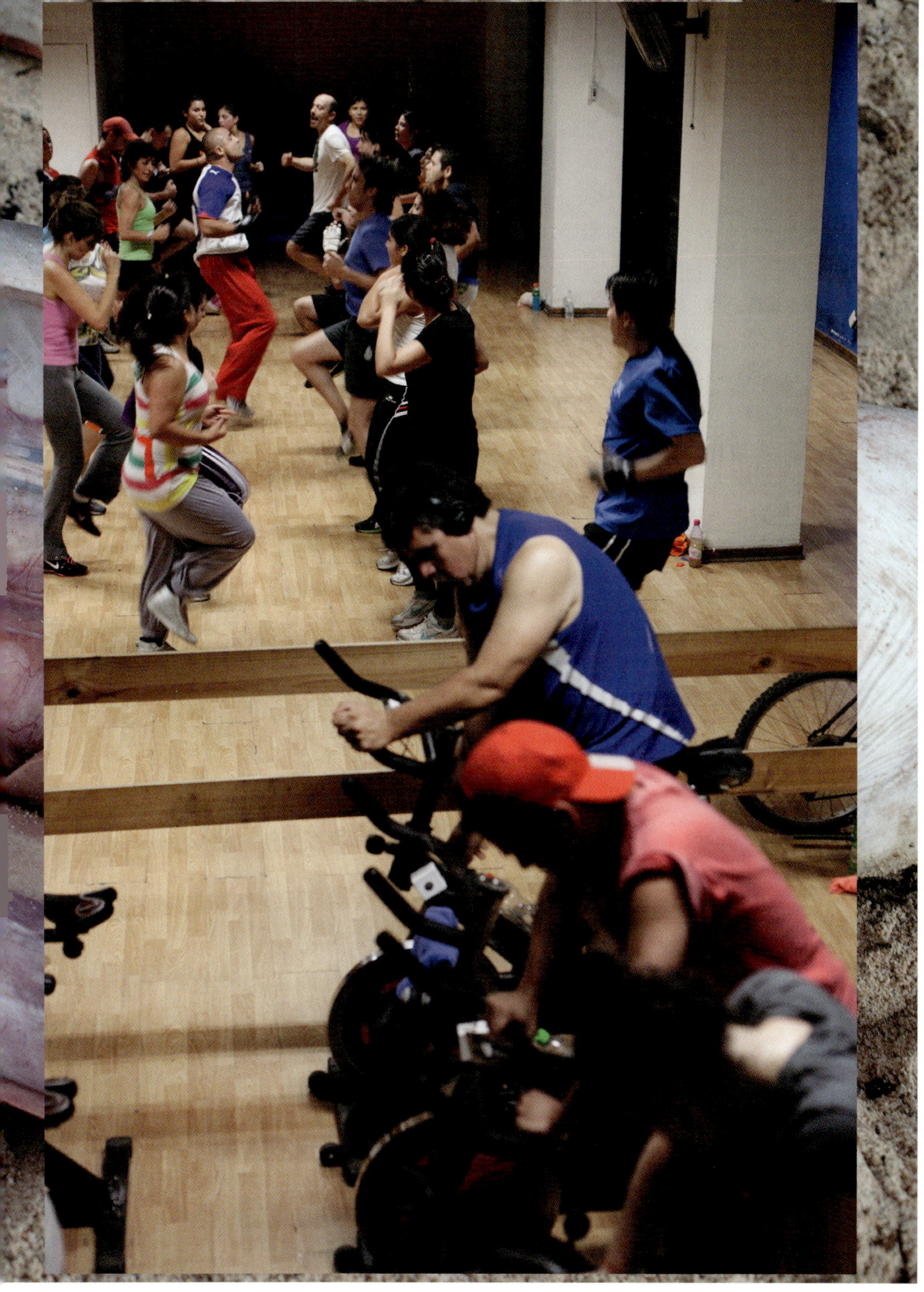

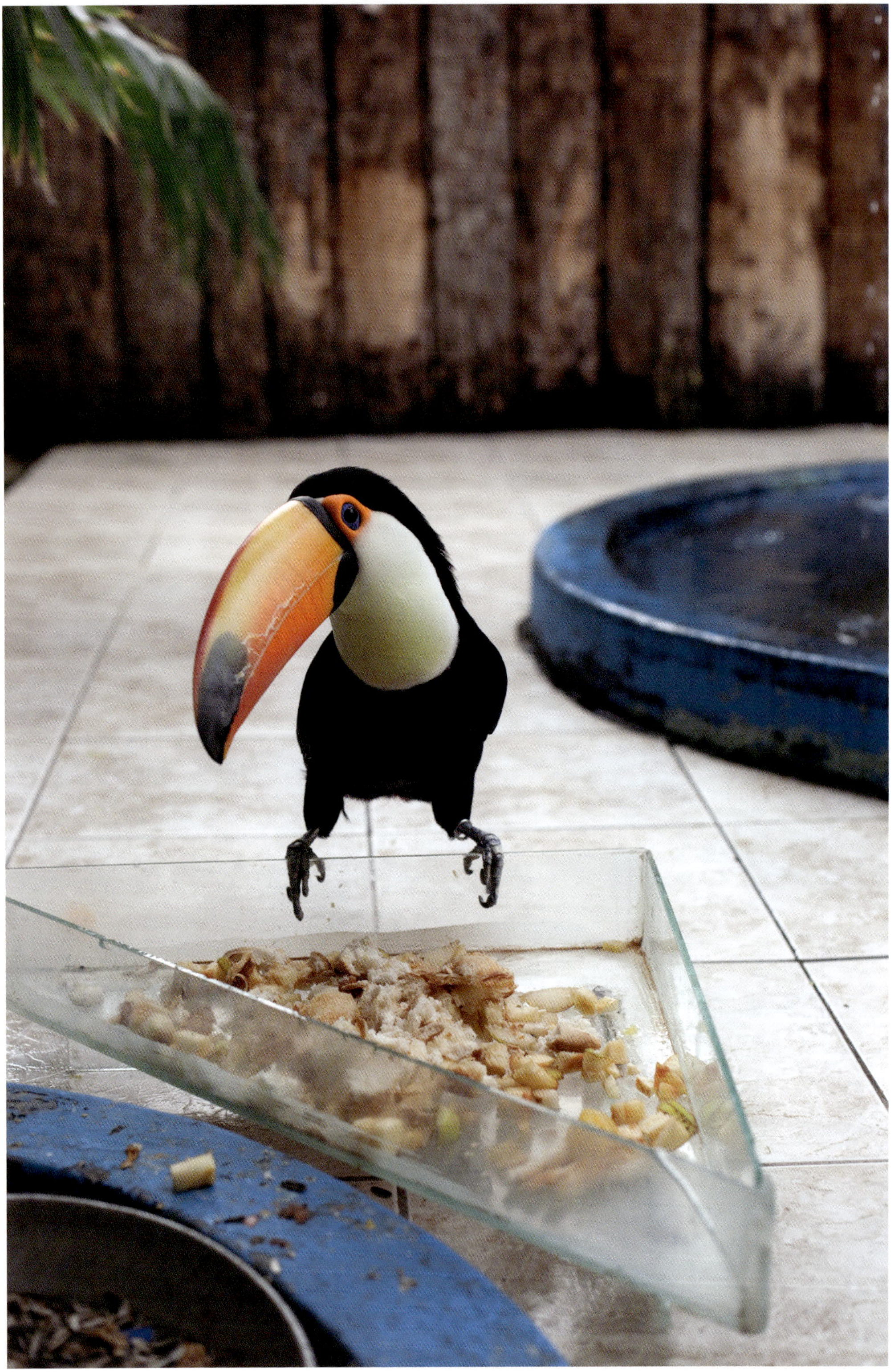

Tukan, 2010   Weed, 2014   Silver 94, 2012

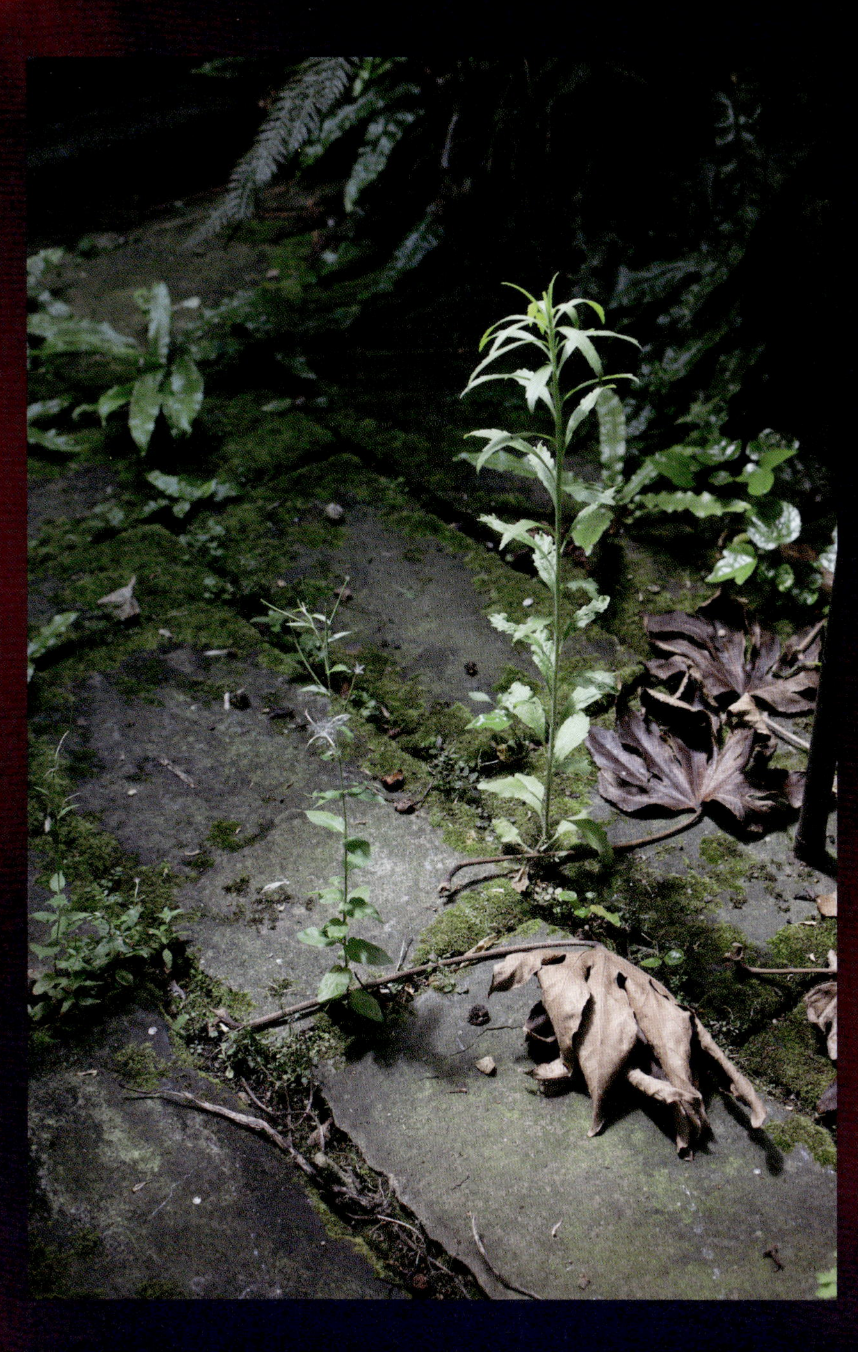

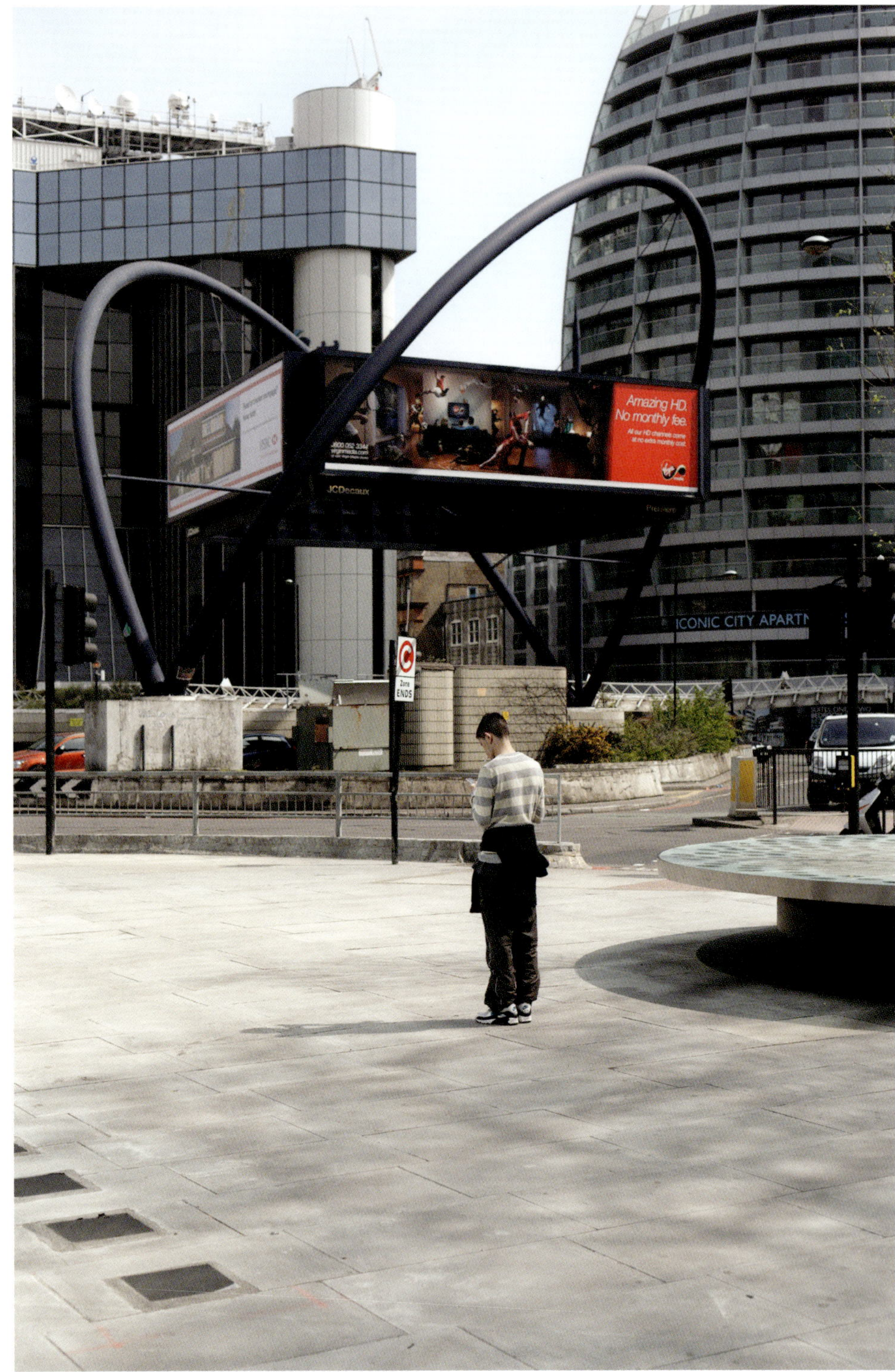

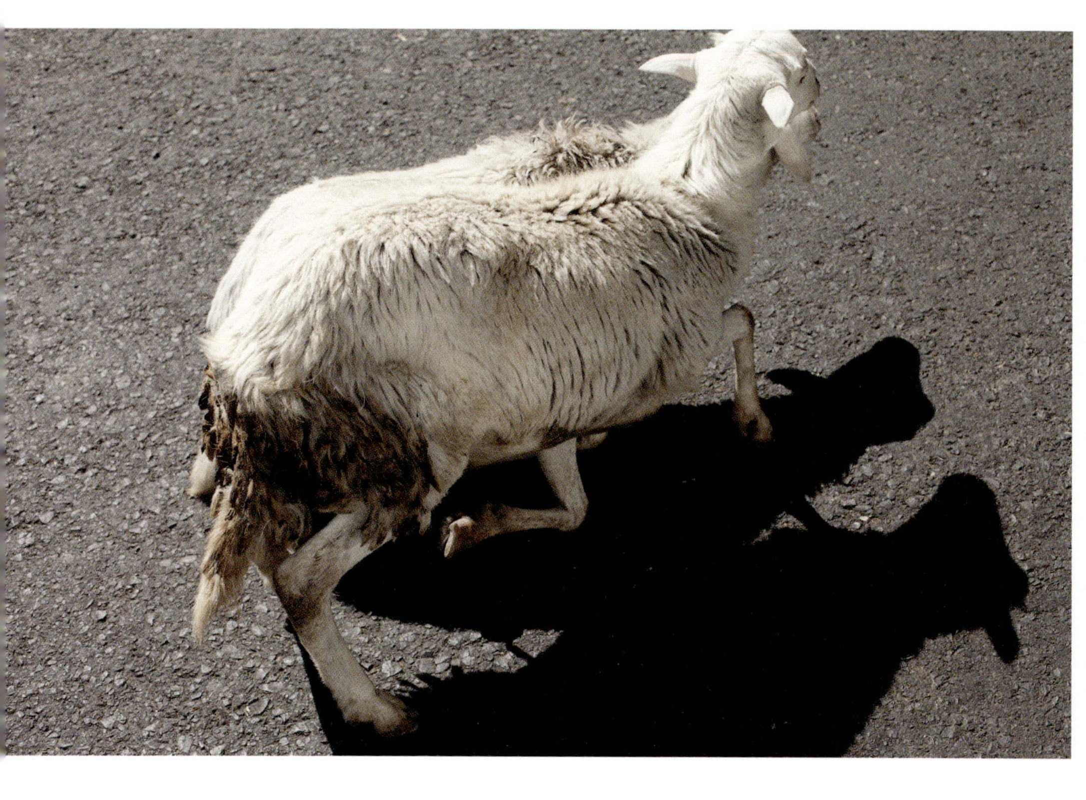

Buenos Aires, 2010   *Sao Paulo*, 2012

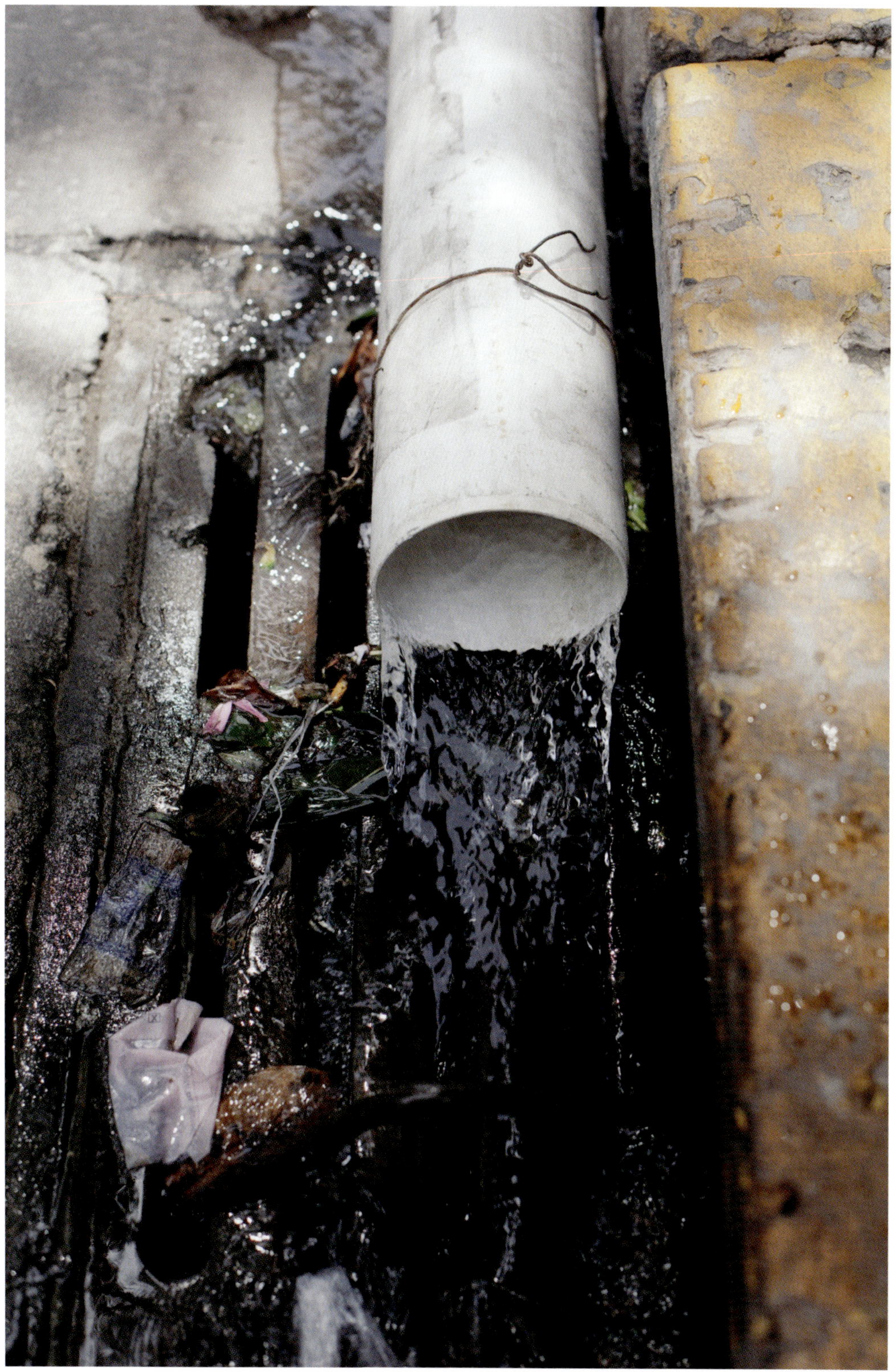

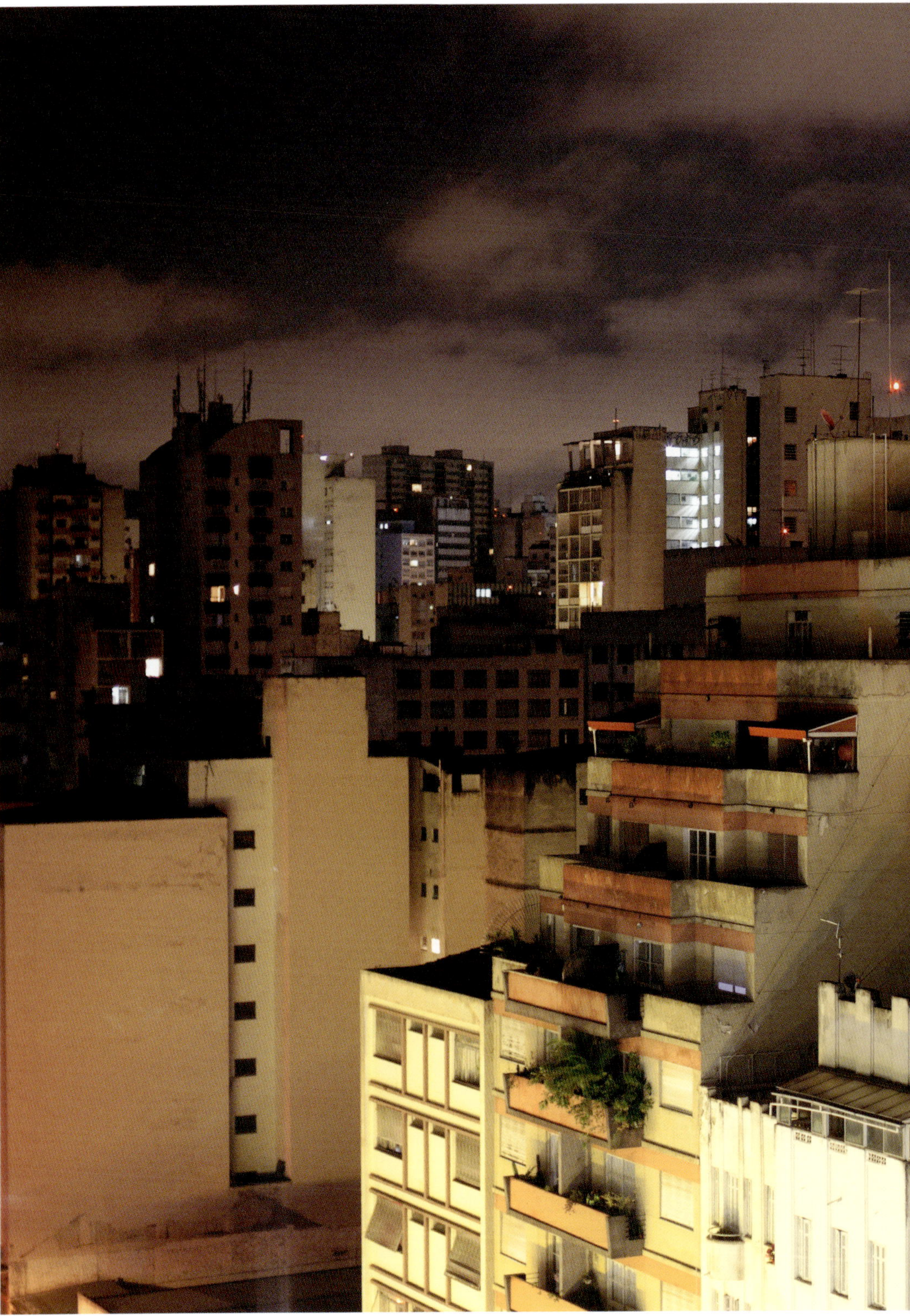

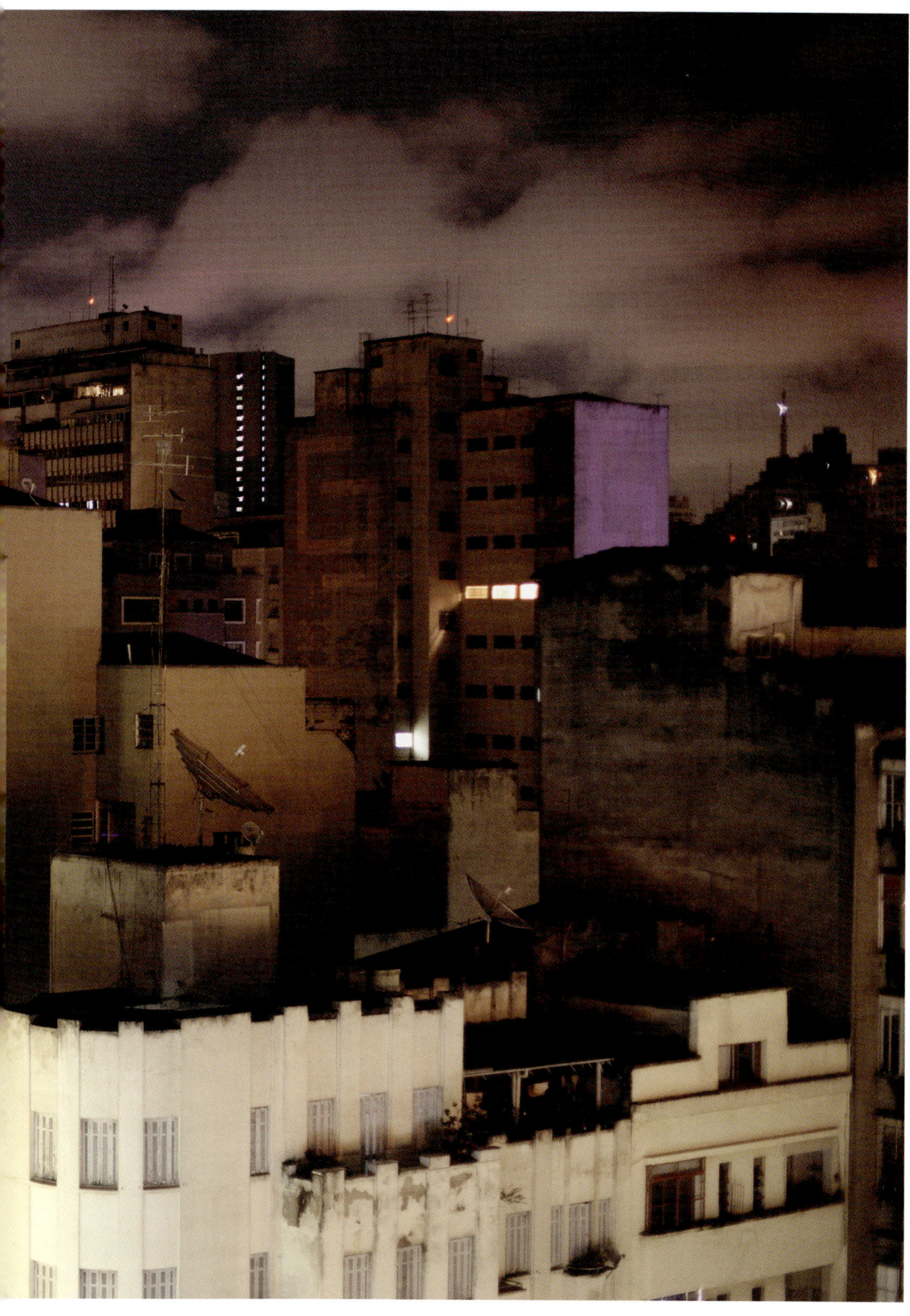

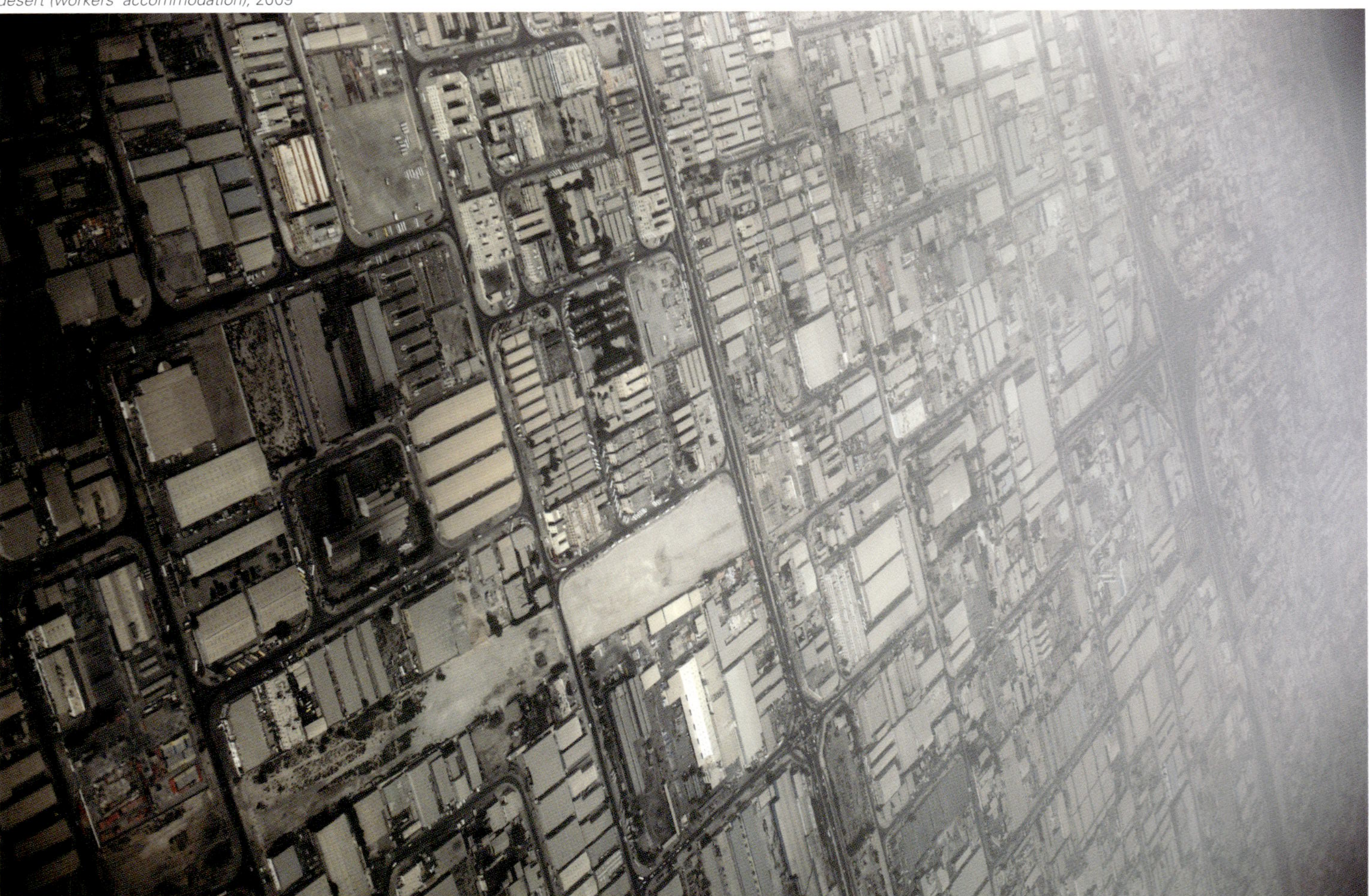

desert (workers' accommodation), 2009

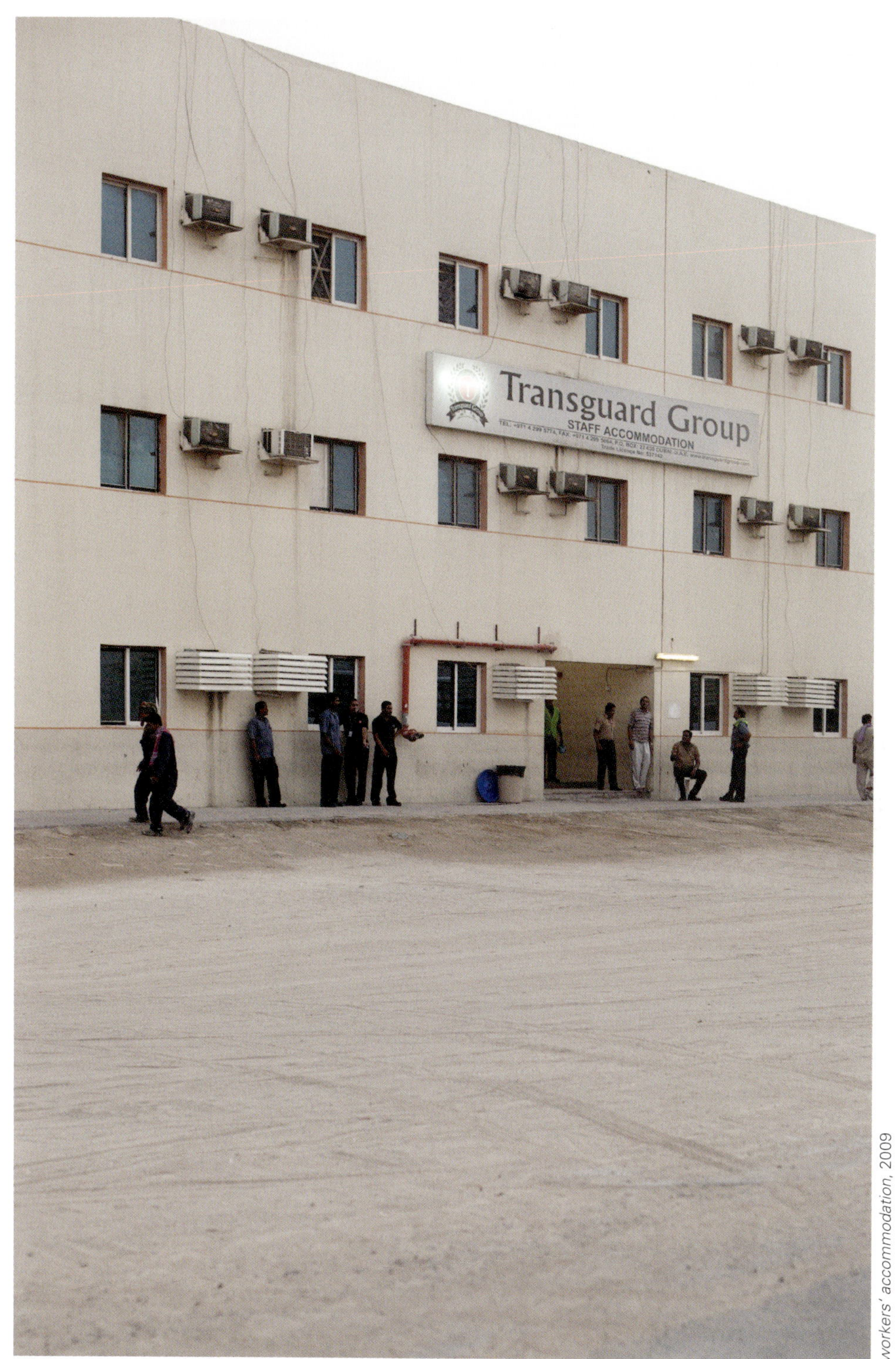

workers' accommodation, 2009

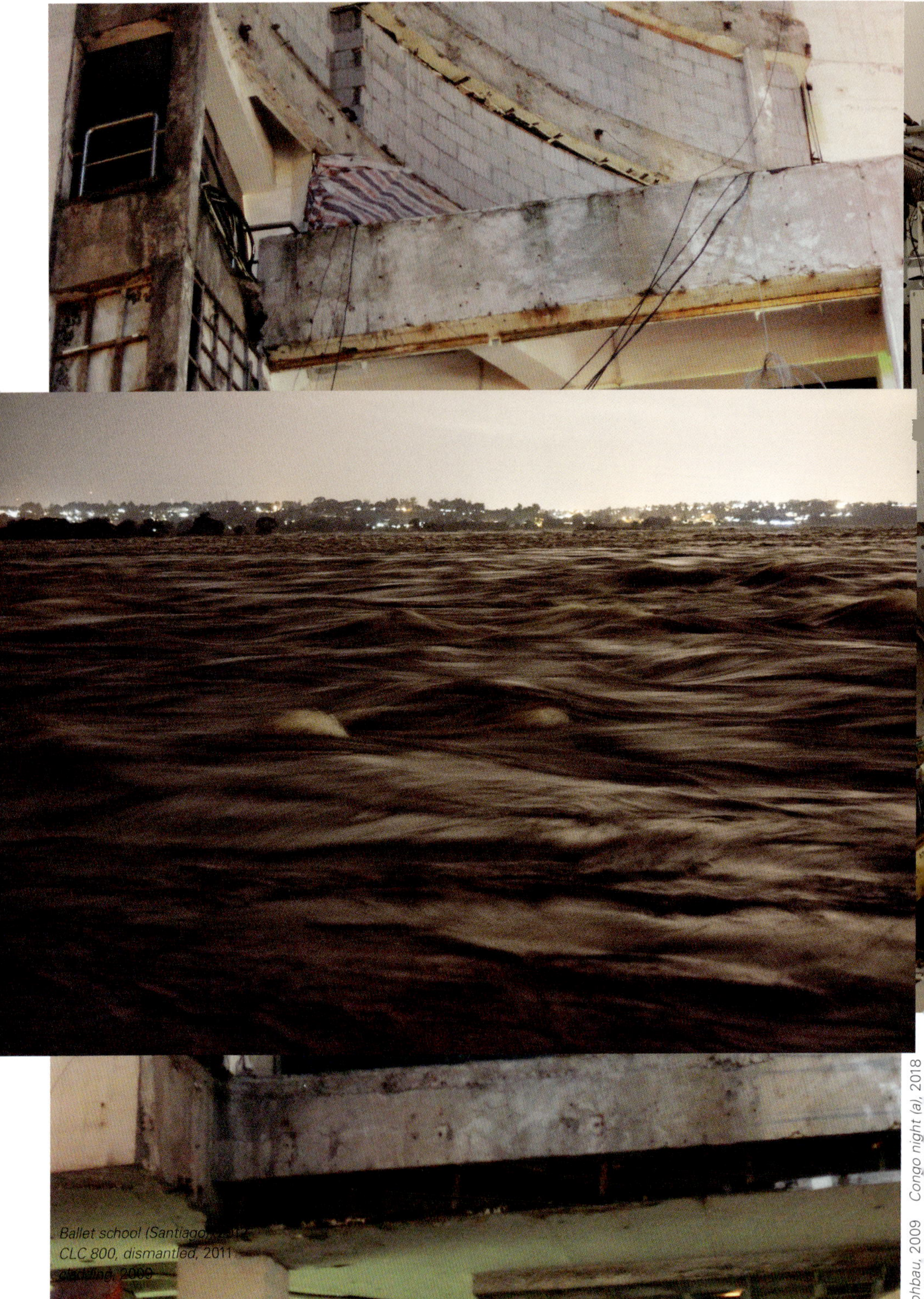

Rohbau, 2009   Congo night (a), 2018

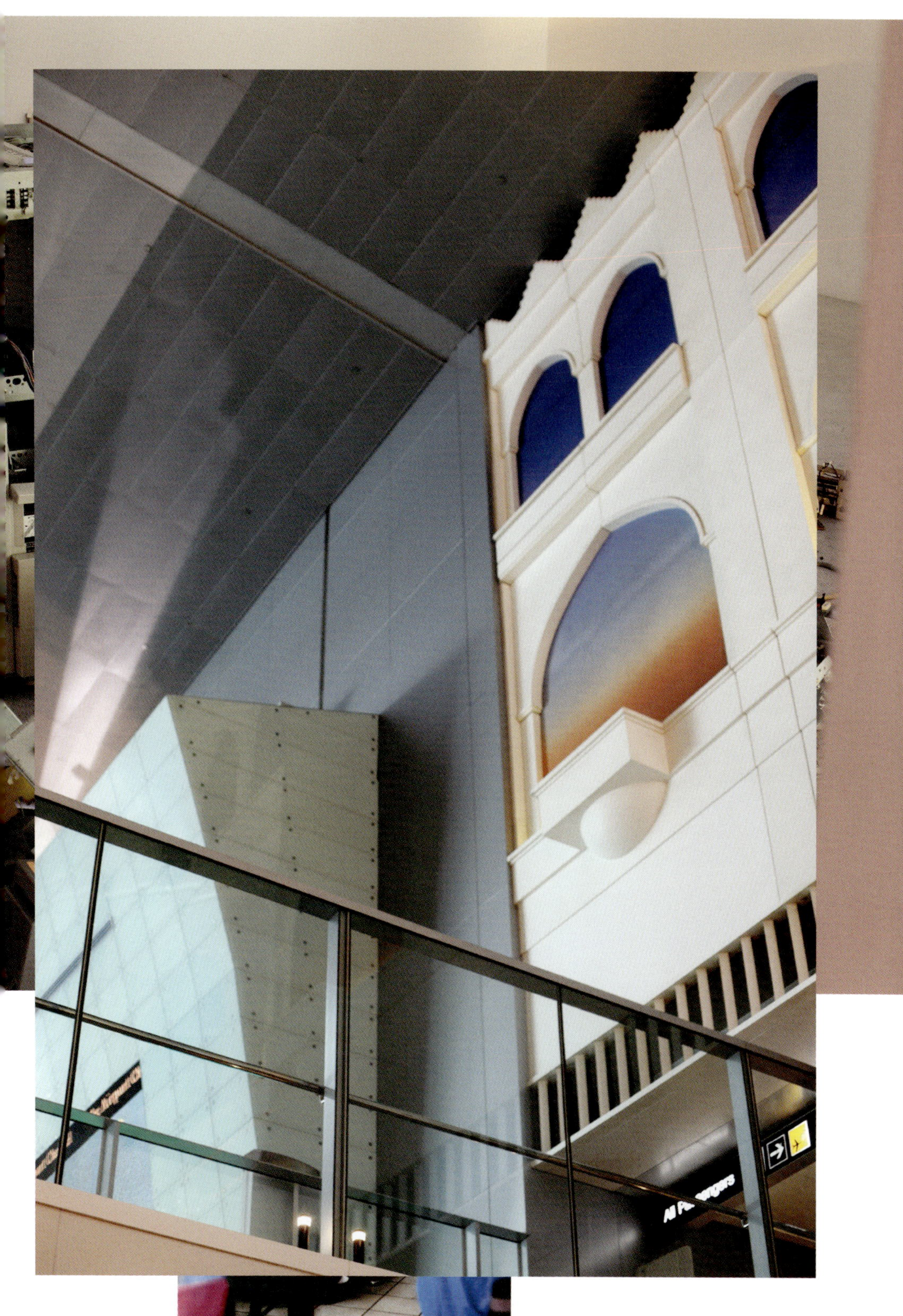

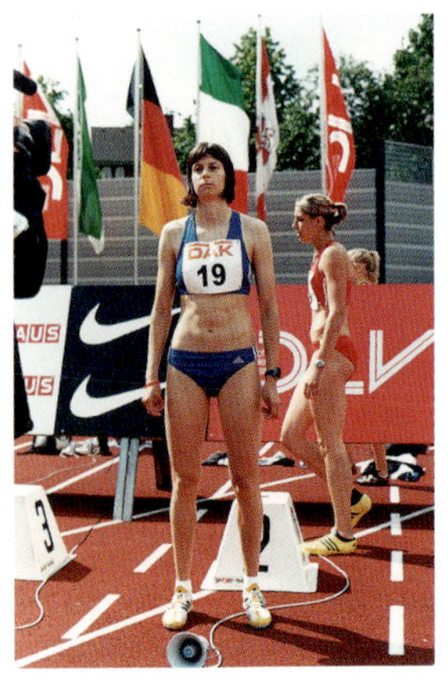
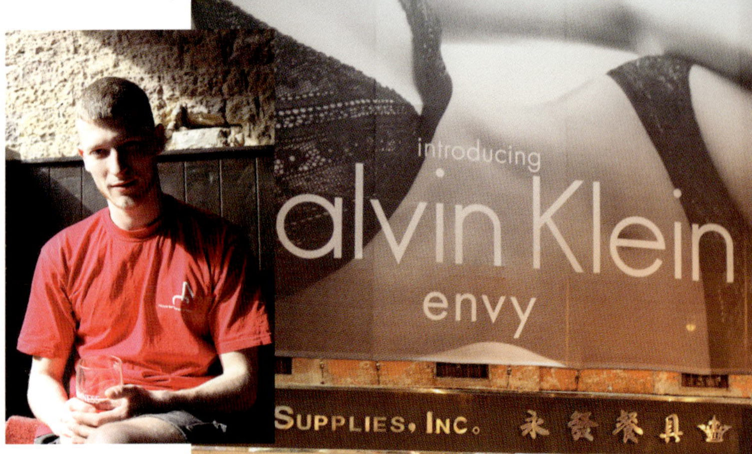

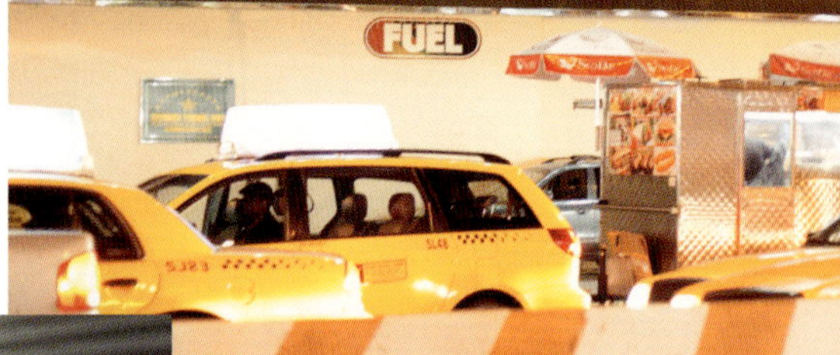

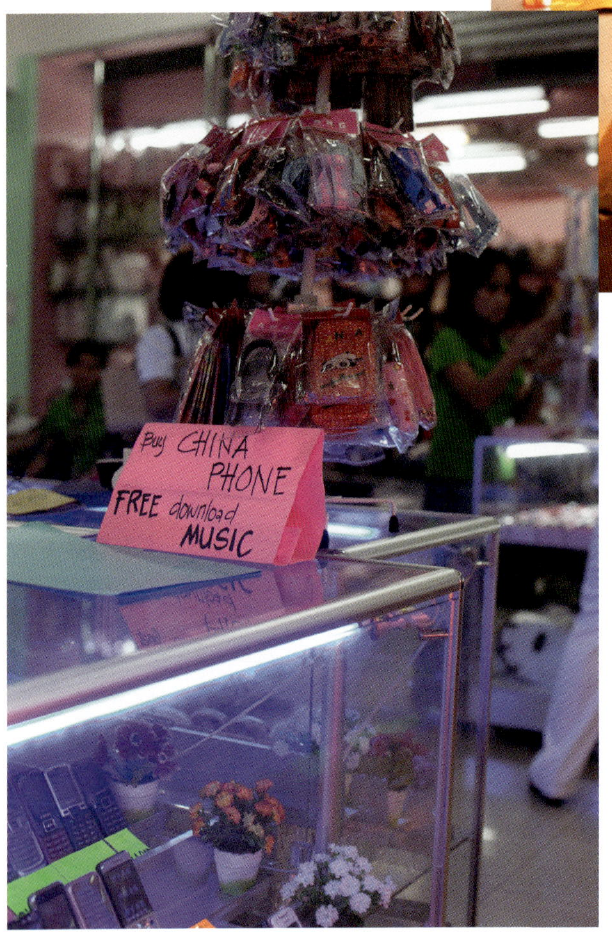

Heptathlon, 2009
China Phone (Cebu), 2009
Karl, sunburst, 2010
Envy, 2010
dusty vehicle, 2012
Tunisia bus, 2009

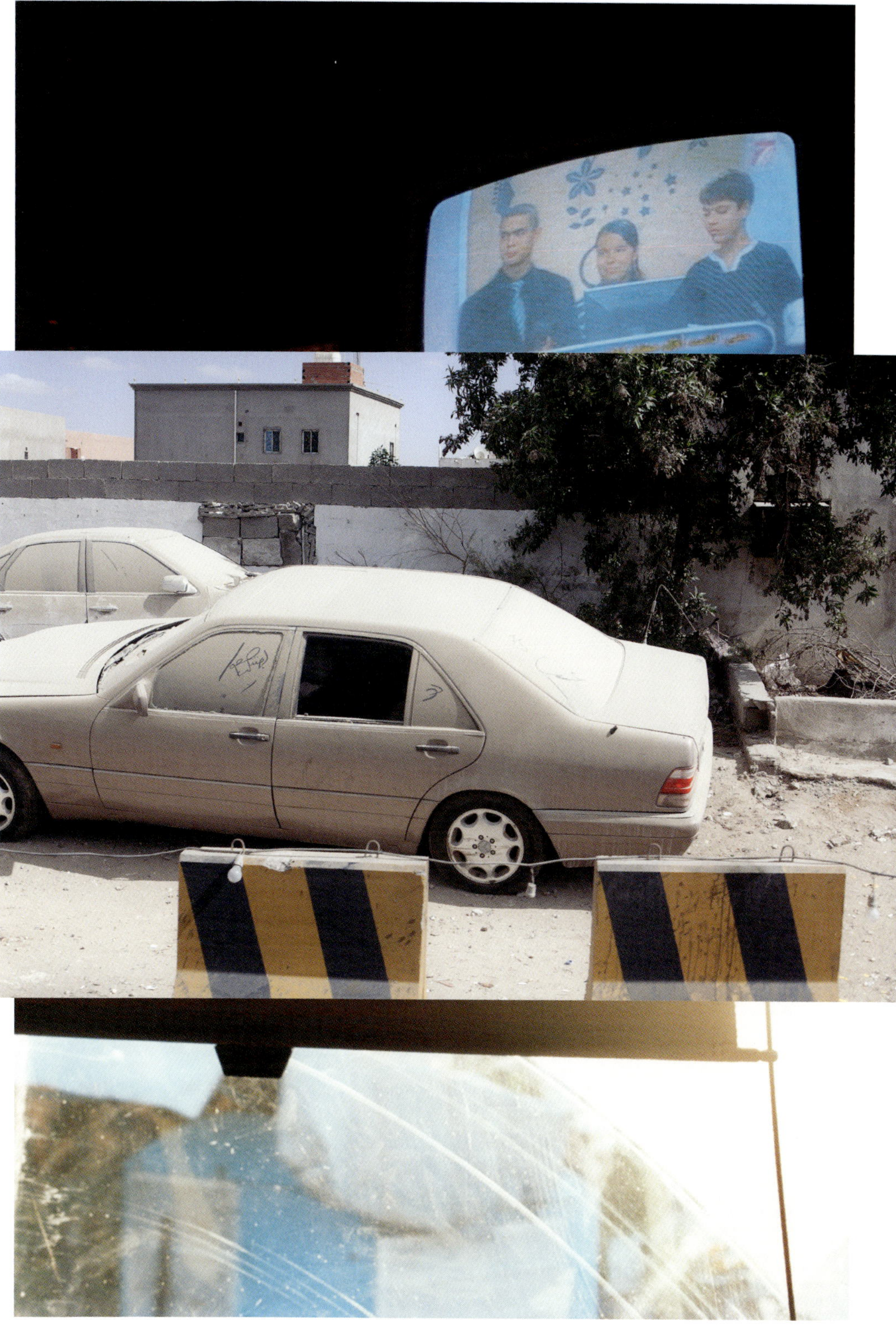

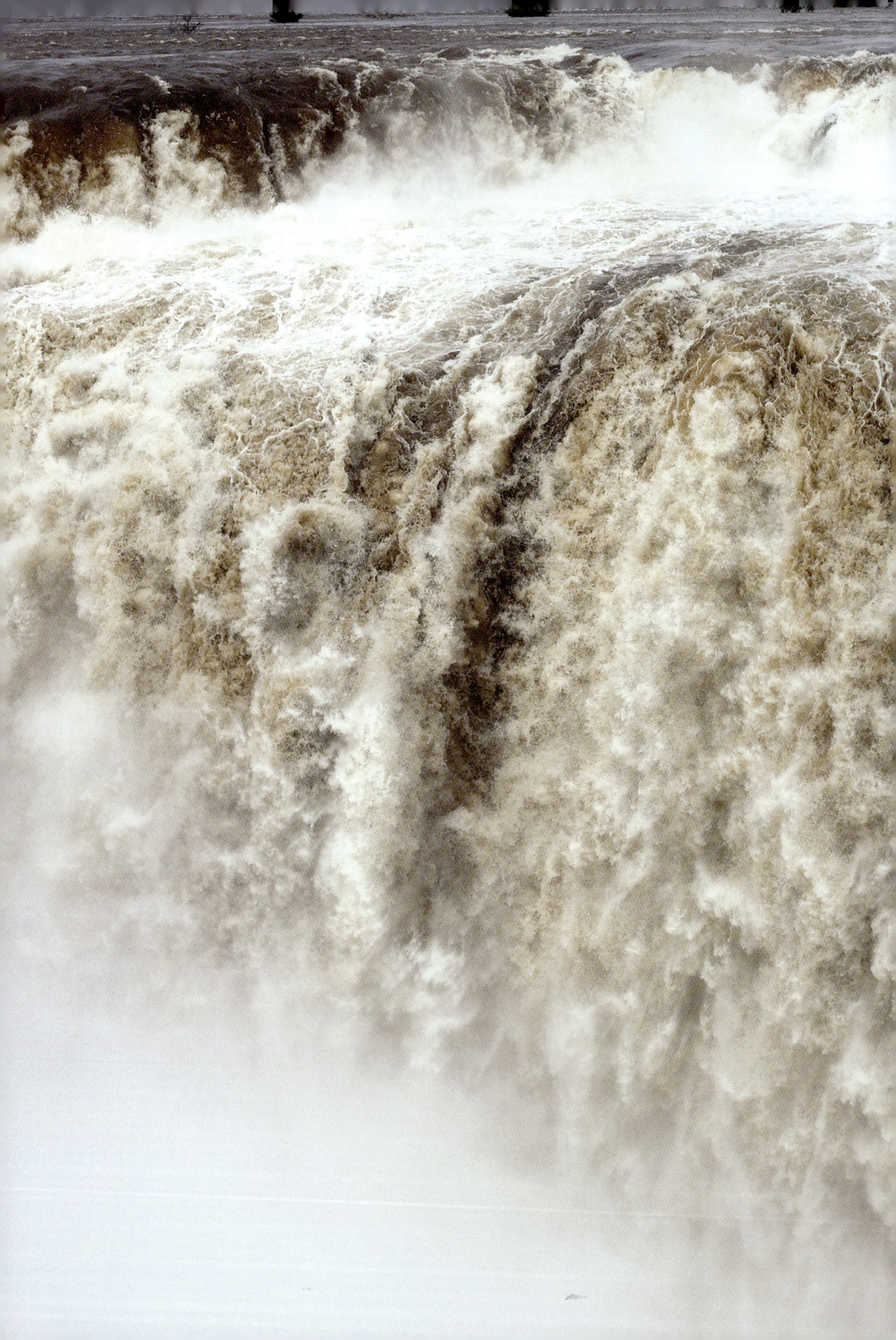

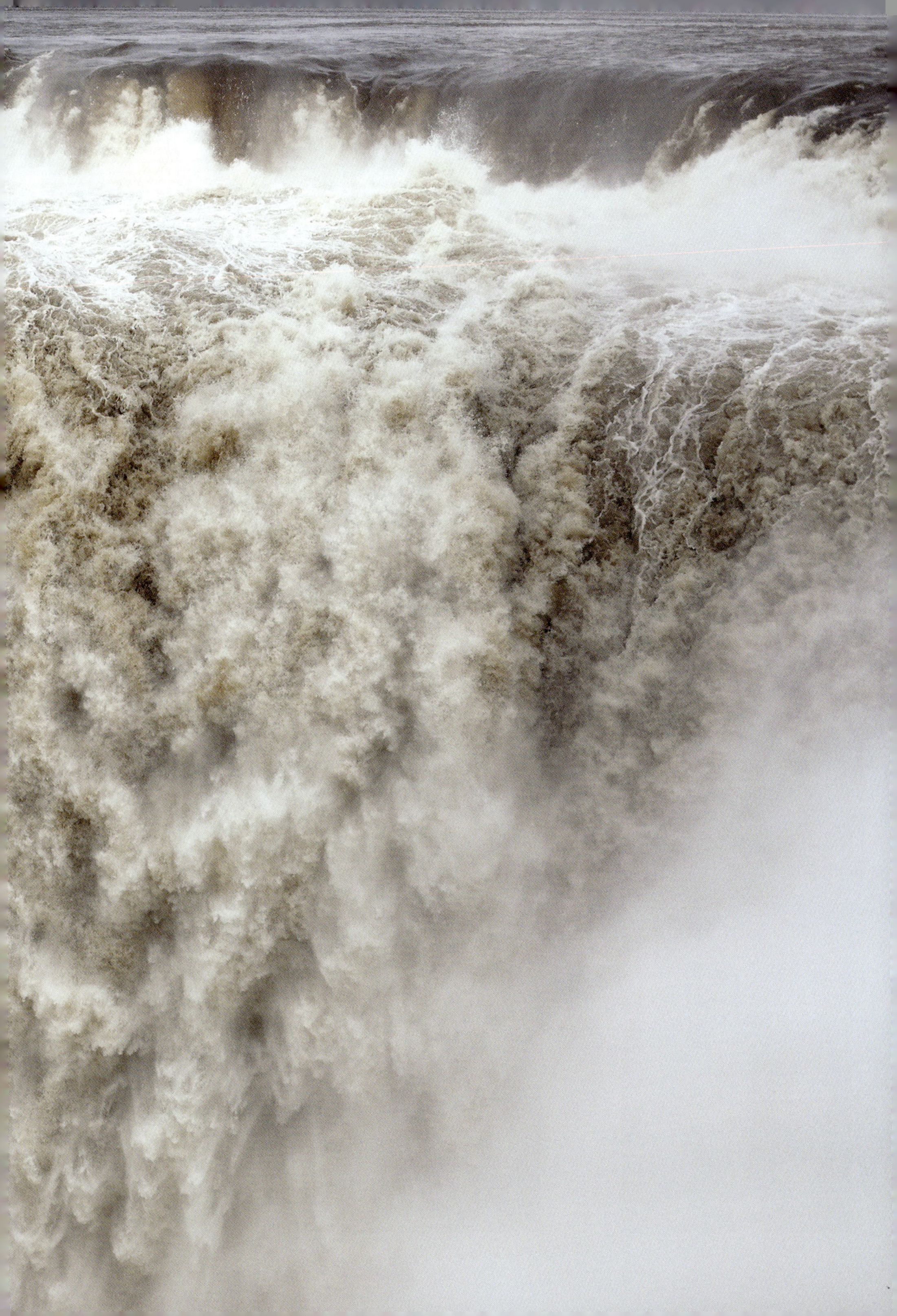

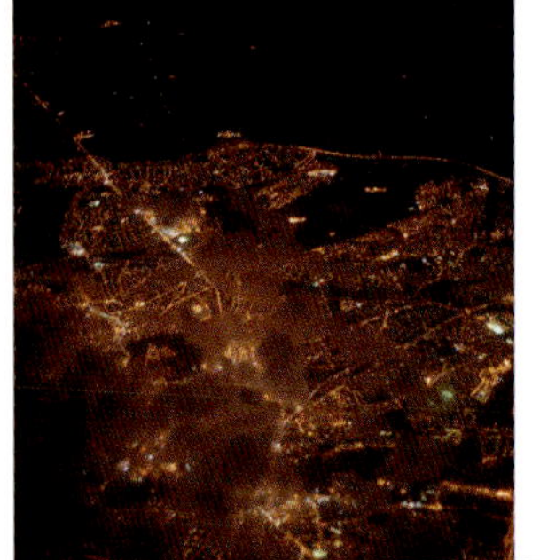

Iguazu, 2010
Aufsicht (night), 2009
Mahalakshmi, Mumbai, a, & c, 2011
Malabar Hill, 2011
non-specific threat, 2005
Sexual Health Clinic, Kakuma Refugee Camp, 2018

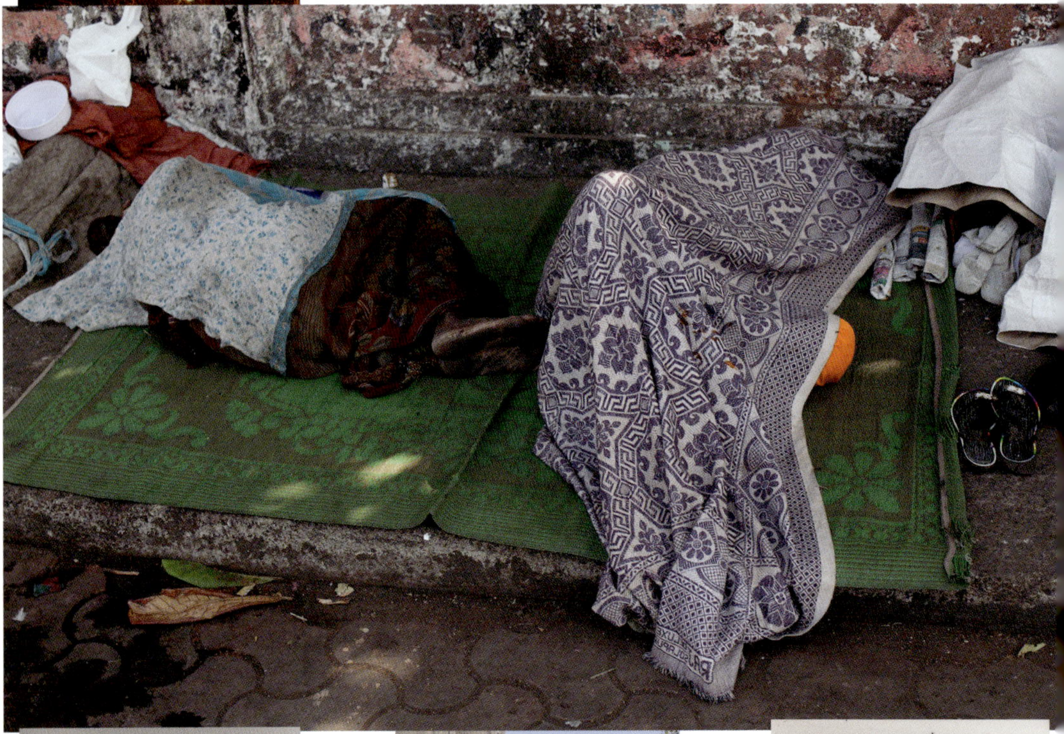

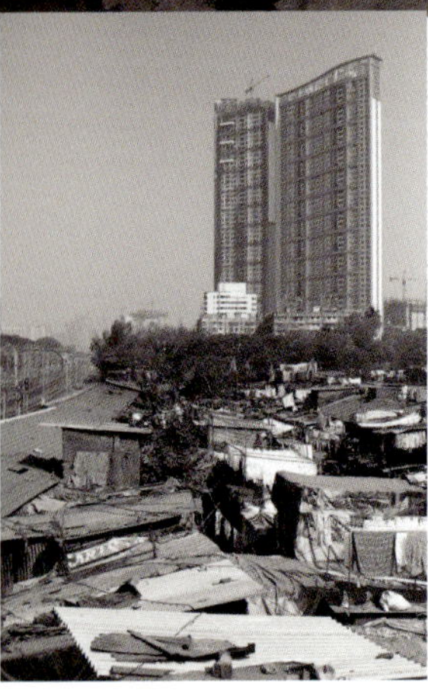

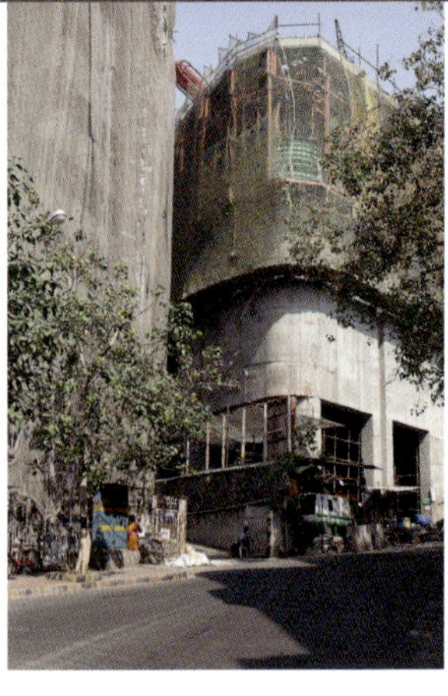

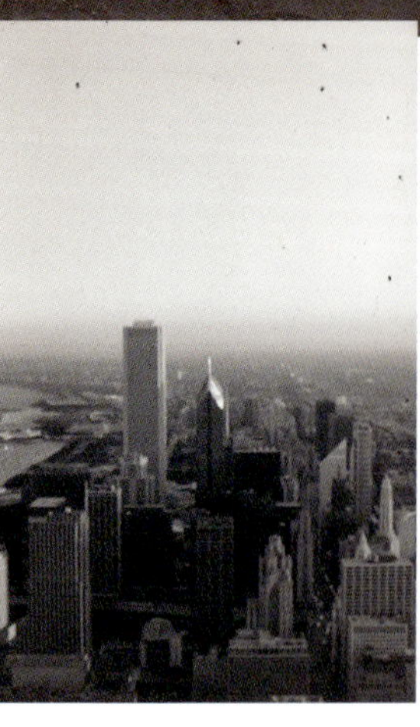

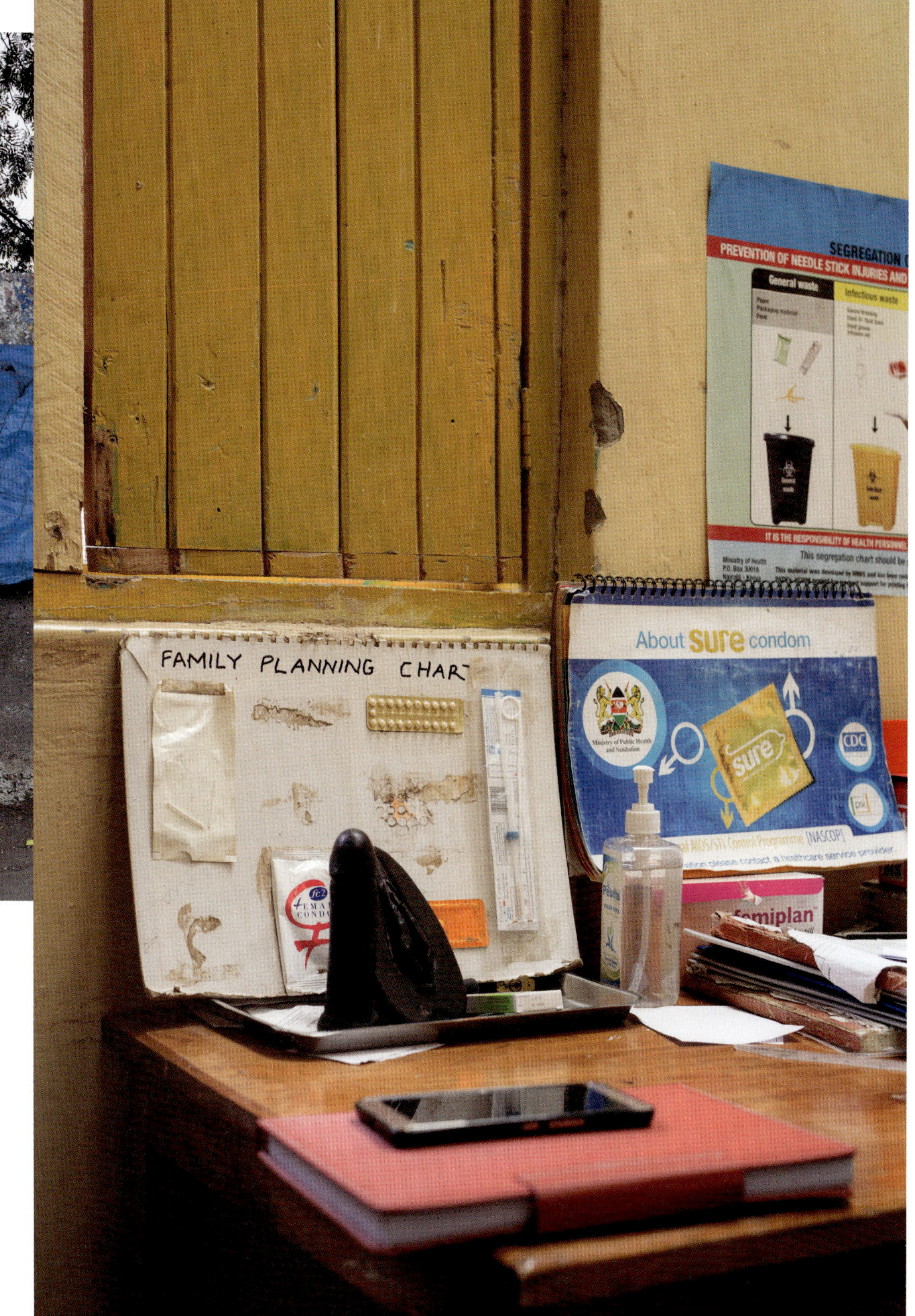
SEGREGATION
PREVENTION OF NEEDLE STICK INJURIES AND
General waste
Infectious waste
IT IS THE RESPONSIBILITY OF HEALTH PERSONNEL
Ministry of Health
P.O. Box 30016
This segregation chart should be
FAMILY PLANNING CHART
FC2
FEMALE CONDOM
About sure condom
Ministry of Public Health and Sanitation
sure
CDC
psi
al AIDS/STI Control Programme (NASCOP)
tion please contact a healthcare service provider
femiplan

Attila with horse, 2011
tube connection, 2010
Andre j, 2010
90 feet Road, 2011

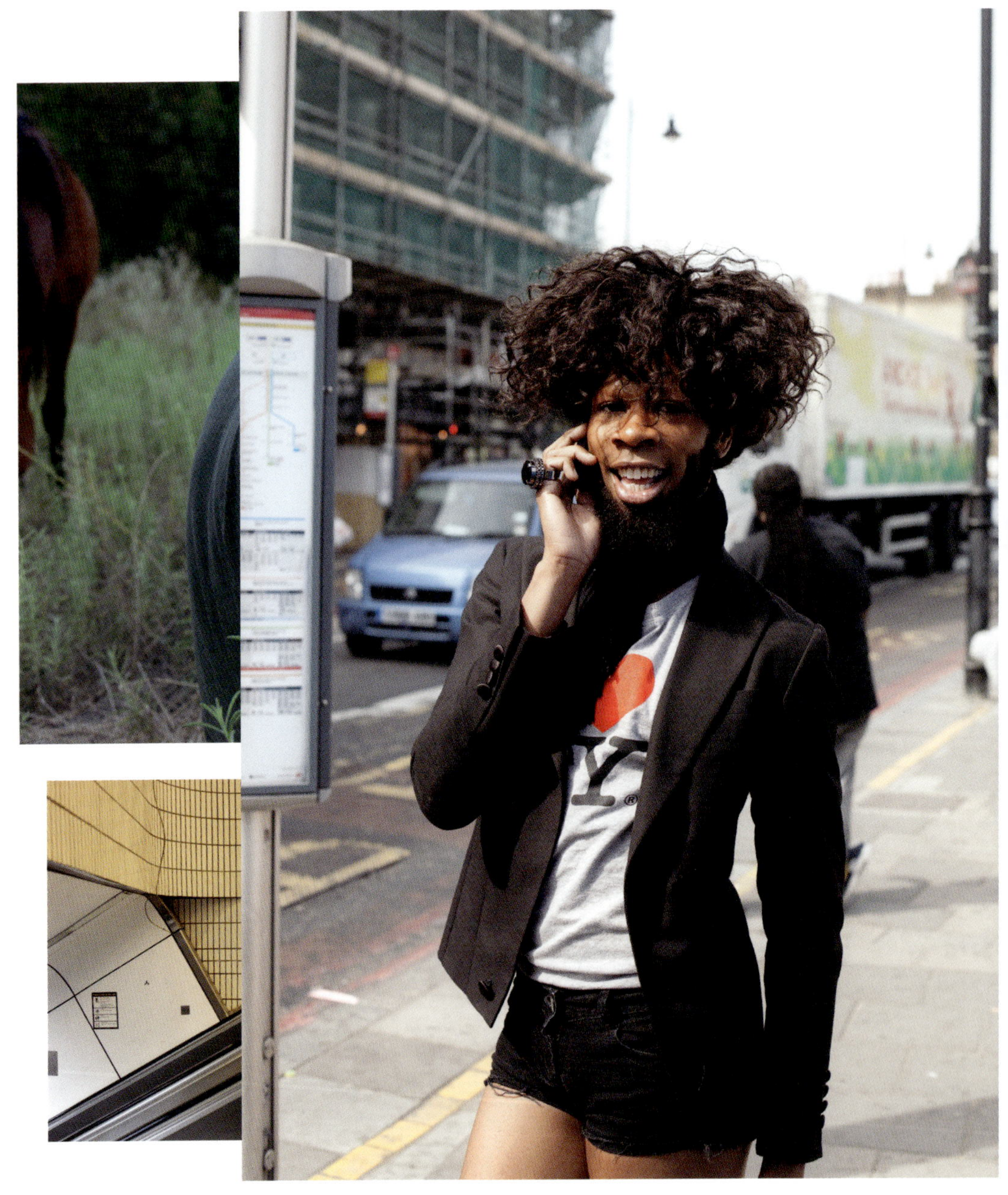

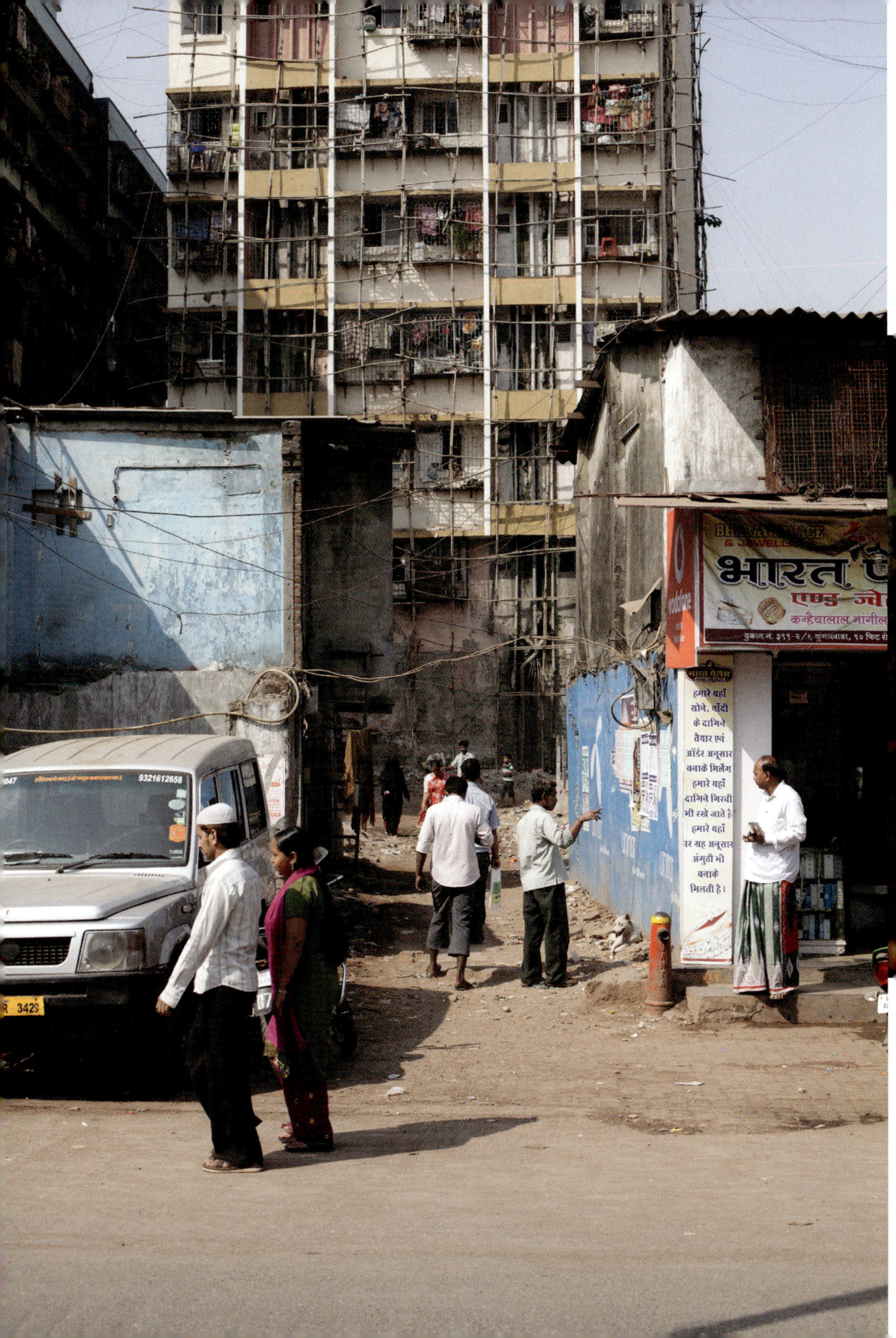
9321612658
BHARAT PALACE
& JEWELLERS
भारत प
एण्ड जे
कन्हैयालाल मांगील
दुकान नं. ३९१-२/१, लुंगादवाडा, ९० फिट रो
भारत पैलेस
हमारे यहाँ
सोने, चाँदी
के दागिने
तैयार एवं
ऑर्डर अनूसार
बनाके मिलेग
हमारे यहाँ
दागिने गिरवी
भी रखे जाते है
हमारे यहाँ
र ग्रह अनूसार
अंगुठी भी
बनाके
मिलती है।

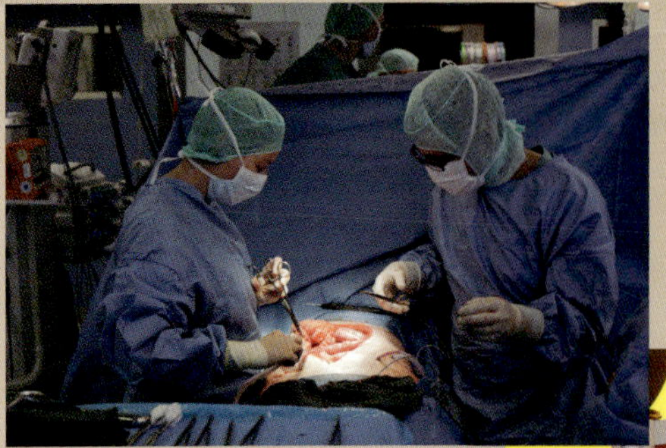

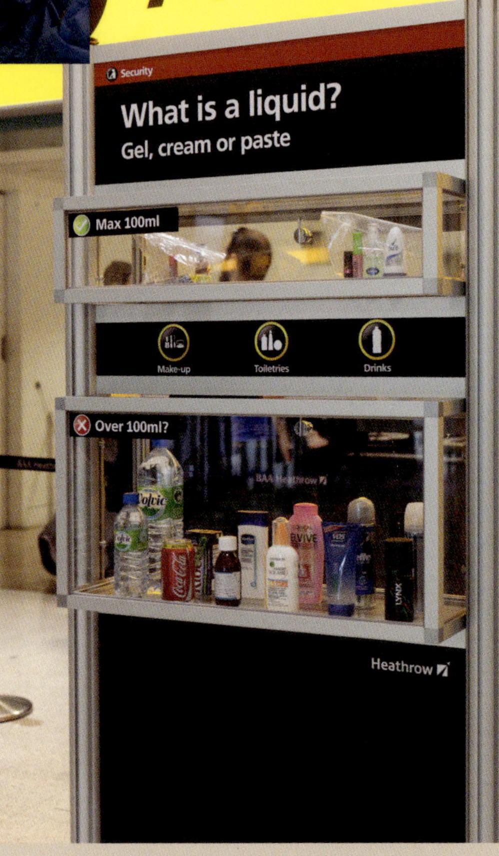

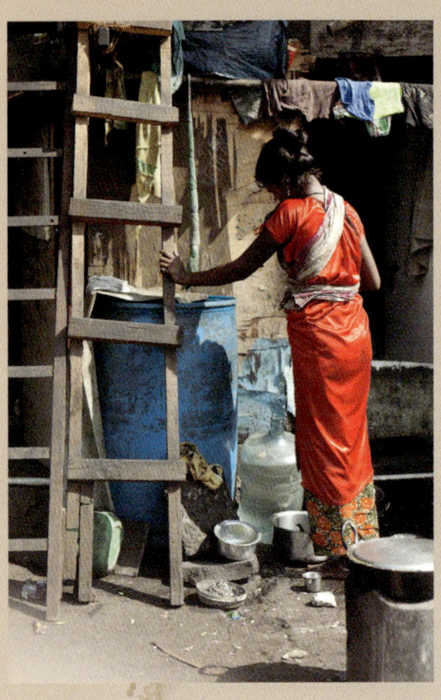

Silver 96, 2012
Reay Road, b, 2011
OP, 2011
What is a liquid?, 2011
Fespa Digital (UV printer), 2012
Fruit Logistica (potato bagging), 2011

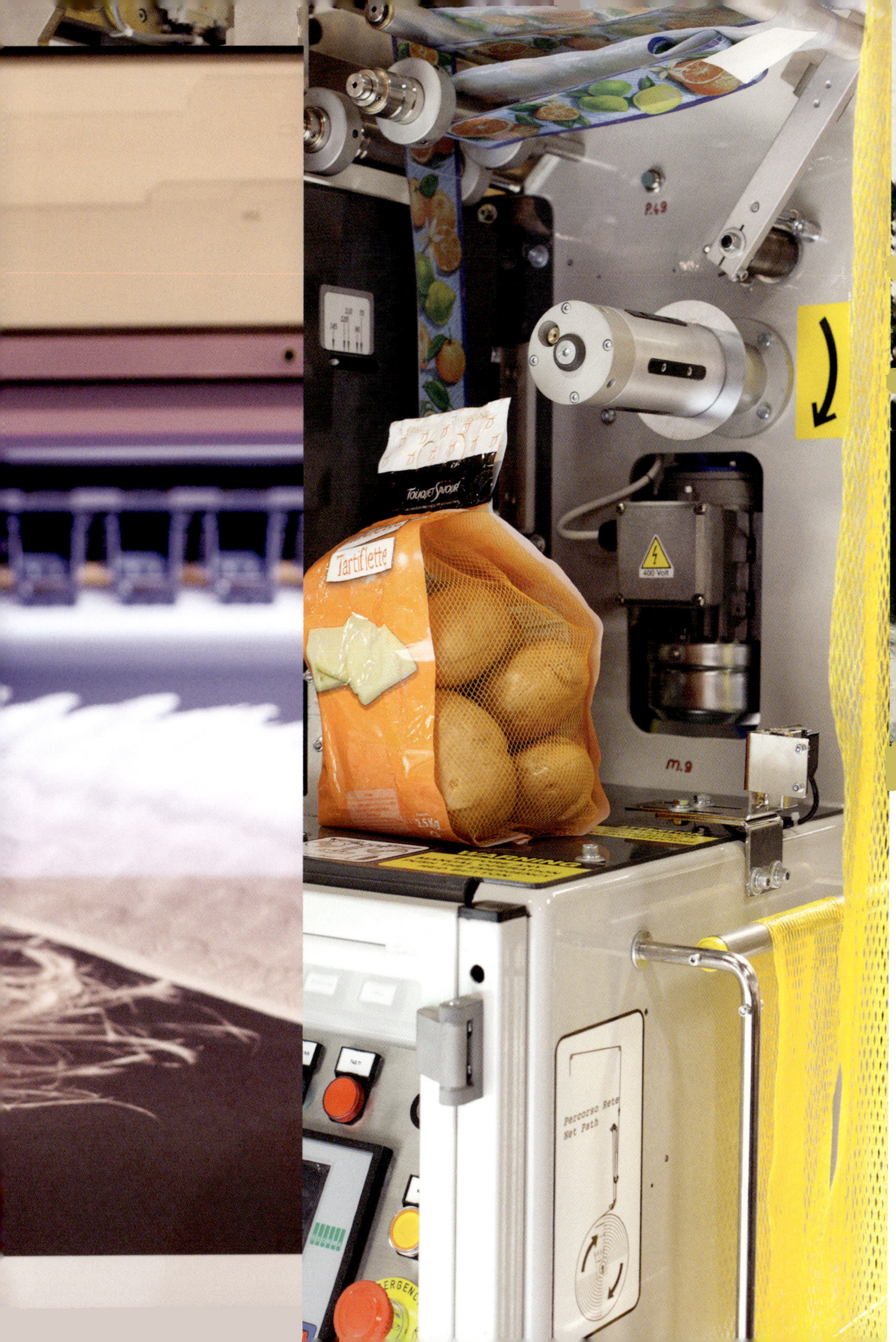

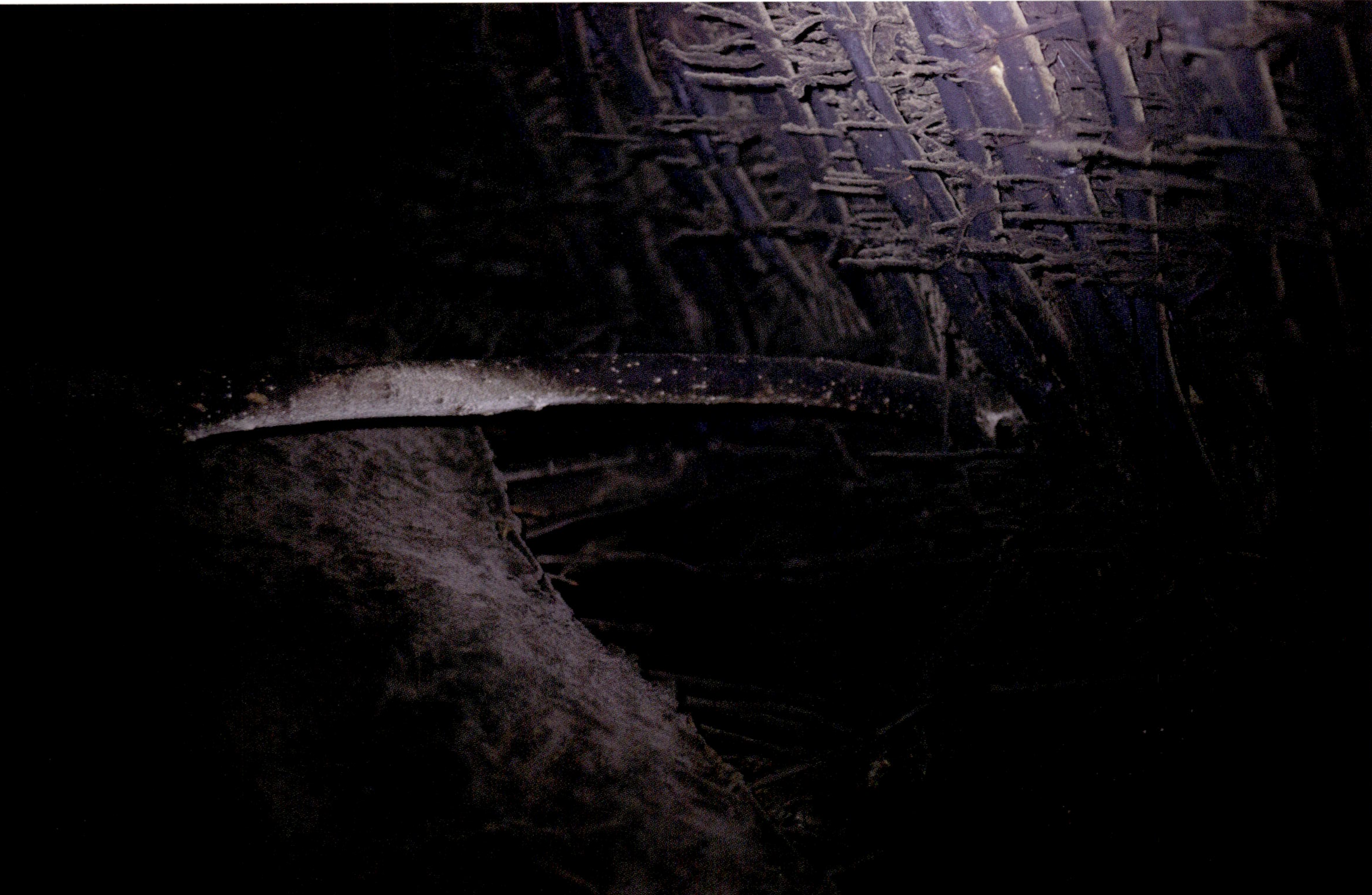

Masai hut, 2012   Mundhöhle, 2012   Greifbar 61, 2017

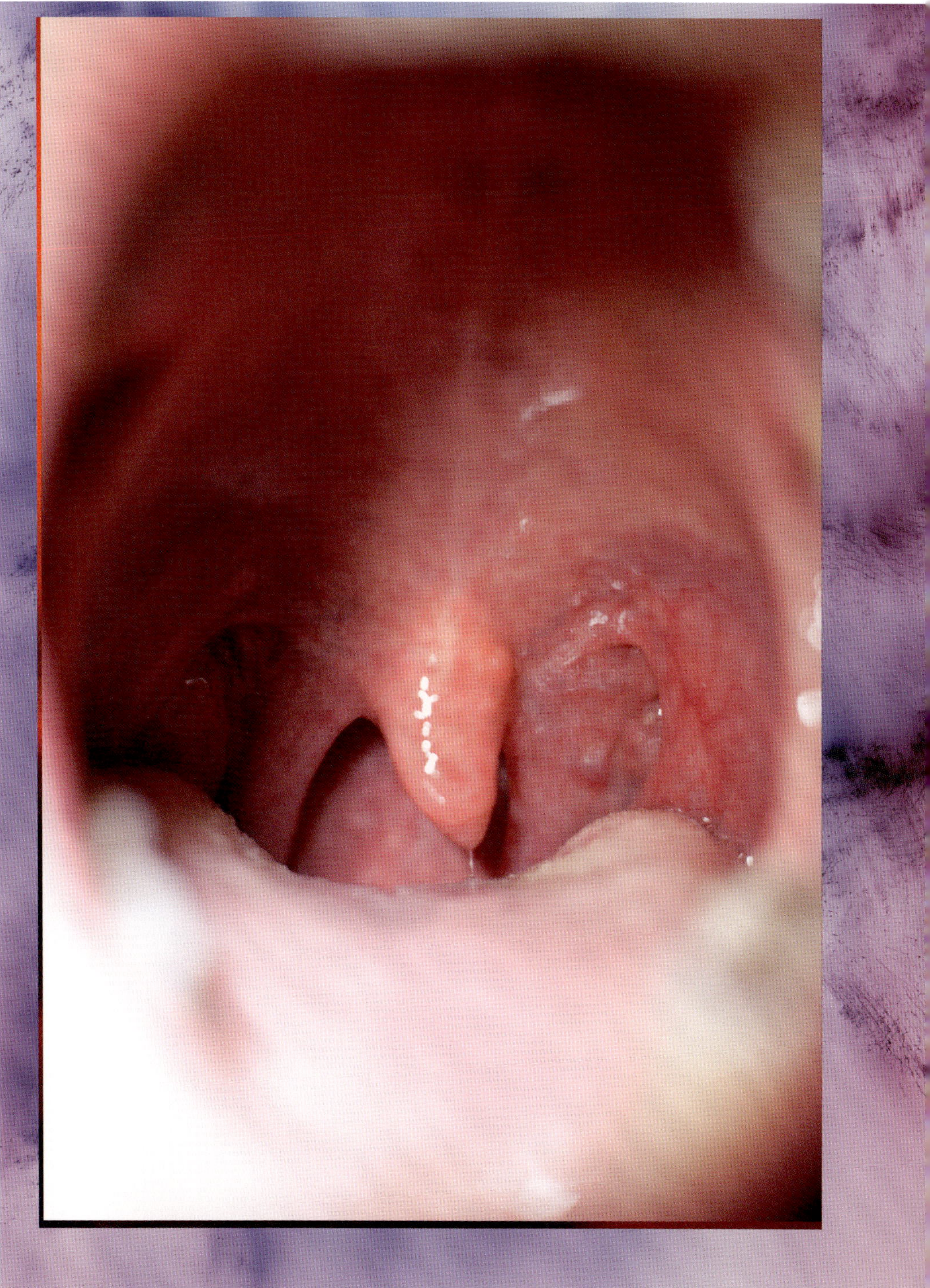

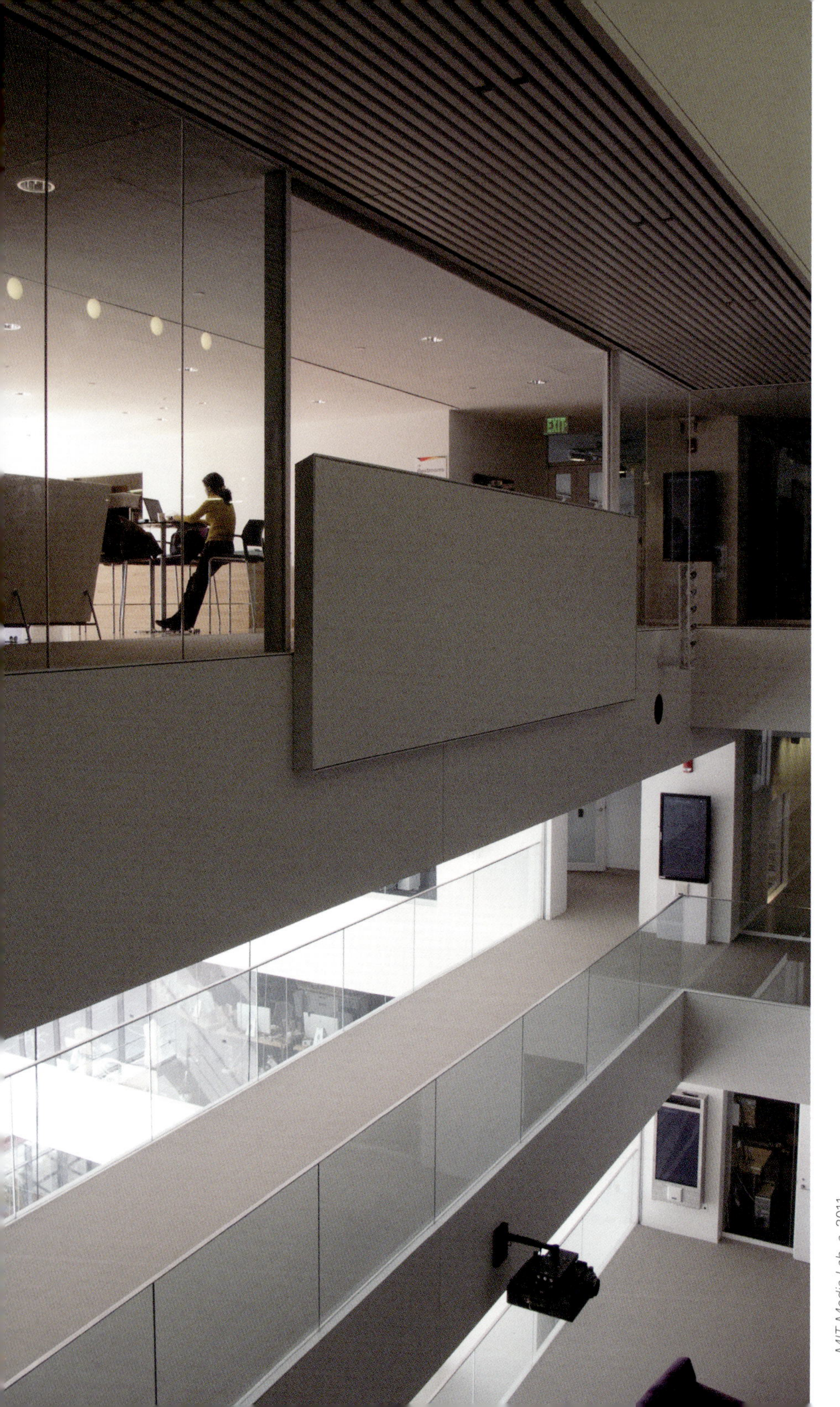

MIT Media Lab, a, 2011

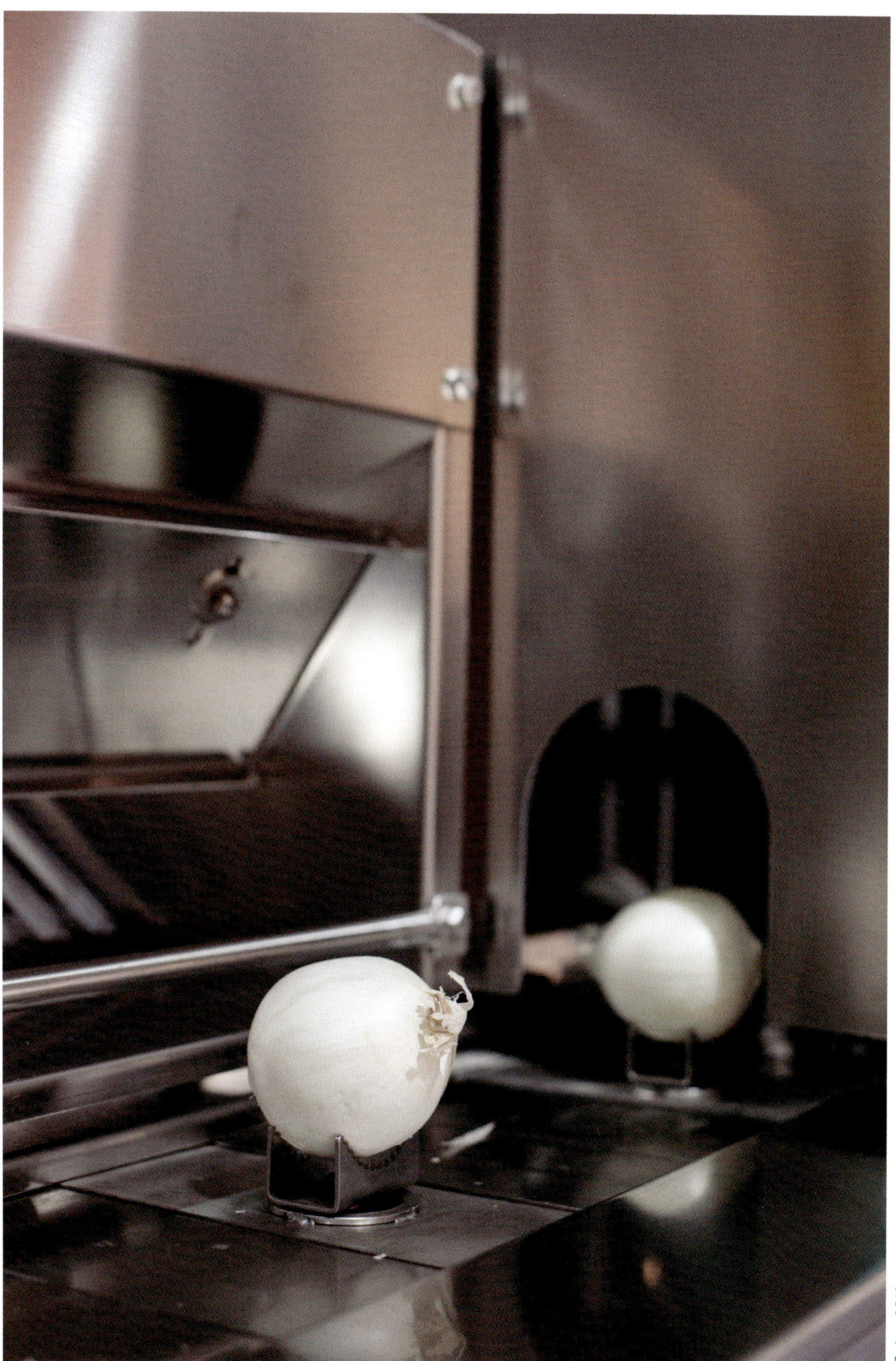

Onion, 2010

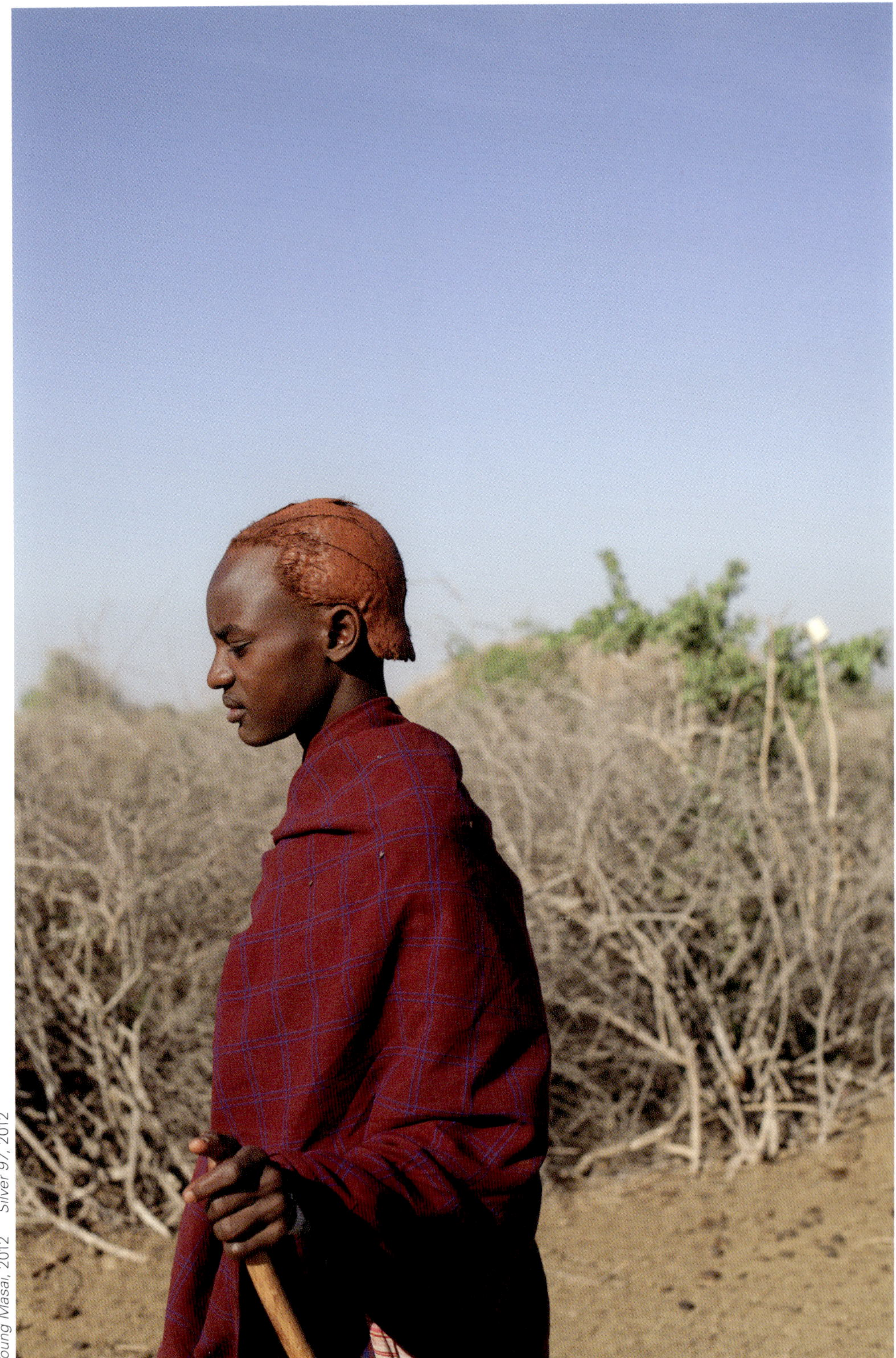

Young Masai, 2012   Silver 97, 2012

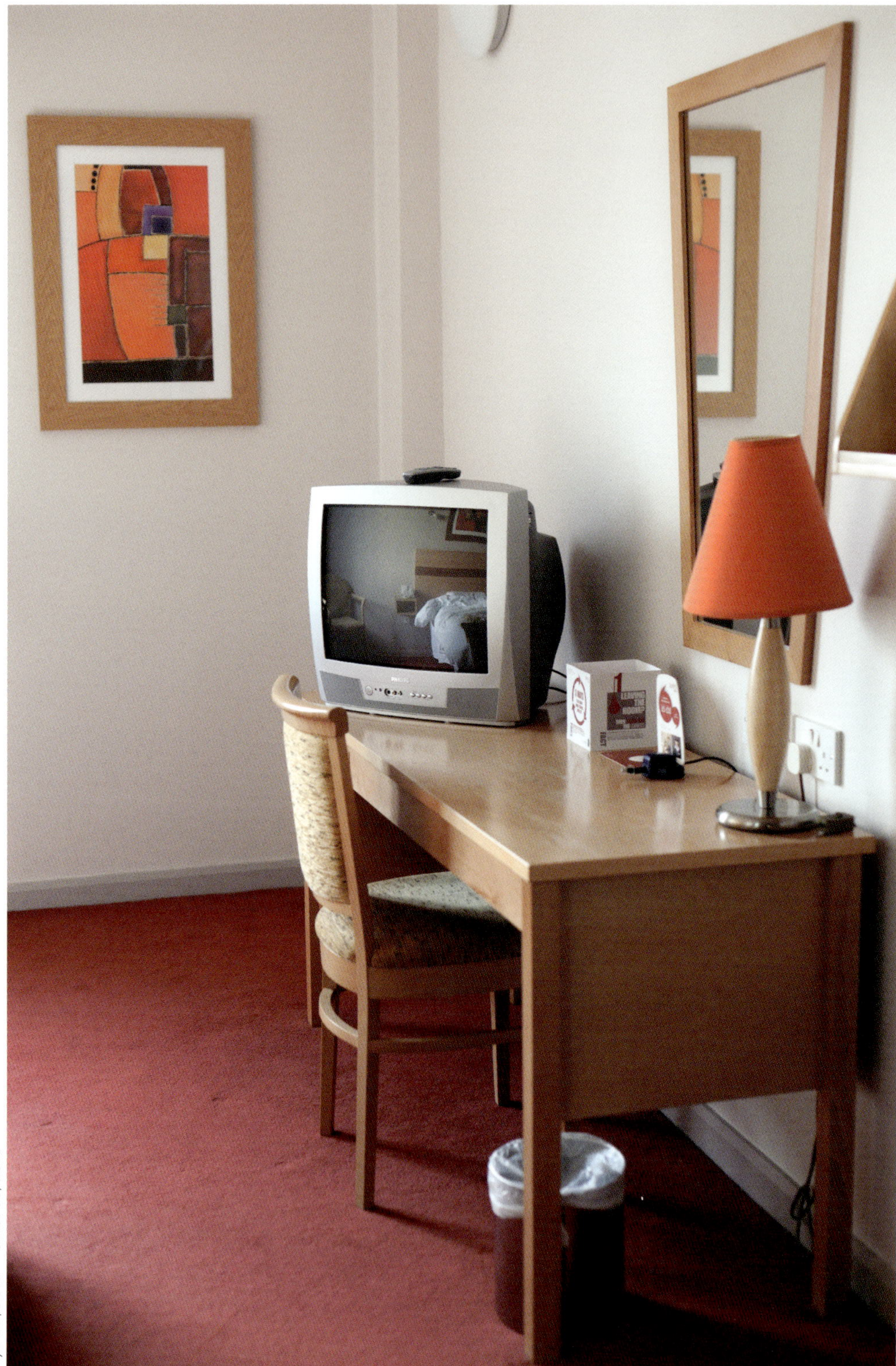

Jurys Inn, 2010   Silver 98, 2012

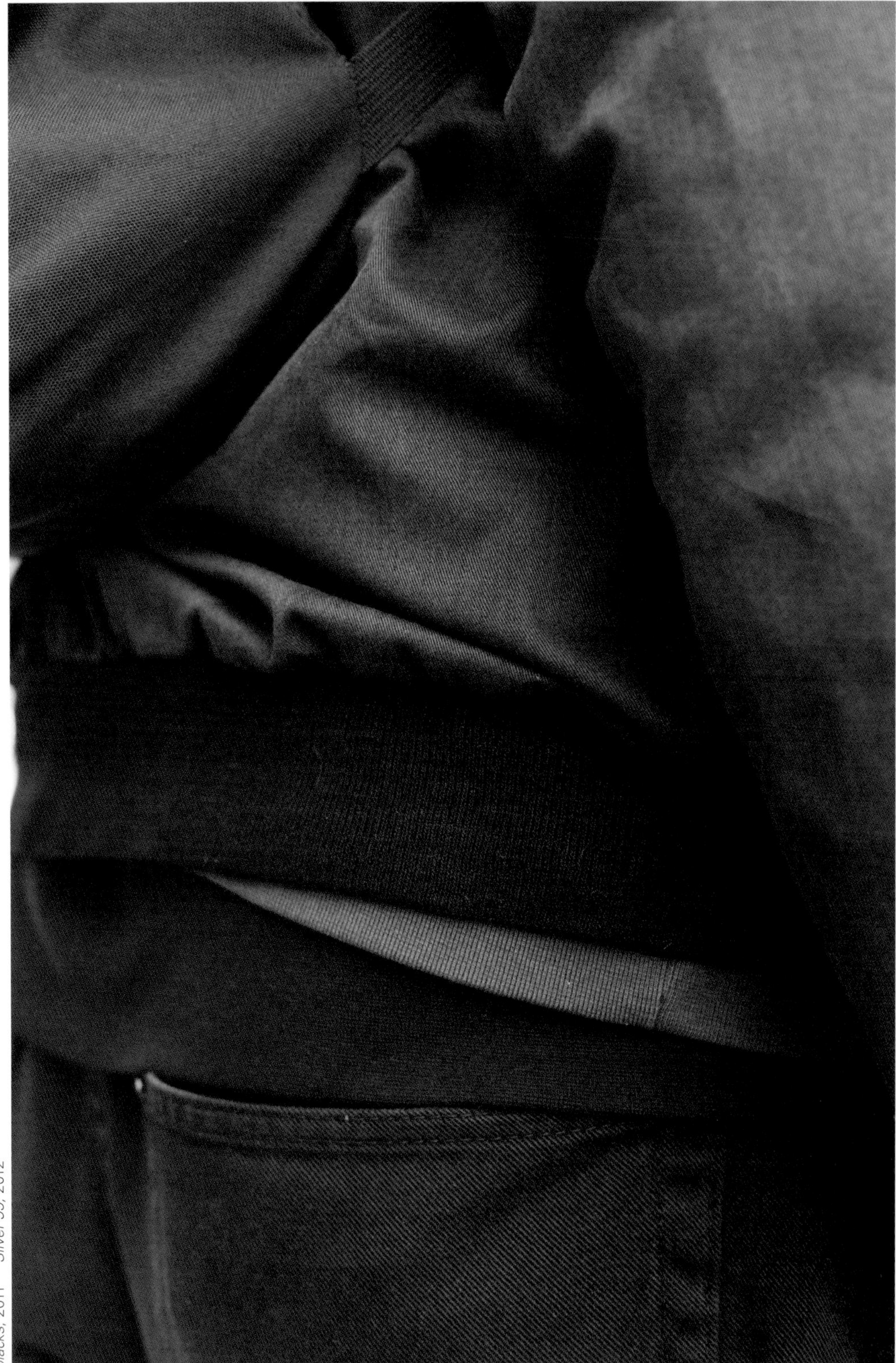

blacks, 2011   Silver 99, 2012

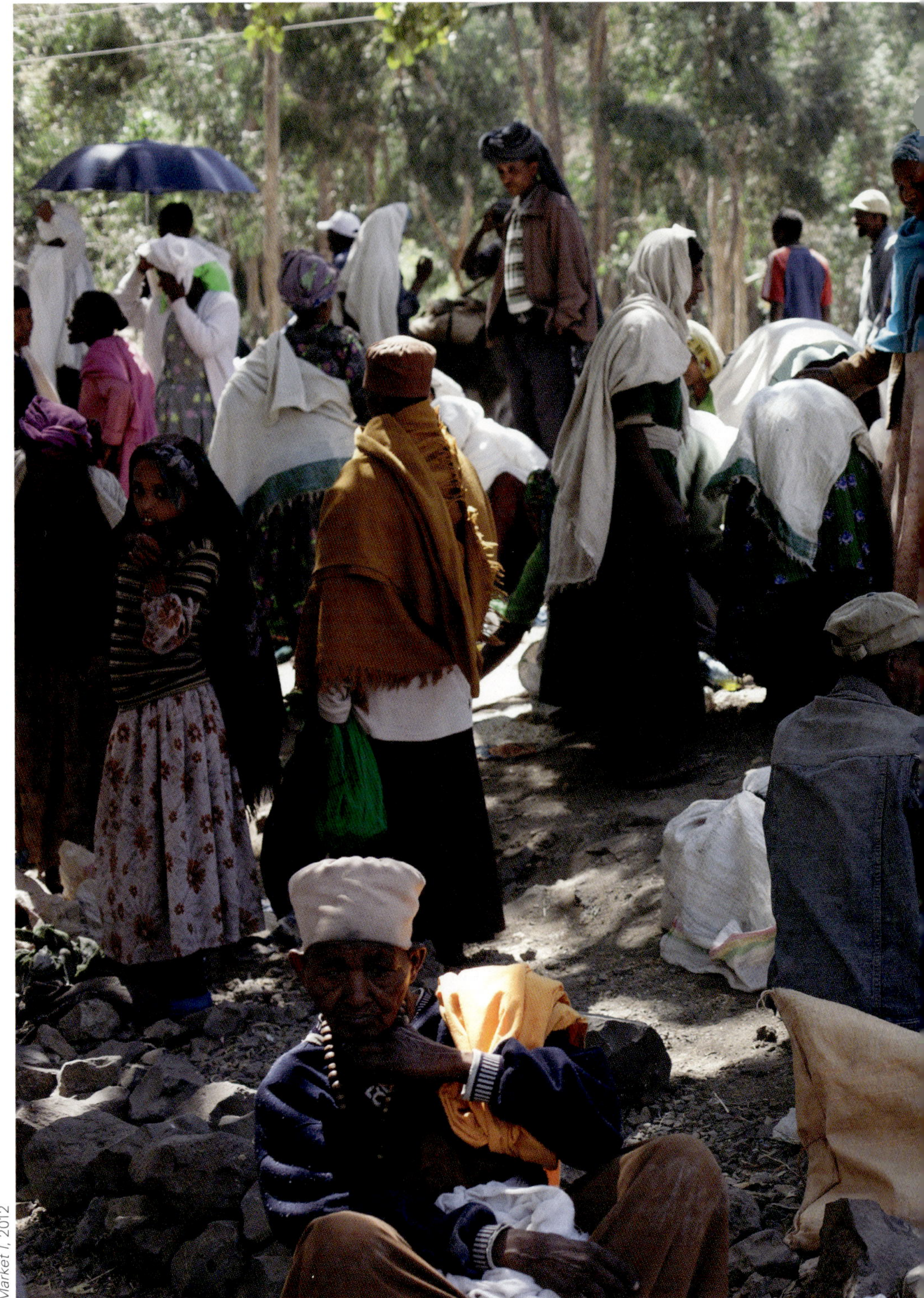

Market I, 2012

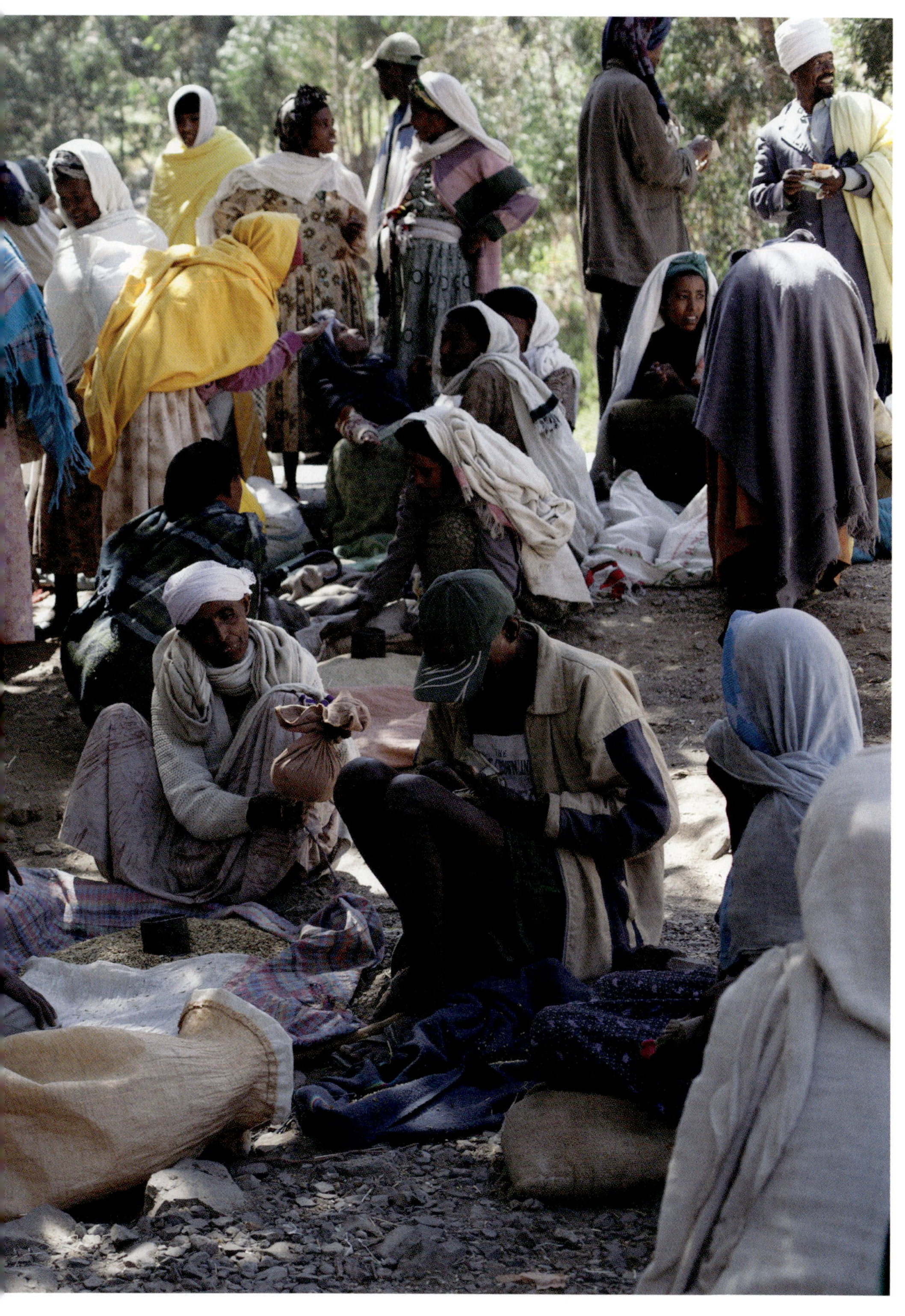

Rest of World Passports
IRIS

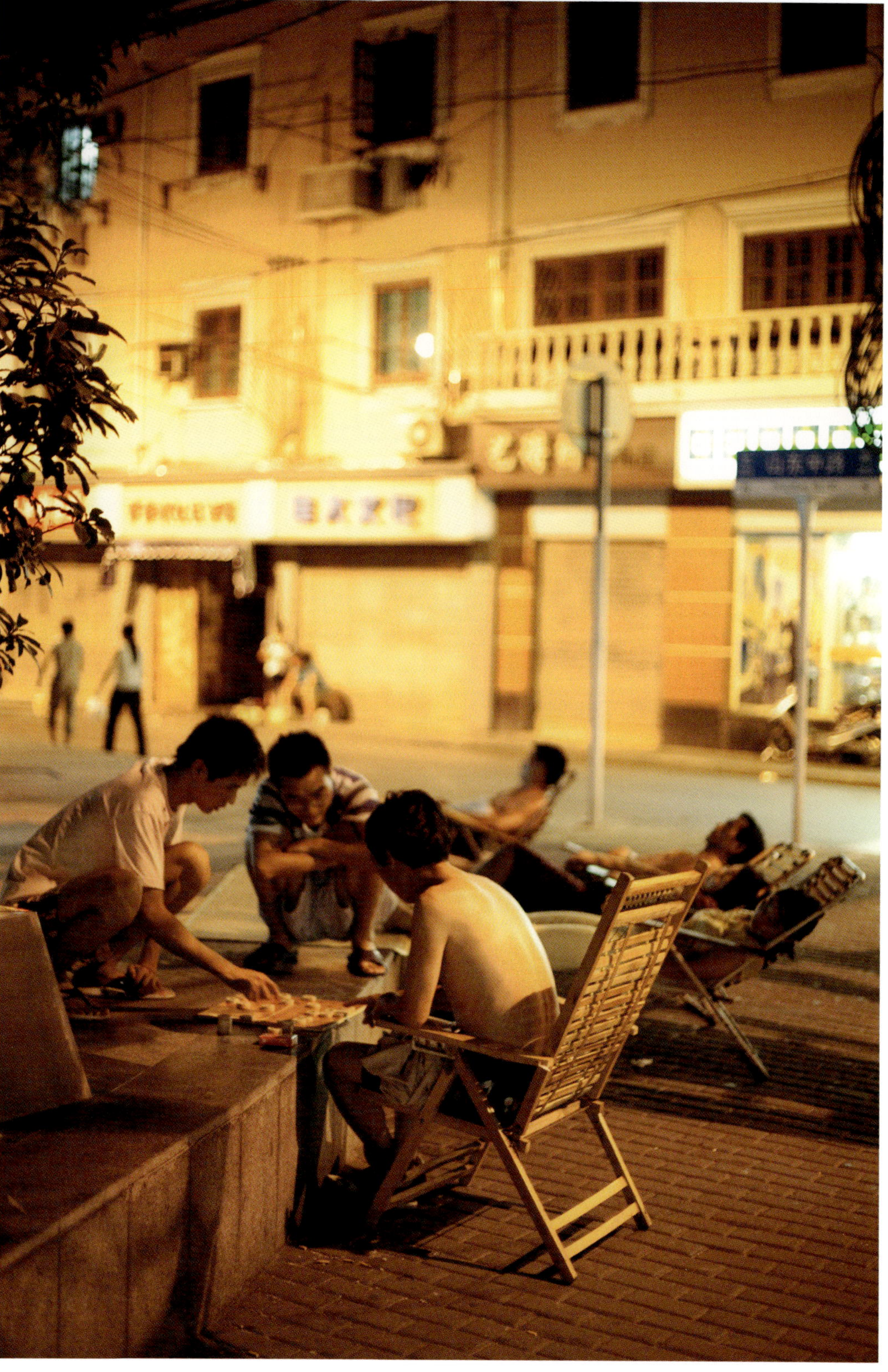

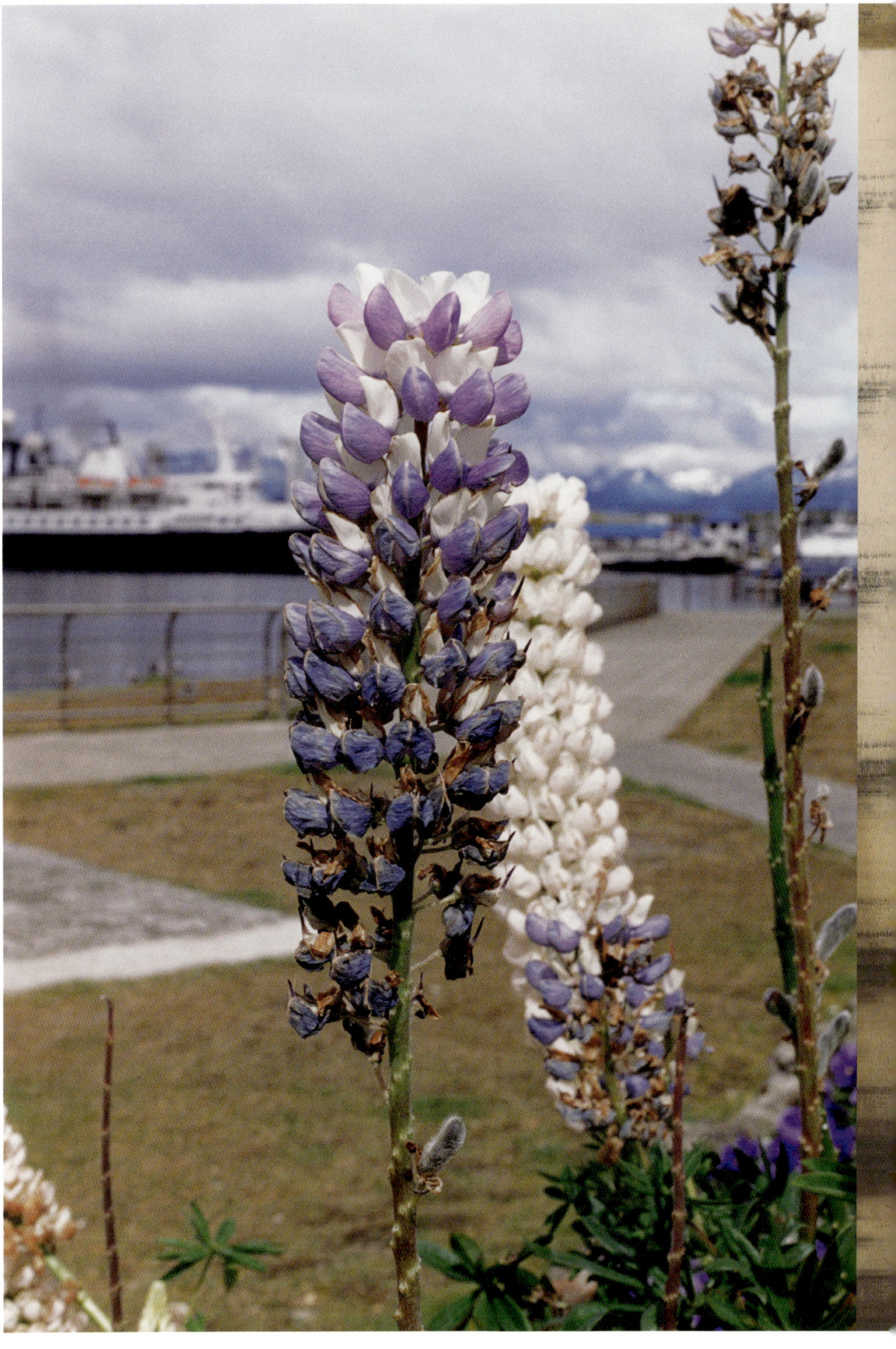

Ushuaia Lupine (a), 2010   Silver 92, 2012   Berlin-Warszawa-Express, 2011

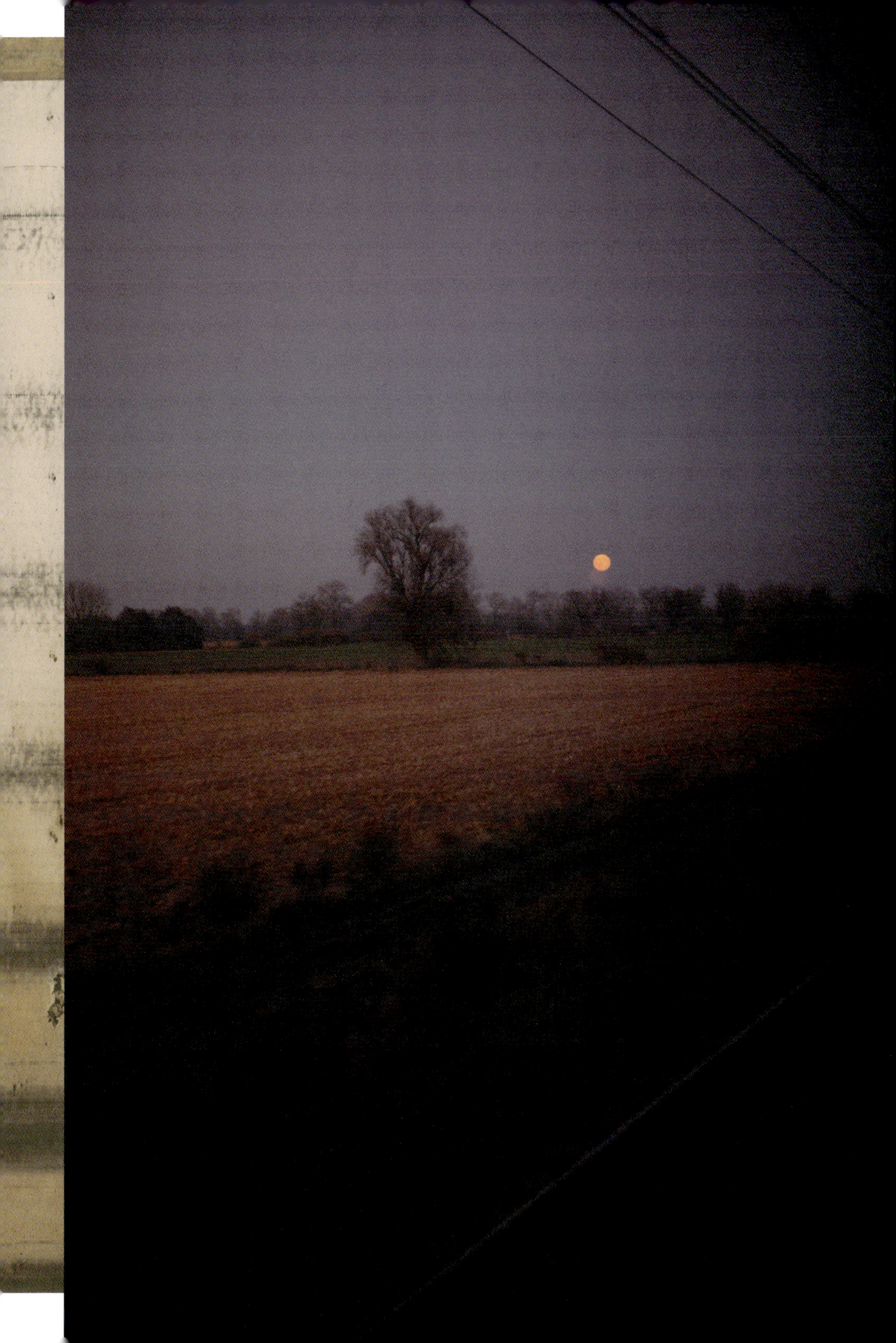

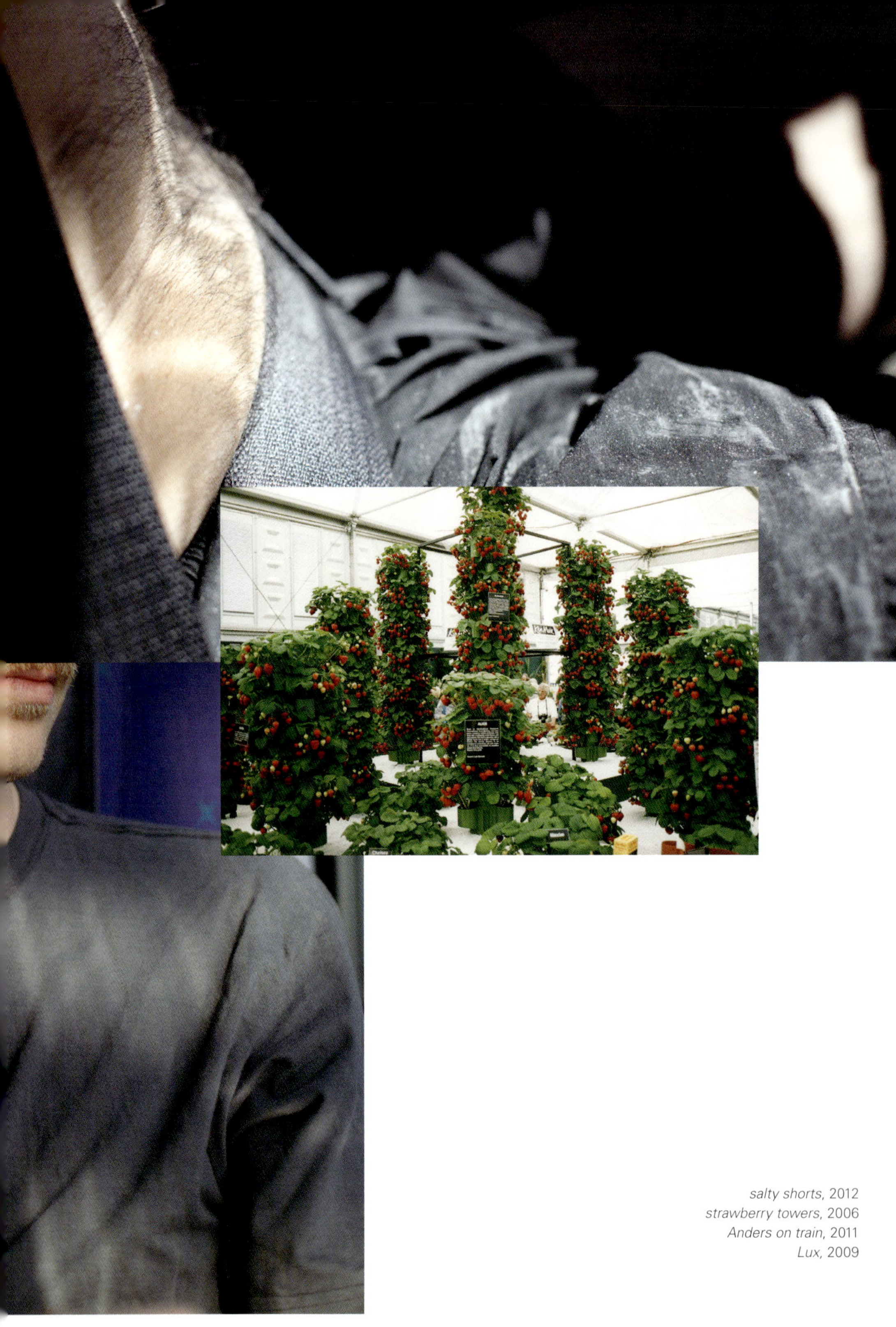

salty shorts, 2012
strawberry towers, 2006
Anders on train, 2011
Lux, 2009

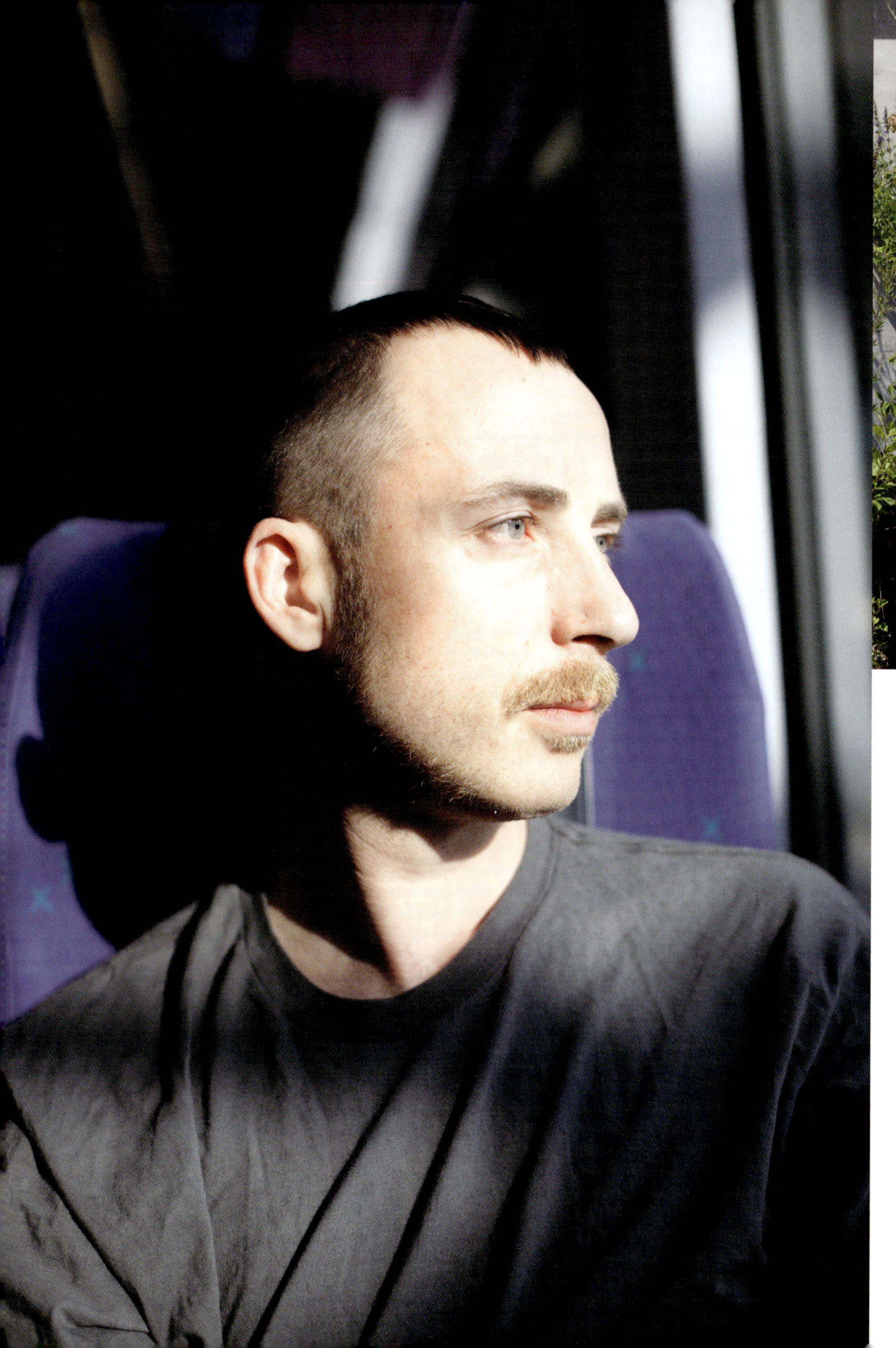

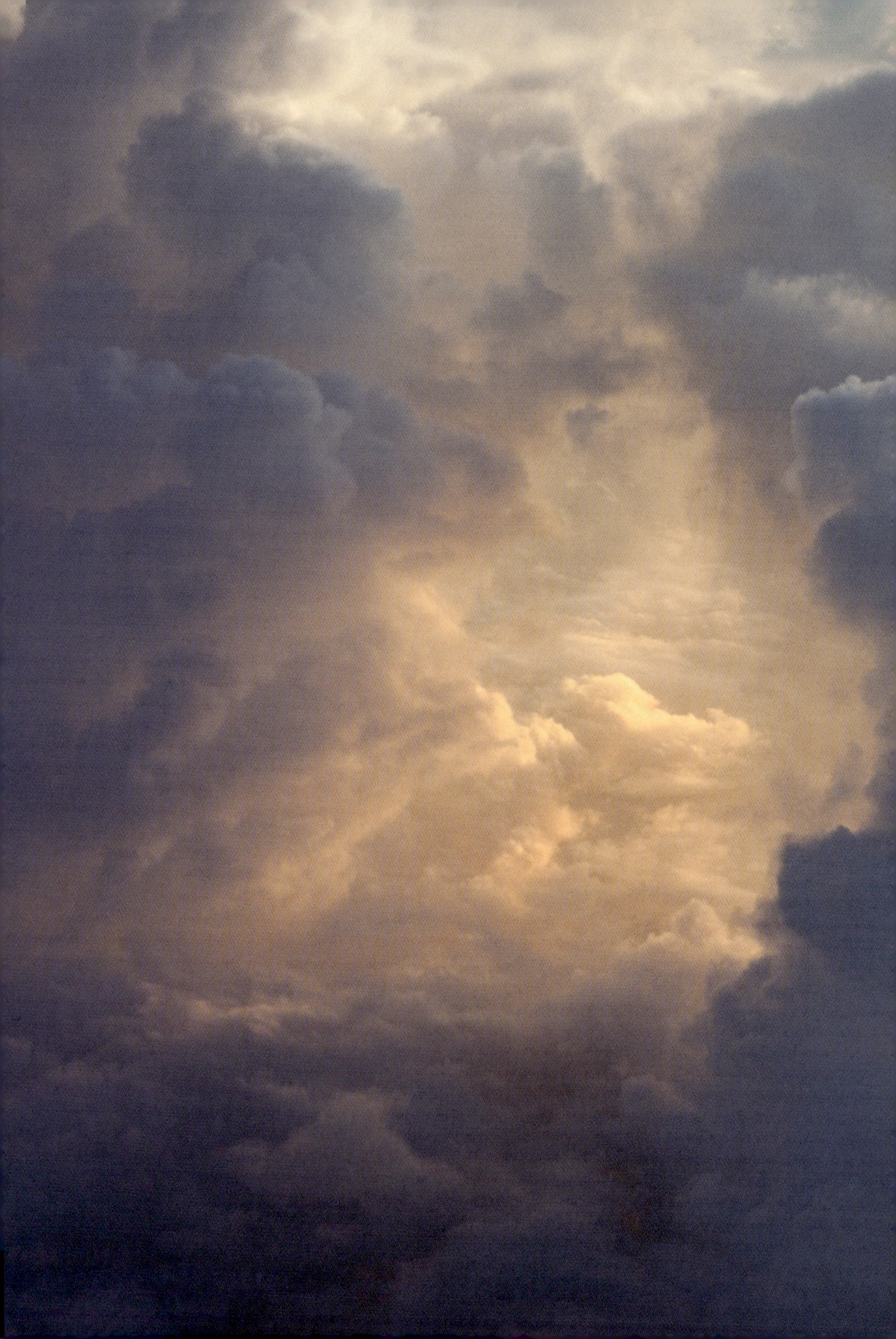

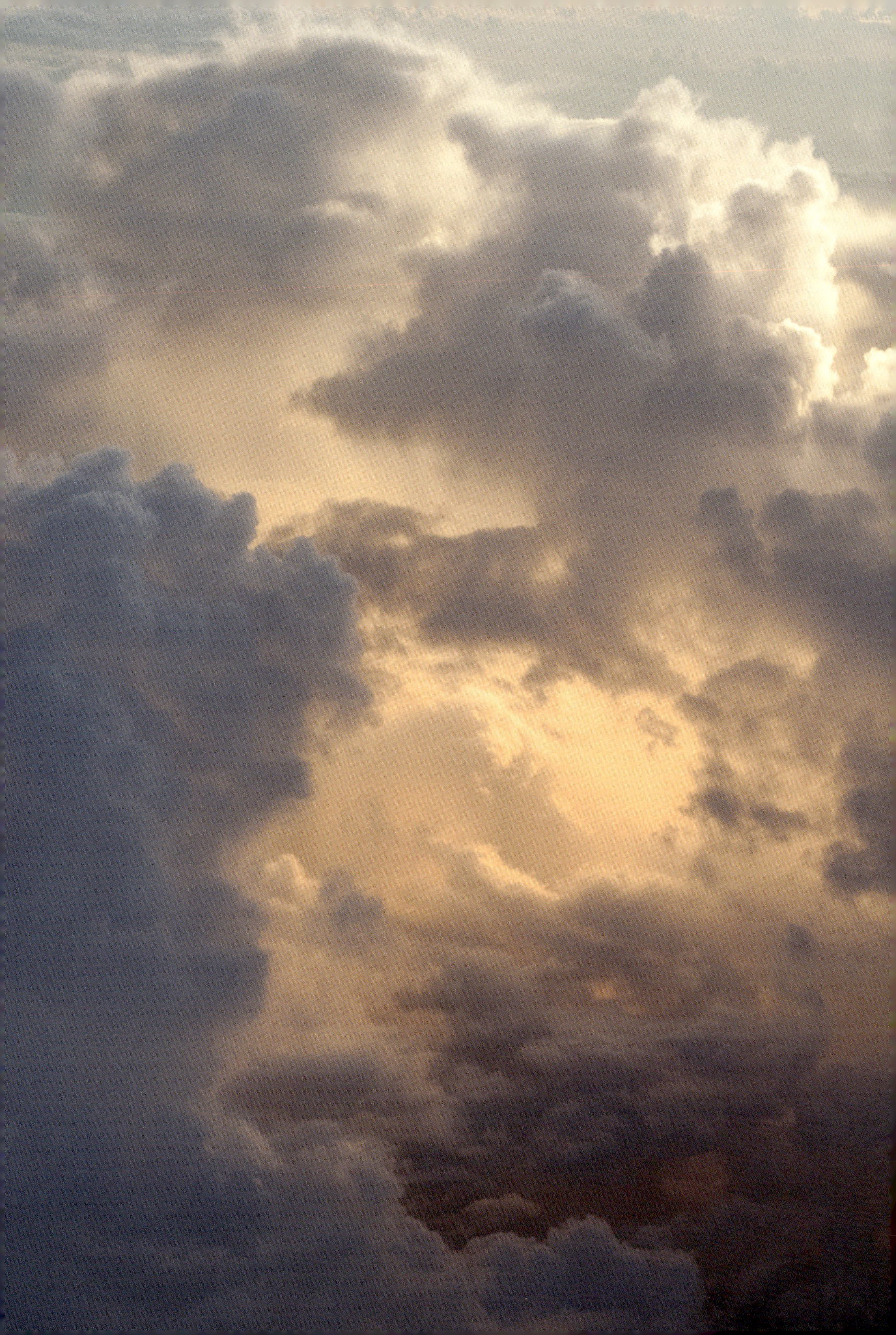

Harvard Astrophysics Institute / European Southern
Observatory, 2012

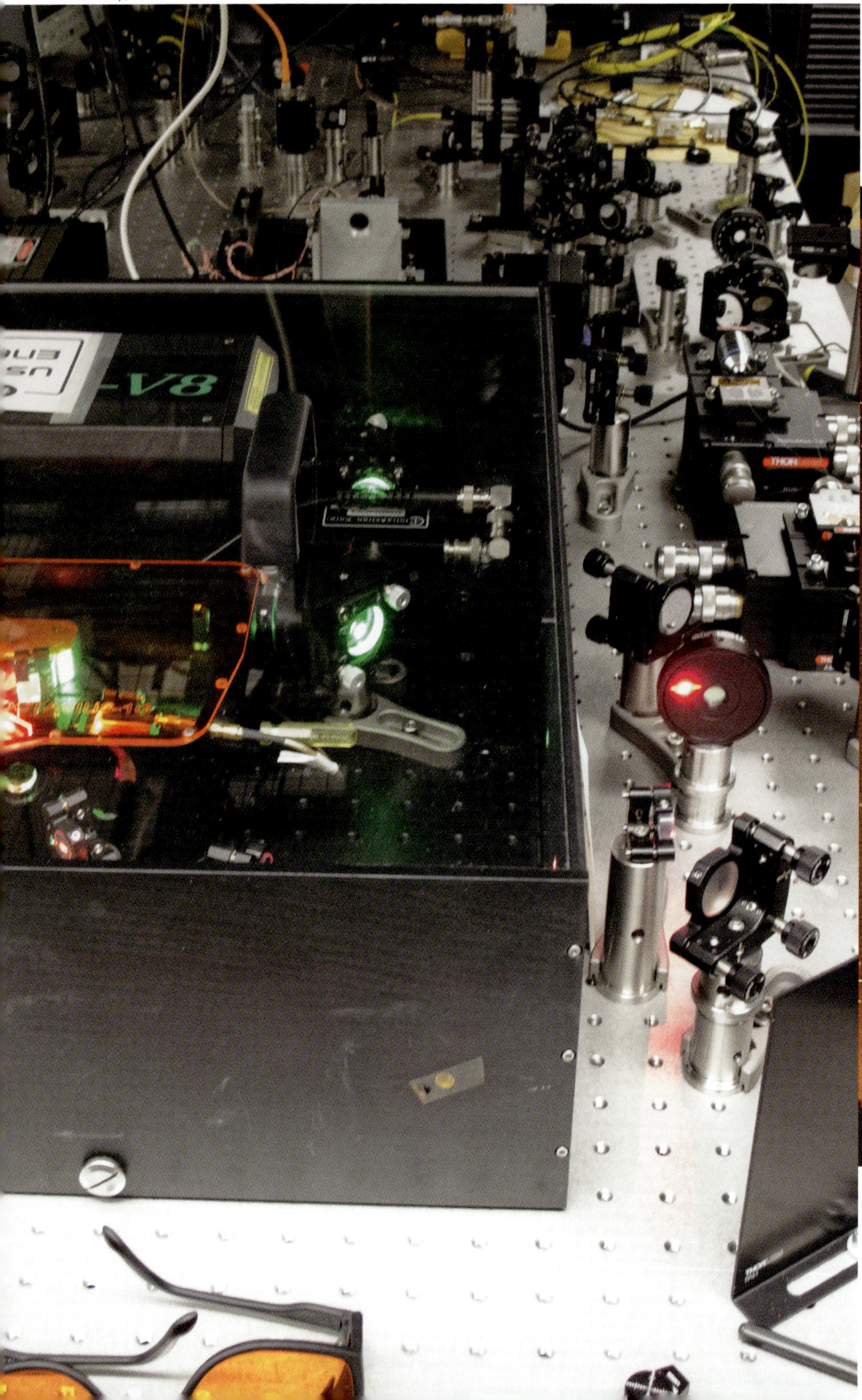

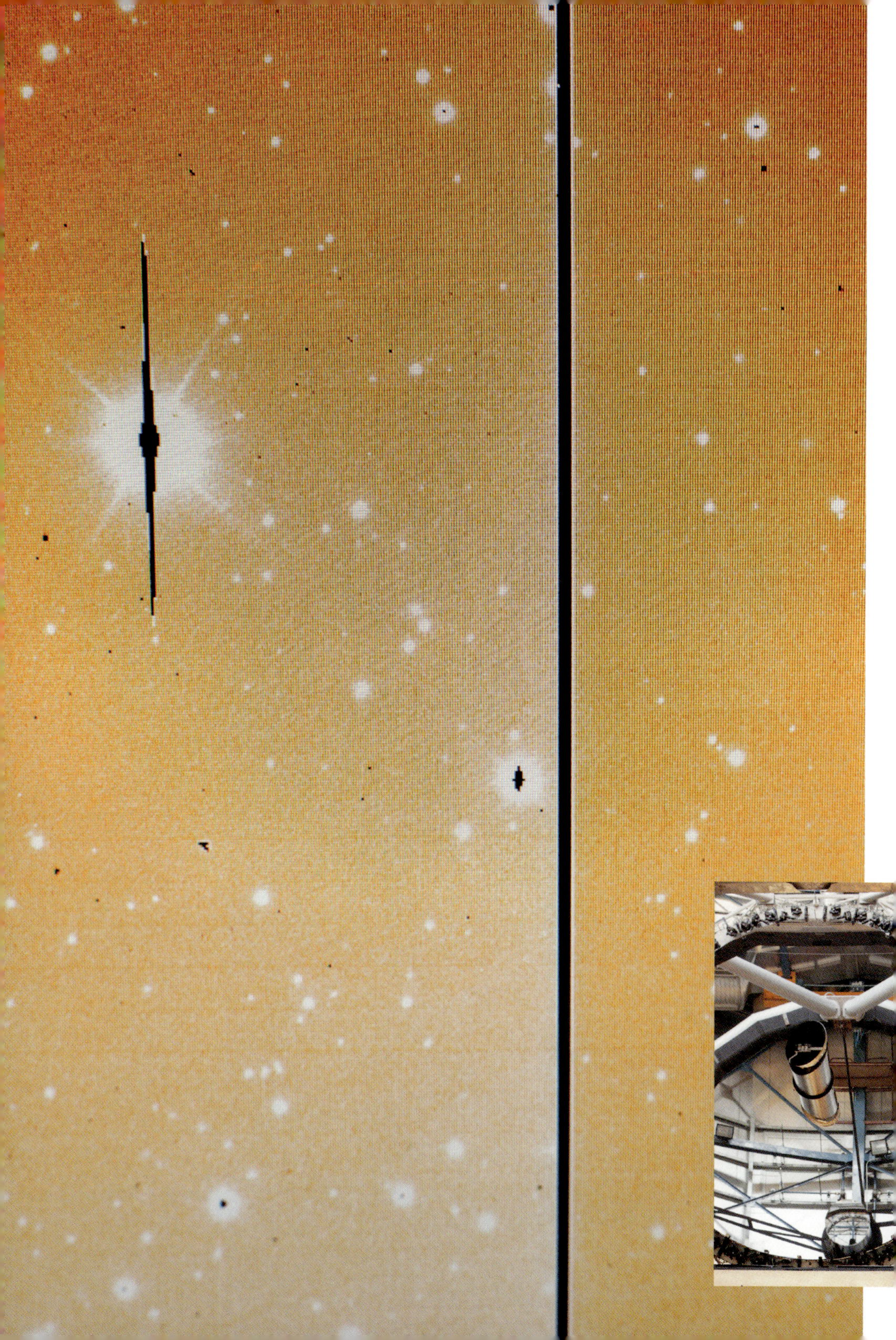

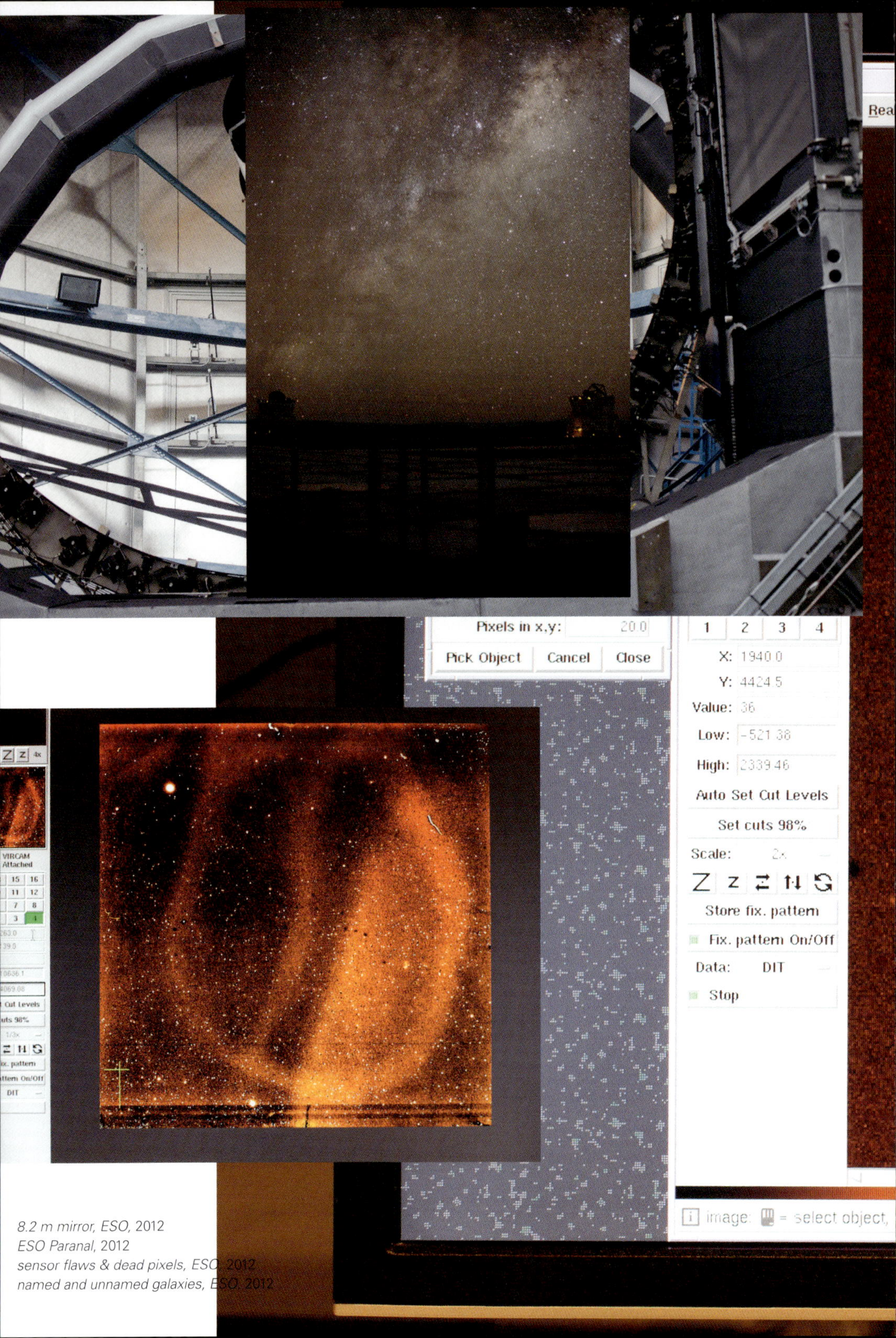

8.2 m mirror, ESO, 2012
ESO Paranal, 2012
sensor flaws & dead pixels, ESO, 2012
named and unnamed galaxies, ESO, 2012

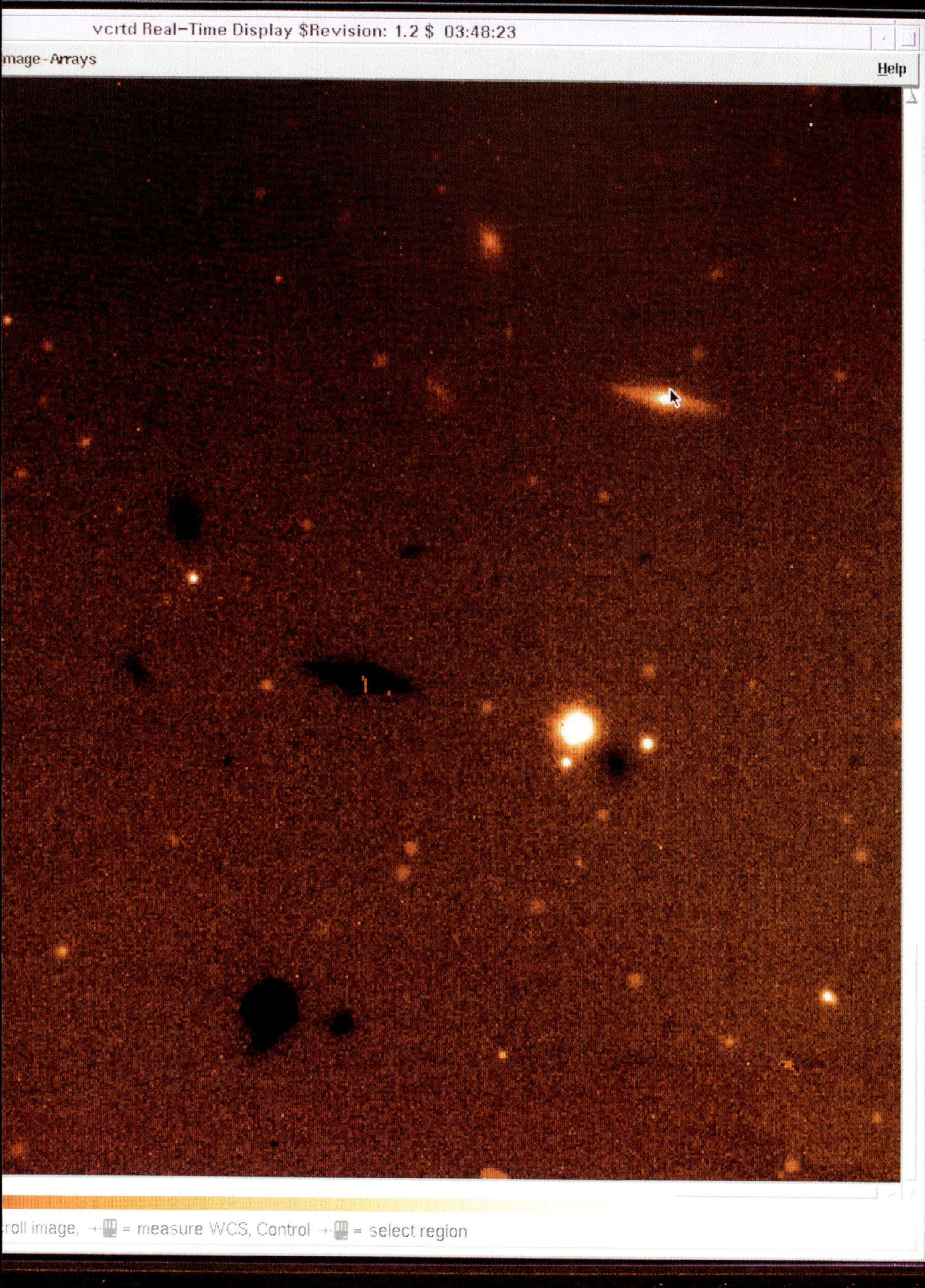

XU63 134.171.230.93 0.1
vcrtd Real-Time Display $Revision: 1.2 $ 03:48:23
Image-Arrays
Help
roll image, →⊞ = measure WCS, Control →⊞ = select region

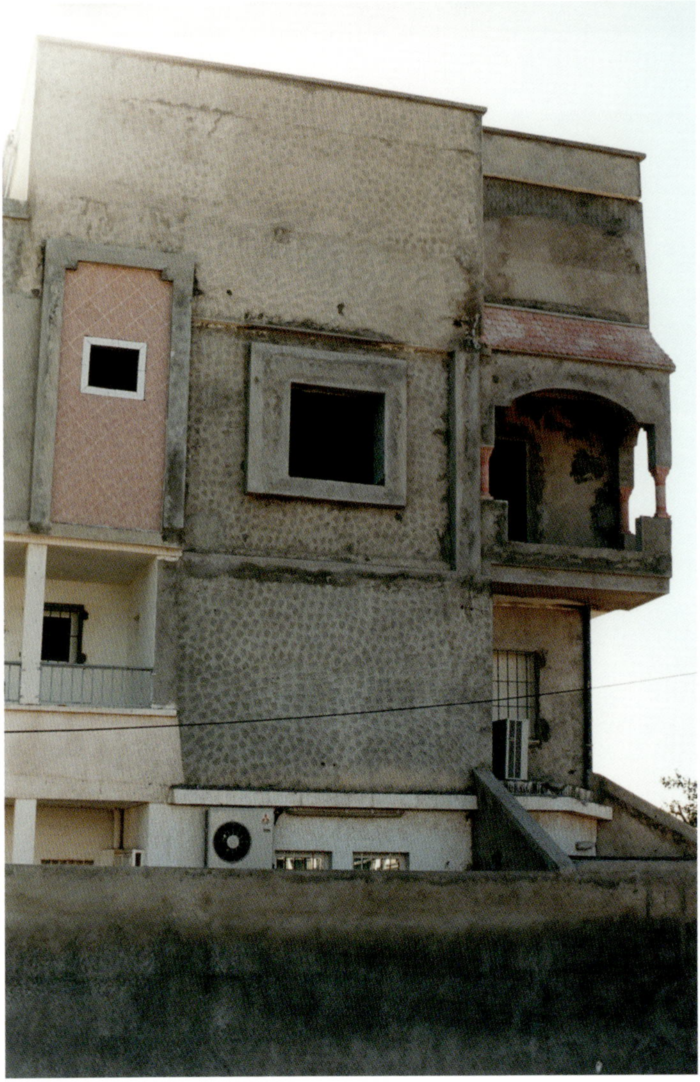

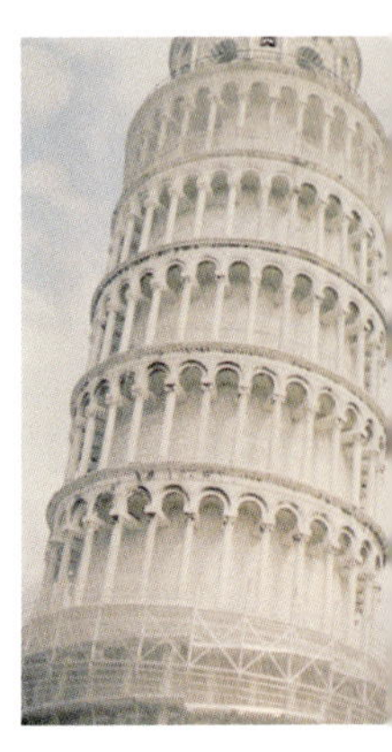

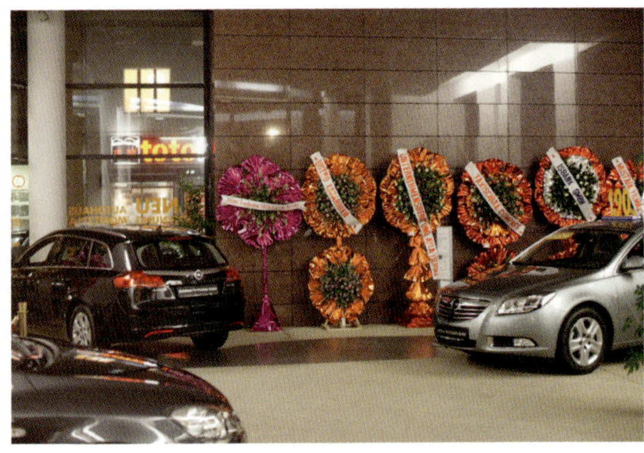

Kelibia, 2009
Neueröffnung, 2010
Turm, 2009
Zona Norte, 2010
CMOS, 2011
O2 Arena (a), 2009
O2 Arena (b), 2009

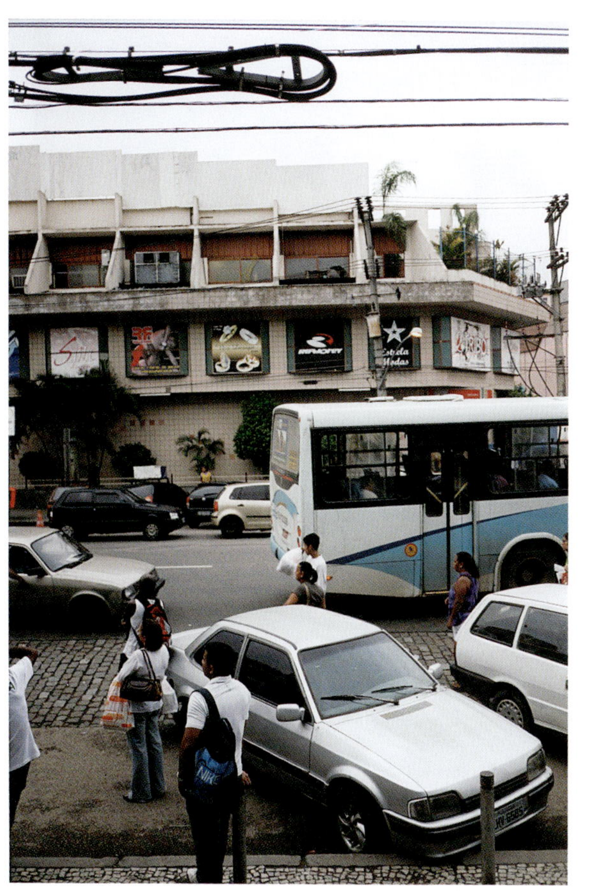
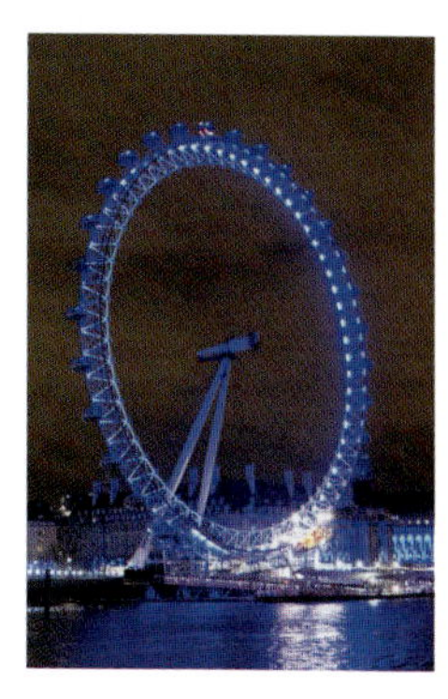
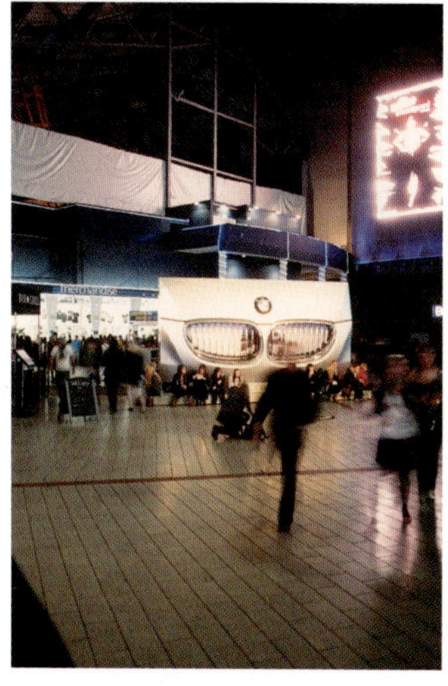
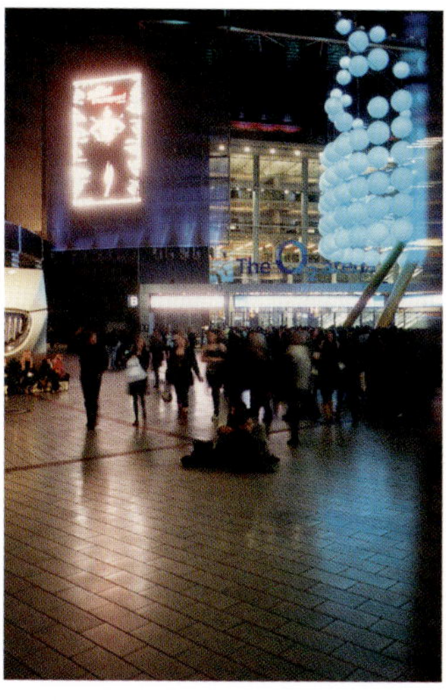

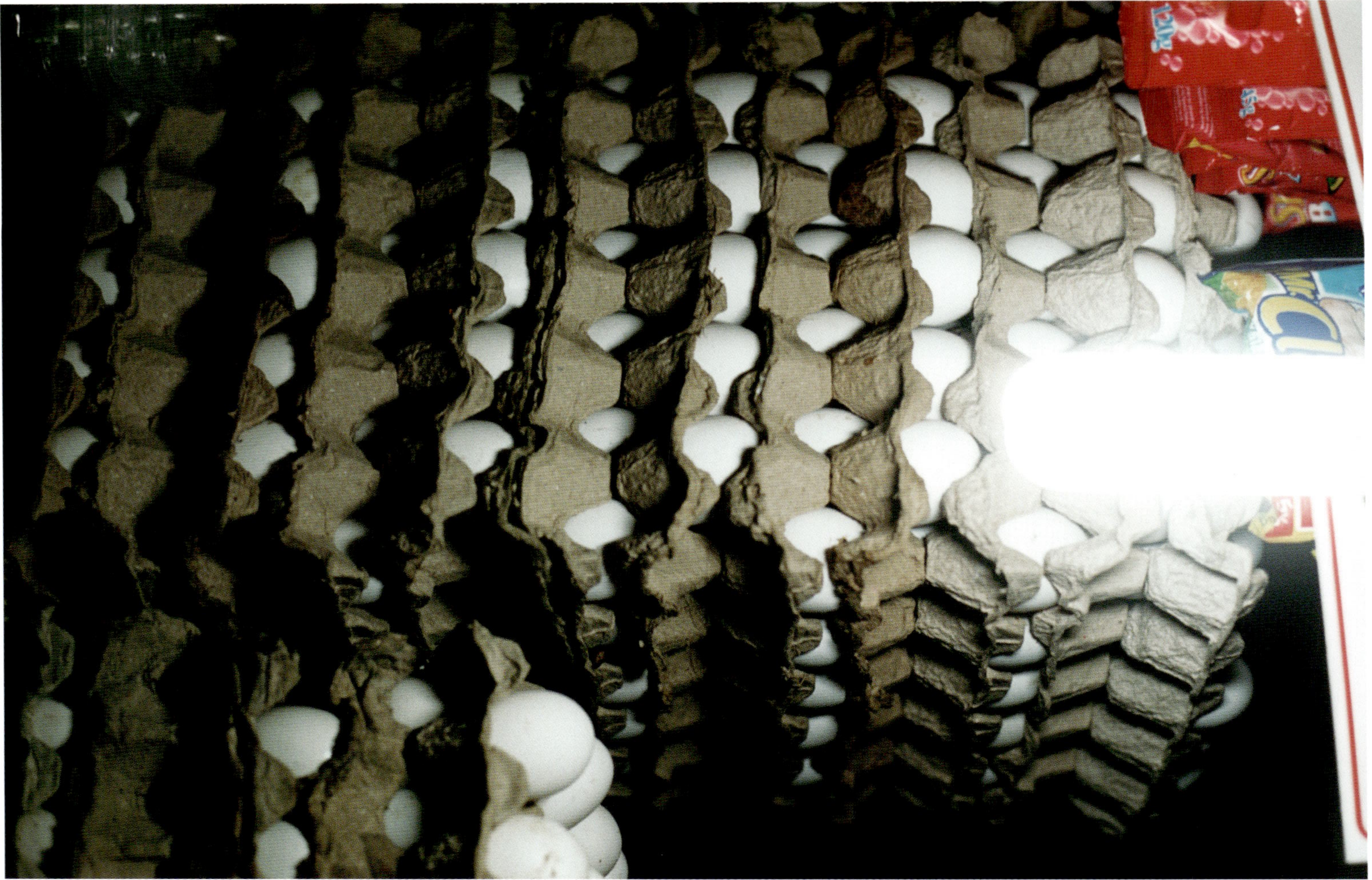

Eierstapel, 2009   *young man, Jeddah, a*, 2012

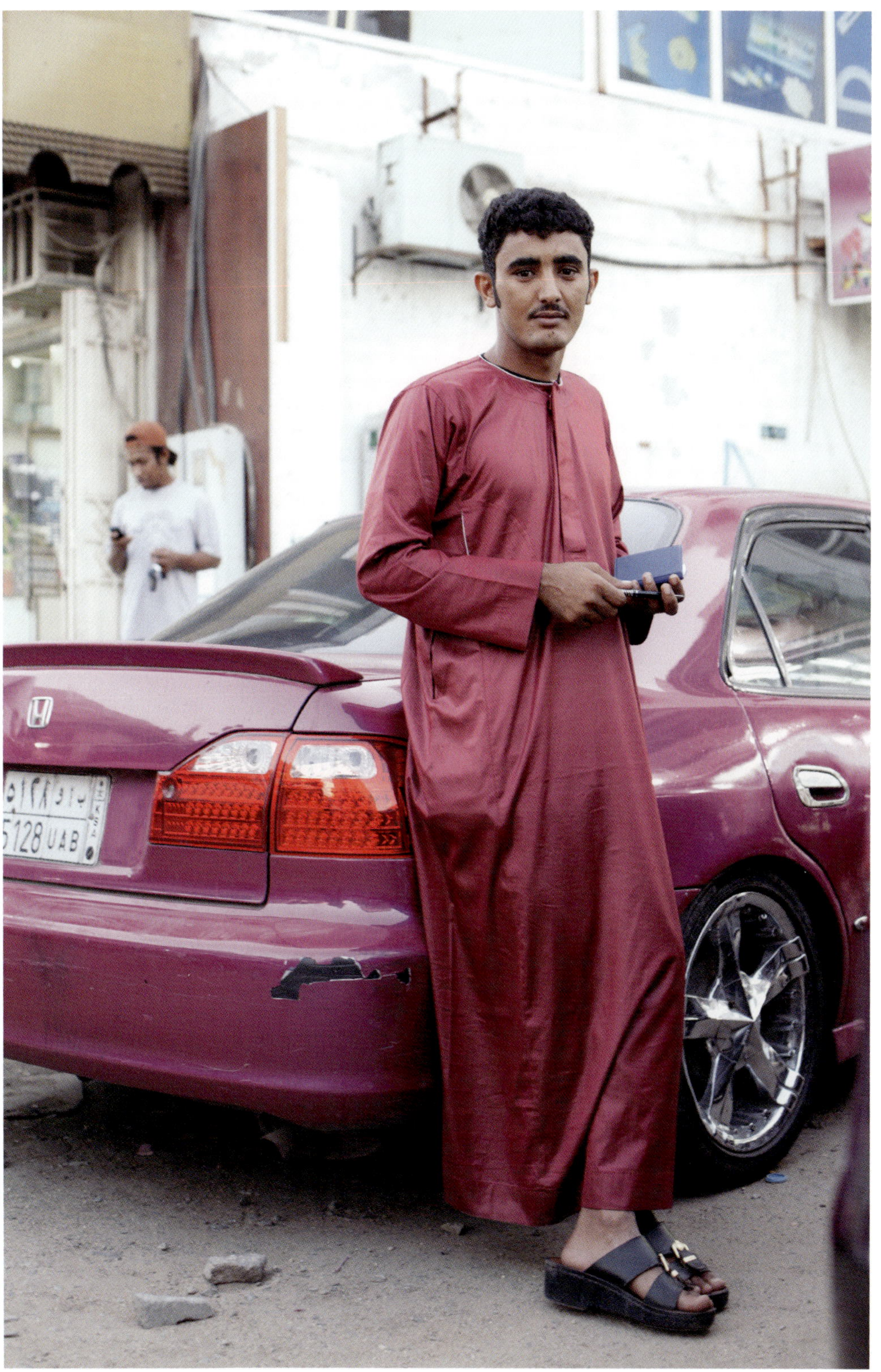

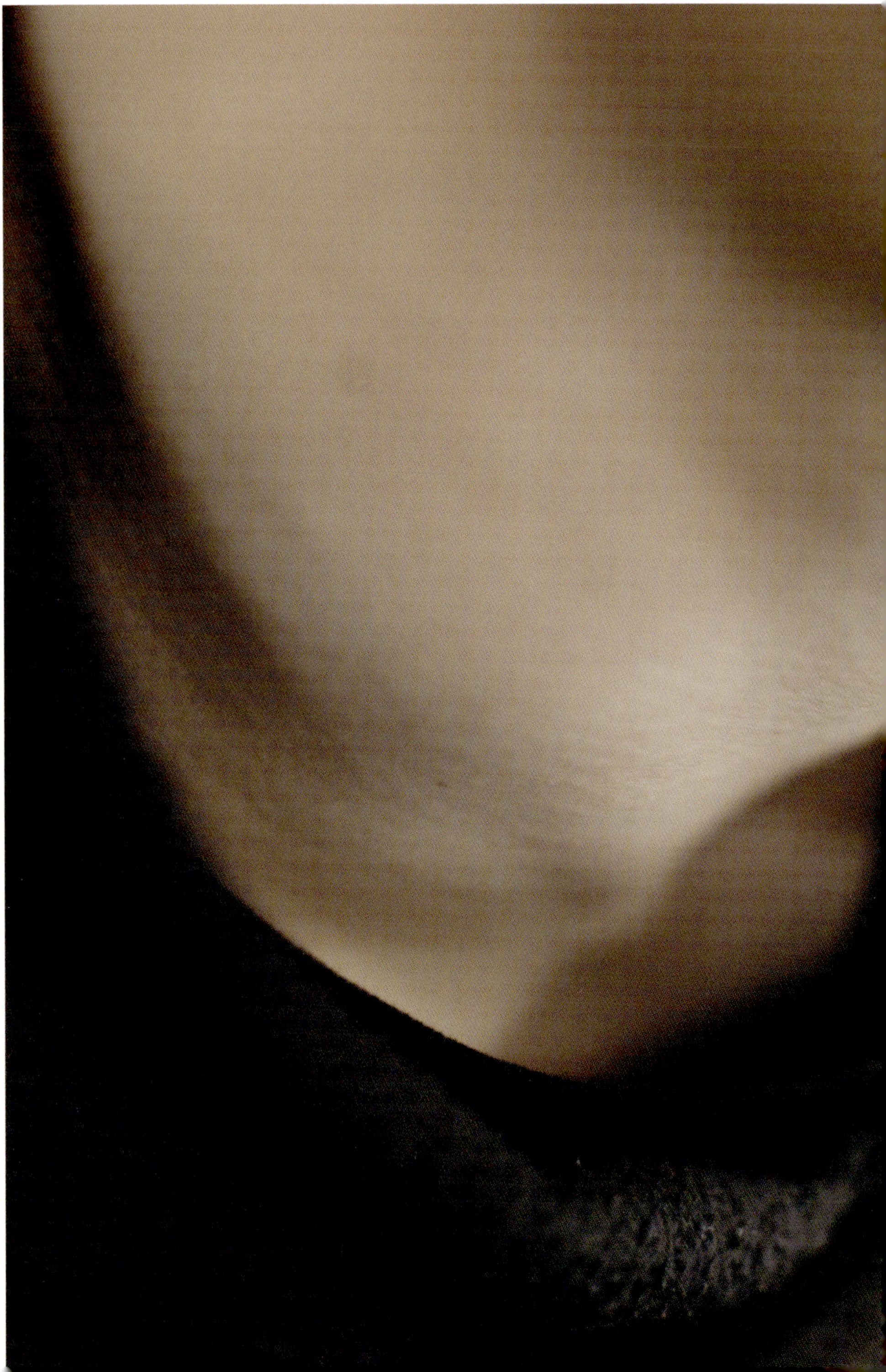

Warmth, 2011   *lovers,* 2009

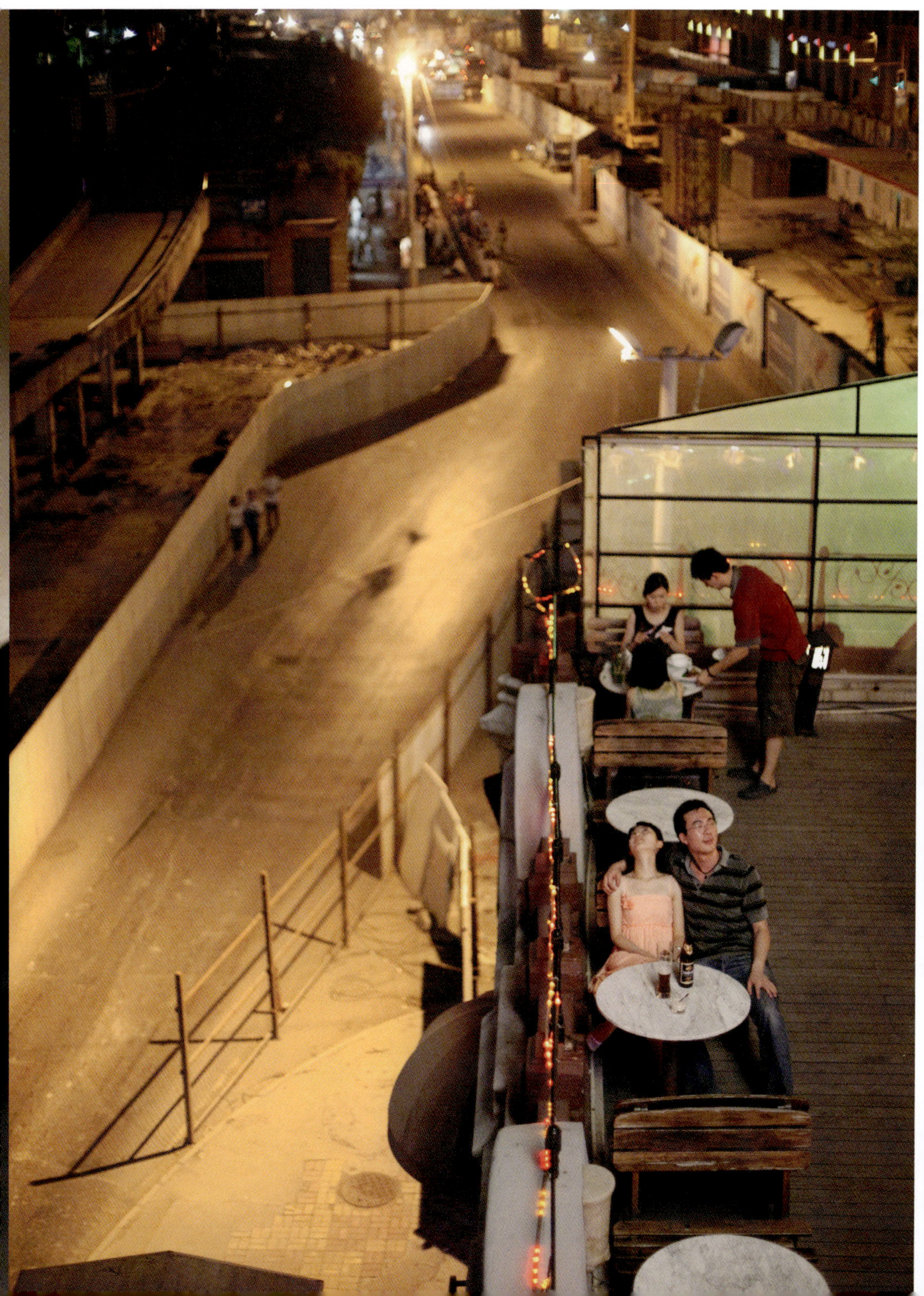

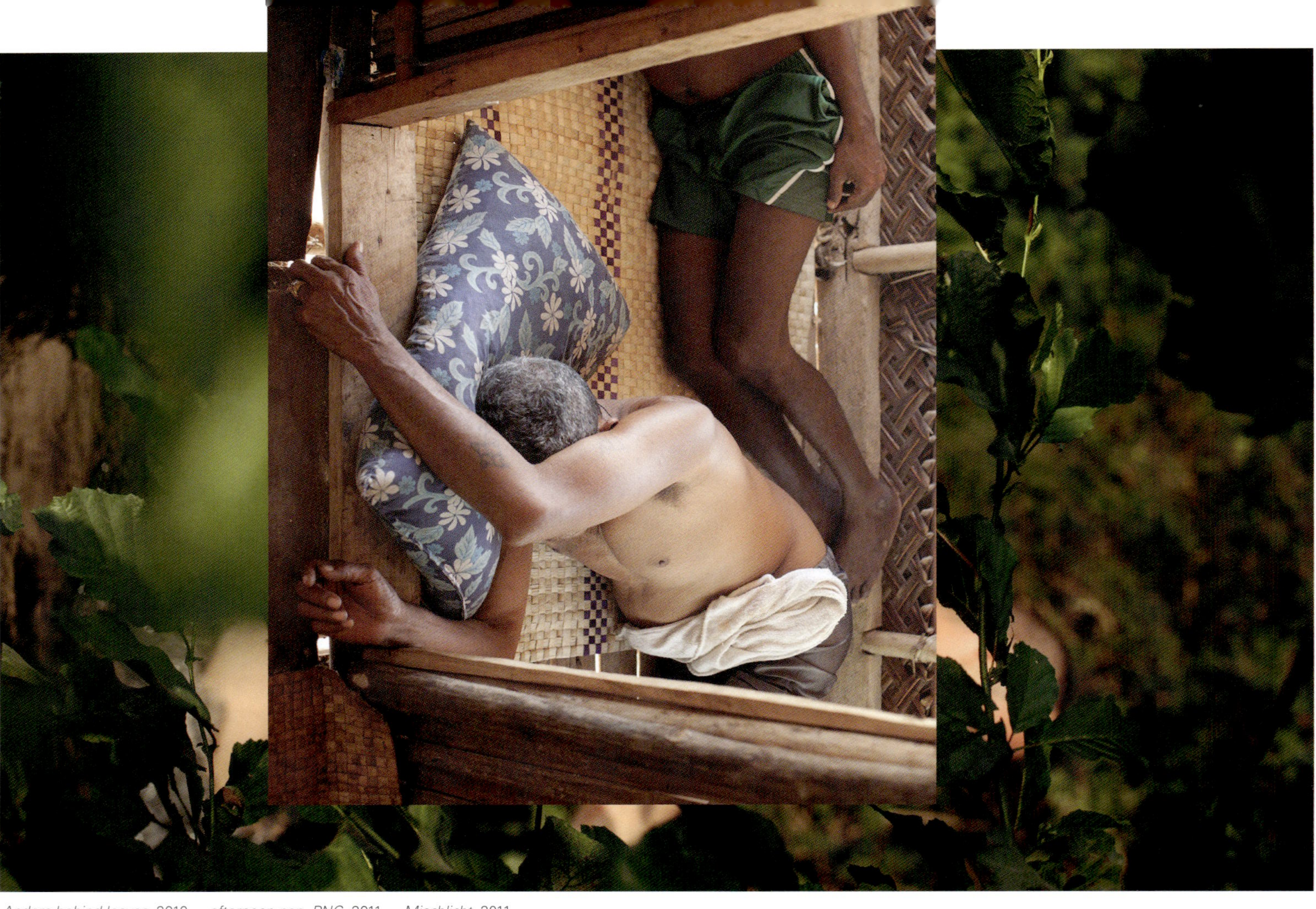

Anders behind leaves, 2010   *afternoon nap, PNG,* 2011   *Mischlicht,* 2011

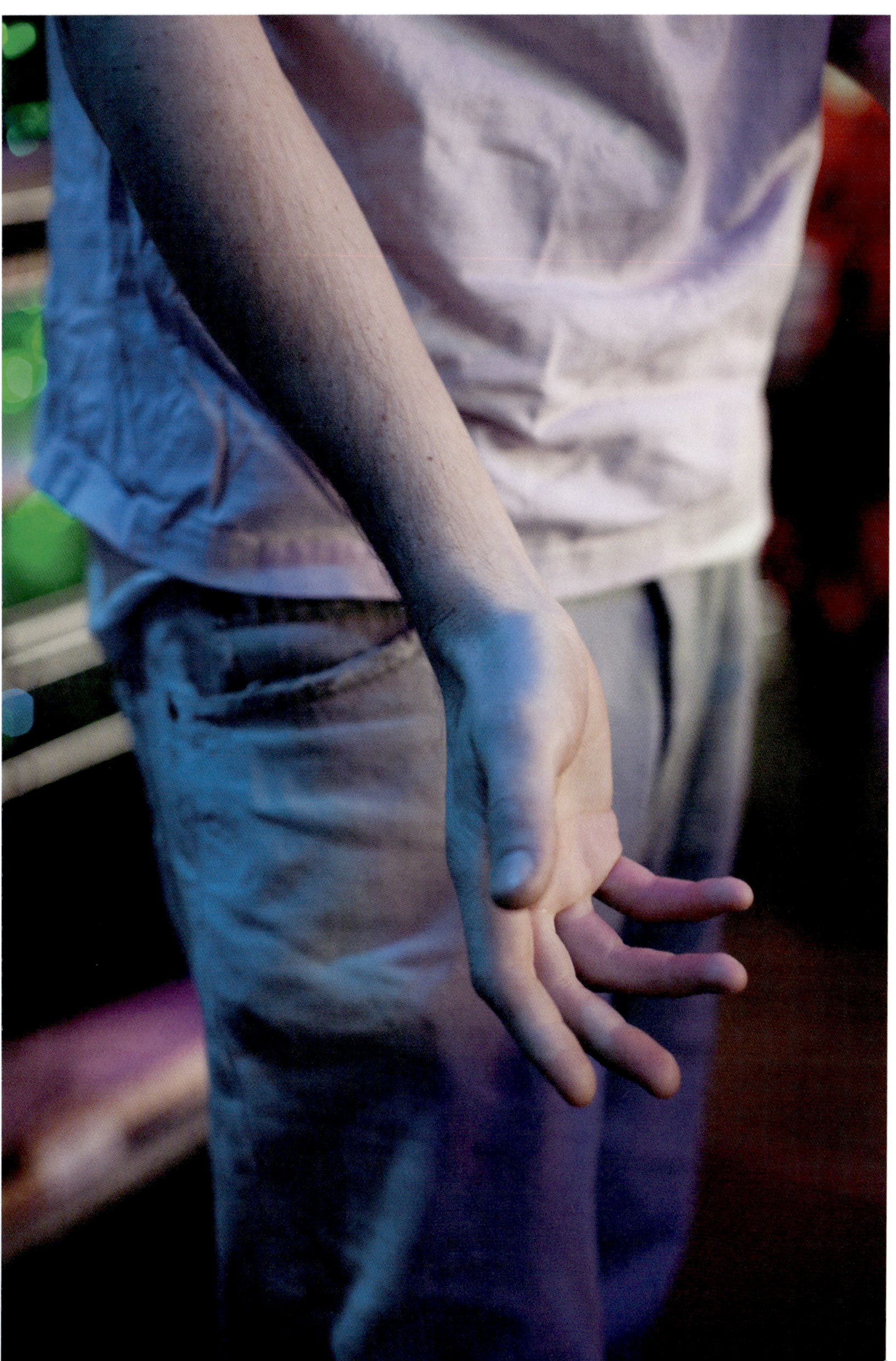

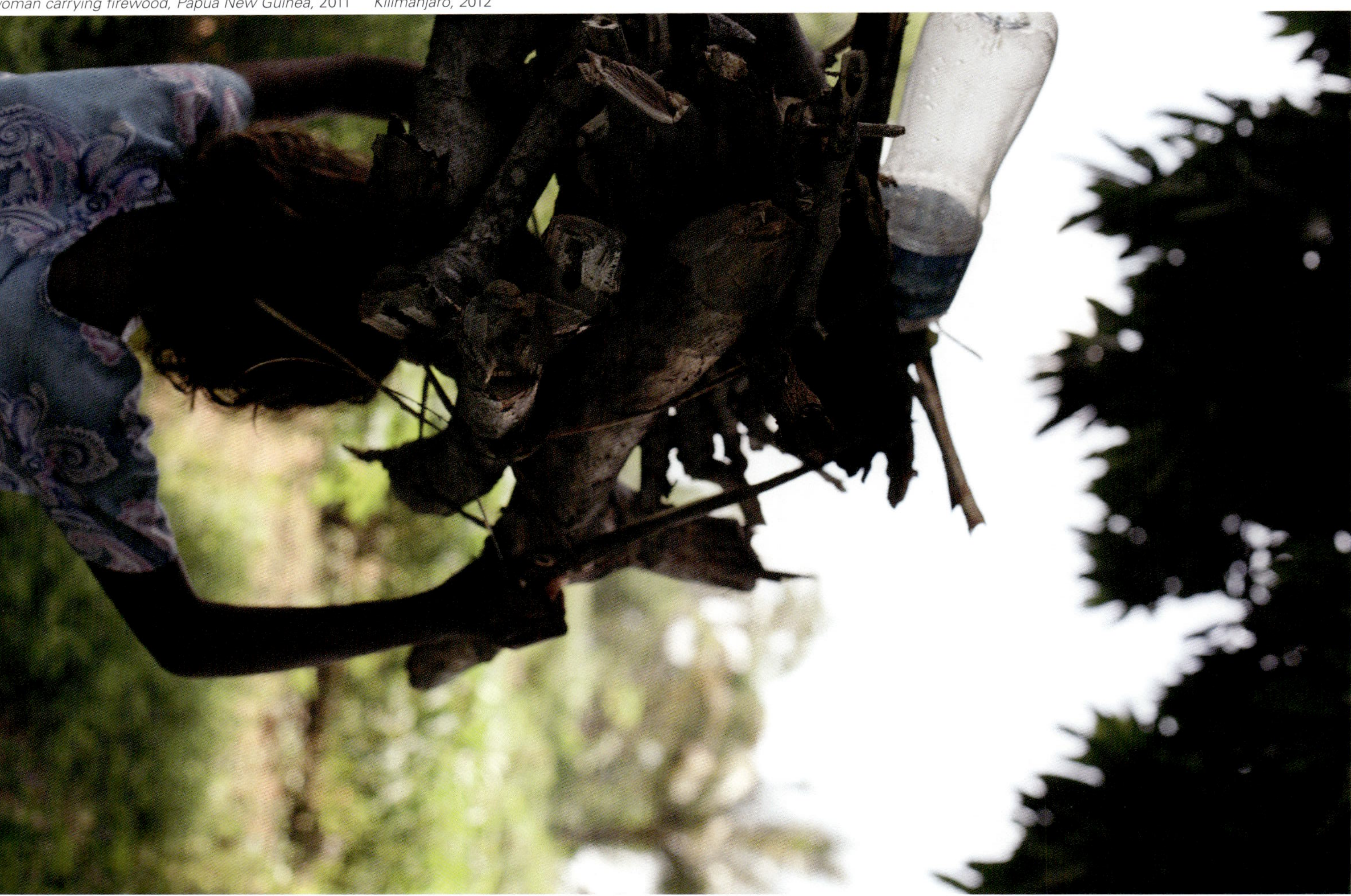

woman carrying firewood, Papua New Guinea, 2011   Kilimanjaro, 2012

astro crusto, a, 2012

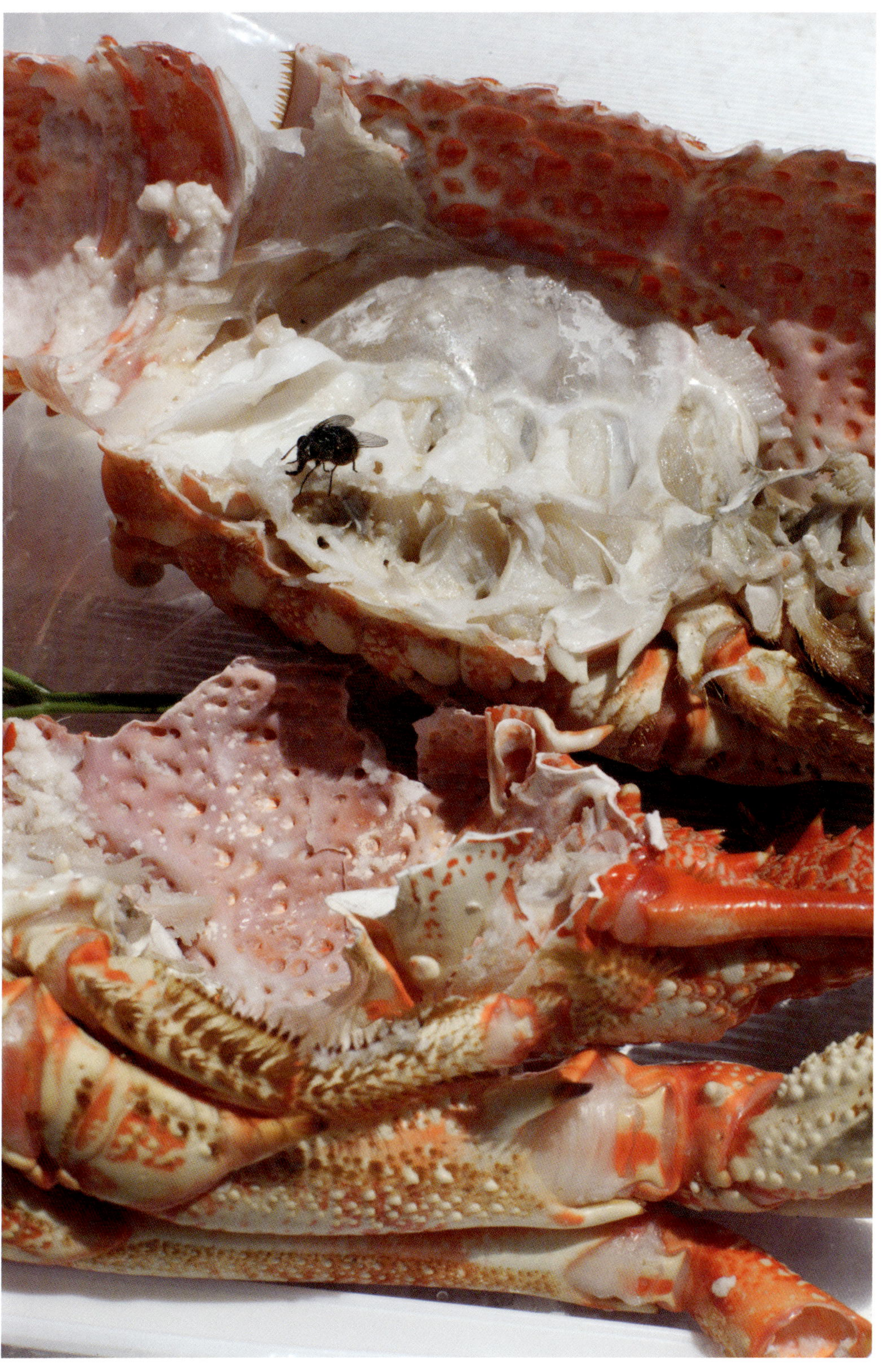

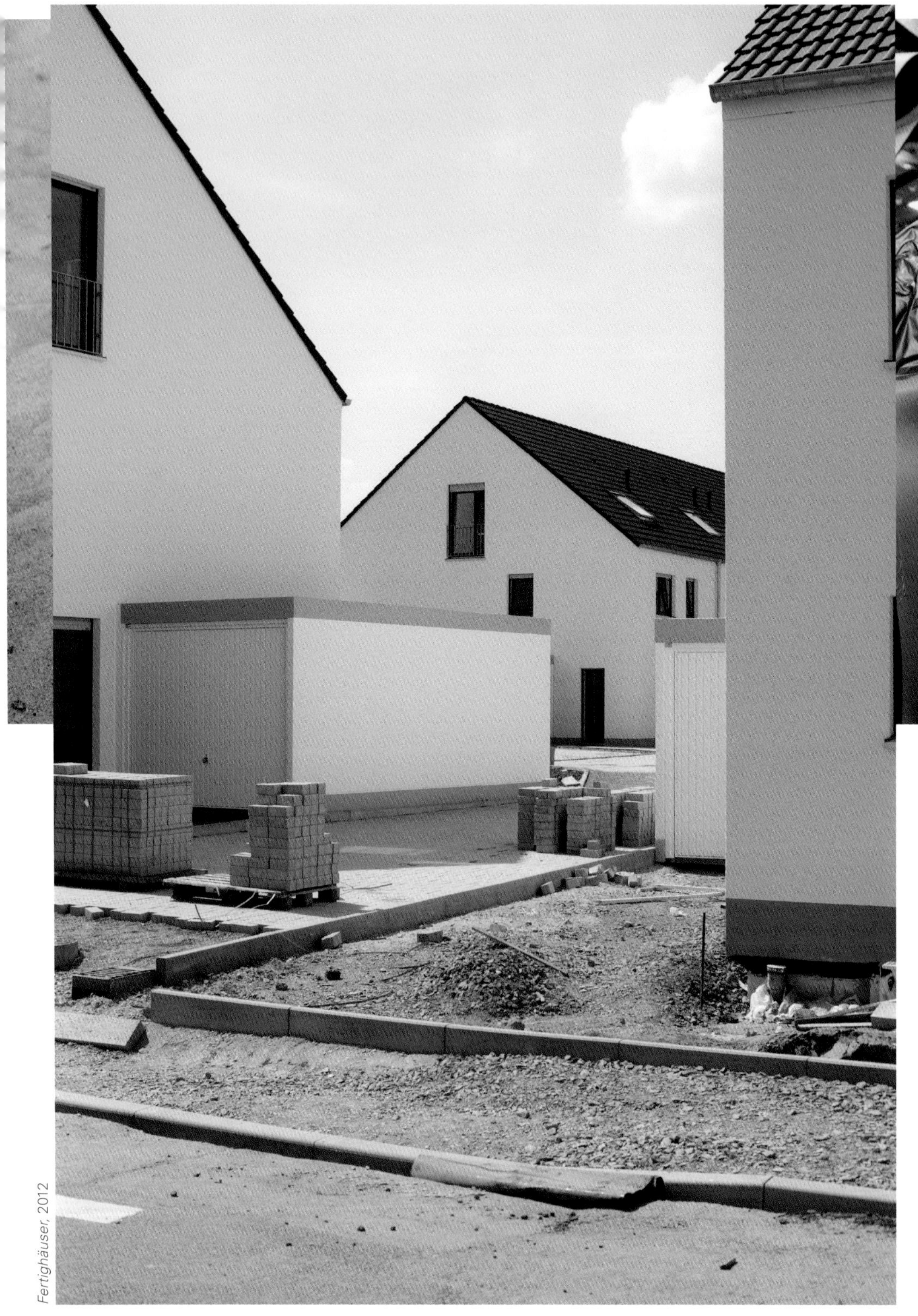

Fertighäuser, 2012

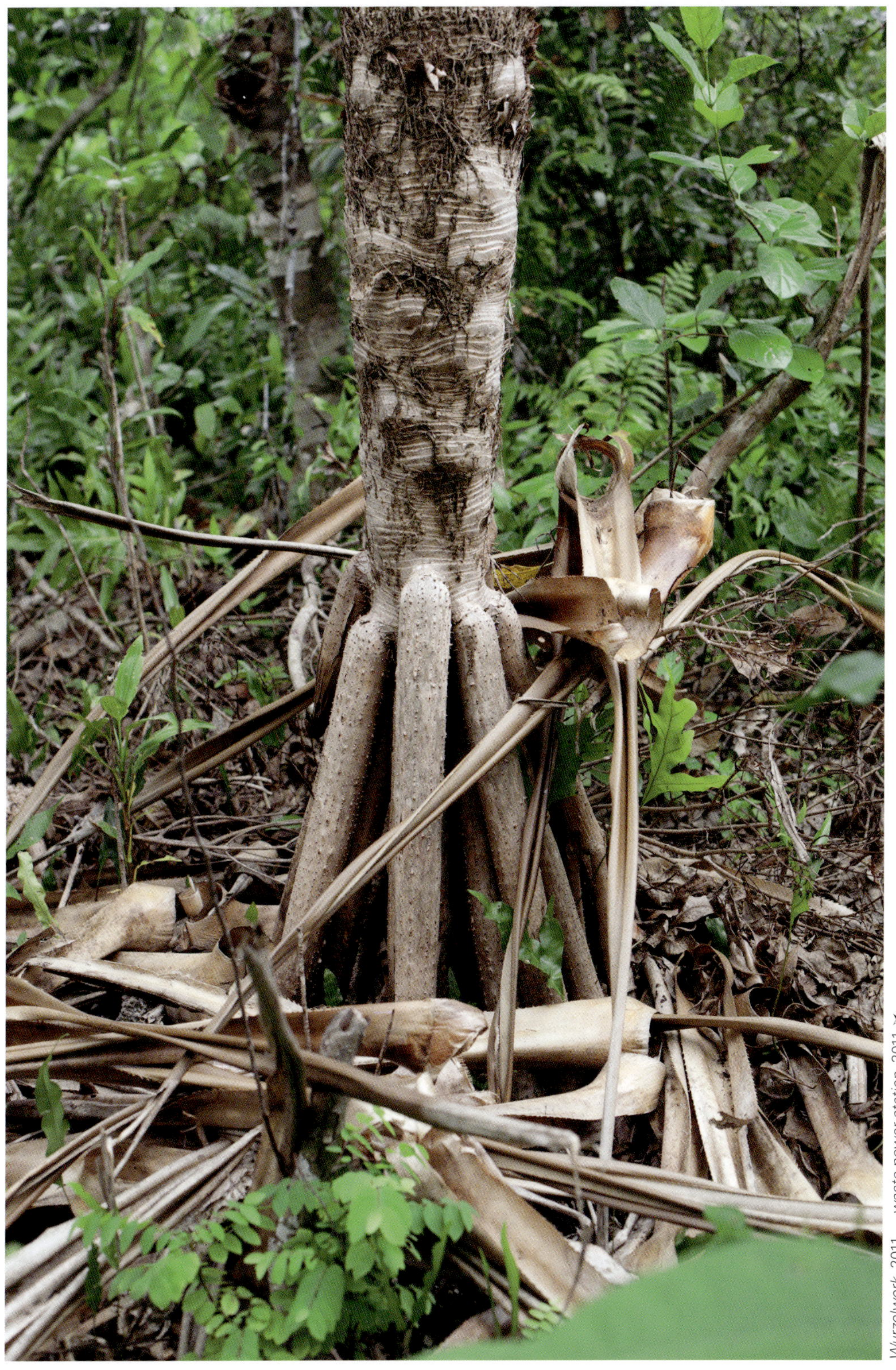

Wurzelwerk, 2011   waste power station, 2011 ⌄

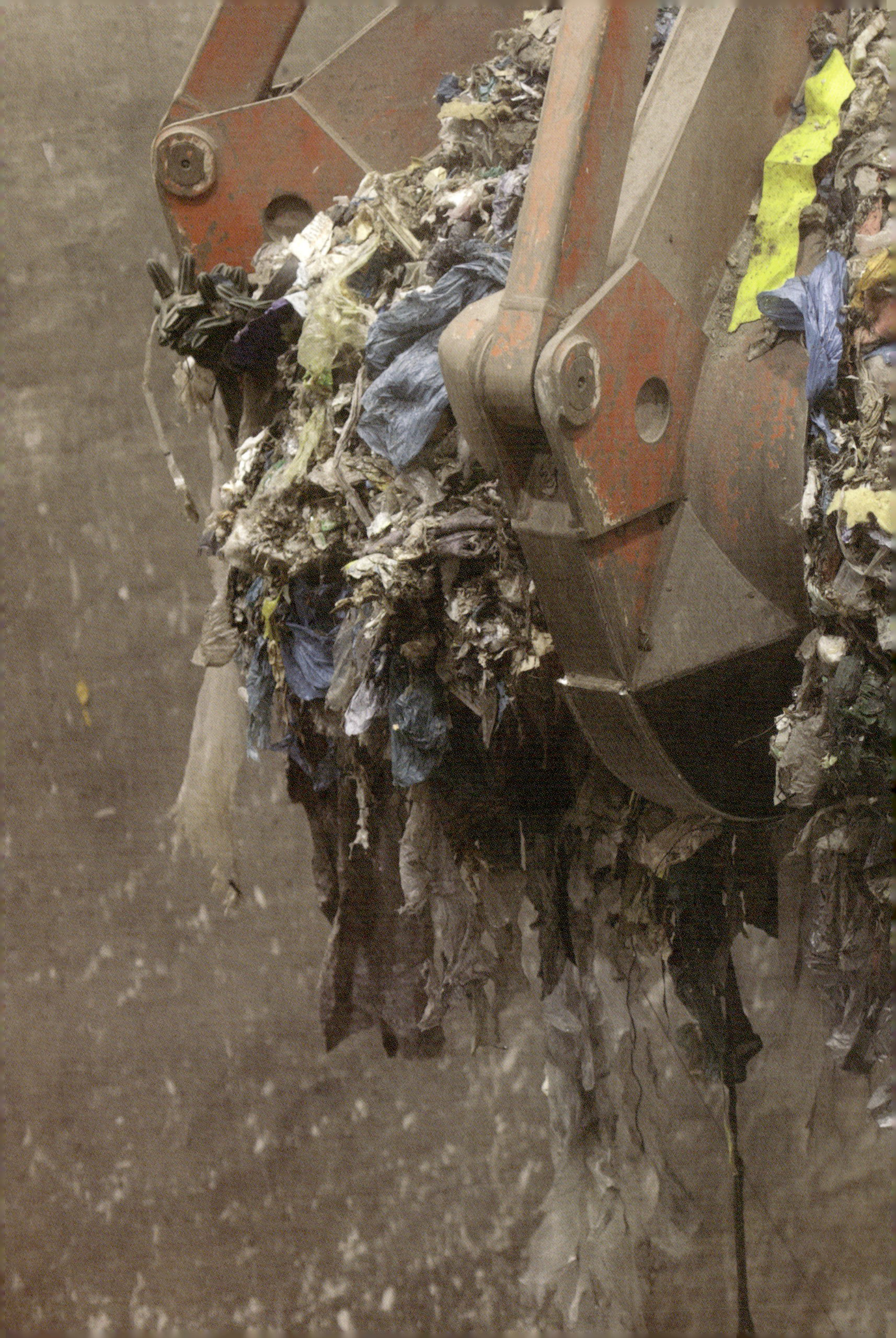

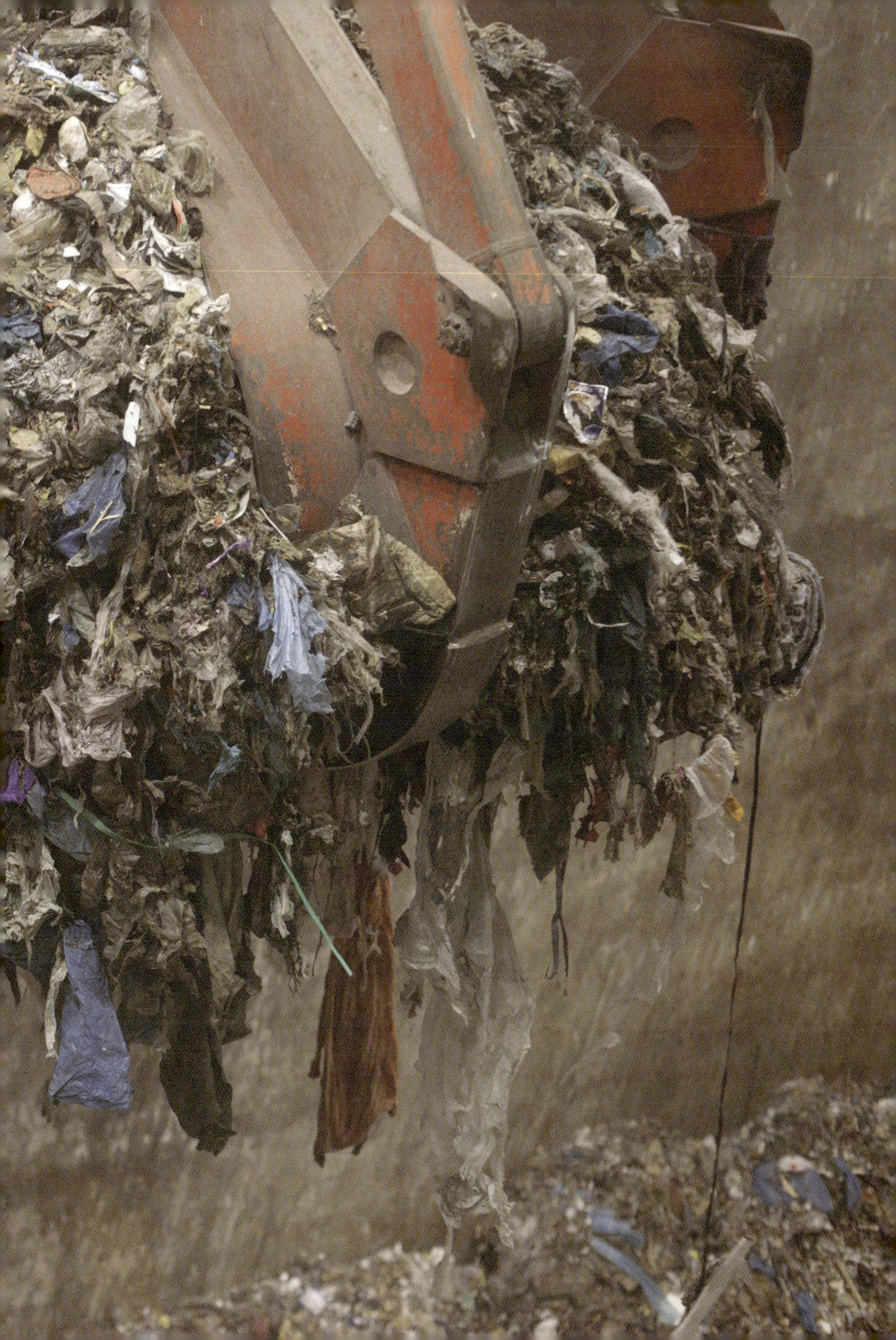

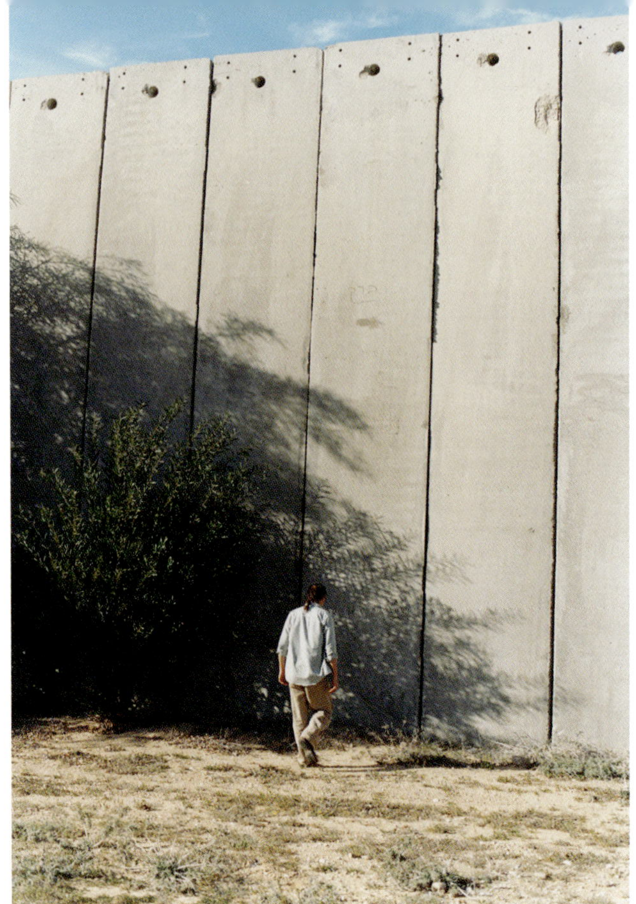
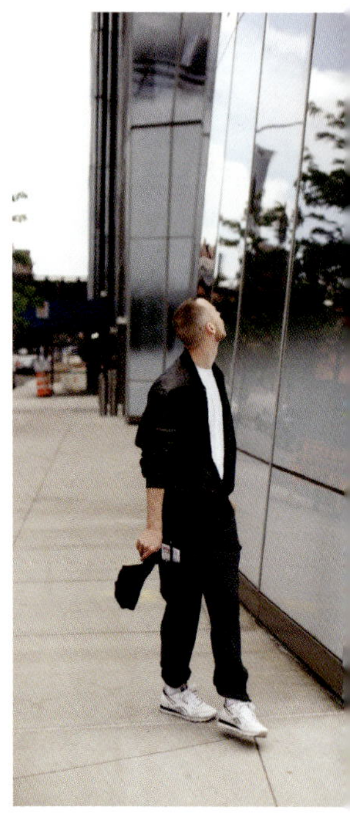
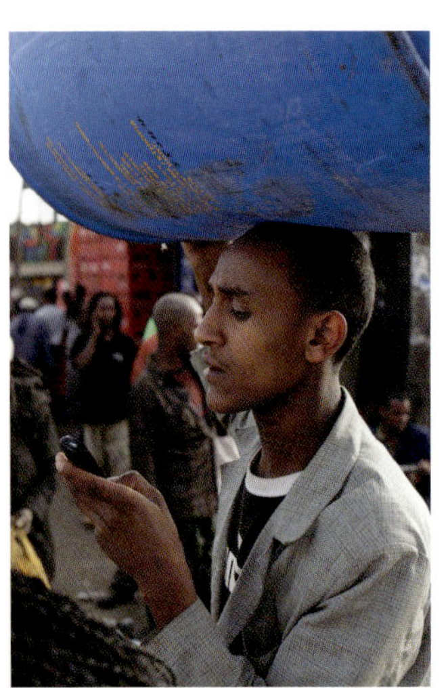

Addis, man texting, 2012
Gaza wall, 2009
Weather, 2010
Nightfall (a), 2010

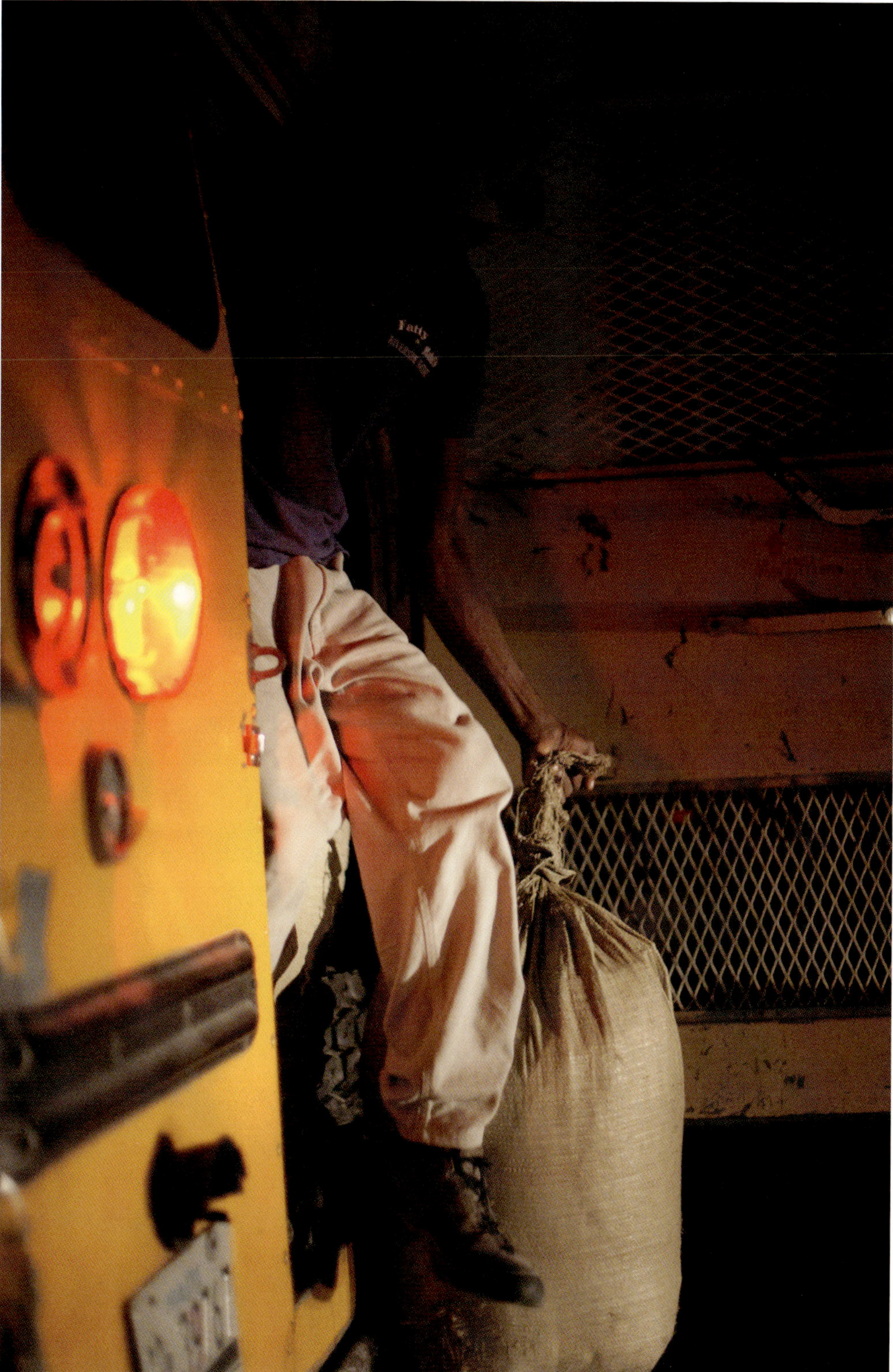

Paranal ESO, sky & ocean, 2012

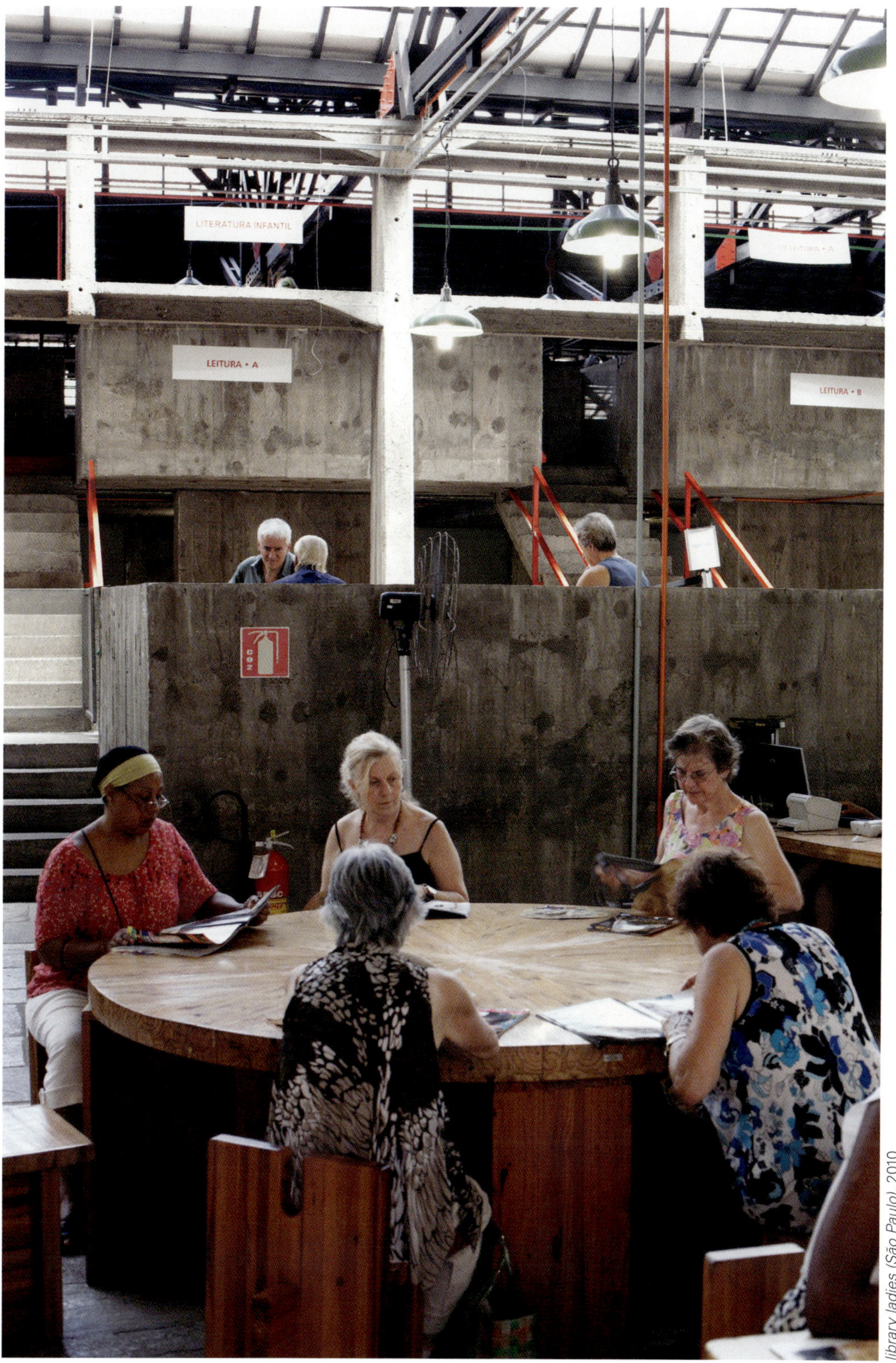

library ladies (São Paulo), 2010

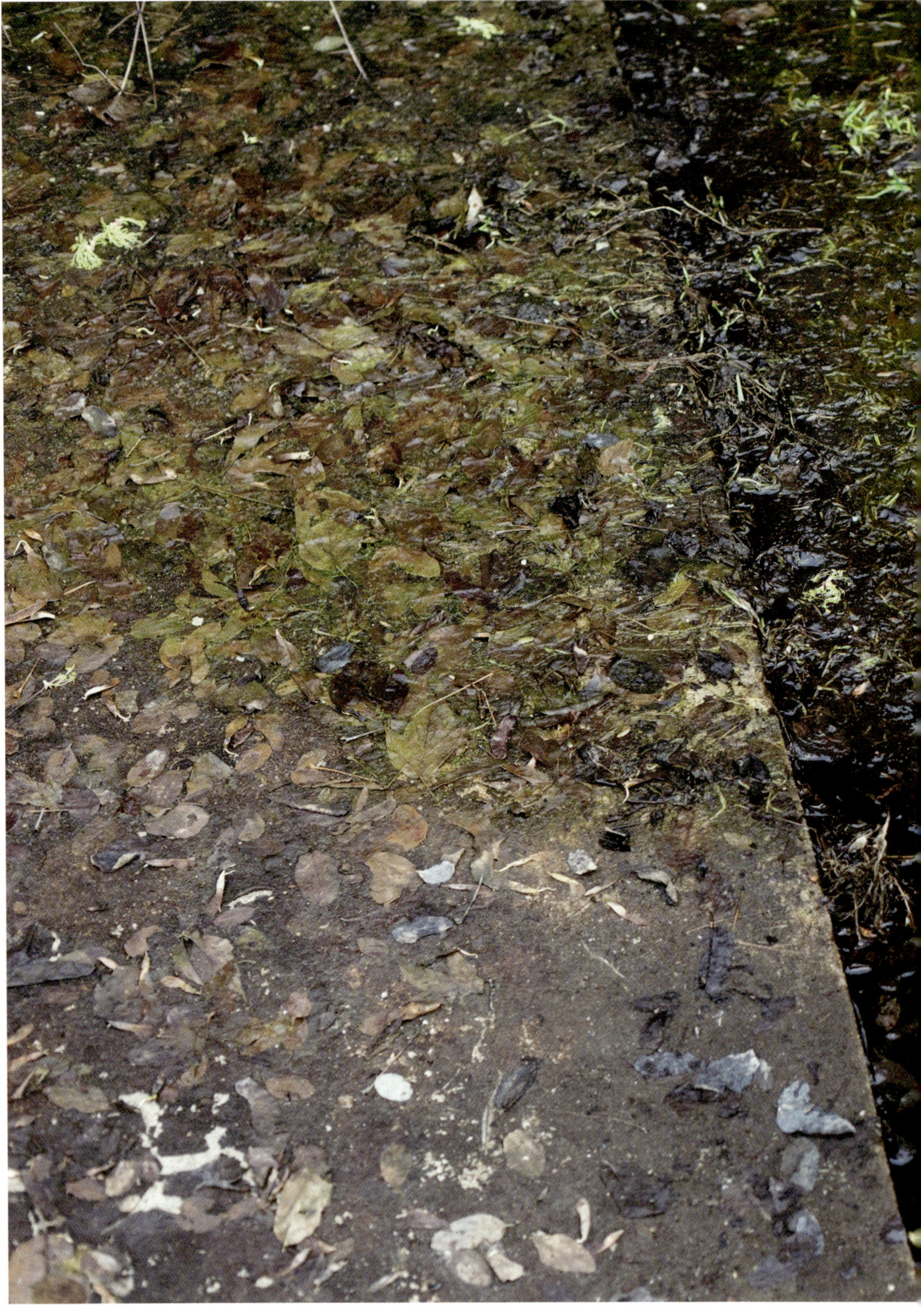

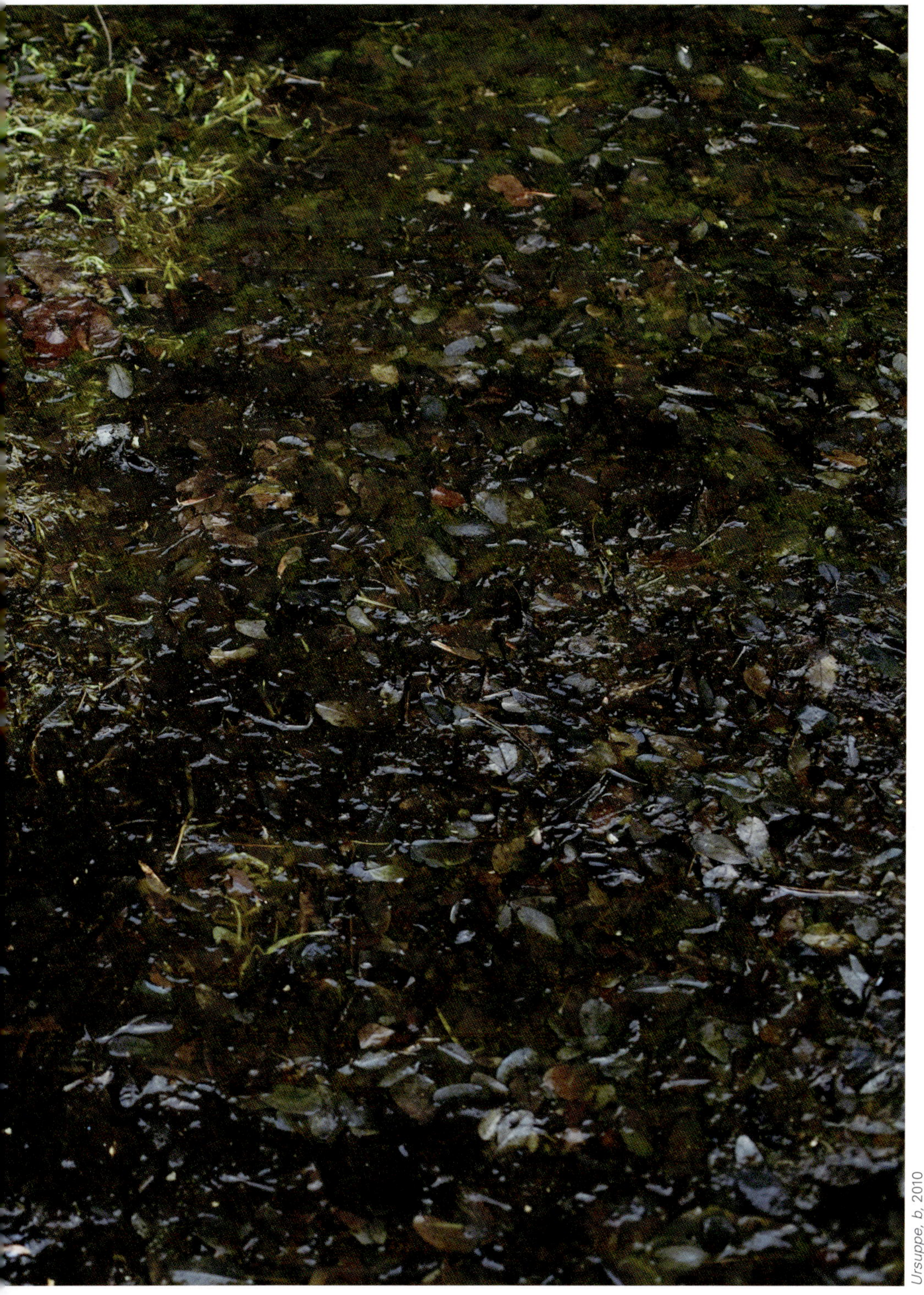

Ursuppe, b, 2010

young man, Jeddah, b, 2012

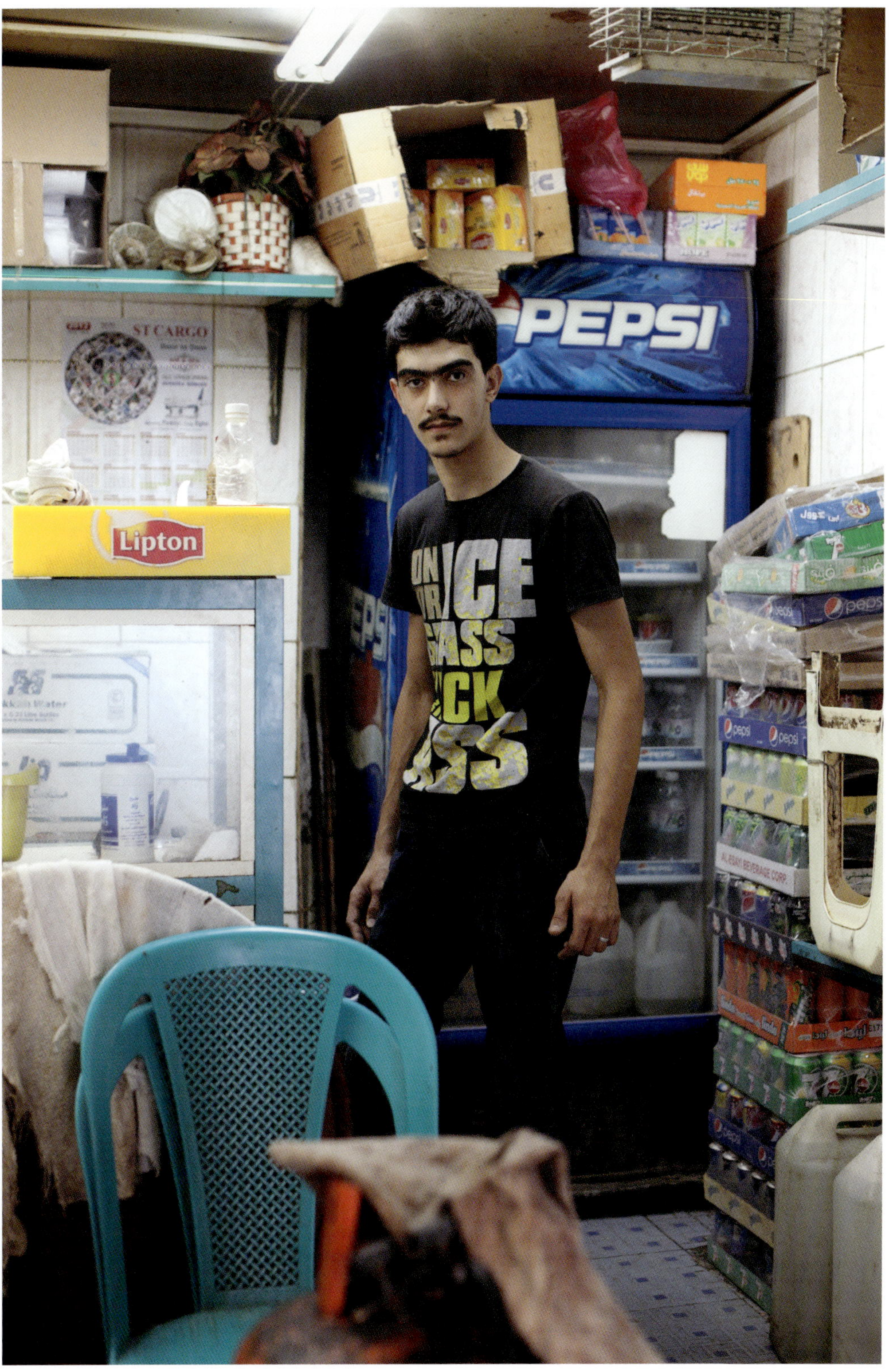
St CARGO
Lipton
PEPSI
PEPSI
pepsi
pepsi
ALBANY BEVERAGE CORP.

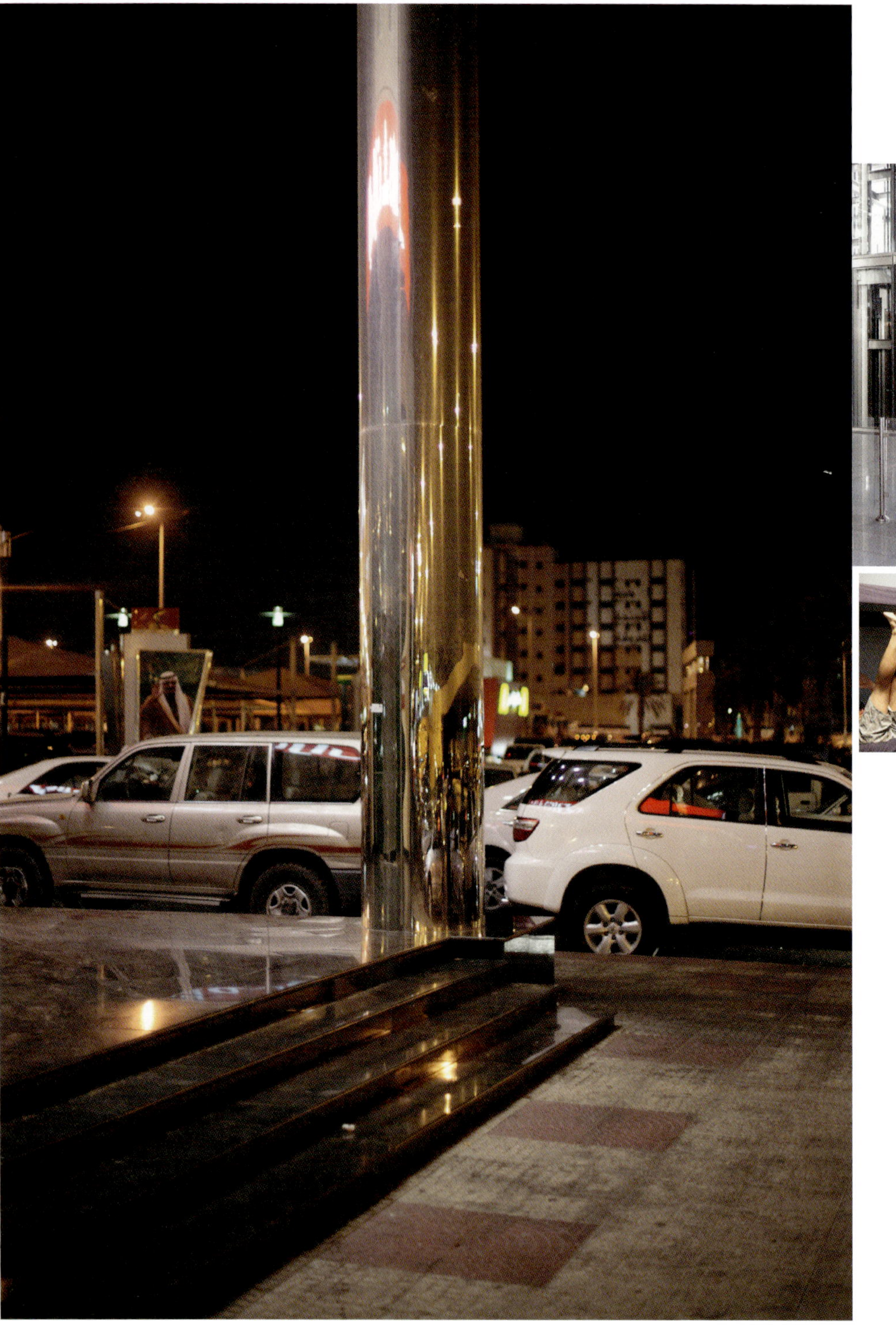

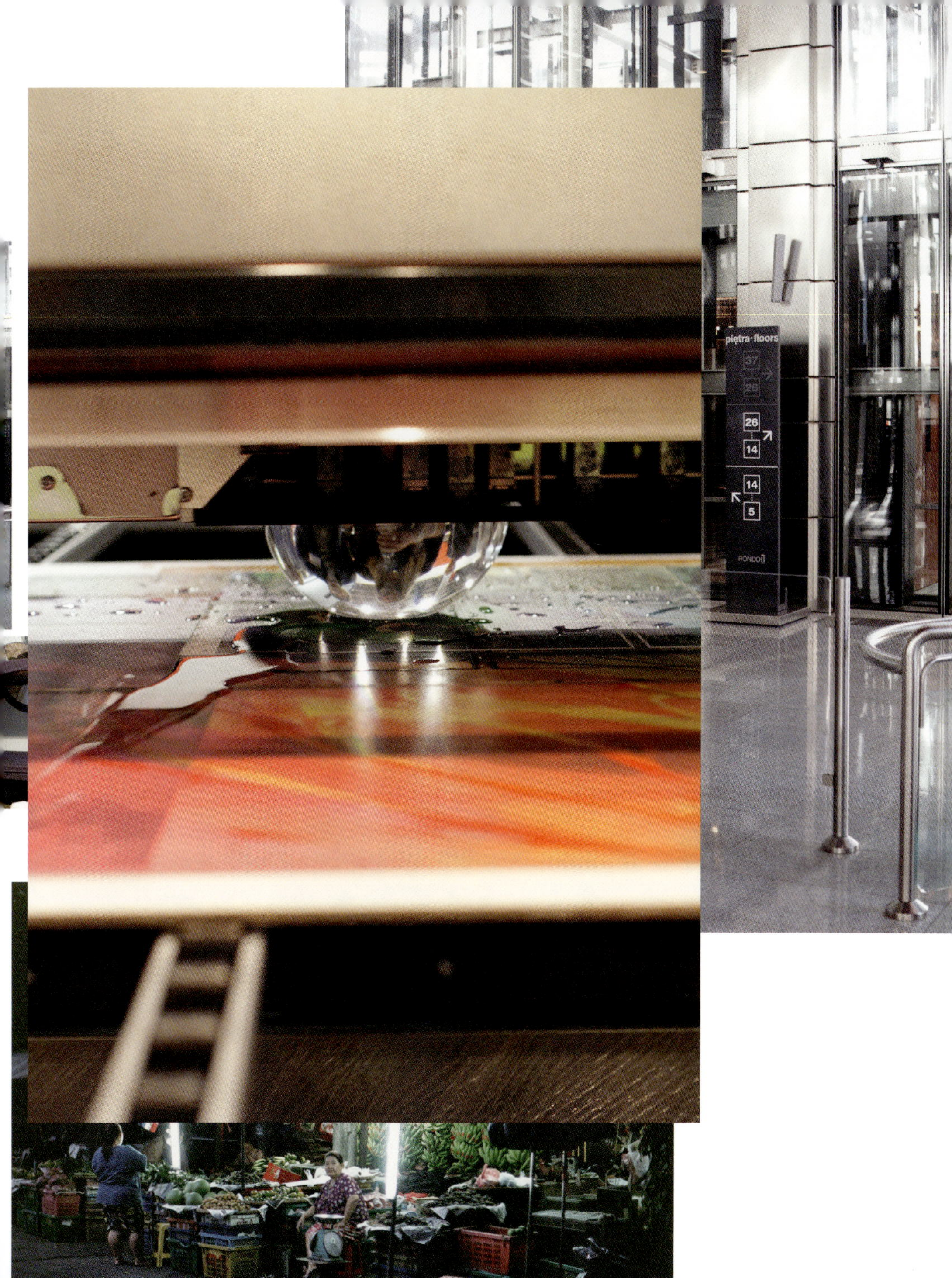

shiny column, 2012
Frontex transparency, 2011
hostel Sydney, 2012
Fespa (inkjet on water), 2012
Bangkok, 2009

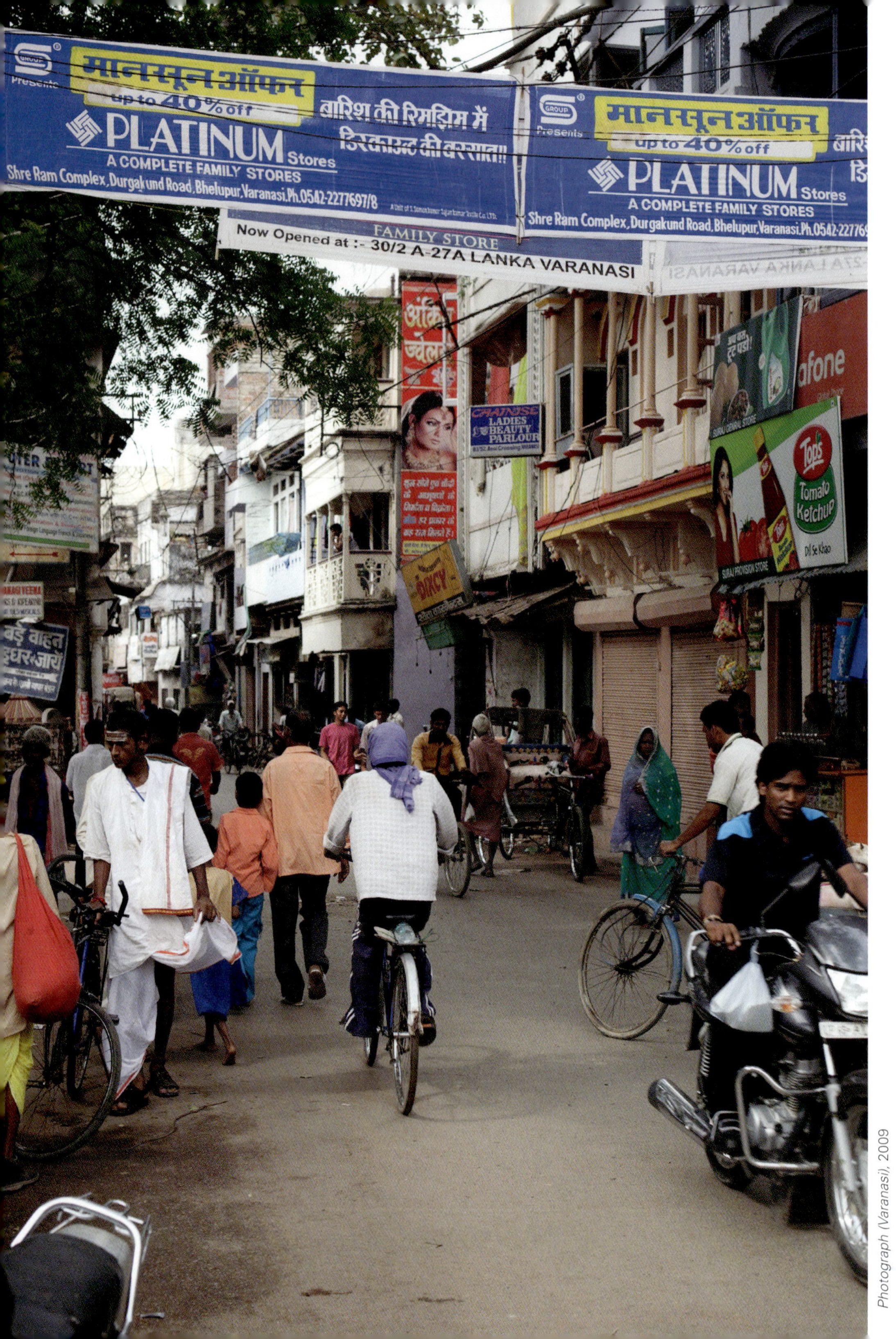
मानसून ऑफर
up to 40% off
बारिश की रिमझिम में
PLATINUM Stores
A COMPLETE FAMILY STORES
Shre Ram Complex, Durgakund Road, Bhelupur, Varanasi. Ph.0542-2277697/8
FAMILY STORE
Now Opened at :- 30/2 A-27A LANKA VARANASI
मानसून ऑफर
up to 40% off
PLATINUM Stores
A COMPLETE FAMILY STORES
Shre Ram Complex, Durgakund Road, Bhelupur, Varanasi. Ph.0542-227769
LANKA VARANASI
LADIES BEAUTY PARLOUR
Tops Tomato Ketchup
Dil Se Khao
SUBAI PROVISION STORE

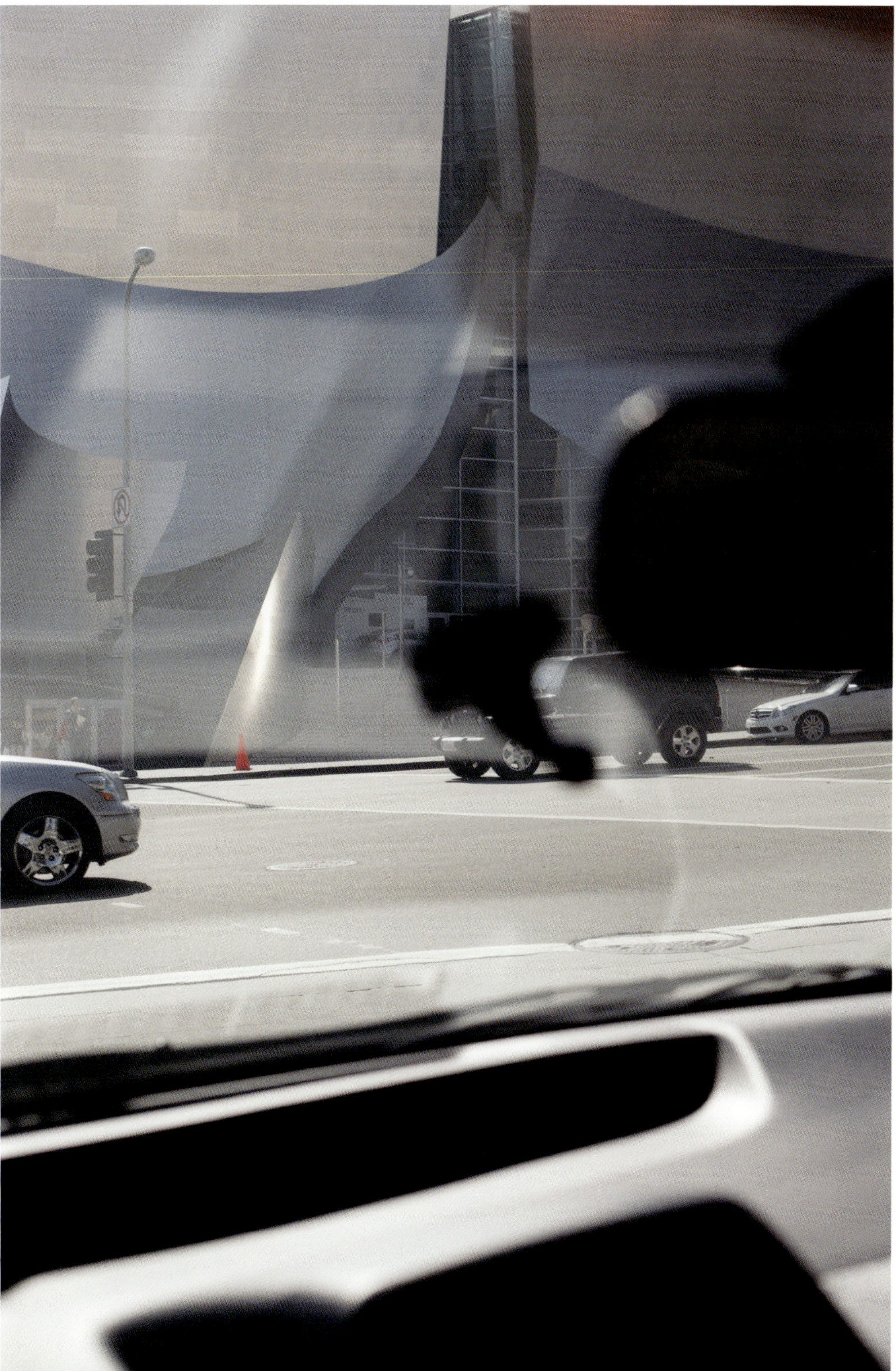

Downtown Los Angeles, 2011

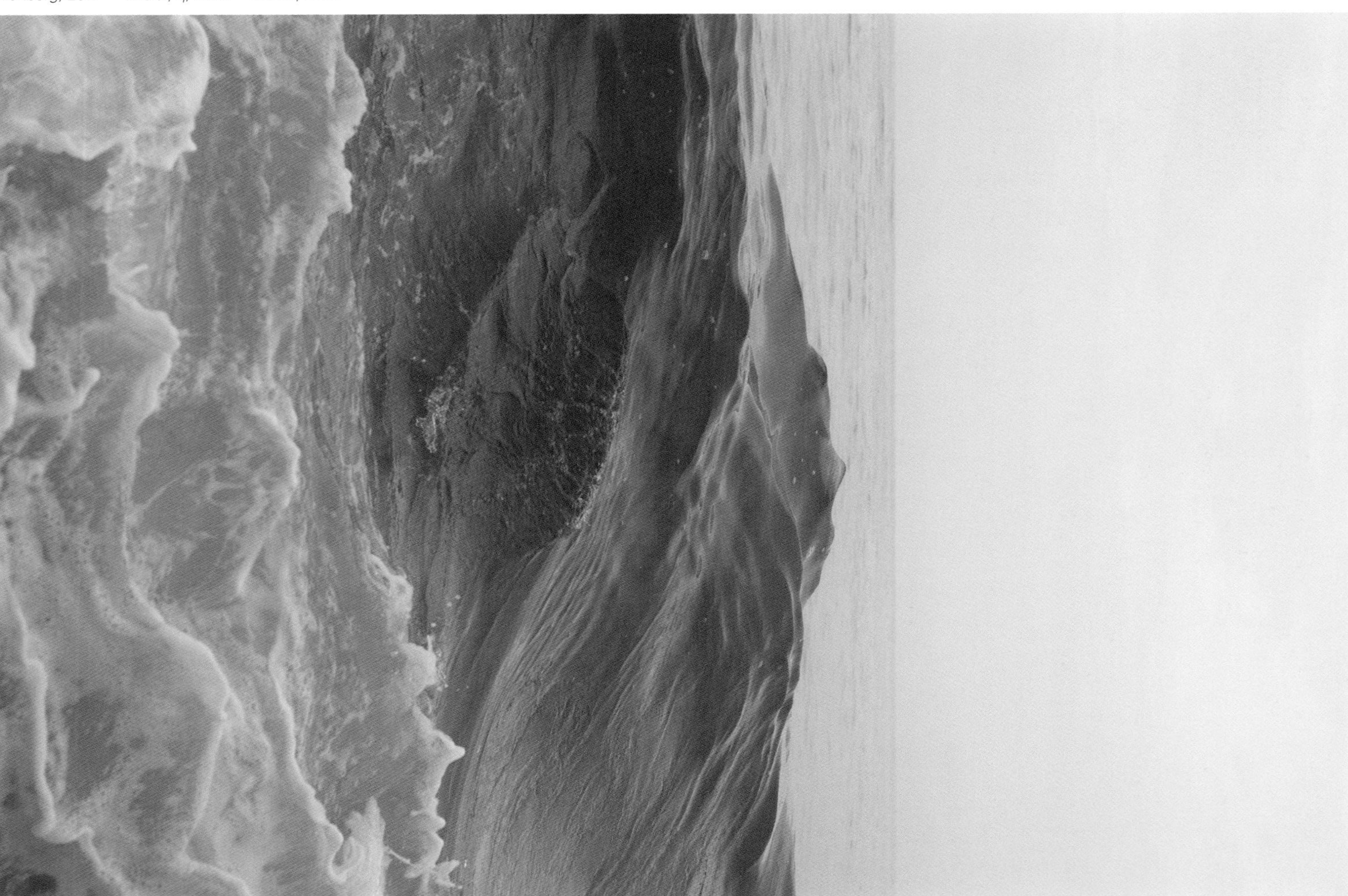

Wellenberg, 2017   Tarsier, q, 2009   Fibres, 2012

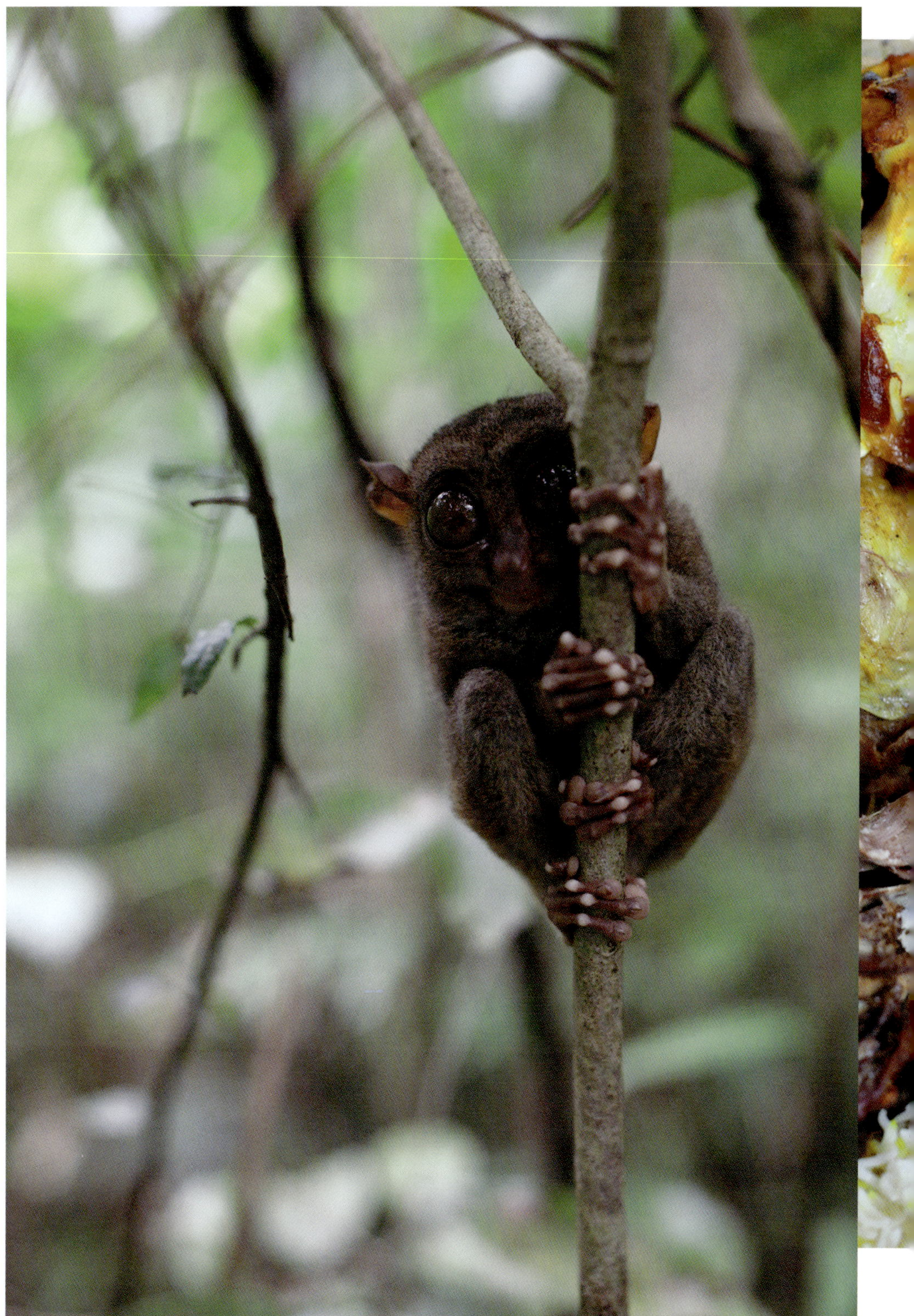

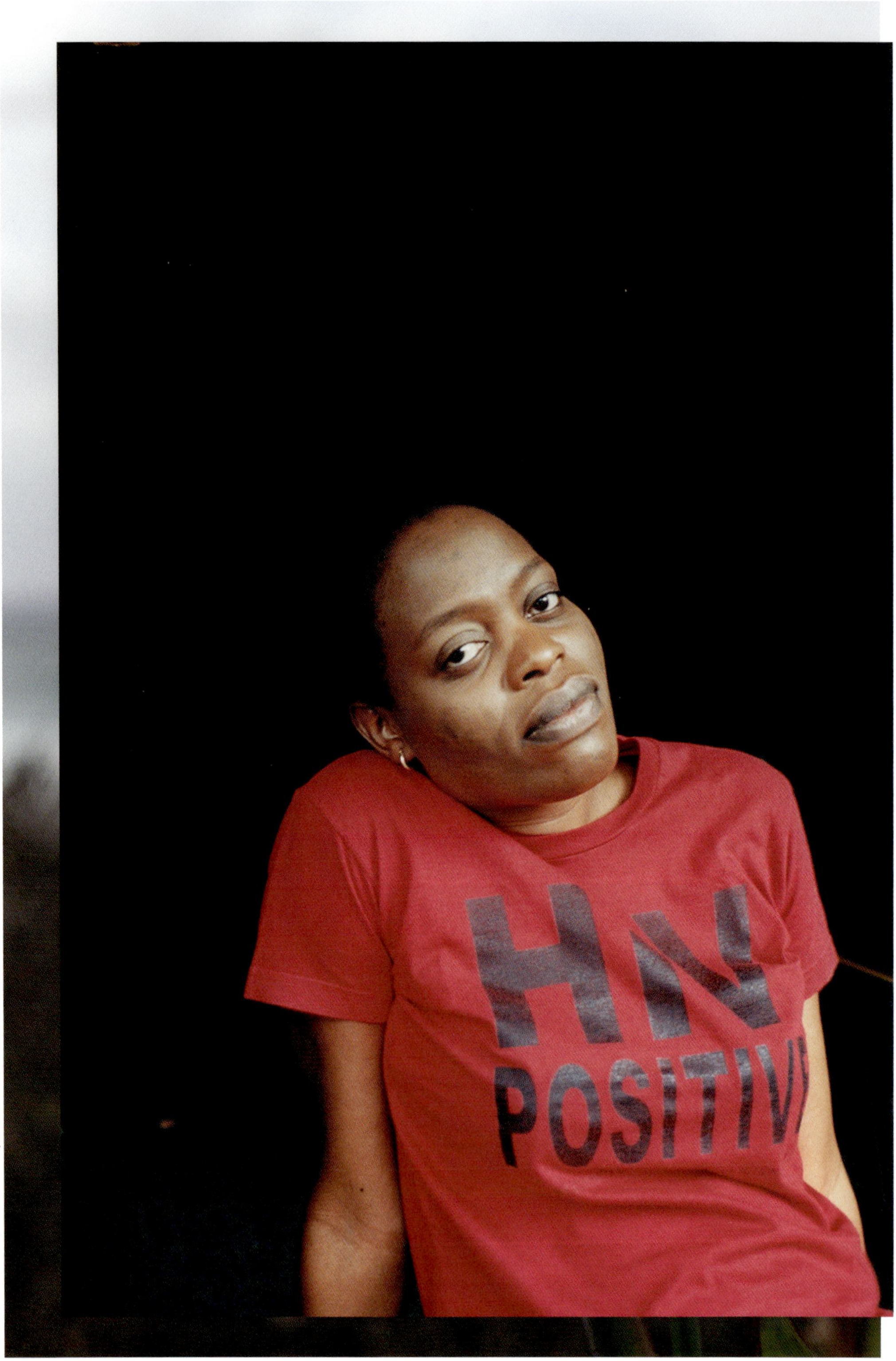

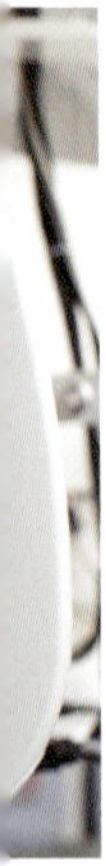

Nonkosi Khumalo, 2008   Aleje Jerozolimskie, 2011

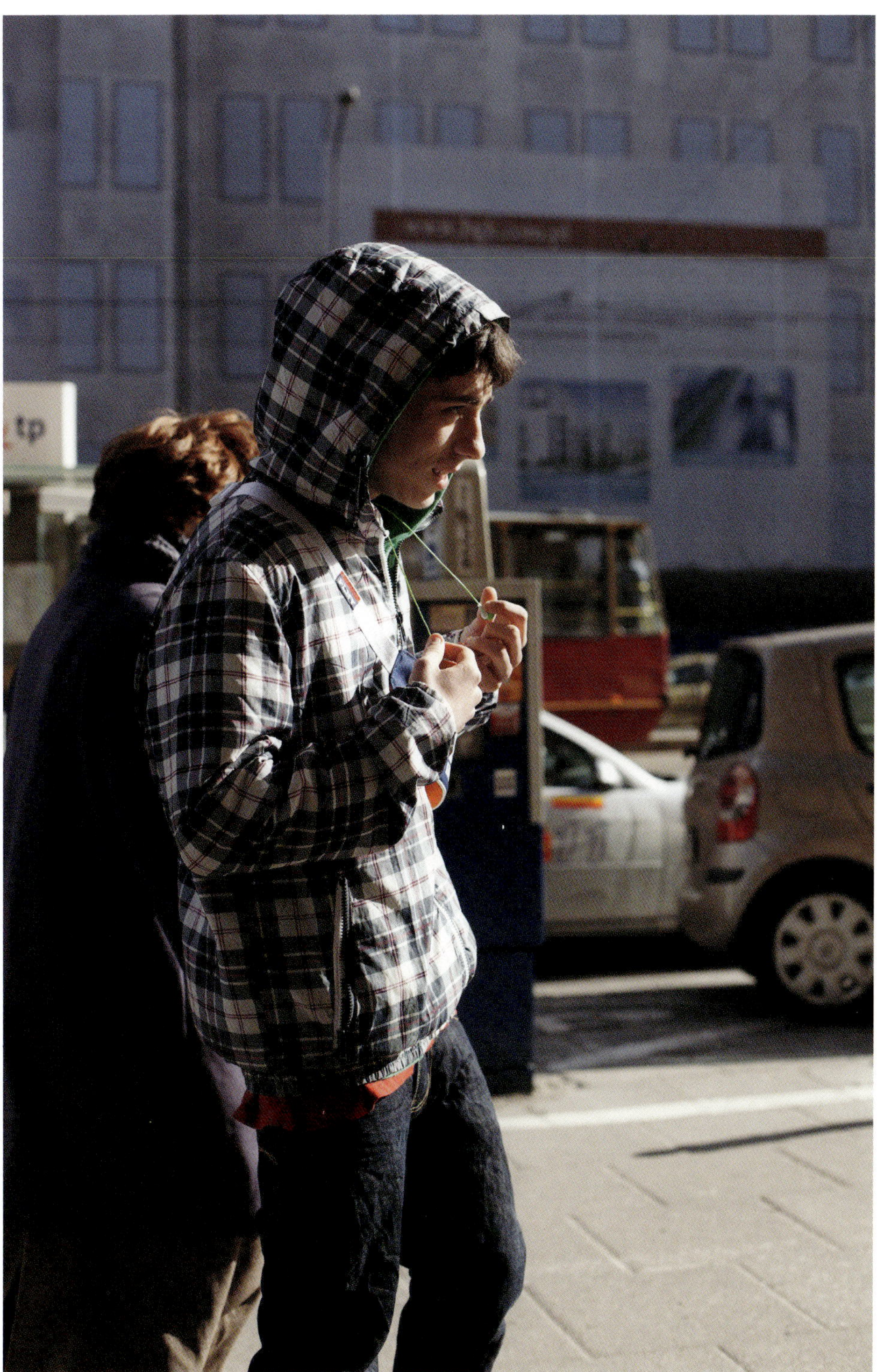

Port-au-Prince, a, 2010

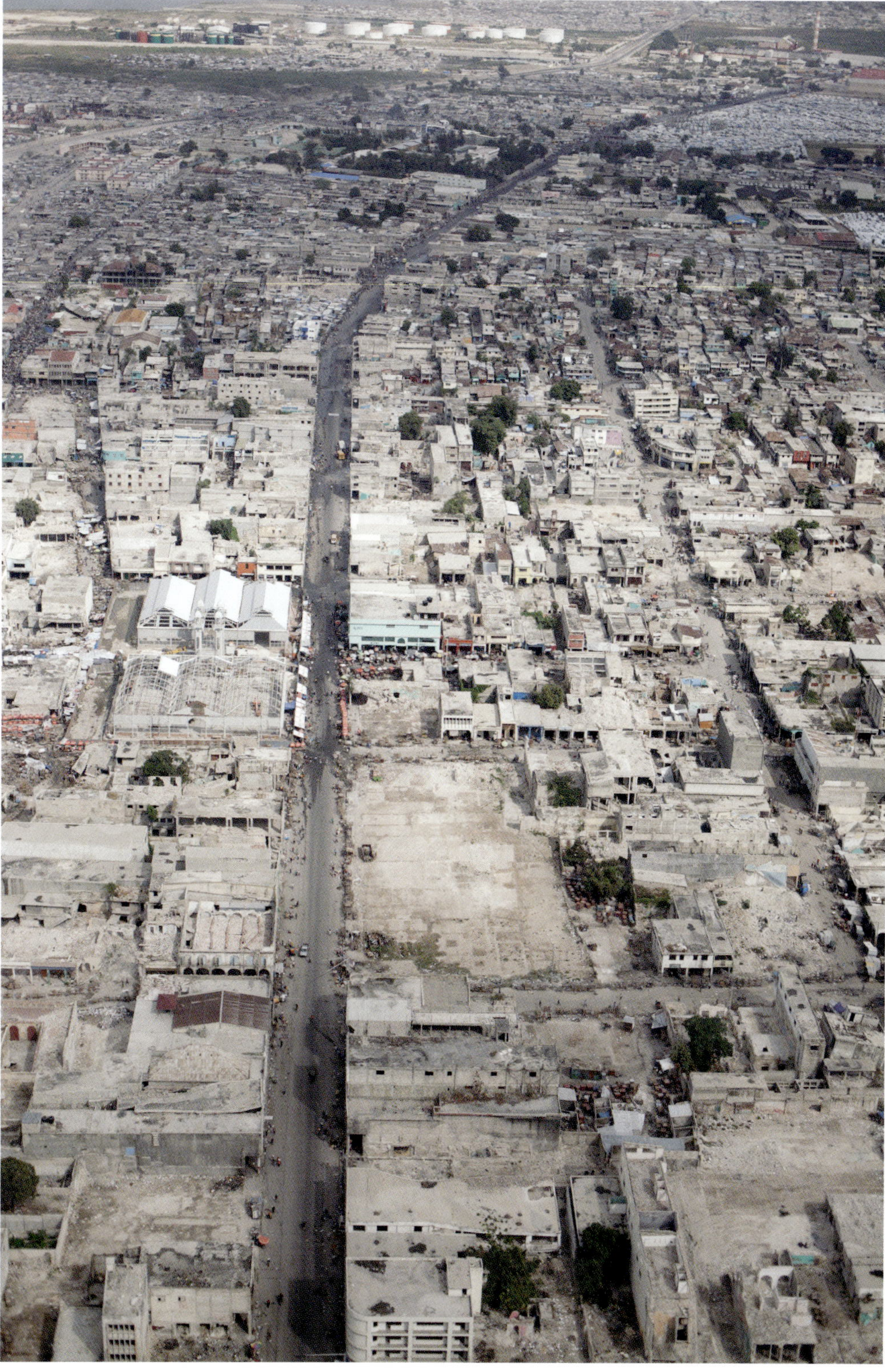

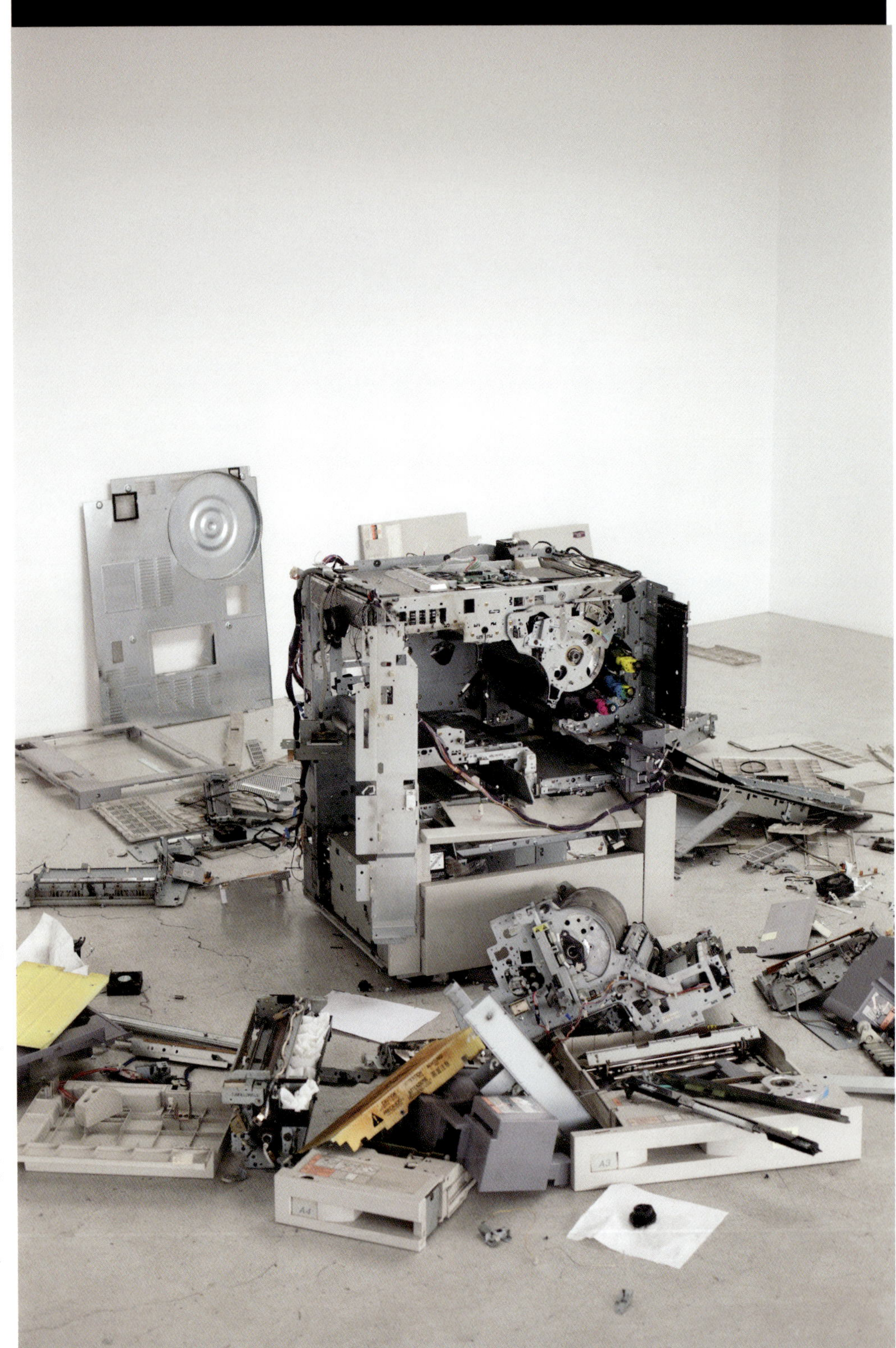

CLC 800, dismantled, a, 2011   The Spectrum / Dagger, 2014

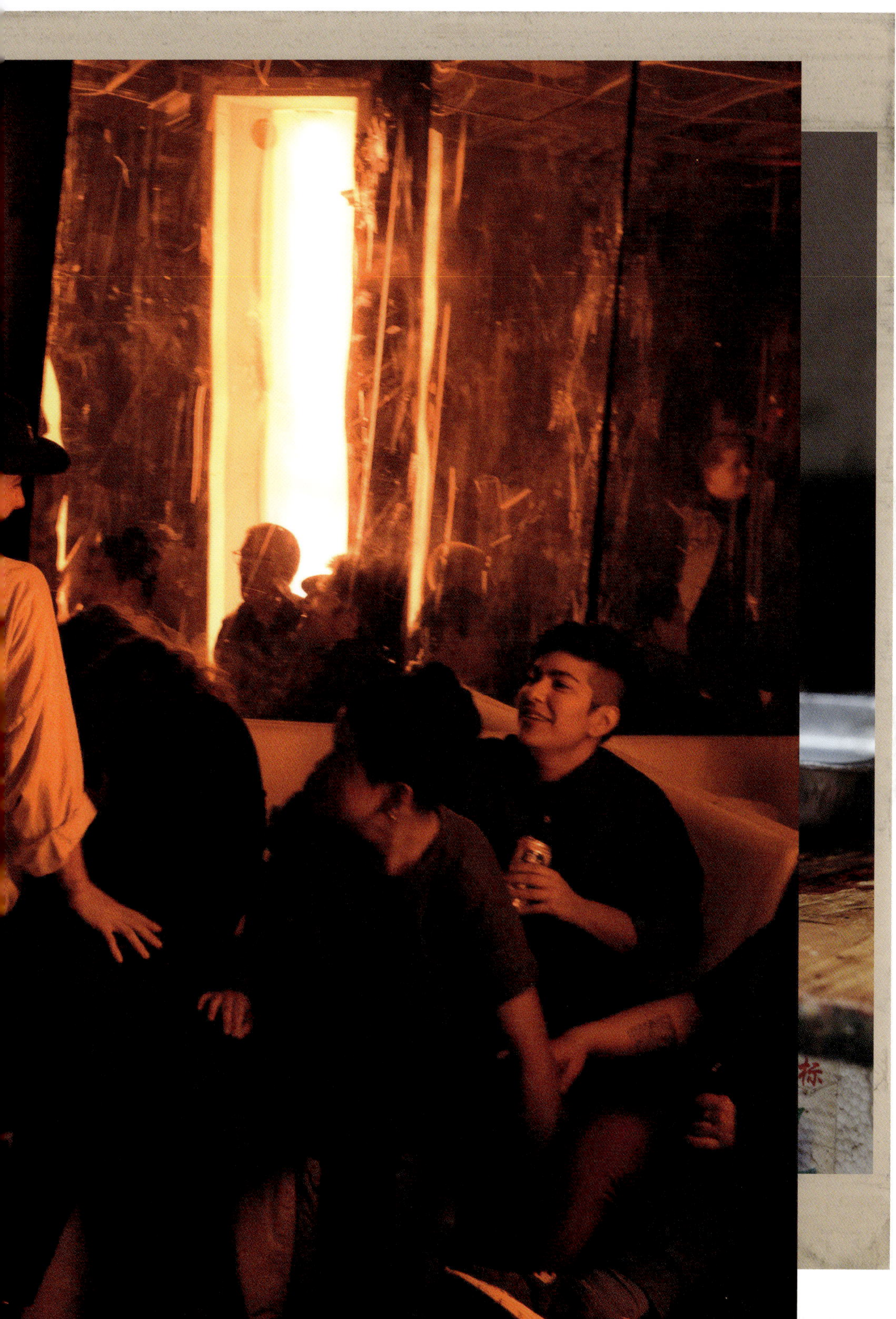

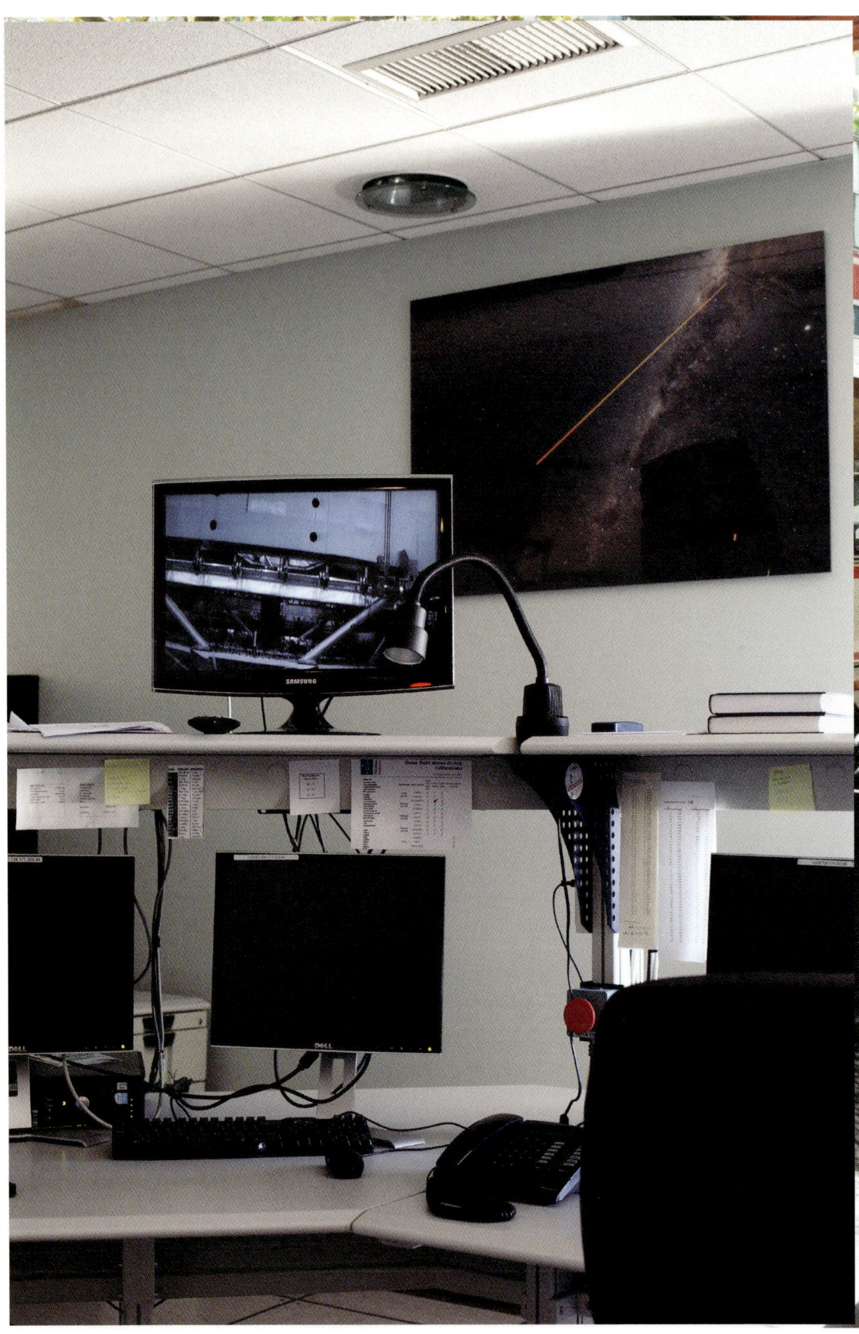

desk space, ESO, 2012

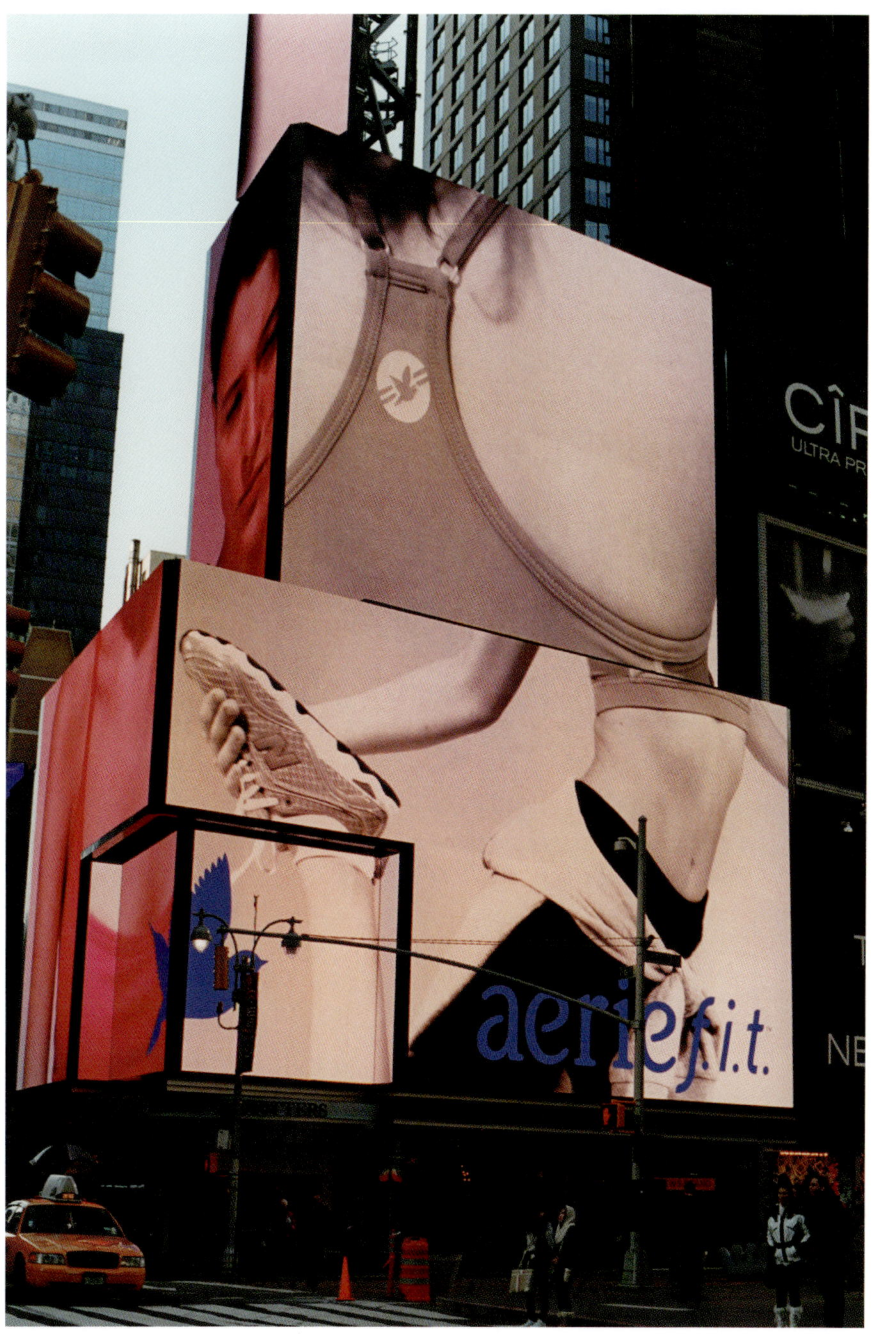

Times Square LED, 2010

Silver 136, 2013   *Tag/Nacht,* 2009

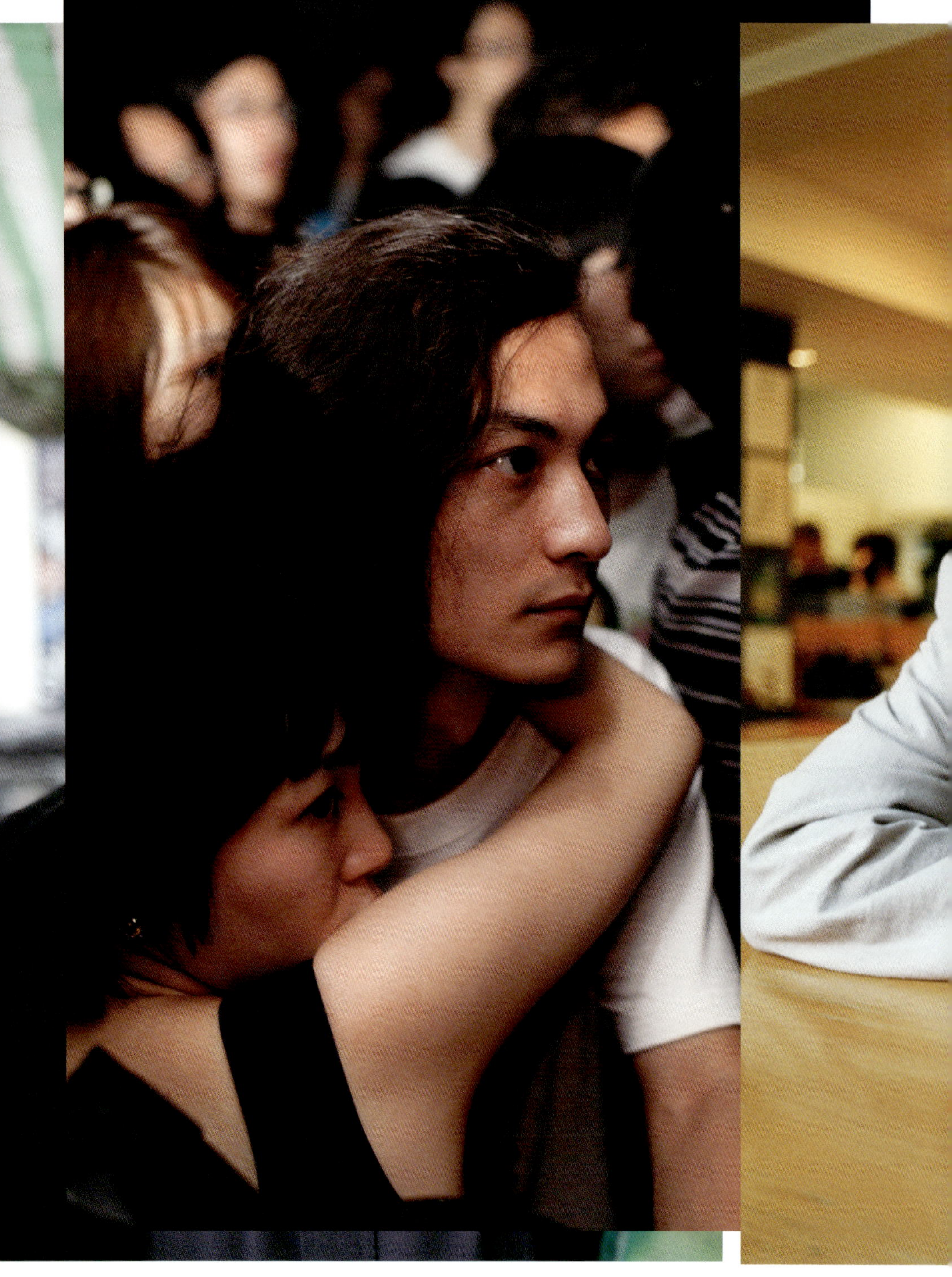

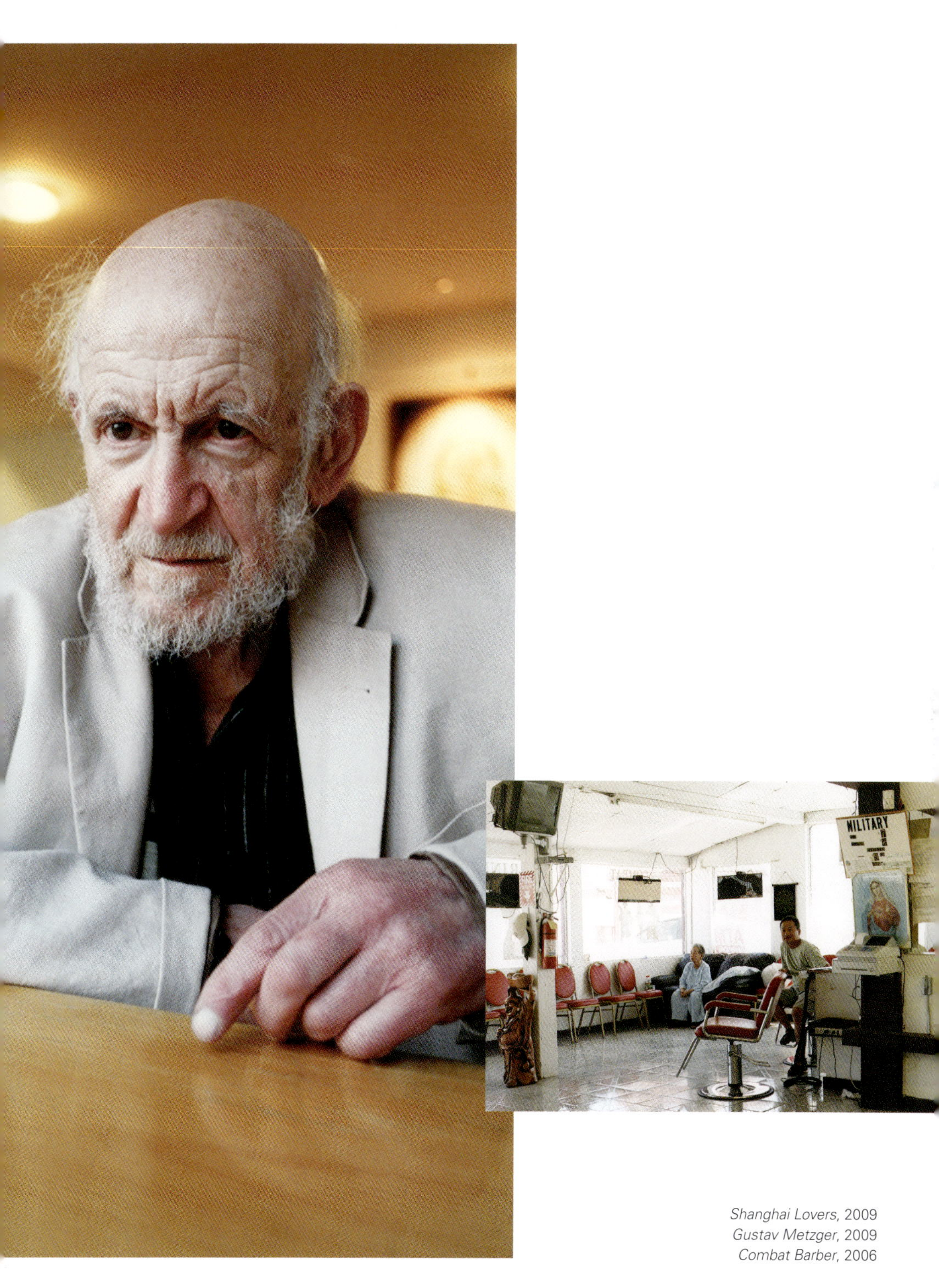

Shanghai Lovers, 2009
Gustav Metzger, 2009
Combat Barber, 2006

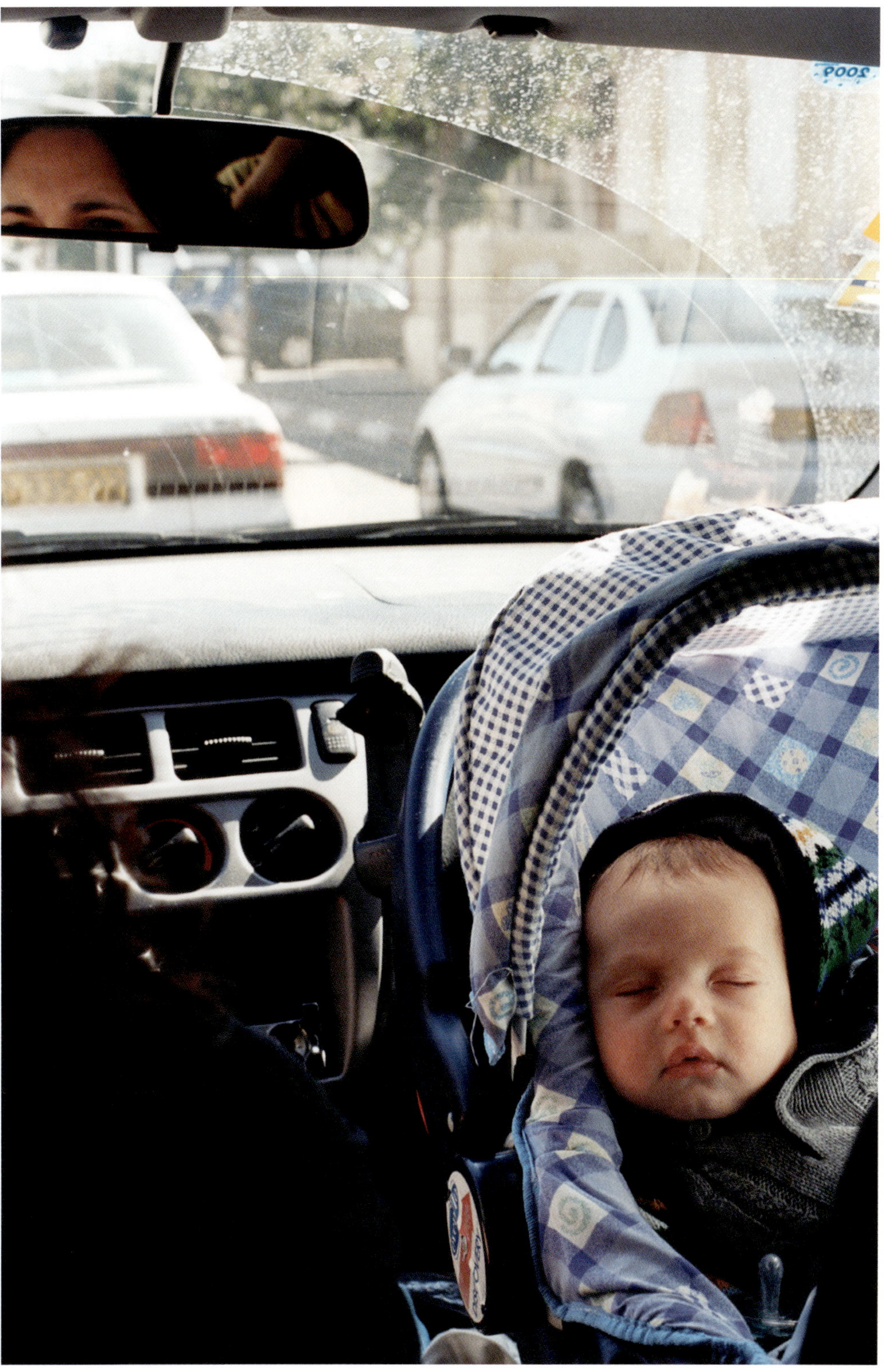

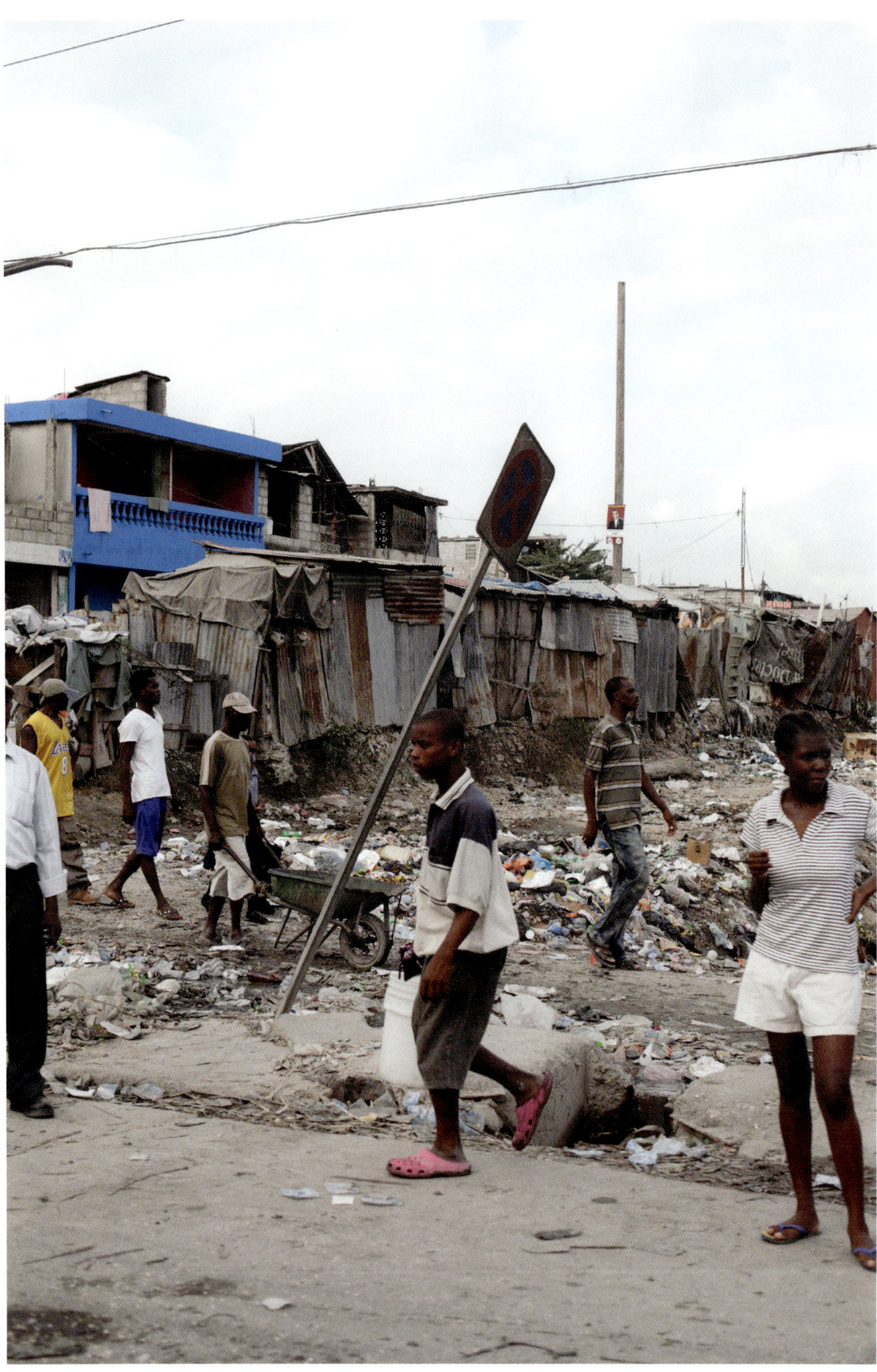

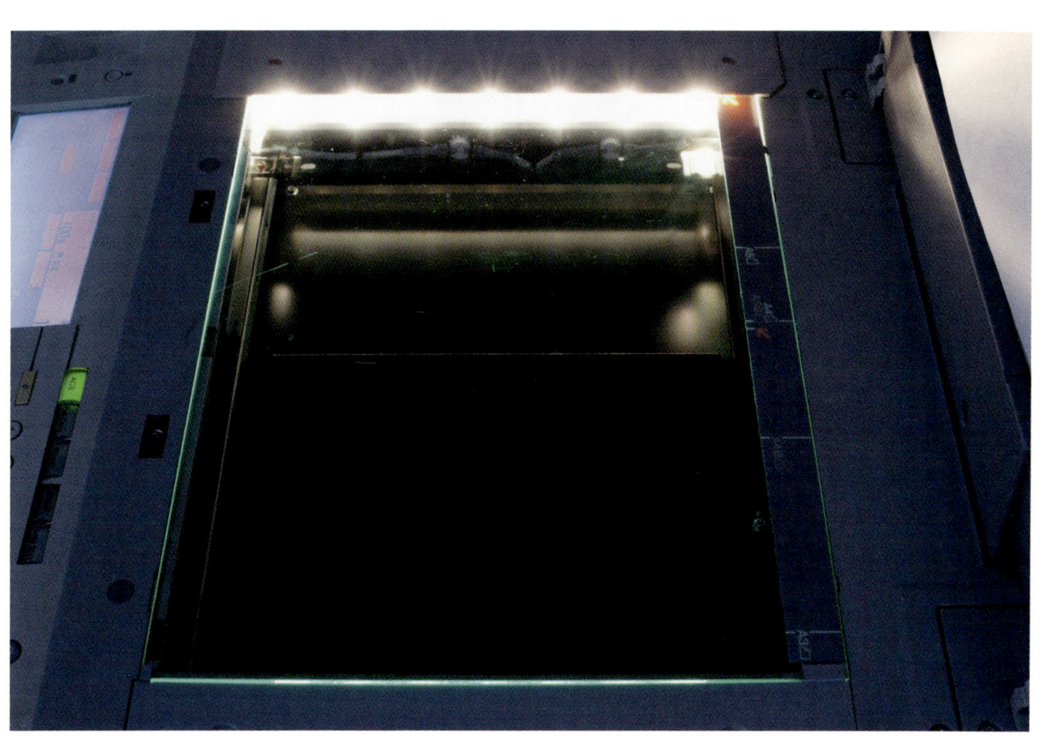

Port-au-Prince, b, 2010
Kopierer, b, 2010

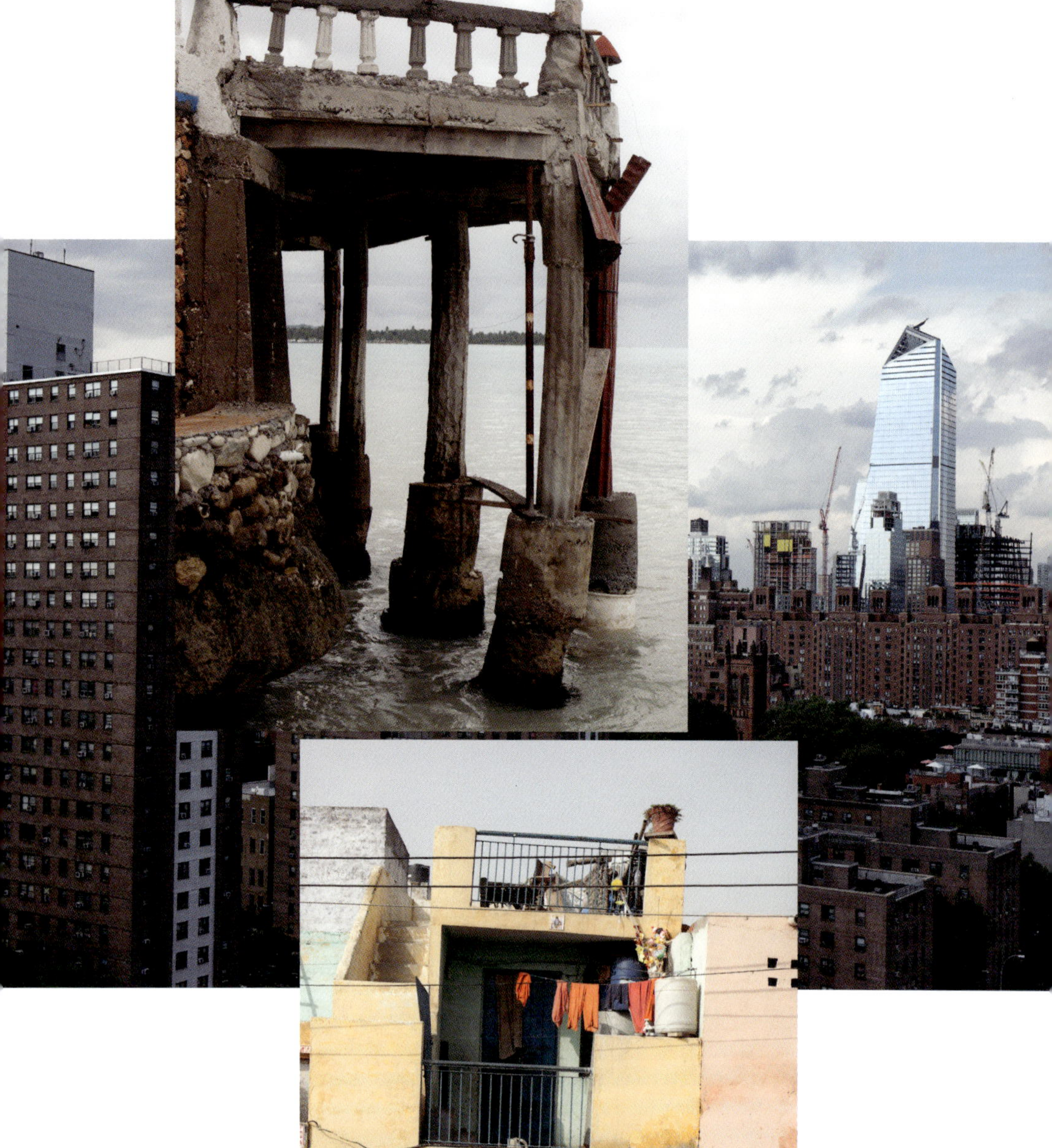

barrel construction, Haiti, 2010
La Dent, 2016
A Day in a Life, 2009

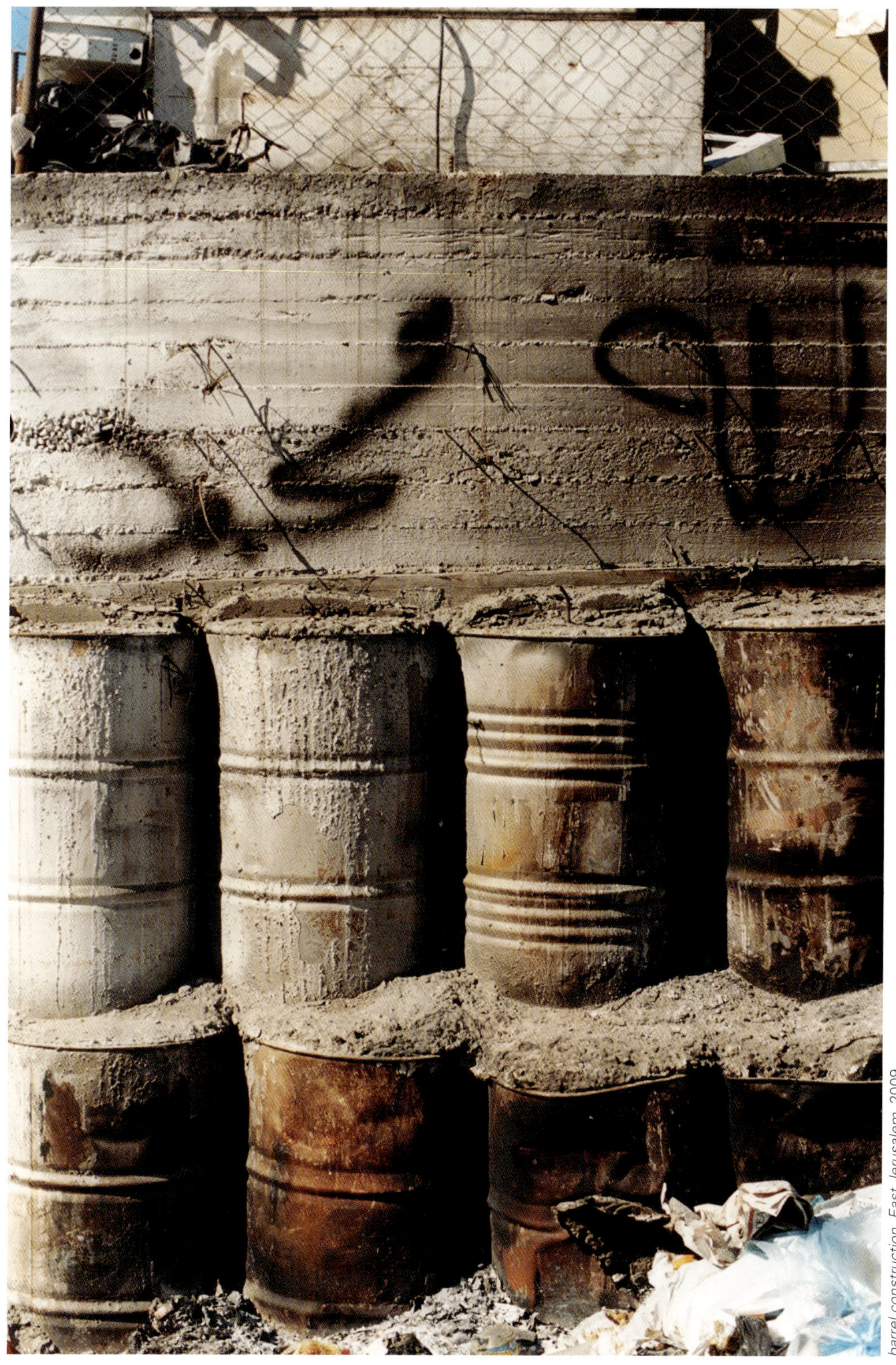

barrel construction, East Jerusalem, 2009

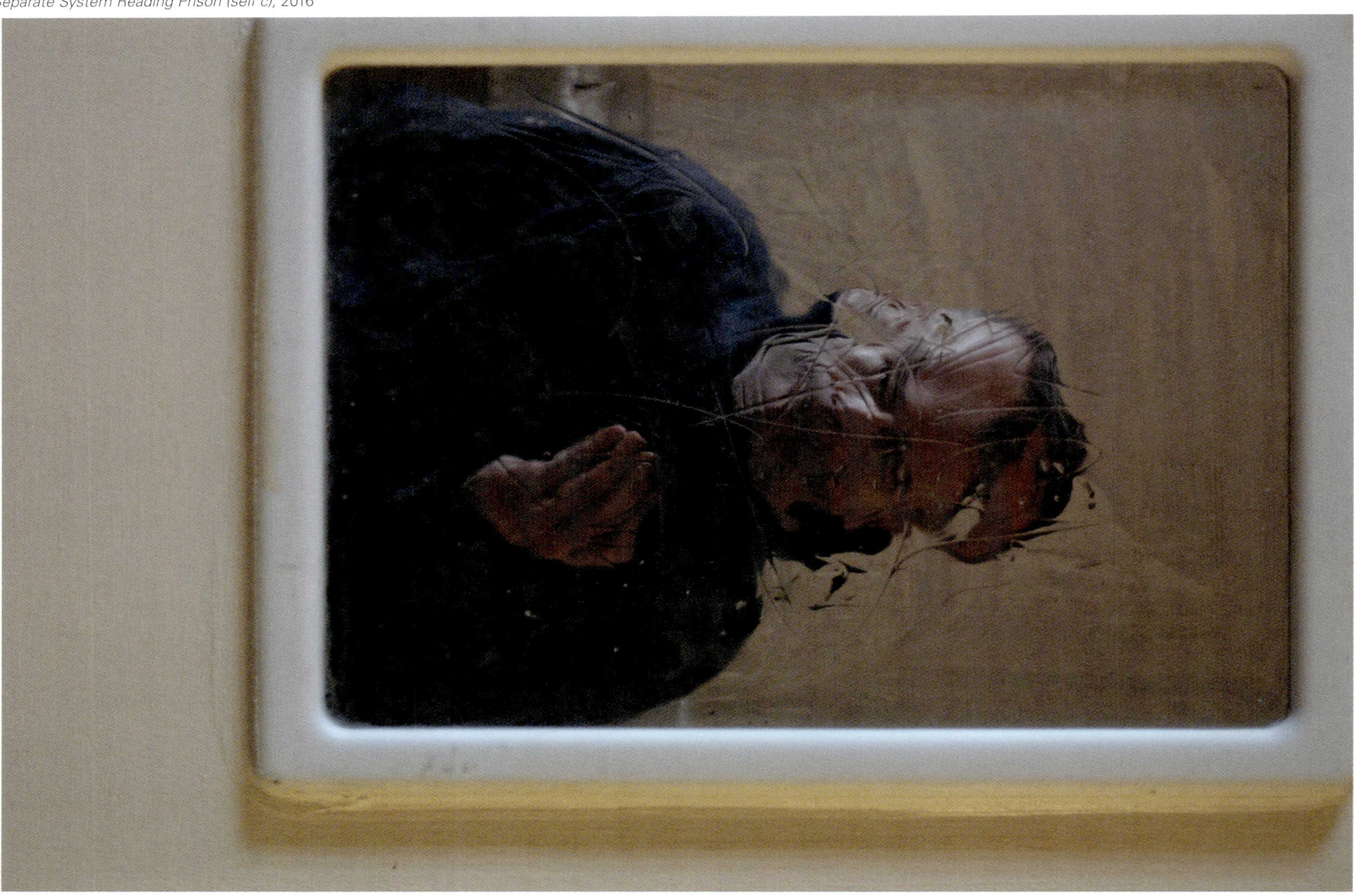

Separate System Reading Prison (self c), 2016

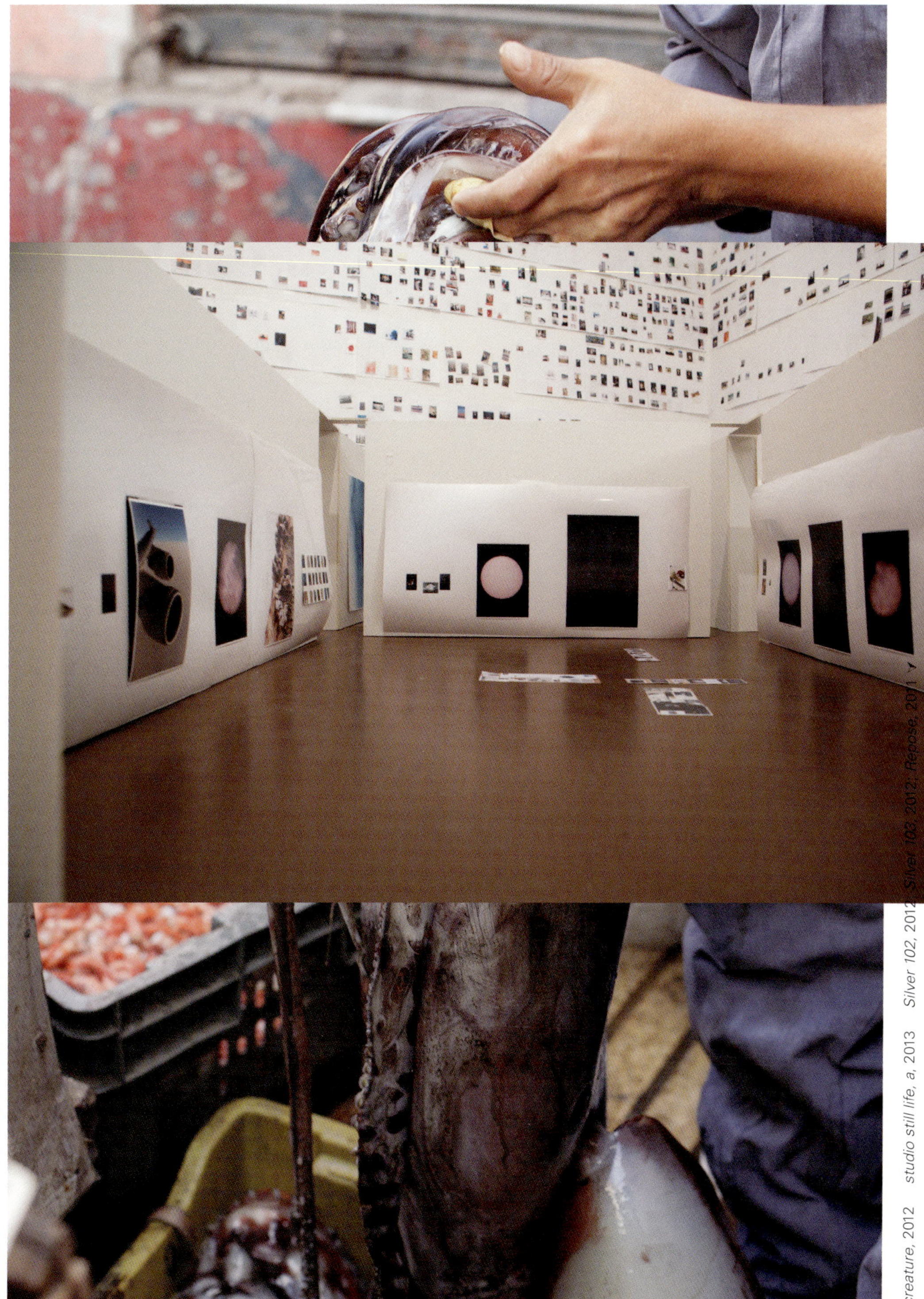

Valparaiso creature, 2012   studio still life, a, 2013   Silver 102, 2012   Silver 103, 2012; Repose, 2011

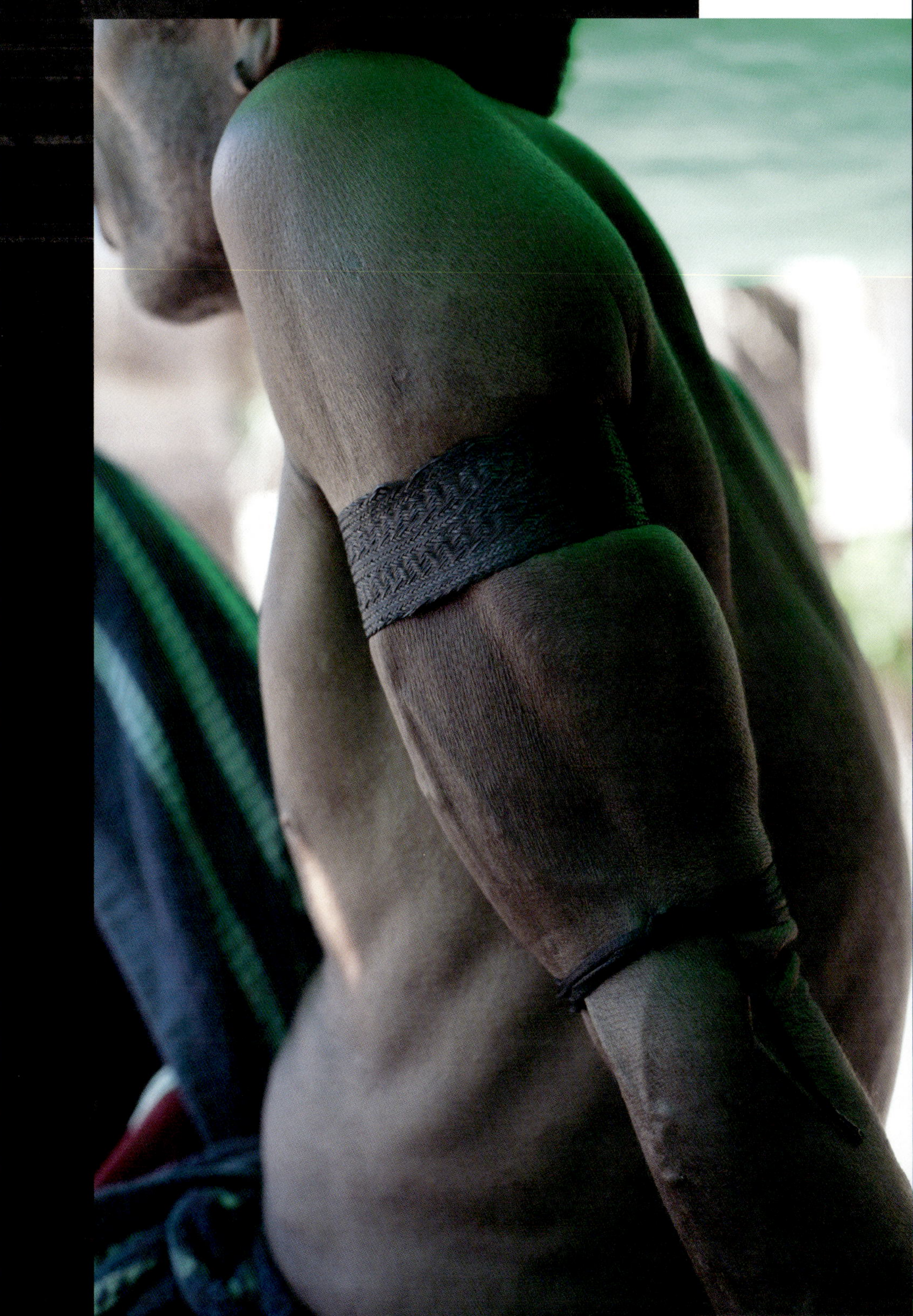

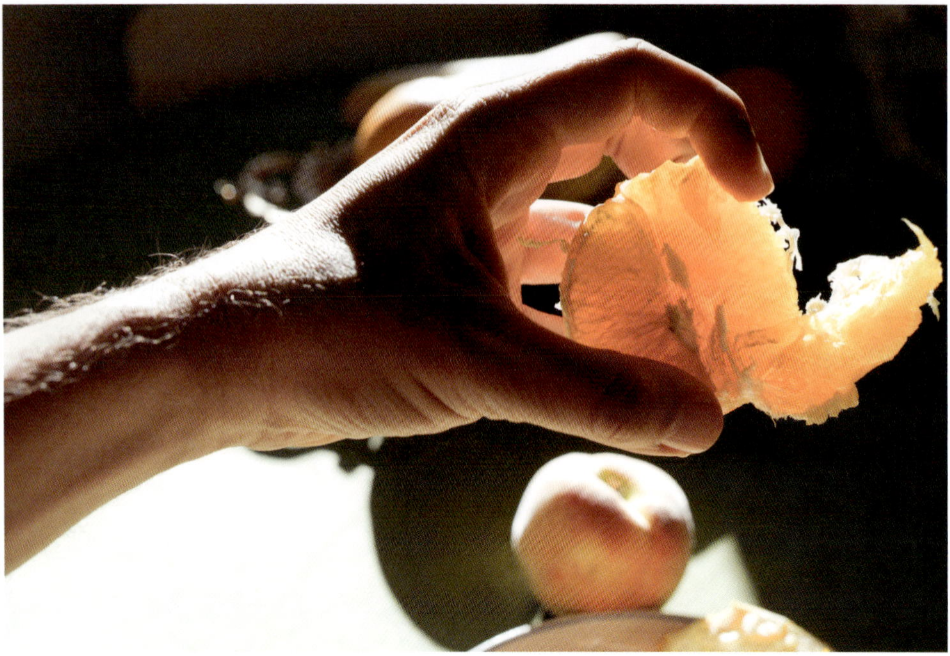

Sicily Morning, 2018   Silver 111, 2013   Oriana & Kayla, Pines, 2016

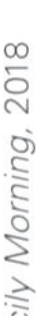

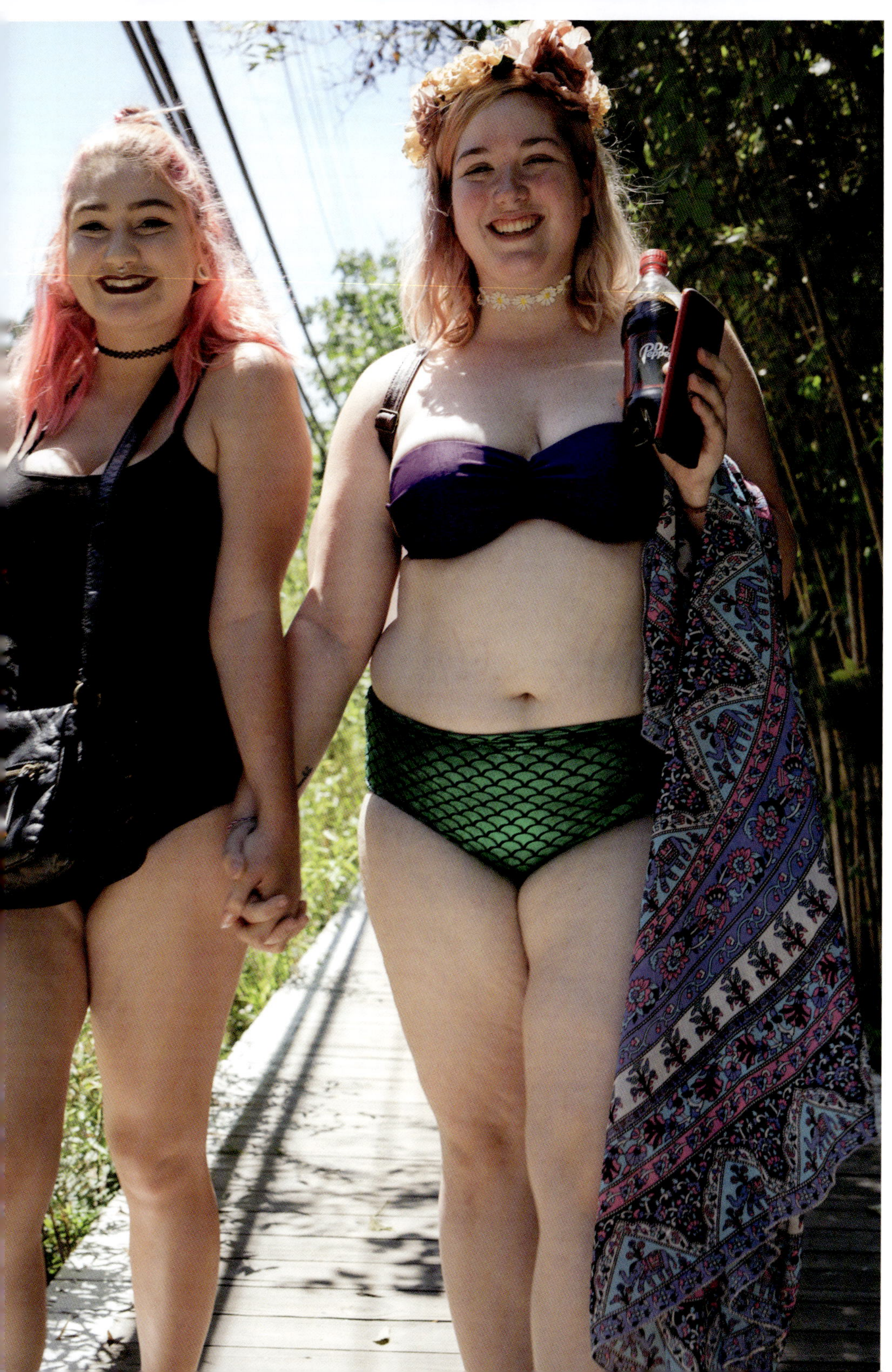

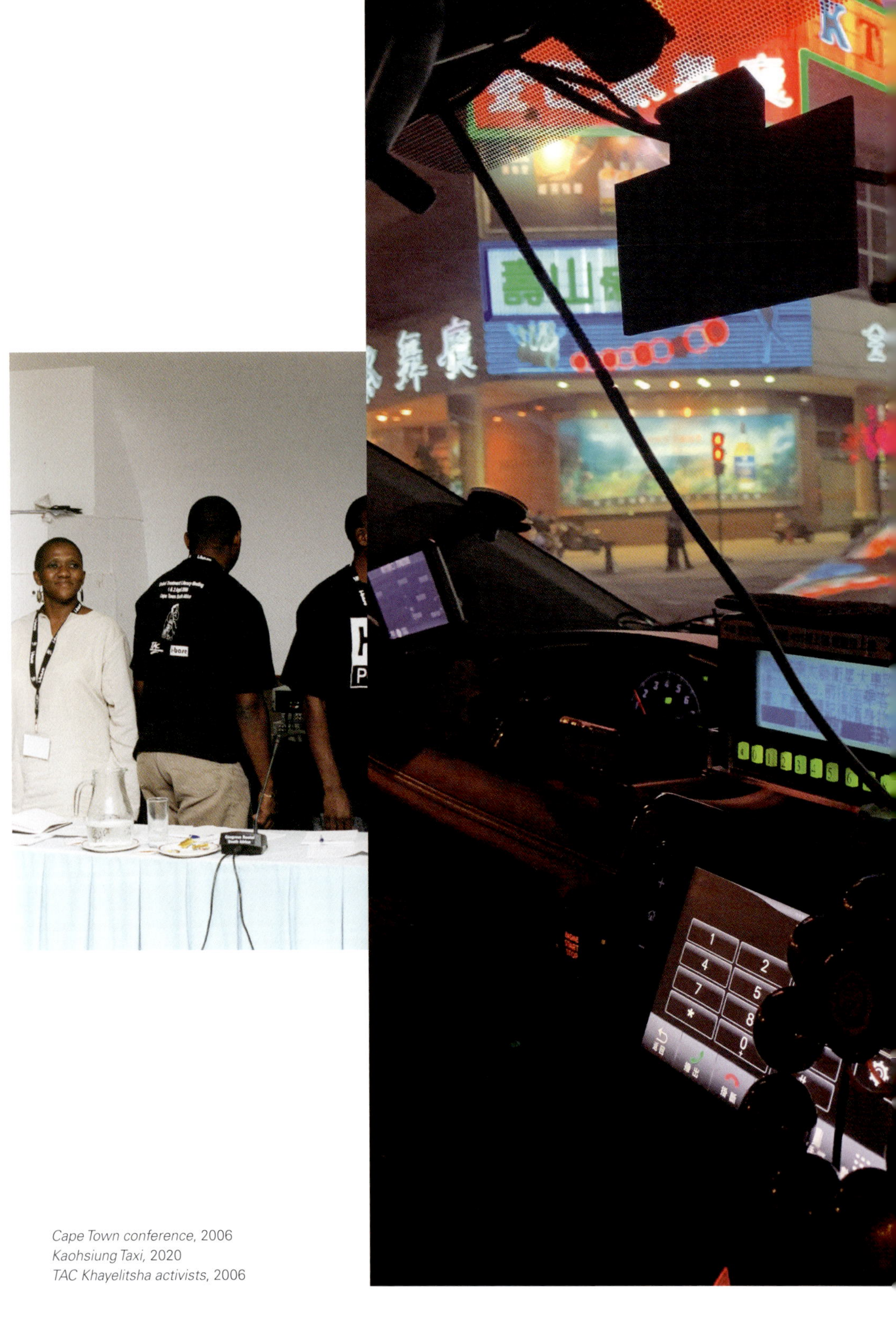

Cape Town conference, 2006
Kaohsiung Taxi, 2020
TAC Khayelitsha activists, 2006

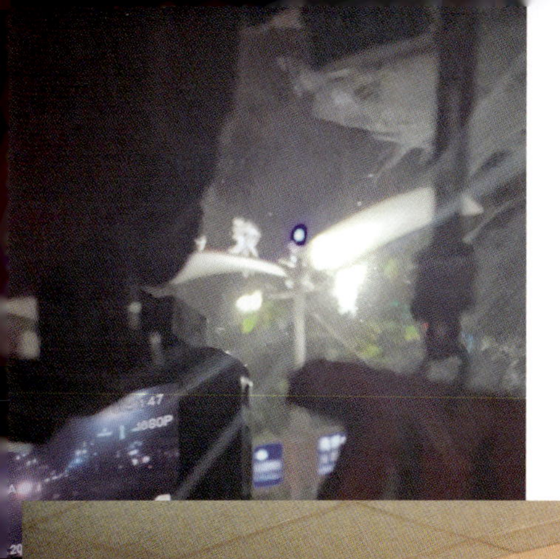

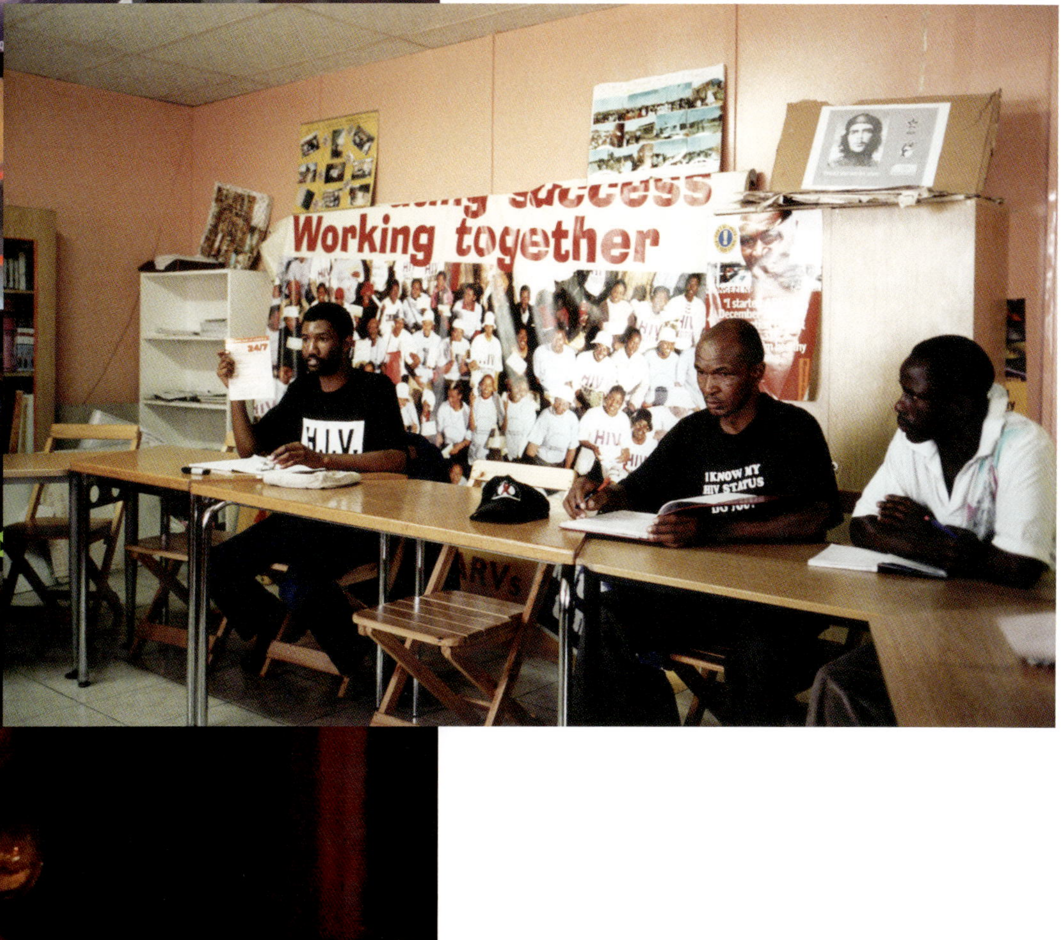

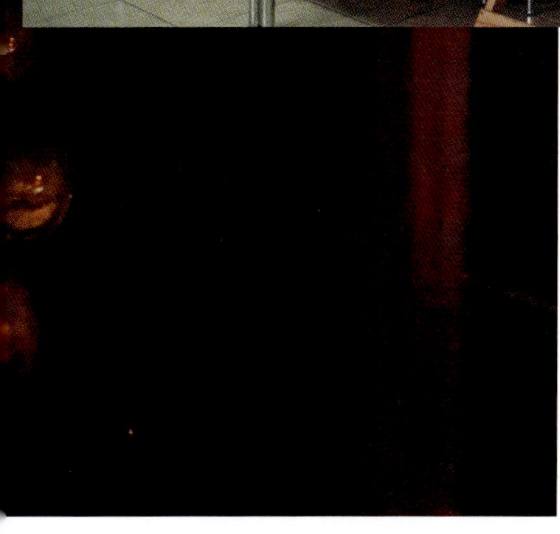

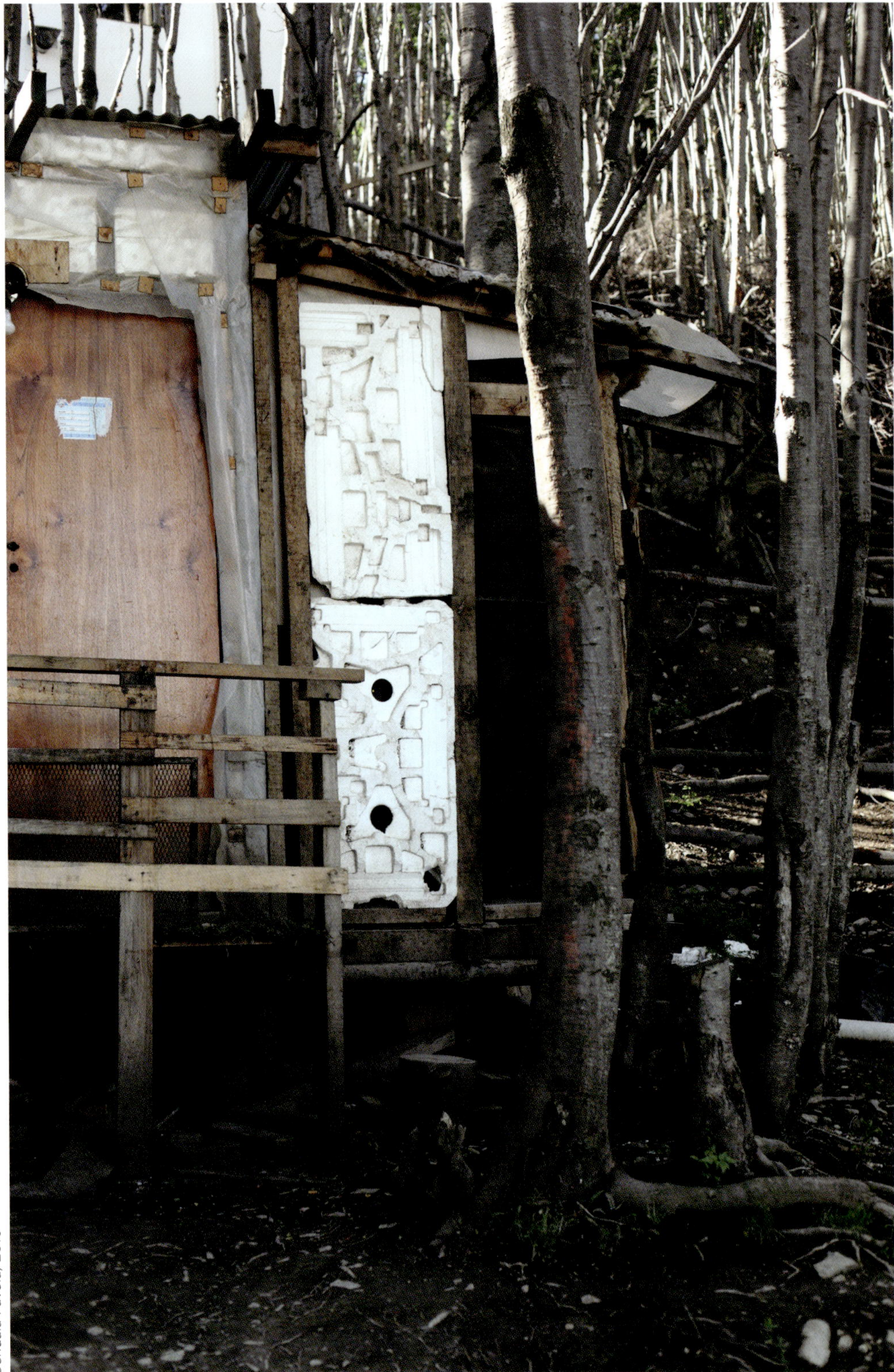

Ushuaia Favela, 2010

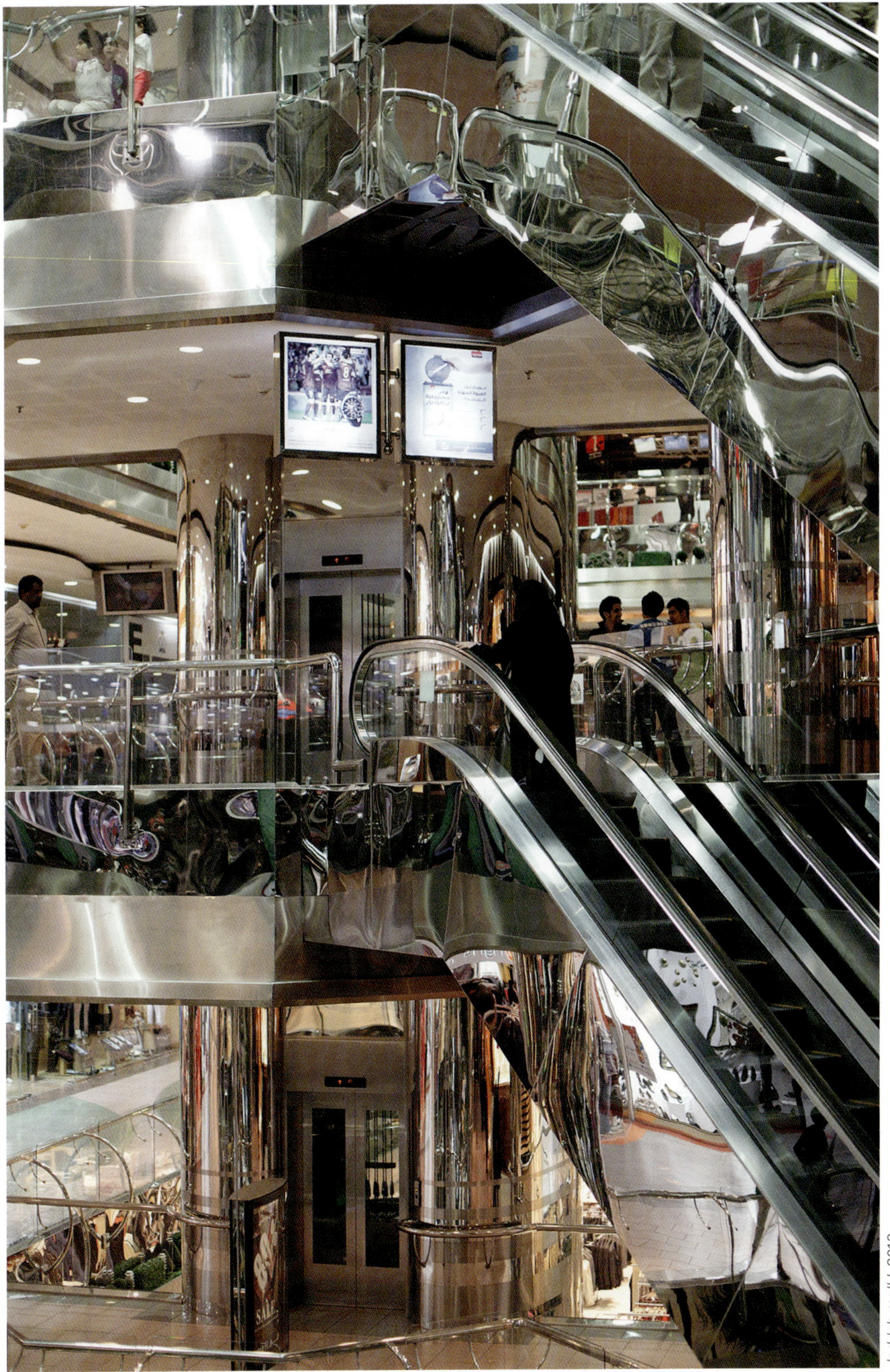

Jeddah mall I, 2012

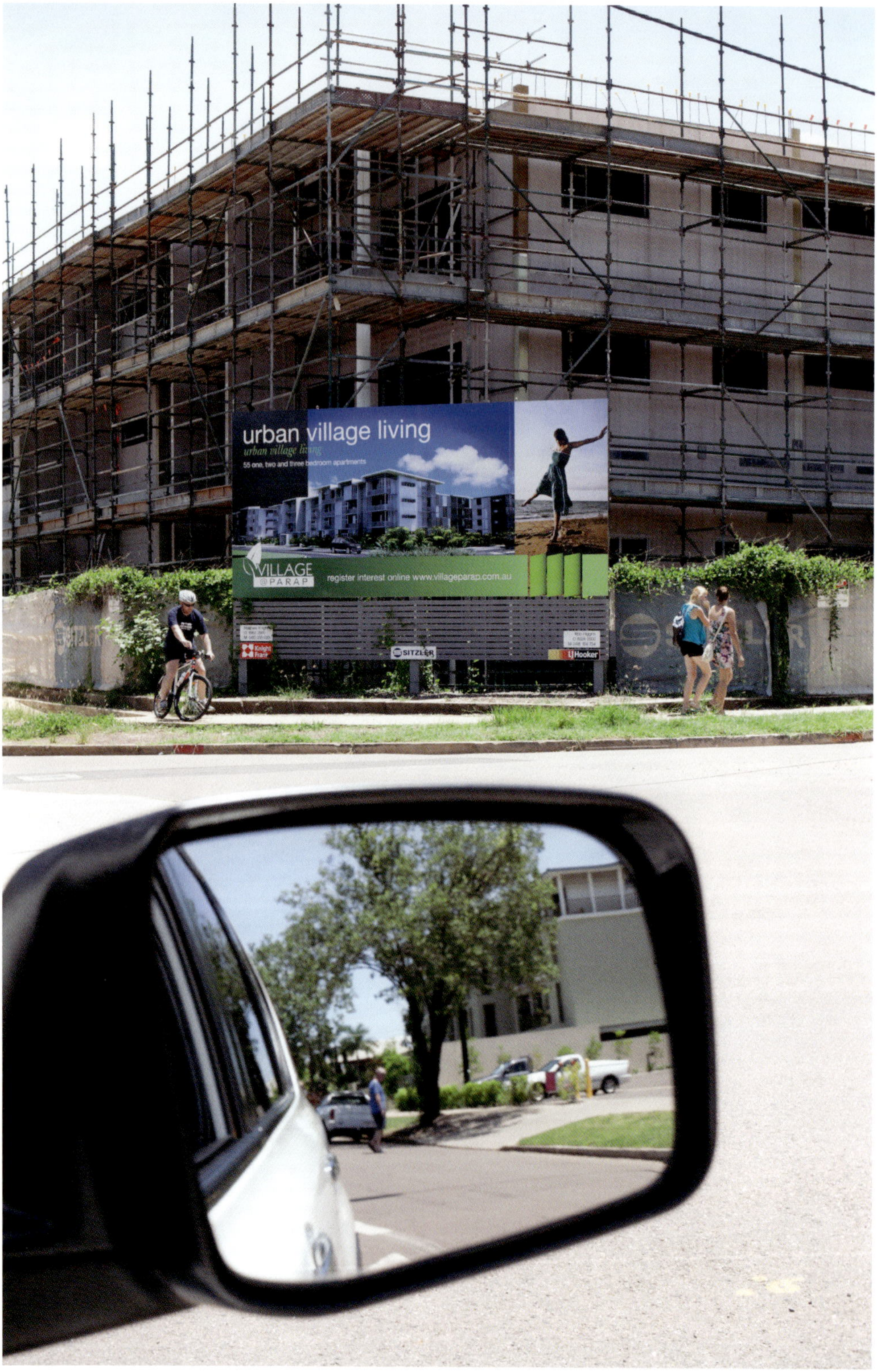

Darwin, NT, 2012   Hermine, a, 2016   branded field, 2012

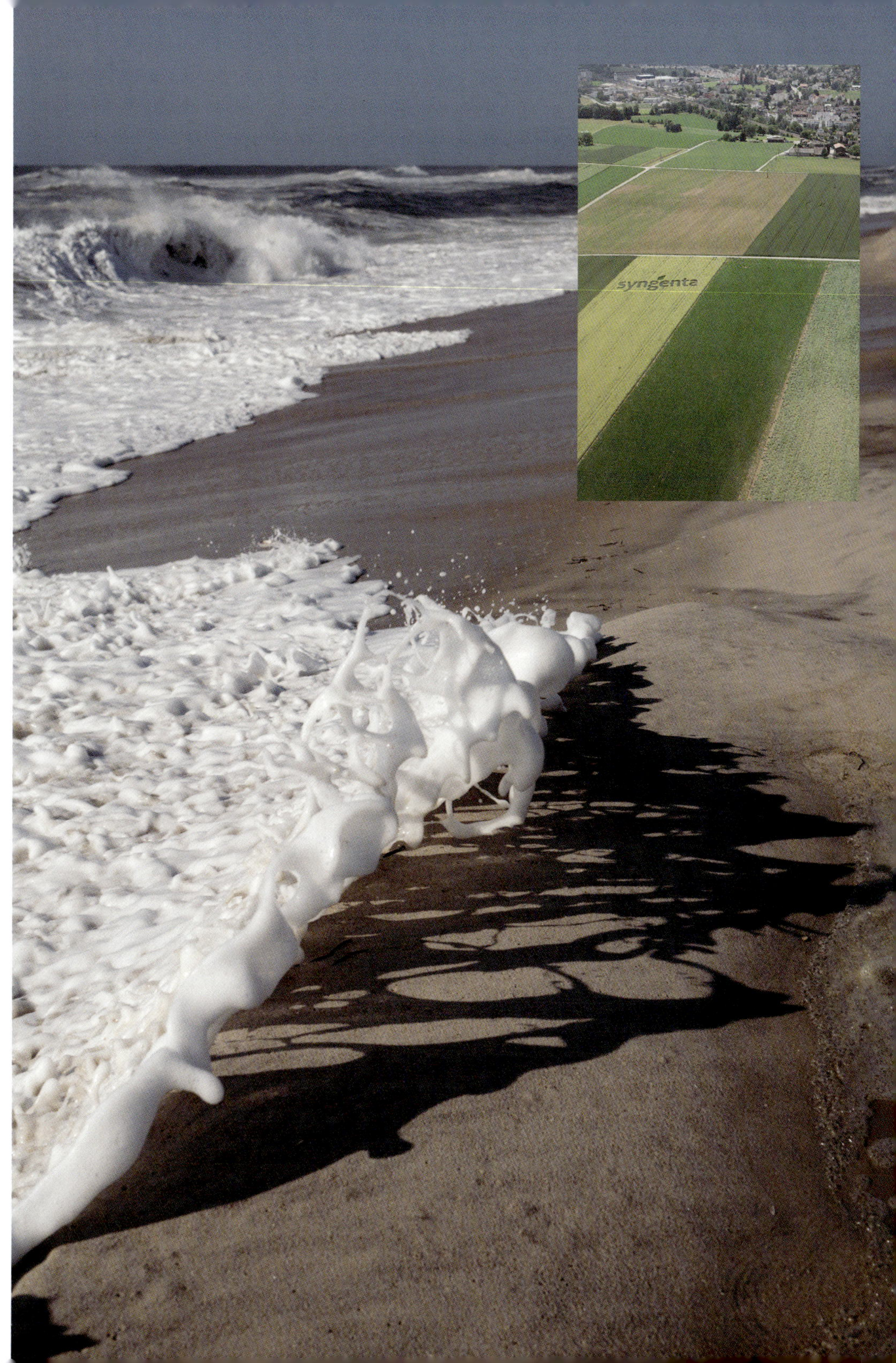

syngenta

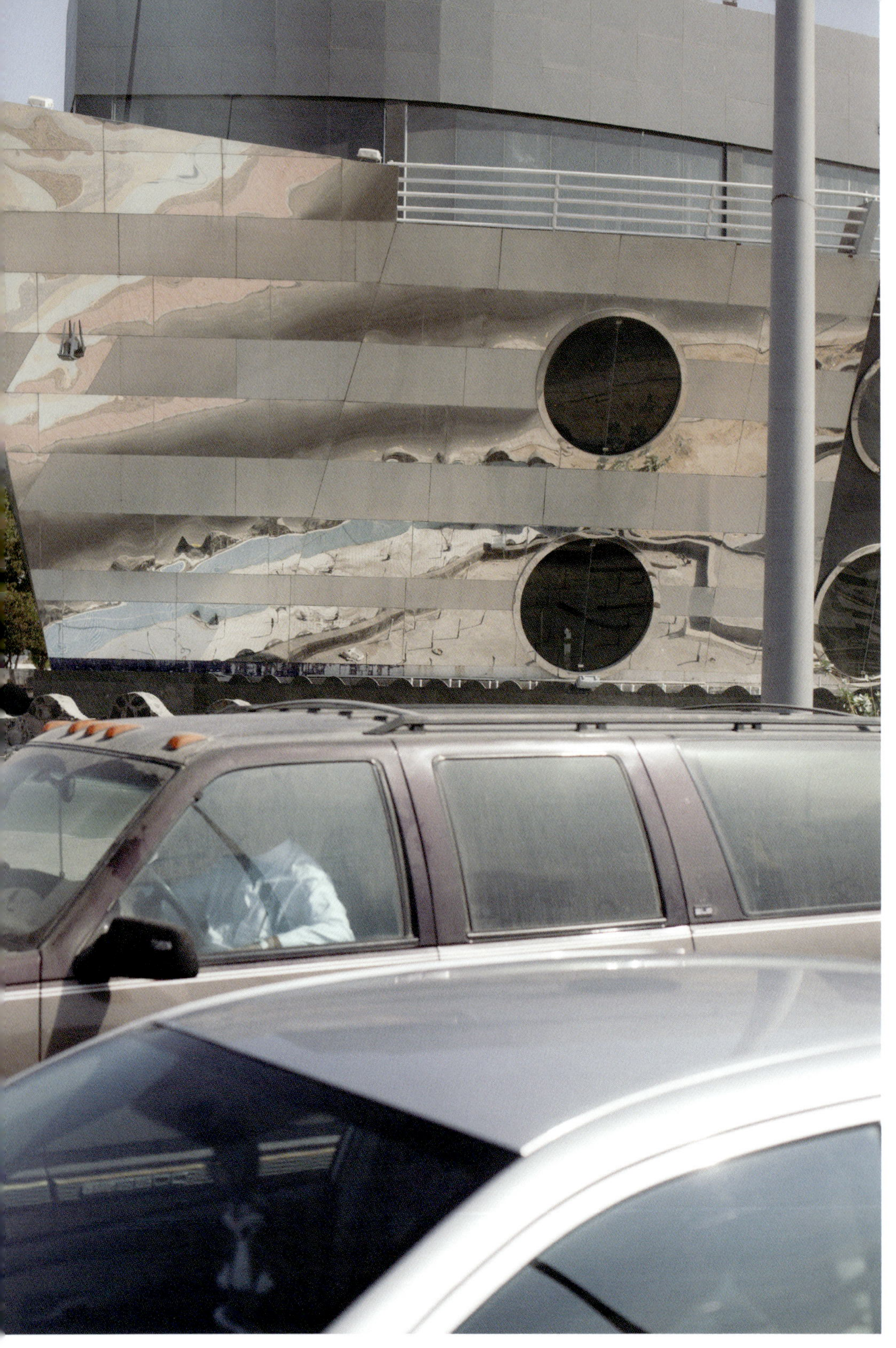

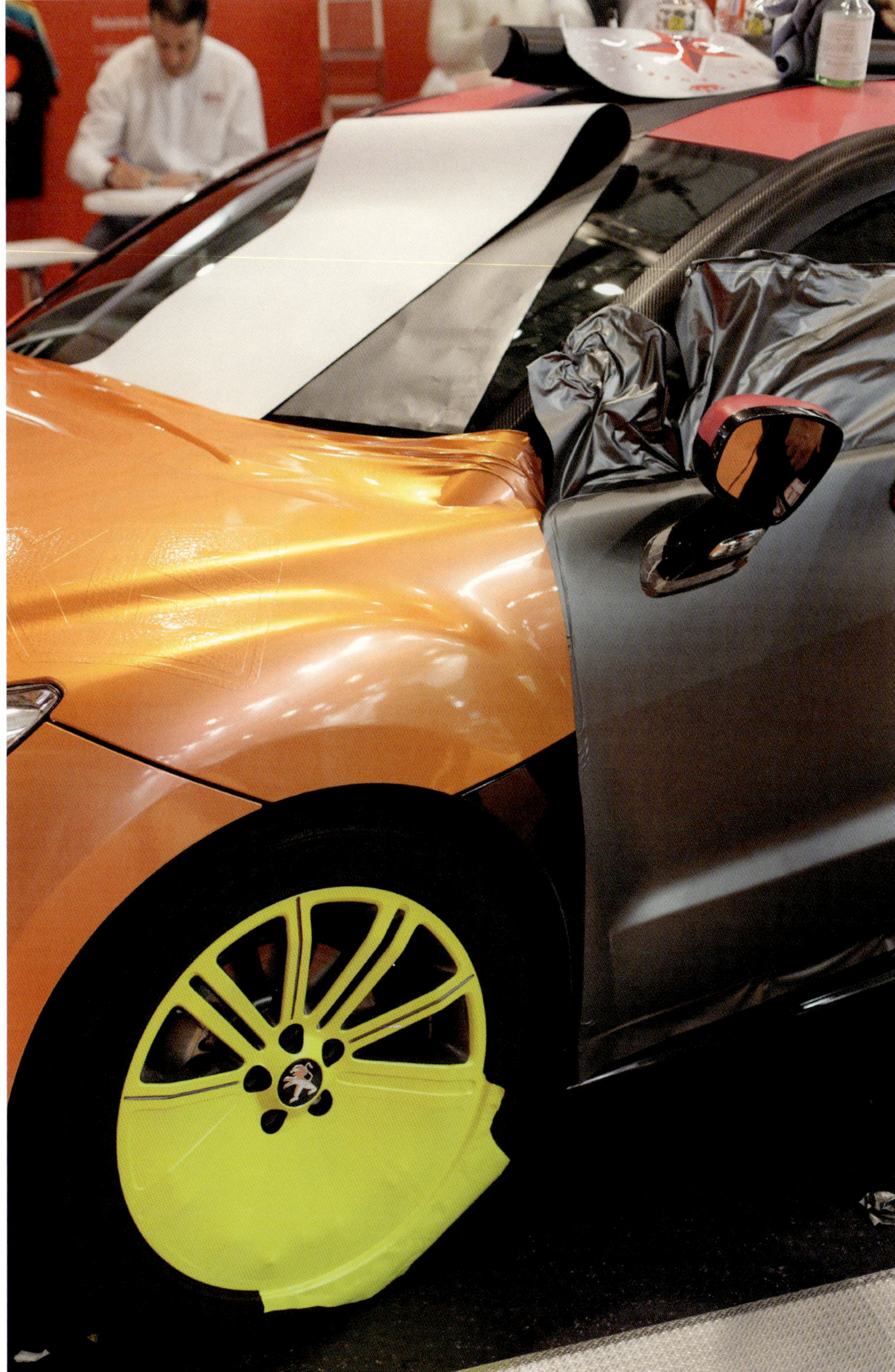

Verschalung, 2012   Fespa Car, 2011

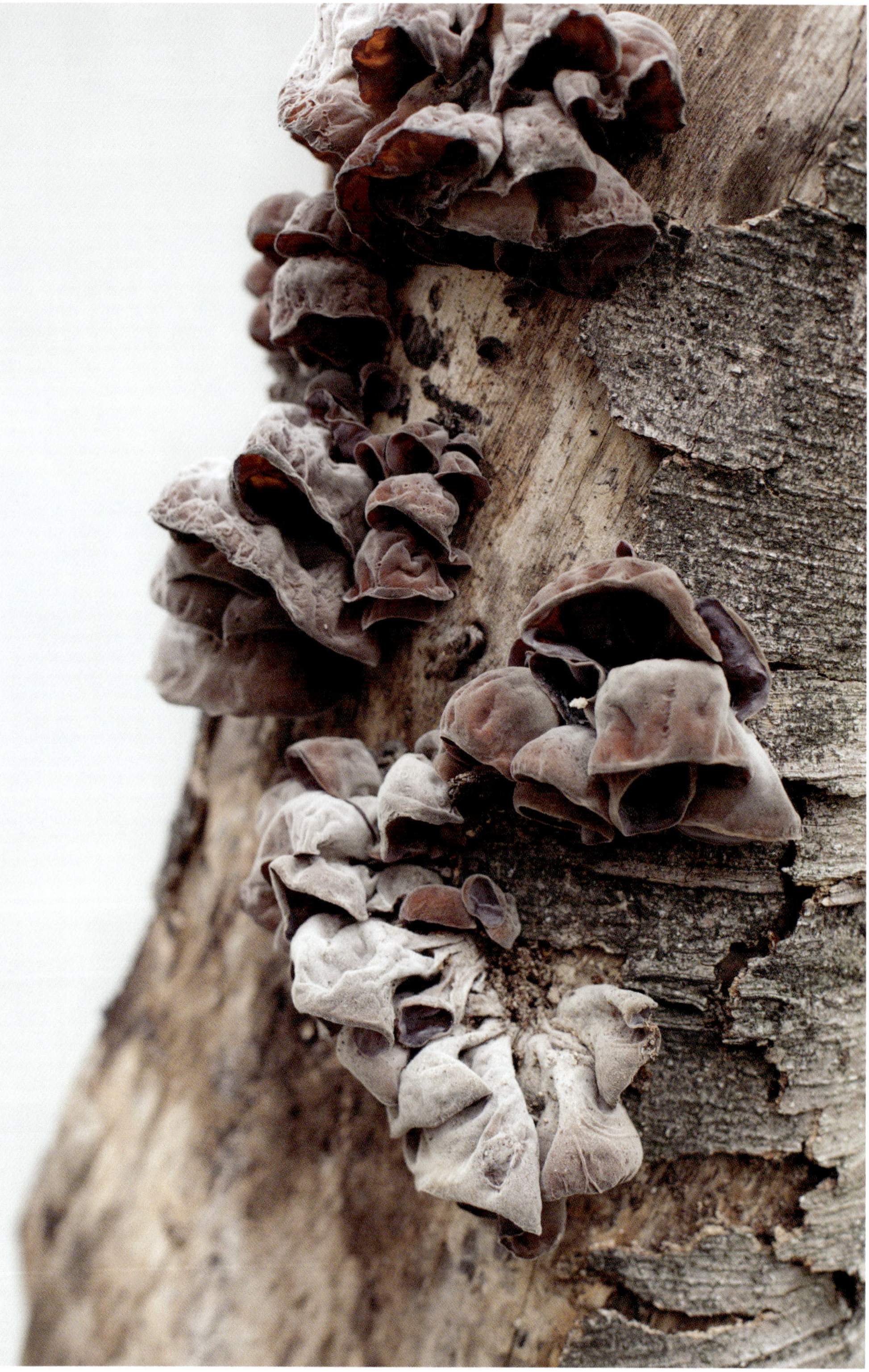

spores, 2012   Greifbar 19, 2015   Frontex flag, 2011

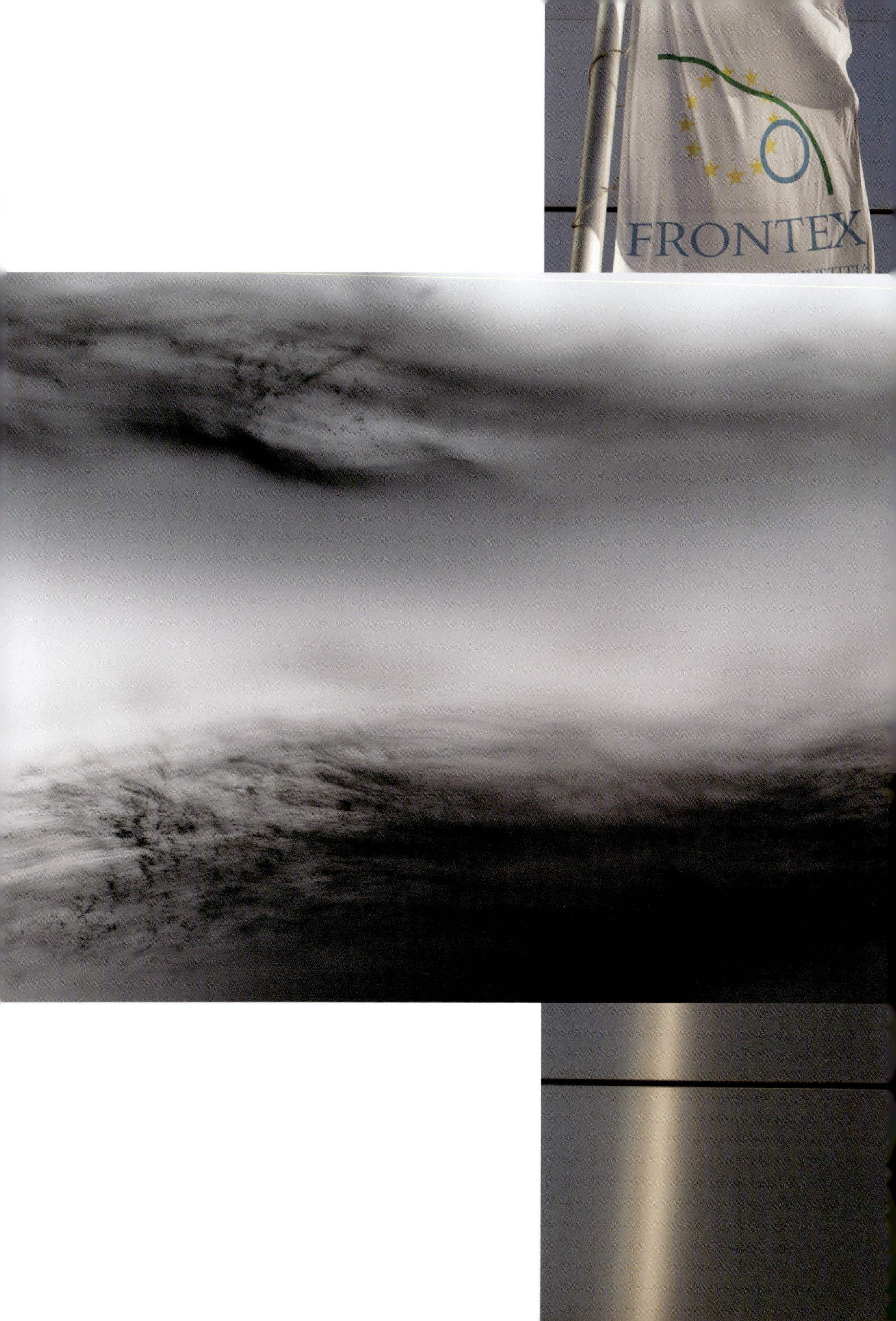

FRONTEX

*Italian Coastal Guard Flying
Rescue Mission off Lampedusa, 2008
Guardia di Finanza, 2008
Lampedusa, 2008*

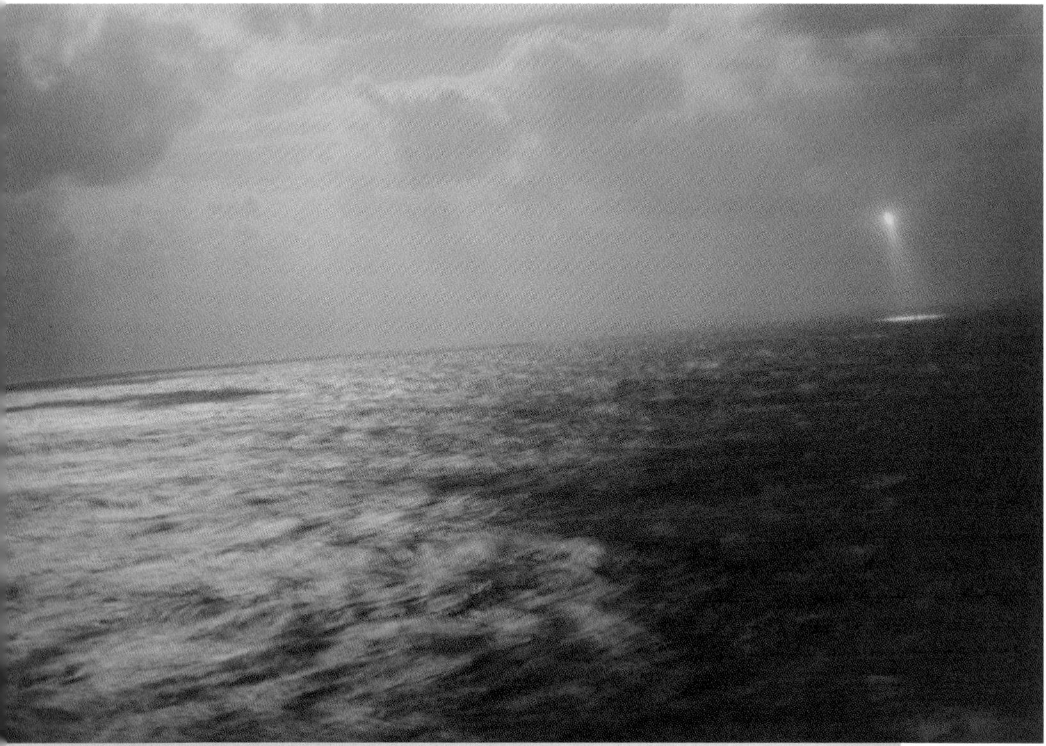

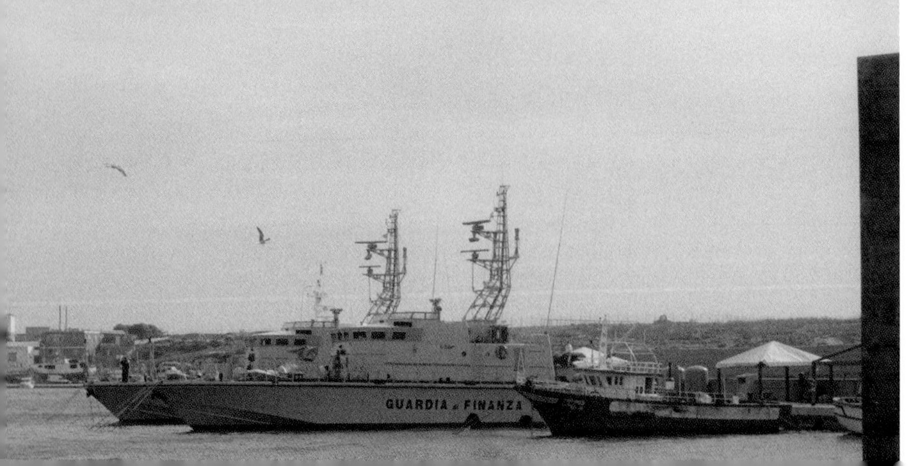

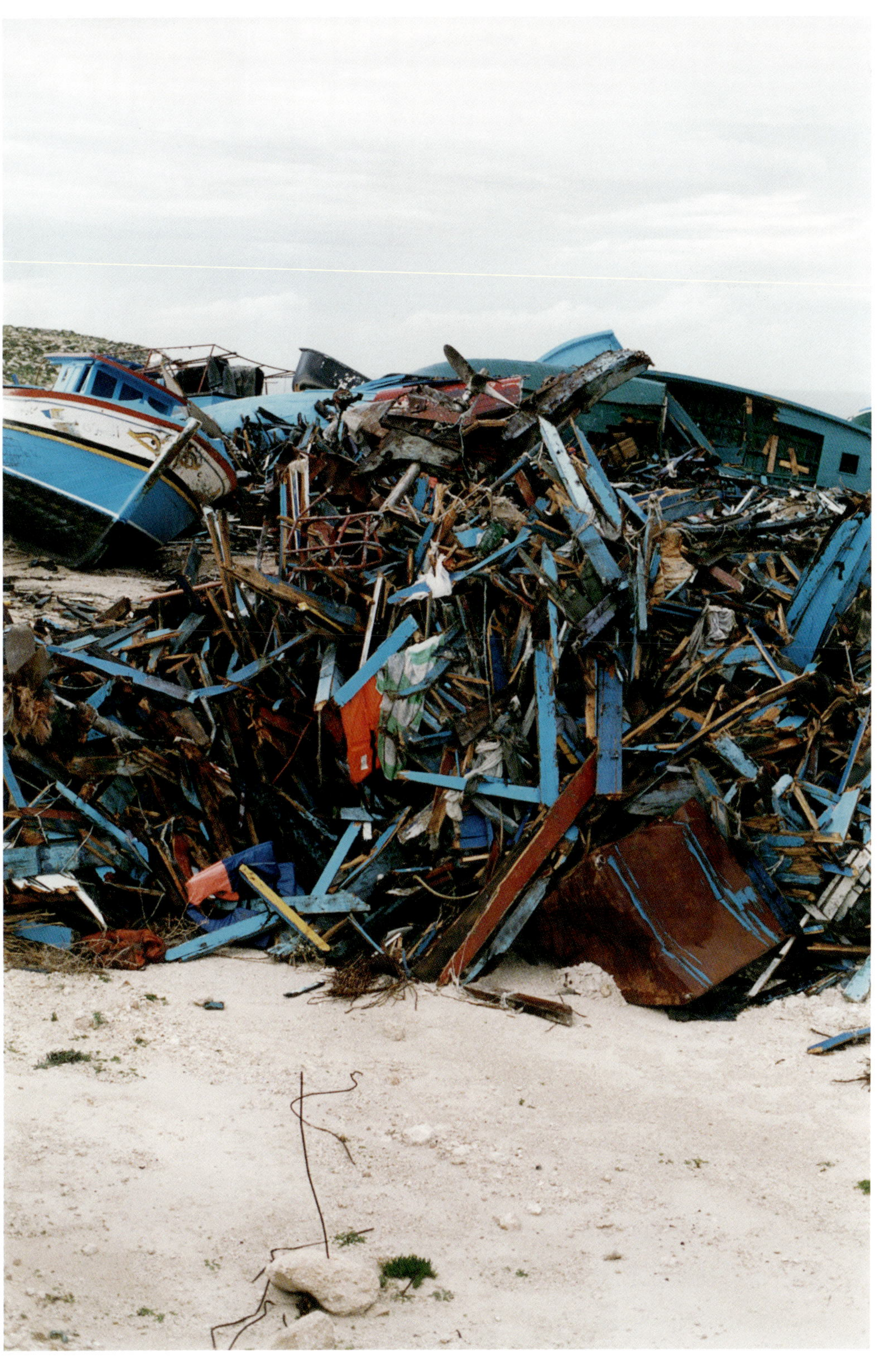

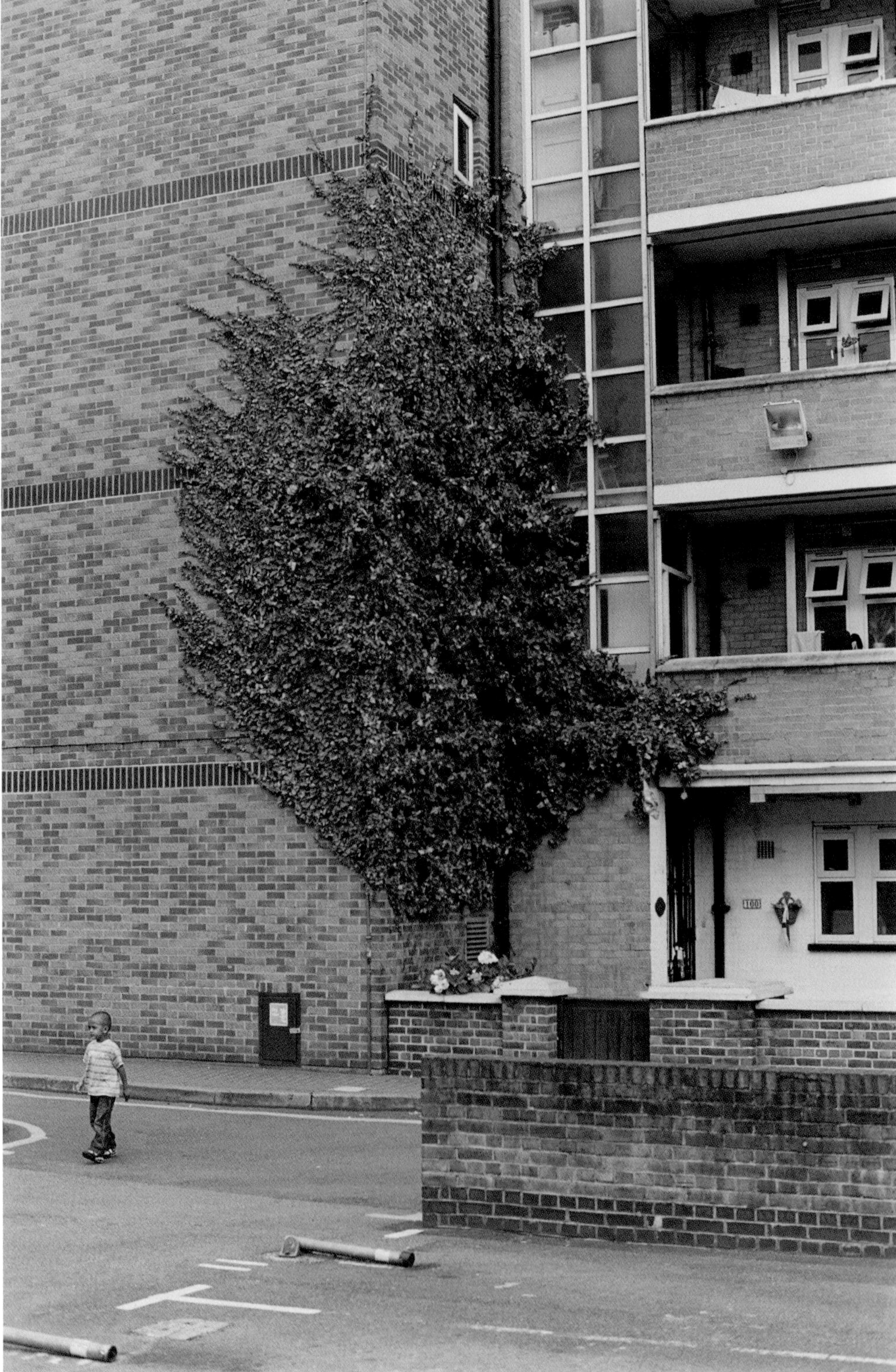

growth, 2006   Black Lives Matter protest, Union Square, b, 2014

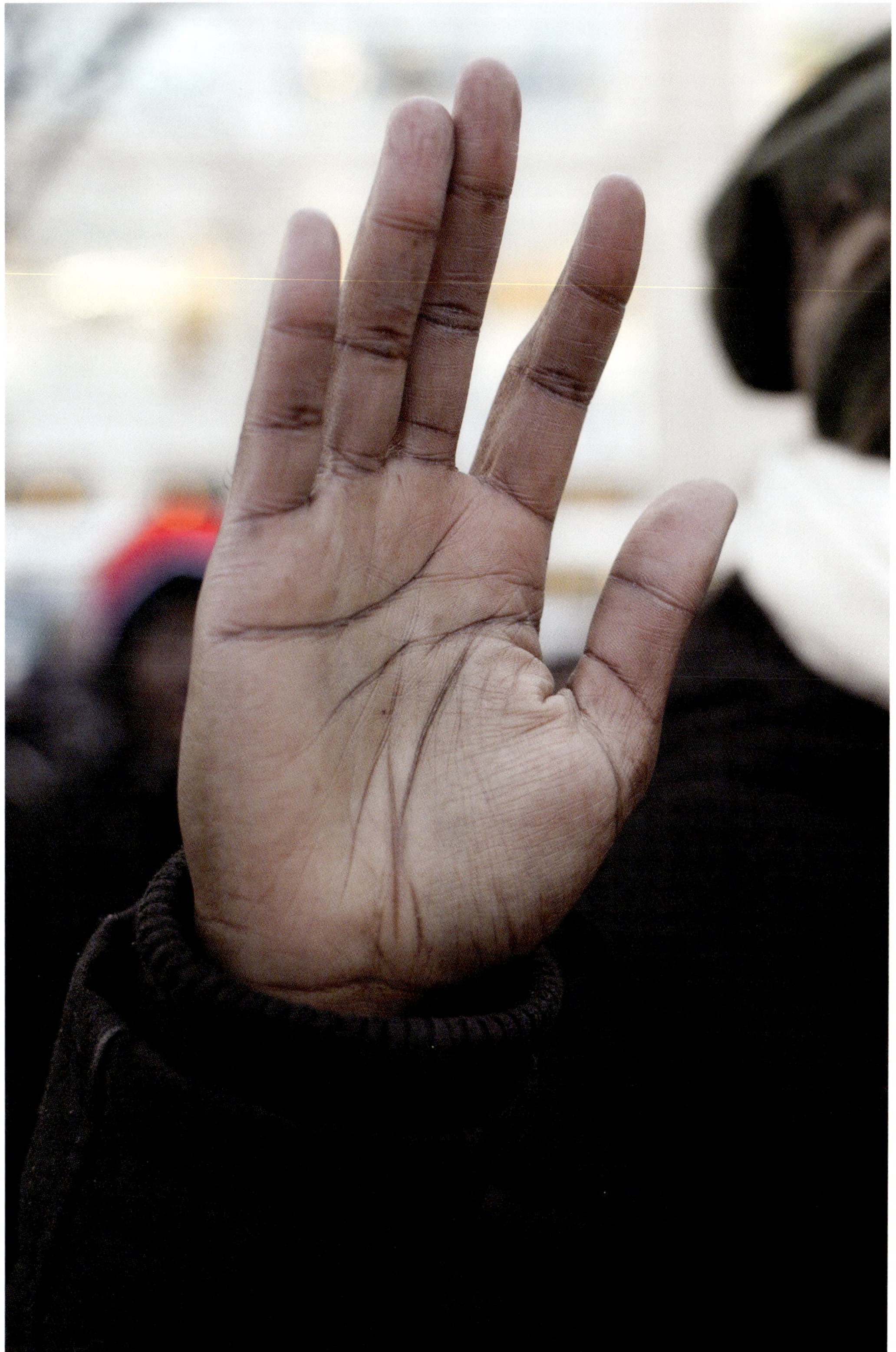

'four books'
Edited and designed by Wolfgang Tillmans, 2020
Additional picture research: Federico Gargaglione

© 2020 TASCHEN GmbH
Hohenzollernring 53, D-50672 Köln
www.taschen.com

© 2020 Wolfgang Tillmans, Berlin/London

Printed in Bosnia-Herzegovina
ISBN 978–3–8365–8253–7